N CRIMINOLOGY

Social Structure Approaches

Social Disorganization

1920 **Thomas and Znaniecki** Displaced immigrants

1920s-1930s **Park & Burgess** Social ecology, social pathology, concentric zones (Chicago School)

1929 **Shaw & McKay** Cultural transmission (Chicago School)

1982 **James Q. Wilson & George L. Kelling** Broken windows, defensible space, criminology of place

1987 **Rodney Stark** Theory of deviant neighborhoods

Culture Conflict

1927 **Frederic Thrasher** Gangs and gang typologies

1938 **Thorsten Sellin** Conduct norms, primary conflict, secondary conflict

1943 **William F. Whyte** Subcultures

1955 **Albert Cohen** Gangs, reaction formation

1957 **Sykes & Matza** Techniques of neutralization

1958 **Walter B. Miller** Focal concerns

1960s **Cloward & Ohlin** Illegitimate opportunity structure, delinquent subcultures

1967 **Ferracuti & Wolfgang** Violent subcultures

Strain Theory

1938 **Robert Merton** Anomie, conformity, innovation, ritualism, retreatism, rebellion

1982 **Blau & Blau** Relative deprivation, frustration, distributive justice

1992 **Robert Agnew** General Strain Theory

1994 **Messner & Rosenfeld** American Dream

Social Process Theories

Social Learning Theory

1939 **Edwin Sutherland** Differential association

1960 **Daniel Glaser** Differential identification theory

1966 **Burgess & Akers** Differential association-reinforcement

Social Control Theory

1950s **Walter Reckless** Containment theory, inner and outer containment

1969 **Travis Hirschi** Social bond and self control: attachment, commitment, belief, involvement

1970s **Howard Kaplan** Self degradation

1990 **Hirschi & Gottfredson** Social bonds and self control

1995 **Charles Tittle** Control-balance, control surplus, control deficit

Labeling Theory

1938 **Frank Tannenbaum** Tagging, dramatization of evil

1951 **Edwin Lemert** Primary deviance, secondary deviance

1963 **Howard Becker** Outsiders, moral enterprise

1997 **John Braithwaite** Reintegrative shaming, stigmatic shaming

Dramaturgy

1960s **Erving Goffman** Dramaturgy, impression management, discrediting information, total institutions, disculturation

Social Conflict Theories

1848 **Karl Marx** The Communist Manifesto

1916 **Willem Bonger** Class struggle

1938 **Thorsten Sellin** Culture conflict

1939 **Rusche & Kircheimer**

Radical Criminology

1958 **George Vold** Political conflict between groups, conflict is normal

1959 **Ralf Dahrendorf** conflict is normal, destructive change

1969 **Austin Turk** Social order= pattern of conflict, laws serve to control

1970s **William Chambliss** Power gaps, crime reduces surplus labor

1974 **Richard Quinney** Contradictions of capitalism, socialist principles

Feminist Criminology

1975 **Adler & Simon** Gender socialization

1977 **Carol Smart** Gender bias in criminology

1988 **Daly & Chesney-Lind** Androcentricity, crime may not be normal

1989 **John Hagan** Power-control theory

Peacemaking Criminology

1986 **Pepinsky & Quinney** Restorative justice, participatory justice

1989 **Lozoff & Braswell** New Age principles

Convict Criminology

2001 **John Irwin, K.C. Carceral, Thomas J. Bernard** Insights from convicted offenders

Criminology TODAY

KALAMAZOO VALLEY

COMMUNITY COLLEGE

A Gift to the KVCC Libraries from

Jeff Shouldice

Annotated Instructor's Edition
Sixth Edition

Criminology TODAY

AN INTEGRATIVE INTRODUCTION

Frank Schmalleger, Ph.D.

Distinguished Professor Emeritus, The University of North Carolina at Pembroke

Prentice Hall

Boston   Columbus   Indianapolis   New York   San Francisco   Upper Saddle River
Amsterdam   Cape Town   Dubai   London   Madrid   Milan   Munich   Paris   Montréal   Toronto
Delhi   Mexico City   São Paulo   Sydney   Hong Kong   Seoul   Singapore   Taipei   Tokyo

Editorial Director: Vernon R. Anthony
Senior Editor: Eric Krassow
Assistant Editor: Megan Heintz
Editorial Assistant: Lynda Cramer
Director of Marketing: David Gesell
Senior Marketing Manager: Adam Kloza
Senior Marketing Coordinator: Alicia Wozniak
Marketing Assistant: Les Roberts
Senior Managing Editor: JoEllen Gohr
Project Manager: Steve Robb
Senior Operations Supervisor: Patricia A. Tonneman
Operations Specialist: Deidra M. Skahill

Director of Design: Christy Mahon
Art Director: Diane Y. Ernsberger
Text and Cover Designer: Candace Rowley
Cover Art: iStockphoto
Media Editor: Michelle Churma
Media Project Manager: Karen Bretz
Full-Service Project Management: Janet Bolton, Milford Publishing Services
Composition: S4Carlisle Publishing Services
Printer/Binder: R.R. Donnelley/Willard
Cover Printer: Lehigh-Phoenix Color/Hagerstown
Text Font: Bembo, 10/13

Chapter Opening Photo Credits
Sonja Flemming/CBS/Courtesy Everett Collection, p. 1; CrimeMapping.com/Courtesy of The Omega Group, p. 25; David Levenson/Alamy, p. 53; Jon Smyth/SuperStock, p. 85; mrtphotos/NewsCom.com, p. 121; LHB Photo/Alamy, p. 149; Photofusion Picture Library/Alamy, p. 175; Gary Coronado/*The Palm Beach Post/*ZUMA Press/NewsCom.com, p. 209; © Alexander Majewski/CORBIS All Rights Reserved, p. 233; Fernando Cortes/Shutterstock.com, p. 277; Everett Collection, p. 301; mediablitzimages (uk) Limited/Alamy, p. 333; ZUMA Press/NewsCom.com, p. 369; NOTIMEX/PHOTO/LUIS SORIAN/NewsCom.com, p. 395; TM & Copyright Twentieth Century Fox and DreamWorks LLC/Courtesy Everett Collection, p. 421.

Credits and acknowledgments for other content borrowed from other sources and reproduced, with permission, in this textbook appear on the appropriate page within the text.

10 9 8 7 6 5 4 3 2 1

Prentice Hall
is an imprint of

www.pearsonhighered.com

ISBN 13: 978-0-13-707486-0
ISBN 10: 0-13-707486-7

For Nicole and Jason

Brief Contents

Contents

WHO'S TO BLAME—The Individual or Society?

The Video Game Killer

In early 2011, 17-year-old Jason Sutter was pulled over in a small Midwestern town for various traffic offenses, including going 70 mph in a 35-mph zone, running a red light, failing to yield for a blue light and siren, and driving recklessly. When officers discovered that he didn't have a driver's license, Sutter was handcuffed, briefly searched, placed in the back of a patrol car, and driven to the local police station for booking.

After he was photographed and fingerprinted, detective Joe Lockman sat down with him in a small interrogation room. Lockman, a 25-year veteran of the force, was working late and was in the station at 2:00 A.M. when Sutter arrived. The building was nearly empty, so Lockman decided to remove Sutter's handcuffs for what he hoped would be an informal chat. Sutter, who stood only 5 feet 4 inches tall and weighed 135 pounds, reminded Lockman of his son, and the detective hoped that he could teach the boy something about right and wrong.

As Lockman leaned forward to unshackle Sutter, a number of unfortunate details came together with deadly results. Sutter was a high school dropout and video game fanatic who spent most of his waking hours playing violence-themed games—including three in which the "heroes" killed pursuing police officers. Sutter had been improperly handcuffed with his hands in front, giving him easy access to Lockman's service revolver. Lockman carried an older model 38-caliber revolver (instead of a 9mm semiautomatic pistol), which was loaded with deadly hollow-point ammunition and did not have a safety. When Sutter grabbed the weapon, he was able to immediately pull the trigger and fire two shots into Lockman's chest, killing him instantly.

Sutter fled out the front door of the police station past the surprised desk sergeant. The sergeant, realizing what had happened, pursued Sutter through the front door, and the two exchanged shots. Sutter was wounded in the exchange and captured; he was taken to an area hospital where he underwent surgery and recovered. He was charged with the murder of Detective Lockman, and the district attorney said that he would seek to have Sutter put away for the rest of his life.

Sutter's parents hired an attorney to defend their son. The lawyer held a press conference during which he announced his defense strategy—that Sutter had been brainwashed by video games and that at the time of the shooting he had been unable to distinguish reality from fantasy. "Jason was playing a game," the attorney said. "He didn't realize that someone might really get hurt." He also announced that he was filing a lawsuit against the two media companies that had made the games Sutter played.

Think about it:

1. Who is primarily responsible for the murder of Detective Lockman, Sutter or the video game manufacturers? Do both bear at least some responsibility?

2. What role, if any, did society play in Detective Lockman's death? Should government regulations control the content of video games?

3. What role did free will and individual choice play in Sutter's quick decision to take Lockman's gun and shoot him? How much control did Sutter have over his own behavior, and how much of his behavior was merely a response to experiences he had in the past?

Who's to Blame Boxes

Author-created hypothetical cases and critical thinking questions help students to focus on the theme of the text (social problems versus social responsibility).

PART TWO   Crime Causation

CHAPTER 3 | Classical and Neoclassical Thought   53

THEORY | versus **REALITY**
The Unabomber and Domestic Terrorism

In April 1996, 52-year-old Harvard-educated Theodore Kaczynski, a Lincoln (Montana) recluse, was arrested and charged with the infamous Unabomber terrorist bombings. Kaczynski admitted responsibility for the bombings in early 1998 and was sentenced to life in prison without parole. The Unabomber's 18-year-long mail-bomb campaign had targeted universities, airlines, and researchers, killing three people and injuring 23 others in 16 separate bombing incidents. Prior to Kaczynski's arrest, a 56-page "manifesto" was mailed to the offices of the *New York Times*, the *Washington Post*, and *Penthouse* magazine. Titled "Industrial Society and Its Future," the Unabomber manifesto was a rambling thesis condemning American social institutions and high technology, blaming many of the world's existing problems on the Industrial Revolution, forecasting an Orwellian future in which helpless humans would be controlled by computers, and calling for a new social order based on a return to simpler times. Excerpts from the manifesto were widely published and helped lead to Kaczynski's capture. This box contains the introductory paragraphs of the Unabomber's manifesto. Read the Unabomber's entire manifesto online at **Web Extra 8–1**. A Profiles in Crime box later in this chapter provides more details about Kaczynski's life and crimes.

The Industrial Revolution and its consequences have been a disaster for the human race. They have greatly increased the life-expectancy of those of us who live in "advanced" countries, but they have destabilized society, have made life unfulfilling, have subjected human beings to indignities, have led to widespread psychological suffering (in the Third World to physical suffering as well) and have inflicted severe damage on the natural world. The continued development of technology will worsen the situation. . . .

The industrial-technological system may survive or it may break down. If it survives, it MAY eventually achieve a low level of physical and psychological suffering, but only after passing through a long and very painful period of adjustment and only at the cost of permanently reducing human beings and many other living organisms to engineered products and mere cogs in the social machine. . . .

If the system breaks down the consequences will still be very painful. But the bigger the system grows the more disastrous the results of its breakdown will be, so if it is to break down it had best break down sooner rather than later.

We therefore advocate a revolution against the industrial system. This revolution may or may not make use of violence; it may be sudden or it may be a relatively gradual process spanning a few decades. We can't predict any of that. But we do outline in a very general way the measures that those who hate the industrial system should take in order to prepare the way for a revolution against that form of society.

Discussion Questions

1. What motivated the Unabomber? Why did he advocate a revolution against the industrial system?

2. Do you think the Unabomber really believed his bombings would create a better world? If so, how did he think they would bring about such change?

Theory versus Reality Boxes
These boxes showcase selected issues and theories in the field of criminology and invite discussion through thought-provoking questions for consideration.

**Questions for Review/
Questions for Reflection**

These questions at the end of each chapter follow up on the learning objectives at the beginning of the chapter.

CHAPTER 4 | Biological Roots of Criminal Behavior 85

Criminal Profiles Boxes

These profiles offer insights into the lives and criminal motivations of notorious offenders, such as Ted Kaczynski (the "Unabomber").

Theory in Perspective Boxes

Summary boxes outline the main points of various theories throughout the chapters in Parts 2 and 3 for easy reference and study.

Crime in the News Boxes

These news articles present case examples and pose analytical discussion questions about connections between examples and the chapter topics.

CHAPTER 10 | Crimes against Property   277

CHAPTER 11 | White-Collar and Organized Crime 301

The Professor Speaks Boxes

Criminology instructors have contributed lecture-style explanations of challenging topics in criminology that have helped their students understand these difficult concepts.

CHAPTER 12 | Public Order and Drug Crimes   333

CHAPTER 13 | Technology and Crime 369

CHAPTER 14 | Globalization and Terrorism 395

New to This Edition

The sixth edition of *Criminology Today: An Integrative Introduction* continues to offer students a clear, contemporary, and comprehensive introduction to criminology that encourages critical thinking about the causes of crime and crime-prevention strategies. The text's hallmark thematic approach of social problems versus social responsibility (Is crime a matter of individual responsibility or a symptom of a dysfunctional society?) prompts students to think critically about the causes of crime and helps them see the link between crime theories and crime policies.

New Features in the Sixth Edition
There are many important new features in this sixth edition:

- The Professor Speaks boxes appear throughout the text. Because students often find concepts and theories in criminology difficult to comprehend, teaching criminologists from around the country were asked to provide their personal insights into helping students understand these materials. The Professor Speaks boxes are unique among criminology texts and provide helpful viewpoints in addition to that of the author.

- Links are provided to full-text articles of relevance to the field of criminology from the Web-based Social Science Research Network (SSRN). Articles on crime causation, crime-control policy, and research and theory are included. Visit the SSRN on the Web at **http://ssrn.com**.

- Start-of-chapter learning objectives are now *learning outcomes*, which are stated as questions and align with each top-level heading within the chapter. Learning outcomes are also now reiterated in the end-of-chapter discussion questions.

- End-of-chapter summaries are now bulleted, and each bullet relates directly to start-of-chapter learning outcomes in order to help students focus on the important material covered in each section.

- Circle quotes now appear throughout the chapters, punctuating important learning opportunities.

- Most boxed items, including Crime in the News boxes, have been shortened to 600 words or less in order to enhance their focus and promote reader comprehension.

New Chapter Content in the Sixth Edition
Chapter 1: What Is Criminology?
The difference between crime and deviance is now illustrated through the use of a "baggy pants" example and via a story about an attempt by the New York State Assembly to ban the use of salt in restaurant kitchens throughout the state. Older Crime in the News boxes have been replaced with a new Crime in the News box titled "Muslim Countries Seek Blasphemy Ban." The section on "What Is Criminology?" has been simplified and reduced in size.

Chapter 2: Where Do Theories Come From?
The old Chapter 2 on crime statistics has been deleted, and some of its content has been moved to other chapters throughout the book so that crime data now appear with the discussion of the crimes to which they relate. This better integration makes for easier student comprehension. Chapter 2 now focuses on the relationship between theory and research in criminology, especially on the new and emerging concept of evidence-based criminology. Lawrence Sherman's "10 principal elements of a viable model for keeping the promise of experimental criminology" are included, and the theory-building process is diagrammed in an added figure. The relevance of the Stockholm Prize in Criminology to evidence-based criminology is reiterated, and this year's recipient (David Weisburd) is recognized.

Chapter 3: Classical and Neoclassical Thought
This chapter begins with a new introductory story, and a previous Crime in the News box has been replaced with one on the important issue of wrongful imprisonment. A number of new studies exploring the deterrent effect of punishment are now included; one was published in 2005, and two of them are from 2009. New line art shows the ethnicities of defendants executed and of murder victims in the United States as well as exoneration data; statistics on the U.S. incarceration rates have been updated.

Chapter 4: Biological Roots of Criminal Behavior
This chapter now builds on the idea that biological theories are theories of criminality, not of crime; criminality is also defined. The text clarifies the dominant point of view today among biocriminologists, who hold that it is the interaction of genes and the behavioral possibilities that they represent, with features of the social and physical environments, that produces meaningful human activity and that may lead to criminality. A new section, "Biosocial and Psychosocial Criminology," emphasizes the importance of recognizing the interaction of biology and the environment in the formation of behavioral responses to given situations. A number of new studies highlighting the relationship of biology and criminality are discussed, and the coverage of Terrie E. Moffitt's biosocial theory has been expanded and moved to this chapter. A Crime in the News box

discusses the possible link between childhood lead exposure and adult crime.

Chapter 5: Psychological and Psychiatric Foundations of Criminal Behavior

Discussion of Hans Eysenck has been removed from this chapter and is now summarized in Chapter 4. A new figure shows the various types of social control. The Crime in the News box has been removed from the chapter.

Chapter 6: Social Structure Theories

The chapter now opens with a new story. A new key term, *human ecology*, is defined and described within the chapter. Two Crime in the News boxes have been replaced. A new box describes the broken windows theory and hot-spot policing; another discusses youth violence and its prevention. A new figure depicts techniques of neutralization.

Chapter 7: Theories of Social Process and Social Development

A replacement Crime in the News box focuses on crime trending in families, and a new figure highlights aspects of criminal careers. Moffitt's dual taxonomic theory was moved from this chapter to the section discussing biosocial and psychosocial criminology in Chapter 4. A discussion of resilience has been added to the life course section; resilience has been defined and added as a key term. Research findings that indicate positive developmental pathways are now summarized near the conclusion of the chapter.

Chapter 8: Social Conflict Theories

A new introductory story opens the chapter, and information on the Unabomber has been revised. The complicated table showing class structure in the United States has been removed. A new perspective on feminist theory begins the discussion of feminist criminology, and the various types of feminist theory are more clearly presented. Statistics on women's involvement in crime have been updated.

Chapter 9: Crimes against Persons

The chapter now contains information about the Uniform Crime Reporting (UCR) Program of the FBI and the Bureau of Justice Statistics (BJS) National Crime Victimization Survey (NCVS) on violent crime. Much of this information has been adapted from what had been Chapter 2 in the previous edition. Crime statistics from the previous Chapter 2 have also been updated and integrated throughout the chapter. Both measures

make it easier for readers to associate crime statistics with other aspects of the criminal offenses under discussion in this chapter. The case of serial killer Anthony Sowell has been added, as has a discussion of pseudocommando mass murderers. A new Crime in the News box on violence on campus replaces an earlier box on child sexual abuse. The 2010 attack on the U.S. Holocaust Museum in Washington, D.C., is now part of the section on hate crimes. New line art shows robbery locations and murders by relationships. Workplace violence, hate crimes, and stalking are now discussed in this chapter.

Chapter 10: Crimes against Property

As in Chapter 9, this chapter now contains UCR and NCVS data on violent crime. Similarly, Chapter 10 borrows from the fifth edition's Chapter 2, with updating and integrating of statistics. These enhancements help readers associate the statistics with other aspects of crime. New line art depicts larceny-theft distribution and the percent of property crimes cleared. The section on shoplifting has been updated and expanded, and a Crime in the News box on shoplifting has been added.

Chapter 11: White-Collar and Organized Crime

A new chapter opening is now in place. The section on the history of white-collar crime has been shortened, but information on Bernie Madoff and other recent white-collar offenders has been added, as has a new Crime in the News box on President Obama's efforts to crack down on white-collar crime. The Criminal Profiles box in this chapter now highlights the criminal activities of Bernard Madoff. A new section on financial crimes describes the FBI's classification of financial crimes, including mortgage and health-care fraud, and provides information about each. Coverage of environmental crimes has been expanded and offers additional examples of such offenses. The link between terrorism and white-collar crime is now discussed in a separate section. The section on organized crime has been significantly expanded to include a number of contemporary organized criminal groups of Eurasian, Balkan, Asian, African, and other nationalities.

Chapter 12: Public Order and Drug Crimes

The chapter opening story is new. The link between Mexican drug trafficking and criminal activity in the United States has been clarified, drug addiction is now defined and explained, and a new table describes the various uses and effects of illicit drugs. Restrictions on the sale of pseudoephedrine under the 2006 Combat Methamphetamine Epidemic Act are discussed. New illustrations depict binge drinking, driving under the influence, illicit drug use, and drugs used when initiating illicit drug use. A replacement Crime in the News box describes the growing and sale of opium in Afghanistan. Changes in federal policy on the use of medical marijuana are discussed, as are possible plans in California to legalize and tax the personal use of marijuana. A new Crime in the News box discusses child prostitutes.

Chapter 13: Technology and Crime

The chapter opens with a new story describing cyberbanging, or the use of the Internet by organized street gangs, and a new Crime in the News box describes the use of the Internet by street gangs seeking to extend their influence to the Web. The list of the most damaging computer viruses and worms, as well as the statistics on identity theft, have been revised and updated. The new position of White House Cybersecurity Coordinator is discussed, as are recommendations from the Comprehensive National Cybersecurity Initiative; line art new to this chapter depicts a global cyberthreat map.

Chapter 14: Globalization and Terrorism

The 2008 report of the Commission on the Prevention of Weapons of Mass Destruction Proliferation and Terrorism is discussed, and a new Crime in the News box describes the recruitment of terrorists within the United States. New illustrations show the countries most involved in human trafficking, worldwide terrorism attacks by method, and worldwide deaths from terrorist attacks.

Supplements

Instructor Supplements

The following supplementary materials are available to support instructors' use of the main text:

- Annotated Instructor's Edition
- Instructor's Manual with Test Bank
- PowerPoint presentations
- MyTest computerized test bank
- Test Item File for Blackboard/Course Compass
- Test Item File for WebCT
- CourseSmart e-book version of the text

Download Instructor Resources from the Instructor Resource Center

To access supplementary materials online, instructors need to request an instructor access code. Go to **www.pearsonhighered .com/irc** to register for an instructor access code. Within 48 hours of registering, you will receive a confirming e-mail including an instructor access code. Once you have received your code, locate your text in the online catalog and click on the Instructor Resources button on the left side of the catalog product page. Select a supplement, and a log-in page will appear. Once you have logged in, you can access instructor materials for all Prentice Hall textbooks. If you have any difficulties accessing the site or downloading a supplement, please contact Customer Service at **http://247.prenhall.com**.

Alternative Book Versions

Alternative versions to traditional printed textbooks, such as our "Student Value Editions" and e-book versions of the text in the "CourseSmart" platform, will be offered.

Preface

The opening decade of the twenty-first century was filled with momentous events in the United States, including the destruction of the World Trade Center and an attack on the Pentagon by Islamic terrorists, a fearsome recession, and corporate scandals that cost Americans billions of dollars in lost investments. The crimes committed by terrorists set a tone for the start of the new century unlike any in living memory. Homeland security became an important buzzword at all levels of American government while pundits questioned just how much freedom people would be willing to sacrifice to enhance security. Americans felt both physically and economically threatened as stock market losses were traced to the unethical actions of a surprising cadre of corporate executives who had previously been held in high regard in the business world and in the communities where they lived. Soon the media were busily showing a parade of business leaders being led away in handcuffs to face trial on charges of crooked accounting.

Added to the mix by the beginning of 2011 were shocking acts of criminality that emanated from all corners of the world: depravities of sex tourism involving human trafficking, sex acts with minors streaming across the Internet in real time, claims of successful human cloning by a fringe religious sect, stem-cell controversies involving Korean scientists said to be in league with Russian organized crime, and thefts of hundreds of thousands of personal identities. This last issue constitutes a very intimate crime that can literally cause a person to face the loss of his or her social self in a complex culture that increasingly defines someone's essence in terms of an economic, educational, and ever more complex social nexus. The Gulf oil spill of 2010, which may have been an environmental crime, and the shooting of a number of Army soldiers at Ft. Hood, Texas, were also featured prominently in news coverage.

Criminologists found themselves wondering what new laws might be enacted to control the potential misuse of technology by energy companies, along with emerging computer capabilities and biotechnologies that, while they seem to hold amazing promise to cure disease and reshape humanity's future, threaten the social fabric in a way not seen since the birth of the atomic bomb or the harnessing of electricity. Similarly, climate changes, violent storms such as Hurricane Katrina, the Gulf oil spill, our nation's desperate need for alternative energy sources, and the instability in the Middle East contribute to a growing awareness that the challenges facing criminologists in the twenty-first century are unlike any they have previously faced.

It was against this backdrop that the need for a comprehensive revision of *Criminology Today* emerged. This new edition addresses the poignant question of how security and freedom interface in an age of increasing globalism. Chapter 14, in particular, provides substantially enlarged coverage of terrorism and cyberterrorism, including an overview of many types of terrorist groups such as nationalist, religious, state-sponsored, left-wing, right-wing, and anarchist groups. The findings and recommendations of special committees and government bodies that have focused on terrorism in recent years are also discussed, and online links to the full text of their reports are provided. Included here are the reports of the 9/11 Commission, the Gilmore Commission, the three-phased report of the U.S. Commission on National Security in the 21st Century (also known as the Hart-Rudman Commission), the National Commission on Terrorism (also known as the Bremmer Commission), and the 2008 report of the Commission on the Prevention of WMD Proliferation and Terrorism.

In the past few years, crime and criminals have changed in ways that few people had previously imagined would occur, and these changes hold considerable significance for each one of us and for our nation as a whole. It is my hope that this new edition will help today's students both to understand the nature of these changes and to find a meaningful place in the social world that is to come.

FRANK SCHMALLEGER, PH.D.
Distinguished Professor Emeritus
The University of North Carolina at Pembroke

Acknowledgments

A book like *Criminology Today* draws on the talents and resources of many people and is the end result of much previous effort. This text could not have been written without the groundwork laid by previous criminologists, academics, and researchers; hence, a hearty thank-you is due everyone who has contributed to the development of the field of criminology throughout the years, especially to those theorists, authors, and social commentators who are cited in this book. Without their work, the field would be that much poorer. I would like to thank, as well, all the adopters—professors and students alike—of my previous textbooks, for they have given me the encouragement and fostered the steadfastness required to write this new edition of *Criminology Today*.

The Pearson Prentice Hall team members, many of whom I have come to know very well and all of whom have worked so professionally with me on this and other projects, deserve special thanks. The team includes Leah Jewell, Vern Anthony, Zina Arabia, Karen Bretz, Michelle Churma, Lynda Cramer, Diane Ernsberger, JoEllen Gohr, David Gesell, Adam Kloza, Eric Krassow, Christy Mahon, Les Roberts, Steve Robb, Karen Sanatar, Deidra Skahill, Pat Tonneman, Rita Wenning, and Alicia Wozniak. I would especially like to thank Elisa Rogers at Pearson Prentice Hall for her commitment and attention to this project. My thanks also to text and cover designer Candace Rowley and to photo researcher Jerry Marshall, whose efforts have helped make *Criminology Today* both attractive and visually appealing. Finally, my sincere thanks to production coordinator Janet Bolton for her very capable handling of numerous details.

My friends and professional colleagues Ellen Cohn at Florida International University, Cassandra Renzi at Keiser University, and Karel Kurst-Swanger at Oswego State University helped in many ways. Dr. Cohn graciously used her deep personal creativity in enhancing the supplements package and creating quality products; she has the exceptional ability of building intuitively on concepts in the text. Thanks to Carolyn Dennis for developing the companion Web site and Venessa Garcia for developing the PowerPoint slides. Thanks also to Bob Winslow at California State University–San Diego for insight and encouragement on a number of important issues and to Jack Humphrey at St. Anselm College and Stephen J. Schoenthaler for their valuable suggestions in the preparation of this new edition.

This book has benefited greatly from the quick availability of information and other resources through online services and in various locations on the Internet's World Wide Web. I am grateful to the many information providers who, although they are too numerous to list, have helped establish such useful resources.

I am thankful as well for the assistance of Bill Tafoya (now retired) and Nancy Carnes of the Federal Bureau of Investigation; William Ballweber at the National Institute of Justice; David Beatty, director of public affairs with the National Victim Center; Kris Rose at the National Criminal Justice Reference Service; Marilyn Marbrook and Michael Rand at the Office of Justice Programs; Mark Reading at the Drug Enforcement Administration; and Barbara Maxwell at *USA Today*.

Many manuscript reviewers have contributed to the development of *Criminology Today*:

Reed Adams, East Carolina State University
Michael P. Brown, Ball State University
Gregg Buchholz, Keiser University
Bryan D. Byers, Ball State University
Dianne Carmody, Old Dominon University
Steven M. Christiansen, Joliet Junior College
Myrna Cintron, Texas A&M University
Patrick G. Donnelly, University of Dayton
Ronald D. Hunter, State University of West Georgia
Steven Johnson, Eastern Arizona College
Daniel D. Jones, University of Washington
John Kirkpatrick, University of New Hampshire
Joan Luxenburg, University of Central Oklahoma
M. Joan McDermott, Southern Illinois University
William McGovern, Sussex County Community College
Darrell K. Mills, Pima Community College (East Campus)
Robert Mutchnick, Indiana University of Pennsylvania
Michael Pittaro, Lehigh Valley College
Glen E. Sapp, Central Carolina Community College
Jennifer L. Schulenberg, Sam Houston State University
Louis Shepard, West Georgia Technical College
John Siler, Georgia Perimeter College
Tamson L. Six, Lock Haven University
Dianne Williams, North Carolina A&T State University
Jeffrey Zack, Fayetteville Technical Community College
Anthony W. Zumpetta, West Chester University

Finally, but by no means least, I am indebted to a small but very special group of contemporary criminologists who have laid the foundation for our discipline's presence on the Internet. Among them are Cecil Greek at Florida State University, whose online lecture notes (**www.criminology.fsu.edu/crimtheory**) are massively informative; Tom O'Connor of Austin Peay State

University, whose Megalinks in Criminal Justice (**http://www .drtomocconor.com**) provide an amazingly comprehensive resource; Matthew Robinson at Appalachian State University, whose Crime Theory links (**www.appstate.edu/∼robinsnmb/ theorylinks.htm**) allow visitors to vote on what they think are the causes of crime; and Bruce Hoffman, whose Crime Theory site (**http://crimetheory.com**) at the University of Washington offers many great insights into the field. All of these excellent resources are referred to throughout this book—and it is to these modern-day visionaries that *Criminology Today* owes much of its technological depth.

About the Author

Frank Schmalleger, Ph.D., is Professor Emeritus at The University of North Carolina at Pembroke, where he also was recognized as Distinguished Professor. Dr. Schmalleger holds degrees from the University of Notre Dame and The Ohio State University; he earned both a master's (1970) and a doctorate (1974) in sociology, with a special emphasis in criminology, from The Ohio State University. From 1976 to 1994, he taught criminal justice courses at The University of North Carolina at Pembroke, and for the last 16 of those years, he chaired the university's Department of Sociology, Social Work, and Criminal Justice. As an adjunct professor with Webster University in St. Louis, Missouri, Schmalleger helped develop the university's graduate program in security administration and loss prevention and taught courses in that curriculum for more than a decade. Schmalleger has also taught in the New School for Social Research's online graduate program, helping build the world's first electronic classrooms in support of distance learning through computer telecommunications.

Schmalleger is the author of numerous articles as well as many books: *Criminal Justice Today: An Introductory Text for the 21st Century* (Prentice Hall, 2011), now in its eleventh edition; *Juvenile Delinquency* (with Clemmens Bartollas; Prentice Hall, 2011); *Criminal Justice: A Brief Introduction*, ninth edition (Prentice Hall, 2012); *Criminal Law Today*, fourth edition (Prentice Hall, 2011); *Crime and the Justice System in America: An Encyclopedia* (Greenwood Publishing Group, 1997); *Trial of the Century: People of the State of California vs. Orenthal James Simpson* (Prentice Hall, 1996); *Career Paths: A Guide to Jobs in Federal Law Enforcement* (Regents/Prentice Hall, 1994); *Computers in Criminal Justice* (Wyndham Hall Press, 1991); *Criminal Justice Ethics* (Greenwood Press, 1991); *Finding Criminal Justice in the Library* (Wyndham Hall Press, 1991); *Ethics in Criminal Justice* (Wyndham Hall Press, 1990); *A History of Corrections* (Foundations Press of Notre Dame, 1983); and *The Social Basis of Criminal Justice* (University Press of America, 1981). He is also founding editor of the journal *Criminal Justice Studies* (formerly *The Justice Professional*).

Schmalleger's philosophy of both teaching and writing can be summed up in these words: "In order to communicate knowledge we must first catch, then hold, a person's interest—be it student, colleague, or policymaker. Our writing, our speaking, and our teaching must be relevant to the problems facing people today, and they must—in some way—help solve those problems."

Criminology
TODAY

Instructor's Annotations

CHAPTER 1

What Is Criminology?

Introduction

▓ **Classroom Activity**

Ask students to write down three ideas they immediately think of when they hear the terms *crime* and *criminology*. Discuss their responses with the class.

▓ **Classroom Activity**

Ask students to define the four perspectives on crime that this book talks about and identify ways in which each aligns with the democratic principles of our society.

▓ **Lecture Note**

Crime covers a limited number of wrongs. Explain that because crime is concerned with the social control of wrongs, crime is fundamentally an issue of morality.

▓ **Thematic Question**

Why is there so much public interest (as evidenced by all the crime shows on TV) in crime and justice?

▓ **Thematic Question**

Are crime and wrongdoing the same? Explain.

▓ **Thematic Question**

Unless defined by law, there can be no crime, but can there, nonetheless, be harm?

What Is Crime?

▓ **Classroom Activity**

Ask students whether a random act of violence has recently occurred in their community. You can also ask about an event they might have heard about recently on the news or read about in the newspaper. Ask them to discuss their initial response, and ask whether they are concerned about possibly becoming a victim of such random violence.

▓ **Lecture Note**

Explain why the legalistic approach dominates this textbook as well as most thinking on criminal justice issues. Inform students that an emphasis on the legal definition of crime can limit the development of theory and crime policy.

▓ **Lecture Note**

Have students make a list of criminal justice facts (for example, low clearance rate for crimes) and then create a list of questions that come to mind about those facts. Ask students if they regularly watch any of the numerous crime television shows. Then ask them to respond to questions that have been developed based on the list of facts: Do the police solve most crimes? The majority? One half? Have a compare-and-contrast discussion of the reality with the media representation.

▓ **Lecture Note**

Explain that deviance is a broad area whose boundaries both encompass much crime and extend beyond crime.

▓ **Thematic Question**

What reasons does the text give for the limits said to be inherent in the legal definitions of crime?

Crime and Deviance

▓ **Classroom Activity**

Ask students to create a list of behaviors they consider deviant. Instruct them that half of the list should be minor violations and the other half should be what they consider major violations. Emphasize the similarities and differences in the student responses. Which of the behaviors are crimes?

▓ **Classroom Activity**

Ask students to come up with three examples showing how the question "What is crime?" differs from the question "What should be criminal?"

▓ **Lecture Note**

Note that deviance is defined relative to the norms and values of a particular group and society. Explain that what is considered deviant for one group may not be so for another group. Select a group and discuss how its behavior may be considered deviant by comparison with another group.

▓ **Thematic Question**

Why is it easier for members of our society to reach a consensus as to right and wrong on certain behaviors than on others?

What Should Be Criminal?

▓ **Lecture Note**

Compare and contrast the consensus and pluralist perspectives on defining crime by discussing how both of these are consistent with a democratic system of criminal justice.

▓ **Lecture Note**

Demonstrate the complexity of the consensus and pluralist perspectives on crime by illustrating that there can be societal consensus that murder is wrong, despite disagreement over the kinds of acts that make one criminally liable for the killing of a human being. The Kevorkian case might serve as an example.

What Do Criminologists Do?

▓ **Lecture Note**

Share with the class how you first became interested in criminology. You might also want to share your current research or writing activities with your students.

▓ **Lecture Note**

Ask students about their possible interest in a career in criminology, and ask why they might want to pursue this occupation.

▓ **Thematic Question**

What is the difference between a criminologist and a criminalist?

What Is Criminology?

▓ **Lecture Note**

Discuss Edwin Sutherland's definition of crime, and compare this to other definitions included in the text.

▓ **Lecture Note**

Point out that the text states that the word *theory* "is only loosely applicable to some of the perspectives we will discuss." Ask, "If this is the case, why are theories useful?"

▓ **Thematic Question**

What is a general theory of crime? Why do we say it is "general"?

▓ **Thematic Question**

What is an integrated theory? Why do we say that such a theory is "integrated"?

Criminology and Social Policy

▦ Classroom Activity

Ask students, "How might violence in the media influence actual occurrences of violence?"

▦ Classroom Activity

Ask students to write about whether they prefer the social problems perspective or the social responsibility perspective on crime. Have them support their choice by giving two reasons for it. Repeat this exercise several times throughout the semester.

▦ Classroom Activity

Have students respond to the question "Why are reactions to crime important?"

▦ Lecture Note

Emphasize that effective crime-control policies must be directly linked to explanations of crime.

▦ Lecture Note

Focus on how crime and crime control have become increasingly politicized.

▦ Lecture Note

Discuss the social problems and social responsibility perspectives, and emphasize that these are not necessarily contrasting or mutually exclusive perspectives. Ask questions like: "Does a responsible society allow social problems that may contribute to crime and then still have the right to punish individuals who violate the law?"

▦ Thematic Question

Why does crime remain a concern among the public despite declining crime rates? Are they right to be concerned?

▦ Thematic Question

Why has workplace homicide increased in recent years?

▦ Thematic Question

What is the basic rationale underlying the social responsibility perspective on crime?

The Theme of This Book

▦ Thematic Question

What are the assumptions inherent in the social problems perspective on crime?

The Social Context of Crime

▦ Classroom Activity

Ask students to respond to the question "What is sociology?" How does it differ from criminology?

▦ Lecture Note

Discuss how a public-health approach to crime is closely aligned with crime prevention rather than crime fighting.

▦ Lecture Note

Ask how the concept of social relativity fits with the social problems and social responsibility perspectives that guide this text.

▦ Lecture Note

Give an example not found in the text to illustrate crime as a social event. Emphasize to students that saying that the victim and the criminal justice system play a part in the social construction of crime does not amount to blaming; it is a more complex situation.

▦ Thematic Question

Do most media reports of criminal events present the perspectives of the offender, the victim, the criminal justice system, and society equally? Is it important to do so?

▦ Thematic Question

Is crime primarily a public-health issue or a criminal justice issue? What's the difference?

▦ Thematic Question

What is involved in taking a three-dimensional integrative view of crime as a social event? What does such a view add to our understanding of crime?

▦ Thematic Question

Ask students what the author means when he says that criminal activity is diversely created and variously interpreted.

The Primacy of Sociology?

▦ Lecture Note

Explain to students that many of the theorists they will learn about in this text either are primarily based in sociology or have been influenced by the writings of sociologists. Emile Durkheim is a good example of the latter because his work on modern society and social change has influenced a number of different criminological theories.

▦ Thematic Question

What does society contribute to the interpretation of criminal offenses?

CHAPTER 2
Where Do Theories Come From?

Introduction

▦ Lecture Note

Ask students what, if any, of the other courses they have taken discuss research methods.

▦ Thematic Question

Why is it important to understand the research methods used by criminologists?

Evidence-Based Criminology

▦ Thematic Question

Ask students to explain the difference between the kind of evidence gathered by law enforcement authorities in seeking to prosecute criminal offenders and the kind of evidence used in evidence-based criminology.

The Evolving Science of Criminology

▦ Classroom Activity

Ask students to discuss how they use scientific information or knowledge in their everyday lives.

▦ Lecture Note

Explain to students that the scientific method provides one means of understanding aspects of our society, including crime. Although it is not the only such means, it is the one that guides criminology as a discipline.

▓ **Thematic Question**

What is the difference between using scientific knowledge versus personal experience to understand and explain patterns of crime?

▓ **Thematic Question**

We often hear it said that "facts speak for themselves." Is that so?

Theory Building

▓ **Lecture Note**

Explain the difference between social science generalizations and stereotypes.

▓ **Lecture Note**

Explain that the search for patterns does not mean that criminologists are not interested in exceptions to the patterns they identify.

▓ **Thematic Question**

What is a theory? What purposes do theories serve?

The Role of Research and Experimentation

▓ **Classroom Activity**

Break students into groups. Give them the same general research question, and tell them to modify it as needed to develop a way to address it with all of the techniques of data collection that are described in the text.

▓ **Lecture Note**

Explain applied research and show that the centrality of applied research has increased in recent years.

▓ **Lecture Note**

Discuss the politicized nature of problem identification in criminological research.

▓ **Lecture Note**

Ask students to think of research designs as blueprints for the research process.

▓ **Lecture Note**

Discuss threats to external validity.

▓ **Lecture Note**

Discuss the link between causation and experimental designs.

▓ **Lecture Note**

Discuss the benefits of experiments conducted in natural settings. Might these benefits be outweighed by other factors? If so, what?

▓ **Lecture Note**

Inform students that data-collection methods should always be selected in light of the questions to be researched.

▓ **Lecture Note**

Discuss examples of research subjects that might be difficult to study through participant observation.

▓ **Lecture Note**

Discuss the kinds of research questions that would be better answered through a case study rather than any other research method.

▓ **Lecture Note**

Discuss the use of one or more methods of data collection in a research project.

▓ **Lecture Note**

Discuss the extent to which secondary analysis is used in the social sciences and why.

▓ **Lecture Note**

Explain why replication is important in science.

▓ **Lecture Note**

Discuss correlations and tests of significance.

▓ **Lecture Note**

Explain why measures of central tendency must always be considered alongside measures of variability.

▓ **Lecture Note**

Explain that descriptive statistics are used in all kinds of research, including qualitative research.

▓ **Thematic Question**

According to Kenneth R. Hoover, what are the four uses of theory in social scientific thinking?

▓ **Thematic Question**

According to John Laub, what are the three central eras in theory development?

▓ **Thematic Question**

Would applied or pure research better inform public policy on crime? Why?

▓ **Thematic Question**

What is a hypothesis? How can researchers develop useful hypotheses to guide practical research?

▓ **Thematic Question**

What is operationalization? What would be one example of operationalization?

▓ **Thematic Question**

What is a research design? When would a research design be used?

▓ **Thematic Question**

What is a confounding effect? Give an example.

▓ **Thematic Question**

How would you compare and contrast internal and external validity? What are some examples of each?

▓ **Thematic Question**

What is a controlled experiment? How can controlled experiments be useful in the field of criminology?

▓ **Thematic Question**

What is a quasi-experimental design? How do such designs differ from "pure" experimental designs?

▓ **Thematic Question**

What is randomization? What is its usefulness in criminological research?

▓ **Thematic Question**

How do surveys collect data? What kinds of data can be gathered through the use of surveys?

▓ **Thematic Question**

When is it appropriate to use case studies? When might case studies not work?

▓ **Thematic Question**

How are data collected using participant observation? What should be the limits imposed on participant observers in criminological research?

▓ **Thematic Question**

How is self-reporting a subjective way of obtaining data? When is it most useful?

▓ **Thematic Question**

What is involved in secondary data-gathering techniques? When are they most useful?

■ Thematic Question

What is intersubjectivity? How can it be achieved?

■ Thematic Question

What is the difference between descriptive and inferential statistics?

Quantitative versus Qualitative Methods

■ Lecture Note

Explain that quantitative and qualitative research methods are used to address different kinds of research questions. Neither one of these is innately superior to the other; the main issue is which method is better suited for the research problem under consideration.

Values and Ethics in the Conduct of Research

■ Lecture Note

Illustrate the ethical dilemmas of research by discussing whether members of vulnerable populations, such as welfare recipients or incarcerated prisoners, can truly give informed consent.

■ Thematic Question

Why are ethical concerns a fundamental part of the research process?

■ Thematic Question

In what ways may a researcher's role as a scientist both interfere with and facilitate his or her ability to engage in participant observation research?

■ Thematic Question

How can researchers reduce pressures that they might face to produce findings in line with the current political stance on crime policy?

Social Policy and Criminological Research

■ Classroom Activity

Have students view the Web Extras in this chapter that contain the ethical guidelines of both the ASC and the ACJS and compare the two codes. What differences can they identify?

■ Lecture Note

Explain how punishment strategies always involve a political component.

■ Lecture Note

Discuss your own publication experiences or recent research or writing.

■ Thematic Question

In what ways has NIJ research funding influenced social policy?

The Research Report

■ Thematic Question

Ask students to list and describe the various sections typically found in a research report in the field of criminology.

CHAPTER 3

Classical and Neoclassical Thought

Major Principles of the Classical School

■ Lecture Note

Explain how assumptions associated with the Classical School of criminology are still a major part of criminological thought today.

■ Thematic Question

What are the major assumptions that underlie classical theories of crime causation?

■ Movies/Television

The series *Law and Order* can be used to illustrate the process of dealing with murder cases from the police through the trial process. Also use the program to illustrate how the social problems and social responsibility perspectives are both represented in the media.

Forerunners of Classical Thought

■ Classroom Activity

Ask students to use the Internet to gain further information on why the Code of Hammurabi is important to understanding modern criminal law.

■ Lecture Note

Explain that while common law formed the basis for the evolution of most statutory and case laws in the United States, certain states (such as Louisiana and Texas) were primarily influenced by the Napoleonic Code. Tell how some differences include a historically broader leeway in these states to use deadly force in the defense of property.

■ Lecture Note

Discuss how, during the Enlightenment, religion gave way to science as the dominant way of understanding social life. Give students examples that show why rationality is a superior way to approach social life.

■ Lecture Note

Note that several disciplines, including sociology, trace their early development to the Enlightenment thinkers.

■ Thematic Question

What are mores and folkways? How do they relate to formal legal notions of right and wrong?

■ Thematic Question

What are the differences between *mala in se* and *mala prohibita* offenses?

■ Thematic Question

Could there ever be one version of right and wrong that would be applicable to all societies and to all cultures? Why or why not?

■ Thematic Question

What are the four sources of the origins of law discussed in this chapter? Why is each important?

■ Thematic Question

What are the Twelve Tables? How do the Twelve Tables relate to the development of law?

■ Thematic Question

Whose version of human nature do you find more sensible: Thomas Hobbes's or John Locke's?

■ Thematic Question

What is natural law? How do atrocities like those committed by the 9/11 attackers relate to natural law? Can crimes against humanity be successfully identified and prosecuted without some notion of natural law?

The Classical School

■ Classroom Activity

Identify each assumption underlying classical theories that is stated in this chapter. Ask students to write down whether they agree or disagree with the assumptions identified, and ask them to tell why in one or two sentences. Return the students' responses at various points throughout the semester, and ask them whether they want to revise any of their original statements.

▓ Classroom Activity
Ask students to examine the U.S. Constitution and to report back on specific places where they see the influence of Beccaria's ideas.

▓ Classroom Activity
Break students into groups, and have them discuss Bentham's different types of punishment. Which of these types continue to operate in our current justice system? Why have some of the others become obsolete?

▓ Classroom Activity
Break students into groups, and ask them to come up with several examples of how crime prevention has become a routine part of everyday life.

▓ Lecture Note
Link structures like the Panopticon to evolving ideas about social control. For example, the Panopticon was characterized by enhanced visibility for those in control and by centralized management—all of which were facilitated through the use of technology and architectural design rather than intensive human labor.

▓ Thematic Question
What are the five principles derived from the Classical School that continue to characterize modern thinking about crime? In terms of criminal justice practice and policy, does fulfilling any one principle present problems in fulfilling another?

▓ Thematic Question
According to Cesare Beccaria, in what ways can punishment be effective? What elements are the most important for effective punishment?

▓ Thematic Question
What is the basic principle that underlies utilitarianism?

▓ Thematic Question
What are the five principles by which the Classical School operated?

Neoclassical Criminology
▓ Classroom Activity
Ask students to visit the Web Extras in this chapter that relate to the death penalty and to evaluate the kinds of information available.

▓ Lecture Note
Explain that positivism can be reconciled with notions of free will if one accepts soft determinism.

▓ Lecture Note
Use a hypothetical crime incident to illustrate the basic logic and key elements of Lawrence Cohen and Marcus Felson's routine activities theory.

▓ Lecture Note
Criminologists other than Jack Katz have examined the extent to which breaking the rules becomes a source of thrills. Describe other research that describes the extent to which delinquency is fun.

▓ Lecture Note
Give examples of access control and target hardening by focusing on the increased popularity of devices that individuals in our society use to protect their homes and themselves.

▓ Lecture Note
Use a hypothetical situation to illustrate the four objectives of situational crime prevention that this chapter discusses.

▓ Lecture Note
Discuss with students the problem of how situational crime prevention and strategies like target hardening can lead to displacement of crime.

▓ Lecture Note
Discuss how social disorganization links to rational choice theory.

▓ Thematic Question
What factors undermined some of the assumptions of positivism during the 1970s?

▓ Thematic Question
To what extent does your everyday routine make you susceptible to becoming the victim of certain crimes? What kinds of crimes might you be most vulnerable to?

▓ Thematic Question
What are the benefits of focusing crime-prevention efforts on places rather than on people?

▓ Thematic Question
Why is the failure to consider emotional states a problem with rational choice theory?

▓ Thematic Question
How is crime rewarding for those who commit it? How can rewards be reduced?

▓ Thematic Question
What might be some situational factors that precipitate criminal incidents? Use the Web Extras in this chapter for help answering this question.

▓ Thematic Question
What are the key strengths and weaknesses of situational crime prevention?

▓ Thematic Question
What is displacement? What are its implications for crime-control policy?

▓ Movies/Television
The Sopranos was a long-running series that dealt with a modern-day Mafia family. The "head" of the family and some other characters are complex, and the story lines follow their enjoyment of their criminal lifestyle as well as the consequences of their life choices.

Punishment and Neoclassical Thought
▓ Classroom Activity
Have students relate and then discuss their perspectives on capital punishment.

▓ Lecture Note
Distinguish between specific and general deterrence by focusing on which one has the greater potential to reduce crime.

▓ Lecture Note
Explore with students why the just deserts approach appears to be such a popular approach to punishment.

▓ Lecture Note
Explain that while *recidivism* can be defined simply as a return to crime, precise measures of this concept vary across research studies. Although this is problematic in that it limits the ability to compare findings across research studies, explain that it can be turned into an asset as well. If research studies tailor recidivism measures to the evaluation of specific programs, crime policy could proceed more effectively.

▓ Lecture Note
Use the crime funnel (Figure 3–2) to illustrate the due process safeguards of our criminal justice system and the priority attached to democratic principles.

Lecture Note

Note the fallibility of the criminal justice system by pointing out how a significant number of wrongful convictions have been shown to occur in capital punishment cases. Ask why it is, given such mistakes, that our society continues to support capital punishment.

Lecture Note

Discuss with students the due process implications of speeding up the process of carrying out death sentences.

Lecture Note

Explain that the relevance of the *McCleskey* v. *Kemp* case was that it was based on claims of a systemic effort of racism in the imposition of the death sentence. Explain why such an argument is difficult to make in a legal system like ours that looks at the particulars of a given case.

Thematic Question

How would you compare and contrast the general perspectives on punishment held by the classical and neoclassical thinkers? What differences can you identify?

Thematic Question

The just deserts model is concerned with punishment that is proportional to the offense committed. How is consensus on proportionality achieved?

Thematic Question

From a deterrence perspective, under what conditions is punishment the most effective deterrent?

Thematic Question

How would you evaluate the claims made by advocates and opponents of the death penalty? Which arguments do you find the most compelling?

Thematic Question

What do research studies reveal about the just application of capital punishment?

Thematic Question

Are there elements of racism in the imposition of capital punishment today? Explain your response.

Movies/Television

The Executioner's Song details the true-life story of serial killer Gary Gilmore.

Movies/Television

Dead Man Walking offers a compelling and gritty view of the moral implications of using capital punishment.

Policy Implications of the Classical School

Lecture Note

Discuss with students the difficulty in predicting the future dangerousness of a particular person in terms of criminal behavior. Ask about the feasibility of incapacitation if the ability to predict dangerousness is faulty.

Lecture Note

Note that the work of Marvin Wolfgang involving chronic offenders has had enormous implications for the direction of criminal justice research and policy.

Lecture Note

Explain how Wolfgang's research demonstrated the benefits of longitudinal research and supported the claim that the propensity for offending is not spread equally across the population of offenders.

Thematic Question

How would you compare and contrast determinate sentencing and truth-in-sentencing practices? How would the social problems and social responsibility perspectives argue for one or the other?

Thematic Question

How does the text critique classical theory? What is your response to this critique?

Thematic Question

What is meant by the term *law-and-order advocate*?

A Critique of Classical Theories

Thematic Question

How did Beccaria, the Enlightenment and classical thinkers influence the creation of the U.S. Constitution?

CHAPTER 4
Biological Roots of Criminal Behavior

Introduction

Thematic Question

If we are serious about addressing explanations for crime in a holistic manner, shouldn't we explore all possible avenues of explanation? With this point in mind, what is your reaction to biological theories of crime?

Major Principles of Biological Theories

Lecture Note

Students may be skeptical of the usefulness of biologically based theories of crime. Make it clear to them that the scientific methodology that guides current research on biology and criminality is sound and rigorous and is not characterized by the same racist motivations that characterized past efforts.

Thematic Question

What are the basic assumptions that underlie biological theories of crime? Do you find any of these assumptions to be problematic? Explain your response.

Biological Roots of Human Aggression

Classroom Activity

Have students research studies linking testosterone levels and crime commission. Then ask them if the researchers they identified would have focused on the role of testosterone as a possible explanation for crime if they did not already know from other sources, such as arrest rates, that males have greater involvement in crime than females. What does this say about the direction of science and explanations for crime?

Classroom Activity

Break students into groups, and have them consider this question: "Are violence and aggression the same? If not, can biological theories of crime explain one better than the other? Explain your response."

Classroom Activity

Break students into groups, and ask them to consider what evidence supports the belief that disproportionate involvement of men in crime is more culturally than biologically based. Are they persuaded by these points? Ask them to explain.

▓ Lecture Note

Explain that certain forms of schizophrenia can be controlled through diet. If a mental illness can be so controlled, it is equally plausible that crime could be so controlled.

▓ Lecture Note

Provide several examples that illustrate how factors like social integration may mediate the effect of biological entities on behavior. Illustrate by using the scenario that opens this chapter as a basis for your speculation. What mediating factors might have changed the life course of the man studied by Russell Swerdlow and Jeffrey Burns?

▓ Lecture Note

Discuss Lombroso's notion of a "born criminal."

▓ Lecture Note

Lombroso argued that female offenders were particularly vile because their essential nature was opposed to criminality, so women involved in crime were "enormously wicked." Discuss the many biases that factored into Lombroso's "scientific research."

▓ Lecture Note

Explain that most of the research linking biology to criminal behavior is based on correlational research studies—studies that are quite weak in demonstrating a causal role of biology with crime. Link this information back to Chapter 2 by reminding students that correlation is not causation.

▓ Lecture Note

Discuss the ways in which lead exposure has been linked to crime.

▓ Thematic Question

Are there particular types of crimes that are best addressed through biologically based crime theories? Explain.

▓ Thematic Question

What contributions did Cesare Lombroso make to biological theories of crime? How did Charles Darwin's work influence Lombroso?

▓ Thematic Question

What did the research of Earnest Hooton contribute to biological theories of crime? Discuss criticisms of Hooton's research.

▓ Thematic Question

What was the body-type typology developed by William H. Sheldon?

▓ Thematic Question

How is sugar consumption possibly linked with crime?

▓ Thematic Question

How might chemical imbalances in the body contribute to criminal activity?

▓ Thematic Question

Are the research studies linking testosterone to aggression saying that there is a link between testosterone and criminal activity? Explain.

▓ Thematic Question

What hormones, other than testosterone, has research linked with delinquent and criminal behavior?

Genetics and Crime

▓ Lecture Note

In February 2001, a resolution to express profound regret by the state for the eugenics movement was passed by the House of Delegates and the Senate in Virginia, making Virginia the first state to denounce this history. Point out that such efforts to discredit past practices serve to further current biological initiatives that are based on sound scientific methods.

▓ Lecture Note

Explore the extent to which the XYY "supermale" is still part of the public consciousness.

▓ Lecture Note

An extreme conclusion to reach from exploring the genetic basis for crime is that society plays no role in the production of crime. Discuss the implications of this conclusion with students by applying the social problems and social responsibility perspectives that characterize this text.

▓ Lecture Note

Discuss the culturally based reasons for women's involvement in crime.

▓ Lecture Note

Explain that race is primarily a social rather than scientific category.

▓ Thematic Question

Who were the Juke and Kallikak families? What significance does study of these families hold for criminology?

▓ Thematic Question

How is the possession of an extra Y chromosome said to be related to criminal activity? Is this argument primarily based on science? Explain.

▓ Thematic Question

What is the focus of the field of behavioral genetics?

▓ Thematic Question

What have studies of identical and fraternal twins revealed about the role of genetics in crime causation?

▓ Thematic Question

What is the Human Genome Project? What is its relevance to the field of criminology?

▓ Thematic Question

What are some of the key problems facing researchers who link genetics to criminal behavior?

▓ Thematic Question

How does gender affect involvement in crime?

▓ Thematic Question

What was Freda Adler's argument regarding women's involvement in crime?

▓ Movies/Television

The film *Jackie Brown* features an odd assortment of criminals, each of whom has some connection to a half-million dollars. The title character is the one "playing both sides of the fence" in this cat-and-mouse game of who has the money now.

Sociobiology

▓ Lecture Note

Ask students to consider how insights drawn from sociobiology might be applied to the principles of natural law.

▓ Thematic Question

What is sociobiology? According to the work of Edward O. Wilson, what are the primary assumptions that underlie this perspective?

▓ Thematic Question

What are the primary criticisms of sociobiological perspectives on crime? How would you evaluate these criticisms?

Biosocial and Psychosocial Criminology

▓ Thematic Question

What constitutional factors did James Q. Wilson and Richard Herrnstein cite for their contributions to crime?

▨ Thematic Question
Why might the perspective of Hans Eysenck be labeled *biopsychology*?

▨ Thematic Question
What is the basic premise of Terrie Moffitt's two-path theory of criminality?

Policy Implications of Biological Theories
▨ Thematic Question
How does C. Ray Jeffery characterize a model program on crime derived from the insights of biology?

▨ Thematic Question
How would you evaluate Jeffery's insights about replacing the philosophy of the "right to punishment" with the "right to treatment" from either the social responsibility or the social problems perspective?

▨ Thematic Question
Lee Ellis and Anthony Walsh contend that criminal behavior is too complex to be accounted for by a gene and that biological links to criminal behavior are indirect. After reading this chapter, do you believe that studying these indirect biological links to crime is worthwhile? Why or why not?

Critiques of Biological Theories
▨ Thematic Question
What are some of the key problems found in the research linking biological factors to crime? Do these factors invalidate the importance of examining biology as an explanatory source of crime? Explain.

CHAPTER 5

Psychological and Psychiatric Foundations of Criminal Behavior

Introduction
▨ Thematic Question
Ask students to answer the question raised in the introduction to this chapter: How can many killers seem so "normal" before exploding into criminality, giving no hints of the atrocities they are about to commit?

Major Principles of Psychological Theories
▨ Thematic Question
What distinguishes psychological explanations of crime from other explanations?

▨ Lecture Note
Explain that the effect of antisocial personality on criminal behavior is not always direct; that is, antisocial personality might contribute to criminality, but it is not necessarily the *cause* of crime commission.

▨ Thematic Question
What are the general assumptions that underlie the majority of psychological theories of crime? Might some of these assumptions be shared with other perspectives on crime causation? Explain.

▨ Movies/Television
The film *Pulp Fiction* investigates several interrelated stories of criminals who exhibit both good and evil tendencies. The extreme depictions of violence in this film were upsetting to many viewers.

Early Psychological Theories
▨ Thematic Question
What are the differences between psychological criminology and psychiatric criminology?

▨ Classroom Activity
Have students go to the Web sites provided in the text on antisocial personality. Ask students to bring back information on treatment approaches and to be prepared to discuss whether they think that these approaches would prevent or inhibit the link with criminal behavior.

▨ Lecture Note
Explain that changes in terminology that appear in publications like the American Psychiatric Association's DSM-IV reflect ongoing scientific research relevant to psychological classification. Mention, as an example, that in 1974 the APA voted to remove homosexuality from its list of diseases.

▨ Lecture Note
Inform students that some of the theories they will encounter in later chapters have a psychological component. Travis Hirschi's social control theory, for example, includes a key component that he labels "attachment," which is essentially the development of a conscience.

▨ Lecture Note
Explain that Freud had many interests but did not engage in the systematic study of criminals. Ask whether the study of psychiatric patients who exhibit patterns of abnormality that do not intersect with crime can assist in the understanding of criminal behavior.

▨ Thematic Question
What does it mean to say that "twin threads ran through early psychological theories"? What are some examples of each thread?

▨ Thematic Question
What is a psychopath? Why is a psychopath difficult to identify?

▨ Thematic Question
Why are individuals who are diagnosed as having antisocial personalities at an increased risk of involvement in criminal behavior?

▨ Thematic Question
Is it a significant problem that most research on the link between antisocial personality and criminal behavior has involved primarily male subjects? Explain.

▨ Thematic Question
How do you think the philosopher John Locke might respond to the fact that forensic psychology gives little attention to the role of the social environment on individual behavior after a certain point in the life course?

▨ Movies/Television
The film *Natural Born Killers* examines two serial killers who become media sensations.

▨ Movies/Television
The film *Reservoir Dogs* focuses on a group of criminals organized to pull off a major robbery. The robbery goes wrong, and the film follows the characters as they try to identify who among them is the traitor.

▨ Movies/Television
Fargo deals with a kidnapping plot by an inept husband that goes wrong in the hands of dangerous yet incompetent criminals. The suspense of the film is offset by its comic aspects and its stark Midwestern setting.

Criminal Behavior as Maladaptation

▓ Classroom Activity

Ask students to break into groups and come up with examples to support Dollard's assertion that "aggression is a natural consequence of living." Have the students provide healthy ways in which they experience this on a daily basis.

▓ Lecture Note

Discuss Freud's work on personality, and review the concepts of id, ego, and superego.

▓ Lecture Note

Explain that most neurotics do not become involved in criminal behavior. Discuss with students how such a form of mental illness may contribute to criminality in some instances but not in others.

▓ Lecture Note

Explain that some forms of schizophrenia may be controlled through diet and nutrition. Link this back to the material from Chapter 4 on the role of biology in human behavior.

▓ Lecture Note

Explain the psychoanalytical term *displacement,* to include that type of violence that is vented on something or someone who is not the source of the original frustration. Discuss the relationship between displacement and crime.

▓ Thematic Question

How is criminal behavior viewed from the perspective of psychoanalytic theory?

▓ Thematic Question

What are Freud's three components to personality? How do they relate to criminal behavior?

▓ Thematic Question

If Freud's concept of sublimation is a primary explanation for criminal motivation, would sociological explanations of crime still be possible?

▓ Thematic Question

What is psychosis? How does it relate to criminality?

▓ Thematic Question

What is the link between frustration and aggression?

▓ Thematic Question

What is displacement? How does it relate to criminality?

▓ Thematic Question

What evidence has been offered to explain why individuals may displace aggression?

Crime as Adaptive Behavior

▓ Lecture Note

Provide examples to illustrate why some forms of behavior other than crime may serve the same adaptive needs as crime. Illustrate how these choices may vary due to factors such as environment and opportunity.

▓ Thematic Question

In what ways can crime be understood as adaptive behavior? As maladaptive behavior?

▓ Thematic Question

Can you see any parallels in the thinking of Seymour Halleck on crime as adaptive behavior and Jack Katz's work, which is also discussed in the chapter?

Modeling Theory

▓ Classroom Activity

Ask students if they play video games such as *Quake.* Break them into groups where at least part of the group consists of players. Have them discuss with the other members of the group the type of television shows they watch, sports they play, and so forth. Is there a pattern? Do they think that video games and TV influence their worldview? Might it create a propensity toward violence in some people?

▓ Lecture Note

Explain that according to modeling theory, aggressive behavior may be learned through the modeling process. Ask whether this process is just as powerful in the case of impersonal entities (for example, television, movies, and video games) that might provide behavioral models as it is with personal entities (for example, other individuals). Does this distinction present a problem for modeling theory?

▓ Lecture Note

Tell the class that males continue to be rewarded in our society for being macho. Explain how technology to some extent has changed some culturally defined acceptable characteristics so that the computer nerd is now viewed differently than he or she used to be at one time. Ask students if they think that such an understanding can be effectively linked to rewards for crime.

▓ Thematic Question

What are the three laws of intimidation and suggestion that characterize Gabriel Tarde's theory of human behavior? Can you provide some examples for the law of insertion not included in the text?

▓ Thematic Question

What is the central contribution to criminology of Albert Bandura's modeling theory of aggression?

▓ Thematic Question

How is the acquiring of aggressive patterns of behavior distinct from the activation of such patterns? What implications does this distinction have for criminology?

▓ Thematic Question

What does Bandura mean by the term *disengagement*? How might this occur?

Behavior Theory

▓ Classroom Activity

Have students discuss how rewards and punishments might apply to some of their roles and daily activities. Ask whether they feel their behavior has been influenced by the rewards and punishments that they've personally experienced.

▓ Lecture Note

Discuss the relationship of crime to behavior theory. Ask how rewards might reinforce criminal behavior.

▓ Thematic Question

What are the basic ideas behind the stimulus–response approach to human behavior? How can reward and punishment explain crime?

▓ Thematic Question

How does behavior theory address both the origins of criminal behavior and the changes in already existing behavior? How might the principles of behavior theory be used to reform offenders?

▓ Thematic Question
Does behavior theory discount the role of cognition in human behavior? If so, why?

Attachment Theory
▓ Classroom Activity
Have students visit the Web Extra related to attachment theory. What are some of the most recent developments regarding the effectiveness of such approaches in explaining violent or destructive behavior in adulthood based on childhood difficulties?

▓ Lecture Note
Discuss the various forms that attachment can take.

▓ Thematic Question
According to John Bowlby's work on attachment theory, how can attachment take both healthy forms and unhealthy forms? How does delinquency fit into this schema?

Self-Control Theory
▓ Lecture Note
Explain to students that many theories of crimes that are primarily sociological in nature contain psychological elements. This is true of Michael Gottfredson and Travis Hirschi's general theory of crime and other theories such as Merton's strain theory.

▓ Lecture Note
Tell the class that Gottfredson and Hirschi's assumptions about human nature can be traced to Hobbes's ideas. Explain to students that the central question from this position is "Why don't people engage in crime?" rather than "Why do they engage in crime?" Ask why this distinction is important.

▓ Thematic Question
What is self-control? What are the four types that have been identified within the field of psychology?

▓ Thematic Question
How do Gottfredson and Hirschi argue for the role of self-control in generating crime?

Insanity and the Law
▓ Lecture Note
Tell the class that insanity is a legal rather than a medical concept. Explain the difference to students.

▓ Lecture Note
Link the insanity defense to the concept of *mens rea*, and explain the notion of criminal intent.

▓ Lecture Note
Explain how the concept of "guilty but mentally ill" conflicts with conventional understanding about the *mens rea* component of criminal intent.

▓ Thematic Question
Why is insanity a defense in cases of criminal prosecution? How do legal notions of insanity differ from psychiatric ones?

▓ Thematic Question
What is the Insanity Defense Reform Act? What are its origins?

▓ Thematic Question
How would you evaluate the verdict of "not guilty by reason of insanity" from both the social problems and social responsibility perspectives?

▓ Thematic Question
Is there only one type of insanity defense to criminal prosecution used across the United States? Explain.

▓ Thematic Question
What standard for insanity is used in the Model Penal Code of the American Law Institute?

▓ Thematic Question
How does the justice system handle those found "guilty but mentally ill"?

Social Policy and Forensic Psychology
▓ Lecture Note
Tell the class that we often use our knowledge about the past behavior of others to predict their future behavior. Ask how confident we want to be about our predictions before we make judgments. Also ask how past knowledge can lead to crime-control policies applicable to those who are known to have committed crimes.

▓ Thematic Question
If aggressiveness is stable over time, does this diminish the importance of the environmental context in understanding criminal behavior?

▓ Thematic Question
What is selective incapacitation? How does the concept of career criminals fit into this strategy?

▓ Thematic Question
Given the difficulty of identifying potentially violent offenders, how much faith do you have in the ability of selective incapacitation as an effective strategy to reduce and control crime?

Criminal Psychological Profiling
▓ Classroom Activity
Ask students to visit the FBI Web site at www.FBI.gov and to compare the information they find there on criminal profiling with the students' own ideas about criminal profiling taken from their everyday knowledge or exposure to the media.

▓ Lecture Note
Distinguish between the "reality" and the "myth" of criminal profiling.

▓ Thematic Question
What is psychological profiling, and how effective is it as a tool for the apprehension of criminal suspects?

▓ Movies/Television
The film *The Silence of the Lambs* deals with the connection between a cannibalistic serial killer, Dr. Hannibal Lecter, and an FBI profiler who seeks his help on another serial killer's case. This film started the public fascination with profiling.

▓ Movies/Television
Copycat deals with a psychiatrist who has been housebound ever since she was almost killed by a serial killer whom she testified against in court. Two homicide detectives working another serial killer's case bring her in to assist with finding the killer.

CHAPTER 6
Social Structure Theories

Introduction
▓ Lecture Note
Explain social structure to students by using simple examples to show that the institutional arrangements that constitute social structure are diverse and varied, ranging from the simple to the complex. Link this to the distinction between micro and macro levels of social life.

Major Principles of Sociological Theories

Thematic Question

What general assumptions underlie the sociological approach to crime causation?

Thematic Question

What are the three key sociological explanations for crime?

Thematic Question

What one factor do all social structure theories of crime causation have in common? Why do you think this is the case?

Movies/Television

New Jack City explores the cocaine underworld by examining the lives of drug dealers. The luxury of the dealers' lifestyles is depicted alongside violence and a constant sense of urgency.

Definitions of Social Structure Theories

Lecture Note

As you go through the different social structure theories, give examples of the types of societal changes that were going on during the development of particular theories (for example, social disorganization theory focused on increased urbanization and immigration).

Movies/Television

TV series such as *Law and Order* explore the background factors involved in murder cases that come to the attention of the police and the prosecutors.

Types of Social Structure Theories

Classroom Activity

Break the class into groups, and have them identify ways in which their everyday activities are consistent with concepts of defensible space (for example, factors that make it hard to break into dorm rooms or physically access protected computers).

Lecture Note

Emile Durkheim noted that even a society of saints would find it necessary to define certain acts as deviant. Use this to explain what Durkheim meant by the statement that "crime is normal."

Lecture Note

Mention to the students that the University of Chicago emerged as the most influential department of sociology during the middle of the twentieth century. Link this to Jane Addams's work at Hull House.

Lecture Note

Explain to students the important role that social research played in the work of criminologists and sociologists at the University of Chicago during the 1930s.

Lecture Note

Explain that the concept of community was an essential part of the crime perspective of the Chicago School.

Lecture Note

Use the example of your own campus to discuss the concept of environmental criminology.

Lecture Note

Robert Merton stated that the best solution to the crime problem was to raise the opportunity structure of society. Relate this to both the social problems and social responsibility perspectives.

Lecture Note

Explain to the class that Merton's theory was developed in order to explain deviance in general, not just crime. Note that the academic community's faith in grand theories has shifted since Merton's time.

Lecture Note

Explain to students that while the factors producing strain in Merton's model are sociological, strain itself is essentially a psychological concept.

Lecture Note

Explain to students that Merton conceptualized financial success as *the* goal prescribed for all. Tell them that this has always been problematic; after all, is it really the main goal for all members of such a diverse society as ours?

Lecture Note

Tell the class that the original article that Merton wrote offering his theory on structural strain is the most quoted article in sociology.

Lecture Note

Mention that Merton's original article detailing his theory lay dormant for many years until Albert Cohen commented on the article. Note that Cohen's ideas concerning reaction formation are built on an acceptance of Merton's basic premise.

Lecture Note

Provide students with examples of how subcultures characterize all types of social life, such as NASCAR fans or fans of rap music.

Lecture Note

Explain that Richard Cloward and Lloyd Ohlin were involved in public-policy efforts to change the opportunity structure of society in a way that few academics ever do. Discuss with students the problematic nature of such involvement (for example, sociologists realize real social change takes time, whereas politicians are driven by wanting results in a short interval of time).

Lecture Note

Explain that while Merton's structural strain theory focused only on the absence of legitimate opportunity structure, Cloward and Ohlin introduced the concept of the availability of illegitimate opportunity structures. Note that this addresses one problem in Merton's analysis—why some individuals who are strained choose one adaptation to anomie over another.

Lecture Note

Cohen stated that the "delinquent is a rogue male." Link Cohen's ideas back to Bandura's ideas from Chapter 5 that some individuals, such as males, may be rewarded for aggressive behavior.

Lecture Note

Discuss how the gang image has become part of popular culture.

Thematic Question

What were the major sources of social disorganization identified in early social ecology perspectives?

Thematic Question

What is the ecological school of criminology? How does the concept of social pathology fit into this model?

Thematic Question

According to Clifford Shaw and Henry McKay, why does delinquency exhibit remarkably stable rates over time in the same locales?

Thematic Question

What is meant by the "Chicago School" of criminology?

Thematic Question

How did the Chicago School researchers pioneer the use of particular types of research?

Thematic Question

How is it that particular locales can have characteristics conducive to crime?

▦ Thematic Question
What is the broken windows perspective?

▦ Thematic Question
What is *anomie*, and how does it lead to deviance?

▦ Thematic Question
What is relative deprivation? How does it relate to distributive justice?

▦ Thematic Question
What are the basic insights offered by Robert Agnew's general strain theory?

▦ Thematic Question
What type of research support can be found for Agnew's general strain theory?

▦ Thematic Question
What are the basic assumptions of culture conflict? What are the two types of culture conflict described by Thorsten Sellin?

▦ Thematic Question
How might adherence to the everyday routines of one culture present problems for the individual when he or she enters another culture?

▦ Thematic Question
What is a subculture? How is it related to crime?

▦ Thematic Question
What did Walter Miller mean by the use of the term *focal concerns*? How do they contribute to delinquent subcultures?

▦ Thematic Question
What is drift, and how does it contribute to delinquency? How does the concept of "techniques of neutralization" fit into this approach?

▦ Thematic Question
What is the central point of Marvin Wolfgang and Franco Ferracuti's work on violent subcultures? What evidence supports the utility of this position?

▦ Thematic Question
To what extent, if at all, does the southern part of the United States represent a violent subculture?

▦ Thematic Question
What are "wholesale" and "retail" costs for homicide? How does this idea relate to violent subcultures?

▦ Thematic Question
How do illegitimate opportunity structures assist in explaining delinquency and criminal behavior? How is this associated with different types of subcultures?

▦ Thematic Question
What does Cohen mean by the term *reaction formation*? How does this influence the formation and content of delinquent subcultures?

▦ Thematic Question
What is the National Youth Gang Survey? What do the latest findings reveal about gangs?

▦ Movies/Television
Robert De Niro stars in *Casino*, the story of the Mafia's hold on Las Vegas gambling that centers on Sam "Ace" Rothstein, whose character was based on the real Frank Rosenthal.

▦ Movies/Television
Menace II Society chronicles life in the Los Angeles hood. While the lead character has a conventional value system, the violent and socially repressive nature of ghetto life is portrayed as an all-encompassing force.

▦ Movies/Television
Scarface stars Al Pacino as a modern-day Al Capone, in this case a Cuban refugee who rises to the top of the cocaine trade in Miami. Driven by his own character flaws and his growing addiction to his own product, the title character is assassinated in an extremely bloody final scene.

▦ Movies/Television
Gotti presents the rise and fall of real-life New York crime boss John Gotti, who rose through the ranks of the Gambino crime family.

▦ Movies/Television
Growing Up Gotti was a reality-based television show that followed the daily life of John Gotti's daughter, Victoria, and her three sons.

▦ Movies/Television
In the film *Gang Related*, Jim Belushi and rapper Tupac Shakur are two corrupt cops who rob and kill drug dealers, until one of their victims is revealed to be an undercover agent for the Drug Enforcement Administration. The cops then have to struggle to build a murder case to cover their tracks.

▦ Movies/Television
Released in 1990, *State of Grace* focuses on members of an Irish American mob known as the Westies.

Policy Implications of Social Structure Theories
▦ Lecture Note
Find current examples of activities such as the Chicago Area Project, and offer information that you glean from those Web sites to students.

▦ Thematic Question
What was the Chicago Area Project? What were its objectives?

Critique of Social Structure Theories
▦ Lecture Note
Tell the class that the title of the 1960s report issued by the President's Commission on Law Enforcement and Administration of Justice was "The Challenge of Crime in a Free Society." Explain how well that title captured the issue of policing deviance within a democratic society.

▦ Lecture Note
Explain that a problem with Merton's strain theory is an overreliance on wealth as the goal driving American society. Might there be other goals equally valued? Are all of us actually socialized to strive for wealth?

▦ Lecture Note
Explain that one problem with Merton's strain theory is that it does not account for the lower offending rates of women who by virtue of their disadvantaged social structural position should experience more strain and hence more deviance.

▦ Thematic Question
Do you think that social structure theories can only be used to argue from a social problems perspective? How could they form the basis of a social responsibility perspective?

▦ Thematic Question
What critiques of the Ecological School are offered in the text?

▦ Thematic Question
What are some criticisms of subcultural theories?

▦ Thematic Question
What factors are identified in the text as the primary deficits of social structure theories in general? How might you evaluate these deficits?

CHAPTER 7
Theories of Social Process and Social Development

Introduction
▧ Thematic Question
Ask what students know about the shooting at Columbine High School, which took place in 1999. What might have led to the shootings?

The Social Process Perspective
▧ Classroom Activity
Have students discuss the various factors that have been identified in both this chapter and previous chapters as "pushes toward crime" and "pulls toward crime."

▧ Thematic Question
What are social process theories?

▧ Thematic Question
What are the most prominent examples of theories under the umbrella of social process?

▧ Movies/Television
Boyz n the Hood involves both a father trying to teach his son right from wrong and a group of friends who are living in a neighborhood characterized by violence, unemployment, and poverty. All of the friends are using different means to leave their South Central Los Angeles neighborhood.

Types of Social Process Approaches
▧ Classroom Activity
Break the students into groups, and have them list ways in which they have been exposed to definitions both favorable to violating the law and unfavorable to violating the law. Link this to Edwin Sutherland's sixth proposition to explain how it is not simply exposure to criminal peers that leads to involvement in crime.

▧ Classroom Activity
Ask students to identify examples of current actions and programs associated with moral entrepreneurs.

▧ Classroom Activity
Have students analyze a particular social interaction from a dramaturgical perspective, paying special attention to what went on in the back and front regions.

▧ Lecture Note
Explain to students that the sixth and seventh of Sutherland's proposition are considered to be the most essential in terms of the theory's contributions.

▧ Lecture Note
Hold a discussion of how Sutherland's theory might explain the Virginia Tech or Columbine school shootings.

▧ Lecture Note
Explain how psychological variables were important in Robert Burgess and Ronald Akers's work.

▧ Lecture Note
Discuss the "symbolic process of identification" that is a central part of Daniel Glaser's theory.

▧ Lecture Note
Emphasize the influence of psychology on crime causation theory by pointing to Walter Reckless's notion of internal containment.

▧ Lecture Note
Connect the Virginia Tech and Columbine school shootings to Howard Kaplan's theory.

▧ Lecture Note
Discuss the influence of Emile Durkheim's work on the development of Travis Hirschi's theory.

▧ Lecture Note
Explain that Hirschi's social control theory has more empirical support than any other theory of crime or delinquency.

▧ Lecture Note
Explain that Hirschi adopts the view of human nature that was articulated by Thomas Hobbes. Consequently, he asks the question "Why don't people violate the rules more often than they do?" rather than "Why do people violate the rules?"

▧ Lecture Note
Discuss the connection of rational choice theory to the general theory of crime.

▧ Lecture Note
Tell students that Hirschi's theory of choice focuses on variation in the process of socialization (for example, some people are not as well bonded to society as others), whereas Sutherland's differential association theory focuses on variation in the content of socialization (for example, learning more definitions favorable to violating the law than definitions unfavorable).

▧ Lecture Note
Remind students that Hirschi's notion of "attachment" is akin to a conscience.

▧ Lecture Note
Explain that a significant problem in Hirschi's social control theory is the role of delinquent peer groups. Hirschi contends that the role of peer groups in producing delinquency is basically the idea that "birds of a feather flock together." Research supports a stronger role for peer groups than this and also suggests strongly that peer groups can disrupt already strong bonds.

▧ Lecture Note
Discuss what Howard Becker means by moral entrepreneurs and what role they play in his approach to labeling theory.

▧ Lecture Note
Discuss the relationship between primary and secondary deviance.

▧ Lecture Note
Explain that the process of labeling by the justice system may actually "shock" someone into stopping his or her offending.

▧ Lecture Note
Tell the class that rather than being a theory of crime causation, the focus of societal reaction is the development of a criminal career, the adoption of a deviant identity.

▧ Lecture Note
Tell the class that in his published works, Howard Becker has said that sociology was his hobby as a graduate student—something that he did for fun. Becker's "real" job was working as a jazz musician.

Lecture Note

Conduct a discussion to consider whether the process of shaming is possible in today's society.

Lecture Note

Discuss Erving Goffman's concept of stigma. Relate this to deviance.

Lecture Note

Explain that Goffman's work on total institutions was quite influential in the development of subcultural research in prisons.

Thematic Question

What is your initial response to the idea that criminal behavior is learned?

Thematic Question

What are the essential principles of Sutherland's differential association theory?

Thematic Question

To what extent does Burgess and Akers's theory of differential reinforcement expand on the original insights of Sutherland's differential association theory?

Thematic Question

How does Glaser's differential identification theory extend Sutherland's ideas expressed in differential association theory?

Thematic Question

Glaser places less emphasis on the intensity of association than did Sutherland, so what does he offer instead?

Thematic Question

What basic premise underlies Reckless's containment theory? What is the difference between internal and external containment?

Thematic Question

What is Kaplan's self-derogation theory?

Thematic Question

How are findings regarding self-derogation theory contradictory?

Thematic Question

According to Hirschi, what is the social bond? What are the four elements of the social bond, and how do they relate to involvement in crime?

Thematic Question

Can you identify some psychological elements in Hirschi's social control theory? How are they linked to social factors and conditions?

Thematic Question

Can low self-control as a primary factor in explaining criminal involvement be reconciled with the importance of social structure in explanation?

Thematic Question

What is Charles Tittle's control–balance perspective?

Thematic Question

According to Frank Tannenbaum, how do individuals come to see themselves as criminal or deviant? Is this perception possible without the comment of formal agents of social control?

Thematic Question

According to Edwin M. Lemert, what is the distinction between primary and secondary deviance, and how does this guide the adoption of a deviant identity?

Thematic Question

What is a self-fulfilling prophecy? What role does this play in continued deviance?

Thematic Question

In general, what unique ideas did labeling theory contribute to our understanding of crime?

Thematic Question

What is Becker's typology of delinquents, and what are some unique examples?

Thematic Question

In what key sense is John Braithwaite's theory of reintegrative shaming different from traditional labeling theory?

Thematic Question

What does the acronym RISE stand for?

Thematic Question

What two kinds of shaming form the core of Braithwaite's experimental research?

Thematic Question

How does Goffman use "discreditable disclosure" to apply a dramaturgical perspective to deviance?

Movies/Television

GoodFellas is a 1990 Martin Scorsese film that tells the story of real-life gangster Henry Hill. The film follows Hill's early days, his association with the Mafia during the 1950s, and his eventual entry into the Witness Protection Program.

Movies/Television

Based on the real-life case of undercover police officer Joe Pistone, *Donnie Brasco* tells his story of infiltrating the New York mob scene. Guided by a low-level member of the organized-crime world, the title character moves through the dangerous and often incompetent world of the Mafia hierarchy.

Policy Implications of Social Process Theories

Classroom Activity

Have students visit the Web sites provided in the text related to social control–based programs and bring additional information back for class discussion.

Thematic Question

What are some criticisms of labeling theory?

Critique of Social Process Theories

Lecture Note

Explain to students that labeling theory does not consider the possibility that contact with the criminal justice system may interrupt the process of deviance escalation.

Thematic Question

What are some criticisms of Sutherland's differential association theory?

The Social Development Perspective

Thematic Question

What is the basic insight into criminal behavior offered by the social development perspective?

Concepts in Social Development Theories

Classroom Activity

Have students go to the Web site for the Chicago Human Development Project and report back on some of the project's latest happenings.

▓ Lecture Note

Explain that several examples of classic research studies in criminology (for example, Marvin Wolfgang's *Delinquency in a Birth Cohort*) were concerned with factors consistent with a social development perspective.

▓ Lecture Note

Include in your discussion of developmental theories the notion that one strong recommendation made by the Panel on the Understanding and Control of Violent Behavior was multicommunity designs that focused on developmental studies of aggressive and violent behavior that integrated biological, individual, and social levels of analysis.

▓ Lecture Note

Explain trajectories and transitions by asking students to identify such items in their own progression from adolescence to adulthood.

▓ Lecture Note

Discuss the concept of social capital. Ask where the term came from.

▓ Lecture Note

Explain that Robert Sampson and John Laub's use of the concept of social capital builds strongly on the work of William Julius Wilson, a leading sociologist and scholar on urban poverty. Students can find Wilson's work on the Internet.

▓ Thematic Question

What are the seven development tasks that confront adolescents within our society according to life course researchers? Why are developmental changes important for understanding involvement in crime and delinquency?

▓ Thematic Question

What is a criminal career, and what are the four dimensions of criminal careers discussed in the text?

▓ Thematic Question

What is a trajectory within the context of life course theory, and what is its significance? How would you relate trajectories to the concept of turning points?

▓ Thematic Question

What three sets of dynamics are important to the life course perspective?

▓ Thematic Question

How does the concept of informal social control figure prominently in the work of Sampson and Laub?

▓ Thematic Question

In their reanalysis of the Gluecks' data, what two events in the life course did Sampson and Laub find to be especially important in reducing the likelihood of criminal offending in adulthood?

▓ Thematic Question

What is the basic premise of Terrie Moffitt's two-path theory of criminality?

▓ Thematic Question

What are persistence and desistance? How do they relate to each other?

▓ Thematic Question

What do research findings reveal about the factors that support positive development pathways?

▓ Thematic Question

How do the concepts of persistence and desistance factor into David Farrington's delinquent development theory?

▓ Thematic Question

What are the basic findings from the Cambridge Study in Delinquent Development?

▓ Thematic Question

What are the four components of desistance according to Rolf Loeber and Marc LeBlanc?

▓ Thematic Question

What is the goal of the Program of Research on the Causes and Correlates of Delinquency?

▓ Thematic Question

What were the three separate developmental pathways found in the Causes and Correlates study? How can such pathways converge?

▓ Movies/Television

To Live and Die in LA contends that a thin line may separate the good guys from the bad guys. Focusing on law enforcement, specifically a pair of Secret Service agents chasing a counterfeiter, this film offers a harsh look at the relationships of cops and informants.

▓ Movies/Television

Made during the 1980s, *At Close Range* stars Sean Penn as the son of a career criminal. The increasing involvement of father and son in crime comes to have deadly consequences.

Policy Implications of Social Development Theories

▓ Lecture Note

Explain that social development theories heavily utilize longitudinal research but that one problem with this is that data are not immediately available. Discuss the implications of this unavailability for the policy uses of research.

▓ Thematic Question

What types of existing programs reflect the perspective of social development theories?

▓ Thematic Question

Effective policy uses of research based on social development theories require the cooperation of various agencies including but not limited to criminal justice agencies and child protective services, so in what ways could such coordination be both essential to sound policy initiatives and problematic to implement?

▓ Thematic Question

What types of problems have been identified with social development theories? In what ways might research designs address these problems?

CHAPTER 8
Social Conflict Theories

Introduction

▓ Classroom Activity

Ask students to visit the Web site containing the Unabomber's manifesto and to retrieve sample text and comment on the manifesto.

Law and Social Order Perspectives

■ **Lecture Note**

Explain that a consensus perspective underlies certain theories such as Travis Hirschi's social control theory.

■ **Lecture Note**

Tell the class that Karl Marx's notion of social class was basically economic in that it was defined by relationship to means of production. Discuss how current stratification research has built more on Max Weber's use of status and power as also crucial to social class formation.

■ **Thematic Question**

Should the *New York Times* have published the Unabomber's manifesto? Why or why not?

■ **Thematic Question**

How would you compare and contrast the consensus, pluralist, and conflict perspectives? Which one do you support and why?

■ **Thematic Question**

How are the three perspectives on social organization compatible with a social problems and a social responsibility perspective?

■ **Thematic Question**

What are the four principles that characterize the consensus perspective?

■ **Thematic Question**

According to a pluralist perspective on social organization, how is conflict resolved?

■ **Thematic Question**

What is the role of law according to the conflict perspective on social organization?

■ **Thematic Question**

How was the differentiation between proletariat and bourgeoisie important for Marx's theory?

■ **Movies/Television**

In *Carlito's Way*, Al Pacino plays a Puerto Rican ex-con trying to go straight, but he has a difficult time due to both friends and enemies on the street that make for difficult choices.

Radical Criminology

■ **Classroom Activity**

Have students construct some crime-control policy initiatives that would likely flow from radical theory.

■ **Lecture Note**

Explain that while not advocating the end of capitalism, the logic of Robert Merton's strain theory purported that the way to attack crime was by altering the opportunity structure of society. Use this to illustrate that elements of radical theory exist in other theories.

■ **Lecture Note**

Explore the extent to which students believe that money buys justice. Use examples such as the O. J. Simpson trial, the murder trial of music producer Phil Spector, and Paris Hilton's ordered jail time to discuss whether a quality legal defense is available to individuals regardless of social class.

■ **Lecture Note**

Discuss how the collapse of the Soviet Union affected radical theory.

■ **Thematic Question**

What three historical circumstances contributed to the development of radical criminology?

■ **Thematic Question**

According to George Vold, what role does conflict play in contributing to crime?

■ **Thematic Question**

How did the early work of William Chambliss and Robert T. Seidman differ from the more traditional radical approach to criminology?

■ **Thematic Question**

How did Chambliss's work develop toward a more Marxist approach to criminology?

■ **Thematic Question**

What basic propositions did Richard Quinney develop as crucial for understanding crime?

■ **Thematic Question**

How can current radical criminology be divided into two schools?

■ **Thematic Question**

Is radical criminology more consistent with a social problems or a social responsibility perspective?

■ **Thematic Question**

What criticisms have been levied against radical criminology?

■ **Thematic Question**

What basic insights does critical criminology offer?

■ **Thematic Question**

According to Elliott Currie, what mechanisms operate in a market society to create crime?

Emerging Conflict Theories

■ **Classroom Activity**

Break students into groups, and ask them to identify ways in which gender significantly organizes elements of social life. Ask them to link these to the likelihood of criminal behavior.

■ **Lecture Note**

Discuss how researchers such as Walter DeKeseredy redirected leftist theories concerning the issues of crime.

■ **Lecture Note**

Explain that the development of feminist perspectives within criminology was furthered by the failure of radical theory to give attention to the role of gender in the production of crime and the response of the state to crime.

■ **Lecture Note**

Emphasize that as an explanatory variable, gender is a strong predictor of many aspects of criminal behavior, especially offending.

■ **Lecture Note**

Explain that, contrary to Freda Adler's proposed ideas, a careful review of the data did not support a convergence in offending patterns of men and women over time. Note that Adler's arguments concerning this kind of convergence were predicated on the assumption that biology was not a sound basis to argue for gender variations in crime.

■ **Lecture Note**

Explain that one of the problems in Adler's data analysis was the use of heterogeneous offense categories that ignored the specific offenses for which arrests of women were increasing (for example, simple assaults under violent crime).

▨ Lecture Note

Link the five major contributions of feminist thought offered by Susan Caulfield and Nancy Wonders to key propositions from other theories already discussed.

▨ Lecture Note

Explain to students that many of the classic theories of crime causation (for example, Cohen's reaction formation and Hirschi's social control theory) were formulated with only males in mind and furthermore were only tested with male samples.

▨ Lecture Note

Expand upon the idea of women's "ways of knowing" by discussing how gender structures almost every facet of our everyday lives.

▨ Lecture Note

Explain to students that to the extent that the chivalry hypothesis ever had any validity, it was not universally applied to all women (for example, white middle-class women certainly benefited more from this than women of color).

▨ Lecture Note

Tell the class that there are a broad variety of perspectives subsumed under the label of postmodern criminology, yet they all share a common belief that the ideas that guided thinking about modernity (especially the reliance on science) were problematic for understanding the nature of the social world after World War II.

▨ Lecture Note

Refer back to material related to the insanity defense in Chapter 5 to illustrate the application of semiotics to the study of law. Remind the class that insanity as a legal defense does not have a corresponding medical equivalent.

▨ Lecture Note

Illustrate how the application of semiotics inherent in constitutive criminology has strong implications for understanding from a social problems perspective.

▨ Lecture Note

A certain segment of postmodern approaches to criminology is argued to be critiques of other approaches in the absence of offering anything new of relevance or practicality. As academic criminology increases its applied focus and partnerships with practitioners, many of the insights of postmodern criminology seem too vague and obtuse to be of use.

▨ Lecture Note

Explain how the scientific method fits into postmodern theories of crime.

▨ Lecture Note

Peacemaking criminology and restorative justice have their roots in a humanist approach to sociology and other disciplines.

▨ Lecture Note

Ask students to what extent the system would have to change if restorative justice ideals guided more programs, practices, and policies within the criminal justice system.

▨ Lecture Note

Discuss the implications for crime policy that are suggested by the application of principles from radical criminology.

▨ Thematic Question

How do realist criminologists critique radical criminology?

▨ Thematic Question

How would you explain the ways that the perspective of left realism contains ideas consistent with both a social problems and a social responsibility perspective?

▨ Thematic Question

What types of policies derive from a left-realist perspective?

▨ Thematic Question

What is meant by the term *androcentricity*?

▨ Thematic Question

According to Kathleen Daly and Meda Chesney-Lind, what are the five elements of feminist thought?

▨ Thematic Question

Can men be feminists? Why or why not?

▨ Thematic Question

Which brand of feminism, if any, appeals most to you and why?

▨ Thematic Question

What evidence supports John Hagan's power-control theory?

▨ Thematic Question

According to postmodern criminology, what has been the key failing of past criminological approaches?

▨ Thematic Question

Why do approaches such as constitutive criminology focus on the sociology of law?

▨ Thematic Question

How is crime a "social construct"?

▨ Thematic Question

How is crime control socially constructed?

▨ Thematic Question

What is peacemaking criminology? Do you see any connection to elements of radical criminology discussed in this chapter? Explain.

▨ Thematic Question

What is restorative justice? What are some examples of programs based on this model?

▨ Thematic Question

Can restorative justice ideals support both a social problems and a social responsibility perspective? Why or why not?

▨ Thematic Question

Based on two of the theoretical perspectives discussed in this chapter, how would you compare and contrast the applications of their key principles in terms of implications for crime policy?

▨ Thematic Question

Based on two of the theoretical perspectives discussed in this chapter, how would you compare and contrast their applicability to a social problems or a social responsibility perspective?

▨ Movies/Television

Kill Bill, Vol. 1 and *Vol. 2*, follow the revenge of "the bride," a woman whose husband is murdered on her wedding day. The film is characterized by violence, action, humor, and sword fighting. It also challenges conventional notions of revenge as a male activity.

Policy Implications of Social Conflict Theories

■ **Thematic Question**

What are some of the policy implications of social conflict theories?

CHAPTER 9

Crimes against Persons

Introduction

■ **Thematic Question**

How are crime statistics valuable to policymakers?

The National Crime Victimization Survey (NCVS)

■ **Thematic Question**

How does the NCVS differ from the UCR Program?

The Uniform Crime Reporting (UCR) Program

■ **Thematic Question**

What is NIBRS? How is it an improvement over previous data-gathering strategies of the UCR Program?

Changing Crime Patterns

■ **Thematic Question**

What significant shifts in offense statistics does the chapter identify? What might have caused them?

Violent Crime Typologies

■ **Lecture Note**

Emphasize that typologies in general are conceptual devices used to organize complex information. Tell the class that a given typology will be more or less accurate depending on how it was created.

■ **Lecture Note**

Refer students back to discussions on data sources in the UCR/NIBRS and the NCVS, and emphasize that all such data sources rely on typologies to measure crime.

■ **Lecture Note**

Ask what kinds of distinctions are made between types of homicides and what additional distinctions might be made (whether there are certain kinds of homicides that are not enumerated but should be).

■ **Thematic Question**

What are typologies? What are violent-crime typologies?

■ **Thematic Question**

How do homicides differ in terms of factors such as victim–offender relationship, weapon used, and gender?

Murder

■ **Classroom Activity**

Ask students to identify ways in which the behavior, lifestyle, or actions of victims may contribute to victimization.

■ **Lecture Note**

Talk about the historically high homicide rates in the South, and ask why rates have been so high there.

■ **Lecture Note**

Refer students back to Chapter 6 and subcultural theory. Ask how the discussion in that chapter is relevant here.

■ **Lecture Note**

Clarify for students that offense categories such as homicide, rape, and robbery contain a heterogeneous group of behaviors, some of which are very dissimilar.

■ **Lecture Note**

Explain how victim precipitation is not about blaming the victim.

■ **Lecture Note**

Explain to students that understanding the role of weapons in homicides requires the simultaneous consideration of other factors such as intent and community medical resources.

■ **Lecture Note**

Examine why alcohol is so closely connected to violent crime.

■ **Lecture Note**

Refer students back to the information on gangs from the National Youth Gang Survey presented in Chapter 6. Ask how it is relevant here.

■ **Lecture Note**

Remind students of Sigmund Freud's notion of the death instinct explained in Chapter 5, and remind them that this is more myth than fact based on what is known about serial killers.

■ **Thematic Question**

According to the subculture of violence thesis, what is the primary motivation underlying homicide?

■ **Thematic Question**

How would you distinguish between primary and nonprimary homicides by applying the concepts of expressive and instrumental crimes to this two-part typology?

■ **Thematic Question**

What is the exposure-reduction theory of intimate homicide? How does it explain homicide?

■ **Thematic Question**

Why is it necessary to distinguish homicides by type if we are to better understand the factors that caused them?

■ **Thematic Question**

What is meant by the term *sibling offense*, and how has the term been used to explain patterns of homicide?

■ **Thematic Question**

How are guns a factor in homicide, and would gun control likely lead to fewer homicides in this country?

■ **Thematic Question**

How does Robert Nash Parker explain the role that alcohol plays in homicide?

■ **Thematic Question**

In what ways are alcohol and illicit drug use linked to crime?

■ **Thematic Question**

What typologies have been offered to highlight the role that gang membership may play in homicide?

■ **Thematic Question**
What distinguishes serial killing from mass murder?

■ **Thematic Question**
To what extent do you believe that the typologies offered for serial killers are useful for understanding these types of offenders and offenses?

■ **Thematic Question**
Is gender an important variable in understanding patterns of serial killers? Why or why not?

■ **Thematic Question**
Why is the apprehension of serial killers so difficult?

■ **Movies/Television**
Shows such as *Law and Order: Criminal Intent* follow the investigation of major crimes including but not limited to murder.

■ **Movies/Television**
Face/Off is a John Woo film in which the hero and villain exchange identities by literally swapping faces through plastic surgery.

■ **Movies/Television**
Blow chronicles the rise and fall of George Jung (Johnny Depp), who built an empire in the 1960s by selling marijuana and then cocaine.

■ **Movies/Television**
Gangs of New York documents the street warfare of rival gangs as they battle for turf in mid-nineteenth-century New York.

■ **Movies/Television**
Collateral stars Tom Cruise as a contract killer who recruits a cab driver named Max to drive him through Los Angeles one night. During the course of his cab ride, Cruise's character will execute five people in a ten-hour spree.

Rape

■ **Lecture Note**
If the role of law reflects only the position of the most powerful in society as radical criminology asserts, ask students how legislation that empowers female victims of violence, such as the VAWA, comes to be.

■ **Lecture Note**
Discuss with students the fact that change in the wake of legislative initiatives is normally slow to occur and requires some time to permeate society.

■ **Lecture Note**
Discuss with students the possible reasons behind forcible rape. What role does lust play?

■ **Lecture Note**
Focus on the assumptions underlying the psychopathological perspective on rape.

■ **Lecture Note**
Expand on the link between social disorganization and rape.

■ **Lecture Note**
Discuss why some writers claim that all men benefit from existing rape myths.

■ **Lecture Note**
Discuss how rape can be reduced in a society characterized by gender inequality.

■ **Thematic Question**
What are rape myths, and how do they contribute to violence against women?

■ **Thematic Question**
What was problematic about the common law definition of *rape*? How has the definition been changed by statute?

■ **Thematic Question**
Why was rape-law reform necessary? What needed reforming?

■ **Thematic Question**
What were the essential goals of rape-law reform? Have they been achieved?

■ **Thematic Question**
What are rape shield laws, and what is their relevance to rape-law reform?

■ **Thematic Question**
What are some of the findings that have been reported in research on the effectiveness of rape-law reform?

■ **Thematic Question**
Why is acquaintance rape referred to as a "hidden crime"?

■ **Thematic Question**
What was the importance of the Rideout case?

■ **Thematic Question**
Do you believe that addressing same-sex rape within male prisons should be a higher priority for criminal justice policy? Why or why not?

■ **Thematic Question**
What do feminists mean by the term *rape culture*? How does this contribute to the presence and prevalence of rape in our society?

■ **Thematic Question**
What is Nicholas Groth's typology of rape?

■ **Thematic Question**
What is the integrated theory of rape? How does it differ from other perspectives on rape?

■ **Thematic Question**
How is rape explained from an evolutionary perspective?

■ **Thematic Question**
What is the typology of rape offered by Robert Hazelwood and Ann Burgess?

■ **Thematic Question**
According to Dennis Stevens, what role does lust play in the motivations of rapists? Is Stevens's work totally inconsistent with a feminist perspective on rape? Explain.

■ **Thematic Question**
What is the feminist sociocultural perspective on rape offered by Diana Scully?

■ **Movies/Television**
The series *Law and Order: Special Victims Unit* follows the investigation of sexually based crimes by a squad in New York.

■ **Movies/Television**
In *The Accused*, Jodie Foster plays a woman who, while out on the town one night, is raped by a group of men in a bar. The efforts of the prosecutor to bring this case to trial and the difficulty of finding witnesses who will come forward are explored.

▓ Movies/Television

The film *Heat* follows the core members of a crew who specialize in large-scale robberies. The members are about to pull one last score before they all retire, but it does not go as simply as planned.

Robbery

▓ Lecture Note

Bring in previous material on the criminology of place, and use it to illustrate how personal and institutional robbery can be explained in different ways.

▓ Lecture Note

Link the material on homicide with that on robbery, and show how some homicide victims are also victims of robbery.

▓ Lecture Note

Explain that most robbers are generalists rather than specialists, and ask if there might be some offenders who specialize in just one kind of robbery.

▓ Lecture Note

Link target-hardening strategies with the material on robbery and public transport discussed here.

▓ Lecture Note

Discuss the extent to which robbers are rational actors.

▓ Lecture Note

Examine the extent to which street values inform the dynamics of drug robberies.

▓ Lecture Note

Remind students of the idea of subcultures, which give substantial context to the lives of drug robbers.

▓ Lecture Note

Ask why robbery is typically understood as a "male" crime and why there aren't more female robbers.

▓ Thematic Question

Are the distinctions between personal and institutional robbery important? Why or why not?

▓ Thematic Question

How is robbery associated with other crimes?

▓ Thematic Question

What is the distinction between robbers as specialists and generalists?

▓ Thematic Question

According to Martha J. Smith and Ronald V. Clarke, what are the possible motivations for robbery in public-transport settings?

▓ Thematic Question

Do you agree with the ruling of the New York Court of Appeals regarding the policies of the Taxi-Livery Task Force? Why or why not?

▓ Thematic Question

According to the research of Richard Wright and his colleagues at the University of Missouri, what is the basic motivational context of street robbery?

▓ Thematic Question

How does the rationality of street robbers require an understanding of their everyday environments?

▓ Thematic Question

What are the different ways in which drugs figure prominently in street robbery?

▓ Thematic Question

Why are drug dealers attractive targets for robbery?

▓ Thematic Question

In what ways are street robberies gendered?

▓ Movies/Television

The Italian Job centers on a group of big-time thieves who are going for the largest score of their lives. Betrayal by one of the members and the path to revenge take up most of the film's time.

▓ Movies/Television

In *The Score*, Robert De Niro plays a professional thief who is lured into carrying out one last job by an old associate.

Assault

▓ Classroom Activity

Ask students to discuss ways in which random violence and stranger violence are linked to the everyday view of crime that most people have.

▓ Lecture Note

Discuss the importance of victim–offender relationships in any examination of assault.

▓ Lecture Note

Ask why the family context in which many assaults occur is so important from a public-policy perspective on crime.

▓ Lecture Note

Focus on the concept of separation assault, including its nature and its consequences.

▓ Thematic Question

Why is it important to study assault?

▓ Thematic Question

According to Marc Riedel, what are the two primary types of relationships found in stranger violence?

▓ Thematic Question

What are some of the reasons that criminal justice practitioners and academic criminologists were reluctant to focus on family violence?

▓ Thematic Question

What was the data source for early studies of family violence?

▓ Thematic Question

What do available FBI/NIBRS data reveal about the patterns of family violence? How do characteristics of family violence differ from overall violence?

▓ Thematic Question

What is the NVAW Survey? What purpose does it serve?

▓ Thematic Question

Why are simplistic responses such as "if you're hit, just leave" to the problem of intimate-partner violence inappropriate?

▓ Thematic Question

Based on James Ptacek's research on battered women in the courtroom, what are the types of control strategies used by men?

▨ Thematic Question
What are some characteristics of individuals and locales that are associated with a greater likelihood of intimate-partner violence?

▨ Movies/Television
Set It Off follows a group of young African American women in Los Angeles who are trying to turn their lives around and achieve their dreams. A series of events places them in a situation where they decide to start robbing banks to solve their problems.

Other Forms of Interpersonal Violence

▨ Lecture Note
Explain that not all workplaces have the same likelihood of experiencing violence, and ask why.

▨ Lecture Note
Ask why it is so difficult to identify and measure hate crimes. How do we know for sure when a hate crime has taken place?

▨ Lecture Note
Explain to students that antistalking laws may function well to prevent the escalation of violence among individuals.

▨ Lecture Note
Focus on how fear factors into the definition of *stalking* used in the NVAW Survey.

▨ Lecture Note
Discuss the association between stalking and ending a relationship.

▨ Lecture Note
Focus on the responses of women to stalking, and discuss how this is a life-changing event.

▨ Lecture Note
Discuss cyberspace-security initiatives.

▨ Thematic Question
What types of violent crime are found in the workplace?

▨ Thematic Question
How are hate groups tied to hate crimes? Is the link between such groups and crime inevitable?

▨ Thematic Question
Why is it so difficult to develop hate-crime laws that satisfy everyone?

▨ Thematic Question
To what extent is stalking both old and new behavior?

▨ Thematic Question
What are the key elements of the variation in state statutes on stalking?

▨ Thematic Question
To what extent is stalking a crime problem?

▨ Thematic Question
What definition of *stalking* is used in the NVAW Survey?

▨ Thematic Question
How does gender factor into the stalking experience?

▨ Thematic Question
What are some of the key characteristics of both stalking offenders and victims? Do any of these characteristics run counter to existing stereotypes concerning stalking?

▨ Thematic Question
What other behaviors often accompany stalking activity?

▨ Thematic Question
What reasons are frequently offered for not reporting stalking victimization to the police?

▨ Thematic Question
Generally speaking, how satisfied are stalking victims with police response?

▨ Thematic Question
What aspects of cyberstalking make it difficult to effectively control?

▨ Movies/Television
American History X tells the story of Derek Vinyard (Edward Norton), a neo-Nazi leader of a skinhead gang of Venice Beach, California. Sent to prison for murdering a black man, Norton's character has an epiphany in prison; when released, he rejects his former affiliation and attempts to change the course of his younger brother's life. Use this movie to stimulate a discussion on the role of hate groups in the commission of hate crimes.

CHAPTER 10
Crimes against Property

Introduction
▨ Lecture Note
Mention that this chapter says, "Professional criminals are rare in the world of theft." Ask why that is the case.

▨ Lecture Note
Discuss the fact that Bernard Welch was not a typical burglar.

▨ Movies/Television
Entrapment features a lead character who is a master thief thought to be long retired, while a hotshot insurance investigator assigned to his case is his foil.

▨ Movies/Television
The Thomas Crown Affair portrays a sophisticated thief who steals art.

Persistent and Professional Thieves
▨ Classroom Activity
Ask students to analyze the decision-making context of a recent life event (for example, coming to college, breaking up with a girlfriend or boyfriend). Have them diagram the key turning points in a flow chart, giving particular attention to the temporal sequence of events. Discuss these in class, and identify where bounded rationality is at work in most decisions we make.

▨ Lecture Note
Relate the material on the sporadic nature of most property offending back to the lack of rigid specialization also found among robbery offenders.

▨ Lecture Note
Have students review the material on life course theories from Chapter 7, and ask them if concepts of the life cycle apply to thieves.

▨ Lecture Note
Discuss what Malcolm Klein means by "cafeteria-style offending." Relate this to John Hepburn's concept of "occasional offenders."

▓ Lecture Note
Describe offense specialization, and ask whether persistent or professional thieves are more likely to engage in such specialization.

▓ Lecture Note
Focus on the problematic nature of applying the career concept to criminal offenders.

▓ Lecture Note
Discuss how rationality enters into the decision making of most property offenders.

▓ Thematic Question
What is the basic distinction between a persistent and a professional thief?

▓ Thematic Question
What are some of the descriptions of professional thieves that have been offered?

▓ Thematic Question
What is your first impression when you hear the term *criminal career*?

▓ Thematic Question
According to Alfred Blumstein, what are the phases of a criminal career?

▓ Thematic Question
What types of diverse behaviors are included under the general term *larceny-theft*?

▓ Movies/Television
Steven Spielberg's *Catch Me If You Can* tells the true story of Frank W. Abagnale, Jr., who began writing bad checks in his teenage years and quickly progressed to successfully posing as a pilot, a doctor, and a lawyer. He was pursued by the FBI, and Abagnale's story as a criminal was over by the time he was in his early twenties. Abagnale now tours the country giving talks on protection against theft.

▓ Movies/Television
The Thief portrays a jewel thief who has spent most of his life in and out of prisons, where he was apprenticed to a master thief.

Larceny-Theft

▓ Classroom Activity
Ask students to discuss personal experiences of theft on campus or to describe instances of campus theft that they have heard about.

▓ Lecture Note
Explain that employee theft is a big problem in small businesses where such behavior can dramatically affect the financial stability of the businesses.

▓ Lecture Note
Discuss the kinds of things that distinguish the typical shoplifter from shoplifters like Winona Ryder.

▓ Lecture Note
Bring the material on life cycle theories into the discussion of offenses such as joyriding and shoplifting that are strongly associated with adolescence. Ask the class what turning points or trajectories could halt the participation of youths in such offenses.

▓ Lecture Note
Explain that the notion of gateway activity is applied in the drug-use literature to argue that one rationale for criminalizing a drug such as marijuana is that it is a gateway drug. Note that if it is based on sound research, this reflects a preventive approach to crime in line with a public-health perspective.

▓ Lecture Note
Ask the class how typologies help criminologists to prevent shoplifting.

▓ Lecture Note
Discuss crimes that have a "thrill factor." Ask what such crimes might be.

▓ Lecture Note
Link the material on environmental criminology to the nature of theft on college campuses.

▓ Thematic Question
Are crime-prevention techniques aimed at employee theft also effective in preventing shoplifting?

▓ Thematic Question
Which causes a greater loss to retail establishments, shoplifting or employee theft?

▓ Thematic Question
What are the characteristics of shoplifting offenders? Is there a typical profile?

▓ Thematic Question
How are the offenses of joyriding and shoplifting associated with adolescence in general? How would life cycle theorists such as Robert Sampson explain this association?

▓ Thematic Question
What is a gateway offense? Are you for or against the view of shoplifting as a gateway offense to more serious property offending? Explain.

▓ Thematic Question
To what extent has research established particular typologies of shoplifting?

▓ Thematic Question
How does Jack Katz's concept of "sneaky thrills" apply to property offending? What is your assessment of Katz's ideas?

▓ Thematic Question
What facts indicate that larceny is a significant problem on college campuses?

Motor Vehicle Theft

▓ Lecture Note
Focus on how the car is often seen as an extension of one's self image and how its theft can be experienced as a personal violation.

▓ Lecture Note
Discuss how cars and motor vehicle technology have changed in response to vehicle theft.

▓ Lecture Note
Ask students whether they believe joyriders cause harm. Also ask them to explain their response.

▓ Thematic Question
Because motor vehicle theft is not a homogeneous crime, what are some different forms of that type of theft?

▓ Thematic Question
Why is motor vehicle theft given special attention by the criminal justice system?

▓ Thematic Question
Why is it important to have specific information regarding the nature of the recovery of stolen vehicles?

▓ Thematic Question
What types of cars do joyriders usually steal?

▓ Thematic Question
Is car theft for profit primarily an activity associated with professional or persistent thieves?

▓ Movies/Television
Gone in 60 Seconds features a lead character, a former jockey, who must steal 50 designated cars in a 24-hour period to save his brother from death by unscrupulous characters.

▓ Movies/Television
Get Shorty stars John Travolta as a successful loan shark who has decided to leave the mob business and try to make movies.

Burglary

▓ Lecture Note
Given what we know about the social ecology of burglary, ask the class how we might use this knowledge to reduce burglary.

▓ Lecture Note
Relate knowledge of specific locales, like the south side of Chicago or south-central Los Angeles, to fear of crime.

▓ Lecture Note
Link the motivation for fast cash expressed by the burglars interviewed by Richard Wright and Scott Decker to subcultural identification. Explore the utility of addressing concepts such as motivation and rationality by reference to their cultural context. Link this to Edwin Sutherland's basic insight that the content of socialization is a key factor in patterns of offending.

▓ Lecture Note
Explore the extent to which the target-hardening strategies function as effective deterrents for burglaries.

▓ Lecture Note
When discussing the costs of crime, emphasize to students that while a conventional understanding of cost translates into money, there are other ways to assess costs. Explain that fear is often identified as one of the most detrimental costs of crime.

▓ Lecture Note
Discuss the extent to which the association of burglary with drug use is a consequence of the "war on drugs."

▓ Lecture Note
Note that while traditional UCR data have not allowed the assessment of circumstances connected with burglaries or sexual assaults, newer UCR/NIBRS data will allow an investigation of the extent to which sexual offenses occur during burglaries. Ask why that might be important.

▓ Thematic Question
What does it mean to refer to burglary as a "victim-avoiding crime"? How does this relate to rationality in decision making?

▓ Thematic Question
What features characterize residential burglaries?

▓ Thematic Question
To what extent is the pursuit of status and a street lifestyle associated with burglary offending?

▓ Thematic Question
Can it be argued that burglary is exclusively an offense in which the victim and offender are strangers?

▓ Thematic Question
Applying the logic of routine activities theory, how is offender motivation independent of changing crime patterns?

▓ Thematic Question
According to the logic of routine activities theory, how are changes in technology related to patterns of property crime?

▓ Thematic Question
What is Mike Maguire's typology of burglars?

▓ Thematic Question
To what extent does burglary vary by locales? How does this relate to the criminology of place?

▓ Thematic Question
According to the research of Wright and Decker, what motivates burglars?

▓ Thematic Question
How do residential burglars typically select their targets?

▓ Thematic Question
How are commercial burglars different from residential burglars?

▓ Thematic Question
To what extent do changes in the drug trade affect the pattern of burglary offenses?

▓ Thematic Question
How can burglary be argued as a unique context of sexual offending?

▓ Movies/Television
As a thriller, *Panic Room* presents the ultimate example of urban fear of crime, panic rooms built into houses and apartments whereby the inhabitants can retreat in safety from intruders. As a mother and daughter move into their new home, their first evening is shattered by the intrusion of burglars who don't just want something from the house but want something housed in the panic room.

Receivers of Stolen Property

▓ Lecture Note
Note that case studies are often used in research on rare populations, such as the professional fence.

▓ Lecture Note
Describe the different types of fences.

▓ Thematic Question
What differentiates the fence from the more typical criminal receiver?

▓ Thematic Question
Would stolen property be able to move without the cooperation of "honest" citizens? Explain.

▓ Thematic Question
How is the offense specialization of the burglar associated with the type of criminal receiver used?

Arson

▓ Lecture Note
Discuss why information on juvenile involvement in arson is crucial to understanding that particular offense.

Lecture Note
Discuss why arson is a problematic crime for the criminal justice system to investigate.

Thematic Question
What is the purpose of the Church Arson Prevention Act of 1996?

Thematic Question
How prevalent is arson for profit?

Thematic Question
Why do you think that juvenile arson isn't covered more by the media?

Movies/Television
Backdraft portrays the story of two brothers who are firefighters, but it also involves a veteran fire inspector who is tracking a series of arsons and interacts with an imprisoned pyromaniac.

CHAPTER 11
White-Collar and Organized Crime

A Brief History of White-Collar Crime

Classroom Activity
Have students discuss their reactions to celebrated white-collar crime cases of recent years, like the Bernie Madoff, Martha Stewart, Enron, and WorldCom cases.

Classroom Activity
Ask students to visit the Web site of the National Check Fraud Center (www.ckfraud.org) and report back to the class on some of the key points they found on the site.

Lecture Note
Direct students back to Edwin Sutherland's differential association theory, and emphasize how the key elements of that theory would be strengthened by a focus on white-collar crime.

Lecture Note
Discuss the reasons why the public has become outraged at corporate wrongdoing.

Thematic Question
What are the various types of offenses that fall under the label of white-collar crime?

Thematic Question
Why did initial attention to white-collar offending focus more on the offender than the offense?

Thematic Question
Do you think that social problems or the social responsibility perspective might better explain white-collar crime?

Understanding White-Collar Crime

Classroom Activity
Ask students to visit the FBI Web site (www.fbi.gov) and bring back information on some of the reasons for the difficulties of enforcement of white-collar offenses.

Lecture Note
Discuss the link between social status and white-collar crime.

Lecture Note
A great deal of corporate misconduct is covered by civil rather than criminal law. Explain the implications of this for addressing harm issues.

Lecture Note
Several of the research studies that support or refute liability for corporate products were financially supported by groups with a vested interest in production. Discuss how this violates ethical principles in terms of scientific research.

Lecture Note
Relate white-collar crime to our society's system of values.

Lecture Note
Explain why the control of white-collar crime is problematic from a policy perspective.

Thematic Question
How did Sutherland define *white-collar crime*?

Thematic Question
What facts support the claim that white-collar offenses represent a significant cost to society?

Thematic Question
What are some of the alternate labels for white-collar crime that have emerged in the literature?

Thematic Question
In what sense is corporate crime a distinct form of white-collar crime?

Thematic Question
What are environmental crimes? Who commits them?

Thematic Question
What do Travis Hirschi and Michael Gottfredson say are the causes of white-collar crime?

Thematic Question
How is corporate culture a factor in John Braithwaite's theoretical perspective on white-collar crime?

Thematic Question
To what extent is money laundering a significant problem within the United States? How can it be curtailed?

Thematic Question
Why is policing organized crime dependent on the statutory definition applied to such activities?

Policy Issues to Curtail White-Collar and Corporate Crime

Lecture Note
Explain how crime-control efforts toward street crime differ from those directed toward white-collar crime.

Thematic Question
How effective has federal legislation been in curtailing white-collar and corporate crime?

■ **Thematic Question**

Why are white-collar offenses difficult to investigate and prosecute?

■ **Thematic Question**

What four areas of reform does James Coleman suggest that directly address white-collar crime?

Organized Crime

■ **Classroom Activity**

Discuss why people had little interest in organized crime in the United States following World War II.

■ **Classroom Activity**

Ask students to discuss the usefulness of understanding the cultural context of organized crime. Have them relate this to ethnographic research as discussed in earlier chapters.

■ **Classroom Activity**

Ask students to relate the elements of the code of conduct of organized crime to conventional conduct norms.

■ **Lecture Note**

Inform students that Robert Merton offered Al Capone as the ideal example of someone adopting the innovator adaptation to strain.

■ **Lecture Note**

Tell students that the concept of ethnic succession can be found in other areas, such as sports. If you look at the history of boxing, for example, the ethnic background of boxing champions follows the assimilation process of various immigrant groups.

■ **Lecture Note**

Explain to students that Prohibition illustrates the difficulty of trying to criminalize behavior that has widespread social acceptance, especially behavior that was at one time legal. Aside from the issue of debates over marijuana as a gateway offense to more serious drug use, opponents of legalizing marijuana are aware that it is difficult to change course once a behavior has been legalized.

■ **Lecture Note**

Remind students that Prohibition also opened the door of opportunity for widespread corruption of local government and law enforcement.

■ **Lecture Note**

Emphasize to students that the association of Prohibition with the rise of organized crime is not an isolated case. Quite often, resistance to changes in the norm (that is, laws in this case) produces resistance in the form of deviance. Changes in technology produce opportunities for new types of deviance, so laws must be developed to counter these new forms.

■ **Lecture Note**

Link notions of a code of conduct among organized-crime members back to subcultural ideas about the normative structure of all groups, even deviant groups.

■ **Lecture Note**

Ask students to identify and elaborate upon media images that they have seen portraying the Russian *Mafiya*.

■ **Lecture Note**

Focus on the link between American activities and the Russian *Mafiya*.

■ **Thematic Question**

Which of the theories that have been offered in this text on crime causation do you feel best explains organized crime?

■ **Thematic Question**

What were the sources for early ideas about the Mafia?

■ **Thematic Question**

What kinds of crimes and criminal groups preceded the development of organized crime?

■ **Thematic Question**

How does the concept of ethnic succession relate to the development of organized crime?

■ **Thematic Question**

Why was organized crime within the United States during the last century primarily seen as the province of Italian American immigrants and their descendants? How is it different today?

■ **Thematic Question**

How did the passage of the Eighteenth Amendment to the U.S. Constitution contribute to the development of organized crime in the United States?

■ **Thematic Question**

What is the importance of the Kefauver Committee for understanding organized crime?

■ **Thematic Question**

What type of information on organized crime emerged from the report of the 1967 President's Commission on Law Enforcement and Administration of Justice?

■ **Thematic Question**

What does a contemporary examination of organized crime reveal about the motivations of such offenders?

■ **Thematic Question**

How are lotteries related to organized crime?

■ **Thematic Question**

What is omertà?

■ **Thematic Question**

What organized criminal groups exist in the United States today? What distinguishes these groups from the traditional Sicilian American criminal enterprise?

■ **Thematic Question**

What factors distinguish those involved in organized crime within the former Soviet Union and in the United States?

■ **Thematic Question**

Why is Russian organized crime of importance to American criminologists today?

■ **Thematic Question**

What is transnational organized crime? Provide examples.

■ **Thematic Question**

What is the importance of RICO statutes as they pertain to the activities of organized crime?

■ **Movies/Television**

The three *Godfather* films follow the rise and fall of a fictional organized-crime family, the Corleones.

■ **Movies/Television**

Growing Up Gotti is a reality series that follows the daily life of crime boss John Gotti's daughter.

■ **Movies/Television**

The Sopranos, now in reruns, details the daily family and business life of a modern-day crime family.

Policy Issues: The Control of Organized Crime

■ **Thematic Question**

What approach to the control of organized crime does Howard Abadinsky recommend?

CHAPTER 12
Public Order and Drug Crimes

Introduction

■ **Classroom Activity**

Break students into groups, and ask them to respond to the following question: "If, according to some sources such as the NSDUH survey, drug abuse is significantly less of a problem today than in previous years, why do you think drugs continue to be at the forefront of crime control policy?"

■ **Classroom Activity**

Ask students to discuss reasons why campus settings are prone to higher rates of binge drinking than most other settings are.

■ **Lecture Note**

Refer students back to Chapter 2, which discussed research methods, and ask them to consider ways in which the measures used in a survey can greatly influence its findings.

■ **Lecture Note**

If your college or university participates in the Harvard CAS, get the latest available findings and share them with students.

■ **Lecture Note**

Use the Internet to find video on events from the 1960s. Show videos that highlight the role of drugs during the period.

■ **Lecture Note**

Explain that men appear to have higher rates of illicit drug use than women. Ask why that is.

History of Drug Abuse in the United States

■ **Lecture Note**

Ask students if they recall participating in the *Monitoring the Future* study in high school. If so, what was the experience like? Did they tell the truth?

■ **Lecture Note**

Remind students that rural areas are generally considered low-crime settings, especially when compared to urban areas. But the reality is that the nature of crime varies by setting. Explain that marijuana production is an increasing problem in rural areas where economics have influenced increases in the production and use of this drug.

■ **Thematic Question**

How is drug use associated with particular subcultural groups in our society?

■ **Thematic Question**

How extensive is drug abuse in the United States? Which drugs seem to be the most abused?

■ **Thematic Question**

How are sociodemographic variables—like age, race, and income—associated with patterns of drug use and abuse?

■ **Thematic Question**

What is the *Monitoring the Future (MTF)* survey? What can it tell us?

■ **Thematic Question**

What are some of the key findings of the *MTF* survey? According to the survey, how have patterns of drug use changed over time?

■ **Thematic Question**

What are some of the costs to society of illegal drug use?

Illegal Drugs and Drug Addiction

■ **Classroom Activity**

Break students into groups, and ask them to explain how certain drug-abuse categories, such as the abuse of anabolic steroids, inhalants, and designer drugs, are associated with particular social groups.

■ **Lecture Note**

Select scenes from the movie *Traffic* to illustrate aspects of drug trafficking.

■ **Thematic Question**

What types of drugs are considered stimulants? What are some of the typical effects of these drugs?

■ **Thematic Question**

What types of drugs are considered depressants? What are some of the typical effects of these drugs?

■ **Thematic Question**

What types of drugs are considered narcotics? What are some of the typical effects of these drugs?

■ **Thematic Question**

What are gateway drugs? Why are they called that?

■ **Movies/Television**

The movie *Traffic* presents a fictional account of drug trafficking from several perspectives.

Drug Trafficking

■ **Thematic Question**

What does the term *drug trafficking* mean from a law enforcement perspective?

■ **Thematic Question**
Based on one drug that mostly comes from another country, how would you explain the methods typically used to smuggle that drug into the United States?

■ **Thematic Question**
What is the Heroin Signature Program (HSP), and how does it influence the policing of drug trafficking?

Drugs and Crime

■ **Classroom Activity**
Break students into groups, and have them discuss and critique the type of drug-education programs that operated in their high schools. Have them attempt to access the effectiveness of this kind of education.

■ **Lecture Note**
Explain to students that surveys of drug use among those in jail or under arrest will be problematic for generalizing the study results back to the relationship between drug use and crime in the general population.

■ **Lecture Note**
Link possible issues of drug money and corruption of public figures back to the relationship between Prohibition and the rise of organized crime.

■ **Lecture Note**
Ask students to consider whether the reality and potential for corruption inherent in policing a lucrative commodity such as drugs are worth the benefits of the "war on drugs."

■ **Thematic Question**
Why is the distinction between drug-defined crimes and drug-related crimes important for crime-control policy initiatives?

■ **Thematic Question**
What evidence exists about drug use among arrestees?

■ **Thematic Question**
What do statistics from jail inmates reveal about drug use?

■ **Thematic Question**
What is the importance of the Mollen Commission?

■ **Movies/Television**
Clockers is a 1995 crime drama directed by Spike Lee. It follows Strike, who is a "clocker" (a drug dealer) in a New York housing project. As Strike works to leave his life of crime behind, the murder of a local restaurant owner places him at the center of the police investigation.

Social Policy and Drug Abuse

■ **Classroom Activity**
Break students into groups, and have them evaluate the goals of the *National Drug-Control Strategy*.

■ **Classroom Activity**
Ask students to formulate responses to whether the association between drugs and crime would go away if drugs were either legalized or decriminalized.

■ **Classroom Activity**
Break students into groups, and have them discuss their knowledge of the drug Rohypnol and similar drugs.

■ **Lecture Note**
Emphasize to students that practices associated with asset forfeiture may raise questions about civil liberties.

■ **Lecture Note**
Given the strong association of peer groups with adolescent activities, including drug use, explain that the most effective drug education needs to be peer directed.

■ **Lecture Note**
Refer students back to information on the connection between robbery and drug offenses contained in Chapter 10. The "war on drugs" assumes a strong deterrence stance, but available information on robbery and drugs supports the idea that deterrence policies may have little impact on most offenders.

■ **Lecture Note**
As you discuss drug legalization, ask students to consider what everyday social life would be like if drugs that are currently illegal were legalized.

■ **Lecture Note**
Have a police officer who has been involved in D.A.R.E. programs speak to the class.

■ **Lecture Note**
Discuss the possible medical uses of marijuana. Ask the class if they think such uses should be legal.

■ **Lecture Note**
Ask students to consider whether, given the number of resources that are poured into the "war on drugs," alternative strategies really have a chance to work.

■ **Thematic Question**
What elements characterized early drug-control policy within the United States? What was the effect of the Food and Drug Act of 1906?

■ **Thematic Question**
What federal drug-control legislation has been enacted over the past few decades?

■ **Thematic Question**
What legislative actions have resulted from introduction of the drug Rohypnol and other similar drugs into the illicit market?

■ **Thematic Question**
How do portions of the Violent Crime Control and Law Enforcement Act of 1994 address drug control?

■ **Thematic Question**
Over the years, what five forms have characterized antidrug policies?

■ **Thematic Question**
What are the strategies and successes for two of the five forms of antidrug policies discussed in this chapter? How are they similar, and how are they different?

■ **Thematic Question**
What is the mission of the Office of National Drug Control Policy?

■ **Thematic Question**
What are some of the criticisms that can be made of the nation's "war on drugs"?

■ **Thematic Question**
Does the ongoing national "war on drugs" make sense from either a social problems or social responsibility perspective?

■ **Thematic Question**
How did the 1994 Violent Crime Control and Law Enforcement Act attempt to exercise control over drugs?

■ **Thematic Question**
What is the Federal-Wide Drug Seizure System?

■ **Thematic Question**
How successful has interdiction been in our nation's efforts to combat drugs?

■ **Thematic Question**
What is asset forfeiture? What is its purpose?

■ **Thematic Question**
What is the focus of the national drug-control strategy?

■ **Thematic Question**
How expensive is the nation's antidrug initiative?

■ **Thematic Question**
How do decriminalization and legalization approaches differ?

■ **Thematic Question**
What are the arguments in favor of legalizing drugs?

■ **Thematic Question**
How would you analyze the possible legalization of drugs from a social problems and a social responsibility perspective?

■ **Movies/Television**
The movie *Blow* tells the true story of George Jung, who went into the cocaine business with Pablo Escobar.

Prostitution
■ **Classroom Activity**
Break students into two groups, and have one group argue in favor of legalizing prostitution while the other group argues against it. It might be interesting to break the groups down along gender lines and have them take turns offering arguments favoring both perspectives.

■ **Lecture Note**
Identify the various types of prostitutes the book discusses, and ask if there might be other types or if the book's typology might be further refined.

■ **Thematic Question**
What are the consequences of the possible legalization of prostitution from a social problems and a social responsibility perspective?

CHAPTER 13
Technology and Crime

Introduction
■ **Lecture Note**
Tell the class that regulating child pornography has been difficult for lawmakers as well as for law enforcement agencies. Ask why it's so difficult.

■ **Thematic Question**
How did COPA intend to change the Web? Is it still effective today?

■ **Movies/Television**
The film *Sneakers* is an interesting, often funny look at a band of private investigators who get involved in trying to keep a valuable technological tool from the bad guys.

The Advance of Technology
■ **Lecture Note**
Emphasize the paradoxical relationship between technology and crime. Explain how technology has both been a tool for crime control and provided opportunities for new forms of crime to emerge.

■ **Lecture Note**
Refer students back to the information on routine activities theory in Chapter 3, and ask them how technological developments would be taken into account by this theory.

■ **Lecture Note**
Comment on the fact that technology facilitates new forms of behavior and social practices in a wide variety of ways. For example, technological developments can make manual labor easier, less hazardous, and also obsolete.

■ **Lecture Note**
Relate the fact that different motivations underlie cybercrime to Jack Katz's notion about the seductions of crime. How might cybercrime or mischief be seductive?

■ **Thematic Question**
Is technology new in the fight against crime?

■ **Thematic Question**
Of all the theories of crime causation that you have read about in this book, which (if any) do you think best explains crime committed with technology?

High Technology and Criminal Opportunity
■ **Classroom Activity**
Break students into groups, and have them discuss whether regulating activity on the Internet should be left to individuals (for example, parents, industry trade groups) or should be a realm for government control.

■ **Lecture Note**
Note that because of the rapid increase in Internet use among organizations, businesses, and individuals, it is not surprising that computer viruses or other forms of malware could become a weapon of terrorists.

■ **Lecture Note**
Discuss how computer viruses and other types of malware have affected the workplace.

■ **Lecture Note**
Explain how the dynamics of technology development drive the creation of new laws.

■ **Thematic Question**
What different ways of direct and indirect access are used by high-tech criminals to gain access to computerized information?

■ **Thematic Question**
What is TEMPEST?

■ Thematic Question

How does David L. Carter classify cybercrime?

■ Thematic Question

How does SIIA conceptualize software piracy? Do you think the distinctions that it makes are necessary?

■ Thematic Question

To what extent do phone phreaks represent a concern for both businesses and individuals? Are they still a threat in today's world of voice-over IP (Internet phones)?

■ Thematic Question

How do both economic and noneconomic motivations underlie cybercrime and mischief?

■ Thematic Question

How would you apply concepts from Edwin Sutherland's differential association to cybercrime? To what extent are these concepts useful for understanding the reality of cybercrime today?

■ Thematic Question

What are some ways in which viruses work? Does this diversity make them easier or more difficult to control?

■ Thematic Question

How might there be a "thrill" factor to the creation of computer viruses?

■ Thematic Question

What is *phishing*? Have you ever been a victim of phishing or known someone who was?

■ Thematic Question

What are some pieces of the federal legislation directed at computer-related crimes?

■ Thematic Question

What are the implications of having considerable variation in state statutes on cybercrime?

■ Thematic Question

Using the example of the Communications Decency Act (CDA), what are the difficulties of developing legislation to police the Internet?

■ Thematic Question

What is the Cyber Security Enhancement Act (CSEA)?

■ Movies/Television

The film *Hackers*, starring Angelina Jolie, offers an interesting look at the hacker subculture.

A Profile of Cybercriminals

■ Classroom Activity

Ask students to identify examples of cyberpunk subculture and to discuss the dominant themes those examples contain. Sources might be books, videos, or Web materials.

■ Lecture Note

Discuss some of the characteristics of the hacker subculture. Ask what kinds of crimes are likely to emanate from such a subculture.

■ Lecture Note

Discuss whether cybercrime is another form of white-collar crime.

■ Thematic Question

What two basic features characterize malicious hackers?

■ Thematic Question

Do all hackers share a common psychological profile?

■ Thematic Question

To what extent is cybercrime among adolescent hackers mainly a form of electronic trespass?

■ Thematic Question

What forms of high-tech crime are committed without the use of computers?

■ Thematic Question

To what extent can it be argued that cybercrime is really a form of white-collar crime?

Identity Theft

■ Thematic Question

Do you agree with the statement that identity theft is really just another form of larceny? How can you protect yourself against identity theft?

Technology in the Fight against Crime

■ Classroom Activity

Break the class into groups, and ask them to identify ways in which forms of technology have made the fight against crime easier.

■ Lecture Note

Detail the opportunities in computer forensics as a field of study and employment.

■ Lecture Note

Discuss DNA evidence, and ask the class if they feel that DNA evidence can be an effective tool in criminal trials involving personal crimes of violence. If so, why was such evidence not effective in the trial of O. J. Simpson in convincing the jury of the former football star's guilt?

■ Lecture Note

Discuss the pros and cons of the federal DNA Identification Act of 1994.

■ Thematic Question

What were some of the first forms of technology to be used in the fight against crime?

■ Thematic Question

What are some examples of innovative crime-fighting techniques? Do any of these involve a loss of individual rights?

■ Thematic Question

What are some examples of crime-related databases? How are they used?

■ Thematic Question

With further advances in DNA technology, do you think that we could effectively solve much crime by requiring submission to a DNA bank at birth? Explain.

■ Thematic Question

How has the introduction of DNA evidence made a difference to criminal offenders? To cybercriminals?

■ Thematic Question

What is the U.S. Supreme Court's position on the use of DNA evidence?

■ **Thematic Question**

How extensive are DNA criminal databases across the United States?

■ **Movies/Television**

Films such as *Judge Dredd* and *RoboCop* offer interesting looks at one possible—if improbable—way that technology can be used in the fight against crime.

Combating Cybercrime

■ **Lecture Note**

Point out that larger businesses and government agencies are better able to prevent and detect criminal use via computer than are smaller ones.

■ **Lecture Note**

Point out that small police departments are rarely able to dedicate significant resources to the enforcement of computer-related crimes. Ask whether specialized law enforcement agencies should be created to investigate such crimes.

■ **Lecture Note**

Discuss FBI involvement in cybercrime investigation.

■ **Lecture Note**

Explain that free speech is not absolutely protected by the First Amendment and that exceptions have long existed. Discuss what this might mean in terms of the future of the Internet.

■ **Lecture Note**

Discuss the idea that information has always been a valuable resource but that with the special role that computer technology plays in a service-based economy, it has taken on an even more heightened significance.

■ **Lecture Note**

Point out that during the Enlightenment, religion gave way to science, with knowledge and information being the means to various ends. People ended up questioning things that they had long taken for granted, including existing forms of government. Building on this example, relate to students how information for the sake of information has become an expectation of citizens today.

■ **Lecture Note**

Discuss the idea that modern telecommunications services might be as much a hindrance to the continued growth of democracy as a catalyst. For example, will technological skills and access increase the divide between social classes? Will the Internet give terrorists and anti-Western forces the tools needed to curtail the growth of democracy throughout the world?

■ **Lecture Note**

Point out the centrality of the Internet to businesses and individual lives today, and ask whether we as a society can afford not to regulate it. Discuss what forms regulation might take.

■ **Lecture Note**

Discuss why international law is the better domain for much emerging law dealing with regulating the Internet.

■ **Lecture Note**

Focus on the concept of technology as a double-edged sword.

■ **Thematic Question**

What is threat analysis? In what kinds of scenarios might it be used?

■ **Thematic Question**

What types of specialized units and squads have been formed to address computer fraud and other high-technology crimes?

■ **Thematic Question**

What is an audit trail? How is it used?

■ **Thematic Question**

Would you agree that the typical police department today is unsuited to the task of cybercrime investigation? Why or why not?

■ **Thematic Question**

How is the FBI involved in cybercrime fighting?

■ **Thematic Question**

How is the shift in the occupational structure of our society related to the increased incidence of cybercrime?

■ **Thematic Question**

What was the purpose of the Commission on Critical Infrastructure Protection?

■ **Thematic Question**

What is the United States Computer Emergency Readiness Team (US–CERT)?

Policy Issues: Personal Freedoms in the Information Age

■ **Lecture Note**

Ask students whether they think that today's criminal law will be able to keep pace with changing technologies.

■ **Thematic Question**

What is the Electronic Frontier Foundation (EFF)? What is its purpose?

CHAPTER 14

Globalization and Terrorism

Globalization

■ **Thematic Question**

Why is comparative criminology a useful approach to the study of crime?

Globalization and Comparative Criminology

■ **Classroom Activity**

Request that students visit the Web site of the *World Factbook of Criminal Justice* and bring information back to class. Develop a focus for this exercise by selecting a country, a global area, or an issue such as crime rates for student exploration.

■ **Lecture Note**

Discuss how comparative criminology can provide insights into the study of crime.

■ **Lecture Note**

Ethnocentrism is applicable to many areas of social life. Have students think about this and describe these areas.

■ **Lecture Note**

Focus on the variations in measuring crime and the differences in reporting practices among countries.

■ **Thematic Question**

Why do you think American students of criminology were slow to study crime in other cultures?

Terrorism

■ Classroom Activity

Form students into small groups. Ask them to develop responses to the question: "What are the implications of the USA PATRIOT Act (and associated reauthorizing legislation) and the Homeland Security Act for civil liberties?"

■ Classroom Activity

Ask students to compare and contrast the social problems and the social responsibility perspectives on the question: "What are the long-term implications for civil liberties of the Homeland Security Act and the USA PATRIOT Act?"

■ Lecture Note

Discuss cyberspace and infrastructure security initiatives.

■ Lecture Note

Discuss biological terrorism, and ask whether the United States is ready to mount an effective response to acts of biological terrorism.

■ Lecture Note

Mention that the idea of terrorism centers on the commission of crimes (usually acts of violence) for political or ideological ends. Ask students whether they would expand that definition. Ask whether they believe that acts of terrorism will increase in frequency throughout the rest of the twenty-first century.

■ Thematic Question

What differentiates terrorist acts from criminal acts?

■ Thematic Question

Which represents the larger threat to the United States, international or domestic terrorism?

■ Thematic Question

How does international terrorism affect daily life in the United States?

■ Thematic Question

What kinds of solutions would best address domestic versus international terrorism?

■ Thematic Question

How serious a problem is cyberterrorism?

■ Thematic Question

What is the Gilmore Commission? What were its findings?

■ Thematic Question

Overall, what are the findings of the most recent reports on terrorism?

■ Thematic Question

What is a hybrid terrorist structure?

■ Thematic Question

What are the criteria for foreign terrorist organization (FTO) designation?

Epilogue: Future Directions

Introduction

■ Lecture Note

Explain how effective the social problems and social responsibility perspectives might be in understanding crime in the future.

■ Lecture Note

Discuss the work of individuals such as Alvin Toffler and organizations such as the World Future Society in terms of their importance to forecasting the future of criminology.

■ Lecture Note

Ask the students why some predictions about the future and crime might be more credible than others.

■ Thematic Question

Based on material already presented throughout this text, what are some of the key issues to be addressed regarding crime in the future?

■ Thematic Question

What were the primary social characteristics affecting crime identified by the Foresight's Crime Prevention Panel?

Techniques of Futures Research

■ Thematic Question

What are some of the techniques of futures research?

■ Thematic Question

What are the basic principles for research from a futurist perspective?

■ Thematic Question

What will be the concerns of the U.S. Department of Justice in the future?

■ Movies/Television

Many media depictions of crime in the future take a science fiction perspective. These include films such as *Demolition Man* and *Judge Dredd*.

Future Crimes

■ Lecture Note

Focus on what behaviors you believe will be the most problematic in the future.

■ Thematic Question

Will future concerns about crimes still focus on street crimes such as murder, rape, and robbery?

■ Thematic Question

According to Richter H. Moore, Jr., what are some of the crimes that will occupy our society in the future?

■ Thematic Question

What are the coming changes in patterns of crime predicted by Georgette Bennett?

■ Movies/Television

Running Man presents a view of the future in the year 2017 where Los Angeles has become a police state. Watching convicted criminals compete for their freedom on a television game show is one of the most popular forms of entertainment.

New Criminologies

■ Thematic Question

How does interdisciplinary research hold a unique role for crime research and policy in the future? What other material has been covered in previous chapters that supports this perspective?

■ Thematic Question

Based on the predictions made by L. Edward Wells about the future of criminological theorizing, which ones fit more of a social problems perspective and which better fit a social responsibility perspective?

Crime-Control Policies of the Future

▧ Classroom Activity

Request that students write an essay on their possible future role in criminology and integrate how the concerns mentioned in this chapter may alter that role. Alternatively, you can ask students to consider how the concerns mentioned in this chapter might help them to further define their future role in criminology or in whatever occupational sector they plan to enter.

▧ Lecture Note

Much of Gene Stephens's discussion of the effects of homogeneity and heterogeneity has direct parallels to Emile Durkheim's insight into social cohesion in modern societies.

▧ Lecture Note

Discuss the role of interest groups in the policy-making forum regarding crime. Ask the students to consider whether politics can ever be completely divorced from crime.

▧ Lecture Note

Give some examples of how criminal events may be distorted by the media.

▧ Thematic Question

What does Gene Stephens state about the future of crime in countries outside the United States?

▧ Thematic Question

How are the concepts of homogeneity and heterogeneity important to the insights of Gene Stephens?

▧ Thematic Question

Which of the issues for future crime-control planners identified by Moore do you find the most compelling and why?

▧ Thematic Question

What does Hermanus Bianchi mean by the difference between criminology and *Kriminalpolitik*?

▧ Thematic Question

Of all the current and possible standards aimed at crime, which ones do you find the most persuasive and why?

▧ Thematic Question

In what sense might crime policies be symbolic political gestures?

CHAPTER 1

WHAT IS CRIMINOLOGY?

LEARNING OUTCOMES

After reading this chapter, you should be able to answer the following questions:

- What is crime? What is the definition of *crime* that the author of this textbook has chosen to use?

- What is deviance? How are crime and deviance similar? How do they differ?

- Who decides what should be criminal? How are such decisions made?

- What is criminology? What do criminologists do?

- How is social policy in the area of crime control determined? What role does criminological research play in the establishment of such policy?

- What is the theme of this book? Upon what two contrasting viewpoints does it build?

- What does it mean to say that "criminal activity is diversely created and variously interpreted"?

- What discipline has contributed the most to theoretical understandings of crime causation over the past century?

WEB EXTRA 1-1
WEB EXTRA 1-2

■ **crime**
Human conduct in violation of the criminal laws of the federal government, a state, or a local jurisdiction that has the power to make such laws.

Introduction

In 2010, the CBS-TV megahit series *NCIS* (Naval Criminal Investigative Service) was recognized by Los Angeles's Paley Center for Media as the most popular scripted TV show in the world.[1] With over 20 million dedicated viewers in the United States alone, the show has achieved heights that most other shows can't even dream of. Another immensely popular series on the same network, *CSI: Miami*, has more than 50 million regular viewers in 55 countries,[2] with programming that extends well beyond its Miami-based series. The *CSI* franchise, which follows teams of crime-scene investigators, now includes shows featuring New York City and other locales and is available to a global audience of nearly 2 billion viewers in 200 countries around the globe.[3]

The popularity of prime-time television crime shows is not limited to *NCIS* or *CSI*, as other widely followed series demonstrate. Included are shows like *Criminal Minds* (CBS), *Without a Trace* (CBS), *Numb3rs* (CBS), *White Collar* (USA), *The Unit* (CBS), *The District* (CBS), *The Shield* (FX), *The Wire* (HBO), *Cold Case* (CBS), *CIS* (CBS), and *Law and Order* (NBC)—along with the *Law and Order* spin-offs, *Law and Order: Criminal Intent* and *Law and Order: Special Victims' Unit*. Social commentators note that the plethora of crime shows bombarding the airwaves today reveals a penchant among American TV viewers for crime-related entertainment and a fascination with criminal motivation and detective work.

The public's interest in real-life stories of criminal victimization, revenge, and reformation has given birth to reality-TV crime shows, including *America's Most Wanted* (which premiered on Fox in 1988), *COPS* (Fox), *Crime and Punishment* (NBC), and *World's Wildest Police Videos* (SPIKE). Similarly, video magazine shows like *60 Minutes* (CBS), *20/20* (ABC), and *Nightline* (ABC) frequently focus on justice issues, and any number of movies—including films like *Sherlock Holmes*, *Cop Out*, *SWAT*, *Training Day*, *2 Fast 2 Furious*, *The Green Mile*, *Runaway Jury*, *The Shawshank Redemption*, *The Collector*, *Whiteout*, and *Minority Report*—play off the public's fascination with crime and the personal drama it fosters.

Like this textbook, many of today's television shows deliver content across a variety of media. View the *CSI* show's Web site at **Web Extra 1-1**, or become a fan of *NCIS* on Facebook via **Web Extra 1-2**.

What Is Crime?

Before we begin the discussion of criminology in earnest, we need to consider just what the term *crime* means. Crime can be defined in a variety of ways, and some scholars have suggested that at least four definitional perspectives can be found in contemporary criminology. These diverse perspectives see crime from (1) legalistic, (2) political, (3) sociological, and (4) psychological viewpoints. How we see any phenomenon is crucial because it determines the assumptions that we make about how that phenomenon should be studied. The perspective that we choose to employ when viewing crime determines the kinds of questions we ask, the nature of the research we conduct, and the type of answers that we expect to receive. Those answers, in turn, influence our conclusions about the kinds of crime-control policies that might be effective.

Seen from a legalistic perspective, **crime** is *human conduct in violation of the criminal laws of a state, the federal government, or a local jurisdiction that has the power to make such laws.* Without a law that circumscribes a particular form of behavior there can be no crime, no matter how deviant or socially repugnant the behavior in question may be.

The notion of crime as behavior[4] that violates the law derives from earlier work by criminologists like Paul W. Tappan, who defined crime as "an intentional act in violation of the criminal law . . . committed without defense or excuse, and penalized by the state as a felony or misdemeanor."[5] Edwin Sutherland, regarded by many as a founding figure in American criminology, said of crime that its "essential characteristic . . . is that it is behavior which is prohibited by the State as an injury to the State and against which the State may react . . . by punishment."[6]

> Without a law that circumscribes a particular form of behavior, there can be no crime.

A serious shortcoming of the legalistic approach to crime is that it yields the moral high ground to powerful individuals who are able to influence the making of laws and the imposition of criminal definitions on lawbreakers. By making their own laws, powerful but immoral individuals can escape the label "criminal." While we have chosen to adopt the legalistic approach to crime in this book, it is important to realize that laws are social products, so crime is socially relative in the sense that it is created by legislative

■ **criminalize**
To make illegal.

■ **statute**
A formal written enactment of a legislative body.

■ **statutory law**
Law in the form of statutes or formal written strictures made by a legislature or governing body with the power to make law.

LIBRARY EXTRA 1–1
WEB EXTRA 1–3

A still image from the highly popular CBS-TV show *CSI: Crime Scene Investigation*. Cast members appearing in this image from the "Lab Rats" episode are Hodges (Wallace Langham, far left), Archie (Archie Kao, far right), Henry (Jon Wellner), and Mandy (Sheeri Rappaport). Why do many people like to watch TV crime shows like *CSI*?
Source: CBS/Ron Jaffe/Landov © 2007 CBS Broadcasting, Inc. All Rights Reserved

activity. Hence, sociologists are fond of saying that "crime is whatever a society says it is." In Chapter 8, we will explore this issue further and will focus on the process of criminalization, which is the method used to **criminalize** some forms of behavior—or make them illegal—while other forms remain legitimate.

Another problem with the legalistic perspective is its insistence that the nature of crime cannot be separated from the nature of law, as the one explicitly defines the other. Not always recognized by legalistic definitions of crime, however, is the social, ethical, and individual significance of fundamentally immoral forms of behavior. Simply put, some activities not yet contravened by **statute** still call out for a societal response, sometimes leading commentators to proclaim, "That ought to be a crime!" or "There should to be a law against that!"

The legalistic definition of crime also suffers from its seeming lack of recognition that formalized laws have not always existed. Undoubtedly, much immoral behavior occurred in past historical epochs, and contemporary laws probably now regulate most such behavior. English common law, for example, upon which much of American **statutory law** is based, judged behavior in terms of traditional practice and customs and did not make use of written

statutes. Although all American jurisdictions have enacted comprehensive legal codes, many states still adhere to a common law tradition. In such "common law states," individuals may be prosecuted for violating traditional notions of right and wrong, even though no violation of written law took place. Such prosecutions rarely occur, and when they do, they are not often successful.[7] Common law is discussed in more detail in Chapter 3. You can also learn more about common law at **Web Extra 1–3**.

Changes in the laws will undoubtedly continue to occur, perhaps even legitimizing former so-called crimes where fundamentally moral or socially beneficial forms of behavior have been unduly criminalized. Over the last few years, for example, state legislatures along with members of the general public have debated the pros and cons of same-sex marriages and certain forms of biomedical research, especially those involving human cloning and the use of human stem cells.

A second perspective on crime is the political one, where crime is the result of criteria that have been built into the law by powerful groups and are then used to label selected undesirable forms of behavior as illegal. Those who adhere to this point of view say that crime is a definition of human conduct created by authorized agents in a politically organized society. Seen this way, laws serve the interests of the politically powerful, and crimes are merely forms of behavior that are perceived by those in power as direct or indirect threats to their interests. Thus, the political perspective defines crime in terms of the power structures that exist in society and asserts that criminal laws do not necessarily bear any inherent relationship to popular notions of right and wrong.

Even though political processes that create criminal definitions are sometimes easier to comprehend in totalitarian societies, the political perspective can also be meaningfully applied to American society. John F. Galliher, a contemporary criminologist, summarized the political perspective on crime when he wrote, "One can best understand crime in a class-structured society such as the United States as the end product of a chain of interactions involving powerful groups that use their power to establish criminal laws and sanctions against less powerful persons and groups that may pose a threat to the group in power."[8] Galliher points out that since legal definitions of criminality are arrived at through a political process, the subject matter of criminality will be artificially limited if we insist on seeing crime solely as a violation of the criminal law.

Some criminologists insist that the field of criminology must include behaviors that go beyond those defined as crimes through the political process; not doing so, they say, restricts rather than encourages inquiry into relevant forms of human behavior.[9]

Adherents of our third perspective, the sociological (also called "sociolegal") viewpoint, would likely agree with this statement, seeing crime as "an antisocial act of such a nature that its repression is necessary or is supposed to be necessary to the preservation of the existing system of society."[10] Some criminologists have gone so far as to claim that any definition of crime must include all forms of antisocial behavior.[11] Ron Claassen, a modern-day champion of restorative justice (discussed in more detail in Chapter 8), suggested, for example, that "crime is primarily an offense against human relationships, and secondarily a violation of a law—since laws are written to protect safety and fairness in human relationships."[12] A more comprehensive sociological definition of crime was offered by Herman Schwendinger and Julia Schwendinger in 1975: Crime encompasses "any harmful acts," including violations of "the fundamental prerequisites for well-being, [such as] food, shelter, clothing, medical services, challenging work and recreational experiences, as well as security from predatory individuals or repressive and imperialistic elites."[13] The Schwendingers have challenged criminologists to be less constrained in what they see as the subject matter of their field, saying that violations of human rights may be more relevant to criminological inquiry than many acts that have been politically or legally defined as crime. "Isn't it time to raise serious questions about the assumptions underlying the definitions of the field of criminology," asked the Schwendingers, "when a man who steals a paltry sum can be called a criminal while agents of the State can, with impunity, legally reward men who destroy food so that price levels can be maintained whilst a sizable portion of the population suffers from malnutrition?"[14] Jeffrey H. Reiman, another contemporary criminologist, asked similar questions.

> Doesn't a crime by any other name still cause misery and suffering?

"The fact is that the label 'crime' is not used in America to name all or the worst of the actions that cause misery and suffering to Americans," said Reiman. "It is primarily reserved for the dangerous actions of the poor." Writing about unhealthy and unsafe workplaces, Reiman asked, "Doesn't a crime by any other name still cause misery and suffering? What's in a name?"[15] While a sociolegal approach to understanding crime is attractive to many, others claim that it suffers from wanting to criminalize activities that cause only indirect harm, that is, it is easier for most people to appreciate the criminality involved in a holdup or a rape than in cost-cutting efforts made by a businessperson.

Finally, a psychological (or maladaptive) perspective states that "crime is a form of social maladjustment which can be designated as a more or less pronounced difficulty that the individual has in reacting to the stimuli of his environment in such a way as to remain in harmony with that environment."[16] Seen this way, crime is problem behavior, especially human activity that contravenes the criminal law and results in difficulties in living within a framework of generally acceptable social arrangements. According to Matthew B. Robinson, "The maladaptive view of crime does not require any of the [traditional] elements . . . in order for an act to be a crime: no actual harm to others; no prohibition by law before the act is committed; no arrest; and no conviction in a court of law. Any behavior which is maladaptive . . . would be considered crime. If criminologists adopted this view of crime," said Robinson, "the scope of criminology would be greatly expanded beyond its current state. All actually or even potentially harmful behaviors could be examined, analyzed, and documented for the purpose of gaining knowledge about potentially harmful behaviors and developing strategies to protect people from all harmful acts, not just those that are called 'crime' today."[17]

As this discussion shows, a unified or simple definition of crime is difficult to achieve. The four points of view that we have discussed here form a kind of continuum, bound on one end by strict legalistic interpretations of crime and on the other by much more fluid behavioral and moralistic definitions.

Crime and Deviance

Sociologically speaking, many crimes can be regarded as deviant forms of behavior—that is, as behaviors that are in some way abnormal. Piers Beirne and James Messerschmidt, two contemporary criminologists, defined deviance as "any social behavior or social characteristic that departs from the conventional norms and standards of a community or society and for which the deviant is sanctioned."[18] Their definition, however, does not count as deviant any sanctionable behavior that is not punished or punishable. Hence, we prefer another approach to defining deviance. The definition of **deviant behavior** that we

the **PROFESSOR** | **SPEAKS**
What Is Crime?

ELLEN G. COHN

Florida
International
University

FIU | FLORIDA INTERNATIONAL UNIVERSITY

Put simply, *crime* is an act that violates a law. So if there is a law against a certain behavior and you engage in it, you have committed a crime. On the other hand, if there is no law against a behavior, then it's not a crime, no matter how socially unacceptable it might be. An omission can be a crime, too; if you don't do something the law requires you to do, that's a crime. Sometimes the situation affects whether a behavior is considered a crime. Gambling is illegal in some states while playing the lottery is not.

Laws are constantly changing, creating new crimes and eliminating old ones. Because not everyone agrees with the law, there are illegal behaviors that are commonplace. There are laws against speeding, but when I drive to work, it's rare to see anyone obeying the speed limit!

This definition basically says that a behavior is a crime only because the law says so. However, some people see crime as a broader concept—behavior that violates prevailing social standards of acceptable behavior. This helps to explain why laws keep changing: as social attitudes about behaviors change over time, the laws are changed to conform to new social views. For example, marijuana was criminalized in the early twentieth century, after drug use became less socially acceptable. In the late twentieth century, social attitudes changed again, and many states legalized or decriminalized marijuana use.

Source: Reprinted by permission of Ellen G. Cohn, Ph.D. Photo courtesy of Ellen G. Cohn. Logo courtesy of Florida International University.

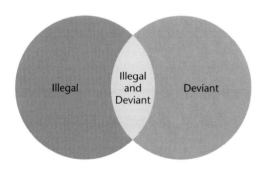

FIGURE 1-1 | The Overlap between Deviance and Crime

will use in this book is as follows: *Deviant behavior is human activity that violates social norms.*

Abnormality, deviance, and crime are concepts that do not always easily mesh. Some forms of deviance are not violations of the criminal law, and the reverse is equally true (see Figure 1–1). Deviant styles of dress, for example, although perhaps outlandish to the majority, are generally not circumscribed by criminal law unless (perhaps) decency statutes are violated by a lack of clothing. Even in such cases, laws are subject to interpretation and may be modified as social norms change over time.

In 2009, for example, a judge in Palm Beach County, Florida, held that a city ordinance barring the wearing of baggy pants was unconstitutional.[19] County Judge Laura Johnson ruled that no matter how "tacky or distasteful" baggy pants might be to others, they are merely a fashion statement and that wearing them, especially when no nudity is involved, is a freedom protected under the Fourteenth Amendment to the U.S. Constitution. The ordinance had been overwhelmingly approved by voters only two years earlier.

Some types of behavior, although quite common, are still against the law even though those who engage in them might not think of them as deviant. Speeding on interstate highways, for example, although probably something that most motorists engage in at least from time to time, is illegal. Complicating matters still further is the fact that certain behaviors are illegal in some jurisdictions but not in others. For example, commercialized gambling, especially that involving slot machines and games of chance, is against the law in most parts of the United States but has been legitimized in Nevada, on some Indian reservations, on cruise ships operating outside of U.S. territorial waters, and on some Mississippi riverboats. Even state governments, seeking to enhance revenues, have gotten into the gambling business through state lotteries, which now operate in 38 states, and many states have laws specifically forbidding participation in online gambling, due largely to their interest in protecting their own lottery revenues. Similarly, prostitution, which is almost uniformly illegal in the United States, is an activity that is fully within the law in parts of Nevada as long as it occurs within licensed brothels and as long as those engaged in the activity meet state licensing requirements and abide by state laws that require condom use and weekly medical checkups.

A young man wearing baggy pants is seen at a pay phone in Nashville, Tennessee. Some jurisdictions have attempted to outlaw the wearing of baggy pants. Should the wearing of such clothing be criminalized?

Source: AP Photo/Mark Humphrey

What Should Be Criminal?

As you have probably realized by now, the question "What is crime?" is quite different from the question "What should be criminal?" Although most people agree that certain forms of behavior, such as murder, rape, burglary, and theft, should be against the law, there is far less agreement about the appropriate legal status of things like drug use, abortion (including the use of "abortion pills" like RU-486, or Mifeprex), gambling, "deviant" forms of consensual adult sexual

> The consensus viewpoint holds that laws should be enacted to criminalize given forms of behavior when members of society generally agree that such laws are necessary.

behavior, and even the use of salt. In 2010, for example, New York State Assemblyman Felix Ortiz introduced a bill to completely ban the use of salt in restaurant kitchens throughout the state.[20] Ortiz argued that reducing the use of salt would lead to healthier lifestyles and would save the state money on health-care bills while reducing the number of deaths from cardiovascular disease. Chefs who added salt to their preparations would be fined $1,000 per serving under the proposed legislation.

While the question "What should be criminal?" can be answered in many different ways, the social and intellectual processes by which an answer is reached can be found in two contrasting points of view: (1) the consensus perspective and (2) the pluralist perspective. The consensus viewpoint holds that laws should be enacted to criminalize given forms of behavior when members of society generally agree that such laws are necessary. The consensus perspective, reflected in the actions of Islamic protestors described in a Crime in the News box in this chapter (and described in greater detail in Chapter 8), is most applicable to homogeneous societies, or those characterized by shared values, norms, and belief systems. In a multicultural and diverse society like the United States, however, a shared consensus may be difficult to achieve. In such a society, even relatively minor matters may lead to complex debates over the issues involved, and these debates show just how difficult it is to achieve a consensus over even relatively minor matters in a society as complex as our own.

Finally, the question of what should be criminal should be distinguished from issues arising from excessive enforcement of the law. In one surprising case of what many saw as an overreaction by law enforcement officers, a 12-year-old student, Alexa Gonzalez, was arrested in New York City in 2010 for doodling on her junior high school desk with a washable felt-tipped marker.[21] School safety officers took the girl into custody for defacing school property and for creating graffiti—both against the law in New York City. Upon being turned over to New York Police Department (NYPD) officers as required by school policy, Alexa was handcuffed and taken to a police station. After spending hours in confinement, the girl was released into the custody of her mother. Eventually, she was ordered to perform eight hours of community service and assigned to write an essay on what she had learned from the experience. The question in this case was not whether defacing public property is wrong and if there should be a law against it but how the police should react to such situations.

The second perspective, the pluralist view of crime (also described in more detail in Chapter 8), recognizes the importance

CRIME | in the NEWS

Muslim Countries Seek Blasphemy Ban

[NEW YORK]—Islamic nations are mounting a campaign for an international treaty to protect religious symbols and beliefs from mockery—essentially a ban on blasphemy that would put them on a collision course with free speech laws in the West.

Documents obtained by The Associated Press show that Algeria and Pakistan have taken the lead in lobbying to eventually bring the proposal to a vote in the U.N. General Assembly. If ratified in countries that enshrine freedom of expression as a fundamental right, such a treaty would require them to limit free speech if it risks seriously offending religious believers. The process, though, will take years and no showdown is imminent.

The proposal faces stiff resistance from Western countries, including the United States, which in the past has brushed aside other U.N. treaties, such as one on the protection of migrant workers. . . .

The countries that form the 56-member Organization of the Islamic Conference are now lobbying a little-known Geneva-based U.N. committee to agree that a treaty protecting religions is necessary. . . .

The proposal may have some support in the General Assembly. For several years the Islamic Conference has successfully passed a non-binding resolution at the General Assembly condemning "defamation of religions."

If the treaty [is] approved, any of the U.N.'s 192 member states that ratified it would be bound by its provisions. Other countries could face criticism for refusing to join.

Just last month, the Obama administration came out strongly against efforts by Islamic nations to bar the defamation of religions, saying the moves would restrict free speech.

"Some claim that the best way to protect the freedom of religion is to implement so-called anti-defamation policies that would restrict freedom of expression and the freedom of religion," Secretary of State Hillary Rodham Clinton said. "I strongly disagree. . . ."

Marghoob Saleem Butt, a Pakistani diplomat in Geneva, . . . confirmed the campaign's existence and has lobbied for the ban. "There has to be a balance between freedom of expression and respect for others," Butt said in a telephone interview. "Taking the symbol of a whole religion and portraying him as a terrorist," said Butt, referring to the Muhammad cartoons, "that is where we draw the line."

One American expert with more than 20 years [of] experience of the U.N. human rights system said the treaty could have far-reaching implications.

"It would, in essence, advance a global blasphemy law," said Felice Gaer, a member of the U.S. Commission on International Religious Freedom. The independent, congressionally mandated panel issued a report last week warning that existing laws against blasphemy, including in Pakistan, "often have resulted in gross human rights violations. . . ."

More broadly, introducing laws to protect religions from criticism would weaken the whole notion of human rights, said Sweden's ambassador to the U.N. in Geneva, Hans Dahlgren. "Religions as such do not have rights—it's people who have rights," he said, adding that the European Union, whose presidency Sweden currently holds, would oppose attempts to limit freedom of speech.

Discussion Questions

1. What do you think of the argument made by Pakistani diplomat Marghoob Saleem Butt, who stated, "There has to be a balance between freedom of expression and respect for others"? Might such a balance be achieved without a law or treaty supporting it?

2. What's the difference between the consensus and pluralistic perspectives? How is the concept of dueling perspectives relevant to the story in this box?

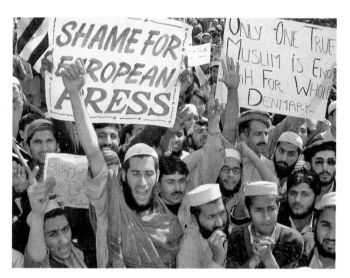

Members of the Muslim League demonstrate against perceived blasphemy in Kashmir, Pakistan. Why would Western countries have difficulty criminalizing the act of blasphemy?

Source: AP Photo/Shakil Adil

of diversity in societies like ours. It says that behaviors are typically criminalized through a political process only after debate over the appropriate course of action. The political process often takes the form of legislation and may involve appellate court action (by those who don't agree with the legislation). After the horrific shootings that occurred on the campus of Virginia Tech University in 2007, for example, legislatures at both the state and federal levels began to reexamine gun laws to see if new laws were needed to keep guns out of the hands of potential mass killers. Given the diversity of perspectives that characterize our society, however, agreement was not easy to reach—and gun-control proponents vigorously debated those who sought to protect existing laws supporting gun ownership and making the purchase of guns relatively easy for most Americans. For the law's

■ **criminologist**
One who is trained in the field of criminology; also, one who studies crime, criminals, and criminal behavior.

■ **criminalist**
A specialist in the collection and examination of the physical evidence of crime.

WEB EXTRA 1–4
WEB EXTRA 1–5
WEB EXTRA 1–6
LIBRARY EXTRA 1–3
LIBRARY EXTRA 1–4

perspective on another issue, see the Who's to Blame box in this chapter. Learn more about both sides of the gun-control debate via **Web Extras 1–4** and **1–5**.

What Do Criminologists Do?

A typical dictionary definition of a **criminologist** is "one who studies crime, criminals, and criminal behavior."[22] Occasionally, the term *criminologist* is used broadly to describe almost anyone who works in the criminal justice field, regardless of formal training. There is a growing tendency, however, to reserve application of the term *criminologist* to academics, researchers, and policy analysts with advanced degrees who are involved in the study of crime and crime trends and in the analysis of societal reactions to crime. Hence, it is more appropriate today to describe specially skilled investigators, crime-laboratory technicians, fingerprint experts, crime-scene photographers, ballistics experts, and others who work to solve particular crimes as criminalists. A **criminalist** is "a specialist in the collection and examination of the physical evidence of crime."[23] Police officers, corrections professionals, probation and parole officers, judges, district attorneys, criminal defense attorneys, and others who do the day-to-day work of the criminal justice system are best referred to as criminal justice professionals.

Academic criminologists and research criminologists generally hold doctoral degrees (Ph.D.s) in the field of criminology or criminal justice from an accredited university. Some criminologists hold degrees in related fields like sociology and political science but have specialized in the study and control of crime and deviance. Most Ph.D. criminologists teach either criminology or criminology-related subjects in institutions of higher learning, including universities and two- and four-year colleges. Nearly all criminology professors are involved in research or writing projects by which they strive to advance criminological knowledge. Some Ph.D. criminologists are strictly researchers and work for federal agencies like the National Institute of Justice (NIJ), the Bureau of Justice Statistics (BJS), and the National Criminal Justice Reference Service (NCJRS) or for private (albeit often government-funded) organizations with such names as RAND and the Search Group, Inc.

The results of criminological research in the United States are generally published in journals like *Criminology* (the official publication of the American Society of Criminology [ASC]), *Theoretical Criminology, Justice Quarterly* (the Academy of Criminal Justice Sciences), *Crime and Delinquency*, the *American Journal of Criminal Justice* (the Southern Criminal Justice Association), the *Journal of Qualitative Criminology, Social Problems*, and *Victimology*.[24] International English-language journals are numerous and include the *Canadian Journal of Criminology*, the *Australian and New Zealand Journal of Criminology*, and the *British Journal of Criminology*. Read some of these journals and visit the organizations that sponsor them at **Web Extra 1–6**.

People who have earned master's and bachelor's degrees in the field of criminology often find easy entrance into police investigative or support work, probation and parole agencies, court-support activities, and correctional (prison) work. Criminologists also work for government agencies interested in the development of effective social policies intended to deter or combat crime. Many criminologists with master's degrees also teach at two- and four-year colleges and schools.

> Private security provides another career track for individuals interested in criminology and criminal justice.

Private security provides another career track for individuals interested in criminology and criminal justice. The number of personnel employed by private security agencies today is twice that of public law enforcement agencies, and the gap is widening. Many upper- and mid-level private managers working for private security firms hold criminology or criminal justice degrees. The same may soon be true for the majority of law enforcement personnel, especially those in managerial positions.

Anyone trained in criminology has many alternatives (see Table 1–1). Some people with undergraduate degrees in criminology or criminal justice decide to go on to law school. Some teach high school, whereas others become private investigators. Many criminologists provide civic organizations (such as victims' assistance and justice advocacy groups) with much-needed expertise, a few work for politicians and legislative bodies, and some appear on talk shows to debate the pros and cons of various kinds of social policies designed to fight crime. Some criminologists even write books like this one! For more thoughts on the role of criminologists in the twenty-first century, read **Library Extra 1–4**.

■ **social policy**
A government initiative, program, or plan intended to address problems in society. The "war on crime," for example, is a kind of generic (large-scale) social policy—one consisting of many smaller programs.

TABLE 1–1 | **What Do Criminologists Do?**

The term *criminologist* is usually applied to credentialed individuals, such as those holding advanced degrees in the field, who engage in the study of crime, criminal behavior, and crime trends. The word *criminalist* is used to describe people who specialize in the collection and examination of the physical evidence associated with specific crimes. Others working in the criminal justice system are called *criminal justice professionals*. This table lists the activities of all three.

Some Activities of Criminologists

Data gathering	Public service
Data analysis	Analysis of crime patterns and trends
Theory construction	Scholarly presentations and publications
Hypothesis testing	Education and training
Social policy creation	Threat assessment and risk analysis
Public advocacy	

Some Jobs in the Field of Criminalistics

Forensics examiner	Crime-scene photographer
Crime-laboratory technician	Polygraph operator
Ballistics expert	Fingerprint examiner
Crime-scene investigator	

Some Jobs in the Field of Criminal Justice

Law enforcement officer	Judge
Probation or parole officer	Defense attorney
Corrections officer	Prosecutor
Prison program director	Jailer
Cybercrime investigator	Private security officer
Juvenile justice worker	Victims' advocate

What Is Criminology?

The attempt to understand crime and deviance predates written history. Prehistoric evidence, including skeletal remains showing signs of primitive cranial surgery, seems to indicate that preliterate people explained deviant behavior by reference to spirit possession. Primitive surgery was an attempt to release unwanted spiritual influences. In the thousands of years since, many other theoretical perspectives on crime have been advanced. This book describes various criminological theories and covers some of the more popular ones in detail.

Definition of Terms

Before beginning any earnest discussion, however, it is necessary to define the term *criminology*. As our earlier discussion of the nature of crime and deviance indicates, not only must criminologists deal with a complex subject matter—consisting of a broad range of illegal behaviors committed by frequently unknown or uncooperative individuals—but they also must manage their work under changing conditions mandated by ongoing revisions of the law and fluctuating **social policy**. In addition, as we have already seen, a wide variety of perspectives on the nature of crime abound. All this leads to considerable difficulties in defining the subject matter under study.

There is some evidence that the term *criminology* was coined by a Frenchman, Paul Topinard, in 1889;[25] he used it to differentiate the study of criminal body types within the field of anthropology from other biometric pursuits.[26] Topinard, while he may have coined the term, did little to help define it. As with the concept of crime, various definitions of criminology can be found in the literature today. About two decades ago, criminologist Joseph F. Sheley wrote, "There seem to be nearly as many definitions of *contemporary criminology* as there are criminologists."[27]

One straightforward definition can be had from a linguistic analysis of the word *criminology*. As most people know, *-ology* means "the study of something," and the word *crimen* comes from the Latin, meaning "accusation," "charge," or "guilt." Hence, linguistically speaking, the term *criminology* literally means "the study of criminal accusations," that is, "the study of crime." In addition to this fundamental kind of linguistic definition, three other important types of definitions can be found in the literature: (1) disciplinary, (2) causative, and (3) scientific. Each type of definition is distinguished by its focus. Disciplinary definitions are those that, as their name implies, focus on criminology as a discipline. Seen from this viewpoint, criminology is a field of study or a body of knowledge. Some of the earliest criminologists of the past century, including Edwin H. Sutherland, who is often referred to as the "dean of American criminology," offered definitions of their field that emphasized its importance as a discipline of study. Sutherland, for example, wrote in the first edition of his textbook *Criminology* in 1924, "Criminology is the body of knowledge regarding the social problem of crime."[28] Sutherland's text was to set the stage for much of American criminology throughout the rest of the twentieth century. Reprinted in 1934 with the title *Principles of Criminology*,[29] it was to become the most influential textbook ever written in the field of criminology.[30] Although Sutherland died in 1950, his revered text was revised for

WHO'S TO BLAME—The Individual or Society?

Should Polygamy Be a Protected Religious Practice?

Taeler Leon, a member of the Fundamentalist Church of Jesus Christ of Latter Day Saints, an ultraconservative offshoot of the Mormon Church, was arrested in a rural area outside of Salt Lake City, Utah, and charged with polygamy and the rape of a child. The charges came after the parents of a 13-year-old girl, whom Leon had "married" in a ceremony performed by a church elder, complained to the Utah State Bureau of Investigation (SBI) that Leon was holding their daughter against her will. SBI agents visited Leon's compound and learned that six of Leon's wives and 16 of his children were living at the compound. The compound, which consisted of four houses and a communal building containing a small school, chapel, and dining and meeting areas, was set in a secluded location well off the main road.

A follow-up investigation revealed that the children's births had been officially registered at the county courthouse and that the needed homeschooling papers had been filed with the State Board of Education for each of the school-aged children living at the compound—meaning that they were exempt from required attendance at public schools.

Polygamy is a criminal offense in Utah and is banned under the state's constitution. It has been officially repudiated by the mainstream Mormon Church since 1890. After determining that Leon was married concurrently to multiple women, SBI agents took him into custody and interviewed each of his wives. Each told much the same story of how she had been promised by her parents to Leon at an early age, how she had been married in a small ceremony, and how she had borne Leon's children. What surprised investigators, though, was the women's agreement that their way of life, while it might not be common in the wider society, was a matter of choice—and that they should be left alone to practice their faith. "Taeler's committed no crime in the eyes of God," said Adaleen, Leon's first wife, speaking for the others. "We should be free to practice our religion just like others are," she said.

Hendy, another of the wives, pointed out that members of the American Indian Church have been allowed to use peyote in their religious ceremonies, even though it is a banned drug, unavailable to non–Native Americans. "If they can smoke peyote, then why can't we get married and live the way we want to?" she asked. "It's our religion, and it's supposed to be a free country."

Think about it:

1. Not all women involved in polygamous unions would agree with Adaleen and Hendy, and those who oppose polygamy argue not only that it is illegal but that it degrades women, devalues the family, and victimizes young women who are forced into arranged unions. Nonetheless, there are those who would agree with Adaleen and Hendy that the practice should be allowed based on constitutional guarantees of freedom of religion. Which perspective makes more sense to you? Why?

2. Do a bit of historical research and see if you can learn the legal history of the practice of polygamy in the United States. When did it become illegal? Why?

3. What rights, if any, should members of minority faiths have when they advocate or engage in behavior that goes beyond social norms or violates the law? Give some examples.

4. Would the rights you identified above extend to the practice of polygamy? Why or why not?

Polygamist Warren Steed Jeffs is pictured on an FBI Ten Most Wanted poster prior to his arrest in 2006. Jeffs, the fugitive leader of a polygamist Mormon sect, was wanted in Utah and Arizona on charges linked to allegations of arranging marriages between men and underage girls. He was arrested and convicted on those charges in 2007. Why is the practice of polygamy a violation of the criminal law? Should it be?
Source: FBI/AP Wide World Photos

Note: Who's to Blame boxes provide fictionalized critical thinking opportunities, and are not actual cases.

many years by Donald R. Cressey and later by David F. Luckenbill. By 1974, Sutherland's classic definition of criminology had been modified by Cressey: "Criminology is the body of knowledge regarding delinquency and crime as a social phenomenon. It includes within its scope the processes of making laws, of breaking laws, and of reacting toward the breaking of laws."[31]

Causative definitions emphasize criminology's role in uncovering the underlying causes of crime. In keeping with such an

■ criminology
An interdisciplinary profession built around the scientific study of crime and criminal behavior, including their forms, causes, legal aspects, and control.

■ criminality
A behavioral predisposition that disproportionately favors criminal activity.

■ criminal behavior
A way of acquiring valued resources from others by exploiting and deceiving them.

emphasis, contemporary criminologists Gennaro F. Vito and Ronald M. Holmes stated, "Criminology is the study of the causes of crime."[32]

Finally, there are those who point to the scientific nature of contemporary criminology as its distinguishing characteristic. According to Clemens Bartollas and Simon Dinitz, for example, "Criminology is the scientific study of crime."[33] Writing in 1989, Bartollas and Dinitz seemed to be echoing an earlier definition of criminology offered by Marvin E. Wolfgang and Franco Ferracuti, who wrote in 1967, "Criminology is the scientific study of crime, criminals, and criminal behavior."[34]

> There is evidence that the term *criminology* was coined by a Frenchman, Paul Topinard, in 1889.

One of the most comprehensive definitions of the term *criminology* that is available today comes from the European Society of Criminology (ESC), which in its constitution defines *criminology* as "all scholarly, scientific and professional knowledge concerning the explanation, prevention, control and treatment of crime and delinquency, offenders and victims, including the measurement and detection of crime, legislation, and the practice of criminal law, and law enforcement, judicial, and correctional systems."[35] ESC's emphasis is on "knowledge"; even though it mentions the "practice" of what many would call criminal justice (that is, policing, courts, and corrections), it is the study and knowledge of such practice that form the crux of the ESC perspective.

For our purposes, we will use a definition somewhat simpler than that of the ESC but one that brings together the works of previous writers and also recognizes the increasingly professional status of the criminological enterprise. Throughout this book, then, we will say that **criminology** is *an interdisciplinary profession built around the scientific study of crime and criminal behavior, including their forms, causes, legal aspects, and control.* As this definition indicates, criminology includes consideration of possible solutions to the problem of crime. Hence, this text (in later chapters) describes treatment strategies and social policy initiatives that have grown out of the existing array of theoretical explanations for crime.

Our definition is in keeping with the work of Jack P. Gibbs, a notable contemporary criminologist, who writes that the *purpose* of criminology is to offer well-researched and objective answers to four basic questions: (1) "Why do crime rates vary?" (2) "Why do individuals differ as to criminality?" (3) "Why is there variation in reactions to crime?" and (4) "What are the possible means of controlling criminality?"[36] It is important to note that our definition and Gibbs's guiding queries encompass a number of different terms

A criminalist at work. Crime-scene investigators, like the person shown here, can provide crucial clues needed to solve crimes. How does the work of a criminologist differ from that of a criminalist? Would you like either kind of work?
Source: CORBIS–NY

that are sometimes easily confused. Criminology, **criminality**, crime, deviance, and **criminal behavior** are five concepts used in this chapter and throughout this book, and learning the definition of each provides a good start for anyone studying in this field.

As a field of study, criminology in its present form is primarily a social scientific discipline. Contemporary criminologists generally recognize, however, that their field is *interdisciplinary*—that is, it draws upon other disciplines to provide an integrated approach to understanding the problem of crime in contemporary society and to advance solutions to the problems crime creates. Hence, anthropology (especially cultural anthropology or ethnology), biology, sociology, political science, psychology, psychiatry, economics, ethology (the study of character), medicine, law, philosophy, ethics, and numerous other fields all have something to offer the student of criminology, as do the tools provided by statistics, computer science, and other forms of scientific and data analysis (see Figure 1–2).

The interdisciplinary nature of criminology was well stated by Jim Short, past president of the ASC, who said, "The organization

■ **criminal justice**
The scientific study of crime, the criminal law, and components of the criminal justice system, including the police, courts, and corrections.

WEB EXTRA 1-7
LIBRARY EXTRA 1-5
LIBRARY EXTRA 1-6
LIBRARY EXTRA 1-7

FIGURE 1-2 | Criminology's Many Roots

of knowledge by traditional disciplines has become increasingly anachronistic, as the generation of knowledge has become more interdisciplinary. From its earliest beginnings, when philosophers grappled with relationships between human nature and behavior and biologists sought to relate human physiology to behavior, criminology's concerns have reached across virtually all disciplines that focus on the human condition. Additionally, much of the impetus for criminology has come from concerns that crime be controlled. Criminology thus cuts across professions as well as disciplines."[37]

It is important to note that although criminology may be interdisciplinary as well as cross-professional, few existing explanations for criminal behavior have been successfully or fully integrated. Just as physicists today are seeking a unified field theory to explain the wide variety of observable forms of matter and energy, criminologists have yet to develop a generally accepted integrated approach to crime and criminal behavior that can explain the many diverse forms of criminality while also leading to effective social policies in the area of crime control. The attempt to construct criminological theories that are relevant to the problems of today is made all the more difficult because, as discussed earlier, the phenomenon under study—crime—is very wide-ranging and is subject to arbitrary and sometimes unpredictable legalistic and definitional changes.

A successfully integrated criminology must bring together the contributions of various theoretical perspectives and disciplines,

but it also must—if it is to have any relevance—blend the practical requirements of our nation's judicial system with emotional and rational calls for morality and justice. Is the death penalty, for example, justified? If so, on what basis? Is it because it is a type of vengeance and therefore deserved? Can we say that it is unjustified because many sociological studies have shown that it does little to reduce the rate of serious crime such as murder? Just what do we mean by "justice," and what can criminological studies tell us—if anything—about what is just and what is unjust?

The editors of the journal *Theoretical Criminology*,[38] which began publication over a decade ago, wrote in the inaugural issue that "criminology has always been somewhat of a haphazardly-assembled umbrella-like structure which nevertheless usefully shelters a variety of theoretical interests that are espoused and employed by different disciplinary, methodological and political traditions." Such a structure, they said, "has obvious advantages, notably that it facilitates an interdisciplinary and inclusivist formation rather than supposing an exclusive but contentious 'core.' But one of its weaknesses is that its inhabitants, many of whom shuttle backwards and forwards between it and their parent disciplines, tend to communicate honestly and meaningfully only with those who speak the same theoretical language."[39] In other words, while the field of criminology can benefit from the wide variety of ideas available via a multiplicity of perspectives, all of which seek to understand the phenomenon we call "crime," successful cross-disciplinary collaboration can be quite difficult.

As our earlier definition of criminology indicates, however, it is more than a field of study or a collection of theories; it is also a discipline and a profession.[40] More than a decade ago, in his presidential address to the ASC, Charles F. Wellford identified the "primary purposes" of the criminology profession: "Controlling crime through prevention, rehabilitation, and deterrence and ensuring that the criminal justice system reflects the high aspiration we have as a society of 'justice for all' characterize the principal goals that in my judgment motivate the work of our field."[41]

Notably, criminology also contributes to the discipline of **criminal justice**, which emphasizes application of the criminal law and study of the components of the justice system, especially the police, courts, and corrections. As one author stated, "Criminology gives prominence to questions about the *causes of criminality*, while the *control of lawbreaking* is at the heart of criminal justice."[42] Learn more about the interdisciplinary nature of criminology via **Web Extra 1–7**. Read a few articles describing the nature of contemporary criminology at **Library Extras 1–5**, **1–6**, and **1–7**.

theory
A series of interrelated propositions that attempts to describe, explain, predict, and ultimately control some class of events. A theory gains explanatory power from inherent logical consistency and is "tested" by how well it describes and predicts reality.

general theory
A theory that attempts to explain all (or at least most) forms of criminal conduct through a single overarching approach.

unicausal
Having one cause. Unicausal theories posit only one source for all that they attempt to explain.

integrated theory
An explanatory perspective that merges (or attempts to merge) concepts drawn from different sources.

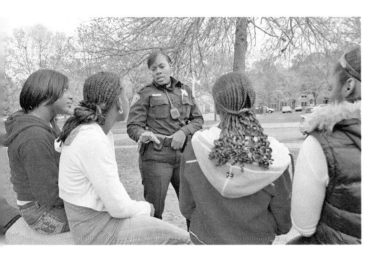

A police officer speaks to a group of young people.
Criminology examines the causes of crime and seeks ways to prevent or control it. Criminal justice examines the criminal justice system, including police, courts, and corrections. How do the two disciplines complement one another?
Source: Peter Casolino/Alamy Images

Theoretical Criminology

Theoretical criminology, a subfield of general criminology, is the type of criminology most often found in colleges and universities. Theoretical criminology, rather than simply describing crime and its occurrence, posits explanations for criminal behavior. As Sutherland stated, "The problem in criminology is to explain the criminality of behavior. . . . However, an explanation of criminal behavior should be a specific part of [a] general theory of behavior and its task should be to differentiate criminal from noncriminal behavior."[43]

To explain and understand crime, criminologists have developed many theories. As we shall see in Chapter 2, a **theory**, at least in its ideal form, is made up of clearly stated propositions that posit relationships, often of a causal sort, between events and things under study. An old Roman theory, for example, proposed that insanity was caused by the influence of the moon and may even follow its cycles—hence the term *lunacy*.

Theories attempt to provide us with explanatory power and help us understand the phenomenon under study. The more applicable a theory is found to be, the more generalizable it is from one specific instance to others—in other words, the more it can be applied to other situations. A **general theory** of crime is one that attempts to explain all (or at least most) forms of criminal conduct through a single overarching approach. Unfortunately, as Don M. Gottfredson, past president of the ASC, observed, "Theories in criminology tend to be unclear and lacking in justifiable generality."[44] When we consider the wide range of behaviors regarded as criminal—from murder to drug use to white-collar crime to cybercrime—it seems difficult to imagine one theory that can explain them all or that might even explain the same type of behavior under varying circumstances. Still, many past theoretical approaches to crime causation were **unicausal** while attempting to be all-inclusive, that is, the approaches posited a single identifiable source for all serious deviant and criminal behavior.

An **integrated theory**, in contrast to a general theory, does not necessarily attempt to explain all criminality but is distinguishable by the fact that it merges (or attempts to merge) concepts drawn from different sources. As noted criminologist Gregg Barak stated, "An integrative criminology . . . seeks to bring together the diverse bodies of knowledge that represent the full array of disciplines that study crime."[45] Hence, integrated theories provide potentially wider explanatory power than narrower formulations. Don C. Gibbons, professor of sociology at Portland State University, noted, "The basic idea of theoretical integration is straightforward; it concerns the combinations of single theories or elements of those theories into a more comprehensive argument. At the same time, it would be well to note that in practice, integration is a matter of degree: some theorists have combined or integrated more concepts or theoretical elements than have others."[46]

Both the general applicability and the theoretical integration of criminological theories to a wide variety of law-violating behaviors are intuitively appealing concepts. Even far more limited attempts at criminological theorizing, however, often face daunting challenges. "As we shall see," noted Gibbons, "criminologists have not managed to articulate a large collection of relatively formalized arguments in a general or integrated form."[47] Hence, although we will use the word *theory* in describing the many explanations for crime covered by this book, it should be recognized that the word is only loosely applicable to some of the perspectives we will discuss.

As we shall learn in Chapter 2, many social scientists insist that to be considered theories, explanations must consist of sets of clearly stated, logically interrelated, and measurable propositions. The fact that only a few of the theories described in this book rise above the level of organized conjecture—and those offer only limited generalizability and have rarely been integrated—is one of the greatest challenges facing criminology today.

LIBRARY EXTRA 1–8
WEB EXTRA 1–8

Experimental criminology uses social scientific techniques to test the accuracy of theories about crime and criminality.

Before leaving this brief discussion of theory, we should mention that a particular aspect of criminology, called *experimental criminology*, consists of the effort to use social scientific techniques to test the accuracy of theories about crime and criminality. Experimental criminology is discussed in more detail in the next chapter.

Criminology and Social Policy

Formulation of Social Policy

Of potentially broader importance than theory testing are social policies based on research findings. Some policy implications, including those relating to the physical environment, may be readily agreed upon and easy to implement—such as the installation of brighter lighting in crime-prone areas in an effort to reduce criminal activity.[48] Other policy innovations, especially those involving calls for cultural or social changes, can be far more complex and difficult to implement, even when there is strong evidence for them. A few years ago, for example, an editorial in the highly regarded British magazine *New Scientist* asked, "Why are we so reluctant to accept that on-screen violence is bad for us?"[49] The article, titled "In Denial," noted that "by the time the average U.S. schoolchild leaves elementary school, he or she will have witnessed more than 8,000 murders and 100,000 other acts of violence on television." If the child has access to computer games and cable TV, the article said, the numbers will be far higher. Scientific studies have consistently demonstrated the detrimental effects of media violence, according to the article, "yet every time a study claims to have found a link between aggression, violence, educational, or behavioral problems and TV programs or computer games, there are cries of incredulity."

A number of professional groups—including the American Medical Association, the American Academy of Pediatrics, the American Psychological Association, and the American Academy of Child and Adolescent Psychiatry—have all said that violence in television, music, video games, and movies leads to increased levels of violent behavior among children. A joint statement issued by those organizations stated that "the effects of violence in the media are measurable and long-lasting . . . based on over 30 years of research . . . that viewing entertainment violence can lead to increases in aggressive attitudes, values and behaviors, particularly in children. [Moreover,] . . . prolonged viewing of media violence can lead to emotional desensitization toward violence in real life."[50] Similarly, some years ago the Federal Trade Commission (FTC) issued a report on teenage violence;[51] it concluded that "Hollywood aggressively markets violent movies, music and electronic games to children even when they have been labeled as appropriate only for adults."[52] The complete 116-page FTC report *Marketing Violent Entertainment to Children* is available at **Web Extra 1–8**.

Even after all the studies that have been done, however, policymakers have been reluctant to curtail the production of violent media, and violence on TV and in video games is still a way of life in the United States. *New Scientist* noted that the profit motives of media vendors interfere with policies aimed at crime reduction, saying that "any criticism of a multibillion-dollar business is bound to provoke a sharp rebuttal."[53]

Professional criminologists are acutely aware of the need to link sound social policy to the objective findings of well-conducted criminological research. A meeting of the ASC, for example, focused on the need to forge just such a link. At the meeting, ASC President Alfred Blumstein, of Carnegie Mellon University, told criminologists gathered there that "an important mission of the ASC and its members involves the generation of knowledge that is useful in dealing with crime and the operation of the criminal justice system, and then helping public officials to use that knowledge intelligently and effectively."[54] Blumstein added, "So little is known about the causes of crime and about the effects of criminal justice policy on crime that new insights about the criminal justice system can often be extremely revealing and can eventually change the way people think about the crime problem or about the criminal justice system."[55]

Social Policy and Public Crime Concerns

Although American crime rates declined steadily for more than a decade beginning in the mid-1990s, concern over national security, crime, immigration, and terrorism (which are also forms of criminal activity) remains pervasive in the United States. About 25 years ago, crime was the number one concern of Americans

WEB EXTRA 1–9
LIBRARY EXTRA 1–9

■ **social problems perspective**
The belief that crime is a manifestation of underlying social problems, such as poverty, discrimination, pervasive family violence, inadequate socialization practices, and the breakdown of traditional social institutions.

A woman peers through a peephole in her front door.
According to pollsters, crime remains one of the American public's top concerns. Given recent statistics showing falling crime rates, is such concern justified?
Source: Peter Alvey People/Alamy

voicing opinions in public polls. In the interim, concern over crime came to be replaced with economic and other worries. However, following a spate of seemingly random violence—including widely publicized shootings, cult-based violence, gang-related drive-by shootings, dramatic instances of kidnapping and human trafficking, terrorist attacks, and highly visible inner-city crime—fear of violence and concern over personal safety have once again moved to the forefront of national issues.

A Gallup poll, for example, found that 67% of respondents believed that crime in the United States is more prevalent than it was a year earlier, and 49% rated the problem of crime in the United States as "extremely serious" or "very serious." While some issues, such as immigration, racial integration, and war, have come and gone from the list of concerns identified by pollsters, others (including crime, education, and the economy) appear to be enduring worries.[56] See **Web Extra 1–9** for recent public opinion polls about crime, concerns about crime, and fear of crime.

Even though crime rates have declined, concern over crime remains an important determinant of public policy. Hence, political agendas that promise to lower crime rates or to keep them low, as well as those that call for changes in the conditions that produce crime, can be quite successful for candidates or incumbents who

promote them in an environment where concern over crime remains high.[57] For more information about measuring the fear of crime, read **Library Extra 1–9**.

The Theme of This Book

This book builds on a social policy theme both by asking questions about the sources of crime and criminality and by asking what we can do to control crime. Our theme contrasts two perspectives now popular in American society and in much of the rest of the world (see Figure 1–3). One point of view, termed the **social problems perspective**, holds that crime is a manifestation of underlying social problems such as poverty, discrimination, inequality of opportunity, breakdown of traditional social institutions, low level of formal education among some disadvantaged groups, pervasive family violence experienced by some during the formative years, and inadequate socialization practices that leave too many young people without the fundamental values necessary to contribute meaningfully to the society in which they live. Advocates of the social problems perspective, while generally agreeing that crime and violence are serious social problems, advance solutions based on what is, in effect, a public health model. Adherents of that model say that crime must be addressed in much the same way as public health concerns like AIDS, herpes, or avian flu.

Social Problems

Social Responsibility

FIGURE 1-3 | The Theme of This Book: Social Problems versus Social Responsibility

■ **social responsibility perspective**
The belief that individuals are fundamentally responsible for their own behavior and that they choose crime over other, more law-abiding courses of action.

At the core of today's thinking about crime exists a crucial distinction between those who believe that crime is a *manifestation of underlying social problems* beyond the control of individuals (the social problems perspective) and those who emphasize that crime is a matter of *individual responsibility* (the social responsibility perspective).

Proponents of the social problems perspective typically foresee solutions to the crime problem as coming in the form of large-scale government expenditures in support of social programs designed to address the issues that are perceived to lie at the root of crime. Government-funded initiatives, designed to enhance social, educational, occupational, and other opportunities, are perceived as offering programmatic solutions to ameliorate most causes of crime. The social problems approach to crime is characteristic of what social scientists term a *macro approach* because it portrays instances of individual behavior (crimes) as arising out of widespread and contributory social conditions that enmesh unwitting individuals in a causal nexus of uncontrollable social forces.

A contrasting perspective lays the cause of crime squarely at the feet of individual perpetrators. This point of view holds that individuals are fundamentally responsible for their own behavior and maintains that they choose crime over other, more law-abiding courses of action. Perpetrators may choose crime, advocates of this perspective say, because it is exciting, because it offers illicit pleasures and the companionship of like-minded thrill seekers, or because it is simply personally less demanding than conformity. This viewpoint, which we shall call the **social responsibility perspective**, has a close affiliation with what is known in criminology as rational choice theory (discussed in detail in Chapter 3). It is also closely associated with a strongly held belief in the importance of free will, which is common to Western societies.[58]

Advocates of the social responsibility perspective, with their emphasis on individual choice, tend to believe that social programs do little to solve the problem of crime because, they say, a certain number of crime-prone individuals, for a variety of personal reasons, will always make irresponsible choices. Hence, advocates of the social responsibility approach suggest highly personalized crime-reduction strategies based on firm punishments, imprisonment, individualized rehabilitation, and increased security as well as a wider use of police powers. The social responsibility perspective characteristically emphasizes a *micro approach* that tends to focus on individual offenders and their unique biology, psychology, background, and immediate life experiences.

Over time, the social responsibility perspective has substantially influenced national crime-control policy. Examples of conservatism in our nation's approach to criminals abound. The Violent Crime Control and Law Enforcement Act of 1994, for example (which is discussed in detail later in this text), expanded the number of capital crimes under federal law from a handful of offenses to 52.[59] The law also made billions of dollars available to municipalities to put 100,000 new police officers on the streets and allocated billions for states to build and operate prisons and incarceration alternatives like "boot camps." Prison funding was intended to ensure that additional prison cells would be available to put—and keep—violent offenders behind bars. A subchapter of the 1994 Violent Crime Control and Law Enforcement Act created a federal "Three Strikes and You're Out" law, mandating life imprisonment for criminals convicted of three violent federal felonies or drug offenses. Similarly, the law increased or created new penalties for over 70 federal criminal offenses, primarily covering violent crimes, drug trafficking, and gun crimes. Since the 1994 federal legislation was passed, many states have moved to toughen their own laws against violent criminals; violent juveniles and repeat offenders have been especially targeted.

> Advocates of the social responsibility approach suggest crime-reduction strategies based on firm punishments, imprisonment, individualized rehabilitation, and increased security.

The USA PATRIOT Act—enacted in 2001 and renewed with modifications in 2006—targets terrorism and crimes committed in support of terrorist activity. The PATRIOT Act has been criticized by many for going too far in limiting individual freedoms and restricting personal choice, although its supporters argue that its provisions are needed to effectively fight the "war on terrorism." The PATRIOT Act and the crime of terrorism are discussed in more detail in Chapter 14.

A note about wording is in order. Although the social responsibility perspective might also be termed the *individual responsibility perspective* because it stresses individual responsibility above all else, we've chosen to use the term *social responsibility perspective* instead, as it holds that individuals must be ultimately responsible to the social group of which they are a part and that they should be held accountable by group standards if they are not. In short, this perspective is characterized by societal demands for the exercise of individual responsibility.

> ■ **social relativity**
> The notion that social events are differently interpreted according to the cultural experiences and personal interests of the initiator, the observer, or the recipient of that behavior.

The Social Context of Crime

Crime does not occur in a vacuum. Every crime has a unique set of causes, consequences, and participants. Crime affects some people more than others, having a special impact on those who are direct participants in the act itself—offenders, victims, police officers, witnesses, and so on. Crime, in general, provokes reactions from its victims, from concerned groups of citizens, from the criminal justice system, and sometimes from society as a whole, which manifests its concerns via the creation of new social policy. Reactions to crime, from the everyday to the precedent-setting, may color the course of future criminal events.[60]

In this book, we shall attempt to identify and examine some of the many social, psychological, economic, biological, and other causes of crime while expounding on the many differing perspectives that have been advanced to explain both crime and criminality. Popular conceptions of criminal motivation are typically shaped by media portrayals of offender motivation, which often fail to take into consideration the felt experiences of the law violators. By identifying and studying this diversity of perspectives on criminality, we will discover the characteristic disjuncture among victims, offenders, the justice system, and society as to the significance that each assigns to the behavior in question—and often to its motivation. It will not be unusual to find, for example, that sociological or psychological initiatives with which the offenders themselves do not identify are assigned to those offenders by theorists and others.

Making Sense of Crime: The Causes and Consequences of the Criminal Event

This book recognizes that criminal activity is diversely created and variously interpreted. In other words, this book depicts crime not as an isolated individual activity but as a *social event*.[61] Like other social events, crime is fundamentally a social construction.[62] To say that crime is a social construction is not to lessen the impact of the victimization experiences that all too many people undergo in our society every day, nor does such a statement trivialize the significance of crime-prevention efforts or the activities of members of the criminal justice system. Likewise, it does not underplay the costs of crime to individual victims and to society

as a whole. It does, however, recognize that although a given instance of criminal behavior may have many causes, it also carries with it many different kinds of meanings—at least one for offenders, another (generally quite a different meaning, of course) for victims, and still another for agents of the criminal justice system. Similarly, a wide range of social interest groups, from victims' advocates to prisoner "rights" and gun-control organizations, all interpret the significance of law-breaking behavior from unique points of view, and each arrives at different conclusions as to what should be done about the so-called crime problem.

For these reasons, we have chosen to apply the concept of social relativity to the study of criminality.[63] **Social relativity** means that social events are interpreted differently according to the cultural experiences and personal interests of the initiator, the observer, or the recipient of that behavior. Hence, as a social phenomenon, crime means different things to the offender who commits it, to the criminologist who studies it, to the police officer who investigates it, and to the victim who experiences it firsthand.

Figure 1–4 illustrates both the causes and the consequences of crime in rudimentary diagrammatic form. In keeping with the theme of this textbook, it depicts crime as a social event. The figure consists of a foreground, which describes those features that immediately determine the nature of the criminal event (including responses to the event as it is transpiring), and a background, in which generic contributions to the crime can be seen along with interpretations of the event after it has taken place. We call the background causes of crime *contributions* and use the word *inputs* to signify the more immediate propensities and predispositions of the actors involved in the situation. Inputs also include the physical features of the setting in which a specific crime takes place. Both background contributions and immediate inputs contribute to and shape the criminal event. The more or less immediate results or consequences of crime are termed *outputs*, whereas the term *interpretations* appears in the diagram to indicate that any crime has a lasting impact both on surviving participants and on society. As Figure 1–4 shows, the criminal event is ultimately a result of the coming together of inputs provided by the following: the offender, the criminal justice system, the victim, and society.

Crime and the Offender

Offenders bring with them certain background features, such as personal life experiences, a peculiar biology (insofar as they are unique organisms), a distinct personality, personal values and beliefs, and various kinds of skills and knowledge (some of which may be useful in the commission of crime). Background contributions to

■ **criminal justice system**
The various agencies of justice, especially the police, courts, and corrections, whose goal it is to apprehend, convict, punish, and rehabilitate law violators.

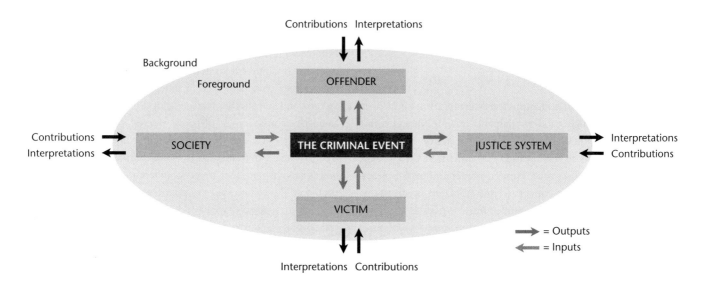

FIGURE 1-4 | The Causes and Consequences of Crime

crime can be vitally important. Recent research, for example, tends to cement the existence of a link between child-rearing practices and criminality in later life. Joan McCord, reporting on a 30-year study of family relationships and crime, found that self-confident, nonpunitive, and affectionate mothers tend to insulate their male children from delinquency and, consequently, later criminal activity.[64] Difficulties associated with the birthing process have also been linked to crime in adulthood.[65] Negative familial relationships and birth trauma are but two of the literally thousands of kinds of experiences individuals may have. Whether individuals who undergo trauma at birth and are deprived of positive maternal experiences will turn to crime depends on many other things, including their own mixture of other experiences and characteristics, the appearance of a suitable victim, the failure of the justice system to prevent crime, and the evolution of a social environment in which criminal behavior is somehow encouraged or valued.

Each of the parties identified in Figure 1–4 contributes immediate inputs to the criminal event. Foreground contributions by the offender may consist of a particular motivation, a specific intent (in many cases), or a drug-induced state of mind.

Crime and the Criminal Justice System

Like the offender, the **criminal justice system** (meaning the various agencies of justice such as the police, courts, and corrections) also contributes to the criminal event, albeit unwillingly, through its failure to (1) prevent criminal activity, (2) adequately identify and inhibit specific offenders prior to their involvement in crime, and (3) prevent the release of convicted criminals who later become repeat offenders. Such background contributions can be seen in prisons (a central component of the justice system) that serve as "schools for crime," fostering anger against society and building a propensity for continued criminality in inmates who have been "turned out." Similarly, the failure of system-sponsored crime-prevention programs—ranging from the patrol activities of local police departments to educational and diversionary programs intended to redirect budding offenders—helps set the stage for the criminal event.

On the other hand, proper system response may reduce crime. A study by Carol W. Kohfeld and John Sprague, for example, found that police response (especially arrest) can, under certain demographic conditions, dramatically reduce the incidence of criminal behavior.[66] Additionally, Kohfeld and Sprague found that arrest "constitutes communication to criminals in general," further supporting the notion that inputs provided by the justice system have the power to either enhance or reduce the likelihood of criminal occurrences. Immediate inputs provided by the justice system typically consist of such features of the situation as the presence or absence of police officers, the ready availability (or lack thereof) of official assistance, the willingness of police officers to intervene in precrime situations, and the response time required for officers to arrive at a crime scene.

> ■ **socialization**
> The lifelong process of social experience whereby individuals acquire the cultural patterns of their society.

Crime and the Victim

Few crimes can occur without a victim. Sometimes the victim is a passive participant in the crime, such as an innocent person killed on the street outside of his or her home by random gunfire from a drive-by shooting. In such cases, the victim is simply in the proverbial wrong place at the wrong time. Even then, however, merely by being present the victim contributes his or her person to the event, thereby increasing the severity of the incident (that is, the random shooting that injures no one may still be against the law but is a far less serious crime than a similar incident in which somebody is killed). Sometimes, however, victims more actively contribute to their own victimization by appearing defenseless (having characteristics such as old age, drunkenness, or disability), by failing to take appropriate defensive measures (leaving doors unlocked or forgetting to remove the key from a car's ignition), by unwisely displaying wealth (flashing large-denomination bills in a public place), or simply by making other unwise choices (walking down a dark alley off of Times Square at 3 A.M.). In a study of Canadian victimization, Leslie W. Kennedy and David R. Forde found that violent personal victimization "is contingent on the exposure that comes from following certain lifestyles," which was especially true "for certain demographic groups, particularly young males."[67]

> Sometimes victims actively contribute to their own victimization by making unwise choices.

Although lifestyles may provide the background that fosters victimization, a more active form of victimization characterizes "victims" who initiate criminal activity, such as the barroom brawler who picks a fight but ends up on the receiving end of the ensuing physical violence. Victim-precipitated offenses are those that involve active victim participation in the initial stages of a criminal event and that take place when the soon-to-be victim instigates the chain of events that ultimately results in the victimization.

Crime and Society

Finally, the general public (termed *society* in Figure 1–4) contributes to the criminal event both formally and informally. Society's formal contributions sometimes take the form of legislation, whereby crime itself is defined. Hence, as we shall discuss in considerable detail in Chapter 14, society structures the criminal event in a most fundamental way by delineating (through legislation and via statute) which forms of activity are to be thought of as criminal.

Society's less formal contributions to crime arise out of generic social practices and conditions like poverty, poor and informal education, and various forms of discrimination by which pathways to success are blocked as well as **socialization** (the process whereby people acquire the cultural patterns of their society). Socialization has an especially important impact on crime causation because it provides the interpretative foundation used to define and understand the significance of particular situations in which we find ourselves, and it is upon those interpretations that we may (or may not) decide to act. Date rape, for example, can occur when a man concludes that his date "owes" him something for the money he has spent on her. That feeling, however inappropriate from the point of view of the victim and the justice system, probably has its roots in early learned experiences—including values communicated from television, the movies, and popular music—about gender-related roles under such circumstances. In other words, society, through the divergent values and expectations it places on people, property, and behavior under particular conditions, may provide the motivational basis for many offenses.

The contributions society makes to the backgrounds of both offender and victim and to the structure of the justice system and the influences each, in turn, has upon the general social order provide for a kind of "feedback loop" in our vision of crime (even though the loop is not shown in Figure 1–4 for fear of unnecessarily complicating it). Through socialization, for example, individuals learn about the dangers of criminal victimization, but when victimization occurs and is publicized, it reinforces the socialization process, leading to an increased wariness of others and so on. An example can be seen in the fact that children throughout the United States are routinely taught to avoid strangers and to be suspicious of people they do not know. A few decades ago, stranger avoidance was not ordinarily communicated to children; it entered cultural awareness following a number of horrendous and well-publicized crimes involving child victims and is now a shared part of the socialization process experienced by countless children every day throughout the United States.

The contributions made by society to crime are complex and far reaching. Some say that the content of the mass media (television, movies, newspapers, popular music, etc.) can lead to crime by exposing young people to inappropriate role models and to the kinds of activity—violence and unbridled sexuality, for example—that encourage criminality.

Society's foreground contributions to crime largely emanate from the distribution of resources and the accessibility of services, which are often the direct result of economic conditions. In a study of the availability of medical resources (especially quality hospital emergency services), William G. Doerner found that serious assaults may "become" homicides when such resources are lacking but that homicides can be prevented through the effective utilization of capable medical technology.[68] Hence, societal decisions leading to the distribution and placement of advanced medical support equipment and personnel can effectively lower homicide rates in selected geographic areas, but homicide rates will be higher in areas where such equipment is not readily available. In Doerner's words, "The causes of homicide transcend the mere social world of the combatants."[69]

The moments that immediately precede any crime are ripe with possibilities. When all the inputs brought to the situation by all those present coalesce into activity that violates the criminal law, a crime occurs. Together, the elements, experiences, and propensities brought to the situation by the offender and the victim, and those that are contributed to the pending event by society and the justice system, precipitate and decide the nature, course, and eventual outcome of the criminal event. As one well-known criminologist explained, "An understanding of crime and criminality as constructed from the immediate interactions of criminals, control agents, victims, and others, and therefore as emerging from a tangled experiential web of situated dangers and situated pleasures, certainly refocuses theories of criminal causality on the criminal moment."[70] While certain circumstances contribute to the criminal event as it unfolds, it is also important to note that some of the inputs brought to the situation may be inhibiting, that is, they may tend to reduce the likelihood or severity of criminal behavior.

As mentioned earlier, the causes of crime, however well documented, tell only half the criminological story. Each and every crime has consequences. Although the immediate consequences of crime may be relatively obvious for those parties directly involved (for example, the offender and the victim), crime also indirectly impacts society and the justice system over the longer term. Figure 1–4 terms the immediate effects of crime *outputs*. As with the causes of crime, however, the real impact of such outputs is mediated by perceptual filters, resulting in what the figure terms *interpretations*. After a crime has taken place, each party to the event must make sense out of what has transpired. Such interpretations consist of cognitive, emotional, and (ultimately) behavioral reactions to the criminal event.

Interpretations are ongoing. They happen before, during, and after the criminal event and are undertaken by all those associated with it. In an interesting and detailed study of the interpretative activity of criminal justice system personnel, James F. Gilsinan documented what happens when callers reach the 9-1-1 operator on police emergency lines.[71] Because many prank calls and calls for information are made to 9-1-1 operators, the operators must judge the seriousness of every call that comes through. What the caller says was found to be only a small part of the informational cues that an operator seeks to interpret before assigning the call to a particular response (or nonresponse) category. Honest calls for help may go unanswered if the operator misinterprets the call. Hence, quite early on in the criminal event, the potential exists for a crucial representative of the justice system to misinterpret important cues and to conclude that no crime is taking place.

Other interpretative activities may occur long after the crime has transpired, but they are at least as significant. The justice system, taken as a whole, must decide guilt or innocence and must attempt to deal effectively with convicted offenders. Victims must attempt to make sense of their victimization in such a way as to allow them to testify in court (if need be) and to pick up the pieces of their crime-shattered lives. Offenders must come to terms with themselves and decide whether to avoid prosecution (if escape, for example, is possible), accept blame, or deny responsibility. Whatever the outcome of these more narrowly focused interpretative activities, society—because of the cumulative impact of individual instances of criminal behavior—will also face tough decisions through its courts and law-making agencies. Society-level decision making may revolve around the implementation of policies designed to stem future instances of criminal behavior, the revision of criminal codes, or the elimination of unpopular laws.

Our perspective takes a three-dimensional integrative view of the social event termed *crime*. We will (1) attempt to identify and understand the multiple causes that give rise to criminal behavior, (2) highlight the processes involved in the criminal event as it unfolds, and (3) analyze the interpretation of the crime phenomenon, including societal responses to it. From this perspective, crime can be viewed along a temporal continuum as an emergent activity that (1) arises out of past complex causes; (2) assumes a course that builds upon immediate interrelationships among the victim, offender, and social order that exist at the time of the offense; and (3) elicits a formal response from the justice system, shapes public perceptions, and (possibly) gives rise to changes in social policy after it has occurred.

The advantages of an integrative perspective can be found in the completeness of the picture that it provides. The integrative point of view results in a comprehensive and inclusive view of crime because it emphasizes the personal and social underpinnings as well as the consequences of crime. The chapters that follow employ the integrative perspective advocated here to analyze criminal events and to show how various theoretical approaches can be woven into a consistent perspective on crime. For a different point of view, one that describes crime in terms of the five dimensions of (1) law, (2) offender, (3) target and/or victim, (4) location, and (5) time of the incident, read **Library Extra 1–10**.

A computerized map showing the incidence of motor vehicle theft for Boston, Massachusetts. What can such maps tell us? What social aspects of criminal offending are not revealed by maps like this?

Source: Copyright & courtesy of Caliper Corporation (Created using Maptitude)

The Primacy of Sociology?

This book recognizes the contributions made by numerous disciplines, including biology, economics, psychology, psychiatry, physiology, and political science, to the study of crime and crime causation. It is important to recognize, however, that the primary perspective from which many contemporary criminologists operate is a sociological one. Hence, a large number of today's theoretical explanations of criminal behavior are routinely couched in the language of social science and fall within the framework of sociological theory. The social problems versus social responsibility theme, around which this book is built, is in keeping with such a tradition.

Many, however, would disagree with those who claim that the sociological perspective should be accorded heightened importance in today's criminological enterprise. Those who argue in favor of the primacy of sociology emphasize the fact that crime, as a subject of study, is a social phenomenon. Central to any study of crime, they say, must be the social context of the criminal event because it is the social context that brings victims and criminals together.[72] Moreover, much of contemporary criminology rests upon a tradition of social scientific investigation into the nature of crime and criminal behavior that is rooted in European and American sociological traditions that are now well over 200 years old.[73]

One of sociology's problems, however, has been its apparent reluctance to accept the significance of findings from other fields as well as its frequent inability to integrate such findings into existing sociological understandings of crime. Another has been its seeming inability to demonstrate conclusively effective means of controlling violent (as well as other forms of) crime. As Diana Fishbein, professor of criminology at the University of Baltimore, said, "Sociological factors play a role. But they have not been able to explain why one person becomes violent and another doesn't."[74]

While sociological theories continue to develop, new and emerging perspectives ask to be recognized. The role of biology in explaining criminal tendencies, for example, appears to be gaining strength as investigations into the mapping of human DNA continue. Charles F. Wellford, past president of the ASC, explained the current state of affairs, saying, "I strongly believe that the future development of causal theory is dependent upon our movement toward integrated theories that involve biological, social, and cultural dimensions. Our failure to achieve much in the way of understanding the causal sequences of crime is in part a reflection of our slowness in moving toward multidisciplinary, integrated theoretical structures. The fact is that for two-thirds of this century, as criminology developed, we remained committed to a small number of sociological models for which there is extensive proof of their important but limited value. Fortunately in the last 20 years, this has begun to change. Today we see under way substantial research efforts that are based upon models of explanation that far exceed the traditional sociological approaches."[75]

Nonetheless, whatever new insights may develop over the coming years, it is likely that the sociological perspective will continue to dominate the field of criminology for some time to come. Such dominance is rooted in the fact that crime—regardless of all the causative nuances that may be identified in its development—occurs within the context of the social world. As such, the primary significance of crime and of criminal behavior is fundamentally social in nature, and any control over crime must stem from effective social policy.

> The primary significance of crime and of criminal behavior is fundamentally social in nature, and any control over crime must stem from effective social policy.

SUMMARY

- At the start of this chapter, the term *crime* was defined as a violation of the criminal law. Near the end of this chapter, we recognized the complexity of crime, calling it an "emergent phenomenon." In the process, crime was redefined as a law-breaking event whose significance arises out of an intricate social nexus involving a rather wide variety of participants.

- Deviance, or deviant behavior, refers to a violation of social norms. Some forms of behavior (such as murder, rape, and most serious crimes) are both criminal and deviant. Others may be deviant but not criminal (for example, nudity under certain circumstances), or may be criminal but not regarded as deviant by many members of society (for example, the use of marijuana).

- Decisions as to what should be criminal are generally made by legislatures, at both the state and federal levels. Such decisions are arrived at through a political process that involves input from social interest groups, including those in favor of criminalizing certain behaviors and those opposed to criminalizing them.

- *Criminology* is "an interdisciplinary profession built around the scientific study of crime and criminal behavior, including their forms, causes, legal aspects, and control." The term *criminologist* is applied to credentialed individuals who engage in the study of crime, criminal behavior, and crime trends. *Criminalist* is used to describe people who specialize in the collection and examination of the physical evidence associated with specific crimes. *Criminal justice professionals* include law enforcement officers, judges, criminal defense attorneys, prosecutors, cybercrime investigators, victims' advocates, jailers, corrections officers, and so on.

- Criminologists are acutely aware of the need to link sound social policy to the objective findings of well-conducted criminological research. Unfortunately, political considerations and long-standing traditional solutions have formed the basis for much crime-control policy in the past, and the situation is only slowly changing.

- This book builds on a social policy theme by asking what the sources of crime and criminality are and what we can do to control crime. The theme contrasts two perspectives: The *social responsibility perspective* holds that crime is a matter of individual responsibility; the *social problems perspective* holds that crime is a manifestation of underlying social problems beyond the control of individuals.

- This book sees crime as a social event, not an isolated individual activity. A given instance of criminal behavior may have many causes and many different kinds of meanings. Social relativity holds that social events are interpreted differently according to the cultural experiences and personal interests of the initiator, the observer, and the recipient of that behavior.

- The discipline of sociology has had the most impact on theoretical understandings of crime and crime causation, so a large number of today's theoretical explanations of criminal behavior are routinely couched in the language of social science and fall within the framework of sociological theory. Nonetheless, it is important to recognize the contributions made by numerous other disciplines (biology, economics, psychology, psychiatry, physiology, political science), making the study of crime and crime causation interdisciplinary.

KEY TERMS

crime, 2	integrated theory, 13
criminal behavior, 11	socialization, 19
criminalist, 8	social policy, 9
criminality, 11	social problems perspective, 15
criminalize, 3	social relativity, 17
criminal justice, 12	social responsibility perspective, 16
criminal justice system, 18	
criminologist, 8	statute, 3
criminology, 11	statutory law, 3
deviant behavior, 4	theory, 13
general theory, 13	unicausal, 13

QUESTIONS FOR REVIEW

1. What is crime? What is the definition of *crime* that the author of this textbook have chosen to use? How might the notion of crime change over time? What impact does the changing nature of crime have on criminology?

2. What is deviance? How are crime and deviance similar? How do they differ?

3. Who decides what should be criminal? How are such decisions made?

4. What is criminology? What do criminologists do? What are some of the employment opportunities available in the field of criminology?

5. How is social policy in the area of crime control determined? What role does criminological research play in the establishment of such policy?

6. What is the theme of this book? Upon what two contrasting viewpoints does it build?

7. What does it mean to say that "criminal activity is diversely created and variously interpreted"?

8. What discipline has contributed the most to theoretical understandings of crime causation over the past century?

QUESTIONS FOR REFLECTION

1. This book emphasizes the theme of social problems versus social responsibility. How would you describe both perspectives? How might social policy decisions based on these perspectives differ?

2. Do you think you might want to become a criminologist? Why or why not?

3. Are there any crimes today that you think should be legalized? If so, what are they and why?

4. Can you think of any advances now occurring in the social or physical sciences that might soon have a significant impact on our understanding of crime and criminality? If so, what would those advances be? How might they impact our understanding of crime and criminal behavior?

5. How would you describe the various participants in a criminal event? How does each contribute to an understanding of the event?

6. In what way is contemporary criminology interdisciplinary? Why is the sociological perspective especially important in studying crime? What other perspectives might be relevant? Why?

7. How does contemporary criminology influence social policy? Do you think that policymakers should address crime as a matter of individual responsibility and accountability, or do you think that crime is truly a symptom of a dysfunctional society? Why?

CHAPTER 2

WHERE DO THEORIES COME FROM?

LEARNING OUTCOMES

After reading this chapter, you should be able to answer the following questions:

- What is evidence-based criminology? How does the meaning of the word *evidence* in evidence-based criminology differ from the evidence found at a crime scene or used in criminal trials?

- What three eras have characterized the field of criminology over the past 100 years?

- What is a theory? What purposes do theories serve? What role do research and experimentation play in theory building in criminology?

- What is the role of criminological research in theory building? What is internal validity? External validity? How can threats to internal and external validity be addressed?

- What are the differences between quantitative and qualitative methods in the social sciences? What are the advantages and disadvantages of each method?

- What are some of the ethical considerations involved in conducting criminological research?

- How do criminological research and experimental criminology impact social policy?

- What sections might a typical research report contain?

Follow the author's tweets about the latest crime and justice news at **http://twitter.com/schmalleger**.

Introduction

Carolyn Risher, the 61-year-old Pentecostal mayor of Inglis, Florida, believes in an unusual crime-reduction strategy. In 2002, she issued an official proclamation banning Satan from Inglis and rendering him powerless over its 1,400 citizens. In the proclamation, issued on official town stationery, Risher wrote, "We exercise our authority over the devil in Jesus' name. By that authority we command all satanic and demonic forces to cease their activities and depart the town of Inglis."[1] While the mayor was undoubtedly well intentioned, Mitchell Billups, the town's police chief, says that crime did not decrease after the mayor took action.[2] Vandalism spiked when someone removed the four hollowed-out wooden posts containing copies of the proclamation that had been placed at town entrances. Following a threatened lawsuit by the American Civil Liberties Union, which accused the mayor and town council of violating our nation's hallowed principle of separation of church and state, the town later rescinded its proclamation and moved the wooden posts, which had been rebuilt and sunk into the ground with concrete, onto private property.[3] The mayor later reimbursed the town for the use of the stationery on which they had been written.[4] Risher was reelected as the town's mayor in 2003, a post she still holds today.[5]

The goings-on in Inglis reminded me of the first criminology class that I taught years ago at a small southern college in the heart of what was then referred to as the Bible Belt. Many of my students were devoutly religious and thoroughly churched in such hallowed concepts as good and evil, sin, salvation, and redemption. When the three-month course was nearly over and a detailed discussion of biological, psychological, and sociological theories of crime causation had ended, I decided to take a survey. I wanted to see which of the theories we had discussed most appealed to the majority of my students. On the last day of class, I took a brief survey. After explaining what I was about to do, I started with the question "How many of you think that most criminal behavior can be explained by the biological theories of crime causation we've studied?" Only one or two students raised their hands. This was a very small number because the class, a popular one, held 131 students and was taught in a small auditorium. "How many

of you," I continued, "think psychological theories explain most crime?" Again, only a handful of students responded. "Well, then, how many of you feel sociological theories offer the best explanation for crime?" I asked. A few more hands went up. Still, the majority of students had not voted one way or the other. Fearing that my teaching had been for naught and not knowing what else to ask, I blurted out, "How many of you believe that 'the devil made him do it' is the best explanation for crime that we can offer?" At that, almost all the students raised their hands.

I realized then that an entire semester spent trying to communicate the best thoughts of generations of criminologists had had little impact on most students in the class. They had listened to what I had to say, considered each of the perspectives I presented, and then dismissed all of them out of hand as so much idle conjecture—assigning them the status of ruminations sadly out of touch with the true character of human nature and lacking in appreciation for the true cosmic temper of human activity.

That class held a lesson for me greater than any that the students had learned: It taught me that contemporary criminological theory cannot be fully appreciated until and unless its fundamental assumptions are comprehended. Until students can be brought to see the value of scientific criminology and unless they can be shown why today's criminologists think and believe the way they do, it is impossible to convince them that the criminological enterprise is worthy of serious attention.

The lesson I learned that day was given voice by noted criminological researcher Lawrence W. Sherman, who, upon realizing that even the best scientific evidence the field has to offer is rarely accorded the significance that it deserves by policymakers, wrote: "The mythic power of subjective and unstructured wisdom holds back every field and keeps it from systematically discovering and implementing what works best."[6]

> Even the best scientific evidence is rarely accorded the significance that it deserves by policymakers.

■ **evidence based**
Built on scientific findings, especially practices and policies founded upon the results of randomized, controlled experiments.

■ **evidence-based criminology**
A form of contemporary criminology that makes use of rigorous social scientific techniques, especially randomized, controlled experiments and the systematic review of research results; also called knowledge-based criminology.

WEB EXTRA 2–1
WEB EXTRA 2–2

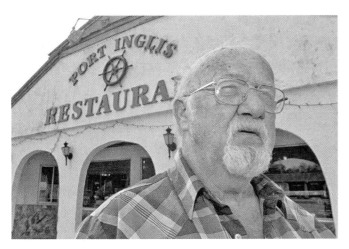

In hopes of keeping crime at bay, the mayor of Inglis, Florida, issued a proclamation in 2002 aimed at keeping Satan and his legions out of town. But Bob Farnan, owner of the Port Inglis Restaurant, isn't convinced that drug dealing and burglary have declined. His restaurant, behind him in this February 20, 2004, photo, has been broken into three times in less than a year. Did the proclamation impact the town's crime rate? Did it keep crime from rising? How can we know?
Source: AP Wide World Photos

Evidence-Based Criminology

This chapter describes how criminologists make use of contemporary social scientific research methods in the development of criminological theories, policies, and practices that are **evidence based**. It is my way of showing to those embarking upon the study of criminology why the modern-day science of criminology has both validity and purpose—that is, to show how it is applicable to the problems and realities of today's world. Were it not, the study of criminology would be pointless, and the criminological enterprise would become irrelevant. However, because contemporary criminology is built on a social scientific approach to the subject matter of crime, criminology—especially **evidence-based criminology** (also

called knowledge-based criminology)—has much to offer as we attempt to grapple with the problems of crime and crime control now facing us.

Evidence-based criminology is an increasing popular form of contemporary criminology that is founded upon the experimental method. The method utilizes the techniques of the social sciences (especially randomized, controlled experiments) in theory testing. When used in this context, the word *evidence* refers to scientific findings, *not* to the kind of evidence gathered by the police or used in criminal trials.

Some authors credit David Farrington, Lloyd Ohlin, and James Q. Wilson with helping to popularize the use of randomized experiments in the field of criminology.[7] In the mid-1980s their influential book, *Understanding and Controlling Crime*, recommended the use of such experiments whenever possible to test assumptions in the justice field.[8] Shortly afterward, the National Institute of Justice (NIJ), under (then) Director James C. Stewart, funded more than two dozen criminology-related experiments.[9] A decade later, Anthony Petrosino and his colleagues found that 267 criminological experiments had been conducted and published in English.[10]

In 2009, in recognition of the growing significance of evidence-based criminology, the executive board of the American Society of Criminology (ASC) established a new division of experimental criminology; the division's purpose is "the promotion and improvement of experimental evidence and methods in the advancement of criminological theory and evidence-based crime policy."[11]

Today, evidence-based criminology is given voice by the Academy of Experimental Criminology, which is based at the University of Pennsylvania, and by a number of important new journals including the *Journal of Experimental Criminology*, which is the first journal in the field of criminology to focus directly on experimental methods.[12] You can reach the Academy of Experimental Criminology via **Web Extra 2–1**. Another important voice in the area can be found at the University of Cambridge's Institute of Criminology in England. Learn more about the growing body of evidence-based findings in the field of criminology from the Institute's experimental criminology webpage at **Web Extra 2–2**.

Follow the author's tweets about the latest crime and justice news at **http://twitter.com/schmalleger**.

The Evolving Science of Criminology

In his seminal 2003 presidential address to the ASC, John H. Laub used the framework of life course theory (discussed in Chapter 7) to describe the history of criminological thought.[13] Laub identified three eras that he says have characterized the field of criminology over the past 100 years. The first era, said Laub, covered the years 1900 to 1930 and can "be thought of as the 'Golden Age of Research.'"[14] It was a time when data on crime and criminal behavior were largely gathered and evaluated independent of any particular ideational framework.

The second era, the period from 1930 to 1960, Laub called the "Golden Age of Theory" and described it as a time when intellectual theorizing "dominated the scene." Strangely, said Laub, during this second period, "there was no systematic attempt to link criminological research to theory."[15]

Era three extended from 1960 to 2000 and was "characterized by extensive theory testing of the dominant theories, using largely empirical methods." In other words, the third era identified by Laub was a time of scientific examination of the accuracy of criminological theories that had been previously advanced. Although he didn't address it directly, Laub indicated that the current era (that is, twenty-first-century criminology) is heir to the first three eras and contains "all possible offspring" of what came before.

As Laub's remarks show, criminologists over the past century have undertaken the task of building a scientific or evidence-based criminology, as distinguished from what had been the "armchair criminology" of earlier times. Armchair criminologists offered their ideas to one another as conjecture—fascinating "theories" that could be debated (and sometimes were) *ad nauseam*. Although the ruminations of armchair criminologists may have achieved a considerable degree of popular acclaim through (1) the involvement of distinguished lecturers, (2) the association of such ideas with celebrated bastions of higher learning, and (3) their publication in prestigious essays, they were rarely founded on anything other than mere speculation.

The ideas of armchair criminologists followed in the intellectual tradition of medieval Christian theologians, who sometimes busied themselves with debates over questions like how many angels could fit on the head of a pin or whether Noah had forgotten to take certain types of insects on board the ark. They were the kinds of things one could probably never know with certainty, no matter how much the ideas were debated, and the ideas being debated were rarely amenable to real-world tests. Under such circumstances, one person's theory was another's fact and still another's wishful thinking.[16]

Although it is easy to dispense with armchair criminology as the relaxed musings of carefree intellectuals undertaken almost as sport, it is far more difficult to agree on the criteria necessary to move any undertaking into the realm of serious scientific endeavor. Present-day criminology is decidedly more scientific, however, than its intellectual predecessor—which means that many of its theories and policy recommendations are amenable to objective scrutiny and systematic testing.

> Criminologists over the past century have undertaken the task of building a scientific or evidence-based criminology.

A variety of criteria have been advanced for declaring any endeavor "scientific." Among them are these:[17]

- The systematic collection of related facts (as in the building of a database)
- An emphasis on the availability and application of the scientific method
- "The existence of general laws, a field for experiment or observation, and control of academic discourse by practical application"
- "The fact that it has been accepted into the scientific tradition"
- An "emphasis on a worthwhile subject in need of independent study even if adequate techniques of study are not yet available" (as in the investigation of paranormal phenomena)

Probably all the foregoing could be said of today's criminology. For one thing, criminologists do gather facts (Laub's "Golden Age of Research"). The mere gathering of facts, however, although it may lead to a descriptive criminology, falls short of offering satisfactory explanations for crime. Hence, most contemporary criminologists are concerned with identifying relationships among the facts they observe and with attempting to understand the many diverse causes of crime. This emphasis on unveiling causality moves criminology beyond the merely descriptive into the realm of conjecture and theory building. A further emphasis on measurement and objectivity gives contemporary criminology its scientific flavor.

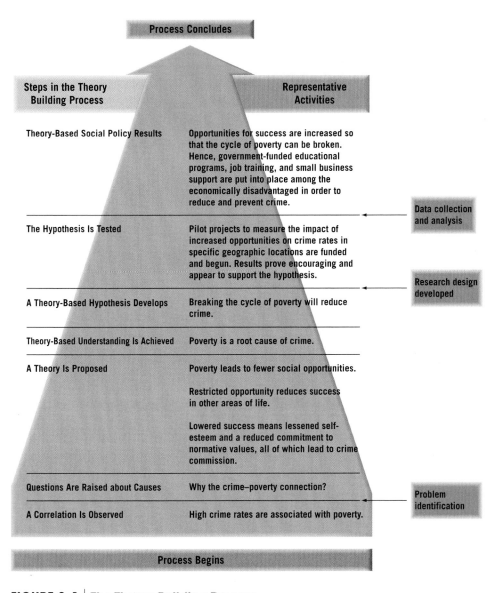

FIGURE 2-1 | The Theory Building Process

Theory Building

A few years ago, Inspector Andy Parr, of the Sussex Police Department in England, reviewed crime statistics for the town of Brighton and found that violent crime was higher on nights when the moon was full.[18] "I compared a graph of full moons and a graph of last year's violent crimes and there is a trend," Parr told the United Kingdom's *Telegraph* newspaper. "People tend to be more aggressive" when the moon is full, Parr concluded. His

findings were supported, he said, by his patrol experience. "When you try to reason with people on a full moon they become more aggressive and less rational," he told reporters. "When you try to reason with them on a full moon they become more argumentative."

Ultimately, the goal of research in criminology is the construction of theories or models that allow for a better understanding of criminal behavior and that permit the development of strategies intended to address the problem of crime. Simply put, a theory consists of a set of interrelated propositions that provides a relatively complete form of understanding (see Figure 2–1). Hence, even if we find that crime is higher when the moon is full, we must still ask why. Is it because the light from a full moon makes it possible for those who want to commit a crime to see better at night? If so, then we would expect crime to be higher in areas where there is no cloud cover than in areas with clouds. Likewise, lighted cities should show less of a rise in crime during a full moon than rural areas and small towns. In any event, a complete lunar theory of crime causation would contain specific propositions about the causal nature of the phenomena involved. For viewpoints on another issue, the influence of violent video games on adolescents' behavior, see the Crime in the News box.

There are many ways to define the word *theory*. One cogent definition comes from Don M. Gottfredson, a well-known criminologist of modern times: "Theories consist of postulates [assumptions], theoretical constructs, logically derived hypotheses, and definitions. Theories can be improved steadily through hypothesis testing, examination of evidence from observations, revisions of the theory, and repetitions of the cycle, repeatedly modifying the theory in light of the

CRIME | in the NEWS
Do Violent Video Games Make Kids Kill?

LOS ANGELES (Reuters)—Do video games kill? The jury is still out on whether violent video games lead to violent behavior in children, but a new study asserts that killer games do not make killer kids.

University of Southern California sociologist Karen Sternheimer, who has been researching the topic since 1999, said blaming video games for youth violence fails to take into account other major factors.

"A symphony of events controls violence," said Sternheimer, who began her research after some experts blamed the video game *Doom* for the gun rampage at Columbine High School in Colorado in which two students killed 13 people and then themselves.

"It was a tragic and, very fortunately, rare event and it was discouraging to see that the conversation often started and stopped at video games."

Sternheimer's article, "Do Video Games Kill?," will appear in the American Sociological Association's *Contexts* magazine as the European Union weighs outlawing certain violent games and harmonizing national penalties for retailers caught selling such products to under-age children.

Her research, which involved analyzing newspaper coverage and FBI statistics detailing trends on youth crime, found that in the 10 years after the release of *Doom*—and many other brutal-sounding titles—juvenile homicide arrest rates in the United States fell 77%.

Students have less than a 7 in 10 million chance of being killed at school, Sternheimer found.

"If we want to understand why young people become homicidal, we need to look beyond the games they play (or) we miss some of the biggest pieces of the puzzle," she said, listing community and family violence, suburban alienation and less parental involvement as other possible factors.

Sternheimer said violent video games have come to carry the baggage of social anxieties over youth violence as the industry has grown into a $10 billion-plus behemoth that rivals Hollywood box office sales.

This also provides a quick fix for when the public demands an explanation for why middle-class children become murderers.

In the United States, the video game industry is self-regulated and retailers decide whether or not to sell M-rated games for mature audiences to minors. These games carry content deemed appropriate for people aged 17 and older.

Sternheimer said putting the blame on video games exonerated the environment in which the child was raised and also removed the culpability of the criminals.

"It's a complicated problem that merits more than a simple solution," she said.

Discussion Questions

1. Do you think that violent video games can have an impact on a player's emotions and influence his or her view of the world? Might they also influence his or her real-life behavior? If so, how?

2. What kind of social scientific experiment might be devised to test the assertion that violent video games influence their players' behavior in the real world?

Amy Brady (right) and Allyson Craghead (left) play Ghost Recon Action War Fighter at the UBI Soft booth at the Electronic Entertainment Exposition in Los Angeles on May 11, 2006. Some say that violent video games can make young people act out their violent fantasies. The studies cited in this article, however, seem to show that that is not the case. What do you think?
Source: Kevork Djansezian/AP Wide World Photos

evidence."[19] (A **hypothesis** is an explanation that accounts for a set of facts and that can be tested by further investigation.) Another well-known methodologist describes theories this way: "A theory is a set of related propositions that suggest why events occur in the manner that they do. The propositions that make up theories are of the same form as hypotheses: they consist of concepts and the linkages or relationships between them."[20]

These definitions both have something to offer. In fact, the definition of the term *theory* that we choose to use in this book combines aspects of both. For our purposes, then, a **theory** is *a series of interrelated propositions that attempts to describe, explain, predict, and ultimately control some class of events.* Theories gain explanatory power from inherent logical consistency and are "tested" by how well they describe and predict reality. In other words, a good theory provides relatively

hypothesis
A tentative explanation accounting for a set of facts that can be tested by further investigation.

theory
A series of interrelated propositions that attempts to describe, explain, predict, and ultimately control some class of events. A theory gains explanatory power from inherent logical consistency and is "tested" by how well it describes and predicts reality.

WEB EXTRA 2–3
WEB EXTRA 2–4

complete understanding, is supported by observations, and stands up to continued scrutiny.

Theories serve a number of purposes. For one thing, they give meaning to observations, explaining what we see in a particular setting by relating it to other things already understood. Hence, a theory of physics can explain the behavior of light by saying that light has properties of both waves and particles. Such a theory is immediately useful because we can easily grasp ideas like waves and particles even if we have trouble conceptualizing light's essence.

Theories within criminology serve the same purpose as those within the physical sciences, but they are often more difficult to test. For example, few people can intuitively understand the motivation of "lust murderers" (a term developed by the Federal Bureau of Investigation and popularized by the media to refer to men who sexually abuse and kill women, often sadistically). Some psychiatric theories (discussed in Chapter 5) suggest that lust murderers kill because of a deep-seated hatred of women. Hate is something that most minds can grasp, and a vision of lust murder as an extreme example of the age-old battle between the sexes provides an intellectual "handle" that at least some people can comprehend.

Theories provide understanding in a number of ways. Kenneth R. Hoover identified four "uses of theory in social scientific thinking":[21]

1. Theories provide patterns for the interpretation of data. Population density, for example, tends to be associated with high crime rates, and maps showing high population density tend to be closely associated with diagrams that reflect rates of crime, so some theorists suggest that overcrowding increases aggression and therefore crime. "People," said Hoover, "like to think in terms of images, analogies, and patterns; this helps to simplify complex realities and to lighten the burden of thought."

2. Theories link one study with another. Some years ago, a case study of women's prisons in California found the existence of artificially constructed "families" around which women's lives centered. A similar but later study of a Chinese prison also found that the female inmates had created family-like groups. As a result, some theorists suggested that women feel a need to nurture and be nurtured and that they carry this need with them into prison. The fact that cross-cultural support was found for this

suggestion provided a linkage between the two studies, which tended to lend further support to it.

3. Theories supply frameworks within which concepts and variables acquire special significance. The death penalty, for example, although especially significant to individuals condemned to die, acquires special significance when seen as a tool employed by the powerful to keep the powerless under their control.

4. Theories allow us to interpret the larger meaning of our findings for ourselves and for others. Hence, the death penalty has become a moral issue for many Americans today, shrouded as it is in ethical considerations and images of national identity and ultimate justice.

Learn more about the nature of modern social scientific thought and theory construction at **Web Extras 2–3** and **2–4**.

The Role of Research and Experimentation

More important than the claims made by theories and by the theorists who create them are findings of fact that either support those claims or leave them without foundation. Hence, theories, once proposed, need to be tested against the real world via a variety of research strategies, including experimentation and case studies. This is equally true whether the proposed theory is relatively simple or dauntingly complex.

> The objective of criminology is the development of a body of general verified principles.
> —Edwin Sutherland and Donald Cressey, *Principles of Criminology*

In his 2009 presidential address to the ASC, incoming president Todd Clear told listeners that "if the evidence-based movement means anything, it means that we want to avoid undertaking programs based on stereotypes and cherished pet theories about crime." Clear described the current state of criminology as focused on the "what works model," and said that "the question '[W]hat works?' might be rewritten as 'How effective is a given program or intervention?'"[22]

Reliable determinations of program effectiveness are made through research. **Research** can be defined as the use of standardized, systematic procedures in the search for knowledge.[23] Some researchers distinguish between applied research and nonapplied, or pure, research. **Applied research** "consists of scientific inquiry that is designed and carried out with practical application in mind."[24] In applied research, the researcher is working toward some more or less practical goal. It may be the reduction of crime, the efficient compensation of victims of crime, or an evaluation of the effectiveness of policies implemented to solve some specific aspect of the crime problem. **Pure research**, on the other hand, is undertaken simply for the sake of advancing scientific knowledge and "does not carry the promise or expectation of immediate, direct relevance."[25]

Another type of research, secondary research or secondary analysis, can be distinguished from primary research.[26] **Primary research** "is characterized by original and direct investigation,"[27] whereas **secondary research** consists of new evaluations of existing information that has already been collected by other researchers.

Scientific research generally proceeds in stages, which can be divided conceptually among (1) problem identification, (2) development of a research design, (3) choice of data-collection techniques, and (4) review of findings (which often includes statistical analysis).

Problem Identification

Problem identification, the first step in any research, consists of naming a problem or choosing an issue to study. Topics may be selected for a variety of reasons. Larry S. Miller and John T. Whitehead, for example, said that "the choice of what criminologists study is influenced by political decisions,"[28] meaning that the availability of government grant monies frequently determines the focus of much contemporary research in the area of crime. It may also be that private foundation monies have become available to support studies in a specific area. Perhaps the researcher has a personal interest in a particular issue and wants to learn more, or maybe a professor or teacher has assigned a research project as part of the requirements for a class. Whatever the reason for beginning research, however, the way in which a research problem is stated and conceptualized will help narrow the research focus and will serve as a guide to the formulation of data-gathering strategies.

Although some criminological research undertaken today is purely descriptive, the bulk of research in criminology is intended to explore issues of causality, especially the claims made by theories purporting to explain criminal behavior. As such, much contemporary research is involved with the testing of hypotheses.

The *American Heritage Dictionary* defines the word *hypothesis* in two ways:[29]

1. "A tentative explanation for an observation, phenomenon, or scientific problem that can be tested by further investigation."
2. "Something that is taken to be true for the purpose of argument or investigation; an assumption."

Within the modern scientific tradition, a hypothesis serves both these purposes. Some criminologists, as mentioned earlier, have observed what appears to be a correlation, or relationship, between the phases of the moon and the rate of crime commission. Such observers may propose the following hypothesis: The moon causes crime. Although this is a useful starting hypothesis, it needs to be further refined before it can be tested. Specifically, the concepts contained within the hypothesis must be translated into measurable variables. A **variable** is simply a concept that can undergo measurable changes.

Scientific precedent holds that only measurable items can be satisfactorily tested. The process of turning a simple hypothesis into one that is testable is called **operationalization**. An operationalized hypothesis is one that is stated in such a way as to facilitate measurement, and it is specific in its terms and in the linkages it proposes. We might, for example, move a step further toward both measurability and specificity in our hypothesis about the relationship between the moon and crime by restating it as follows: Rates of murder, rape, robbery, and assault rise when the moon's fullness increases and are highest when the moon is fullest. Now we have specified what we mean by *crime* (that is, murder, rape, robbery, and assault), rates of which can be calculated. The degree of the moon's fullness can also be measured. Once we have

■ **research design**
The logic and structure inherent in an approach to data gathering.

LIBRARY EXTRA 2-1

The full moon over New York City. It is the job of researchers to determine the validity of such claimed relationships—and of theorists to explain why such relationships hold. Are phases of the moon correlated with changes in the rate of occurrence of certain crimes?
Source: gary718/Shutterstock

operationalized a hypothesis and made the concepts it contains measurable, those concepts have, in effect, become variables.

Once the concepts within our hypothesis are measurable, we can test the hypothesis itself; that is to say, we can observe what happens to crime rates as the moon approaches fullness, as well as what happens when the moon is full, and see whether our observations support our hypothesis. As our dictionary definition tells us, once a hypothesis has been operationalized, it is assumed to be true for purposes of testing. It is accepted, for study purposes, until observation proves it untrue, at which point it is said to be rejected. As two renowned research methodologists have stated, "The task of theory-testing is predominantly one of rejecting inadequate hypotheses."[30]

Development of a Research Design

Research designs structure the research process. They provide a kind of road map to the logic inherent in one's approach to a research problem, and they also serve as guides to the systematic collection of data (see **Library Extra 2-1**).

> The cardinal principle of experimentation is that we must accept the outcome whether or not it is to our liking.
>
> —Abraham Kaplan,
> *The Conduct of Inquiry*

Research designs consist of the logic and structure inherent in any particular approach to data gathering. A simple study, for example, might be designed to test the assertion that the consumption of refined white sugar promotes aggressive or violent tendencies. One could imagine researchers approaching prison officials with the proposal that inmate diets be altered to exclude all refined white sugar. Under the plan, cafeteria cooks would be instructed to prepare meals without the use of sugar. Noncaloric sweeteners would be substituted for sugar in recipes calling for sugar, and sweetened beverages and carbonated drinks containing sugar would be banned. Likewise, the prison canteen would be prohibited from selling items containing sugar for the duration of the experiment.

To determine whether the forced reduction in sugar consumption actually affected inmates' behavior, researchers might look at the recorded frequency of aggressive incidents (sometimes called "write-ups" in prison jargon) occurring within the confines of the prison before the experiment was initiated and compare such data with similar information on such incidents following the introduction of dietary changes. A research design employing this kind of logic can be diagrammed as follows:

$$O_1 \times O_2$$

Here O_1 (termed a *pretest*) refers to the information gathered on inmate aggressiveness prior to the introduction of dietary changes (which themselves are shown as "X," also called the *experimental intervention*), and O_2 (termed the *posttest*) signifies a second set of observations—those occurring after dietary changes have been implemented. Researchers employing a strategy of this type, which is known as a "one-group pretest-posttest," would likely examine differences between the two sets of observations, one made before introduction of the experimental intervention and the other after. The difference, they may assume, would show changes in behavior resulting from changes in diet—in this case, the exclusion of refined white sugar.

■ **confounding effect**
A rival explanation or competing hypothesis that is a threat to the internal or external validity of a research design.

■ **internal validity**
The certainty that experimental interventions did indeed cause the changes observed in the study group.

■ **external validity**
The ability to generalize research findings to other settings.

Although this basic research design well illustrates the logic behind naïve experiments, it does not provide a good research structure because it does not eliminate other possible explanations of behavioral change. For example, during the time between the first and second observations, inmates may have been exposed to some other influence that reduced their level of aggression. A new minister may have begun preaching effective sermons filled with messages of love and peace to the prison congregation; television cable service to the prison may have been disrupted, lowering the exposure inmates received to violent programming; a new warden may have taken control of the facility, relaxing prison rules and reducing tensions; a transfer or release of especially troublesome inmates, scheduled at some earlier time, may have occurred; a new program of conjugal visitation may have been initiated, creating newfound sexual outlets and reducing inmate tensions; and so on. The possibilities for rival explanations (that is, those that rival the explanatory power of the hypothesis under study) are nearly limitless. Rival explanations like these, called by some researchers "competing hypotheses" and **confounding effects** by others, make the results of any single series of observations uncertain.

Validity in Research Designs

Confounding effects, which may invalidate the results of research, are of two general types: those that limit the certainty that internal interventions caused the changes in research findings, which is called **internal validity**, and those that affect the ability of researchers to generalize the research findings to other settings, which is called **external validity**. Often, when external validity is threatened, researchers do not feel confident that interventions that "worked" under laboratory-like or other special conditions will still be effective when employed in the field. Hence, researchers achieving internal validity may be able to demonstrate that diets low in refined white sugar lower the number of instances of overt displays of aggressiveness in a single prison under study. They may not feel confident (for reasons discussed in the paragraphs that follow), however, that similar changes in diet, if implemented in the general nonprison population, would have a similar effect. Most researchers consider internal validity the most vital component of any planned research because without it, considerations of external validity become irrelevant.

Factors that routinely threaten the internal validity of a design for research are said to include the following:[31]

- **History**: Specific events that occur between the first and second observations that may affect measurement. The examples given in the prison study described earlier (the arrival of a new minister or a new warden, for example) are all applicable here.

- **Maturation**: Processes occurring within the respondents or subjects that operate as a result of the passage of time. Fatigue and decreases in response time due to age are examples.

- **Testing**: Effects of taking a test upon the scores of a later testing. When respondents are measured in some way that requires them to respond, they tend to do better (that is, their scores increase) the next time they are tested. In effect, they have learned how to take the test or how to be measured, even though they may not have acquired more knowledge about the subject matter that the test intends to measure.

- **Instrumentation**: Changes in measuring instruments or in survey takers that occur as a result of time. Batteries wear down, instruments need to be recalibrated, interviewers grow tired or are replaced with others, and so on—all of which can change the nature of the observations made.

- **Statistical regression**: Return to more average scores. When respondents have been selected for study on the basis of extreme scores (as may be the case with personality inventories), later testing will tend to show a "regression toward the mean" because some extreme scores are inevitably more the result of accident or luck than anything else.

- **Differential selection**: Built-in biases that result when more than one group of subjects are involved in a study and when the groups being tested are initially somehow different. The random assignment of subjects to test groups greatly reduces the chances that such significant differences will exist.

- **Experimental mortality**: Differential loss of respondents from comparison groups that may occur when more than one group are being tested. For example, one group loses members at a greater rate than another group, or certain kinds of members are lost from one group but not from another.

Threats to external validity include the following:

- **Reactive effects of testing**: Sensitizing effects of initial tests. A pretest may sensitize subjects in such a way that they especially respond to the experimental intervention when it is introduced. Nonpretested subjects (such as those in other locations) may not respond in the same way.

- **Self-selection**: Process whereby subjects are allowed to decide whether they want to participate in a study. Self-selected subjects may be more interested in participation than others, and they may respond more readily to the experimental intervention or treatment.

- **Reactive effects of experimental arrangements**: Sensitizing effects of the setting. People being surveyed or tested may know that they are part of an experiment and therefore may react differently than if they were in more natural settings. Even if they are not aware of their participation in a study, the presence of some investigative paraphernalia (such as observers, cameras, and tape recorders) might change the way they behave.

- **Multiple-treatment interference**: Interaction of multiple exposures or treatments. Sometimes more than one study is simultaneously conducted on the same person or group of people. Under such circumstances, "treatments" to which subjects are exposed may interact, changing what would otherwise be the study's results. Multiple-treatment interference may also result from delayed effects, as when a current study is affected by one that has already been completed.

Experimental and Quasi-Experimental Research Designs

To have confidence that the changes intentionally introduced into a situation are the real cause of observed variations, it is necessary to achieve some degree of control over factors that threaten internal validity. In the physical sciences, controlled experiments often provide the needed guarantees. **Controlled experiments** are those that attempt to hold conditions (other than the intentionally introduced experimental intervention) constant. Some researchers have defined the word *experiment* simply as "controlled observation."

> Self-selected subjects may be more interested in participation than others, and they may respond more readily to experimental treatment.

Whereas constancy of conditions may be possible to achieve within laboratory settings, it is far more difficult to come by in the social world, which by its very nature is in an ongoing state of flux. Hence, although criminologists

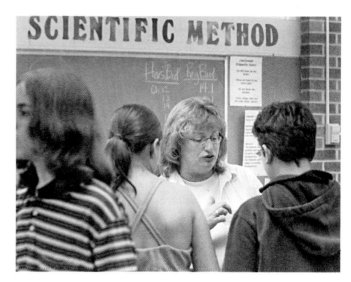

A high school science fair booth pays homage to the scientific method. What is evidence-based criminology? How does it make use of the scientific method?
Source: Orlin Wagner/AP Wide World Photos

sometimes employ true experimental designs in the conduct of their research, they are more likely to find it necessary to use **quasi-experimental designs**, or approaches to research that "are deemed worthy of use where better designs are not feasible."[32] Quasi-experimental designs are especially valuable when aspects of the social setting are beyond the control of the researcher. The crucial defining feature of quasi-experimental designs is that they give researchers control over the "when and to whom" of measurement, even though others decide the "when and to whom" of exposure to the experimental intervention.

Sometimes, for example, legislators enact new laws intended to address some aspect of the crime problem, specifying the kinds of crime-prevention measures to be employed and the segment of the population to receive them. Midnight basketball, intended to keep young people off the streets at night, provides an example of a legislatively sponsored intervention. During debate on the 1994 Violent Crime Control and Law Enforcement Act, midnight basketball became a point of contention, with senators asking whether money spent in support of such an activity would actually reduce the incidence of serious street crime in our nation's inner cities. Unfortunately, no good research data that could answer the question were then available. Now, however, federally funded midnight basketball programs, which have existed for a number of years, could be studied by researchers. Hence, although criminologists were not politically situated so as

---

■ control group
A group of experimental subjects that, although the subject of measurement and observation, is not exposed to the experimental intervention.

■ randomization
The process whereby individuals are assigned to study groups without biases or differences resulting from selection.

---

to be able to enact midnight basketball legislation, they are able to study the effects of such legislation after it has been enacted.[33]

Whether criminologists decide on experimental or quasi-experimental designs to guide their research, they depend on well-considered research strategies to eliminate rival explanations for the effects they observe. One relatively powerful research design that criminologists frequently employ can be diagrammed as follows:

$$\text{Experimental group} \quad O_1 \times O_2$$
$$\text{Control group} \quad O_3 \times O_4$$

The meaning of the notation used here is similar to that of the one-shot case study design discussed earlier. This approach, however, called the "pretest-posttest control group design," gains considerable power from the addition of a second group; it is called a **control group** because it is not exposed to the experimental intervention.

Critical to the success of a research design like this is the use of randomization in the assignment of subjects to both the experimental and the control groups. **Randomization** is the process whereby individuals are assigned to study groups without biases or differences resulting from selection. Self-selection (when some individuals volunteer for membership in either the experimental or the control group) is not permitted, nor are researchers allowed to use personal judgment in assigning subjects to groups.

Control over potential threats to internal validity is achieved by the introduction of a properly selected control group because it is assumed that both experimental and control groups are essentially the same at the start and that any threats to internal validity will affect both groups equally as the experiment progresses—effectively canceling out when final differences between the two groups are measured. If some particular historical event, for example, affects the experimental group and modifies the measurable characteristics of that group, that event should have the same impact on the control group. Hence, in the previous design, when O_4 is subtracted from O_2, the remaining observable *net effects* are assumed to be attributable to the experimental intervention.

In the prison study discussed earlier, randomization would require that all inmates be systematically but randomly divided into two groups. Random assignments are typically made by using a table of random numbers. In this simple study, however, something as easy as the flip of a coin should suffice. Members of one group (the experimental group) would no longer receive refined white sugar in their diets while members of the other group (the control group) would continue eating as before. With this

one exception in diet, both groups would continue to be exposed to the same environment, so it can be assumed that any other influences on the level of violence within the prison will cancel out when final measurements are taken and that measurable differences in violence between the two groups can be attributed solely to the effects of the experimental variable (in this case, removal of sugar from the diet).

According to Shawn Bushway and David Weisburd at the University of Maryland, criminology is the only field within the social sciences to "show a marked increase in the use of experimental designs over the past 40 years."[34] And the movement has powerful friends. No less an authority than Lawrence W. Sherman, professor and chair of the Department of Criminology and Criminal Justice at the University of Maryland and the former director of research at the Police Foundation, says that the use of experimental design in the field of criminology is the "gold standard" to which evaluations of both theory and practice should be held.[35]

> Further development in theoretical criminology will result primarily from making sense out of what we already know.
>
> —George B. Vold and Thomas J. Bernard, *Theoretical Criminology*

Choice of Data-Collection Techniques

It is the combination of (1) hypothesis building, (2) operationalization, and (3) systematic observation in the service of hypothesis testing that has made modern-day criminology scientific and that has facilitated scientific theory building within the field. Hence, once a research problem has been identified, concepts have been made measurable, and a research design has been selected, investigators must then decide on the type of data to be gathered and the techniques of data gathering they wish to employ. Ultimately, all research depends on the use of techniques to gather information, or data, for eventual analysis. Like research designs, which structure a researcher's approach to a problem, data-gathering strategies provide approaches to the accumulation of information needed for analysis to occur.

Many first-time researchers select data-gathering techniques on the basis of ease or simplicity, and some choose according to the cost or the amount of time the techniques require. The most important question to consider when beginning to gather information, however, is whether the data-gathering strategy selected will produce information in a usable form. The kind of information needed depends on the questions to be answered. Surveys of public opinion as to the desirability of the death penalty, for example, cannot address issues of the punishment's effectiveness as a crime-control strategy.

Five major data-gathering strategies typify research in the field of criminology: surveys, case studies, participant observations, self-reporting, and secondary analysis.

Surveys

Survey research typically involves the use of questionnaires, or surveys. Respondents may be interviewed in person or over the telephone or queried via e-mail or fax. Mail surveys are common, although they tend to have a lower response rate than other types of social surveys. The information produced through the use of questionnaires is referred to as "survey data." Polling companies like Gallup, CNN, and Roper gather data on public opinion, voting preferences, and so forth, and the U.S. Census Bureau data are gathered by trained survey takers. Survey data also inform the National Crime Victimization Survey (NCVS) and result in such publications as *Crime and the Nation's Households, Criminal Victimization,* and other NCVS-related reports produced by the Bureau of Justice Statistics. Surveys have also been used to assess fear of crime, attitudes toward the police, and extent of unreported crime.

Case Studies

Case studies are built around in-depth investigations into individual cases. The study of one (perhaps notorious) offender, the scrutiny of a particular criminal organization, and the analysis of a prison camp may all qualify as case studies. Case studies are useful for what they can tell us to expect about other similar cases. If a study of a street gang, for example, reveals the central role of a few leaders, then we would expect to find a similar organizational style among other gangs of the same kind.

When one individual (a single subject) is the focus of a case study, the investigation may take the form of a subjective life history, which involves gathering as much historical data as possible about a given individual and his or her life experiences. Life histories may also be gathered on groups of individuals, and similarities in life experiences that are thereby discovered may provide researchers with clues to current behavior or with points at which to begin further investigations.

Case studies, although they may suffer from high levels of subjectivity in which feelings cannot be easily separated from

fact, provide the opportunity to investigate individual cases—an element lacking in both surveys and participant observations.

Participant Observations

Participant observation "involves a variety of strategies in data gathering in which the researcher observes a group by participating, to varying degrees, in the activities of the group."[36] Some participant researchers operate undercover, whereas others make their identity and purpose known from the outset. As one criminologist stated, participant observation "means that criminologists must venture inside the immediacy of crime."[37]

One of the earliest and best-known participant observers in the field of criminology was William Foote Whyte, who described his 1943 study of criminal subcultures in a slum district that he called "Cornerville" this way:

My aim was to gain an intimate view of Cornerville life. My first problem, therefore, was to establish myself as a participant in the society so that I would have a position from which to observe. I began by going to live in Cornerville, finding a room with an Italian family. It was not enough simply to make the acquaintance of various groups of people. The sort of information that I sought required that I establish intimate social relations. This active participation gave me something in common with them so that we had other things to talk about besides the weather. It broke down the social barriers and made it possible for me to be taken into the intimate life of the group.[38]

It is possible to distinguish between at least two additional kinds of participant observation: (1) the participant as observer and (2) the observer as complete participant. When researchers make their presence known to those whom they are observing without attempting to influence the outcome of their observations or the activities of the group, they fit the category of participants who are observers. But researchers who make their presence known may inadvertently influence outcomes because people tend to act differently when they know they are being watched.

When they become complete participants in the group they are observing, researchers run the risk of influencing the group's direction. As Whyte explained, "I made it a rule that I should try to avoid influencing the actions of the group. I wanted to observe what the men did under ordinary circumstances; I did not want to lead them into different activities."[39] Another problem facing the participant observer is that of "going native," assuming too close an identification with the subjects or the behavior under study (for example, an undercover police officer who may be tempted to participate in the illegalities he or she is supposed to be monitoring). When that happens, all sense of the research perspective may be lost, and serious ethical problems may arise.

■ **intersubjectivity**
A scientific principle that requires that independent observers see the same thing under the same circumstances for observations to be regarded as valid.

■ **replicability**
A scientific principle that holds that valid observations made at one time can be made again later if all other conditions are the same.

On the other hand, some researchers may feel disgust for the subjects of their research. Data gatherers with a particular dislike of drug abuse, for example, may be hard put to maintain their objectivity when working as participant observers within the drug subculture. Hence, as noted social science researcher Frank Hagan observed, "The researcher must avoid not only over identification with the study group, but also aversion to it."[40]

Self-Reporting

Another subjective data-gathering technique is the self-report that investigates aspects of a problem not otherwise amenable to study. When official records are lacking, research subjects may be asked to record and report rates of otherwise secretive behavior. Self-reports may prove especially valuable in providing checks on official reports consisting of statistical tabulations gathered through such channels as police departments, hospitals, and social services agencies.

Self-reports may also be requested of subjects in survey research, so self-reporting is sometimes considered simply another form of survey research. However, many self-reporting techniques require the maintenance of a diary or personal journal and request vigilant and ongoing observations of the study subject's own behavior. Hence, sex researchers may ask subjects to maintain an ongoing record of their frequency of intercourse, the variety of sexual techniques employed, and their preference in partners—items of information that are not easy to come by through other means or that cannot be accurately reconstructed from memory.

Self-reporting enters the realm of the purely subjective when it consists of introspection, or personal reflection. Introspective techniques intended to gather data on secretive feelings and felt motivations are often used by psychologists seeking to assess the mental status of patients. Criminologists have at times used introspective techniques to categorize criminal offenders into types and to initiate the process of developing concepts more amenable to objective study.

Secondary Analysis

Not all data-gathering techniques produce new data. Secondary analysis purposefully culls preexisting information from data that have already been gathered (possibly for another purpose) and examines it in new ways. The secondary analysis of existing data and the use of previously acquired information for new avenues of inquiry are strategies that can save researchers a considerable amount of time and expense.

One important source of data for secondary analysis is the National Archive of Criminal Justice data located in the Institute for Social Research at the University of Michigan. In the words of the U.S. Department of Justice, the archive's sponsoring agency, "The Archive continually processes the most relevant criminal justice data sets for the research community,"[41] maintaining information on victimization, various aspects of the criminal justice system, and juvenile delinquency. Access to archive data is by request, and data sets are available to individual researchers. Visit the archive via **Web Extra 2–5**.

The use of secondary data rarely alerts research subjects to the fact that they (or the data they have provided) are being studied, although they may have been aware of it when the data were first gathered, making secondary analysis "nonreactive." For example, the use of archival records in data analysis constitutes a virtual "goldmine of information waiting to be exploited."[42] Nonetheless, it is important to keep in mind that secondary analysis usually involves the use of information that was collected for a purpose outside of the interests of the current researcher.

Problems in Data Collection

Scientific data gathering builds on observations of one sort or another. Observation is not unique to science—individuals continuously make observations and draw a plethora of personal conclusions based on what they see or hear. Scientific observation, however, generally occurs under controlled conditions and must meet the criteria of intersubjectivity and replicability. **Intersubjectivity** means that for observations to be valid, independent observers must report seeing the same thing under the same circumstances. "Do you see what I see?" is a question that highlights the central role of intersubjectivity in scientific observation. If observers cannot agree on what they saw, then the raw data necessary for scientific analysis have not been acquired. **Replicability** of observations, at

> "Do you see what I see?" is a question that highlights the central role of intersubjectivity in scientific observation.

least in the field of scientific experimentation, means that when the same conditions exist, the same results can be expected to follow; hence, valid experiments can be replicated. The same observations made at one time can be made again at a later time if all other conditions are the same.

In the physical sciences, replicability is easy to achieve. Water at sea level, for example, will always boil at 100° Celsius. Anyone can replicate the conditions needed to test such a contention. When replicability cannot be achieved, it casts the validity of the observation into doubt. Some years ago, for example, a few scientists claimed to have achieved nuclear fusion at room temperature. Their supposed accomplishment was dubbed "cold fusion" and was hailed as a major breakthrough in the production of nuclear energy. However, when scientists elsewhere attempted to replicate the conditions under which cold fusion was said to occur, they could find no evidence that the initial experimenters were correct. Intersubjectivity and replicability are critical to the scientific enterprise, with one researcher stating that "science rests its claim to authority upon its firm basis in observable evidence."[43]

It is important to recognize, however, that some observations—even those that stand up to the tests of intersubjectivity and replicability—can lead to unwarranted conclusions. For example, spirit possession, an explanation for deviance that was apparently widely held in primitive times, must have appeared to be well validated by the positive behavioral changes that became apparent in those who submitted to the surgery called for by the theory, which was a craniotomy intended to release offending spirits from the head of the afflicted person. The actual cause of behavioral reformation may have been brain infections resulting from unsanitary surgical conditions, slips of the stone knife, or the intensity of pain endured by those undergoing the procedure without anesthetics. To the uncritical observer, however, the theory of spirit possession as a cause of deviance and cranial surgery as a treatment technique would probably appear to have been supported by the evidence of induced behavioral change.

Some methodologists noted that "theories are as much involved in the determination of fact as facts are in establishing a theory."[44] Theories are intimately involved in the process of data

Social science research within a correctional setting. Inmate surveys may increase our knowledge of crime causation. Specifically, what might such surveys tell us?
Source: Rick Friedman/Black Star

collection: They determine what kinds of data we choose to gather, what we look for in the data, and how we interpret the information we have gathered. In short, theories determine what we see as well as what we ignore. In the late 1700s, for example, when a meteor shower was reported to the French Academy of Sciences, observers reported that some fragments had struck the ground, causing tremendous explosions. The learned scientists of the academy quickly dismissed these accounts, however, calling them "a superstition unworthy of these enlightened times."[45] Everyone, they said, knows that stones don't fall from the sky.

Review of Findings

Some data, once collected, are simply archived or stored, but most data are subject to some form of analysis. Data analysis generally involves the use of mathematical techniques intended to uncover correlations between variables and to assess the likelihood that research findings can be generalized to other settings. These are statistical techniques, and their use in analyzing data is called *statistical analysis*. Some theorists, for example, posit a link between poverty and crime. Hence, we might suspect that low-income areas would

---

■ **descriptive statistics**
Statistics that describe, summarize, or highlight the relationships within data that have been gathered.

■ **inferential statistics**
Statistics that specify how likely findings are to be true for other populations or in other locales.

■ **correlation**
A causal, complementary, or reciprocal relationship between two measurable variables.

■ **test of significance**
A statistical technique intended to provide researchers with confidence that their results are, in fact, true and not the result of sampling error.

---

be high-crime areas. Once we specify what we mean by "low-income" and "crime," so that they become measurable variables, and we gather data on income levels and the incidence of crime in various locales, we are ready to begin the job of data analysis.

Statistical techniques provide tools for summarizing data and also provide quantitative means for identifying patterns within the data and for determining the degree of correlation that exists between variables. Statistical methods can be divided into two types: descriptive and inferential. **Descriptive statistics** are those that describe, summarize, or highlight the relationships within the data that have been gathered. **Inferential statistics**, on the other hand, attempt to generalize findings by specifying how likely they are to be true for other populations or in other locales.

Descriptive statistics include measures of central tendency, commonly called the mode, median, and mean. *Mode* refers to the most frequently occurring score or value in any series of observations. If, for example, we measure the age of all juvenile offenders held in a state training facility, it may be that they range in age from 12 to 16, with 15 being the most commonly found age; 15, then, would be the modal age for the population under study.

Median defines the midpoint of a data series—half of the scores will be above the mean and the other half will be below. It may be, for example, that in our study of juveniles, we find equal numbers in each age category, so the median age for those offenders would be 14.

Mean is the mathematical average of all scores within a given population and is the most commonly used measure of central tendency. It is calculated by simply adding together all the scores (or ages, in our example) and dividing by the total number of observations. Although calculations of the mode, median, and mean will often yield similar results, such will not be the case with populations that are skewed in a particular direction. If our population of juveniles, for example, consisted almost entirely of 16-year-olds, then the mode for that population would inevitably be 16 while other measures of central tendency would yield somewhat lower figures.

Other descriptive statistics provide measures of the standard deviation of a population (that is, the degree of dispersion of scores about the mean) and the degree of **correlation** or interdependence between variables (that is, the extent of variation in one that can be expected to follow from a measured change in another). Although the degree of correlation may vary, the direction of correlation can be described. We say, for example, that if one variable increases whenever another, upon which it is dependent, does the same, a positive correlation (or positive relationship) exists between

the two; when one variable decreases in value as another rises, a negative correlation (or inverse relationship) exists.

Another statistical technique, one that provides a measure of the likelihood that a study's findings are the results of chance, is commonly found in criminological literature. **Tests of significance** are designed to provide researchers with confidence that their results are, in fact, true and not the result of sampling error. We may, for example, set out to measure the degree of gun ownership. Let's say that the extent of gun ownership in the area under study is actually 50%. (We have no way of knowing this until our study is complete.) We may decide to use door-to-door surveys of randomly selected households because cost prohibits us from canvassing all households in the study area. Even if we have made our best survey effort, however, some slight probability remains that the households we have chosen to interview may all be populated by gun owners. Although it is very unlikely, we may—by chance—have excluded those without guns. Assuming that everyone interviewed answers truthfully, we would come away with the mistaken impression that 100% of the population in the study area is armed!

The likelihood of faulty findings increases as sample size decreases. Were we to sample only one or two households, we would have little likelihood of determining the actual incidence of gun ownership. The larger the sample size, however, the greater the confidence we can have in our findings. In other words, a positive correlation exists between sample size and degree of confidence we can have in our results. Even so, in most criminological research, it is not possible to study all members of a given population, so samples must be taken. Statistical tests of significance, expressed as a percentage, assess the likelihood that our study findings are due to chance. Hence, a study that reflects a 95% confidence level can be interpreted as having a 5% likelihood that the results it reports are mere happenstance. To put it another way, for every hundred such studies, five yield misleading results. The problem is that it would be impossible to know (without further research) which five that would be!

Learn more about statistics and statistical methods from the American Statistical Association and the American Association for the Advancement of Science via **Web Extras 2–6** and **2–7**. Read about statistical tools on the World Wide Web via **Library Extra 2–2**.

> Tests of significance are designed to provide researchers with confidence that their results are, in fact, true.

WEB EXTRA 2-6
WEB EXTRA 2-7
LIBRARY EXTRA 2-2

quantitative method
A research technique that produces measurable results.

WHO'S TO BLAME—The Individual or Society?

Is Criminology Really Just a Form of Academic Excuse Making?

Three teenage boys were arrested in the small town of Hillsboro, Maine, and charged with beating a homeless man to death with a baseball bat in an underground parking garage on a cold January evening. A surveillance camera captured the beating, and the youngsters were identified by residents who watched the video clip on local TV news.

Because the boys were juveniles, a storm of controversy swarmed around a local judge's decision to charge them as adults and to bind them over for trial in criminal court—something that state law allows for serious crimes if the suspected offenders were over 14 years of age at the time of the alleged offense.

Soon opinions were being heard from many quarters, and the news media arranged to interview a criminology professor, Dr. Roy Humbolt, at a local college to see if he might be able to shed some light on the boys' behavior.

The first question came from a reporter holding a digital voice recorder toward Professor Humbolt. "What happened here? How do you explain this kind of senseless killing?"

"Well," Humbolt began, "it's not senseless. Crime is a social event, not just an isolated instance of individual activity. And in much youth crime we see patterns of co-offending."

Humbolt felt as though he was hitting his stride and started lecturing as though he was in the classroom with his undergraduates. "Criminal behavior is often attributable to social failings rather than to individual choice. Consider, for a moment, the backgrounds of these young men. Were they subjected to physical abuse while they were growing up? Was violence what they learned at the hands of older siblings or parents? Were they, in this instance, involved in some adolescent rite of passage, maybe even an initiation into a gang? Did they feel forced to behave this way because of peer pressure? Was it something they saw on television or in video games that they might have played and then decided to reenact?"

"Dr. Humbolt," the reporter asked, bringing the professor back from his reverie, "even if you find that some of those things are true, isn't criminology just an exercise in excuse making for criminals?"

Think about it:

1. What do you think of the explanations offered by Professor Humbolt for the boys' behavior? Which of his explanations, if any, makes the most sense? How can we know for sure if those explanations are accurate?

2. What do you think of the reporter's stinging criticism of the professor? Is the reporter right, that criminology is "just an exercise in excuse making for criminals"? Explain your answer.

3. Generally speaking, does understanding absolve responsibility? In other words, if we can understand why someone does something, then should we hold him or her less responsible for doing it? Why or why not?

Note: Who's to Blame boxes provide fictionalized critical thinking opportunities, and are not actual cases.

Quantitative Versus Qualitative Methods

Years ago, during the Clinton administration, (then) Attorney General Janet Reno addressed researchers, criminologists, and professors gathered at the annual meeting of the ASC in Miami, Florida. "Let's stop talking about numbers," Reno exhorted the crowd, "and start talking about crime in human terms."[46] With her admonition, Reno placed herself squarely on the side of those who feel that there has been a tendency in American criminology over the past half century to overemphasize **quantitative methods** or techniques, that is, those that produce measurable results that can be analyzed statistically. To be sure, as such critics would be quick to admit, a considerable degree of intellectual comfort must be achieved in feeling that one is able to reduce complex forms of behavior and interaction to something countable (as, say, the frequency of an offense). Intellectual comfort of this sort derives from the notion that anything expressible in numbers must be somehow more meaningful than that which is not.

qualitative method
A research technique that produces subjective results, or results that are difficult to quantify.

It is crucial to realize, however, that numerical expression is mostly a result of how researchers structure their approach to the subject matter and is rarely inherent in the subject matter itself. Such is especially true in the social sciences, where attitudes, feelings, behaviors, and perceptions of all sorts are subject to quantification by researchers who impose upon such subjective phenomena artificial techniques for their quantification.

One highly quantitative study, reprinted in the journal *Criminology*, reported on the relationship between personality and crime and found that "greater delinquent participation was associated with a personality configuration characterized by high Negative Emotionality and Weak Constraint."[47] It may seem easy to quantify "delinquent participation" by measuring official arrest statistics (although official statistics may not be a good measure of delinquent behavior because many law violations go undiscovered), but imagine the conceptual nightmares associated with trying to make measurable such concepts as "Negative Emotionality" and "Weak Constraint." In such studies, even those replete with numerical data derived through the use of carefully constructed questionnaires, questions still remain of precisely what it is that has been measured.

Not everyone who engages in social science research labors under the delusion that everything can and must be quantified. Those who do, however, are said to suffer from the "mystique of quantity." As some critics have pointed out, "The failure to recognize this instrumentality of measurement makes for a kind of *mystique of quantity*, which responds to numbers as though they were repositories of occult powers. The mystique of quantity is an exaggerated regard for the significance of measurement, just because it is quantitative, without regard either to what has been measured or to what can subsequently be done with the measure."[48] The "mystique of quantity" treats numbers as having intrinsic scientific value. Unfortunately, this kind of thinking has been popular in the social sciences, where researchers, seeking to make clear their intellectual kinship with physical scientists, have been less than cautious in their enthusiasm for quantification.

Qualitative methods, in contrast to those that are quantitative, produce subjective results, or results that are difficult to quantify. Even though their findings are not expressed numerically, qualitative methods provide yet another set of potentially useful criminological research tools. Qualitative methods are important for the insights they provide into the subjective workings of the criminal mind and the processes by which meaning is accorded to human experience. Introspection, life histories, case studies, and participant observations all contain the potential to yield highly qualitative data.[49]

Consider, for example, how the following personal account of homicidal motivation conveys subjective insights into the life of a Los Angeles gang member that would otherwise be difficult to express:

> Wearing my fresh Pendleton shirt, beige khakis, and biscuits [old men's comfort shoes, the first shoe officially dubbed "Crip shoe"], I threw on my black bomber jacket and stepped out into the warm summer night. I walked up Sixty-Ninth Street to Western Avenue and took a car at gunpoint. Still in a state of indecision, I drove toward the hospital.
>
> I intentionally drove through Sixties' hood. Actually, I was hoping to see one of them before I had made it through, and what luck did I have. There was Bank Robber, slippin' [not paying attention, not being vigilant] hard on a side street. I continued past him and turned at the next corner, parked and waited. He would walk right to me.
>
> Sitting in the car alone, waiting to push yet another enemy out of this existence, I reflected deeply about my place in this world, about things that were totally outside the grasp of my comprehension. Thoughts abounded I never knew I could conjure up. In retrospect, I can honestly say that in those moments before Bank Robber got to the car, I felt free. Free, I guess, because I had made a decision about my future.
>
> "Hey," I called out to Robber, leaning over to the passenger side, "got a light?"
>
> "Yeah," he replied, reaching into his pants pocket for a match or lighter. I never found out which.
>
> I guess he felt insecure, because he dipped his head down to window level to see who was asking for a light.
>
> "Say your prayers, muthaf."
>
> Before he could mount a response I blasted him thrice in the chest, started the car, and drove home to watch *Benny Hill*. Bangin' was my life. That was my decision.[50]

The passage was written by Sanyika Shakur, once known as "Monster Kody" to fellow South Central Los Angeles Crips members. Monster, named for his readiness to commit acts of

verstehen
The kind of subjective understanding that can be achieved by criminologists who immerse themselves in the everyday world of the criminals they study.

data confidentiality
The ethical requirement of social scientific research to protect the confidentiality of individual research participants while preserving justified research access to the information participants provide.

WEB EXTRA 2–8
LIBRARY EXTRA 2–3
LIBRARY EXTRA 2–4

A 22-year-old gang member who identified himself as "Criminal." Some researchers doubt that quantitative methods can adequately assess the subjective experiences of certain kinds of offenders. What is the nature of such "subjective experiences"?
Source: AP Photo/Rodrigo Abd

brutality so extreme that they repulsed even other gang members, joined the Crips at age 11. Sent to a maximum-security prison while still in his teens, Monster learned to write, took on the name Sanyika Shakur, and joined the black nationalist New Afrikan Independence Movement. Shakur's prison-inspired autobiography, *Monster*, provides a soul-searching account of the life of an L.A. gang member. The purpose of the book, said Shakur, is "to allow my readers the first ever glimpse at South Central from my side of the gun, street, fence, and wall."[51]

Although Shakur's book is a purely personal account and may hold questions of generalizability for researchers, imagine the difficulties inherent in acquiring these kinds of data through the use of survey instruments or other traditional research techniques. Autobiographical accounts, introspection, and many forms of participant observations amount to a kind of phenomenological reporting in which description leads to understanding and intuition is a better guide to theory building than volumes of quantifiable data.

Jeff Ferrell of Texas Christian University uses the term **verstehen** to describe the kind of subjective understanding that can be achieved

by criminologists who immerse themselves in the everyday world of the criminals they study. Criminological *verstehen*, a term derived from the early writings of sociologist Max Weber, means, said Ferrell, "a researcher's subjective understandings of crime's situational meanings and emotions—its moments of pleasure and pain, its emergent logic and excitement—within the larger process of research"; Ferrell adds, "It further implies that a researcher, through attentiveness and participation, at least can begin to apprehend and appreciate the specific roles and experiences of criminals, crime victims, crime control agents, and others caught up in the day-to-day reality of crime."[52] Learn more about *verstehen* at "Max Weber's Home Page" via **Web Extra 2–8**. You can learn more about the techniques of social science research at **Library Extra 2–3**.

Values and Ethics in the Conduct of Research

Research, especially research conducted within the social sciences, does not occur in a vacuum. Values enter into all stages of the research process, from the selection of the problem to be studied to the choice of strategies to address it. In short, research is never entirely free from preconceptions and biases, although much can be done to limit their impact.

The most effective way of controlling the effects of biases is to be aware of them at the outset of the research. If, for example, researchers know that the project they are working on elicits strong personal feelings but necessitates the use of interviewers, then it would be beneficial to strive to hire interviewers who are relatively free of biases or who can control the expression of their feelings. Data gatherers who are prejudiced against subgroups of potential respondents can represent a threat to the validity of the research results, and they may turn off some respondents, perhaps through racial innuendo, personal style, mannerisms, and so forth.

Of similar importance are ethical issues. Although they may not affect the validity of research results, these issues can have a significant impact on the lives of both researchers and research subjects. The protection of human subjects from harm, the provision of privacy, the need for disclosure of research methods, and **data confidentiality**—which embraces the principle of

■ **informed consent**
The ethical requirement of social scientific research that research subjects be informed as to the nature of the research about to be conducted, their anticipated role in it, and the uses to which the data they provide will be put.

WEB EXTRA 2–9

protecting the confidentiality of individual research participants while preserving justified research access to needed information provided by them—are all critical ethical issues.

To address these and other concerns, the Academy of Criminal Justice Sciences (ACJS) has adopted an official code of ethics. The ACJS Code of Ethics says that researchers "should seek to anticipate potential threats to confidentiality." It goes on to state, "Techniques such as the removal of direct identifiers, the use of randomized responses, and other statistical solutions to problems of privacy should be used where appropriate. Care should be taken to ensure secure storage, maintenance, and/or destruction of sensitive records."[53]

The ACJS code also says, "Confidential information provided by research participants should be treated as such by members of the Academy, even when this information enjoys no legal protection or privilege and legal force is applied. The obligation to respect confidentiality also applies to members of research organizations (interviewers, coders, clerical staff, etc.) who have access to the information. It is the responsibility of administrators and chief investigators to instruct staff members on this point and to make every effort to [ensure] that access to confidential information is restricted."[54]

Informed consent, a strategy used by researchers to overcome many of the ethical issues inherent in criminological research, means that research subjects are informed as to the nature of the research about to be conducted, their anticipated role in it, and the uses made of the data they provide. Ethics may also require that data derived from personal interviews or the testing of research subjects be anonymous (not associated with the names of individual subjects) and that raw (unanalyzed) data be destroyed after a specified time interval (often at the completion of the research project).

> Ethical issues can have a significant impact on the lives of both researchers and research subjects.

Federal regulations require a plan for the protection of human subjects as part of grant proposals submitted to federal agencies. For example, the NIJ, a major source of grant support for researchers in the area of criminology, has this to say:

> All National Institute of Justice (NIJ) employees, contractors and grant recipients must be cognizant of the importance of protecting the rights and welfare of human subject research participants. In this period of expanding research on criminal justice issues and growing concerns for personal privacy, the protection of human subjects in our research endeavors is extremely important. All research conducted at NIJ or supported with NIJ funds must comply with all Federal, U.S. Department of Justice (DOJ), Office of Justice Programs and NIJ regulations and policies concerning the protection of human subjects and the DOJ confidentiality requirements.[55]

Learn more about NIJ requirements for confidentiality and the protection of human subjects at **Web Extra 2–9**.

Some universities, research organizations, and government agencies have established institutional review boards tasked with examining research proposals to determine whether expectations of ethical conduct have been met before these proposals are submitted to funding organizations. Institutional review boards often consist of other researchers with special knowledge of the kinds of ethical issues involved in criminological research.

Participant observation sometimes entails an especially thorny ethical issue: Should researchers themselves violate the law if their research participation appears to require it? Those researching gang activities, for example, have sometimes been asked to transmit potentially incriminating information to other gang members, to act as drug couriers, and even to commit crimes of violence to help establish territorial claims important to members of the gang. Researchers who refuse may endanger not only their research but also themselves. Compliance with the expectations of criminal groups evokes other kinds of dangers, including the danger of apprehension and prosecution for violations of the criminal law. As one criminologist explained, "Criminological (and other) field researchers cannot conveniently distance themselves from their subjects of study, or from the legally uncertain situations in which the subjects may reside, in order to construct safe and 'objective' studies. Instead criminological field research unavoidably entangles those who practice it in complex and ambiguous relations to the subjects and situations of study, to issues of personal and social responsibility, and to law and legality."[56]

Although the dilemma of a participant observer, especially one secretly engaged in research, is a difficult one, some of the best advice on the subject is offered by Frank E. Hagan: "In self-mediating the potential conflicting roles of the criminal justice researcher, it is incumbent on the investigator to enter the setting with eyes wide open. A decision must be made beforehand on the level of commitment to the research endeavor and the analyst's ability to negotiate the likely role conflicts. Although there are no hard and fast rules *the researcher's primary role is that of a scientist*."[57]

LIBRARY EXTRA 2–5
WEB EXTRA 2–10
WEB EXTRA 2–11
WEB EXTRA 2–12

Hagan also suggested that a code of ethics should guide all professional criminologists in their research undertakings, requiring each researcher to do the following:[58]

- Avoid procedures that may harm respondents.
- Honor commitments to respondents and respect reciprocity.
- Exercise objectivity and professional integrity in performing and reporting research.
- Protect confidentiality and the privacy of respondents.

Hagan's admonition "Exercise objectivity and professional integrity" became especially important in the mid-1990s when supporters of Project D.A.R.E. blocked publication of research results that showed the program to be ineffective.[59] D.A.R.E., a widely popular antidrug program common in the nation's schools, is a favorite of educational administrators because of the funding it provides. The study, a review of most prior D.A.R.E. research, was conducted by the Research Triangle Institute, a respected research firm in North Carolina, and was paid for by the NIJ.[60] When results showed that D.A.R.E. programs did not significantly reduce drug use among student participants, however, NIJ decided not to publish the findings. "We're not trying to hide the study," said NIJ's Ann Voit. "We just do not agree with one of the major findings."[61] In contrast, Research Triangle Institute researcher Susan T. Ennett proposed that results of the study should be used to decide how to spend drug-education money. Other studies have since supported the finding that D.A.R.E. does not have a significant impact on actual drug use, drug-related outcomes, or attitudes toward drugs.[62] Learn more about the D.A.R.E. study via **Library Extra 2–5**.

Scientific research demonstrating that popular—and often widely supported—programs are ineffective will inevitably fuel controversy. Such was the case in 2006, when a group of Italian researchers published findings purporting to show that the 12-step method used by Alcoholics Anonymous (A.A.) to prevent future problem drinking doesn't work. The researchers concluded that "no experimental studies unequivocally demonstrated the effectiveness of A.A. or professional 12-step theory for reducing alcohol dependence or problems."[63] The research left some people claiming that A.A. worked for them and others saying that more (and better) studies were needed.

Because criminological research can affect social policy, which often involves the expenditure of public funds, the ethical code of the ASC mandates that criminologists be "committed to enhancing the *general well-being* of societies and of the individuals and groups within them," further stating that "criminologists have an obligation not to re-create forms of social injustice such as discrimination, oppression, or harassment in their own work."[64]

Learn more about ethics in criminological research directly from the ASC and the ACJS via **Web Extras 2–10** and **2–11**. To read a comprehensive code of ethical standards for general survey research, visit the Council of American Survey Research Organizations via **Web Extra 2–12**.

Social Policy and Criminological Research

Ideally, research results in the field of criminology should have both practical implications that can guide daily practice in relevant areas and a significant impact on those who formulate public crime-control policy. Faye S. Taxman of the University of Maryland's Center for Applied Policy Studies explained that "the normative educative model assumes that a rational use of data by

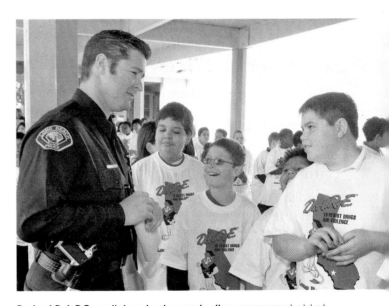

Project D.A.R.E. participants at a graduation ceremony held at Patrick Henry Elementary School in Long Beach, California. A decade ago, studies of Project D.A.R.E. questioned its effectiveness, but government officials decided not to publish the results. How can the objectivity of social scientific research be ensured?

Source: *Kayle Deioma*/Photo Edit

LIBRARY EXTRA 2-6
LIBRARY EXTRA 2-7

policy makers, practitioners, and scientists will be of value to the field."[65] For example, after studies showed that arrests (rather than mere warnings) of domestic violence perpetrators proved effective in reducing the likelihood of reoffending, many police departments across the country began advising their officers to make such arrests, and some state legislators advocated passage of mandatory arrest laws.[66]

Unfortunately, publicly elected officials either are often ignorant of current criminological research or do not heed the advice of professional criminologists, seeking instead to create politically expedient policies, which has led some to proclaim the "irrelevance" of criminology. James Austin of George Washington University bemoaned the lack of attention politicians give to the results of research in criminology: "Despite the annual publication of hundreds of peer-reviewed articles and textbooks proudly displayed at our annual conventions, policy makers are paying little if any attention to us. When Congress or state legislatures debate new crime bill legislation or the effectiveness of past actions, their first question is not, 'What do the criminologists think?' I would venture that one would be hard pressed to cite another discipline that has been so ignored for such a long time."[67]

Research findings may also be ignored because they are at odds with public sentiments. A realistic appraisal must recognize that criminologists are as much to blame for the current situation as anyone else. As Robert M. Bohm explained in his 1993 presidential address to the ACJS, "[M]uch of our work is simply ignored because it is not politically expedient or does not serve the dominant ideology. At the same time, others among us are more than willing to do the bidding of politicians and criminal justice officials in order to feed at the trough of political largess."[68]

> Research results in the field of criminology should have a significant impact on those who formulate public crime-control policy.

One year later, at the 1994 annual meeting of the ASC, (then) Attorney General Janet Reno appealed to the nation's assembled criminologists for urgent assistance in dealing with some of the major crime and criminal justice issues facing the country. She identified 12 important problem areas and challenged ASC members to translate existing research findings into useful recommendations that could benefit practitioners and policymakers throughout the nation who routinely confront issues of crime and justice.

Following her presentation, the ASC National Policy Committee formed 12 task forces—one to investigate each identified problem area. Task force members distilled research findings into policy recommendations that could meaningfully contribute to public debates that were then raging (and still are) over how best to deal with problems of crime, juvenile delinquency, prison overcrowding, and so on. In 1997, after all 12 task forces had submitted final reports, the documents were published by the NIJ and were made available through the National Criminal Justice Reference Service under the title *Critical Criminal Justice Issues: Task Force Reports from the American Society of Criminology*.[69] At the time of publication, Jeremy Travis, then-director of the NIJ, termed the reports a "remarkable contribution to improving our understanding of the issues of crime and the challenge of justice." The task force reports, which have contemporary applicability as well as historical relevance, can be viewed at the *Criminology Today* Web site where the 132-page publication *Critical Criminal Justice Issues* is available in its entirety as **Library Extra 2–7**.

Three-strikes laws provide an example of the kind of dilemma facing criminologists who hope to influence social policy on the basis of statistical evidence. Three-strikes laws, which became popular with legislatures near the end of the twentieth century, require that felons receive lengthy prison sentences (often life without possibility of parole) following their third felony conviction. Such laws are built on the seemingly commonsense notion that "getting tough" on repeat offenders by putting them in prison for long periods should reduce the crime rate; logic seems to say that lengthy prison sentences for recidivists will reduce crime by removing the most dangerous offenders from society.

A study of the three-strikes laws in 22 states, however, concluded that such legislation typically results in clogged court systems and crowded correctional facilities and encourages three-time felons to take dramatic risks to avoid capture.[70] A wider-based study, dubbed "the most comprehensive study ever of crime prevention,"[71] found that "much of the research on prisons was inadequate or flawed, making it impossible to measure how much crime was actually prevented or deterred by locking up more criminals."[72] The central finding of the massive study, sponsored by the federal Office of Justice Programs and carried out by researchers at the University of Maryland's Department of Criminology and Criminal Justice, was that current government-sponsored crime-prevention initiatives—totaling over $3 billion annually—are often poorly evaluated, leading to uncertainty over whether funded

▧ **meta-analysis**
A study that combines the results of other studies about a particular topic of interest; a comprehensive and systematic review of other studies.

THEORY | versus REALITY
The Stockholm Prize in Criminology

On June 15, 2010, during the annual Stockholm Criminology Symposium meeting, world-renowned criminologist David L. Weisburd was awarded the 2010 Stockholm Prize in Criminology at the Stockholm (Sweden) City Hall.

The prize, which carries a cash award of 1.3 million Swedish kronor (about $140,000), was given in recognition of the importance of a series of experiments Weisburd conducted demonstrating that intensified police patrol in high-crime areas does not simply push crime around but can effectively reduce it.

Weisburd, who received a Ph.D. from Yale University, is Professor of Law and Criminal Justice at the Hebrew University Institute of Criminology in Jerusalem, Israel, and Distinguished Professor and Director of the Center for Evidence-Based Crime Policy at George Mason University in Virginia.

Weisburd is also the founder and editor of the *Journal of Experimental Criminology* and co-editor of various other books, including the *Handbook of Quantitative Criminology; Statistics in Criminal Justice; Putting Crime in its Place*; and *The Criminology of White-Collar Crime*. He has published more than 70 scientific articles that cover a wide range of criminal justice research topics, including the criminology of place, violent crime, white-collar crime, and policing.

The Stockholm Prize is financed by the Jerry Lee Foundation in the United States, with support from the Japanese Correctional Association, the Hitachi Mirai Foundation, and the Söderberg Foundation of Sweden. Visit www.criminologyprize.com for further information about the prize and award recipients and to learn more about the annual Stockholm Criminology Symposium.

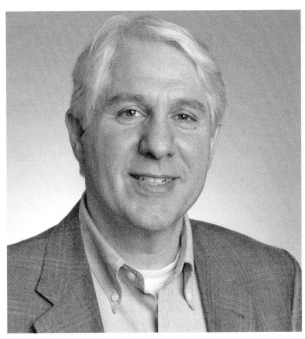

David L. Weisburd of the Jerry Lee Center of Criminology at the University of Pennsylvania. Weisburd was the recipient of the 2010 Stockholm Prize in Criminology. What accomplishments does the prize recognize?
Source: Courtesy of David Weisburd, PhD

programs actually work. The study, a **meta-analysis** (that is, a study of other studies), reviewed more than 500 impact evaluations of local crime-prevention programs and practices throughout the nation. Due to largely ineffective evaluation efforts that are often only loosely tied to funded programs, researchers concluded that "the current [government-sponsored research] plan does not provide effective guidance to the nation about what works to prevent crime." Hence, although the three-strikes laws remain popular with the voting public and lawmakers have been quick to seize upon "get tough" crime-prevention policies in the interest of getting votes, solid and consistent research support showing the efficacy of such laws continues to be elusive.

To draw together much of the discussion in this chapter to this point, consider what the internationally known criminologist Lawrence Sherman identified in 2009 as "the 10 principal elements of a viable model for keeping the promise of experimental criminology":[73]

1. Identify key factual questions about policies.
2. Formulate testable hypotheses about competing answers to those questions.
3. Conduct randomized experiments where possible to compare those answers.
4. Conduct quasi-experiments when better designs are not possible.

WEB EXTRA 2-13
WEB EXTRA 2-14

5. Identify all good evidence on any one question in systematic reviews.

6. Synthesize that evidence, if possible, in single-outcome meta-analyses.

7. Present the research synthesis to committees of practitioners and scientists.

8. Develop succinct operational guidance based on evidence.

9. Communicate or promulgate the guidance.

10. Test and practice methods for obtaining more compliance with that guidance.

One especially important repository of crime- and justice-related literature today can be found at the Campbell Crime and Justice Coordinating Group, a subsidiary project of the Campbell Collaboration which focuses on what works in the areas of education, social welfare, and criminal justice. The Campbell Collaboration began in 2000 to make systematic reviews of research on the effects of social interventions accessible.

For recognition of another researcher and his experiments in criminology, see the Theory versus Reality box.

You can access the Collaboration via **Web Extra 2–13**. The Campbell Collaboration Crime and Justice Coordinating Group, which provides a number of the Library Extras referenced throughout this book, can be reached via **Web Extra 2–14**.

The Research Report

Following the research and analysis of data, findings are typically presented in the form of a report or paper in which suggestions for further study may be made. Policy issues or strategies for addressing the problems identified by the researcher are also frequently discussed. Charts, graphs, and tables may be included in the body of a research report. Most reports are professional-looking documents prepared on a word processor with a grammar and spelling checker and printed on a laser or ink-jet printer. Some are eventually published in professional journals, and a few become staples of the field—frequently cited works that illustrate fundamental criminological or methodological principles.

Most research reports follow a traditional professional format with the following component features:

- **Title page**: The title page contains the names of the report's authors, their institutional or professional affiliations, the date of the report, and its title. Many report titles consist of a main title and a subtitle, which generally gives additional information about the report's subject matter. Some report titles seem all-inclusive: "The Impact of Family Structure and Quality on Delinquency: A Comparative Assessment of Structural and Functional Factors";[74] others are relatively straightforward: "Comparing Criminal Career Models."[75]

- **Acknowledgments**: Often, the author wishes to express appreciation to individuals and organizations that facilitated the study or without whose help the study would not have been possible. Sources of grant support, including funding agencies and foundations, individuals and organizations that either participated in the study or were themselves studied, and people who facilitated various aspects of the study or the production of the report are all frequently acknowledged.

- **Table of contents**: Reports of any length (say, beyond ten pages) often contain a table of contents that helps readers quickly find the needed material and provides structure to the report itself. A good table of contents will reflect section headings within the body of the report.

- **Preface (optional)**: The purpose of a preface is to allow the author to make observations (often of a personal nature) that might not be appropriate within the body of the report. Reasons for choice of the study's subject, observations about the promise held by the field of study, and wide-ranging statements about the future of criminological research are all frequent topics of prefaces found in research reports.

- **Abstract**: An abstract is a brief (usually one-paragraph) summation of the report's findings, allowing readers to gauge whether the subject matter will be of interest to them without reading the entire report. In this day of electronic information, abstracts serve the additional function of providing a quick synopsis that can readily be made available to those searching large databases containing many research articles.

- **Introduction**: Most authors write an introductory section as part of their research report. The introduction describes the aim and purpose of the study, provides a general statement of the problem studied, and furnishes a general conceptual framework for the remainder of the report. The introduction may also outline issues that both are related to the problem under study and could benefit from further investigation.

- **Review of existing literature**: Most research builds on existing knowledge and makes use of previous findings. To cite a few proverbial observations, although it is not true that "there is nothing new under the sun" when conducting research, it is also not necessary to "reinvent the wheel." In other words, the relevant works of other researchers should be discussed in any report, and the bearing that previous studies have on the present one should be explained. Sometimes researchers who are engaged in literature reviews discover that the questions they wish to study have already been answered or that someone else has found a more concise way of stating their concerns. Hence, new investigators can avoid concept development that is merely repetitive and even data gathering that has already been undertaken.

- **Description of existing situation**: Sometimes a description of the existing situation is combined with a report's introduction. If not, then it is appropriate to elaborate on the problem under study by providing details that describe the conditions existing at the beginning of the study.

- **Statement of hypothesis**: Research etiquette in criminology frequently requires the statement of a hypothesis to be tested. Most researchers have an idea of what they expect to find and set out to test a theory or a proposition derived from a theory. Researchers may, for example, wish to test whether the Brady Law, a federal statute which limits handgun sales, has effectively met its goal of reducing the number of deaths by firearms. A hypothesis should be a clear and concise statement of what the study purports to test. As mentioned previously, hypotheses useful in guiding research are always operationalized, or expressed in terms that are in some way measurable. Descriptive studies, on the other hand, are not designed to prove or disprove assumptions (although they may not be free of them), and such studies may not contain hypotheses.

- **Description of research plan**: The research design, data-gathering strategies, and plans for statistical analysis should all be described. This section, although it may be elaborate and lengthy, simply provides an overview of the methodology employed by the researcher and explains how the problem was investigated and why particular research strategies were chosen.

- **Disclaimers/limitations**: All research is subject to limitations. Shortages of money, time, personnel, and other resources impose limitations on research undertakings, as do shortcomings in statistical techniques and restrictions on the availability of data. Limitations should be honestly appraised and presented in the research report so that readers will be able to assess their impact on the results reported.

- **Findings/results**: Along with an overview of the research as it was actually conducted, the findings provide a statement of research results, and many regard this section as the heart of the report. The manner in which results are presented can be crucial for ease of understanding: Bar charts and pie charts are probably the most commonly employed types of diagrams (although the type of data collected will determine the appropriate format for its presentation). Some researchers choose to employ tables containing raw numbers when pictorial forms of representation like charts and graphs would better facilitate comprehension.

- **Analysis/discussion**: Once findings have been presented, they should be analyzed and discussed. Not all analyses need be of a quantitative sort; however, much of today's criminological literature is replete with statistical analyses, some of them quite sophisticated. Unfortunately, poorly conceptualized research cannot be helped by later analysis, no matter how sophisticated that analysis may be. It is therefore of crucial importance to the success of any research endeavor that early planning—including conceptual development, strategies for data collection, and research designs—be undertaken with an eye toward producing data that will lend themselves to meaningful analysis and discussion after data gathering has been completed. The analysis section should also focus on whether the data, as analyzed, support the study's guiding hypothesis.

- **Summary/conclusions**: The summation section encapsulates the study's purpose and findings in a few paragraphs and may also contain suggested improvements or recommended solutions to the problem studied based on the evidence produced by the report. Policy implications are also discussed (if at all) in the conclusion of the report because they are simply broad-based solutions to problems that have been identified.

- **Endnotes/footnotes**: Endnotes or footnotes may be used to reference quoted sources or to refer readers to supporting documents. Sometimes a combination of endnotes and footnotes is employed. Endnotes, as their name

WEB EXTRA 2–15

implies, appear at the conclusion of a report (often after the summary but before the appendixes), whereas foot-notes are found at the bottom of the pages containing the referenced material.

- **Appendixes**: Not all reports contain appendixes. Those that do may place sample questionnaires, accompanying cover letters, concise exhibits from literature reviews, de-tailed statistical tables, copies of letters of support, detailed interview information, and so forth near the end of the document. Appendixes should be used only if they serve the purpose of further explicating the report's purpose, methods, or findings. Otherwise, appendixes may appear to pad the report and can discredit the researcher's efforts in the eyes of readers.

- **List of references**: No report is complete without a list of references or a bibliography used in planning the study and in preparing the document. Although all items listed in the bibliography may not be referenced within the body of the report, source material should still be provided if it was reviewed and served some purpose in study development. Literature that is examined, for ex-ample, may guide the researcher to other material or may provide useful insights during the study's overall conceptual formation.

> The primary medium for research papers consists of refereed professional journals.

Writing for Publication

Criminologists often seek to publish the results of their research to share them with others working in the field. The primary medium for such publication consists of refereed professional journals, those that employ the services of peer reviewers to gauge the quality of the manuscripts submitted to them. Al-though the review process can be time-consuming, it is believed to result in the publication of manuscripts that make worthwhile contributions to the field of criminology and in the rejection of those of lesser quality.

Perhaps the best-known professional journals in the field of criminology today are *American Journal of Criminal Justice, British Journal of Criminology, Crime and Delinquency, Crime and Social Justice, Criminal Justice and Behavior, Criminal Justice Ethics,* *Criminal Justice Policy Review, Criminal Justice Review, Criminology, Criminology and Public Policy, Critical Criminology, Journal of Contemporary Criminal Justice, Journal of Crime and Justice, Journal of Criminal Justice Education, Journal of Criminal Law and Criminology, Journal of Quantitative Criminology, Journal of Research in Crime and Delinquency, Justice Quarterly,* and *Theoretical Criminology.*[76] For a comprehensive list of journals in the field of criminology, including some that are Web-based, visit **Web Extra 2–15**.

Each journal has its own requirements for manuscript sub-mission. Some require a single copy of a manuscript, others ask for multiple copies, a few journals request manuscript files on disk along with hard copies, and still others are moving toward elec-tronic submission via the Internet. An increasing number of jour-nals have established submission fees, usually in the $10 to $20 range, to help defray the costs associated with the review process.

Submission etiquette within the field of criminology demands that an article be sent to only one journal at a time. Simultaneous submissions are discouraged and create difficul-ties for both authors and editors when articles are accepted by more than one publication. Given the complexities of the review and publication processes, it is probably best to write the editor of any journal to which submission is be-ing contemplated to inquire as to that journal's particular expectations.

Most journals require that manuscripts be prepared according to a particular style, meaning that citations, capital-ization, footnoting, abstracts, notes, headings, and subheadings are all expected to conform to the style of other articles pub-lished in the same journal. Two of the most prevalent styles are the American Psychological Association (APA) style and the American Sociological Association (ASA) style.

Most criminological journals, however, utilize a modifica-tion of one of these styles. When considering submission of a manuscript for publication review, it is advisable to write to the editor of the journal in question requesting a style sheet or general style guidelines. Style guides are also available from the APA[77] and the ASA, with third-party publishers making style guides available through university and special-purpose bookstores.

If a research report is not intended for publication, other styles may be acceptable. Answers to general questions about re-port writing and style can be found in publications like William Strunk, Jr., and E. B. White's *The Elements of Style*[78] and Mary-Claire van Leunen's *A Handbook for Scholars.*[79]

SUMMARY

- Criminology is a social science that endeavors to apply the techniques of data collection and hypothesis testing through observation and experimentation. Successful hypothesis testing can lead to theory building and a more complete understanding of the nature of crime and crime causation. Evidence-based criminology offers the promise of building a valuable collection of evidence-based knowledge that can be of service to policymakers and individuals concerned about the fight against crime.

- The three eras that have characterized the field of criminology over the past 100 years are the "Golden Age of Research," the "Golden Age of Theory," and an age characterized by extensive theory testing using empirical methods. The fourth (current) era of evidence-based criminology is heir to the first three eras.

- A theory is a series of interrelated propositions attempting to describe, explain, predict, and ultimately control some class of events. Theories gain explanatory power from inherent logical consistency, are "tested" by how well they describe and predict reality, provide relatively complete understanding, are supported by observations, and stand up to continued scrutiny.

- Research refers to the use of standardized, systematic procedures in the search for knowledge. Determinations of program effectiveness are made through research. Threats to the internal and external validity of research designs refer to confounding effects that might invalidate the results of research.

- Quantitative methods tend to produce results that are easy to measure, whereas qualitative methods produce subjective results that are difficult to quantify. Quantitative methods are useful in objectively assessing hypotheses and measuring the effects of an experimental intervention; qualitative methods are important for the insights they provide into the subjective workings of the criminal mind and the processes by which meaning is accorded to human experience.

- Values enter into all stages of the research process. Protection of human subjects from harm, need for privacy, disclosure of research methods, and data confidentiality are all critical ethical issues. To address these and other concerns, the Academy of Criminal Justice Sciences (ACJS) has adopted an official code of ethics for research in the field of criminology.

- Ideally, research results in the field of criminology should have a significant impact on public crime-control policy. Unfortunately, publicly elected officials either are often ignorant of current criminological research or do not heed the advice of professional criminologists, seeking instead to create politically expedient policies.

- A typical research report might contain the following sections: title page, acknowledgments, table of contents, preface, abstract, introduction, review of existing literature, description of existing situation, statement of hypothesis, description of research plan, disclaimers/limitations, findings/results, analysis/discussion, summary/conclusion, endnotes/footnotes, appendixes, and list of references. Research findings in the field of criminology are published in professional journals.

KEY TERMS

applied research, 32	operationalization, 32
confounding effect, 34	participant observation, 37
control group, 36	primary research, 32
controlled experiment, 35	pure research, 32
correlation, 40	qualitative method, 42
data confidentiality, 43	quantitative method, 41
descriptive statistics, 40	quasi-experimental design, 35
evidence based, 27	randomization, 36
evidence-based criminology, 27	replicability, 38
	research, 32
external validity, 34	research design, 33
hypothesis, 31	secondary research, 32
inferential statistics, 40	survey research, 37
informed consent, 44	test of significance, 40
internal validity, 34	theory, 31
intersubjectivity, 38	variable, 32
meta-analysis, 47	*verstehen*, 43

QUESTIONS FOR REVIEW

1. What is evidence-based criminology? How does the meaning of the word *evidence* in evidence-based criminology differ from the evidence found at a crime scene or used in criminal trials?

2. What three eras have characterized the field of criminology over the past 100 years? Describe each.

3. What is a theory? What purposes do theories serve? What role do research and experimentation play in theory building in criminology?

4. What is a hypothesis? How can a hypothesis be tested? What is internal validity? External validity? How can threats to internal and external validity be addressed?

5. What are the differences between quantitative and qualitative methods in the social sciences? What are the advantages and disadvantages of each method?

6. What are some ethical considerations involved in conducting criminological research? How can researchers make sure that such considerations are met?

7. How do criminological research and experimental criminology impact social policy?

8. What sections might a typical research report contain? Where are research findings in criminology published?

QUESTIONS **FOR REFLECTION**

1. This book emphasizes the theme of social problems versus social responsibility. How might a thorough research agenda allow us to decide which perspective is more fruitful in combating crime?

2. What does it mean to operationalize a hypothesis? Why is operationalization necessary?

3. Why is the task of criminological theory construction so demanding? How do we know if a theory is any good?

4. What is a meta-analysis? For what purposes might a meta-analysis be conducted?

5. What are the various types of data-gathering strategies discussed in this chapter? Describe them. Is any one technique better than another? Why? Under what kinds of conditions might certain types of data-gathering strategies be most appropriate?

6. A few years ago, the Bureau of Justice Statistics announced findings that male military veterans were less than half as likely as male nonveterans of the same age to be in prison (the rates reported were 630 versus 1,390 per 100,000 male prisoners, respectively). Does this mean that we can say with confidence that military service decreases a male's likelihood of committing a criminal offense? What other influences might be operating to lower the likelihood of crime commission by male military veterans? (See the full report at www.justicestudies.com/pubs/veterans.pdf.)

CHAPTER 3

CLASSICAL AND NEOCLASSICAL THOUGHT

LEARNING OUTCOMES

After reading this chapter, you should be able to answer the following questions:

- What are the major principles of the Classical School of criminology?

- What were some forerunners of classical thought in criminology?

- Who were some important thinkers of the Classical School of criminology, and what heritage did their way of thinking provide?

- What is neoclassical criminology, and how does it differ from the classical perspective? How does it build on it?

- What is the role of punishment in neoclassical criminology?

- What are the policy implications of the Classical School?

- How can classical perspectives on crime be criticized?

▦ **mores**	▦ **folkways**
Behavioral proscriptions covering potentially serious violations of a group's values. Examples include strictures against murder, rape, and robbery.	Time-honored customs. Although folkways carry the force of tradition, their violation is unlikely to threaten the survival of the group.

Introduction

On February 5, 2010, a 34-year-old man with the unlikely name of Johnny B. Goode (aka, Johnathan Bartholomew Goode) was arrested for the forty-ninth time in Palm Beach County, Florida.[1] Goode's arrest came on four outstanding warrants for failure to appear in court on trespassing charges. Goode, who still lives in Florida, is homeless and mentally ill, and all of his arrests have been for misdemeanors, including disorderly conduct. Goode's history shows that when he finally makes a court appearance, he is usually sentenced to the time he's already served while waiting in jail. Mug shots from each of Goode's 49 arrests were still available on the Web at http://tinyurl.com/yhs74sm at the time this book went to press.

This chapter examines the belief that at least some illegal activity is the result of rational choices made by individuals seeking various kinds of illicit rewards. The perspectives analyzed in this chapter form the basis for strict policies of social control—those based on punishment as a primary means for curtailing continued criminality. As you read through this chapter, however, you might ask yourself how the theoretical approaches that it describes can account for the behavior of people like Johnny B. Goode.

> Some illegal activity is the result of rational choices made by individuals seeking various kinds of illicit rewards.

Major Principles of the Classical School

This section summarizes the central features of the Classical School of criminological thought. Each of the points listed in this discussion is covered in more detail elsewhere in this chapter; this overview is intended to provide a summation and to be a guide to the rest of this chapter.

Most classical theories of crime causation make the following basic assumptions:

- Human beings are fundamentally rational, and most human behavior is the result of free will coupled with rational choice.

- Pain and pleasure are the two central determinants of human behavior.

- Punishment, a necessary evil, is sometimes required to deter law violators and to serve as an example to others who would also violate the law.

- Root principles of right and wrong are inherent in the nature of things and cannot be denied.

- Society exists to provide benefits to individuals that they would not receive in isolation.

- When men and women band together for the protection offered by society, they forfeit some of the benefits that accrue from living in isolation.

- Certain key rights of individuals are inherent in the nature of things, and governments that contravene those rights should be disbanded.

- Crime disparages the quality of the bond that exists between individuals and society and is therefore an immoral form of behavior.

Forerunners of Classical Thought

The notion of crime as a violation of established law did not exist in most primitive societies. Lack of law-making bodies, absence of formal written laws, and loose social bonds precluded the concept of crime as law violation, but all human societies, from the simplest to the most advanced, did evidence their own widely held notions of right and wrong. Sociologists call such fundamental concepts of morality and propriety *mores* and *folkways*. *Mores, folkways*, and *law* are terms used by **William Graham Sumner** to describe the three basic forms of behavioral strictures imposed by social groups upon their members.[2] Mores and folkways govern behavior in relatively small primitive societies, whereas in large complex societies, they are reinforced and formalized through written laws.

Mores consist of proscriptions covering potentially serious violations of a group's values (for example, murder, rape, and robbery). **Folkways** are time-honored customs; although they carry the force of tradition, their violation is less likely to threaten the survival of the social group. The fact that American men have traditionally worn little jewelry illustrates a folkway that has given way in recent years to various types of male adornment, including earrings, gold chains, and even makeup. Mores and folkways, although they may

■ *mala in se*
An act that is thought to be wrong in and of itself.

■ *mala prohibita*
An act that is wrong only because it is prohibited.

■ **Code of Hammurabi**
An early set of laws established by the Babylonian king
Hammurabi, who ruled the ancient city from 1792 to 1750 B.C.

WEB EXTRA 3–1

■ **retribution**
The act of taking revenge upon a criminal perpetrator.

Demons torment a man in this historical rendition. Crime and
other social evils have always begged for explanation. What
would today's criminologists think of the claim that "the devil
made him do it"?
Source: CORBIS–NY

be powerful determinants of behavior, are nonetheless informal
because only laws have been codified into formal strictures wielded
by institutions and created specifically for enforcement purposes.

Another method of categorizing socially proscriptive rules is
provided by some criminologists who divide crimes into the dual
categories of *mala in se* and *mala prohibita*. Acts that are **mala in se**
are said to be fundamentally wrong, regardless of the time or
place in which they occur (for example, forcing someone to have
sex against his or her will and the intentional killing of children).
Those who argue for the existence of *mala in se* offenses usually
point to some fundamental rule, such as religious teachings (the
Ten Commandments, the Koran, and so on), to support their belief that some acts are inherently wrong.

Offenses termed **mala prohibita** are said to be wrong in areas where they are prohibited (for example, prostitution, gambling, drug use, and premarital sexual behavior). The status of
such behaviors as *mala prohibita* is supported by the fact that they
are not necessarily crimes in every jurisdiction; prostitution, for
example, is legal in parts of Nevada, as is gambling.

The Demonic Era

Since time began, humankind has been preoccupied with what
appears to be an ongoing war between good and evil. Oftentimes
evil has appeared in impersonal guise, as when the great bubonic

plague (the "black death") ravaged Europe and Asia in the fourteenth century, leaving as much as three-quarters of the population dead in a span of 20 years. At other times, evil has seemed
to wear a human face, as when the Nazi Holocaust claimed millions of Jewish lives during World War II.

Whatever its manifestation, the very presence of evil in the
world has begged for interpretation, and sage minds throughout
human history have advanced many explanations for the evil
conditions that individuals and social groups have at times been
forced to endure. Some forms of evil, like the plague and the
Holocaust, appear cosmically based, whereas others—including
personal victimization, criminality, and singular instances of
deviance—are the undeniable result of individual behavior.
Cosmic-level evil has been explained by ideas as diverse as divine punishment, karma, fate, and vengeful activities of offended
gods. Early explanations of personal deviance ranged from
demonic possession to spiritual influences to temptation by
fallen angels.

Early Sources
of Criminal Law

Code of Hammurabi

Modern criminal law is the result of a long evolution of legal
principles. The **Code of Hammurabi** is one of the first known
bodies of law to survive for study today. King Hammurabi ruled
the ancient city of Babylon from 1792 to 1750 B.C. and created a
legal code consisting of strictures that were originally intended to
establish property and other rights and that were crucial to the
continued growth of Babylon as a significant commercial center.
Hammurabi's law spoke to issues of theft, property ownership,
sexual relationships, and interpersonal violence. Well-known criminologist Marvin Wolfgang observed, "In its day, 1700 B.C.,
the Hammurabi Code, with its emphasis on retribution, amounted
to a brilliant advance in penal philosophy mainly because it represented an attempt to keep cruelty within bounds."[3] Prior to
the code, captured offenders often faced barbarous **retribution**,
frequently at the hands of revenge-seeking victims, no matter how
minor their transgressions had been. Learn more about the Code
of Hammurabi at **Web Extra 3–1**.

Early Roman Law

Of considerable significance for our own legal tradition is
early Roman law. Roman legions under Emperor Claudius I

Twelve Tables
Early Roman laws written circa 450 B.C. that regulated family, religious, and economic life.

common law
Law originating from usage and custom rather than from written statutes. The term refers to nonstatutory customs, traditions, and precedents that help guide judicial decision making.

WEB EXTRA 3–2
WEB EXTRA 3–3

Enlightenment
A social movement that arose during the eighteenth century and that built upon ideas like empiricism, rationality, free will, humanism, and natural law.

(10 B.C.–A.D. 54) conquered England in the middle of the first century, and Roman customs, law, and language were forced upon the English population during the succeeding three centuries under the Pax Romana—a peace imposed by the military might of Rome.[4]

Early Roman law derived from the **Twelve Tables**, a collection of basic rules regulating family, religious, and economic life written around 450 B.C. They appear to have been based on common and fair practices generally accepted among early tribes existing prior to the establishment of the Roman Republic; only fragments of the tables survive today.

The best-known legal period in Roman history occurred during the reign of Emperor Justinian I (A.D. 527–565). By the end of the sixth century, the Roman Empire had declined substantially in size and influence and was near the end of its life. Possibly to preserve Roman values and traditions, Justinian undertook the laborious process of distilling Roman laws into a set of writings. This Justinian Code consisted of three lengthy legal documents—the Institutes, the Digest, and the Code itself—and distinguished between two major legal categories: public laws and private laws. Public laws dealt with the organization of the Roman state, its Senate, and governmental offices; private law concerned itself with contracts, personal possessions, legal status of various people (citizens, free people, slaves, freedmen, guardians, husbands, and wives), and injuries to citizens. It contained elements of our modern civil and criminal law, and it influenced Western legal thought up through the Middle Ages. Learn more about early Roman law at **Web Extra 3–2**.

Common Law

Common law refers to a traditional body of unwritten legal precedents that was created through everyday practice in English society, was based on shared traditions and standards, and was supported by court decisions during the Middle Ages. As novel situations arose and were handled by British justices, their declarations became the start for any similar future deliberations.

Common law was given considerable legitimacy in the eleventh century with the official declaration that it was the law of the land by King Edward the Confessor (A.D. 1042–1066). The authority of common law was further reinforced by the decision of William the Conqueror to use popular customs as the basis for judicial action following his subjugation of Britain in A.D. 1066.

Eventually, court decisions were recorded and made available to barristers (English trial lawyers) and judges. As criminologist Howard Abadinsky wrote, "Common law involved the transformation of community rules into a national legal system.

The controlling element [was] precedent."[5] Today, common law forms the basis for much of our statutory and case law and has been called *the* major source of modern criminal law in English-speaking countries around the world. Learn more about common law at **Web Extra 3–3**.

Magna Carta

The Magna Carta (literally, "great charter"), another important source of modern laws and legal procedure, was signed on June 15, 1215, by King John of England at Runnymede, under pressure from British barons who took advantage of his military defeats to demand a pledge to respect their traditional rights and to be bound by law. At the time of its signing, the Magna Carta (63 chapters in length) was little more than a feudal document listing specific royal concessions.[6] Its original purposes were to ensure feudal rights, to guarantee the king would not encroach on landowning barons' privileges, to guarantee the freedom of the church, and to ensure respect for the customs of towns.

> Common law refers to a traditional body of unwritten legal precedents that was created through everyday practice in English society.

Its wording, however, was later interpreted during a judicial revolt in 1613 to support individual rights and jury trials. Sir Edward Coke, chief justice under James I, held that the Magna Carta guaranteed basic liberties for all British citizens and ruled that any acts of Parliament that contravened common law would be void, a famous ruling that possibly became the basis for the rise of the U.S. Supreme Court, with its power to nullify laws enacted by Congress.[7] Similarly, a specific provision of the Magna Carta, designed originally to prohibit the king from prosecuting the barons without just cause, was expanded into the concept of due process of law, a fundamental cornerstone of modern legal procedure. Because of these later interpretations, the Magna Carta has been called "the foundation stone of our present liberties."[8]

The Enlightenment

The **Enlightenment** (or the Age of Reason), a highly significant social movement occurring during the seventeenth and eighteenth centuries, was built upon ideas developed by many important thinkers. Because of their indirect contributions to classical criminological thought, it will be worthwhile to spend a

WEB EXTRA 3-4

■ **social contract**
The Enlightenment-era concept that human beings abandon their natural state of individual freedom to join together and form society. In the process of forming a social contract, individuals surrender some freedoms to society as a whole, and government, once formed, is obligated to assume responsibilities toward its citizens and to provide for their protection and welfare.

The Magna Carta, an important source of modern Western laws and legal procedure. What are some other important sources of modern criminal law?
Source: CORBIS-NY

few paragraphs discussing the writings of a few of these historical figures. Learn more about the Enlightenment and the intellectual figures who gave it life at **Web Extra 3-4**.

Thomas Hobbes

English philosopher **Thomas Hobbes** (1588–1679) developed what many writers regard as an extremely negative view of human nature and social life, which he described in his momentous work, *Leviathan* (1651). Fear of violent death, he said, forces human beings into a **social contract** with one another to create a state that demands the surrender of certain natural rights and submission to the absolute authority of a sovereign while offering protection and succor to its citizens. The social contract concept significantly influenced many of Hobbes's contemporaries, but much of his writing was condemned for an overly pessimistic view of both human nature and existing governments.

John Locke

In 1690, English philosopher **John Locke** (1632–1704) published his *Essay Concerning Human Understanding*, putting forth the idea that the natural human condition at birth is like a blank slate upon which interpersonal encounters and other experiences indelibly inscribe the traits of personality. In contrast to earlier thinkers, who assumed that people are born with certain innate propensities and rudimentary intellectual concepts and ideas, Locke ascribed the bulk of adult human qualities to life experiences.

In the area of social and political thought, Locke further developed the Hobbesian notion of the social contract and contended that human beings, through a social contract, abandon their natural state of individual freedom and lack of interpersonal responsibility to join together and form society. Although individuals surrender some freedoms to society, government—once formed—is obligated to assume responsibilities toward its citizens, to provide for their protection and welfare, and to guarantee them certain inalienable rights such as the right to life, health, liberty, and possessions. A product of his times (the dictatorial nature of monarchies and the Roman church were being much disparaged), Locke stressed the duties that governments have toward their citizens while paying very little attention to the responsibilities of individuals to the societies of which they are a part, and he argued that political revolutions, under some circumstances, might become an obligation incumbent upon citizens.

Locke also developed the notion of checks and balances between divisions of government, a doctrine elaborated on by French jurist and political philosopher **Charles-Louis de Secondat Montesquieu** (1689–1755). In *The Spirit of Laws* (1748), Montesquieu wove Locke's notions into the concept of a separation of powers between divisions of government. Both ideas later found a place in the U.S. Constitution.

Jean-Jacques Rousseau

Swiss-French philosopher and political theorist **Jean-Jacques Rousseau** (1712–1778) further advanced the notion of the social contract in his treatise of that name (*Social Contract*, 1762), stating that human beings are basically good and fair in their natural state but historically were corrupted by the introduction of shared concepts and joint activities like property, agriculture, science, and commerce. As a result, the social contract emerged when civilized people agreed to establish governments and systems of education to correct the problems and inequalities brought on by the rise of civilization.

> ▨ **natural law**
> The philosophical perspective that certain immutable laws are fundamental to human nature and can be readily ascertained through reason. Human-made laws, in contrast, are said to derive from human experience and history—both of which are subject to continual change.

> ▨ **natural rights**
> Rights that, according to natural law theorists, individuals retain in the face of government action and interests.

Rousseau also contributed to the notion of **natural law**, a concept originally formulated by Saint Thomas Aquinas (1225–1274), Baruch Spinoza (1632–1677), and others to provide an intuitive basis for the defense of ethical principles and morality. Submissive to the authority of the church, secular rulers were pressed to reinforce church doctrine in any laws they decreed. Aquinas wrote in his *Summa Theologica* that any human-made law that contradicts natural law is corrupt in the eyes of God. Hence, natural law was incorporated into English common law throughout the Middle Ages.

Rousseau agreed with earlier writers that certain immutable laws are fundamental to human nature and can be readily ascertained through reason. Human-made law, in contrast, derives from human experience and history, both of which are subject to continual change, so human-made law (or "positive law") changes from time to time and from epoch to epoch. Rousseau expanded the concept of natural law to support emerging democratic principles.

Natural Law and Natural Rights

Thomas Paine (1737–1809), an English-American political theorist and the author of *The Rights of Man* (1791 and 1792), defended the French Revolution, arguing that only democratic institutions could guarantee individuals' **natural rights**. At the Second Continental Congress, Thomas Jefferson (1743–1826) and other congressional representatives (many well versed in the writings of Locke and Rousseau) built the U.S. Constitution around an understanding of natural law as they perceived it. Hence, when Jefferson wrote of inalienable rights to "life, liberty, property," he was following in the footsteps of his intellectual forebears and meant that such rights were the natural due of all men and women because they were inherent in the social contract between citizens and their government.

Natural law and natural rights have a long intellectual history. In a *National Review* article subtitled "If Natural Law Does Not Permit Us to Distinguish between Men and Hogs, What Does?" Harry V. Jaffa, director of the Claremont Institute's Center for the Study of the Natural Law, called an 1854 speech given by Abraham Lincoln "the most moving and compelling exhibition of natural-law reasoning in all political history."[9] In that speech, Lincoln argued in favor of freedom for slaves by succinctly pointing out there is no difference between people, whatever their color: "Equal justice to the South, it is said, requires us to consent to the extending of slavery to new countries. That is to say, inasmuch as you do not object to my taking my hog to Nebraska, therefore I must not object to your taking your slave. Now, I admit this is perfectly

logical, if there is no difference between hogs and Negroes."[10] Lincoln's point, of course, was that there is a huge difference between human beings and animals by virtue of their nature and that such a difference cannot be denied by logic.

Other commentators have cited the "crimes against humanity" committed by Nazis during World War II as indicative of natural law principles. The chilling testimony of Rudolf Hess,[11] Hitler's deputy, during the 1945 war crimes trial in Nuremberg, Germany, as he recalled the Fuehrer's order to exterminate millions of Jews indicates the extent of the planned "final solution": "In the summer of 1941, I was summoned to Berlin to Reichsfuehrer SS Himmler to receive personal orders. He told me something to the effect—I do not remember the exact words—that the Fuehrer had given the order for a final solution of the Jewish question. We, the SS, must carry out that order. If it is not carried out now then the Jews will later on destroy the German people. He had chosen Auschwitz on account of its easy access by rail and also because the extensive site offered space for measures ensuring isolation."[12] Who could argue against the premise, natural law supporters ask, that Hitler's final solution to the Jewish "question" was inherently wrong?

Although the concept of natural law has waned somewhat in influence over the past half century, many people today still hold that the basis for various existing criminal laws can be found in immutable moral principles or some other identifiable aspect of the natural order. Modern-day advocates of natural law claim that it comes from outside the social group and that it is knowable through some form of revelation, intuition, or prophecy.

The present debate over abortion is an example of the modern-day use of natural law arguments to support both sides in the dispute. Antiabortion forces, frequently called "pro-lifers" or "right-to-lifers," claim that an unborn fetus is a person, that he or she is entitled to all the protection we would give to any other living human being, and that such protection is basic and humane and lies in the natural relationship of one human being to another within the relationship of a society to its children. Abortion (also called "pro-choice") advocates, who are striving for passage of a law or for a reinterpretation of past Supreme Court precedent which would support their position, maintain that abortion is a right of any pregnant woman because she is the only one who should be in control of her body and claim that the legal system must address the abortion question by offering protection for this natural right.

Perhaps the best-known modern instance of a natural law debate occurred during confirmation hearings for U.S. Supreme

> ■ **Classical School**
> A criminological perspective of the late 1700s and early 1800s that had its roots in the Enlightenment and that held that humans are rational beings, that crime is the result of the exercise of free will, and that punishment can be effective in reducing the incidence of crime to the degree it negates the pleasure to be derived from crime commission.

WEB EXTRA 3–5

Thomas Paine (1737–1809), an important contributor to the concept of natural law. What are the central tenets of natural law?
Source: CORBIS-NY

Court Justice Clarence Thomas. Thomas, who was confirmed in 1991, once wrote an opinion in which he argued from a natural law point of view, but that opinion was later challenged by Senate Judiciary Committee members who felt it reflected an unbending judicial attitude. Learn more about natural law at **Web Extra 3-5**.

The Classical School

The Enlightenment fueled the fires of social change, leading eventually to the French and American Revolutions and providing many of the intellectual underpinnings of the U.S. Constitution, and also inspired other social movements and freed innovative thinkers from the chains of convention. As a direct consequence of Enlightenment thinking, superstitious beliefs were discarded and

men and women began to be perceived, for the first time, as self-determining entities possessing a fundamental freedom of choice; free will and rational thought came to be recognized as the linch-pins of all significant human activity. In effect, the Enlightenment inspired the reexamination of existing doctrines of human behavior from the point of view of rationalism.

Within criminology, the Enlightenment led to the development of the **Classical School** of criminological thought. Crime and deviance, which had previously been explained by reference to mythological influences and spiritual shortcomings, took their place in Enlightenment thought alongside other forms of human activity as products of the exercise of free will. Once people were seen as having control over their own lives, crime came to be explained as a particularly individualized form of evil—that is, as moral wrongdoing fed by personal choice.

Cesare Beccaria

Cesare Beccaria (1738–1794) was born in Milan, Italy, the eldest of four children; he was trained at Catholic schools and had earned a doctor of laws degree by the time he was 20. In 1764, Beccaria published his *Essay on Crimes and Punishments*, which consisted of 42 short chapters covering a few major themes to communicate his observations on the laws and justice system of his time. In the *Essay*, Beccaria distilled the notion of the social contract into the idea that "laws are the conditions under which independent and isolated men united to form a society."[13] More than anything else, his writings consisted of a philosophy of punishment. Beccaria claimed that purpose of punishment should be deterrence rather than retribution, and punishment should be imposed to prevent offenders from committing additional crimes. Beccaria saw punishment as a means to an end, not an end in itself, and crime prevention was more important to him than revenge.

> The more promptly and the more closely punishment follows upon the commission of a crime, the more just and useful will it be.
> —Cesare Beccaria, *Essay on Crimes and Punishments*

To help prevent crimes, Beccaria argued, adjudication and punishment should both be swift, and once punishment is decreed, it should be certain: "The more promptly and the more closely punishment follows upon the commission of a crime, the

WEB EXTRA 3-6
LIBRARY EXTRA 3-1

▓ **hedonistic calculus**
The belief, first proposed by Jeremy Bentham, that behavior holds value to any individual undertaking it according to the amount of pleasure or pain it can be expected to produce for that person. See also *utilitarianism*.

▓ **utilitarianism**
Another term for Jeremy Bentham's concept of hedonistic calculus.

more just and useful it will be." Punishment that is imposed immediately following crime commission, claimed Beccaria, is connected with the wrongfulness of the offense, both in the mind of the offender and in the minds of others who might see the punishment imposed and thereby learn of the consequences of involvement in criminal activity.

Beccaria concluded that punishment should be only severe enough to outweigh the personal benefits to be derived from crime commission and that any additional punishment would be superfluous. "In order," he said, "for punishment not to be, in every instance, an act of violence of one or of many against a private citizen, it must be essentially public, prompt, necessary, the least possible in the given circumstances, proportionate to the crimes, [and] dictated by the laws."

Beccaria distinguished among three types of crimes: those that threaten the security of the state, those that injure citizens or their property, and those that run contrary to the social order. Punishment should fit the crime—theft should be punished through fines, personal injury through corporal punishment, and serious crimes against the state (such as inciting revolution) via application of the death penalty. (Beccaria was opposed to the death penalty in most other circumstances, seeing it as a kind of warfare waged by society against its citizens.)

Beccaria condemned the torture of suspects, a practice still used in the eighteenth century, saying that it was a device that ensured that weak suspects would incriminate themselves, whereas strong ones would be found innocent. Torture was also unjust because it punished individuals before they had been found guilty in a court of law. In Beccaria's words, "No man can be called guilty before a judge has sentenced him, nor can society deprive him of public protection before it has been decided that he has in fact violated the conditions under which such protection was accorded him. What right is it then, if not simply that of might, which empowers a judge to inflict punishment on a citizen while doubt still remains as to his guilt or innocence?"

Beccaria's *Essay* also touched upon a variety of other topics. He distinguished between two types of proof: "perfect proof," where there was no possibility of innocence, and "imperfect proof," where some possibility of innocence remained. Beccaria also believed in the efficacy of a jury of one's peers, recommending that half of any jury panel consist of the victim's peers and half consist of the accused's peers.

Beccaria's ideas were widely recognized as progressive by his contemporaries. His principles were incorporated into the French penal code of 1791 and significantly influenced the

justice-related activities of European leaders like Catherine the Great of Russia, Frederick the Great of Prussia, and Emperor Joseph II of Austria. Evidence suggests that Beccaria's *Essay* influenced framers of the U.S. Constitution, and some scholars claim that the first ten amendments to the Constitution, known as the Bill of Rights, might not have existed were it not for Beccaria's emphasis on individuals' rights in the face of state power. Perhaps more than anyone else, Beccaria is responsible for the contemporary beliefs that criminals have control over their behavior, that they choose to commit crimes, and that they can be deterred by the threat of punishment. Learn more about Cesare Beccaria at **Web Extra 3-6** and **Library Extra 3-1**.

Jeremy Bentham

Jeremy Bentham (1748–1832), another founder of the Classical School, wrote in his *Introduction to the Principles of Morals and Legislation* (1789) that "nature has placed mankind under the governance of two sovereign masters, pain and pleasure."[14] To reduce crime or, as Bentham put it, "to prevent the happening of mischief," the pain of crime commission must outweigh the pleasure to be derived from criminal activity. Bentham's claim rested upon his belief, spawned by Enlightenment thought, that human beings are fundamentally rational and that criminals will weigh in their minds the pain of punishment against any pleasures thought likely to be derived from crime commission.

> Nature has placed mankind under the governance of two sovereign masters, pain and pleasure.
>
> —Jeremy Bentham, *Introduction to the Principles of Morals and Legislation*

Bentham advocated neither extreme nor cruel punishment—only punishment sufficiently distasteful to the offender that the discomfort experienced would outweigh the pleasure to be derived from criminal activity. The more serious the offense is, the more reward it holds for its perpetrator and therefore the more weighty the official response must be. "Pain and pleasure," said Bentham, "are the instruments the legislator has to work with" in controlling antisocial and criminal behavior.

Bentham's approach has been termed **hedonistic calculus** or **utilitarianism** because of its emphasis on the worth any action holds for an individual undertaking it. Bentham stated, "By the principle of utility is meant that principle which approves or

> ■ **Panopticon**
> A prison designed by Jeremy Bentham that was to be a circular building with cells along the circumference, each clearly visible from a central location staffed by guards.

the **PROFESSOR** | **SPEAKS**
Classical Theories of Crime

STACEY NOFZIGER

University of Akron

The University of Akron

Imagine a pair of two-year-olds. Although they will not be arrested, they often engage in many "criminal" behaviors: They take what they want when they want it (theft); hit, kick, or bite others (assault); and have no compunctions about running around nude (indecent exposure).

Positivist theories search for differences between criminals and non-criminals to identify the causes of law violation. In contrast, classical and neoclassical theories argue that this search is unnecessary because the answer lies within human nature. According to the classical perspectives, all human activity is motivated by the pursuit of pleasure and avoidance of pain. Therefore, the question for these theories is not *why* people engage in crime but what *prevents* all of us from engaging in crime.

The answer to this question varies across different classical theories, and includes fear of legal repercussions, social and internal controls, and our everyday routines. What such theories have in common is the assertion that there is no need to be pushed or pulled into criminal behavior. Instead, these theories argue, our human nature must be in some way controlled so we do not continue to act like two-year-olds all of our lives.

Source: Reprinted by permission of Stacey Nofziger, Ph.D. Photo courtesy of Stacey Nofziger. Logo courtesy of The University of Akron.

disapproves of every action whatsoever, according to the tendency which it appears to have to augment or diminish the happiness of the party whose interest is in question; or, what is the same thing to promote or to oppose that happiness." In other words, Bentham believed that individuals could be expected to weigh the consequences of their behavior before acting to maximize their pleasure and minimize their pain, based on intensity, duration, certainty, and immediacy (or remoteness) in time.

Like Beccaria, Bentham focused on the potential held by punishment to prevent crime and to act as a deterrent for those considering criminal activity. Regarding criminal legislation, he wrote that "the evils of punishment must be made to exceed the advantage of the offence." Bentham distinguished among 11 types of punishment:

1. Capital punishment (death)
2. Afflictive punishment (whipping and starvation)
3. Indelible punishment (branding, amputation, and mutilation)
4. Ignominious punishment (public punishment involving use of stocks or pillory)
5. Penitential punishment (censure by the community)
6. Chronic punishment (banishment, exile, and imprisonment)
7. Restrictive punishment (license revocation and administrative sanction)
8. Compulsive punishment (restitution and appointment with probation officer)
9. Pecuniary punishment (fine)
10. Quasi-pecuniary punishment (denial of services otherwise available)
11. Characteristic punishment (mandates such as wearing prison uniforms)

Utilitarianism is a practical philosophy, and Bentham was quite practical in his suggestions about crime prevention. He recommended the creation of a centralized police force focused on crime prevention and control—a recommendation that resulted in the English Metropolitan Police Act of 1829 establishing London's New Police under the direction of Sir Robert Peel.

Bentham's other major contribution to criminology was his suggestion that prisons be designed along the lines of what he called a "Panopticon House." The **Panopticon** was to be a circular building with cells along the circumference, each clearly visible from a central location staffed by guards, constructed near or within cities so that it might serve as an example to citizens of what would

■ **positivism**
The application of scientific techniques to the study of crime and criminals.

■ **hard determinism**
The belief that crime results from forces beyond the control of the individual.

WEB EXTRA 3–7

Jeremy Bentham (1748–1832), whose work is closely associated with the Classical School of criminology. What are the key features of the Classical School?
Source: CORBIS-NY

happen to them should they commit crimes. He also wrote that prisons should be managed by contractors who could profit from the labor of prisoners and that each contractor should "be bound to insure the lives and safe custody of those entrusted to him." Although a Panopticon was never built in Bentham's England, French officials funded a modified version of such a prison, which was eventually built at Lyons, and three prisons modeled after the Panopticon concept were constructed in the United States.

Bentham's critics have been quick to point out that punishment often does not seem to work and that even punishment as severe as death appears not to have any effect on the incidence of crimes like murder (discussed in greater detail later in this chapter). Such critics forget Bentham's second tenet: For punishment to be

effective, "it must be swift and certain." Learn more about Jeremy Bentham from the Bentham Project via **Web Extra 3-7**.

Heritage of the Classical School

The Classical School was to influence criminological thinking for a long time to come, from the French Revolution and the U.S. Constitution to today's emphasis on deterrence and crime prevention. The heritage left by the Classical School is still operative today in the following five principles:

1. **Rationality**. Human beings have free will, and the actions they undertake are the result of choice.

2. **Hedonism**. Pleasure and pain, or reward and punishment, are the major determinants of choice.

3. **Punishment**. Criminal punishment is a deterrent to unlawful behavior, and deterrence is the best justification for punishment.

4. **Human rights**. Society is made possible by individuals cooperating together. Hence, society owes to its citizens respect for their rights in the face of government action and for their autonomy insofar as such autonomy can be secured without endangering others or menacing the greater good.

5. **Due process**. An accused should be presumed innocent until proved otherwise, and an accused should not be subject to punishment before guilt is lawfully established.

Neoclassical Criminology

By the end of the 1800s, classical criminology, with its emphasis on free will and individual choice as the root causes of crime, had given way to another approach known as positivism. **Positivism** (discussed in greater detail in Chapter 4) made use of the scientific method in studying criminality and was based on an acceptance of **hard determinism**, the belief that crime results from forces beyond the control of the individual. The original positivists

Positivism made use of the scientific method in studying criminality.

■ neoclassical criminology
A contemporary version of classical criminology that emphasizes deterrence and retribution, with reduced emphasis on rehabilitation.

■ nothing-works doctrine
The belief popularized by Robert Martinson in the 1970s that correctional treatment programs have little success in rehabilitating offenders.

■ justice model
A contemporary model of imprisonment in which the principle of just deserts forms the underlying social philosophy.

■ three-strikes legislation
A criminal statute that mandates life imprisonment for criminals convicted of three violent felonies or serious drug offenses.

completely rejected the notion of free will and turned their attention to the impact of socialization, genetics, economic conditions, peer group influences, and other factors that might determine criminality. Acceptance of the notion of hard determinism implied that offenders were not entirely (if at all) responsible for their crimes and suggested that crime could be prevented by changing the conditions that produced criminality (see Figure 3–1).

While positivism remains an important component of contemporary criminology, many of its assumptions were undermined in the 1970s by (1) studies that seemed to show that offenders could not be rehabilitated no matter what was tried, (2) a growing and widespread public fear of crime that led to "get tough on crime" policies, and (3) a cultural reaffirmation of the belief that human beings had a rational nature. The resulting resurgence of classical ideals, called **neoclassical criminology**, focused on the importance of character (a kind of middle ground between total free will and hard determinism) and the dynamics of character development, as well as the rational choices that people make when faced with opportunities for crime. The neoclassical movement appears to have started with a number of publications produced in the 1970s, such as Robert Martinson's national survey of rehabilitation programs.[15] Martinson found that when it came to the rehabilitation of offenders, nothing seemed to work, as most resumed their criminal careers after release from prison. "Nothing works!" became a rallying cry of conservative policymakers, and the **nothing-works doctrine** received much public attention. Many conservative politicians and some criminologists began calling existing notions of crime prevention and rehabilitation into question amid claims that enhanced job skills, increased opportunities for employment, and lessened punishment did nothing to stem what was a rising tide of crime.

In 1975, Harvard political scientist James Q. Wilson wrote *Thinking about Crime*, suggesting that crime is not a result of poverty or social conditions and cannot be affected by social programs;[16] he argued for the lengthy incarceration of offenders and

An architect's rendering of Jeremy Bentham's Panopticon design for a prison. What did Bentham mean when he said that for punishment to be effective, "it must be swift and certain"?
Source: University College London (Bentham papers 119a/119)

Free Will	Soft Determinism	Hard Determinism
Classical Criminology		19th-Century Positivist Criminology

FIGURE 3-1 | Classical Criminology versus Positivism—The Role of Free Will

the elimination of criminal opportunity. Also in 1975, David Fogel published a book called *We Are the Living Proof: The Justice Model of Corrections.*[17] His **justice model**, predicated on the growing belief that prisons do not rehabilitate or cure and that criminal offenders *deserve* punishment because of the choices they make, was proposed to the Illinois state legislature as a model for prison reform. Fogel argued that for the criminal justice process to work, offenders must be treated "as responsible as well as accountable, that is, volitional."[18] **Three-strikes legislation**, a reflection of the justice model, is discussed in the Theory versus Reality box.

■ **rational choice theory**
A perspective that holds that criminality is the result of conscious choice and that predicts that individuals choose to commit crime when the benefits outweigh the costs of disobeying the law.

■ **routine activities theory**
A brand of rational choice theory posited by Lawrence Cohen and Marcus Felson that suggests that lifestyles contribute significantly to both the volume and the type of crime found in any society; also called *lifestyle theory*.

WEB EXTRA 3–8

■ **situational choice theory**
A brand of rational choice theory that views criminal behavior "as a function of choices and decisions made within a context of situational constraints and opportunities."

THEORY | versus REALITY
Three-Strikes Legislation

Throughout the 1990s, many states jumped on the "get tough on crime" bandwagon and adopted the justice model in their approach to crime-control legislation. In the spring of 1994, for example, California legislators passed the state's now-famous "three strikes and you're out" law. Amid much fanfare, (then) Governor Pete Wilson signed the three-strikes legislation into law, calling it "the toughest and most sweeping crime bill in California history." California's law, which is retroactive (in that it counts offenses committed before the date the legislation was signed), requires a 25-year-to-life sentence for three-time felons with convictions for two or more serious or violent prior offenses. Criminal offenders facing a "second strike" can receive up to double the normal sentence for their most recent offense. Under the law, parole consideration is not available until at least 80% of an offender's sentence has been served.

In 2003, in two separate cases, the U.S. Supreme Court upheld the three-strikes California convictions of Gary Ewing and Leandro Andrade.[i] Ewing, who had four prior felony convictions, had received a 25-year-to-life sentence in a California courtroom following his conviction for felony grand theft of three golf clubs. Andrade, who also had a long record, had been sentenced to 50 years in prison for two petty-theft convictions.[ii] In writing for the Court in the *Ewing* case, Justice Sandra Day O'Connor noted that states should be able to decide when repeat offenders "must be isolated from society to protect the public safety," even when nonserious crimes trigger the lengthy sentence.

In deciding these two cases, both of which were based on Eighth Amendment claims, the Court found that it is *not* cruel and unusual punishment to impose a possible life term for a nonviolent felony when the defendant has a history of serious or violent convictions.

In 2004, Californians voted down Proposition 66, a ballot initiative that would have changed the state's three-strikes law so that only specified serious or violent crimes could be counted as third strikes. Passage of the proposition would also have meant that only previous convictions for violent or serious felonies, brought and tried separately, would have qualified for second- and third-strike sentence increases.

California's three-strikes law remains firmly in place today. In its current form, it punishes anyone who commits a third felony, regardless of its severity, with a mandatory sentence of 25 years to life if the first two felonies were violent or serious. Learn more about crime-control policy at the Center for Law and Social Policy via **Web Extra 3–8**.

Discussion Questions

1. Some people suggest that three-strikes sentences should be imposed only on offenders who commit violent crimes, such as murder, rape, armed robbery, and certain types of arson. What do you think?

2. How is three-strikes legislation in keeping with the spirit of the justice model described in this chapter?

Notes

i. *Ewing* v. *California*, 583 U.S. 11 (2003); *Lockyer* v. *Andrade*, 583 U.S. 63 (2003).

ii. Under California law, a person who commits petty theft can be charged with a felony if he or she has prior felony convictions. The charge is known as "petty theft with prior convictions." Andrade's actual sentence was two 25-year prison terms to be served consecutively.

Rational Choice Theory

Rational choice theory, a product of the late 1970s and early 1980s, mirrors many of the principles found in classical criminology. The theory rests upon the belief that criminals make a conscious, rational, and at least partially informed choice to commit crime and employs cost–benefit analysis (as in the field of economics), viewing human behavior as the result of personal choices made after weighing both the costs and benefits of available alternatives. "[Rational choice] predicts that individuals choose to commit crime when the benefits outweigh the costs of disobeying the law. Crime will decrease when opportunities are limited, benefits are reduced, and costs are increased."[19]

Two varieties of rational choice theory can be identified. One builds on an emerging emphasis on victimization and is called **routine activities theory**; the second, largely an extension of the rational choice perspective, is called **situational choice theory**.

Routine activities theory (also termed *lifestyle theory*) was proposed by **Lawrence Cohen** and **Marcus Felson** in 1979.[20] Cohen and Felson said that lifestyles contribute significantly to both the volume and the type of crime found in any society and suggested that changes in American society during the 1960s and 1970s (increased personal affluence and greater involvement in social activities outside the home) brought about increased rates of household theft and personal victimization by strangers. Central to the routine activities approach is the claim that crime

■ **capable guardian**
One who effectively discourages crime.

■ **soft determinism**
The belief that human behavior is the result of choices and decisions made within a context of situational constraints and opportunities.

LIBRARY EXTRA 3–2

is likely to occur when a motivated offender and a suitable target come together in the absence of a **capable guardian**, one who effectively discourages crime, and that a person who has taken crime-prevention steps is less likely to be victimized. Cohen and Felson stated, "The risk of criminal victimization varies dramatically among the circumstances and locations in which people place themselves and their property."[21] For example, a person who routinely uses an automated teller machine late at night in an isolated location is far more likely to be preyed upon by robbers than someone who stays home after dark. Lifestyles that contribute to criminal opportunities are likely to result in crime because they increase the risk of potential victimization.[22]

Although noncriminal lifestyles at a given point in one's lifetime are partly the result of unavoidable social roles and assigned social positions, those who participate in a given lifestyle generally make rational decisions about specific behaviors (such as going to a given automated teller machine at a certain time). The same is true of criminal lifestyles. Hence, the meshing of choices made by both victims and criminals contributes significantly to both the frequency and the type of criminal activity observed in society. Learn more about the routine activities approach, including its implications for crime control, via **Library Extra 3–2**.

> Central to the routine activities approach is the claim that crime is likely to occur when a motivated offender and a suitable target come together in the absence of a capable guardian.

In a later work, Felson suggested that a number of "situational insights" might combine to elicit a criminal response from individual actors enmeshed in a highly varied social world, pointing out that "individuals vary greatly in their behavior from one situation to another" and that criminality might flow from temptation, bad company, idleness, or provocation.[23] Convenience stores, for example, create temptations toward theft when they display their merchandise within easy reach of customers. Other authors have defined the term *situation* to mean "the perceptive field of the individual at a given point in time" and have suggested that it can be described "in terms of who is there, what is going on, and where it is taking place."[24]

Situational choice theory provides an example of **soft determinism**, which views criminal behavior "as a function of choices and decisions made within a context of situational constraints and opportunities."[25] The theory holds that "crime is not simply a matter of motivation; it is also a matter of opportunity."[26] Situational choice theory suggests that the probability of criminal activity can be reduced by changing the features of the environment. **Ronald V. Clarke** and **Derek B. Cornish**, collaborators in the development of the situational choice perspective, analyzed the choice-structuring properties of a potentially criminal situation, defining them as "the constellation of opportunities, costs, and benefits attaching to particular kinds of crime."[27] Clarke and Cornish suggested the use of situational strategies to lower the likelihood of criminal victimization in given instances. They also recognized that the rationality of criminal offenders is inevitably bounded or limited, as it is for all of us, by the amount and accuracy of information available to them at the time they are weighing the costs and consequences of future actions.[28]

In brief, rational choice theorists concentrate on "the decision-making process of offenders confronted with specific contexts, . . . [shifting] the focus of the effort to prevent crime from broad social programs to target hardening, environmental design or any impediment that would [dissuade] a motivated offender from offending."[29] The 25 techniques of situational crime control can be identified, and each can be classified according to the five objectives of situational prevention: (1) increase the effort involved in crime, (2) increase the risks associated with crime commission, (3) reduce the rewards of crime, (4) reduce the provocations that lead to criminal activity, and (5) remove the excuses that facilitate crime commission. Table 3–1 outlines the 25 techniques and provides examples of each.[30]

Earlier approaches focused largely on the balance between pleasure and pain as the primary determinant of criminal behavior, whereas rational choice theory tends to place less emphasis on pleasure and emotionality and more on rationality and cognition. Some rational choice theorists distinguish among the types of choices offenders make as they move toward criminal involvement. One type of choice, known as involvement decisions, has been described as "multistage" and is said to "include the initial decision to engage in criminal activity as well as subsequent decisions to continue one's involvement or to desist."[31] Another type of choice, event decisions, relates to particular instances of criminal opportunity (such as the decision to rob a particular

TABLE 3-1 | Twenty-Five Techniques of Situational Crime Control, with Examples

INCREASE THE EFFORT	INCREASE THE RISKS	REDUCE THE REWARDS	REDUCE PROVOCATIONS	REMOVE THE EXCUSES
1. Harden targets • Steering column locks and immobilizers • Antirobbery screens • Tamperproof packaging	6. Extend guardianship • Routine precautions • Presence in group at night • Signs of occupancy and cell phones • "Cocoon" neighborhood watches	11. Conceal targets • Off-street parking • Gender-neutral phone directories • Unmarked bullion trucks	16. Reduce frustration and stress • Efficient queues and polite service • Expanded seating • Soothing music/muted lights	21. Set rules • Rental agreements • Harassment codes • Hotel registrations
2. Control access to facilities • Entry phones • Electronic card access • Baggage screening	7. Assist natural surveillance • Improved street lighting • Defensible space designs • Whistle-blowers	12. Remove targets • Removable car radios • Women's shelters • Prepaid phone cards	17. Avoid disputes • Separate enclosures for rival fans • Reduced crowding in pubs • Fixed cab fares	22. Post instructions • "No parking" signs • "Private property" signs • "Extinguish campfires" signs
3. Screen exits • Tickets needed for exit • Export documents • Electronic merchandise tags	8. Reduce anonymity • Taxi driver IDs • "How's my driving?" decals • School uniforms	13. Identify property • Property markings • Vehicle licensing and parts markings • Cattle branding	18. Reduce emotional arousal • Controls on violent pornography • Enforced good behavior on sports fields • Prohibition of racial slurs	23. Alert conscience • Roadside speed signs • Signatures for customs declarations • "Shoplifting is stealing" signs
4. Deflect offenders • Street closures • Separate bathrooms for women • Dispersal of pubs	9. Utilize place managers • CCTV for double-decker buses • Two clerks for convenience stores • Rewards for vigilance	14. Disrupt markets • Monitoring of pawn shops • Controls on classified ads • Licensed street vendors	19. Neutralize peer pressure • Slogans ("Idiots drink and drive") • Rules ("It's OK to say NO") • Dispersal of troublemakers at school	24. Assist compliance • Easy library checkouts • Public lavatories • Litter bins
5. Control tools/weapons • "Smart" guns • Disabling of stolen cell phones • Restriction of spray paint sales to juveniles	10. Strengthen formal surveillance • Red light cameras • Burglar alarms • Security guards	15. Deny benefits • Ink merchandise tags • Graffiti cleaning • Speed bumps	20. Discourage imitation • Rapid repairs of vandalism • V-chips in TVs • Censored details of *modus operandi*	25. Control drugs/alcohol • Breathalyzers in bars • Server interventions • Alcohol-free events

Source: Center for Problem Oriented Policing, http://www.popcenter.org/25techniques.htm. Reprinted by permission.

WEB EXTRA 3-9
LIBRARY EXTRA 3-3
LIBRARY EXTRA 3-4
WEB EXTRA 3-10

person or let him or her pass); in contrast to involvement decisions, which may take months or even years to reach, these are usually made quickly. Learn more about rational choice theories via **Web Extra 3-9**. You can read about the use of environmental design techniques to reduce crime at **Library Extra 3-3**. Learn more about crime prevention in general via **Library Extra 3-4**.

The Seductions of Crime

One criminologist who focuses on the relationship between the decision to commit crime and the rewards that such a decision brings is **Jack Katz**, whose book *Seductions of Crime* explains crime as the result of the "often wonderful attractions within the lived experience of criminality."[32] Crime, Katz said, is often pleasurable for those committing it, and pleasure of one sort or another is the major motivation behind crime, even if the kind of pleasure to be derived from crime is not immediately obvious. According to Katz, criminologists have often depicted crime as something to be avoided and have failed to understand just how good crime *feels* to those who commit it:

> The social science literature contains only scattered evidence of what it means, feels, sounds, tastes, or looks like to commit a particular crime. Readers of research on homicide and assault do not hear the slaps and curses, see the pushes and shoves, or feel the humiliation and rage that may build toward the attack, sometimes persisting after the victim's death. How adolescents manage to make the shoplifting or vandalism of cheap and commonplace things a thrilling experience has not been intriguing to many students of delinquency. The description of "cold-blooded, senseless murders" has been left to writers outside the social sciences. Neither academic methods nor academic theories seem to be able to grasp how it makes sense to them to kill when only petty cash is at stake. Sociological and psychological studies of robbery rarely focus on the distinctive attractions of robbery, even though research has now clearly documented that alternative forms of criminality are available and familiar to many career robbers.[33]

For criminal offenders, crime is indeed rewarding, according to Katz. It is exciting and feels good: "The particular seductions and compulsions [which criminals] experience may be unique to crime," he stated, "but the sense of being seduced and compelled is not. To grasp the magic in the criminal's sensuality, we must acknowledge our own."[34] Katz described the almost sexual attraction shoplifting held for one young offender: "The experience was almost orgasmic for me. There was a buildup of tension as I contemplated the danger of a forbidden act, then a rush of excitement at the moment of committing the crime, and finally a delicious sense of release."[35]

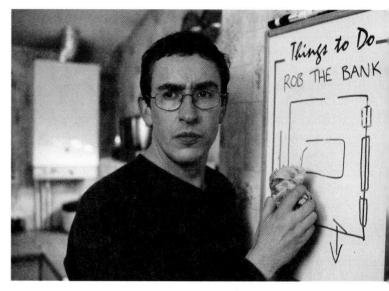

Steve Coogan in the movie *The Parole Officer*. Rational choice theory says that offenders make a conscious, rational choice to commit crimes. Might some crimes also be irrational?
Source: Stephen Morley/DNA Films/Picture Desk, Inc./Kobal Collection

Katz's approach stresses the sensual dynamics of criminality, arguing that crime is sensually compelling for many people. As one writer noted, "Jack Katz argues for a redirection of the criminological gaze—from the traditional focus on background factors such as age, gender, and material conditions to foreground or situational factors that directly precipitate criminal acts and reflect crimes' sensuality."[36] Learn more about the seductions of crime at **Web Extra 3-10**.

> Criminologists have often depicted crime as something to be avoided and have failed to understand just how good crime *feels* to those who commit it.

Situational Crime-Control Policy

Building on the work of rational and situational choice theorists, Israeli criminologist David Weisburd described the advantages of a situational approach to crime prevention. "Crime prevention research and policy have traditionally been concerned with offenders

■ situational crime prevention
A social policy approach that looks to develop a greater understanding of crime and more effective crime-prevention strategies through concern with the physical, organizational, and social environments that make crime possible.

■ target hardening
The reduction in criminal opportunity for a particular location, generally through the use of physical barriers, architectural designs, and enhanced security measures.

or potential offenders. Researchers have looked to define strategies that would deter individuals from involvement in crime or rehabilitate them so they would no longer want to commit criminal acts. In recent years, crime prevention efforts have often focused on the incapacitation of high-rate or dangerous offenders so they are not free to victimize law-abiding citizens. In the public debate over crime prevention policies, these strategies are usually defined as competing approaches."[37] However, Weisburd said that "they have in common a central assumption about crime prevention research and policy: that efforts to understand and control crime must begin with the offender. In all of these approaches, the focus of crime prevention is on people and their involvement in criminality."

A new approach developed in large part as a response to the failures of traditional theories and programs. "Although this assumption [the focus on people] continues to dominate crime prevention research and policy," said Weisburd, "it has begun to be challenged by a very different approach that seeks to shift the focus of crime prevention efforts." For many scholars and policymakers, this meant having to rethink assumptions about criminality and the ways offenders might be prevented from participating in crime, with some suggesting that a more radical reorientation of crime-prevention efforts was warranted. They argued that the shift must come not in terms of the specific strategies or theories that were used but in terms of the unit of analysis that formed the basis of crime-prevention efforts and called for a focus not on people who commit crime but on the context in which crime occurs.

This approach, which is called **situational crime prevention**, looks to develop greater understanding of crime and more effective crime-prevention strategies through concern with the physical, organizational, and social environments that make crime possible.[38] The situational approach does not ignore offenders; it merely sees them as one part of a broader crime-prevention equation centered on the context of crime. It demands a shift in the approach to crime prevention from one concerned primarily with why people commit crime to one looking primarily at why crime occurs in specific settings. It moves the context of crime into central focus and sees the offender as only one of a number of factors that affect it. Situational crime prevention is closely associated with the idea of a "criminology of place," which is discussed in the Theory versus Reality box in Chapter 7.

Weisburd suggested that a "reorientation of crime prevention research and policy from the causes of criminality to the context of crime provides much promise. . . . At the core of situational prevention is the concept of opportunity."[39] In contrast to offender-based approaches to crime prevention that usually focus on the dispositions of criminals, situational crime prevention begins with the opportunity structure of the crime situation, meaning the immediate situational and environmental components of the context of crime. This approach to crime prevention tries to reduce the opportunities for crime in specific situations, which involves efforts as simple and straightforward as **target hardening** or access control.

The value of a situational approach lies in the fact that criminologists have found it difficult to identify who is likely to become a serious offender and to predict the timing and types of future offenses that repeat offenders are likely to commit. Weisburd explained that "legal and ethical dilemmas make it difficult to base criminal justice policies on models that still include a substantial degree of statistical error." Weisburd added that "if traditional approaches worked well, of course, there would be little pressure to find new forms of crime prevention. If traditional approaches worked well, few people would possess criminal motivation and fewer still would actually commit crimes."

Situational prevention advocates argue that the context of crime provides a promising alternative to traditional offender-based crime-prevention policies.[40] They assume that situations provide a more stable and predictable focus for crime-prevention efforts than do people, based on commonsense notions of the relationship between opportunities and crime. Shoplifting, for example, is by definition clustered in stores and not residences, and family disputes are unlikely to be a problem outside the home. High-crime places, in contrast to high-crime people, cannot flee to avoid criminal justice intervention, and crime that develops from the specific characteristics of certain places cannot be easily transferred to other contexts.

In short, situational crime control works by removing or reducing criminal opportunity. Felson and Clarke reminded us that "accepting opportunity as a cause of crime also opens up a new vista of crime prevention policies focused upon opportunity-reduction. [Such policies] do not merely complement existing efforts to diminish individual propensities to commit crime through social and community programs or the threat of criminal sanctions. Rather, the newer policies operate on circumstances much closer to the criminal event and thus have a much greater chance to reduce crime immediately."[41]

If we accept that opportunity is a cause of crime equal in importance to the personal and social characteristics that other researchers point to as causes, then, stated Felson and Clarke, we have a "criminology that is not only more complete in its theorizing, but also more relevant to policy and practice."[42] If Felson and Clarke are correct in what they say, then much of the crime-prevention work that is already being done by police agencies, private security, and businesses aimed at reducing criminal opportunity directly impacts the basic causes of crime.

WEB EXTRA 3-11

THEORY | in PERSPECTIVE
The Classical School and Neoclassical Thinkers

The Classical School is a criminological perspective developed in the late 1700s and early 1800s. It had its roots in the Enlightenment and held that men and women are rational beings and that crime is the result of the exercise of free will and personal choices based on calculations of perceived costs and benefits. Hence, punishment can be effective in reducing the incidence of crime when it negates the rewards to be derived from crime commission.

Classical Criminology

Approach: Application of Classical School principles to problems of crime and justice

Period: 1700s–1880

Theorists: Cesare Beccaria, Jeremy Bentham, others

Concepts: Free will, deterrence through punishment, social contract, natural law, natural rights, due process, Panopticon

Neoclassical Criminology

Approach: Modern-day application of classical principles to problems of crime and crime control in contemporary society, often in the guise of "get tough" social policies

Period: 1970s–present

Theorists: Lawrence Cohen, Marcus Felson, Ronald V. Clarke, Derek B. Cornish, Jack Katz, many others

Concepts: Rational choice, routine activities theory, capable guardians, situational crime prevention, target hardening, just deserts, determinate sentencing, specific deterrence, general deterrence

---

Learn more about situational crime prevention and target hardening via **Web Extra 3-11**.

Critique of Rational Choice Theory

Rational choice theory (as well as situational choice and routine activities theories) can be criticized for an overemphasis on individual choice and a relative disregard for the role of social factors in crime causation, such as poverty, poor home environment, and inadequate socialization. In one study, for example, Laura J. Moriarty and James E. Williams found that the routine activities approach explained 28% of property crimes committed in socially disorganized (high-crime) areas of a small Virginia city and explained only 11% of offenses committed in low-crime areas.[43] In the words of the authors, "This research demonstrates more support for routine activities theory in socially disorganized areas than in socially organized areas."[44] Hence, although one could argue that the kinds of routine activities supportive of criminal activity are more likely to occur in socially disorganized areas, it is also true that the presence (or absence) of certain ecological characteristics (that is, the level of social disorganization) may enhance (or reduce) the likelihood of criminal victimization. The authors stated, "Those areas characterized by low socioeconomic status will have higher unemployment rates, thus creating a larger pool of motivated offenders. Family disruption characterized by more divorced or separated families will result in more unguarded living structures, thus making suitable targets more available. Increased residential mobility will result in more non-occupied housing, which creates a lack of guardianship over the property and increases the number of suitable targets."[45]

Similarly, according to M. Lyn Exum of the University of North Carolina at Charlotte, rational choice theory does not adequately consider the impact of emotional states on cognitive ability and the role of psychopharmacological agents in decision making.[46] Exum studied the effects of alcohol and anger on aggression and found that "alcohol diminishes individuals' perceptions of the costs associated with aggression and, in some instances, actually increases the perceived benefits." Similarly, high arousal levels, such as those associated with anger and other emotions, appear to impair judgment. Hence, when acting under the influence of alcohol or when experiencing strong emotions, "the individual's capacity to anticipate gratification and aversion, success and failure, and cost is diminished."[47] As Exum noted, other studies show that approximately 40% of offenders are under the influence of alcohol when committing the crimes for which they are arrested, and she suggested that future research involving the rational choice perspective should include the role of emotions and the potential impact of psychopharmacological agents such as drugs or alcohol.

> Rational choice theory can be criticized for an overemphasis on individual choice and a relative disregard for the role of social factors in crime causation.

▨ **displacement**
A shift of criminal activity from one location to another.

One 2005 study that explored the deterrent effect of punishment offers insight into the potential that rational choice theory holds for social policy. In that study, David Lee and Justin McCrary, both at the University of California–Berkeley, examined how juvenile offenders respond to the likelihood of significantly higher sanctions associated with criminality when they reach adulthood.[48] They found that a 230% increase in expected sentence length was associated with only a 1.8% reduction in the likelihood of arrest, so they reasoned that even enormous increases in sentence length seem to do little to reduce the probability of repeat offending: "The small behavioral responses that we estimate suggest that potential offenders are extremely impatient, myopic, or both."[49]

A 2009 study conducted by Italian researchers focused on the large number of Italian inmates who were released in 2006 as efforts were made to reduce the prison population in that country.[50] A condition of release was that anyone who reoffended would face new sanctions *and* have to finish the term they were serving at the time of their release. The possibility of added time was found to have a "substantial effect" on the average prisoner, but the most serious offenders (those whose original sentences were 69 months or longer) appeared not to be deterred by the threat of enhanced sentences. The researchers concluded that career offenders were far less likely to be impacted by penalty enhancements than offenders who were not as far down the path of criminality.

Rational choice theory seems to assume that everyone is equally capable of making rational decisions when such is probably not the case. Some individuals are more logical than others by virtue of temperament, personality, or socialization, whereas others are emotional, hotheaded, and unthinking. Empirical studies of rational choice theory have added scant support for the perspective's underlying assumptions, tending to show instead that criminal offenders are often unrealistic in their appraisals of the relative risks and rewards facing them.[51] Similarly, rational and situational choice theories seem to disregard individual psychology and morality with their emphasis on external situations; moral individuals, when faced with easy criminal opportunities, may rein in their desires and turn their backs on temptation, say critics.

Finally, the emphasis of rational and situational choice theories on changing aspects of the immediate situation to reduce crime has been criticized for resulting in the **displacement** of crime from one area to another.[52] Target hardening,[53] a key crime-prevention strategy among such theorists, has sometimes caused criminals to find new targets of opportunity in other areas.[54]

Punishment and Neoclassical Thought

Punishment is a central feature of both classical and neoclassical thought. Whereas punishment served the ends of deterrence in classical thought, its role in neoclassical thinking has been expanded to support the ancient concept of retribution, with those advocating retribution seeing the primary utility of punishment as revenge.

If a person is attracted to crime and chooses to violate the law, modern neoclassical thinkers argue, then he or she *deserves* to be punished because the consequences of crime were known to the offender before the crime was committed. Moreover, the criminal *must* be punished so that future criminal behavior can be curtailed.

> **Punishment is a central feature of both classical and neoclassical thought.**

Notions of revenge and retribution are morally based, built on a sense of indignation at criminal behavior and on the righteousness inherent in Judeo-Christian notions of morality and propriety. Both philosophies of punishment turn a blind eye to the mundane and practical consequences of any particular form of punishment. Hence, advocates of retributive philosophies of punishment easily dismiss critics of the death penalty, who frequently challenge the efficacy of court-ordered capital punishment on the basis that such sentences do little to deter others. Wider issues, including general deterrence, become irrelevant when a person focuses narrowly on the emotions that crime and victimization engender in a given instance. From the neoclassical perspective, some crimes cry out for vengeance while others demand little more than a slap on the wrist or an apology from the offender.

■ **just deserts model**
The notion that criminal offenders deserve the punishment they receive at the hands of the law and that punishments should be appropriate to the type and severity of the crime committed.

■ **deterrence**
The prevention of crime.

■ **specific deterrence**
A goal of criminal sentencing that seeks to prevent a particular offender from engaging in repeat criminality.

■ **general deterrence**
A goal of criminal sentencing that seeks to prevent others from committing crimes similar to the one for which a particular offender is being sentenced.

LIBRARY EXTRA 3–5
LIBRARY EXTRA 3–6
LIBRARY EXTRA 3–7

■ **recidivism**
The repetition of criminal behavior.

■ **recidivism rate**
The percentage of convicted offenders who have been released from prison and who are later rearrested for a new crime, generally within five years following release.

Just Deserts

The old adage "He got what was coming to him" well summarizes the thinking behind the **just deserts model** of criminal sentencing, which refers to the concept that criminal offenders deserve the punishment they receive at the hands of the law and that any punishment imposed should be appropriate to the type and severity of the crime committed. The idea of just deserts has long been part of Western thought, dating back at least to Old Testament times. The Old Testament dictum of "an eye for an eye, and a tooth for a tooth" has been cited by many as divine justification for strict punishments, although some scholars believe that "an eye for an eye" was intended to *reduce* the barbarism of existing penalties, whereby an aggrieved party might exact the severest of punishments for only minor offenses (even petty offenses were often punished by whipping, torture, and sometimes death).

One famous modern-day advocate of the just deserts philosophy was Christian thinker C. S. Lewis:

> The concept of desert is the only connecting link between punishment and justice. It is only as deserved or undeserved that a sentence can be just or unjust. I do not here contend that the question: "is it deserved?" is the only one we can reasonably ask about a punishment. We may very properly ask whether it is likely to deter others and to reform the criminal. But neither of these two last questions is a question about justice. There is no sense in talking about a "just deterrent" or a "just cure"—we demand of a deterrent not whether it is just but whether it will deter. We demand of a cure not whether it is just but whether it succeeds. Thus when we cease to consider what the criminal deserves and consider only what will cure him or deter others, we have tacitly removed him from the sphere of justice altogether.[55]

According to the neoclassical perspective, doing justice ultimately comes down to an official meting out of what is deserved. Justice for an individual is nothing more or less than what that individual deserves when all the circumstances surrounding that person's situation and behavior are taken into account.

Deterrence

True to its historical roots, **deterrence** is a hallmark of modern neoclassical thought. In contrast to early thinkers, however, today's neoclassical writers distinguish between general and specific deterrence: **Specific deterrence** is a goal of criminal sentencing seeking to prevent a particular offender from engaging in repeat criminality. **General deterrence** works by way of example, seeking to prevent others from committing crimes similar to the one for which a particular offender is being sentenced.

Following their classical counterparts, modern-day advocates of general deterrence frequently stress that for punishment to be an effective impediment to crime, it must be swift, certain, and severe enough to outweigh the rewards flowing from criminal activity. Unfortunately, those who advocate punishment as a deterrent are often frustrated by the complexity of today's criminal justice system and by the slow and circuitous manner in which cases are handled and punishments are meted out. Punishments today, even when imposed by a court, are rarely swift in their imposition; the wheels of modern criminal justice are relatively slow to grind to a conclusion, given the many delays inherent in judicial proceedings and the numerous opportunities for delay and appeal available to defense counsel. Certainty of punishment is also anything but a reality. Certain punishments are those that cannot be easily avoided, but today even when punishments are ordered, they are frequently not carried out—at least not fully. In contemporary America, offenders sentenced to death, for example, are unlikely to ever have their sentences finalized; for those who do, an average of nearly 12 years passes between the time a death sentence is imposed and the time it is carried out.[56]

If the neoclassicists are correct, criminal punishments should ideally prevent a repetition of crime, but punishments in America rarely accomplish that goal, as high rates of contemporary **recidivism** (repetition of criminal behavior by those already involved in crime) indicate. Recidivism, when used to measure the success of a given approach to the problem of crime, is referred to as a **recidivism rate**, expressed as the percentage of convicted offenders who have been released from prison and who are later rearrested for a new crime, generally within five years following release. Studies show that recidivism rates are high indeed, reaching levels of 80% to 90% in some instances, meaning that eight or nine of every ten criminal offenders released from confinement are rearrested for new law-breaking activity within five years of being set free. Such studies do not measure the numbers

■ **capital punishment**
The legal imposition of a sentence of death upon a convicted offender.

LIBRARY EXTRA 3–8
LIBRARY EXTRA 3–9

of released offenders who return to crime but who are not caught and ignore those who return to crime more than five years after release from prison; if such numbers were available, recidivism rates would likely be even higher.

One reason American criminal justice seems so ineffectual at preventing crime and reducing recidivism may be that punishments that contemporary criminal law provides are rarely applied to the majority of offenders. Statistics show that few lawbreakers are ever arrested and that of those who are, fewer still are convicted of the crimes with which they have been charged. After a lengthy court process, most offenders processed by the justice system are released, fined, or placed on probation. Relatively few are sent to prison, although short of capital punishment, prison is the most severe form of punishment available to authorities today. To represent this situation, criminal justice experts often use a diagram known as a "crime funnel." See Figure 3–2 for the 2009 crime funnel, which shows that less than 1% of criminal law violators in America can be expected to spend time in prison as punishment for their crimes.

Exacerbating the situation is the fact that few people sent to prison ever serve anything close to the sentences that have been imposed on them. Many inmates serve only a small fraction of their sentences due to early release made possible by time off for good behavior, mandated reentry training, and practical considerations necessitated by prison overcrowding.

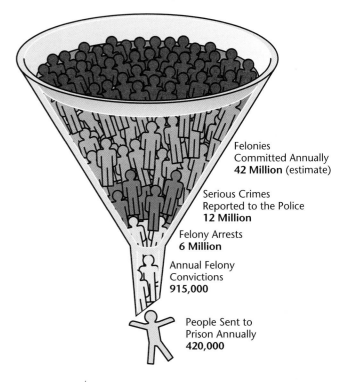

Felonies
Committed Annually
42 Million (estimate)

Serious Crimes
Reported to the Police
12 Million

Felony Arrests
6 Million

Annual Felony
Convictions
915,000

People Sent to
Prison Annually
420,000

FIGURE 3–2 | The Crime Funnel
Note: Includes drug crimes.
Source: Statistics derived from the Bureau of Justice Statistics, *Sourcebook of Criminal Justice Statistics, 2009* (Washington, DC: National Institute of Justice, 2010).

Capital Punishment

Notions of deterrence, retribution, and just deserts all come together in **capital punishment**, the legal imposition of a death sentence. The many different understandings of crime and crime control, along with arguments over free will and social determinism, combine with varying philosophies of punishment to produce considerable disagreement over the efficacy of death as a form of criminal sanction.

Opponents of capital punishment make ten claims:

1. Capital punishment does not deter crime.

2. The death penalty has been imposed on innocent people, and no workable system is currently in place to prevent the accidental execution of innocents.

3. Human life, even the life of a murderer, is sacred.

4. State-imposed death lowers society to the same moral (or amoral) level as the murderer.

5. The death penalty has been (and may still be) imposed in haphazard and seemingly random fashion.

6. The death penalty is imposed disproportionately upon ethnic minorities.

7. Capital punishment goes against the most fundamental precepts of almost every organized religion.

8. The death penalty is more expensive than imprisonment.

9. Capital punishment is widely viewed as inhumane and barbaric internationally.

10. There is a better alternative (usually said to be life in prison without possibility of parole). Read more about arguments against the death penalty at **Library Extras 3–8** and **3–9**.

Advocates of capital punishment generally discount each of these claims, countering abolitionist arguments with the proposition that death is *deserved* by those who commit especially heinous acts and that anything short of capital punishment under certain circumstances is an injustice in itself; some people deserve to die for what they have done. Such arguments have evolved from a natural law perspective, are sometimes supported on religious grounds, and are based on the notion of just deserts (discussed earlier).

LIBRARY EXTRA 3–10
LIBRARY EXTRA 3–11
LIBRARY EXTRA 3–12
WEB EXTRA 3–12

Strong feelings on both sides of the issue have generated a plethora of studies of the efficacy and fairness of capital punishment as a criminal sanction. Although one might expect study results to have produced some agreement, just the opposite seems to have happened—and a relative impasse exists as to how those death-penalty studies that have been conducted should be interpreted. The extent to which the death penalty acts as a general deterrent has been widely examined. Some researchers have compared murder rates between states that have eliminated the death penalty and those that retain it, finding little variation in the rate at which murders are committed.[57] Others have looked at variations in murder rates over time in jurisdictions that have eliminated capital punishment, with similar results.[58] A now-classic 1988 Texas study provided a comprehensive review of capital punishment by correlating homicide rates with the rate of executions within the state between 1930 and 1986;[59] the study, which was especially important because Texas has been quite active in the capital punishment arena, failed to find any support for the use of death as a deterrent.

Similarly, in an important study of the deterrent effect of capital punishment published in 2009, Tomislav V. Kovandzic and colleagues found "no empirical support for the argument that the existence or application of the death penalty deters offenders from committing homicide."[60] Kovandzic's study made use of homicide data from all 50 states and the District of Columbia between the years 1977 and 2006, and the study's design allowed researchers to both assess the impact of changes in capital punishment laws and compare murder rates in death-penalty jurisdictions with those without capital punishment laws.

Regardless of studies to the contrary, many death-penalty advocates remain unconvinced that the sanction cannot be an effective deterrent, stating that a death penalty that is swift and certain is likely to deter others. A thought experiment proposed by Gordon Tullock seems to prove the point.[61] Imagine, said Tullock, that a person is pointing a gun at another and is about to shoot him, intending to kill him, when a police officer appears and points a shotgun at the would-be killer's head. The officer says, "You can go ahead and shoot him, but if you do so, I will then shoot and kill you." Tullock pointed out that, under these circumstances, most potential murderers would be immediately dissuaded from following through on their plans. Tullock's thought experiment shows that punishments that are both swift and certain hold the potential to prevent even the most serious crimes. However, modern-day capital

> **Punishments that are both swift and certain hold the potential to prevent even the most serious crimes.**

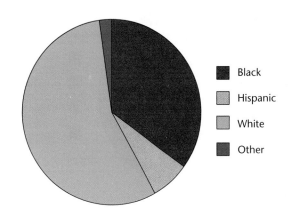

FIGURE 3-3 | Ethnicity of Defendants Executed in the United States, 1976–2010

Source: Death Penalty Information Center, http://www.deathpenaltyinfo.org/race-death-row-inmates-executed-1976 (data current as of March 30, 2010). Reprinted by permission.

Legend: Black, Hispanic, White, Other

punishment practices rarely meet these requirements because appellate processes are long and drawn out and offenders sentenced to death are unlikely to ever have their sentences finalized. Even if the threat of death does not effectively deter others, advocates of capital punishment say, it will ensure that the people who are put to death will never commit another crime. Learn more about how capital punishment is seen in contemporary America from the Death Penalty Information Center at **Web Extra 3-12**. Read about the current state of the death penalty at **Library Extra 3-11**. A balanced approach to the subject can be read at **Library Extra 3-12**.

Capital Punishment and Race

According to the Washington-based Death Penalty Information Center, the death penalty has been imposed disproportionately on racial minorities throughout most of American history.[62] Statistics maintained by the center show that "since 1930 nearly 90% of those executed for the crime of rape in this country were African Americans. Currently, about 50% of those on the nation's death rows are from minority populations representing 20% of the country's population." The center, a fervent anti–capital punishment organization, claims that "evidence of racial discrimination in the application of capital punishment continues. Nearly 40% of those executed since 1976 have been black, even though blacks constitute only 12% of the population. And in almost every death penalty case, the race of the victim is white." In 1996 alone, "89% of the death sentences carried out involved white victims, even though 50% of the homicides in this country have black victims. Of the 229 executions that have occurred since the death penalty was reinstated [in 1972], only one has involved a white defendant for the murder of a black person." Figures 3–3 and 3–4 show the

Follow the author's tweets about the latest crime and justice news at **http://twitter.com/schmalleger**.

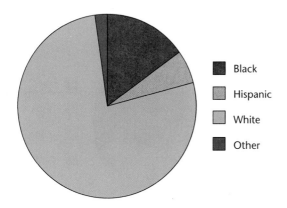

FIGURE 3-4 | **Ethnicity of Murder Victims in the United States, 1976–2010**

Source: Death Penalty Information Center, http://www.deathpenaltyinfo .org/race-death-row-inmates-executed-1976 (data current as of March 30, 2010). Reprinted by permission.

ethnicity of defendants executed in the United States, as well as the ethnicity of murder victims, over the past 35 years.

A 1994 congressional report by the Subcommittee on Civil and Constitutional Rights titled *Racial Disparities in Federal Death Penalty Prosecutions 1988–1994* reached much the same conclusion:

> Racial minorities are being prosecuted under federal death penalty law far beyond their proportion in the general population or the population of criminal offenders. Analysis of prosecutions under the federal death penalty provisions of the Anti-Drug Abuse Act of 1988 reveals that 89% of the defendants selected for capital prosecution have been either African-American or Mexican-American. Moreover, the number of prosecutions under this Act has been increasing over the past two years with no decline in racial disparities. All ten of the recently approved federal capital prosecutions have been against black defendants. This pattern of inequality adds to the mounting evidence that race continues to play an unacceptable part of the application of capital punishment in America today.[63]

The report was prepared with the assistance of the Death Penalty Information Center.

On the other hand, capital punishment advocates say that the real question is not whether ethnic differences exist in the rate of imposition of the death penalty but whether the penalty is *fairly* imposed. They argue that if 50% of all capital punishment–eligible crimes were committed by members of a particular (relatively small) ethnic group, then anyone anticipating fairness in imposition of the death penalty would expect to see 50% of death-row populations composed of members of that group (no matter how small the group). In like manner, one would also expect to see the same relative ethnicity among those executed. In short, if fairness is to be a guide, those committing capital crimes should be the ones sentenced to death regardless of race, ethnicity, gender, or other social characteristics.

Although evidence may suggest that African Americans and other minorities in the United States have in the past been unfairly sentenced to die,[64] the present evidence is not so clear. For an accurate appraisal to be made, any claims of disproportionality must go beyond simple comparisons with racial representation in the larger population and must somehow measure both the frequency and the seriousness of capital crimes between and within racial groups. Following that line of reasoning, the Supreme Court, in the 1987 case of *McCleskey* v. *Kemp*,[65] held that a simple showing of racial discrepancies in the application of the death penalty does not amount to a constitutional violation.

In order to reduce the likelihood that capital punishment decisions will be influenced by a defendant's race, the Washington-based Constitution Project[66] recommended that "all jurisdictions that impose the death penalty should create mechanisms to help ensure that the death penalty is not imposed in a racially discriminatory

Ronell Wilson (right), age 24, is escorted past a corrections officer in New York City. Wilson was convicted in 2007 of shooting two undercover police officers during a buy-and-bust drug operation that took place in 2003. A Brooklyn jury recommended that Wilson be sentenced to die by lethal injection—making him the first person in more than 50 years to be sentenced to death in a federal case in New York State. Why is the number of death sentences being handed out in the United States declining?
Source: Ed Betz/AP Wide World Photos

WEB EXTRA 3-13

manner."[67] The project said that two approaches are especially appropriate in building such mechanisms: (1) the gathering of statistical data on the role of race in the operation of a jurisdiction's capital punishment system, and (2) the active involvement of members of all races in every level of the capital punishment decision-making process. Read the entire report of the Constitution Project at **Web Extra 3-13**.

Is the System Flawed?

In 1996, researchers at the Institute for Law and Justice in Alexandria, Virginia, published *Convicted by Juries, Exonerated by Science*, a report funded by the National Institute of Justice providing a detailed review of 28 cases in which postconviction DNA evidence conclusively exonerated defendants who had been sentenced to lengthy prison terms.[68] The 28 cases were selected on the basis of a detailed examination of records indicating that the convicted defendants actually might have been innocent. The men in the study had served, on average, seven years in prison, and most had been tried and sentenced prior to the widespread availability of reliable DNA testing—although eyewitness testimony and other forensic evidence had led to their convictions. In each case, the DNA results unequivocally demonstrated that the defendants had been wrongfully convicted, and each defendant was ultimately set free. Although the study did not specifically involve the death penalty, *Convicted by Juries* showed just how fallible the judicial process can be. See the Crime in the News box for another story of exoneration.

More recent studies have focused on claimed injustices inherent in the sentencing process that leads to imposition of the death penalty. In 2000, for example, the nonprofit Texas Defender Service examined hundreds of capital trials and appeals, including every published death-penalty decision handed down by the Texas Court of Criminal Appeals (the state's highest criminal court) since 1976.[69] The study found that (1) poor clients routinely received bad representation by court-appointed attorneys, (2) race has a pervasive influence on the administration of capital punishment because prosecutors are far more likely to ask for imposition of the death sentence in cases in which the victim is white as opposed to black, and (3) blacks and Hispanics are often excluded from capital juries. The report also identified instances in which prosecutors intentionally distorted truth in order to win convictions, cases that involved the use of courtroom testimony from disbarred psychiatrists, and examples where unreliable "jailhouse informers" were used in capital cases.

A U.S. Department of Justice (DOJ) study in 2000 found significant racial and geographic disparities in the imposition of federal death sentences.[70] The study revealed that 80% of the 682 defendants who have faced capital charges in federal courts since 1995 have been black and that U.S. attorneys in only 49 of the nation's 94 judicial districts have prosecuted defendants for capital crimes. Critics of the study noted that such numbers are meaningless unless compared with the actual proportion of minority defendants qualifying for capital prosecution. Similarly, the absence in some jurisdictions of crimes that might qualify for prosecution as capital offenses—rather than the supposed exercise of prosecutorial discretion—may explain the lack of death-penalty prosecutions.

A potentially more significant study was conducted by Columbia University Law School professor James Liebman and his colleagues and published at about the same time as the DOJ review. Liebman's group examined 4,578 death-penalty appeals during the years 1973–1995 and found that most cases were seriously flawed—with many having to be retried.[71] A state or federal court threw out the conviction or death sentence in 68% of the cases analyzed, which means that appellate courts found serious reversible errors in almost seven out of every ten cases involving capital sentences; 82% of defendants whose death sentences were overturned by state appellate courts due to serious error were found to deserve a sentence less than death, and 7% were found to be innocent of the capital crime with which they had been charged. According to the study's authors, "Our 23 years' worth of findings reveal a capital punishment system collapsing under the weight of its own mistakes."

> Many years' worth of findings reveal a capital punishment system collapsing under the weight of its own mistakes.

According to the Death Penalty Information Center, 138 people in 26 states were released from death row across the United States between 1973 and mid-2009 after proof of their innocence became available.[72] Figure 3–5 shows such releases on a state-by-state basis.

Studies like the ones cited here have led to official rethinking of the death penalty in some parts of the country, contributing to what some have called a moratorium movement focused on reform of capital punishment laws.[73] In January 2000, for example, Illinois Governor George Ryan suspended executions in his state after DNA results showed conclusively that 13 death-row prisoners were innocent. Ryan appointed a commission to study capital punishment in Illinois and to determine what reforms, if any, could ensure a fair and impartial capital punishment system. In 2002, after 24 months of discussions, the governor's commission concluded

CRIME | in the NEWS

University of Texas–Arlington Student Worked Tirelessly to Free Men from Wrongful Imprisonment

DALLAS—When Claude Simmons and Chris Scott walked out of a courtroom Friday morning as free men, Natalie Ellis dabbed tears from her face.

"I'd never seen them in anything before except prison clothes," she said of the two men who were released after a judge apologized for the wrongful murder conviction that sent them to prison 12 years ago.

"Seeing them walk out the first time in normal clothes, and the looks on their faces, was probably the best thing."

Simmons and Scott said they probably wouldn't have been in the courtroom Friday to bask in the cheers, applause and pats on the back from friends and relatives if not for Ellis and other students from the University of Texas at Arlington's little-known Innocence Network.

"She's an amazing woman," Scott, 39, said of Ellis, "and I love her to death."

The students, led by Ellis, helped reopen the case of a 1997 home invasion robbery that resulted in the shooting death of Alfonso Aguilar. Their work, along with that of students from the University of Texas Actual Innocence Clinic, persuaded the Dallas County district attorney's office to take another look at the case.

Earlier this week, another man, Don Michael Anderson, was charged with the murder. A second man, Alonzo Hardy, was identified as a participant.

Hardy has confessed and implicated Anderson.

The case, which prosecutor Mike Ware said boiled down to mistaken eyewitness testimony, is a rare exoneration that does not include DNA evidence. "The mistakes made in 1997 have had a profound impact on these men and their families' lives, and we are asking the court to set it right," Ware said Friday.

Judge Robert Burns did, releasing the men. "I want to extend to each of you, on behalf of the state of Texas, my most sincere apologies for the injustice," he said, while encouraging them to overcome any bitterness....

Friday's hearing was the Holy Grail for Ellis and her fellow UTA students, the first exoneration since the project was started in 2005 by Dr. John Stickels, a former prosecutor and criminal justice professor.

Unlike many innocence groups, such as the one at the University of Houston or the University of Texas at Austin, the UTA program is not affiliated with a law school....

Stickels persuaded the university to let him start a class and a club devoted to investigating innocence claims after joining the faculty in 2004. The class includes about two dozen students, while the club has about 35 more who work on cases outside of class.

Many are criminal justice majors or pre-law. Some put in a few hours a week; others, like Ellis, are obsessed with the work, spending almost every waking hour for the cause.

Most cases examined by the students do not result in exonerations. Either the convict is guilty or there isn't enough evidence to prove innocence. So Friday's rare victory made the long hours worthwhile.

By the time the exonerees made their way to the House of Blues for a celebratory lunch Friday, Ellis was winding down. She plans to take a few days off to catch her breath, then jump into another case.

For Julpa Dave, past president of the Innocence Network and now a law student at Texas Wesleyan, attending exoneration proceedings is always bittersweet.

"Each time I go to an exoneration, I kind of hope it's the last one," she said. "Because I hope everyone else in prison is actually guilty."

Discussion Questions

1. What are your feelings about capital punishment? Provide reasons to support the way you feel.

2. What do you think are the most significant arguments against the death penalty? What do you consider to be the most convincing arguments in favor of it?

3. How do cases of exoneration, like the ones described in this box, impact public opinion about capital punishment?

John Stickels (right), director of the Innocence Network at the University of Texas–Arlington, looks on as Patrick Waller reacts to the in-court announcement that his criminal conviction has been overturned. Waller had spent more than 15 years in prison before his July 3, 2008, exoneration. He became the nineteenth man in Dallas County, Texas, to have his innocence demonstrated by DNA evidence since 2001. How can innocent people be convicted of such serious crimes?
Source: Tony Gutierrez/AP Wide World Photos

LIBRARY EXTRA 3-13

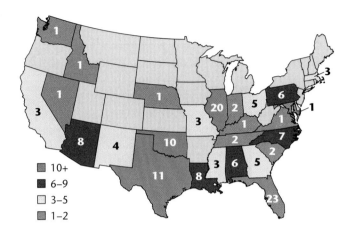

FIGURE 3-5 | Death-Row Prisoners Exonerated and Freed Since 1973, by State

Source: Death Penalty Information Center Web site, http://www.deathpenaltyinfo .org/innocence-and-death-penalty#inn-st.

that "if capital punishment is to continue to be imposed in Illinois, achieving a higher degree of confidence in the outcomes will require a significant increase in public funding at virtually every level, ranging from investigation through trial and its aftermath"; the commission's report contained 85 recommendations intended to reform what the members of the commission saw as a broken system.[74] Recommendations included videotaping all police questioning of a capital suspect and revising procedures for police lineups intended to lead to eyewitness identification. Capital punishment, said the commission, should not be available when a conviction is based solely upon the testimony of a single eyewitness or on evidence provided by an in-custody informant.

On May 9, 2002, Maryland became the second state to declare a moratorium on executions, on order of Governor Parris N. Glendening after the governor decided that "reasonable questions have been raised in Maryland and across the country about the application of the death penalty."[75] Glendening wanted to have an opportunity to consider the results of a two-year University of Maryland study (which was about to be released) examining the effects of racial and jurisdictional factors on the imposition of capital punishment before deciding on a future course of action.

In May 2000, the New Hampshire legislature voted in favor of abolishing the death penalty. In doing so, it became the first state legislature to cast such a vote since the U.S. Supreme Court's 1976 decision in *Gregg* v. *Georgia*,[76] which invalidated the manner in which capital punishment was imposed in a number of jurisdictions. New Hampshire's governor subsequently vetoed the legislation.

Not all state governors are convinced that the death penalty should be abolished. Some, like Massachusetts Governor Mitt

Romney, believe that capital punishment should be revived. Massachusetts has long been one of the 12 states where capital punishment is not a sentencing option for the crime of murder. The state abolished the death penalty in 1984 and has not carried out an execution since 1947.[77] In 2003, however, Governor Romney, after having campaigned in favor of the death penalty, established the Governor's Council on Capital Punishment in an effort to restore the death penalty in his state, telling constituents that he was seeking to avoid the problems that have cast the death-sentencing systems of other states into doubt. The council's report, issued in 2004, included a recommended requirement that physical or scientific evidence like DNA be used to corroborate guilt during the sentencing phase of trial. Jurors would also be informed of the demonstrated fallibility of human evidence and eyewitness testimony. Were the state to follow the council's recommendations, jurors would be told that in order to impose a sentence of death, they must find that there is "no doubt" about the defendant's guilt—a much higher standard of proof than the reasonable doubt standard used elsewhere. The council's complete report is available as **Library Extra 3-13**.

In 2006, the New Jersey legislature voted to suspend use of the death penalty until a state task force made its report on whether capital punishment is fairly imposed.[78]

In 2004, in recognition of the power that DNA testing holds to exonerate the innocent, President George W. Bush signed into law the Innocence Protection Act.[79] It provides federal funds to eliminate the backlog of unanalyzed DNA samples in the nation's crime laboratories;[80] it also sets aside money to improve the capacity of federal, state, and local crime laboratories to conduct DNA analyses.[81] The act facilitates access to postconviction DNA testing for those serving time in state[82] or federal prisons or on death row and sets forth conditions under which a federal prisoner asserting innocence may obtain postconviction DNA testing of specific evidence. Similarly, the legislation requires the preservation of biological evidence by federal law enforcement agencies for any defendant under a sentence of imprisonment or death.

Not all claims of innocence are supported by DNA tests. In 2006, for example, DNA test results confirmed the guilt of Roger Keith Coleman, a Virginia coal miner who had steadfastly maintained his innocence until he was executed in 1992. Coleman, executed for the rape and murder of his sister-in-law, Wanda McCoy, in 1981, died declaring his innocence and proclaiming that he would one day be exonerated. His case became a cause célèbre for death-penalty opponents, who convinced Virginia Governor Mark Warner to order DNA tests on surviving evidence. Coleman's supporters claimed that the tests would provide

■ determinate sentencing
A criminal punishment strategy that mandates a specified and fixed amount of time to be served for every offense category. Under the strategy, for example, all offenders convicted of the same degree of burglary would be sentenced to the same length of time behind bars.

WEB EXTRA 3-14

■ truth in sentencing
A close correspondence between the sentence imposed upon those sent to prison and the time actually served prior to prison release.

the first scientific proof that an innocent man had been executed in the United States. Results from the tests, however, conclusively showed that blood and semen found at the crime scene had come from Coleman.[83] View more than 1,000 capital punishment-related Web links at **Web Extra 3-14**.

Policy Implications of the Classical School

A few years ago, Lawrence W. Sherman of the University of Pennsylvania described four paradigms of justice shown in Figure 3–6.[84] As the figure illustrates, each form of justice can be described in terms of whether it presumes a rational or an emotional basis for crime as well as a rational or an emotional societal response to criminality. According to Sherman, two types of justice—one rational (focused on deterrence) and the other emotional (focused on retribution)—"have competed for primacy" since the dawn of the modern era. Combining those two perspectives on justice with notions of either a rational or an emotional offender yields the four paradigms in the figure.

The first paradigm, which Sherman termed *expressive economics*, assumes that crime is a rational act but that the justice philosophy that undergirds it uses "punishment as a symbolic *expression* of the emotions of anger and outrage by the state and society at the act of a criminal." Expressive economics finds an emotional society using the criminal law and the justice system as a combined means of expressing its feelings and inflicting retribution on offenders who have made the decision to violate the law. This, said Sherman, is the "paradigm that dominates current practice." It is also, he explained, the reason that so many people come away from the justice process feeling unfulfilled: "Few of us expect much justice from an expressive state that dramatizes its outrage at a rational offender who coolly calculates costs and benefits."[85] According to Sherman, it was Beccaria's attacks on expressive punishment as immoral that led to abolition of the death penalty in many European countries.

Another important justice paradigm is a kind of *rational economics*, under which an assumed-to-be-purposeful offender encounters a justice system based on rational—rather than emotional—principles. Such a system employs punishment to make the economics of crime more favorable to law-abiding than to law-breaking behavior. This kind of rational economics

FIGURE 3-6 | Lawrence W. Sherman's Paradigms of Justice

Source: Lawrence W. Sherman, "Reason for Emotion: Reinventing Justice with Theories, Innovations, and Research: The American Society of Criminology 2002 Presidential Address," *Criminology*, Vol. 41, No. 1 (2003), pp. 1-37. Reprinted with permission.

favors deterrence and most closely mirrors the principles of classical and neoclassical thought.

During the past 30 years or so, a mixed American justice philosophy of expressive and rational economics has led to the advent of such seemingly rational punishment practices as determinate sentencing and truth in sentencing and to such emotional consequences as long prison terms and a rebirth of interest in the use of capital punishment.

Determinate sentencing is a strategy that mandates a specified and fixed amount of time to be served for every offense category. Under determinate sentencing schemes, for example, judges might be required to impose seven-year sentences on armed robbers, but only one-year sentences on strong-armed robbers (who use no weapon). Determinate sentencing schemes build upon twin notions of classical thought: (1) The pleasure of a given crime can be somewhat accurately assessed, and (2) a fixed amount of punishment necessary for deterrence can be calculated and specified. **Truth in sentencing** requires judges to assess and make public the actual time an offender is likely to serve, once sentenced to prison, and many recently enacted truth-in-sentencing laws require that offenders serve a large portion of their sentence (often 80%) before they can be released.

> Truth in sentencing requires judges to assess and make public the actual time an offender is likely to serve, once sentenced to prison.

■ incapacitation

The use of imprisonment or other means to reduce the likelihood that an offender will be capable of committing future offenses.

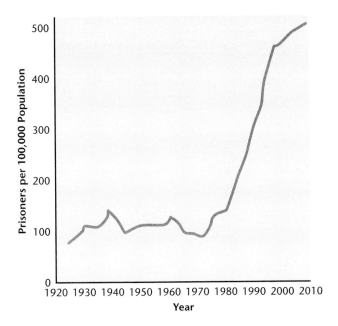

FIGURE 3-7 | Growth in U.S. Incarceration Rate, 1924-2010

Source: Heather C. West, *Prisoners at Yearend 2009-Advance Counts* (Washington, DC: Bureau of Justice Statistics, 2010); and *Correctional Forum*, by Alfred Blumstein, December 2005, p. 10. Reprinted with permission from Alfred Blumstein, Heinz School, Carnegie Mellon University.

Partially as a result of the widespread implementation of determinate sentencing strategies and the passage of truth-in-sentencing laws during the last quarter century, prison populations today are larger than ever before. By January 1, 2010, the nation's state and federal prison population (excluding jails) stood at 1,613,656 inmates, representing an increase of more than 700% over 1970.[86] Figure 3–7 shows the U.S. prison population growth rate from 1924 to 2010.

Imprisonment is one component of a strategy of **incapacitation** (the use of imprisonment or other means to reduce the likelihood that an offender will be capable of committing future offenses). Proponents of modern-day incapacitation often distinguish between the terms *selective incapacitation*, in which crime is controlled via the imprisonment of specific individuals, and *collective incapacitation*, whereby changes in legislation and/or sentencing patterns lead to the removal from society of entire groups of individuals judged to be dangerous. Advocates of selective incapacitation as a crime-control strategy point to studies that show the majority of crimes are perpetrated by a small

number of hard-core repeat offenders. The most famous of those studies, conducted by University of Pennsylvania Professor Marvin Wolfgang, focused on 9,000 men born in Philadelphia in 1945.[87] By the time this cohort of men had reached age 18, Wolfgang was able to determine that 627 "chronic recidivists" were responsible for the large majority of all serious violent crimes committed by the group. Other, more recent studies have similarly shown that a small core of criminal perpetrators is probably responsible for most criminal activity in the United States.

Such thinking has led to the development of incapacitation as a modern-day treatment philosophy and to the creation of innovative forms of incapacitation that do not require imprisonment—such as home confinement, use of halfway houses or career training centers for convicted felons, and psychological and/or chemical treatments designed to reduce the likelihood of future crime commission. Similarly, such thinkers argue, the decriminalization of many offenses and the enhancement of social programs designed to combat what they see as the root causes of crime—including poverty, low educational levels, general lack of skills, and inherent or active discrimination—will lead to a much reduced incidence of crime in the future, making high rates of imprisonment unnecessary.

Before leaving our discussion of Sherman, however, it should be pointed out that the figure implies the existence of two other justice paradigms. One of these, which he termed quite simply *expression*, results from the combination of an emotional offender and an emotional society. In this particular interface—of emotion upon emotion—Sherman explained that "the state is morally obliged to take an explicitly *emotional* stance towards a presumably emotional offender, without regard for harm to the state's self-interest in the effects of its action on the offender's future behavior."[88] See the Who's to Blame box for an inside look at crime and emotion.

It is the fourth paradigm—*emotional intelligence*—in which Sherman placed the most hope for the future. Under such a paradigm, actors within the criminal justice system would control their emotions and would work with offenders and victims to bring about a reasonable resolution of the situation that would repair the harm caused by the crime. Sherman cited the 32% drop in executions that occurred nationwide following the growing availability of DNA evidence that helped to exonerate those wrongfully convicted of capital crimes as evidence of how intelligence and reason can ameliorate emotions in even the most egregious crimes.

WHO'S TO BLAME—The Individual or Society?

The Excitement of Crime

Following his arrest for the theft of a police car, Moonbeam Kittaro met with one of his friends in the visiting area of the local jail. Here's what he said:

I stole a cop car and s***, was it exciting!

I mean, the thing was just sitting there running in the parking lot with the keys in it. Who wouldn't take it?

I've never been so high on pure adrenaline. It was an adrenaline rush being behind the wheel of that f***ing car.

It turned my girlfriend on too.

I drove over to her place with the lights and siren on, and as soon as she saw the car she wanted to go for a ride.

We must have hit 140 on the Interstate!

Then we pulled into a rest stop and made love in the back seat.

It was the whole illegal thing that got her so excited.

But that's when we got arrested.

The cops surrounded the car, guns drawn and all that s***. We didn't even hear them coming.

Think about it:

1. Why did Kittaro steal the car? Do you think he knew, before he stole it, that the theft would lead to so much excitement?

2. Can the desire for excitement explain crimes like Kittaro's? Can the same desire explain other kinds of crimes? If so, what might they be?

3. If excitement explains crime commission, then why doesn't everyone commit crime for the excitement it brings?

4. What kinds of crime-prevention programs might be based on the principles illustrated here?

Note: Who's to Blame boxes provide fictionalized critical thinking opportunities, and are not actual cases.

A Critique of Classical Theories

Classical and neoclassical thought represents more a philosophy of justice than it does a theory of crime causation. As Randy Martin, Robert J. Mutchnick, and W. Timothy Austin have observed, "The true test of Beccaria's essay can be judged by the influence it has had over time on our justice system."[89] The influence of Beccaria, the Enlightenment, and classical thinkers can be found today in the U.S. Constitution, in "get tough" approaches to crime, and in a continuing emphasis on individual rights. Martin and colleagues concluded that the Classical School "has left behind a legacy that we see in almost every aspect of our present-day justice system."[90]

As we observed in Chapter 2, any perspective gains credence if actions taken on the basis of its assertions appear to bear fruit. Not surprisingly, advocates of today's neoclassical approaches to crime control take much of the credit for the recent drop-off in crime rates. After all, following the implementation of "get tough on crime" policies like the determinate sentencing schemes called for by the just deserts model, official rates of crime have shown substantial declines. **Dangerousness** (the likelihood that an individual will later harm people or society) is one of many criteria that could be used to decide whether to incarcerate someone and for how long; see the Theory versus Reality box. The extent of crime's decline, however, might not be as substantial as many people think. Publicized statistical declines may be largely an artifact of the measuring process or may be due to demographic changes in the American population.

Critics charge that classical and neoclassical thought lacks comprehensive explanatory power over criminal motivation,

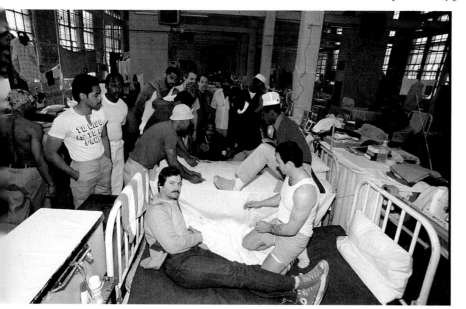

Rahway (New Jersey) State Prison. Today's "law and order" approach has led to dramatically overcrowded prisons. How can overcrowding be reduced?
Source: J. P. Laffont/CORBIS-NY

▓ **dangerousness**
The likelihood that a given individual will later harm society or others. Dangerousness is often measured in terms of recidivism, or the likelihood of new crime commission or rearrest for a new crime within a five-year period following arrest or release from confinement.

CRIMINAL | PROFILES
Gary Steven Krist

Born in Aberdeen, Washington, in 1945, Gary Steven Krist was raised in the small fishing village of Pelican, Alaska. His father was a poor salmon fisherman, and Krist himself described his mother as "a well-intentioned scatterbrain."[i]

During his parents' absence, Gary and his brother, Gordon, were left in the care of others. As a preteen, Gary showed a propensity for violence, and he once fired a shotgun over his babysitter's and brother's heads because the babysitter made him angry.

He soon became known throughout the tiny Pelican community as a troublemaker. Krist's parents, however, seemed to view this behavior as simply displays of typical youthful exuberance.

As he entered his teens, Krist's delinquency bloomed into full-fledged criminality. At the age of 14, Krist was arrested with a friend for a series of burglaries, various sexual conquests, and much drinking. He later wrote in a memoir that their "crimes arose, I believe, more from an overpowering hungry curiosity coupled with excess physical energy than from any defined hostility or malice toward others."

While on probation for these offenses, Krist stole a car, which got him sent to a reform school in Ogden, Utah. He unsuccessfully tried to escape on two different occasions yet later recalled that he was "happy" in this reform school because he was "accepted."

After being released in 1961, Krist served a series of short jail terms for crimes such as auto theft. In 1965, he married; then he was arrested a year later, again for auto theft. Eight months into a five-year sentence, he engineered an escape during which guards shot his accomplice to death. Since California law permitted capital punishment when an escape led to someone's death, Krist worried that he'd get the gas chamber if he were found, so he moved his young family to Boston and created a new identity as George Deacon, an aspiring scientist.

The undeniably intelligent Krist obtained a job as a lab technician at MIT, which led to his participation in a September 1968 marine science expedition where the still-married Krist began an affair with a female student named Ruth Eisemann Schier. Before the expedition was over Krist confessed his true identity and criminal past to her, and they formed a plan to run off to Australia.

To finance their planned new life together, Krist and Eisemann Schier plotted to kidnap Emory University student Barbara Jane Mackle, the daughter of a prominent Miami family, and bury her in a homemade box, where she would remain until they received a $500,000 ransom.

Krist and Eisemann Schier did abduct and bury Mackle, who ultimately survived 83 hours underground before police, informed by Krist

A bearded Gary Steven Krist is escorted from an elevator by a DeKalb County (Georgia) deputy sheriff en route to jail in 1969. Krist had been found guilty for his part in the kidnapping of Barbara Jane Mackle and was sentenced to life in prison. Paroled after ten years, he entered a new life of crime. Why didn't he reform?
Source: © Bettmann/CORBIS. All Rights Reserved.

of the burial site, were able to find and release her. The kidnappers were subsequently caught and tried in Decatur, Georgia, in May 1969.

Before his trial, Krist's intellect was evaluated by a psychiatrist as "if not at the genius level, then certainly in the near genius category." Found guilty, the 23-year-old Krist received a life sentence.

Paroled after ten years, Krist set about lobbying for a complete pardon, which he eventually obtained in 1989. He then enrolled in a medical school in the West Indies and completed his M.D. degree. Several states denied him a medical license before the state of Indiana finally granted him a probationary license in 2001.[ii] That license was revoked two years later when Krist's past criminal record and allegations of sexual assaults on patients surfaced.[iii]

In January 2007, 61-year-old Gary Krist, who once described himself as the "Einstein of crime," was on his way back to prison to serve a five-year, five-month sentence. A federal sting operation busted Krist and his 41-year-old stepson in early 2006 for conspiracy to bring cocaine and illegal aliens into the United States.[iv]

Notes
i. Steve Fennessy, "The Talented Dr. Krist." *Atlanta Magazine* Online, http://www.atlantamagazine.com/article.php?id=299, (accessed May 21, 2007).
ii. *Cincinnati Enquirer, The Enquirer* Online Edition, "Doctor Found to Have Been Imprisoned for Kidnapping," November 16, 2002, http://www.enquirer.com/editions/2002/11/16/loc_in-felondoc16.html (accessed July 10, 2007).
iii. Wishtv.com, "Doctor's License Revoked," August 29, 2003, http://www.wishtv.com/Global/story.asp?S=1423007 (accessed May 21, 2007).
iv. MSNBC, "Georgia Man in 1960s Buried Alive Case Gets 5 Years in Drug Case," http://www.msnbc.msn.com/id/16710294/ (accessed May 21, 2007).

THEORY | versus REALITY

Assessing Dangerousness

Dangerousness is a difficult concept to comprehend. Indicators of dangerousness have yet to be well defined in the social scientific literature, and legislators who attempt to codify any assessment of future dangerousness often find themselves frustrated. On the individual level, however, dangerousness might be more easily assessed. What follows is a description of the criteria one judge, Lois G. Forer, used in deciding whether an offender needed to spend a long time away from society.

I had my own criteria or guidelines—very different from those established by most states and the federal government—for deciding on a punishment. My primary concern was public safety. The most important question I asked myself was whether the offender could be deterred from committing other crimes. No one can predict with certainty who will or will not commit a crime, but there are indicators most sensible people recognize as danger signals:

- First, was this an irrational crime? If an arsonist sets a fire to collect insurance, that is a crime but also a rational act. Such a person can be deterred by being made to pay for the harm done and the costs to the fire department. However, if the arsonist sets fires just because he likes to see them, it is highly unlikely that he can be stopped from setting others, no matter how high the fine. Imprisonment is advisable even though it may be a first offense.
- Second, was there wanton cruelty? If a robber maims or slashes the victim, there is little likelihood that he can safely be left in the community. If a robber simply displays a gun but does not fire it or harm the victim, then one should consider his life history, provocation, and other circumstances in deciding whether probation is appropriate.
- Third, is this a hostile person? Was his crime one of hatred, and does he show any genuine remorse? Most rapes are acts of

hostility, and the vast majority of rapists have a record of numerous sexual assaults. I remember one man who raped his mother. I gave him the maximum sentence under the law—20 years—but with good behavior, he got out fairly quickly. He immediately raped another elderly woman.
- Fourth, is this a person who knows he is doing wrong but cannot control himself? Typical of such offenders are pedophiles. One child abuser who appeared before me had already been convicted of abusing his first wife's child. I got him on the second wife's child and sentenced him to the maximum. Still, he'll get out with good behavior, and I shudder to think about the children around him when he does. This is one case in which justice is not tough enough.
- By contrast, some people who have committed homicide present very little danger of further violence—although many more do. Once a young man came before me because he had taken aim at a person half a block away and then shot him in the back, killing him. Why did he do it? "I wanted to get me a body." He should never get out.

Discussion Questions

1. How are public safety and criminal punishment related?
2. Do you agree that the criteria used by Judge Forer to identify dangerousness are useful? Why?
3. Do you believe that offenders who are identified as dangerous should be treated differently from other offenders? If so, how?
4. What elements of classical or neoclassical thought are apparent in Judge Forer's writing?

Source: Lois G. Forer, "Justice by the Numbers: Mandatory Sentencing Drove Me from the Bench," *Washington Monthly*, April 1992, pp. 12–18. Reprinted with permission from *The Washington Monthly*. Copyright by The Washington Monthly Company, 1611 Connecticut Ave., N.W., Washington, D.C. 20009; 202–462-0128. Web site: www.washingtonmonthly.com.

other than to advance the relatively simple claim that crime is the result of free will, the personal attractions of crime, and individual choice (see the Criminal Profiles box). Such critics point out that classical theory is largely bereft of meaningful explanations as to how a choice for or against criminal activity is made. Similarly, classical theory lacks any appreciation for the deeper fonts of personal motivation, including those represented by aspects of human biology and psychology as well as the social environment. Moreover, the Classical School, as originally detailed in the writings of Beccaria and Bentham, lacked any scientific basis for the claims it made. Although neoclassical writers have advanced the scientific foundation of classical claims (via studies like those showing the effectiveness of particular forms of deterrence), many still defend their way of thinking by referring to what are purely philosophical ideals, such as just deserts.

> Critics charge that classical and neoclassical thought lacks comprehensive explanatory power over criminal motivation.

SUMMARY

- The Classical School in criminology posits that at least some illegal activity is the result of rational choices made by individuals seeking various kinds of illicit rewards. The classical perspective sees human beings as fundamentally rational, portrays pain and pleasure as the two central determinants of human behavior, and sees punishment as necessary to deter law violators and to serve as an example.

- The Classical School grew out of the Enlightenment. Notions of free will, individual choice, deterrence as a goal of the justice system, and punishment as a natural consequence of crime owe much of their contemporary influence to the Classical School. Influential thinkers of the Enlightenment era include Thomas Hobbes, John Locke, Thomas Paine, Montesquieu, and Rousseau.

- Two important thinkers of the Classical School of criminology, Cesare Beccaria and Jeremy Bentham, saw crime as providing pleasure to those who commit it and believed in punishment as the way to prevent it.

- Neoclassical criminology is a contemporary perspective built on classical principles emphasizing the importance of character and character development as well as the choices people make when faced with opportunities for crime. Rational choice theory recognizes the opportunities for crime and the important role that capable guardians play in preventing it.

- In neoclassical criminology, punishment is seen as providing both a deterrent and just deserts. Just deserts implies that criminal offenders deserve the punishment they receive and that any criminal punishment meted out should be appropriate to the type and severity of the crime committed.

- Policy implications of the Classical School revolve around the idea of a rational offender punished by a system working purposefully toward the goals of crime reduction and prevention of recidivism. Determinate sentencing and truth in sentencing as well as capital punishment are all strategies developed from Classical School principles.

- Classical perspectives can be criticized for their lack of comprehensive explanatory power over criminal motivation, and they also largely lack both meaningful explanations as to how a choice for or against criminal activity is made and any appreciation for the deeper fonts of personal motivation.

KEY TERMS

capable guardian, 65

capital punishment, 72

Classical School, 59

Code of Hammurabi, 55

common law, 56

dangerousness, 81

determinate sentencing, 78

deterrence, 71

displacement, 70

Enlightenment, 56

folkways, 54

general deterrence, 71

hard determinism, 62

hedonistic calculus, 60

incapacitation, 79

just deserts model, 71

justice model, 63

mala in se, 55

mala prohibita, 55

mores, 54

natural law, 58

natural rights, 58

neoclassical criminology, 63

nothing-works doctrine, 63

Panopticon, 61

positivism, 62

rational choice theory, 64

recidivism, 71

recidivism rate, 71

retribution, 55

routine activities theory, 64

situational choice theory, 64

situational crime prevention, 68

social contract, 57

soft determinism, 65

specific deterrence, 71

target hardening, 68

three-strikes legislation, 63

truth in sentencing, 78

Twelve Tables, 56

utilitarianism, 60

KEY NAMES

Cesare Beccaria, 59

Jeremy Bentham, 60

Ronald V. Clarke, 65

Lawrence Cohen, 64

Derek B. Cornish, 65

Marcus Felson, 64

Thomas Hobbes, 57

Jack Katz, 67

John Locke, 57

Charles-Louis de Secondat Montesquieu, 57

Thomas Paine, 58

Jean-Jacques Rousseau, 57

William Graham Sumner, 54

QUESTIONS FOR REVIEW

1. What are the major principles of the Classical School of criminology?

2. What were some forerunners of classical thought in criminology?

3. Who were the important thinkers of the Classical School of criminology, and what heritage did their way of thinking provide?

4. What is neoclassical criminology, and how does it differ from the classical perspective? How does it build on it?

5. What is the role of punishment in neoclassical criminology?

6. What are the policy implications of the Classical School, and what kinds of punishment might work best to prevent crime?

7. What are the shortcomings of the Classical School? Of neoclassical thinking about crime and crime control?

QUESTIONS FOR REFLECTION

1. This book emphasizes a theme of social problems versus social responsibility. Which perspective is more clearly supported by classical and neoclassical thought? Why?

2. How would you define *natural law*? Do you believe that natural law exists? If so, what types of behaviors would be contravened by natural law? If not, why not?

3. What is meant by a social contract? How does the concept of a social contract relate to natural law?

4. What are the central concepts that defined the Classical School of criminological thought? Which of those concepts are still alive? Where do you see evidence for the survival of those concepts?

5. How would you define *recidivism*? What is a recidivism rate? Why are recidivism rates so high today? What can be done to lower them?

CHAPTER 4
BIOLOGICAL ROOTS OF CRIMINAL BEHAVIOR

LEARNING OUTCOMES

After reading this chapter, you should be able to answer the following questions:

- What basic principles characterize biological theories of crime causation?

- How might biological perspectives explain human aggression?

- How strong are research findings linking genetics and crime?

- What is sociobiology? What contributions has sociobiology made to the study of criminality?

- How is criminality explained from a biosocial perspective?

- What modern-day social policies reflect the biological and biosocial approaches to crime causation?

- What are the shortcomings of biological theories of criminal behavior?

Introduction

At a recent annual meeting of the American Neurological Association, Russell Swerdlow and Jeffrey Burns, neuroscience researchers at the University of Virginia Medical School, reported on the case of a man with no history of pedophilia who began molesting children after developing an egg-sized brain tumor.[1] According to Swerdlow and Burns, friends of the man told investigators that the 40-year-old married teacher had never previously exhibited abnormal impulses but suddenly started visiting prostitutes, making sexual advances toward children, and spending time on Web sites selling child pornography. Soon, they reported, his wife left him, and he was arrested and convicted on child molestation charges. Although he entered a treatment program for pedophiles, he propositioned women at the facility and was expelled from treatment. About the same time, he began having headaches and went to a hospital emergency room where he reported experiencing strong sexual urges and said that he feared he would rape his landlady. Attending neurologists noticed other symptoms indicative of neurological problems, such as poor balance and the inability to copy simple drawings. An MRI scan conducted at the hospital showed that the man had a large tumor in the right frontal cortex of his brain; the tumor was removed, and the man's abnormal urges disappeared. Later, however, they reoccurred, and another scan showed that the tumor had returned. Once again it was removed, and the man's behavior returned to normal.

Swerdlow and Burns reported that the tumor was located in the part of the brain associated with social judgments and self-control, and they speculated that it was the cause of the man's pedophiliac urges. "We're dealing with the neurology of morality here," said Swerdlow. The case was reminiscent of the 1966 University of Texas bell tower sniper shootings, which left 14 students dead and many others injured. An autopsy conducted on Charles Whitman, the shooter, after he had been killed by police officers who stormed the tower, revealed that he had a tumor in the amygdala—a portion of the brain involved with controlling emotions.[2]

Can a brain tumor cause crime? Many biological theories have been advanced to explain criminality. Abnormalities of the brain,[3] brain damage,[4] head trauma,[5] genetic predispositions, vitamin deficiencies, an excess of hormones like testosterone, hypoglycemia (low blood sugar), fetal alcohol syndrome (FAS),[6] a relative lack of neurotransmitters like serotonin in the brain, and blood abnormalities are among the many biological explanations of crime available today.

The field of criminology has been slow to give credence to biological theories of deviant behavior. One reason for this, as noted in Chapter 1, is that

> The field of criminology has been slow to give credence to biological theories of deviant behavior.

contemporary criminology's academic roots are firmly grounded in the social sciences. As well-known biocriminologist **C. Ray Jeffery**, commenting on the historical development of the field, observed, "The term *criminology* was given to a social science approach to crime as developed in sociology. Sutherland's [1924] text *Criminology* was pure sociology without any biology or psychology; beginning with publication of that text, criminology was offered in sociology departments as a part of sociology separate from biology, psychology, psychiatry and law. Many of the academicians who call themselves criminologists are sociologists."[7]

Another problem with biological theories is that the link between biology and crime is rarely as clear as the example that opened this chapter. The influence of biology on behavior of any kind is more often the result of an *interaction* among genetic, hormonal, and other biological features of an individual and his or her social and physical environments. Noted biosocial researcher and writer Anthony Walsh observed that "biological theories are theories of criminality, not crime."[8] Walsh explained that crime is a "legal label" that is placed on specific behaviors violating criminal law. Criminality, on the other hand, said Walsh, "is a property of individuals, a continuous trait that is itself an amalgam of other continuous traits, and thus belongs to a more inclusive kind of criminology."[9] According to Walsh, criminality can be seen as the willingness to violate individual rights and social norms, whether or not such behavior is against the law. Criminality, said Walsh, consists of "a relative lack of empathy, conscience, self-control, and fear, as well as self-centeredness, and a penchant for risky behavior."[10] Seen this way, biological explanations of criminality are more likely to be couched in terms of a propensity for violence, aggression, deceit, recklessness, fearlessness, and so on.

The cancellation of a previously scheduled 1992 National Institutes of Health–sponsored conference focusing on biology and crime made clear the strong bias against biological explanations for crime that then existed. The conference was canceled after critics charged that the meeting would, by virtue of its biological focus, be racist and might intentionally exclude sociological perspectives on the subject.[11] Dr. Peter Breggin,

> ■ **biological theory**
> A theory that maintains that the basic determinants of human behavior, including criminality, are constitutionally or physiologically based and often inherited.

A mother reads to her child. The following question forms the essence of the "nature versus nurture" controversy: Are the choices that people make determined more by their biology or by what they have learned?
Source: J. Carini/The Image Works

director of the Center for the Study of Psychiatry in Bethesda, Maryland, and leader of the opposition to the conference, argued that "the primary problems that afflict human beings are not due to their bodies or brains; they are due to the environment. Redefining social problems as public health problems is exactly what was done in Nazi Germany."[12] Three years later, when the conference was finally held at a site selected to discourage demonstrations, Jeffery pointed out that "when ideology replaces rational thought there is little hope for a better understanding of human problems."[13]

Society shies away from biological explanations for criminality and disordered behavior because of phrases like "genetic determinism," which have come to be synonymous with inevitability. Hence, people tend to believe that "biological" equals "hopeless"[14]—since the physical makeup of a person is hard to change. Yet, as this chapter will show, genes may be more facilitators than determinants of behavior. Moreover, biologically based interventions may be some of the easiest to

implement, and new possibilities in the treatment arena are emerging daily.

Major Principles of Biological Theories

This brief section summarizes the central features of most **biological theories** of crime causation. Each of these points can be found elsewhere in this chapter, so this section is meant to function as a guide.

Biological theories of crime causation make certain fundamental assumptions:

- The brain is the organ of the mind and the locus of personality. In the words of C. Ray Jeffery, "The brain is the organ of behavior; no theory of behavior can ignore neurology and neurochemistry."[15]

- Basic determinants of human behavior, including criminal tendencies, are constitutionally or genetically based to a considerable degree.

- Observed gender and racial differences in rates and types of criminality may be at least partially the result of biological differences between the sexes and between racially distinct groups.

- Basic determinants of human behavior, including criminality, may be passed on from generation to generation, that is, a penchant for crime may be inherited.

- Much of human conduct is fundamentally rooted in instinctive behavioral responses, such as territoriality, condemnation of adultery, and acquisitiveness, that are characteristic of biological organisms everywhere.

- Biological roots of human conduct have become increasingly disguised, as modern symbolic forms of indirect expressive behavior have replaced more primitive and direct ones.

- At least some human behavior is the result of biological propensities inherited from more primitive developmental stages in the evolutionary process, meaning that some human beings may be further along the evolutionary ladder than others, and their behavior may reflect that fact.

- The interplay among heredity, biology, and the social environment provides the nexus for any realistic consideration of crime causation.

Follow the author's tweets about the latest crime and justice news at **http://twitter.com/schmalleger**.

The brain is indeed "the organ of the mind," as early criminologists claimed. Here a computer-enhanced image shows areas of activity within the brain. Do you think biology may play a significant role in crime?
Source: Scott Camazsine/Photo Researchers, Inc.

Biological Roots of Human Aggression

In 1966, **Konrad Lorenz** published his now-famous work *On Aggression*.[16] In it, Lorenz described how aggression permeates the animal kingdom and asked, "What is the value of all this fighting?" He wrote, "In nature, fighting is such an ever-present process, its behavior mechanisms and weapons are so highly developed and have so obviously arisen under the pressure of a species-preserving function, that it is our duty to ask this question."[17]

Lorenz accepted the evolutionary thesis of nineteenth-century biologist **Charles Darwin** that intraspecies aggression favored the strongest and best animals in the reproductive process, but he concluded that aggression serves a variety of other purposes as well. Aggression, said Lorenz, ensures an "even distribution of animals of a particular species over an inhabitable area"

> ## The evidence is very firm that there is a genetic factor involved in crime.
> —Sarnoff A. Mednick

and provides for a defense of the species from predators.[18] Human aggression, he claimed, meets many of the same purposes but can take on covert forms, and the drive to acquire wealth and power, which was so characteristic of Western men at the time of his writing, is part of the human mating ritual whereby a man might "win" a prized woman through displays of more civilized forms of what could otherwise be understood as intraspecies aggression.

Lorenz's greatest contribution to the study of human behavior may have been his claim that all human behavior is, at least to some degree, "adapted instinctive behavior"; in other words, much of human conduct is fundamentally rooted in instinctive behavioral responses characteristic of biological organisms everywhere and present within each of us in the form of a biological inheritance from more primitive times. Even rational human thought derives its motivation and direction from instinctual aspects of human biology, and the highest human virtues, such as the value placed on human life, "could not have been achieved," said Lorenz, "without an instinctive appreciation of life and death."[19]

Building on the root functions of aggression, Lorenz concluded that much of what we today call "crime" is the result of overcrowded living conditions combined with a lack of legitimate opportunity for the effective expression of aggression. Crowding increases the likelihood of aggression while contemporary socialization works to inhibit it. In the words of Lorenz, "In one sense we are all psychopaths, for each of us suffers from the necessity of self-imposed control for the good of the community."[20] When people break down, said Lorenz, they become neurotic or delinquent, and crime may be the result of stresses that have been found to typically produce aggression throughout the animal kingdom.

Lorenz's explanations, like many of the biologically based theories we will encounter in this chapter, appear to be more applicable to violent crime than to other forms of criminal offense, but it is important to recognize that modern frustrations and concomitant manifestations of aggression may be symbolically—rather than directly—expressed. Hence, a stockbroker who embezzles a client's money, spurred on by the need to provide material goods for an overly acquisitive family, may be just as criminal as a robber who beats his victim and steals her purse to have money to buy liquor.

■ **criminal anthropology**
The scientific study of the relationship between human physical characteristics and criminality.

■ **phrenology**
The study of the shape of the head to determine anatomical correlates of human behavior.

WEB EXTRA 4–1

■ **atavism**
A term used by Cesare Lombroso to suggest that criminals are physiological throwbacks to earlier stages of human evolution.

Charles Darwin (1809–1882), founder of modern evolutionary theory. How might evolutionary theory relate to criminality?
Source: Julia Cameron/CORBIS-NY

Early Biological Theories

Numerous perspectives on criminal biology predate Lorenz's work. Some of the perspectives fall into the category of **criminal anthropology**, the scientific study of the relationship between human physical characteristics and criminality. Criminal anthropology probably derives from earlier subjective feelings, prominent for millennia, that unattractiveness, deformity, and disfigurement are somehow associated with evil, spiritual malaise, and general uncleanliness.

One of the earliest criminological anthropologists was **Franz Joseph Gall** (1758–1828). Gall hypothesized, in his theory of **phrenology** (also called *craniology*), that the shape of the human skull was indicative of the personality and could be used to predict criminality. Gall's approach contained four themes:

1. The brain is the organ of the mind.

2. Particular aspects of personality are associated with specific locations in the brain.

3. Portions of the brain that are well developed cause personality characteristics associated with them to be more prominent in the individual under study, whereas poorly developed brain areas lead to a lack of associated personality characteristics.

4. The shape of a person's skull corresponds to the shape of the underlying brain and is therefore indicative of the personality.

Gall was one of the first Western writers to firmly locate the roots of personality in the brain. Prior to his time, it was thought that aspects of personality resided in various organs throughout the body—a fact reflected in linguistic anachronisms that survive to the present day (for example, when someone is described as being "hard-hearted" or having "a lot of gall"). Greek philosopher Aristotle was said to believe that the brain served no function other than to radiate excess heat from the body, so Gall's perspective, although relatively primitive by today's standards, did much to advance physiological understandings of the mind–body connection in Western thought.

Although Gall never tested his theory, it was widely accepted by many of his contemporaries because it represented something of a shift from the theological perspectives prevalent at the time toward scientific understanding—a trend that was well under way by the time of his writings. Phrenology also provided systematic evaluation of suspected offenders and was intriguing for its ease of use. One of Gall's students, **Johann Gaspar Spurzheim** (1776–1853), brought phrenological theory to America and helped to spread its influence through a series of lectures and publications on the subject. Phrenology's prestige in America extended into the twentieth century, finding a place in classification schemes used to evaluate newly admitted prisoners. Even Arthur Conan Doyle's fictional character Sherlock Holmes was described as using phrenology to solve a number of crimes. It is still popular today among palm readers and fortune-tellers, some of whom offer phrenological "readings"—although a few states have outlawed such activities. Learn more about phrenology at **Web Extra 4–1**.

Positivist School

One of the best-known early scientific biological theorists—nineteenth-century Italian army prison physician **Cesare Lombroso** (1836–1909)—coined the term **atavism** to suggest

THEORY | in PERSPECTIVE
Types of Biological Theories

Biological theories adhere to the principle that many predispositions relating to human behavior, including criminality, are constitutionally or physiologically influenced and inherited.

Early Positivism

These biological approaches, built on evolutionary principles, were the first to apply scientific techniques to the study of crime and criminals. Early positivistic theories saw criminals as throwbacks to earlier evolutionary epochs.

Period: 1880s–1930

Theorists: Franz Joseph Gall, Johann Gaspar Spurzheim, Cesare Lombroso, Charles Buckman Goring, Earnest A. Hooton

Concepts: Phrenology, atavism, born criminals, criminaloids

Constitutional Theories

These biological theories explain criminality by reference to offenders' body types, inheritance, genetics, or external observable physical characteristics.

Period: Classical constitutional theories, 1930s–1940s; modern constitutional theories, 1960s–present

Theorists: Ernst Kretschmer, William H. Sheldon, Richard Louis Dugdale, Arthur H. Estabrook, Henry Herbert Goddard

Concepts: Somatotyping, mesomorph, ectomorph, endomorph, XYY supermale, twin studies, behavioral genetics, heritability

Body Chemistry Theories

These biological theories utilize chemical influences, including hormones, food additives, allergies, vitamins, and other chemical substances, and the impact of weather to explain criminal behavior.

Period: 1940s–present

Theorists: Various ones, including Ellen G. Cohn and James Rotton

Concepts: Weather and crime, hypoglycemia, vitamins, food allergies, serotonin, premenstrual syndrome (PMS), monoamine oxidase inhibitors (MAOIs)

Sociobiology

This theoretical perspective developed by Edward O. Wilson includes the systematic study of the biological basis of all social behavior, which is a branch of evolutionary biology and particularly of modern population biology.

Period: 1975–present

Theorist: Edward O. Wilson

Concepts: Altruism, tribalism, survival of the gene pool

Biosocial Criminology

This theoretical perspective sees the interaction between biology and the environment as key to understanding human behavior, including criminality.

Period: 1987–present

Theorists: Terrie E. Moffitt, Hans J. Eysenck, Anthony Walsh, H. Hilger Ropers, Han Brunner

Concepts: Biopsychology, life course persisters, adolescence-limited offenders

---

that criminality was the result of primitive urges that survived the evolutionary process in modern-day human throwbacks. He described "the nature of the criminal" as "an atavistic being who reproduces in his person the ferocious instincts of primitive humanity and the inferior animals."[21]

At about this time, Charles Darwin was making a substantial impact on the scientific world with his theory of biological evolution. Darwin proposed that human beings and other contemporary living organisms were the end products of a long evolutionary process governed by such rules as natural selection and survival of the fittest. Lombroso adapted elements of Darwin's theory to suggest that primitive traits survived in present-day human populations and led to heightened criminal tendencies among individuals who harbored them. Darwin himself had proposed this idea when he wrote, "With mankind some of the worst dispositions which occasionally without any assignable cause make their appearance in families, may perhaps be reversions to a savage state, from which we are not removed by very many generations."[22]

Lombroso has been called "the father of modern criminology" because he was the first criminologist of note to employ the scientific method—particularly measurement, observation, and generalization—in his work. Other writers have referred to him as "the father of the Italian School" of criminology in recognition of the fact that nineteenth-century positivism began in Italy.

Positivism, as mentioned in Chapter 3, was built on two principles: (1) unflagging acceptance of social determinism, or the belief that human behavior is determined not by the exercise of free choice but by causative factors beyond the control of the individual, and (2) application of scientific techniques to the study of crime and criminology. The term *positivism* had its roots in the writings of Auguste Comte (1798–1857), who proposed use of the scientific method in the study of society in his 1851 work *A System of Positive Polity*.[23] Positivism holds that social phenomena are observable, explainable, and measurable in quantitative terms. For a strict positivist, reality consists of a world of objectively

■ **born criminal**
An individual who is born with a genetic predilection toward criminality.

■ **criminaloid**
A term used by Cesare Lombroso to describe the occasional criminal who is enticed into criminality primarily by environmental influences.

WEB EXTRA 4-2

■ **masculinity hypothesis**
The belief that, over time, men and women will commit crimes that are increasingly similar in nature, seriousness, and frequency. Increasing similarity in crime commission was predicted to result from changes in the social status of women.

defined facts, which can be scientifically measured and—ultimately—controlled.[24]

Lombroso's scientific work consisted of postmortem studies of the bodies of executed offenders and deceased criminals, measuring the bodies in many different ways. The body of one such wellknown criminal, named Vilella, provided Lombroso with many of his findings and reinforced his belief that most offenders were biologically predisposed to criminality. When he examined Vilella's brain, Lombroso found an unusual depression, which he named "the median occipital fossa," and identified features of Vilella's brain as being similar to those found in lower primates. Study of another offender, an Italian soldier whom Lombroso called Misdea in his writings and who "attacked and killed eight of his superior officers and comrades," supported his conclusions.[25]

Atavism implies that criminals are born that way. Lombroso was continuously reassessing his estimates of the proportion, from among all offenders, of **born criminals**. At one point, he asserted that fully 90% of offenders committed crimes because of atavistic influences; he later revised the figure downward to 70%, admitting that normal individuals might be pulled into lives of crime. In addition to the category of born criminal, Lombroso described other categories of offenders, including the insane, "criminaloids," and criminals incited by passion. The insane were said to include mental and moral degenerates, alcoholics, drug addicts, and so forth. **Criminaloids**, also called "occasional criminals," were described as people who were enticed into breaking the law by virtue of environmental influences. Nevertheless, most criminaloids were seen by Lombroso as exhibiting some degree of atavism and hence were said to "differ from born criminals in degree, not in kind." Those who became criminals by virtue of passion were said to have surrendered to intense emotions, including love, jealousy, hatred, or an injured sense of honor.

To read excerpts of a positivist criticizing the classical criminology viewpoint, see the Theory versus Reality box in this chapter.

In 1893, Lombroso published *The Female Offender.*[26] In that book, he expressed his belief that women exhibited far less anatomical variation than do men, but he insisted that criminal behavior among women, as among men, derived from atavistic foundations. Violence among women, although a rarity in the official statistics of the late 1800s, was explained by the

Cesare Lombroso coined the term atavism to suggest that criminality was the result of primitive urges that survived the evolutionary process.

masculinity hypothesis, or the belief that criminal women exhibited masculine features and mannerisms. Lombroso saw the quintessential female offender, however, as a prostitute, who was "the genuine typical representative of criminality" among women.[27] Prostitutes, he claimed, act out atavistic yearnings and, in doing so, return to a form of behavior characteristic of humankind's primitive past. Learn more about Lombroso and the theory of atavism via **Web Extra 4–2**.

Evaluations of Atavism

Following in Lombroso's positivistic footsteps around the turn of the twentieth century, English physician **Charles Buckman Goring** (1870–1919) conducted a well-controlled statistical study of Lombroso's thesis of atavism. Using newly developed but advanced mathematical techniques to measure the degree of correlation between physiological features and criminal history, Goring examined nearly 3,000 inmates at Turin prison beginning in 1901. Enlisting the aid of London's Biometric Laboratory, he concluded that "the whole fabric of Lombrosian doctrine, judged by the standards of science, is fundamentally unsound."[28] Goring compared the prisoners with students at Oxford and Cambridge Universities, British soldiers, and noncriminal hospital patients and published his findings in 1913 in his lengthy treatise *The English Convict: A Statistical Study.*[29]

A similar study was conducted between 1927 and 1939 by **Earnest A. Hooton**, a professor of anthropology at Harvard University. In 1939, Hooton published *Crime and the Man,*[30] in which he reported having evaluated 13,873 inmates from ten states, comparing them along 107 physiological dimensions with 3,203 nonincarcerated individuals who formed a control group; his sample consisted of 10,953 prison inmates, 2,004 county jail prisoners, 743 criminally insane, 173 "defective delinquents," 1,227 "insane civilians," and 1,976 "sane civilians."

Hooton distinguished among regions of the country, saying that "states have favorite crimes, just as they have favorite sons."

THEORY | versus REALITY
Positivism: The Historical Statement

In 1901, Enrico Ferri, one of the fathers of positivist criminology, was invited to deliver a series of lectures at the University of Naples. Ferri used the occasion to admonish classical criminologists and to advance the principles of positivism. Following are excerpts from those lectures:

> Let us speak of this new science, which has become known in Italy by the name of the Positive School of Criminology. The 19th century has won a great victory over mortality and infectious diseases by means of the masterful progress of physiology and natural science. But while contagious diseases have gradually diminished, we see on the other hand that moral diseases are growing more numerous. And this makes it very evident that the science which is principally, if not exclusively, engaged in studying these phenomena of social disease should feel the necessity of finding a more exact diagnosis of these moral diseases of society, in order to arrive at some effective and more humane remedy.
>
> The science of positive criminology arose in the last quarter of the 19th century. [T]he positive school of criminology arises out of the very nature of things, the same as every other line of science. It is based on the conditions of our daily life.
>
> The general opinion of classic criminalists and of the people at large is that crime involves a moral guilt, because it is due to the free will of the individual who leaves the path of virtue and chooses the path of crime, and therefore it must be suppressed by meeting it with a proportionate quantity of punishment. And the illusion of a free human will (the only miraculous factor in the eternal ocean of cause and effect) leads to the assumption that one can choose freely between virtue and vice. How can you still

> believe in the existence of a free will, when modern psychology armed with all the instruments of positive modern research denies that there is any free will and demonstrates that every act of a human being is the result of an interaction between the personality and the environment of man?
>
> And how is it possible to cling to that obsolete idea of moral guilt, according to which every individual is supposed to have the free choice to abandon virtue and give himself up to crime? The positive school of criminology maintains, on the contrary, that it is not the criminal who wills; in order to be a criminal it is rather necessary that the individual should find himself permanently or transitorily in such personal, physical and moral conditions, and live in such an environment which become for him a chain of cause and effect, externally and internally, that disposes him toward crime. This is our conclusion and it constitutes that vastly different and opposite method, which the positive school of criminology employs as compared to the leading principle of the classic school of criminal science.

Discussion Questions

1. Why does Ferri link control over contagious diseases with the study of crime?

2. If Ferri was asked to define *positive criminology*, what kind of definition do you think he would offer?

3. How are notions of moral guilt and free will associated in Ferri's line of thought?

Source: Ernest Unterman, trans., *The Positive School of Criminology: Three Lectures Given at the University of Naples, Italy, on April 22, 23, and 24, 1901,* by Enrico Ferri (Chicago: Charles H. Kerr, 1912).

He was drawn to the conclusion that "crime is not an exclusively sociological phenomenon, but is also biological."[31]

Hooton stated that "it is impossible to improve and correct environment to a point at which these flawed and degenerate human beings will be able to succeed in honest social competition,"[32] making it clear that he did not believe that rehabilitation programs could have much effect on most offenders, and he suggested banishing them to a remote location. Hooton concluded that criminals showed an overall physiological inferiority to the general population and that crime was the result of "the impact of environment upon low grade human organisms."[33] Learn more about the life and work of Earnest Hooton at **Web Extra 4–3**.

Hooton, an example of whose work is provided in Figure 4–1, was quickly criticized along a number of dimensions. Stephen Schafer, a well-known contemporary criminologist, said, "The major criticisms were that his criminal population was not a representative sample of all criminals, that his control group was a fantastic conglomeration of noncriminal civilians, that he emphasized selected characteristics and disregarded others, that he gave no convincing evidence that the criminal's 'inferiority' was inherited, and that he failed to explore other important data that were available."[34] Perhaps even more significant, Hooton failed to recognize that members of his noncriminal control group may, in fact, have been involved in crime but had managed to elude capture and processing by the criminal justice system; in other

Seattle police officer Diana Boggs identifying a picture of the gun she found in Maurice Clemmons's possession the night he was shot and killed by another officer while she testifies during an inquest into the shooting. Clemmons, an ex-con, walked into a coffee shop in Tacoma, Washington, on the morning of November 28, 2009, pulled out a handgun, and opened fire without warning on four uniformed police officers who were working on laptop computers and preparing for their shift. Two days later, Clemmons was confronted by a lone officer and was killed. Might any of the theories discussed in this chapter explain Clemmons's violence? If so, which ones?

Source: AP Photo/Mike Siegel

anthropometric, psychophysiological, neuropsychological, and psychiatric evaluations of 1,037 boys who had attended kindergarten in 1984 in a socially and economically disadvantaged area of Montreal.[35] Using evaluations provided years later by parents, teachers, classmates, and the children themselves, Arseneault and Tremblay concluded that subtle physical abnormalities, including minor abnormalities in the shape of the ears, tongue, and teeth, were associated with an increased risk of behavioral and psychiatric problems in later years. The researchers suggested that such minor physical abnormalities might have resulted from genetic problems or prenatal insults associated with exposure to toxins, concluding that "both the total count of minor physical anomalies and the total count of minor physical anomalies of the mouth were significantly associated with an increased risk of violent delinquency in adolescence, beyond the effects of childhood physical aggression and family adversity." Arseneault and Tremblay recognized, however, that abnormalities of the type they identified might be associated with neurological deficits and that abnormalities of the mouth could lead to feeding problems in the first months after birth, which might somehow cause problems in development or socialization.

FIGURE 4-1 | **Earnest A. Hooton's "Massachusetts Criminal"**

Source: Reprinted by permission of the publisher from "Old American Criminals—Massachusetts: Mosaic of Cranial, Facial, and Morphological Features" in *Crime and the Man* by Earnest Albert Hooton, p. 57, Cambridge, Mass.: Harvard University Press, Copyright © 1939 by the President and Fellows of Harvard College. Copyright © renewed 1967 by Mary C. Hooton.

Biological theories are theories of criminality, not crime.

—Anthony Walsh

words, most successful criminals may not have appeared in Hooton's study group of inmates because they had eluded the law, thereby making their way into his supposedly noncriminal control group. His study may have simply demonstrated that "inferior" criminal specimens are the ones who get caught and end up in prison.

Nonetheless, claims that physical abnormalities may be linked to crime persist into the present day. In a study of teenage boys reported in 2000, for example, Canadian researchers L. Arseneault, Richard E. Tremblay, and colleagues conducted hormonal,

■ **constitutional theory**
A theory that explains criminality by reference to offenders' body types, inheritance, genetics, or external observable physical characteristics.

■ **somatotyping**
The classification of human beings into types according to body build and other physical characteristics.

■ **cycloid**
A term developed by Ernst Kretschmer to describe a particular relationship between body build and personality type. The cycloid personality, which was associated with a heavyset, soft type of body, was said to vacillate between normality and abnormality.

■ **schizoid**
A person characterized by schizoid personality disorder. Such disordered personalities appear to be aloof, withdrawn, unresponsive, humorless, dull, and solitary to an abnormal degree.

the PROFESSOR | SPEAKS
Biological Theories of Crime

NANA DERBY

Virginia State University

William Sheldon's theory of somatotype, which argues that there is a relationship between body types and mental disorders or temperaments, sprang from Cesare Lombroso's earlier perspective that low sloping forehead, prominent chin, fleshy lips, high cheekbones, and several other traits attributable to prehuman stages of evolution are suggestive of criminal behavioral tendencies. Sheldon categorized human bodies into ectomorph (skinny), endomorph (round), and mesomorph (athletic and muscular) and concluded that mesomorphs have the highest probability of crime commission. Stanley Tookie Williams, founder of the Crips street gang and convicted and executed for multiple murders, was a mesomorph; Dennis Rader (the so-called BTK), a convicted serial killer, looks something like a mesomorph. Based on these two criminals, we might want to affirm Sheldon's theory, but that could be deceptive because several other examples suggest otherwise. Consider the more ectomorphic physique of Osama bin Laden, the "son of Sam" David Berkowitz, Timothy McVeigh, and all the 9/11 hijackers. Moreover, consider that there are fluctuations in people's weights and sizes: Dennis Rader looked mesomorphic at the time of his arrest; nevertheless, he was ectomorphic when he committed those crimes in his youth. If you look at yourself and the people around you today, in class or elsewhere, they may not fit well within any of these three body types. What, then, is your conclusion about this particular biological theory?

Source: Reprinted by permission of C. Nana Derby, Ph.D., Associate Professor of Criminal Justice, Virginia State University. Photo courtesy of C. Nana Derby. Logo courtesy of Virginia State University.

Endomorphs on the march. A group of would-be actors line up to audition for roles in the movie *Fat Chance*. How might body type relate to criminal activity?
Source: AP Wide World Photos

Body Types

Constitutional theories explain criminality by reference to offenders' body types, genetics, or external observable physical characteristics. A constitutional, or physiological, orientation that found its way into the criminological mainstream during the early and mid-twentieth century was that of **somatotyping** (classifying according to body types), primarily associated with the work of **Ernst Kretschmer** and **William H. Sheldon**. Kretschmer, a professor of psychiatry at the German University of Tubingen, proposed a relationship between body build and personality type and created a rather detailed "biopsychological constitutional typology" that revolved around three basic mental categories: cycloids (also called "cyclothymes"), schizoids (or "schizothymes"), and displastics. **Cycloids**, who were associated with a heavyset, soft type of body, vacillated between normality and abnormality, lacked spontaneity and sophistication, and committed mostly nonviolent property offenses. **Schizoids**, who

displastic
A mixed group of offenders described by constitutional theorist Ernst Kretschmer as highly emotional and often unable to control themselves. They were thought to commit mostly sexual offenses and other crimes of passion.

endomorph
A body type originally described as soft and round or overweight.

mesomorph
A body type described as athletic and muscular.

LIBRARY EXTRA 4–1
WEB EXTRA 4–4

ectomorph
A body type originally described as thin and fragile, with long, slender, poorly muscled extremities and delicate bones.

hypoglycemia
A medical condition characterized by low blood sugar.

tended to possess muscular athletic bodies but could also be thin and lean, were seen as more likely to be schizophrenic and to commit violent types of offenses. **Displastics** were a mixed group described as highly emotional and often unable to control themselves, and they were thought to commit mostly sexual offenses and other crimes of passion.

Influenced by Kretschmer, Sheldon utilized measurement techniques to connect body type with personality.[36] Sheldon felt that Kretschmer had erred in including too large an age range in his work, so he limited his study to 200 boys between the ages of 15 and 21 at the Hayden Goodwill Institute in Boston and concluded that four basic body types characterized the entire group:

1. The **endomorph** is soft and round, with "digestive viscera [that] are massive and highly developed" (the person is overweight and has a large stomach).

2. The **mesomorph** is muscular and athletic, with "somatic structures [that] are in the ascendancy" (the person has larger bones and considerable muscle mass).

3. The **ectomorph** is thin and fragile and has "long, slender, poorly muscled extremities, with delicate, pipestem bones."

4. The balanced type is a person of average build, not overweight, thin, or exceedingly muscular.[37]

Individuals (excluding the balanced type) were ranked along each of the three major dimensions using a 7-point scale. A score of 1–1–7, for example, would indicate that a person exhibited few characteristics of endomorphology or mesomorphology but was predominantly ectomorphic. Sheldon claimed that varying types of temperaments and personalities were closely associated with each of the body types he identified: Ectomorphs were said to be "cerebrotonic," or restrained, shy, and inhibited; endomorphs were "viscerotonic," or relaxed and sociable. Mesomorphs, or muscular body types, were most likely to be associated with delinquency or "somatotonia," which he described as "a predominance of muscular activity and vigorous bodily assertiveness." Sheldon's work was supported by constitutional studies of juvenile delinquents conducted by Sheldon Glueck and Eleanor Glueck and reported in 1950.[38] The Gluecks compared 500 known delinquents with 500 nondelinquents, matching both groups on age,

general intelligence, ethnic-racial background, and place of residence. Like Sheldon, the Gluecks concluded that mesomorphy was associated with delinquency. Learn more about early theories of body types via **Library Extra 4–1** and **Web Extra 4–4**.

Early biological theorists like Gall, Lombroso, and Sheldon provide an interesting footnote in the history of criminological thought. Today, however, their work is mostly relegated to the dustbins of academic theorizing. Modern biological theories of crime are far more sophisticated than their early predecessors, and it is to these that we now turn.

Chemical and Environmental Precursors of Crime

Recent research in the area of nutrition has produced some limited evidence that the old maxim "You are what you eat" may contain more than a grain of truth. Biocriminology has made some significant strides in linking violent or disruptive behavior to eating habits, vitamin deficiencies, genetic inheritance, and other conditions that affect the body. Studies of nutrition, endocrinology, and environmental contaminants have all contributed to advances in understanding such behavior.

> "You are what you eat" may contain more than a grain of truth.

One of the first studies to focus on chemical imbalances in the body as a cause of crime was reported in the British medical journal *Lancet* in 1943.[39] The authors of the study linked murder to **hypoglycemia**, or low blood sugar. Low blood sugar, produced by too much insulin in the blood or by near-starvation diets, was said to reduce the mind's capacity to reason effectively or to judge the long-term consequences of behavior. More recent studies have linked excess consumption of refined white sugar to hyperactivity, aggressiveness, excitability, and impairment of the ability to make reasoned decisions, and popular books like *Sugar Blues* provide guides for individuals seeking to free themselves from the negative effects of excess sugar consumption.[40]

To some degree, even courts have accepted the notion that excess sugar consumption may be linked to crime. In the early 1980s, for example, Dan White, a former San Francisco police officer, was given a reduced sentence after his lawyers used what

Follow the author's tweets about the latest crime and justice news at **http://twitter.com/schmalleger**.

came to be known as the "Twinkie Defense."[41] They argued that White's nightlong binge on large numbers of Coca-Colas and Twinkies before he murdered San Francisco Mayor George Moscone and City Councilman Harvey Milk was evidence of White's unbalanced mental state; the consumption of junk food was presented as evidence of depression since White was normally very health conscious.

More than ten years later, however, a well-conducted 1994 study reported in the *New England Journal of Medicine* seemed to contradict the notion that sugar may lead to hyperactivity;[42] similarly, neither sugar nor artificial sweeteners were shown to have any link to an increase in learning disabilities. In the study, researchers at Vanderbilt University and the University of Iowa varied the diets of supposedly sugar-sensitive youngsters from a diet that was high in sugar to a diet that was low in sugar but that contained the artificial sweetener aspartame, and a third experimental diet contained very little sugar but had added saccharin. After surveying parents, teachers, and babysitters and testing the study group for changes in memory, concentration, and math skills, the researchers concluded, "We couldn't find any difference in terms of their behavior or their learning on any of the three diets."[43] Hence, to date, the evidence concerning sugar's impact on behavior is less than clear.

While dietary levels of refined sugar may or may not affect behavior, studies using positron emission tomography (PET), which can measure the uptake of glucose by the brain, of the prefrontal cortex of subjects' brains were analyzed and showed interesting results. In a study conducted by Adrian Raine and his colleagues in 1994, PET scans of the brains of 22 murderers (including some who had only attempted murder) revealed that the murderers showed much lower levels of glucose uptake in the prefrontal cortex than did the controls.[44] "The differences were not related to age, gender, handedness, ethnicity, motivation, history of head injury, or presence of schizophrenia. In addition, no subjects were taking psychoactive drugs at the time of the test."[45] Raine and his colleagues said that their data strongly suggested that "deficits localized to the prefrontal cortex may be related to violence" in some offenders; they also noted that "frontal damage is associated with impulsivity, loss of self-control, immaturity, lack of tact, inability to modify and inhibit behavior appropriately, and poor social judgment."[46] The researchers explained, however, that prefrontal cortex dysfunction must be evaluated in terms of how individuals who exhibit the condition interact with environmental conditions, including social and psychological influences. Because prefrontal cortex dysfunction may result in

A man undergoes an MRI of his brain. Some companies like No Lie MRI, which currently offers testing services in California, have developed guilty knowledge tests using MRI brain scans. Trained operators are said to be able to identify lies by looking for areas of the brain that are known to undergo enhanced activity when subjects are lying. What might such scans tell us about truth or falsehood? What do they say, if anything, about the biological basis of morality?
Source: James Steidl/iStockphoto.com

failure in school, inability to hold a job, problems in relationships, and so forth, it may not be a direct cause of crime but might predispose someone afflicted with the condition to "a criminal and violent way of life."[47]

Allergic reactions to common foods have been reported as the cause of violence and homicide by a number of investigators.[48] Some foods—including milk, citrus fruit, chocolate, corn, wheat, and eggs—are said to produce allergic reactions in sensitive individuals, leading to a swelling of the brain and the brain stem; such swelling is also thought to impede the higher faculties, reducing people's sense of morality and creating conditions that support impulsive behavior. Involvement of the central nervous system in such allergies may reduce the amount of learning that occurs during

> **PET scans of the brains of murderers showed much lower levels of glucose uptake in the prefrontal cortex than did the controls.**

CRIME | in the NEWS

Childhood Lead Exposure Linked to Adult Crime

In what may be the strongest link yet between lead exposure and crime rates, researchers at the University of Cincinnati on Tuesday released new evidence, spanning more than 20 years, that draws a direct relationship between the amount of lead in a child's blood and the likelihood he or she will commit crimes as an adult.

Research has shown before that lead has harmful effects on judgment, cognitive function and the ability to regulate behavior. But until now the best research focused on juveniles, not adults.

Now, researchers have collected data from as early as 1979 when pregnant women and their healthy babies had their blood drawn regularly at four Cincinnati medical clinics. By the time the children were 7, researchers had a complete portrait of lead levels.

Nearly two decades later, the researchers tracked down 250 of the subjects, ages 19–24. Controlling for a host of factors, including parental IQ, education, income and drug use, the team found that the more lead in a child's blood from birth through age 7, the more likely he or she was to be arrested as an adult. The tie between high lead levels and violent crime was particularly strong.

"We need to be thinking about lead as a drug and a fairly strong one," says Kim Dietrich, a professor of environmental health at the University of Cincinnati College of Medicine and the principal investigator for the study in the journal *Public Library of Science Medicine*. "These kids have been exposed to this drug, chronically, since before birth."

For nearly 50 years, researchers have known about the relationship between children's impulsivity and high levels of lead in their bodies. As recently as 2007, economist Rick Nevin tied violent crime rates to historic use of leaded gasoline.

Children in poor neighborhoods are often exposed to high levels of lead from old lead paint in dilapidated homes.

Fordham University School of Law criminologist Deborah Denno, who has studied the effects of lead, calls the findings' ties to adult criminal behavior "very important." Denno studied National Institutes of Health statistics of nearly 1,000 children in Philadelphia and found that a high blood lead level at 7 years old was among the strongest predictors

that a child would have both learning difficulties and disciplinary problems in school. High blood lead also strongly predicted whether a child would have a juvenile or adult criminal record.

Denno says Tuesday's data are newer than hers by 20 years. "It's still a huge problem," she says, "and it's still a huge problem among African-American communities and poorer neighborhoods."

Discussion Questions

1. What does this article say is the likely link between childhood lead consumption and later criminality?

2. What steps can be taken to reduce childhood exposure to environmental lead? What steps have already been taken?

Leaky water pipes in an older home. Pipes like these sometimes contain lead, which can contaminate the water they carry. What role might childhood lead consumption play in the development of delinquency and antisocial behavior?
Source: AP Wide World Photos

Source: Greg Toppo, "Childhood Lead Exposure Linked to Adult Crime," *USA Today*, May 28, 2008. Reprinted by permission.

---

childhood and may contribute to delinquency as well as to adult criminal behavior.

Some studies have implicated food additives, such as the flavor enhancer monosodium glutamate, dyes, and artificial flavorings, in producing criminal violence.[49] Other research has found that coffee and sugar may trigger antisocial behavior;[50] researchers were led to these conclusions through finding that inmates consumed considerably greater amounts of coffee, sugar, and processed foods than others.[51] It is unclear, however, whether inmates drink more coffee because of boredom or whether "excitable" personalities feel a need for the kind of stimulation available through coffee consumption. On the other hand, habitual coffee drinkers in nonprison populations have not been linked to crime, and other studies, like the one conducted by Mortimer Gross of the University of Illinois, showed no link between the

amount of sugar consumed by inmates and hyperactivity.[52] Nonetheless, some prison programs have been designed to limit intake of dietary stimulants through nutritional management and substitution of artificial sweeteners for refined sugar.

Vitamins have also been examined for their impact on delinquency. At least one researcher found that disruptive children consumed far less than optimal levels of vitamins B_3 and B_6 than did nonproblem youths.[53] Some researchers have suggested that the addition of these vitamins to the diets of children who are deficient in them could control unruly behavior and improve school performance.

Other nutrients have been studied to assess their possible behavioral impact. In 2003, for example, Ingrid Bergliot Helland reported that maternal diet during pregnancy can strongly affect IQ and early infant behavior and concluded that it might also

LIBRARY EXTRA 4-2

determine the risk of delinquency and criminality in later life.[54] Helland and her colleagues supplemented the diets of pregnant and lactating women with either omega-3 (DHA) or omega-6 fatty acids and followed the development of their offspring for years after the supplementation program had ended; they found that children receiving dietary omega-3 supplementation had significantly higher IQ levels by age four and performed better on problem-solving tests than those receiving omega-6 fatty acids.

A year later, a study of the relationship between omega-3 intake levels and chronic hostility among 3,600 urban young adults concluded that higher consumption of omega-3 fatty acids was related to significantly lower levels of hostility, with researchers stating that "high dietary intake of DHA and consumption of fish rich in omega-3 fatty acids may be related to lower likelihood of high hostility in young adulthood."[55] Similarly, a 2007 study conducted in the United Kingdom found that antisocial behavior could be reduced in children through dietary supplementation with polyunsaturated fatty acids.[56]

In a study designed to test the hypothesis that dietary supplementation could reduce violence among prison populations, C. Bernard Gesch and colleagues supplemented the diets of 115 English young adult prisoners and compared their behavior with 116 inmates receiving placebos.[57] The experiment lasted 142 days, and supplements included vitamins, minerals, and essential fatty acids. Researchers found a 35.1% reduction in offense rates in the supplement group, with the greatest reduction for the most serious problems such as violence. The Gesch study supported the earlier findings of Stephen Schoenthaler and his colleagues, who found that nutritional supplementation reduced antisocial acts by incarcerated offenders in California, citing a 30% decrease in the rate of serious rule violations for persons receiving dietary supplements similar to those used in the Gesch study.[58] Read more about diet and its possible contribution to criminal behavior at **Library Extra 4–2**.

High dietary intake of DHA and consumption of fish rich in omega-3 fatty acids may be related to lower likelihood of high hostility in young adulthood.

In 1997, British researchers Roger D. Masters, Brian Hone, and Anil Doshi published a study purporting to show that industrial and other forms of environmental pollution cause people to commit violent crimes.[59] The study used statistics from the FBI's Uniform Crime Reporting Program and data from the U.S. Environmental Protection Agency's Toxic Release Inventory. A comparison between the two data sets showed a significant correlation between juvenile crime and high environmental levels of both lead and manganese. Masters and his colleagues suggested an explanation based on a neurotoxicity hypothesis. Another author stated, "According to this approach, toxic pollutants—specifically the toxic metals lead and manganese—cause learning disabilities, an increase in aggressive behavior, and—most importantly—loss of control over impulsive behavior. These traits combine with poverty, social stress, alcohol and drug abuse, individual character, and other social and psychological factors to produce individuals who commit violent crimes."[60] See the Crime in the News box for more information on lead exposure and its effects.

According to Masters, the presence of excess manganese lowers brain levels of serotonin and dopamine, both of which are associated with impulse control and planning, and low brain levels of serotonin are known to cause mood disturbances, poor impulse control, and increases in aggressive behavior.[61] Masters also claimed that children raised from birth on infant formula rather than breast milk will absorb five times as much manganese as breast-fed infants; calcium deficiency is known to increase the absorption of manganese, and "a combination of manganese toxicity and calcium deficiency adds up to 'reverse' Prozac."[62]

In defense of his thesis, Masters cited other studies, the largest of which was an examination of 1,000 black children in Philadelphia that showed that the level of exposure to lead was a reliable predictor of the number of juvenile offenses among the exposed male population, the seriousness of juvenile offenses, and the number of adult offenses. More recent studies, including many that Masters was unaware of, seem to support his thesis.[63]

Masters reasoned that toxic metals affect individuals in complex ways. Because lead diminishes a person's normal ability to detoxify poisons, it may heighten the effects of alcohol and drugs; industrial pollution, automobile traffic, lead-based paints, and aging water-delivery systems are all possible sources of lead contamination. In a recent interview, Masters said, "The presence of pollution is as big a factor [in crime causation] as poverty. It's the breakdown of the inhibition mechanism that's the key to violent behavior."[64] When brain chemistry is altered by exposure to heavy metals and other toxins, people lose the natural restraint that holds their violent tendencies in check.

In 1999, researchers set out to test the hypothesis that enhancing brain levels of serotonin might reduce aggression and

WEB EXTRA 4–5
LIBRARY EXTRA 4–3
LIBRARY EXTRA 4–4

■ **testosterone**
The primary male sex hormone. It is produced in the testes, and its function is to control secondary sex characteristics and sexual drive.

impulsivity in aggressive male criminals.[65] In the volunteer-only study, ten young male offenders were given daily injections of d,l-fenfluramine, a drug that makes serotonin more available to brain cells. Findings showed that "the drug produced a significant, dose-dependent decrease in aggressive responding 2 to 4.5 hours after dosing . . . [and that] all ten subjects decreased their aggressive responding following the highest 0.8 mg/kg dose."[66] Subjects exhibiting the highest rates of aggression showed the greatest decreases in aggression levels after being treated with d,l-fenfluramine; impulsivity similarly decreased.

In addition to chemical substances likely to be ingested that may impact behavior, other environmental features have been linked to the likelihood of aggressive behavior. During the early 1980s, for example, Alexander G. Schauss and his followers were able to show that use of a specific shade of pink could have a calming effect on people experiencing feelings of anger and agitation.[67] Findings indicated that exposure to pink produced an endocrine change, which caused a tranquilizing effect on the muscles which was not subject to conscious control. As a result of such studies, jail cells in a number of locales—including Seattle, San Bernardino (California), San Mateo County (California), Southbridge (Massachusetts), New Orleans, and Charlotte (North Carolina)—were painted pink in hopes that aggressive tendencies among inmates might be reduced. Researchers supported such measures, saying that "the use of pink color in reducing aggression and causing muscular relaxation of inmates is humane and requires no medication or physical force."[68]

More recent studies have focused on prenatal exposure to substances like marijuana, tobacco smoke, and alcohol. In 2000, for example, L. Goldschmidt and colleagues reported the results of a ten-year study that monitored the development of children of more than 600 low-income women. The study, which began during the women's pregnancies, found that prenatal marijuana use was significantly related to increased hyperactivity, impulsivity, inattention, increased delinquency, and externalizing problems;[69] the findings remained significant even when researchers controlled for other lifestyle features.

In 1998, David Fergusson and colleagues, in a study of 1,022 New Zealand children who had been followed for 18 years, found that "children whose mothers smoked one pack of cigarettes or more per day during their pregnancy had mean rates of conduct disorder symptoms that were twice as high as those found among children born to mothers who did not smoke during their pregnancy."[70] The observed relationship was twice as strong among male teens as among females. Similar relationships between prenatal smoking and both aggression and

hyperactivity in later life have been reported by Dutch researchers.[71] A similar 2006 meta-analysis by researchers at Washington State University found that smoking by pregnant mothers contributed slightly to their children's subsequent antisocial behavior.[72]

Prenatal alcohol exposure also seems to be linked to delinquency and psychiatric problems later in life. A 1999 study of 32 children by Tresa M. Roebuck and colleagues found that alcohol-exposed children exhibited greater delinquency and less intelligence than a control group of children who had not suffered from alcohol exposure while in the womb. The researchers concluded that their findings, which are consistent with the work of other researchers,[73] showed that "alcohol-exposed children, although less impaired intellectually, are more likely than children with mental retardation to exhibit antisocial behaviors, lack of consideration for the rights and feelings of others, and resistance to limits and requests of authority figures."[74]

One 2010 study found that the brains of monkeys whose mothers had the flu while they were pregnant exhibited physical changes similar to those in people with schizophrenia.[75] Researchers noted that their findings supported the suggestion that flu in human mothers-to-be can impact brain development. Learn more about the role of environmental contaminants, fetal alcohol exposure, and other factors and their contributions to criminality at **Web Extra 4–5**. Read about pollution's possible link to crime and toxic threats to child development at **Library Extras 4–3** and **4–4**.

Hormones and Criminality

Hormones have also come under scrutiny as potential behavioral determinants. The male sex hormone **testosterone** has been linked to aggression. Most studies on the subject have consistently shown a relationship between high blood testosterone levels and increased aggressiveness in men. More focused studies have unveiled a direct relationship between the amount of the chemical present and the degree of violence used by sex offenders;[76] other researchers have linked steroid abuse among bodybuilders to destructive urges and psychosis.[77] Some contemporary investigations have demonstrated a link between testosterone levels and aggression in teenagers,[78] and others have shown that adolescent problem behavior and teenage violence rise in proportion to the amount of testosterone in the blood of young men.[79] In 1987, for example, a Swedish researcher, Dan Olweus, reported that boys ages 15 to 17 showed levels of both verbal and physical

Follow the author's tweets about the latest crime and justice news at **http://twitter.com/schmalleger**.

aggression that correlated with the level of testosterone present in their blood, stating that boys with higher levels of testosterone "tended to be habitually more impatient and irritable than boys with lower testosterone levels."[80] He concluded that high levels of the hormone led to increased frustration and habitual impatience and irritability.

In what may be the definitive work to date on the subject, Alan Booth and D. Wayne Osgood concluded that there is a "moderately strong relationship between testosterone and adult deviance" but suggested that the relationship "is largely mediated by the influence of testosterone on social integration and on prior involvement in juvenile delinquency."[81] In other words, measurably high levels of testosterone in the blood of young men may have some effect on behavior, but that effect is likely to be moderated by the social environment.

Similar conclusions were reached in 1998 by Swedish researchers who evaluated 61 men undergoing forensic psychiatric examinations for blood levels of free testosterone, total testosterone, and sex hormone–binding globulin (SHBG).[82] SHBG is known to determine the level of testosterone concentration in the blood and in body tissue. The Swedish researchers found that blood levels of total testosterone and SHBG were closely related to the extent of antisocial personality, alcoholism, and criminality exhibited by the subjects under study.

A 1997 study by Paul C. Bernhardt found that testosterone might not act alone in promoting aggression.[83] Bernhardt discovered that aggressive behavior in men may be influenced by

> Aggressive behavior in men may be influenced by high testosterone levels combined with low brain levels of the neurotransmitter serotonin.

high testosterone levels combined with low brain levels of the neurotransmitter serotonin and postulated that testosterone's true role is to produce dominance-seeking behavior, but not necessarily overt aggression. According to Bernhardt, when individuals are frustrated by their inability to achieve dominance, serotonin acts to reduce the negative psychological impact of frustration, producing calmer responses; men whose brains are lacking in serotonin, however, feel the effects of frustration more acutely and therefore tend to respond to frustrating circumstances more aggressively, especially when testosterone levels are high.

A 2007 study by University of Michigan researchers showed a relationship between testosterone, vigilance, and facial expressions of anger (considered to be signals of an impending dominance challenge). People with higher levels of testosterone were more prone to respond aggressively to displays of anger in others. According to the researchers, higher levels of testosterone "may generally decrease aversion to threatening stimuli, and/or may specifically facilitate approach towards signals of dominance challenge . . . [and that] a signal of an impending dominance challenge could be rewarding to individuals [who] have a history of success in such encounters."[84] The researchers concluded that the "relationship between testosterone and dominance appears to be reciprocal: winners of dominance challenges show increases in [testosterone], and in turn, higher [testosterone] leads to a greater likelihood to aggress and/or to pursue further dominance challenges, in nonhuman animals and potentially also in humans."[85] See the Who's to Blame box for a hypothetical example of the possible influence of testosterone on crime causation.

A few limited studies have attempted to measure the effects of testosterone on women. Although women's bodies manufacture roughly one-tenth the amount of the hormone secreted by men, subtle changes in testosterone levels in women have been linked to changes in personality and sexual behavior.[86] One such study showed that relatively high blood levels of testosterone in female inmates were associated with "aggressively dominant behavior" in prison.[87]

Another study whose results were reported in 2003 attempted to measure the impact of high levels of androgens (male hormones, including testosterone) on both males and females.[88] The study examined the "externalizing behavior" of 87 fourteen-year-olds (51 females and 36 males); other data on externalizing behavior, including aggression, were available from information gathered when the children were 8, 11, and 14 years old. Findings showed that boys with the highest blood plasma levels of androgens exhibited the most persistent aggression, but no association was found between aggression and androgen levels in females.

Fluctuations in the level of female hormones may also bear some relationship to law violation. In 1980, a British court exonerated Christine English of charges that she murdered her live-in lover after English admittedly ran him over with her car after an argument; English's defense rested on the fact that she was suffering from PMS at the time of the homicide. An expert witness, Dr. Katharina Dalton, testified at the trial that PMS had caused English to be "irritable, aggressive, and confused, with loss of self-control."[89]

WHO'S TO BLAME—The Individual or Society?

Hormones and Criminal Behavior

Lamont Ridgeway, 22, was arrested and charged with rape after 21-year-old Nicole Bachman called police to her Minneapolis home at 2:00 A.M. Ridgeway and Bachman had met in an evening art class at the local community college, and Bachman invited Ridgeway to her apartment for a glass of wine after the class was over. Officers couldn't help but notice that Bachman was an unusually attractive young woman whose clothes were in disarray and that she was visibly intoxicated and slurred her words as she spoke; Ridgeway was passed out on her couch, apparently after having had far too much to drink.

"He raped me!" Bachman told the two officers who responded to her call for help. "I told him to stop, and he wouldn't," she said.

Ridgeway was roused from sleep, arrested, searched, handcuffed, and taken to jail, where he was booked and charged with rape. After being advised of his rights not to speak and to have a lawyer represent him, he decided to tell the officers who were questioning him that it wasn't really rape. "She came on to me," he said. "She took her blouse off, then her pants. And she gave me a lot to drink. Yeah, she said 'No,' but by then we were already there. I couldn't stop. Why would she want to, anyway?"

When Ridgeway's lawyer arrived, he advised Ridgeway not to say anything more. The lawyer, hired by Ridgeway's wealthy parents, read the statement that he had given to the police and then hired a psychiatrist to help in building a defense that might stand up in court.

When the case went to trial two months later, the psychiatrist testified as an expert witness for the defense. He told the jury that blood tests showed that Ridgeway had abnormally large amounts of testosterone naturally occurring in his blood, that testosterone was the chemical messenger responsible for the male sex drive (which, he said, differed substantially from that of women), and that Ridgeway had consequently been unable to control his behavior on the night of the alleged rape. "The young man was simply doing what his hormones made him do," the psychiatrist testified. "It's my professional opinion," he concluded, "that with that amount of testosterone affecting his judgment, he really didn't have much choice in his behavioral responses once he was offered alcohol and was then visually stimulated by the young woman's removal of her clothes. If this was my patient," the psychiatrist added, "I'd treat him with the testosterone antagonist Depo-Provera, and we would see the strength of his sex drive substantially diminished. You could be sure that this kind of thing wouldn't happen again."

In response, the prosecution called their own expert, a noted biochemist who, citing various studies, said that there was no clearly established link between blood levels of testosterone and aggressive sexual behavior in human beings. "Even if there were," he said, "people are not mindless animals. We have free choice. We are not so driven by our blood chemistry that we cannot decide what we are going to do in any given situation."

Think about it:

1. With which expert witness do you agree more—the psychiatrist or the biochemist? Why?

2. Do you believe that blood chemistry can ever be an explanation for behavior? For crime?

3. If you answered "Yes" to the previous question, then do you think that blood chemistry can ever be an effective excuse for criminality? If you answered "No," then why not?

4. How do our understandings of criminal motivation and crime causality influence our policies on the treatment, punishment, and reformation of those who violate the law?

Note: Who's to Blame boxes provide fictionalized critical thinking opportunities, and are not actual cases.

Another case involving PMS was decided in 1991 by a Fairfax, Virginia, judge who dismissed drunk-driving and other charges against Dr. Geraldine Richter, an orthopedic surgeon.[90] After being stopped for driving erratically, Richter allegedly kicked and cursed a Virginia state trooper and admitted to having consumed four glasses of wine. A breathalyzer test showed her blood-alcohol level to be nearly 0.13%—above the 0.10% level Virginia law sets for drunk driving. Charges against Dr. Richter were dismissed after a gynecologist testified on her behalf, saying that the behavior she exhibited was likely to have been due primarily to PMS.

Although evidence linking PMS to violent or criminal behavior is far from clear, some researchers believe that a drop in serotonin levels in the female brain just before menstruation might explain the agitation and irritability sometimes associated with PMS. Serotonin has been called a "behavior-regulating chemical," and animal studies have demonstrated a link between low levels of the neurotransmitter present in the brain and aggressive behavior. For example, monkeys with low serotonin levels in their brains have been found to be more likely to bite, slap, and chase others of their kind. Studies at the National Institute on Alcohol Abuse and Alcoholism have linked low serotonin levels in humans to

Follow the author's tweets about the latest crime and justice news at **http://twitter.com/schmalleger**.

impulsive crimes. Men convicted of premeditated murder, for example, have been found to have normal serotonin levels, whereas those convicted of crimes of passion had lower levels.[91]

One 1998 study of 781 men and women age 21 found a clear relationship between elevated *blood* levels of serotonin (which correspond to lower *brain* levels of the chemical) and violence in men.[92] The study controlled for a host of possible intervening factors, including gender, diet, psychiatric medications, illicit drug use, season of the year (during which the blood test was done), plasma levels of tryptophan (dietary precursor of serotonin), alcohol and tobacco use, psychiatric diagnoses, platelet count, body mass, socioeconomic status, IQ, and history of suicide attempts. The relationship held true when both court records and self-reports of violence were assessed. No relationship between serotonin levels and aggression was seen in female subjects. According to the study's authors, "This is the first study to demonstrate that a possible index of serotonergic function is related to violence in the general population. The epidemiological serotonin effect was not small [but rather] indicated a moderate effect size in the population."[93]

Wrestler Umaga (top) putting Bobby Lashley on the ropes during their match at Wrestlemania 23 at Ford Field in Detroit, Michigan, on April 1, 2007. The match featured a bet between Donald Trump and WWE Chairman Vince McMahon. Sex hormones, such as testosterone, have been linked to aggressive behavior; testosterone also enhances secondary sexual characteristics like body hair and muscle mass in males. What kinds of crimes might be hormonally influenced?
Source: Carlos Osorio/AP Wide World Photos

Similar research by Swedish neuropsychiatrists in 2003 found that a "dysregulation of serotonin" in the brain and central nervous system could lead to increased impulsivity, irresponsibility, aggression, and need for stimulation.[94] The researchers examined the cerebrospinal fluid (CSF) of 28 violent and sexual offenders and noted that an imbalance between levels of serotonin and dopamine was highly associated with psychopathic traits.

Other hormones, such as cortisol and the thyroid hormone T_3, have also been implicated in delinquency and poor impulse control. In 2000, for example, Keith McBurnett and colleagues reported the results of a study that evaluated 38 boys between the ages of seven and 12 who had been referred to a clinic for the management of behavioral problems.[95] The children were studied for four years, using various medical and psychological assessment tools. McBurnett and fellow researchers found that the "meanest" boys had the lowest levels of the hormone cortisol in their saliva: "Low cortisol levels were associated with persistence and early onset of aggression. Boys with lower cortisol concentrations exhibited triple the number of aggressive symptoms and were named as most aggressive by peers three times as often as boys who had higher cortisol concentrations." Although the researchers did not explain why low cortisol levels might be linked to aggression, they suggested that "children with persistent conduct disorder may have genes that predispose them to produce certain hormones differently, or their hormone production may have been altered before or soon after birth."[96]

> Low cortisol levels were associated with early onset of aggression.

A few years ago, two separate Swedish studies found evidence suggesting that elevated levels of the thyroid hormone T_3 were related to alcoholism, psychopathy, and criminality.[97] Blood serum levels of the thyroid hormone T_4 (thyroxine), on the other hand, were negatively related to antisocial behavior. The researchers concluded that the results of their studies indicate an intimate relationship between T_3 and T_4 and abuse and antisocial behavior. They emphasize the importance of further studies on T_3 as a biological marker for abuse, social deviance, and repeated violent behavior.

A few years ago a different kind of link between hormones and crime was identified when Swiss researchers published a study in the prestigious journal *Nature* identifying what they called a trust hormone.[98] Greater quantities of the hormone, a small protein called oxytocin, appear to make people more trusting, and the researchers showed that trust levels could be manipulated by having men inhale oxytocin. (Oxytocin has also

WEB EXTRA 4–6

been called the "love hormone" because its levels in the brain spike when people make love as well as when women breast-feed.) Those commenting on the research suggested that confidence schemes might one day be perpetrated by con men (or women) spraying oxytocin in the air.[99] Learn more about the possible role of hormones in criminality at **Web Extra 4–6**.

Weather and Crime

Weather may also have an influence on human behavior. Research on crime and meteorological variables has looked at everything from sunshine and humidity to wind speed, barometric pressure, and rainfall. After reviewing both published and unpublished research in this area, James Rotton and Ellen G. Cohn of Florida International University concluded that temperature is the only weather variable that is consistently and reliably related to criminal behavior[100] (see Figure 4–2). In general, field research has found a definite positive correlation between temperature and violent crime—more violent crime is reported to the police on warm days than on cold days. However, the relationship between temperature and criminal behavior is more complex than it first appears. Rotton and Cohn's research incorporated not only temperature but also a variety of time-based variables, such as time of the day and day of the week. Their findings suggested that relationships between temperature and various types of criminal behavior are affected, or moderated, by time of the day, day of the week, and season of the year.

In a study of assaults in Minneapolis, Cohn and Rotton found that relationships between temperature and assaults were strongest during evening and early hours of the night.[101] A replication conducted in Dallas also found that temperature's correlation with assaults was strongest during evening hours, which are usually the coolest time of day.[102] Other studies conducted in Minneapolis found that temperature was significantly correlated with certain property crimes (burglary, larceny, and robbery),[103] with domestic violence,[104] and with disorderly conduct.[105]

Cohn and Rotton's findings are consistent with predictions that might be derived from routine activities theory (discussed in Chapter 3). They suggested that uncomfortably hot and cold temperatures keep people apart, resulting in less opportunity for victims and motivated offenders to come in contact with one another. Temporal variables, such as time of the day and day of the week, moderate the relationship between temperature and crime by also affecting opportunity; offenders and victims are more likely to come in contact with each other during evening and weekend hours than during the day, when many people are busy at work or school or are engaged in other routine activities.

Other researchers have found an apparent link between barometric pressure and violent criminal offending. Using data on suicides and violent crimes during 1999 in the Louisville, Kentucky, area, Thomas J. Schory and colleagues discovered that "the total number of acts of violence and emergency psychiatry visits are significantly associated with low barometric pressure";[106] low pressure appears to be associated with changes in cerebral blood flow and may lead to increased impulsivity.

FIGURE 4-2 | Assault as a Function of Temperature

Source: E. G. Cohn and J. Rotton, "Assault as a Function of Time and Temperature: A Moderator-Variable Time-Series Analysis," *Journal of Personality and Social Psychology*, Vol. 72 (1997), pp. 1322–1334. Data used with permission.

Genetics and Crime

Criminal Families

Some scholars have suggested that a penchant for crime may be inherited and that criminal tendencies are genetically based. Beginning in the late 1800s, researchers in the field of criminal anthropology focused on criminal families, or families that appeared to exhibit criminal tendencies through several generations.

LIBRARY EXTRA 4–5
LIBRARY EXTRA 4–6
LIBRARY EXTRA 4–7
WEB EXTRA 4–7

▓ **Juke family**
A well-known "criminal family" studied by Richard L. Dugdale.

▓ **Kallikak family**
A well-known "criminal family" studied by Henry H. Goddard.
▓ **eugenics**
The study of hereditary improvement by genetic control.
▓ **eugenic criminology**
A perspective that holds that the root causes of criminality are passed from generation to generation in the form of "bad genes."

In 1877, **Richard Louis Dugdale** (1841–1883) published a study of one such family—the **Juke family**.[107] Dugdale traced the Juke lineage back to a notorious character named Max, a Dutch immigrant who arrived in New York in the early 1700s. Two of Max's sons married into the notorious "Juke family of girls," six sisters, all of whom were said to be illegitimate. Max's male descendants were reputed to be vicious, and one woman named Ada had an especially bad reputation and came to be known as "the mother of criminals." By the time of the study, Dugdale was able to identify approximately 1,200 of Ada's descendants; included among their numbers were seven murderers, 60 habitual thieves, 90 or so other criminals, 50 prostitutes, and 280 paupers. Dugdale compared the crime-prone Jukes with another family, the pure-blooded progeny of Jonathan Edwards, a Puritan preacher and one-time president of Princeton University. Descendants of Edwards included American presidents and vice presidents as well as many successful bankers and businesspeople, and no one was identified among the Edwards lineage who had had a run-in with the law. In 1916, **Arthur H. Estabrook** published a follow-up to Dugdale's work in which he identified an additional 715 Juke descendants, including 378 more prostitutes, 170 additional paupers, and 118 other criminals.[108] **Library Extras 4–5** to **4–7** contain more information about genetics and crime.

> A penchant for crime may be inherited.

Following in the tradition of family tree researchers, **Henry Herbert Goddard** (1866–1957) published a study of the **Kallikak family** in 1912.[109] Goddard attempted to place the study of deviant families within an acceptable scientific framework via the provision of a kind of control group, so for comparison purposes he used two branches of the same family. One branch began as the result of a sexual liaison between Martin Kallikak, a Revolutionary War soldier, and a barmaid whose name is unknown; as a result of this union, an illegitimate son (Martin, Jr.) was born. After the war, Kallikak returned home and married a righteous Quaker girl, and a second line of descent began. The legitimate branch produced only a few minor deviants, but the illegitimate line resulted in 262 feebleminded births and various other epileptic, alcoholic, and criminal descendants. (The term *feebleminded*, which was much in vogue at the time of Goddard's study, was later recast as "mentally retarded," and today people exhibiting similar characteristics might be referred to as "mentally handicapped" or "mentally challenged.") Because feeblemindedness appeared to occur with some predictability in Goddard's study, but criminal activity seemed to be only randomly represented among the descendants of both Kallikak lines, Goddard concluded that a tendency toward feeblemindedness was inherited but that criminality was not.

Studies like these, which focused on inherited mental degeneration, led to the movement of **eugenics** in the 1920s and early 1930s and to the development of **eugenic criminology**,[110] which held that the root causes of criminality were largely passed from generation to generation in the form of "bad genes." Eugenic criminology replaced the idea of the "feebleminded criminal" with the "defective delinquent," and social policies developed during the eugenics movement called for the sterilization of mentally handicapped women to prevent their bearing additional offspring.[111] Those policies were supported by the federal Eugenics Record Office, which funded studies of "cacogenic," or "bad-gened," families and were endorsed by the 1927 U.S. Supreme Court case of **Buck v. Bell**.[112] In *Buck*, Justice Oliver Wendell Holmes, Jr., writing in support of a Virginia statute permitting sterilization, said, "It is better for all the world, if instead of waiting to execute degenerate offspring for crime, or to let them starve for their imbecility, society can prevent those persons who are manifestly unfit from continuing their kind." Learn about the consequences of *Buck* v. *Bell* at **Web Extra 4–7**.

The eugenics movement continued in the United Kingdom into the 1960s but was largely discredited in this country by intense condemnation of Nazi genetic research, mass sterilization, and eugenics programs, including those that led to the Holocaust. In 1962, Sir Julian Huxley, perhaps striving to rekindle positive interest in eugenics, gave the Galton Lecture to the English Eugenics Society, attesting to his belief that the general level of human abilities and performance could be improved by taking steps to improve on natural selection. Huxley argued that mankind could be improved "simply by encouraging the differential reproduction of human beings exhibiting generally desirable characteristics such as health, physical beauty, manual dexterity, longevity, athletic ability, intelligence, general mental ability, mathematical aesthetic and other special aptitudes, and capacity for leadership and for cooperative effort."[113]

The XYY "Supermale"

More recent developments in the field of human genetics have led to the study of the role of chromosomes, and sex-linked chromosomes in particular, in crime causation. The first well-known study

■ **supermale**
A male individual displaying the XYY chromosome structure.

of this type was undertaken by Patricia A. Jacobs,[114] a British researcher, and her colleagues, who in 1965 examined 197 Scottish prisoners for chromosomal abnormalities through a relatively simple blood test known as karyotyping.[115] Twelve members of the group displayed chromosomes that were unusual, and seven were found to have an XYY chromosome. Normal male individuals possess an XY chromosome structure; normal female individuals are XX. Some other unusual combinations might be XXX, wherein a woman's genetic makeup contains an extra X chromosome, and XXY (also called Klinefelter's syndrome), in which a man might carry an extra X, or female, chromosome. Klinefelter's men often have male genitalia but are frequently sterile and evidence breast enlargement and intellectual retardation. The XYY man, however, whose incidence in the prison population was placed at around 3.5% by Jacobs, was quickly identified as potentially violent and was termed a **supermale**.

Following the introduction of the supermale notion into popular consciousness, a number of offenders attempted to offer a chromosome-based defense. In 1969, for example, Lawrence E. Hannell, who was adjudged a supermale, was acquitted of murder in Australia on the grounds of insanity.[116] Such a defense, however, did not work for Richard Speck, who also claimed to be an XYY man but was convicted of killing eight Chicago nursing students in 1966; it was later learned that Speck did not carry the extra Y chromosome. See the Criminal Profiles box for more on Richard Speck.

To date, there have been nearly 200 studies of XYY males. Although not all researchers agree, these studies as a group tend to show that supermales have the following characteristics:[117]

- Taller than the average height (often 6 feet, 1 inch or taller)
- Acne and other skin disorders
- Below-average intelligence
- Overrepresentation in prisons and mental hospitals
- Family tree with above-average history of crime or mental illness

The supermale phenomenon (also called the XYY syndrome) may have been more sensationalism than fact. Little evidence suggests that XYY men actually commit crimes of greater violence than do other men, although they may commit somewhat more crimes overall. A 1976 Danish study of 4,000 men born in Copenhagen between 1944 and 1947 may have helped put the issue to rest with its finding that the incidence of XYY men was less than 1% in the general male population.[118] More recent researchers have similarly concluded that "studies done thus far are largely in agreement and demonstrate rather conclusively that males of the XYY type are not predictably aggressive."[119]

Chromosomes and Modern-Day Criminal Families

In 1993, Dutch criminologists caught worldwide attention with their claim that they had uncovered a specific gene with links to criminal behavior. Researcher H. Hilger Ropers, geneticist Han Brunner, and collaborators studied what media sources called "the Netherlands' most dysfunctional family."[120] Although members of the unnamed family displayed IQs in the near-normal range, they seemed unable to control their impulses and often ended up being arrested for violations of the criminal law; the arrests, however, were always of men. Tracing the family back five generations, Brunner found 14 men whom he classified as genetically given to criminality, but none of the women in the family displayed criminal tendencies, although they were often victimized by their crime-prone male siblings.

According to Ropers and Brunner, because men have only one X chromosome, they are especially vulnerable to any defective gene, whereas women (with two X chromosomes) have a kind of backup system in which one defective gene may be compensated for by another correctly functioning gene carried in the second X chromosome. After a decade of study, Ropers and Brunner announced that they had isolated the specific mutation that caused the family's criminality. This gene, they said, is responsible for the production of an enzyme called monoamine oxidase A (MAOA), which is crucially involved in the process by which signals are transmitted within the brain by breaking down the chemicals serotonin and noradrenaline—both of which have been linked to aggressive behavior in human beings. Because men with the mutated gene do not produce enough of the enzyme necessary to break down a lot of chemical transmitters, the researchers surmised, their brains are overwhelmed with stimuli, resulting in uncontrollable urges and, ultimately, criminal behavior.

Behavioral Genetics

Sir Francis Galton (1822–1911) was the first Western scientist to systematically study heredity and its possible influence on human behavior.[121] In 1907, Galton wrote that "the

CRIMINAL | PROFILES
Richard Benjamin Speck

In an appalling crime ranked number ten on *Time*'s list of the top 25 crimes of the twentieth century,[i] Richard Speck committed the mass murder of eight nurses from a community hospital in Chicago on the night of July 14, 1966.

Born the seventh of eight children on December 6, 1941, Speck had an early upbringing in Kirkwood, Illinois, that included strict adherence to Baptist religious teachings. When he was just six years old, his father died, and his mother subsequently married a hardfisted drinker with an arrest record. After the family relocated to Dallas, Texas, Speck performed poorly in school and began sinking into increasingly serious delinquent behavior. His drunken stepfather's response was typically the administration of severe physical punishment for each of Speck's continuing transgressions.[ii] Speck himself became a heavy drinker, an affliction that would haunt him for the remainder of his life.

Interspersed with a series of incarcerations for various burglaries, thefts, check forgeries, and other low-level crimes, 18-year-old Speck married 15-year-old Shirley Malone in November 1962. Their brief marriage was marked by his repeated absence while imprisoned, punctuated by his physical abuse of both his wife and his mother-in-law whenever he was not in jail. The abuse of his wife included frequent instances of rape at knifepoint.[iii]

In January 1966, the couple divorced, and Speck left Texas to return by bus to Illinois, ending up in Monmouth, a small town near the Iowa border. Following the rape of a 65-year-old woman in early April and the murder of a barmaid 11 days later, Speck was interrogated. He was let go when he became physically ill, but he promised to return for further questioning. When he failed to show up, investigators who went looking for him found he had fled on a bus headed east, presumably to the Chicago area.

Late on the evening of July 13, 1966, a drunken Speck invaded a town house where nursing students from nearby South Chicago Community Hospital resided. Within the first hour, he was able to capture and tie up nine women. After securing all the victims, Speck spent the next three hours systematically taking each student to another room within the town house and killing her. Each was violently murdered by strangulation, multiple stab wounds, and/or a cut throat; one was also raped.

Speck lost count of the number of women he had captured, and as a result, one of the women survived by rolling under a bed and hiding there. Speck left the town house at approximately 3:30 A.M. The survivor, Corazon Amurao, huddled in terror under the bed until almost 6 A.M. before she finally crawled out a window and began calling for help.[iv]

Mass murderer Richard Speck, hands cuffed and chained, looking down during an interview with the *Chicago Sun-Times* at Stateville Penitentiary in Illinois. Speck killed eight young nurses in 1966, and he admitted during the interview that they would be alive today if one of the women had not spit in his face as he raped her. Speck's case helped popularize the notion of supermales—predators with a distinctive genetic makeup. Do contemporary understandings of biology support the idea of a supermale?
Source: AP Wide World Photos

Speck was soon arrested and tried in Peoria, Illinois. The jury returned a guilty verdict in just 49 minutes, and Speck was sentenced to death.[v]

Speck achieved notoriety in the national press when his lawyers offered the claim that he was an XYY supermale, apparently hoping that the claim could provide a defense to the charges against him. At the time the claim was made, the XYY theory was being debated in academic circles and had become popular with the public. Later tests showed, however, that Speck did not carry the extra Y chromosome.

Speck's death sentence was commuted to 50 to 100 years in prison when the U.S. Supreme Court voided the death penalty in 1972. He died of a heart attack on December 5, 1991.

Notes

i. Howard Chua-Eoan, "The Top 25," *Crimes of the Century, Time,* http://www.time.com/time/2007/crimes/9.html (accessed May 22, 2007).

ii. David Lohr, "Richard Speck," *Crime Magazine: An Encyclopedia of Crime,* August 2003, http://crimemagazine.com/03/richardspeck,0820.htm (accessed May 22, 2007).

iii. Connie Fillippelli, "Richard Speck: Born to Raise Hell," Chapter 11, CourtTV Crime Library, 2007, http://www.crimelibrary.com/serial_killers/predators/speck/hell_11.html (accessed May 22, 2007).

iv. Ibid., Chapter 16, http://www.crimelibrary.com/serial_killers/predators/speck/hell_16.html (accessed May 22, 2007).

v. Fillippelli, Chapter 16.

perpetuation of the criminal class by heredity is a question difficult to grapple with on many accounts. It is, however, easy to show that the criminal nature tends to be inherited. . . . The criminal population receives steady accessions from those

who, without having strongly marked criminal natures, do nevertheless belong to a type of humanity that is exceedingly ill suited to play a respectable part in our modern civilization, though it is well suited to flourish under half-savage

behavioral genetics
The study of genetic and environmental contributions to individual variations in human behavior.

dizygotic twin
A twin who develops from a separate ovum and who carries the genetic material shared by siblings.

LIBRARY EXTRA 4-8

monozygotic twin
One of two twins who develop from the same egg and who carry virtually the same genetic material.

conditions, being naturally both healthy and prolific."[122] Galton's work contributed to the development of the field of **behavioral genetics**, the study of genetic and environmental contributions to individual variations in human behavior. See **Library Extra 4–8** for more about behavioral genetics and crime.

More recently, studies of the criminal tendencies of fraternal and identical twins have provided a methodologically sophisticated technique for ferreting out the role of heredity in crime causation. Fraternal twins, or **dizygotic (DZ) twins**, develop from different fertilized eggs and share only the genetic material common among siblings; identical twins, or **monozygotic (MZ) twins**, develop from the same egg and carry virtually the same genetic material. Hence, if human behavior has a substantial heritable component, twins would display similar behavioral characteristics despite variations in their social environment, with any observed relationship being stronger among MZ twins than among DZ twins.

One of the first studies to link MZ twins to criminality was published in the 1920s by German physician Johannes Lange.[123] Examining 13 pairs of MZ twins and 17 pairs of DZ twins, he found that in 10 of the 13 MZ twins both were criminal, whereas only 2 of the 17 DZ twins exhibited such similarity. Lange's findings drew considerable attention, even though his sample was small and he was unable to adequately separate environmental influences from genetic ones. A much larger twin study was begun in 1968 by European researchers Karl O. Christiansen and Sarnoff Mednick, who analyzed all twins (3,586 pairs) born on a selected group of Danish islands between 1881 and 1910.[124] Christiansen and Mednick found significant statistical support for the notion that criminal tendencies are inherited: 52% of identical twins and 22% of fraternal siblings displayed the same degree of criminality within the twin pair. Such similarities remained apparent even among twins separated at birth and raised in substantially different environments.

The Minnesota Twin Family Study began in 1983.[125] The study's original goal was to establish a registry of all twins born in Minnesota from 1936 to 1955 for psychological research purposes but expanded to include twins born between 1961 and 1964. The Minnesota registry conducted personality and interests tests with more than 8,000 twin pairs and family members (by mail), and its findings seemed to show that MZ twins reared apart are about as similar as MZ twins reared together in personality and temperament, occupational and leisure-time interests, and social attitudes. Study authors warned, however, that "this evidence for the strong heritability of most psychological traits, sensibly construed, does

not detract from the value or importance of parenting, education, and other propaedeutic interventions."[126]

In 1994, Dutch researchers reported finding substantial genetic influences on delinquent and aggressive behavior in a study comparing 221 pairs of biologically unrelated siblings in adoptive families with 111 pairs of biologically related siblings in similar settings.[127] Using a sophisticated study design, the researchers concluded that genetics accounted for 70% in the variance of aggressiveness while predicting only 39% of delinquency and 47% of attention-related problems.

In 1996, British researchers studying 43 MZ and 38 DZ same-sex twins through the use of self-report questionnaires stated that "common bad behaviors of the sort admitted to by the majority of adolescents have a substantially heritable component. Additive genetic effects account for most of the variation, with no evidence of a contribution from shared environment."[128] The researchers also determined that genetic effects on behavior appear to increase with age. The British research was supported by the findings of a joint U.S.–Australian examination of 2,682 adult twin pairs; in that study, researchers found "a substantial genetic influence on risk for conduct disorder" (defined to include chronic stealing, lying, bullying, arson, property destruction, weapons use, cruelty to animals or people, fighting, aggression, truancy, and running away from home).[129]

> Christiansen and Mednick found significant statistical support for the notion that criminal tendencies are inherited.

In 2003, researchers examined the behavior of 1,116 pairs of five-year-old twins participating in a longitudinal study and asked mothers, teachers, study examiners, and the children themselves to evaluate the degree of the children's level of antisocial behavior.[130] Findings showed that antisocial children can be identified early in life, that their behavior can be nearly impossible to control by the time they reach kindergarten, and that heredity plays a far greater role in determining such behavior than does home life or parenting. The researchers concluded that genetic influences were extremely powerful determinants of antisocial behavior across diverse social settings, writing that "research and theory on the etiology of childhood antisocial behavior must look beyond the current focus on socioeconomic contexts and parenting processes, to incorporate genetic explanations and develop new theories of nature-nurture interplay."[131] Also in 2003, Florida State University researcher Jeanette Taylor

■ **genetic determinism**
The belief that genes are the major determining factor in human behavior.

and colleagues studied two separate groups of teenage male twins—142 MZ and 70 DZ twin pairs—and concluded that antisocial traits among study subjects existed prior to adulthood and that they stemmed to a significant degree from genetic factors.[132]

Twin studies appear to point to criminal genes that, once inherited, inevitably produce antisocial behavior. Such a conclusion, however, is not necessarily warranted; genes may simply influence the way people respond to their surroundings, that is, so-called criminal genes may essentially be genetic predispositions to respond in certain ways to a criminogenic environment.

Human Genome Project

Many of the questions criminologists have raised about the role of genetics in criminal behavior may be answered by the results of research undertaken by the Human Genome Project (HGP).[133] The HGP, an international research program designed to construct detailed maps of the human genome, began in the United States in 1990 through a joint effort of the Department of Energy and the National Institutes of Health. Its purpose was to determine the complete nucleotide sequence of human DNA, to localize the nearly 100,000 genes within the human genome, and to determine the sequences of the 3 billion chemical base pairs that make up human DNA. Successors to the HGP store the information developed by the HGP in databases, with the goal of eventually transferring that information and associated technologies to the private sector to stimulate the multibillion-dollar U.S. biotechnology industry and to foster the development of new medical treatments and technologies. The HGP was officially declared completed on April 14, 2003[134]—almost exactly 50 years after James Watson and Francis Crick published their historic findings on the double helix three-dimensional structure of DNA.[135]

The use of genetic knowledge developed by the HGP is likely to have momentous implications for both individuals and society. In the area of crime-control policy, HGP-developed information is expected to provide choices for public and professional deliberation, so the analysis of the ethical, legal, and social implications of genetic knowledge and the development of policy options for public consideration are central components of the human genome research effort.

Some scientists had previously been confident that advances in the field of behavioral genetics would support the idea of behavioral **genetic determinism**, or the belief that genes are the major determining factor in human behavior. Others, however, warn that discoveries in behavioral genetics need to be interpreted in terms of what is already known about social and psychological influences on behavior. The dominant point of view today holds that it is the interaction of genes and the behavioral possibilities that they represent, with features of the social and physical environments, that produce meaningful human activity.

Early studies associated with the HGP results are interesting. Researchers at the University of Texas Health Science Center in San Antonio announced the discovery of a pleasure-seeking gene that, they suspected, plays a role in deviant behavior, addictions, and maybe even murder and violence. The gene, called "DRD2 A1 allele," is normally involved in controlling the flow of dopamine (a powerful brain chemical that gives people a sense of well-being). When defective, however, the DRD2 A1 allele diminishes dopamine function, which may drive a person to take drugs, drink, or engage in activity that provides a dopamine-like experience. "We think they're seeking out ways of fixing the lack of pleasure," said researcher Kenneth Blum. "You might be a pleasure seeker for alcohol, drugs, sex or maybe you get it from violence or murder."[136]

In 2007, researchers at the University of Texas Southwestern Medical Center discovered that mice carrying certain mutations in what is called the clock gene exhibited manic

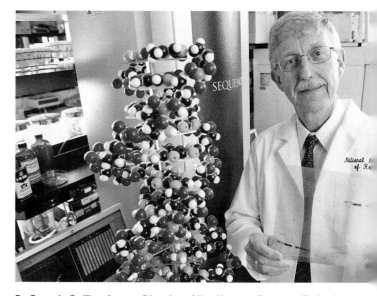

Dr. Francis Collins, former Director of the Human Genome Project and current Director of the National Institutes of Health. The National Center for Human Genome Research at the National Institutes of Health supported the international Human Genome Project, a research program that determined the complete nucleotide sequence of human DNA. What ethical, legal, and social implications are inherent in such a project?
Source: Michael Ventura/Alamy

WEB EXTRA 4–8
WEB EXTRA 4–9
LIBRARY EXTRA 4–9
LIBRARY EXTRA 4–10
LIBRARY EXTRA 4–11

■ **heritability**
A statistical construct that estimates the amount of variation in the traits of a population that is attributable to genetic factors.

behaviors, such as recklessness and hyperactivity, and also displayed a preference for addictive substances, such as cocaine, but that treatment with the antipsychotic medicine lithium caused them to behave normally. A month later, Francis McMahon of the National Institute of Mental Health in Bethesda, Maryland, reported finding a number of specific genes that act by influencing how the brain responds to neurotransmitters such as dopamine and that might be associated with bipolar disorder.[137]

In 2010, researchers from Columbia University's Medical Center were able to show how a gene defect that leads to a communications breakdown in the brain predisposes people with the defect to schizophrenia.[138] Maria Karayiorgou, who first noticed the relationship between the genetic variant and schizophrenia more than ten years earlier, was able to identify a definite pathophysiological mechanism of how the risk of schizophrenia is enhanced by a small deletion of genetic material on a specific chromosome shared by all human beings—30% of people with the missing genetic material will go on to develop schizophrenia, making it one of the biggest genetic risk factors for the disease.

> The interaction of genes and the behavioral possibilities that they represent, with features of the social and physical environments, produce meaningful human activity.

Two years before the Columbia University study, researchers with the National Institute on Drug Abuse announced that "as much as half of an individual's risk of becoming addicted to nicotine, alcohol, or other drugs depends on his or her genes."[139] The researchers stated, "Pinning down the biological basis for this risk is an important avenue of research for scientists trying to solve the problem of drug abuse."

The HGP and studies like those cited here notwithstanding, behavioral geneticists examining the crime problem face some daunting issues: coming up with a generally acceptable definition of criminality, determining how best to measure criminality once it has been defined, separating the influences of the social and physical environments from genetic influences on behavior, and distinguishing among the multiple and potentially interrelated influences of many genes. In the final analysis, the explanatory power of **heritability**, a statistical construct estimating the amount of variation in the traits of a population attributable to genetic factors, appears to be limited by the fact that it may apply only to specific environments that existed at the time of a given study. For example, red roses grown under optimal conditions will likely all be similar in size, shape, and color, but grow the same roses in a desert or put food coloring in their water, and their appearance is likely to change substantially. As one noted geneticist says, "If the population or the environment changes, the heritability most likely will change as well. Most important, heritability statements provide no basis for predictions about the expression of the trait in question in any given individual."[140] In other words, even red roses watered with blue food coloring are unlikely to end up being red.

New understandings about how genes operate also seem to call into question previous notions that genes are strong determinants of human behavior. Researchers in the field of neurobiology, for example, have found 17 genes, known as CREB genes, that are switched on and off in response to environmental influences. The CREB genes lay down neural pathways in the brain and form the basis of memory; the act of learning turns the CREB genes on and is made possible by them.[141] Hence, the CREB genes respond to human experience rather than determine it. One writer said, "These genes are at the mercy of our behavior, not the other way around."[142] The FOXP2 gene on chromosome 7 allows the development of language skills in human beings. The CREB and FOXP2 genes have taught researchers that genes are not just carriers of heredity; they are active during life and respond to the environment. Genes are both the cause and the consequence of our actions—they do not so much *cause* human action as *enable* it. Some writers have suggested that such insights will soon allow us to fully appreciate the roles of both genetics and environment in eliciting specific forms of human behavior and thereby leave the nature–nurture argument behind.[143]

Learn more about the HGP by visiting the National Human Genome Research Institute via **Web Extra 4–8**; you might also want to visit the U.S. Department of Energy's Human Genome Program site at **Web Extra 4–9**. You can read about how DNA and genetics might influence human behavior at **Library Extras 4–9, 4–10**, and **4–11**.

Male–Female Differences in Criminality

A number of contemporary writers propose that criminologists must recognize that "the male is much more criminalistic than the female."[144] With the exception of crimes like prostitution and shoplifting, the number of crimes committed by men routinely far exceeds the number of crimes committed by women in almost all categories, and when women commit crimes, they are far more likely to assume the role of followers than leaders.[145] The data on the extent of male–female criminality show surprising regularity over time: The proportion of homicides committed by men versus women has remained more or less constant for decades (see Table 4–1), and the proportion of men murdered by men versus the proportion of women murdered by women has been consistent, with men having a much greater propensity to murder one another.

If culture exercises the major role in determining criminality, as many social scientists today suggest, then we would expect to see recognizable increases in the degree and nature of female criminality over time, especially as changes in socialization practices, cultural roles, and other ethnographic patterns increase the opportunity for women to commit what had previously been regarded as traditionally male offenses. With the exception of a few crimes, such as embezzlement, drug abuse, and liquor-law violations, such has not been the case. Although women comprise 51% of the population of the United States, they are arrested for only 19% of all violent crimes and 37% of property crimes[146]—a proportion that has remained surprisingly constant since the FBI began gathering crime data more than half a century ago—in spite of all the cultural changes creating new possibilities for women to commit crimes. These gender differences also can be seen in cross-cultural studies.

Such findings contrast with the suggestions of authors like Freda Adler, who, in her 1975 book *Sisters in Crime*, proposed that as women entered nontraditional occupations and roles, there "would be a movement toward parity with men in the commission of crime in terms of both incidence and type."[147] Darrell J. Steffensmeier, who studied changes in women's criminality following publication of Adler's book, found almost no evidence to support the belief that a new female criminal is emerging or that female criminality is undergoing the kind of increase Adler might have expected.[148] The lack of contemporary validation for Adler's thesis suggests that something else is occurring, that some element other than cultural inhibition or equality of opportunity is preventing women from taking their place alongside men as equals in crime. Biological criminologists suggest that the organic correlates of gender provide the needed explanation.

In evaluating the criminality of women based on statistics alone, causal factors operative in the behavior itself may be misidentified. Although men consistently commit more murders than women, we should not jump to the conclusion that this bit of evidence shows a genetic predisposition toward interpersonal violence in men that is absent in women because to do so would fail to recognize the role of other causal factors. For example, observable racial variations in crime rates have caused certain writers to claim that some racial groups are disproportionately violent, attributing such violence to genetics. A look at the statistics appears to show that in the United States, African Americans are more than six times as likely as whites to commit murder, three times as likely to commit rape, seven times as likely to rob, and twice as likely to commit any kind of crime.[149]

Such statistics, however, can be inherently misleading because—unlike the undeniable and easily observable biological differences that exist between men and women—racial groupings are defined more by convention than by genetics. Some writers suggest that "pure" racial groups no longer exist and that even historical racial distinctions were based more on political considerations and social convention than on significant genetic differences.

The criminality of women (or its lack) may be culturally determined to a considerable degree, but data consistently show that women are far less likely than men to be involved in most property crimes and less likely still to commit violent crimes.

> Genetically based behavioral differences between men and women are moderated by aspects of the social environment.

We have already evaluated the role that testosterone may play in increasing the propensity toward violence and aggression among men. A few authors have suggested that testosterone is the agent primarily responsible for male criminality and that

TABLE 4-1 | Male and Female Murder Perpetrators as a Percentage of All Arrests for Homicide, 1960-2009

1960	1975	1980	1990	2000	2009
MALE v. FEMALE	MALE v. FEMALE	MALE v. FEMALE	MALE v. FEMALE	MALE v. FEMALE	MALE v. FEMALE
82.5% v. 17.5%	84.7% v. 15.3%	87.2% v. 12.8%	89.6% v. 10.4%	87.5% v. 12.5%	89.6% v. 10.4%

Source: Adapted from Federal Bureau of Investigation, *Crime in the United States*, various years.

> ■ **sociobiology**
> The systematic study of the biological basis of all social behavior.
>
> ■ **paradigm**
> An example, a model, or a theory.

Uruguayan female boxer Chris Namus (left) and Colombian Leli Luz Flores fight in Montevideo, Uruguay, on August 8, 2009, for the WBC super lightweight title. Flores knocked out Namus in the first round. Women's boxing, a relatively new sport, reflects women's changing social roles. Male-female differences in criminality, however, seem to display considerable regularity over time. Does this mean that men and women have inherently different behavioral tendencies?
Source: AFP Photo/Martin Bernetti/NewsCom.com

its relative lack in women leads them to commit fewer crimes, and some evidence supports just such a hypothesis. Studies have shown, for example, that female fetuses exposed to elevated testosterone levels during gestation develop masculine characteristics, including a muscular build and a demonstrably greater tendency toward aggression later in life.[150] However, genetically based behavioral differences between men and women are moderated by aspects of the social environment, including socialization, the learning of culturally prescribed roles, and the expectations of others, so definitive conclusions are difficult to reach.

One proposed social-psychological explanation for homicidal behavior among women, for example, suggested that men who kill tend to do so out of a need to control a situation, whereas women who kill tend to do so because they have lost control over themselves.[151] The theorists stated that "women as a group are more 'controlled' than men, particularly with respect to their experience and expression of anger" and that such control emanates from the fact that "men are always the subjects and women the objects in [a] male-centric universe."[152] As a consequence of our culture's emphasis on women's looks rather than

their performance, women internalize a self-image based on their appearance rather than their character, resulting in low self-esteem and low self-confidence; low self-esteem necessitates greater self-control and results in lower criminality among women. Such a perspective suggests that women tend to commit homicides only when driven past the brink of self-control, thus offering an explanation for why homicides committed by women are generally spontaneous rather than planned, why they usually involve the killing of intimates, and why they generally occur in the home. "Women generally view themselves as part of a collective of relationships around them," said these theorists, "and evaluate their self-worth based on the value and success of these relationships."[153] Hence, when relationships break down, a woman's self-worth may be negated, resulting in a lessening of control—and homicide may ensue.

Sociobiology

In the introduction to his insightful article summarizing sociobiology, Arthur Fisher wrote, "Every so often, in the long course of scientific progress, a new set of ideas appears, illuminating and redefining what has gone before like a flare bursting over a darkened landscape."[154] To some, **sociobiology**—a theoretical synthesis of biology, behavior, and evolutionary ecology brought to the scientific community by **Edward O. Wilson** in his seminal 1975 work *Sociobiology: The New Synthesis*[155]—holds the promise of just such a new **paradigm**, or model. In his book, Wilson defined *sociobiology* as "the systematic study of the biological basis of all social behavior [that is] a branch of evolutionary biology and particularly of modern population biology." Through his entomological study of social insects (especially ants), Wilson demonstrated that particular forms of behavior could contribute to the long-term survival of the social group. Wilson focused on altruism (selfless, helping behavior); contrary to the beliefs of some evolutionary biologists, he found that helping behavior facilitated the continuity of the gene pool among altruistic individuals and that the primary determinant of behavior, including human behavior, was the need to ensure the survival and continuity of genetic material from one generation to the next.

Territoriality, according to Wilson's writings, explained many of the conflicts, including homicide, warfare, and other forms of aggression, between and among human beings. In Wilson's words, "Part of man's problem is that his intergroup responses are still crude and primitive, and inadequate for the extended extraterritorial relationships that civilization has thrust

WEB EXTRA 4–10
WEB EXTRA 4–11

upon him." The "unhappy result," as Wilson terms it, may be "tribalism," expressed through the contemporary proliferation of street gangs, racial tension, and hardened encampments of survivalist and separatist groups.

Sociobiological theory not only tells us that the violence and aggressiveness associated with territoriality are often reserved for strangers but also explains intragroup aggression (violence occurring within groups). Wilson's theory suggested that within the group "a particularly severe form of aggressiveness should be reserved for actual or suspected adultery. In many human societies, where sexual bonding is close and personal knowledge of the behavior of others detailed, adulterers are harshly treated. The sin is regarded to be even worse when offspring are produced."[156] Hence, territoriality and acquisitiveness extend to location, possessions, and even other people. Human laws, explained Wilson, are designed to protect genetically based relationships that people have with one another, as well as their material possessions and their claimed locations in space, so violations of these intuitive relationships result in crime and in official reactions by the legal system.

Wilson's writings generated a flurry of studies intended to test the validity of his assertions. A Canadian study of violence in the homes of adoptive children found that stepchildren run a risk 70 times greater of being killed by their adoptive parents than do children living with their natural parents.[157] Some writers concluded that "murderous behavior, warfare, and even genocide were unavoidable correlates of genetic evolution, controlled by the same genes for territorial behavior that had been selected in primate evolution."[158] Others have suggested that biological predispositions developed during earlier stages of human evolution color contemporary criminal activity; male criminals, for example, tend toward robbery and burglary—crimes in which they can continue to enact their "hunter" instincts developed long ago—but the criminality of women often involves shoplifting and simple theft, more typical of "gatherer" instincts.

Human behavioral predilections can be studied in a variety of ways. In the 1989 book *Evolutionary Jurisprudence*, John H. Beckstrom reported on his examination of over 400 legal documents, as well as legal claims and court decisions spanning over 300 years of judicial activity, that showed support for Wilson's contentions that humans tend to act to preserve their territorial claims, their likelihood of successful reproduction, and the continuation of their own particular genetic material.[159] Other theorists have gone so far as to imply that, among humans, there may be a gene-based tendency to experience guilt and to develop a conscience and that notions of right and wrong, whether embodied in laws

Two Alpine Ibex bucks fight over territory in the Swiss Alps. Sociobiologists tell us that certain traits, such as territoriality, are common to both animals and humans. How might territoriality lead to crime?
Source: blickwinkel/Alamy

or in social convention, may flow from such a naturalistic origin. Learn more about sociobiology in general and the sociobiology of sociopathy at **Web Extras 4–10** and **4–11**.

As sociobiology began to receive expanded recognition from American investigators, some social scientists, believing the basic tenets of their profession to be challenged by the movement, began to treat it as "criminology's anti-discipline."[160] Contemporary criminologist John Madison Memory wrote, "By the early 1980s sociobiology presented such a significant threat to American criminology that it could no longer be ignored."[161] Criticisms were quick to come, and Memory identified many of them:

- Sociobiology fails to convey the overwhelming significance of culture, social learning, and individual experiences in shaping the behavior of individuals and groups.

- Sociobiology is fundamentally wrong in its depiction of the basic nature of humans; there is no credible evidence of genetically based or determined tendencies to act in certain ways.

- Sociobiology is just another empirically unsupported rationale for the authoritative labeling and stigmatization of despised, threatening, powerless minorities.

- Humans are so thoroughly different from other animal species, even other primates, that there is no rational basis for the application to humans of findings from animal studies.

> ■ **biosocial criminology**
> A theoretical perspective that sees the interaction between biology and the environment as key to understanding human behavior, including criminality.

Many such criticisms were advanced by old-guard academics in an effort to prevent their own discipline's decline in influence in the face of otherwise convincing sociobiological claims. In the words of one observer, "Most criminologists, like most academicians, were wedded to a paradigm, ... the idea that one great problem solution can permit the explanation of nearly all the unexplained variation in the field."[162] Today, many open-minded scholars are beginning to sense the growing need for a new synthesis, a way to integrate the promise of biological theories like sociobiology with other long-accepted perspectives like sociology and psychology. As a result, the field of criminology appears ripe for a new multicausal approach, with some saying that this approach can be found in contemporary biosocial explanations of criminal behavior (discussed next).

Biosocial and Psychosocial Criminology

In the mid-1980s, Arnold L. Lieber delivered an address at the annual meeting of the American Psychological Association in Denver, Colorado.[163] He used that forum to describe his research on biology and crime, which linked phases of the moon to fluctuations in the incidence of violence among human beings (nights around full moons show a significant rise in crime).

Shortly after Lieber's presentation, criminologist **James Q. Wilson** and psychologist **Richard J. Herrnstein** teamed up to write *Crime and Human Nature*, a book-length treatise that restates and refines many of the arguments proposed by biological criminologists over the previous century.[164] Part of their purpose was to reopen discussion of biological causes of crime. "We want to show," Herrnstein said, "that the pendulum is beginning to swing away from a totally sociological explanation of crime."[165] Their avowed goal was "not to state a case just for genetic factors, but to state a comprehensive theory of crime that draws together all the different factors that cause criminal behavior."[166]

Wilson and Herrnstein cited several constitutional factors contributing to crime:[167]

- **Gender.** "Crime has been predominantly male behavior."

- **Age.** "In general, the tendency to break the law declines throughout life."

- **Body type.** "A disproportionate number of criminals have a mesomorphic build."

- **Intelligence.** Criminality is said to be clearly and consistently associated with low intelligence.

- **Personality.** Criminals are typically aggressive, impulsive, and cruel.

Although personality, behavioral problems, and intelligence may be related to environment, the authors said that "each involves some genetic inheritance." Wilson and Herrnstein recognized social factors in the development of personality but suggested that constitutional factors predispose a person to specific types of behavior and that societal *reactions* to such predispositions may determine, to a large degree, the form of continued behavior. One of today's most vocal proponents of **biosocial criminology**, Anthony Walsh of Boise State University, emphasized the importance of recognizing the *interaction* of biology and the environment in the formation of behavioral responses to given situations: "Biological factors do not operate in an environmental vacuum, nor do environmental factors operate in a biological vacuum, and we must cease formulating our theories as if they do."[168]

> Biological factors do not operate in an environmental vacuum, nor do environmental factors operate in a biological vacuum.

More recently, some scientists have advanced the term *neuroplasticity* (sometimes called *brain plasticity* or *cortical plasticity*), meaning that the brain can alter its structure and function in response to experience, to explain why some people experience significant changes in personality when undergoing new experiences. It is well known, for example, that when portions of the brain are physically damaged through trauma, stroke, or other types of injury, adjacent parts of the brain can assume some of the psychological or motor functions that would have otherwise been lost. In 2003, Harvard University Medical School researchers discovered that the normally thick cable of nerve cells (the corpus collosum) connecting the right and left hemispheres in the brain is generally smaller in children who have been abused than in children who were free from abuse.[169] Brain scans showed that neglect also reduced the size of the connector, as did constant and severe verbal abuse. According to Martin Teicher, associate professor of psychiatry at Harvard Medical School, "These changes are not limited to physical and sexual abuse; there's growing evidence that even verbal assault can alter the way a developing brain is wired." Teicher and other psychiatrists who conducted the scans concluded that "a smaller *corpus collosum*

> ▥ **life course persisters**
> An offender who, as a result of neuropsychological deficits combined with poverty and family dysfunction, displays patterns of misbehavior throughout life.
>
> ▥ **adolescence-limited offenders**
> A juvenile offender who abandons delinquency upon maturity.

leads to less integration of the two halves of the brain, and that this can result in dramatic shifts in mood and personality."[170]

In a more positive direction, researchers found that the neural circuitry in the brains of practiced meditators changes—apparently in response to thousands of hours spent meditating—as evidenced by the fact that the brain waves of meditators were significantly different than those of nonmeditators.[171] Scientists who study neuroplasticity now believe not only that the brain changes in response to external stimuli or physical trauma but also that it is malleable in response to internal stimuli (thoughts). If true, simple self-improvement techniques—like positive thinking and silently repeated self-affirmations—may foster positive alterations in personality and produce an increased likelihood of socially approved behaviors. A few years ago, for example, UCLA psychiatrist Jeffrey M. Schwartz and Sharon Begley demonstrated that patients suffering from obsessive-compulsive disorder (OCD) are capable of consciously rechanneling compulsive urges into more socially acceptable activities and that by doing so they could actually alter their brains' neuronal circuitry.[172] Hence,

Looters leaving a supermarket with stolen groceries in Pueco, Chili, in 2010 one day after an 8.8-magnitude earthquake rocked the area, killing at least 300 people. The South American nation saw looters ransacking numerous stores following the quake, taking everything from boxes of food to plasma TVs. Is the tendency toward certain kinds of criminal offenses natural to human beings? Might it be so only under certain circumstances?
Source: AFP Photo/Pablo Porciuncula/NewsCom.com

physical changes to the brain in response to experiences that were once thought possible only in the very young also can characterize adults in some situations. One writer explained that "the brain physically 'captures' the environment as it wires itself in response to environmental experience."[173] The same writer noted, however, that "the brain has many assumptions built into it over eons of evolutionary time; it is no *tabula rasa*."[174] With these considerations in mind, some suggest that the interplay among heredity, biology, and the social and physical environments may be much more complicated than once thought and may provide the key nexus in any consideration of crime causation.

Moffitt's Biosocial Theory

In what some criminologists have called "the most widely recognized biosocial theory of crime,"[175] psychologist **Terrie E. Moffitt** developed a two-path (dual taxonomic) theory of criminality that helps to explain the long-standing observation that most antisocial children do not become adult criminals.[176] While adult criminality is almost always preceded by antisocial behavior during adolescence, most adolescents who engage in delinquency do not go on to later lives of crime.

Moffitt's two-path biosocial theory contends that as a result of neuropsychological deficits (specifically, early brain damage or chemical imbalances), combined with poverty and family dysfunction, some people come to display more or less constant patterns of misbehavior throughout life.[177] These people are called **life course persisters** (LCPs) or "life course–persistent offenders." LCPs tend to fail in school and become involved in delinquency at an early age, so their opportunities for legitimate success are increasingly limited with the passage of time.

Others, said Moffitt, go through limited periods where they exhibit high probabilities of offending, which are generally greatest during their mid-teen years; this second group, called **adolescence-limited offenders** (ALs), is led into offending primarily by structural disadvantages. The most significant of these disadvantages is the status anxiety of teenagers that stems from modern society's inadequacy at easing the transition from adolescence to adulthood for significant numbers of young people.

In blending biological factors with environmental influences, Moffitt hypothesized that a significant source of adolescent strain arises from the fact that biological maturity occurs at a relatively early age (perhaps as early as age 12) and brings with it the desire for sexual and emotional relationships, as well as personal autonomy;[178] however, society does not permit the assumption of autonomous adult roles until far later (around age 18 or even 21). As adolescents begin to desire autonomy, they are prevented from achieving it because of preexisting societal expectations and societally limited opportunities, resulting in what Moffitt called a "maturity gap." They might be told, "You're too young for that," or "Wait until you grow up." Lacking the resources to achieve autonomy on their own, adolescents are drawn into delinquent roles by LCPs who have already achieved autonomy and who serve as role models for others seeking early independence. Hence, the association with LCPs makes an appearance of autonomy achievable for ALs by allowing them to engage in actions mimicking those routinely undertaken by LCPs. Once ALs realize the substantial costs of continuing misbehavior, however, they abandon such social mimicry and the participation in delinquent acts that characterizes it; as they mature, ALs begin to aspire to achieve legitimate autonomy. Those who fail to successfully make the transition add to the ranks of the LCP population.

Moffitt noted that ALs display inconsistencies in antisocial behavior from one place to another. They might, for example, participate in illicit drug use with friends or shoplift in stores and might also experiment sexually. Still, their school behavior is likely to remain within socially acceptable bounds, and they will probably act with respect toward teachers, employers, and adults. LCPs, on the other hand, consistently engage in antisocial behavior across a wide spectrum of social situations.

Study authors Avshalom Caspi and Terrie E. Moffitt and their colleagues recognized that childhood maltreatment appears to be a "universal risk factor for antisocial behavior" in adulthood but noted that not all maltreated children grow up to become criminal.[179] In an effort to identify vulnerability factors that might predispose some abused children to antisocial behavior,

Childhood maltreatment appears to be a "universal risk factor for antisocial behavior" in adulthood.

Caspi and Moffitt hypothesized that the development of antisocial behavior was mediated by an interaction between a gene responsible for the production of the enzyme MAOA and an environment variable (maltreatment). At the conclusion of the study, researchers determined that maltreatment "has lasting neurochemical correlates in human children" and found that deficient MAOA activity may cause "neural hyperreactivity" in children in response to threats; "childhood maltreatment predisposes most strongly to adult violence among children whose MAOA is insufficient to constrain maltreatment-induced changes to neurotransmitter systems."[180] Maltreated children with high MAOA activity did not develop antisocial behavior. The finding was supported by two separate Swedish studies published in 2007.[181]

Similar results came from the Dunedin Multidisciplinary Health and Development Study—a longitudinal study of 1,037 children born in the maternity hospital in Dunedin, New Zealand, between April 1, 1972, and March 31, 1973—and pointed to what appears to be significant biosocial interaction between MAOA and early child abuse, leading to violence later in life.[182] Children who experience abuse—especially those exposed to erratic, coercive, and punitive parenting—frequently develop conduct disorders and display antisocial personality symptoms, and they are known to be at greater risk of becoming violent adult offenders than children who do not experience such maltreatment.[183] (Previous research had demonstrated that the earlier children experience maltreatment, the more likely they are to display such problems in later life.)

A 2008 analysis of data from the National Longitudinal Study of Adolescent Health (also known as Add Health) by Kevin M. Beaver of Florida State University and associates found that low MAOA activity can interact with neuropsychological deficits (defined in this study as poor scores on verbal skills tests) to produce low self-control and delinquency. Hence, according to Beaver, findings from the data analysis "are supportive of an interdisciplinary scientific approach to the study of crime and delinquency, which views antisocial behavior as a multifactorial phenotype that is the result of genetic factors, neural substrates, and environmental factors working independently and synergistically."[184] In other words, in at least some cases, genetic predispositions and their interaction with the surrounding social and physical environments combine to produce delinquency.

Psychosocial Criminology

In 1964, **Hans J. Eysenck**, a British psychiatrist, published *Crime and Personality*, a book-length treatise in which he explained crime as the result of fundamental personality characteristics.[185] Eysenck described three personality dimensions with links to criminality: psychoticism, extroversion, and neuroticism.

Psychoticism, which Eysenck said "is believed to be correlated with criminality at all stages,"[186] is defined by such characteristics as lack of empathy, creativeness, tough-mindedness, and antisociability. Psychoticism, according to Eysenck, is also frequently characterized by hallucinations and delusions, leading to the personality type described as psychotic. Extroverts, the second personality group, are described as carefree, dominant, and venturesome, operating with high levels of energy. "The typical

■ **biopsychology**
A field of study that combines the principles of psychology with those of neuroscience and biology. It examines how thoughts and behavior are mediated by interaction between the brain (especially neurotransmitters) and the environment. Also called *behavioral psychology* and *behavioral neuroscience*.

extrovert," Eysenck wrote, "is sociable, likes parties, has many friends, needs to have people to talk to, and does not like reading or studying by himself."[187] Neuroticism, the third of the personality characteristics Eysenck described, is said to be typical of people who are irrational, shy, moody, and emotional.

According to Eysenck, psychotics are the most likely to be criminal because they combine high degrees of emotionalism with similarly high levels of extroversion; individuals with such characteristics are especially difficult to socialize and to train and do not respond well to the external environment. Eysenck cited many studies in which children and others who harbored characteristics of psychoticism, extroversion, and neuroticism performed poorly on conditioning tests designed to measure how quickly they would respond appropriately to external stimuli. Conscience, according to Eysenck, is fundamentally a conditioned reflex, so an individual who does not take well to conditioning will not fully develop a conscience and will continue to exhibit the asocial behavioral traits of a very young child.

Central to Eysenck's approach was his belief that personality traits are fundamentally dependent upon physiology, specifically upon the individual's autonomic nervous system (ANS). Some individuals possess nervous systems that cannot handle a great deal of stimulation, and these introverts shun excitement, are easily trained, and rarely become criminal. However, those who possess nervous systems in need of constant stimulation seek excitement and are far more likely to turn to crime. Up to two-thirds of all behavioral variance, claimed Eysenck, could be strongly attributed to genetics. Because Eysenck believed that it was the ANS that underlay "the behavioral trait of emotionality or neuroticism,"[188] his approach has been termed **biopsychology** (also called *behavioral psychology* and *behavioral neuroscience*).

> Up to two-thirds of all behavioral variance, claimed Eysenck, could be attributed to genetics.

Policy Implications of Biological Theories

In 1992 the term *standard social science model* (SSSM) was introduced to the general public by Jerome H. Barkow and his colleagues in the edited volume *The Adapted Mind*.[189] The SSSM—which assumes that human beings come into this world like blank slates and acquire almost all of their values, behavioral patterns, and modes of thought through socialization into their surrounding cultures—was identified as the perspective that had characterized much social scientific thought during the twentieth century. According to Barkow, the SSSM provided the underpinnings for the work of many famous sociologists, social psychologists, and social anthropologists of the 1900s, including anthropologists Margaret Mead and Leslie White and sociologist Ellsworth Faris.

Only in the last decade or two has the SSSM largely given way to broader perspectives that include an examination of the role of biology and genetic influences on human behavior. In a more recent book, *The Blank Slate: The Modern Denial of Human Nature*,[190] MIT cognitive scientist Steven Pinker told readers that today's social scientists still continue to unjustly ignore the biological basis of human behavior, replacing it instead with three myths: (1) the myth of the blank slate, (2) the myth of the Noble Savage, and (3) the myth of the Ghost in the Machine. The blank slate myth (mentioned above) holds that the human mind has no innate traits and that the human personality is fully malleable by society, the Noble Savage myth says that human nature is essentially good, and the Ghost in the Machine myth holds that each person has an individual soul-like quality that can make choices that can be completely independent of any biological predispositions. These three myths, according to Pinker, comprise the SSSM of the modern era and have led to misguided social and political policies, but it is only when the impact of biology on human behavior is fully recognized that effective social policies—including those aimed at controlling crime—can be developed.

C. Ray Jeffery proposed the following as part of a comprehensive biologically based program of crime prevention and crime control:[191]

- "Pre- and postnatal care for pregnant women and their infants" is needed to monitor and address potentially detrimental developmental conditions that could lead to heightened aggression and crime later in life.
- Monitoring of children throughout the early stages of their development would identify "early symptoms of behavioral disorder."
- Monitoring of children in their early years would reduce the risk of exposure to violence-inducing experiences like child abuse as well as violence committed by other children.

LIBRARY EXTRA 4–12

- Neurological examinations, including CAT, PET, and MRI scans, should be used "when the need is evident."
- Biological research should be conducted in prisons and treatment facilities to better identify the root causes of aggression and violence, and laws that prevent the experimental use of prison subjects, the analysis of bodies of executed prisoners, and other similar types of biological investigations must change.

Jeffery added that the fundamental orientation of our legal system must also change to acknowledge contributions of biological criminologists, replacing or supplementing our current "right to punishment" doctrine with a "right to treatment" philosophy. Jeffery concluded his analysis by saying, "If legal and political barriers prevent us from regarding antisocial behavior as a medical problem, and if we do not permit medical research on criminal behavior, how can we ever solve the crime problem?"[192]

The dangers of too great a dependence on biological approaches to crime, however, raise the specter of an Orwellian bogeyman in charge of every aspect of human social life—from conception to the grave—and include the possible abortion of defective fetuses, capital punishment in lieu of rehabilitation, and enforced sterilization. Precedent for such fears can be found in cases like *Buck* v. *Bell*,[193] (discussed earlier), in which the U.S. Supreme Court, influenced by the genetically based perspectives of the times, sanctioned state-enforced sterilization statutes.

Potential links between race and crime, suggested by some researchers, are especially repugnant to many who criticize biological criminology, seeing it as a reemergence of the eugenics movement of the early twentieth century. Ronald Walters, a political scientist at Howard University, for example, observed that "seeking the biological and genetic aspects of violence is dangerous to African-American youth. When you consider the perception that black people have always been the violent people in this society, it is a short step from this stereotype to using this kind of research for social control."[194] University of Maryland criminologists Gary LaFree and Katheryn K. Russell stated, "A major reason for moving away from studies of differential crime rates by race, beginning in the 1960s, was to avoid negative associations between race and crime: blacks already were disadvantaged by the economy and the society. Thus, to imply that crime problems were more serious for blacks than for others seemed to be double victimization"; they added that "no group has suffered more than African-Americans by our failure to understand and control street crime."[195]

Although biological theories of crime may have problems, some criminologists believe that to ignore the potential contributions of biological theorists because of hypothetical policy consequences or because of the supposed danger of racial prejudice does a disservice to the science of criminology and denies the opportunity for compassionate and objective researchers to realistically assist in the process of crime reduction. In 1993, for example, the Youth Violence Initiative, begun under President George Bush to study problem behavior among American youth, was canceled by the Clinton administration because indications were that it might identify a disproportionate number of racial and ethnic minorities as delinquent.

In 1997, in an attempt to bring biological theorizing into the criminological mainstream, Lee Ellis and Anthony Walsh expanded on the theme of genetic predispositions, noting that "in the case of behavior, nearly all of the effects of genes are quite indirect because they are mediated through complex chains of events occurring in the brain. This means that there are almost certainly no genes for something as complex as criminal behavior. Nevertheless, many genes may affect brain functioning in ways that either increase or reduce the chances of individuals learning various complex behavior patterns, including behavior patterns that happen to be so offensive to others that criminal sanctions have been instituted to minimize their recurrence."[196]

Critiques of Biological Theories

In a critique of biological theories of crime, Nicole Hahn Rafter, a noted criminologist at Northeastern University, argued against the possible development of a contemporary eugenics movement based on the findings of modern-day genetics. In *Creating Born Criminals*, Rafter attempted to demonstrate the need for contemporary researchers and policymakers to know how eugenics reasoning worked in the past so that they would be able to recognize the dangers posed by any theory that interprets social problems in biological terms and that sees what might be innate differences as evidence of biological inferiority.[197] While genetic solutions to human problems may seem to offer a near-future panacea, Rafter warned that policymakers must always be on their guard against the danger of oversimplifying social issues as complex as crime.

Rafter's comments, however, may be more applicable to older biological theories in which biology was portrayed as having a direct and unavoidable impact on behavior; under those approaches, one's biology was one's destiny. Today's more sophisticated biological approaches to criminality stress the interaction between biology and the environment, holding that neither one fully determines behavior.

One focused critique of biological perspectives on crime causation is provided by Glenn D. Walters and Thomas W. White, who contended that "genetic research on crime has been poorly designed, ambiguously reported, and exceedingly inadequate in addressing the relevant issues."[198] Walters and White highlighted these specific shortcomings of research studies in the area of genetics:

- Few biological studies adequately conceptualize criminality. "Several studies have defined criminality on the basis of a single arrest."[199]

- Twin studies, in particular, have sometimes failed to properly establish whether a pair of twins is MZ or DZ because some MZ twins are not identical in appearance, and only a few twin studies have depended on biological testing rather than on a simple evaluation of appearances.

- Problems in estimating the degree of criminality among sample populations are rife in biological (and many other) studies of criminality. Interview data are open to interpretation, and existing statistical data on the past criminality of offenders are not always properly appreciated.

- Methodological problems abound in many studies attempting to evaluate the role of genetics in crime: lack of control groups or comparison groups, small sample sizes, dropping out of subjects from study groups, biased sampling techniques, and use of inappropriate forms of statistical analysis.

- Results obtained outside the United States may not be applicable within this country. Twin studies conducted in Sweden and Denmark provide an example of this potential lack of generalizability.

> Investigators of the link between biology and crime find themselves caught in one of the most bitter controversies to hit the scientific community in years.
>
> —*Time*

Walters and White nonetheless concluded that "genetic factors are undoubtedly correlated with various measures of criminality," adding that "the large number of methodological flaws and limitations in the research should make one cautious in drawing any causal inferences at this point in time."[200]

SUMMARY

- Biological theories of crime causation adhere to the principle that many behavioral predispositions, including aggression and criminality, are constitutionally or physiologically influenced and inherited. Early proponents of biological theories argued that at least some human behavior is the result of biological propensities inherited from more primitive developmental stages in the evolutionary process.

- According to some, human behavior is, to some degree, adapted instinctual behavior, and aggression is a form of biological inheritance from more primitive times. Aggression today may manifest as criminal behavior when environmental conditions conspire to elicit such instinctive responses.

- Some scholars have suggested that a penchant for crime may be inherited and that criminal tendencies are genetically based. Beginning in the late 1800s, researchers in the field of criminal anthropology focused on criminal families. More recently, developments in the field of genetics have led to the study of the role of chromosomes in crime causation. One of the first ideas to make use of chromosomes as an explanation for violent crime was the XYY, or supermale, notion of criminality.

- Sociobiology is a theoretical perspective developed by Edward O. Wilson that can be described as "the systematic study of the biological basis of all social behavior." Wilson believed that the primary determinant of human behavior was the need to ensure the survival and continuity of genetic material from one generation to the next. Sociobiologists often focus on explaining the violence and aggression associated with territoriality. Sociobiology has been employed to explain intergroup and intragroup aggression.

- The biosocial perspective sees the interaction between biology and environment as key to understanding human behavior, including criminality, and genetic predispositions and their interaction with the surrounding social and physical environments may combine to produce criminality. Neuroplasticity may influence and facilitate much of human behavior.

- In the past, one's biology was often seen as deterministic. The eugenics movement, Nazi extermination programs, and enforced sterilization all resulted from an inaccurate assessment of the power of genes to determine behavior. At the same time, the once widely held belief that the human organism was a blank slate at birth appears now to be a fallacy. A contemporary crime-prevention program needs to be based on modern understandings of the link between biology and crime. A medical perspective could replace the current legalistic interpretation of criminality, leading to the right to treatment for criminal offenders.

- Establishing a workable definition of criminality has been a problem. Few biological studies adequately conceptualize criminality, methodological problems have been found in many studies attempting to evaluate the role of genetics in crime, and results obtained outside the United States may not be applicable within this country. Many criminologists have concluded that while biology provides a context for human behavior, biological predispositions are overshadowed by the role of volition, mechanisms of human thought, and undeniable influences of socialization and acculturation.

KEY TERMS

adolescence-limited offender, 114

atavism, 89

behavioral genetics, 107

biological theory, 87

biopsychology, 116

biosocial criminology, 113

born criminal, 91

constitutional theory, 94

criminal anthropology, 89

criminaloid, 91

cycloid, 94

displastic, 95

dizygotic twins, 107

ectomorph, 95

endomorph, 95

eugenic criminology, 104

eugenics, 104

genetic determinism, 108

heritability, 109

hypoglycemia, 95

Juke family, 104

Kallikak family, 104

life course persister, 114

masculinity hypothesis, 91

mesomorph, 95

monozygotic twins, 107

paradigm, 111

phrenology, 89

schizoid, 94

sociobiology, 111

somatotyping, 94

supermale, 105

testosterone, 99

KEY NAMES

Charles Darwin, 88

Richard Louis Dugdale, 104

Arthur H. Estabrook, 104

Hans J. Eysenck, 115

Franz Joseph Gall, 89

Sir Francis Galton, 105

Henry Herbert Goddard, 104

Charles Buckman Goring, 91

Richard J. Herrnstein, 113

Earnest A. Hooton, 91

C. Ray Jeffery, 86

Ernst Kretschmer, 94

Cesare Lombroso, 89

Konrad Lorenz, 88

Terrie E. Moffitt, 114

William H. Sheldon, 94

Johann Gaspar Spurzheim, 89

Edward O. Wilson, 111

James Q. Wilson, 113

QUESTIONS FOR REVIEW

1. What basic principles characterize biological theories of crime causation? How do such theories differ from other perspectives that attempt to explain the same phenomena?

2. How might biological perspectives explain human aggression?

3. How strong are research findings linking genetics and crime? What have research studies in the field of genetics had to say about possible causes of crime?

4. What is sociobiology? What contributions has sociobiology made to the study of criminality?

5. How is criminality explained from a biosocial perspective?

6. What are the social policy implications of biological and biosocial theories of crime? What modern-day social policies reflect the biological and biosocial approaches to crime causation?

7. What are the shortcomings of biological theories of criminal behavior? Why have biological approaches to crime causation encountered stiff criticism?

QUESTIONS FOR REFLECTION

1. This book emphasizes the theme of social problems versus social responsibility. Which perspective is better supported by biological theories of crime causation? Why?

2. What does C. Ray Jeffery mean when he writes, "Open inquiry requires objective consideration of all points of view and an unbiased examination of each for its ability to shed light on the subject under study"? Do you agree or disagree with this assertion? Why?

CHAPTER 5
PSYCHOLOGICAL AND PSYCHIATRIC FOUNDATIONS OF CRIMINAL BEHAVIOR

LEARNING OUTCOMES

After reading this chapter, you should be able to answer the following questions:

- What are the major principles of psychological perspectives on criminal behavior?
- What were some early psychological and psychiatric theories offered to explain criminality?
- How can criminality be seen as a form of maladaptive behavior?
- How can criminality be seen as a form of adaptive behavior?
- How does the modeling theory of aggression explain how aggressive patterns of behavior, once acquired, can be activated?

- How does behavior theory explain the role of rewards and punishments in shaping behavior?
- How does attachment theory explain behavior, and what are the three forms of attachment?
- What is self-control, and how can a lack of self-control lead to crime?
- How does the legal concept of insanity differ from behavioral definitions of the same concept?
- What types of crime-control policies might be based on psychological understandings of criminality?
- What are some assumptions underlying the practice of criminal psychological profiling?

Introduction

Some crimes cry out for explanation. Shortly after midnight on July 22, 1991, a handcuffed man flagged down a police car in suburban Milwaukee.[1] Officers soon learned that the man was Tracy Edwards, a 32-year-old city resident. The lurid story of homosexual abuse and physical attack that Edwards told led investigators to the apartment of a 31-year-old loner named Jeffrey Dahmer. Dahmer was quickly arrested, and a search of his apartment revealed the body parts of at least 11 people. In a confession to police, Dahmer told of how he had repeatedly lured men and boys to his apartment, murdered them, and then dismembered their bodies. Soon police investigations implicated Dahmer in a ten-year killing spree spanning several states and possibly reaching as far as Europe. Edwards, whom Dahmer had met in a shopping mall, explained that he went to Dahmer's apartment because Dahmer "seemed so normal."[2] One of Dahmer's victims, a 15-year-old boy, had earlier been discovered by police dazed and bleeding—and was returned to Dahmer's apartment after officers concluded that the situation involved nothing but a dispute between homosexual lovers.

Dahmer pleaded insanity as a defense to charges of murder, but an expert witness at his trial, psychiatrist Park Dietz, testified that

Jeffrey Dahmer, perhaps the most infamous serial killer of the twentieth century. What explains the public's fascination with serial killers?
Source: Rosemary Jensen /*Milwaukee Journal*/SIPA Press

although Dahmer suffered from various psychological disorders, he could have chosen not to kill. Comparing Dahmer's sexual desires with someone who wants money but chooses not to rob, Dietz said, "The choice is exactly the same. The freedom to make it is exactly the same."[3] In contrasting testimony, another expert witness claimed that Dahmer "had uncontrollable urges to kill and have sex with dead bodies."[4] Dahmer was sentenced to 15 consecutive life terms—1 each for the murders of his 15 victims[5]—but was himself murdered in prison by another inmate in late 1994.

What motivates people to kill or maim or to commit other serious offenses? How can many killers seem so "normal" before exploding into criminality, giving no hints of the atrocities they are about to commit? How can a mother kill her own children and seemingly feel little or no remorse? For answers to questions like these, many people turn to psychological theories. Psychologists are the pundits of the modern age of behaviorism, offering explanations rooted in determinants lying within individual actors. Psychological determinants of deviant or criminal behavior may be couched in terms of exploitative personality characteristics, poor impulse control, emotional arousal, an immature personality, and so on. Two contemporary commentators observed that "the major sources of theoretical development in criminology have been—and continue to be—psychological. A theory of criminal conduct is weak indeed if uninformed by a general psychology of human behavior."[6] Other writers go so far as to claim that any criminal behavior is only a symptom of a more fundamental psychiatric disorder.[7]

Before beginning a discussion of psychological theories, however, it is necessary to provide a brief overview of the terminology used to describe the psychological study of crime and criminality. **Forensic psychology**, one of the fastest growing subfields of psychology, is the application of the science and profession of psychology to questions and issues relating to law and the legal system.[8] (See the Theory versus Reality box for its definition, areas of specialty, and qualifications.) Forensic psychology is sometimes referred to as **criminal psychology**, and forensic psychologists are also called "criminal psychologists," "correctional psychologists," and "police psychologists." Unlike forensic psychologists (who generally hold Ph.D.s), forensic psychiatrists are medical doctors, and **forensic psychiatry** is a branch of psychiatry having to do with the study of crime and criminality. It's practitioners apply psychiatry to the needs of crime prevention and solution, criminal rehabilitation, and issues of the criminal law.[9]

> ▨ **psychological theory**
> A theory derived from the behavioral sciences that focuses on the individual as the unit of analysis. Psychological theories place the locus of crime causation within the personality of the individual offender.

THEORY | versus REALITY
What Is Forensic Psychology?

The American Academy of Forensic Psychology defined *forensic psychology* as "the application of the science and profession of psychology to questions and issues relating to law and the legal system," including the following:

- Psychological evaluation and expert testimony regarding criminal forensic issues like trial competence, waiver of *Miranda* rights, criminal responsibility, death-penalty mitigation, battered woman syndrome, domestic violence, drug dependence, and sexual disorders

- Testimony and evaluation regarding civil issues like personal injury, child custody, employment discrimination, mental disability, product liability, professional malpractice, civil commitment, and guardianship

- Assessment, treatment, and consultation regarding individuals with a high risk for aggressive behavior in the community, in the workplace, in treatment settings, and in correctional facilities

- Research, testimony, and consultation on psychological issues affecting the legal process, such as eyewitness testimony, jury selection, children's testimony, repressed memories, and pretrial publicity

- Specialized treatment services to individuals involved with the legal system

- Consultation to lawmakers about public-policy issues with psychological implications

- Consultation and training for law enforcement, criminal justice, and correctional system personnel

- Consultation and training for mental health system practitioners on forensic issues

- Analysis of issues related to human performance, product liability, and safety

- Court-appointed monitoring of compliance with settlements in class-action suits affecting mental health or criminal justice settings

- Mediation and conflict resolution

- Policy and program development in the psychology–law arena

- Teaching, training, and supervision of graduate students, psychology and psychiatry interns/residents, and law students

Psychologists who already hold Ph.D.s and who are interested in the practice of forensic psychology may apply for certification by the American Board of Professional Psychology (ABPP), which awards a "Diplomate in Forensic Psychology" to those who function "at the highest level of excellence in his or her field of forensic competence." The diploma is generally recognized by the American judicial system as the definitive standard of professional competence in forensic psychology.

Source: Adapted with permission from the American Board of Forensic Psychology's Web page, http://www.abfp.com/brochure.asp (accessed August 5, 2010).

What is the fundamental distinguishing feature of psychological approaches as opposed to other attempts to explain behavior? Criminologists Cathy Spatz Widom and Hans Toch offered the following insight: "Theories are psychological insofar as they focus on the individual as the unit of analysis."[10] Another writer, Curt R. Bartol, defined *psychology* as "the science of behavior and mental processes"; he went on to say, "psychological criminology is the science of the behavior and mental processes of the criminal."[11]

> **Forensic psychiatry is a branch of psychiatry having to do with the study of crime and criminality.**

Major Principles of Psychological Theories

This brief section summarizes the central features of **psychological theories** of crime causation.[12] This cursory overview, however, is intended to provide more than a summary; it is meant to be a guide to the rest of this chapter.

Most psychological theories of crime causation make the following fundamental assumptions:

- The individual is the primary unit of analysis.

- Personality is the major motivational element because it is the seat of drives and the source of motives.

LIBRARY EXTRA 5-1

■ **conditioning**
A psychological principle that holds that the frequency of any behavior can be increased or decreased through reward, punishment, or association with other stimuli.

■ **psychopathy**
A personality disorder characterized by antisocial behavior and lack of affect.

- Crimes result from abnormal, dysfunctional, or inappropriate mental processes within the personality.

- Criminal behavior may be purposeful for the individual insofar as it addresses certain felt needs. Behavior can be judged "inappropriate" only when measured against external criteria purporting to establish normality.

- *Normality* is generally defined by social consensus (what the majority of people in any social group agree is "real," appropriate, or typical).

- Defective, or abnormal, mental processes may have a variety of causes, including a diseased mind, inappropriate learning or improper conditioning, the emulation of inappropriate role models, and poor adjustment to inner conflicts.

Early Psychological Theories

Twin threads ran through early psychological theories and constituted the early field of psychological criminology. One strand emphasized behavioral **conditioning**; the other focused mostly on personality disturbances and diseases of the mind. The concept of conditioned behavior was popularized through the work of Russian physiologist Ivan Pavlov (1849–1936), whose work with dogs won the Nobel Prize in physiology and medicine in 1904. The dogs, which salivated when food was presented to them, were always fed in the presence of a ringing bell. Soon, the dogs salivated when the bell alone was rung—no food was present. Hence, Pavlov demonstrated that animal behavior could be predictably altered via association with external changes arising from the environment surrounding the organism.

> The concept of conditioned behavior was popularized through the work of Russian physiologist Ivan Pavlov.

The Psychopath

The other thread winding its way through early psychological theories was that of mental disease, or **psychopathy**. Psychologists and psychiatrists distinguish between the terms *psychopathology* and *psychopathy*. In the psychological literature, the word *psychopathology* "refers to any sort of psychological disorder that causes distress either for the individual or for those in the individual's life."[13] Depression, schizophrenia, attention deficit/hyperactivity disorder, alcoholism, and bulimia can all be considered forms of psychopathology. The term *psychopathy* "refers to a very specific and distinctive type of psychopathology"[14]—a personality disorder characterized by antisocial behavior and a lack of feelings, especially empathy for or sensitivity to others.

The concept of psychopathy, called "one of the most durable, resilient and influential of all criminological ideas,"[15] may have evolved from the work of French physician Philippe Pinel (1745–1826), who described a form of "insanity without delirium." The concept is summarized in the words of Nolan D. C. Lewis, who wrote that "the criminal, like other people, has lived a life of instinctive drives, of desires, of wishes, of feelings, but one in which his intellect has apparently functioned less effectually as a brake upon certain trends. His constitutional makeup deviates toward the abnormal, leading him into conflicts with the laws of society and its cultural patterns."[16] Learn more at **Library Extra 5–1**.

The term *psychopathy* comes from the Greek words *psyche* (meaning "soul" or "mind") and *pathos* ("suffering" or "illness"). The word, which appears to have been coined by German

Marc Hauser, professor of psychology and biological anthropology at Harvard University. Hauser, who says that we instinctually know right from wrong, also directs the university's Cognitive Evolution Laboratory. Do you believe that we naturally know right from wrong, or is the difference between right and wrong something that we learn?
Source: John Soares

psychopath
An individual who has a personality disorder, especially one manifested in aggressively antisocial behavior, and who is lacking in empathy; also called *sociopath*.

sociopath
An individual who has a personality disorder, especially one manifested in aggressively antisocial behavior, and who is lacking in empathy; also called *psychopath*.

neurologist Richard von Krafft-Ebing (1840–1902),[17] made its way into English psychiatric literature through the writings of Polish-born American psychiatrist Bernard H. Glueck (1884–1972)[18] and British psychiatrist William Healy (1869–1963).[19] The **psychopath**, also called a **sociopath**, has been historically viewed as perversely cruel, often without thought or feeling for his or her victims.[20]

The concept of a psychopathic personality, which by its very definition is asocial, was fully developed by Georgian neuropsychiatrist **Hervey M. Cleckley** in his important 1941 book *The Mask of Sanity*.[21] He described the psychopath as a "moral idiot," as one who does not feel empathy with others even though that person may be fully cognizant of what is objectively happening around him or her. The central defining characteristic of a psychopath came to be "poverty of affect," or the inability to accurately imagine how others think and feel, so it becomes possible for a psychopath to inflict pain and engage in cruelty without appreciation for the victim's suffering. In *The Mask of Sanity*, Cleckley described numerous characteristics of the psychopathic personality:

- Superficial charm and "good intelligence"
- Absence of delusions, hallucinations, or other signs of psychosis
- Absence of nervousness or psychoneurotic manifestations
- Inability to feel guilt or shame
- Unreliability
- Chronic lying
- Ongoing antisocial behavior
- Poor judgment and inability to learn from experience
- Self-centeredness and incapacity to love
- Unresponsiveness in general interpersonal relations
- Impersonal, trivial, and poorly integrated sex life
- Failure to follow any life plan

Cleckley stated that "psychopathy was defined by a constellation of dysfunctional psychological processes as opposed to specific behavioral manifestations."[22] Even though psychopaths have a seriously flawed personality, they can easily fool others into trusting them—hence the title of Cleckley's book.

According to Cleckley, indicators of psychopathy appear early in life, often in the teenage years, and include lying, fighting, stealing, and vandalizing. Even earlier signs may be found, according to some authors, in bed-wetting, cruelty to animals, sleepwalking, and fire setting.[23]

A definitive modern measure of psychopathy can be found in the Psychopathy Checklist (PCL), developed by Robert Hare.[24] This series of ratings by qualified experts using information from subject interviews and official records assesses degree of psychopathy using two kinds of indicators: affective and interpersonal traits (glibness, emotional detachment, egocentricity, superficial charm, shallow affect) and traits associated with a chronic unstable and antisocial lifestyle (irresponsibility, impulsivity, criminality, proneness to boredom).[25] Hence, psychopathy has both emotional and behavioral components.

A 2004 study of eight Canadian maximum-security male prisoners classified as psychopaths according to the PCL found that the men were not only impaired emotionally but also unable to efficiently process abstract words, perform abstract categorization tasks, understand metaphors, and process emotionally weighted words and speech.[26] During a test on abstract concepts, the men's brains were scanned using functional magnetic resonance imaging (fMRI), and scans showed that a section of each of their brains did not activate as it should have. The researchers concluded that their findings "support the hypothesis that there is an abnormality in the function of the right anterior superior temporal gyrus in psychopathy."[27] Other studies in neurobiology have linked this part of the brain with abstract problem solving and insight.[28] Deficiencies in this part of the brain may also be associated with autism and the development of childhood schizophrenia.[29]

Some have questioned whether psychopaths merely lack empathy or really don't know the difference between right and wrong. Recent research by Harvard professor and director of the Cognitive Evolution Laboratory at Harvard Marc Hauser seems to show that the ability to tell right from wrong is something that human beings are born with, that the human brain is hard-wired to make moral distinctions, and that the same distinctions tend to be made across cultures. "The question," explained Hauser, "is whether emotions are causally necessary for moral judgment. Take psychopaths: we know they have some kind of emotional deficit because they don't seem to feel remorse or empathy for their victims. Does this deficit corrupt their moral judgment because emotions are necessary to make the right decision? Or is their moral judgment actually intact, but their behavior is screwed up because their emotions don't stop them from doing the wrong thing? My guess is the latter—that emotions flow from moral judgments and control behavior."[30] You can test your own

WEB EXTRA 5–1
WEB EXTRA 5–2
LIBRARY EXTRA 5–2
LIBRARY EXTRA 5–3

■ **antisocial (asocial) personality**
An individual who is unsocialized and whose behavior pattern brings him or her into repeated conflict with society.

■ **antisocial personality disorder (ASPD)**
A psychological condition exhibited by individuals who are basically unsocialized and whose behavior pattern brings them repeatedly into conflict with society.

■ **electroencephalogram (EEG)**
The electrical measurement of brain wave activity.

sense of right and wrong by taking the Moral Sense Test (MST) online. The MST, which researchers are using to detail the nature of moral psychology, is accessible through Harvard University's Cognitive Evolution Laboratory online at **Web Extra 5–1**.

Traditionally, psychopathology has been regarded as difficult or impossible to treat. But a 2006 study of adolescent psychopaths found that "youth with psychopathic features who received intensive treatment had significantly lower rates of violent recidivism and a longer time to rearrest for violent behavior" than those who received treatment in a typical juvenile correctional facility.[31] In 2007, the United Kingdom launched an unprecedented treatment and research program focused on "Dangerous People with Severe Personality Disorder" (DPSPD).[32] To be eligible, participants had to be diagnosed with a severe personality disorder, and there had to be a demonstrable link between that disorder and the risk of violent offending. Some stated that the program "holds the best chance yet of showing whether violent psychopaths can be reformed." Learn more about the concept of the psychopath as a clinical construct by visiting the Society for Research in Psychopathology via **Web Extra 5–2**. Read about the issues involved in identifying criminal psychopaths via **Library Extras 5–2** and **5–3**.

Antisocial Personality Disorder

In the attempt to identify sociopathic individuals, some psychologists started to place greater emphasis on the type of behavior exhibited rather than on identifiable personality traits. By 1968, the American Psychiatric Association (APA) had completely discontinued using the words *sociopath* and *psychopath* in its *Diagnostic and Statistical Manual of Mental Disorders*, replacing them with the terms *antisocial* and *asocial personality*.[33] In that year, the APA manual changed to a description of **antisocial (asocial) personality** types as "individuals who are basically unsocialized and whose behavior pattern brings them repeatedly into conflicts with society. They are incapable of significant loyalty to individuals, groups, or social

> Individuals exhibiting an antisocial personality are said to be suffering from antisocial personality disorder.

values. They are grossly selfish, callous, irresponsible, impulsive, and unable to feel guilt or to learn from experience and punishment. Frustration tolerance is low. They tend to blame others or offer plausible rationalization for their behavior."[34] In most cases, individuals exhibiting an antisocial personality are said to be suffering from **antisocial personality disorder (ASPD)** (sometimes referred to in clinical circles as APD or ANPD).

The World Health Organization, in its *Classification of Mental and Behavioral Disorders*, described ASPD this way:

> [It is a] personality disorder usually coming to attention because of a gross disparity between behavior and the prevailing social norms, [which is] characterized by at least three of the following: (a) callous unconcern for the feelings of others; (b) gross and persistent attitude of irresponsibility and disregard for social norms, rules and obligations; (c) incapacity to maintain enduring relationships, though having no difficulty in establishing them; (d) very low tolerance to frustration and a low threshold for discharge of aggression, including violence; (e) incapacity to experience guilt and to profit from experience, particularly punishment; [and] (f) marked proneness to blame others, or to offer plausible rationalizations, for the behavior that has brought the patient into conflict with society.[35]

Other features of ASPD have been identified as lack of empathy, inflated and arrogant self-appraisal, and glib, superficial charm.[36]

Individuals manifesting the characteristics of ASPD are likely to run afoul of the law. As one writer stated, "The impulsivity and aggression, the selfishness in achieving one's own immediate needs, and the disregard for society's rules and laws bring these people to the attention of the criminal justice system."[37] Individuals who score high on psychological inventories designed to measure degree of psychopathy have been found to exhibit high rates of both criminality and recidivism;[38] psychopaths who have also been diagnosed as schizophrenics display even higher levels of criminality.[39]

The causes of ASPD are unclear. Somatogenic causes (those based on physiological features) are said to include a malfunctioning of the central nervous system, which is characterized by a low state of arousal driving the sufferer to seek excitement, and brain abnormalities, which may have been present since birth. Some studies show that an **electroencephalogram (EEG)** taken of an individual diagnosed as having ASPD is frequently abnormal, reflecting

THEORY | in PERSPECTIVE
Types of Psychological and Psychiatric Theories

Psychological and psychiatric theories of criminology are derived from the behavioral sciences and focus on the individual as the unit of analysis.

Psychiatric Criminology

This approach envisions a complex set of drives and motives operating from recesses deep within the personality to determine behavior; it is also known as *forensic psychiatry*.

Period: 1930s–present

Theorists: Hervey M. Cleckley, many others

Concepts: Psychopath, sociopath, antisocial and asocial personality

Psychoanalytic Criminology

This psychiatric approach, developed by Austrian psychiatrist Sigmund Freud, emphasizes the role of personality in human behavior and sees deviant behavior as the result of dysfunctional personalities.

Period: 1920s–present

Theorists: Sigmund Freud, others

Concepts: Id, ego, superego, sublimation, psychotherapy, Thanatos, neurosis, psychosis, schizophrenia, the Oedipus complex

Frustration–Aggression Theory

Frustration is a natural consequence of living and a root cause of crime in this theory, and criminal behavior can be a form of adaptation when it results in stress reduction.

Period: 1940s–present

Theorists: J. Dollard, Albert Bandura, Richard H. Walters, S. L. Halleck

Concepts: Frustration, aggression, displacement, catharsis, alloplastic and autoplastic adaptation

Modeling Theory

This theory states that people learn how to behave by modeling themselves after others whom they have the opportunity to observe.

Period: 1950s–present

Theorists: Gabriel Tarde, Albert Bandura, others

Concepts: Imitation, interpersonal aggression, modeling, disengagement

Behavior Theory

A psychological perspective, this theory posits that individual behavior that is rewarded will increase in frequency while that which is punished will decrease.

Period: 1940s–present

Theorists: B. F. Skinner, others

Concepts: Operant behavior, conditioning, stimulus–response, reward, punishment

Self-Control Theory

This approach sees the root cause of crime as a person's inability to exercise socially appropriate controls over him- or herself.

Period: 1940s–present

Theorists: Michael R. Gottfredson, Travis Hirschi, Harold G. Grasmick

Concepts: Self-control, general theory, criminal opportunity

"a malfunction of some inhibitory mechanisms" that makes it unlikely that someone characterized by ASPD will "learn to inhibit behavior that is likely to lead to punishment."[40] It is difficult, however, to diagnose ASPD through physiological measurements because similar EEG patterns show up in patients with other types of disorders. Psychogenic causes (those rooted in early interpersonal experiences) include inability to form attachments to parents or other caregivers early in life, sudden separation from the mother during the first six months of life, and other forms of insecurity during the first few years of life. In short, a lack of love or the sensed inability to unconditionally depend upon one central loving figure (typically the mother in most psychological literature) immediately following birth is often posited as a major psychogenic factor contributing to the development of ASPD.

Most studies of ASPD have involved male subjects. Only rarely have researchers focused on women with antisocial personalities, and it is believed that only a small proportion of those afflicted with ASPD are women.[41] What little research there is suggests that females with ASPD possess many of the same definitive characteristics as their male counterparts and that they assume their antisocial roles at similarly early ages.[42] The lifestyles of antisocial females, however, appear to include sexual misconduct and abnormally high levels of sexual activity, but such research can be misleading because the cultural expectations of female sexual behavior inherent in early studies may not always have been in keeping with reality, that is, early researchers may have had so little accurate information about female sexual activity that the behavior of women judged to possess antisocial personalities may have actually been far closer to the norm than originally believed.

More recent studies that attempted to classify criminal offenders by type of mental disorder have determined that ASPD characterizes 46.6% of all inmates; schizophrenics, 6.3%; manic-depressives, 1.6%; drug-disordered persons, 18.6%; depressed individuals, 8.1%; and alcohol abuse–related sufferers, 33.1%.[43] A review of 20 such studies found great variation in the degree and type of disorders said to be prevalent among incarcerated

WEB EXTRA 5–3
WEB EXTRA 5–4

■ **psychiatric criminology**
A theory that is derived from the medical sciences (including neurology) and that, like other psychological theories, focuses on the individual as the unit of analysis. Psychiatric theories form the basis of psychiatric criminology.

■ **psychoanalysis**
The theory of human psychology founded by Sigmund Freud on the concepts of the unconscious, resistance, repression, sexuality, and the Oedipus complex.

■ **psychotherapy**
A form of psychiatric treatment based on psychoanalytical principles and techniques.

offenders.[44] The studies categorized 0.5% to 26% of all inmates as psychotic, 2.4% to 28% as mentally subnormal, 5.6% to 70% as ASPD, 2% to 7.9% as neurotic, and 11% to 80% as suffering from mental disorders induced by alcoholism or excessive drinking. Such studies usually concluded that few convicted felons are free of mental impairment of one sort or another.

Learn more about ASPD at the National Library of Medicine via **Web Extra 5–3**; possible forms of treatment for the disorder can be found at **Web Extra 5–4**.

Early Psychiatric Theories

Psychological criminology, with its historical dual emphasis on early forces shaping personality and conditioned behavior, can be distinguished from **psychiatric criminology** (also called *forensic psychiatry*), which envisions a complex set of drives and motives operating from hidden recesses deep within the personality to determine behavior. Psychiatrist David Abrahamsen explained crime this way: "Antisocial behavior is a direct expression of an aggression or may be a direct or indirect manifestation of a distorted erotic drive. Crime may be considered a product of a person's tendencies and the situation of the moment interacting with his mental resistance."[45] The key questions to be answered by psychiatric criminology, according to Abrahamsen, are "What creates the criminal impulse?" and "What stimulates and gives it direction?" A later forensic psychiatrist answered the questions this way: "Every criminal is such by reason of unconscious forces within him."[46] Forensic psychiatry explains crime as being caused by biological and subconscious psychological urges that are mediated through consciousness; little significance is placed on the environment after the first few formative years of life. Psychiatric theories are derived from the medical sciences, including neurology, and focus on the individual as the unit of analysis.

> Psychiatric criminology envisions a complex set of drives and motives operating from hidden recesses deep within the personality to determine behavior.

Criminal Behavior as Maladaptation

The Psychoanalytic Perspective

Perhaps the best-known psychiatrist of all time is **Sigmund Freud** (1856–1939), who coined the term **psychoanalysis** in 1896 and based an entire theory of human behavior on it. From the point of view of psychoanalysis, criminal behavior is maladaptive, the product of inadequacies inherent in the offender's personality. Significant inadequacies may result in full-blown mental illness, which in itself can be a direct cause of crime. The psychoanalytic perspective encompasses diverse notions like personality, neurosis, and psychosis and more specific concepts like transference, sublimation, repression, and the Oedipus complex (the desire to have sexual intercourse with the parent of the opposite sex and to kill the parent of the same sex). **Psychotherapy** is the attempt to relieve patients of their mental disorders through the application of psychoanalytic principles and techniques.

According to Freud, the personality is made up of three components: the id, the ego, and the superego (see Figure 5–1).

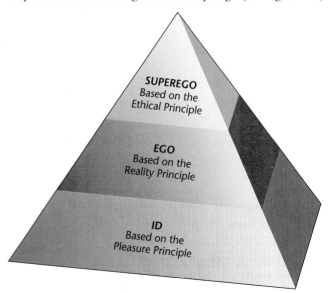

FIGURE 5–1 | The Psychoanalytic Structure of Personality

■ **id**
The aspect of the personality from which drives, wishes, urges, and desires emanate. More formally, this division of the psyche is associated with instinctual impulses and demands for immediate satisfaction of primitive needs.

■ **ego**
The reality-testing part of the personality; also called the *reality principle*. More formally, this personality component is conscious, most immediately controls behavior, and is most in touch with external reality.

■ **superego**
The moral aspect of the personality, much like the conscience. More formally, this division of the psyche develops by the incorporation of the perceived moral standards of the community, is mainly unconscious, and includes the conscience.

■ **sublimation**
The psychological process whereby one aspect of consciousness comes to be symbolically substituted for another.

■ **Thanatos**
A death wish.

The **id** is the fundamental aspect of the personality from which drives, wishes, urges, and desires emanate and operates according to the pleasure principle, seeking full and immediate gratification of its needs. From the Freudian perspective, we carry within our id the prerequisite motivation for criminal behavior—we are all potential murderers, sexual aggressors, and thieves, and our drives and urges are kept in check only by other controlling aspects of our personalities.

A second component of the personality, the **ego**, is primarily charged with reality testing. (Freud's use of the word *ego* should not be confused with popular usage, whereby a person might talk about an "inflated ego" or an "egotistical person.") For Freud, the ego is primarily concerned with how objectives might be best accomplished and effects strategies that maximize pleasure and minimize pain, laying out various paths of action for wish fulfillment, but the ego inherently recognizes that it may be necessary to delay gratification to achieve a more fulfilling long-term goal.

The **superego**, the third component of the personality, is like a moral guide to right and wrong. If properly developed, it assays the ego's plans, dismissing some as morally inappropriate while accepting others as ethically viable. When the dictates of the superego are not followed, feelings of guilt may result. The superego also contains what Freud called the "ego-ideal" (a symbolic representation of what society values), which differs from the conscience in that it is less forceful in controlling behavior in the absence of the likelihood of discovery.

Although Freud wrote little about crime per se, he did spend much of his time attempting to account for a variety of abnormal behaviors, many of which might lead to violations of the criminal law. One way in which a person might be led into crime is as the result of a poorly developed superego: His or her mind is left to fall back on the ego's reality-testing ability, and the ego, operating without a moral guide, may select a path of action that, although expedient at the time, violates the law. Individuals suffering from poor superego development are likely to seek immediate gratification without giving much thought to the long-term consequences.

Freud held that many outstanding accomplishments of the human species are due to **sublimation** (the psychological process whereby one item of consciousness is symbolically substituted for another), when powerful sexual and aggressive drives

Sigmund Freud (1856–1939) examining a manuscript in the office of his Vienna home, circa 1930. How have Freud's theories influenced contemporary criminology?
Source: CORBIS-NY

are channeled into socially constructive activity, but that inadequate sublimation can be another cause of crime. For example, a man may hate his mother, his hatred being perhaps the faulty by-product of the striving for adult independence. If he is unable to give voice to that hatred directly, he may act out this hatred by attacking other women whom he symbolically substitutes in his mind for his mother. Sublimation, like many other psychoanalytical concepts, is a slippery idea. Mother hatred, for example, is difficult to demonstrate, and the link between such hidden feelings and adult action is impossible to prove.

Freud also postulated the existence of a death instinct, which he called **Thanatos**. According to Freud, all living things have a fundamental desire to descend into an inanimate state, or death. Living takes energy and cunning; death, at least at some level, is an easier choice because it releases the organism from the need for continued expenditure of energy. Thanatos was seen as

▓ **neurosis**
A functional disorder of the mind or of the emotions involving anxiety, phobia, or other abnormal behavior.

▓ **psychosis**
A form of mental illness in which sufferers are said to be out of touch with reality.

contributing to many advances of the human species because if there was no wish to die at some instinctual level, according to Freud, few people would have the courage to take risks, and without risks, little progress would be possible in any sphere of life. An innate death wish has been used to explain why some offenders seem to behave in ways that ensure their eventual capture—serial killers sending taunting messages to the police, terrorists telling the media of their planned activities or taking credit for public attacks, rapists "accidentally" leaving their wallets at the scene, and burglars breaking into occupied dwellings.

> Sublimation is the psychological process whereby one item of consciousness is symbolically substituted for another.

From the Freudian perspective, **neurosis** is a minor form of mental illness. Neurotic individuals are in touch with reality but may find themselves anxious, fearful of certain situations, or unable to help themselves; fear of heights, compulsive hand washing, and eating disorders are examples. Most neuroses do not lead to crime, but some can. In 1991, for example, Stephen Blumberg of Des Moines, Iowa, was sentenced in federal court to nearly six years in prison and fined $200,000 for the theft of more than 21,000 rare books from hundreds of libraries.[47] Blumberg, whose compulsive interest in rare books began with yard sales and searches in trash receptacles, may have seen himself as being involved in a messianic mission to preserve recorded history. Well-heeled individuals may be manifesting a compulsive neurosis when a powerful need to steal drives them to risk arrest and jail by shoplifting.

Freudian theory was very popular during the middle part of the twentieth century, but by the 1980s, the notions of ego and id were considered antiquated by most psychiatrists. Attention shifted to the study of chemical imbalances in the brain, and psychopharmacology supplemented—if not replaced—the earlier ideas of Freud and his followers. Marti Olsen Laney, a neuroscience researcher in Portland, Oregon, found that the brains of introverted children functioned somewhat differently from those of extroverts. Brain scans of introverted kids found much more overall activity—especially in the brain's frontal lobes, which are areas associated with problem solving, introspection, complex thinking, and planning.[48]

The field of psychiatry has seen a rekindling of interest in Freudian psychology, however, because psychopharmacology (the use of drugs to treat psychiatric symptoms and disorders) has been unable to provide an alternative grand theory of personality, emotion, and motivation.[49] Moreover, today's neuroscientists are busily creating a chemical map of the mind that seems to validate the general sketch that Freud provided decades ago, and soon a new unified perspective that reconciles the work of neurologists and psychiatrists may emerge. The recognition of just such a possibility prompted Eric R. Kandel of Columbia University, the 2000 Nobel laureate in physiology and medicine, to say that psychoanalysis is "still the most coherent and intellectually satisfying view of the mind."[50] Read more about the life and work of Sigmund Freud at **Library Extra 5–4**.

The Psychotic Offender

For many law-abiding citizens, extreme forms of criminal behavior are often difficult to understand, as the gruesome story of Gary Heidnik illustrates.[51] At his double-murder trial in 1988, Heidnik claimed insanity after he admittedly killed two women and tortured four others.

A jury rejected Heidnik's claim of insanity and convicted him on two charges of first-degree murder, and he was executed in July 1999. Assistant District Attorney Charles Gallagher, who prosecuted Heidnik, called the case one of the most complicated he has ever taken to court. "He's an evil man and he did evil things. That's what the death penalty is for."

Some seemingly inexplicable forms of criminality may be the result of **psychosis**. Neurotic individuals often face only relatively minor problems in living. Psychotic people are out of touch with reality in some fundamental way, possibly suffering from hallucinations, delusions, or other breaks with reality. Psychoses may be either organic (resulting from physical damage to or abnormalities in the brain) or functional (having no known physical cause). Canadian criminologist Gwynn Nettler said, "Thought disorder is the hallmark of psychosis. People are called crazy when, at some extremity, they cannot 'think straight.'"[52] She identified three characteristics of psychotic individuals: "(1) a grossly distorted conception of reality, (2) moods, and swings of mood, that seem inappropriate to circumstance, and (3) marked inefficiency in getting along with others and caring for oneself."[53] Psychotics have also been classified as schizophrenic or paranoid schizophrenic.

■ **schizophrenic**
A mentally ill individual who is out of touch with reality and who suffers from disjointed thinking.

■ **paranoid schizophrenic**
A schizophrenic individual who suffers from delusions and hallucinations.

Gary Heidnik (left), executed by the Commonwealth of Pennsylvania in 1999. Heidnik wanted to die for his crimes. Should he have been executed? Was he insane?
Source: AP Photo/George Widman

Schizophrenics are characterized by disordered or disjointed thinking, in which the types of logical associations they make are atypical of other people; **paranoid schizophrenics** suffer from delusions and hallucinations.

Unfortunately, psychiatrists have not been able to agree on definitive criteria for schizophrenia that would allow for convenient application of the term. One prominent psychiatrist wrote about "how varying schizophrenia may appear, ranging from no striking symptoms at all to conspicuous psychotic features. Thus on the surface the schizophrenic may appear normal and, to some extent, lead a conventional life."[54] The same author later explained, "Schizophrenia is not a clearly defined disease. It is characterized rather by a kind of alteration of thinking or feeling."[55] Schizophrenia is a disorganization of the personality, and in its most extreme form, it may manifest itself in seemingly irrational behavior as well as hallucinations and delusions.

Psychoses may lead to crime in a number of ways. Following the Vietnam War, for example, several American soldiers suffering from a kind of battlefield psychosis killed friends and family members, thinking they were Vietcong soldiers (the enemy). These men, who had been traumatized by battlefield experiences in Southeast Asia, relived their past on American streets. In other crimes committed by psychotics, thought disorders may be less obvious or may exist only temporarily.

Link between Frustration and Aggression

In his early writings, Freud suggested that aggressive behavior is a natural response to frustration and limitations imposed upon a person. The frustration–aggression thesis was later developed more fully in the writings of J. Dollard, Albert Bandura, Richard H. Walters, and others. Dollard's frustration–aggression theory held that although frustration can lead to various forms of behavior—including regression, sublimation, and aggressive fantasy—direct aggression toward others is its most likely consequence.[56] Because everyone suffers frustration at times in life (beginning with weaning and toilet training), aggression is a natural consequence of living, but that aggression can be manifested in socially acceptable ways (contact sports, military or law enforcement careers, simple verbal attacks) and/or engaged in vicariously by observing others who are acting violently (in movies, on television, in fiction). Dollard applied the psychoanalytical term *displacement* to the type of violence that is vented on something or someone who is not the source of the original frustration and suggested that satisfying one's aggressive urges via observation was a form of "catharsis."

The story of Paul Calden, a former insurance company executive, provides an example of the frustration–aggression theory applied to real-life crime. In January 1993, the 33-year-old Calden, carrying a 9mm semiautomatic handgun, opened fire on his former bosses in the Island Center Cafe in Tampa, Florida, killing three and injuring two others. Calden went up to the table where the five were eating, showed them the gun, shouted, "This is what you get for firing me!" and pulled the trigger.[57] He had been let go from his position as an underwriter with Fireman's Fund Insurance Company in March 1992. Calden then killed himself.

Some psychologists have tried to identify what it is that causes some individuals to displace aggression or to experience it vicariously (through catharsis) while others respond violently and directly toward the immediate source of their frustrations. Andrew F. Henry and James F. Short, Jr., for example, suggested that child-rearing practices are a major determining factor in such a causal nexus.[58] Restrictive parents who both punish and love their children, said Henry and Short, will engender in their

Follow the author's tweets about the latest crime and justice news at http://twitter.com/schmalleger.

children the ability to suppress outward expressions of aggression, but when one parent punishes and the other loves, or when both punish but neither shows love, children can be expected to show anger directly and perhaps even immediately because they will not be threatened with the loss of love. Physical punishment rarely threatens the loss of love, and children so punished cannot be expected to refrain from direct displays of anger.

In 1960, Stewart Palmer studied murderers and their siblings to determine the degree of frustration to which they had been exposed as children.[59] He found that male murderers had experienced much more frustration than their brothers and that more than twice as many frustrating experiences—ranging from difficult births to serious illnesses, childhood beatings, severe toilet training, and negative school experiences—were reported by the murderers than by their law-abiding siblings.

Crime as Adaptive Behavior

Some psychiatric perspectives have held that "crime is a compromise, representing for the individual the most satisfactory method of adjustment to inner conflicts which he cannot express otherwise. Thus, his acting out the crime fulfills a certain aim or purpose."[60] One pressing need of many criminals, according to psychiatric theory, is the need to be punished, which arises from a sense of guilt. Psychiatrists who suggest that the need to be punished is a motivating factor in some criminal behavior are quick to point out that this need may be a closely guarded secret, unknown even to the offender, because many drives, motives, and wishes are unconscious or repressed by people who harbor them. (Repression occurs when the mind chooses to keep certain aspects of itself out of consciousness, possibly because of shame, self-loathing, or a simple lack of adequate introspection—but the desire for punishment sometimes comes to the fore.) In 1993, for example, Westley Alan Dodd was hanged by authorities in Washington State for the kidnapping, rape, and murder of three little boys four years earlier. Dodd, who said he had molested dozens of children over the course of a decade, sought the death penalty after he was convicted, saying he deserved to die and

> The need to be punished is a motivating factor in some criminal behavior.

Westley Alan Dodd, hanged in 1993 in Washington State for murdering young boys whom he molested. "People need to know it's the only thing that will stop me," he said of his execution. Might there have been some other alternative?
Source: Benjamin Benschneider/*Seattle Times*

vowing to sue the American Civil Liberties Union or anyone else who sought to save him.[61]

Crime can be adaptive in other ways, such as an adaptation to life's stresses. According to Seymour L. Halleck, a psychiatrist and adjunct professor of law at the University of North Carolina–Chapel Hill, turning to crime can provide otherwise disenfranchised individuals with a sense of power and purpose.[62] In Halleck's words, "During the planning and execution of a criminal act the offender is a free man. The value of this brief taste of freedom cannot be overestimated. Many of the criminal's apparently unreasonable actions are efforts to find a moment of autonomy."[63]

■ **alloplastic adaptation**
A form of adjustment that results from changes in the
environment surrounding an individual.

■ **autoplastic adaptation**
A form of adjustment that results from changes within an
individual.

When the choice of crime reduces stresses that the
individual faces by producing changes in the environment
(empowerment), it is referred to as **alloplastic adaptation**.
When crime leads to stress reduction as a result of internal
changes in beliefs, value systems, and so forth, it is called
autoplastic adaptation. The offender who is able to deny
responsibility for other failures by turning to crime is said to
be seeking autoplastic adaptation. Because other forms of
behavior may also meet the same needs as crime does, Halleck
pointed out, individuals may choose crime only when no reasonable alternatives are available or when criminal behavior
has inherent advantages, as under instances of economic or
social oppression; for example, individuals who are actively dis-
criminated against may find personal and political significance
in violating the laws of the oppressing society.

From Halleck's point of view, crime "has many advantages
even when considered independently of the criminal's conscious
or unconscious needs for gratification."[64] Even though crime can
be immediately rewarding or intensely pleasureful, such a reward
is more like a "fringe benefit"; its central significance is that it "is
an action which helps one survive with dignity."[65] Halleck
explained that "we cannot understand the criminal unless we
appreciate that his actions are much more than an effort to find
a specific gratification."[66]

In another approach to stress as a causative agent in crime commission, Arnold S. Linsky, Ronet Bachman, and Murray A. Straus
suggested that stress may lead to aggression toward others and
toward oneself (self-destructive behavior like suicide, smoking, and
abuse of alcohol).[67] Linsky and his colleagues measured stress at the
societal level, arguing that although the relationship between stress
and aggression has been studied at the individual level, "the neglect
of social stress as an explanation for society-to-society differences in
aggression may be partially due to a lack of an objective means
of comparing the stressfulness of life in different societies."[68]
Concluding that societal stress levels heighten levels of aggression,
the authors suggested that social policies should be created to
reduce the impact of such stressful events as having to stop work,
foreclosing on a mortgage, and dropping out of school.

People's perceptions vary, so although criminal behavior
may appear to be a valid choice for some individuals who are
seeking viable responses to perceived stresses and oppression,
their perceptions may not be wholly accurate. Misperceived
stress and oppression may lead to crime even when far simpler
solutions may be found in a more realistic appraisal of a
situation.

Modeling Theory

On December 1, 1997, 14-year-old Michael Carneal walked up
to a student prayer group in his Kentucky high school and
opened fire with a .22-caliber pistol. Like a trained marksman, he
squeezed off eight shots, killing three students and wounding five
others. Lieutenant Colonel Dave Grossman, a retired Army
Ranger and former West Point assistant professor of psychology,
was amazed at the accuracy of Carneal's shooting. "He got eight
hits on eight different targets, five of them head shots, [a] truly,
truly stunning" feat of marksmanship.[69]

Grossman reviewed Carneal's psychiatric records and found
that the teenager had spent hundreds of hours playing violent
computer games (including *Quake, Redneck Rampage*, and
Resident Evil) for months before the shooting. Grossman called
the games "hypnotic murder simulators," likening them to military combat-training programs. "This boy was doing exactly
what he was drilled to do. [Young men like Carneal] play these
video games not twice a year, but hours every night, and they
shoot every living creature in sight until they run out of bullets
or run out of targets."[70]

Do violent computer games lead to violent crime? While the
jury is still out on that question, some courts have acted to ensure
the continued availability of such software. In 2009, for example,
the Ninth U.S. Circuit of Appeals ruled that a California law that
sought to ban the sale or rental of violent video games to minors
was unconstitutional.[71]

While the court looked at the constitutionality of a single
state statute, it largely ignored the broader significance of imitation and modeling in shaping behavior. One of the earliest
attempts to explain crime and deviance as learned behavior can
be found in the work of Gabriel Tarde (1843–1904), a French social theorist who discounted the biological theories of Lombroso
and others so prevalent in his day and suggested that it was possible to infer certain laws that appeared to govern the social
world. The basis of any society, Tarde believed, was imitation, and
he developed a theory of human behavior built on three laws of
imitation and suggestion.[72] Tarde's first law held that individuals
in close intimate contact with one another tend to imitate each
other's behavior (children tend to imitate their parents). His
second law stated that imitation moves from the top down (poor
people tend to imitate wealthy people, youngsters tend to emulate older people). The third law was the law of insertion, meaning that new acts and behaviors tend to either reinforce or replace
old ones (the music of each generation replaces the music of the

■ **modeling theory**
A form of social learning theory that asserts that people learn
how to act by observing others.   LIBRARY EXTRA 5–5

WHO'S TO BLAME—The Individual or Society?

The Video Game Killer

In early 2011, 17-year-old Jason Sutter was pulled over in a small Midwestern town for various traffic offenses, including going 70 mph in a 35-mph zone, running a red light, failing to yield for a blue light and siren, and driving recklessly. When officers discovered that he didn't have a driver's license, Sutter was handcuffed, briefly searched, placed in the back of a patrol car, and driven to the local police station for booking.

After he was photographed and fingerprinted, detective Joe Lockman sat down with him in a small interrogation room. Lockman, a 25-year veteran of the force, was working late and was in the station at 2:00 A.M. when Sutter arrived. The building was nearly empty, so Lockman decided to remove Sutter's handcuffs for what he hoped would be an informal chat. Sutter, who stood only 5 feet 4 inches tall and weighed 135 pounds, reminded Lockman of his son, and the detective hoped that he could teach the boy something about right and wrong.

As Lockman leaned forward to unshackle Sutter, a number of unfortunate details came together with deadly results. Sutter was a high school dropout and video game fanatic who spent most of his waking hours playing violence-themed games—including three in which the "heroes" killed pursuing police officers. Sutter had been improperly handcuffed with his hands in front, giving him easy access to Lockman's service revolver. Lockman carried an older model .38-caliber revolver (instead of a 9mm semiautomatic pistol), which was loaded with deadly hollow-point ammunition and did not have a safety. When Sutter grabbed the weapon, he was able to immediately pull the trigger and fire two shots into Lockman's chest, killing him instantly.

Sutter fled out the front door of the police station past the surprised desk sergeant. The sergeant, realizing what had happened, pursued Sutter through the front door, and the two exchanged shots. Sutter was wounded in the exchange and captured; he was taken to an area hospital where he underwent surgery and recovered. He was charged with the murder of Detective Lockman, and the district attorney said that he would seek to have Sutter put away for the rest of his life.

Sutter's parents hired an attorney to defend their son. The lawyer held a press conference during which he announced his defense strategy—that Sutter had been brainwashed by video games and that at the time of the shooting he had been unable to distinguish reality from fantasy. "Jason was confused by all that happened. He thought that he was playing a game," the attorney said. "He didn't realize that someone might really get hurt." He also announced that he was filing a lawsuit against the two media companies that had made the games Sutter played.

Think about it:

1. Who is primarily responsible for the murder of Detective Lockman, Sutter or the video game manufacturers? Do both bear at least some responsibility?

2. What role, if any, did society play in Detective Lockman's death? Should government regulations control the content of video games?

3. What role did free will and individual choice play in Sutter's quick decision to take Lockman's gun and shoot him? How much control did Sutter have over his own behavior, and how much of his behavior was merely a response to experiences he had in the past?

Note: Who's to Blame boxes provide fictionalized critical thinking opportunities, and are not actual cases.

preceding one, the politics of young people eventually become the politics of the nation).

Albert Bandura developed a comprehensive **modeling theory** of aggression. Bandura stated that "a complete theory of aggression must explain how aggressive patterns are developed, what provokes people to behave aggressively, and what sustains such actions after they have been initiated."[73] Although everyone is capable of aggression, "people are not born with repertories of aggressive behavior. They must learn them. The specific forms that aggressive behavior takes, the frequency with which it is expressed, the situation in which it is displayed, and the specific targets selected for attack are largely determined by social learning factors."[74]

Modeling theory, a form of social learning theory, asserts that people learn how to act by observing others. Early on, Bandura experimented with children who observed adult role models striking inflatable cartoon characters. When these children were observed following their encounter with adult behavior, they exhibited similarly aggressive behavior. Bandura also studied violence on television and concluded that "television is an effective tutor. (See **Library Extra 5–5**.) Both laboratory and controlled field studies in which young children and adolescents are

■ **behavior theory**
A psychological perspective that posits that behavior that is rewarded will increase in frequency and behavior that is punished will decrease.

■ **operant behavior**
Behavior that affects the environment so as to produce responses or further behavioral cues.

■ **punishment**
An undesirable behavioral consequence likely to decrease the frequency of occurrence of that behavior.

■ **reward**
A desirable behavioral consequence likely to increase the frequency of occurrence of that behavior.

repeatedly shown either violent or nonviolent fare, disclose that exposure to film violence shapes the form of aggression and typically increases interpersonal aggressiveness in everyday life."[75] A later study by other researchers showed that even after ten years, the level of violence engaged in by young adults was directly related to the degree of violent television they had been exposed to as children[76] (see the Who's to Blame box). One 2010 meta-analysis (a study of other studies) by Craig Anderson, director of the Center for the Study of Violence at Iowa State University, and his colleagues found that playing violent video games increases the frequency of aggressive thoughts and behaviors and leads to a decrease in empathy.[77] Anderson's team analyzed data from studies of more than 130,000 gamers in the U.S., Europe, and Japan from elementary school through college.

> Modeling theory, a form of social learning theory, asserts that people learn how to act by observing others.

Once aggressive patterns of behavior have been acquired, it becomes necessary to show how they can be activated. Aggression can be provoked, Bandura suggested, by people experiencing physical assaults as well as verbal threats and insults and by having their hopes thwarted or their goal-seeking behavior obstructed. Deprivation and other adversities in life are also potential triggers of aggression.

Bandura stated that individuals sometimes become aggressive because they are rewarded for doing so. The early-twentieth-century American concept of a macho (virile and masculine) male figure was often associated with the expectation of substantial reward—he won the most respect, came away with the greatest honors (on the playing field, in school, from the community), and eventually married the most desirable woman.

Another reward flowing from aggression is what Bandura called "reduction of aversive treatment." For example, standing up to a bully is the most effective way of dealing with harassment, and "the squeaky wheel gets the grease"—aggressive people often get what they go after.

Bandura recognized that everyone has self-regulatory mechanisms that can ameliorate the tendency toward aggression and that people reward or punish themselves according to internal standards for their own behavior. Hence, aggression may be inhibited in people who value religious, ethical, or moral standards of conduct like compassion, thoughtfulness, and courtesy. People who devalue aggression may still engage in it via a process he called "disengagement," whereby rationalizations are constructed that overcome internal inhibitions: (1) placement of blame on their victim; (2) dehumanization through bureaucratization, automation, urbanization, and high social mobility; (3) vindication of aggressive practices by legitimate authorities; and (4) desensitization resulting from repeated exposure to aggression.

Modeling theory has been criticized for lacking comprehensive explanatory power. How can striking differences in sibling behavior be explained when early childhood experiences were similar? Why do apparent differences exist between the sexes in degree and type of criminality, irrespective of social background and early learning experiences? More recent versions of modeling theory, sometimes called "cognitive social learning theory,"[78] attempt to account for such differences by hypothesizing that reflection and cognition play a significant role in interpreting what is observed and in determining responses. Few people behave precisely as others do because they have their own ideas about both the meanings of observed behavior and the consequences of emulation.

Behavior Theory

Behavior theory has sometimes been called the stimulus–response approach to human behavior. "At the heart of behavior theory is the notion that behavior is determined by environmental consequences which it produces for the individual concerned."[79] When an individual's behavior results in rewards or feedback seen as pleasurable and desirable, the behavior is reinforced and will likely become more frequent, but when punishment follows the behavior, the frequency of that behavior will probably decrease.

The individual's responses are termed **operant behavior** because his or her choices effectively operate on the surrounding environment to produce consequences for him or her. Similarly, stimuli provided by the environment become behavioral cues eliciting conditioned responses from the individual. Behavior theory is often employed by parents seeking to control their children through a series of **punishments** and **rewards**. Young children may be punished with a spanking, the temporary loss of a favored toy, or a turned-off television; older children are often told what rules to obey and what rewards to anticipate if they adhere to those rules and what punishment to expect if they do not.

■ **attachment theory**
A social-psychological perspective on delinquent and criminal behavior that holds that the successful development of secure attachment between a child and his or her primary caregiver provides the basic foundation for all future psychological development.

In behavior theory, rewards and punishments have been divided into four conceptual categories: (1) positive rewards that increase the frequency of approved behavior by adding something desirable to the situation (a "good" child is given a toy); (2) negative rewards that increase the frequency of approved behavior by removing something distressful (a "good" child is permitted to skip the morning's chores); (3) positive punishments that decrease the frequency of unwanted behavior by adding something undesirable (a "bad" child is spanked); and (4) negative punishments that decrease the frequency of unwanted behavior by removing something desirable (a "bad" child has candy taken away). It is through the application of rewards and punishments that behavior is shaped.

Behavior theory differs from other psychological theories in that the major determinants of behavior are envisioned as existing in the environment surrounding the individual rather than in the individual. **B. F. Skinner** (1904–1990), the best-known proponent of behavior theory, rejected unobservable psychological constructs, focusing instead on patterns of responses to external rewards and stimuli. Skinner did extensive animal research involving behavioral concepts and created programmed instruction, which allows students to work at their own pace and provides immediate rewards for learning accomplishments.

Although behavior theory has much to say about the reformation of criminal offenders through the imposition of punishment, the approach is equally significant for its contributions to understanding the genesis of such behavior. One writer explained, "It is the balance of reinforcement and punishment in an individual's learning history which will dictate the presence or absence of criminal behavior."[80] According to the behavioral model, crime results when individuals "receive tangible rewards (positive reinforcement) for engaging in delinquent and criminal behavior, particularly when no other attractive alternative is available."[81]

Behavior theory has been criticized for ignoring the role that cognition plays in human behavior. A martyr, for example, persists in what society may define as undesirable behavior even in the face of severe punishment, including the loss of his or her own life; no punishment deters a martyr from answering this higher calling. Criminals who are punished for law violations may find that their social group interprets their punishment as status enhancing. According to behavior theory, criminal punishments are in danger of losing sway over many forms of human behavior today because society's fragmented value system leads to various interpretations of criminal punishments, thereby changing the significance of arrest, conviction, and

imprisonment. In the past, criminal offenders were often shunned and became social outcasts, but today those who have been adjudicated criminal may find their new status holds many rewards.

Attachment Theory

Another psychological approach to explaining crime and delinquency is **attachment theory**, first proposed by English child psychiatrist John Bowlby (1907–1990) who observed children during his tenure at the London Child Guidance Clinic after World War II.[82] Bowlby was especially interested in the maladjusted behavior of children who lacked a solid relationship with a mother figure, and he concluded that for healthy personality development to occur, "the infant and young child should experience a warm, intimate, and continuous relationship with his mother (or permanent mother substitute) in which both find satisfaction and enjoyment."[83]

Bowlby identified three forms of attachment: secure attachment, anxious-avoidant attachment, and anxious-resistant attachment.[84] Only the first is healthy, and it develops early in life when a child is confident that the mother figure will be responsible and available when needed. The successful development of secure attachment between children and their primary caregivers, Bowlby said, provides the basic foundation for all their future psychological development, with children developing a secure psychological base when they are "nourished physically and emotionally, comforted if distressed [and] reassured if frightened."[85]

> The successful development of secure attachment provides the basic foundation for future psychological development.

According to attachment theory, delinquent behavior arises when nonsecure attachments are created. Anxious-avoidant attachment develops when children feel rejection and lack confidence concerning parental support and care. Anxious-resistant attachment develops from similar experiences and results in feelings of uncertainty, causing the child (and later, the adult) to feel anxious, to be fearful of his or her environment, and to cling to potential caregivers or partners. Bowlby called delinquents "affectionless," meaning they did not form intimate attachments as children and cannot form such attachments later in life.

WEB EXTRA 5–5
LIBRARY EXTRA 5–6

■ **self-control**
A person's ability to alter his or her own mental and emotional states and behavioral responses.

Attachment theory predicts that the most problematic individuals will be those who were abandoned at an early age, who experienced multiple placements (in foster homes and so on), who had to deal with the early absence of one or both parents, and who faced traumatic conditions (physical, sexual, or other abuse) in early childhood.

Tests of attachment theory seem to confirm that difficulties in childhood (especially before the age of eight) produce criminality later in life.[86] Studies have shown that children who were raised in insecure environments are likely to engage in violent behavior as adults and that childhood insecurity leads to a relative lack of empathy.[87] Some attachment theorists believe that the development of empathy is the single most important factor leading to conformity. When children do not receive empathy from those around them, they appear to also be unable to see others as deserving of empathy and become more likely to inflict injury on others. Learn more about attachment theory by visiting the Attachment Research Center via **Web Extra 5–5**, and read about the development of attachment theory at **Library Extra 5–6**.

Self-Control Theory

Many people are able to exercise **self-control** (the ability to alter mental and emotional states and behavioral responses[88]) sufficiently to keep themselves from getting into trouble with the law, even under the most challenging circumstances. Psychologists have suggested that "the capacity to override and alter the self's responses is a vital characteristic that sets human beings apart from other species."[89] Self-control is most obvious when exercised in the face of adversity and is both key to adaptive success and central to virtuous behavior.

In the field of psychology, four types of self-control have been identified (see Figure 5–2). The first type is impulse control;

people resist temptations and refrain from acting on impulses considered socially or personally undesirable (taking drugs, acting violently or aggressively, engaging in sexual activity). A second type of self-control is exercised over the contents of the mind and includes suppression of unwanted thoughts, focused thoughts and concentration, reasoning and analysis, and inference and guided intuition. A third type exerts self-control over emotional and mood states, and a fourth type controls performance (persisting in the face of adversity or physical challenges). Self-control enables people to adjust to a much wider range of circumstances than they otherwise could. Psychologists sometimes argue that the majority of today's personal and social problems (drug abuse, violence, school failure, alcoholism, unwanted pregnancy, venereal disease, irresponsible money management, underachievement, poor eating habits and obesity, lack of exercise, cigarette smoking, and delinquency and criminality) stem from deficiencies in self-control.[90]

A somewhat different perspective on self-control is offered by criminologists Michael R. Gottfredson and Travis Hirschi as part of their general theory of crime (also discussed in Chapter 7). "Gottfredson and Hirschi's general theory of crime claims to be *general*, in part, due to its assertion that the operation of a single mechanism, low self-control, accounts for 'all crime, at all times'; acts ranging from vandalism to homicide, from rape to white-collar-crime."[91] Gottfredson and Hirschi defined *self-control* as the degree to which a person is vulnerable to temptations of the moment.[92] They proposed that self-control is acquired early in life and that low self-control is the premier individual-level cause of crime. It develops by the end of childhood and is fostered through parental emotional investment in the child, monitoring the child's behavior, recognizing deviance when it occurs, and punishing the child.

Some researchers have called the argument that self-control develops early in childhood and persists over time the *stability thesis*. In research reported in 2006, Florida State University criminologists Carter Hay and Walter Forrest conducted a test of the stability thesis, finding moderately strong support for it:[93] Levels of self-control that developed early in childhood tended to persist, but not as strongly as the general theory of crime would suggest; 16% of the study population showed changes in levels of self-control over time, and those individuals demonstrating the greatest stability in self-control started at the highest levels.

Gottfredson and Hirschi recognized the sociological dimensions of criminality by noting that the link between self-control and crime depends substantially upon criminal opportunity, which in itself is a function of the structural or situational circumstances that an individual encounters. They suggested that

impulse control	control over the contents of the mind
control over emotions and moods	controlling performance

FIGURE 5-2 | The Four Types of Self-Control

> ■ **insanity (legal)**
> A legally established inability to understand right from wrong or to conform one's behavior to the requirements of the law.

"the link between self-control and crime is not deterministic, but probabilistic, affected by opportunities and other constraints."[94]

More recent research appears to show that low self-control tends to lead to peer rejection and isolation—especially among juveniles.[95] Consequently, young people with low self-control tend to associate with their deviant peers, meaning that those with low levels of self-control are essentially self-selected into groups of people who share their characteristics. Constance L. Chapple of the University of Nebraska explained that "the delinquent peer group may provide increased opportunities for crime or exert situational pushes towards delinquency" because of the lack of self-control that characterizes its members.[96]

Gottfredson and Hirschi rejected the notion that some people have an enduring propensity to commit crime or that any such propensity compels people to do so.[97] Crimes require "no special capabilities, needs, or motivation; they are, in this sense, available to everyone."[98] However, some people have a tendency to ignore the long-term consequences of their behavior; they tend to be impulsive, reckless, and self-centered, and they often end up committing crime because of such tendencies.[99]

Building on the work of Gottfredson and Hirschi, Harold G. Grasmick identified some characteristics of individuals with low levels of self-control.[100] Such people are impulsive and seek immediate gratification, whereas those with higher levels of self-control tend to defer gratification in favor of long-term gains. People with less self-control lack diligence, tenacity, and persistence; prefer simple tasks; and want "money without work, sex without courtship, [and] revenge without court delays."[101] Grasmick believed that risk seeking is an important determinant of self-control and that people with little self-control are drawn to adventurous and exciting activities. They also prefer physical activity over contemplation or conversation, tend to be indifferent or insensitive to the needs of others, and are predisposed to being self-centered. According to Grasmick, self-control is inversely associated with a low frustration tolerance and an inclination to handle conflict through confrontation.

A meta-analysis (a summary analysis of other research) of 21 studies of self-control theory conducted by Travis Pratt and Francis Cullen in 2000 found considerable support for the thesis that lack of self-control plays a central role in crime and deviance.[102] Looking at various studies that explored self-control as a delinquency preventative—including those on self-reported juvenile delinquency, self-reported and projected crime and deviance among college students, adult criminal behavior, and official delinquency—Pratt and Cullen concluded that low self-control is "one of the strongest known correlates of crime."

Carter Hay of Washington State University studied the role that parenting plays in the development of self-control and concluded that effective parenting can contribute to the development of self-control in children.[103] He pointed out that although Gottfredson and Hirschi recognized the importance of parenting in the development of self-control, they failed to adequately consider the nature of effective parenting, which must involve fair and nonphysical forms of discipline; harsh or unfair discipline did not appear to contribute to the development of children's self-control. Hay stated, "The sort of discipline that teaches children to control their behavior is not simply that which consistently occurs in the wake of deviance; other factors may be consequential as well, including the extent to which discipline is perceived as fair and is not reliant on physical force."[104]

In 2002, Karen L. Hayslett-McCall and Thomas J. Bernard of Pennsylvania State University proposed a new theory of disproportionate male offending that combined elements of Gottfredson and Hirschi's theory of low self-control with ideas from attachment theory.[105] Hayslett-McCall and Bernard examined the strong relationship between gender and criminality (men are more likely than women to offend in almost all offense categories) and concluded that gender-based differences in offending are caused by disruptions in attachments to primary caregivers early in childhood and that such disruptions are more likely to occur in the lives of boys than girls because of cultural differences in the way boys are treated. Boys are held less, comforted less when they cry, and spoken to less than girls in their early years because of child-rearing patterns that are thoroughly ingrained in our culture—"boys disproportionately experience disruptions of early attachment and these disruptions are causally related to elements of what is often described as the masculine gender role." Low self-control among males, concluded Hayslett-McCall and Bernard, is the final result of gendered differences in attachment disruptions.

Insanity and the Law

Unfortunately for criminologists, psychological conceptions of mental illness, ASPD, and even psychopathy are not readily applicable to the criminal justice system, which relies instead on the legal concept of **insanity**.[106] Seen this way, *insanity* is a term that refers to a type of defense allowable in criminal courts. While the legal concept of insanity is based upon claims of mental illness, it has no precise counterpart in the jargon of contemporary psychologists or psychiatrists, who speak in terms of mental status or psychosis or personality disorder, so legal and

LIBRARY EXTRA 5-7
LIBRARY EXTRA 5-8

■ **insanity (psychological)**
A persistent mental disorder or derangement.

psychiatric understandings of mental impairment rarely coincide. In the 1992 case of ***Foucha* v. *Louisiana***, the U.S. Supreme Court recognized this problem: "It is by now well established that insanity as defined by the criminal law has no direct analog in medicine or science. The divergence between law and psychiatry is caused in part by the legal fiction represented by the words 'insanity' [and] 'insane,' which are a kind of lawyer's catchall and have no clinical meaning."[107]

> The legal concept of insanity has no precise counterpart in the jargon of psychologists.

Because insanity is a defense to criminal prosecution, a criminal defendant may be found "not guilty by reason of insanity" (NGBRI) and avoid punitive sanctions, even when it is clear that he or she committed a legally circumscribed act, but the burden of proving a claim of NGBRI falls on the defendant.[108] Just as a person is assumed to be innocent at the start of any criminal trial, so, too, is the person assumed to be sane.

A defendant has a right to the opportunity to prove a claim of insanity in court and cannot be forced to take medications during trial that might control the condition. In 1992, the U.S. Supreme Court, in the case of *Riggins* v. *Nevada*,[109] held that the "forced administration of antipsychotic medication" may have impaired the accused's ability to defend himself and violated due process guarantees. In 2003, in the case of *Sell* v. *United States*,[110] the Court placed additional limits on the government's power to forcibly medicate some mentally ill defendants to make them competent to stand trial, ruling that the use of antipsychotic drugs on a nonviolent offender who does not represent a danger while institutionalized must be in the defendant's best medical interest and be "substantially unlikely" to cause side effects that might compromise the fairness of the trial.

In 1984, the U.S. Congress enacted the Insanity Defense Reform Act (IDRA), part of the 1984 Crime Control and Prevention Act.[111] Congress had been spurred to action by John Hinckley's attempted assassination of (then) President Ronald Reagan. At trial, Hinckley's lawyers claimed that their client's history of schizophrenia left him unable to control his behavior, and Hinckley was acquitted of the criminal charges that had been brought against him. Although Hinckley was institutionalized to prevent him from harming others, his release is mandated by federal law that existed at the time of his trial if or when he recovers.

Through the IDRA, Congress intended to prohibit the presentation at trial in federal court of evidence of mental disease or defect, short of legal insanity, to excuse conduct.[112] **Insanity** under the act is defined as a condition in which the defendant can be shown to have been suffering under a "severe mental disease or defect [and as a result] was unable to appreciate the nature and quality or the wrongfulness of his acts."[113] The IDRA also placed the burden of proving insanity squarely on the defendant—a provision that has been unsuccessfully challenged a number of times since the act was passed.

The IDRA created a special verdict of "not guilty by reason of insanity."[114] Through a comprehensive civil commitment procedure, a defendant found NGBRI can be held in custody pending a court hearing, and the hearing must occur within 40 days of the verdict. At the conclusion of the hearing, the court determines whether the defendant should be hospitalized or released. In the words of the U.S. Supreme Court, "The Insanity Defense Reform Act of 1984 ensures that a federal criminal defendant found not guilty by reason of insanity will not be released onto the streets."[115]

The IDRA is especially significant because it contains a provision that permits mentally ill individuals to be held for trial in the hopes that they will recover sufficiently to permit their trial to proceed. The law allows for an initial hearing to determine the mental status of the defendant. If the defendant is found incompetent to stand trial, he or she will be committed to a hospital "for such a reasonable period of time, not to exceed four months, to determine whether there is a substantial probability that in the foreseeable future he will attain the capacity to permit the trial to proceed; and for an additional reasonable period of time until his mental condition is so improved that trial may proceed." The law sets no maximum period of confinement, implying only that the defendant will undergo periodic review while institutionalized "if the court finds that there is a substantial probability that within such additional period of time he will attain the capacity to permit the trial to proceed."[116] Learn more about insanity and the law at **Library Extras 5–7** and **5–8**.

The M'Naughten Rule

One of the first instances within the Western legal tradition where insanity was accepted as a defense to criminal liability can be found in the case of Daniel M'Naughten (also spelled "McNaughton" or "M'Naghton"). M'Naughten was accused of the 1843 killing of Edward Drummond, the secretary of British Prime Minister Sir Robert Peel. M'Naughten had intended to kill Peel, but because he was suffering from mental disorganization, he shot Drummond instead, mistaking him for Peel. At his trial, the defense presented information to show that M'Naughten was suffering from delusions, including the belief that Peel's political party was, in some vague way, persecuting him. The court accepted his lawyer's claims,

■ **M'Naughten rule**
A standard for judging legal insanity that requires that offenders not know what they were doing, or if they did, that they not know it was wrong.

■ **irresistible-impulse test**
A standard for judging legal insanity that holds that a defendant is not guilty of a criminal offense if the person, by virtue of his or her mental state or psychological condition, was not able to resist committing the crime.

■ **Durham rule**
A standard for judging legal insanity that holds that an accused is not criminally responsible if his or her unlawful act was the product of mental disease or mental defect.

and the defense of insanity was established in Western law. Other jurisdictions were quick to adopt the **M'Naughten rule**, as the judge's decision in the case came to be called, which holds that individuals cannot be held criminally responsible for their actions if at the time of the offense either (1) they did not know what they were doing or (2) they did not know that what they were doing was wrong.

Today the M'Naughten rule is still followed by many states when insanity is at issue in criminal cases. Critics of the M'Naughten rule say that although the notion of intent inherent within it appeals greatly to lawyers, "it is so alien to current concepts of human behavior that it has been vigorously attacked by psychiatrists. An obvious difficulty with the *M'Naughten* rule is that practically everyone, regardless of the degree of his criminal disturbance, knows the nature and quality and rightness or wrongness of what he is doing."[117]

The Irresistible-Impulse Test

The M'Naughten ruling opened the floodgates for other types of insanity claims offered as defenses to charges of criminal activity. The **irresistible-impulse test**—employed by 18 states—holds that a defendant is not guilty of a criminal offense if the person, by virtue of his or her mental state or psychological condition, was not able to resist committing the action in question.

It is difficult for anyone to really know whether a person in a given situation was able to control his or her behavior. In 1994, Lorena Bobbitt was found not guilty by virtue of temporary insanity of charges of maliciously wounding her husband by cutting off his penis with a kitchen knife. Her attorneys successfully employed the irresistible-impulse defense, convincing the jury that Bobbitt acted on an irresistible impulse after years of abuse (physical, verbal, and sexual) at the hands of her husband. Her attorneys maintained that while committing the crime, she had a brief psychotic breakdown and could not resist the impulse to maim her husband.

Scientific advances combined with the irresistible-impulse test offer a number of intriguing possibilities. For example, colognes and perfumes combine the usual scents with pheromones, chemical substances that (at least in insect form) have been shown to produce very predictable, and apparently

Insanity can be used as a defense against criminal charges. Lorena Bobbitt sobs on the witness stand before acquittal on charges she severed her husband's penis with a kitchen knife; Bobbitt claimed a kind of irresistible impulse. Should she have been acquitted?
Source: Gary Hershorn/CORBIS-NY

uncontrollable, behavior by stimulating the olfactory nerves to produce specific chemicals targeting neuroreceptors in the brain and directly altering brain chemistry. Most uses of pheromones have been in the area of pest control; sexual pheromones that attract specific types of male insects are released into the atmosphere to confuse the insects' mating behavior or to lure the pests into a trap. But might these new toiletries lead to claims of uncontrollable sexual desire? Will toiletries containing human pheromones lead to instances of sexual attack? If so, will the attackers be held blameless on claims of irresistible impulse, and what will be the civil liability of the companies that make them?

The Durham Rule

In 1954, Judge David Bazelon of the U.S. Court of Appeals for the District of Columbia announced a new rule—now called the **Durham rule**—in the case of Monte Durham: "The rule we now hold is simply that an accused is not criminally responsible

■ **substantial-capacity test**
A standard for judging legal insanity that requires that a person lack the mental capacity needed to understand the wrongfulness of his or her act or to conform his or her behavior to the requirements of the law.

■ **Brawner rule**
A somewhat vague rule for determining insanity created in the 1972 federal court case of *United States* v. *Brawner* (471 F.2d 969), since superseded by statute, that asks the jury to decide whether the defendant could be justly held responsible for the criminal act with which he or she stands charged in the face of any claims of insanity or mental incapacity.

■ **guilty but mentally ill (GBMI)**
A finding that offenders are guilty of the criminal offense with which they are charged, but because of their prevailing mental condition, they are generally sent to psychiatric hospitals for treatment rather than to prison. Once they have been declared cured, such offenders can be transferred to correctional facilities to serve out their sentences.

if his unlawful act was the product of mental disease or mental defect. We use 'disease' in the sense of a condition which is considered capable of improving or deteriorating. We use 'defect' in the sense of a condition which is not considered capable of either improving or deteriorating and which may be congenital or the result of injury or the residual effect of a physical or mental disease."[118]

Although the Durham rule was intended to simplify the adjudication of mentally ill offenders, it has resulted in additional confusion. Many criminal defendants suffer from mental diseases or defects—some show retarded mental development, others are dyslexic, a few are afflicted with Down's syndrome, others have cerebral palsy, and a vast number show some degree of neurosis or psychosis. The link between any of these conditions and criminal behavior in specific cases, however, is far from clear: Some people struggle with psychological disabilities or mental illnesses all their lives but never violate the criminal law; others, with similar conditions, are frequent law violators. The Durham rule provides no way of separating one group from the other.

Some observers have noted the "danger of circularity" in the Durham rule. If a person exhibits unusual behavior during the commission of a crime, the criminal behavior itself may be taken as a sign of mental disease, automatically exonerating the offender of criminal culpability.

The Substantial-Capacity Test

In the determination of insanity for purposes of criminal prosecution, 19 U.S. states adhere to the **substantial-capacity test**, a standard embodied in the Model Penal Code of the American Law Institute which blends elements of the M'Naughten rule with the irresistible-impulse standard. Insanity is said to be present when a person lacks "the [substantial] mental capacity needed to understand the wrongfulness of his act, or to conform his behavior to the requirements of the law."[119] A lack of mental capacity does not require total mental incompetence, nor does it mandate that the behavior in question meet the standard of total irresistibility, so the problem of determining just what constitutes "substantial mental capacity," or its lack, has plagued this rule from its inception.

The Brawner Rule

The **Brawner rule**, created in 1972 in the case of *United States* v. *Brawner*,[120] is unique among standards of its type. It delegates responsibility to the jury to determine what constitutes insanity by asking it to decide whether the defendant could be *justly* held responsible for the criminal act with which he or she stands charged in the face of any claims of insanity or mental incapacity. Under the Brawner rule, which has not seen wide applicability, juries are left with few rules to guide them other than their own sense of fairness.

Guilty but Mentally Ill

Frustrated by the seeming inability of criminal courts to effectively adjudicate mentally ill offenders and by the abuse of insanity claims by offenders seeking to avoid criminal punishments, several states have enacted legislation permitting findings of "guilty but insane" or **guilty but mentally ill (GBMI)**. In 1997, Pennsylvania multimillionaire John E. du Pont was found GBMI in the shooting death of former Olympic gold medalist David Schultz during a delusional episode. Although defense attorneys were able to show that du Pont sometimes thought he saw Nazis in his trees, heard the walls talking, and had cut off pieces of his own skin in efforts to remove bugs from outer space, he was held criminally liable for Schultz's death and was sentenced to 13–30 years in confinement.

> Several states permit findings of guilty but mentally ill (GBMI).

A GBMI verdict means that a person can be held responsible for a specific criminal act even though a degree of mental incompetence may be present. In most GBMI jurisdictions, a jury must return a finding of GBMI if (1) every statutory element necessary for a conviction has been proved beyond a reasonable doubt, (2) the defendant is found to have been *mentally ill* at the time the crime was committed, and (3) the defendant was not found to have been *legally insane* at the time the crime was committed. The difference between mental illness and legal insanity is crucial because a defendant can be mentally ill by standards of the medical profession but sane for purposes of the law.

Upon return of a GBMI verdict, a judge may impose any sentence possible under the law for the crime in question.

LIBRARY EXTRA 5-9

CRIMINAL | PROFILES
Andrea Yates

Few crimes have shocked American society as deeply as the drowning of five young children by their mother, Andrea Pia (Kennedy) Yates, in a bathtub in their suburban Houston, Texas, home on June 20, 2001. Her subsequent trial, conviction, life sentence, successful appeal, and second trial brought the insanity defense based on a claim of postpartum psychosis under intense scrutiny. Ultimately, it is difficult to find a national consensus on the emotional issues involved in this horrifying event.

Yates's early life showed promise for future success. After obtaining a job as a registered nurse, she met Rusty Yates. Their shared deep Christian faith was a significant factor in their attraction to one another.

When Andrea and Rusty finally married after three years of dating, they planned on having as many children as God intended them to have. The birth of their first child, Noah, a year after their marriage brought unexpected difficulties.

Unaware of the extent to which mental illness had plagued her own family, the new mother was understandably tormented when she began to have violent visions of stabbings and came to believe that Satan was speaking directly to her. Yates hid these frightening experiences from everyone, including her husband.

Events over the next few years led Andrea deeper into depression. The Yateses had two more children, after which she miscarried. She then had their fourth child, but the birth was followed by pronounced depressive manifestations. She began a series of psychiatric counseling sessions with various doctors, and a wide variety of drug therapies were tried.

Despite extensive hospitalizations and medications for her ongoing depression and emerging psychosis and against the advice of her psychiatrist, Yates became pregnant again, delivering her fifth child, Mary, in November 2000. The pregnancy had resulted from the urging of her husband, who also ignored the strong medical opposition to the birth of another child.[i]

When Yates's father died just four and a half months after her fifth child was born, her mental health declined dramatically.[ii] Yates returned to the hospital again for ten days in May. Upon her release, she was advised to think positive thoughts and to see a psychologist. Two days later, she systematically drowned each of her five children.

Andrea Yates (center), who admitted drowning her five children in a bathtub at the family home, leaving the Harris County (Texas) Criminal Justice Center with her attorney, George Parnham, after being found NGBRI in a second trial. Yates was sent to a maximum-security mental hospital where she will be held until she is cured. What do you think should have been done with Yates?
Source: David J. Phillip/AP Wide World Photos

Following a sensational trial that was widely followed by the media, Yates was convicted and sentenced to life in prison. That conviction was subsequently overturned because of the false testimony of forensic psychologist Park Dietz.[iii] In July 2006, Yates was retried, but this time she was acquitted of capital murder charges and found NGBRI. She was immediately ordered to commitment in a mental hospital, where she will remain until she is no longer considered to be a threat to herself or others.[iv]

Notes
i. Charles Montaldo, "Profile of Andrea Yates," About: Crime/Punishment, 2007, http://crime.about.com/od/current/p/andreayates.htm (accessed June 16, 2007).
ii. Ibid.
iii. "Court Lets Stand Ruling That Tossed Andrea Yates' Murder Conviction," CourtTV News, November 9, 2005, http://www.courttv.com/trials/yates/110905_cnn.html (accessed June 16, 2007).
iv. "Jury: Yates Not Guilty by Reason of Insanity," July 26, 2006, MSNBC/Associated Press, http://www.msnbc.msn.com/id/14024728 (accessed June 16, 2007).

Offenders adjudicated GBMI are found guilty of the criminal offense with which they are charged but are generally sent to psychiatric hospitals for treatment rather than to prison. Once they have been declared "cured," however, such offenders can be transferred to correctional facilities to serve out their sentences. Learn more about GBMI at **Library Extra 5–9**.

Confinement of Individuals Found NGBRI

Federal law provides for confinement in a "suitable facility" of criminal defendants found NGBRI.[121] The law mandates a "psychiatric or psychological examination and report" and a hearing to

LIBRARY EXTRA 5–10
LIBRARY EXTRA 5–11

■ **selective incapacitation**
A social policy that seeks to protect society by incarcerating individuals deemed to be the most dangerous.

be held within 40 days after the not guilty verdict. If the hearing court finds that the person's release would "create a substantial risk of bodily injury to another person or serious damage of property of another due to a present mental disease or defect, the court shall commit the person." To be released later, the person "has the burden of proving by clear and convincing evidence that his release would not create a substantial risk of bodily injury to another person or serious damage of property of another due to a present mental disease or defect." The person can be discharged "when the director of the facility in which an acquitted person is hospitalized determines that the person has recovered from his mental disease or defect to such an extent that his release, or his conditional release under a prescribed regimen of medical, psychiatric, or psychological care or treatment, would no longer create a substantial risk of bodily injury to another person or serious damage to property of another." See the Criminal Profiles box for a case of NGBRI.

The federal statute has been used as a model by many of the states. A few laws that differ from the federal model have been held to be unconstitutional, especially when they permit the continued confinement of offenders who have been declared "well," even though they may still be dangerous. In 1992, the U.S. Supreme Court, in the case of *Foucha* v. *Louisiana*, ordered the release of Terry Foucha, who had been adjudicated NGBRI in the state of Louisiana. In effect, the Supreme Court struck down a provision of the Louisiana law that made possible continued confinement of recovered persons who had once been deemed NGBRI when their continued confinement is predicated solely on the basis of the belief that they might represent a continuing danger to the community. Learn more about psychiatry and the law via **Library Extras 5–10** and **5–11**.

Social Policy and Forensic Psychology

Psychological theories continue to evolve. Research in the field has shown a stability of aggressiveness over time, that is, children who display early disruptive or aggressive behavior are likely to continue their involvement in such behavior as adults.[122] Some researchers have found that aggressiveness appears to stabilize over time.[123] Children who demonstrate aggressive traits often evidence increasingly frequent episodes of such behavior until it becomes a major component

> **Problem children are likely to become problem adults.**

of their adolescent or adult personality, so it is possible to conclude that problem children are likely to become problem adults.

This research holds considerable significance for those who are attempting to assess dangerousness and to identify personal characteristics that would allow for the prediction of dangerousness in individual cases, which is of great concern to today's policymakers. In 1993, Michael Blair, a convicted child molester paroled after serving 18 months of a ten-year prison sentence, was charged with the kidnap-slaying of young Ashley Estell, who disappeared from a soccer match in Plano, Texas. Ashley was found dead the next day.[124] In November of that year, Anthony Cook was executed in Huntsville, Texas, for the slaying of law student Dirck Van Tassel, Jr.[125] Cook robbed Van Tassel of his wallet, watch, and wedding ring and shot him four times in the head, killing him only 13 days after being paroled. Less than a month later, Richard Allen Davis, a twice-convicted kidnapper, was arrested for the kidnap-murder of 12-year-old Polly Klaas, who was abducted from a slumber party in her Petaluma, California, home as her mother slept in the next room.[126] Davis had been paroled only a few months earlier after serving an eight-year prison term for a similar offense.

Can past behavior predict future behavior? Do former instances of criminality presage additional ones? Are there other identifiable characteristics that violent offenders might manifest that could serve as warning signs to criminal justice decision makers faced with the dilemma of whether to release convicted felons? One study found a strong relationship between childhood behavioral difficulties and later problem behavior: "Early antisocial behavior is the best predictor of later antisocial behavior. It appears that this rule holds even when the antisocial behavior is measured as early as the preschool period."[127] Using children as young as three years old, researchers were able to predict later delinquency, leading them to conclude that "some antisocial behavioral characteristics may be components of temperament." A second study, tracking a sample of male offenders for over 20 years, found that stable but "unmeasured individual differences" account for the positive association that exists between past criminal behavior and the likelihood of future recurrence.[128] A 1996 analysis of recidivism studies by Canadians Paul Gendreau, Tracy Little, and Claire Goggin found that criminal history, preadult antisocial behavior, and "criminogenic needs" (measurable antisocial thoughts, values, and behavior) were all predictors of recidivism.[129]

Prediction requires more than generalities; it necessitates the ability to predict which specific individuals will engage in future violations of criminal law. **Selective incapacitation** is a policy based on the notion of career criminality.[130] Career criminals (also called "habitual offenders") are people who repeatedly violate the

■ **correctional psychology**
The branch of forensic psychology concerned with the diagnosis and classification of offenders, the treatment of correctional populations, and the rehabilitation of inmates and other law violators.

LIBRARY EXTRA 5–12
WEB EXTRA 5–6

criminal law. Research has shown that only a small percentage of all offenders account for most of the crimes reported to the police—some studies found as few as 8% of all offenders committing as many as 60 serious crimes each per year.[131] A Wisconsin study found that imprisonment of individuals determined to be career offenders saved the state approximately $14,000 per year per offender when the cost of imprisonment was compared with the estimated cost of new crimes, concluding that "prison pays," and suggested that the state continue pursuing a policy of aggressive imprisonment of career offenders, even in the face of escalating costs and vastly overcrowded prisons.[132] The strategy of selective incapacitation has been criticized by some authors for yielding a rate of "false positives" of over 60%.[133] Potentially violent offenders are not easy to identify, even on the basis of past criminal records, and sentencing individuals to long prison terms simply because they are thought likely to commit crimes in the future would no doubt be unconstitutional.

The 1984 federal Comprehensive Crime Control Act,[134] which established the U.S. Sentencing Commission, targeted career offenders. Commission guidelines contained a "criminal history" dimension substantially increasing the amount of punishment an offender faces based on his or her history of law violations. The sentencing guidelines classified a career offender as follows: "(1) [T]he defendant was at least 18 years old at the time of the offense, (2) the offense is a crime of violence or trafficking in a controlled substance, and (3) the defendant has at least two prior felony convictions of either a crime of violence or a controlled substance offense."[135] The definition later came under fire for putting individuals with a history of minor drug trafficking in the same category as serial killers.

Definitions of *dangerousness* are fraught with difficulty because "dangerousness is not an objective quality like obesity or brown eyes; rather it is an ascribed quality like trustworthiness."[136] Dangerousness is not necessarily a personality trait that is stable or easily identifiable, but even if it were, some studies of criminal careers seem to show that involvement in crime decreases with age.[137] One author stated that if "criminality declines more or less uniformly with age, then many offenders will be 'over the hill' by the time they are old enough to be plausible candidates for preventive incarceration."[138]

No discussion of social policy relating to the insights of criminal psychology would be complete without mention of **correctional psychology,** which is concerned with the diagnosis and classification of offenders, the treatment of correctional populations, and the rehabilitation of inmates and other law violators. One of the most commonly used classification instruments in correctional facilities today is the Minnesota

> Dangerousness is not an objective quality like obesity or brown eyes; rather it is an ascribed quality like trustworthiness.

Multiphasic Personality Inventory (MMPI). Based on the results of the MMPI, an offender may be assigned to a security level, a correctional program, or a treatment program. Psychological treatment typically takes the form of individual or group counseling, such as psychotherapy, guided group interaction, cognitive therapy, behavioral modification, and various forms of interpersonal therapy. Learn more about forensic psychology via **Library Extra 5–12**, and visit the American Association for Correctional and Forensic Psychology (AACFP) at **Web Extra 5–6**.

Social Policy and the Psychology of Criminal Conduct

A practical synthesis of psychological approaches to criminal behavior is offered by Donald A. Andrews and James Bonta in their book *The Psychology of Criminal Conduct*.[139] Andrews and Bonta prefer the term *psychology of criminal conduct (PCC)* to distinguish their point of view from what they call "the weak psychology represented in mainstream sociological criminology and clinical/forensic psychology."[140] Any useful synthesis of contemporary criminal psychology should be fundamentally objective and empirical, and they dislike many well-accepted perspectives that have "placed higher value on social theory and political ideology than [on] rationality and/or respect for evidence."[141] Andrews and Bonta explained, "The majority of perspectives on criminal conduct that are most favored in mainstream criminology reduce people to hypothetical fictions whose only interesting characteristics are their location in the social system. Almost without exception, the causal significance of social location is presumed to reflect inequality in the distribution of social wealth and power, [which] is a major preoccupation of mainstream textbook criminology, even though such a focus has failed to significantly advance understanding of criminal conduct."[142]

In *The Psychology of Criminal Conduct*, Andrews and Bonta did not attempt to develop a new behavior theory but asked for objective application of what is understood about the psychology of crime, criminal behavior, and criminal offenders possible through

---

psychological profiling
The attempt to categorize, understand, and predict the behavior of certain types of offenders based on behavioral clues they provide; also called *criminal profiling* and *behavioral profiling*.

---

the application of readily available high-quality psychological findings. Based on nearly 500 published reports on "controlled evaluations of community and correctional interventions," they concluded that treatment reduces recidivism "to at least a mild degree."[143] Targeting higher-risk cases and using treatments outside of formal correctional settings (such as an offender's family and peers) are elements of the most effective treatment strategies. Along with objective measures of the success of rehabilitation programs and strategies, effective intervention and treatment services based on the use of psychological assessment instruments that have already demonstrated their validity, empirically established risk factors that can be accurately assessed, and accurately measured community crime rates are all ready and waiting to make a practical psychology of criminal conduct available to today's policymakers. In the words of Andrews and Bonta, "There exists now an empirically defensible general psychology of criminal conduct (PCC) that is of practical value. It should speak to policy advisors, policy makers and legislators who must come to see that human science is not just [a] relic of a positivistic past."[144] They concluded that the major remaining issue "on which work is only beginning is how to make use of what works."[145]

Scott Glenn, starring as Jack Crawford in the crime thriller *Silence of the Lambs.* The movie publicized the practice of criminal profiling. How can psychological profiling assist criminal investigations?
Source: Photo by Orion Pictures Corporation/ZUMA Press. © Copyright 1991 by Orion Pictures Corporation

Criminal Psychological Profiling

During World War II, the U.S. War Department recruited psychologists and psychiatrists in an attempt to predict the future moves that enemy forces might make, and psychological and psychoanalytic techniques were applied to the study of German leader Adolf Hitler, Italian leader Benito Mussolini, Japanese general and prime minister Hideki Tojo, and other Axis leaders. Such psychological profiling of enemy leaders may have given the Allies the edge in battlefield strategy.

Today, **psychological profiling** (also called *criminal profiling* and *behavioral profiling*) is used to assist police investigators seeking to better understand individuals wanted for serious offenses. During an interview, famed profiler John Douglas, the retired FBI special agent who became the model for the Scott Glenn character in Thomas Harris's *Silence of the Lambs*, described criminal profiling: "It is a behavioral composite put together of the unknown subject after analyzing the crime scene materials, to include the autopsy protocol, autopsy and crime scene photographs, as well as the preliminary police reports. It is also a detailed analysis of the victim and putting that information together. To me, it's very much like an internist in medicine who

now attempts to put a diagnosis, say, on an illness; I'm trying to put a diagnosis on this particular case that's relative to motive, as well as the type of person(s) who would perpetrate that type of crime."[146]

Profilers develop a list of typical offender characteristics and other useful principles by analyzing crime-scene and autopsy data, in conjunction with interviews and studies of past offenders, in the belief that almost any form of conscious behavior (including behavior engaged in by the offender during a criminal episode) is symptomatic of the individual's personality. The way a kidnapper approaches victims, the type of attack used by a killer, and the specific sexual activities of a rapist might all help paint a picture of the offender's motivations, personal characteristics, and likely future behavior. Sometimes psychological profiles can provide clues as to what an offender might do following an attack: Some offenders have been arrested after returning to the crime scene, a behavior typically predicted by specific behavioral clues left behind, and a remorseful type can be expected to visit the victim's grave, permitting fruitful stakeouts of a cemetery.

While criminal profiling is not necessarily useful in every case, it can help narrow the search for an offender in repetitive crimes involving one offender, such as serial rape or murder. Knowledge gleaned from profiling can also help in the interrogation of suspects and can be used to identify and protect possible victims before the offender has a chance to strike again.

Profilers have also contributed significantly to the scientific literature in criminology. In a well-known study of lust murderers

> **Profilers have contributed significantly to the scientific literature in criminology.**

(men who kill and often mutilate victims during or following a forced sexual episode), FBI Special Agents Robert R. Hazelwood and John E. Douglas distinguished between the organized nonsocial and the disorganized asocial types.[147] The organized nonsocial lust murderer exhibits complete indifference to the interests of society and is completely self-centered, methodical, cunning, and "fully cognizant of the criminality of his act and its impact on society."[148] The disorganized asocial lust murderer was described this way: "[He] exhibits primary characteristics of societal aversion. This individual prefers his own company to that of others and would be typified as a loner. He experiences difficulty in negotiating interpersonal relationships and consequently feels rejected and lonely. He lacks the cunning of the nonsocial type and commits the crime in a more frenzied and less methodical manner. The crime is likely to be committed in close proximity to his residence or place of employment, where he feels secure and more at ease."[149]

During the 1980s, the FBI led the movement to develop psychological profiling through its concentration on violent sex offenders and arsonists, and much of that work continues at the FBI's Training Academy in Quantico, Virginia, in the Behavioral Science Unit (BSU), whose official mission is to develop and provide programs of training, research, and consultation in the behavioral and social sciences for the FBI and the law enforcement community to improve or enhance their administration, operational effectiveness, and understanding of crime. Visit the FBI's BSU via **Web Extra 5–7**.

SUMMARY

- Psychological and psychiatric theories of criminal behavior emphasize individual propensities and characteristics in explaining criminality. Whether the emphasis is on conditioned behavior, development of parental attachment, or psychoanalytic structure of the human personality, these approaches see the wellsprings of human motivation, desire, and behavioral choice as being firmly rooted in the personality.

- Early psychological theories used the concept of behavioral conditioning to explain most human activity. Criminality was seen as a form of mental disease, or psychopathy. Psychiatric criminology, or forensic psychiatry, saw crime as caused by biological and subconscious psychological urges mediated through consciousness.

- From the point of view of psychoanalysis, criminal behavior is maladaptive, the product of inadequacies in the offender's personality. The psychoanalytic perspective, advanced by Sigmund Freud in the early 1900s, encompasses diverse notions like personality, neurosis, and psychosis as well as transference, sublimation, and repression.

- Some psychiatric perspectives see criminality as a form of adaptive behavior to stresses, holding that law violation represents an individual's most satisfactory method of adjustment to inner conflicts that he or she cannot otherwise express.

- Modeling theory asserts that people learn how to act by observing others. Once aggressive patterns of behavior have been thus acquired, aggression can be activated when someone is experiencing physical assaults or verbal threats and insults as well as by thwarting his or her hopes or obstructing his or her goal-seeking behavior.

- Behavior theory (or the stimulus–response approach to human behavior) holds that behavior is directly determined by the environmental consequences it produces for the individual exhibiting the behavior. When an individual's behavior results in rewards or positive feedback, that behavior will increase in frequency; when punishment follows behavior, that behavior will decrease.

- Attachment theory says that the successful development of secure attachment between a child and his or her primary caregiver, believed to form early in childhood, provides the basic foundation for all future psychological development and that delinquent behavior arises whenever nonsecure attachments are created. Three forms of attachment are secure attachment, anxious-avoidant attachment, and anxious-resistant attachment.

- Self-control refers to a person's ability to alter his or her own mental and emotional states and behavioral responses. Gottfredson and Hirschi's general theory of crime says that self-control is acquired early in life and that low self-control is the primary individual-level cause of crime.

- Psychological and psychiatric conceptions of mental illness, antisocial personality, and even psychopathy are not readily applicable to the criminal justice system, which relies instead on the legal concept of insanity. While the legal concept of insanity is based upon claims of mental illness, it has no precise counterpart in the jargon of contemporary psychologists or psychiatrists.

- Some theorists now consider that psychological criminology can be used for the development of consistent and dependable social policy in the prediction of dangerousness and the rehabilitation of offenders and that selective incapacitation may be a workable policy to prevent future criminality.

- Psychological profiling of criminal offenders, based on the belief that almost any form of conscious behavior is symptomatic of the individual's personality, is a serious crime-fighting undertaking that may change the nature of localized crime-prevention strategies.

KEY TERMS

alloplastic adaptation, 133	electroencephalogram (EEG), 126
antisocial (asocial) personality, 126	forensic psychiatry, 122
antisocial personality disorder (ASPD), 126	forensic psychology, 122
attachment theory, 136	guilty but mentally ill (GBMI), 141
autoplastic adaptation, 133	id, 129
behavior theory, 135	insanity (legal), 138
Brawner rule, 141	insanity (psychological), 139
conditioning, 124	irresistible-impulse test, 140
correctional psychology, 144	M'Naughten rule, 140
criminal psychology, 122	modeling theory, 134
Durham rule, 140	neurosis, 130
ego, 129	operant behavior, 135

paranoid schizophrenic, 131	reward, 135
psychiatric criminology, 128	schizophrenic, 131
psychoanalysis, 128	selective incapacitation, 143
psychological profiling, 145	self-control, 137
psychological theory, 123	sociopath, 125
psychopath, 125	sublimation, 129
psychopathy, 124	substantial-capacity test, 141
psychosis, 130	superego, 129
psychotherapy, 128	Thanatos, 129
punishment, 135	

KEY NAMES

Albert Bandura, 134	Sigmund Freud, 128
Hervey M. Cleckley, 125	B. F. Skinner, 136

QUESTIONS FOR REVIEW

1. What are the major principles of psychological perspectives on criminal behavior?

2. What were some early psychological and psychiatric theories offered to explain criminality?

3. How can criminality be seen as a form of maladaptive behavior?

4. How can criminality be seen as a form of adaptive behavior?

5. How does the modeling theory of aggression explain how aggressive patterns of behavior, once acquired, can be activated?

6. How does behavior theory explain the role of rewards and punishments in shaping behavior?

7. How does attachment theory explain behavior, and what are the three forms of attachment?

8. What is self-control, and how can a lack of self-control lead to crime?

9. How does the legal concept of insanity differ from behavioral definitions of the same concept?

10. What types of crime-control policies might be based on psychological understandings of criminality?

11. What are some assumptions underlying the practice of criminal psychological profiling?

QUESTIONS **FOR REFLECTION**

1. This book emphasizes the theme of social problems versus social responsibility. Which perspective is better supported by psychological theories of crime causation? Why?

2. How do psychological theories of criminal behavior differ from other types of theories presented in this book? How do the various psychological and psychiatric approaches presented in this chapter differ from one another?

3. How would the perspectives discussed in this chapter suggest that offenders might be prevented from committing additional offenses? How might they be rehabilitated?

4. How can crime be a form of adaptation to one's environment? Why would an individual choose such a form of adaptation over others that might be available?

5. Which of the various standards for judging legal insanity discussed in this chapter do you find the most useful? Why?

CHAPTER 6

SOCIAL STRUCTURE THEORIES

LEARNING OUTCOMES

After reading this chapter, you should be able to answer the following questions:

- What is the nature of sociological theorizing, and what are the assumptions upon which sociological perspectives on crime causation rest?

- What do sociologists mean by the term *social structure*, and how might the organization and structure of a society contribute to criminality?

- What three key sociological explanations for crime are discussed in this chapter, and what are the characteristics of each?

- What are the policy implications of the theories discussed in this chapter?

- What are the shortcomings of the social structure approaches to understanding and preventing crime?

Follow the author's tweets about the latest crime and justice news at **http://twitter.com/schmalleger.**

Introduction

There's an old saying something to the effect that you can take the criminal out of a bad environment, but you can't take the bad environment out of the criminal. While we don't necessarily believe this to be true, some suggest that negative influences of the social environment—especially things like poverty, lack of education, broken families, disorganized neighborhoods, episodes of discrimination, and socialization into unproductive values—predispose certain people to lives of crime and that such negative influences may remain active even when people's circumstances change. Central to this perspective is the idea that crime is a social phenomenon, and central to any understanding of crime is the role that society, social institutions, and social processes play in its development and control.

In 2009, the California Dropout Research Project at the University of California–Santa Barbara announced study findings showing that the state's high school dropouts were significantly more likely to commit crimes than students who graduated.[1] "Research," wrote the study's authors, "has established a robust link between dropping out of high school and juvenile crime."[2] The project, which acknowledged that not all dropouts become offenders, estimated that crimes committed by one cohort of high school dropouts (ages 12–17) cost the state $8.9 billion annually for each year before they reached the age of 18, that cutting the dropout rate in half would prevent 30,000 juvenile crimes and save $900 million every year in enforcement costs alone, and that much more would be saved in terms of prevented victimizations. Project Director Russell W. Rumberger asserted, "If California could reduce the dropout rate, it could subsequently reduce the juvenile crime rate and its staggering impact on the state budget."[3]

Every year, 19% of students drop out of high school before graduation in Los Angeles County; in some schools within the system, the rate is much higher. Fresno Police Chief Jerry Dyer

> **Cutting California's dropout rate in half would prevent 30,000 juvenile crimes and save $900 million yearly in enforcement costs.**

Ecological theories suggest that crime shows an unequal geographic distribution. Why might certain geographic areas be associated with identifiable patterns of crime?
Source: Peter Turnley/CORBIS-NY

noted, "The connection between dropping out of school and juvenile crime is very clear. The simple fact is if kids aren't in school, they're much more likely to be on the streets causing trouble, engaging in criminal activities such as burglary, thefts, graffiti, and arsons."[4] In an interesting aside, an earlier report by the same group found that the economic cost to the state from wages lost by high school dropouts came to $46.4 billion over the lifetime of those dropouts. Because each cadre of students loses that much in wages, the accumulated wages lost over a generation (20 years of dropouts) comes to more than a trillion dollars in Los Angeles County alone.

A sociological analysis undertaken to identify the reasons why kids drop out of school would likely point to elements of the social world in which potential dropouts live as risk factors for quitting school: poverty, family demands on students' time that take away from studies, lack of opportunities to seek remedial help, socialization into value systems that focus on alternative means to success, overexposure to negative media, and involvement with neighborhood and other social groups that stress adolescent peer values and alternative social roles over the importance of schooling. At the time of the 2009 study,

■ **sociological theory**
A perspective that focuses on the nature of the power relationships that exist between social groups and on the influences that various social phenomena bring to bear on the types of behaviors that tend to characterize groups of people.

■ **social structure**
The pattern of social organization and the interrelationships among institutions characteristic of a society.

■ **social process**
The interaction between and among social institutions, groups, and individuals.

■ **social life**
The ongoing (typically) structured interaction—including socialization and social behavior in general—that occurs between persons in a society.

■ **social structure theory**
A theory that explains crime by reference to the economic and social arrangements in society. This type of theory emphasizes relationships among social institutions and describes the types of behavior that tend to characterize groups of people rather than individuals.

Los Angeles County Sheriff Lee Baca pointed out, "Schools need better tools for identifying potential dropouts so they can target interventions at the kids who need them the most."

Major Principles of Sociological Theories

Theories that explain crime by reference to social structure are only one of three major sociological approaches to crime causation. (We describe the other two in Chapters 7 and 8.) But first, consider some of the general features and assumptions of the sociological viewpoint:

- Social groups, social institutions, arrangements of society, and social roles all provide the proper focus for criminological study.
- Group dynamics, group organization, and subgroup relationships form the causal nexus out of which crime develops.
- Society's structure and its relative degree of organization or disorganization are important factors contributing to the prevalence of criminal behavior.
- Specific behavior of a given individual cannot be predicted, but statistical estimates of group characteristics and of the probability that a member of a given group will engage in a specific type of crime are possible.

Sociological theories examine both institutional arrangements within a **social structure** (i.e., interrelationships among society's institutions) and **social processes** (i.e., interactions between and among different social institutions, groups, and individuals) as they affect socialization and have an impact on **social life** (i.e., social interaction). In contrast to more individualized psychological theories, which have what is called a micro focus, sociological approaches utilize a macro perspective, stressing the type of behavior likely to be exhibited by group members rather than attempting to predict the behavior of specific individuals. As noted in Chapter 1, sociological thought has influenced criminological theory construction more significantly than any other perspective during the past half century, due (at least in part) to a widespread concern with social problems including civil rights, the women's movement, issues of poverty,

and the decline in influence experienced by many traditional social institutions, such as the family, government, organized religion, and educational systems.

Although all sociological perspectives on crime share some characteristics, particular theories give greater or lesser weight to selected components of social life. We can identify three key sociological explanations for crime:

1. **Crime is the result of an individual's location within the structure of society**. This approach focuses on the social and economic conditions of life, including poverty, alienation, social disorganization, weak social control, personal frustration, relative deprivation, differential opportunities, alternative means to success, and deviant subcultures and subcultural values that conflict with conventional values. (These are the primary features of *social structure theories*, which are discussed in this chapter.)

2. **Crime is the end product of various social processes**. This approach stresses inappropriate socialization and social learning as well as interpersonal relationships, strength of the social bond, lack of self-control, and personal and group consequences of societal reactions to deviance as they contribute to crime. (These are the primary characteristics of *social process theories* and *social development theories*, which are discussed in Chapter 7.)

3. **Crime is the product of class struggle**. This perspective emphasizes existing power relationships between social groups, distribution of wealth within society, ownership of the means of production, and economic and social structures of society as they relate to social class and social control. (These are the primary features of *social conflict theories*, which are discussed in Chapter 8.)

Definition of Social Structure Theories

The theories in this chapter are termed **social structure theories**. These theories look at the formal and informal economic and social arrangements (or structure) of society as the root causes of crime and deviance. These theories also see the negative aspects of societal structure, such as disorganization within the family, poverty

> ■ **social disorganization theory**
> A perspective on crime and deviance that sees society as a kind of organism and crime and deviance as a kind of disease, or social pathology. This type of theory is often associated with the perspective of social ecology and with the Chicago School of criminology, which developed during the 1920s and 1930s.

the **PROFESSOR** | **SPEAKS**

Characterizing Social Structural Theories

JENNIFER HUCK

Indiana
University of
Pennsylvania

Social structural theories explain crime at a macro level, positing that societal institutions create crime because they limit individual behavior. For instance, our society divides social classes due to its economic structure,

so your family's social class impacts your choice of college, likely marriage partners, and so on. Certain people engage in crime because their social class and other institutional factors (such as their neighborhood) limit their legitimate opportunities.

Merton's strain theory measures the disjuncture between aspirations and expectations. One cause of strain is poor grades (expectation) when you want to graduate from college (aspiration). When taking a final exam, you can respond to this strain in different ways:

* *Conformity.* Study hard, take the final, and hope for an A.
* *Innovation.* Steal a copy of the exam, and take the final.
* *Ritualism.* Study, take the final, and hope for a C.
* *Retreatism.* Party hard, and maybe take the final.
* *Rebellion.* Quit school, and speak out against college education.

Social disorganization theory examines the physical decay (property), social decay (people), and social ties (connections) of a neighborhood. Think of the typical American suburban neighborhood; now think of the typical poor ghetto neighborhood. What do these areas look like, and what are some differences? How do these differences connect to crime rates?

Source: Reprinted by permission of Jennifer Huck. Photo courtesy of Jennifer Huck. Logo courtesy of Indiana University of Pennsylvania.

or income inequality, and disadvantages due to lack of success in the educational process, as producers of criminal behavior.

Although different kinds of social structure theories have been advanced to explain crime, they all have one thing in common: They highlight those arrangements within society that contribute to the low socioeconomic status of identifiable groups as significant causes of crime. Social structure theorists view members of socially and economically disadvantaged groups as being more likely to commit crime, and they see economic and social disenfranchisement as fundamental causes of crime. Poverty, lack of education, absence of salable skills, and subcultural values conducive to crime are all thought to be predicated on the social conditions surrounding early life experiences, and they provide the causal underpinnings of social structure theories. Environmental influences, socialization, and traditional and accepted patterns of behavior are all used by social structuralists to portray the criminal as a product of his or her social environment, and the immediate social environment is viewed as a consequence of the structure of the society to which the offender belongs. Although criminality is recognized as a form of acquired behavior, it is depicted as the end result of social inequality, racism, and feelings of disenfranchisement to which existing societal arrangements give rise. When these arrangements are unfair and relatively unchangeable, they perpetuate the fundamental conditions that cause crime.

Crime is seen largely as a lower-class phenomenon, and the criminality of the middle and upper classes is generally discounted as less serious, less frequent, and less dangerous.

Types of Social Structure Theories

This chapter describes three major types of social structure theories: (1) social disorganization theory (also called the *ecological approach*), (2) strain theory, and (3) culture conflict theory (also called *cultural deviance theory*). All have a number of elements in common, and the classification of a theory into a subcategory is often a matter of which aspects a writer chooses to emphasize rather than any clear-cut definitional elements inherent in that theory (see the Theory in Perspective box).

Social Disorganization Theory

Social disorganization theory (which depicts social change, social conflict, and lack of social consensus as the root causes of crime and deviance) is closely associated with the ecological school of criminology. Much early criminology in the United States was

■ **human ecology**
The interrelationship between human beings and the physical and cultural environments in which they live.

■ **social disorganization**
A condition said to exist when a group is faced with social change, uneven development of culture, maladaptiveness, disharmony, conflict, and lack of consensus.

THEORY | in PERSPECTIVE
Types of Social Structure Theories

Social structure theories emphasize poverty, lack of education, absence of marketable skills, and deviant subcultural values as fundamental causes of crime. These theories, which portray crime as the result of an individual's location within the structure of society and focus on the social and economic conditions of life, are divided into three types.

Social Disorganization

Depicts social change, social conflict, and the lack of social consensus as the root causes of crime and deviance; an offshoot, social ecology, sees society as a kind of organism and crime and deviance as a disease or social pathology.

Period: 1920s–1930s

Theorists: Robert Park, Ernest Burgess, W. I. Thomas, Florian Znaniecki, Clifford Shaw, Henry McKay

Concepts: Social ecology, ecological theories, social pathology, social disorganization, Chicago School, Chicago Area Project, demographics, concentric zones, delinquency areas, cultural transmission (criminology of place, environmental criminology, defensible space, and the broken windows thesis represent, at least in part, a contemporary reinterpretation of early ecological notions).

Strain Theory

Points to a lack of fit between socially approved success goals and the availability of socially approved means to achieve those goals.

As a consequence, according to the perspective of strain theory, individuals who are unable to succeed through legitimate means turn to other avenues (crime) that promise economic and social recognition.

Period: 1930s–present

Theorists: Robert K. Merton, Steven F. Messner, Richard Rosenfeld, Peter Blau and Judith Blau, Robert Agnew

Concepts: Anomie, goals, means, innovation, retreatism, ritualism, rebellion, differential opportunity, relative deprivation, distributive justice, general strain theory (GST)

Culture Conflict

Sees the root cause of crime in a clash of values between variously socialized groups over what is acceptable or proper behavior.

Period: 1920s–present

Theorists: Thorsten Sellin, Frederic M. Thrasher, William F. Whyte, Walter Miller, Gresham Sykes, David Matza, Franco Ferracuti, Marvin Wolfgang, Richard A. Cloward, Lloyd E. Ohlin, Albert Cohen, many others

Concepts: Subculture, violent subcultures, socialization, focal concerns, delinquency and drift, techniques of neutralization, illegitimate opportunity structures, reaction formation, conduct norms

rooted in the study of urban settlements and communities[5] as well as the human ecology movement of the early twentieth century. *Ecology* is a term borrowed from biology that describes the interrelationships between living organisms and their environment, and social scientists use the term **human ecology** to describe the interrelationship between human beings and the physical and cultural environments in which they live.[6] Pioneers in the human ecology movement saw cities as superorganisms that incorporated areas adapted to specific groups, including ethnic groups ("Little Italy," "Chinatown"), which were functional enclaves within a larger organized whole that possessed its own dynamics.

The idea of the community as a functional whole that directly determines the quality of life for its members was developed and explored around the beginning of the twentieth century by sociologists like Emile Durkheim (1858–1917),[7] Ferdinand Toennies (1855–1936),[8] and Georg Simmel (1858–1918).[9] Durkheim believed that crime was a normal part

of all societies and that law was a symbol of social solidarity, so an act was "criminal when it offends strong and defined states of the collective conscience."[10]

Some of the earliest sociologists to study American communities were **W. I. Thomas** and **Florian Znaniecki**. In *The Polish Peasant in Europe and America*, Thomas and Znaniecki described the problems Polish immigrants faced in the early 1900s when they left their homeland and moved to American cities.[11] The authors noted that crime rates rose among displaced people and hypothesized that the cause was the **social disorganization** that resulted from immigrants' inability to successfully transplant guiding norms and values from their

> If we would change the amount of crime in the community, we must change the community.
> —Frank Tannenbaum

■ **social ecology**
An approach to criminological theorizing that attempts to link the structure and organization of a human community to interactions with its localized environment.

■ **social pathology**
A concept that compares society to a physical organism and that sees criminality as an illness.

LIBRARY EXTRA 6–1
WEB EXTRA 6–1
WEB EXTRA 6–2

home cultures into the new one (see **Library Extra 6–1**). Learn more about early social disorganization perspectives via **Web Extra 6–1;** read more about classical sociological theory at **Web Extra 6–2**.

Chicago School

Some of the earliest sociological theories to receive widespread recognition can be found in the writings of **Robert Park** and **Ernest Burgess**. In the 1920s and 1930s at the University of Chicago, they developed what became known as **social ecology** or the ecological school of criminology.[12] The social ecology movement, influenced by the work of biologists on the interactions of organisms with their environments, concerned itself with how the structure of society adapts to the quality of natural resources and to the existence of other human groups.[13] One writer stated that social ecology is "the attempt to link the structure and organization of any human community to interactions with its localized environment."[14] Because ecological models build on an organic analogy, it is easy to portray social disorganization as a disease or pathology.[15] Hence, social ecologists who studied crime developed a disease model built around the concept of **social pathology**, defined as "those human actions which run contrary to the ideals of residential stability, property ownership, sobriety, thrift, habituation to work, small business enterprise, sexual discretion, family solidarity, neighborliness, and discipline of will."[16] Over time, the concept of social pathology changed and came to represent the idea that some aspects of society are pathological, or "sick," and produce deviant behavior among groups and individuals who are exposed to such social conditions.

Social disorganization and social pathology may arise when a group is faced with "social change, uneven development of culture, maladaptiveness, disharmony, conflict, and lack of consensus."[17] Due to the rapid influx of immigrant populations at the beginning of the twentieth century, American cities were caught up in swift social change, and Park and Burgess saw in them an ideal focus for the study of social disorganization. They viewed cities as having five concentric zones, much like the circles on a target, each with unique characteristics and populations (see

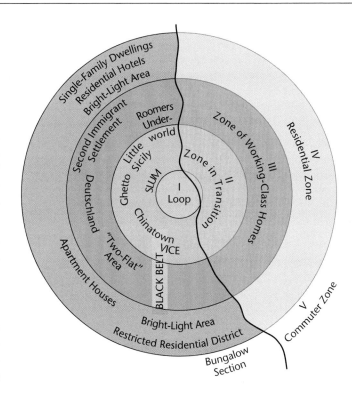

FIGURE 6-1 | Chicago's Concentric Zones
Source: Robert E. Park, Ernest W. Burgess, and R. D. McKenzie, *The City* (Chicago: University of Chicago Press, 1925), p. 55. Copyright © 1925 University of Chicago Press. Reprinted by permission.

Figure 6–1): Zone I, or the "loop," contained retail businesses and light manufacturing; Zone II, surrounding the city center, was in transition from residential to business uses, was home to recent immigrant groups, and was characterized by deteriorating houses and factories and abandoned buildings; Zone III contained mostly working-class tenements; Zone IV was occupied by middle-class citizens with single-family homes; and Zone V, the suburbs, was called the "commuter zone." Park and Burgess noticed that residents of the inner zones tended to migrate to outer zones as their economic positions improved.

Clifford Shaw and **Henry McKay**, other early advocates of the ecological approach, applied the concentric zones to the

> ▨ **cultural transmission**
> The idea that delinquency is transmitted through successive generations of people living in an area through the same process of social communication by which languages, social roles, and attitudes are transmitted.
>
> ▨ **ecological theory**
> A type of sociological approach that emphasizes demographics (the characteristics of population groups) and geographics (the mapped location of such groups relative to one another) and that sees the social disorganization that characterizes delinquency areas as a major cause of criminality and victimization.
>
> ▨ **Chicago School of criminology**
> An ecological approach to explaining crime that examines how social disorganization contributes to social pathology.

WEB EXTRA 6–3

> ▨ **criminology of place**
> A perspective that emphasizes the importance of geographic location and architectural features as they are associated with the prevalence of criminal victimization; also called *environmental criminology*.
>
> ▨ **environmental criminology**
> A perspective that emphasizes the importance of geographic location and architectural features as they are associated with the prevalence of criminal victimization; also called *criminology of place*.

study of juvenile delinquency, conducting empirical studies of Chicago juveniles' arrest rates in 1900–1906, 1917–1923, and 1927–1933 (years associated with high rates of neighborhood transition). Shaw and McKay found that rates of offending remained relatively constant over time within zones of transition and concluded that delinquency was caused by the nature of the environment in which immigrants lived rather than by characteristics of the immigrant groups themselves.[18] Shaw and McKay saw social disorganization as the inability of local communities to solve common problems and believed that the degree of disorganization in a community was largely predicated upon the extent of residential mobility and racial heterogeneity present in that community. As a result of their studies, they developed the idea of **cultural transmission**: Traditions of delinquency were transmitted to successive generations in the same zone in the same way that languages, roles, and attitudes were communicated.

> Cultural transmission theory says that delinquency is transmitted to new generations in the same way that languages, roles, and attitudes are.

Because early **ecological theories** focused on selected geographic areas, their methodology came to be known as "area studies." Because 1920s Chicago served as the model for most such studies, they became collectively referred to as the **Chicago School of criminology**. Although the applicability of these early studies to other cities or other time periods was questionable, the Chicago School had demonstrated the tendency for criminal activity to be associated with urban transitional zones, which were typified by social disorganization, turmoil, lower property values, poverty, and lack of privacy.

The greatest contribution the ecological school made to criminological literature can be found in its claim that society wields a major influence on human behavior.[19] Ecological theorists of the Chicago School used two sources of information: (1) population statistics and official crime and (2) ethnographic data. Population statistics (demographics), when combined with crime information, provided empirical material that gave scientific weight to ecological investigations; ethnographic information, gathered in the form of life stories (ethnographies), described the lives of city inhabitants. By comparing one set of data with the other—demographics with ethnographies—ecological investigators were able to show that life experiences varied from one location to another and that personal involvement in crime was strongly associated with place of residence. Learn more about the Chicago School of criminology at **Web Extra 6–3**.

Criminology of Place

Ecological approaches to crime causation have found a modern rebirth in the **criminology of place** (also called **environmental criminology**), which builds on the contributions of routine activities theory and situational crime prevention (both of which were discussed in Chapter 3). It emphasizes the importance of geographic location and architectural features in terms of prevalence of victimization. Hot spots of crime can include neighborhoods, specific streets, and even individual houses and businesses. Lawrence W. Sherman and colleagues cited a study that revealed that 3% of places (addresses and intersections) in Minneapolis produce 50% of all calls to the police and noted that crime in Minneapolis, although relatively rare, is geographically concentrated.[20]

Reflecting the questions first addressed by Shaw and McKay, researcher, Rodney Stark asked, "How is it that neighborhoods can remain the site of high crime and deviance rates despite a complete turnover in their populations? There must be something about places as such that sustains crime."[21] Stark developed a theory of deviant neighborhoods consisting of 30 propositions, including the following:[22]

- To the extent that neighborhoods are dense and poor, homes will be crowded.

- Where homes are more crowded, there will be a greater tendency to congregate outside the home in places and circumstances that raise levels of temptation and offer opportunity to deviate.

■ **broken windows thesis**
A perspective on crime causation that holds that physical deterioration in an area leads to increased concerns for personal safety among area residents and to higher crime rates in that area.

■ **defensible space**
The range of mechanisms that combine to bring an environment under the control of its residents.

WEB EXTRA 6-4
LIBRARY EXTRA 6-2

- Where homes are more crowded, there will be lower levels of supervision of children.
- Reduced levels of child supervision will result in poor school achievement, with a consequent reduction in stakes in conformity and an increase in deviant behavior.
- Poor, dense neighborhoods tend to be mixed-use neighborhoods.
- Mixed use increases familiarity with and easy access to places offering the opportunity for deviance.

Central to the criminology of place is the **broken windows thesis**, which holds that physical deterioration such as increases in unrepaired buildings leads to greater concerns for personal safety among area residents.[23] These concerns lead to further decreases in maintenance and repair; to increased delinquency, vandalism, and crime; and to even further deterioration in safety and the physical environment—all resulting in offenders from other neighborhoods being increasingly attracted by the area's perceived vulnerability. Physical disorder, left unchecked, leads to crime by driving residents indoors and sending a message to would-be offenders that a neighborhood is out of control.[24]

The broken windows perspective, first advanced in a 1982 article by James Q. Wilson and George L. Kelling titled "Broken Windows: The Police and Neighborhood Safety,"[25] led to an increase in the use of "order maintenance policing" and a crackdown on quality-of-life offenses, such as panhandling, graffiti, littering, and prostitution, in some of our nation's cities. In 2000 in New York City, (then) Mayor Rudolph Giuliani announced a new police campaign using computer mapping to track crime and to target offenses such as jaywalking, public urination, panhandling, graffiti, public drinking, and prostitution.

Even within high-crime neighborhoods and neighborhoods characterized by urban decay, crimes tend to be concentrated at specific locations, such as street blocks or multiple-family dwellings, and some units within specific apartment buildings are more likely to be the site of criminal occurrences. Therefore, the criminology of place employs the concept of **defensible space** (evolving from a 1994 conference at Washington University in St. Louis, Missouri[26]), meaning "the range of mechanisms—real and symbolic

> The broken windows thesis says that neighborhood physical deterioration leads to increased delinquency, vandalism, and crime.

barriers, strongly defined areas of influence, and improved opportunities for surveillance—that combine to bring an environment under the control of its residents."[27] The St. Louis conference brought criminologists, police officers, and architects face-to-face and focused on crime problems characteristic of public-housing areas. Conference findings demonstrated that specific architectural changes that enhanced barriers, defined boundaries, and removed criminal opportunity could do much to reduce the risk of crime—even in the middle of high-crime neighborhoods.

The criminology of place holds that location can be as predictive of criminal activity as lifestyles of victimized individuals or social features of victimized households. (*Place* has been defined by researchers as "a fixed physical environment that can be seen completely and simultaneously, at least on its surface, by one's naked eyes."[28]) Places can be criminogenic because they have certain routine activities associated with them or because they provide the characteristics that facilitate crime commission.

Recognizing the importance of criminology of place, New York City police developed a program called Operation Padlock designed to close businesses with repeated crime problems; it appeared to be successful in reducing the incidence of certain kinds of crime. Author Sherman pointed out that "neither capital punishment of places (as in arson of crack houses) nor incapacitation of the routine activities of criminal hot spots (as in revocation of liquor licenses) seems likely to eliminate crime. But since the routine activities of places may be regulated far more easily than the routine activities of persons, a criminology of place would seem to offer substantial promise for public policy as well as theory."[29]

Some crime-prevention programs are combining ideas derived from the criminology of place with spatial-mapping techniques to fight crime (the Theory versus Reality box provides information about crime-mapping techniques). Visit the National Institute of Justice's MAPS program via **Web Extra 6–4** to learn more about crime mapping, and read more about the broken windows thesis at **Library Extra 6–2**.

More recent studies of the broken windows concept have cast doubt on the assertion, made by Wilson and Kelling, that police intervention into the process that links disorder and crime can be effective in reducing crime.[30] It may be that disorder and crime have common roots and that one is more associated with the other than produced by it.[31] Hence, efforts to target quality-of-life offenses in urban areas experiencing high levels of social disorganization may not have the desired effect of reducing crime. David Thacher, professor of public policy and urban planning at the University of Michigan, explained that "these challenges to

▓ **strain theory**
A sociological approach that posits a disjuncture between socially and subculturally sanctioned means and goals as the cause of criminal behavior.

WEB EXTRA 6-5

▓ **anomie**
A social condition in which norms are uncertain or lacking.

THEORY | versus REALITY

The Criminology of Place, Routine Activities, and Crime Mapping

Today's law enforcement agencies are using the criminology of place and routine activities theories (discussed in Chapter 3) to develop situational crime-prevention techniques that combine technology with crime mapping. One proponent of this approach is the Mapping and Analysis Program (MAPS) of the National Institute of Justice. Crime mapping, used in conjunction with geographic information systems (GIS), makes effective use of law enforcement resources by helping police administrators direct patrols to places where they are most needed.

In the routine activities interpretation, crimes are seen as needing three ingredients: a likely offender, a suitable target, and the absence of a guardian capable of preventing the criminal act. Then comes the term *density paradox*: On the one hand, high population densities create a high potential for crime because people and property are crowded in small spaces, resulting in many likely offenders and suitable targets; on the other hand, surveillance is plentiful, so criminal acts in public spaces are likely to be observed by others (guardians). Crime can be reduced or prevented by making people less likely to offend (by increasing guilt and fostering development of the "inner policeman" who tames criminal impulses), by making targets less available (also called *situational crime prevention*), and by making guardians more numerous or effective. Putting the routine activities approach and situational crime prevention into a geographic context involves asking how each element is distributed in geographic space. Where are the likely offenders? (What is the geography of the youthful male population?) Where are the suitable targets? (What is the geography of convenience stores, malls, ATMs, poorly illuminated pedestrian areas?) Where are the guardians? (What is the potential for surveillance, both formal and informal, of targets or areas that may contain targets?)

The perspective that focuses on criminal spatial behavior develops a scenario in which the motivated (potential) criminal uses cues, or environmental signals, to assess victims or targets. Clusters and sequences of cues relating to the social and physical aspects of the environment are seen as a *template*, which the offender uses to evaluate victims or targets; tied to this process is the concept of *activity space*, the area where the offender customarily moves about that is familiar to him or her.

Activity spaces vary with demographics. Historically, younger persons tended to have more constricted activity spaces, not having resources to travel far, and women had more geographically limited activity areas than men because men worked farther from home and their jobs gave them greater mobility; both are less true today.

Analysts considering crime patterns from a theoretical perspective might ask some "filter" questions: How important is geography in explaining a pattern? Is the pattern random or not? If not, why not? Can routine activities theory or criminal spatial behavior theory help explain this pattern? Is this pattern normal or unusual for this area? If the pattern is an anomaly, why is this? What resources can be used to better understand the social and other environmental dynamics of the area of interest?

For a list of Web sites displaying active crime maps, see **Web Extra 6-5**.

Discussion Questions

1. How does routine activities theory support the concepts involved in the spatial analysis of crime?

2. What is the density paradox? What implications does it have for crime prevention?

3. What "filter" questions are discussed in this box? Can you think of any others that might be asked?

Source: National Institute of Justice, "Mapping and Analysis for Public Safety (MAPS)," http://www.ojp.gov/nij/maps (accessed May 28, 2007); and Keith Harries, *Mapping Crime: Principles and Practice* (Washington, DC: National Institute of Justice, 1999), http://www.ojp.usdoj.gov/cmrc (accessed December 15, 2005).

the broken windows theory have not yet discredited order maintenance policing with policymakers or the public. But among criminologists, order maintenance is clearly under siege."[32] See the Crime in the News box in this chapter for more on broken windows theory.

Strain Theory

The second type of social structure theory discussed in this chapter is strain theory. *Strain* can be defined as the pressure that individuals feel to reach socially determined goals.[33] The classic statement of **strain theory**—which depicts delinquency as a form of adaptive problem-solving behavior committed in response to problems involving frustrating and undesirable social environments—was offered in 1938 by **Robert K. Merton**, who also developed the concept of **anomie** (a French word meaning "normlessness").

Anomie was popularized by Emile Durkheim in his 1897 book *Suicide*, in which he used the term to explain how a breakdown of predictable social conditions can lead to feelings of personal loss, dissolution, and lack of a sense of belonging.[34] Merton's use of the term *anomie* was somewhat different and meant a disjunction between socially approved means to success and legitimate goals.[35] Merton maintained that legitimate goals, such as wealth,

CRIME | in the NEWS

Broken Windows and Crime

LOWELL—The year was 2005 and Lowell (Massachusetts) was being turned into a real-life crime-fighting laboratory.

Researchers, working with police, identified 34 crime hot spots. In half of them, authorities set to work—clearing trash from the sidewalks, fixing street lights, and sending loiterers scurrying. Abandoned buildings were secured, businesses forced to meet code, and more arrests made for misdemeanors. Mental health services and homeless aid referrals expanded.

In the remaining hot spots, normal policing and services continued.

Then researchers from Harvard and Suffolk University sat back and watched, meticulously recording criminal incidents in each of the hot spots.

The results, just now circulating in law enforcement circles, are striking: A 20% plunge in calls to police from the parts of town that received extra attention. It is seen as strong scientific evidence that the long-debated "broken windows" theory really works—that disorderly conditions breed bad behavior, and that fixing them can help prevent crime. . . .

Many police departments across the country already use elements of the broken windows theory, or focus on crime hot spots. The Lowell experiment offers guidance on what seems to work best. Cleaning up the physical environment was very effective; misdemeanor arrests less so, and boosting social services had no apparent impact. . . .

The broken windows theory was first put forth in a 1982 *Atlantic* article by James Q. Wilson, a political scientist then at Harvard, and George L. Kelling, a criminologist. The theory suggests that a disorderly environment sends a message that no one is in charge, thus increasing fear, weakening community controls, and inviting criminal behavior. It further maintains that stopping minor offenses and restoring greater order can prevent serious crime.

That theory has been hotly debated even as it has been widely deployed.

Critics have pointed out that defining "disorder" is inherently subjective. Some challenge "broken windows" success stories, questioning, for example, whether New York City's decrease in crime in the 1990s could have been caused by the decline in the use of crack cocaine or other factors. . . .

Discussion Questions

1. How would you describe the broken windows theory of policing?

2. What implications does the broken windows theory hold for crime-prevention policy? Do you know of any communities in which you'd like to see it applied?

A playground next to an abandoned apartment building. What does broken windows theory say about places like this?
Source: Jim West/Alamy

status, and personal happiness, are generally portrayed as desirable for everyone, but the widely acceptable means to these goals, such

Robert K. Merton popularized the term anomie, a French word meaning *normlessness.*

as education, hard work, and financial savings, are not equally available. As a consequence, crime and deviance tend to arise as alternative means to success when individuals feel the strain of being pressed to succeed in socially approved ways but find that the tools necessary for such success are not available to them, and that strain increases as the gulf between the goals and the means available to achieve them widens. Merton's emphasis on the felt strain resulting from a lack of fit between goals and means led to his approach being called *strain theory.*

Complicating the picture further, Merton maintained that not everyone accepts the legitimacy of socially approved goals. Merton diagrammed possible combinations of goals and means as shown in Table 6–1. The first row, labeled *conformity,* signifies acceptance of the goals that society holds as legitimate for everyone, with ready availability of the means approved for achieving those goals; the mode of adaptation associated with this combination of goals and means typifies most middle- and upper-class individuals.

Innovation arises when an emphasis on approved goal achievement combines with a lack of opportunity to participate fully in socially acceptable means to success, which is experienced by many lower-class individuals who have been socialized to desire traditional success symbols (expensive cars, large homes, big bank accounts) but do not have ready access to approved means of acquiring them (educational opportunity); innovative

■ **relative deprivation**
A sense of social or economic inequality experienced by those who are unable, for whatever reason, to achieve legitimate success within the surrounding society.

London's Metropolitan Police officers view displays from CCTV cameras around London in the Special Operations Room of their Central Communications Command. Defensible space can be defined in terms of barriers to crime commission and preventive surveillance opportunities. How might such features be enhanced in high-crime areas?
Source: Oli Scarff/Liaison/Getty Images, Inc.

TABLE 6-1 | Goals and Means Disjuncture

	GOALS	MEANS
Conformity	+	+
Innovation	+	−
Ritualism	−	+
Retreatism	−	−
Rebellion	±	±

Source: Adapted from Robert K. Merton, "Social Structure and Anomie," *American Sociological Review*, Vol. 3, No. 5 (Oct. 1938), pp. 672–682.

behavioral responses, including crime, can be expected to develop when individuals find themselves deprived. Merton said that "poverty as such, and consequent limitation of opportunity, are not sufficient to induce a conspicuously high rate of criminal behavior. Even the often mentioned 'poverty in the midst of plenty' will not necessarily lead to this result."[36] It is when those who find themselves in poverty are pressured to achieve material success and acquire other associated symbols of status that innovation results.

The third row, *ritualism*, refers to the type of behavior arising when members of society participate in socially desirable means but show little interest in goal achievement. A ritualist may get a good education, work every day in an acceptable occupation, and appear to be leading a solid middle-class lifestyle yet care little for the symbols of success, choosing to live an otherwise independent lifestyle.

Retreatism describes the behavior of those who reject both the socially approved goals and the means. They may become dropouts, drug abusers, or homeless persons or participate in alternative lifestyles, like communal living; they are often socially and psychologically quite separate from the larger society around them.

Merton's last category, *rebellion*, describes the actions of a person who wishes to replace socially approved goals and means with some other system, and political radicals, revolutionaries, and antiestablishment agitators fit into this category. Merton believed that conformity is the most common mode of adaptation prevalent in society and that retreatism is the least common.

A 2006 study by sociologists Thomas M. Arvanites and Robert H. Defina at Villanova University tested a prediction based on Merton's theory: that negative economic conditions and declining business cycles can increase social strain, resulting in heightened rates for certain kinds of crimes, especially property crimes. By comparing society's economic conditions over time with rates for such crimes, the researchers concluded that "an improving economy has a negative and statistically significant effect on all four index property crimes and robbery." Because financial gain is the primary purpose of robbery, they noted that "a finding that robbery is the only violent crime to be influenced by the business cycle was not surprising."[37]

Relative Deprivation

Another version of Merton's anomie theory has been proposed by Steven F. Messner and Richard Rosenfeld, who suggested that inconsistencies in the American Dream are to be blamed for most criminal activity: "Our thesis is that the American Dream itself exerts pressures toward crime by encouraging an anomic cultural environment, an environment in which people are encouraged to adopt an 'anything goes' mentality in the pursuit of personal goals."[38]

It is often said that Americans are the richest people on earth and that even the poorest Americans are far richer than the average citizen of many Third World nations, but even if such an assertion is true, it means little to someone who is living in the United States and is poor when judged in terms of U.S. standards. Deprivation has an important psychological component and cannot be accurately assessed in absolute terms.

Relative deprivation refers to the economic and social gaps that exist between rich and poor who live in close proximity to one another. According to sociologists Judith Blau and

■ **distributive justice**
The rightful, equitable, and just distribution of rewards within a society.

■ **general strain theory (GST)**
A perspective that suggests that law-breaking behavior is a coping mechanism that enables those who engage in it to deal with the socioemotional problems generated by negative social relations.

Peter Blau, two proponents of the relative deprivation concept, people assess their position in life by way of comparison with things and people they already know.[39] According to the Blaus, relative deprivation creates feelings of anger, frustration, hostility, and social injustice on the part of those who experience it. According to **distributive justice**, which refers to people's perceptions of their rightful place in the reward structure of society, even wealthy and socially privileged individuals may feel slighted or shortchanged if they feel inadequately rewarded for their behavior or accomplishments. But the perception of the rightful distribution of rewards appears to be highly dependent upon cultural expectations; for example, even successful Americans sometimes feel they deserve more, whereas studies show that Japanese society has been able to accommodate rapid socioeconomic growth without generating a felt sense of economic injustice, even among its least successful members, and without experiencing a substantial increase in crime.[40]

Surveys provide evidence for distinguishing between two types of relative deprivation: personal and group.[41] Personal relative deprivation is characteristic of individuals who feel deprived compared with other people; group relative deprivation is a communal sense of injustice that is shared by members of the same group. People who experience personal deprivation are likely to feel socially isolated and personally stressed, and those who believe their entire social group is deprived relative to other groups are more prone to participate in social movements and may actively attempt to change the social system, making group relative deprivation a powerful force for social change.

General Strain Theory

In 1992, strain theory was reformulated by **Robert Agnew** and others who molded it into a comprehensive perspective called

> GST sees law-breaking as a coping mechanism for dealing with socioemotional problems.

general strain theory (GST).[42] GST sees law-breaking behavior as a coping mechanism enabling those who engage in it to deal with the socioemotional problems generated by negative social relations.

In 2006, Agnew restated the six central propositions of GST:[43]

1. Strains refer to events and conditions disliked by individuals. There are three major types of strain: Individuals may (a) lose something they value, (b) be treated in an aversive or negative manner by others, and (c) be unable to achieve their goals.

2. Strains increase the likelihood of *particular* crimes primarily through their impact on a range of negative emotional *states*. Certain kinds of strains might lead some to seek revenge, whereas others cause those who experience them to steal things of value.

3. Those strains most likely to cause crime (a) are perceived as high in magnitude, (b) are seen as unjust, (c) are associated with low self-control, and (d) create some pressure or incentive to engage in criminal coping.

4. The likelihood that an individual will react to strains with criminal behavior depends on a range of factors influencing the individual's (a) ability to engage in legal coping, (b) costs of crime, and (c) disposition of crime.

5. Patterns of offending over the life course, group differences in crime, and community and societal differences in crime can be partly explained in terms of differences in the exposure to strains conducive to crime (males, for example, are more often exposed to strains conducive to crime and are more likely than females to cope with strains through crime).

6. Crime can be reduced by reducing individuals' exposure to strains conducive to crime and by reducing individuals' likelihood of responding to strains with crime.

Agnew explained that the strains most likely to cause crime in Western societies include child abuse and neglect; negative secondary school experiences; abusive peer relations; chronic unemployment; marital problems; parental rejection; erratic, excessive, and or/harsh supervision or discipline; criminal victimization; homelessness; racial, ethnic, or gender discrimination; and failure to achieve selected goals. Factors that increase the likelihood of criminal coping include poor conventional coping skills and resources; availability of criminal skills and resources; low levels of conventional social support; routine association with criminal others; personal beliefs and values favorable to crime; frequent exposure to situations where the costs of crime are low; low levels of social control, including weak bonds to conventional others; and lack of investment in conventional institutions. Agnew's strategies for reducing exposure to strains include eliminating strains conducive to crime, altering strains to make them less conducive to crime, removing individuals from exposure to strain, and equipping individuals with the traits and skills needed to avoid strains conducive to crime.

GST expands on traditional strain theory in several ways. First, it significantly widens the focus of strain theory to include

WEB EXTRA 6-6
LIBRARY EXTRA 6-3

■ **negative affective state**
An adverse emotion such as anger, fear, depression, or disappointment that derives from the experience of strain.

■ **culture conflict theory**
A sociological perspective on crime that suggests that the root cause of criminality can be found in a clash of values between variously socialized groups over what is acceptable or proper behavior; also called *cultural deviance theory*.

all types of negative relations between an individual and others; second, GST maintains that strain is likely to have a cumulative effect on delinquency after reaching a certain threshold; third, general strain theory provides a more comprehensive account of the cognitive, behavioral, and emotional adaptations to strain than traditional strain approaches; and finally, GST more fully describes the wide variety of factors affecting the choice of delinquent adaptations to strain.

Agnew saw the crime-producing effects of strain as cumulative and concluded that whatever form it takes, "strain creates a predisposition for delinquency in those cases in which it is chronic or repetitive."[44] Predispositions may be manifested in the form of **negative affective states**, meaning emotions such as anger, fear, depression, and disappointment.

An analysis by Agnew of other strain theories found that all such theories share at least two central explanatory features.[45] Agnew said that strain theories focus on (1) "explicitly on negative relationships with others, relationships in which the individual is not treated as he or she wants to be treated," and he argued that (2) "adolescents are pressured into delinquency by the negative affective states—most notably anger and related emotions—that often result from negative relationships."[46]

In 1994, Raymond Paternoster and Paul Mazerolle tested some of the assumptions underlying GST through an analysis of data from the National Youth Survey.[47] They found partial support for GST and discovered that negative relations with adults, feelings of dissatisfaction with friends and school life, and experiences of stressful events were positively related to delinquency, as was living in an unpleasant neighborhood (with social problems and physical deterioration). When conceived of more broadly as exposure to negative stimuli, general strain was found to be significantly related to delinquency.

Contrary to Agnew's hypothesis, however, Paternoster and Mazerolle found no evidence that the effects of strain were enhanced when they were experienced for longer periods of time or that they were diminished when adolescents classified the area of their life in which they experienced strain as "unimportant." Consistent with earlier findings,[48] Paternoster and Mazerolle found that feelings of general strain were positively related to later delinquency—regardless of the number of delinquent peers, moral beliefs, self-efficacy, and level of conventional social support—and that general strain leads to delinquency by weakening the conventional social bond and strengthening the unconventional bond with delinquent peers.

In a more recent test of GST, Lisa M. Broidy of the University of New Mexico examined the intervening role of negative emotions and legitimate coping strategies as they impact the relationship between strain and crime and found that strain can produce anger and other negative emotions and that different sources of strain tend to produce different emotions.[49] "Hence, although evidence of a relationship exists between strain and negative emotions, the nature of this relationship depends on the specific type of strain and negative emotions considered."[50] Strain-induced anger was more likely to lead to criminal outcomes among men than among women, even though members of both genders experienced anger equally under certain specific types of strained circumstances. Broidy also discovered that "negative emotional responses to strain other than anger are associated with a significant increase in legitimate coping and significant decrease in illegitimate/criminal outcomes."[51]

A 2002 study by Robert Agnew and associates further refined GST by explaining why some individuals are more likely than others to react to strain with delinquency.[52] They found that juveniles who measured high in negative emotionality and low in constraint were more likely to react to strain with delinquency and noted that the "incorporation of such traits into GST represents an integration between strain theory and the rapidly growing research on behavioral genetics and crime."[53] Hence, it may be that certain biological factors make some individuals particularly susceptible to the effects of strain in their lives. Learn more about strain theory via **Web Extra 6-6**.

Culture Conflict Theory

The third type of social structure theory discussed in this chapter is **culture conflict theory** (also called *cultural deviance theory*), which suggests that the root cause of criminality can be found in a clash of values between differently socialized groups over what is acceptable or proper behavior. The culture conflict concept is inherent in ecological criminology (discussed earlier in this chapter) and its belief that zones of transition tend to be in flux and harbor groups of people whose values are often at odds with those of the larger society.

The culture conflict perspective found its clearest expression in the writings of **Thorsten Sellin** in his 1938 book *Culture Conflict and Crime*, where he stated that the root cause of crime could be found in different values for what is acceptable or

■ **conduct norms**
Shared expectations of a social group relative to personal conduct.
■ **subculture**
A collection of values and preferences that is communicated to subcultural participants through a process of socialization.
■ **subcultural theory**
A sociological perspective that emphasizes the contribution made by variously socialized cultural groups to the phenomenon of crime.

■ **focal concerns**
The key values of any culture, especially a delinquent subculture.

proper behavior.[54] According to Sellin, **conduct norms**, which provide the valuative basis for human behavior, are acquired early in life through childhood socialization, and it is the clash of norms between variously socialized groups that results in crime. Because crime is a violation of laws established by legislative decree, the criminal event itself is nothing other than a disagreement over what should be acceptable behavior.

Sellin described two types of culture conflict. *Primary conflict* arises when a fundamental clash of cultures occurs, as when an immigrant father kills his daughter's lover following an Old World tradition that demands a family's honor be kept intact.[55] *Secondary conflict* occurs, according to Sellin, when smaller cultures within the primary one clash, as when middle-class values (on which most criminal laws are based) find fault with inner-city or lower-class norms, resulting in the social phenomenon we call *crime*.

> Conduct norms are acquired early in life through childhood socialization.

Subcultural Theory

Fundamental to the notion of culture conflict is the idea of **subculture**, a collection of values and preferences that is communicated to subcultural participants through a process of socialization. Subcultures differ from the larger culture in that they claim the allegiance of smaller groups of people. For example, the wider American culture may proclaim that hard work and individuality are valuable, but a particular subculture may espouse the virtues of deer hunting, male bonding, and recreational alcohol consumption. Countercultures, which tend to reject and invert the values of the surrounding culture, and criminal subcultures, which actively espouse deviant activity, represent extremes. **Subcultural theory** is a sociological perspective that emphasizes the contribution made by variously socialized cultural groups to the phenomenon of crime.

Early writings on subcultures include *The Gang* by **Frederic M. Thrasher**.[56] Thrasher studied 1,313 gangs in Chicago in 1927, and his descriptive work led to a typology in which he described different types of gangs. In 1943, **William F. Whyte**, drawing on Thrasher's work, published *Street Corner Society*.[57] Whyte, in describing his three-year study of the Italian slum he called "Cornerville," further developed the subcultural thesis, showing that lower-class residents of a typical slum could achieve success through the opportunities afforded by slum culture, including racketeering and bookmaking.

Focal Concerns

In 1958, **Walter Miller** attempted to detail the values that drive members of lower-class subcultures into delinquent pursuits, describing lower-class culture as "a long established, distinctively patterned tradition with an integrity of its own."[58] According to that article, titled "Lower Class Culture as a Generating Milieu of Gang Delinquency," a large body of systematically interrelated attitudes, practices, behaviors, and values characteristic of lower-class culture are designed to support and maintain the basic features of the lower-class way of life. In areas where these differ from features of middle-class culture, action oriented to the achievement and maintenance of the lower-class system may violate norms of the middle class and be perceived as deliberately nonconforming. "This does not mean, however, that violation of the middle-class norm is the dominant component of motivation; it is a by-product of action primarily oriented to the lower-class system."

Miller also outlined what he termed the **focal concerns** (key values) of delinquent subcultures: trouble, toughness, smartness, excitement, fate, and autonomy. Miller concluded that subcultural crime and deviance are not the direct consequences of poverty and lack of opportunity but emanate from specific values characteristic of such subcultures. According to Miller, *trouble* is a dominant feature of lower-class culture. Getting into trouble, staying out of trouble, and dealing with trouble when it arises become focal points in the lives of many members of lower-class culture. Miller recognized that getting into trouble is not necessarily valued in and of itself but is seen as a necessary means to valued ends.

Like many theorists of the time, Miller was primarily concerned with the criminality of men. The lower-class masculine concern with *toughness* may have been due to many men in the groups he examined being raised in female-headed families and may have reflected an almost obsessive concern with masculinity as a reaction to the perceived threat of overidentification with female role models.

Miller described *smartness* as the "capacity to outsmart, outfox, outwit, dupe, take, [or] con another or others and the concomitant capacity to avoid being outwitted, taken or duped oneself. In its essence, smartness involves the capacity to achieve a valued entity—material goods, personal status—through a maximum use of mental agility and a minimum of physical

■ **techniques of neutralization**
Culturally available justifications that can provide criminal offenders with the means to disavow responsibility for their behavior.

effort." *Excitement* was seen as a search for thrills—often necessary to overcome the boredom inherent in lower-class lifestyles. Fighting, gambling, picking up women, and making the rounds were all described as derivative aspects of the lower-class concern with excitement. *Fate* is related to the quest for excitement and to the concept of luck. As Miller stated, "Many lower-class persons feel that their lives are subject to a set of forces over which they have relatively little control. These are not supernatural forces or organized religion but relate more to a concept of 'destiny' or man as a pawn. This often implicit worldview is associated with a conception of the ultimate futility of directed effort toward a goal."

Autonomy, manifested in statements like "I can take care of myself" and "No one's going to push me around," produces behavioral problems from the perspective of middle-class expectations when it surfaces in work environments, public schools, or other social institutions built on expectations of conformity.

Miller's work on subcultures and their focal concerns is derived almost entirely from his study of black inner-city delinquents in the Boston area in the 1950s and may have less relevance to members of lower-class subcultures in other places or at other times.

Delinquency and Drift

Members of delinquent subcultures are, to varying degrees, participants in the larger culture that surrounds them. Why do subcultural participants choose behavioral alternatives that seemingly negate the norms and values of the larger society? How can a person give allegiance to two seemingly different sets of values—those of the larger culture and those of a subculture—at the same time? **Gresham Sykes** and **David Matza** provided an answer to this question in their 1957 article "Techniques of Neutralization."[59] Sykes and Matza suggested that offenders and delinquents are aware of conventional values, understand that their offending is wrong, but engage in neutralizing self-talk before offending to mitigate the anticipated shame and guilt associated with violating societal norms.[60] Offenders can overcome feelings of responsibility when involved in crime commission by using five types of justification:

1. **Denying responsibility**. They point to their background of poverty, abuse, and lack of opportunity: "The trouble I get into is not my fault."

2. **Denying injury**. They explain that everyone does it or that individuals or companies can afford it: "They're so rich, they'll never miss it." (See Figure 6–2.)

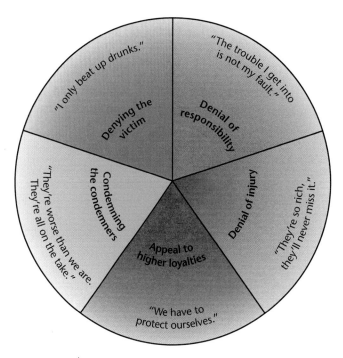

FIGURE 6-2 | Techniques of Neutralization

3. **Denying the victim**. They justify the harm done by claiming that the victim deserved the victimization: "I only beat up drunks."

4. **Condemning the condemners**. They assert that authorities are corrupt or are responsible for their own victimization and that society has made them what they are and must now suffer the consequences: "They're worse than I am. They're all on the take."

5. **Appealing to higher loyalties**. They use defense of their family honor, gang, girlfriend, or neighborhood: "I have to protect myself."

In the words of Sykes and Matza, "It is our argument that much delinquency is based on what is essentially an unrecognized extension of defenses to crimes, in the form of justifications for deviance that are seen as valid by the delinquent but not by the legal system or society at large."[61]

A few years later, Matza went on to suggest that delinquents tend to drift into crime when available **techniques of neutralization** combine with weak or ineffective values espoused by the controlling elements in society, stating that the delinquent "drifts between criminal and conventional action,"[62] choosing whichever is more expedient at the time. By employing techniques of

Follow the author's tweets about the latest crime and justice news at **http://twitter.com/schmalleger.**

neutralization, delinquents need not be fully alienated from the larger society because these techniques provide an effective way of overcoming their feelings of guilt so that they can commit crimes. Matza used the phrase "soft determinism" to describe drift, saying that delinquents are neither forced to make choices because of fateful experiences early in life nor entirely free to make choices unencumbered by the realities of their situation.

More recent studies have found that whereas "only a small percentage of adolescents generally approve of violence or express indifference to violence, [a] large percentage of adolescents accept neutralizations justifying the use of violence in particular situations."[63] Studies have found that young people who disapprove of violence but associate with delinquent peers often use neutralization techniques as justifications for violence in which they personally engage.[64]

Hard-core, active, noninstitutionalized drug dealers, street robbers, and carjackers have also used neutralization techniques.[65] Sociologist Ken Levi found that professional contract killers, or hit men, tend to begin adapting to the role of professional killer by learning to view killing as "just a job" or as "just business," which allows them to deny responsibility for contracted killings and to view themselves as "hired guns," and their victims as "targets" rather than people.[66]

A 2003 study by sociologist Lois Presser of the University of Tennessee on remorse and neutralization among violent male offenders, based on interviews with 27 men who had committed serious violent crimes, found that the men excused or justified their violent actions through five rationalizations: (1) Victims were to blame for harms that resulted from provoking the offender, (2) victims were themselves offenders or deserving of harm, (3) harm to a victim that was not premeditated or intended carried no blame, (4) the legal sanctioning of an offender negated any harm, and (5) harms to the offender and his or her family stemming from the crime negated any harms caused by the offender.[67]

In innovative research published in 2008, Orly Turgeman-Goldschmidt of Israel's Bar-Ilan University conducted 54 unstructured, in-depth face-to-face interviews with malicious Israeli computer vandals (hackers) in order to determine what kinds of neutralization techniques they employ and found that the hackers used neutralization techniques common to other offenders, although their language reflected the cyber-realm.[68] Some hackers were found to be like political criminals, assuming responsibility by means of internal justifications (by attacking al-Qaeda Web sites or bringing down computers of the Arab news network Al-Jazeera and seeing the activity as a positive contribution to their sociopolitical environment); these "hacktivists" defined themselves as hackers with political consciences.[69] Other hackers justified illegal hacking as simply being fun, rewarding, or self-fulfilling

and argued that anyone or anything affected (financial institutions) could afford it and that no one was physically hurt.

Violent Subcultures

Some subcultures are decidedly violent and built around themes and values supporting violent activities. In 1967, **Franco Ferracuti** and **Marvin Wolfgang** published their seminal work, *The Subculture of Violence: Toward an Integrated Theory of Criminology,*[70] which drew together many of the sociological perspectives previously advanced to explain delinquency and crime. Ferracuti and Wolfgang's main thesis was that violence is a learned form of adaptation to certain problematic life circumstances and that learning to be violent takes place within the context of a subcultural milieu emphasizing the advantages of violence over other forms of adaptation. These subcultures of violence both expect violence from their members and legitimize it when it occurs: "The use of violence is not necessarily viewed as illicit conduct, and the users do not have to deal with feelings of guilt about their aggression."[71]

Ferracuti and Wolfgang based their conclusions on an analysis of data that showed substantial differences in the rates of homicides between racial groups in the Philadelphia area—nonwhite men had a homicide rate of 41.7 per 100,000 versus a homicide rate of only 3.4 for white men, and nonwhite women showed a homicide rate of 9.3 versus 0.4 for white women. Explaining these findings, Ferracuti and Wolfgang stated, "Homicide is most prevalent, or the highest rates of homicide occur, among a relatively homogeneous subcultural group in any large urban community. The value system of this group . . . constitutes a subculture of violence. From a psychological viewpoint, we might hypothesize that the greater the degree of integration of the individual into this subculture, the higher the probability that his behavior will be violent in a variety of situations."[72]

Ferracuti and Wolfgang extended their theory of subcultural violence with the following "corollary propositions":[73]

- No subculture can be totally different from or totally in conflict with the society of which it is a part.

- To establish the existence of a subculture of violence does not require that the actors sharing in these basic value elements should express violence in all situations.

- The potential resort or willingness to resort to violence in a variety of situations emphasizes the penetrating and diffusive character of this culture theme.

- The subcultural ethos of violence may be shared by all ages in a subsociety, but this ethos is most prominent in a limited age group, ranging from late adolescence to middle age.

- The counternorm is nonviolence.

■ illegitimate opportunity structure
A subcultural pathway to success that the wider society disapproves of.

- The development of favorable attitudes toward violence and its use in a subculture usually involves learned behavior and a process of differential learning, association, or identification.

- The use of violence in a subculture is not necessarily viewed as illicit conduct, and the users therefore do not have to deal with feelings of guilt about their aggression.

Other writers have commented on geographic distinctions among violent subcultures in different parts of the United States. For example, there are claims that certain forms of criminal violence are more acceptable in the southern United States than in northern portions of the country.[74] Some writers referred to variability in the degree to which interpersonal violence has been accepted in the South over time, whereas others suggested that violence in the South might be a traditional tool in the service of social order.[75]

In 1998, James W. Clarke, a political science professor at the University of Arizona, posited that the high rate of black underclass homicide in the United States flows from a black subculture of violence created by generations of white-on-black violence that first emerged with the "generation of black males that came of age after emancipation."[76] According to Clarke, many black males learned from earlier generations to seek status through their ability to "harm, intimidate, and dominate others."[77]

The wider culture often recognizes a violent subculture's internal rules, so when one member of such a subculture kills another, the wider society may take the killing less seriously than if someone outside the subculture had been killed. Franklin Zimring and his associates described what they called "wholesale" and "retail" costs for homicide: Killings that are perceived to occur within a subculture of violence (when both the victim and the perpetrator are seen as members of a violent subculture) generally result in a less harsh punishment than do killings that occur outside that subculture.[78] Punishments relate to the perceived seriousness of the offense; if members of the subculture in which a crime occurs accept the offense as part of the landscape, so will members of the wider culture.

Differential Opportunity Theory

In 1960, **Richard A. Cloward** and **Lloyd E. Ohlin** published *Delinquency and Opportunity*.[79] Their book, a report on the nature and activities of juvenile gangs blends the subcultural thesis with ideas derived from strain theory, and identified two types of socially structured opportunities for success: legitimate and illegitimate. Legitimate opportunities are generally available to individuals born into middle-class culture, but participants in lower-class subcultures are often denied access to them, so

illegitimate opportunities for success are often seen as quite acceptable by participants in so-called illegitimate subcultures.

Cloward and Ohlin used the term **illegitimate opportunity structure** to describe preexisting subcultural paths to success not approved of by the wider culture. Where illegitimate paths to success are not already in place, alienated individuals may undertake a process of ideational evolution through which "a collective delinquent solution" or a "delinquent means of achieving success" may be decided upon by members of a gang. Because the two paths to success—legitimate and illegitimate—differ in their availability to members of society, Cloward and Ohlin's perspective has been called "differential opportunity."

According to Cloward and Ohlin, delinquent behavior may result from the ready availability of illegitimate opportunities and the effective replacement of the norms of the wider culture with expedient and "legitimate" subcultural rules. "A delinquent subculture is one in which certain forms of delinquent activity are essential requirements for the performance of the dominant roles supported by the subculture."[80] Its most critical elements are the "prescriptions, norms, or rules of conduct that define the activities required of a full-fledged member."[81] They continued, "A person attributes legitimacy to a system of rules and corresponding models of behavior when he accepts them as binding on his conduct."[82] They concluded, "Delinquents have withdrawn their support from established norms and invested officially forbidden forms of conduct with a claim to legitimacy."[83]

Cloward and Ohlin noted that there are two necessary parts to a delinquent act—"It is behavior that violates basic norms of the society, and, when officially known, it evokes a judgment by agents of criminal justice that such norms have been violated."[84] For Cloward and Ohlin, however, crime and deviance are just as normal as any other form of behavior supported by group socialization: "Deviance and conformity generally result from the same kinds of social conditions, [and] deviance ordinarily represents a search for solutions to problems of adjustment." In their view, deviance is just as much an effort to conform (albeit to subcultural norms and expectations) as conformity to the norms of the wider society. "[I]t has been our experience that most persons who participate in delinquent subcultures, if not lone offenders, are fully aware of the difference between right and wrong, between conventional behavior and rule-violating behavior. They may

> *Illegitimate opportunity structures are preexisting subcultural paths to success not approved of by the wider culture.*

WHO'S TO BLAME—The Individual or Society?
Like Father, Like Son

Reginald Barfield, age 22, was arrested for DUI (alcohol) and taken to jail. A judge set bail at $500, and his mother came to the jail to post bond for her son. She didn't have much money, so she used the services of a bondsman, who charged her a $70 fee and arranged for Reginald's release. As she drove her son home, she began yelling at him, telling him that he had turned out just like his father, who had had a long-standing problem with alcohol.

"You're just like your father, and if you don't change, you'll end up just like him—dead."

Reginald became angry and blurted out that he drank because that was all he had known as a child. "What do you mean?" his mother asked.

"Whenever Dad had a problem or when you two fought," Reginald said, "Dad broke open a bottle and killed the pain. It worked for him. It works for me. So you're right. I'm just like him. But it's not my fault. I learned it from him. You didn't stop him. And you didn't stop me."

Think about it:

1. Is Reginald right? Did he learn his problem behavior from his father? What other factors might have contributed to his excessive use of alcohol?

2. Might the concept of reaction formation help explain Reginald's behavior? If so, how?

3. If you were Reginald's mother, to what degree would you hold your son responsible for his problem drinking? To what degree would you hold him responsible if you were a judge hearing his case in court?

4. Are questions about responsibility merely exercises in blame shifting? Is blame shifting ever appropriate when assessing criminal responsibility?

Note: Who's to Blame boxes provide fictionalized critical thinking opportunities, and are not actual cases.

not care about the difference, or they may enjoy flouting the rules of the game, or they may have decided that illegitimate practices get them what they want more efficiently than legitimate practices."[85]

Cloward and Ohlin described three types of delinquent subcultures: (1) criminal subcultures, in which criminal role models are readily available for adoption by those being socialized into the subculture; (2) conflict subcultures, in which participants seek status through violence; and (3) retreatist subcultures, in which drug use and withdrawal from the wider society predominate. These delinquent subcultures have at least three identifiable features: "acts of delinquency that reflect subcultural support are likely to recur with great frequency, access to a successful adult criminal career sometimes results from participation in a delinquent subculture, and the delinquent subculture imparts to the conduct of its members a high degree of stability and resistance to control or change."[86]

Cloward and Ohlin divided lower-class youths into four types based on degree of commitment to middle-class values and material achievement: Type I youths desire entry to the middle class via improvement in their economic position, Type II youths desire entry to the middle class but not improvement in their economic position, Type III youths desire wealth but not entry to the middle class and are seen as the most crime-prone; Type IV youths are dropouts who retreat from the cultural mainstream through drug and alcohol use (see the creative example in the Who's to Blame box).

Reaction Formation

Another criminologist whose work is often associated with both strain theory and the subcultural perspective is **Albert Cohen**, whose work focused primarily on the gang behavior of delinquent youths: "When we speak of a delinquent subculture, we speak of a way of life that has somehow become traditional among certain groups in American society. These groups are the boys' gangs that flourish most conspicuously in the 'delinquency neighborhoods' of our larger American cities. The members of these gangs grow up, some to become law-abiding citizens and others to graduate to more professional and adult forms of criminality, but the delinquent tradition is kept alive by the age-groups that succeed them."[87] Cohen argued that youths from all backgrounds are generally held accountable to the norms of the wider society through a "middle-class measuring rod" of expectations related to school performance, language proficiency, cleanliness, punctuality, neatness, nonviolent behavior, and allegiance to other similar standards but noted that not everyone is prepared, by birth circumstances and subsequent socialization, to effectively meet such expectations.

In an examination of vandalism, Cohen found that "non-utilitarian" delinquency, in which things of value are destroyed rather than stolen or otherwise used for financial gain, is the result of middle-class values turned upside down.[88] Delinquent youths, often alienated from middle-class values and lifestyles

■ **reaction formation**
The process by which a person openly rejects that which he or she wants or aspires to but cannot obtain or achieve.

through deprivation and limited opportunities, can achieve status among their subcultural peers via vandalism and other forms of delinquent behavior.

Children from deprived backgrounds turn to delinquency because they experience status frustration when judged by adults and others according to middle-class standards and goals that they are unable to achieve, Cohen claimed. Because it is nearly impossible for them to succeed in middle-class terms, they also may overcome anxiety through the process of **reaction formation**, in which hostility toward middle-class values develops. (Cohen adapted reaction formation from psychiatric perspectives and used it to mean "the process in which a person openly rejects that which he wants, or aspires to, but cannot obtain or achieve."[89])

Cohen discovered the roots of delinquent subcultures in what he termed the "collective solution to the problem of status."[90] When youths who experience the same kind of alienation from middle-class ideals band together, they achieve a collective and independent solution and create a delinquent subculture. "The delinquent subculture, we suggest, is a way of dealing with the problems of adjustment. These problems are chiefly status problems: certain children are denied status in the respectable society because they cannot meet the criteria of the respectable status system. The delinquent subculture deals with these problems by providing criteria of status which these children can meet."[91]

Cohen's approach is effectively summarized in a theoretical scenario offered by Donald J. Shoemaker, who said that lower-class youths undergo a working-class socialization combining lower-class values and habits with middle-class success values.[92] Lower-class youths experience failure in school because they cannot live up to the middle-class norms operative in American educational institutions, suffer a consequent loss of self-esteem and increased feelings of rejection, drop out of school and associate with delinquent peers, and experience hostility and resentment toward middle-class standards through

> Reaction formation means the process in which a person openly rejects that which he wants, or aspires to, but cannot obtain or achieve.

reaction formation. Such alienated youths achieve status and a sense of improved self-worth through participation in a gang of like-minded peers; delinquency and crime are the result.

Code of the Street

Work by Elijah Anderson, who studied African American neighborhoods along Philadelphia's Germantown Avenue and published the results in his book titled *The Code of the Street*, offered a subcultural ethnography of the social mores operating in some American inner cities today.[93] In *Code*, Anderson detailed aspects of street code that stress a hyperinflated notion of manhood resting squarely on the idea of respect: "At the heart of the code is the issue of respect, loosely defined as being treated 'right' or being granted one's 'props' (or proper due) or the deference one deserves." In street culture, a man's sense of worth is determined by the respect he commands when in public.

A crucial distinction between both families and individuals in inner-city neighborhoods like Germantown are expressed by what residents call the "decent family" and the "street family," marking people as either trying to uphold positive values or being oriented toward the street. Street life, Anderson explained, involves displays of physical strength and intellectual prowess meant to demonstrate that "I can take care of myself" and "I can take care of my own." Those who wholeheartedly embrace the street code are proud to live the "thug life," they identify with role models like Tupac Shakur and Young Jeezy, and they see people and situations as obstacles to be subdued or overcome, learning to outsmart or hustle others while avoiding being hustled themselves. See the Criminal Profiles box on gang member Sanyika Shakur, aka Monster Kody Scott.

Gangs Today

Gangs have become a major source of concern in contemporary American society. Although the writings of investigators like Cohen, Thrasher, and Cloward and Ohlin focused on the illicit activities of juvenile gangs in the nation's inner cities, most gang-related crimes involved vandalism, petty theft, and battles over turf. Today the ethnic distinctions that gave rise to gang culture in the 1920s through the 1950s are largely forgotten, and Italian, Hungarian, Polish, and Jewish immigrants, whose children made up many of the early gangs, have been successfully integrated into modern America.

Today's gangs are quite different. The 2008 National Gang Center (NGC) survey (conducted annually by the Office of Juvenile Justice and Delinquency Prevention), found that gang activity remains a widespread problem across the United States, with prevalence rates remaining significantly elevated in 2008 compared with recorded lows in the early 2000s.[94] Approximately one-third of the jurisdictions in the National Youth Gang Survey (NYGS) study population reported gang problems in

CRIMINAL | PROFILES

Sanyika Shakur, aka Monster Kody Scott

It is tempting to rely on Sanyika Shakur's compelling autobiography, *Monster: The Autobiography of an L.A. Gang Member*, as the primary reference for this box. But while much of the material is drawn from his memoir—Shakur is undeniably the world's expert on his alter ego Monster Kody Scott—there is more to this story than can be gleaned from his own writings.

Shakur repeatedly justifies brutal assaults he has committed as being the only reasonable solution "[w]hen the police and other government agencies don't seem to care about what is going on in our communities, those of us who live in them must take responsibility for their protection and maintenance."[i] Yet he also chillingly recounts other assaults, and even murders, as being a form of self-administered therapy to relieve his tensions from such terrible pressures as his mother telling him she disapproved of his lawless lifestyle and use of drugs.

For example, his need "to shoot somebody, eager to vent my anger," after being scolded by his mother for his criminality and marijuana use compelled him (at age 16) to go on the prowl on a bicycle, looking for suitable victims. Upon encountering "three cats who looked about my age leaning against a van, talking and drinking beer," he circled past them and opened fire with a .45-caliber pistol, leaving one victim "motionless in the street." Shakur said he went home, "put the bike in the garage, went to my room [and] fell asleep. I slept very well."[ii]

Born in the tumultuous 1960s (1963), 11-year-old Kody Scott (he adopted the name Sanyika Shakur in prison years later) earned initiation into the infamous Crips street gang with eight blasts from a shotgun at a group of the notorious Bloods, a rival gang. His teen years were an odyssey of violent crime, interspersed with repeated stays in various juvenile detention centers and, ultimately, the California State Penitentiary.

His "Monster" moniker came from one such crime. After being robbed and beaten, the victim had the audacity to strike Shakur in the face, so Shakur "beat him, and stomped him and disfigured him," leaving the young man in a coma.[iii] The severity of the damage caused one investigating police officer to use the word *monster* to refer to the perpetrator, and Shakur decided to adopt the name. "[I]t was just power," he says, proudly. "And I felt it. And I just took that name."[iv]

Feared even by his fellow Crips, Shakur rose through the gang's leadership ranks until he eventually became one of its top leaders and achieved status as an Original Gangster (O.G.), the highest "honor" a gang member can receive.

Sanyika Shakur (born Kody Scott), aka Monster Kody Scott, photographed at Pelican Bay prison in June 1993 through Plexiglas. The gangster thug of the literary set was sent back to prison in 2008 for beating a man and stealing his car while out on parole. Is Shakur a villain or a hero?
Source: Susan Ragan/AP Wide World Photos

Shakur calls his behavior inevitable, asserting there are no other options available to him and those like him to achieve success legitimately, portraying himself as the "inevitable product of a hellish environment."[v]

Shakur has been dubbed an "iconic figure" of the hip-hop culture by independent filmmaker Billy Wright, stating that Shakur's "real life encapsulates what hip hop imagery is all about."[vi] Wright's current project, titled *Can't Stop, Won't Stop*, tells Shakur's life story.

In December 2006, out on parole from yet another term in the California State Penitentiary, Shakur broke into a man's home and beat him in order to steal his car. In May 2008, as a result of those charges, he was sentenced to six years in prison. He had faced a possible life sentence without the possibility of parole as a persistent felon under California's three-strikes law.[vii]

Notes

i. Sanyika Shakur, *Monster: The Autobiography of an L.A. Gang Member* (reprint, New York: Grove Press, 2004), p. 379.

ii. Ibid., pp. 173–174.

iii. Mandalit Del Barco, "Gang Member Turned Author Arrested in L.A.," *Morning Edition*, National Public Radio, March 9, 2007, http://www.npr.org/templates/story/story.php?storyId=7793148 (accessed July 14, 2007).

iv. Ibid.

v. Mark Horowitz, "In Search of a Monster," *Atlantic Monthly*, December 1993, http://www.theatlantic.com/doc/199312/monster (accessed July 14, 2009).

vi. "America's O. G. Gangster—Monster Kody (aka Sanyika Shakur)," http://www.rapindustry.com/monster_cody.htm (accessed September 14, 2009).

vii. Del Barco, "Gang Member Turned Author Arrested in L.A."

2008. The National Gang Center estimates that 32.4% of all cities, suburban areas, towns, and rural counties in the United States experienced gang problems in 2008. This represents a 15% increase over 2002. Approximately 774,000 gang members and 27,900 gangs are estimated to have been active in the United

States in 2008. From 2002 to 2008 the number of gangs increased by 28%, and the number of gang members increased by 6%. Among agencies reporting a gang problem in 2008, 45% characterized their gang problem as "getting worse." In contrast, less than 1 in 10 respondents said their gang problem was "getting

WEB EXTRA 6–7
WEB EXTRA 6–8

better." Suburban counties and rural counties reported higher percentages of "getting worse" compared with the other population categories.

In addition to conducting surveys, the NGC provides a compilation of gang-related legislation, maintains a repository of gang-related literature, analyzes gang-related data and statistics, and coordinates the activities of the Youth Gang Consortium; you can visit the NGC via **Web Extra 6–7**. Another group of special interest to anyone wanting to know more about gangs is the National Alliance of Gang Investigators Associations; see **Web Extra 6–8**.

> Gangs have become a major source of concern in contemporary American society.

Although its data are older than data available through the NYGS, the National Gang Crime Research Center's Project Gangfact provided a profile of gangs and gang members nationwide, based on data collected by 28 researchers in 17 states:[95]

- The average age for joining a gang nationally is 12.8 years of age.
- Over half who joined gangs have tried to quit.
- More than two-thirds of gangs have written rules for members to follow.
- Over half of all gangs hold regular weekly meetings.
- Nearly 30% of gangs require their members to pay dues.
- Approximately 55% of gang members were recruited by other gang members; the remainder sought out gang membership.
- Most gang members (79%) say they would leave the gang if given a second chance at life.
- Four-fifths of gang members report that their gangs sold crack cocaine.
- Most gangs (70%) are not racially exclusive and consist of members drawn from a variety of ethnic groups.
- One-third of gang members report that they have been able to conceal their gang membership from their parents.
- Most gangs (83%) report having female members, but few allow female members to assume leadership roles.
- Many gang members (40%) report knowing male members of their gangs who had raped females.

Three young men in the Sunset Park section of Brooklyn, New York, showing off gang signs. What would ecological theories say about gangs?
Source: David Grossman/Alamy

Gangs can also be big business. In addition to traditional criminal activities like burglary, extortion, vandalism, and protection rackets, drug dealing has become a mainstay of many inner-city gangs. Los Angeles police estimate that at least four city gangs earn over $1 million each per week through cocaine sales.[96] The potential for huge drug-based profits appears to have changed the nature of the gangs, making them more prone to violence and cutthroat tactics; gang killings, including the now-infamous drive-by shootings, have become commonplace in our nation's cities.

Rodney Dailey, a self-avowed former Boston-area drug dealer and gun-wielding gang member who is now the founder of Gang Peace, an outreach group that tries to reduce gang-related violence, said of today's gang world that "shoot before you get shot is the rule" and that today "things that normally people would have had fistfights about can get you shot or stabbed."[97]

Contemporary researchers are drawing some new distinctions between gangs and violence. G. David Curry and Irving A. Spergel, in a study of Chicago communities, distinguished between juvenile delinquency and gang-related homicide.[98] They found that communities characterized by high rates of delinquency do not necessarily experience exceptionally high rates of crime or of gang-related homicides, and they concluded that although gang activity may be associated with homicide, "gang homicide rates and delinquency rates are ecologically distinct

CRIME | in the NEWS
Addressing Youth Violence

Every year scores of Chicago children are shot, knifed, and beaten on the city's streets. Almost as frequently, new policing strategies are rolled out, antiviolence programs launched, and private and public money thrown at the problem. But youth violence acts like a disease, and researchers and experts, who say the cure lies in evidence-based practices and in more targeted scientific treatment of the cause, are coalescing around the idea that violence should be seen as a public health issue and treated like other diseases. . . .

That approach sounds promising, but its success depends on something that Chicago and the nation lacks—rigorous evaluation of which programs work and which ones waste time and money. "Despite all the money and all the pilot programs that have been started, we are floundering around," said Jens Ludwig, a criminologist and head of the University of Chicago Crime Lab, which is evaluating antiviolence programs. "We should do more of what they do in medicine. . . ."

Many researchers, psychiatrists, and others say that interventions should come during critical stages in human development such as early childhood if they are to make a difference. "There is no question that if we intervene early by identifying developmental, medical and behavioral problems and put in services, it would be so cost-effective," said Dr. Jill Glick, medical director of child protective services at University of Chicago Medical Center. "If we invest in our children early on, long term it will pay off."

Because children raised in violence tend to be more violent adults, experts point to parenting classes as one way to help break that cycle. One national study found that children of mothers in high-quality parenting programs had an arrest rate 60% lower than their peers.

Experts say a child who cannot read proficiently by the end of third grade is destined to a lifetime of educational failures and is more likely to end up in prison. The National Institutes of Health considers the nation's reading problem so pernicious that researchers there have labeled it a major threat to public health.

Chicago school officials and law enforcement have tried various strategies to deal with violent teens—more police, more video cameras in schools, tougher curfew laws—all with little success. But Chicago Public Schools Chief Ron Huberman has a new strategy based on current research: His $30 million antiviolence campaign, funded through federal stimulus funds, rolls back zero-tolerance school policies and focuses on softer strategies, such as intensive mentoring for the 200 most at-risk high school students and additional school counselors, social workers and sympathetic school security personnel for the 38 most dangerous schools, to target underlying causes of violence. "There is one chain of thought that 'Hey, this is

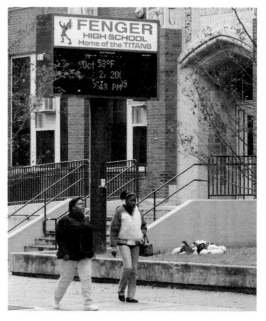

Two women walking past a memorial to slain student Derrion Albert outside Christian Fenger Academy High School in Chicago in late 2009. Albert, an honor student at the school, was attacked on September 24, 2009, and died as a result of being kicked and beaten with splintered railroad ties. Four teens have been charged in his death. How can youth violence be prevented?
Source: AP Photo/David Banks

about getting tough on kids so we need zero tolerance,'" Huberman said. "Our data showed the exact opposite. We need to engage kids in conflict resolution, get them in front of social workers, deal with their emotional needs. . . ."

Discussion Questions

1. What does it mean to say that "violence should be seen as a public health issue and treated like other diseases"? Is violence a disease?

2. This news article mentions the idea of "evidence-based practices" in preventing crime. What are "evidence-based practices"?

community problems." Gang-related homicide seems to be well explained by classical theories of social disorganization and is especially prevalent in city areas characterized by in-migration and the "settlement of new immigrant groups." In their study, high rates of juvenile delinquency seemed to correlate more with poverty, which they defined as "social adaptation to chronic deprivation." According to Curry and Spergel, "Social disorganization and poverty rather than criminal organization and conspiracy may

better explain the recent growth and spread of youth gangs to many parts of the country. Moreover, community organization and social opportunity in conjunction with suppression, rather than simply suppression and incapacitation, may be more effective policies in dealing with the social problem."[99] In proposing a national gang strategy, Finn-Aage Esbensen reminded policymakers that many gang members are delinquent before they become associated with gangs.[100] Esbensen stated that "concerns with gang

■ **Chicago Area Project**
A program originating at the University of Chicago during the 1930s that focused on urban ecology and that attempted to reduce delinquency, crime, and social disorganization in transitional neighborhoods.

LIBRARY EXTRA 6–4
LIBRARY EXTRA 6–5

suppression should not supplant efforts to implement effective delinquency intervention and prevention strategies."[101]

The term *co-offending* refers to the fact that youthful offenders tend to commit crimes in the company of their peers and is especially prevalent in the lives of gang members—about 40% of juvenile offenders commit most of their crimes with others. Co-offenders are also more likely to be recidivists; when young co-offenders were compared with young solo offenders, the co-offenders had high recidivism rates and committed high numbers of violent crimes. In a 2005 study of co-offending made with grant support from the National Institute of Justice, Temple University Professor Joan McCord and fellow researchers found that violence appears to be learned in the company of others: "Co-offending actually may increase the likelihood that offenders will commit violent crimes. When young offenders affiliate with offenders who have previously used violence, the result appears to be an increase in the likelihood that they will subsequently commit a violent crime. . . . [Y]oung offenders pick up attitudes and values from their companions."[102] Learn more about gangs from Professor Mike Carlie's online book *Into the Abyss* via **Library Extra 6–4**, and read a report on co-offending at **Library Extra 6–5**.

Policy Implications of Social Structure Theories

Theoretical approaches that fault social structure as the root cause of crime point in the direction of social action as a panacea. In the 1930s, for example, Clifford Shaw, in an effort to put his theories into practice and to reduce delinquency in transitional neighborhoods, established the **Chicago Area Project**. Shaw analyzed oral histories gathered from neighborhood citizens to determine that delinquents were essentially normal youngsters who entered into illegal activities at early ages, often through street play, so he worked to increase opportunities for young people to embark on successful work careers.

The Chicago Area Project attempted to reduce social disorganization in slum neighborhoods through the creation of community committees staffed with local residents rather than professional social workers. The project had three broad objectives: (1) improving the physical appearance of poor neighborhoods, (2) providing recreational opportunities for youths, and (3) involving project members directly in the lives of troubled youths through school and courtroom mediation. Although no effective assessment programs were established to evaluate the Chicago Area Project during the program's tenure, in 1984 RAND Corporation published a 50-year review of the program, declaring it "effective in reducing rates of juvenile delinquency."[103]

Mobilization for Youth (a programmatic outgrowth of Cloward and Ohlin's theory of differential opportunity) provides a bold example of the treatment implications of social structure theories, seeking not only to provide new opportunities but also through direct social action to change the fundamental arrangements of society and thereby address the root causes of crime and deviance. Leaders of Mobilization for Youth decided that "what was needed to overcome formidable barriers to opportunity was not community organization but community action" that attacked entrenched political interests, so the program promoted "boycotts against schools, protests against welfare policies, rent strikes against 'slum landlords,' lawsuits to ensure poor people's rights, and voter registration."[104] A truly unusual government-sponsored program for its time, Mobilization for Youth was eventually disbanded amid protests that "the mandate of the President's Committee was to reduce delinquency, not to reform urban society or to try out sociological theories on American youths."[105]

The War on Poverty declared by the Kennedy and Johnson administrations during the 1960s and subsequent federal and state-run welfare programs that provided supplemental income assistance have been cited[106] as examples of programs that at least held the potential to reduce crime rates by redistributing wealth in American society.[107] Such programs, however, came under fire for perpetuating injustices and for financially penalizing responsible citizens who had to fund the programs. The federal Welfare Reform Reconciliation Act of 1996[108] reduced or eliminated long-term benefits that had previously been available through avenues like the federal Aid to Families with Dependent Children (AFDC) program and established stricter work requirements for welfare recipients through a new Welfare-to-Work program under the Personal Responsibility and Work Opportunity Reconciliation Act of 1996.[109]

> The Chicago Area Project attempted to reduce social disorganization in slum neighborhoods through the creation of community committees.

Critique of Social Structure Theories

The fundamental assumption of social structure approaches is that social inequality, racism, and poverty are the root causes of crime. Hence, the social structure perspective is intimately associated with the first part of this textbook's theme, the social problems approach (described in Chapter 1). If the assumptions that inform social structure theories are true, they largely negate the claims of those who advocate our theme's other part, the social responsibility perspective.

Social structural explanations for criminality received an enormous boost during the 1960s with the report of President Lyndon B. Johnson's Commission on Law Enforcement and Administration of Justice, a widely disseminated and highly influential document that portrayed social inequality and stifled opportunity as fundamental causes of crime. Later, a number of social commentators began to question the nature of the relationship among poverty, apparent social inequities, and crime.[110] Some argued the inverse of the root causes argument: Poverty and social inequality are produced by crime rather than the other way around; disorder, fear, and crime undermine positive social and economic institutions; and families, schools, churches, businesses, and other institutions cannot function properly in social settings where crime is a taken-for-granted part of the social landscape. If this proposed inverse relationship is even partially true, then addressing poverty and social inequality as the root causes of crime is not only an ineffective crime prevention strategy but also an unnecessarily costly one.

This chapter has identified three types of social structure theory, and each can be critiqued. Some authors have suggested that ecological theories give too much credence to the notion that spatial location determines crime and delinquency because the nature of any given location changes over time, and evolutions in land-use patterns (such as movement away from homeownership and toward rental or low-income housing) may seriously affect the nature of a neighborhood and the concomitant quality of its social organization. Rates of neighborhood crime and delinquency may be "an artifact of police decision-making practices" and may bear little objective relationship to the actual law violations in an area.[111] If police bias (focus on low-income inner-city areas) exists, it may seriously mislead researchers into categorizing certain areas as high in crime when enforcement decisions made by police administrators merely make them appear that way.

Another critique of the ecological school can be found in its seeming inability to differentiate between the condition of

> The fundamental assumption of social structure approaches is that social inequality, racism, and poverty are the root causes of crime.

social disorganization and the things it is said to cause. What is the difference between social disorganization and high rates of delinquency? Isn't delinquency a form of the very thing said to cause it? Stephen J. Pfohl observed that early ecological writers sometimes used the incidence of delinquency as "both an example of disorganization and something caused by disorganization,"[112] making it difficult to gauge the efficacy of their explanatory approach.

Similarly, those who criticize the ecological approach noted that many crimes occur outside of geographic areas said to be characterized by social disorganization. Murder, rape, burglary, drug use, and assault all occur in affluent, well-established neighborhoods; white-collar crime, cybercrime, and environmental crime may actually occur *more often* in well-established neighborhoods. Hence, the ecological approach is clearly not an adequate explanation for all crime or for all types of crime.

From a social responsibility perspective, those who criticize strain theory noted that Merton's strain theory is probably less applicable to American society today than it was in the 1930s because in the ensuing decades considerable effort has been made toward improving success opportunities for all Americans, regardless of ethnicity, race, or gender. Travis Hirschi criticized contemporary strain theory for its inability "to locate people suffering from discrepancy" and noted that human beings are naturally optimistic—a fact that "overrides [the] aspiration-expectation disjunction," concluding that "expectations appear to affect delinquency, but they do so regardless of aspirations, and strain notions are neither consistent with nor required by the data."[113] More recent studies have found that "delinquents do not report being more distressed than other youth."[114] Delinquent youths who are not afforded the opportunities for success available to others appear to be well shielded from sources of stress and despair through their participation in delinquency, so "although strain theorists often have portrayed the lives of delinquents in grim terms, this depiction does not square well with the lived world of delinquency."[115]

Subcultural approaches (the last of the three types of social structure explanations for crime discussed in this chapter) have been questioned by some criminologists who see them lacking explanatory power. Canadian criminologist Gwynn Nettler called the notion of violent subcultures tautological, or circular, arguing that saying that people "are murderous because they live violently" does little to explain their behavior and that attributing fighting to "other spheres of violence" may be true but that it is fundamentally "uninformative."[116]

The subcultural approach has also been criticized for being racist because many so-called violent subcultures are said to be populated primarily by minorities. Margaret Anderson stated that "the problem with this explanation is that it turns attention away from the relationship of black communities to the larger society and it re-creates dominant stereotypes about blacks as violent, aggressive, and fearful. Although it may be true that rates of violence are higher in black communities, this observation does not explain the fact."[117] In sociological jargon, an observed correlation between race and violence does not necessarily provide a workable explanation for the relationship.

There are other problems with social structure theories that routinely link low levels of socioeconomic status to high levels of delinquency. Empirical studies have consistently found weak or nonexistent correlations between an individual's economic standing and his or her self-reported delinquency.[118] While low socioeconomic status may promote delinquency by increasing social alienation and financial strain and by decreasing educational opportunity and occupational aspiration, high socioeconomic status may also promote delinquency by increasing a person's willingness to take risks and by decreasing the influence of conventional values. Parental monitoring (knowing where the child is and what he or she is doing) and parental discipline are far more effective predictors of the degree of delinquent involvement.[119]

According to Nettler, social structure theories suffer from another shortcoming that generally affects most other sociological perspectives on crime causation: "The conceptual bias of social scientists emphasizes environments—cultures and structures—as the powerful causes of differential conduct. This bias places an intellectual taboo on looking elsewhere for possible causes as, for example, in physiologies. This taboo is strongly applied against the possibility that ethnic groups may have genetically transmitted differential physiologies that have relevance for social behavior."[120] In other words, social scientists unnecessarily downplay the causative role of nonsociological factors. Many outside of sociology believe that such factors are important, but since sociological theorizing has captured the lion's share of academic attention over the past few decades, the role of other causative factors in the etiology of criminal behavior is in danger of being shortchanged.

Some also see the inability of social structure theories to predict which individuals—or what proportion of a given population—will turn to crime as a crucial failure of such perspectives. Although the large majority of people growing up in poverty-ridden inner-city areas probably experience an inequitable opportunity structure firsthand, only a relatively small number of them become criminal. Even if substantially more people living under such conditions become criminal compared to those living in other types of social environments, a large proportion of people being raised in deviant subcultures and experiencing strain still embrace noncriminal lifestyles. In his book *The Moral Sense*, James Q. Wilson suggested that most people—regardless of socialization experiences and structural aspects of their social circumstances—may still carry within them an inherent sense of fairness and interpersonal morality.[121] If what Wilson suggested is even partially true, then the explanatory power of social structure theories will inevitably be limited by human nature itself. Read a PBS interview with Wilson at **Library Extra 6–6**.

SUMMARY

- Sociological theories explore relationships among groups and institutions and envision crime as the result of social processes, as the natural consequence of aspects of social structure, or as the result of economic and class struggle. Sociological theories examine institutional arrangements within society and interactions among individuals, groups, and social institutions that affect socialization and have an impact on social behavior.

- Although different kinds of social structure theories have been advanced to explain crime, they all have one thing in common: They highlight those arrangements within society that contribute to the low socioeconomic status of identifiable groups—poverty, lack of education, absence of marketable skills, and subcultural values—as significant causes of crime and view members of socially and economically disadvantaged groups as being more likely to commit crime.

- Three subtypes of social structure theories can be identified: social disorganization theory, strain theory, and culture conflict theory. Social disorganization theory encompasses social pathology, seeing society as a kind of organism and crime and deviance as a kind of disease (or social pathology), and is often associated with social ecology and the Chicago

School of criminology. Strain theory points to a lack of fit between socially approved success goals and availability of socially approved means to achieve those goals, so individuals unable to succeed through legitimate means turn to other avenues (crime) that promise economic and social recognition. Culture conflict theory suggests that the root cause of criminality can be found in a clash of values between differently socialized groups over what is acceptable or proper behavior.

- Because theories of social structure look to the organization of society for their explanatory power, intervention strategies based on them typically seek to alleviate the social conditions thought to produce crime through social programs that increase socially acceptable opportunities for success and availability of meaningful employment.

- Social structure theories are open to criticisms. Social structure approaches assume that social inequality, racism, and poverty are the root causes of crime, but some argue the inverse: Poverty and social injustices are produced by crime rather than the other way around. If this proposed inverse relationship is even partially true, then addressing poverty and social inequality as the root causes of crime is not only an ineffective crime-prevention strategy but also an unnecessarily costly one.

KEY TERMS

anomie, 157	negative affective state, 161
broken windows thesis, 156	reaction formation, 167
Chicago Area Project, 171	relative deprivation, 159
Chicago School of criminology, 155	social disorganization, 153
conduct norm, 162	social disorganization theory, 152
criminology of place, 155	social ecology, 154
cultural transmission, 155	social life, 151
culture conflict theory, 161	social pathology, 154
defensible space, 156	social process, 151
distributive justice, 160	social structure, 151
ecological theory, 155	social structure theory, 151
environmental criminology, 155	sociological theory, 151
focal concern, 162	strain theory, 157
general strain theory (GST), 160	subcultural theory, 162
	subculture, 162
human ecology, 153	technique of neutralization, 163
illegitimate opportunity structure, 165	

KEY NAMES

Robert Agnew, 160	Robert Park, 154
Ernest Burgess, 154	Thorsten Sellin, 161
Richard A. Cloward, 165	Clifford Shaw, 154
Albert Cohen, 166	Gresham Sykes, 163
Franco Ferracuti, 164	W. I. Thomas, 153
David Matza, 163	Frederic M. Thrasher, 162
Henry McKay, 154	William F. Whyte, 162
Robert K. Merton, 157	Marvin Wolfgang, 164
Walter B. Miller, 162	Florian Znaniecki, 153
Lloyd E. Ohlin, 165	

QUESTIONS FOR REVIEW

1. What is the nature of sociological theorizing? What are the assumptions on which sociological perspectives on crime causation rest?

2. What do sociologists mean by the term *social structure*? How might the organization and structure of a society contribute to criminality?

3. What are the three types of social structure theories that this chapter describes? What are the major differences among them?

4. What are the policy implications of the theories discussed in this chapter? What kinds of changes in society and in government policy might be based on the theories discussed here? Would they be likely to bring about a reduction in crime?

5. What are the shortcomings of the social structure approaches to understanding and preventing crime? Can these shortcomings be overcome?

QUESTIONS FOR REFLECTION

1. This book emphasizes the theme of social problems versus social responsibility. Which of the theoretical perspectives discussed in this chapter best support the social problems approach? Which support the social responsibility approach? Why?

2. What do we mean by the term *ecological*? Do you believe that ecological approaches have a valid place in contemporary criminological thinking? Why?

3. How does the notion of a criminology of place differ from more traditional ecological theories? Do you see the approach of criminology of place as capable of offering anything new over traditional approaches? If so, what?

4. What is a violent subculture? Why do some subcultures seem to stress violence? How might participants in a subculture of violence be turned toward less aggressive ways?

CHAPTER 7

THEORIES OF SOCIAL PROCESS AND SOCIAL DEVELOPMENT

LEARNING OUTCOMES

After reading this chapter, you should be able to answer the following questions:

- How does the process of social interaction contribute to criminal behavior?
- What are the various social process perspectives discussed in this chapter?
- What kinds of social policy initiatives might be based on social process theories of crime causation?
- What are the shortcomings of the social process perspective?
- What are the various social development perspectives discussed in this chapter?
- What are the central concepts of social development theories?
- What kinds of social policy initiatives might be suggested by social development perspectives?
- What are the shortcomings of social development perspectives on criminality?

Introduction

On a chilly February day in 2004, two huge rooms at the Jefferson County Fairgrounds near Golden, Colorado, were turned into a public showcase to hold the evidence that Jefferson County Sheriff's Office deputies had gathered from Columbine High School in Littleton—scene of one of the nation's deadliest school shootings.[1] The 1999 rampage by 17-year-old Dylan Klebold and 18-year-old Eric Harris resulted in the deaths of 15 people, including the shooters, who took their own lives; more than 20 other people were wounded. The evidence included pipe bombs, guns used in the attack, bullet fragments, more than 700 spent shell casings, blood-stained furniture, knives carried by the attackers, and clothing worn by Klebold and Harris during their destructive rampage as well as more mundane items, such as a computer screen with a bullet hole in it and a lost shoe abandoned by a student attempting to flee the carnage.

Also available to the public was a newly released videotape of the attackers that had been made in the hallways of Columbine High School five months before the killings. On the tape, Klebold and Harris are seen wearing trench coats and sunglasses, portraying hit men offering their services to students who had been victimized by bullies.[2]

Attendees at the display were provided with a document prepared by Colorado Attorney General Ken Salazar on the two years leading up to the attacks. The report revealed that Jefferson County officers had had 15 contacts with Klebold and Harris, most of them based on complaints filed by neighbors. Investigators had once considered asking for a warrant to search Harris's home because of his threats on the Internet and because of a pipe bomb found along a bike path that Harris used. The warrant was never sought, however, after officers concluded that they lacked enough evidence to procure it.

"In the end," Salazar told reporters, "none of the many efforts to open up the Columbine records, including today's activity, will mean much beyond passing curiosity if we cannot learn from this tragedy."[3] What we learn will be different depending on who we are. Criminologists continue to debate the influences in the lives of Harris and Klebold that led up to the Columbine shootings. One report, released three years after the shootings, indicated that Klebold and Harris were victims of bullying by other teenagers and might have

Victims' family members looking over evidence from the Columbine (Colorado) High School shootings that took place in 1999. The display was presented by the Jefferson County Sheriff's Office in 2004, prior to the evidence being archived. The evidence on display included the shotguns and pistols that Eric Harris and Dylan Klebold used to kill their schoolmates in the Columbine High School library and cafeteria. Might the killings have been prevented?
Source: Gary Caskey/Reuters/CORBIS-NY

been suffering from the depression, loneliness, and suicidal urges that victims of bullying can experience.[4] The killings, the report suggested, may have been the end result of those feelings.

We might also ask how others caught up in the Columbine tragedy found the courage to confront the shooters. Darrell Scott, whose daughter Rachel was killed in the shootings and who was present at the fairgrounds, told CBS News that "one moment for me was when I saw the picture of Dave Sanders who was one of my heroes, who was the teacher [who] was killed at Columbine. There is a still shot of him as he's going up the stairs to confront the two boys and everyone else is running out of the cafeteria. And you can see in his stride, it's a purposeful stride toward his own death. He knew that he was going to possibly die when he confronted those boys. And he'll always be a hero of mine."[5]

LIBRARY EXTRA 7–1
LIBRARY EXTRA 7–2

▓ **social process theory**
A theory that asserts that criminal behavior is learned in interaction with others and that socialization processes that occur as the result of group membership are the primary route through which learning occurs; also called *interactionist theory*.

▓ **social learning theory**
A perspective that places primary emphasis on the role of communication and socialization in the acquisition of learned patterns of criminal behavior and the values that support that behavior; also called *learning theory*.

▓ **differential association**
The sociological thesis that criminality, like any other form of behavior, is learned through a process of association with others who communicate criminal values.

Social process theories draw their explanatory power from the process of interaction between individuals and society.

A 2007 shooting spree at Virginia Tech University by a student suffering from mental problems resulted in the deaths of 33 people, claiming the record for the nation's deadliest school shooting ever (this is discussed more fully in Chapter 9). Learn more about school shooters and how they might be identified before they act from the FBI's National Center for the Analysis of Violent Crime by reading **Library Extra 7–1**, and read the federal *Report to the President on Issues Raised by the Virginia Tech Tragedy* at **Library Extra 7–2**.

The Social Process Perspective

The theories discussed in the first part of this chapter are called **social process theories**, or *interactionist perspectives*, because they depend on the process of interaction between individuals and society for their explanatory power. Social process theories of crime causation assume that everyone has the potential to violate the law and that criminality is not an innate human characteristic; instead, criminal behavior is learned in interaction with others, and the socialization process occurring as the result of group membership is seen as the primary route through which learning occurs. Among the most important groups contributing to the process of socialization are the family, peers, work groups, and reference groups with which one identifies because they instill values and norms in their members and communicate their acceptable worldviews and patterns of behavior.

Social process perspectives hold that the process through which criminality is acquired, deviant self-concepts are established, and criminal behavior results is active, open-ended, and ongoing throughout a person's life. They suggest that individuals who have weak stakes in conformity are more likely to be influenced by the social processes and contingent experiences that lead to crime and that criminal choices tend to persist because they are reinforced by the reaction of society to those whom it has identified as deviant.

Types of Social Process Approaches

A number of theories can be classified under the social process umbrella: social learning theory, social control theory, labeling theory, reintegrative shaming, and dramaturgical perspective. A social learning theory places primary emphasis on the role of communication and socialization in the acquisition of learned patterns of criminal behavior and the values supporting that behavior, whereas a social control theory focuses on the strength of the bond people share with individuals and institutions around them, especially as those relationships shape their behavior. Labeling theory points to the special significance of society's response to the criminal and sees the process through which a person comes to be defined as a criminal, along with society's imposition of the label *criminal*, as a significant contributory factor in future criminality. Reintegrative shaming, a contemporary offshoot of labeling theory, emphasizes possible positive outcomes of the labeling process; the dramaturgical perspective focuses on how people can effectively manage the impressions they make on others. It is to different social learning theories that we now turn our attention.

Social Learning Theory

A **social learning theory** (also called *learning theory*) says that all behavior is learned in much the same way and that such learning includes the acquisition of norms, values, and patterns of behaviors conducive to crime, meaning that crime is also learned and that people learn to commit crime from others. Criminal behavior is a product of the social environment, not an innate characteristic of particular people.

Differential Association

One of the earliest and most influential forms of social learning theory was advanced by **Edwin Sutherland** in 1939, who stated that criminality is learned through a process of **differential association** with others who communicate criminal values and who advocate the commission of crimes.[6] He emphasized the role of social learning as an explanation for crime because he believed that many concepts popular in the

THEORY | in PERSPECTIVE
Types of Social Process Theories

Social process theories (also called *interactionist theories*) depend on the process of interaction between individuals and society for their explanatory power. They assume that everyone has the potential to violate the law and that criminality is not an innate human characteristic; instead, criminal behavior is learned in interaction with others, and the socialization process that occurs as the result of group membership is seen as the primary route through which learning occurs.

Social Learning Theory

Social learning theory (also called *learning theory*) says that all behavior is learned in much the same way and that crime is also learned. It places primary emphasis on the roles of communication and socialization in the acquisition of learned patterns of criminal behavior and the values supporting that behavior.

Period: 1930s–present

Theorists: Edwin Sutherland, Robert Burgess, Ronald L. Akers, Daniel Glaser

Concepts: Differential association, differential association–reinforcement (including operant conditioning), differential identification

Social Control Theory

Social control theory focuses on the strength of the bond people share with the individuals and institutions around them, especially as those relationships shape their behavior, and seeks to identify those features of the personality and of the environment that keep people from committing crimes.

Period: 1950s–present

Theorists: Walter C. Reckless, Howard B. Kaplan, Travis Hirschi, Michael Gottfredson, Charles R. Tittle, others

Concepts: Inner and outer containment, self-derogation, social bond, control–balance

Labeling Theory

Labeling theory (also called *social reaction theory*) points to the special significance of society's response to the criminal and sees continued crime as a consequence of limited opportunities for acceptable behavior that follow from the negative responses of society to those defined as offenders.

Period: 1938–1940, 1960s–1980s, 1990s

Theorists: Frank Tannenbaum, Edwin M. Lemert, Howard Becker, John Braithwaite, others

Concepts: Tagging, labeling, outsiders, moral enterprise, primary and secondary deviance, reintegrative shaming, stigmatic shaming

Dramaturgical Perspective

The dramaturgical perspective depicts human behavior as centered around the purposeful management of impressions and seeks explanatory power in the analysis of social performances.

Period: 1960s–present

Theorists: Erving Goffman, others

Concepts: Total institutions, impression management, back and front regions, performances, discrediting information, stigma, spoiled identity

---

field of criminology at the time—including social pathology, genetic inheritance, biological characteristics, and personality flaws—were inadequate to explain the process by which an otherwise normal individual turns to crime. Sutherland was the first well-known criminologist to suggest that all significant human behavior is learned and that crime is not substantively different from any other form of behavior.

Sutherland's nine principles of differential association were presented in complete form three years before his death in the fourth edition of his famous book, *Principles of Criminology*:[7]

1. Criminal behavior is learned.

2. Criminal behavior is learned in interaction with others in a process of communication.

3. The principal part of the learning of criminal behavior occurs within intimate personal groups.

4. When criminal behavior is learned, the learning includes (a) techniques of committing the crime, which are sometimes very complicated and sometimes very simple, and (b) the specific direction of motives, drives, rationalizations, and attitudes.

5. The specific direction of motives and drives is learned from definitions of the legal codes as favorable or unfavorable.

6. A person becomes delinquent because of an excess of definitions favorable to law violation over definitions unfavorable to law violation.

7. Differential associations may vary in frequency, duration, priority, and intensity.

8. The process of learning criminal behavior by association with criminal and anti-criminal patterns involves all mechanisms involved in any other learning.

9. While criminal behavior is an expression of general needs and values, it is not explained by those general needs and values because non-criminal behavior is also an expression of the same needs and values.

Differential association found considerable acceptance among mid-twentieth-century theorists because it combined then-prevalent psychological and sociological principles into a coherent perspective on criminality. Crime as a form of learned behavior became the catchword, and biological and other perspectives were largely abandoned by those involved in the process of theory testing.

Differential Association–Reinforcement Theory

In 1966, **Robert Burgess** and **Ronald L. Akers** published an article titled "A Differential Association–Reinforcement Theory of Criminal Behavior."[8] The perspective, often termed *differential reinforcement theory* or *sociological learning theory*, expands on Sutherland's original idea of differential association by adding the idea of reinforcement, the concept of the power of punishments and rewards to shape behavior (see the heading "Behavior Theory" in Chapter 5). In developing their perspective, Burgess and Akers integrated psychological principles of operant conditioning with sociological notions of differential association, and they reorganized Sutherland's nine principles into seven, the first of which stated, "Criminal behavior is learned according to the principles of operant conditioning."[9] Fundamental to this perspective is the belief that human beings learn to define behaviors that are rewarded as positive and that an individual's criminal behavior is rewarded at least sometimes by individuals and groups that value such activity.

Although the 1966 Burgess–Akers article only alluded to the term *social learning*, Akers began to apply that term to differential association–reinforcement theory with the 1973 publication of his book *Deviant Behavior: A Social Learning Approach*.[10] According to Akers, "The basic assumption in social learning theory is that the same learning process, operating in a context of social structure, interaction, and situation, produces both conforming and deviant behavior."[11] Akers identified two primary learning mechanisms: differential reinforcement (also called *instrumental conditioning*), in which behavior is a function of the frequency, amount, and probability of experienced and perceived contingent rewards and punishments, and imitation, in which the behavior of others and its consequences are observed and modeled. These learning mechanisms, said Akers, operate in a process of differential association involving direct and indirect verbal and nonverbal communication, interaction, and identification with others. As with Sutherland's theory of

> Differential association theory says that criminality is learned through a process of association with criminal others.

differential association, the relative frequency, intensity, duration, and priority of associations remain important because they determine the amount, frequency, and probability of reinforcement of behavior that is either conforming or deviant. Interpersonal association also plays an important role because it can expose individuals to deviant or conforming norms and role models.

Akers continued to develop learning theory and in 1998 published the book *Social Learning and Social Structure*, in which he explained crime rates as a function of social learning that occurs within a social structure.[12] He called this explanation of the model of crime the *social structure–social learning model* (SSSL) and summarized it in seven concise propositions:[13]

1. Deviant behavior is learned according to the principles of operant conditioning.

2. Deviant behavior is learned both in nonsocial situations that are reinforcing or discriminating and through social interaction in which the behavior of others is reinforcing or discriminating for such behavior.

3. The principal part of the learning of deviant behavior occurs in those groups that comprise or control the individual's major source of reinforcements.

4. The learning of deviant behavior, including specific techniques, attitudes, and avoidance procedures, is a function of the effective and available reinforcers and the existing reinforcement contingencies.

5. The specific class of behavior learned and its frequency of occurrence are a function of the effective and available reinforcers and the deviant or nondeviant direction of the norms, rules, and definitions that in the past have accompanied the reinforcement.

6. The probability that a person will commit deviant behavior is increased in the presence of normative statements, definitions, and verbalizations that, in the process of differential reinforcement of such behavior over conforming behavior, have acquired discriminative value.

LIBRARY EXTRA 7–3
LIBRARY EXTRA 7–4

■ **differential identification theory**
An explanation for crime and deviance that holds that people pursue criminal or deviant behavior to the extent that they identify themselves with real or imaginary people from whose perspective their criminal or deviant behavior seems acceptable.

■ **social control theory**
A perspective that predicts that when social constraints on antisocial behavior are weakened or absent, delinquent behavior emerges. Rather than stressing causative factors in criminal behavior, social control theory asks why people actually obey rules instead of breaking them.

7. The strength of deviant behavior is a direct function of the amount, frequency, and probability of its reinforcement. The modalities of association with deviant patterns are important insofar as they affect the source, amount, and scheduling of reinforcement.

Akers's SSSL theory says that social learning is the social-psychological mediating process through which social structural aspects of the environment work to cause crime and that it integrates two levels of explanation—social structure and social learning—by specifying the links between the larger social context and the individual relationships that lead to criminal behavior.[14] Hence, a person's location in the social structure—defined by age, gender, ethnicity, place of residence, and so on—is seen as a major determinant of how that person is socialized and what he or she will learn.

Differential Identification Theory

Like Akers, **Daniel Glaser** built on Sutherland's notion of differential association, and Glaser offered a **differential identification theory**.[15] The central tenet of Glaser's differential identification theory is that "a person pursues criminal behavior to the extent that he identifies himself with real or imaginary persons from whose perspective his criminal behavior seems acceptable."[16] Glaser proposed that the process of differential association leads to an intimate personal identification with lawbreakers, resulting in criminal or delinquent acts. Glaser recognized that people will identify with various people and that some of these identifications will be relatively strong and others weaker—hence the term *differential identification*.

Identification with noncriminals offers the possibility of rehabilitation.

According to Glaser, it is not the frequency or intensity of association that determines behavior (as Sutherland believed) but the symbolic process of identification. Identification with a person or with an abstract understanding of what that person might be like can be more important than actual associations with real people. Role models can consist of abstract ideas as well as actual people, so an individual might identify with a serial killer or a terrorist bomber even though he or she has never met that person. Glaser also recognized the role of economic conditions, frustrations with one's place in the social structure, learned moral creeds, and group participation in producing differential identifications. Alternatively, identification with noncriminals offers the possibility of rehabilitation. Learn more about social learning and adolescent development via **Library Extras 7–3** and **7–4**.

Social Control Theories

According to Charles R. Tittle, a prominent sociologist at Washington State University with a specialty in crime and deviance, a **social control theory** emphasizes "the inhibiting effect of social and psychological integration with others whose potential negative response, surveillance, and expectations regulate or constrain criminal impulses."[17] In other words, social control theorists seek to identify those features of the personality (see Chapter 5) and the environment (see Chapter 6) that keep people from committing crimes. According to Tittle, social control theorists take a step beyond static aspects of the personality and physical features of the environment in order to focus on the *process* through which social integration develops. The extent of a person's integration with positive social institutions

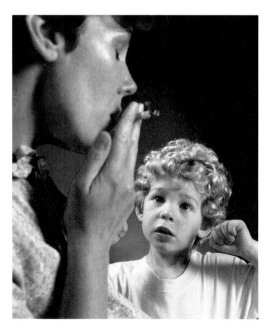

A child watching his mother smoke a cigarette. Social learning theory says that social behavior is learned. Will this child grow up to be a smoker?
Source: James King-Holmes/Science Photo Library/Photo Researchers, Inc.

> ■ **containment theory**
> A form of control theory that suggests that a series of both internal and external factors contributes to law-abiding behavior.

> ■ **containment**
> An aspect of the social bond that acts as a stabilizing force to prevent individuals from committing crimes and that keeps them from engaging in deviance.

and with significant others determines that person's resistance to criminal temptations, and social control theorists focus on the process through which such integration develops. Rather than stressing causative factors in criminal behavior, social control theories tend to ask why people actually obey rules instead of breaking them.[18]

Containment Theory

In the 1950s, a student of the Chicago School of criminology, **Walter C. Reckless**, wrote *The Crime Problem*.[19] He tackled head-on the realization that most sociological theories, although conceptually enlightening, offered less-than-perfect predictability, being unable to predict which individuals (even those exposed to various "causes" of crime) would become criminal. Reckless thought that prevalent sociological perspectives offered only half of a comprehensive theoretical framework, writing that crime was the consequence of both social pressures to become involved in violations of the law and failures to resist such pressures. Reckless called his approach **containment theory** and compared it with a biological immune response, saying that only some people exposed to a disease actually come down with it and that both sickness and crime result from the failure of control mechanisms, some internal and others external.

In the case of crime, Reckless wrote that *external containment* consists of "the holding power of the group."[20] Under most circumstances, Reckless said that "the society, the state, the tribe, the village, the family, and other nuclear groups are able to hold the individual within the bounds of the accepted norms and expectations."[21] In addition to setting limits, he saw society as providing individuals with meaningful roles and activities, also important factors of external containment.

Reckless stated that *inner containment* "represents the ability of the person to follow the expected norms, to direct himself."[22] This ability was enhanced by a positive self-image, a focus on socially approved goals, personal aspirations in line with reality, a tolerance for frustration, and a general adherence to society's norms and values.

In Figure 7–1 (a diagram of containment theory), "Pushes toward Crime" represents those factors in an individual's background that might propel him or her into criminal behavior and include a criminogenic background or upbringing involving participation in a delinquent subculture, deprivation, biological propensities toward deviant behavior, and psychological maladjustment. "Pulls toward Crime" signifies all the perceived rewards, including financial gain, sexual satisfaction, and higher status, that crime may offer. **Containment** is a stabilizing force that blocks such pushes and pulls from leading the individual into crime.

Reckless believed that inner containment was far more effective than external containment in preventing law violations. "As social relations become more impersonal, as society

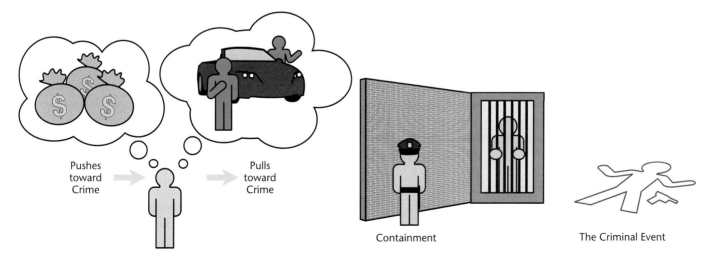

Pushes toward Crime → Pulls toward Crime

Containment

The Criminal Event

FIGURE 7-1 | A Diagrammatic Representation of Containment Theory

> **■ social bond**
> The link, created through socialization, between individuals and the society of which they are a part.

becomes more diverse and alienated, as people participate more and more for longer periods of time away from a home base, the self becomes more and more important as a controlling agent."[23]

Delinquency and Self-Esteem

Social control theory predicts that when social constraints on antisocial behavior are weakened or absent, delinquent behavior will emerge. An innovative perspective on social control was offered by **Howard B. Kaplan** in the mid-1970s, when he proposed that people who are ridiculed by their peers suffer a loss of self-esteem, assess themselves poorly, and abandon the motivation to conform.[24] This approach has come to be known as the *self-derogation theory of delinquency*.

A number of studies appear to support the idea that low self-esteem fosters delinquent behavior.[25] However, it appears that delinquency can also enhance self-esteem, at least for some delinquents;[26] for example, one study found that delinquent behavior enhances self-esteem in adolescents whose self-esteem is already very low.[27]

Some researchers have examined ethnic identification as both a factor in low self-esteem and a precursor to delinquent behavior. In 1986, K. Leung and F. Drasgow tested Kaplan's self-derogation theory using white, African American, and Hispanic youth groups.[28] They concluded that while all three groups reported low self-esteem, only among white youths were low levels of self-esteem related to delinquent behavior. Other researchers found no differences in self-esteem and delinquency between white and African American delinquents and nondelinquents.[29]

In 1990, in an effort to explain some contradictory findings of self-derogation research, Daphna Oyserman and Hazel Rose Markus proposed that "possible selves," rather than self-esteem, might be a major explanatory factor in delinquency.[30] According to this approach, the degree of disjuncture between what people want to be and what they fear they might become is a good potential predictor of delinquency.[31] For example, an adolescent who is confused about what he or she wants to be or is fearful about what he or she could become may resort to delinquency in order to resolve the conflict. Oyserman and Markus suggested that the highest levels of delinquency can be found among youths who lack balance between their expected selves and their feared selves.

Social Bond Theory

An important form of social control theory was popularized by **Travis Hirschi** in his 1969 book *Causes of Delinquency*.[32]

Hirschi's approach was well received by criminologists and "epitomized social control theorizing for nearly three decades."[33] Hirschi argued that through successful socialization, a bond forms between individuals and the social group, but when that bond is weakened or broken, deviance and crime may result (see the Crime in the News box). Hirschi described four components of the **social bond**:

1. Attachment (a person's shared interests with others)
2. Commitment (the amount of energy and effort put into activities with others)
3. Involvement (the amount of time spent with others in shared activities)
4. Belief (a shared value and moral system)

Regarding *attachment*, Hirschi cited the psychopath as an example of the kind of person whose attachment to society is nearly nonexistent.[34] Other relatively normal individuals may find their attachment to society loosened through "the process of becoming alienated from others [which] often involves or is based on active interpersonal conflict. Such conflict could easily supply a reservoir of socially derived hostility sufficient to account for the aggressiveness of those whose attachments to others have been weakened."[35]

> A social bond forms between individuals and society; but when that bond is weakened or broken, deviance and crime may result.

The second component of the social bond—*commitment*—reflects a person's investment of time and energies into conforming behavior and the potential loss of the rewards that he or she has already gained from that behavior. In Hirschi's words, "The idea, then, is that the person invests time, energy, himself, in a certain line of activity—say, getting an education, building up a business, acquiring a reputation for virtue. Whenever he considers deviant behavior, he must consider the costs of this deviant behavior, the risk he runs of losing the investment he has made in conventional behavior."[36] For such a traditionally successful person, committing petty theft is stupid because the potential loss far exceeds the possible gains. Recognizing that his approach applies primarily to individuals who have been successfully socialized into conventional society, Hirschi added, "The concept of commitment assumes that the organization of society is such that the interests of most persons would be endangered if they were to engage in criminal acts."[37]

CRIME | in the NEWS

For Many Inmates, Crime Runs in the Family

ANGOLA, LA.—The fates of the three Caston brothers may well have been fixed at their births.

Obsessed with the lore of the outlaw James Gang, James "Tokie" Caston decided that his first two boys would bear the names of his heroes: Jesse and Frank James. By the time the third son, Sonny, arrived in 1967, the boys' futures were clear. At an early age, Frank Caston recalls, most people in tiny Lake Providence, La., referred to the brothers not as the Castons, but as the "James Gang."

"To be named after the worst outlaw in the country, I think you put a stamp on a person," says Jesse James Caston, 42, who was on the FBI's 10 Most Wanted list in 2000. "We never had a chance."

Their names were symbolic of a troubled upbringing that Jesse and Frank Caston say was marked by abuse and neglect. Today, all three brothers are convicted killers serving life sentences at Louisiana's state prison.

Their story is extraordinary but emblematic of what social scientists and law enforcement officials see as an increasingly complex and persistent problem: people who become criminals in part because of the influence of family members. . . .

Social scientists and law enforcement authorities say the influence of family members may be one of the most important and largely unaddressed factors in determining whether people adopt lives of crime. . . .

James Caston couldn't read very well, but that didn't stop him from collecting every book he could find on the criminal exploits of Jesse James, the legendary outlaw who along with his brother and other members of the "James Gang" robbed banks, trains and stagecoaches after the Civil War.

One of Frank Caston's most vivid memories is of his father asking him to read passages from those books aloud until the elder Caston's curiosity was satisfied for the night.

Those were the good times. The bad times are what the Caston brothers say scarred them for life.

In separate interviews . . . at the Louisiana State Penitentiary, Jesse and Frank Caston, 41, described Gothic-like childhoods during which their father beat them, and after their parents separated, they often were left at early ages to find their own food and places to sleep. . . .

Both men characterized the breakup of their parents' marriage as perhaps the most life-altering event of their childhood. . . .

Although the three boys lived briefly with their sickly grandfather, they spent most of their time with their father. From that point on, they say, their lives were marked by near-constant misery. . . .

The brothers say they spent five to six nights a week locked out of the house. Some nights were spent with sympathetic neighbors. Other nights, they sought refuge in a local cemetery or in an alley near a commercial laundry, where a sympathetic manager would leave the dryers running so the boys could warm themselves under the outside vents. . . .

"That can put a lot of hate in a person," Jesse Caston says of their upbringing.

At 13, Frank Caston says, he crossed the line, when he and Sonny burglarized a neighbor's home. "We just didn't care anymore," he says. Before they were caught, they splurged on a meal of pork chops and rice with money they took from the home. "It was the first time we ate like that" in a month, he says.

Shortly afterward, Frank Caston says, he and Sonny served two stints in juvenile detention for separate thefts of a truck and a bicycle.

"Daddy said we would end up at Angola by the time we were 18," Frank Caston says.

As it turned out, James Caston wasn't off by very much.

In 1988, Frank, then 22, and Sonny, 21, were sentenced to life in prison in connection with the murder of a local sheriff's deputy during an attempted jail break. The brothers had been jailed on lesser charges when a third suspect helped engineer the escape.

Discussion Questions

1. This article seems to say that crime runs in families. Is that assertion likely to be true? If so, why?

2. What kinds of social policies might be built on the ideas expressed in this article?

Frank Caston, one of the Caston brothers. Frank killed a sheriff's deputy during a jail break while in prison on a minor charge in 1988. Does criminality run in families?
Source: Misty Leigh McElroy

Source: Kevin Johnson, "For Many of USA's Inmates, Crime Runs in the Family," *USA Today*, January 29, 2008. Reprinted by permission.

Involvement, the third aspect, means "engrossment in conventional activities"[38] and is similar to Reckless's concept of meaningful roles. In explaining the importance of involvement in determining conformity, Hirschi cited the colloquial saying that "idle hands are the devil's workshop"—time and energy are limited, so if a person is busy at legitimate pursuits, he or she will have little opportunity for crime and deviance.

Belief (the last of Hirschi's four aspects of the social bond) sets his control theory apart from subcultural approaches because "control theory assumes the existence of a common value

■ **general theory of crime**
The assertion that the operation of a single mechanism, low self-control, accounts for "all crime, at all times," including acts ranging from vandalism to homicide, from rape to white-collar crime.

■ **control ratio**
The amount of control to which a person is subject versus the amount of control that person exerts over others.

system within the society or group whose norms are being violated. We not only assume the deviant has believed the rules [but also] assume he believes the rules even as he violates them."[39] How can a person simultaneously believe it is wrong to commit a crime and still commit it? Hirschi's answer would be that "many persons do not have an attitude of respect toward the rules of society."[40] Although they know the rules exist, they basically do not care and invest little of their sense of self in moral standards.

In 1990, **Michael Gottfredson**, in collaboration with Hirschi, proposed a **general theory of crime** (GTC) based on the concepts advanced earlier in control theory.[41] (Control theory and the general theory of crime are also discussed in Chapter 5.) Gottfredson and Hirschi began by asking, "What is crime?" Because nearly all crimes are mundane, simple, trivial, easy acts aimed at satisfying desires of the moment, their general theory is built on a classical or rational choice perspective—the belief that crime is a natural consequence of unrestrained human tendencies to seek pleasure and avoid pain. They concluded that crime is little more than a subset of general deviant behavior and bears little resemblance to

> GTC holds that crime is a natural consequence of unrestrained human tendencies to seek pleasure and avoid pain.

the explanations offered in the media, by law enforcement officials, or by most academic thinkers on the subject.

According to Gottfredson and Hirschi, the offender is neither the diabolical genius of fiction nor the ambitious seeker of the American Dream often portrayed by other social scientists. Offenders appear to have little control over their own desires, so when personal desires conflict with long-term interests, those who lack self-control often opt for the desires of the moment, thus contravening legal restrictions and becoming involved in crime.[42] Central to Gottfredson and Hirschi's thesis is the belief that a well-developed social bond will result in the creation of effective mechanisms of self-control. "For Gottfredson and Hirschi, self-control is the key concept in the explanation of all forms of crime as well as other types of behavior. Indeed, they believe that all current differences in rates of crime between groups and categories may be explained by differences in the management of self-control."[43]

Control–Balance Theory

Traditional control theories posit that deviance and crime result from either weak social bonds or low levels of self-control, but a novel form of control theory can be found in the control–balance theory of **Charles R. Tittle**.[44] Tittle's control–balance approach resulted from blending the social bond and containment perspectives, and he argued that too much control can be just as dangerous as too little. The crucial concept in Tittle's approach is what he called the **control ratio**—the amount of control to which a person is subject versus the amount of control that person exerts over others—which predicts not only the probability that a person will engage in deviance but also the specific form that deviance will take (Figure 7–2).

High levels of control (or overcontrol) are termed *control surplus*; low levels are called *control deficit*. Individuals with control surpluses are able to exercise a great deal of control over others and will work to extend their degree of control even further. Their efforts lead to deviant actions involving exploitation, plunder, and decadence—frequently seen in cases of white-collar crime and political corruption.[45] Tittle explained that control surpluses build on "the fundamental drive toward autonomy," which involves "a desire to extend control as far as possible" and results in forms of deviance that he called "autonomous."[46]

A control deficit exists for people unable to exercise much control over others (and who are hence overly controlled) and results in deviance as an attempt to escape repressive controls. Deviance engendered by control deficit takes the form of predation (physical violence, theft, sexual assault, robbery), defiance

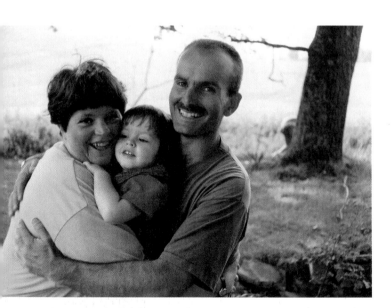

An example of a social bond forming early in life. What might this child be learning?
Source: Steve Rubin/The Image Works

■ **tagging**
The process whereby an individual is negatively defined by agencies of justice.

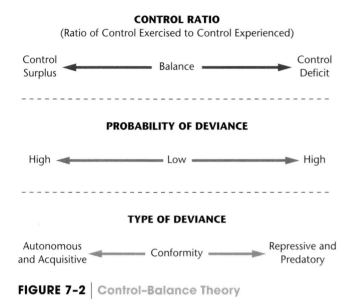

CONTROL RATIO
(Ratio of Control Exercised to Control Experienced)

Control Surplus ← Balance → Control Deficit

PROBABILITY OF DEVIANCE

High ← Low → High

TYPE OF DEVIANCE

Autonomous and Acquisitive ← Conformity → Repressive and Predatory

FIGURE 7-2 | Control-Balance Theory

(challenges to conventional norms, including vandalism, curfew violations, and sullenness), or submission ("passive, unthinking, slavish obedience to the expectations, commands, or anticipated desires of others"[47]). According to Tittle, control imbalance only sets the stage for deviance: Deviance ultimately occurs once a person realizes, at some level, that acts of deviance can reset the control ratio in a favorable way. Opportunity also plays a significant role in Tittle's theory. "No matter how favorable the motivational and constraint configuration," said Tittle, "the actual likelihood of deviance occurring depends on there being an opportunity for it to happen."[48]

Labeling Theory

In the early 1990s, James Hamm, a convicted murderer who had served 18 years for shooting a man in the head over a drug deal gone bad, found himself at the center of a vicious controversy. While in prison, Hamm had earned a bachelor's degree in sociology and had been active in Middle Ground Prison Reform, Inc., a prisoner rights group. He was paroled after Arizona's parole board had judged him "rehabilitated" and was about to enter Arizona State University School of Law. Students at the university challenged his access to law school, saying that a convicted murderer did not deserve to be admitted. Mark Killian, (then) Arizona Republican house speaker, said, "There are a lot of hard-working young people out there who could not get into law school because he did."[49] Members of the Arizona Board of Regents, which runs the state's public universities, called for a

review of policies admitting ex-convicts to the schools. Nonetheless, Hamm, who scored in the top 5% of all applicants taking the law school admissions test nationwide, was eventually admitted to law school and graduated in 1997. Following graduation, he passed the bar exam and applied to be allowed to practice law in Arizona, but the state's parole board refused to terminate his parole, leaving him ineligible to work as an attorney, so he is presently working as a paralegal in the areas of criminal defense, civil rights, and appellate law.[50]

The case of James Hamm provides an example of how society's continued reaction to criminal behavior can change the course of an offender's life—even after he has paid his dues. While there are plenty of ex-cons, there is no such thing as an "ex-ex-con" ("once a con, always a con"). Society seems to never forget. Society's response to known or suspected offenders is important not only because it determines the future of those who are labeled as criminals but also because it may contribute to a heightened incidence of criminality by reducing the behavioral options available to labeled offenders.

Tagging

An early description of societal reaction to deviance can be found in the work of **Frank Tannenbaum**, whose 1938 book *Crime and the Community* popularized the term **tagging** to explain what happens to offenders following arrest, conviction, and sentencing. Tannenbaum told his readers that crime is essentially the result of two opposing views—those of the delinquent and those of the community at large. "This conflict over the situation is one that arises out of a divergence of values. As the problem develops, the situation gradually becomes redefined. The attitude of the community hardens definitely into a demand for suppression. There is a gradual shift from the definition of the specific acts as evil to a definition of the individual as evil, so that all his acts come to be looked upon with suspicion. From the community's point of view, the individual who used to do bad and mischievous things has now become a bad and unredeemable human being.... There is a persistent demand for consistency in character. The community cannot deal with people whom it cannot define."[51]

After the process whereby an offender comes to be seen as ultimately and irrevocably bad has been completed, Tannenbaum said, the offender "now lives in a different world. He has been tagged. The process of making the criminal, therefore, is a process of tagging."[52] Once the offender has been defined as bad, he or she finds that few legitimate opportunities remain open and that only other people who have been similarly defined by society as bad are available to associate with him or her, and this continued association with negatively defined others leads to continued crime.

■ **primary deviance**
The initial deviance often undertaken to deal with transient problems in living.

■ **secondary deviance**
The deviant behavior that results from official labeling and from association with others who have been so labeled.

■ **labeling theory**
An interactionist perspective that sees continued crime as a consequence of limited opportunities for acceptable behavior that follow from the negative responses of society to those defined as offenders; also called *social reaction theory*.

■ **moral enterprise**
The efforts made by an interest group to have its sense of moral or ethical propriety enacted into law.

Primary and Secondary Deviance

Using terminology developed by **Edwin M. Lemert**, it became fashionable to call an offender's initial acts of deviance *primary deviance* and his or her continued acts of deviance (especially those resulting from forced association with other offenders) *secondary deviance*. **Primary deviance** may be undertaken to solve some immediate problem or to meet the expectations of one's subcultural group. For example, the robbery of a convenience store by a college student temporarily desperate for tuition money may be the first serious criminal offense he or she has ever committed, and he or she may well intend for it to be the last, but if arrest ensues and the student is tagged with the status of a criminal, then secondary deviance may occur as a means of adjustment to the negative status. In Lemert's words, "When a person begins to employ his deviant behavior or a role based upon it as a means of defense, attack, or adjustment to the overt and covert problems created by the consequent societal reaction to him, his deviation is secondary."[53]

Secondary deviance is especially important due to the forceful role it plays in causing tagged individuals both to internalize the negative labels applied to them and to assume the role of the deviant. According to Lemert, "Objective evidences of this change will be found in the symbolic appurtenances of the new role, in clothes, speech, posture, and mannerisms, which in some cases heighten social visibility, and which in some cases serve as symbolic cues to professionalization."[54]

Labeling

The person most often associated with labeling theory is **Howard Becker**, who published *Outsiders: Studies in the Sociology of Deviance*, the work in which the perspective of **labeling theory** (the idea that society's response to the criminal and the process through which a person comes to be defined as a criminal and labeled *criminal* are significant contributory factors in future criminality) found its fullest development.[55] In *Outsiders*, Becker described the deviant subculture in which jazz musicians live and the process by which an individual becomes a marijuana user, but his primary focus was explaining how a person becomes labeled as an outsider, as "a special kind of person, one who cannot be trusted to live by the rules agreed on by the group."[56] The central fact is that society creates both deviance and the deviant person by responding to circumscribed behaviors. In Becker's words, "Social groups create deviance by making the rules whose infraction constitutes deviance, and by applying those rules to

particular people and labeling them as outsiders. From this point of view, deviance is not a quality of the act the person commits, but rather a consequence of the application by others of rules and sanctions. The deviant is one to whom that label has been successfully applied."[57] For Becker and other labeling theorists, no act is intrinsically deviant or criminal but must be defined as such by others; becoming deviant involves a sequence of steps that eventually leads to commitment to a deviant identity and participation in a deviant career.

> Becker said that society creates both deviance and the deviant person by responding negatively to circumscribed behaviors.

In developing labeling theory, Becker attempted to explain how some rules carry the force of law while others have less weight or apply only within the context of marginal subcultures. His explanation centered on the concept of **moral enterprise**, meaning all the efforts a particular interest group makes to have its sense of propriety embodied in law. "Rules are the products of someone's initiative, and we can think of the people who exhibit such enterprise as moral entrepreneurs."[58] An early example of moral enterprise can be found in the Women's Christian Temperance Union (WCTU), a group devoted to the prohibition of alcohol.

Becker was especially interested in describing deviant careers and the processes by which individuals become members of deviant subcultures and take on the attributes associated with the deviant role. Becker argued that most deviance is likely to be transitory but that transitory deviance can be effectively stabilized in a person's behavioral repertoire through the labeling process. Once a person is labeled deviant, opportunities for conforming behavior are seriously reduced and behavioral opportunities that remain open are primarily deviant ones; the budding deviant increasingly exhibits deviant behavior because his or her choices are restricted by society. Successful deviants must acquire the techniques and resources necessary to undertake the deviant act (drug use, bank robbery) and develop the mind-set characteristic of others like them. Near the end of a deviant career, the person labeled a deviant has internalized society's negative label, has assumed a deviant self-concept, and is likely a member of a deviant subgroup. "A drug addict once told me that the moment she felt she was really 'hooked' was when she realized she no longer had any friends who were not drug addicts."[59] In this way, explained Becker, deviance becomes a self-fulfilling prophecy, so labeling is a cause of crime insofar as the actions of society in defining the rule breaker as deviant push the person further in the direction of continued deviance.

Contributions of Labeling Theory

Labeling theory contributed a number of unique ideas to criminological literature:

- Deviance is the result of social processes involving the imposition of definitions rather than the consequence of any quality inherent in human activity itself.
- Deviant individuals achieve their status by virtue of social definition rather than inborn traits.
- The reaction of society to deviant behavior and to those who engage in such behavior is the major element in determining the criminality of the behavior and the person in question.
- Negative self-images follow processing by the formal criminal justice system rather than precede delinquency.
- Labeling by society and handling by the justice system tend to perpetuate crime and delinquency rather than reduce them.

Becker's typology of delinquents—the pure deviant, the falsely accused deviant, and the secret deviant—helped explain the labeling approach (Figure 7–3). The pure deviant is one who commits norm-breaking behavior and is accurately appraised by society, who is tried and convicted, and who gets what he or she deserves. The falsely accused individual is one who is not guilty but is labeled deviant nonetheless, who experiences the impact of conviction and of the experiences that attend prison life, and who is left with a negative self-concept and with group associations practically indistinguishable from those of a true deviant. This person demonstrates the power of social definition—the life of the falsely accused is changed just as thoroughly as the life of the pure deviant by the process of labeling. The secret deviant violates social norms, but his or her behavior is not noticed, so negative societal reactions do not follow; a secret deviant again demonstrates the power of societal reaction, but in this case by the lack of consequences.

Although labeling theory fell into disregard during the late 1970s and early 1980s due to accusations that it was vague and ambiguous, some criminologists have recast the approach as a developmental theory of structural disadvantage.[60] The theory is now seen as one that points out the cumulative effects over time of official intervention on future life chances and opportunities for approved success. Robert J. Sampson and John H. Laub observed that labeling theory is "truly developmental in nature because of its explicit emphasis on processes over time."[61] Contemporary proponents of the labeling perspective generally see labeling as only one factor contributing to cumulative disadvantages in life chances. In 2003, Jon Gunnar Bernburg and Marvin D. Krohn studied the impact of negative official interventions on young men in Rochester, New York, from the time they were about 13.5 years old until they reached the age of 22. In keeping with what labeling theory would predict, Bernburg and Krohn found that official intervention during adolescence led to increased criminality in early adulthood because it reduced life chances for educational achievement and successful employment and that poor people were more negatively impacted by official processing, probably because they were already disadvantaged along other important social dimensions.[62]

Negative labels can carry significant visible liabilities as well as hidden ones. A 2004 study by the Legal Action Center, a crime and justice policy group, found that all 50 states have laws that hamper

Pure deviant

Falsely accused

Secret deviant

FIGURE 7–3 | Becker's Types of Delinquents

WEB EXTRA 7–1
LIBRARY EXTRA 7–5

■ **reintegrative shaming**
A form of shaming, imposed as a sanction by the criminal justice system, that is thought to strengthen the moral bond between the offender and the community.

■ **stigmatic shaming**
A form of shaming, imposed as a sanction by the criminal justice system, that is thought to destroy the moral bond between the offender and the community.

the ability of former offenders to reenter society.[63] Four states—Colorado, Georgia, South Carolina, and Virginia—were rated as places where ex-offenders have the least chance to become productive citizens. According to the center, many states prohibit ex-offenders from obtaining professional licenses to work in businesses as diverse as real estate, medicine, and law; 27 states, in keeping with a requirement imposed by Congress on states seeking federal highway funds, revoke or refuse to issue driver's licenses to former drug felons, effectively prohibiting access to many job sites.

Mike S. Adams proposed a general sociological learning theory of crime and deviance that incorporated components of labeling theory and differential association.[64] Adams contended that "labeling effects are mediated by associations with delinquent peers," concluding that labeling is not a direct cause of delinquency and crime but "appears to cause delinquency indirectly via the effects of associations with delinquent peer groups" and that "the causal chain linking primary to secondary deviance must incorporate links that account for the effects of associations with delinquent [peers]."[65] Learn more about labeling theory at **Web Extra 7–1**, and read about the postprison consequences of a criminal label at **Library Extra 7–5**.

Reintegrative Shaming

In a more contemporary offshoot of labeling theory, **John Braithwaite** and colleagues at the Australian National University (ANU) reported initial results of studies in 1997 on **reintegrative shaming**, which describes processes by which a deviant is labeled and sanctioned but then is brought back into a community of conformity through words, gestures, or rituals.[66]

Called RISE (for Reintegrative Shaming Experiments), the project assessed the efficacy of each approach using several criteria: (1) prevalence and frequency of repeat offending, (2) victim satisfaction with the process, (3) estimated cost savings within the justice process, (4) changes in drinking or drug use among offenders, and (5) perceptions of procedural justice, fairness, and protection of rights.[67]

At the core of the study was Braithwaite's belief that two different kinds of shame exist. **Stigmatic shaming** is thought to destroy the moral bond between the offender and the community, whereas reintegrative shaming is thought to strengthen the moral bond between the offender and the community. According to Braithwaite and Strang, "Stigmatic shaming is what American

judges employ when they make an offender post a sign on his property saying 'a violent felon lives here,' or a bumper sticker on his car saying 'I am a drunk driver.' Stigmatic shaming sets the offender apart as an outcast—often for the rest of the offender's life. By labeling him or her as someone who cannot be trusted to obey the law, stigmatic shaming says the offender is expected to commit more crimes."[68]

Their alternative to stigmatic humiliation is "to condemn the crime, not the criminal."[69] Through carefully monitored diversionary conferences, Braithwaite and Strang hoped to give offenders the opportunity to rejoin the community as law-abiding citizens, but to earn the right to a fresh start, offenders must express remorse for their past conduct, apologize to any victims, and repair the harm caused by the crime.

Preliminary results from the RISE studies supported the claimed value of reintegrative shaming, but most of these results have been measured using interviews with offenders following diversionary conferences and consist primarily of anecdotal evidence based on the reported feelings of respondents. These findings showed that offenders are far more likely to feel ashamed

Minor offenders in Hillsborough County, Florida, performing court-ordered duties in public view. Some people believe that shaming can be an effective rehabilitative tool. What different kinds of shaming can you identify?
Source: ZUMA Press/NewsCom.com

LIBRARY EXTRA 7–6
LIBRARY EXTRA 7–7
WEB EXTRA 7–2

■ **dramaturgical perspective**
A theoretical point of view that depicts human behavior as centered around the purposeful management of interpersonal impressions.

■ **impression management**
The intentional enactment of practiced behavior that is intended to convey to others one's desirable personal characteristics and social qualities.

■ **discrediting information**
Any information that is inconsistent with the managed impressions being communicated in a given situation.

■ **total institution**
A facility from which individuals can rarely come and go and in which communal life is intense and circumscribed. Individuals in total institutions tend to eat, sleep, play, learn, and worship together.

> Reintegrative shaming is thought to strengthen the moral bond between the offender and the community.

of their crimes if they are handled through conferences rather than through formal court processing and that both offenders and victims find conferences fairer than official court proceedings. Learn more about reintegrative shaming experiments at **Web Extra 7–2** and **Library Extras 7–6** and **7–7**.

Dramaturgical Perspective

Another social process approach to the study of criminology can be found in the work of **Erving Goffman** in his 1959 book *The Presentation of Self in Everyday Life*, which introduced students of criminology to dramaturgy.[70] The **dramaturgical perspective** says that individuals play a variety of nearly simultaneous social roles—such as mother, teacher, daughter, wife, and part-time real estate agent—and that such roles must be sustained in interactions with others. Goffman argued that social actors present themselves more or less effectively when acting out a particular role and that role performances basically consist of managed impressions. Criminals, through a similar process of managed impressions and by the fear engendered in their victims, may likewise achieve cooperation.

Impression management, according to Goffman, is a complex process involving a never-ending give-and-take of information. When it has been successful, said Goffman, dramatic realization has occurred: "Together, the participants contribute to a single overall definition of the situation which involves not so much a real agreement as to what exists but rather a real agreement as to whose claims concerning what issues will be temporarily honored."[71]

Deviant behavior finds its place in the dramaturgical perspective through the concept of discreditable disclosure. Some actors, said Goffman, may find themselves targeted by the introduction of **discrediting information**, information they have sought to hide that is inconsistent with managed impressions. The flow of interaction is then disrupted, and the nature of the performance may be altered substantially.

Goffman's work takes on considerable relevance for criminology in his later writings, especially his book *Stigma: Notes on the Management of Spoiled Identity*, in which he advanced the notion that discredited or stigmatized individuals differ significantly from "normals" in the way that society responds to them.[72] By definition, he said that "we believe that a person with a stigma is not quite human. On this assumption, we exercise varieties of discrimination, through which we effectively, if often unthinkingly, reduce his life chances. We construct a stigma-theory, an ideology to explain his inferiority and account for the danger he represents. We tend to impute a wide range of imperfections on the basis of the original one."[73] A stigma may be physical (birthmarks), behavioral (theft), or ideational (low rank in the pecking order).

In *Stigma*, Goffman was primarily concerned with how "normals" and stigmatized individuals interact. At times, discredited individuals are known to others before they come in contact with them, and when that happens, normal people approach the stigmatized ones with expectations of encountering further stigmatizing behavior. When discrediting information does not precede interpersonal encounters, the stigmatized individuals may attempt to pass as normal by using various techniques of concealment, including aliases and misrepresentation.

According to Goffman, societal reactions, although they may forcibly create social identities, are also instrumental in the formation of group identities. When similarly discredited individuals come together in like-minded groups, they may align themselves against the larger society; in so reacting, they may justify their own deviant or criminal behavior. At the conclusion of *Stigma*, Goffman reminded us, "The normal and the stigmatized are not persons, but rather perspectives. These are generated in social situations during mixed contacts by virtue of the unrealized norms that are likely to play upon the encounter."[74]

In his book titled *Asylums*, Goffman described **total institutions**—facilities from which individuals can rarely come and go and in which communal life is intense and circumscribed.[75] Individuals in total institutions tend to eat, sleep, play, learn, and worship together; military camps, seminaries, convents, prisons, rest homes, and mental hospitals are all types of total institutions. Goffman believed that residents of total institutions bring "presenting cultures" with them to their

■ **prosocial bond**
A bond between the individual and the social group that strengthens the likelihood of conformity. Prosocial bonds are characterized by attachment to conventional social institutions, values, and beliefs.

LIBRARY EXTRA 7–8
LIBRARY EXTRA 7–9
WEB EXTRA 7–3

respective facilities, so some inmates would carry street culture into correctional facilities. However, residents undergo a period of "disculturation," during which they drop aspects of their native culture that are not consistent with existing institutional culture—a culture that they must acquire. Read about jails as total institutions at **Library Extra 7–8**.

Policy Implications of Social Process Theories

Social process theories suggest that crime-prevention programs should work to enhance self-control and to build **prosocial bonds** (bonds that strengthen conformity). One program that seeks to build strong prosocial bonds while attempting to teach positive values to young people is the Juvenile Mentoring Program (JUMP) of the Office of Juvenile Justice and Delinquency Prevention (OJJDP), funded by Congress in 1992 under an amendment to the Juvenile Justice and Delinquency Prevention Act of 1974.[76] JUMP programs, commencing in 1996, place at-risk youths (those at risk of delinquency, gang involvement, educational failure, or dropping out of school) in a one-on-one relationship with favorable adult role models.

A 2010 performance of the musical *The Addams Family* at the Lunt-Fontanne Theater in New York City. Some criminologists suggest that people, like actors on a stage, intentionally present themselves to others in ways calculated to produce predictable social responses. How might criminals manipulate impressions?
Source: Sara Krulwich/*The New York Times*/Redux

Data in 2007 showed 9,200 youths (average age just under 12) enrolled in more than 200 JUMP programs nationwide. Based on evaluation data, both youths and mentors were very positive when rating various aspects of their mentoring experiences.[77] Learn more about JUMP at **Library Extra 7–9**.

Another social control–based program is Preparing for the Drug Free Years (PDFY), designed to increase effective parenting as part of the Strengthening America's Families Project.[78] PDFY works with parents of children in grades four to eight in an effort to reduce drug abuse and behavioral problems in adolescents, seeks to teach effective parenting skills as a way to decrease the risks that juveniles face, and incorporates both behavioral skills training and communication-centered approaches into parent training. Through a series of 10 one-hour sessions, parents learn to (1) increase their children's opportunities for family involvement, (2) teach needed family participation and social skills, and (3) provide reinforcement for positive behavior and appropriate consequences for misbehavior. Early studies showed that program participation (session attendance) tends to be high and that the program is effective at improving general child-management skills among parents.[79] Learn more about PDFY at **Web Extra 7–3**.

A program emphasizing the development of self-control is the Montreal Preventive Treatment Program, which addresses early-childhood risk factors for gang involvement by targeting boys from poor socioeconomic backgrounds who display disruptive behavior while in kindergarten.[80] The program offers training sessions for parents designed to teach family crisis management, disciplining techniques, and other parenting skills while the boys participate in training sessions emphasizing the development of prosocial skills and self-control. At least one evaluation of the program showed that it was effective at keeping boys from joining gangs.[81]

Critique of Social Process Theories

Criticisms of social process theories are many and varied. Perhaps the most potent criticism of association theory is the claim that Sutherland's initial formulation of differential association is not applicable at the individual level because even people who experience an excess of definitions favorable to law violation may still not become criminal and those who rarely associate with recognized deviants may still turn to crime. Also, the theory is untestable because most people experience a multitude of definitions—both favorable

■ **human development**
The relationship between the maturing individual and his or her changing environment, as well as the social processes that the relationship entails.

■ **social development perspective**
An integrated view of human development that examines multiple maturational levels, including psychological, biological, familial, interpersonal, cultural, societal, and ecological, simultaneously.

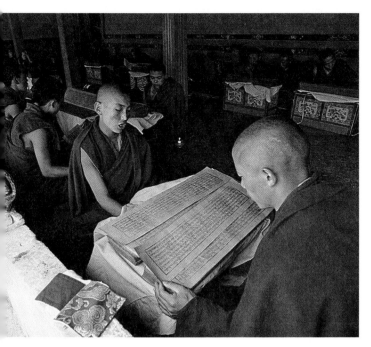

Monks in a Buddhist monastery. People in total institutions share all aspects of their lives. How is a prison like a monastery?
Source: Woodfin Camp & Associates, Inc.

and unfavorable to law violation—and it is up to them to interpret what those experiences mean, so classifying experiences as either favorable or unfavorable to crime commission is difficult at best.

Other critics suggest that differential association alone is not a sufficient explanation for crime. In effect, association theory does not seem to provide for free choice in individual circumstances, nor does it explain why some individuals, even when surrounded by associates committed to lives of crime, are still able to hold on to noncriminal values. Finally, association theory fails to account for the emergence of criminal values, addressing only the communication of those values.

Although the labeling approach successfully points to the labeling process as a reason for continued deviance and as a cause of stabilization in deviant identities, it does little to explain the origin of crime and deviance, and few studies seem to support the basic tenets of the theory. Critics of labeling have pointed to its "lack of firm empirical support for the notion of secondary deviance, [and] many studies have not found that delinquents or criminals have a delinquent or criminal self-image."[82] There is also a lack of empirical

> The labeling approach does little to explain the origin of crime and deviance.

support for the claim that contact with the justice system is fundamentally detrimental to the personal lives of criminal perpetrators, but even if that were true, one must ask whether it would ultimately be better if offenders were not caught and forced to undergo the rigors of processing by the justice system. Although labeling theory hints that official processing makes a significant contribution to continued criminality, it seems unreasonable to expect that offenders untouched by the system would forgo the rewards of future criminality. Finally, labeling theory has little to say about secret deviants (people who engage in criminality but are never caught). Can they be expected to continue in lives of deviance if never caught?

Goffman's work has been criticized as providing a set of "linked concepts" rather than a consistent theoretical framework.[83] Other critics have faulted Goffman for failing to offer suggestions for institutional change or for not proposing treatment modalities based on his assumptions. Goffman's greatest failing may be taking the analogy of the theater too far and convincing readers that real life is but a form of playacting; according to George Psathas, "Performing and being are not identical."[84]

The Social Development Perspective

Over the past 25 years, an appreciation for the process of **human development** (the relationship between the maturing individual and his or her changing environment and the social processes that relationship entails) has played an increasingly important role in understanding criminality.[85] Students of human development recognize that the process of development occurs through reciprocal dynamic interactions that take place between individuals and various aspects of their environment, and the **social development perspective** posits that development, which begins at birth (and perhaps even earlier), occurs primarily within a social context. Unlike social learning theory (discussed earlier in this chapter), social development sees socialization as only one feature of that context. If socialization were the primary determinant of criminality, then we might expect that all problem children would become criminals as adults, but since that doesn't happen, there must be other aspects to the developmental process that social learning theories don't fully cover.

WEB EXTRA 7–4
WEB EXTRA 7–5

■ **life course perspective**
A perspective that draws attention to the fact that criminal behavior tends to follow a distinct pattern across the life cycle; also called *life course criminology*.

■ **criminal career**
The longitudinal sequence of crimes committed by an individual offender.

■ **life course**
The different pathways through the age-differentiated life span; the course of a person's life over time.

According to the social development perspective, human development simultaneously occurs on many levels—psychological, biological, familial, interpersonal, cultural, societal, and ecological—so social development theories tend to be integrated theories combining various points of view. The rest of this chapter describes life course criminology, the major social development perspective; various ideas contributing to the life course perspective, along with other perspectives on social development, are also described. You can learn more about such perspectives at **Web Extra 7–4**.

Concepts in Social Development Theories

Most sociological explanations for crime involve the study of groups and the identification of differences among groups of offenders, but social development theories focus more on individual rates of offending and seek to understand both increases and decreases in rates of offending over the individual's lifetime. Social development theories generally employ longitudinal (over time) measurements of delinquency and offending, and they pay special attention to the transitions that people face as they move through the life cycle.

Most theories of social development recognize that a critical transitional period occurs as a person moves from childhood to adulthood, and life course theorists have identified at least seven developmental tasks that American adolescents must confront: (1) establishing identity, (2) cultivating symbiotic relationships, (3) defining physical attractiveness, (4) investing in a value system, (5) obtaining an education, (6) separating from family and achieving independence, and (7) obtaining and maintaining gainful employment.[86] Youths are confronted with many obstacles or risks in their attempts to resolve these issues as they work to make a successful transition to adulthood. Figure 7–4 provides a conceptual model of the developmental processes that a maturing youth experiences during adolescence. Learn more about the transitional process leading to adulthood at **Web Extra 7–5**.

The Life Course Perspective

Traditional explanations for crime and delinquency often lack a developmental perspective because they generally ignore developmental changes throughout the life course and frequently fail to distinguish between different phases of criminal careers.[87] In contrast, developmental theories draw attention to the fact that criminal behavior tends to follow a distinct pattern across the life cycle: Criminality is relatively uncommon during childhood, tends to begin as sporadic instances of delinquency during late adolescence and early adulthood, and then diminishes and sometimes completely disappears from a person's behavioral repertoire by age 30 or 40. Of course, some people never commit crimes or do so only rarely, whereas others become career criminals and persist in lives of crime (see the Criminal Profiles box).

> Developmental theories draw attention to the fact that criminal behavior tends to follow a distinct pattern across the life cycle.

The **life course perspective** (also called *life course criminology*) shifted the traditional focus away from the reasons why people begin offending to questions about what the dimensions of criminal offending are over the entire life course.[88] It has its roots in a 1986 National Academy of Sciences (NAS) panel report prepared by Alfred Blumstein, Jacqueline Cohen, Jeffrey Roth, and Christy Visher that emphasized the importance of the study of criminal careers and of crime over the life course.[89] The NAS panel defined a **criminal career** as "the longitudinal sequence of crimes committed by an individual offender."[90] The report was especially important for its analysis of "offending development," a concept that underlies the life course perspective (see the Theory in Perspective box).

The panel noted that criminal careers could be described in terms of four dimensions: participation, frequency, duration, and seriousness (Figure 7–5). *Participation*, the fraction of a population that is criminally active, depends on the scope of criminal acts considered and the length of the observation period.[91] *Frequency* refers to the number of crimes committed by an individual offender per unit of time and generally varies over the life course, even for habitual offenders. *Duration* is the length of the criminal career, and *seriousness* ranges from petty crimes to a high degree of seriousness.

Life course criminology was given its name in a seminal book written by **Robert J. Sampson** and **John H. Laub** in 1993.[92] Earlier, the concept of **life course** had been defined as "pathways through the life span involving a sequence of culturally defined, age-graded roles and social transitions enacted over time."[93] Life course theories, which build on social learning and social control principles, recognize that criminal careers may develop as the result of various criminogenic influences that affect individuals over the course of their lives.

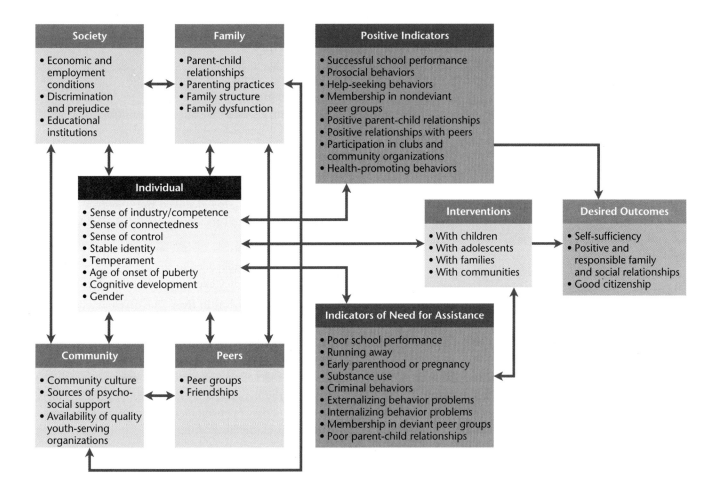

FIGURE 7-4 | A Conceptual Model of Adolescent Development

Source: Family and Youth Services Bureau, *Understanding Youth Development: Promoting Positive Pathways of Growth* (Washington, DC: U.S. Department of Health and Human Services, 2000).

Researchers who focus on the life course as it leads to delinquency, crime, and criminal identities are interested both in evaluating the prevalence, frequency, and onset of offending and in identifying different developmental pathways to delinquency. Life course researchers ask a variety of questions: How do early-childhood characteristics (for example, antisocial behavior) lead to adult behavioral processes and outcomes? How do life transitions (for example, shifts in relationships from parents to peers, transitions from same-sex peers to opposite-sex peers, moves from school to work, marriage, divorce) influence behavior and behavioral choices? How do offending and victimization interact over the life cycle?[94]

Life course researchers examine "trajectories and transitions through the age-differentiated life span."[95] According to Sampson

FIGURE 7-5 | Aspects of Criminal Careers

▓ **human agency**
The active role that people take in their lives; the fact that people are not merely subject to social and structural constraints but actively make choices and decisions based on the alternatives they see before them.

THEORY | in **PERSPECTIVE**
Social Development Theories

Social development theories are integrated theories of human development that simultaneously examine many different levels of development—psychological, biological, familial, interpersonal, cultural, societal, and ecological.

Life Course Perspective

The life course perspective highlights the development of criminal careers, which are seen as the result of various criminogenic influences that affect individuals throughout the course of their lives.

Period: 1980s–present

Theorists: Alfred Blumstein, John H. Laub, Robert J. Sampson, David P. Farrington, Donald J. West, Lawrence E. Cohen, Richard Machalek, Terence Thornberry

Concepts: Criminal career, life course, trajectory, turning points, age grading, social capital, human agency, developmental pathways, life course persisters, persistence, desistance, resilience, cohort, cohort analysis, longitudinal research, evolutionary ecology

---

and Laub, "Trajectories refer to longer-term patterns and sequences of behavior, whereas transitions are marked by specific life events (for example, first job or the onset of crime) that are embedded in trajectories and evolve over shorter time spans."[96] The concept of age differentiation (or age grading) recognizes the fact that certain forms of behavior and some experiences are more appropriate (in terms of their social consequences) in certain parts of the life cycle than in others. Life course theorists search for evidence of continuity between childhood or adolescent experiences and adult outcomes or lifestyles.

Three sets of dynamic concepts are important to the life course perspective: (1) activation, (2) aggravation, and (3) desistance.[97] *Activation*, the way that delinquent behaviors are stimulated and the processes by which the continuity, frequency, and diversity of delinquency are shaped, comes in three types: (1) acceleration (increased frequency of offending over time), (2) stabilization (increased continuity over time), and (3) diversification (propensity of individuals to become involved in more diverse delinquent activities). *Aggravation*, the second dynamic process, refers to the existence of a developmental sequence of activities that escalates or increases in seriousness over time. *Desistance*, the third process which is discussed in greater detail later in this chapter, describes a slowing down in the frequency of offending (deceleration), a reduction in its variety (specialization), or a reduction in its seriousness (de-escalation).[98]

> **The life course perspective highlights the development of criminal careers.**

Another central organizing principle of life course theories is linked lives, a concept meaning that human lives "are typically embedded in social relationships with kin and friends across the life span";[99] these relationships exercise considerable influence on the life course of most people.

Glen H. Elder, Jr., has identified five important life course principles that provide a concise summary of life course theory:[100]

1. **Principle of historical time and place**. The life course of individuals is embedded in and shaped by the historical times and places they experience over their lifetime.

2. **Principle of timing in lives**. The developmental impact of a succession of life transitions or events is contingent on when they occur in a person's life.

3. **Principle of linked lives**. Lives are lived interdependently, and social and historical influences are expressed through this network of shared relationships. When there is a serious illness, opportunities that might have been otherwise available are likely to be lost.

4. **Principle of human agency**. **Human agency** refers to the fact that individuals construct their own life course through the choices they make and the actions they take within the opportunities and constraints of history and social circumstances.

5. **Principle of human development and aging as lifelong processes**. Human behavior cannot be fully explained by restricting analysis to one life stage, whether it be adolescence, mid-life, or old age.

Life course theories are supported by research dating back over three-quarters of a century. During the 1930s, **Sheldon Glueck** and **Eleanor Glueck** studied the life cycles and careers of 500 nondelinquent and 500 known delinquent boys in an effort to identify the causes of delinquency.[101] Study group participants were matched on age, intelligence, ethnicity, and neighborhood residence. Data was collected through psychiatric interviews with subjects, parent and teacher reports, and official records obtained from police, court, and correctional files, and surviving subjects were interviewed again between 1949 and 1965.

CRIMINAL | PROFILES

Seung-Hui Cho

Seung-Hui Cho was born January 18, 1984. He rarely talked and possessed a disassociated manner, displaying little reaction to what was occurring around him. Cho came to America from the Republic of Korea when he was just eight years old, a sullen, withdrawn, brooding child, but he is remembered today as the campus shooter who took the lives of 27 students and five professors at Virginia Tech University in 2007.

Interviewed after the tragic events at Virginia Tech, Cho's 84-year-old great-aunt Yang-Soon Kim said: "When I told his mother that he was a good boy, quiet but well behaved, she said she would rather have him respond to her when talked to than be good and meek."[i]

After coming to America and moving to the tight-knit Korean community in Centreville, Virginia, the family maintained an "uncommonly private" existence.[ii] Cho's progression through elementary school was unremarkable; at nearby Westfield High School, Cho was teased and bullied, especially about his poor English and deep-throated voice;[iii] he remained a quiet and aloof loner who acted, a neighbor observed, "like he had a broken heart."[iv]

While others (including his own sister, Sun-Kyung) in the success-oriented community were heralded in the community newspaper for making the selection lists at some of the most elite Ivy League universities, Cho's less-than-stellar grades kept him off such lists, so he went to Virginia Tech in the Blue Ridge Mountains.

Cho's freshman, sophomore, and junior years as an English major at Virginia Tech were noteworthy for the palpable anger of his writings, and the disturbingly violent nature of his papers caused the chairwoman of the English Department to remove him from a creative writing class. She attempted to teach him one on one and then sought assistance from the university's counseling department and other university officials.[v]

The anger within Cho was also of concern to his fellow students, who openly discussed whether he could become a school shooter.[vi] *New York Times* columnist Benedict Carey eloquently explained afterwards that "the tragedy illustrates how human social groups, whether in classrooms, boardrooms or dormitories, are in fact exquisitely sensitive to a threat in their midst."[vii]

The attacks on the Virginia Tech campus were planned and executed with near-military precision. Weeks before the shooting, Cho acquired two handguns, extra magazines, ammunition, and lengths of chain to

Seung-Hui Cho, age 23, of South Korea, identified by police as the shooter in a massacre that left 33 people dead at Virginia Tech in Blacksburg, Virginia, on April 16, 2007. The shooting is said to be the deadliest killing by a single gunman in modern U.S. history. How can crimes like Seung-Hui's be understood?

Source: Virginia State Police/AP Wide World Photos

secure the doors of classroom buildings so that potential victims would be unable to escape. Days before the killings, he videotaped a raging manifesto-like diatribe/suicide note blaming society for making him into what he'd become.[viii]

Shortly after 7 A.M. on April 16, 2007, Cho killed his first two victims, which police mistakenly believed was the result of a lovers' quarrel. Their error gave Cho the time he needed to make his last preparations for another attack.[ix]

Entering Norris Hall around 9:30 A.M., Cho secured the interior door handles with chains and then systematically slaughtered everyone he encountered. During the next 15 minutes, he fired more than 175 rounds of ammunition from two weapons, leaving 30 people dead. When Cho heard police blast through the entrance doors to gain access to the building, Cho turned the gun on himself. His rampage is the worst of its kind in U.S. history, leaving a total of 32 victims.

Notes

i.   N. R. Kleinfield, "Before Deadly Rage, a Life Consumed by Troubling Silence," *New York Times*, April 22, 2007, http://www.nytimes.com/2007/04/22/us/22vatech .html?_r=1&n=Top%2fReference%2fTimes%20Topics%2fPeople%2fC%2fCho%2c%20Seung%2dHui&oref=slogin (accessed July 1, 2007).

ii.   Ibid.

iii. "High School Classmates Say Gunman Was Bullied," MSNBC, April 19, 2007, http://www.msnbc.msn.com/id/18169776/ (accessed July 1, 2007).

iv.   Kleinfield, "Before Deadly Rage."

v.   "Professor: Shooter's Writing Dripped with Anger," Cable News Network, April 18, 2007, http://www.cnn.com/2007/US/04/17/vtech.shooting/index.html (accessed July 1, 2007).

vi.   Kleinfield, "Before Deadly Rage."

vii. Benedict Carey, "When the Group Is Wise," *New York Times*, April 22, 2007, http://www.nytimes.com/2007/04/22/weekinreview/22carey.html?_r=1&ref =weekinreview&oref=slogin (accessed July 1, 2007).

viii. Ned Potter et al., "Killer's Note: You Caused Me to Do This," ABC News, April 28, 2007, http://abcnews.go.com/US/Story?id=3048108&page=1 (accessed July 1, 2007).

ix.   Ibid.

x.   Aamer Madhani, E. A. Torriero, and Rex W. Huppke, "Danger Signs Festered below Aloof Surface," *Chicago Tribune*, April 17, 2007, http://www.chicagotribune.com/news/nationworld/chi-070417vtech-shootings,0,1137509.story?page=1&coll=chi-homepagepromo440-fea (accessed July 1, 2007).

LIBRARY EXTRA 7-10
LIBRARY EXTRA 7-11

■ **social capital**
The degree of positive relationships with others and with social institutions that individuals build up over the course of their lives.

The Gluecks investigated possible contributions to crime causation on four levels: sociocultural (socioeconomic), somatic (physical), intellectual, and emotional-temperamental and concluded that family dynamics played an especially significant role in the development of criminality—"the deeper the roots of childhood maladjustment, the smaller the chance of adult adjustment."[102] Delinquent careers, said the Gluecks, tend to carry over into adulthood and frequently lead to criminal careers. Read more about the life course perspective at **Library Extra 7–10**, and review a paper comparing the life course perspective to other theories discussed in this book at **Library Extra 7–11**.

Laub and Sampson's Age-Graded Theory

John H. Laub and Robert J. Sampson dusted off 60 cartons of nearly forgotten data that had been collected by the Gluecks and stored in the basement of the Harvard Law School.[103] Upon re-analysis of the data, Laub and Sampson found that children who turned to delinquency were frequently those who had trouble at school and at home and who had friends who were already involved in delinquency. They also discovered that two events in the life course—marriage and job stability—seemed to be especially important in reducing the frequency of offending in later life.

Using a sophisticated cyberanalysis of the Gluecks' original data, Laub and Sampson developed an "age-graded theory of informal social control."[104] Like Hirschi (discussed earlier), Laub and Sampson suggested that delinquency is more likely to occur when an individual's bond to society is weak or broken, but they also recognized that "social ties embedded in adult transitions (for example, marital attachment, job stability) explain variations in crime unaccounted for by childhood deviance."[105] Hence, although it incorporated the concept of social bonds, Laub and Sampson's perspective also emphasized the significance of continuity and change over the life course.

Central to Laub and Sampson's approach is the idea of turning points in a criminal career—"the interlocking nature of trajectories and transitions may generate turning points or a change in the life course."[106] Turning points were first identified by G. B. Trasler in 1980 when he wrote, "As they grow older, most young men gain access to other sources of achievement and social satisfaction—a job, a girlfriend, a wife, a home and eventually children—and in doing so become gradually less dependent upon peer-group support."[107] Given the importance of turning points—which

> Delinquency is more likely to occur when an individual's bond to society is weak or broken.

may turn a person toward or away from criminality and delinquency—a clear-cut relationship between early delinquency and criminality later in life cannot be assumed. Sampson and Laub also identified two significant turning points: employment and marriage. Other important turning points can occur in association with leaving home, having children, getting divorced, graduating from school, and receiving a financial windfall. According to Laub and Sampson, even chronic offenders can be reformed when they experience the requisite turning points, whereas individuals with histories of conventionality can begin offending in response to events and circumstances that undermine previously restraining social bonds.[108]

Because transitions in the life course are typically associated with age and because transitional events either enhance or weaken the social bond, Sampson and Laub contended that "age-graded changes in social bonds explain changes in crime"; since these events are not the result of "purposeful efforts to control," they are dubbed "informal social controls."[109]

In 2001, an examination of data from the Dunedin Study (referred to in Chapter 4) suggested the idea of life course interdependence, in which "the effects of social ties on crime vary as a function of criminal propensity."[110] In other words, prosocial ties that deter crime (education, marriage, steady employment) are more likely to discourage criminality among those who are already predisposed to avoid it than among those who are not; researchers dubbed this the "social-protection effect." Conversely, a "social-amplification effect" could be identified in antisocial ties (delinquent friends) that promote crime among individuals predisposed to criminality. The researchers concluded that certain features of the social environment could serve as positive turning points in the lives of antisocial individuals, but the social-amplification effect could produce negative turning points in the lives of the same people.

Another important concept in Laub and Sampson's theory is **social capital**, which refers to the degree of positive relationships with other people and with social institutions that individuals build up over the course of their lives.[111] Social capital directly impacts life course trajectories: The greater a person's social capital, the less chance there is of criminal activity.[112]

A study of how two primary constituents of social capital—marriage and full-time employment—impact life course trajectories was reported by Matthew G. Yeager in 2003. He examined the lives

LIBRARY EXTRA 7–12

■ **persistence**
A person's continuity in crime or continual involvement in offending.

■ **desistance**
A person's cessation of criminal activity or termination of a period of involvement in offending behavior.

■ **Cambridge Study in Delinquent Development**
A longitudinal (life course) study of crime and delinquency tracking a cohort of 411 boys born in London in 1953.

of 773 adult male prisoners released from the Canadian federal prison system between 1983 and 1984, following them for a period of three years.[113] He found that being married reduced the likelihood of return to prison, but an even stronger indicator of post-prison success was full-time employment, which Yeager described as having "a strong suppression effect on general criminal recidivism." Because employment is something for which prisoners can be prepared and because it can be offered by the state or federal government, Yeager suggested that it provides a rare opportunity for successful intervention in the lives of released prisoners.

In 2006, Sampson and Laub reported on the application of sophisticated data-analysis techniques to subjects from the Gluecks' original study group who were reinterviewed at age 70. The 2006 study supported the conclusion that "being married is associated with an average reduction of approximately 35 percent in the odds of crime compared to nonmarried status for the same man."[114]

An interesting evaluation of social capital—commitment to a romantic partner, strong job attachment, and nature of close friends among adult subjects—was reported by a group of criminologists in 2002.[115] They found that adolescent delinquency tended to result in involvement with an antisocial romantic partner for both males and females and that such a relationship tended to influence the nature of adult relationships and to increase the likelihood of later criminality. Conventional romantic partners and friends, along with strong job attachment, were found to be especially likely to reduce the chance of criminality among young adult women, but only conventional adult friends had the same effect among males. Learn more about the concept of social capital via **Library Extra 7–12**.

Persistence and Desistance

Life course theorists use the term **persistence** to describe continuity in crime or continual involvement in offending; **desistance** refers to the cessation of criminal activity or the termination of a period of involvement in offending behavior. Desistance (mentioned briefly earlier in this chapter) can be unaided or aided: *Unaided desistance* refers to desistance that occurs without the formal intervention or assistance of criminal justice agencies like probation or parole agencies, the courts, or prison or jail, and *aided desistance*, involving agencies of the justice system, is generally referred to as rehabilitation. Delinquents often mature successfully and grow out of offending; even older persistent offenders may tire of justice system interventions, lose the personal energy required for continued offending, and "burn out."

A number of early criminologists noted the desistance phenomenon. Marvin Wolfgang described the process as one of "spontaneous remission,"[116] although it was recognized far earlier—in 1833, Adolphe Quetelet argued that the penchant for crime diminished with age "due to the enfeeblement of physical vitality and the passions."[117] The Gluecks later developed the concept of maturational reform to explain the phenomenon and suggested that the "sheer passage of time" caused delinquents to "grow out" of this transitory phase and to "burn out" physiologically, concluding, "Ageing is the only factor which emerges as significant in the reformative process."[118]

In 1985, Walter R. Grove proposed a maturational theory of biopsychosocial desistance that sees the desistance phenomenon as a natural or normal consequence of the aging process.[119] "As persons move through the life cycle, (1) they will shift from self-absorption to concern for others; (2) they will increasingly accept societal values and behave in socially appropriate ways; (3) they will become more comfortable with social relations; (4) their activities will increasingly reflect a concern for others in their community; and (5) they will become increasingly concerned with the issue of the meaning of life."[120] Some criminologists argued, however, that the claim that aging causes desistance is meaningless because it doesn't explain the actual mechanisms involved.

Longitudinal studies of crime over the life course conducted by **David P. Farrington** and **Donald J. West** have shown far greater diversity in the ages of desistance than in the ages of onset of criminal behavior.[121] In 1982, in an effort to explain the considerable heterogeneity of developmental pathways, Farrington and West began tracking a cohort of 411 boys born in London in 1953 in an ongoing study known as the **Cambridge Study in Delinquent Development**, which uses self-reports of delinquency as well as psychological tests and in-depth interviews. To date, participants have been interviewed eight times, with the earliest interviews being conducted at age eight.

The Cambridge study reveals that life course patterns found in the United States are also characteristic of English delinquents. Farrington found that the study's persistent offenders suffered from "hyperactivity, poor concentration, low achievement, an antisocial father, large family size, low family income, a broken family, poor parental supervision, and parental disharmony."[122] Other risk factors for delinquency included harsh discipline, negative peer influences, and parents with offense histories of their own. Chronic offenders were found to have friends and peers who were also offenders, and offending was found to begin with early

■ **resilience**
The psychological ability to successfully cope with severe stress and negative events.

■ **cohort analysis**
A social scientific technique that studies a population with common characteristics over time. Cohort analysis usually begins at birth and traces the development of cohort members until they reach a certain age.

■ **evolutionary ecology**
An approach to understanding crime that draws attention to the ways people develop over the course of their lives.

■ **interactional theory**
A theoretical approach to exploring crime and delinquency that blends social control and social learning perspectives.

antisocial behavior, including aggressiveness, dishonesty, problems in school, truancy, hyperactivity, impulsiveness, and restlessness. Consistent with other desistance studies, Farrington found that offending tends to peak around the age of 17 or 18 and then declines. By age 35, many subjects were found to have conforming lifestyles, although they were often separated or divorced and had poor employment records and patterns of residential instability. Many former offenders were also substance abusers and consequently served as very poor role models for their children.

While studies of desistance are becoming increasingly common, one of the main methodological problems for researchers is determining when desistance has occurred. Some theorists conceptualize desistance as the complete or absolute stopping of criminal behavior of any kind, while others see it as the gradual cessation of criminal involvement.[123] In 1990, Rolf Loeber and Marc LeBlanc identified four components of desistance:[124] (1) *deceleration*—a slowing down in the frequency of offending, (2) *specialization*—a reduction in the variety of offenses, (3) *deescalation*—a reduction in the seriousness of offending, and (4) *reaching a ceiling*—remaining at a certain level of offending and not committing more serious offenses.

Resilience, another important concept in life course research, refers to the psychological ability to successfully cope with severe stress and negative events and has important implications for the development of delinquency and criminal offending.[125] One 2009 study of resilience among teenage girls exposed to a number of risk factors associated with delinquency development (physical and sexual assault, neglect, poverty, unemployed parents, female-headed households) found a number of protective factors that could enhance resilience among girls. Included were things like religiosity, school connectedness and success, and presence of a caring adult; the latter offered the most protection against delinquency. "The most consistent protective effect . . . was the extent to which a girl felt she had caring adults in her life."[126]

> Resilience is the psychological ability to successfully cope with severe stress and negative events and has important implications for the development of delinquency and criminal offending.

Evolutionary Ecology

Because life course theory uses a developmental perspective in the study of criminal careers, life course researchers typically use longitudinal research designs involving **cohort analysis**, which usually begins at birth and traces the development of a population whose members share common characteristics until they reach a certain age. One well-known analysis of a birth cohort, undertaken by **Marvin Wolfgang** during the 1960s, found that a small nucleus of chronic juvenile offenders accounted for a disproportionately large share of all juvenile arrests.[127] Wolfgang studied male individuals born in Philadelphia in 1945 until they reached age 18 and concluded that a small number of violent offenders were responsible for most of the crimes committed by the cohort—6% of cohort members accounted for 52% of all arrests. A follow-up study found that the seriousness of the offenses among the cohort increased in adulthood but that the actual number of offenses decreased as the cohort aged.[128] Wolfgang's analysis has since been criticized for its lack of a second cohort, or control group, against which the experiences of the cohort under study could be compared.[129]

The ecological perspective on crime control, pioneered by **Lawrence E. Cohen** and **Richard Machalek**, provides a more contemporary example of a life course approach.[130] **Evolutionary ecology** builds on the approach of social ecology while emphasizing developmental pathways encountered early in life. Criminologist Bryan Vila stated that "the evolutionary ecological approach draws attention to the ways people develop over the course of their lives. Experiences and environment early in life, especially those that affect child development and the transmission of biological traits and family management practices across generations, seem particularly important."[131] According to Vila, evolutionary ecology "attempts to explain how people acquire criminality—a predisposition that disproportionately favors criminal behavior—when and why they express it as crime, how individuals and groups respond to those crimes, and how all these phenomena interact as a dynamic self-reinforcing system that evolves over time."[132]

Thornberry's Interactional Theory

Terence Thornberry proposed what he called an **interactional theory** regarding crime, which integrates social control and social learning explanations of delinquency.[133]

THEORY | versus REALITY
Social Influences on Developmental Pathways

A report by the Family and Youth Services Bureau (an agency of the U.S. Department of Health and Human Services) identified five "aspects of the social context" that can either promote or block the development of prosocial behavior among adolescents:

1. **Biophysical aspects of the individual**. Biophysical characteristics found to influence developmental pathways during adolescence include temperament, gender, cognitive development, and age of onset of puberty. The influence of these factors on development depends to a large extent on how others in the social context react to them. Individuals bring these aspects of self to the interactions in which they are engaged, and the reaction of the social context to these aspects determines the quality and nature of the interactions.

2. **Aspects of the society**. Society may be understood as the economic and institutional structures, values, and mores that constitute a national identity. Some of the aspects of society that influence the development of a sense of competency, connectedness, control, and identity are current economic and employment conditions, discrimination and prejudice, and educational institutions. Societal factors influence adolescent development directly and indirectly through their effects on communities and families. The societal factors of prejudice and discrimination often present barriers to positive developmental pathways for minority and economically disadvantaged youths, so for these youths, community and family contexts are particularly important for moderating the potentially negative influences of societal factors.

3. **Aspects of the community**. The community context (neighborhood or town) incorporates where individuals spend their time and with whom they spend it. The aspects of the community context that have been studied with respect to their effects on adolescent development include community culture, availability of sources of support to parents and youths, and availability of quality community institutional or organizational resources for children and youths. As with societal factors, community factors have both direct and indirect influences on developmental pathways during adolescence. Formal and informal broad-based community institutions and organizations, in particular, influence adolescent development directly by teaching and encouraging prosocial behaviors and indirectly by supporting parents in their parenting efforts.

4. **Aspects of the family**. The following aspects of the family context have received considerable research attention with respect to their influences on developmental pathways: quality of the parent–child relationship, parenting styles or practices, family structure, and family dysfunction. In general, family practices that serve to monitor and control adolescents' behaviors in a caring and consistent manner, provide support and encouragement to adolescents, and allow them psychological and emotional independence appear to be most effective in fostering the development of a sense of competency, connectedness, control over one's fate in life, and identity.

5. **Aspects of peer relationships**. Research findings do not support the popular notion that adolescent problem behaviors are the result of peer pressure; instead, it has been shown that peers do not direct adolescents to new behaviors as much as they reinforce existing dispositions that helped direct the adolescent to a particular peer group in the first place. Close friendships with peers during adolescence have been found to promote positive growth because they foster the development of conceptions of fairness, mutual respect, empathy, and intimacy, through which youths are able to develop a sense of connectedness to others and a stable sense of identity.

The information in the Family and Youth Services Bureau report suggested that interventions designed to assist youths in making successful transitions to adulthood will need to provide adolescents, either directly or through parents and community resources, with opportunities to engage in interactions that foster the development of a sense of competency, connectedness, control, and identity and that interventions must address children, families, and communities as a unit if they are to be effective for large numbers of children and their families.

Discussion Questions

1. How would you rank the five aspects of the social context identified in this box as impacting the development of prosocial behavior among adolescents in order of relative importance? Why would you choose such a ranking?

2. How might the five aspects of the social context interact?

3. Are there other important aspects of the social context that can be identified? If so, what might they be?

Source: Family and Youth Services Bureau, *Understanding Youth Development: Promoting Positive Pathways of Growth* (Washington, DC: U.S. Department of Health and Human Services, January 1997).

In constructing his approach, Thornberry was attentive to the impact of social structure on behavior and noted how delinquency and crime seem to develop within the context of reciprocal social arrangements. Reciprocity was especially important to Thornberry because he believed that too many other theories were overly simplistic in their dependence on simple unidirectional causal relationships (see the Theory versus Reality box).

The fundamental cause of delinquency according to interactional theory is a weakening of a person's bond to conventional society.[134] Thornberry pointed out that adolescents who are strongly attached to their parents and family and who strive to achieve within the context of approved social arrangements, such as education, rarely turn to serious delinquency. It takes more than weak conventional bonds, however, for delinquency to develop; it requires the presence of an environment in which delinquency can be learned and in which rule-violating behavior can be positively rewarded. Delinquent peers are especially important in providing the kind of environment necessary for criminal behavior to develop, and gang membership can play a highly significant role in the development and continuation of such behavior. Associating with delinquent peers, said Thornberry, leads to delinquent acts but also involves a causal loop such that those who commit delinquent acts are likely to continue associating with others like themselves—creating a mechanism of social reinforcement and resulting in ever-escalating levels of criminal behavior. Thornberry also predicted that delinquents will seek out association with ever-more delinquent groups if their delinquency continues to be rewarded, so delinquency is seen as a process that unfolds over the life course.

In a test of interactional theory, Thornberry used data drawn from the Rochester Youth Development Study, a multiwave panel study designed to examine drug use and delinquent behavior among adolescents in the Rochester, New York, area.[135] Study findings (discussed in more detail later) supported the loop-type aspects of interactional theory and showed that delinquency is part of a dynamic social process, not merely the end result of static conditions. The study also found that the development of beliefs supportive of delinquent behavior tends to follow that behavior in time. In other words, commitment to delinquent values may be more a product of delinquent behavior that is rewarded than an initial cause of such behavior.

Thornberry also found that childhood maltreatment (based on official records) could be an important element of the developmental process leading to delinquency and that the degree of

> # Childhood maltreatment is an important element of the developmental process leading to delinquency.

maltreatment experienced in childhood bore some relationship to the extent of delinquent involvement later in life.[136] While maltreatment appears to weaken the bond to conventionality, it also weakens the family bond. Suman Kaker of Florida International University, in an extension of interactional theory, noted that delinquency also puts stress on the family, resulting in a further weakening of the familial bond.[137]

Developmental Pathways

Researchers have found that manifestations of disruptive behaviors in childhood and adolescence are often age dependent, reflecting a developing capability to display different behaviors with age.[138] Budding behavioral problems can often be detected at an early age. In 1994, Rolf Loeber and Dale F. Hay described the emergence of opposition to parents and aggression toward siblings and peers as a natural developmental occurrence during the first two years of life.[139] As toddlers develop the ability to speak, they become increasingly likely to use words to resolve

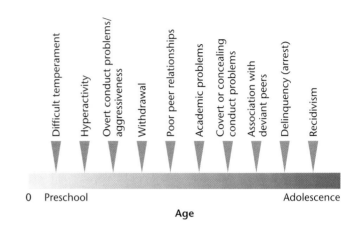

FIGURE 7-6 | Manifestations of Disruptive and Antisocial Behaviors in Childhood and Adolescence

Source: Barbara Tatem Kelley et al., *Developmental Pathways in Boys' Disruptive and Delinquent Behavior* (Washington, DC: Office of Juvenile Justice and Delinquency Prevention, December 1997).

conflicts, with oppositional behaviors declining between ages three and six as children acquire greater verbal skills for expressing their needs and for dealing with conflict, but children who are unable to develop adequate verbal coping skills commit acts of intense aggression, initiate hostile conflict, and are characterized by parents as having a difficult temperament.[140] Figure 7–6 shows the order in which disruptive and antisocial childhood behaviors tend to manifest between birth and late adolescence, and Figure 7–7 shows the order of development of skills and attitudes

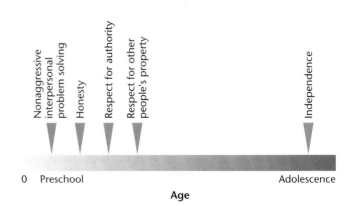

FIGURE 7-7 | Developmental Tasks Necessary for Prosocial Development during Childhood and Adolescence

Source: Barbara Tatem Kelley et al., *Developmental Pathways in Boys' Disruptive and Delinquent Behavior* (Washington, DC: Office of Juvenile Justice and Delinquency Prevention, December 1997).

deemed necessary for successful prosocial development during childhood and adolescence.

One of the most comprehensive studies to date attempting to detail life pathways leading to criminality began in 1986, is called the Program of Research on the Causes and Correlates of Delinquency, sponsored by the U.S. Department of Justice's Office of Juvenile Justice and Delinquency Prevention. The program, a longitudinal study producing ongoing results, aims to better understand serious delinquency, violence, and drug use by examining how youths develop within the context of family, school, peers, and community.[141] It has compiled data on 4,500 youths from three distinct but coordinated projects: the Denver Youth Survey, conducted by the University of Colorado; the Pittsburgh Youth Study, undertaken by University of Pittsburgh researchers; and the Rochester Youth Development Study, fielded by professors at the State University of New York at Albany.

The Causes and Correlates projects, using a similar research design, are longitudinal investigations involving repeated contacts with youths during a substantial portion of their developmental years. Researchers conduct individual face-to-face interviews with inner-city youths considered to be at high risk for involvement in delinquency and drug abuse. Multiple perspectives on each child's development and behavior were obtained through interviews with the child's primary caretakers and with teachers. In addition to interview data, the studies collect extensive information from official agencies, including police, courts, schools, and social services.[142] Following are some program results:

1. Delinquency is related to individual risk factors like impulsivity.

2. The more seriously involved in drugs a youth is, the more seriously that juvenile will be involved in delinquency.

3. Children who are more attached to and involved with their parents are less involved in delinquency.

4. Greater risks exist for violent offending when a child is physically abused or neglected early in life.

5. Students who are not highly committed to school have higher rates of delinquency, and delinquency involvement reduces commitment to school.

6. Poor family life, especially poor parental supervision, exacerbates delinquency and drug use.

7. Affiliation with street gangs and illegal gun ownership are both predictive of delinquency.

8. Living in a bad neighborhood doubles the risk for delinquency.

9. A family being on public assistance (welfare) is associated with the highest risk of delinquency (followed by a family having low socioeconomic status).[143]

Results showed that "peers who were delinquent or used drugs had a great impact on [other] youth" and that "the best predictors of success were having conventional friends, having a stable family and good parental monitoring, having positive expectations for the future, and not having delinquent peers."[144]

Research findings indicated that positive developmental pathways are fostered when adolescents are able to develop (1) a sense of industry and competency, (2) a feeling of connectedness to others and to society, (3) a belief in their ability to control their future, and (4) a stable identity.[145] Competency, connectedness, control, and identity develop through youths' interactions with their community, family, school, and peers. Adolescents who develop these characteristics appear more likely than others to engage in prosocial behaviors, exhibit positive school performance and be members of nondeviant peer groups. The following interactions appear to promote these characteristics:

- Children engage in productive activities and win recognition for their productivity.

- Parents and other adults control and monitor adolescents' behaviors in a consistent and caring manner while allowing them a substantial degree of psychological and emotional independence.

- Parents and other adults provide emotional support, encouragement, and practical advice to adolescents.

- Adolescents are accepted as individuals with unique experiences based on their temperament, gender, and biosocial development as well as family, cultural, and societal factors.

Perhaps the most significant result of the Causes and Correlates study is the finding that three separate developmental pathways to delinquency (shown in Figure 7–8) exist:[146]

1. **Authority conflict pathway**. Subjects appear to begin quite young (three or four years of age) on the authority conflict pathway. "The first step," said the study authors, "was stubborn behavior, followed by defiance around age 11, and authority avoidance—truancy, staying out late at night, or running away."

2. **Covert pathway**. "Minor covert acts such as frequent lying and shoplifting usually [start] around age 10." Delinquents following the covert pathway quickly progress "to acts of property damage, such as fire starting or vandalism, around age 11 or 12, followed by moderate and serious forms of delinquency."

WEB EXTRA 7–6
LIBRARY EXTRA 7–13
LIBRARY EXTRA 7–14
LIBRARY EXTRA 7–15

■ **Project on Human Development in Chicago Neighborhoods (PHDCN)**
An intensive study of Chicago neighborhoods employing longitudinal evaluations to examine the changing circumstances of people's lives in an effort to identify personal characteristics leading toward or away from antisocial behavior.

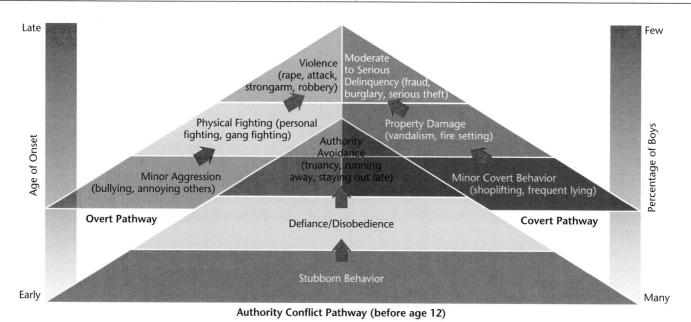

FIGURE 7-8 | Three Pathways to Disruptive Behavior and Delinquency

Source: Barbara Tatem Kelley et al., *Developmental Pathways in Boys' Disruptive and Delinquent Behavior* (Washington, DC: Office of Juvenile Justice and Delinquency Prevention, December 1997).

3. **Overt pathway.** The first step on the overt pathway is minor aggression such as "annoying others and bullying—around age 11 or 12." Bullying was found to escalate into "physical fighting and violence as the juvenile progressed along this pathway." The overt pathway eventually leads to violent crimes like rape, robbery, and assault.

Researchers have found that these three different pathways are not necessarily mutually exclusive and can at times converge (see Figure 7–9). Self-report data have shown that simultaneous progression along two or more pathways leads to higher rates of delinquency.[147] Learn more about the Causes and Correlates study and view results from each study site at **Web Extra 7–6**. Read more about the Program of Research on the Causes and Correlates of Delinquency at **Library Extra 7–13**, and review literature on developmental pathways at **Library Extras 7–14** and **7–15**.

Project on Human Development in Chicago Neighborhoods (PHDCN)

The **Project on Human Development in Chicago Neighborhoods (PHDCN)**, begun in 1990, is jointly sponsored by the National Institute of Justice and the John D. and Catherine T.

MacArthur Foundation.[148] PHDCN is directed by physician Felton J. Earls, professor of human behavior and development at Harvard University's School of Public Health; also involved are Robert Sampson, professor of sociology at the University of Chicago, and Stephen Raudenbush, professor of education at Michigan State

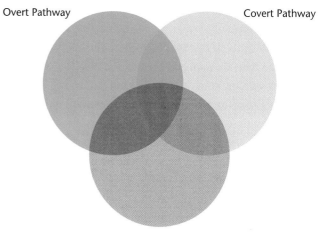

FIGURE 7-9 | Single or Multiple Disruptive Pathways

Source: Barbara Tatem Kelley et al., *Developmental Pathways in Boys' Disruptive and Delinquent Behavior* (Washington, DC: Office of Juvenile Justice and Delinquency Prevention, December 1997).

WHO'S TO BLAME—The Individual or Society?

Sexual Abuser Claims Victim Status

Mortimer Rataway was arrested after authorities received a report of a man struggling with a boy in a Short Stop food and beverage store. A police officer on nearby patrol arrived at the scene within minutes and observed Rataway forcing the boy, nine-year-old Justin, into an old sedan outside the convenience store. When the officer asked Rataway what was going on, the boy blurted out that he had been kidnapped.

The officer had heard reports on his radio describing the kidnapping of a nine-year-old boy from a school bus stop in an adjacent city two days earlier, and he quickly took Rataway into custody on suspicion of kidnapping.

Justin was taken to a special area reserved for juveniles in the local police station where he told detectives that he was the boy who had been kidnapped. Although he was physically okay, he told police that Rataway had forced him to engage in repeated masturbation and that Rataway had taken many photographs of him naked.

A search of Rataway's apartment uncovered a number of digital cameras and a computer Web server hosting a child pornography site. The camera and computer contained photos of many other young boys; some of the photos had probably been purchased over the Internet, but Rataway later admitted taking others.

"I never hurt anybody," Rataway told investigators. "Most of the boys agreed to serve as models after I paid them. But I got carried away and grabbed Justin because I thought he'd make one of my best models.

"Yeah, I'm gay," Rataway told the police in a recorded statement. "And sure, I like boys. But it isn't my fault. When I was growing up as a young Catholic I was taught to enjoy my body and to like other men by the parish priest. Now I know that most priests are good men and that the crisis in the Church has been way overblown by the media. But if that hadn't happened to me, I know I would have been straight, and I'm sure I would have gotten married and had kids of my own. Because of what happened to me when I was a kid, I'm as much a victim as anybody. It doesn't matter how much you punish me, I'm never going to change my sexual orientation."

Think about it:

1. Do you see Rataway as a criminal or a victim (as he claims)? Might he be both?

2. Some people describe child molesters as "sick." Is Rataway "sick"? If so, how can he be cured?

3. Will sending Rataway to prison rehabilitate him? Why or why not? How can you ensure that he won't pose a future threat if he is released back into society someday?

4. How does this case illustrate the way our understandings of criminal motivation and crime causality influence our notions of fairness and justice in the treatment of offenders?

Note: Who's to Blame boxes provide fictionalized critical thinking opportunities, and are not actual cases.

University. Earls and Albert J. Reiss described the ongoing research as "the major criminologic investigation of this century."[149]

PHDCN, consisting of a longitudinal analysis of how individuals, families, institutions, and communities evolve together, is now "tracing how criminal behavior develops from birth to age 32."[150] It involves experts from a wide range of disciplines, including psychiatry, developmental and clinical psychology, sociology, criminology, public health and medicine, education, human behavior, and statistics.

> The Project on Human Development in Chicago Neighborhoods (PHDCN) has been called "the major criminologic investigation of the century."

The project is actually two studies combined into a single comprehensive design: One is an intensive study of Chicago's neighborhoods that evaluates the social, economic, organizational, political, and cultural components of each neighborhood and seeks to identify changes that have taken place in the neighborhoods over the study's eight-year data-gathering period. The second study consists of a series of coordinated longitudinal evaluations of 7,000 randomly selected children, adolescents, and young adults that looks at the changing circumstances of people's lives and attempts to identify personal characteristics leading toward or away from antisocial behavior (see the Who's to Blame box). Researchers explore a wide range of variables—from prenatal drug exposure, lead poisoning, and nutrition to adolescent growth patterns, temperament, and self-image—as they try to identify which individuals might be most at risk for crime and delinquency. They also study children's exposure to violence and its consequences and evaluate child care and its impact on early childhood development. A variety of study methodologies, including self-reports, individualized tests and examinations, direct observations, examination of existing records, and reports by informants, are being used. Following are some areas and questions being explored:[151]

- **Communities**. Why do some communities experience high rates of antisocial behavior while apparently similar communities are relatively safe?

WEB EXTRA 7-7
LIBRARY EXTRA 7-16

A drawing found on the masthead of the Project on Human Development in Chicago Neighborhoods (PHDCN). The multidisciplinary project, consisting of a longitudinal analysis of how individuals, families, institutions, and communities evolve together, is jointly sponsored by the National Institute of Justice and the John D. and Catherine T. MacArthur Foundation. What results has the study produced?
Source: Hyde Park Bank Foundation

- **Schools**. Some children have achievement problems early in school, and others have behavioral or truancy problems; some exhibit both kinds of problems, and others neither kind. Why do these differences exist? What are their causes and effects?

- **Peers**. Delinquent youths tend to associate with delinquent peers and usually act in groups. Does this association lead to delinquency, or is it simply a case of "like finding like"? Are the influences of peers equally important for girls and for boys, or are their developmental pathways entirely different?

- **Families**. Poor parenting practices are strongly associated with substance abuse and delinquency, but are they the cause of such behaviors? If so, then social programs in parenting skills could make a difference. But what if there are underlying factors, such as temperamental characteristics or social isolation, that cause problems in both parents and children?

- **Individual differences**. What health-related, cognitive, intellectual, and emotional factors in children promote positive social development? What factors put them at risk of developing antisocial behaviors?

PHDCN is already producing results and has led to targeted interventions intended to lower rates of offending. According to Sampson, "Instead of external actions (for example, a police crack-down), we stress in this study the effectiveness of 'informal'

mechanisms by which residents themselves achieve public order. In particular, we believe that collective expectations for intervening on behalf of neighborhood children [are] a crucial dimension of the public life of neighborhoods."[152] Life course perspectives, like one informing PHDCN, often point to the need for early intervention with nurturant strategies that build self-control through positive socialization. As Vila pointed out, "There are two main types of nurturant strategies: those that improve early life experiences to forestall the development of strategic styles based on criminality, and those that channel child and adolescent development in an effort to improve the match between individuals and their environment."[153] Nurturant crime-control strategies are discussed in more detail in Chapter 14. Learn more about the PHDCN at **Web Extra 7-7**. **Library Extra 7-16** discusses cultural mechanisms involved in neighborhood violence.

Policy Implications of Social Development Theories

Social development strategies have been widely applied to juvenile justice and human services settings. The OJJDP adopted the social development model as the foundation for its Comprehensive Strategy for Serious, Violent, and Chronic Juvenile Offenders program, which provides participating communities with a framework for preventing delinquency, intervening in early delinquent behavior, and responding to serious, violent, and chronic offending. It assists communities in establishing or modifying a juvenile justice continuum of care through risk-focused prevention, risk and needs assessment, structured decision making, and graduated sanctions training and technical assistance. The OJJDP's Comprehensive Strategy program centers around the following six components:

1. Strengthening families in their role of providing guidance and discipline and instilling sound values as the first and primary teacher of children

2. Supporting core social institutions, including schools, churches, and other community organizations, so that they can reduce risk factors and help children develop their full potential

3. Promoting prevention strategies that enhance protective factors and reduce the impact of negative risk factors affecting the lives of young people at risk for high delinquency

4. Intervening immediately and constructively when delinquent behavior first occurs

WEB EXTRA 7–8

5. Identifying and controlling a small segment of violent and chronic juvenile offenders

6. Establishing a broad spectrum of sanctions that ensure accountability and a continuum of services

A few years ago the OJJDP began a national evaluation of the Comprehensive Strategy Program. Learn more about the program via **Web Extra 7–8**, where you can keep abreast of the ongoing evaluation.

OJJDP adopted the social development model as the foundation for its Comprehensive Strategy for Serious, Violent, and Chronic Juvenile Offenders program.

Another contemporary example of social intervention efforts tied to a developmental model is Targeted Outreach, a program operated by Boys and Girls Clubs of America.[154] The program has its origins in the 1972 implementation of a youth development strategy based on studies undertaken at the University of Colorado, which showed that at-risk youths could be effectively diverted from the juvenile justice system through the provision of positive alternatives. Using a wide referral network made up of local schools, police departments, and various youth services agencies, club officials work to end what they call the "inappropriate detention of juveniles."[155]

The program's primary goal is to provide a positive and productive alternative to gangs for the youths who are most vulnerable to their influences or are already entrenched in gang activity. It recruits at-risk youngsters (as young as seven years old) and diverts them into activities intended to promote a sense of belonging, competence, usefulness, and self-control: A sense of belonging is fostered through clubs that provide familiar settings where each child is accepted; competence and usefulness are developed through opportunities for meaningful

activities, which young people in the club program can successfully undertake; self-control is developed as youthful participants have a chance to be heard and to influence decisions affecting their future. To date, Targeted Outreach has served more than 10,000 at-risk youths and hopes to eventually involve more than 1.5 million youngsters between the ages of seven and 17. Mobilization for Youth and Targeted Outreach are the kinds of programs that theorists who focus on the social structure typically seek to implement.

Critique of Social Development Theories

Social development theories have been criticized for definitional issues. What, for example, do life course concepts like turning point, pathway, risk factor, persistence, desistance, and criminal career really mean? Precise definitions of such concepts are necessary if hypotheses derived from life course theories are to be tested. Some writers have identified "associated problems of how to develop risk/needs assessment devices and how to use these both in fundamental research (to maximize the yield of serious offenders while still making it possible to draw conclusions about the general population) and in applied research (to decide which populations should be targeted by interventions)."[156]

Like the social structural approaches discussed in Chapter 6, social development theories are intimately associated with the first prong of this textbook's theme—the social problems approach (described in Chapter 1). For policymakers, important questions include: What role (if any) does individual choice play in human development? Do people actively select components of the life course? Do they influence their own trajectories? Since so many important life course determinants are set in motion in early childhood and during adolescence, should those who make wrong choices be held accountable?

SUMMARY

- According to social process theories, criminal behavior is learned in interaction with others. The socialization process occurring as the result of group membership—in families, peer groups, work groups, and reference groups—is seen as the primary route through which

learning occurs. Social process theories suggest that individuals who have weak stakes in conformity are more likely to be influenced by the social processes and contingent experiences that lead to crime and that criminal choices tend to persist because they are reinforced by the reaction of society to those whom it has identified as deviant.

- A number of theories can be classified under the social process umbrella: social learning theory, social control theory, labeling theory, reintegrative shaming, and dramaturgical perspective.

- Social process theories suggest that crime-prevention programs should enhance self-control and build prosocial bonds. Preparing for the Drug Free Years (PDFY) is designed to increase effective parenting and is part of the Strengthening America's Families Project.

- Criticisms of social process theories are many and varied. Differential association theory is not applicable at the individual level; in addition, the theory is untestable. The labeling approach does little to explain the origin of crime and deviance. Dramaturgical perspective's greatest failing may be in taking the analogy of the theater too far and convincing readers that real life is but a form of playacting.

- The life course perspective is the major social development perspective discussed in this chapter and emphasizes turning points in a criminal career. Age-graded theory incorporates the element of social bonds and also stresses the idea of turning points in a criminal career. The delinquent development approach places an emphasis on desistance and persistence over the life course, and interactional theory points to a weakening of a person's bond to conventional society as the fundamental cause of delinquency.

- The central concepts of social development theories include: criminal careers, the life course, trajectory, turning points, age grading, social capital, human agency, developmental pathways, life course persisters, persistence, desistance, resilience, cohort, cohort analysis, longitudinal research, and evolutionary ecology.

- Social development strategies have been widely applied to juvenile justice and human services settings. The OJJDP has adopted the social development model as the foundation for its Comprehensive Strategy for Serious, Violent, and Chronic Juvenile Offenders program, which provides participating communities with a framework for preventing delinquency, intervening in early delinquent behavior, and responding to serious, violent, and chronic offending.

- Social development theories have been criticized for definitional issues. What do life course concepts like turning point, pathway, risk factor, persistence, desistance, and criminal career really mean? Precise definitions of such concepts are necessary if hypotheses derived from life course theories are to be tested.

KEY TERMS

KEY NAMES

QUESTIONS FOR REVIEW

1. How does the process of social interaction contribute to criminal behavior?

2. What are the various social process perspectives discussed in this chapter? Describe each.

3. What kinds of social policy initiatives might be based on social process theories of crime causation?

4. What are the shortcomings of the social process perspective?

5. What are the various social development perspectives discussed in this chapter? Describe each.

6. What are the central concepts of social development theories? Explain each.

7. What kinds of social policy initiatives might be suggested by social development perspectives?

8. What are the shortcomings of social development perspectives on criminality?

QUESTIONS FOR REFLECTION

1. This chapter describes both social process and social development perspectives. What are the significant differences between these two perspectives? What kinds of theories characterize each?

2. This textbook emphasizes the theme of social problems versus social responsibility. Which of the perspectives discussed in this chapter (if any) best support the social problems approach? Which (if any) support the social responsibility approach? Why?

3. This chapter contains a discussion of the labeling process. What are a few examples of the everyday imposition of positive (rather than negative) labels? Why is it so difficult to impose positive labels on individuals who were previously labeled negatively?

4. Do you believe that Erving Goffman's dramaturgical perspective, which sees the world as a stage and individuals as actors on that stage, provides any valuable insights into crime and criminality? If so, what are they?

5. Examine your personal life course. What turning points did you experience that led to where you are today?

SOCIAL CONFLICT THEORIES

LEARNING OUTCOMES

After reading this chapter, you should be able to answer the following questions:

- What three analytical perspectives on law and social order are described in this chapter?

- What are the central tenets of radical criminology?

- What five emerging conflict perspectives discussed in this chapter purport to explain crime and criminality?

- What are the crime-control implications of social conflict theories?

LIBRARY EXTRA 8–1

Introduction

On March 11, 2010, 53-year-old software engineer Joseph A. Stack launched a suicide attack on the Austin, Texas, offices of the Internal Revenue Service by crashing his small private plane into an office building containing nearly 200 IRS employees.[1] In preparation for the attack, Stack had filled a number of gasoline drums and added them to the passenger compartment of his airplane, causing a huge explosion upon impact. The raging fire that resulted almost completely destroyed the office building and sent workers running for their lives; two people were killed and almost two dozen injured.

Before taking off, Stack had set his house on fire and posted a long antigovernment diatribe on his Web site ranting about government bailouts, corporate America's "thugs and plunderers," and the IRS (which he said had ruined his life). "How can any rational individual explain . . . our tax system?" he asked. "Here we have a system that is, by far, too complicated for the brightest . . . to understand. Yet, it mercilessly 'holds accountable' its victims, claiming that they're responsible for fully complying with laws not even the experts understand. . . . If this is not the measure of a totalitarian regime, nothing is. . . . I have had all I can stand," he wrote, adding, "I choose not to keep looking over my shoulder at 'big brother' while he strips my carcass." The entire text of Stack's online letter can be found at **Library Extra 8–1**. See the Theory versus Reality box for another example of someone with antiestablishment thinking and his resulting actions.

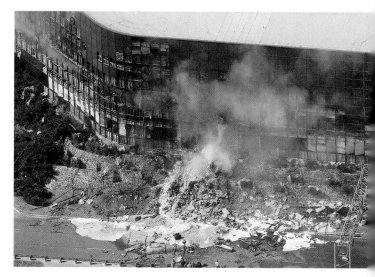

A photo of the destroyed Austin, Texas, IRS office building. Joseph Andrew Stack was angry with the U.S. government—and particularly the IRS—and decided to set fire to his house and then take a small private plane and fly it into this building on February 18, 2010. What characteristics do Theodore Kaczynski and Andrew Stack share?
Source: Alberto Martinez/Austin American-Statesman/PSG/NewsCom.com

Law and Social Order Perspectives

Antiestablishment thinking like Stack's, which saw government working in league with big business at the expense of the working man and woman, existed throughout parts of Europe during the middle to late 1800s. Among the most important thinkers of that period were **Karl Marx** (discussed in more detail later) and Friedrich Engels. In 1848, in *The Communist Manifesto*, Marx and Engels advanced the idea that communism would inevitably replace capitalism as the result of a natural historical process, or dialectic. Their egalitarian ideals fed the communist ideology that led to the Marxist-inspired Bolshevik Revolution of 1917, the fall of the Romanov dynasty in Russia, the coming to power of Vladimir Lenin and (later) Joseph Stalin in Russia, and the rise of the Soviet Union. But communism soon came to denote a repressive totalitarian system in which a single political party controlled the government, which owned the means of production and supposedly distributed wealth with the professed aim of establishing a classless society.[2]

The decline of European monarchies during the first half of the twentieth century, the rise of socialist ideals, and the advent of Marxist-inspired revolutions all conspired to change laws and create new kinds of criminal activity. An understanding of the interplay between law and social order is critical to any study of social change and of theories of criminology that emphasize the role of social conflict as it underlies criminality. Three analytical perspectives shed some light on this subject: the consensus perspective, the pluralist perspective, and the conflict perspective.

> **Communism came to denote a repressive totalitarian system in which a single political party controlled the government.**

WEB EXTRA 8–1

▓ **consensus perspective**
An analytical perspective on social organization that holds that most members of society agree about what is right and wrong and that the various elements of society work together toward a common vision of the greater good.

THEORY versus **REALITY**

The Unabomber and Domestic Terrorism

In April 1996, 52-year-old Harvard-educated Theodore Kaczynski, a Lincoln (Montana) recluse, was arrested and charged with the infamous Unabomber terrorist bombings. Kaczynski admitted responsibility for the bombings in early 1998 and was sentenced to life in prison without parole. The Unabomber's 18-year-long mail-bomb campaign had targeted universities, airlines, and researchers, killing three people and injuring 23 others in 16 separate bombing incidents. Prior to Kaczynski's arrest, a 56-page "manifesto" was mailed to the offices of the *New York Times*, the *Washington Post*, and *Penthouse* magazine. Titled "Industrial Society and Its Future," the Unabomber manifesto was a rambling thesis condemning American social institutions and high technology, blaming many of the world's existing problems on the Industrial Revolution, forecasting an Orwellian future in which helpless humans would be controlled by computers, and calling for a new social order based on a return to simpler times. Excerpts from the manifesto were widely published and helped lead to Kaczynski's capture. This box contains the introductory paragraphs of the Unabomber's manifesto. Read the Unabomber's entire manifesto online at **Web Extra 8–1**. A Criminal Profiles box later in this chapter provides more details about Kaczynski's life and crimes.

> The Industrial Revolution and its consequences have been a disaster for the human race. They have greatly increased the life-expectancy of those of us who live in "advanced" countries, but they have destabilized society, have made life unfulfilling, have subjected human beings to indignities, have led to widespread psychological suffering (in the Third World to physical suffering as well) and have inflicted severe damage on the natural world. The continued development of technology will worsen the situation. . . .

The industrial-technological system may survive or it may break down. If it survives, it MAY eventually achieve a low level of physical and psychological suffering, but only after passing through a long and very painful period of adjustment and only at the cost of permanently reducing human beings and many other living organisms to engineered products and mere cogs in the social machine. . . .

If the system breaks down the consequences will still be very painful. But the bigger the system grows the more disastrous the results of its breakdown will be, so if it is to break down it had best break down sooner rather than later.

We therefore advocate a revolution against the industrial system. This revolution may or may not make use of violence; it may be sudden or it may be a relatively gradual process spanning a few decades. We can't predict any of that. But we do outline in a very general way the measures that those who hate the industrial system should take in order to prepare the way for a revolution against that form of society.

Discussion Questions

1. What motivated the Unabomber? Why did he advocate "a revolution against the industrial system"?

2. Do you think the Unabomber really believed his bombings would create a better world? If so, how did he think they would bring about such change?

The Consensus Perspective

The **consensus perspective** of social organization (described briefly in Chapter 1) posits that most members of society agree on what is right and wrong and that the various elements of society—including institutions like churches, schools, government agencies, and businesses—work together toward a shared vision of the greater good. According to **Raymond J. Michalowski**, whose work is used to describe each of the three major approaches discussed in this section, the consensus perspective is characterized by four principles:[3]

1. **Most members of a society believe in the existence of core values**. The consensus perspective holds that shared notions of right and wrong characterize the majority of society's members.

2. **Laws reflect the collective will of the people**. Law is seen as the result of a consensus, achieved through legislative action, and represents a kind of social conscience.

3. **Law serves all people equally**. From the consensus point of view, the law not only embodies a shared view of justice but also is perceived to be just in its application.

4. **Law violators represent a unique subgroup with distinguishing features**. The consensus approach holds that law violators must somehow be improperly socialized or psychologically defective or must suffer from some other lapse that leaves them unable to participate in what is otherwise widespread agreement on values and behavior.

The consensus perspective was operative in American politics and characterized social scientific thought in this country

> **pluralist perspective**
> An analytical approach to social organization that holds that a multiplicity of values and beliefs exists in any complex society but that most social actors agree on the usefulness of law as a formal means of dispute resolution.

throughout much of the early 1900s and found its greatest champion in **Roscoe Pound**, former dean of Harvard School of Law and one of the greatest legal scholars of modern times. Pound developed the notion that the law is a tool for engineering society, meets the needs of men and women living together in society, and can be used to fashion society's characteristics and major features. Pound distilled his ideas into a set of jural postulates explaining the existence and form of all laws insofar as laws reflect shared needs:[4]

- In civilized society, men and women must be able to assume that others will commit no intentional aggressions upon them.[5]

- In civilized society men and women must be able to assume that they may control for beneficial purposes what they have discovered and appropriated to their own use, what they have created by their own labor, and what they have acquired under the existing social and economic order.

- In civilized society men and women must be able to assume that those with whom they deal in the general intercourse of society will act in good faith. . . .

- In civilized society men and women must be able to assume that those who are engaged in some course of conduct will act with due care not to cause an unreasonable risk of injury upon others.

- In civilized society men and women must be able to assume that those who maintain things likely to get out of hand or to escape and do damage will restrain them or keep them within their proper bounds.

The Pluralist Perspective

Contrary to the assumptions made by consensus thinkers, it has become quite plain to most observers of the contemporary social scene that not everyone agrees on what the law should say and that society is rife with examples of conflicting values and ideals—consensus is hard to find. Modern debates center on issues like abortion, euthanasia, the death penalty, purposes of criminal justice agencies in a diverse society, social justice, rights and responsibilities of minorities and other underrepresented groups, women's issues, the proper role of education, economic policy, social welfare, functions of the military in a changing world, environmental concerns, and appropriate uses of high technology. There exists within America today a great diversity of social groups, each with its own point of view regarding right and wrong, each with its own agenda. Add to that the plethora of self-proclaimed individual experts busily touting their own points of view, and anything but a consensus of values seems characteristic of society today.

Such a situation is described by some writers as "pluralist." A **pluralistic perspective** (described briefly in Chapter 1) mirrors the thought that a multiplicity of values and beliefs exists in any complex society and that each different social group will have its own set of beliefs, interests, and values. A crucial element of this perspective is the assumption that although different viewpoints exist, most individuals agree on the usefulness of law as a formal means of dispute resolution, so from a pluralist perspective, the law exists as a peacekeeping tool that allows officials and agencies within the government to effectively settle disputes between individuals and among groups. It also assumes that whatever settlement is reached will be acceptable to all parties because of their agreement on the fundamental role of law in dispute settlement. Following are five basic principles of the pluralist perspective:[6]

1. Society consists of many diverse social groups. Differences in age, gender, sexual preference, ethnicity, and the like often provide the basis for much naturally occurring diversity.

2. Each group has its own set of values, beliefs, and interests. Variety in gender, sexual orientation, economic status, and ethnicity, as well as other forms of diversity, produces interests that may unite like-minded individuals but may also place them in natural opposition to other social groups.

3. A general agreement exists on the usefulness of formalized laws as a mechanism for dispute resolution. People and groups accept the role of law in the settlement of disputes and accord decisions reached within the legal framework at least a modicum of respect.

4. The legal system is value neutral, that is, free of petty disputes and above the level of general contentiousness that may characterize relationships among groups.

5. The legal system is concerned with the best interests of society. Legislators, judges, prosecutors, attorneys, police officers, and correctional officials are assumed to perform idealized functions beyond the reach of the everyday interests of self-serving groups, so official functionaries

■ conflict perspective
An analytical perspective on social organization that holds that conflict is a fundamental aspect of social life and can never be fully resolved.

■ bourgeoisie
The "haves," or the class of people who own the means of production in Marxist theory.

LIBRARY EXTRA 8–2
WEB EXTRA 8–2
WEB EXTRA 8–3

■ proletariat
The "have-nots," or the working class in Marxist theory.

can be trusted to act in accordance with the greater good, to remain unbiased, and to maintain a value-free system for the enforcement of laws.

According to the pluralist perspective, conflict is essentially resolved through the peacekeeping activities of unbiased government officials exercising objective legal authority.

The Conflict Perspective

A third point of view, the **conflict perspective**, maintains that conflict is a fundamental aspect of social life that can never be fully resolved. Formal agencies of social control merely coerce the unempowered and disenfranchised to comply with the rules established by those in power. Laws are a tool of the powerful, useful in keeping others from wresting control over important social institutions. Rather than being the result of any consensus or process of dispute resolution, social order rests on the exercise of power through law. Those in power must work ceaselessly to remain there, although the structures they impose on society—including the patterns of wealth building that they define as acceptable and the circumstances under which they authorize the exercise of legal power and military might—give them all the advantages they are likely to need. See the Criminal Profiles box on the Unabomber, someone who fits the conflict perspective. **Library Extra 8–2** provides related information.

> The conflict perspective maintains that conflict is a fundamental aspect of social life and can never be fully resolved.

One of the best-known writers on social conflict was Karl Marx, whose writings on the conflicts inherent in capitalism led to the formulation of communist ideals and the rise of communist societies in the twentieth century. According to Marx, two fundamental social classes exist in any capitalist society: the haves or the **bourgeoisie**, who are capitalists and wealthy owners of the means of production (factories, businesses, land, natural resources), and the have-nots or the **proletariat**, who are relatively uneducated workers without power.

According to Marx, members of the proletariat, possessing neither capital nor means of production, must earn their living by selling their labor, and the powerful bourgeoisie oppose the proletariat in an ongoing class struggle. Marx saw such a struggle between classes as inevitable in the evolution of any capitalist society and believed that the natural outcome of such a struggle would be the overthrow of the capitalist social order and the birth of a truly classless, or communist, society. Learn more about the life and writings of Karl Marx at **Web Extras 8–2** and **8–3**.

Conflict theory in the social sciences has a long history. In 1905, the writings of **Willem Bonger** echoed Marxist principles by describing the ongoing struggle between the haves and the have-nots as a natural consequence of capitalist society;[7] he advanced the notion that in such societies only those who lack power are routinely subject to the criminal law. Georg Simmel's 1908 text *Conflict and the Web of Group Affiliations* highlighted the role of social conflict in two- and three-person groups, which Simmel called diads and triads.[8] Thorsten Sellin's notion of culture conflict (discussed in Chapter 6) also incorporated the notion of social conflict. Since Sellin's day, many other thinkers have contributed to the development of conflict theory, but before discussing specific ideas, it is important to understand six key elements of the conflict perspective:[9]

1. Society is made up of diverse social groups, and diversity is based on distinctions that people hold to be significant, such as gender, sexual orientation, and social class.

2. Each group holds to differing definitions of right and wrong, so moralistic conceptions and behavioral standards vary from group to group.

3. Conflict between groups is both socially significant and unavoidable because groups defined by characteristics such as ethnicity, gender, and social class compete for power, wealth, and other forms of recognition.

4. The fundamental nature of group conflict centers on the exercise of political power, which is the key to the accumulation of wealth and other forms of power.

5. Law is a tool of power and furthers the interests of those powerful enough to make it. Laws allow those in control to gain what they define as legitimate access to scarce resources and to deny such access to the politically disenfranchised.

6. Those in power are inevitably interested in maintaining their power against those who would usurp it.

CRIMINAL | PROFILES

Theodore John "Ted" Kaczynski (the Unabomber)

Born in Chicago on May 22, 1942, Kaczynski recalled his childhood as "uneventful." (Interestingly, he claimed to have been the victim of verbal and emotional abuse—but those claims never surfaced until he was in his twenties.) An introspective child and youth, Ted Kaczynski did not socialize easily or well and periodically underwent episodes of intense brooding and withdrawal. As he grew older, the episodes were increasingly accompanied by a seething rage.[i] Consumed with obsessions and emotionally crippled, the reclusive Kaczynski would eventually resolve his contempt for society's technological advances by mounting a bombing campaign that killed three people and injured 29 others.

His academic abilities enabled him to skip both the sixth and eleventh grades, start undergraduate studies at Harvard at age 16, and earn his doctoral degree at the age of 25, but the promise of his remarkable early academic achievements foundered quickly.[ii] Upon completing his Ph.D., Kaczynski accepted an assistant professorship in mathematics at the University of California–Berkeley in 1967, but in June 1969, declaring there was "no relevance" to what he was doing, he quit his teaching post and then worked only sporadically out of financial necessity, living off the land in a hermit's existence of self-exile in a ramshackle cabin in the remote Montana wilderness for almost 25 years.[iii]

Kaczynski also experienced lifelong difficulties with sexual relationships. He struggled with his own sexuality, came to believe he should undergo a sex-change operation, and initiated the process, but when finally seen by a doctor, he claimed to be there for an entirely different reason and then left in a rage; subsequently, he described the experience as shameful and humiliating.[iv] In the ensuing years, he attempted to establish meaningful relationships with women but was never able to do so.

As he retreated deeper into his isolationist lifestyle, Kaczynski handwrote a lengthy manifesto railing against contemporary life, stating "The Industrial Revolution and its consequences have been a disaster for the human race."[v]

Between May 25, 1978, and April 24, 1995, Kaczynski left or sent a total of 16 homemade pipe bombs to various targets, primarily associated with universities and airlines. (The FBI's designation of the investigation as the "Unabomb" case derives from these early university targets.) The first ten bombs caused serious injuries to numerous people; the eleventh resulted in the first death.[vi]

Kaczynski's intermittent attacks were anonymous, a trait inexplicably broken when he began sending letters to a newspaper threatening to bomb an airplane. He also stated that he would stop the bombings if his 35,000-word manifesto was published in the *Washington Post*,[vii] and its subsequent publication eventually led to his capture.

Former University of California-Berkeley math professor Theodore John Kaczynski—aka the Unabomber—being led to an interview at the Federal Administrative Maximum Prison in Florence, Colorado in 1999. What motivated Kaczynski?
Source: John Youngbear/AP Wide World Photos

Upon reading the manifesto, David Kaczynski (Ted's younger brother) immediately realized that "the tone of the language, the approach, almost had the feeling for me of one of Ted's angry letters over the years. Some of those letters were addressed to the theme of technology just as the manifesto was."[viii] The content and wording of the manifesto led David Kaczynski to contact the FBI. The FBI went to Kaczynski's cabin in the isolated Montana wilderness and found overwhelming evidence that he was the Unabomber: a live bomb, meticulous notes of past bombings, bomb-making materials, and the original copy of his infamous manifesto.

On January 22, 1998, after reaching a plea agreement, Kaczynski pleaded guilty to four bombings that occurred in 1985, 1993, and 1995. Kaczynski also admitted to the three deaths his bombings had caused, and all other charges against him were resolved; he was sentenced to a life term without parole.[ix] Kaczynski remains imprisoned at the maximum-security federal prison in Florence, Colorado. On January 22, 2007, he filed suit against the federal government and a group of his victims, seeking to prevent the sale of more than 40,000 pages of his original writings and correspondence.[x]

Notes

i. Paul Ferguson, "A Loner from Youth," CNN Interactive, http://www.cnn.com/SPECIALS/1997/unabomb/accused/early (accessed May 28, 2007).

ii. Ted Ottley, "Ted Kaczynski: The Unabomber," CourtTV Crime Library, http://www.crimelibrary.com/terrorists_spies/terrorists/kaczynski/1.html (accessed May 28, 2007).

iii. CNN and Time Interactive, "The Unabomb Case," Cable News Network, http://www.cnn.com/SPECIALS/1997/unabomb/index.html (accessed May 28, 2007).

iv. Ottley, "Ted Kaczynski."

v. "The Unabomber's Manifesto: Industrial Society and Its Future," *Sacramento Bee*, http://www.unabombertrial.com/manifesto/index.html (accessed May 28, 2007).

vi. CNN and Time Interactive, "The Unabomb Case."

vii. Paul Ferguson, "Tracking the Unabomber: More Luck Than Computer Analysis," CNN Interactive, http://www.cnn.com/SPECIALS/1997/unabomb/investigation/puzzle/index.html (accessed May 28, 2007).

viii. "When Your Brother Is the Unabomber," MSNBC, December 29, 2006, http://www.msnbc.msn.com/id/16304477 (accessed May 28, 2007).

ix. "Kaczynski Admits He Is Unabomber, Sentenced to Life Without Parole," CNN Interactive, January 22, 1998, http://www.cnn.com/US/9801/22/unabomb.plea (accessed June 16, 2007).

x. Serge F. Kovaleski, "Unabomber Wages Legal Battle to Halt Sale of Papers," *New York Times*, January 22, 2007, http://www.nytimes.com/2007/01/22/us/22unabomber.html?ex=1327122000&en=3fda08d949905a96&ei=5088&partner=rssnyt&emc=rss (accessed May 28, 2007).

■ **social class**
A distinction made between individuals based on important social characteristics.

THEORY | in PERSPECTIVE
Social Conflict Theories

Social conflict theories emphasize the power of conflict within society, which is thought to be based largely on inequities between social classes.

Radical Criminology

Radical criminology holds that the causes of crime are rooted in social conditions empowering the wealthy and the politically well organized but disenfranchising those less successful.

Period: 1960s–present

Theorists: Karl Marx, Ralf Dahrendorf, George B. Vold, Richard Quinney, William J. Chambliss, Raymond J. Michalowski, Austin Turk

Concepts: Social class, bourgeoisie, proletariat

Left-Realist Criminology

This branch of radical criminology posits that crime is a real social problem experienced by the lower classes.

Period: 1980s–present

Theorists: Walter DeKeseredy, Jock Young

Concepts: Radical realism, critical realism, street crime, social justice, crime control

Feminist Criminology

This radical criminological approach to the explanation of crime sees the conflict and inequality present in society as being based primarily on gender.

Period: 1970s–present

Theorists: Freda Adler, Rita J. Simon, Kathleen Daly, Meda Chesney-Lind, John Hagan

Concepts: Power-control issues, gender socialization, empowerment

Peacemaking Criminology

Peacemaking criminology holds that crime-control agencies and citizens must work together to alleviate social problems, including crime.

Period: 1980s–present

Theorists: Harold E. Pepinsky, Richard Quinney

Concepts: Compassionate criminology, restorative justice

Convict Criminology

Convict criminology consists of writings and musings on criminology by convicted felons and ex-inmates who have acquired academic credentials or are associated with credentialed others.

Period: 2001–present

Theorists: Ian Ross, Stephen Richards

Concepts: Issues-based writings, personal experience as valid information, critical of system

---

Central to the conflict perspective is the notion of **social class** (distinctions made between individuals based on characteristics such as race, religion, education, profession, income, wealth, family background, housing, artistic tastes, aspirations, cultural pursuits, child-rearing habits, speech, and accent). Some authors maintain that "class is nothing but an abbreviation to describe a way of living, thinking, and feeling."[10] Individuals are assigned to classes by others and by themselves on the basis of characteristics that are both ascribed and achieved: Ascribed characteristics are those a person is born with, such as race or gender; achieved characteristics are acquired through personal effort or chance over the course of a person's life and include level of education, income, place of residence, and profession.

> Marx saw a struggle between classes as inevitable in the evolution of any capitalist society.

Although Marx concerned himself with only two social classes, most social scientists today talk in terms of at least three groups—the upper, middle, and lower classes. Some, such as Vance Packard, have distinguished among five hierarchically arranged classes (the real upper, semiupper, limited-success, working, and real lower classes) while further subdividing classes horizontally according to ascribed characteristics like race and religion.[11]

In his 1958 book *Theoretical Criminology*, **George B. Vold** described crime as the product of political conflict between groups, an ongoing struggle for power, control, and material well-being.[12] Conflict is "a universal form of interaction," and groups are naturally in conflict because their interests and purposes "overlap, encroach on one another and [tend to] be competitive."[13] Vold's most succinct observation of the role conflict plays in contributing to crime stated: "The whole political process of law making, law breaking, and law enforcement becomes a direct reflection of deep-seated and fundamental conflicts between interest groups. Those who produce legislative

The tomb of Karl Marx in Highgate Cemetery, London. Marxist thought underpins the writings of many radical criminologists. How did Marxism influence criminology?

Source: Rex Features USA Ltd.

presence but the absence of conflict is surprising and abnormal, and we have good reason to be suspicious if we find a society or social organization that displays no evidence of conflict."[16]

From Dahrendorf's perspective, power and authority were most at issue between groups and the cause of class conflicts. It is out of conflict that change—either destructive or constructive—arises. Destructive change brings a lessening of social order, whereas constructive change increases cohesiveness within society.

Another mid-twentieth-century conflict theorist, **Austin Turk**, said that in the search for an explanation of criminality, "one is led to investigate the tendency of laws to penalize persons whose behavior is more characteristic of the less powerful than of the more powerful and the extent to which some persons and groups can and do use legal processes and agencies to maintain and enhance their power position vis-à-vis other persons and groups."[17] In his 1969 seminal work, *Criminality and Legal Order*, Turk wrote that in any attempt to explain criminality, "it is more useful to view the social order as mainly a pattern of conflict" rather than to offer explanations for crime based on behavioral or psychological approaches.[18] Turk, like most other conflict criminologists, saw the law as a powerful tool of prominent social groups seeking continued control over others and crime as the natural consequence of such intergroup struggles, resulting from definitions imposed by the laws of the powerful on the disapproved strivings of the unempowered.

Radical Criminology

The conflict perspective is today thoroughly entrenched in **radical criminology**, which holds that the causes of crime are rooted in social conditions empowering the wealthy and the politically well organized but disenfranchising those less fortunate; it is also called *new criminology* and *critical criminology* as well as **Marxist criminology** (when based on Marx's writings). Radical criminology is the intellectual child of three important historical circumstances: (1) the ruminations of nineteenth-century social utopian thinkers, including Karl Marx, Friedrich Engels,

> Radical criminology holds that the causes of crime are rooted in social conditions empowering the wealthy.

Georg Wilhelm Friedrich Hegel, Georg Simmel, Willem Bonger, and Max Weber; (2) the rise of conflict theory in the social sciences; and (3) the dramatic radicalization of American academia in

majorities win control over the power and dominate the policies that decide who is likely to be involved in violation of the law."[14]

From Vold's point of view, the body of laws that characterizes any society is a political statement, and crime is a political definition imposed on those whose interests lie outside those that the powerful, through the law, define as acceptable.

Conflict theorists of the early and mid-1900s saw in the concept of social class the rudimentary ingredients of other important concepts like authority, power, and conflict. **Ralf Dahrendorf** wrote that "classes are social conflict groups the determinant of which can be found in the participation in or exclusion from the exercise of authority."[15] For Dahrendorf, conflict was ubiquitous, fundamental, and coextensive: "Not the

the **PROFESSOR** | **SPEAKS**
Social Conflict Theories

ZACHARY MINER

University
at Albany

UNIVERSITY
AT ALBANY
State University of New York

When studying crime, social conflict theorists examine how powerful groups use their influence to make sure that the things they value are protected, often at the expense of what less powerful groups want. These theorists see law and justice as two parts of a larger struggle—almost like a game in which each team is trying to get more benefit for its members. But in this "game," the ultimate winners get a better prize than any sports trophy: the power to create and enforce the kinds of laws that benefit them most.

A historical example relevant to social conflict theory is the post–Civil War passage of Jim Crow laws. During that time, many Southern whites feared that their social and political power would be threatened by newly emancipated African Americans; so whites responded by creating laws that harshly restricted African Americans' ordinary aspects of life—voting, owning property, using public transportation, and going to school. Because African Americans had little political or social power at the time, they were unable to resist the passage of these laws that helped whites maintain control over their lives.

the 1960s and 1970s. **William J. Chambliss**, a well-known spokesperson for radical thinkers, succinctly summarized the modern perspective: "What makes the behavior of some criminal is the coercive power of the state to enforce the will of the ruling class."[19]

In 1971, Chambliss, along with Robert T. Seidman, published a critically acclaimed volume titled *Law, Order, and Power*, which represented a bridge between earlier conflict theorists and the more radical approach of the Marxists. Through its emphasis on social class, class interests, and class conflict, *Law, Order, and Power* presented a Marxist perspective stripped of any overt references to capitalism as the root cause of crime. "The more economically stratified a society becomes, the more it becomes necessary for the dominant groups in the society to enforce through coercion the norms of conduct which guarantee their supremacy."[20] Chambliss and Seidman outlined their position in four propositions:[21]

1. The conditions of one's life affect one's values and norms.

2. Complex societies are composed of groups with widely different life conditions and highly disparate and conflicting sets of norms.

3. The probability of a given group having its particular normative system embodied in law is not distributed equally but is closely related to the political and economic position of that group.

4. The higher a group's political or economic position is, the greater the probability that its views will be reflected in laws.

Chambliss also believed that middle- and upper-class criminals are more apt to escape apprehension and punishment, not because they are any smarter or more capable of hiding their crimes than lower-class offenders but because of a "very rational choice on the

Deteriorating factories in Novokuznetsk, Siberia. Radical criminology has its origins in the writings of Karl Marx, whose thinking was strongly influenced by the social conditions of the industrial era. How did the downfall of the Soviet Union impact radical thought in criminology?
Source: Peter Turnley/CORBIS-NY

part of the legal system to pursue those violators that the community will reward them for pursuing and to ignore those violators who have the capability for causing trouble for the agencies."[22]

By the 1970s, Chambliss's writings assumed a much more Marxist flavor. In a 1975 article, Chambliss once again recognized the huge power gap separating the haves from the have-nots, saying that crime is created by the ruling class, who define as criminal any undertakings and activities contravening their interests yet sometimes violate the criminal law with impunity because it is their own creation.[23]

WEB EXTRA 8–4

■ **structural Marxism**
A perspective that holds that the structural institutions of society influence the behavior of individuals and groups by virtue of the type of relationships created.

■ **instrumental Marxism**
A perspective that holds that those in power intentionally create laws and social institutions that serve their own interests and keep others from becoming powerful.

Soon the Marxist flavor of Chambliss's writing became undeniable. "As capitalist societies industrialize and the gap between the bourgeoisie and the proletariat widens, penal law will expand in an effort to coerce the proletariat into submission."[24] For Chambliss, the economic consequences of crime within a capitalist society were partially what perpetuated it. Socialist societies, he wrote, should reflect much lower crime rates than capitalist societies because a "less intense class struggle should reduce the forces leading to and the functions of crime."[25] Learn more about the writings of William J. Chambliss at **Web Extra 8–4**.

Although Chambliss provided much of the intellectual bedrock of contemporary radical criminology, that school of thought found its most eloquent expression in the writings of **Richard Quinney**, who attempted to challenge and change American social life for the better by setting forth in 1974 his six Marxist propositions for an understanding of crime:[26]

1. American society is based on an advanced capitalist economy.

2. The state is organized to serve the interests of the dominant economic class—that is, the capitalist ruling class.

3. Criminal law is an instrument of the state and ruling class used to maintain and perpetuate the existing social and economic order.

4. Crime control in a capitalist society is accomplished through a variety of institutions and agencies established and administered by a governmental elite, representing ruling-class interests, for the purpose of establishing domestic order.

5. The contradictions of advanced capitalism—the disjunction between existence and essence—require that the subordinate classes remain oppressed by whatever means necessary, especially through the coercion and violence of the legal system.

6. Only with the collapse of the capitalist society and the creation of a new society, based on socialist principles, will there be a solution to the crime problem.

Later, Quinney published *Class, State, and Crime*, in which he argued that almost all crimes committed by members of the lower classes are necessary for the survival of individual members of those classes and are actually an attempt by the socially disenfranchised "to exist in a society where *survival* is not assured by other, collective means."[27] He concluded, "Crime is inevitable under capitalist conditions [because crime is] a response to the material conditions of life. Permanent unemployment—and the acceptance of that condition—can result in a form of life where criminality is an appropriate and consistent response."[28] The solution offered by Quinney to the problem of crime is the development of a socialist society: "The *ultimate meaning* of crime in the development of capitalism is the need for a socialist society."[29]

Contemporary radical criminology attributes much existing propensity toward criminality to differences in social class, especially those societal arrangements that maintain class differences. Quinney explained, "Classes are an expression of the underlying forces of the capitalist mode of production."[30]

Today's radical criminologies can be divided into two schools: structuralist and instrumentalist. **Structural Marxism** sees capitalism as a self-maintaining system in which the law and the justice system work to perpetuate the existing system of power relationships. Even the rich are subject to certain laws designed to prevent them from engaging in forms of behavior that might undermine the system of which they are a part, and laws regulating trade practices and monopolies regulate the behavior of the powerful and ensure survival of the capitalist system. **Instrumental Marxism** sees the criminal law and the justice system as tools that the powerful use to control the poor and to keep them disenfranchised. The legal system serves not only to perpetuate the power relationships that exist within society but also to keep control in the hands of those who are already powerful. A popular book by **Jeffrey H. Reiman** titled *The Rich Get Richer and the Poor Get Prison* is built on this premise, contending that the criminal justice system is biased against the poor from start to finish and that well-to-do members of society control the criminal justice system from the definition of crime through the process of arrest, trial, and sentencing.[31]

Reiman also claimed that many actions undertaken by well-off people, such as refusal to make workplaces safe, refusal to curtail deadly industrial pollution, promotion of unnecessary surgery, and prescription of unnecessary drugs, should be defined as criminal but aren't. This kind of self-serving behavior creates occupational and

> Crime is created by the ruling class, who define as criminal any undertakings and activities contravening their interests, yet sometimes violate the criminal law with impunity because it is their own creation.

■ **critical criminology**
A perspective that holds that crime is the natural product of a capitalist system.

LIBRARY EXTRA 8–3
LIBRARY EXTRA 8–4
WEB EXTRA 8–5

WHO'S TO BLAME—The Individual or Society?

Human Trafficking, Illegal Aliens, and the American Dream

Jose Gonzales, a naturalized U.S. citizen who worked for a Houston-based trucking company, was driving a tractor trailer through a U.S. Customs checkpoint on the Mexican border near San Diego when his truck was searched and found to contain 45 illegal immigrants concealed in Brazilian-made caskets that were being shipped to Los Angeles. Each of the immigrants had been supplied with plastic bottles containing water, and a few even had portable radios to keep them entertained on what had been planned as an hours-long trip.

The illegal immigrants were interrogated and fingerprinted and then taken back across the border to the Mexican border town of Tijuana in a U.S. Customs and Border Protection van. They were released into the custody of a Mexican Federal Investigative Agency official at a local police station, with instructions not to attempt an illegal return into the United States.

Gonzales's fate was quite different. Arrested and charged under the federal Immigration and Nationality Act with attempting to bring unauthorized aliens into the United States, he was held in a federal jail in southern California, where he met with his court-appointed lawyer. The lawyer, Felix Alverez, told Gonzales that agents had him cold, and that he might as well confess in return for a plea bargain that might get him only a brief stint in a federal correctional facility. "Why confess?" Gonzales replied. "I was only trying to help those people have

better lives. Many of them were my friends. I didn't even take money for what I was doing."

"Why you were doing what you were doing doesn't matter," Alverez said. "You broke the law, and they are going to punish you."

"No," Gonzales replied. "I am a citizen. I want a trial. You can show them that I was only trying to help unfortunate people live the American Dream. Most of the people who live here and are going to be on a jury have immigrant ancestors. A lot of them were illegal. They won't dare find me guilty." **Library Extras 8–3 and 8–4** relate to this box.

Think about it:

1. Why did Gonzales attempt to smuggle illegal immigrants into the United States? Do you think it was primarily for money or for altruistic motives?

2. How likely would Gonzales have been to commit this offense if he had a different ancestry—say, African American or European?

3. What do you think of Gonzales's claim that a jury won't find him guilty? Should he be held responsible for violating the law? Why or why not?

Note: Who's to Blame boxes provide fictionalized critical thinking opportunities, and are not actual cases.

environmental hazards for the poor and those less well-off and produces as much death, destruction, and financial loss as the so-called crimes of the poor. Learn more about radical criminology at **Web Extra 8–5**.

Critical Criminology

Some writers distinguish between critical criminology and radical criminology, saying that the former is simply a way of critiquing social relationships that lead to crime, whereas the latter constitutes a proactive call for a radical change in the social conditions that lead to crime. Gresham M. Sykes explained **critical criminology** this way: "It forces an inquiry into precisely how the normative content of the criminal law is internalized in

different segments of society, and how norm-holding is actually related to behavior."[32] As David A. Jones stated in his insightful *History of Criminology*, "Sometimes, it may be difficult to distinguish 'critical' from a truly Marxist criminology. One basis, advanced by Marvin Wolfgang, is that 'critical' criminology is 'more reactive than proactive,' meaning that 'critical' criminology does not aim to overthrow the 'ruling class' so much as it may criticize the way it believes such a group dominates society."[33] See the Who's to Blame box for a present-day issue regarding whether something should be "criminal."

A cogent example of the critical perspective in contemporary criminology can be seen in the work of Elliott Currie, who claimed that "'market societies'—those in which the pursuit of private gain becomes the dominant organizing principle of social and economic life—are especially likely to breed high levels of violent crime."[34] Market societies are characterized by more than free enterprise and a free market economy; they are societies in which striving after personal economic gain runs rampant and becomes the hallmark of social life, and this striving leads to high crime rates because it undercuts and overwhelms more traditional principles that "have historically sustained individuals, families, and communities." The United States is the world's premier market society, and its culture provides "a particularly fertile breeding ground for serious violent crime." According to Currie, seven "profoundly criminogenic and closely intertwined mechanisms" operate in a market society to produce crime:

1. "The progressive destruction of livelihood," which results from the long-term absence of opportunities for stable and rewarding work and is a consequence of the fact that market societies view labor "simply as a cost to be reduced" rather than as an asset with intrinsic value

2. "The growth of extremes of economic inequality and material deprivation," which causes many children to spend their developmental years in poverty

3. "The withdrawal of public services and supports, especially for families and children," which results from the fact that "it is a basic operating principle of market society to keep the public sector small"

4. "The erosion of informal and communal networks of mutual support, supervision, and care," which is brought about by the high mobility of the workforce characteristic of market societies

5. "The spread of a materialistic, neglectful, and 'hard' culture," which exalts brutal forms of individualized competition

6. "The unregulated marketing of the technology of violence," which includes ready availability of guns, emphasis on advancing technologies of destruction (such as the military), and mass-marketed violence on television and in other media

7. "The weakening of social and political alternatives," which leaves people unable to cope effectively with the forces of the market society, undermines their communities, and destroys valuable interpersonal relationships

Currie suggested that as more nations emulate the "market society" culture of the United States, crime rates throughout the world will rise, and that an increasing emphasis on punishment and the growth of huge prison systems will consequently characterize most of the world's nations in the twenty-first century.

Radical-Critical Criminology and Policy Issues

According to more contemporary writers on radical criminology, "Marxist criminology was once dismissed as a utopian perspective with no relevant policy implication except revolution. At best, revolution was considered an impractical approach to the problems at hand. Recently, however, many radicals have attempted to address the issues of what can be done under our current system."[35] Most radical-critical criminologists today have come to terms with the collapse of the Soviet Union, a society representing utopian Marxism in practice, and have recognized that a sudden and total reversal of existing political arrangements within the United States is highly unlikely. Such theorists have begun to focus instead on promoting a gradual transition to socialism and to socialized forms of government activity, including "equal justice in the bail system, the abolition of mandatory sentences, prosecution of corporate crimes, increased employment opportunities, and promoting community alternatives to imprisonment."[36] Programs to reduce prison overcrowding, efforts to highlight injustices in the current system, elimination of racism and other forms of inequality in handling both victims and offenders, and increased equality in criminal justice system employment are all frequently mentioned as midrange strategies for bringing about a justice system that is more fair and closer to the radical ideal.

Michalowski summarized well the policy directions envisioned by today's radical-critical criminologists: "We cannot be free from the crimes of the poor until there are no more poor; we cannot be free from domination of the powerful until we reduce the inequalities that make domination possible; and we cannot live in harmony with others until we begin to limit the competition for material advantage over others that alienates us from one another."[37] Even so, few radical-critical criminologists seem to expect to see dramatic changes in the near future. Michael J. Lynch and W. Byron Groves explained, "In the end, the criminal justice system has failed as an agent of social change because its efforts are directed at an individual as opposed to social remedies. For these reasons, radicals suggest that we put our efforts into the creation of economic equality or employment opportunities to combat crime."[38]

Critique of Radical-Critical Criminology

Radical-critical criminology has been criticized for its nearly exclusive emphasis on methods of social change at the expense of well-developed theory. William V. Pelfrey stated, "It is in the Radical School of Criminology that theory is almost totally disregarded, except as something to criticize, and radical methods are seen as optimum."[39] Radical-critical criminology can also be criticized for failing to recognize what appears to be a fair degree of public consensus about the nature of crime—that crime is undesirable and that criminal activity should be controlled. If criminal activity was a true expression of the sentiments of the politically and economically disenfranchised, as some radical criminologists claim, then public opinion might be expected to offer support for at least certain forms of crime, but even the sale of illicit drugs (a type of crime that may provide an alternative path to riches for the otherwise disenfranchised) is frequently condemned by residents of working-class communities.[40]

An effective criticism of Marxist criminology centers on the fact that Marxist thinkers appear to confuse issues of personal politics with social reality, allowing personal values and political leanings to enter the criminological arena and sacrificing their objectivity. Jackson Toby claimed that Marxist and radical thinkers are simply building on an "old tradition of sentimentality toward those who break social rules."[41] Such sentimentality can be easily discounted when we realize that "color television sets and automobiles are stolen more often than food and blankets."[42] The Marxist perspective also fails to recognize that personal success in any society often comes as the result of hard work and preparation and is not merely the result of luck, so wording characterizing social failures as less "fortunate" than others does not take into account the efforts made by those who have succeeded and seems to blame them for the failures of others who have not expended equal effort.

Marxist criminology has also been refuted by contemporary thinkers who find that it falls short in appreciating the multiplicity of problems that contribute to the problem of crime. Astute criminologist Hermann Mannheim critiqued Marxian assumptions by showing how "subsequent developments" have shown that "Marx was wrong in [his] thinking" in several areas: (1) "that there could be only two classes in a capitalist society," (2) that "class struggle was entirely concerned with the question of private property in the means of production," (3) "that the only way in which fundamental social changes could be effected was by violent social revolution," and (4) "that all conflicts were class conflicts and all social change could be explained in terms of class conflicts."[43] Mannheim also pointed out that the development of a semiskilled workforce along with the advent of highly skilled and well-educated workers has led to the creation of a multiplicity of classes within contemporary capitalist societies and that their growth effectively spreads the available wealth in those societies where such workers are employed and reduces the likelihood of revolution.

A now-classic critique of radical criminology was offered in 1979 by Carl Klockars.[44] Klockars charged that Marxists are unable to explain low crime rates in some capitalist countries, such as Japan, and seem equally unwilling to acknowledge or address the problems of communist countries, which often have terrible human rights records. Writing more than 20 years ago, Klockars claimed that Marxist criminologists behaved more like "true believers" in a "new religion" who were unwilling to objectively evaluate their beliefs.[45]

> Marxist criminologists are unable to explain low crime rates in some capitalist countries.

Marxist criminology has suffered a considerable loss of prestige among many would-be followers in the wake of the collapse of the former Soviet Union and its client states in Eastern Europe and other parts of the world and seems to have lost some of its impetus. Many would argue that the work of writers like Quinney and Chambliss presaged the decline of Soviet influence and had already moved Marxist and radical criminology into new areas. The work of Currie and others has since led in a post-Marxist direction while retaining a critical emphasis on the principles out of which radical criminology was fashioned. Today's radical criminologists have largely rescinded calls for revolutionary change and escalated their demands for the eradication of gender, racial, and other inequalities in the criminal justice system; the elimination of prisons; the abolition of capital punishment; and an end to police misconduct.

Emerging Conflict Theories

The radical ideas associated with mid-twentieth-century Marxist criminology contributed to the formation of new and innovative approaches to crime and criminology such as left-realist criminology, feminist criminology, postmodern criminology, peacemaking criminology, and convict criminology. It is to these perspectives that we now turn our attention.

Left-Realist Criminology

Left-realist criminology, a natural outgrowth of concerns with street crime, the fear of crime, and everyday victimization, approaches criminology based on the ideas of **left realism**, which uses a pragmatic assessment of crime and its problems. Left-realist criminology faults radical-critical criminologists for romanticizing street crime and the criminals who commit it. It does not reject the conflict perspective inherent in radical-critical criminology but shifts the focus to the assessment of crime and the needs of crime victims, seeking to portray crime in terms understandable to those most affected by it—victims and their families, offenders, and criminal justice personnel. The test insisted on by left-realist criminology is not whether a particular perspective on crime control or an explanation of crime causation complies with rigorous academic criteria but whether it speaks meaningfully to those faced with crime on a routine basis. "For realists crime is no less harmful to its victims because of its socially constructed origins."[46]

Left-realist criminology is generally considered synonymous with left realism (also called *radical realism* or *critical realism*) but tends to distance itself from some of the more visionary claims of early radical and Marxist theory.[47] Daniel J. Curran and Claire M. Renzetti portrayed left realism as a natural consequence of increasingly conservative attitudes toward crime and criminals in both Europe and North America: "Though not successful in converting many radicals to the right, this new conservatism did lead a number of radical criminologists to temper their views a bit and to take what some might call a less romanticized look at street crime."[48]

Some authors credit **Walter DeKeseredy**[49] with popularizing left-realist notions in North America, and **Jock Young**[50] is identified as a major source of left-realist writings in England. Prior to the writings of DeKeseredy and Young, radical criminology, with its emphasis on the crime-inducing consequences of existing power structures, tended to portray the ruling class as the "real criminals" and saw street criminals as social rebels who were acting out of felt deprivation; DeKeseredy and Young were successful in refocusing leftist theories on the serious consequences of street crime and on the crimes of the lower classes. Left realists argued that victims of crime are often the poor and disenfranchised who fall prey to criminals with similar backgrounds and saw the criminal justice system and its agents not as pawns of the powerful but as institutions that could offer useful services if modifications were made to reduce their use of force and to increase their sensitivity toward the public.

A central tenet of left realism is that radical ideas must be translated into realistic social policies if contemporary criminology is to have any practical relevance. Concrete suggestions with respect to community policing models are indicative of the direction left realists are headed. Instead of seeing the police as oppressors working on behalf of the state, left realists recommend that the police work with, and answer to, the communities they serve.[51] The major goal of left realism is to achieve a just and orderly society through a practical emphasis on social justice.[52]

Critique of Left-Realist Criminology

Left-realist criminology has been convincingly criticized for being more of an ideological emphasis than a theory. As Don C. Gibbons explained, "Left realism can best be described as a general perspective centered on injunctions to 'take crime seriously' and to 'take crime control seriously' rather than as a well-developed criminological perspective."[53] Realist criminologists appear to build on preexisting theoretical frameworks but rarely offer new testable propositions or hypotheses, but they do suggest crime-control approaches in keeping with the needs of the victimized. Policies promulgated by left realists understandably include an emphasis on community policing, neighborhood justice centers, and dispute-resolution mechanisms, whereas right realists are more punitive in their policy suggestions. Piers Beirne and James W. Messerschmidt summarized

> Left-realist criminology has been criticized for being more ideology than a theory.

LIBRARY EXTRA 8–5
LIBRARY EXTRA 8–6
LIBRARY EXTRA 8–7
LIBRARY EXTRA 8–8

■ **feminist criminology**
A corrective model intended to redirect the thinking of mainstream criminologists to include gender awareness.

■ **liberal feminism**
A feminist perspective in criminology that sees gender-role socialization as the primary source of women's oppression.

■ **radical feminism**
A perspective that sees patriarchy as the cause of women's oppression.

■ **Marxist feminism**
A perspective in feminist criminology that sees the oppression of women as caused by their subordinate class status within capitalist societies.

■ **socialist feminism**
A perspective in modern criminology that sees gender oppression as a consequence of the interaction between the economic structure of society and gender-based roles.

the situation this way: "What left realists have essentially accomplished is an attempt to theorize about conventional crime realistically while simultaneously developing a 'radical law and order' program for curbing such behavior."[54] Read some original writings in the area of critical criminology via **Library Extras 8–5** and **8–6**, and access an online version of the *Red Feather Dictionary of Critical Social Science* via **Library Extra 8–7.**

Feminist Criminology

As some have observed, "Women have been virtually invisible in criminological analysis until recently and much theorizing has proceeded as though criminality is restricted to men."[55] Others put it this way: "Criminological theory assumes a woman is like a man."[56] But beginning in the 1970s, advances in feminist theory were applied to criminology, resulting in what has been called a **feminist criminology** (a model redirecting criminologists' thinking to include gender awareness).

Feminism is a way of seeing the world, not a sexual orientation. To be a feminist is to "combine a female mental perspective with a sensitivity for those social issues that influence primarily women."[57] Central to understanding feminist thought is the realization that feminism views gender in terms of power relationships. According to feminist approaches, men have traditionally held much more power in the patriarchal structure of Western society than women and have excluded women from much decision making in socially significant areas, and sexist attitudes—deeply ingrained notions of male superiority—have perpetuated inequality between the sexes. The consequences of sexism and the unequal gender-based distribution of power have been far-reaching, affecting fundamental aspects of social roles and personal expectations at all levels.

Five strands of feminist thought inform feminist criminology today: liberal feminism, radical feminism, Marxist feminism, socialist feminism, and postmodern feminism. Each of these perspectives argues that conflict in society is based on inequalities focused around issues of gender. Learn more at **Library Extra 8–8.**

Liberal Feminism

Liberal feminism sees gender-role socialization as the primary source of women's oppression.[58] Liberal feminists describe a power-based and traditional domination of women's bodies and minds by men throughout history and blame present inequalities on the development within culture and society of "separate and distinct spheres of influence and traditional attitudes about the appropriate role of men and women."[59] Liberal feminists call for elimination of traditional divisions of power and labor between the sexes as a way of eliminating inequality and promoting social harmony.

Radical Feminism

Radical feminism sees patriarchy, or male dominance, as the cause of women's oppression, depicting men as being fundamentally brutish, aggressive, and violent and controlling women through sexuality by taking advantage of both women's biological dependence during childbearing years and their lack of physical strength relative to men. The exploitation of women by men triggers women's deviant behavior, because young women who are sexually or physically exploited may run away or abuse substances and become criminalized, so the elimination of male domination should reduce crime rates for women and "even precipitate a decrease in male violence against women."[60]

Marxist Feminism

The oppression of women caused by their subordinate working-class status in capitalist societies is the main tenet of **Marxist feminism.** Within capitalist society, women may be drawn into crime commission in an effort to support themselves and their children; men commit violent street crimes more often, whereas women commit property and vice crimes.[61]

Social Feminism

Socialist feminism, a fourth perspective, sees gender oppression as a consequence of the interaction between the economic structure of society and gender-based roles. Egalitarian societies would be built around socialist or Marxist principles with the aim of creating a society that is free of gender and class divisions.

Postmodern Feminism

The social construction of concepts typically used in any discussion of criminology—including concepts like justice and

■ **postmodern feminism**
A perspective in modern criminology that questions the social construction of concepts typically used in discussions of crime and justice.

■ **patriarchy**
The tradition of male dominance.

■ **androcentricity**
A male-dominated perspective, as in the case of criminologists who study only the criminality of males.

crime—are questioned by **postmodern feminism**. According to criminologist Amanda Burgess-Proctor, postmodern feminism departs from the other feminist perspectives by questioning the existence of any one "truth," including "women's oppression," and that "postmodern feminists reject fixed categories and universal concepts in favor of multiple truths and as such examine the effects of discourse and symbolic representation on claims about knowledge."[62]

Proponents of Feminist Criminology

Feminist criminology points out the inequities inherent in patriarchal forms of thought. According to James W. Messerschmidt, **patriarchy** (male dominance) is a "set of social relations of power in which the male gender appropriates the labor power of women and controls their sexuality."[63]

Early works in the field of feminist criminology include *Sisters in Crime* by **Freda Adler**[64] and *Women and Crime* by **Rita J. Simon**,[65] both published in 1975. In these books, the authors attempted to explain existing divergences in crime rates between men and women as being due primarily to socialization rather than biology. Women were taught to believe in personal limitations, faced reduced socioeconomic opportunities, and suffered from lowered aspirations. As gender equality increased, they said, it could be expected that male and female criminality would take on similar characteristics, but such has not been the case, and the approach of Adler and Simon has not been validated by observations surrounding increased gender equality over the past few decades (Table 8–1). Another early work, *Women, Crime and Criminology*, was published in 1977 by British sociologist Carol Smart;[66] it sensitized criminologists to sexist traditions within the field and led to recognition of women's issues. Smart pointed out that men and women experience and perceive the world in different ways, and she showed how important it is for women to have a voice in interpreting the behavior of other women as opposed to having women's behavior interpreted from a man's standpoint.

Early feminist theorizing may not have borne the fruit that some researchers anticipated, but it has led to a heightened awareness of gender issues within criminology. Two of the most

TABLE 8-1 | Male and Female Involvement in Crime: Offense Patterns, 2009

UCR CRIME	PERCENTAGE OF ARRESTS	
	MALES	FEMALES
Murder and nonnegligent manslaughter	89.6	10.4
Rape	98.7	1.3
Robbery	88.2	11.8
Aggravated assault	78.0	22.0
Burglary	85.1	14.9
Larceny-theft	56.3	43.7
Motor vehicle theft	82.2	17.8
Arson	83.0	17.0
Forgery and counterfeiting	62.3	37.7
Fraud	57.2	42.8
Embezzlement	49.1	50.9

Source: Federal Bureau of Investigation, *Crime in the United States, 2009* (Washington, DC: U.S. Department of Justice, 2010).

insightful contemporary proponents of the need to apply feminist thinking to criminological analysis are **Kathleen Daly** and **Meda Chesney-Lind**, who are concerned about the existence of an **androcentricity** (male-dominated) perspective in criminology and point out that "gender differences in crime suggest that crime may not be so normal after all."[67] Traditional understandings of what is typical about crime are derived from the study of men, especially that small group of men who commit most crimes. The relative lack of criminality exhibited by women is rarely acknowledged as having criminological significance, which calls into question many traditional assumptions about crime—especially the assumption that crime is somehow a "normal" part of social life. Daly and Chesney-Lind have identified the following five elements of feminist thought that set it apart from other types of social and political thought:[68]

1. Gender is not a natural fact but a complex social, historical, and cultural product that is related to, not simply derived from, biological sex differences and reproductive capacities.

2. Gender and gender relations order social life and social institutions in fundamental ways.

3. Gender relations and constructs of masculinity and femininity are not symmetrical but are based on an organizing principle of men's superiority and their social, political, and economic dominance over women.

4. Systems of knowledge reflect men's views of the natural and social world; the production of knowledge is gendered.

■ **power–control theory**
A perspective that holds that power relationships existing in the wider society are reflected in domestic settings and in everyday relationships among men, women, and children in the context of family life

5. Women should be at the center, not the periphery, of intellectual inquiry; they should not be invisible or treated as appendages to men.

In a more recent analysis of feminist criminology, Susan Caulfield and Nancy Wonders described "five major contributions that have been made by feminist scholarship and practice" to criminological thinking: (1) a focus on gender as a central organizing principle of contemporary life, (2) an awareness of the importance of power in shaping social relationships, (3) a heightened sensitivity to the way in which social context helps shape human relationships, (4) the recognition that social reality must be understood as a process and that the development of research methods should take this into account, and (5) a commitment to social change as a crucial part of feminist scholarship and practice.[69]

> Gender differences in crime suggest that crime may not be so normal after all.

John Hagan built on defining features of power relationships in his book *Structural Criminology*, in which he explained that power relationships existing in the wider society are effectively "brought home" to domestic settings and are reflected in everyday relationships among men, women, and children within the context of family life.[70] Hagan's approach, termed **power–control theory**, suggested that "family class structure shapes the social reproduction of gender relations, and in turn the social distribution of delinquency."[71]

In a cogent analysis encompassing much of contemporary feminist theory, Daly and Chesney-Lind suggested that feminist thought is more important for the way it informs and challenges existing criminology than for the new theories it offers. Theories of crime causation and prevention must include women, and more research on gender-related issues in the field is badly needed. Daly and Chesney-Lind explained that "criminologists should begin to appreciate that their discipline and its questions are a product of white, economically privileged men's experiences" and that rates of female criminality, which are lower than those of males, may highlight the fact that criminal behavior is not as "normal" as once thought.[72] Because modern-day criminological perspectives were mostly developed by white middle-class men, the perspectives failed to take into consideration women's "ways of knowing."[73] Feminist criminologists Daly and Chesney-Lind asked: Given the current situation in theory development, do existing theories of crime causation apply as well to women as they do to men, or "do theories of men's crime apply to women?"[74]

Other feminists have analyzed the process by which laws are created and legislation passed and have concluded that modern-day statutes frequently represent characteristically masculine modes of thought and that existing criminal laws are overly rational and hierarchically structured, reflecting traditionally male ways of organizing the social world.[75] Until recently, many jurisdictions viewed assault victims differently based on the gendered relationships involved in the offense. *Assault* (or *battery*) is defined as an attack by one person on another, but until the last few decades of the twentieth century, domestic violence statutes tended to downplay the seriousness of the attacks involved, giving the impression that because they occurred within the home and the victims were typically women, they weren't as important to the justice system as other forms of assault. Some analysts have suggested that existing laws need to be replaced by "a system of justice based upon the specifically feminine principles of care, connection and community."[76]

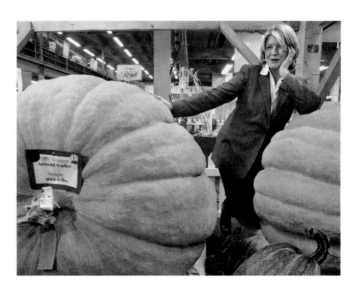

Homewares icon Martha Stewart, age 62, prior to her arrest and prosecution. In 2004, Stewart was sentenced to five months in prison for obstructing a federal investigation into her 2001 sale of shares of the biotechnology company ImClone Systems, Inc.; was ordered to spend two years on probation, including five months of monitored home detention; and was fined $30,000. She was released from prison in 2005 after spending five months at the federal prison for women in Alderson, West Virginia. Some say that the criminality of women is beginning to rival that of men. Might Stewart serve as an example of just such a trend? Why or why not?
Source: AP Wide World Photos

WEB EXTRA 8–6
WEB EXTRA 8–7
LIBRARY EXTRA 8–9
LIBRARY EXTRA 8–10
LIBRARY EXTRA 8–11

■ **gender gap**
The observed differences between male and female rates of criminal offending in a given society.

■ **postmodern criminology**
A brand of criminology that builds on the tenets inherent in postmodern social thought.

■ **deconstructionist theory**
A postmodern perspective that challenges existing criminological theories in order to debunk them and that works toward replacing traditional ideas with concepts seen as more appropriate to the postmodern era.

In the area of social policy, feminist thinkers have pointed to the need for increased controls over men's violence toward women, the creation of alternatives (to supplement the home and traditional family structures) for women facing abuse, and the protection of children. They also questioned the role of government, culture, and the mass media in promulgating pornography, prostitution, and rape and portrayed ongoing crimes against women as characteristic of continuing traditions in which women are undervalued and controlled. Many radical feminists have suggested the replacement of men with women in positions of power, especially within justice system and government organizations, but others noted that replacement still would not address needed changes in the structure of the system itself, which is gender biased due to years of male domination. Centrists, on the other hand, have offered a more balanced approach, believing that individuals of both genders have much to contribute to a workable justice system.[77] Learn more about feminist criminology at **Web Extras 8–6** and **8–7**.

Critique of Feminist Criminology

Some would argue that feminist criminology has yet to live up to its promise because few comprehensive feminist theories of crime were proposed; feminist criminology focused instead on descriptive studies of female involvement in crime.[78] Male violence against women was seen as adding support to the central tenet of feminist criminology (that the relationship between the sexes is primarily characterized by the exercise of power), but that did not make for broad theory building. As one writer explained, "Feminist theory is a theory in formation."[79]

Feminist criminology has faced criticism from many other directions. Predicted increases in female crime rates have failed to materialize as social opportunities available to both genders have become more balanced, and the **gender gap** in crime—with males accounting for much more law violation than females—continues to exist. Criminologist Karen Heimer noted that the gender gap is "virtually a truism in criminology. The relationship holds, regardless of whether the data analyzed are arrest rates, victimization incidence reports on characteristics of offenders, or self-reports of criminal behavior.... [A]s far as we can tell, males have always been more criminal than females, and gender differences emerge in every society that has been studied systematically."[80] Other critics have pointed to fundamental flaws in feminist thought, asking such questions as "If men have more power than women, then why are so many more men arrested?"[81]

Some critics have even argued that a feminist criminology is impossible. Daly and Chesney-Lind agreed that although feminist thought may inform criminology, "a feminist criminology cannot exist because neither feminism nor criminology is a unified set of principles and practices."[82] A criminology built solely on feminist principles is unlikely because neither feminist thought nor criminology meets the strict requirements of formal theory building. Read more about feminist perspectives on crime and criminology at **Library Extras 8–9, 8–10, and 8–11**.

> Some would argue that feminist criminology has yet to live up to its promise.

Postmodern Criminology

Some significant new approaches now emerging within criminology are largely the result of postmodern social thought and can be lumped together under the rubric **postmodern criminology**, which applies understandings of social change inherent in postmodern philosophy to criminological theorizing and to issues of crime control.

Postmodern thought, which developed primarily in Europe after World War II, represents "a rejection of the enlightenment belief in scientific rationality as the main vehicle to knowledge and progress."[83] One of its important aspects can be found in its efforts to demonstrate the systematic intrusion of sexist, racist, capitalist, colonialist, and professional interests into the very content of science. Contemporary feminist scholar Joycelyn M. Pollock put it this way: "Post-modernism questions whether we can ever 'know' something objectively; so-called neutral science is considered a sham and criminology's search for causes is bankrupt because even the question is framed by androcentric, sexist, classist, and racist definitions of crime, criminals, and cause."[84]

All postmodern criminologies build on the feeling that past criminological approaches have failed to realistically assess the true causes of crime and have failed to offer workable solutions for crime control. Hence, much postmodern criminology is deconstructionist, and its theories are sometimes called **deconstructionist theories**, meaning approaches that challenge existing criminological perspectives to debunk them and to work toward replacing them with approaches more relevant to the postmodern era.

Two notable authors in the field of postmodern criminology are **Stuart Henry** and **Dragan Milovanovic**,[85] whose constitutive criminology, rooted in phenomenology, claimed that

WEB EXTRA 8-8
LIBRARY EXTRA 8-12

■ **peacemaking criminology**
A perspective that holds that crime-control agencies and the citizens they serve should work together to alleviate social problems and human suffering and thus reduce crime; also called *compassionate criminology*.

crime and crime control are not "object-like entities" but are constructions produced through a social process in which offender, victim, and society are all involved.[86] A central feature of their constitutive criminology is its assertion that individuals shape their world while also being shaped by it.

Semiotics, or the study of signs and symbols, is another important concept in constitutive criminology. Semiotics can be applied to the notion of crime, itself a socially constructed category or sign. In the words of Henry and Milovanovic, crime "is a categorization of the diversity of human conflicts and transgressions into a single category 'crime,' as though these were somehow all the same. It is a melting of differences reflecting the multitude of variously motivated acts of personal injury into a single entity."[87] Crime should be understood as an integral part of society, not as something separate from it.

From this perspective, a kind of false consciousness, or lack of awareness, gives rise to criminal activity. According to Werner Einstadter and Stuart Henry, crime is seen to be the culmination of certain processes that allow persons to believe they are somehow not connected to other humans and society, that place others in categories or stereotypes, and that make them different or alien, denying their humanity; this results in the denial of responsibility for other people and to other people.[88] Learn more about postmodern criminology at **Web Extra 8–8**, and read an interesting paper by Dragan Milovanovic at **Library Extra 8–12**.

Critique of Postmodern Criminology

Ian Taylor is a British sociologist who lent focus to radical-critical criminology in the 1970s with the publication of two well-received books.[89] He criticized postmodern approaches to crime and deviance for their "increasing incoherence."[90] In other words, postmodern criminologists employ vaguely defined terminology. Taylor also explained that the "battle with orthodox criminology" has led postmodern approaches to increasingly obfuscate their most basic claims, so a second result of the postmodern influence on criminology "has been the development of a social account of crime that entirely lacks a value or ethical foundation."[91] Deconstructionism may challenge traditional theories, but unless it offers viable alternatives for crime control and prevention, it does little good.

Peacemaking Criminology

Throughout much of history, formal agencies of social control—the police, officials of the courts, and corrections personnel—have been seen as pitted against criminal perpetrators and would-be wrongdoers, and crime control has been depicted as an epic struggle in which diametrically opposed antagonists continuously engage one another but in which only one side can emerge victorious. Another point of view has come to the fore: **Peacemaking criminology** (also called *compassionate criminology*), a form of postmodern criminology with roots in Christian and Eastern philosophies, advances the notion that social control agencies and the citizens they serve should work together to alleviate social problems and human suffering and thus reduce crime.[92] Peacemaking criminology includes the notion of service and suggests that "compassion, wisdom, and love are essential for understanding the suffering of which we are all a part and for practicing a criminology of nonviolence."[93]

Peacemaking criminology is popularized by the works of **Harold E. Pepinsky**[94] and Richard Quinney.[95] Both Pepinsky and Quinney restated the problem of crime control from one of how to stop crime to one of how to make peace within society and between citizens and criminal justice agencies. Peacemaking criminology draws attention to many issues: (1) perpetuation of violence through continuation of social policies based on dominant forms of criminological theory, (2) role of education in peacemaking, (3) commonsense theories of crime, (4) crime control as human rights enforcement, and (5) conflict resolution within community settings.[96]

Richard Quinney and John Wildeman summarized the underpinnings of peacemaking criminology by stating that "a criminology of peacemaking—a nonviolent criminology of compassion and service—seeks to end suffering and thereby eliminate crime."[97]

Other contributors to the peacemaking movement include Bo Lozoff, Michael Braswell, and Clemens Bartollas. In *Inner Corrections*, Lozoff and Braswell claimed that "we are fully aware by now that the criminal justice system in this country is founded on violence. It is a system which assumes that violence can be overcome by violence, evil by evil. Criminal justice at home and warfare abroad are of the same principle of violence. This principle sadly dominates much of our criminology."[98] *Inner Corrections* provides meditative techniques and prayers for those seeking to become more compassionate and includes a number of letters from convicts who demonstrate the book's philosophy.

In a work titled "Correctional Treatment, Peacemaking, and the New Age Movement," Bartollas and Braswell applied New Age principles to correctional treatment:[99] "Most offenders suffered abusive and deprived childhoods. Treatment that focuses on

■ **peace model**
An approach to crime control that focuses on effective ways for developing a shared consensus on critical issues that can seriously affect the quality of life.

■ **participatory justice**
An informal type of criminal justice case processing that makes use of local community resources rather than requiring traditional forms of official intervention.

WEB EXTRA 8–9
LIBRARY EXTRA 8–13

■ **restorative justice**
A postmodern perspective that stresses solutions and restoration rather than imprisonment, punishment, and neglect of victims; also called *reparative justice.*

the inner child and such qualities as forgiveness and self-esteem could benefit offenders."[100] In a fundamental sense, peacemaking criminologists exhort their colleagues to transcend personal dichotomies to end the political and ideological divisiveness that separates people.

Restorative Justice

Peacemaking criminology suggests that effective crime control can best be achieved by the adoption of a **peace model** of crime control based on cooperation rather than retribution and focused on effective ways of developing a shared consensus on critical issues that could seriously affect people's quality of life. Major issues include crimes like murder and rape but also extend to property rights, rights to the use of new technologies, and ownership of information; minor issues, including sexual preference, nonviolent sexual deviance, gambling, drug use, noise, child-custody claims, and publicly offensive behavior, can be dealt with in ways that require few resources beyond those immediately available in the community.

Alternative-dispute resolution plays an important role in peacemaking perspectives.[101] Mediation programs, such as dispute-resolution centers and neighborhood justice centers, are characterized by cooperative efforts to reach dispute resolution rather than adversarial proceedings now characteristic of most American courts. Dispute-resolution programs, now operating in over 200 areas throughout the country, are based on **participatory justice**—all parties to a dispute accept a kind of binding arbitration by neutral parties, often utilize administrative hearings and ombudsmen, and are staffed by volunteers who work to resolve disputes without assigning blame.

Miami's drug court, a local judicial initiative begun in 1989, provides an example of dispute-resolution programs. It diverts nonviolent drug users from the traditional path of streets to court to jail. Officially called the Dade County Diversion and Treatment Program, the drug court "channels almost all nonviolent defendants arrested on drug possession charges into an innovative court-operated rehabilitation program as an alternative to prosecution."[102] Drug-court processing appears to be successful at reducing the incidence of repeat offenses, does not result in a criminal record for those completing the program, and offers drug-dependent offenders a second chance at gaining control over substance abuse problems.

Alternative-dispute resolution is not without its critics, who charge that this type of program is often staffed by poorly qualified individuals who are ill-prepared to mediate disputes effectively. But as case-processing expenses continue to rise and minor cases continue to flood justice system agencies, we can expect that an emphasis on alternative-dispute resolution will continue.

Many dispute-resolution strategies are really a form of **restorative justice** (also called *reparative justice*), "a new system based on remedies and restoration rather than on prison, punishment and victim neglect."[103] It is "a system rooted in the concept of a caring community," and adherents hope it leads to social and economic justice and increased concern and respect for both victims and victimizers.[104]

But restorative justice is more than a system—it is a modern social movement to reform the criminal justice system that stresses healing rather than retribution.[105]

Restoration (repairing the harm done by crime and rebuilding relationships in the community) is the primary goal of restorative justice, and its effectiveness is measured by how many relationships are healed rather than by how much punishment is inflicted on the offender. Table 8–2 highlights some of the significant differences between traditional retributive justice and restorative justice. Learn more about restorative justice at **Web Extra 8–9**, and read a paper on restorative justice at **Library Extra 8–13**.

> Restorative justice is a modern social movement that stresses healing rather than retribution.

Critique of Peacemaking Criminology

Peacemaking criminology has been criticized as being naïve and utopian and for failing to recognize the realities of crime control and law enforcement because few victims would expect to gain much from attempting to make peace with their victimizers (although such strategies do occasionally work). Such criticisms may be improperly directed at a level of analysis that peacemaking criminologists have not assumed. While it involves work with individual offenders, peacemaking criminology envisions positive change on the societal and institutional levels and does not suggest to victims that they attempt to effect personal changes in offenders.

■ **convict criminology**

A radical paradigm consisting of writings on criminology by convicted felons and ex-inmates who have acquired academic credentials or who are associated with credentialed others; also called *alternative criminology*.

TABLE 8-2 | Differences between Retributive and Restorative Justice

RETRIBUTIVE JUSTICE	RESTORATIVE JUSTICE
Crime is an act against the state, a violation of a law, an abstract idea.	Crime is an act against another person or the community.
The criminal justice system controls crime.	Crime control lies primarily with the community.
Offender accountability is defined as taking punishment.	Offender accountability is defined as assuming responsibility and taking action to repair harm.
Crime is an individual act with individual responsibility.	Crime has both individual and social dimensions of responsibility.
Victims are peripheral to the process of resolving a crime.	Victims are central to the process of resolving a crime.
The offender is defined by deficits.	The offender is defined by the capacity to make reparation.
The emphasis is on adversarial relationships.	The emphasis is on dialogue and negotiation.
Pain is imposed to punish, deter, and prevent.	Restitution is a means of restoring both parties; the goal is reconciliation.
The community is on the sidelines, represented abstractly.	The community is the facilitator in the restorative process by the state.
The response is focused on the offender's past behavior.	The response is focused on harmful consequences of the offender's behavior; the emphasis is on the future and on reparation.
There is dependence on proxy professionals.	There is direct involvement by both the offender and the victim.

Source: Adapted from Gordon Bazemore and Mark S. Umbreit, *Balanced and Restorative Justice: Program Summary* (Washington, DC: Office of Juvenile Justice and Delinquency Prevention, 1994), p. 7.

Convict Criminology

A new radical paradigm emerging in the field of criminology is **convict criminology** (also called *alternative criminology*), which is not so much a school of thought as it is a body of writings and musings on criminology by convicted felons and ex-inmates who have acquired academic credentials or who are associated with credentialed others. It was formalized in 2001 with the publication of the article "Introducing the New School of Convict Criminology" by Stephen C. Richards in the journal *Social Justice*.[106] With the publication of "Convict Criminology" by Ian Ross and Stephen Richards in 2002,[107] the writings of convict criminologists went mainstream and began garnering attention from those in the discipline as well as the media. Today convict criminology (sometimes referred to as the New School of Convict Criminology) offers a blend of writings by credentialed ex-inmates and critical criminologists who have joined forces in distrust of mainstream criminology.[108] Convict criminology is largely issues based and personal; it has an agenda and tends to assume a critical perspective with regard to the justice system—especially corrections. The language of convict criminologists is different from that of academic criminologists who do not share their convict background (the latter use words like *convicts* instead of *offenders* and *inmates* instead of *prisoners*). The distinction is an important one, because the terminology used by academic criminologists is "managerial," consistent with the language of controlling agents in the justice system such as police officers, correctional officers, probation and parole officers, and court officials. By using the language of convict insiders, convict criminologists signify their allegiance to an insider's perspective and refer to traditional criminology as *managerial criminology*.[109]

The method used by convict criminologists is based in ethnography, a branch of anthropology that studies other cultures

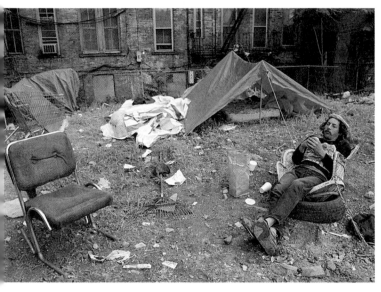

A homeless man in New York City. Peacemaking criminology holds that the alleviation of social problems and the reduction of human suffering will lead to a truly just world and thus reduce crime. What do you think?
Source: Photo by Susan Rae

(in this case, inmate society). Ethnographers (discussed in Chapter 2) depend on lived experiences and oral communications about them (interviews, stories, conversations of study subjects). The advantage of convict criminologists is that they are their own subjects, so the long hours needed to gather experiences have already been spent—usually in prison or in personal interactions with the justice system.

The prototype convict criminologist is John Irwin, who spent five years in California's Soledad Prison in the 1950s for armed robbery. While imprisoned, Irwin earned college credits and after release went on to attend San Francisco State College and then UCLA. "The point is, I made my transition from the life of a thief, drug addict, and convict to one of a 'respectable' professional." Irwin went on to write *The Felon*, an academic work that shared the career criminal's point of view with interested readers.[110]

More recent works in convict criminology result from the collaboration between traditional criminologists and ex-convicts: *Behind Convict's Eyes*[111] and *Prison, Inc.: A Convict Exposes Life inside a Private Prison*,[112] both by the author team of K. C. Carceral (a convict serving

> Convict criminology is largely issues based and personal.

life in prison who holds an associate's degree in paralegal studies), Thomas J. Bernard (a criminologist at Penn State University), and others.

Convict criminology is the source of a number of recommendations for improving the justice system that stem not from traditional forms of social scientific research but from "personal research" based on the lived experiences of the convict criminologists:[113]

1. Prisons hold far too many people, do not effectively reduce crime, and hold far too many people who have committed minor crimes.

2. Prison expansion has disproportionately and unfairly impacted the nation's poor—especially young men of color—who have made bad decisions in their lives and committed relatively harmless and bothersome crimes.

3. A substantial reduction in the number of federal and state prisoners is needed. Many of today's prisoners are nonviolent drug offenders who committed property crimes in support of drug habits or who were caught with drugs in their possession for either personal use or resale; diversion and treatment are viable alternatives to incarceration. The nation's "war on drugs"—seen as having a negative impact on all society—should be terminated.

4. Corrections today can benefit significantly from the use of smaller prisons instead of large institutions that now characterize many state facilities because they are less dangerous than large ones and tend to result in heightened rates of rehabilitation.

5. Treatment should be given precedence over security because most inmates will eventually return to society, and treatment offers the best hope for desistance from crime. Institutional priorities should be reversed—treatment programs need to receive top-level funding.

Critique of Convict Criminology

Not everyone agrees that convict criminology offers an edge over traditional criminology. Critics say that having been in prison might actually distort a criminologist's view of the field rather than enhance it and that personal experience rarely gives anyone the entire picture needed to understand a phenomenon. Focusing on the injustices of prison life might keep someone from appreciating the reformative effects of punishment. Read more about convict criminology at **Library Extra 8–14**.

Policy Implications of Social Conflict Theories

The policy implications of social conflict theory are fairly clear: Bring about social change and redistribute the wealth in society, and crime rates will fall. At one extreme, radical-Marxist criminologists argue that the only effective way of reducing conflict is through a total dismantling of the existing capitalist system in the United States and its replacement by a socialist economic structure. At the other extreme are the calls of peacemaking criminologists for a practical application of the principles of conflict resolution. Between these two extremes lie left realism and feminist criminology, although the solutions they offer vary from the reduction of paternalism in all its forms to a practical recognition of the consequences of crime to victims.

SUMMARY

- Three analytical perspectives on law and social order are discussed in this chapter: the consensus perspective, the pluralist perspective, and the conflict perspective. The consensus perspective is built around the notion that most members of society agree on what is right and wrong and that various elements of society work together toward a shared vision of the greater good. The pluralistic perspective holds that a multiplicity of values and beliefs exists in any complex society and that each different social group will have its own set of beliefs, interests, and values. The conflict perspective maintains that conflict is a fundamental aspect of social life itself that can never be fully resolved.

- Radical criminology holds that the root causes of crime are found in social conditions empowering the wealthy and the politically well organized but disenfranchising the less successful and that law is a tool of the powerful, who use it to control the less fortunate.

- Five perspectives offer explanations of crime and criminality: left-realist criminology, feminist criminology, postmodern criminology, peacemaking criminology, and convict criminology. Left-realist criminology is concerned with street crime, fear of crime, and everyday victimization and embraces radical and Marxist criminology. Feminist criminology believes that sexism and an unequal gender-based distribution of power in our patriarchal society affect both crime and its understanding in the field of criminology. Postmodernist criminologists doubt that an objective study of crime is possible and believe that criminology's search for the causes of crime is doomed because its questions are framed by sexist, class-specific, and racist assumptions. Peacemaking criminology restates the problem of crime control from how to stop crime to how to make peace within society and between citizens and criminal justice agencies. Convict criminology is a body of writings on criminology by convicted felons and ex-inmates who have acquired academic credentials or who are associated with credentialed others.

- Conflict theories hold that social conflict and its manifestations are the root causes of crime; the crime-control implications involve redressing injustices to end the marginalization of the politically and economically disadvantaged.

KEY TERMS

androcentricity, 224

bourgeoisie, 213

conflict perspective, 213

consensus perspective, 211

convict criminology, 229

critical criminology, 219

deconstructionist theory, 226

feminist criminology, 223

gender gap, 226

instrumental Marxism, 218

left realism, 222

left-realist criminology, 222

liberal feminism, 223

Marxist criminology, 216

Marxist feminism, 223

participatory justice, 228

patriarchy, 224

peacemaking criminology, 227

peace model, 228

pluralistic perspective, 212

postmodern criminology, 226

postmodern feminism, 224

power-control theory, 225

proletariat, 213

radical criminology, 216

radical feminism, 223

restorative justice, 228

social class, 215

socialist feminism, 223

structural Marxism, 218

KEY NAMES

Freda Adler, 224

Willem Bonger, 213

William J. Chambliss, 217

Meda Chesney-Lind, 224

Ralf Dahrendorf, 216

Kathleen Daly, 224

Walter DeKeseredy, 222

John Hagan, 225

Stuart Henry, 226

Karl Marx, 210

Raymond J. Michalowski, 211

Dragan Milovanovic, 226

Harold E. Pepinsky, 227

Roscoe Pound, 212

Richard Quinney, 218

Jeffrey H. Reiman, 218

Rita J. Simon, 224

Austin Turk, 216

George B. Vold, 215

Jock Young, 222

QUESTIONS FOR REVIEW

1. What three analytical perspectives on law and social order are described in this chapter?

2. What are the central tenets of radical criminology? What are its shortcomings?

3. What five emerging conflict perspectives discussed in this chapter purport to explain crime and criminality?

4. What are the crime-control implications of social conflict theories?

QUESTIONS FOR REFLECTION

1. This book emphasizes the theme of social problems versus social responsibility. Which of the theoretical perspectives discussed in this chapter (if any) support the social problems approach? Which (if any) support the social responsibility approach? Why?

2. What are the differences among the consensus, pluralist, and conflict perspectives? Which comes closest to your way of understanding society? Why?

3. What is Marxist criminology? How (if at all) does it differ from radical criminology? From critical criminology?

4. Does the Marxist perspective hold any significance for contemporary American society? Why?

5. What are the fundamental propositions of feminist criminology? How would feminists change the study of crime?

6. What does it mean to say that traditional theories of crime need to be "deconstructed"? What role does deconstructionist thinking play in postmodern criminology?

CHAPTER

CRIMES AGAINST PERSONS

■ **National Crime Victimization Survey (NCVS)**
A survey conducted annually by the Bureau of Justice Statistics that provides data on surveyed households that report they were affected by crime.

■ **Uniform Crime Reporting Program (UCR)**
A Federal Bureau of Investigation data-gathering initiative that provides an annual tally of statistics consisting primarily of information on crimes reported to the police and on arrests.

■ **National Incident-Based Reporting System (NIBRS)**
An enhanced statistical reporting system to collect data on each incident and arrest within 22 crime categories.

Introduction

The government-sponsored gathering of crime data for the nation as a whole began in the United States around 1930. Before then, the gathering of statistics was random at best, and most accounts were anecdotal and either spread by word of mouth or printed in local newspapers (or both). Today's official U.S. crime statistics come from the Bureau of Justice Statistics (BJS), which conducts the annual **National Crime Victimization Survey (NCVS)**, and from the Federal Bureau of Investigation (FBI), which publishes yearly data under its summary-based **Uniform Crime Reporting Program (UCR)** and its more detailed **National Incident Based Reporting System (NIBRS)**; the latter provides a more complete picture of crimes reported and committed.

NCVS data appear in a number of annual reports, the most important of which is *Criminal Victimization in the United States*, and FBI data take the form of the annual publication *Crime in the United States*. Numerous other surveys and reports are made available through the BJS and cover not only the incidence of crime and criminal activity in the United States but also many other aspects of the criminal justice profession, including justice system expenditures, prisons and correctional data, probation and parole populations, jail inmate information, law enforcement agencies and personnel data, and information on state and federal courts. These and other reports are generally made available free of charge to interested parties through the National Criminal Justice Reference Service (NCJRS).[1] The largest collection of facts about all aspects of U.S. crime and criminal justice is the *Sourcebook of Criminal Justice Statistics*, compiled yearly by the BJS and made available in various formats.

The UCR/NIBRS and the NCVS both use their own specialized definitions in deciding which events should be scored as crimes. Sometimes the definitions vary considerably between programs, and none of the definitions used by the reporting agencies is strictly based on federal or state statutory crime classifications.

The National Crime Victimization Survey (NCVS)

The NCVS, which began collecting data in 1972, differs from FBI-sponsored programs in one significant way: Rather than depending on reports of crimes to the police, the NCVS data consist of information from interviews with members of randomly selected households throughout the nation. Hence, the NCVS uncovers a large number of crimes that may not have been reported and is regarded by many researchers as a more accurate measure of the actual incidence of crime in the United States than the UCR/NIBRS.

NCVS interviewers ask questions about the incidence of rape, personal robbery, aggravated and simple assault, household burglary, personal and household theft, and motor vehicle theft as they have affected household members during the past six months. Information is gathered on victims (sex, age, race, ethnicity, marital status, income, educational level), offenders (sex, age, race, relationship to the victim), and crimes (time and place of occurrence, use of weapons, nature of injury, economic consequences for the victim). Questions also cover protective measures used by victims, the possibility of substance abuse by offenders, and the level of previous experience victims may have had with the criminal justice system.

The number of victimizations counted by the NCVS for any single reported criminal occurrence is based on the number of people victimized by the event, so if a robbery has more than one victim, that will be reported in NCVS data. Although this distinction is applied to personal crimes, households are treated as individual units, so all household crimes are counted only once, no matter how many members the household contains.

According to the NCVS, on average only 49% of violent victimizations and 38% of property crimes are reported to the police.[2] While violent crimes are most likely to be reported to the police, personal thefts are the least likely crimes to be reported.

> On average only 49% of violent victimizations and 38% of property crimes are reported to the police.

NCVS data show that around 80% of motor vehicle thefts are reported to the police, making this the most highly reported of crimes; larcenies, at 32%, are least likely to be reported. Recovering property or receiving insurance payments motivates many victims of property crimes to report their victimization to the police. The two most common reasons for not reporting violent victimizations are that the crime is a personal or private matter and that the offender was unsuccessful (the crime was only attempted).

Critique of the NCVS

Just as the UCR/NIBRS has been criticized for underestimating the actual incidence of criminal activity within the United States, the NCVS can be criticized for possible overreporting.

No comprehensive attempt is made to verify the actual occurrence of any of the crimes reported to NCVS interviewers, so no reliable measure exists of the number of crimes falsely reported or underreported in NCVS data. Although the proportion is not known, it is also likely that some individuals, when approached by NCVS interviewers, may be unable to resist embellishing crime reports pertaining to their households and may even concoct criminal incidence data for purposes of self-aggrandizement or in an attempt to please the interviewer by providing copious amounts of data.

The NCVS program is much newer than the FBI's UCR Program, and comparisons between the programs are not available for the years before 1973. As with the UCR/NIBRS, definitions of crimes measured by the NCVS do not necessarily correspond to any federal or state statutes or to definitions used for other purposes, making comparisons with other state and federal crime records difficult. Complicating matters still further, changes in NCVS categories have resulted in the inability to easily compare NCVS findings of even a decade ago with current NCVS data.[3]

The Uniform Crime Reporting (UCR) Program

The UCR Program was created by the FBI in 1929 as an official crime data–gathering program covering the entire United States. It came from a national initiative by the International Association of Chiefs of Police (IACP), whose goal was to develop a set of uniform crime statistics for use by police agencies and policymakers. The FBI was designated to serve as a national clearinghouse on crime facts, and police agencies around the country began submitting data under the UCR Program. In its initial year of operation, 400 police departments representing cities and towns in 43 states participated in the program.

Early UCR data were structured in terms of seven major offense categories: murder, rape, robbery, aggravated assault, burglary, larceny, and motor vehicle theft. These crimes, called Part I offenses, formed the FBI's Crime Index, which provided a crime rate that could be compared over time and from one geographic location to another. Rates of crime under the UCR/NIBRS Program are generally expressed as "x number of offenses per 100,000 people." The 2009 rate of criminal homicide, for example, was 5.0 murders for every 100,000 people in the U.S. population. In 1979, Congress

TABLE 9-1 | Violent Crimes Known to the Police, 2009

OFFENSE	NUMBER	RATE PER 100,000	CLEARANCE RATE (%)
Murder	15,241	5.0	66.6
Forcible rape	88,097	56.6[a]	41.2
Robbery	408,217	133	28.2
Aggravated assault	806,843	262.8	56.8

[a]Rate shown is per 100,000 females.
Source: Federal Bureau of Investigation, *Crime in the United States, 2009.*

mandated that arson be added to the list of major offenses, but the inclusion of arson as an eighth index offense made it difficult to compare pre- and post-1979 Crime Indexes. For this and other reasons, the FBI officially discontinued use of the term *crime index* beginning with its report of crime data for 2005.[4]

In today's UCR/NIBRS reports, Part I offenses are subdivided into two categories: violent personal crimes consisting of murder, rape, robbery, and aggravated assault (which will be specifically discussed in this chapter) and property crimes consisting of burglary, larceny, motor vehicle theft, and arson (which will be discussed in subsequent chapters). Table 9–1 lists violent personal crimes, showing the number of offenses reported to the police in 2009. UCR/NIBRS trend data for personal crimes over the past 50 years are shown graphically in Figure 9–1.

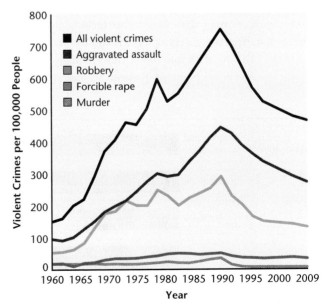

FIGURE 9-1 | Violent Crime Trend Data, 1960-2009
Source: Federal Bureau of Investigation, *Crime in the United States* (Washington, DC: FBI, various years).

Each year, when the FBI issues its annual report titled *Crime in the United States*, it includes information within each Part I offense category on the percentage of *cleared crimes*, those for which an arrest has been made or for which the perpetrator is known but an arrest is not possible (as when the offender is deceased or is out of the country); cleared crimes are also referred to as *solved crimes*. Those charged with a crime that is scored as cleared by the FBI may not yet have been adjudicated. In official UCR/NIBRS terminology, a Part I offense is regarded as cleared or solved when (1) "a law enforcement agency has charged at least one person with the offense" or (2) "a suspect has been identified and located and an arrest is justified, but action is prevented by circumstances outside law enforcement control."[5] Clearance rates (proportions of reported or discovered crimes within a given offense category that are solved) are reported for each Part I crime category. Figure 9–2 shows 2009 clearance rates for violent crimes.

The most significant feature of the UCR Program is indicated by its description—it is a *reporting* program. Only crimes that are reported to the police (or discovered by the police or by others who then report them to the police) are included in the statistics compiled by the program; most complaints are made by victims.

Because UCR/NIBRS data are based on reported crime, the program has been criticized for seriously underestimating the true incidence of criminal activity within the United States—a measurement that would also include unreported crimes. Some experts say that rape is the most underreported crime in the FBI data, with four to five times as many rapes occurring each year as are reported. Reasons for not reporting a

> Cleared crimes are those for which an arrest has been made or for which the perpetrator is known but an arrest is not possible.

crime like rape are numerous: fear of the perpetrator, shame, fear the victim may have of not being believed, and fear of participation in the justice system. Although rape is seriously underreported (a conclusion drawn from comparison of NCVS and UCR/NIBRS rape statistics), many other crimes like larceny (theft of small items that may never make it into official police reports) are underreported as well.

NIBRS: The New UCR Data Format

The NIBRS revises the definitions of a number of offenses for reporting purposes, but its incident-driven nature is its most important feature. The term *incident-driven* means that the FBI uses the NIBRS system to collect detailed data on the circumstances surrounding each serious criminal incident and that NIBRS reports are much more detailed than those previously provided under the UCR Program.

The NIBRS data-collection format focuses on each single incident and arrest within 22 crime categories, with incident, victim, property, offender, and arrestee information being gathered when available. The 22 NIBRS crime categories are made up of 46 specific crimes called "Group A offenses" (as compared with only 8 major offenses on which the old UCR Program gathered data); in addition, there are 11 Group B offense categories for which only arrest data are reported. The goal of NIBRS is to make data on reported crime more useful by relating them more completely than the old system did to other available information, such as victim and offender characteristics.

Because the UCR Program is currently undergoing a transition in format that involves more complete use of NIBRS data, we refer to UCR information cited in this and the following chapters as UCR/NIBRS data.

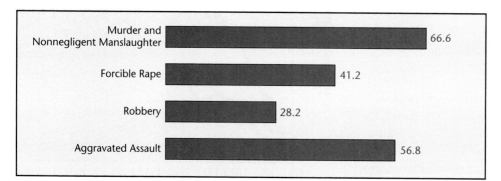

FIGURE 9–2 | Percent of Violent Crimes Cleared, 2009
Source: Federal Bureau of Investigation, *Crime in the United States, 2009* (Washington, DC: FBI, 2010).

Changing Crime Patterns

Since official crime statistics were first gathered around 1930, there have been three major shifts in crime rates. The first occurred during the early 1940s at the outbreak of World War II when crime decreased sharply due to the large number of young men who entered military service. Because young males make up the most crime-prone segment of the population, their participation in the war abroad lowered crime rates at home; from 1933 to 1941, the Crime Index declined from 770 to 508 offenses per every 100,000 members of the U.S. population.[6]

The second significant shift in offense statistics was a dramatic increase in most forms of crime that began in the 1960s and ended in the 1990s. Many criminologists believe that this shift also had a link to World War II. With the end of the war and the return of millions of young men to civilian life, birth rates skyrocketed between 1945 and 1955, creating a postwar baby boom. By 1960, baby boomers were entering their teenage years, and a disproportionate number of young people in the U.S. population produced a dramatic increase in most major crimes.

Other factors contributed to the increase in reported crime during this period. Crimes that went undetected in the past began to figure more prominently in official statistics, and the growing professionalization of police departments resulted in more accurate and increased data collection—which made the most progressive departments appear to be associated with the largest crime increases.[7] The 1960s were also tumultuous years: the Vietnam War, a vibrant civil rights struggle, the heady growth of secularism, dramatic increases in the divorce rate, diverse forms of "liberation," and the influx of psychedelic and other drugs. Social norms were blurred, and group control over individual behavior declined substantially. According to the FBI, from 1960 to 1980 crime rates rose from 1,887 to 5,950 offenses per every 100,000 members of the U.S. population.

Crime rates recorded by the FBI continued their upward swing (with the exception of a brief decline in the early 1980s) until postwar boomers began to "age out" of the crime-prone years, and U.S. society emerged from the cultural drift that had characterized the previous 20 years. But then an increase in drug-related criminal activity led crime rates, especially in the area of violent crime, to soar again.

Crime rates peaked about 1991 and have since shown a third major shift, with decreases in the rates of most major crimes being reported since that time. Between 1991 and 2009, the crime rate decreased from 5,897 to 3,466 offenses per every 100,000 citizens, sending it down to levels not seen since 1975. These decreases in crime since the mid-1990s may have been due to an "aging out" of the post–World War II baby-boom generation (members of which are now mostly too old to continue active criminal lifestyles), new strict laws, expanded justice system and police funding, changes in crime-fighting technologies, and economic factors.

While the two-decade-long decline in crime that took place beginning in 1991 is noteworthy, it did not begin to bring the overall crime rate in this country down to the low crime rates characteristic of the early 1940s and the 1950s. From a long-term perspective, even with recent declines, crime rates in this country remain more than seven times what they were in 1940.

Recent evidence may indicate that the decline in crime is ending and that we may be on the cusp of a new cycle of increased crime. Some criminologists think that recent economic uncertainty, an increased jobless rate among unskilled workers, the growing number of ex-convicts who are back on the streets, the recent growth in the teenage population in this country, the increasing influence of gangs, copycat crimes, and the lingering social disorganization brought on by natural disasters like Hurricane Katrina in 2005 and the nearby Haitian earthquake of 2010 (which led to increased immigration, both legal and illegal) may soon lead to sustained increases in crime. See **Library Extra 9–1** for more information.

Unreported Crime

As the NCVS shows, many crimes are not reported, leading criminologists to talk about the "dark figure of crime";[8] it refers to the large number of unreported crimes that never make it into official crime statistics. Crime's dark figure is sometimes glimpsed through offender self-reports (also known as offender self-report surveys), in which anonymous respondents are asked to report confidentially any violations of the criminal law they have committed. Unfortunately for researchers, self-reports of crime are too often limited to asking questions only about petty offenses (shoplifting, simple theft), are usually conducted among young people like high school or college students (not representative of the wider population), typically focus on juvenile delinquency rather than adult criminality, and cannot guarantee that respondents have told the truth. Limitations aside, some criminologists believe that "the development and widespread use of the self-report method of collecting data on delinquent and criminal

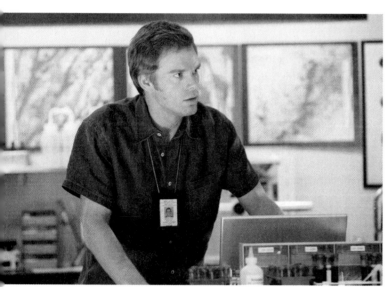

A still image from the Showtime TV series "Dexter." Dexter, a serial killer who strives to eliminate evil, works as a blood-spatter expert in a police department. What kinds of criminal offenses are likely to be self-reported? Which ones are unlikely to be self-reported? Why?

Source: Peter Lovino/Showtime/Courtesy: Everett Collection

behavior was one of the most important innovations in criminological research in the twentieth century."[9]

Some of the more recent and best-known self-report surveys include the National Youth Survey (NYS) and the *Monitoring the Future* study. Begun in 1976, the NYS surveyed a national sample of 1,725 youths between the ages of 11 and 17; 12 members of the group (or panel) were interviewed each year for five years between 1977 and 1981 and later at three-year intervals. The survey, last conducted in 1993, followed the original respondents into their thirties. Self-report data were compared with official data over time, and information was gathered on a wide variety of variables. Among other things, researchers found that (1) females were involved in a much higher proportion of crime than previously thought, (2) race differentials in crime were smaller than traditional data sources (the UCR/NIBRS) indicated, and (3) violent offenders began lives of crime much earlier than previous estimates provided by official statistics; the NYS also found a consistent progression from less serious to more serious acts of delinquency over time.

Monitoring the Future is an ongoing national self-report study of the behaviors, attitudes, and values of U.S. secondary school

students, college students, and young adults.[10] The study began in 1975, and each year a total of almost 50,000 eighth-, tenth-, and twelfth-grade students are surveyed. (Twelfth-graders have been surveyed since 1975, eighth- and tenth-graders since 1991.) In addition, annual follow-up questionnaires are mailed to a sample of each graduating class for a number of years after their initial participation.

Violent Crime Typologies

Criminologists use crime typologies to make sense of patterns that characterize criminal offending. A **crime typology** categorizes offenses using a set of defined characteristics, such as legal categories, offender motivation, victim behavior, situational aspects of the criminal event, and offender peculiarities. Statutory definitions of crimes based on legal categories allow for the creation of crime typologies, which "are designed primarily to simplify social reality by identifying homogeneous groups of crime behaviors that are different from other clusters of crime behaviors."[11] To be useful, the basis around which a typology is organized should serve a particular purpose. Some criminology typologies use a single variable as the primary explanation for variations in criminal offending; other typologies offer a number of variables thought to interact to produce certain patterns in violent offending. An example of a single-variable typology can be found in the general theory of crime advanced by Michael R. Gottfredson and Travis Hirschi (see Chapter 7), who emphasized low self-control as the crucial determinant of variations in offending. Other theories, such as developmental and life course theories, focus on different explanatory variables or on a combination of factors.

Some relatively straightforward typologies are built around data-gathering strategies in an attempt to provide useful information about different kinds of violent crime, but no one typology can perfectly capture all violent offending. This chapter relies on UCR/NIBRS and NCVS crime-reporting categories as the basis on which to distinguish among types of violent crimes; we

A crime typology categorizes offenses using a set of defined characteristics.

■ **homicide**
The killing of one human being by another.

■ **murder**
An unlawful homicide; also called *criminal homicide*.

■ **felony murder**
An unlawful homicide that occurs during the commission or attempted commission of a felony, or certain felonies specified by law.

WEB EXTRA 9–1
LIBRARY EXTRA 9–2

will also discuss some motivational factors associated with each category of violent offending.

Murder

The terms **homicide**—the willful killing of one human being by another—and **murder**—an unlawful homicide—are often used interchangeably, although they are not the same. Some homicides, such as those committed in defense of oneself or one's family, may be justifiable and therefore legal. The term used by most courts and law enforcement agencies to describe murder is *criminal homicide*, which means causing the death of another person without legal justification or excuse.

According to the UCR/NIBRS, 15,241 murders were committed throughout the United States in 2009; the rate was 5.0 people murdered for every 100,000 individuals.[12] Jurisdictions generally distinguish among various types of murder: first-degree murder (also called *premeditated murder*), second-degree murder, and third-degree murder (also called *negligent homicide*).

First-degree murder differs from the other two types in that it is planned; it involves what some statutes call "malice aforethought," which could entail someone lying in wait for a victim or a murderer going into an adjacent room to find a weapon and using it to kill someone. Any activity in preparation to kill that demonstrates the passage of time, however brief, between the formation of intent to kill and the act of killing itself is technically sufficient to establish the legal requirements needed for a first-degree murder prosecution.

Second-degree murder is a true crime of passion, an unlawful killing in which the intent to kill and the killing itself happen almost simultaneously. A person who kills in a fit of anger is likely to be charged with second-degree murder, as is one who is provoked into killing by insults or physical abuse. For a murder to be second-degree, the killing must immediately follow the insults or abuse; time that elapses between the insults or abuse and the murder itself allows the opportunity for thought to occur and hence for premeditation.

Both first- and second-degree murderers intend to kill, but third-degree murder most often refers to homicides resulting from someone's action that is unlawful or negligent, so it is frequently called *negligent homicide*, *negligent manslaughter*, *manslaughter*, or *involuntary manslaughter*. Under negligent-homicide statutes, for example, a drunk driver who causes a fatal accident may be charged with third-degree murder even though that person had not the slightest intent to kill.

Some jurisdictions have created a special category of **felony murder**, whereby an offender who commits a crime during which someone dies can be found guilty of first-degree murder, even though the person committing the crime had no intention of killing anyone. For example, a bank robbery in which one of the robbers is shot to death by police or a bank patron succumbs to a fear-induced heart attack may leave a surviving robber subject to the death penalty under the felony-murder rule.

Significant contributions to the understanding of homicide are being made today by the Homicide Research Working Group (HRWG). Prior to its creation, work in lethal violence had been scattered among numerous disciplines and was largely uncoordinated. To address this lack of coordination, homicide experts from various disciplines (criminology, public health, demography, medicine, sociology, criminal justice) joined together to create the HRWG. You can visit HRWG on the Internet at **Web Extra 9–1** and view the group's annual meetings proceedings at **Library Extra 9–2**.

Homicide offenders include men and women, young and old, rich and poor, with members of some groups disproportionately represented. Distinctive patterns of homicide can be identified through sociodemographics using individual characteristics, cultural norms, community characteristics, geographic regions, availability of weapons and weapons used, gang activities and affiliations, and victim–offender relationships. All of these sociodemographic features have been used to further our understanding of homicide patterns and to create typologies surrounding homicide.

The Subculture of Violence Thesis

Within the United States, there has been strong research interest in the subculture of violence thesis originally formulated by Marvin Wolfgang and Franco Ferracuti, who stressed the role of norms and values characteristic of certain groups in lifestyles of violence (discussed in Chapter 6).[13] Ethnic and racial differences in criminal activity reflect distinctive patterns of interaction with others characterized by a shared sense of history, language, values, and beliefs. The existence of a subculture necessitates a sufficient number of people who share not only values and beliefs but also a forum (even something as elusive as a street corner) that expresses

LIBRARY EXTRA 9–3
LIBRARY EXTRA 9–4

■ **primary homicide**
A murder involving a family member, friend, or acquaintance.

■ **expressive crime**
A criminal offense that results from acts of interpersonal hostility, such as jealousy, revenge, romantic triangles, and quarrels.

■ **nonprimary homicide**
A murder that involves a victim and an offender who have no prior relationship and that usually occurs during the course of another crime, such as robbery.

■ **instrumental crime**
A goal-directed offense that involves some degree of planning by the offender and little or no precipitation by the victim.

membership, and it is primarily this subtlety associated with subcultural theory that makes it difficult to test empirically. The subculture of violence thesis has been the primary theoretical perspective used to explain the similarity between homicide victims and offenders. First, homicide statistics reveal that victims and offenders share similar sociodemographic characteristics such as age, gender, and race, with African Americans disproportionately represented in the homicide statistics as both victims and offenders.[14] Second, victims and offenders who are intimately known to each other are disproportionately represented in homicide statistics; an analysis of supplemental homicide reports shows that approximately 55% of victims and offenders have some prior relationship.[15]

The subculture of violence thesis has also been explored at the community level, where the emphasis is on the importance of "critical masses" as support for the existence of subcultures.[16] Early research argued that the disproportionate rate at which African Americans commit homicide is associated with the presence of a large African American population, the "critical mass" necessary for the "transmission of violence-related models" and subcultural behavior patterns.[17] However, most of the research that found higher homicide rates to be associated with higher percentages of African Americans in the population did not take into consideration things like socioeconomic status and level of education.[18] Research by Robert Sampson using more sophisticated measures and stronger research designs revealed that the racial composition of an area alone did not have a significant effect on the homicide rates for either whites or blacks.[19]

> Homicide statistics reveal that victims and offenders share similar sociodemographic characteristics.

Structural Explanations for Homicide

Other researchers have focused on regional variations, particularly in the South, in patterns of violent crimes. The South has a long history of high homicide rates.[20] Subcultural theorists have proposed that the high rate of violent crime in the South reflects adherence to a set of violence-related norms that were generally accepted in earlier times but that have since become outdated in other regions.[21] Some researchers found that southern origin had a significant effect on the production of high homicide rates in particular areas;[22] other researchers challenged subcultural theories for their inability to control for noncultural factors that might explain the findings.[23] Specifically, Colin Loftin and R. H. Hill concluded that the influences of structural variables, especially poverty, must be considered as alternative explanations for regional differences in homicide rates.[24] While no definitive answers exist on whether the high rates of violence in the South are attributable to a specific subculture of violence or to structural factors, there still remains evidence (arrest statistics) that the South differs from other regions in terms of the frequency of homicides. Read more about serious violent crime and its characteristics via **Library Extras 9–3** and **9–4**.

The Victim–Offender Relationship

Marvin Wolfgang's 1958 study of homicides in Philadelphia revealed that approximately 25% of all homicides were between family members and that women were far more likely than men to be both offenders and victims in this category than in any other.[25] Males were more likely to be killed by friends and strangers than by their family members, but when a male was killed by a female, the offender was most likely to be his spouse.[26] Other researchers have emphasized qualitative differences in the pattern of homicide within the victim–offender relationship. The work of **Robert Nash Parker** and Dwayne Smith represented the first systematic research that focused on differentiating homicide according to the victim–offender relationship.[27] Their work used two classifications of homicide: primary and nonprimary. **Primary homicides** are the most frequent and involve family members, friends, and acquaintances, and they are usually characterized as **expressive crimes** because they often result from interpersonal hostility, based on jealousy, revenge, romantic triangles, and minor disagreements.[28]

Nonprimary homicides involve victims and offenders who have no prior relationship and usually occur in the course of another crime such as robbery; these are referred to as **instrumental crimes** because they involve some degree of premeditation by the offender and are less likely to be precipitated by the victim (see the Criminal Profiles boxes). The difference between expressive and instrumental motives for homicide continues to be important in criminological research, and we will return to this shortly. Figure 9–3 shows the relationship between killers and their victims.

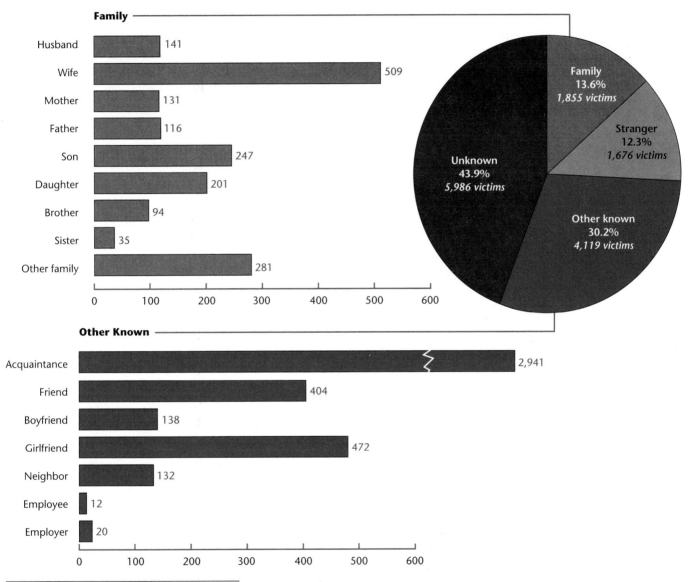

NOTE: Relationship is that of victim to offender. Percentages may not total 100 due to rounding.

FIGURE 9-3 | Murder by Relationship, 2009

Source: Federal Bureau of Investigation, *Crime in the United States, 2009* (Washington, DC: FBI, 2010).

Further attention to the heterogeneous nature of homicide is found in the work of K. R. Williams and R. L. Flewelling, who disaggregated homicide rates according to two criteria: (1) the nature of the circumstances surrounding the homicide, which included whether there was some indicator of a fight or argument precipitating the homicide, and (2) the victim–offender relationship, distinguishing between victims and offenders who were family members, acquaintances, or strangers.[29] By comparing how factors like poverty and population size have different effects on different types of homicide, Williams and Flewelling found that some factors are more important in explaining certain forms of homicide. Poverty is a stronger predictor of family homicide, population size is more important in explaining stranger homicide, and both the victim–offender relationship and the context

LIBRARY EXTRA 9-5

■ **exposure-reduction theory**
A theory of intimate homicide that claims that a decline in domesticity, accompanied by an improvement in the economic status of women and a growth in domestic-violence resources, explains observed decreases in intimate-partner homicide.

■ **sibling offense**
An offense or incident that culminates in homicide. The offense or incident may be a crime, such as robbery, or an incident with a less stringent criminal definition, such as a lovers' quarrel involving assault or battery.

■ **victim precipitation**
A contribution made by the victim to the criminal event, especially one that led to its initiation.

Armin Meiwes (right) standing next to his lawyer, Harald Ermel, in the district court in Kassel, Germany, on January 30, 2004. Meiwes confessed to killing, dismembering, and cannibalizing a 43-year-old computer specialist from Berlin whom he had met over the Internet. Meiwes was convicted of manslaughter and sentenced to eight years in prison. The case was complicated by a series of e-mail messages written by the mentally ill victim in which he repeatedly expressed a wish to be killed and eaten. How might the Internet contribute to violent victimization?
Source: AP Wide World Photos

of the homicide (for example, the end result of a robbery) are crucial factors in explaining patterns of homicide.

Beginning in the 1980s, the intimate-partner homicide rate began to decline, a decline that has continued to the present day. Using homicide data from a sample of 29 large cities in the United States from 1976 to 1992, Laura Dugan, Daniel S. Nagin, and Richard Rosenfeld offered an **exposure-reduction theory** of intimate-partner homicide.[30] These researchers examined the ability of the "decline in domesticity, improved economic status of women, and growth in domestic violence resources" to explain decreases in intimate-partner homicide in urban areas.[31] Analysis of the data did support the major hypotheses offered by Dugan, Nagin, and Rosenfeld—as resources supporting a nonviolent exit from a violent relationship increase, rates of

intimate-partner homicide decrease. Read more about intimate-partner violence at **Library Extra 9–5**.

Sibling Offenses

Not all homicide offenders intend to kill their victims. For example, an incident may begin as a robbery motivated by instrumental ends, such as getting money, but end in someone's death. The term **sibling offense** refers to the incident that initiates the homicide. A sibling offense may be a crime, such as robbery, or another incident, such as a lovers' quarrel. It is crucial to take these sibling offenses into account because they help explain why some robberies end in murder and others do not.

Victim Precipitation

When discussing homicide, **victim precipitation** focuses on the characteristics of victims that may have precipitated their victimization. This seems to blame the victim, so it has been quite controversial, but from a scholarly point of view, the thrust of victim precipitation is not to blame the victim but to examine both individual and situational factors that may have contributed to and initiated the crime. This is especially important in studying patterns of homicide because often a homicide begins as a fight or an argument between people who know each other, and the circumstances of the encounter determine whether the event will end as an assault or a homicide. In his classic 1958 work on homicide, Marvin Wolfgang designated as many as 60% of cases where women had killed their husbands as victim precipitated but only 9% of incidents where men had killed their wives as victim precipitated.[32] The gendered patterns of victim precipitation have not changed significantly since Wolfgang's investigation: Based on data on intimate-partner homicides in St. Louis, Missouri, Richard Rosenfeld analyzed data from 1980 to 1993 and designated slightly more than 50% of all homicides committed by women and only 12% of those committed by men as victim precipitated.[33]

Wolfgang also identified alcohol use as a factor in homicide cases where the "victim is a direct, positive precipitator in the crime."[34] He concluded that the significant association between alcohol and victim-precipitated homicides may be explained by the fact that the victim was the "first to slap, punch, stab, or in some other manner commit an assault" and

WEB EXTRA 9–2
LIBRARY EXTRA 9–6

Victim precipitation focuses on the characteristics of victims that may have precipitated their victimization.

that if the victim had not been drinking, he or she would have been less violent.[35] Wolfgang's research on homicide revealed that most victims of spousal homicide had been drinking at the time of the incident, a situation that did not apply to homicide offenders.[36] Learn more about victim precipitation at the Howard League for Penal Reform via **Web Extra 9–2**.

Weapon Use

As previously noted, there are different perspectives on the role that weapons play in crime, with most of the discussion centering on the role of firearms in homicide. In examining the relationship between guns and homicide, Philip J. Cook and Mark H. Moore differentiated between instrumentality and availability. *Instrumentality* refers to the fact that the type of weapon used in a particular encounter has an effect on whether the encounter ends in death. For example, the involvement of a gun may mean the difference between a criminal event ending as an assault or as a homicide—when guns are used in robberies, the fatality rate is "three times as high as for robberies with knives and 10 times as high as for robberies with other weapons."[37] However, Cook and Moore warned, an examination of fatality rates in isolation does not necessarily support the idea that the involvement of a gun caused the fatality because other factors, such as the intent of the offender, must be considered; offenders may select a weapon on the basis of their intent, and those who take more lethal weapons to a crime may be more prepared to use deadly force.

Availability refers to issues surrounding how access to guns may increase their presence in all types of interactions, including criminal ones. As Cook and Moore argued, "Availability can be thought of relative to time, expense, and other costs."[38] The ease of availability of guns is important both at the individual level, because some violent encounters are relatively spontaneous, and at the community level, because a greater presence of guns in a neighborhood provides easier access for individuals outside their immediate households. Cook and Moore explained that gun availability is a much stronger factor in explaining lethal violence than gun instrumentality and recommended that "rather than a general effort to get guns off the streets, a more focused effort can

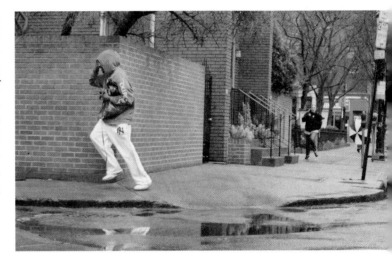

A purse snatcher (green jacket) running off with his loot. Why do victimologists suggest that some people contribute to their own victimization?
Source: AP Photo/The Inquirer/Elizabeth Robertson

be directed at prohibiting guns in particularly dangerous locations such as homes with histories of domestic violence, bars with histories of drunken brawls, parks in which gang fights tend to break out, and schools in which teachers and students have been assaulted."[39] See **Library Extra 9–6** for more information.

Alcohol and Drug Use

An important conceptual typology detailing the relationship between alcohol or drugs and crime was developed by Paul J. Goldstein in an article first published in 1985.[40] According to Goldstein, the association of alcohol and illicit drugs with violent offending generally takes one of three forms: psychopharmacological use, economic compulsion, and systemic violence. Drugs may be linked to violent offending through *psychopharmacological use*, whereby infrequent or chronic use of certain drugs produces violent behavior by lowering inhibitions or elevating aggressive tendencies; however, not all drugs produce such effects, and the relationship appears to hold only for people with certain types of personalities using certain substances in certain settings.

When crimes are committed to support a drug habit, Goldstein said that the concept of *economic compulsion* best describes the relationship between crime and drug use. He used the idea of *systemic violence* to describe the connection between drugs and

CRIMINAL | PROFILES
Dennis Rader (the BTK Killer)

He "hid for more than 30 years in plain sight."[i] That's how a leading news service described Wichita, Kansas, serial killer Dennis Rader's evasion of capture for more than three decades. Rader, the self-proclaimed BTK killer ("BTK" being a nickname he gave himself to denote his propensity to "Bind, Torture, and Kill" his victims), lived a normal, rather mundane existence with his wife and two children, all the while concealing his second persona: a murderous predator. His "front" included his ordinance enforcement officer job in the Wichita suburb of Park City, service as a Cub Scout troop leader, and active participation in his Lutheran church.[ii]

Rader was born March 9, 1945, the eldest of four brothers. After high school, he did a four-year stint in the U.S. Air Force before returning to Park City, where he completed an undergraduate degree in administration of justice at Wichita State University in 1979. Beginning in 1974, Rader worked in a variety of positions at ADT Security Services over the next 14 years.[iii] It was also in 1974 that Rader committed the first of what eventually became ten grisly murders.

His initial murderous foray occurred mid-morning on January 15, 1974, when Rader killed four members of the Otero family: dad Joseph, mom Julie, 11-year-old Josephine, and 9-year-old Joseph II. Each victim was subjected to various acts of torture before ultimately being strangled. The bodies were discovered when 15-year-old Charlie Otero returned from school later that afternoon.[iv]

The shocking murders were only the start of a long criminal career. Kathryn Bright, 20, was stabbed to death just three months later, on April 4, 1974. Amazingly, her 19-year-old brother, Kevin, survived the attack despite being shot twice in the head.

Almost three years elapsed before BTK struck again on March 17, 1977, by strangling 26-year-old Shirley Vian. Uncharacteristically, BTK locked the three young Vian children in the closet and allowed them to survive. Just nine months later, on December 8, 1977, police found Nancy Jo Fox, 25, dead in her bedroom, strangled with a nylon stocking. BTK's final three killings occurred on April 27, 1985 (Marine Hedge), September 16, 1986 (Vicki Wegerle), and January 18, 1991 (Dolores Davis); all were strangled.[v]

A strange component of the BTK murders was the way the killer periodically wrote taunting letters to the local police and newspapers.[vi] The frequency of the BTK letters decreased by the end of the 1980s, as he apparently became dormant. In 1991, Rader became a Park City Compliance Officer,[vii] where he developed a reputation as a by-the-book "bureaucratic bully."[viii]

In March 2004, new BTK letters began surfacing. Over the course of the next year, a total of 11 communications were received. One, a computer floppy disk, was forensically identified as having been used by

Convicted BTK killer Dennis Rader listening during a court proceeding on October 12, 2005, at the El Dorado Correctional Facility in El Dorado, Kansas. A judge recommended that Rader receive treatment as a sexual offender and have restrictions placed on what he can receive or do in prison while he serves the rest of his life in prison. Rader, a 60-year-old former church congregation president and Cub Scout leader, pleaded guilty in 2005 to ten murders that haunted Wichita over three decades. Why wasn't he caught sooner?
Source: Travis Heying/AP Wide World Photos

Rader's church and containing residue that included the name "Dennis." That disk directly led to Rader's arrest on February 25, 2005. At his arraignment on May 3, Rader stood mute, and a trial date of June 27 was set.

Rader subsequently surprised everyone when, on June 27, he confessed in open court to the murders of ten people. In response to direct questioning from the judge, Rader recounted in chillingly graphic and dispassionate detail exactly how he had killed each of the ten victims.

At a sentencing hearing on August 17 and 18, 2005, Rader received the harshest possible sentence under Kansas law when Judge Gregory Waller gave him ten life sentences to be served consecutively. The consecutive service provision means that Rader must serve a minimum of 175 years before becoming eligible for parole consideration.[ix]

Notes

i. "Neighbors Paint Mixed Picture of BTK Suspect," MSNBC, February 27, 2005, http://www.msnbc.msn.com/id/7036219 (accessed June 16, 2007).

ii. Ibid.

iii. Ibid.

iv. Marilyn Bardsley, Rachael Bell, and David Lohr, "BTK—Birth of a Serial Killer," CourtTV Crime Library, http://www.crimelibrary.com/serial_killers/unsolved/btk/index_1.html (accessed June 16, 2007).

v. Ibid.

vi. "Neighbors Paint Mixed Picture of BTK Suspect," MSNBC.

vii. "Report: Daughter of BTK Suspect Alerted Police," Cable News Network, April 19, 2005.

viii. Bardsley.

ix. *State of Kansas* v. *Dennis Rader*, Office of the Sedgwick County, Kansas, District Attorney Web site, February 1, 2006, http://www.sedgwickcounty.org/da (accessed June 16, 2010).

■ **selective disinhibition**
A loss of self-control due either to the social setting or to drugs
or alcohol, or a combination of both.

trafficking, and it can take several forms, ranging from rival drug wars to robberies of drug dealers. Although distinct types of relationships between drugs and violence can be described, these are not necessarily mutually exclusive, with one or more relationships present in a single criminal incident.

Researchers from the Drug Relationships in Murder Project (DREIM), which analyzed incarcerated homicide offenders in New York State, found that in the majority of homicide cases involving both alcohol and illicit drugs, the primary basis for the connection with the crime was psychopharmacological, which is not in line with Goldstein's research in New York.[41]

One theoretical approach focused on explaining the role that alcohol plays in homicide as social in nature rather than biochemical is **selective disinhibition**, advanced by Robert Nash Parker and others.[42] In particular situations or interactions, the "disinhibiting" effect of alcohol may operate to suspend certain factors that could restrain the occurrence of violence and may operate to put into play certain factors that could increase the occurrence or degree of violence. This perspective relies on the existence of norms operating both to prohibit and to proscribe the use of violence in particular situations. Because alcohol can reduce both forms of constraint, "the selective nature of alcohol-related homicide is dependent on the interaction of an impaired rationality and the nature of the social situation."[43] Parker and his colleagues tested this model by analyzing data on homicides in several cities in 1980, in several cities between 1960 and 1980, and in several states from 1976 to 1983. One key finding from this research was the ability of alcohol to significantly predict primary homicide. In relationships between individuals who are known to each other, alcohol may operate to disinhibit restraints against violence, but the norms that operate to govern interactions between strangers are more rigid in terms of the type of conduct that is proscribed. The use of violence against those known to us is treated with greater tolerance—tolerance that can be increased even more in the presence of alcohol.[44]

> The selective nature of alcohol-related homicide is dependent on the interaction of an impaired rationality and the nature of the social situation.

In his research using state-level data, Parker tested several hypotheses derived from competing theoretical perspectives about the effect of alcohol on homicide.[45] Based on the victim–offender relationship, five types of homicides were identified: "robbery, other felony, family intimate, family other, and primary nonintimate."[46] Poverty had a stronger effect on both robbery and other felony

homicides in states with "above average rates of alcohol consumption";[47] alcohol consumption had direct effects on two of the three types of primary homicide.

Gangs

Gang membership may influence homicide in a number of ways. Analyzing data from Los Angeles, researchers found several differences between homicides involving gang members and those involving nongang members: Gang homicides were more likely to involve minority males, to make use of guns, to occur in public places, and to involve victims and offenders with no prior relationship.[48] Richard Rosenfeld and colleagues stated that the association of gangs and homicide may be one of two general types: (1) gang-motivated violence, in which violent crime is the direct result of gang activity, and (2) gang-affiliated violence, in which individual gang members are involved in crime but not as a purposeful result of gang activity.[49] Using data from St. Louis, these researchers compared cases of gang-motivated homicide with gang-affiliated homicide and nongang youth homicide. Across all three homicide types, African American males were more likely to be participants, and there was very little difference in the neighborhood context because all three types of homicides clustered in disadvantaged communities whose populations were predominantly African American. While gang-motivated homicides declined in the early 1990s, gang-affiliated homicides rose, leading the researchers to conclude that their continued increase

Los Angeles gang members showing off their weapons. Scott Decker applied Colin Loftin's theory of violence as a contagion to the processes that are put in play as more gang members begin to carry guns. How does Loftin view assaultive violence as a contagious social process?
Source: Daniel Laine/CORBIS-NY

■ **serial murder**
A type of criminal homicide that involves the killing of several victims in three or more separate events.

■ **mass murder**
The illegal killing of four or more victims at one location within one event.

"results from increased involvement of gang members—not gangs—in the drug trade."[50]

Serial Murder

In 2009, 50-year-old Cleveland resident Anthony Sowell was arrested and charged with luring eleven women into his house, raping, and then killing them.[51] As this book goes to press, Sowell faces 85 counts of murder, rape, and kidnapping but has pleaded not guilty by reason of insanity. In 1989, 20 years before his latest arrest, Sowell had pleaded guilty to attempted rape, had served 15 years in prison before being released in 2005, and had been living as a registered sex offender after his release.[52]

Serial murder is a criminal homicide that "involves the killing of several victims in three or more separate events."[53] Our fascination with serial killers is based on our disbelief that seemingly ordinary individuals could commit such atrocities. Both seedy losers and charismatic, charming, handsome college men (like Ted Bundy) are found among serial killers, but "there is one trait that appears to separate serial killers from the norm: many are exceptionally skillful in their presentation of self so that they are beyond suspicion and thus are difficult to apprehend."[54] One

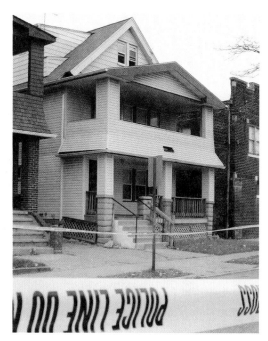

The home of alleged serial killer Anthony Sowell on Imperial Avenue in Cleveland. In 2009, the remains of 11 murder victims were found in and around Sowell's house. Why did it take so long to stop Sowell's string of homicides?
Source: Jason L. Nelson/AdMedia/NewsCom.com

factor that makes it difficult to identify serial killers, even with modern technology, is that these individuals often change the pattern of their offending, including their method of killing.[55]

James Alan Fox and **Jack Levin** have written extensively on both serial killing and **mass murder** (the illegal killing of four or more victims at one location in one event). They offer ten myths of serial murder: (1) Serial murder is at epidemic proportions, (2) serial killers have a distinct appearance, (3) all serial killers are insane, (4) all serial killers are sociopaths, (5) serial killers are primarily motivated by pornography, (6) traumatic childhoods are at the root of most serial killers' problems, (7) identification of serial killers prior to killing occurs is a straightforward task, (8) serial killers are primarily sexual sadists, (9) the victim's resemblance to a family member (usually the killer's mother) is the primary source of victim selection, and (10) serial killers want to be apprehended.[56] While annual figures as high as 5,000 victims of serial killers have been cited, this figure was based on both the erroneous assumption that killings without a motive were attributable to serial killers and an accumulation of cases over time;[57] more reasonable estimates suggest that perhaps 100 murders each year are the result of serial killings.[58] While serial killers have been found in different age groups and races and both genders, the more typical serial killer is "a white male in his late twenties or thirties who targets strangers at or near his place of residence or work."[59] While acknowledging that the motivations for serial homicide are numerous, Fox and Levin contended that "murder is a form of expressive rather than instrumental violence."[60] Unlike homicide generally, serial killing is more likely to involve strangers and rarely involves the use of guns.

Many serial killers are diagnosed as *sociopaths*, a term for those with antisocial personalities who lack a conscience. Sociopaths do not consider the needs or basic humanity of others, do not see themselves as being bound by conventional rules or the expectations of others, and view other people as "tools to be manipulated for the purpose of maximizing their personal pleasure."[61] However, many sociopaths are not serial killers or involved in violent crime, even though "they may lie, cheat, or steal."[62] (Sociopaths are also discussed in Chapter 5.)

Although not an exclusive characteristic of serial killers, sexual sadism is a strong pattern and often forms the basis for a type of serial killer. Ronald Holmes and J. DeBurger developed a taxonomy based on an analysis of 400 cases that had four different types of serial killers differentiated by offender motivation, selection of victim, expected gain, and method of murder.[63]

Refining the typology of Holmes and DeBurger, Fox and Levin offered a three-part typology for serial murderers: thrill motivated, mission oriented, or expedience directed. *Thrill-motivated serial killers*, the most common type of serial

DeFronzo, show a positive relationship with the incidence and location of serial killings.

Female Serial Killers

Although the vast majority of serial killers are male, there have been female serial killers, and the patterns of their activities are sometimes distinct from those of male serialists.[66] Female serial killers typically select their victims from among people known to them, but male serial killers tend to target strangers.[67] A type of serial killer found primarily among women is the *disciple killer*, who murders as the result of the influence of a charismatic personality; women who killed at the behest of Charles Manson were this type. The geographic area in which serial killers operate may be either stable or transient, with no clear preference among male serial killers, but geographic stability characterizes almost all known female serial killers.[68]

Michael D. Kelleher and C. L. Kelleher researched female serial killers from a historical perspective. Arguing that there are two broad categories of female serial killers—those who act alone and those who work in partnership with others—Kelleher and Kelleher presented a typology based on distinct motivation, selection of victim, and method of killing.[69] The categories include the *black widow*, who generally kills a spouse (usually for economic profit), and the *angel of death*, who generally kills "those in her care or who rely on her for some form of medical attention or similar support."[70] The typical career of a female serial killer is longer than that of her male counterpart, possibly because she tends to approach her crimes in a systematic fashion.[71]

> Female serial killers typically select their victims from among people known to them.

Apprehension of Serial Killers

Fox and Levin contended that it is extremely difficult to identify and apprehend serial killers because of the cautiousness and skill with which they operate—the very factors that allow them to kill often enough to be labeled *serial killers*. The FBI established the **Violent Criminal Apprehension Program (VICAP)** in 1985 to increase the efficiency and effectiveness of serial killer apprehension. Although Fox and Levin called VICAP an "excellent concept in theory," they noted several practical problems with the program.[72] First, the data complexity and the associated record keeping have limited compliance by law enforcement officials, seriously affecting VICAP's potential usefulness; second, the recognition of patterns among serial killers, even with the assistance of powerful computers, is not easily achieved; and third, VICAP functions more as a detection tool than an apprehension tool.

Gary L. Ridgway, age 54, the self-confessed Green River strangler. Ridgway, reputed to be the nation's worst captured serial killer, admitted to killing 48 women over a 20-year period in the Pacific Northwest. He is now serving life in prison without possibility of parole. Why did it take so long to stop Ridgway?
Source: *Elaine Thompson/AP Wide World Photos*

killer, may be either a sexual sadist or a dominance killer. *Mission-oriented serial killers* generally have either a reformist or a visionary orientation. Reformists want to rid the world of evil; visionaries, who are quite rare and tend to be genuinely psychotic, hear voices commanding them to do certain activities. *Expedience-directed serial killers* are driven by profit or protection. Profit-driven killers may kill for financial or material gain, and protection-oriented killers commit murder to mask other crimes, such as robbery.[64]

Although many studies of serial killers have highlighted their psychological characteristics, James DeFronzo and his coresearchers pointed out that the incidence of male serial killers varies widely among the U.S. states—ranging from a high of 18.6 serial killers per 10 million residents in California to a low of 3.4 per 10 million in Pennsylvania.[65] A sociological examination of demographic factors—the availability of vulnerable targets, the percentage of a state's population living in urban areas, the percentage of the state's divorced population, and the percentage of households with only one person—could help explain such differences. These kinds of sociological variables, according to

In addition to VICAP, the FBI employs profilers who assist local law enforcement. Employing classification system based on two prongs, FBI profiling theory distinguishes between organized social killers and disorganized asocial killers. Organized social killers have a higher level of intelligence, better social skills, and a greater ability to function in all areas of life than do disorganized killers. These two types also differ in their method of killing—although variation exists among them, the "organized/disorganized continuum is used as an overall guideline for drawing inferences from the crime scene to the behavioral characteristics of the killer."[73] More recent attempts to identify serial killers rely on geomapping techniques to approximate the killer's probable location.[74] Learn more about serial killers from the FBI's Behavioral Analysis Unit via **Web Extra 9–3**.

Mass Murder

Mass murder refers to the killing of more than three individuals at a single time.[75] Mass murder can be based on either political motivations, as when Timothy McVeigh carried out the 1995 Oklahoma City bombing, or personal reasons, like the mass killing at L'Ecole Polytechnique in Montreal on December 6, 1989, by Marc Lepine, who hated women (feminists in particular). Mass murders are a shock because they often occur in everyday locales that are thought of as safe and because they erupt spontaneously. Although mass murders do not occur with great frequency, they cause great concern because they shatter the sense of safety that characterizes everyday life.

Levin and Fox offered a four-part typology of mass murder—revenge, love, profit, and terror—that differentiates these crimes by motive and further subdivides them by "victim–offender relationship, degree of planning, and randomness and state of mind of the perpetrator."[76] Mass murders motivated by *revenge* represent the largest category and may be against either particular individuals or groups of individuals. For example, George Hennard hated "all of the residents of the county in which he lived," so in 1991 he drove his truck through the front window of Luby's Cafeteria in Killeen, Texas, and then "indiscriminately opened fire on customers as they ate their lunch, killing 23."[77]

Serial killer Aileen Wuornos, who was executed by the state of Florida in 2002 after refusing further appeals. Although some women are moving into areas of traditional male criminality, the number of women committing violent crimes is still far smaller than the number of men. How does the criminality of women appear to differ from that of men?
Source: *Daytona Beach News Journal*/CORBIS-NY

Some mass murders are motivated by *love* (but not in the way most individuals would define *love*), whereas mass murders motivated by *profit* may result when the killer wants to eliminate witnesses to a crime. Mass murders motivated by *terror* include the killings by people like those in the Charles Manson family. Levin and Fox explained that mass murders motivated by revenge or love are expressive in nature and those motivated by profit and terror are more instrumental because there is some concrete goal to be achieved through the killings.[78]

Although most mass murders strike the public as senseless acts of a crazy person, Levin and Fox contended that "most massacrers are not madmen."[79] Yet why would someone like James Huberty, a former security guard, walk calmly into a fast-food restaurant in

■ **Violence against Women Act (VAWA)**
A federal law enacted as a component of the 1994 Violent Crime Control and Law Enforcement Act intended to address concerns about violence against women. The law focused on improving the interstate enforcement of protection orders, providing effective training for court personnel involved with women's issues, improving the training and collaboration of police and prosecutors with victim-services providers, strengthening law enforcement efforts to reduce violence against women, and increasing services to victims of violence. VAWA was reauthorized by Congress in 2000 and 2005.

■ **National Violence against Women (NVAW) Survey**
A national survey of the extent and nature of violence against women conducted between November 1995 and May 1996 funded through grants from the National Institute of Justice and the U.S. Department of Health and Human Services National Center for Injury Prevention and Control.

1984 and fatally shoot 21 victims at random, most of whom were children? Why would Patrick Edward Purdy shoot and kill 5 children and wound 30 others at Cleveland Elementary School in Stockton, California, in 1989?[80] Levin and Fox argued that factors like frustration, isolation, blame, loss, and failure, as well as other external and internal motivations and situational elements, help make sense of these mass murders, and they delineate three types of contributing factors: "*predisposers*, long-term and stable preconditions that become incorporated into the personality of the killer, which are nearly always present in his biography; *precipitants*, short-term and acute triggers, i.e., catalysts; and *facilitators*, conditions, usually situational, which increase the likelihood of a violent outburst but are not necessary to produce that response."[81] Using this typology to explain why most mass murderers are middle-aged, Levin and Fox contended that it takes a long time to accumulate the kind of rage and frustration that set off some mass murderers. Mass murderers also select targets that have some significance for them, such as workers at a site of former employment. "A majority of mass killers target victims who are specially chosen, not just in the wrong place at the wrong time. The indiscriminate slaughter of strangers by a 'crazed' killer is the exception to the rule."[82] Unlike serial murderers, mass murderers are easy to apprehend because they rarely leave the scene of their crime—either they commit suicide after the killings or they stay long enough to be detected.

In 2010, Australian forensic psychiatrist Paul Mullen identified a type of mass murderer whom he referred to as a *pseudocommando*.[83] Pseudocommandos, according to Mullen, are driven by strong feelings of anger and resentment and can be thought of as "collectors of injustices," retreating into a life of fantasy filled with dreams of violence and revenge.[84] Although most pseudocommandos plan their attacks (usually with an arsenal of powerful weapons), they have no plan of escape and generally believe they will die in the attack they plan to carry out. Mullen examined five pseudocommandos who were caught before they could take their own lives and found that these people seek to indiscriminately kill members of the public and that they may kill their own family members as well. Public attacks were designed as payback for perceived injustices and often targeted the source of the injustice; Joseph A. Stack, the software engineer who demonized the IRS and flew his gasoline-laden private airplane into an IRS-occupied building in Austin, Texas, in 2010 would be categorized as a pseudocommando (see his story in Chapter 7).

Rape

The violent crime of rape has generated much discussion and controversy over the years. To understand why, we must examine the changing legal definitions of *rape*, our societal understanding of it, variations in the ways in which theoretical explanations of rape have evolved, and the development of rapist typologies. Concerns with improving the social, legal, medical, and social service response to rape were at the forefront of changes that have brought greater awareness of the extent and nature of violence against women. The significant evolution of this awareness is evidenced by federal legislation first enacted in 1994 and known as the **Violence against Women Act (VAWA)**, which was reauthorized in 2000 and 2005. (Additional information on VAWA is available in Chapter 14.)

Attempts to measure the extent of rape have occupied many different researchers across various disciplines, which explains why findings vary across research studies. There is no agreement on the number of women who are raped each year;[85] the final number is determined by how rapes are counted and what data sources are used. According to the FBI's UCR Program, 88,097 completed or attempted rapes were reported to the police in 2009, and an estimated 56.6 of every 100,000 females in the country were reported victims of forcible rape.[86] However, the ability of official statistics to accurately assess the incidence of rape is hampered by lack of victim reporting—most rapes are not reported to the police. Information reported from victims in the NCVS reveals 198,850 rape incidents during 2006, or almost 2 attempted or completed rapes for every 1,000 residents age 12 or older.[87] Other problems with both measurement of rape and disclosure to researchers by victims also characterize the NCVS data and have led several researchers to question the accuracy of rape incidence based on these data.[88] The best measure of the prevalence of rape comes from the **National Violence against Women (NVAW) Survey**, which reported that 17.6% of women experienced either a completed or an attempted rape at some point during their lifetime; the prevalence rate for one year was 0.3% for attempted and completed rapes combined, translating to slightly

> Almost 18% of women are sexually assaulted at some point during their lifetime.

LIBRARY EXTRA 9–7

■ **rape myth**
A false assumption about rape, such as "When a woman says no, she really means yes." Rape myths characterize much of the discourse surrounding sexual violence.

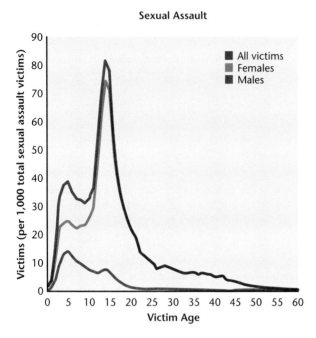

FIGURE 9–4 | Sexual Assault Victimization Rates by Age and Sex

Source: Office of Juvenile Justice and Delinquency Prevention, *Juvenile Offenders and Victims: 2006 National Report* (Washington, DC: OJJDP, 2006), p. 31.

more than 300,000 rape victims and 876,064 rape incidents annually in the population.[89] As Figure 9–4 shows, the risk of sexual assault varies greatly by age as well as sex. The lifetime likelihood of being the victim of a violent crime or the victim of a particular violent crime is higher because risk accumulates over time. See **Library Extra 9–7**.

Rape Myths

The ability to capture the extent of sexual violence against women remains hampered by sociocultural factors that contribute to underreporting. **Rape myths** are false assumptions about rape that continue to characterize much of the discourse surrounding sexual violence: that women bring false rape charges to get even with men, that women bring rape upon themselves by wearing provocative clothing, that women are "asking for it" by going to bars alone, and that women say no when they really mean yes. In 1980, Martha R. Burt first began re-

> Rape myths are false assumptions about rape that characterize much of the discourse surrounding sexual violence.

searching rape myth ideology;[90] since then, numerous other studies have supported widespread acceptance of these myths.[91] Rape myths serve to undermine the traumatic nature of this offense. As feminists have long argued, rape myths serve to discount the experiences of women by placing stereotypical parameters around who can and who cannot be raped. Rape myths inhibit the reporting of rape and normalize rape as a crime of violence.[92] Largely as a result of such myths, women continue to report that the criminal justice system does not respond with sensitivity and compassion toward their victimization.

The Common Law Definition of Rape

Rape myths both fueled and supported the common law understanding of rape. Until the 1970s in the United States, rape was a common law offense, the "carnal knowledge of a woman not one's wife by force or against her will." Although rape was clearly understood as a crime under the common law, it was a crime in which the legitimacy of the victim as a victim was challenged. The common law did not recognize men as victims, did not recognize rape within marriage, did not allow for acts of sexual penetration other than vaginal penetration by a penis, and did not allow for various means by which force could occur. Moreover, the rules of evidence required that the victim who brought a rape charge must demonstrate physical resistance to the attack and must have some form of corroboration that the rape occurred, and the victim's previous sexual history could be admitted as relevant information.

Rape-Law Reform

Rape-law reform aimed to make the legal understanding of rape compatible with other violent crimes. Characterized as the "second rape," rape investigations (especially at the trial stage) too often exposed the victim to further trauma rather than focusing on assessing offender culpability.[93] Feminist groups, at the forefront of organized efforts to bring about rape-law reform, were joined by law enforcement officials and prosecutors who supported efforts "to remove obstacles to the apprehension and conviction of offenders."[94] In 1975, Michigan became the first state to dramatically redefine *rape* to encompass a broader range of sexually assaultive behaviors, circumstances, and victims; other states followed Michigan's lead, and by 1992, all states had made significant statutory changes to the common law offense defini-

■ **rape shield law**
A statute providing for the protection of rape victims by ensuring that defendants do not introduce irrelevant facts about victims' sexual history into evidence.

WEB EXTRA 9–4
LIBRARY EXTRA 9–8

the **PROFESSOR** | **SPEAKS**
Crime Statistics and Patterns

MARY ALTANI KARPOS

Vanderbilt University

VANDERBILT UNIVERSITY

People frequently argue that statistics can be made to say anything, and to some degree, that may be true. The Uniform Crime Report (UCR) is widely considered a valuable resource for quantifying crime in the United States, but its method of counting crimes makes it vulnerable to manipulation. The UCR collects the number of "known" crimes from law enforcement agencies across the country; however, all agencies have the right to "unfind" (not count) any activities they believe are not credible. Simply put, agencies have the ability to increase and decrease the "known" crimes in their jurisdiction by changing their "finding" process. This can make a particular agency appear to be highly efficient at stopping crime or to be in need of more resources to stop crime waves.

tion of *rape*.[95] **Cassia Spohn** and **Julie Horney**, two of the most prolific researchers in the area of rape-law reform, identified four common themes in all rape-law reforms:[96]

1. Redefining *rape* and replacing the single crime of rape with a series of graded offenses defined by the presence or absence of aggravating conditions

2. Changing the consent standard by eliminating the requirement that the victim physically resist the attacker

3. Eliminating the requirement that the victim's testimony be corroborated

4. Placing restrictions on the introduction of evidence of the victim's prior sexual conduct

In some states, sweeping changes were made to existing rape statutes.[97] Michigan was considered the model for rape-law reform; in other states (like Texas), legal reform was more gradual, with slight changes being made to statutes in a step-by-step fashion. Jurisdictions also varied in how the legal redefinition of *rape* occurred, with many states adopting a tiered approach, renaming the offense *sexual assault* of varying levels, intended to more fully capture the violent nature of the crime.

Individual rape-law reform in states and at the federal level proceeded in different routes via **rape shield laws**, intended to protect rape victims by ensuring that defendants did not introduce irrelevant facts about victims' sexual past into evidence.

Prior to the 1970s, no guidelines prevented the defense from bringing into evidence a victim's sexual history as a way to discredit her and to use to rape myth ideology. The rape shield laws varied in the amount of a judge's discretion regarding the type of evidence that could be introduced but were necessary and sent the message that the courts would no longer be party to a "second rape" on the victim.[98]

A number of expectations attached to rape-law reform. Spohn and Horney identified four general changes that were anticipated in the wake of rape law reform.[99] First, an increase in the reporting of rapes was expected because legal reforms would mean that victims would receive more sympathetic and effective treatment within the criminal justice system. Second, the reforms were expected to produce symbolic change that would emphasize the violent nature of rape. Third, legal reforms were expected to alter the decision-making structure of the criminal justice system by eliminating the consideration of extralegal evidence (for example, what the victim was wearing). Finally, reform was expected to remove the barriers preventing more effective prosecution and higher conviction rates for rape. Learn more about rape-law reform at **Web Extra 9–4** and **Library Extra 9–8**.

Effects of Rape-Law Reform

What have been the effects of rape-law reform? Have the reforms changed the way rape cases are handled by the criminal justice system? Have legal changes altered the social landscape

CRIMINAL | PROFILES
Karla Homolka

On October 17, 1987, then-17-year-old Karla Homolka met then-23-year-old Paul Bernardo in an Ontario hotel restaurant.[i] Their physical attraction was immediate and intense, and two hours later the couple had sex in one of the hotel's rooms.

Unbeknownst to Homolka, handsome, boy-next-door Paul Bernardo had already embarked on a clandestine career as a serial rapist. In May of 1987, Bernardo raped a young woman in Scarborough, a small suburban town northeast of Toronto on the shores of Lake Ontario. Hers was to be the first of at least 14 rapes that the man dubbed the "Scarborough Rapist" would admit to committing during the next five years. Additionally, he was convicted of murdering two of his rape victims.[ii]

As the relationship between Bernardo and Homolka evolved, Bernardo began to assert increasingly outrageous sexual demands with which Homolka willingly complied. Eventually, he expressed his annoyance that she had not been a virgin when he first met her. To resolve the problem, Homolka arranged to present Bernardo her own virgin younger sister, Tammy, as a Christmas gift. On December 23, 1990, then 15-year-old Tammy was fed alcohol laced with the sedative Halcion. When Tammy passed out, Bernardo raped and sodomized her while Homolka kept a drug-laced rag over Tammy's face to maintain her unconscious state. Both Bernardo and Homolka videotaped the rape as it was occurring, including Tammy's death at the end of the incident.[iii]

When Bernardo later complained to Homolka that she had cost him future sexual opportunities with Tammy by allowing her to die, Homolka found a replacement virgin whom she offered to Bernardo as a prewedding gift. Homolka invited a 15-year-old family acquaintance to dinner at the house she had rented with Bernardo. As with Tammy, the girl was fed Halcion until she became unconscious. Bernardo then videotaped Homolka performing sexual acts on the sleeping girl, then raped and brutally sodomized the girl as Homolka videotaped his acts.[iv]

On June 14, 1991, Bernardo abducted 14-year-old Leslie Mahaffy and brought her back to the house he shared with Homolka. After stripping and blindfolding the terrified girl, Bernardo woke his future wife and proceeded to act as a movie director while videotaping Homolka performing lesbian sexual acts on Mahaffy. Homolka then took over the camera while Bernardo initiated a violent assault on the young girl, including brutal anal rape. Bernardo's violence continued to escalate until Mahaffy finally died. The two then dismembered her body and dumped the parts into Lake Ontario.[v]

Bernardo and Homolka married on June 29, 1991, and Bernardo continued his campaign of rape, often with Homolka's encouragement and assistance. At least one victim recalled seeing a woman videotaping her rape.

On April 16, 1992, the married rapists/killers abducted 16-year-old Kristen French from the parking lot outside of French's church. They

A courtroom sketch of notorious Canadian sex criminal Karla Homolka as she appeared in court in Joliette, Quebec, on June 3, 2005. She was set free after having served 12 years in prison for helping her former husband rape and murder three teenage girls, including her younger sister. Homolka remarried following release and is the mother of a baby boy; she lives under the name Leanne Teale. Why are female sex killers so rare?

Source: Reuters/Marianne Boucher/Landov Media

then raped, tortured, and murdered the pretty young girl and left her nude body in a roadside ditch.

DNA evidence finally led to Bernardo's arrest on February 17, 1993. Homolka agreed to testify against him in exchange for a sentence of just 12 years for her role as an accomplice.

In July 1993, Homolka pleaded guilty and her sentence, as agreed to in the plea bargain, was pronounced. Controversy exploded, however, when the numerous videotapes of the rapes and murders surfaced in September 1994, and the public became aware of the full extent of Homolka's willing participation in the atrocities.[vi]

Bernardo was convicted of the two murders on September 15, 1995, and was sentenced to life in prison without possibility of parole. Public ire again boiled over following Homolka's release from prison on parole on July 4, 2005, when it became known that Homolka was complaining about the postrelease restrictions to which she was subjected. In February 2007, the Canadian media reported that Homolka, with a new husband and a new name—Leanne Teale—had given birth to a baby boy.[vii]

Notes

i. Posted by Her Karma on Vancouver Forum, the Discover Vancouver Bulletin Board, July 3, 2005, http://www.discovervancouver.com/forum/topic.asp?TOPIC_ID521791&whichpage52 (accessed May 28, 2007).

ii. Marilyn Bardsley, "Paul Bernardo and Karla Homolka." CourtTV Crime Library, http://www.crimelibrary.com/serial_killers/notorious/bernardo/index_1.html (accessed May 28, 2007).

iii. Anne M. Griffy, "The Evil Within: The Twisted Minds of Paul Bernardo and Karla Homolka," Justice Junction, http://www.justicejunction.com/judicial_injustice_the_evil_within.htm (accessed May 27, 2007).

iv. Ibid.

v. Ibid.

vi. iLinda Diebel, "Professor Alan Young on Karla Homolka's Deal," Toronto Star, May 28, 2005, http://osgoode.yorku.ca/media2.nsf/83303ffe5af03ed585256ae6005379c9/47f95c9ce0cae54385257011007096ca!OpenDocument (accessed May 28, 2007).

vii. "Victims' Families 'Distressed' Over Homolka Baby: Lawyer," CBC News, February 13, 2007, http://www.cbc.ca/canada/montreal/story/2007/02/13/homolka-baby.html (accessed May 28, 2007).

■ **acquaintance rape**
A rape characterized by a prior social, though not necessarily intimate or familial, relationship between the victim and the perpetrator.

enough to affect the reporting behavior of rape victims? Questions like these, which highlight some of the goals of rape-law reform, have been addressed in research by Spohn and Horney focused on rape-law reform.[100] The researchers selected six urban jurisdictions—three areas of strong legal reform and three areas of weaker reform—in which to evaluate rape-law reform, expecting that the effects would be most dramatic in areas where reforms had been comprehensive and strong (where the entire rape statute had been revised and where elements of reform, such as the rape shield laws, offered little discretion to judges). Spohn and Horney analyzed data from court records of all processed rape cases and collected all police reports of rape in the six jurisdictions from 1970 through 1984. To assess the impact of rape-law reform, the researchers looked at changes in several outcome measures: the reporting of rapes to the police, the indictment of rape cases by prosecutors, and the conviction rates for offenders. In addition to statistical analysis of cases and reports, the researchers conducted interviews with a sample of more than 150 judges, prosecutors, and defense attorneys.[101]

While their findings supported the hypothesis that the impact of rape-law reform would be most pronounced in jurisdictions characterized by strong reform, there was far from uniform support. Detroit, Michigan, one of the three jurisdictions with strong reforms, did accomplish some expected ends, such as an increase in reports, indictments, and convictions, but other expected outcomes of reform, such as a greater percentage of convicted rape offenders being sentenced to incarceration, did not materialize. In jurisdictions like Illinois, where reform efforts were less strong, the effects of reform were weak to nonexistent on all outcome measures used. Jurisdictions with weak reforms, like Houston, saw significant increases in reports of rape following reform implementation—an effect not seen in Philadelphia, a jurisdiction implementing stronger reforms.[102]

One of the common findings in this type of study is that new legislation has only a limited effect on changing the behavior of courtroom work groups unless they embrace the reforms or unless the reforms actually force instrumental changes.[103] Spohn and Horney stated that "reformers should find encouragement in some evidence for the effectiveness of rape shield laws. Officials in all jurisdictions rated evidence relating to a complainant's sexual history low in importance."[104] Spohn and Horney concluded with the key observation that legal reforms take time to produce large-scale change and that rape-law reforms must be continually evaluated for evidence of how much change is occurring.

The Social Context of Rape

Although rape can occur in almost any social context, certain social situations are characterized by a higher prevalence of rape and by a difference in the offender's motivation; they are described in this section.

Acquaintance Rape

The vast majority of rapes are **acquaintance rapes**, meaning the victim and the offender have some prior relationship (though not necessarily an intimate or a familial one); this type of rape is often referred to as a "hidden crime" because it represents a type of sexual assault that is not reported to the police and that is quite susceptible to rape myth ideology.

Among adults, acquaintance rape usually occurs within the context of a dating relationship, so a great deal of empirical research has focused on the college setting, and researchers have identified college campuses as places that typically have a high incidence of rape. E. J. Kanin reported in a 1957 *American Journal of Sociology* article that as many as 20% of college women had experienced either a completed or an attempted rape;[105] however, societal awareness and concern for rape on college campuses did not emerge until the 1980s. Helping to publicize the problem have been a number of high-profile rape cases on college campuses in which the victims not only went public with their experiences but also grabbed headlines and the covers of major publications like *Time, Newsweek*, and *People*.[106] Media publicity has emphasized the reality of the college setting as a site of rape, and in 1992 the Campus Sexual Assault Victims' Bill of Rights Act became law.[107] It requires campus authorities to "conduct appropriate disciplinary hearings, treat sexual assault victims and defendants with respect, making their rights and legal options clear, and cooperate with them in fully exercising those rights."[108]

One of the most prolific researchers on rape (especially among college students) is **Mary P. Koss**; she and her colleagues found that approximately 28% of women reported having experienced an attempted or a completed rape since the age of 14.[109] Based on incidents occurring in the last 12 months, Koss calculated an incidence rate of 76 per 1,000 women, which was ten to 15 times the rate obtained with NCVS data.[110] Approximately 57% of the rapes involved dating partners, and 73% of the rape victims reported that the offender was drinking. Other studies on college campuses have found similarly high levels of rape and sexual assault.[111]

Much research on rape in college settings has focused on

> The vast majority of rapes are acquaintance rapes.

WEB EXTRA 9–5
WEB EXTRA 9–6
WEB EXTRA 9–7

■ **spousal rape**
A rape of one spouse by the other. The term usually refers to the rape of a woman by her husband.

identifying the unique factors of campus life conducive to rape. Some researchers contended that college fraternities "create a sociocultural context in which the use of coercion in sexual relations with women is normative and in which the mechanisms to keep this pattern of behavior in check are minimal at best and absent at worst."[112] Rather than focusing on the pathological nature of individual males in fraternities, these researchers identified characteristics of the social organization of fraternities that contribute to the formation of attitudes and behaviors that objectify women and normalize sexual coercion: "a preoccupation with loyalty, group protection and security, use of alcohol as a weapon, involvement in violence and physical force, and an emphasis on competition and superiority."[113] Learn more about campus rape at **Web Extra 9–5**. You can visit the National Coalition against Violent Athletes via **Web Extra 9–6** and Mentors in Violence Prevention via **Web Extra 9–7**.

Marital Rape

As previously mentioned, under common law there was no such crime as **spousal rape**, so one of the most challenging aspects of rape-law reform was the elimination of the marital exemption for rape. In 1978, one year after Oregon removed the marital exemption from its rape statutes, John Rideout became the first American husband indicted for raping his wife.[114] Lisa M. Cuklanz examined the Rideout case and argued that the central issue in this case was the credibility of the new law.[115] The first case that goes to court under any new law should be as strong as possible, but the Rideout case did not fit this scenario. At the time of the Rideout case, evidence of the victim's sexual history was allowed, and such evidence damaged Greta Rideout's credibility as a rape victim and illustrated that "she was on trial as much as her husband." Cuklanz noted that in this case, the victim was tried first, "the law second, and the defendant third."[116] At the trial's conclusion, John Rideout was acquitted, and the Rideouts briefly reconciled before finally divorcing.

As Cuklanz noted in her analysis, media coverage of the Rideout case did not include commentary about the nature of marital rape that could have helped the audience understand the interactional dynamics of the case, so "character evidence underscored the validity of the traditional interpretation that posited confusion, manipulation, and personal gain as motives."[117]

In an article published in 1982, David Finkelhor and Kersti Yllo said that "the marriage license is a raping license."[118] The first research to systematically examine spousal rape was based on a random sample of 930 women in San Francisco in 1990 by **Diana E. H. Russell**:[119] Approximately 14% of women who had ever been married reported at least one attempted or completed rape by

their husbands. Based on an analysis of the interview data, Russell developed a four-part typology of men who rape their wives:[120]

1. Husbands who prefer raping their wives to having consensual sex with them
2. Husbands who are able to enjoy both rape and consensual sex with their wives or who are indifferent to which it is
3. Husbands who would prefer consensual sex with their wives but are willing to rape them when their sexual advances are refused
4. Husbands who might like to rape their wives but do not act out these desires

Rather than being one-dimensional, rape within marriage has several forms reflecting the various nuances of motivation on the part of offenders.

Rape in Prison

Correctional institutions provide a setting in which same-sex rape can be common. Charles Crawford, professor of sociology at Western Michigan University, referred to males who are sexually assaulted in prison as the "forgotten victims."[121] While the high prevalence of rape within prisons has been documented by prison researchers for some time, the victimization of prisoners does not raise the type of societal outrage reserved for crimes against "law-abiding" victims. Rape has been documented in both women's and men's prisons, but the patterns differ: Rape within women's prisons primarily takes the form of male staff attacking female inmates, whereas in men's prisons, the assaults involve only inmates. While precise estimates of the extent of rape in prison are difficult to develop because of lack of data, researchers who studied three prisons in Nebraska found that 22% of respondents reported to have been sexually assaulted.[122]

Theoretical Perspectives on Rape

Several theoretical perspectives have been offered to explain what the individual motivations for rape are, why rape is more prevalent in particular contexts, and how certain cultural values may reinforce rape. Many of these perspectives attempt to explain how rape is patterned according to the context, the victim–offender relationship, and the motivations of the rapist.

Feminist Perspectives

There is no one feminist perspective on rape, but some common elements run through the various feminist perspectives (also discussed in Chapter 8). Feminists view gender as a social construct rather than a biological given and regard as problematic the way in which gender is used to structure social relations and institutions. The patriarchal relations and structures within our society contributing to the privileged status of men are inseparable from rape itself because rape serves as a social control mechanism. Rape is viewed as an act of power or domination in which the "tool" used to subordinate is sexual—rape is a crime of violence that is sexual in nature, but this aspect is considered secondary to the power dynamics that occur in rapes.[123]

Socialization patterns, cultural practices, structural arrangements, media images, sexuality norms, and women's status in society all combine to create a rape culture in which both men and women come to view male aggression as normal, even in sexual relations.[124] Within this culture, women are blamed for their own rape by virtue of the fact that males are naturally incapable of controlling their sexual desire. For feminists like **Catherine MacKinnon**[125] and **Andrea Dworkin**,[126] rape and sex are not easily distinguishable under patriarchy because the male dominance that characterizes patriarchy is inherent in both the act of rape and the social construction of sex. Who women are and what women choose for themselves become problematic in the perspectives of these feminists because heterosexuality is "compulsory" under patriarchy. The views of feminists like MacKinnon and Dworkin are often met with resistance by others and are misunderstood as "male bashing." MacKinnon and Dworkin did not focus on individual males as somehow being either "good" or "bad" but on the construction of gender and all that flows from it under patriarchy. The work of Dworkin, MacKinnon, and others also stressed the existence of a rape culture that has the effect of equating sex with violence and objectifying women to the point that they lack an identity separate from that which is defined by men.

Pornography is often thought to contribute to the manner in which women are objectified because violence and sex are combined in a manner that makes the association normative. In an essay first published in 1974, Robin Morgan asserted that "pornography is the theory, and rape the practice."[127] Susan Brownmiller also discussed both pornography and prostitution as institutions that encourage and support social patterns and responses to rape.[128] While not everyone shares the same view of the role of pornography in supporting the inequality of women and justifying violence against women, pornography is frequently associated with rape in the writings and research of many prominent feminists.

James W. Messerschmidt acknowledged the positive contributions of feminist thought but critiqued these perspectives for their often one-dimensional view of masculinity.[129] Ngaire

Naffine also shared Messerschmidt's positive evaluation of this body of work, saying that "Dworkin is trying to shatter our complacency about everyday life for women, to get us to see the daily criminal violence and injustice done to women that has been rendered utterly ordinary and so invisible."[130] Messer-schmidt also contended that the response of the state to violence against women is not monolithic; while there are limits to how the state will respond in behalf of women, the state is viable as a site for positive change in terms of women and feminist ideals, and the emergence of rape crisis centers and changes in institutional protocol regarding rape victims illustrate that a state that is basically patriarchal in nature can be pushed to respond to women in ways that are positive and that increase women's autonomy.

> Pornography and prostitution are institutions that support social patterns and responses to rape.

Psychopathological Perspective

The psychopathological perspective on rape is based on two assumptions: (1) Rape is the "result of idiosyncratic mental disease," and (2) "it often includes an uncontrollable sexual impulse."[131] Acknowledgment that rape is connected to issues like power and anger is found in the frequently cited work of **Nicholas Groth**[132] (other works also contained elements of this psychopathological perspective).[133] Some researchers claimed that Groth's model does not appear to successfully characterize the majority of men who rape, yet this model has been applied as if that were the case.[134] However, Russell did find elements of Groth's model to be useful in developing her own typology for men who rape within marriage.[135] Several of the factors that Groth identifies as important to understanding the motivation and pattern of rapes are found in other typologies of rapists.

Integrated Theory of Rape

Larry Baron and **Murray A. Straus** offered what they termed an "integrated theory of rape."[136] They combined elements from other theoretical explanations of rape into one model that posits that (1) support for legitimate violence, (2) higher levels of gender inequality, and (3) social disorganization combine to produce higher rape rates at the state level. The phrase "support for legitimate violence" refers to norms and institutional arrangements that serve to justify the expression of violence in certain contexts as normative.

"Higher levels of gender inequality" are related to rates of rape because as women's status in society improves, rape is challenged as a mechanism of social control over women. This occurs as socialization patterns change and as women attain positions of power within society. The connection between gender inequality and rape is supported in cross-cultural and anthropological research.[137]

The wording "social disorganization" refers to the inability of communities to sustain viable social institutions—institutions that serve as a buffer to all sorts of social ills, including criminal activity. Poverty alone is not enough to directly produce crime, but in the absence of other factors that strengthen institutional structures within communities, poverty is linked to crime by virtue of its association with other factors.

In a test of their theory at the state level, Baron and Straus found support for the direct effect of gender inequality on rape rates: The higher the level of gender inequality—a combination of several measures relating to economic indicators—the higher was a state's rape rate. They examined the direct effect of pornography and found that higher rates of pornography were associated with higher rates of rape within the state; high levels of social disorganization, measured by such things as residential mobility, percentage of female-headed households, and divorce rates, were also tied to increased rates of rape.[138]

Evolutionary/Biological Perspectives

Within the evolutionary perspective, "humanity is a product of evolution in which both physical and social traits conducive to survival are selected and survive through a process of natural selection. Propagation is the key to survival of a trait, as a genetic predisposition can be passed on only through offspring."[139] Natural selection favors those traits that are most adaptive, and over several generations these traits survive. An evolutionary perspective does not identify rape as an adaptation but focuses on certain motives and ends that are conducive to rape. The environment is also thought to play a role because "genes cannot make traits without environmental causes acting in concert."[140] According to **Randy Thornhill** and **Craig T. Palmer**, "Selection favored different traits in females and males, especially when the traits were directly related to mating.

Although some of these differences could have arisen from what Darwin called natural selection, most of them are now believed to have evolved through sexual selection."[141] *Sexual selection* refers to the observation that some traits appear to survive, not because they are related to survival but because they further the attainment of mates or defense against competition over mates; this is said to apply primarily to males because "male fitness is limited by access to the opposite sex much more directly than is female fitness, with the result that females compete for mates much less than do males."[142]

The specialized jargon and knowledge that inform evolutionary perspectives make it difficult to understand how they apply to social behaviors like rape, and these perspectives have been severely criticized for justifying rape as "natural." Proponents of the usefulness of evolutionary perspectives on rape contended that evolutionary perspectives can explain why rape is so prevalent and why it takes the forms that it does, arguing that "biology provides understanding, not justification, of human behavior."[143] Evolutionary perspectives contend that the feminist position on rape that equates it primarily with expressions of violence diminishes the fact that there is a biologically based sexual motivation and that ignoring this eliminates one avenue by which rape may be understood and prevented. Rather than being counter to the agenda of feminists, evolutionary psychologists offered their perspective as another avenue through which rape can be approached, understood, and thereby prevented.

> Evolutionary perspectives have been criticized for justifying rape as "natural."

Typologies of Rapists

Several researchers have attempted to develop typologies of rapists. Nicholas Groth's work represented one of the first systematic attempts to do this based on empirical evidence, gathered in his capacity as a prison psychologist. **Robert R. Hazelwood** and **Ann Burgess** developed a four-part typology of rapists based on the motivation of the offender and revolving around the themes of power, anger, and sadism:[144] power–assertive, power–reassurance, anger–retaliatory, and anger–excitation.

Based on interviews with 61 serial rapists (all incarcerated in a South Carolina maximum-security prison for the crime of rape), Dennis J. Stevens offered a typology of his own based on motivations. Using Groth's "Protocol for the Clinical Assessment of the Offender's Sexual Behaviors" to structure the interview, Stevens explored the areas of premeditation, victim selection, style of attack, degree of violence associated with the rape, accompanying fantasies, and role of aggression. One of his major findings was the role of lust as a primary motive among a large proportion of the rapists (42%). While acknowledging that "lust is not a new idea concerning predatory rape," Stevens believed it to be a primary rather than a secondary motive for rapists.[145] A constant theme emerging throughout Stevens's interviews with the rapists was that for most of them, the amount of force that

LIBRARY EXTRA 9–9
LIBRARY EXTRA 9–10

WHO'S TO BLAME—The Individual or Society?

Exotic Dancer Claims Rape

Twenty-one-year-old Carla Maybe-Love called 9-1-1 from her cell phone at 3:00 A.M. on a Sunday morning, telling the 9-1-1 operator who answered that she had just been raped.

"Ma'am, are you injured? Are you in need of immediate medical assistance?" the operator asked.

"No, no, I'm okay," Carla told her.

"Are you safe? Is anyone threatening you? Is anyone there with you?" the operator continued.

"I'm okay. I'm back home. Alone," Carla said.

Carla gave her address, and the operator dispatched a patrol car to the location.

The female officer who arrived encouraged Carla to go with her to the hospital for an examination and for evidence collection. Once Carla had been signed in at the emergency room, the officer took a report of the incident.

Carla described herself as an exotic dancer and for-hire personal companion, who spent her evenings entertaining men of all ages. "I show them a good time," she said, "and there's nothing illegal about that. But that don't give them the right to rape me," she told the officer.

Carla then went on to tell the officer how she had been hired by two men who were attending a local convention to come to their hotel room with a friend and put on a show. "Dancing, that's all we were supposed to do," she said. The men, she said, called a number of their friends in to their room to watch the show. At some point, Carla told the officer, she had to go to the bathroom. That's when, she said, a man followed her and pushed her into the small room, locking the door behind them. "That's when it happened," she said. "He put his hand around my throat, and he raped me."

Think about it:

1. Assuming that Carla is telling the truth about what happened, how would you explain this crime? That is, why did it happen, and how might it have been prevented?

2. In your opinion, does Carla bear any responsibility for her own victimization? Why or why not?

Note: Who's to Blame boxes provide fictionalized critical thinking opportunities, and are not actual cases.

---

accompanied the rape was just enough to accomplish the victim's submission, but in cases in which extreme violence accompanied all stages of the rape, the violence would have been present regardless of the level of victim resistance. Therefore, one of the conclusions reached by Stevens is that advocating the idea that women should not resist their attackers is ill-advised.

Another way to approach a typology of men who rape is represented in the work of **Diana Scully**, a professor at Virginia Commonwealth University.[146] Scully's research involved intensive interviews with 114 convicted rapists in seven prisons, all of whom volunteered to be interviewed. Scully rejected the psychopathological perspective on rape and instead employed a feminist sociocultural perspective premised on several assumptions. First, rape is "socially learned behavior," involving "not only behavioral techniques, but also a host of values and beliefs, like rape myths, that are compatible with sexual aggression against women."[147] This premise is based on the assumption that both positive and negative forms of social behavior are learned "socially through direct association with others as well as indirectly through cultural context."[148] Second, Scully viewed rape not as a reflection of pathology but as a reflection of a continuum of

normality in which it is important to understand "how sexual violence is made possible in a society [and] what men who rape gain from their sexually violent behavior."[149] Scully thus approached these interviews with convicted rapists from the feminist perspective of wanting to understand the explanations given by the rapists and their sociocultural beliefs about women and sexual violence. Scully identified several patterns to the rationalizations used by men who rape, and she organized these according to two broad types of rapists: admitters and deniers.

In the interviews, Scully explored how these two groups could operate from an understanding of reality that justified their behavior and tended to normalize it as well as what they gained from such behavior. While some of the rapists in the admitter group relied on rape myth ideology, this was a more prevalent pattern among the deniers. The rape myths' definition of a very narrow group of individuals as legitimate rape victims was a common theme in the interviews given by these rapists. While variations existed, the majority of rapists in both groups expressed little guilt or empathy for their victims. Read more about the violent criminal victimization of women in America via **Library Extras 9–9** and **9–10**.

> ▉ **child sexual abuse**
> A term encompassing a variety of criminal and civil offenses in which an adult engages in sexual activity with a minor, exploits a minor for purposes of sexual gratification, or exploits a minor sexually for purposes of profit.

LIBRARY EXTRA 9–11

Child Sexual Abuse

In what is a very sad case, 75-year-old Dr. William Ayres, a child psychiatrist who once headed the American Academy of Child and Adolescent Psychiatry, was arrested in 2007 and charged with molesting three male children who were his patients in the 1960s.[150] Prosecutors said that they would present evidence showing that Ayers had molested young boys in his care for decades.

Child sexual abuse is a term encompassing a variety of criminal and civil offenses in which an adult engages in sexual activity with a minor, exploits a minor for purposes of sexual gratification, or exploits a minor sexually for purposes of profit. The term encompasses a variety of activities and motivations, including child molestation, child sexual exploitation, and the commercial sexual exploitation of children (CSEC).

The National Institute of Justice (NIJ) observed that "few criminal offenses are more despised than the sexual abuse of children, and few are so little understood in terms of incidence (the number of offenses committed), prevalence (the proportion of the population who commit offenses), and reoffense risk."[151] Moreover, studies on the psychology, behavior, treatment, and recidivism rates of child molesters have often yielded inconsistent findings.

NIJ also noted that the assumption that sexual crimes against children and teenagers are underreported is now commonly accepted, and sexual offenses are apparently more likely than other types of criminal conduct to elude the attention of the criminal justice system—self-reports from both sex offenders and sexually abused children revealed far more abuse than officially reported.[152] The Child Molestation Research and Prevention Institute (based in Atlanta, Georgia) estimated that at least two out of every ten girls and one out of every ten boys are sexually abused by the time they turn age 14.[153]

One of the most informative offender self-report studies on the adult sexual victimization of children comes from research conducted slightly more than two decades ago.[154] In that study, investigators recruited 561 adult subjects who had engaged in what the researchers described as "child-focused sexual behavior." The subjects, who were guaranteed anonymity, were recruited through health care workers, media advertising, presentations at meetings, and other ways, and all were free from confinement at the time of the interviews. The interviewees reported a total of 291,737 paraphiliac acts over the course of their adult lives committed against 195,407 victims under the age of 18. The five most commonly reported acts involved criminal conduct:

1. Nonincestuous child molestation with a female victim (224 of the 561 subjects reported 5,197 acts against 4,435 victims)

2. Nonincestuous child molestation with a male victim (153 of the 561 subjects reported 43,100 acts against 22,981 victims)

3. Incest with a female victim (159 of the 561 subjects reported 12,927 acts against 286 victims)

4. Incest with a male victim (44 of the 561 subjects reported 2,741 acts against 75 victims)

5. Rape (126 of the 561 subjects reported 907 acts against 882 victims)

These five categories included 64,872 self-reported acts, although the total number of individual victims could not be determined since many subjects reported multiple kinds of acts across different categories. The results of this study made it clear that, in cases of child sexual abuse, a relatively small number of offenders can commit a large number of crimes. Learn more at **Library Extra 9–11**.

Typology of Abusers

Almost all pedophiles are male, with one study of more than 4,400 offenders finding fewer than 0.5% of convicted child sex offenses committed by females.[155] Other than that, little can be said about similarities among child sexual abusers. As individuals, they tend to be highly dissimilar in terms of personal characteristics, life experiences, and criminal histories, so no single "molester profile" exists.[156] Child molesters appear to arrive at deviancy via multiple pathways and engage in many different sexual and nonsexual acting-out behaviors. Figure 9–5 shows the number of registered predatory child sex offenders by state.

> **Almost all pedophiles are male.**

Typologies of child sex offenders are many and varied. One typology, developed at the Massachusetts Treatment Center (MTC) for Sexually Dangerous Persons, classified offenders along a number of dimensions: (1) the amount of contact with children, (2) the kinds of sexual acts engaged in, (3) the relationship of the offender to the victim, (4) the amount of physical injury to the victim, and (5) the amount of planning in offenses.[157] The MTC model produces six offender types (shown in Table 9–2).

In 1983 Nicholas Groth and his associates proposed a different kind of typology—a simple two-part distinction whereby offenders were classified as either "regressed" or "fixated."[158] According to Groth, a regressed offender is attracted sexually primarily to his own age group but is passively aroused by minors, and the use of alcohol, drugs, or other

CRIME | in the NEWS
Violent Crime on Campus

KANSAS CITY, MO—A disturbing pattern of violent crime has erupted across the nation's campuses — from Yale University, where a female graduate student was strangled, to the University of California at Los Angeles, where a chemistry student was stabbed repeatedly in a lab.

While saying that campuses almost always are safer than their surrounding communities, Jonathan Kassa of Security On Campus Inc. acknowledged that the headlines can create the opposite impression.

"This has been a very uniquely deadly and brutal first semester, so there is concern," said Kassa, the executive director of the nonprofit organization that seeks to reduce campus crime.

"This month at Sacramento State University in California, a student was beaten to death in his dormitory by a bat-wielding roommate. A football player was fatally knifed at the University of Connecticut. In September, a Kansas City woman was killed by a stray bullet on a campus in Atlanta. In May, a student was shot down while working in the bookstore cafe at Wesleyan University in Connecticut.

"Those big incidents do worry me, but I worry more about the more regular types of crimes," said Elise Higgins, a senior at the University of Kansas whose friend was mugged on campus a year ago. "That made me really aware that I can be vulnerable even when I'm on campus around buildings I'm familiar with."

Kassa said that sensational tragedies not only distort the college picture but can distract students from the bigger problems of theft, assault, stalking, sex offenses, and alcohol abuse.

"Deadly crime is rare on campuses," Kassa said, "and statistics give no indication it is increasing."

Since 1990, all colleges and universities in federal financial aid programs annually report crimes on and near their campuses to the U.S. Department of Education. The data are passed to the Justice Department.

In 2007, the latest year for which national numbers are available, 48 killings occurred on the nation's four-year campuses. That year, however, a mentally ill student gunned down 32 people at Virginia Tech. The year before, eight people died violently on the nation's more than 4,000 campuses, down from 11 in 2005.

Since the Virginia Tech rampage, all universities have tried to prepare for the rare incident of a person on campus with a gun.

Robbery is a far more common campus crime. Hundreds occur each year.

According to Security On Campus Inc., sexual assault is increasing. The numbers don't show it, but officials think it often goes unreported.

Thieves commit most of the crimes at area schools. Crimes of opportunity are most prevalent, campus police said, because students walk away from a laptop or iPod or leave their cars or dorm rooms unlocked.

Whether a school is nestled among cornfields or next to inner-city neighborhoods can affect the amount of crime.

The Web site The Daily Beast recently analyzed 4,000 reports from public and private four-year schools and reported the New York Institute of Technology in Old Westbury, Long Island, with 11,831 students, was the safest in the country.

The least safe campus on the list was Emerson College, an arts-focused school in Boston. In The Daily Beast's survey, many urban campuses fared poorly, including Harvard University, the Massachusetts Institute of Technology, the University of Maryland at Baltimore, and Tufts University in Medford, Mass., outside Boston.

"Campus crime is not new," said Kassa of Security On Campus Inc. "You can't stop it all. You can't control everything, search everyone, but you can reduce the risks and strengthen the response. Be prepared."

Discussion Questions

1. What kinds of crimes are most likely to occur on college campuses?

2. What can college students do to protect themselves from being victimized while on campus?

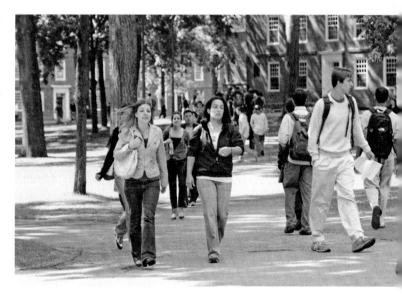

Students on the campus of Harvard University in Cambridge, Massachusetts. Why are some college campuses likely to be more free of crime than others?
Source: Kevin Galvin/Alamy

inhibition-lowering substances, combined with social circumstances providing opportunity, can cause the regressed offender to act out his interest in having sexual encounters with children; a fixated offender is an adult pedophile who engages in planned sexual acts with children and whose behavior is not necessarily influenced by drugs or alcohol.

A U.S. Department of Justice publication representing a compilation of studies produced by the NIJ showed that most victims of childhood sexual abuse do not go on to become child molesters.[159] However, sexual victimization as a child, if accompanied by other intervening factors—such as the co-occurrence of physical and verbal abuse—may contribute to the

Follow the author's tweets about the latest crime and justice news at **http://twitter.com/schmalleger**.

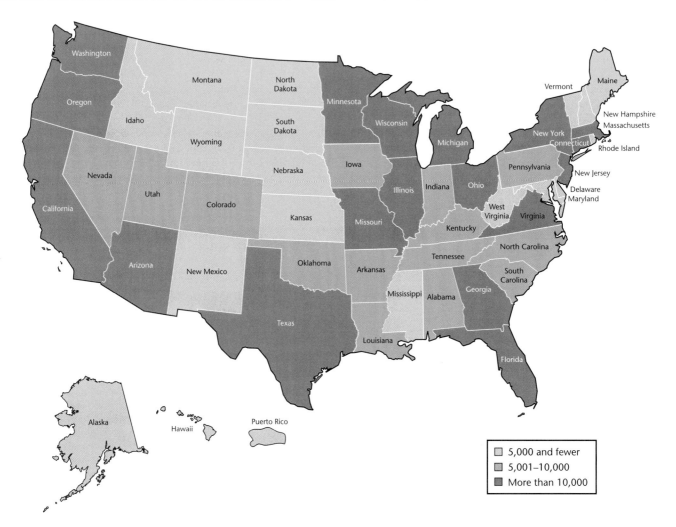

FIGURE 9-5 | Registered Sex Offenders by State

Source: Wendy Koch, "Developments Bar Sex Offenders; Restrictions Boosts Sales, but Some Predict Problems," *USA Today*, June 16, 2006, p. A.3. © USA Today. Reprinted with permission.

child-victim's development as a perpetrator of child sexual abuse later in life. Also, social competence deficits are significant in child molestation, but an individual's inadequate social and interpersonal skills do not, by themselves, make his sexual abuse of children inevitable.

NIJ researchers did find that a history of impulsive antisocial behavior is a well-documented risk factor for certain predatory extrafamilial child molesters and that offenders who have this background and who began their offending careers in adolescence tend to demonstrate higher degrees of nonsexual aggression. Other possible factors contributing to an adult with a predisposition to the sexual abuse of children include certain

early childhood experiences, including a high turnover in primary caregivers or "caregiver inconstancy," a strong predictor of adult sexual violence because it may interfere with the development of viable age-appropriate adult relationships, making it more likely that children will be selected as sexual targets.[160]

Some evidence has suggested that child molestation may be related to an offender's restaging of his own childhood sexual victimization.[161] Tests of the restaging theory on a sample of 131 rapists and child molesters revealed that child molesters who committed their first assault when they were age 14 or younger were sexually victimized at a younger age than offenders who committed their first assault in adulthood; they

LIBRARY EXTRA 9–12

TABLE 9-2 | Hypothetical Profiles of Child Sex Predators

	INTERPERSONAL	NARCISSISTIC	EXPLOITATIVE	MUTED SADISTIC	NONSADISTIC AGGRESSIVE	SADISTIC
Amount of Contact with Children	High	High	Low	Low	Low	Low
Sexual Acts	Fondling, caressing, frottage (nonphallic sex)	Phallic nonsadistic sex	Phallic nonsadistic sex	Sodomy, "sham" sadism[a]	Phallic non-sadistic sex	Sadism
Relationship of Offender to Victim	Known	Known or stranger	Stranger	Stranger	Stranger	Stranger
Amount of Physical Injury to Victim	Low	Low	Instrumental[b]	Instrumental[b]	High	High
Amount of Planning in Offenses	High[c]	Moderate	Low	Moderate	Low	High

[a]"Sham" sadism implies behaviors or reported fantasies that reflect sadism without the high victim injury present in the sadistic type.
[b]Instrumental aggression implies only enough force to gain victim compliance.
[c]Interpersonal types know their victims and may spend a considerable amount of time "grooming" them (setting them up), but the offenses often appear to be unplanned or spontaneous.
Source: Adapted from Robert A. Prentky, Raymond A. Knight, and Austin F. S. Lee, *Child Sexual Molestation: Research Issues* (Washington, DC: National Institute of Justice, 1997).

also experienced more severe sexual abuse than offenders with adult onset of sexual aggression.[162]

Nonetheless, sexual victimization alone is unable to fully explain child molestation because studies have shown that most victims of childhood sexual abuse do not go on to become perpetrators.[163] As is true for other kinds of maltreatment, childhood sexual victimization may be one critical element in the presence or absence of a variety of other factors.

Not all adults involved in the sexual abuse of children pursue personal sexual gratification. Some have a profit motive, as in instances of CSEC, which refers to all offenses in which an adult victimizes a child sexually for profit, including the prostituting of a child and creating or trafficking in child pornography. Read a comprehensive report on the commercial sexual exploitation of children in the United States, Canada, and Mexico via **Library Extra 9–12**.

Robbery

In 2010, 31-year-old Indiana resident Brian Kendrick was convicted of shooting a pregnant Indianapolis bank teller named Katherine Shuffield in the abdomen during a robbery that took place in 2008.[164] The shooting, which critically injured Shuffield, resulted in the deaths of twin girls that she was carrying. Kendrick was convicted of attempted murder, robbery, feticide, and illegal possession of a handgun and was sentenced to 53 years in prison. At sentencing, Shuffield told the court about the sorrow she felt at the loss of her daughters-to-be: "We will never hear them laugh," she said, "or speak their first words or take their first steps." Kendrick could have received a sentence of up to 87 years in prison.

> **Robbery is classified as a violent crime because it involves the threat or use of force.**

Robbery is classified as a violent crime because it involves the threat or use of force, but it is also a property crime because its express purpose is to take the property of another.[165] Robberies

The home page of the U.S. Department of Justice's National Sex Offender Public Registry at www.nsopr.gov. Community notification laws frequently result in the posting of online offender databases. How do such databases help victims?
Source: U.S. Department of Justice-Office of Justice Programs

■ **personal robbery**
A robbery that occurs on a highway or a street or in a public place (also called a *mugging*) or a robbery that occurs in a residence.

LIBRARY EXTRA 9-13

■ **institutional robbery**
A robbery that occurs in a commercial setting, such as a convenience store, gas station, or bank.

can occur in different locations and are quite often categorized in this manner by both law enforcement agencies and social science researchers. Robberies that occur on the highway or street are often referred to as highway robberies or muggings; muggings and robberies that occur in residences are types of **personal robbery**. While residential robberies are certainly deterred by the presence of security precautions, the effectiveness of deterrents depends on the type of neighborhood in which the residence is located. Terance D. Miethe and David McDowall found that security precautions that tend to be effective in neighborhoods characterized by a viable social control structure are ineffective in socially disorganized neighborhoods.[166] Security precautions, such as not leaving the home unoccupied, are not enough in socially disorganized neighborhoods to compensate for the strong effect that neighborhood context has on increasing the likelihood of robbery. Homes and persons do not exist as potential targets for motivated offenders in a vacuum but appear as more or less attractive targets based on their perceived vulnerability and the social context of the surrounding neighborhood in which they are found. The FBI reported that an estimated 408,217 robberies occurred in 2009.

Robberies that occur in commercial settings (Figure 9–6), such as convenience stores, gas stations, and banks, are **institutional robberies**.[167] Several research studies have found that institutional

robberies may be prevented through environmental and policy changes. Scott A. Hendricks and his colleagues found in a study of convenience store robberies that "the robber chooses a target based on various situational crime prevention factors";[168] these factors include staffing, hours of operation, cash-handling policies, and characteristics of the surrounding neighborhood. Many of the precautions that lower the risk of robbery are costly, so not all businesses can afford them. As Richard T. Wright and Scott H. Decker noted, "This puts businesses located in high-crime neighborhoods in a no-win situation because their clientele frequently are too poor to bear increased prices to support crime prevention measures."[169] Additionally, if the business fails as a result of robberies, the community loses again because the exodus of businesses that are forced to relocate makes the community less viable. Most of the robbers interviewed by Wright and Decker in their ethnographic study of robbers who selected commercial targets generally selected liquor stores, taverns, and pawnshops, because of the large amount of cash available, and targeted businesses with low levels of customer activity, because they viewed customers as an unpredictable risk factor. The robbers interviewed as part of Floyd Feeney's research in California during the 1970s reported very little planning overall, but those who engaged in commercial robbery were much more likely to report planning than those who engaged in personal robberies (60% compared with 30%).[170]

The Lethal Potential of Robbery

Robbery carries the threat of injury—often lethal injury—for the victim. Reported injuries were found among one in every three robbery victims whose data were entered into the NIBRS.[171] Robbery provides the context for 6% of all homicides annually. In 2009, approximately 15% of all homicides occurred during the commission of another felony, and among these cases, robbery was the most likely felony to result in homicide, accounting for almost one-half (42%) of all felony murders.[172] The weapon most often used in robbery homicides is a firearm, accounting for 42% of all cases; the type of firearm used in the vast majority of these cases (85%) is a handgun.[173] See **Library Extra 9–13**.

Criminal Careers of Robbers

Are robbers specialists (specialize in only robbery) or generalists (vary the types of crimes they commit)? The majority of robbery offenders are generalists who have fairly lengthy but varied

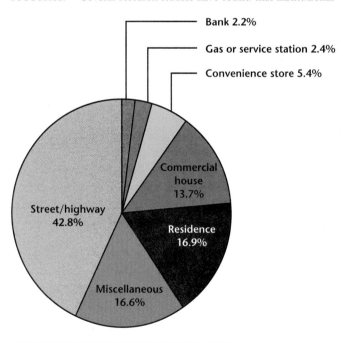

Bank 2.2%

Gas or service station 2.4%

Convenience store 5.4%

Commercial house 13.7%

Street/highway 42.8%

Residence 16.9%

Miscellaneous 16.6%

Note: Due to rounding, the percentages may not add to 100.0

FIGURE 9-6 | Robbery Locations

Source: Federal Bureau of Investigation, *Crime in the United States, 2009* (Washington, DC: FBI, 2010).

criminal careers.[174] Research on a sample of inmates in California prisons found that less than 10% of convicted robbers could be labeled specialists who engaged solely in robbery to the exclusion of other offenses;[175] in a survey of inmates sponsored by RAND Corporation, approximately 18% of offenders were primarily involved in only one type of offense.[176] Diversity in offense type appears to be the norm for the vast majority of offenders, based on both ethnographic and survey data.

> The majority of robbers are generalists who have fairly lengthy but varied criminal careers.

Robbery and Public Transportation

One setting in which crime-prevention strategies can be quite effective is public transportation. According to Martha J. Smith and Ronald V. Clarke, "Robbery on mass transit is a rare event, even in systems with relatively high numbers of incidents such as New York City."[177] Viewing instances of robbery on public transportation as reflecting a "lack of supervision," Smith and Clarke contended that the majority of these robberies follow one of three scenarios: (1) Offenders purposefully select their victims from among passengers in isolated areas of large subway stations, especially when the station is not crowded, meaning that security measures (such as using closed-circuit television and closing off unused parts of the station) may serve to effectively deter these offenders;[178] (2) offenders select their victims outside the station at particular locales and times that are relatively isolated; and (3) offenders act on opportunity and often lie in wait for passengers leaving public transportation.[179] Prevention strategies to deter these types of robberies include a variety of surveillance techniques. In addition to targeting public transportation customers, robbers also target the staff in order to steal the fare money; Smith and Clarke stated that policies such as exact fare and other similar changes "led to a dramatic fall in the number of bus robberies in New York City."[180]

According to Smith and Clarke, "Transit workers with perhaps the greatest risk of robbery are taxicab drivers, who carry cash, travel by themselves around cities with strangers, and do not choose their destinations."[181] Derek Cornish offered several strategies, ranging from having a weapon to screening passengers for potential threats, that taxicab drivers can use to prevent robberies.[182] While "drivers can use informal passenger screening practices such as refusing to pick up fares at certain locations," such screening practices "can discriminate against those who live in poorer areas or are from certain racial or age groups, making it difficult for them to use the service."[183] These very practices have recently been the subject of debate because of claims of discrimination.

Other strategies, such as the installation of protection partitions between the driver and passenger, can be quite effective in deterring crime. Under the New York City Police Department's special Taxi-Livery Task Force, created in 1992, police in unmarked cars stop taxis in particular neighborhoods, often according to some strategy such as every fifth taxi. A similar strategy was also adopted in Boston, again as a response to the substantial number of violent crimes (especially robberies), experienced by cab drivers. While the Boston statute withstood court review, the New York Court of Appeals ruled in December 1999 that the policy of the police department "gave officers too much discretion to stop taxis carrying passengers when they had no reason to suspect any crime was afoot."[184] The U.S. Supreme Court was asked to review both rulings and declined, allowing the rulings of the lower courts to stand. Policies like those in New York and Boston clearly illustrate the tension involved in policing a democratic society; measures that might prevent certain forms of crime must be weighed against the potential violation of individual liberties.

The Motivation of Robbers

Research tends to support the idea that most robberies, of both people and places, involve very little planning on the part of the offender. Floyd Feeney's research in California during the early 1970s found little evidence that the majority of bank robbers had even been in the bank before the robbery.[185] Most of the robbers Feeney studied did very little planning, no matter what the target, and the planning that did occur was minor and "generally took place the same day as the robbery and frequently within a few hours of it."[186] The motivation and decision making of street robbers were evaluated in a series of research studies conducted by Bruce A. Jacobs, Richard Wright, and others at the University of Missouri at St. Louis involving 86 active robbers in St. Louis. Jacobs and Wright found that the decision to offend occurs as part of ongoing social action that is "mediated by prevailing situations and subcultural conditions."[187] Fast cash was the direct need that robbery satisfied, but this need can be properly understood only against the backdrop of street culture. Jacobs and Wright hypothesized that street culture was the intervening force that connected background factors (such as low self-esteem, deviant peer relations, and weak social bonds) to the motivation to

A bank photo (bottom) showing Ashley Nicole Miller (top left) and Heather Lyn Johnston (top right), both age 19, as they robbed a bank located in a grocery store in Acworth, Georgia, in 2007. Cameras caught the fashionably dressed unarmed teenagers smiling and giggling as they produced a holdup note and were handed money. Some news outlets were quick to christen the pair the "Barbie Bandits." Mug shots (top) show the two following their arrest after it was discovered that the robbery was an inside job aided by Benny Herman Allen, a 22-year-old bank employee. Why are female bank robbers the exception rather than the rule?
Source: Courtesy Cobb County Sheriff's Office

offend, and they found that the majority of robbers gave little thought to planning robberies until they found themselves needing money. For less than half the robbers, the financial need was for basic necessities; mostly, it was connected to a fairly hedonistic lifestyle.

Jacobs and Wright considered three alternatives that these individuals could have employed for money: (1) performing legitimate work, (2) borrowing, and (3) committing other crimes. Legitimate employment was not a viable option for these individuals for several reasons. Most of the robbers had neither the skills nor the education to obtain decent-wage jobs, and even if they did have such resources, their perceived need for cash was too immediate for legitimate work to satisfy; additionally, legitimate work was viewed as an impediment to their "every night is a Saturday night" lifestyle. Borrowing money was not a viable route because many had no one to turn to for a loan, and for those who did, borrowing was not part of the self-sufficient code of the streets. Robbery was preferable to committing other crimes because it was perceived to be safer than burglary and quicker than fencing stolen goods. Other research has found that some robberies do begin as another crime, such as burglary, and become robberies more by accident than design.[188] Jacobs and Wright concluded that the economic motivation behind robbery should not be interpreted as "genuine financial hardship" but as an ongoing crisis situation experienced as a result of the logic of the street context of robbers' daily lives.[189] For the individuals whom Jacobs and Wright interviewed, "being a street robber . . . is a way of behaving, a way of thinking, an approach to life."[190] Such individuals are unlikely to be easily deterred by legal sanctions, and the rationality of their decision making is unlikely to be adequately explained outside the context of their street culture.

In 2006, Trevor Bennett and Fiona Brookman interviewed 120 English robbery offenders in a study funded by Britain's Economic and Social Research Council (ESRC).[191] Bennett and Brookman found that financial gain was only one of many motivations reported by robbers. Others included having a "sheer desire to fight," desiring to set right a perceived injustice, enhancing one's street credibility, and doing it "just for kicks." Some offenders participating in the study had been arrested as many as 50 times and reported that they were addicted to robbery. One told the researchers, "I was more addicted to robbing than I was to drugs" (drug connections were mentioned in 60% of all robberies studied).

> Being a street robber is a way of behaving, a way of thinking, an approach to life.

Drug Robberies

In their ethnographic research on armed robbers, Richard T. Wright and Scott H. Decker found that "six out of every ten offenders who specialized in street robbery—forty-three of seventy-three—said that they usually preyed on individuals who themselves were involved in lawbreaking."[192] These are generally not reflected in official statistics on crime because the victims do not report their victimization to the police due to their own illegal

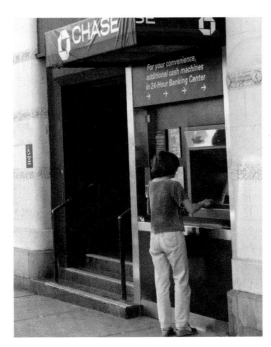

A possible robbery victim. Some robbers seem to give little thought to planning their crimes until they need fast cash. Why might this person be an attractive target for such robbers?
Source: Ed Bailey/AP Wide World Photos

behavior, so they can be victimized with relative impunity. Because the overriding motivation behind the robberies for many offenders in Wright and Decker's research was to get high, it follows that drug dealers would be an obvious target. Among offenders who stated that they selected victims involved in crime, the vast majority targeted drug dealers, though rarely major drug dealers. "Almost all of these offenders targeted young, street-level dealers who sold quantities of crack cocaine directly to consumers."[193] According to one robber, the attraction of robbing drug dealers was twofold: "It satisfies two things for me; my thirst for drugs and the financial aspect."[194] The neighborhoods in which these robbers lived and conducted their routine activities were generally characterized by an abundance of drug dealers, which increased their suitability as targets. Because they were also unlikely to report their victimization to the police, drug customers were perceived as ideal targets. Additionally, offenders were well aware that the police did not take drug robberies seriously. However, these factors do not consider the one element that makes robbing drug dealers very risky: "There always is a possibility of violent retaliation."[195]

Further analysis of the ethnographic research on the armed robbers in St. Louis by Bruce A. Jacobs, Volkan Topalli, and Richard Wright explored the issue of retaliation by asking, "Why should offenders elect to reduce their chances of getting arrested at the cost of increasing their odds of being killed?"[196] To answer this, the researchers looked at the findings from 25 in-depth interviews with active drug robbers conducted as part of the larger study of robbers in St. Louis. The researchers conceptualized retaliation as an informal sanction "capable of deterrence in its own right; to be sure, it may be the sole sanction offenders face."[197] Drug dealers who are victimized are cut off from one avenue of redress, the formal sanctions provided by police, and "have a strong incentive to retaliate."[198]

The drug robbers interviewed in the St. Louis study were completely aware of the risk involved in targeting drug dealers and sought to minimize it by selecting one of three strategies: intimidation, anonymity, or hypervigilance. Drug robbers primarily targeted dealers "whose retributive potential was weak."[199] Some of the offenders stated that "some street corner dealers simply dismissed robberies as an occupational hazard and accepted their losses with equanimity."[200]

The second strategy used by robbers who targeted drug dealers, anonymity, involved robbing only those dealers with whom they were totally unfamiliar so that "retaliation becomes moot" because the victim does not know the robber.[201] Hypervigilance, the third strategy, refers to how offenders consciously "devoted a significant portion of their day-to-day cognitive resources to minimizing the prospect of postoffense victim contact."[202] For offenders engaged in a substantial volume of robberies, the chances of running into a victim were increased even if the victim was initially unknown to them, so offenders avoided the sites of previous robberies until they could be fairly sure that the threat of recognition or retaliation had subsided, and the nomadic lifestyle of drug robbers allowed them to easily do this.

Circumstances and situations bring offenders and victims together in unexpected ways—"the more members of a network there are, and the denser that network is, the more likely run-ins become. Bus stops, mini-malls, grocery stores, bars, theaters, and fast-food restaurants emerge as contexts fraught with potential risk."[203] This not only hinders the offender's ability to manage the risk of retaliation but also increases the potential for violence within the entire community itself, based on the extent of drug robberies. Jacobs and his colleagues concluded that this community effect represents the "contagion-like processes through which violence is contracted and contained," and if "street justice" is stronger than the formal justice represented by law enforcement, the community becomes increasingly unstable.[204] They explained, "The more entrenched informal justice becomes, and the more likely formal authorities will 'look the other way,'" the more the community becomes disorganized and violence spreads beyond robbers and their victims.[205] This becomes one set of dynamics that creates and sustains the "tangled web of violence we see in so many high-crime urban locales across the country."[206]

The Gendered Nature of Robbery

According to researcher **Jody Miller**, "With the exception of forcible rape, robbery is perhaps the most gender differentiated serious crime in the United States."[207] Women represent robbery offenders in approximately 11% of all incidents.[208] Miller's research goal was to assess the extent to which gender impacts robbery offending, so she analyzed a subset of the interviews with active robbers from the research data used by Jacobs and Wright consisting of 37 robbers, 14 women and 23 men. The two groups were matched on current age and age at first robbery. In her examination of motivations for robbery, Miller found that economic incentives were the primary mo-

> With the exception of forcible rape, robbery is the most gender differentiated serious crime in the United States.

tivation for both men and women but that there were significant differences in the way in which men and women carried out street robberies. Men exhibited a fairly uniform pattern. Their robberies were characterized by "using physical violence and/or a gun placed on or at close proximity to the victim in a confrontational manner";[209] the presence of a gun was almost a constant in robberies conducted by men. While perceiving women to be easier targets, male robbers tended to rob other men rather than women because of another perception—that men tended to carry more money. The majority of males targeted as victims were those involved in "street life."

Female robbers tended to fall into one of three patterns. The robbery of other women in a "physically confrontational manner" was the most prevalent way in which female robbers worked, but they also used their sexuality to attract male victims and acted as accomplices to male robbers in offenses against other men.[210] Except when they were robbing men, female robbers generally did not use guns. While similar cultural and structural forces can drive men and women to offend in the same way, gender continues to exert an influence on shaping the nature of robbery incidents. Learn more about the crime of robbery at **Web Extra 9–8**.

Assault

Assault is the "prototype of violent crime."[211] Not only is assault the most common violent crime, but it is also the starting point for more serious incidents of interpersonal violence. So it is important to understand that assaults can kill, "even if they don't actually end a human life."[212]

The profile of typical offenders in aggravated assault mirrors those involved in homicide—disproportionate involvement of males, African Americans, 15- to 34-year-olds, those of lower socioeconomic status, those with prior arrest records, and those with little evidence of offense specialization.[213] Also consistent with most homicides, aggravated assaults are "spontaneous, triggered by a trivial altercation or argument that quickly escalates in the heat of passion."[214]

Based on statistics from the NCVS, the overall decline in the crime rate between 1993 and 2009 was primarily due to decreases in the rate of simple assault. In 2009, victims reported 2,860,410 victimizations, a rate of 11.3 per 1,000 residents age 12 or older, with the majority of assaults reported by victims being simple rather than aggravated assault. (The definition of *aggravated assault* used by the NCVS is "attack or attempted attack with a weapon, regardless of whether or not an injury occurred and attack without a weapon when serious injury results.")[215] Aggravated assaults are divided into those with injury and those without injury, and the victims and offenders are equally likely to be strangers and nonstrangers. When you look at the gender of the victim, a pattern emerges: A slight majority of male victims are assaulted by a stranger, whereas slightly more than one-third (39%) of female victims are assaulted by a stranger in aggravated assaults; simple assaults are more likely in general to involve nonstrangers (58%), with almost one-half (47%) of male victims assaulted by nonstrangers and 71% of female victims assaulted by nonstrangers in these cases. Whether an aggravated or a simple assault, the largest category of nonstranger offenders of female victims is represented by friends and acquaintances, followed by intimate partners. Weapons are present in less than one-fourth (23%) of all assaults, and when a weapon is present, it is most likely to be something other than a gun or a knife.[216]

Stranger Assault

The possibility of stranger violence elicits a great deal of fear and concern among most members of the population. Based on research using victimization data in both the United States and Great Britain, Robert Sampson said that "the probability of suffering a serious personal crime by strangers is very low," with this likelihood varying by demographic characteristics like gender, age, marital status, and lifestyle.[217] For example, individuals who have an active social life away from home are far more likely to be victimized in the evening by strangers, but this effect depends very much on the community context in which the individuals engage in their leisure pursuits.

Marc Riedel and Roger K. Przybylski proposed that stranger violence consists of two primary types.[218] One type of violence between strangers results from the "exploitation of a setting," as is often the case in a robbery in which the offender cases the store in advance.[219] Other encounters between strangers are less calculated, and violence can "emerge from more spontaneous encounters between strangers in routine settings such as bars or sporting events."[220] This is the situation of the typical assault, where something as benign as an offensive remark escalates into violence; because "confrontational stranger violence occurs in [certain types of] public settings," there is a strong likelihood that assault victims and offenders will be about the same age, but settings in which assaults frequently occur, such as bars, are generally restricted on the basis of age, and they "acquire local reputations that attract a clientele that is usually homogeneous in age."[221] Thus, compared with assaults within the family, stranger assaults are more likely to involve victims and offenders of similar ages.

Assault within Families

As the statistics from several sources reveal, the majority of assaults involve victims and offenders who are known to each other, quite often in a familial or an intimate relationship. In the sections that follow, the familial context of assault is examined, with a special emphasis on how key variables like weapons and alcohol help us understand the patterns of these crimes.

Family Privacy

While statistics on homicide have long supported the violent potential of families, criminologists were not the pioneers in studies centered on the violent aspects of our society's most basic institution. Richard J. Gelles, a leading family-violence researcher, correctly asserted in the 1970s that violence within the family concerned criminologists only when someone was killed.[222] Criminology as a discipline began to give more attention to violent behavior within the family just as societal attention turned to viewing the halo of privacy that has long surrounded the family with a bit more scrutiny. Empirical research concerning the phenomenon of family violence encounters several problems.

The family as a social institution is intensely private, and the discussion of physical, emotional, and sexual violence among family members violates this privacy; these types of abuse also represent extremely sensitive parts of a person's experience, which an individual may be reluctant to discuss. Michael Hindelang conducted research on crime-reporting behavior and found that two of the most common reasons for not reporting crimes to the police were that it was a private matter and that there might be reprisal from the offender.[223] Current research has shown that such rationales supporting nonreporting continue to characterize incidents involving violence among family members.

Early Studies of Family Violence

The initial research on violence within the family came from small clinical studies and official records, the latter consistently revealing that women were much more likely than men to become victims of domestic violence. Based on an examination of emergency room victims in the late 1970s, Evan Stark and colleagues found that approximately 25% of all women who had been injured had been the victim of a spousal attack.[224] Murray Straus and colleagues at the University of New Hampshire were the first to develop a survey methodology for the study of family violence nationally and conducted the first National Survey on Family Violence (NSFV) in 1975 with a representative sample of 2,146 families; the second NSFV was conducted in 1985 with a sample of 4,032 households.[225] In both surveys, the key tool developed for measuring family violence was the Conflict Tactics Scale, containing a series of 18 items that range from calm discussion to the use of a potentially lethal weapon. By the time a respondent reaches the questions concerning spousal behavior, Straus reasoned that familiarity with the questions would diminish the respondent's uneasiness about answering whether he or she had ever hit a spouse.[226] The rate of violence between spouses in the 1985 NSFV was 161 per 1,000 couples.[227] While this rate was lower than that reported in 1975, it still remained higher than estimates produced from other studies not specifically directed at family violence, such as the NCVS.

Current Survey Information on Family Violence

In the years since survey research was first used to estimate violence against family members, other surveys have emerged to assess this phenomenon, and existing data sources have improved. The FBI has released specialized reports based on available NIBRS data; 19 states submitted data in NIBRS format for 2006, and the FBI compiled a special report on these data based on an

WEB EXTRA 9–9

> ■ **intimate-partner assault**
> A gender-neutral term used to characterize assaultive behavior that takes place between individuals involved in an intimate relationship.

> ■ **separation assault**
> A type of violence inflicted by a partner on a significant other who attempts to leave an intimate relationship.

analysis of family incidents. Using a measure of violent crime that includes murder, rape, robbery, and assault, NIBRS data revealed that 51% of violent crimes involved victims and offenders who were related. Among all offenses involving family members that came to the attention of the police, the overwhelming majority (94%) were assaults, a percentage that is "4 points higher than the frequency of assault offenses in overall crimes of violence."[228] Thus, while assault is the most frequently occurring violent crime both among the general population and within the family, the percentage is even higher within the family. While aggravated assault accounted for 18% of all violent offenses, the percentage of all family violence offenses involving aggravated assaults is slightly smaller, at 15%.[229]

Compared with aggravated assaults, firearms are less likely to be used in family assaults; fists, hands, and knives are more common, and a slight majority of aggravated assaults involve some type of injury both in the general population (57.5%) and within the family (60.8%). Women are more likely to be the victims of both aggravated assaults and simple assaults within the family than in the general population (60% versus 41% and 72% versus 60%, respectively).[230] Learn more about family violence and the crimes it engenders via **Web Extra 9–9**.

Intimate-Partner Assault

Intimate-partner assault is a term used to characterize assaultive behavior that takes place between individuals involved in an intimate relationship. Based on research using various data sources, the overwhelming majority of victims of marital violence within heterosexual relationships are women. This does not deny that men can be the victims of violence at the hands of their wives but merely states that based on official records, self-reports, emergency room records, and small clinical samples, it is women who emerge as victims. In line with this empirical reality, Neil Websdale titled his ethnographic exploration of violence in rural areas of Kentucky *Rural Woman Battering and the Justice System*.[231] However, the terms *woman battering* and *wife assault* are biased in terms of heterosexual relationships, so some researchers now use the term *intimate-partner assault* to avoid this bias. We will also use this term in our discussion because it now frequently appears in the literature on assault among intimates and because it reflects the changing nature of most sexual assault laws and mandatory arrest laws, which are becoming gender neutral and moving away from the legal relationship as the criterion that defines an intimate relationship.

> Intimate-partner assault refers to assaultive behavior that takes place between individuals involved in an intimate relationship.

For many individuals, the notion of assault between intimate partners gives rise to the response "If I was hit, I would leave," but this places the burden on the victim to justify why she stays and takes the burden off the offending partner. More crucially, this type of response ignores the reality that when most women do leave violent relationships, that behavior may trigger a particularly violent response by the male partner, labeled **separation assault** by Martha R. Mahoney.[232] A woman who attempts to leave a violent relationship is seen as violating the right of her husband to control her, and even if she does manage to leave, many times the husband will follow her and attempt to take her back.

Violent relationships between intimate partners are characterized by a cycle of violence in which numerous forms of social control may be used. Men in Websdale's research disconnected telephone lines, disabled cars, and threatened women at their place of work, actions which narrowed the abused partner's options to leave, especially in the case of women in rural settings where powerful notions of family loyalty and gender roles work against leaving as an option. As Websdale noted in his research, many women who are battered by their husbands must face the fact that if they leave their husbands, they will be leaving their communities. Physical assaults often involve other tactics of abuse, such as emotional abuse and attacks or threats against children—most women who have reported abuse by intimate partners also had dependent children.[233]

In analyzing the cases of women in two counties in Massachusetts who applied for restraining orders during 1992 and 1993, as well as observations in the courtroom, **James Ptacek** developed a typology of the strategies men used to control women in violent relationships.[234] He analyzed both the types of abuse that women reported in their petitions for restraining orders and the rationales that women provided in their affidavits that "gave some indication of the objectives behind the men's violence and abuse."[235] In 18% of the cases, the woman reported that her male partner had used violence to prevent her from leaving, and in 22% of the cases, the woman reported that

WEB EXTRA 9–10

■ **workplace violence**
The crime of murder, rape, robbery, or assault committed against someone who is at work or on duty.

violence was used to get back at her for leaving. Ptacek argued that women are assaulted in the process of leaving their abusers, and some of the incidents of separation assault had occurred more than a year following legal separation or divorce. Men also used "punishment, coercion, and retaliation against women's actions concerning children," which could take several forms.[236] Some men attacked their wives during pregnancy, other men attacked women who challenged their parental authority over the children, and still others attacked partners who had requested child support through the courts. In about 12% of the cases, the affidavits of women revealed that men used violence in response to other types of legal action. Ptacek labeled this "retaliation or coercion against women's pursuit of court or police remedies," in which the men responded with violence to actions that women were thought to have taken, whether those actions were real or imaginary. The final motivation for the violence of males was "retaliation for other perceived challenges to authority." These challenges included comments that the woman made concerning her male partner's behavior, ranging from drinking behavior to financial matters. As with the other motivational categories, the challenge to male authority was viewed as actionable, and violence was considered a justified course of action.[237] Ethnographic research like that of Websdale and Ptacek is an important avenue for increasing our knowledge of intimate-partner violence.

Another source of information is survey research such as the NVAW Survey (mentioned earlier), which had the goal of estimating both the extent and the nature of physical abuse among intimate partners. At some point during their lifetime, 22% of women and slightly more than 7% of men reported having been physically assaulted by an intimate partner, and during the study year, slightly more than 1% of women and less than 1% of men reported physical assault by an intimate partner. The vast majority of behaviors considered to be physical assault were acts like grabbing and shoving rather than acts using a gun or knife. In both same-sex and opposite-sex relationships, males more often perpetrate intimate-partner violence.

On the extent of injury in intimate-partner assaults, the NVAW Survey revealed that women are more likely than men to report injuries and that most of the injuries received are minor in nature. More findings from the NVAW Survey are presented in the section of this chapter examining stalking. Learn more about intimate-partner violence via **Web Extra 9–10**.

Other Forms of Interpersonal Violence

This chapter concludes with an overview of three special forms of interpersonal violence: workplace violence, hate crimes, and stalking.

Workplace Violence

On November 5, 2009, U.S. Army Major Nidal Malik Hasan opened fire on a group of unarmed soldiers and civilians at Fort Hood, near Kileen, Texas—13 people died and 30 others were wounded before Hasan was shot and wounded by responding local police officers. Hasan, a devout Muslim who had been born in Virginia after his parents emigrated from Jordan, was a psychiatrist who had been scheduled to deploy to Afghanistan and had been in communication with a radical Middle Eastern Muslim cleric via e-mail. The shootings apparently resulted from Hasan's closely held religious and ideological beliefs, including the belief that the "war on terror" was actually a war against Islam.[238]

In another incident of workplace violence, three professors were killed and another three wounded on February 12, 2010, during a routine faculty meeting of the Biology Department at the University of Alabama–Huntsville.[239] The alleged shooter, Amy Bishop, a professor being reconsidered for tenure in the department, apparently opened fire with a 9mm handgun she had concealed on her person. Bishop, who was arrested a few minutes after the shooting, denied involvement. "It didn't happen; there's no way," she told arresting officers.

Workplace violence (murder, rape, robbery, and assault committed against persons who are at work or on duty) is a significant problem in America today, with incidents of workplace violence becoming common. The FBI stated that "workplace violence is now recognized as a specific category of violent crime that calls for distinct responses from employers, law enforcement, and the community."[240] On average, 1.7 million nonfatal violent workplace victimizations are committed every year: Assaults, both simple and aggravated, account for the largest number of workplace violence incidents, affecting approximately 11.7 out of every 1,000 persons in the workforce annually, and another 900 work-related homicides occur annually. Workplace violence

Follow the author's tweets about the latest crime and justice news at http://twitter.com/schmalleger.

accounts for approximately 18% of all violent crime that occurs in the United States. As might be expected, police officers experience workplace violence at rates higher than persons employed in any other occupation, whereas college or university professors are among persons least likely to be victimized (Figure 9–7).

Workplace violence falls into four broad categories:

1. Violent acts by criminals who have no other connection with the workplace but who enter to commit robbery, acts of terrorism, or another crime

2. Violence directed at employees by customers, clients, patients, students, inmates, or any others for whom an organization provides services

3. Violence against coworkers, supervisors, or managers by a present or former employee

4. Violence committed in the workplace by someone who doesn't work there but who has a personal relationship with an employee, such as an abusive spouse or domestic partner

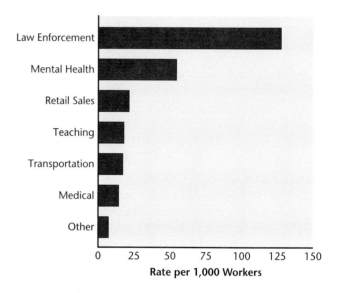

FIGURE 9-7 | Annual Rate of Violent Workplace Victimization by Occupation

Source: Detis T. Duhart, *Violence in the Workplace, 1993-99* (Washington, DC: Bureau of Justice Statistics, 2001), p. 4.

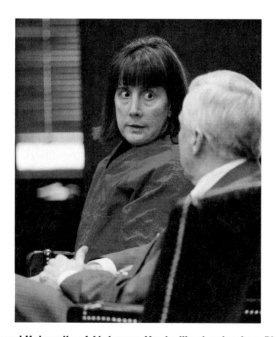

Accused University of Alabama–Huntsville shooter Amy Bishop conferring with her lawyer in Madison Circuit Court (Alabama). Bishop, age 45, is charged with killing three fellow UAH biology faculty members and wounding three others during a shooting rampage at a faculty meeting on campus on February 12, 2010. Can anything be done to reduce the number of incidents of workplace violence?

Source: ZUMA Press/NewsCom.com

Violence committed by criminals otherwise unconnected to the workplace accounts for nearly 80% of all workplace homicides.[241] In such incidents, the motive is usually theft, and in a great many cases, the criminal is carrying a gun or other weapon, increasing the likelihood that the victim(s) will be killed or seriously wounded. This type of violence falls heavily on particular occupational groups whose jobs make them vulnerable: taxi drivers, late-night retail or gas station clerks and others on duty at night, workers in isolated locations or dangerous neighborhoods, and workers with cash or access to it.

The second type of workplace violence typically involves assaults on an employee by a customer, patient, or someone else receiving a service.[242] In general, the violent acts occur as workers are performing their daily tasks. In some occupations (police officers, correctional officers, security guards, and mental health workers), dealing with dangerous people is a part of the job. In other occupations, violent reactions by a customer or client are unpredictable, possibly triggered by an argument, anger at the quality of service or denial of service, a delay, or some other precipitating event. Employees experiencing the largest number of these assaults are those in health care occupations—nurses in particular, as well as doctors, and aides who deal with psychiatric patients; members of

Workplace violence is a significant problem in America today.

WEB EXTRA 9-11
LIBRARY EXTRA 9-14
LIBRARY EXTRA 9-15
LIBRARY EXTRA 9-16
LIBRARY EXTRA 9-17

■ **hate crime**
A criminal offense in which the motive is hatred, bias, or prejudice based on the actual or perceived race, color, religion, national origin, ethnicity, gender, or sexual orientation of another individual or group of individuals.

emergency medical response teams; and hospital employees working in admissions, emergency rooms, and crisis or acute care units.

The third and fourth types of violence—incidents of violence by past or present employees and acts committed by domestic abusers and other personal relational issues that follow an employee into the workplace—are often the kind of workplace violence reported in the media. Violence in these categories is no less damaging than any other violent act, but when the violence comes from an employee or someone close to an employee, there is a much greater chance that some warning sign will have reached the employer prior to the violent act.

A BJS study revealed the following facts about workplace violence:[243]

- Private-sector and federal government employees are victimized at similar rates.

- More than 80% of all workplace homicides are committed with a firearm.

- Rape and sexual assault, robbery, and homicide account for a small percentage (6%) of all workplace violent crime; the majority of workplace violent incidents (almost 19 of every 20) are aggravated or simple assaults.

- Males experience more workplace violence (except for rape and sexual assault) than females, with about two-thirds of all robberies, aggravated assaults, and simple assaults in the workplace being committed against males.

- People ages 20–34 experience workplace violence at a rate higher than any other age group.

- The workplace violent crime rate for whites (13 per 1,000 in the workforce) is 25% higher than the rate for blacks (10 per 1,000) and 59% higher than the rate for other races (8 per 1,000); whites experience more than four-fifths of all rapes and sexual assaults (88%), robberies (81%), aggravated assaults (86%), and simple assaults (89%) occurring in the workplace, but blacks have the highest rates of overall violent crime (including both workplace and nonworkplace violence).

- Most workplace victimizations are intraracial—about six in ten white and black victims of workplace crime perceive their assailant to be of the same race.

- Almost four of every ten robberies occurring while the victim is at work or on duty are committed against someone in retail sales or transportation.

- About 12% of all workplace violence victims sustain injuries from the incident; of those injuries, about ten out of 11 are minor injuries.

The National Institute for Occupational Safety and Health (NIOSH)[244] recommended a number of prevention strategies to lower the incidence of workplace violence, including environmental design factors that physically separate workers from customers: bullet-resistant barriers or enclosures, high counters to prevent customer access to workers and goods, and limited avenues of access and egress.[245] Also recommended were enhanced administrative controls such as staffing plans and work practices that include the prescreening of patients or customers and the training and education of employees in conflict-resolution strategies.

Visit NIOSH's Occupational Violence Center to learn more about workplace violence and techniques to prevent it at **Web Extra 9–11**. Read two articles about workplace violence at **Library Extras 9–14** and **9–15**, and learn about recommendations for curtailing workplace violence from the FBI at **Library Extra 9–16**; a Canadian perspective on workplace violence is available at **Library Extra 9–17**.

Hate Crimes

At 12:49 P.M. on June 10, 2009, the U.S. Holocaust Memorial Museum in Washington, D.C., became the scene of a violent **hate crime** (crime whose motive is hatred, bias, or prejudice). James von Brunn, an 88-year-old Maryland resident who had served five years in a federal prison for a 1981 attempted armed kidnapping, entered the museum with a .22-caliber rifle and opened fire.[246] One security officer was killed before von Brunn, a known white supremacist and gun rights activist, was shot and seriously wounded by two other officers.

The collection of hate-crime statistics was mandated by the U.S. Congress with passage of the Hate Crime Statistics Act of 1990.[247] Under the law, the FBI is required to serve as a repository for data collected on crimes motivated by religious, sexual orientation, ethnic, or racial prejudice. The Violent Crime Control and Law Enforcement Act of 1994 mandated the addition to the category of hate crimes any crimes motivated by biases against people with disabilities, and the UCR Program began reporting such crimes in 1997.[248]

According to the BJS, hate crimes (also called *bias crimes*) are characterized by "manifest evidence of prejudice based on race, religion, sexual orientation, or ethnicity, including where appropriate the crimes of murder, non-negligent manslaughter, forcible rape, aggravated assault, simple assault, intimidation, arson, and destruction, damage, or vandalism of property."[249] In 2009, President Barack Obama signed into law a bill that enhances the federal protection of gays by specifically adding acts of

WEB EXTRA 9–12
WEB EXTRA 9–13
LIBRARY EXTRA 9–18
LIBRARY EXTRA 9–19
LIBRARY EXTRA 9–20

■ **stalking**
A course of conduct directed at a specific person that involves repeated visual or physical proximity; nonconsensual communication; verbal, written, or implied threats; or a combination thereof that would cause a reasonable person fear.

Glass doors damaged by gunfire being examined at the U.S. Holocaust Memorial Museum in Washington, D.C. On June 10, 2009, James van Brunn, an 88-year-old anti-Semite, opened fire on security officers inside the museum; he killed one officer before he was injured and detained. What are hate crimes?
Source: Olivier Douliery/AbacaPress/MCT/NewsCom.com

violence against gay, lesbian, bisexual, and transgender people to the list of federal hate crimes.[250]

Based on FBI statistics on hate crimes, 7,783 hate-crime incidents were reported in 2008; these incidents involved 9,683 victims, with 70% of the incidents involving a single victim.[251] (Since a single incident may involve multiple offenses, it is important to state also that the 7,783 reported incidents accounted for a total of 9,168 chargeable offenses.) Slightly more than one-half of these incidents were motivated by racial bias (51.3%), 19.5% by religious bias, 16.7% by bias based on sexual orientation, and 11.5% by bias based on ethnicity or national origin. Crimes against the person represented 61.4% of all reported offenses, with intimidation being the most commonly reported personal offense at 29.5%, followed by simple assault at 19.4%; in the category of crimes against property, vandalism or destruction of property was the most frequently occurring type of hate offense. Murder accounted for only 0.1% of all hate crimes, with a total of 7 people killed in 2008 because the offender was motivated by hate.

Role of Hate Groups

Hate groups like the Ku Klux Klan (KKK), the Aryan Nations, the National Alliance, and the Identity church movement have existed for many years and have long been associated with acts of violence. It is easy to classify groups in the hate-group category when their fundamental purpose is grounded in prejudice, but in the case of some other organizations, classification is not as easy. Are all militia groups hate groups? Given its anti-Semitic position, does the Nation of Islam, led by Louis Farrakhan, qualify as a hate group?

Are hate groups a necessary feature of hate crimes? Citing a wide array of research studies, James B. Jacobs and Kimberly A. Potter found that "the vast majority of reported hate crimes are not committed by organized hate groups and their members, but by teenagers, primarily white males, acting alone or in a group."[252] Visit the NCJRS Hate Crime Resources page via **Web Extra 9–12** and the Anti-Defamation League's Combating Hate page at **Web Extra 9–13** and read **Library Extras 9–18** and **9–19** to learn more about hate crimes. View the latest FBI statistics on hate crimes via **Library Extra 9–20**.

> The collection of hate-crime statistics was mandated by the U.S. Congress in 1990.

Stalking

While **stalking**—conduct directed at a specific person involving repeated visual or physical proximity, nonconsensual communication, and threats—is not new, making this behavior worthy of societal concern and undesirable enough to be criminalized is relatively new. Several high-profile cases have illustrated the dangerous potential of stalking behavior. John Hinkley was obsessed with actress Jodie Foster and thought he could capture her attention and admiration by shooting President Ronald Reagan in 1981. Mark David Chapman, the man who shot John Lennon in 1980, considered himself to be one of Lennon's biggest fans. Talk-show host David Letterman was stalked from 1988 to 1993 by a woman who professed her love for him by breaking into his house repeatedly, trespassing on his property, and stealing his car. Michael David Barrett, a 47-year-old divorced Chicago-area man, pleaded guilty in 2009 to interstate stalking for filming ESPN reporter Erin Andrews through a peephole while she undressed in her neighboring hotel room.[253] That same year, Michael Lawrence Kozelka of Townsend, Maryland, was arrested on charges of stalking singer-songwriter Jewel at her Texas ranch; at the time of his arrest, Kozelka, age 50, told authorities that he had been on a mission from God.[254] While these high-profile cases may capture media attention because they involve celebrities, stalking often involves average individuals as they go about their lives.

The first antistalking statute was passed in 1990 in California;[255] now all states and the federal government have antistalking laws. Rather than being an offense that occurs once, stalking is conceptualized as a pattern of behavior that causes victims to fear for their personal safety. The definition used in the Model Antistalking Code for States, developed by the NIJ, is "a course of conduct directed at a specific person that involves repeated visual or physical proximity, nonconsensual communication, or verbal, written or implied threats, or a combination thereof, that would cause a reasonable person fear"[256] (*repeated* is defined to mean at least two occasions).

Statutory definitions of *stalking* encompass a number of diverse but interrelated behaviors: making phone calls, following the victim, sending letters, making threats in some manner, vandalizing property, and watching the victim. Rather than viewing these behaviors in isolation from one another, antistalking laws take into account the totality of the circumstances so that seemingly benign behaviors are seen in light of how they are connected to other behaviors. For example, sending unwanted letters might be seen as innocuous behavior, but when this activity is combined with following the victim and standing outside his or her place of work or residence, the behavior takes on a more threatening tone and may be the precursor for more serious offenses like assault, rape, and murder.[257]

Extent of Stalking

Recent data on stalking, which came from the 2009 BJS report, *Stalking Victimization in the United States*, showed that during a recent 12-month period, an estimated 3.4 million persons age 18 or older were victims of stalking.[258] The BJS report, derived from data accumulated under the NCVS, identified seven types of harassing or unwanted behaviors consistent with conduct experienced by stalking victims: (1) receiving unwanted phone calls; (2) receiving unsolicited or unwanted letters or e-mails; (3) being followed or spied upon; (4) having the stalker show up at places without a legitimate reason; (5) having the stalker wait at places for the victim; (6) receiving unwanted items, presents, or flowers; and (7) having the stalker post information or spread rumors about the victim on the Internet, in a public place, or by word of mouth. BJS noted that these acts, taken individually, may not be criminal, but "collectively and repetitively these behaviors may cause a victim to fear for his or her safety or the safety of a family member."

The BJS report found the following during the 12-month data-gathering period:[259]

- An estimated 14 in every 1,000 persons age 18 or older were victims of stalking.

- About half (46%) of stalking victims experienced at least one unwanted contact per week, and 11% of victims said they had been stalked for five years or more.

- The risk of stalking victimization was highest for individuals who were divorced or separated—34 per 1,000 individuals.

- Women were at greater risk than men for stalking victimization; however, women and men were equally likely to experience harassment.

- A pattern of decreasing risk for stalking victimization existed for persons residing in households with higher incomes.

- Male (37%) and female (41%) stalking victimizations were equally likely to be reported to the police.

- Approximately one in four stalking victims reported some form of cyberstalking such as e-mail (83%) or instant messaging (35%).

- About 46% of stalking victims felt fear of not knowing what would happen next.

- Nearly three in four stalking victims knew their offender in some capacity.

- More than half of stalking victims lost five or more days from work as a result of experiencing stalking.

The most common reasons victims perceived as the cause of stalking behavior were retaliation, anger, spite (37%), or desire to control the victim (33%). About one in six victims believed the stalking started to keep him or her in the relationship with the offender, and one in ten reported the stalking began while living with the offender. About a tenth of victims did not know why the stalking began.

For stalking victims, the most common fear cited was not knowing what would happen next; 9% of stalking victims reported their worst fear was death, 29% feared the behavior would never stop, and more than 50% feared bodily harm to themselves, their child, or another family member. More than seven in ten victims felt angry or annoyed at the beginning of the unwanted contacts or as they progressed. Stalking victims were about twice as likely as harassment victims to feel anxious or concerned at the beginning of the unwanted contacts (52.7% versus 25.4%), and as the unwanted contacts progressed, about 15% of stalking victims felt depressed or sick, and 1% reported feeling suicidal.

About 139,000 stalking victims were attacked with a weapon, with stalkers equally likely to use a knife, blunt instrument, or other object; 23% used handguns. Of the 279,000 victims who were injured in an attack, nearly all (99%) sustained

LIBRARY EXTRA 9–21
LIBRARY EXTRA 9–22

minor bruises and other injuries, and about 20% sustained serious injuries, including gunshot or knife wounds, internal injuries, or broken bones.

Examining the behaviors that stalkers engage in, Patricia Tjaden and Nancy Thoennes (principal investigators for the NVAW Survey) concluded that antistalking laws requiring that an overt threat be made against the victim before action can be taken against the stalker are ill-advised and that laws should be strengthened to allow for early action by the justice system to prevent later harm to stalking victims.[260]

Types of Stalkers

A 1999 psychiatric study of 145 Canadian stalkers who had been referred to a forensic psychiatry center for treatment found that most were men (79%) and that many were unemployed (39%).[261] Perhaps not surprisingly, most (52%) had never had an intimate relationship. Five types of stalkers were identified:

1. **Rejected stalkers.** Rejected stalkers pursue their victims in order to reverse, correct, or avenge a felt rejection (for example, divorce, separation, termination).

2. **Intimacy-seeking stalkers.** Wanting to establish an intimate, loving relationship with the victim, intimacy-seeking stalkers may see the victim as a soul mate with whom they are fated to be.

3. **Incompetent suitors.** Incompetent suitors have a romantic or sexual interest in their victim despite having poor social or courting skills.

4. **Resentful vendetta-motivated stalkers.** Vendetta-motivated stalkers act out revenge based on a perceived wrong or a grievance against their victim, and their intent is generally to frighten and distress the victim.

5. **Predatory stalkers.** Predatory stalkers spy on their victim in preparation for an attack, which is usually sexual in nature.

Delusional disorders were found to be common among the stalkers treated, and 30% were determined to suffer consistently from delusions about those they stalked. Stalking behavior among those studied lasted anywhere from four weeks to 20 years, with an average of 12 months. Rejected and intimacy-seeking stalkers tended to persist the longest in stalking behavior. About 63% of stalkers made threats toward their victims, and 36% were assaultive. The researchers concluded, "Stalkers have a range of motivations, from reasserting power over a partner who rejected them to the quest for a loving relationship."[262] Read more about the types of stalkers identified in the social scientific literature and their motivations at **Library Extra 9–21**.

Victim–Offender Relationships in Stalking

The majority of stalking victims identified in the NVAW Survey are women (78%, or four out of every five victims), and the majority of individuals who stalk are men (94% of women and 60% of men identify a male as the stalker). The majority of stalking victims are young, with 52% between the ages of 18 and 29 and 22% between the ages of 30 and 39. Results from the NVAW Survey confirmed previous research that showed that the majority of victims know their stalker—a stranger was identified as the stalker in only 23% of the cases where a woman was stalked and 36% of the cases where a man was stalked. For women who are stalked, the majority (59%) are more likely to be stalked by an intimate partner than by a stranger, an acquaintance, or a relative other than the spouse, but the majority of men are stalked by strangers or acquaintances (70%), usually a male in both cases (90%). Tjaden and Thoennes stated that while there is no clear explanation for this finding, it may be related to a greater risk of stalking among homosexual as opposed to heterosexual men because the survey found that stalking was more often experienced by male respondents who indicated that they had lived as a couple with another male. The belief that stalkers suffer from mental illness or personality disorder was not confirmed by the survey findings, as only 7% of the victims stated that they were stalked by offenders who were "mentally ill or abusing drugs or alcohol."[263] Learn more at **Library Extra 9–22**.

Stalking in Intimate-Partner Relationships

Almost one-fourth (21%) of female respondents in the NVAW Survey who had been stalked by an intimate partner stated that they were stalked before the end of the relationship, 43% indicated that the stalking occurred after the relationship had ended, and slightly over one-third (36%) reported that they were stalked both before and after the end of the relationship with their partner.[264] The survey found that other forms of violence often accompany stalking. For women stalked by an intimate partner, 81% were also physically assaulted, and about 33% were sexually assaulted by their stalker; the percentage of women experiencing assault of either kind by a current or former intimate partner who stalked them was higher than the percentage experiencing some form of assault but no stalking (20% of women who had ever married or lived with a male partner had experienced physical assault by that partner and 5% had experienced sexual assault).[265] Men who stalked their former wives were "significantly more likely than ex-husbands who did not stalk to engage in emotionally abusive and controlling behavior toward their wife."[266]

■ **cyberstalking**
An array of high-technology options, including e-mail and the Internet, that an offender uses to harass or "follow" another individual.

WEB EXTRA 9–14
WEB EXTRA 9–15
LIBRARY EXTRA 9–23
LIBRARY EXTRA 9–24

Consequences of Stalking

Respondents in the NVAW Survey reported a number of consequences of stalking that negatively affected their life, with women who had been stalked reporting a significantly higher level of concern for their personal safety than those who had not been stalked. Almost one-third reported seeking counseling, and slightly more than one-fourth lost time from work. Women took a variety of extra self-protective measures as a response to the stalking: 17% stated they had bought a gun, 11% stated they had changed residences, and 11% stated they had moved out of state. Women who had been stalked were more likely than men to have obtained a protective order against their stalker (23% versus 10%, respectively).[267]

Since the definition used in the NVAW Survey to assess stalking required high levels of fear on the part of victims, it is worthwhile to note the data on whether the victims reported stalking to the

> Women who had been stalked reported a significantly higher level of concern for their personal safety than those who had not been stalked.

police—a higher percentage of women than men reported the stalking to police (55% versus 48%, respectively). When asked their reasons for not reporting stalking to the police, victims consistently gave fairly general reasons: 20% defined it as not a police matter, 17% did not believe the police could do anything, 16% were afraid of reprisal from the stalker, 12% said they resolved it on their own, and smaller percentages reported that the police would not believe them or that it was a private matter.[268] Responses to questions on satisfaction with law enforcement's handling of the

case indicated that about half of respondents approved of police procedure, but in cases where an arrest was made in the stalking, three-fourths of the victims were satisfied with the police handling of the case.[269] Learn more about the crime of stalking at the federal Stalking Resource Center at **Web Extra 9–14**.

Cyberstalking

Cyberstalking (use of electronic communication like e-mail or the Internet to harass individuals) has received attention as efforts progress to better understand the consequences of our increased reliance on electronic communication and the Internet.[270] A 1999 report from (then) Attorney General Janet Reno made the following recommendations to help control cyberstalking:[271]

- A review of all stalking laws at the state level is needed to ensure that provisions for cyberstalking are included.
- An amendment to federal law is needed to make transmission of communication in specified forms of commerce actionable if the intent involves threatening behavior or causes the recipient fear.
- Training on cyberstalking should be offered at all levels of law enforcement.
- A Web site with information on cyberstalking should be created and made available to the public.

Learn more about the crime of cyberstalking from the Stalking Resource Center run by the National Center for Victims of Crime at **Web Extra 9–15**, and read an article describing the growing use of technology and other menacing stalking behaviors at **Library Extra 9–23**. Find out more about the activities of cyberstalkers and how to combat the crime of cyberstalking at **Library Extra 9–24**.

SUMMARY

- Many of today's official U.S. crime statistics come from the BJS, which conducts the annual NCVS based on interviews with members of randomly selected households. The NCVS uncovers a large number of unreported crimes and is regarded as relatively accurate.

- The UCR Program is an official data-gathering program of crimes reported to the police. The incident-driven NIBRS revises the definitions of a number of offenses for reporting purposes, collecting detailed data on circumstances surrounding each serious criminal incident.

- There have been three major shifts in U.S. crime rates: (1) during the early 1940s at the outbreak of World War II,

a sharp decrease in crime due to the large number of young men who entered military service; (2) from the 1960s to the 1990s, a dramatic increase in crime; and (3) from the 1990s to the present, decreases in the rates of most major crimes.

- A crime typology categorizes offenses using a set of defined characteristics such as legal categories, offender motivations, and victim behaviors. The UCR/NIBRS and NCVS crime-reporting categories distinguish among types of violent crimes.

- Criminal homicide, the illegal killing of one human being by another, ranges from serial killing and mass murder to murder in intimate settings. Patterns of murder vary along subcultural and social structural dimensions such as economic inequality and community social disorganization.

- The NCVS defines rape as carnal knowledge through the use of force or the threat of force; statutory rape (without force) is excluded from the definition, but both heterosexual and homosexual rape are included. Accurate assessment of the extent of sexual violence against women is hampered by sociocultural factors contributing to underreporting rape. Rape myths are false assumptions about rape that continue to characterize the discourse surrounding sexual violence.

- The FBI defines robbery as the taking of or attempting to take anything of value from the care, custody, or control of someone by using force or threat of force or violence or by putting the victim in fear. Muggings and robberies in residences are personal robbery, and robberies in commercial settings are institutional robberies. The majority of robbery offenders are generalists with a fairly lengthy but varied criminal career who put very little planning into their robberies.

- Assaults are either simple or aggravated (violent unlawful attacks for the purpose of inflicting severe or aggravated bodily injury). Intimate-partner violence characterizes assaultive behavior between individuals involved in an intimate relationship.

- Workplace violence is a widespread significant problem today and includes murder, rape, robbery, and assault committed against persons who are at work or on duty. Hate crimes are criminal offenses motivated by hatred, bias, or prejudice based on the race, religion, national origin, ethnicity, gender, or sexual orientation of another person. Stalking is repeated visual or physical proximity, nonconsensual communication, and/or threats that would cause someone to be fearful; cyberstalking is a special type of stalking that uses high technology to harass someone.

KEY TERMS

acquaintance rape, 253

child sexual abuse, 258

crime typology, 238

cyberstalking, 275

exposure-reduction theory, 242

expressive crime, 240

felony murder, 239

hate crime, 271

homicide, 239

institutional robbery, 262

instrumental crime, 240

intimate-partner assault, 268

mass murder, 246

murder, 239

National Crime Victimization Survey (NCVS), 234

National Incident-Based Reporting System (NIBRS), 234

National Violence against Women (NVAW) Survey, 249

nonprimary homicide, 240

personal robbery, 262

primary homicide, 240

rape myth, 250

rape shield law, 251

selective disinhibition, 245

separation assault, 268

serial murder, 246

sibling offense, 242

spousal rape, 254

stalking, 272

Uniform Crime Reporting Program (UCR), 234

victim precipitation, 242

Violence against Women Act (VAWA), 249

Violent Criminal Apprehension Program (VICAP), 247

workplace violence, 269

KEY NAMES

Larry Baron, 255

Ann Burgess, 256

Andrea Dworkin, 255

James Alan Fox, 246

Nicholas Groth, 255

Robert R. Hazelwood, 256

Julie Horney, 251

Mary P. Koss, 253

Jack Levin, 246

Catherine MacKinnon, 255

Jody Miller, 266

Craig T. Palmer, 256

Robert Nash Parker, 240

James Ptacek, 268

Diana E. H. Russell, 254

Diana Scully, 257

Cassia Spohn, 251

Murray A. Straus, 255

Randy Thornhill, 256

QUESTIONS FOR REVIEW

1. What kinds of crime data are reported by the NCVS, and how are those data gathered?

2. What is the purpose of the UCR Program, and how is it unique?

3. What three major shifts in crime rates can be identified in the United States since official crime-reporting programs began?

4. What are crime typologies, and what kind of violent crime typology does this chapter employ?

5. What is criminal homicide, and what are the key issues involved in explaining patterns of homicide?

6. How is the crime of rape defined, and what are the key issues involved in explaining the crime of rape?

7. How is the crime of robbery defined, and what are the different kinds of robbery?

8. How is the crime of assault defined, and what are the various kinds of assault?

9. What three additional forms of interpersonal violence does this chapter discuss?

QUESTIONS FOR REFLECTION

1. Why are crime typologies useful for understanding patterns of violent crime?

2. Are violent crimes primarily rational activities?

3. Why was rape-law reform necessary? What have been the beneficial aspects of reform for rape victims?

4. Is robbery primarily a rational activity? Why or why not?

CHAPTER 10

CRIMES AGAINST PROPERTY

LEARNING OUTCOMES

After reading this chapter, you should be able to answer the following questions:

- What are some characteristics of persistent and professional thieves?
- What are the major forms of property crime discussed in this chapter?
- What constitutes the crime of larceny-theft? What forms does it take?

- What is motor vehicle theft? How prevalent is it?
- What constitutes the crime of burglary? What are some of its characteristics?
- What are the typical activities of receivers of stolen property, and how are stolen goods distributed?
- What constitutes the crime of arson?

WEB EXTRA 10-1

■ **professional criminal**
A criminal offender who makes a living from criminal pursuits, is recognized by other offenders as professional, and engages in offending that is planned and calculated.

■ **persistent thief**
One who continues in common law property crimes despite no better than an ordinary level of success.

■ **offense specialization**
A preference for engaging in a certain type of offense to the exclusion of others.

Introduction

The March 18, 1990, theft of several valuable paintings worth more than $300 million from the Isabella Stewart Gardner Museum in Boston remains "the unsolved art crime of the century." Two people disguised as Boston police officers entered the museum, incapacitated security guards, and made off with the paintings as well as surveillance tapes.[1] The Boston art theft was atypical for several reasons. According to Lynne Chafinch, an expert in art theft with the Federal Bureau of Investigation (FBI), the vast majority of "stolen art is lower value" and hence represents works that will not be easily recognized.[2] Even though the FBI maintains a listing of stolen art and cultural property in its National Stolen Art File, the bureau investigates such thefts only if they occur in a "museum as defined by federal statute, [and then] a stolen artwork has to be either more than 100 years old and worth more than $5,000 or less than 100 years old and worth more than $100,000."[3] According to Don Hrycyk, who leads the art theft unit of the Los Angeles Police Department, one of the few of its kind nationally, many people involved in art theft are common burglars who steal art along with any other goods available. Other art thieves do not fit a conventional criminal profile and instead come from the ranks of college professors, gallery owners, and individuals involved in insurance fraud.[4] In more than a decade of such investigation, Hrycyk noted that about the only type of crook that he hasn't come across is the sophisticated, debonair thief portrayed in movies like *Entrapment* and *The Thomas Crown Affair*.[5] Learn more about art theft at **Web Extra 10–1**.

Persistent and Professional Thieves

While legal distinctions separate the offenses of larceny and burglary, both are basically property crimes of theft, so all such offenders are thieves. Before discussing the legal classifications of property crimes, some basic differences between persistent thieves and professional thieves should be noted; while many thieves are persistent, this does not make them professionals. Willie Sutton, a famous bank robber, saw himself as a professional and defined a professional thief quite simply as "a man who wakes up every morning thinking about committing a crime, the same way another man gets up and goes to his job."[6] In a classic study of the professional thief, Edwin H. Sutherland defined this offender as one who "makes a regular business of stealing," plans carefully, possesses "technical skills and methods which are different from those of other professional criminals," and moves from locale to locale in offending pursuits.[7] **Neil Shover** defined **professional criminals** as those "who commit crime with some degree of skill, earn reasonably well from their crimes, and despite stealing over long periods of time, spend rather little time incarcerated."[8] This is certainly not the profile of most offenders, who continue to commit crimes but never exhibit signs of a professional approach to crime; instead of being viewed as professional, they are best understood as persistent.

> Professional criminals commit crime with some degree of skill, earn reasonably well from their crimes, and spend little time incarcerated.

Persistent thieves are those who continue in "common-law property crimes despite their, at best, ordinary level of success."[9] Rather than specializing to any significant degree, the vast majority of persistent thieves alternate between a variety of crimes like burglary, robbery, car theft, and confidence games. Even though they exhibit a generalist approach to offending, persistent thieves may have "crime preferences" that take the form of characteristics like "whether to avoid or to confront their victim(s)."[10]

Similarly, **offense specialization**, a preference for a certain type of offense, is quite limited among property offenders and does not allow the classification of most offenders as professionals or specialists. A significant number of property offenders are fully immersed in a street culture and lifestyle characterized by a hedonistic approach to life and a disregard for conventional pursuits, and their everyday lives are filled with a wide array of petty crimes, including confidence games, gambling, and minor thefts.[11]

Malcolm W. Klein used the term *cafeteria-style offending* in his research to refer to the heterogeneous and unplanned nature of offending among gang members.[12] In analyzing offending among gang members for possible patterns, he likened it to "a cafeteria display with [several] choices of food. Imagine the gang member walking along the display, choosing to try a little petty theft, then a group assault, then some truancy, then two varieties of malicious mischief, and so on."[13] Research using data sources ranging from official crime statistics to offenders' self-reports to

■ **occasional offender**
A criminal offender whose offending patterns are guided primarily by opportunity.

A ransacked home following a burglary. Burglary is a property crime that can turn violent if victims encounter the perpetrator. What are the characteristics of a professional burglar?

Source: Mediacolor's/Alamy

ethnographies confirms that a minimal level of specialization exists among property offenders.[14] Shover, who has studied burglary and professional thieves for more than two decades, suggested that terms like *burglar* have little utility if conceived of in a strict sense of exclusive offending within that crime type. Many offenders engaged in burglary prefer this type of offending to offenses like robbery because burglary does not involve direct contact with victims.[15]

Because of the short-term, sporadic nature of their offending, property offenders are also known as **occasional offenders**[16] (the label "occasional" refers not to the frequency of offending but to the nature and character of offending), whom **John R. Hepburn** defined as those whose crimes "occur on those occasions in which there is an opportunity or situational inducement to commit the crime."[17] This observation (which fits well with rational choice theory discussed in Chapter 3) has been confirmed in subsequent research, such as the work of Richard T. Wright and Scott H. Decker, who stated that the burglars they interviewed are not a "continually motivated group of criminals; the motivation for them to offend is closely tied to their assessment of current circumstances and prospects."[18] This does not mean that offenders plan their crimes carefully or accurately

assess a situation; it means only that they are seeking to achieve some personal benefit through criminal activity. Often offenders don't succeed because they rarely have all the information they need, they do not devote enough time to planning their actions, they take risks, and they make mistakes. This is how we all behave in everyday decision making and is what theorists call *limited* or *bounded rationality*.[19] So while some degree of rationality characterizes the criminal activity of most property offenders, it is only a limited or bounded rationality.

Criminal Careers of Property Offenders

Criminologists have long studied the criminal careers of offenders, both violent offenders and property offenders. Neil Alan Weiner defined a criminal career as "criminal behavior [that] is an integrated, dynamic structure of sequential unlawful acts that advances within a wider context of causal and correlative influences, including among others, those of biological, psychological, and informal social and formal criminal justice origins."[20]

According to Alfred Blumstein and colleagues, a criminal career in property offending consisted of three distinct phases.[21] The first phase is the "break-in" period, which characterizes the early years of an offender's career, a time when young offenders become increasingly committed to criminal careers and explore various kinds of criminality; this initial phase generally lasts for the first ten to 12 years. The second phase, the "stable" period, is the time of highest commitment, the period in an offender's career when he or she identifies most closely with a criminal lifestyle and probably also the period when rehabilitation efforts are most likely to fail. The final phase of a criminal career, the "burnout" period, begins around age 40 and is characterized by increasing dropout rates and a lowered commitment to criminal lifestyles.

In a study of violent offending, D. S. Elliott and fellow researchers examined data from the National Youth Survey and found that the careers of violent offenders were typically quite short—averaging just 1.58 years.[22] Only about 4% of subjects studied by Elliott and others had a violent criminal career of five years or more. However, they defined *career length* as the maximum number of consecutive years the individual was classified as a serious violent offender during the study period.

It was long assumed that offending becomes more serious and more frequent over time, but that assumption was strongly challenged by Michael R. Gottfredson and Travis Hirschi.[23] They

LIBRARY EXTRA 10–1

> ■ **larceny-theft**
> The unlawful taking, carrying, leading, or riding away of property (other than a motor vehicle) from the possession or constructive possession of another (attempts are included), according to the UCR/NIBRS.

posited that while the idea of deviance and crime as an orderly process similar to the rationality of conventional activities may be appealing for social policy purposes, evidence on offense specialization and the trajectories associated with chronic offending offers more support for crime as a fragmented pursuit than as a "career." Other researchers have found that while there is a certain logic to offenders' lifestyles, it is not one that easily complies with "a concept appropriate in a distinctly different culture (lawful society)."[24]

Based on ethnographic research on street criminals in urban settings, **Mark S. Fleisher** argued that the "social maturation" of the street life cycle "allows hustlers at any age to speak and act like adolescents and never acquire responsibilities similar to those marking social maturation in lawful society. In the sociocultural world of hustlers, youth is marked by gang membership, 'kids' crimes,' the onset of drug and alcohol addictions, and juvenile detention."[25] From the cradle to the grave, the lifestyle of street criminals is "created less by design than by default."[26] Fleisher explained that street criminals do not have careers, so thinking of their offenses or the pattern of their lives as following a series of life events similar to those outside this sociocultural environment will do little to increase understanding of the patterns of property offending because there is not enough planning in how the street criminal approaches life and crime to constitute a career. The type of offense specialization existing among property offenders is a loosely based preference for certain types of offending but not necessarily for a particular offense.

> The lifestyle of street criminals is created less by design than by default.

Property Offenders and Rational Choice

Property crimes are often investigated from the perspective of rational choice theories (discussed in Chapter 3). One definition of *rationality* offered by Dermot Walsh was "activities identified by their impersonal, methodical, efficient, and logical components";[27] however, the rationality of the typical criminal offender is not the same as "the rationality used by the civil engineer."[28] Thomas Bennett and Richard Wright researched the rationality surrounding decision making by burglars.[29] Walsh's conclusions agreed with theirs—that offenders employ a "limited, temporal rationality. . . . Not all these men are highly intelligent, and few are equipped to

calculate Bentham-style, even supposing the information were available. Yet it is very common for rationality to be used. Of course it is partial and limited rather than total, but at the time, the actor feels he has planned enough and weighed enough data."[30] While some offenders (especially those closer to the end of the continuum marked professional) use a higher degree of rationality and others may exhibit totally senseless behavior, most expressions of rationality are not dramatically clear. As Neil Shover and David Honaker explained, "Rationality is not a dichotomous variable," so given the extent to which it is shaped by the social context of offenders' lives, researchers must "learn more about the daily worlds that comprise the immediate contexts of criminal decision making behavior."[31] The extent to which property crimes are rational pursuits for either expressive or instrumental gains is a question that can be addressed by examining a wide variety of research on typologies of property crimes. Learn more about trends in property crimes from **Library Extra 10–1**.

Property crimes vary along a continuum from crimes that are so petty in nature that they are not even noticed by the victim to crimes on a scale so large that the associated economic loss can be vast (see the Criminal Profiles box). Both the Uniform Crime Reporting (UCR) Program and the National Crime Victimization Survey (NCVS) report data on property crimes. According to the FBI, the major property crimes are burglary, larceny, motor vehicle theft, and arson (Table 10–1).

Larceny-Theft

The prototypical property crime is usually petty in nature. The UCR defined **larceny-theft** as "the unlawful taking, carrying, leading, or riding away of property from the possession,

TABLE 10–1	Property Crimes Known to the Police, 2009		
OFFENSE	NUMBER	RATE PER 100,000	CLEARANCE RATE (%)
Burglary	2,199,125	726.9	12.5
Larceny	6,327,230	2,060.9	21.5
Motor vehicle theft	794,616	258.8	12.4
Arson	58,871	21.3	34.7
U.S. total	9,379,842	3,067.9	

Source: Federal Bureau of Investigation, *Crime in the United States, 2009* (Washington, DC: U.S. Department of Justice, 2010).

CRIMINAL | PROFILES
Frank W. Abagnale, Jr. ("Catch Me If You Can")

High school dropout Frank Abagnale never met a credential he couldn't cheerfully ignore. He simply assumed any role that needed a credential and let you assume that he had it—or helped you assume he had it by showing you convincing forgeries of qualifying documents. Airline pilot, attorney, pediatrician, college professor, stockbroker, and FBI agent were all roles that Abagnale convincingly assumed at one point or other in his criminal career.[i]

Born April 17, 1948, Abagnale started a life of crime by conning his father out of $2,500 just after the younger Abagnale's sixteenth birthday. Allowed to use his father's gas credit card, Abagnale schemed for spending money by using the card to buy tires from a gas station, then selling them back to the station owner at half price for cash.[ii] The scam was discovered at the same time that Abagnale's parents were divorcing, which gave him an excuse to run off to New York.

He was a 16-year-old runaway when he made his first big score—$40,000—by printing up a bunch of bank deposit slips with his own account number (obtained, of course, under a false name) printed on them in magnetic ink. He then placed them at the service desk in the bank's lobby in place of the generic deposit slips provided by the bank for customer use. Other customers used the slips to make deposits, thinking that the deposit would be credited to their own account. In reality, the automated processing equipment would read Abagnale's account number magnetically encoded on the slip and credit his account for the amount of the deposit. When the account balance reached $40,000, he simply withdrew the funds and closed the account.

After five years of tricking people around the world, Abignale was arrested while pretending to be a licensed commercial airline pilot when an Air France flight attendant recognized him from a wanted poster on the bulletin board in the employee's lounge. Abagnale subsequently served time in prisons in France (six months) and Sweden (six months) before he was finally extradited to the United States. Convicted of federal forgery charges, he received a 12-year sentence to federal prison.[iii]

Abagnale's exploits during that infamous five-year period of nonstop cons were the subject of Steven Spielberg's highly successful film *Catch Me If You Can*, released in 2002.

After Abagnale had served four years of his sentence he received an offer from the U.S. government that changed his life. Wanting to learn

Frank Abagnale, Jr., posing for a photo at the Four Seasons Hotel in Beverly Hills, California. Abagnale, portrayed by actor Leonardo DiCaprio in the film *Catch Me If You Can* is the real-life subject of a book he wrote about his time as a successful con artist. How does Abagnale differ from most other property offenders?
Source: Lucy Nicholson/AP Wide World Photos

how to prevent future Abagnale-like scams, the U.S. government asked Abagnale to teach them how he did the things, and how to prevent others from doing them in the future. Specifically, they wanted to explore his ability to manipulate official documents so as to virtually eliminate any chance of detection. In exchange, the government offered him immediate release from prison.[iv]

And that is how Frank Abagnale, the most successful con man of the twentieth century, morphed into a world-renowned expert on forgery, embezzlement, and document security. Today, he heads Abagnale and Associates, a highly respected secure document consultancy. Abagnale has become an extraordinarily successful author and lecturer whose speeches, according to multiple-Oscar–winner Tom Hanks, "may be the best one-man show you will ever see."[v]

Notes

i. Bernie Alexander, "Frank Abagnale: From Fraud to FBI," AskMen.com, http://www.askmen.com/toys/special_feature/36_special_feature.html (accessed July 10, 2007).

ii. Norman Swan, "Frank Abagnale-New Life," *Life Matters*, March 17, 2000, http://www.abc.net.au/rn/talks/lm/stories/s111098.htm (accessed July 10, 2007).

iii. Rachael Bell, "Skywayman: The story of Frank W. Abagnale Jr.," CourtTV Crime Library, http://www.crimelibrary.com/criminal_mind/scams/frank_abagnale/index.html (accessed July 10, 2007).

iv. Ibid.

v. Keppler Speakers home page, http://www.kepplerspeakers.com/speakers/speakers.asp?1+EV+1175 (accessed May 21, 2007).

or constructive possession, of another."[32] As a form of theft, larceny (as opposed to burglary) does not involve the use of force or other means of illegal entry, so larceny is a crime "less frightening than burglary because to a large, perhaps even to a preponderant, extent it is a crime of opportunity, a matter of

making off with whatever happens to be lying around loose: Christmas presents in an unlocked car, merchandise on a store counter, a bicycle in a front yard."[33] Just about anything can be stolen. In California in November 2000, for example, thieves stole "more than 1,200 young orange trees during

LIBRARY EXTRA 10–2
LIBRARY EXTRA 10–3

nightly raids at the San Joaquin Valley, heartland of the state's citrus crop."[34] The volume and specialized focus of crimes like this are clearly the province of professional thieves; orange trees are not easily bartered on the street corner or the local pawnshop.

Prevalence and Profile of Larceny-Theft

Larceny is the most frequently occurring property offense, according to official data compiled by the FBI and data from both the NCVS and the National Incident Based Reporting System (NIBRS). The FBI reported that during 2009 there were an estimated 6.3 million larceny-thefts nationwide, accounting for an estimated 67.9% of all property crimes. The rate of larceny-theft was 2,061 per every 100,000 people, and on average, larceny-theft offenses cost victims an estimated $5.5 billion in lost property annually.

Within the offenses subsumed under the category of larceny in UCR/NIBRS data, the largest category is theft from

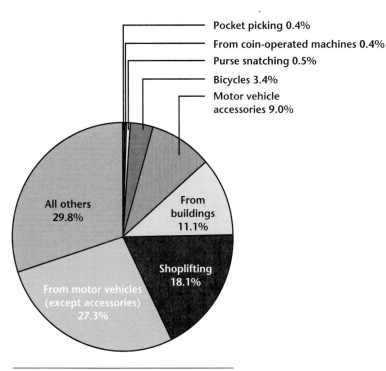

Pocket picking 0.4%
From coin-operated machines 0.4%
Purse snatching 0.5%
Bicycles 3.4%
Motor vehicle accessories 9.0%

All others 29.8%
From buildings 11.1%
Shoplifting 18.1%
From motor vehicles (except accessories) 27.3%

Due to rounding, the percentages may not total 100.

FIGURE 10-1 | Larceny-Theft Distribution, 2009
Source: Federal Bureau of Investigation, *Crime in the United States, 2009.*

motor vehicles, followed by shoplifting and theft from buildings (Figure 10–1).[35] Offenses like pocket picking and purse snatching constitute a small percentage of all larcenies, less than 1% each. Just as rates of different offenses within the category of larceny differ, so do estimated losses to victims.

Data from both the NCVS and the UCR/NIBRS provide some basis to estimate the value of loss due to property crimes. While the aggregate economic loss is quite high, slightly more than one-third of all losses individually are under $50, with personal items like jewelry and camera equipment (the largest category of stolen items) constituting almost one-fourth of all stolen goods. The NCVS category of theft covers items taken from motor vehicles, which account for almost 13% of all items stolen, and firearms and cash, which constitute smaller percentages ranging from less than 1% for firearms to 7% for cash.[36] Learn more about crimes of theft at **Library Extras 10–2** and **10–3**.

Employee Theft and Shoplifting

According to the National Retail Security Survey (NRSS), an annual survey by the University of Florida, thefts cost U.S. retailers a staggering $33.6 billion a year.[37] Much retail theft is committed by store employees: "The theft of merchandise by employees can range from the simple act of walking out the door with stolen goods to complex schemes requiring the manipulation of documents and/or involving several employees."[38] Most of the employees engaging in theft of either cash or merchandise are short-term workers.

Internal theft is typically found in retail establishments with higher-than-average sales and a significant degree of turnover in management, and many retailers perceive it as much costlier than the economic loss caused by customer shoplifting. According to the U.S. Chamber of Commerce, employee theft has become an even more serious problem recently with the advent of hard economic times, with about 75% of employees stealing from their employers at least once during their employment.[39]

Shoplifting is a crime especially prevalent among adolescents. It crosses class lines, and it is thought to be committed primarily by women (but see below). It is infrequently carried out by professionals. Retailers have to consider whether efforts to combat shoplifting could impact sales.

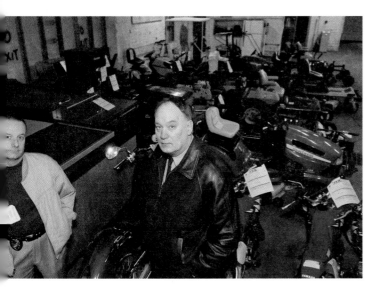

Warren (Ohio) Police Detective Jeff Hoolihan (left) and Canfield (Ohio) Police Detective Sergeant Andy Bodzar standing in front of items seized from members of a theft-to-order burglary ring that operated in and around Youngstown, Ohio. What's the difference between larceny and burglary?
Source: Mark Stahl/AP Wide World Photos

Technology represents one of the best ways to address both employee theft and shoplifting. Computerized inventory counts to track merchandise are quite useful in quickly identifying thefts by employees. The widespread prevalence of shoplifting among youths means that increased security personnel in stores are less successful at detection than are electronic and other devices—store personnel must know whom to target to be successful, whereas security systems make shoplifting more difficult for everyone.[40] The NRSS found that "retailers' loss prevention budget averaged only 0.57 percent of annual retail sales."[41] The technological developments that make managing inventory lists easier also help control the greatest loss to retailers—employee theft—without seriously undermining the attractiveness of shopping (most of us are so familiar with antitheft devices attached to goods that we do not see them as unusual).

Who Shoplifts?

On December 6, 2002, actress Winona Ryder was sentenced to three years of probation and required to perform 480 hours of community service for shoplifting more than $5,500 in merchandise from a Beverly Hills, Calfornia, Saks Fifth Avenue store a year earlier. At sentencing, Superior Court Judge Elden Fox

Shoplifting is a crime prevalent among adolescents.

warned the 31-year-old Ryder that "If you steal again, you will go to jail."[42] The judge also ordered the two-time Academy Award nominee to participate in a court-approved drug-counseling program.

Although actress Winona Ryder's shoplifting case was widely covered by the news media, she is not a typical shoplifter. In self-reports of offending, official arrest data, and store records, juveniles are overrepresented as shoplifters, the frequency of offending varies, and most offending patterns are fairly sporadic across all social classes, even though the most serious and chronic forms are found among the economically disadvantaged.

While females represent the majority of offenders in some shoplifting data sources, this finding has been seriously challenged in research since the 1970s.[43] The research of **Lloyd W. Klemke**, which used self-reports from high school students from four different schools in the Pacific Northwest to assess juvenile shoplifting, revealed that almost two-thirds of the sample had shoplifted at some point in their lifetime and that a significantly higher percentage of males compared with females reported

Two-time Academy Award nominee Winona Ryder is shown in a still frame taken from a surveillance camera that captured her actions at Saks Fifth Avenue in Beverly Hills, California, in 2001. Ryder was found guilty of shoplifting in a 2002 trial, and was sentenced to three years of probation and required to perform 480 hours of community service. The actress was also ordered to participate in a court-approved drug counseling program. Why would someone like Ryder shoplift?
Source: Los Angeles County Courts/ZUMA Press/Newscom

shoplifting during the year considered.[44] Earlier research by **Mary Owen Cameron** using department store records had revealed that females were more likely than males to be apprehended for shoplifting.[45] Klemke, however, found the reverse to be true. The difference in these findings may be attributed to the fact that Klemke's research included only adolescents, whereas Cameron's research also included adults. In line with Cameron's findings, Klemke "found petty theft to be the dominant pattern for shoplifting" and described such theft as infrequent enough to correspond to the "sporadic pilfering" Cameron reported.[46] Klemke found the frequency of shoplifting to vary by the offender's social class.

Youths from lower-income households are more likely to shoplift than their higher-income counterparts, but this relationship is a moderate one. The relationship between social class and likelihood of shoplifting is stronger among adults. While research in this area is sparse, JoAnn Ray's study of shoppers in Spokane, Washington, revealed that out of a random sample, those in lower-income groups were three times more likely to shoplift than those in higher-income brackets.[47]

Among Klemke's other findings was a "maturing out" pattern, whereby "shoplifting activity peaked in the under ten age category" and decreased considerably as the youths entered adolescence.[48] These findings are contrary to other research that supports escalation during late adolescence.

Is Shoplifting an Adolescent Phase?

No one type of youth is most likely to shoplift. A majority of youths report such activity, making shoplifting one of the largest categories of unofficial delinquency (delinquency not detected by authorities). According to a relatively large body of research, adolescence is the period in a person's life when shoplifting is most likely to occur.[49] Shoplifting that assumes the form of "adolescence-limited phasic behavior can be seen as normal for at least three reasons: because of its relatively high prevalence, because adolescents are expected to loosen their ties to social control, and because our culture is full of descriptions under which periodical crises and phases make sense."[50] Adolescence-limited offenders (discussed in Chapter 7) are the largest group of those engaged in delinquency for whom the onset and desistance from deviance can be fairly well predicted.[51] There is still no evidence that intense shoplifting reflects significant psychological problems. Shoplifting appears to be one of several forms of deviant behavior during adolescence, and "a shoplifting phase is one of the many cafeteria items selected by juveniles whose ties to sources of social control have been weakened."[52]

Is Shoplifting a Gateway Offense?

Evidence has long been seen to support the notion that shoplifting is part of the early offense history of a certain segment of property offenders, meaning shoplifting may be a kind of **gateway offense** (an offense that represents a starting point leading to more serious and chronic types of offending). Frederick M. Thrasher's classic study of gangs in Chicago detailed how various forms of property crime were found among boys in gangs. Although shoplifting was quite prevalent, there was no indication that it served as a starting point for more serious offending in any formal sense.[53]

> Offenders often fall back on lesser offenses like shoplifting if the opportunity presents itself.

Shoplifting is not an offense limited by the age of the offender; it requires little skill or training and is accomplished in several different venues. It is perhaps less likely that shoplifting forms an impetus for increasing levels of involvement in more serious forms of property crime than that shoplifting satisfies material and sensational needs among a group of individuals who are fairly nonspecialized in their offending (see the Crime in the News box).

Other research has offered more support for shoplifting as a gateway to more serious offending. In interviews with 60 repeat property offenders in a Tennessee prison, **Kenneth D. Tunnell** found that some offenders had begun with shoplifting, that late offenses reflected a calculated move to more serious property crimes, and that among the majority of persistent property offenders, their careers "consisted of progressive steps, with each step representing a different crime type of specialty."[54] Tunnell offered no direct research, however, that supports the idea that offenders move systematically from lesser to more serious forms of property offending. Offenders often fall back on lesser offenses like shoplifting if the occasion presents itself or if shoplifting appears to be attractive and profitable and do not move in a linear fashion from one type of property offense to another.

CRIME | in the NEWS

Retailers See Rise in Shoplifting

KANSAS CITY, MO.—Stores want strong holiday traffic in a tough economy, but they'd like to avoid some of the foot traffic—a growing number of shoplifters. December is the worst month for shoplifting, experts say, and the crime has been on the increase for about two years.

Shoplifters can be hard to spot but are major players in thefts that cost American retailers about $13 billion a year. And more people are doing it for the first time.

"They can be anyone—your mother, my sister—there is no profile," said Barbara Staib, communications director for the National Association for Shoplifting Prevention.

Most are otherwise normal people, experts say, but some get addicted to the rush of a five-finger discount.

Three-quarters of 27 million people who shoplift act out of impulse related to social or personal pressures, according to the association. They steal anywhere from $2 to $200 in goods at a time and often buy something as well.

Of course, there have been famous thieves such as actresses Winona Ryder and Hedy Lamarr, but shoplifters come from every demographic.

In a recent incident, Overland Park, Kan., charged an assistant county prosecutor with shoplifting about $40 worth of deodorant and liquid bandages.

Not unusual at all, said Terrence Shulman, an author and counselor on the subject who is also a lawyer with a master's degree in social work—and a former shoplifter.

Shulman, who founded Cleptomaniacs and Shoplifters Anonymous in 1991, said lawyers often have been among his clients.

"I've worked with doctors, lawyers, prosecutors, judges, millionaires," he said.

Most amateur shoplifters tend to have middle-class incomes, he said, although that might be shifting in hard economic times.

"Most people are doing it when there is a perceived loss in their lives or a loss of control and a perceived injustice or unfairness," he said. "It's a secret cry for help but also an attempt to regain power or control."

Casey Chroust, an executive vice president with the Retail Industry Leaders Association, said most shoplifters don't do it to feed families.

"These are not Robin Hood stories," he said. "They're stealing iPods and other luxury items; they're trying to maintain a lifestyle they can no longer afford."

The largest recently reported increases in shoplifting were in clothing and electronics, his trade group reported.

During December 2008, more than 80 percent of retailers in Chroust's trade association reported that amateur shoplifting had increased in the previous six months. Not one reported a decline, he said. In a May 2009 update, more than 60 percent reported additional increases, he said, and the trend is worldwide.

A global study that came out recently reported that retail losses related to all thefts increased almost 6 percent on average in 41 countries over the previous year.

The largest part of that $121 billion in increased losses—41 percent—was caused by shoplifting. Overall, the increased losses in the U.S. and 40 other countries cost each family $208 in higher prices for goods.

Retailers are in a bind, Chroust said, because they probably can't afford to hire as many loss-prevention officers as they would like.

"They have to make do with what they have to stymie this," he said.

However, more retailers are using high-tech tools, such as wires with electronic sensors wrapped around boxes of high-end items and smart cameras that send signals over the Internet.

Discussion Questions

1. How does shoplifting differ from other kinds of larceny?

2. What kind of impact might this kind of crime, if it continues to expand, have on retailers?

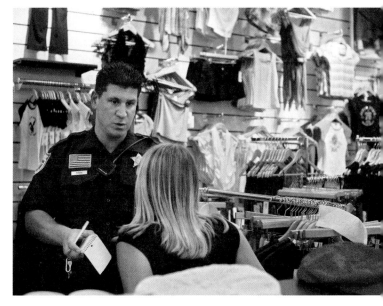

A Palm Beach County (Florida) sheriff's deputy talking with a 15-year-old girl caught shoplifting at The Mall at Wellington Green. Store management decided not to prosecute and called one of her parents to come pay for the blouse. Why do some teens shoplift?
Source: ZUMA Press/NewsCom.com

Source: Joe Lambe, "Retailers See Rise in First-Time Shoplifters," McClatchy Newspapers, December 3, 2009. © McClatchy-Tribune Information Services. All Rights Reserved. Reprinted with permission.

■ **booster**
A frequent shoplifter.
■ **snitch**
An amateur shoplifter.

WEB EXTRA 10-2

What Are Some Meaningful Typologies of Shoplifting?

Several researchers have attempted to use research findings to formulate shoplifting typologies that focus on the motivation and frequency of offending as the primary means of distinguishing among the quite heterogeneous groups that shoplift. Cameron distinguished between those who engaged professionally in shoplifting, the **boosters**, and those who were novices, the **snitches**. The boosters sold the items they stole rather than engaging in shoplifting primarily for their own personal consumption and were a small percentage of all those apprehended for shoplifting. The snitches were a larger group characterized by a tendency to steal for their own personal gratification, quite often stealing items of small monetary value.[55]

Richard H. Moore developed a typology of shoplifters that went beyond the preliminary categorization offered by Cameron and targeted their motivations. *Impulsive shoplifters* were inexperienced, rarely planned the offense in advance, and were quite remorseful upon apprehension. *Occasional shoplifters* (about 15%, similar to the size of the impulsive group) were motivated primarily by peer pressure and committed shoplifting more frequently; the smallest group was the *episodic shoplifters*, who generally had psychological problems. *Amateur shoplifters* (slightly more than 50%) made shoplifting a fairly regular activity, and their offending incidents were calculated to maximize profit and minimize risk. *Semiprofessional shoplifters* (almost 12% of the sample) were the group for whom shoplifting was an integral part of their everyday lives; they possessed the greatest degree of skill and expertise in their offending and showed a clear preference for more expensive items. Moore found that it was only the semiprofessional shoplifters who (like the boosters) stole merchandise for resale to others.[56] Because Moore's sample consisted entirely of convicted shoplifters, the extent to which the typology he developed is applicable to the majority of shoplifters—those who are never apprehended—is unclear.

In another attempt to develop a meaningful typology of shoplifters, **Frank J. McShane** and **Barrie A. Noonan** used a sophisticated statistical technique termed *cluster analysis* to sort shoplifters into groups, taking into account relevant demographic characteristics, prior offending history, psychological factors, and measures of life purpose.[57] Using data on 75 subjects apprehended for shoplifting in a variety of retail stores, McShane and Noonan identified four clusters of shoplifter types. *Rebels* (almost 19% of the sample) were primarily younger females with a significant prior history of offending. *Reactionaries* (slightly more than 27%) were similar to the rebels in that they often had the economic wherewithal to pay for the stolen merchandise, but they were older, had higher levels of education, and were

more likely to be married and to be male, compared with members of other groups—"[a] distinguishing characteristic of these shoplifters was that occupational pressure was found to be the exclusively reported psychosocial stressor."[58] *Enigmas* (41.43%), like reactionaries, were older and slightly more likely to be male, had a low likelihood of prior criminal offending, and "were characterized by a notable lack of apparent psychosocial stressors preceding apprehension."[59] The *infirms* were more likely to be female than male and were most likely to be elderly, which explains another defining characteristic of this group, their tendency to have "experienced more previous episodes of chronic illness."[60]

The Thrill of It All?

Many shoplifters have the economic means to afford the items they steal and/or have significant amounts of money on them at the time of their offenses, so there must be some motivation other than financial that drives shoplifters. Is shoplifting a thrill-seeking activity? Jack Katz (whose work was discussed in Chapter 3) argued that many property crimes, including shoplifting, represent "sneaky thrills"—it is not a desire for the object that leads to the crime but the crime that makes the object desirable.[61] Referring to adolescents in particular, Katz stated that "quite apart from what is taken, they may regard 'getting away with it' as a thrilling demonstration of personal competence, especially if it is accomplished under the eyes of adults."[62] Using self-report data from college students in his classes over a three-year period, Katz concluded that many individuals, once they are apprehended for shoplifting, report feelings of profound degradation, reflecting their basic awareness that shoplifting is wrong. Learn more about the crime of shoplifting at **Web Extra 10–2**.

Theft on College Campuses

Any locale can be the setting for theft. Criminologist Marcus Felson noted, "A college campus is a giant delivery system. It funnels students, faculty, staff, and various products into one general location and moves them from building to building to deliver education. It also delivers crime opportunities."[63]

Larceny is not only the most common index offense but also the most frequent one on college campuses. The Crime Awareness and Campus Security Act of 1990 mandated that institutions of higher learning compile and make public their data on certain index offenses, but crimes of theft are exempt from

WEB EXTRA 10-3

■ **motor vehicle theft**
The theft or attempted theft of a motor vehicle, according to the UCR/NIBRS. In the FBI's definition, this offense category includes the stealing of automobiles, trucks, buses, motorcycles, motor scooters, and snowmobiles.

the requirement.[64] One researcher who investigated theft on college campuses said that "to omit theft is to present a misleading picture of crime on campus."[65]

Some researchers have conducted independent investigations of theft on college campuses. **Magnus Seng** gathered data from incident reports at two different campuses of Loyola University in Chicago during 1993, one being located in an area with higher theft rates. Seng investigated whether the nature and prevalence of crime in the areas surrounding the campuses affected the nature of crime on campus and found that reported thefts were lower on the campuses than in the surrounding areas. Consistent with the value of stolen property in the surrounding area, "over three quarters (77%) of these thefts were classified as involving items worth $300 or less."[66] Members of the university staff had the highest victimization rates for thefts, followed by members of the faculty; students had the lowest rates. To determine exactly where the thefts occurred, he focused on the types of buildings, which was another factor that distinguished the two campuses. Thefts were more frequent on the campus with the larger number of buildings and the larger population of students, faculty, and staff. Approaching theft as primarily a crime of opportunity, Seng found that the larger campus afforded "more targets of opportunity" for theft.[67]

> ## Larceny is the most frequent offense on college campuses.

Elizabeth Ehrhardt Mustaine and Richard Tewksbury, using a probability sample of college students in eight states, examined the importance of both individual lifestyle and community characteristics as they impact the likelihood of being the victim of larceny.[68] As in more sophisticated tests of routine activities theory, their research revealed that both measures of individual lifestyle (such as the way in which an individual spends leisure time) and characteristics of the community where the individual resides are predictors of victimization. Mustaine and Tewksbury emphasized that an individual's lifestyle need not be "unhealthy" to reflect increased risk of victimization. For example, college students who spend a significant amount of time studying away from their residence or who are involved in numerous organizations on campus have an increased risk of theft victimization. Mustaine and Tewksbury concluded that "where you are, what your behaviors are, and what you are doing to protect yourself are the more important aspects of lifestyle influencing victimization risk."[69] Learn more about theft on college campuses at **Web Extra 10–3**.

Motor Vehicle Theft

The UCR defines **motor vehicle theft** as "the theft or attempted theft of a motor vehicle," where the term *motor vehicle* refers to various means of transportation, including automobiles, buses, motorcycles, and snowmobiles.[70] Automobiles are the type of vehicle most often stolen. The theft of a car violates the victim in a way that goes beyond financial loss, as does home-invasion robbery or residential burglary. Besides representing an invasion of the victim's possessions and personal space, auto theft creates a significant inconvenience, making it difficult to get to work and sometimes requiring time away from work to take care of the incident. In 22% of all motor vehicle thefts, the victim reports losing time at work, compared with about 7% for household burglary and 12% for violent crimes like robbery; approximately one-third of the victims of motor vehicle theft miss work for less than one day and about one-half for anywhere from one to five days.[71]

Prevalence and Profile of Motor Vehicle Theft

Approximately 794,616 vehicles were reported stolen in 2009 (an auto theft rate of 258.8 per every 100,000 people), with an estimated total value in excess of $5.2 billion (an average of $6,505 per vehicle stolen). The largest percentages of stolen vehicles were in a parking lot or garage at the time of the theft.[72] A significant percentage of these thefts take place either at or near the victim's residence, with 17% taking place on a street near the home.[73] Marcus Felson contended that the risks posed by parking location are related to population density: "In low-density areas, one finds more personal garages and opportunities to park right near the home or office. Those living or working in high-density areas are more likely to have street parking and higher risk of auto theft."[74]

Based on NCVS data, 81% of all motor vehicle thefts (attempted and completed) are reported to the police, although the reporting percentage is higher for completed thefts (90%) than for attempts (54%).[75] While the rate of motor vehicle victimization is the same for the lowest-income households (under $7,500) as for the highest-income households ($75,000 or more), the rate of reporting increases with the income level of the household.[76]

Approximately 62% of stolen cars are recovered.[77] Both law enforcement agencies and insurance companies keep records of recovered vehicles, but each employs its own definition of *recovered*. No matter what the condition of the vehicle, law enforcement agencies consider any found vehicle to be recovered, but insurance companies use definitions based on how much damage was done to the vehicle relative to its market value. Almost "one-third of the recovered stolen vehicles are completely stripped at 'chop shops' and another third are stripped of easy-to-sell accessories like radios, air bags, and seats."[78] Stripping cars for parts has increased since the 1970s, as has the variety of venues for such activities (an issue to which we will return shortly).

Cars are stolen for a variety of reasons: joyriding, temporary transportation needs, use in a crime, and stripping, and each of these rationales is representative of a fairly distinctive offender profile (for example, teenagers are most likely to take cars for joyriding). Almost any type of car is potentially a target, but thieves tend to prefer certain cars, with Honda Accords and Toyota Camrys leading the list.[79] According to Robert Bryant, chief executive officer of the National Insurance Crime Bureau, "Vehicle thieves follow market trends and target the most popular vehicles because they provide the best market for stolen vehicle parts and illegal export to other countries."[80]

> Vehicle thieves follow market trends and target the most popular vehicles.

A Philadelphia police officer carrying parts of stolen cars out of a chop shop during a raid. A chop shop is a place where stolen cars are disassembled and their parts sold. Why is the sale of parts often more profitable for criminals than the sale of stolen vehicles?
Source: George Widman/AP Wide World Photos

Theft of Car Parts

The theft of car parts is variously motivated. Some car parts are worth significant sums on the illegal market and can be sold easily by even the most inexperienced thieves. Also, novice thieves usually do not have access to the type of network required to sell "hot cars," and stolen car parts are more difficult to identify than entire cars.[81]

The Motor Vehicle Theft Law Enforcement Act, passed by Congress in 1984, made mandatory the marking of the major sheet metal parts of high-theft automobiles with Vehicle Identification Numbers (VINs);[82] this would enhance detection of people engaged in the widespread sale of stolen parts to the autobody industry.[83] While previous legislation had required the marking of the transmission, engine, and frame, the marking of additional parts reflected a presumption "that chopping accounts for the theft of a very high proportion of automobiles, particularly those lines which exhibit high theft rates."[84]

Some researchers report that while theft of vehicle parts constitutes most automobile crime, the exact nature of what is taken from the car has not been the subject of extensive research.[85] Conventional wisdom held that stereo equipment

was the primary target. Using data from the British Crime Survey, Joanna Sallybanks and Nerys Thomas found that "the most frequently stolen items were external parts of the vehicle, such as body panels, windshield wipers, mirrors, luggage racks, antennas, and tires and wheels, followed by stereo equipment and 'other' items (bags, briefcases, cameras, clothing, etc.)."[86] Over the past few years, the theft of stereo equipment has held constant, but the theft of external parts has increased significantly. When vehicle parts are the objects of theft, these incidents are even less likely to be reported to the police than other types of thefts. According to the FBI, 20% of thefts involving car parts and 72% of thefts of stereo equipment are reported to the police.

Car Theft for Fun: Joyriders

Some car thefts are opportunistic in nature, committed by teenagers (usually in groups) for fun or thrills, and are referred to as **joyriding**. Because such thefts generally involve the temporary appropriation of a vehicle primarily to satisfy needs ranging

■ **jockey**
A professional car thief involved in calculated steal-to-order car thefts.

■ **burglary**
The unlawful entry of a structure to commit a felony or a theft.

WEB EXTRA 10-4

from excitement to personal autonomy, joyriding is often characterized as an "expressive act with little or no extrinsic value."[87] The motivation is not characterized by planning and quite often resembles the scenario provided by Michael Gottfredson and Travis Hirschi: "The typical auto theft [involves] a car left unlocked on a public street or in a public parking lot with the keys in the ignition or in plain view [that] is entered by a 16-year-old male or group of males and is driven until it runs out of gas or until the offenders must attend to other obligations."[88]

Most vehicles stolen for joyriding are recovered after being abandoned, often after they have been crashed. Joyriders favor sports cars, particularly American-made cars.[89] While the majority of auto thefts involve victims and offenders who are unknown to each other, cars stolen for joyriding are one of the exceptions to this pattern. When adolescents select a vehicle for joyriding, they are more likely to select the car of a known owner.[90]

Available research offers no definite answer as to whether there is a distinctive social class profile of the joyriding offender. Based on the early work of William W. Wattenberg and James Balliestri, the "favored-group hypothesis" associated higher social class with greater involvement in auto theft because of greater access to cars and an earlier association of cars as status symbols.[91] On the other hand, the "disadvantaged-group hypothesis" contended that youths from lower socioeconomic classes are more likely to be involved in car thefts because conventional means of acquiring status symbols like cars are blocked, so they are left with only the avenue of illegitimate acquisition.[92] Although some support has been found for each of these perspectives, other research has failed to find a link between social class and involvement in auto theft among adolescents.[93]

Car Theft for Profit: Jockeys

Jockey is a slang term for car thieves who are regularly involved in "steal-to-order jobs."[94] For professional car thieves, "the quicker the ride, the more productive the race, and the more races are made, the more productive the jockey."[95]

Professional auto thieves (a less common type) operate in groups that are characterized by much more planning and calculation in target selection—usually luxury cars that can be driven across national borders or shipped overseas. Professional thefts have the lowest recovery rates but are only a small part of the vehicle theft problem. Ronald V. Clark and Patricia M. Harris contended that "successful action against professional theft [would] have less effect on the scale of the overall problem than against thefts for temporary use and much less than against thefts from

the vehicle."[96] Learn more about motor vehicle theft at **Web Extra 10–4**.

Burglary

One of the most serious forms of property crime is **burglary** (the illegal entering of a dwelling or another type of building to commit a felony or theft). More than 40 years ago, the president's Commission on Law Enforcement and Administration of Justice noted that the high prevalence of burglaries and the numerous costs incurred by burglary victims make this offense one of the "major reasons for America's alarm about crime."[97] Today, burglary continues to be a highly prevalent crime: 72% of households in the United States are burglarized at least once over the average lifetime.[98] The risk of burglary in any given year is much lower, but burglary is still feared because it invades the sanctity and privacy of the home as well as threatens the existence of businesses.

Burglary targets structures such as a residence, a business, or some other type of building. Force is not a necessary ingredient of burglary, but burglaries are differentiated by whether force is used. For example, the FBI distinguishes among burglaries involving forcible entry, unlawful entry, and attempted forcible entry.[99] In 2009, the FBI estimated there were 2,199,125 burglaries, accounting for 23.6% of the total number of property crimes committed and costing victims an estimated $4.6 billion in lost property (average dollar loss per burglary offense was $2,096). Burglary of residential properties accounted for 72.6% of all burglary offenses; 36% of residential burglaries occurred during the day, and 56.4% of nonresidential burglaries occurred at night. Only 12.5% of burglaries were cleared by arrest or other means in 2009 (Figure 10–2).

FIGURE 10-2 | Percent of Property Crimes Cleared by Arrest or Exceptional Means, 2009
Source: Federal Bureau of Investigation, *Crime in the United States, 2009* (Washington, DC: U.S. Department of Justice, 2010).

Follow the author's tweets about the latest crime and justice news at **http://twitter.com/schmalleger**.

In contrast to UCR/NIBRS reports, NCVS statistics on burglary painted a different picture—3,134,920 household burglaries and attempted burglaries in 2009, nearly 90% more than UCR/NIBRS estimates. Rates of burglary were generally higher for African American households than for white households, regardless of family income levels, although wealthy African American families had far lower burglary rates than did low-income white families. According to UCR/NIBRS data for 2009, the majority of burglaries involved forcible entry, followed by unlawful entry and attempted forcible entry. In 2009, a slight majority of all burglaries occurred during the day, but residential burglaries were more likely to occur during the evening.[100] In contrast to robbery, burglary is generally "a victim-avoiding crime."[101] Most residential burglars commit their offenses at a time when residents are unlikely to be home, and such information is important in target selection.

The consequences of both residential and commercial burglaries can be significant for the victims. Residential burglaries do not involve a direct confrontation between the victim and the offender, but the fear in the aftermath of the offense can have lasting effects on the victim. In commercial burglaries of smaller, more economically precarious businesses, the loss from burglaries can seriously affect their continued viability.[102]

The Social Ecology of Burglary

Rates of property crimes vary across cities, communities, and states, with higher burglary rates in large metropolitan areas and in particular regions, such as the South. Much research on variations in property crime at the aggregate level has examined how economics influences rates of crime. Lifestyle theory[103] and routine activities theory[104] (described in Chapter 3) have had a significant impact on explanations of how the nature and level of property crime have changed in response to alterations in the structures and routine activities of daily living. Both of these theoretical perspectives emphasize how criminal opportunity is affected by the everyday activities and environments experienced by victims and offenders. For a criminal act to occur, three ingredients are necessary: (1) someone who wants something (a *motivated offender*) coming in direct contact with (2) someone who has that thing (a *suitable target*) and (3) the lack of anything or anyone to inhibit the crime (a *capable guardian*). The basic contention of both lifestyle theory and routine activities theory is that what people do, where they do it, how often they do it, and with whom they do it all influence the risk of criminal victimization, and the

theories explore not why people commit crimes but rather "how the structure of social life makes it easy or difficult for people to carry out these inclinations," which are taken as a given.[105]

In a study of residential burglary, Lawrence E. Cohen and David Cantor set out to test Michael Hindelang's hypothesis that household wealth was a more important factor in selection of burglary targets than was ease of access to the household because they wanted to resolve often contradictory findings of previous research on the relationship between the impact of income and race on burglary victimization.[106] Cohen and Cantor found that, independent of race, the highest-income households and the lowest-income households in areas both within and outside the central city had the greatest victimization risk, which meant that high-income households (with items of special value) and low-income households (with ease of access) were both targeted.

Using data from the British Crime Survey, Robert J. Sampson and John D. Wooldredge estimated the risk for crimes like burglary and personal theft.[107] Given the specific implications of two components of opportunity theory for victimization risk—the proximity of suitable targets and motivated offenders and the spatial structure of community organization—these researchers were concerned with the impact of community context on lifestyle. Sampson and Wooldredge's research revealed that the highest victimization risks for burglary were found in single-adult households, in households with younger adults as heads, and in households left unguarded. Of the seven community-level variables, all but one had moderate to strong effects: The highest victimization risks were for residents in areas characterized by high unemployment, high building density, primary individual households, and single-parent households with children. Even controlling for individual factors of single-person households, the community measure of percentage of single-adult households continues to have a significant effect on increasing the risk of burglary victimization.

> Both the highest- and the lowest-income households have the greatest victimization risk.

Sampson and Wooldredge found that victimization risk for personal theft was less for those who were married, older, and male and higher for individuals with more education and for women.[108] The community factors of (1) the percentage of single adults with children, (2) social cohesion, and (3) street activity were significantly related to victimization risk—areas characterized by a high degree of family disruption, low social cohesion, and a large amount of street activity had higher

WEB EXTRA 10–5
LIBRARY EXTRA 10–4

THEORY | versus **REALITY**

Ethnographic Research on Active Burglars

Ethnographic research involving active burglars attempts to understand a burglar's way of life and hence offers a depth of insight rarely achieved in survey research or research using official data. However, ethnographic research is often dangerous, costly, and time-consuming.

The true benefit that comes from studying active burglars is related to an essential methodological issue common to all research endeavors: the classic issue of how individuals behave when they know they are being studied. In the case of studying burglars who are active versus those who are incarcerated, Richard T. Wright and Scott H. Decker note that individuals behave differently "in the wild" than in the jailhouse. The researchers point to statements made by two pioneers in criminology, Edwin Sutherland and Donald Cressey, more than 30 years ago: "Those who have had intimate contacts with criminals in the open know that criminals are not 'natural' in police stations, courts, and prisons, and that they must be studied in their everyday life outside of institutions if they are to be understood."[i] It is this concern for getting as close as possible to the social world one is studying that marks the tradition of ethnography.

Ethnographic research has already been described in Chapter 9, where research by Richard Wright and Scott Decker on armed robbers was discussed. This chapter presents further ethnographic research by Wright and Decker, this time on residential burglars. During 1989, the researchers located and interviewed 105 active residential burglars in St. Louis, Missouri. To qualify for inclusion in Wright and Decker's research, the offenders had to meet one of three criteria: they had to (1) have committed a residential burglary within two weeks prior to contact, (2) define themselves as residential burglars, or (3) be labeled as residential burglars by other offenders so identified. Research subjects were identified by the field workers whom Wright and Decker employed, most of whom were ex-offenders. The interviews with the subjects were all conducted in the field. Building on previous research on active offenders not currently incarcerated, Wright and Decker provide insight into various facets of the offending of burglars, including an examination of their motivation, target selection, entry method, search for valuable goods, and disposal of goods. In addition to answering questions, the offenders were asked to reconstruct their most recent residential burglary offense.

Defining the eligibility of subjects for research and using field workers are common practices in ethnographic research. Similar strategies were followed in other ethnographic research projects discussed in this chapter. They include research on 30 active burglars in an urban Texas setting by Paul F. Cromwell and his colleagues[ii] and research on the professional fence by Darrell J. Steffensmeier.[iii] As you read through the discussion of research in this chapter, keep in mind the strengths of ethnographic research and the insights to be gained by studying criminal offenders within their native social and cultural contexts.

Discussion Questions

1. What is ethnographic research? How does it differ from other types of research in the field of criminology?

2. Can criminologists learn anything special about burglary by focusing on active burglars who are not currently incarcerated—rather than on burglars who are imprisoned?

Notes

i. Edwin Sutherland and Donald Cressey, *Criminology*, 8th ed. (Philadelphia: Lippincott, 1970), p. 68, cited in Richard T. Wright and Scott H. Decker, *Burglars on the Job: Streetlife and Residential Break-Ins* (Boston: Northeastern University Press, 1994), p. 5.

ii. Paul F. Cromwell, James N. Olson, and D'Aunn Wester Avary, *Breaking and Entering: An Ethnographic Analysis of Burglary* (Newbury Park, CA: Sage, 1991).

iii. Darrell J. Steffensmeier, *The Fence: In the Shadow of Two Worlds* (Savage, MD: Rowman and Littlefield, 1986).

victimization risks for personal theft. You can learn more about burglary trends by visiting the Bureau of Justice Statistics (BJS) via **Web Extra 10–5** and read about the most common targets of burglars at **Library Extra 10–4**. See the Theory versus Reality box for ethnographic research on active burglars.

The Typology of Burglars

A three-part typology of burglary types was offered by **Mike Maguire**: low-level, middle-range, and high-level.[109] Neil Shover determined how the social organization of burglary varied based on Maguire's three types. *Low-level burglars* (primarily juveniles) often commit their crimes "on the spur of the moment," usually work with others, and are easily dissuaded from a particular target by sound locks, alarms, and/or other such security devices, and the rewards are generally not significant, so many desist from burglary as they get older and feel "the pull of conventional relationships and fear of more severe adult sanctions."[110] Members of this group never develop connections that allow them to move large volumes of stolen goods.

Middle-range burglars are a bit older (although they may have begun their offending as juveniles) and go back and forth between legitimate pursuits and involvement in crime, and the use of alcohol and other drugs is more common. These offenders select targets that take into account both the potential payoff and the risk involved; however, they are not as easily dissuaded by security devices as the low-level burglars. While their take from their crimes may be substantial at times, they lack the type of connections that would permit dealing in stolen goods on a large scale.

High-level burglars are professionals who work in organized crews and "are connected with reliable sources of information about targets."[111] Members of this group earn a good living from the proceeds of their crimes, which have carefully planned targets based on the assistance of outside sources (like the art theft described at the beginning of this chapter).

The Locales and Times of Burglary

Burglars may target residences and/or commercial buildings. Although most research has focused on residential burglary, many findings on offender patterns apply to both types. Police reports generally detail the time of the burglary, with nighttime residential burglary and daytime commercial burglary being considered the most serious. Evening hours are the time burglars are most likely to face homeowners, and daytime hours present the greatest risk of confrontation between offenders and customers or workers.[112] According to NCVS data, slightly more residential burglaries take place during the daytime than during the evening hours, but one-third of burglary reports do not contain information on when the burglary occurred, so those incidents could significantly change the temporal pattern of occurrence.[113]

Burglary is known as a "cold" crime because there is usually little physical evidence to link the offender to the offense. By the time the victim realizes there has been a burglary and calls the police, the burglar is long gone. However, commercial buildings are more likely to have alarms or other security devices.

The Motivation of Burglars

Rational choice perspectives (discussed in Chapter 3), which have guided a great deal of research on decision making among property offenders, contend that the decision-making process is not defined by only one objective or shared view of rationality but is guided by the logic and perspective of an individual offender. The way offenders justify their decisions may not make sense objectively, but their decisions have their own logic based on the offenders' social world and reflect the fact that many of them are "limited information processors with various simplifying strategies for resolving decisions."[114]

The most prevalent rationale behind residential burglary is economic: a need for fast cash.[115] Based on ethnographic research conducted in Texas[116] and in St. Louis,[117] active burglars do not have a conventional lifestyle, and most of their everyday concerns revolve around maintaining their street status and supporting a lifestyle of self-indulgence and often gratuitous consumption of drugs. Wright and Decker contended that the need to maintain a party lifestyle, to "keep up appearances," and to provide basic necessities for themselves and their families are all key factors that drive offenders' decisions to commit a burglary.[118]

> The most common rationale behind residential burglary is a need for fast cash.

As in the ethnographic research on the lifestyle of armed robbers (discussed in Chapter 9), Wright and Decker found that the vast majority of residential burglars they interviewed were committed to an "every night is a Saturday night" lifestyle, so when offenders discussed their offending as a means of survival, it had to be interpreted against the backdrop of this lifestyle, for it was only in this context that an understanding of what they meant by "survival" emerged. The vast majority of offenders were committed to street culture, and almost three-fourths of the money they obtained from burglary pursuits went to support their party lifestyle, which included illicit drugs, alcohol, and sexual pursuits. Keeping up appearances resulted in the need to buy things that assisted in maintaining street status (the right clothes, the right car). While some offenders interviewed by Wright and Decker did use the proceeds from their burglaries to pay their bills, the researchers noted that "the bills were badly delinquent because the offenders avoided paying them for as long as possible—even when they had the cash—in favor of buying, most typically, drugs."[119] The lifestyle of these offenders all but guaranteed that "the crimes they commit will be economically motivated," but it is not an economic motivation that results from a desire to satisfy needs as opposed to wants.[120]

Burglaries of commercial establishments are generally thought to be even more associated with instrumental ends—usually economic gain—than residential burglaries. The same is true of professional burglars, who invest more planning and strategy into their offenses, calculating and carefully weighing risks and benefits.

What causes offenders to focus on burglary as their crime of choice? Some offenders selected burglary quite simply because "they regarded burglary as their 'main line.'"[121] Because most of the offenders interviewed by Wright and Decker regarded themselves as hustlers, "people who were always looking to get over by making some fast cash," they would commit offenses other than burglary if an opportunity presented itself; otherwise, they stayed with burglary.[122] For many, burglary was not as risky as selling drugs, which has carried increasingly stiffer penalties that offenders fear. Robbery was perceived as too risky because it involved direct confrontation with the victim and hence a higher likelihood of being injured, and some offenders stated they did not own guns. Because guns can be easily translated into cash in the street economy, "offenders who are in need of immediate cash often are tempted to sell their weapon instead of resorting to a difficult or risky crime."[123]

A small number of offenders in Wright and Decker's research in St. Louis indicated that "they did not typically commit burglaries as much for the money as for the psychic rewards."[124] This is consistent with Katz's concept of sneaky thrills: "If we looked more closely at how [offenders] define material needs, we might get a different image of these 'serious thieves.'"[125] Based on his ethnographic research with property offenders, Kenneth D. Tunnell concluded that "excitement was present but only as a latent benefit—a by-product of the criminal act."[126]

The Target Selection for Burglary

The sites for commercial burglaries are usually selected on the basis of suitability. Retail establishments are four times as likely to be burglarized as other types of establishments, such as wholesale or service businesses.

How do residential burglars select their targets? According to Wright and Decker, most residential burglars already have potential targets in mind before committing their offenses. Generally, burglars select a target by drawing on their knowledge of the occupants, "through receiving a tip," or "through observing a potential target."[127]

While a prior relationship between offenders and victims has long characterized many violent crimes, property crimes generally do not involve known victims, and the pattern of the victim–offender relationship in property crimes does not mirror that of violent crimes; however, there are some interesting dynamics. The residential burglars interviewed by Wright and Decker rarely selected residences of close friends or relatives as targets, but they did quite often purposefully select as targets residences of individuals otherwise known to them.[128] An offender may also target known drug offenders because they can be victimized with relative impunity. A job provides offenders with the opportunity to get to know the occupants of a household and their daily routine as well as to determine their target suitability. When offenders did target residences of friends and loved ones, it was generally in two scenarios: One occurred when an argument or some type of wrongdoing on the victim's part had occurred, and the burglary was as much for revenge as for economic gain; the other involved the offender having such a desperate need for money that anyone was fair game. While many offenders expressed remorse over having burglarized the homes of close family members, this was not universally the case, and burglars' expressions of remorse must be interpreted with the knowledge that "their allegiances seemed forever to be shifting to suit their own ends."[129]

Burglars may also select a target based on information from tipsters, who "regularly pass on intelligence about good burglary opportunities for a fee or a cut of the take."[130] Those who use tipsters do so in a variety of ways, including using individuals who work in service capacities in households and businesses and acting in collusion with insurance agents or other middle-class people who feed the offender information in exchange for money or for some stolen merchandise.

Approximately one-fourth of burglaries do not involve any type of forced entry, "the world affords abundant poorly protected opportunities for burglars."[131] While offenders may not go out actively searching for potential targets, they are "continually 'half looking' for targets."[132]

Target selection is also influenced by other key elements such as signs of occupancy because "most offenders are reluctant to burglarize occupied dwellings," according to Wright and Decker.[133] Burglars have reported that they avoid occupied homes because they want to avoid injury to their victims and to themselves. For some offenders, the fear of their own injury was greater than the fear of apprehension: "I'd rather for the police to catch me versus a person catching me breaking in their house because the person will kill you."[134] To ensure that a residence was unoccupied, offenders would knock on the door (ready to offer some excuse if someone actually answered), phone the residence, or even phone the householder at work.

Most residential burglars also avoid residences with complex security devices because they generally lack the expertise to bypass the system. Dogs also will deter an offender from a potential target because they make noise and could injure the offender. Offenders tended to stay in the same area, sometimes within walking distance, because of lack of a car. As one offender in Wright and Decker's research noted, "It's hard as hell getting on a bus carrying a big picture or a vase."[135]

Follow the author's tweets about the latest crime and justice news at http://twitter.com/schmalleger.

The Costs of Burglary

According to the NCVS, well over three-fourths (86%) of all household burglaries involve some type of economic loss. Approximately 20% of household burglaries involve losses exceeding $1,000, 21% involve losses between $250 and $1,000, 24% involve losses between $50 and $249, and slightly more than 14% involve losses under $50.[136] What do offenders steal from homes? According to self-reports of victims of household burglary, 29% of items stolen from homes are personal in nature, with the largest categories being jewelry and clothing; household furnishings represent 11% of all stolen items, followed by tools (6%) and cash (6%). Another type of crime cost can be gauged by looking at whether victims lose time from work as a result of their victimization: Among all victims of household burglaries, approximately 7% lose some time from work, with 33% of those losing less than one day, slightly over 50% losing from one to five days, and 7% losing six days or more.[137]

Using NCVS data to test the relationship between criminal victimization and a household's decision to move, researcher **Laura Dugan** revealed that property crimes like burglary have a greater effect on the decision to move than violent crimes.[138] Dugan had hypothesized that experiencing a violent crime would have a greater effect on the decision to move—a hypothesis not supported by the data. Instead, she found that a household's likelihood of moving increased after experiencing a criminal victimization near the home, an effect that was significant and strong for property crime but not for violent crime. Communities are also affected because the more affluent households are the ones most likely to relocate after experiencing victimization.

The Burglary–Drug Connection

During the 1980s, the parallel rates of robbery and burglary began to diverge, with robbery increasing and burglary decreasing. Using city-level data from 1984 to 1992, research by Eric Baumer and colleagues linked these changes to the effects of an increased demand for crack cocaine on altering structures of offending.[139] As a stimulant, crack use is characterized by short highs that are "followed by an intense desire for more crack."[140] If users are funding their drug habit through criminal pursuits, they need to rely on offenses that complement the demands of their drug of choice—offenses like robbery—that can net cash quickly, directly, anytime; burglary is more likely to net stolen goods than cash. As the illicit market for crack drove down the street value of stolen property, "dramatically enhancing the attractiveness of cash," burglary became an offense with diminishing rewards.[141] Ethnographic research on active burglars supported the claim that in areas with a strong crack cocaine trade, there was also a "preference for cash-intensive crimes like robbery and a corresponding reduced preference for burglary."[142] This is consistent with research that emphasized that most property offenders are generalists rather than strictly committed to one type of property offense.

The Sexualized Context of Burglary

Although economic gain is the primary motive for the vast majority of burglaries, some criminologists say that there is a category of burglaries with "hidden sexual forces lying at their root."[143] According to Louis B. Schlesinger and Eugene Revitch, the sexual dynamics associated with burglaries may be of two general interrelated types: One type of offender craves fetishes, stealing particular items as an outlet for sexual gratification rather than for their material value.

> A certain number of sexually motivated homicides begin as other offenses, such as burglary.

A voyeuristic burglar has a more subtle sexual dynamic in which the goal may be just to "look around, to inspect the drawers," but not to actually take anything.[144] Schlesinger and Revitch analyzed the clinical records of 52 sexual murderers and found that the majority of these offenders had a history of burglaries, so burglary may serve as a precursor to more serious offenses and may constitute part of a pattern of sexual offending. A certain number of sexually motivated homicides begin as other offenses, such as burglary, and the ability to link the two early in the investigation is important for effective forensic assessment, so details of a burglary should be more purposefully evaluated because they could be related to a progression of events that could culminate in homicide.

Mark Warr investigated the connection of sexual offenses with property crimes from a different perspective.[145] Not only can sexual motives underlie property crimes, Warr argued, but the theoretical perspective of opportunity theory (discussed in Chapter 6) can explain patterns of rape and burglary. Warr said

fence
An individual or a group involved in the buying, selling, and distributing of stolen goods.

that "residential rape and burglary can be viewed as crimes of stealth that involve the unlawful entry of a structure [and] have very similar opportunity structures."[146] Using city arrest data, Warr found support for his contention that both the type of residence and the type of people victimized are similar enough in certain rape and burglary incidents to call into question the idea that rape shares a criminal etiology exclusively with violent offending.

For a certain category of rape termed *home-intrusion rape*, "the traditional distinction between violent crime and property crime may not apply," and such incidents represent a "hybrid offense"; they are "a violent crime with the opportunity structure of a property crime."[147] According to Warr, the correspondence in the opportunity structures of rape and burglary warrants consideration if research and investigative procedures are to identify the "proximate causes of rape."[148]

Receivers of Stolen Property

Darrell J. Steffensmeier posited that "the 1827 English statute—'a person receiving stolen property knowing the same to be stolen is deemed guilty of a felony'—is the prototype of subsequent American law. The exact wording may vary from one state to another, but the basic elements of the crime—'buying and receiving,' 'stolen property,' and 'knowing it to be stolen'—have remained essentially intact."[149] A small number of thieves steal for their own consumption, steal mostly cash, and have no need to translate the goods into cash. In other cases, it is necessary for stolen goods to be translated into cash, and "there are many paths that stolen property may take from thieves to eventual customers."[150] Receiving stolen property is engaged in for profit by individuals and groups with varying skill levels. Some burglars commit their offenses specifically to get something they know someone wants and sell their merchandise directly to a waiting customer.[151] Burglars may sell to people they know or may take stolen goods to places like flea markets or auctions. Other options for disposing of stolen goods "involve the thief and dabbling 'middlemen' who buy and sell stolen property under the cover of a bar, a luncheonette, or an auto service station with the encouragement, if not the active participation, of the proprietor."[152] Some burglars also sell their merchandise to merchants by representing it as legal goods. The most complicated path from the thief to customers is through a **fence** (someone involved in buying, selling, and/or distributing stolen goods); the use of a

fence is the least common method of disposing of stolen goods for the majority of thieves but the most common method used by professional burglars.

Steffensmeier linked the rise of fences to industrialization and the availability of mass-produced goods, which made fencing profitable for significant numbers of people.[153] Steffensmeier used case studies to research the fence, as did **Carl Klockars** in his classic work.[154] Klockars detailed the career of Vincent Swaggi, a successful fence for more than 20 years; Steffensmeier profiled Sam Goodman, a 60-year-old white male whom he began interviewing in early 1980.[155] Building on Klockars's definition, Steffensmeier defined a *fence* as one who "purchases stolen goods both on a regular basis, and for resale."[156] The defining characteristics of the professional fence are that he or she "[has] direct contact with thieves, . . . buys and resells stolen goods regularly and persistently, . . . [and is a] public dealer—recognized as a fence by thieves, the police, and others acquainted with the criminal community."[157] Other variations and distinguishing characteristics exist for those who are part of the puzzle of how stolen goods move from the original owner to the open market.

The Role of Criminal Receivers

In their ethnographic research on residential burglars, **Paul F. Cromwell** and his colleagues offered a three-part typology of criminal receivers: professional receivers, avocational receivers, and amateur receivers.[158] *Professional receivers* fit the definition of *fences* provided by Steffensmeier: those who purchase stolen goods on a regular basis for resale. The use of a professional fence to dispose of stolen goods is uncommon for most residential burglars, who lack "sophisticated underworld connections."[159] Such connections often distinguish "high-level burglars" from the more typical and prevalent residential burglars.[160] Burglars and other thieves who develop access to fences have cited a number of advantages to disposing of stolen goods this way. First, the professional fence offers a safe and quick means of disposing of goods, especially for burglars who commit high-visibility crimes and have easily recognizable goods. In Wright and Decker's ethnographic research on residential burglars, one burglar who had stolen from a local celebrity's house stated, "We couldn't just sell [the jewelry] on the street, it was like too hot to handle."[161] Second, fences are the best outlet for a large volume of stolen goods. Some professional fences are "generalists" who deal in a wide variety of stolen goods, and others are "specialists" who deal only in certain types of goods. Goodman (the professional fence described in Steffensmeier's research) started as a specialist but evolved into a generalist as a "function of greater capital and a growing knowledge of varied merchandise."[162] The vast majority of professional fences are involved in a legitimate business that serves as a cover for their criminal activity and facilitates it. For example, Goodman operated a secondhand store whose inventory partially matched the stolen goods he received, a characteristic that made him quasi-legitimate, a "partly covered fence." Fences who are "fully covered" do not deal in stolen goods that are outside their inventory in the legitimate business, and "noncovered" fences are those whose "illicit lines of goods are distinct from the legitimate commerce."[163] The more a fence is able to cover illicit activities by incorporating them into legitimate enterprises, the safer the fence is from criminal detection and prosecution.

> The professional fence offers a safe and quick means of disposing of goods.

There is a great deal of variety in the businesses that fences use as a front for their criminal activity, ranging from those viewed by the "community-at-large as strictly clean," like restaurants, to businesses that "are perceived as clean but somewhat suspect," like auto parts shops and antique shops, to businesses that are viewed as "quasi-legitimate or marginal," like pawnshops.[164] Some of the residential burglars interviewed by Wright and Decker stated that they avoided marginal businesses like pawnshops when disposing of stolen goods because, given the increasingly strict regulations of pawnshops, owners must often demand identification and take photos of those selling to them, and they have "hot sheets" of recently stolen goods. In addition, pawnshops generally do not provide the greatest return on the merchandise. Given the fact that many residential burglars commit their offenses for fast cash, "pawnshops almost always [have] the upper hand in negotiations."[165] The residential burglars who did regularly use pawnshops reported having an established relationship with the owner that enabled them "to pawn stolen property 'off camera'" because they had made transactions with the owner previously that had not resulted in "bringing additional police pressure to bear on his business."[166]

A second type of fence is *avocational receivers*, who buy stolen property as a part-time endeavor "secondary to, but usually associated with, their primary business activity."[167] This is a fairly diverse group that can include individuals involved in respectable occupations, such as lawyers or bail bondsmen who "provide legitimate professional services to property offenders who cannot pay for these services with anything but stolen property."[168] Others involved in illegitimate occupations, such as drug dealers, may also accept stolen goods.

Amateur receivers are those "otherwise honest citizens who buy stolen property on a relatively small scale, primarily, but not exclusively, for personal consumption. Crime is peripheral rather than central to their lives."[169] These individuals are quite sporadic in their involvement in activities that generate stolen goods. Cromwell and colleagues cited as an example a "public-school teacher who began her part-time fencing when she was approached by a student who offered her a 'really good deal' on certain items."[170] While these individuals do not engage in receiving stolen property at the same level as professional or avocational fences, "they represent a large market for stolen goods" because they "compensate for lack of volume with their sheer numbers."[171] Stuart Henry's study of property crime among ordinary people, which he termed "hidden-economy crime," described the involvement of ordinary citizens in a wide variety of property offenses, including receiving stolen property.[172] Learn more about how fences operate at **Web Extra 10–6**. For an unusual scenario about "fencing," see the Who's to Blame box.

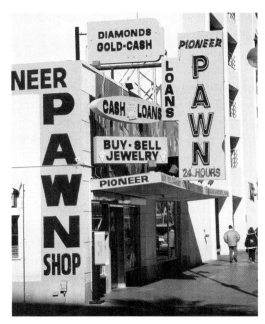

A Las Vegas pawnshop. Could this shop serve as a front for a fencing operation?
Source: Buddy Mays/CORBIS-NY

■ **arson**
The willful or malicious burning (or attempt to burn), with or without intent to defraud, of a house, public building, motor vehicle or aircraft, or personal property of another.

LIBRARY EXTRA 10–5
WEB EXTRA 10–7

WHO'S TO BLAME—The Individual or Society?

Body Parts for Sale

On March 20, 2010, Dr. Paul Sutter, a Palm Beach, Florida, plastic surgeon, was arrested and charged with a federal crime after he allegedly purchased facial bones that he knew had been illegally removed from a cadaver, and implanted them into a wealthy female patient undergoing elective facial reconstructive surgery following a car accident. The doctor and a mortician, who sold him the bones, were both charged with violating the National Organ Transplant Act of 1984, which expressly prohibits interstate trafficking in human tissue for profit.

In an interview the doctor gave after posting bail, Sutter told reporters, "I understand that there's a law against what I did. But it's not my fault that the materials I need to work with are frequently so hard to acquire. There needs to be a better system in place for the distribution of bones and other tissues that are so desperately needed by patients like the woman whose face I reconstructed in this case."

Think about it:

1. Why did Sutter violate the law? What do you think was his primary motivation for what he did?

2. Do you think it would have mattered to Sutter's patient had she known that the bones used in her surgery had been acquired illegally?

3. Can body parts be considered items of property, like a person's other possessions? If so, should he or she have the right to sell them—perhaps to the highest bidder?

Learn more about the illegal trade in body parts at **Library Extra 10–5**.

Note: Who's to Blame boxes provide fictionalized critical thinking opportunities, and are not actual cases.

Arson

The FBI defined **arson** as "any willful or malicious burning or attempt to burn, with or without intent to defraud, a dwelling house, public building, motor vehicle or aircraft, personal property of another, etc."[173] It is only after a fire has been investigated and officially classified as arson by the proper investigative authorities that the FBI records the incident as arson, so fires that are suspicious or of unknown origin are not included in the FBI's arson statistics.[174]

Several diverse motives from profit to thrill seeking to politics may underlie arson. On August 1, 2003, a 206-unit San Diego condominium complex burned down while under construction. A 12-foot banner found at the scene declared, "If you build it, we will burn it," and it was signed *ELF*, letters which stand for the Earth Liberation Front. Less than a month later, ELF arsonists attacked a number of car dealerships in Los Angeles, targeting those that sold gas-guzzling SUVs such as Hummers. Although one person was arrested, he was soon released.

The organization targets what it deems to be threats to the environment—residential and commercial construction in environmentally sensitive areas, bioengineered crops, certain types of animal-research facilities, lumber mills, mink farms, military recruiting offices, and even Starbucks restaurants. The ELF maintains a Web site, which can be seen at **Web Extra 10–7**.

Between 1989 and 1996, a wave of arsons at predominantly African American churches throughout the United States caused enormous concern that these were hate crimes, with some people even contending that the fires were part of an organized effort by "members of various hate groups to start an all-out war between the races."[175] The level of concern about church arsons resulted in President Clinton signing the Church Arson Prevention Act of 1996, legislation designed to increase penalties for church arsons and to accomplish other objectives, such as the rebuilding of destroyed churches.[176] The National Church Arson Task Force arrested 199 suspects in 150 of the 429 arsons under investigation and concluded that most of the arsons were the result of individuals acting alone rather than as part of an organized conspiracy.[177]

Fire Setters

Some people think of arson as "some crooked businessman torching his establishment in order to collect the insurance money," as do some property claims adjusters, argued Ken Brownlee in an article in *Claims* magazine.[178] While representing one part of the reality of arson, arson for profit "has been only a minor part of the loss due to arson for more than a decade"[179] and is atypical of arson in general.

WEB EXTRA 10-8
LIBRARY EXTRA 10-6
LIBRARY EXTRA 10-7

The vast majority of those involved in arson are juveniles.

Whatever the motive, the vast majority of those involved in arson are juveniles, a pattern established for some time. Juveniles are slightly more likely to be involved in arsons in cities than in suburbs or rural areas. Overall, "juveniles account for 21 percent of the clearances for arsons of mobile property, 40 percent of structural arson clearances and 41 percent of clearances for arsons of all other property."[180] Juveniles are involved more often than adults in both residential and commercial fires.

Eileen M. Garry posited that there are three general groups of juvenile fire setters.[181] The first group consists of children younger than age seven who generally start fires either accidentally or out of curiosity. The second group comprises children between the ages of eight and 12 who may start fires out of curiosity, but "a greater proportion of their fire setting represents underlying psychosocial conflicts."[182] The final group of youths between the ages of 13 and 18 has a history of fire setting that usually goes undetected. For more information on the problem of fire setting among juveniles, as well as the prevalence of and issues surrounding arson in the United States, visit the National Fire Data Center online via **Web Extra 10–8**. Learn more about the crime of arson from **Library Extras 10–6** and **10–7**.

SUMMARY

- Professional thieves commit thefts with some degree of skill, earn reasonably good money from their crimes, and spend relatively little time incarcerated. Persistent thieves continue in property crimes despite their ordinary level of success; professional thieves are characterized by greater planning and financial reward. Strict specialization is rarely found among property offenders.

- The major forms of property crime discussed in this chapter are larceny-theft, motor vehicle theft, burglary, and arson.

- Larceny-theft is the unlawful taking or attempted taking, carrying, leading, or riding away of property from the possession or constructive possession of another (motor vehicles are excluded). The largest category is theft from motor vehicles, followed by shoplifting and theft from buildings; pocket picking and purse snatching are much less common.

- Motor vehicle theft is the theft of a motor vehicle and does not include farm equipment, bulldozers, airplanes, construction equipment, or motorboats; almost 1 million motor vehicles are stolen in the United States each year.

- Burglary is the unlawful entry of a structure (residential or commercial) with intent to commit a felony or a theft. Burglars often cross the line to more serious violent crimes like homicide, rape, and robbery, but even in the absence of violent crime, the social costs of burglary to victims and to society are numerous.

- Property crimes usually involve stolen goods that need to be turned into cash. Those who receive stolen goods range from the amateur receiver, who is occasionally involved in fencing, to the professional fence, who buys and sells stolen goods in volume and offers a safe, quick means of disposing of goods, especially for burglars who have committed high-visibility crimes and have easily recognizable goods. Most professional fences are also involved in legitimate businesses that serve as a cover for their criminal activity and facilitate it.

- Arson, the burning or attempted burning of property with or without intent to defraud, has the potential to result in both great economic loss and loss of life. Although arson for profit and for protest certainly occurs, the majority of arsons involve adolescents with various motives for fire setting.

KEY TERMS

arson, 297

booster, 286

burglary, 289

fence, 295

gateway offense, 284

jockey, 289

joyriding, 288

larceny-theft, 280

motor vehicle theft, 287

occasional offender, 279

offense specialization, 278

persistent thief, 278

professional criminal, 278

snitch, 286

KEY NAMES

QUESTIONS FOR REVIEW

1. What are some characteristics of persistent and professional thieves?

2. What are the major forms of property crime discussed in this chapter?

3. What constitutes the crime of larceny-theft? What forms does it take?

4. What is motor vehicle theft? How prevalent is it?

5. What constitutes the crime of burglary? What are some of its characteristics?

6. What are the typical activities of receivers of stolen property, and how are stolen goods distributed?

7. What constitutes the crime of arson?

QUESTIONS FOR REFLECTION

1. To what extent is thrill seeking a motivation behind certain types of property offenses? How might it contribute to the crime of shoplifting?

2. Why is so much attention given to shoplifting among adolescents? Should it be? Why or why not?

3. How are "honest" citizens and professional criminal receivers connected?

4. To what extent are property offenders rational actors? Use examples from larceny, burglary, and receipt of stolen property to illustrate your answer.

5. What does the phrase "sexualized context of burglary" mean? How can burglary have a sexual component or motivation?

6. How are drugs involved in the offending patterns of some burglars? Might effective drug-treatment programs reduce the number of burglaries committed? Why?

CHAPTER 11

WHITE-COLLAR AND ORGANIZED CRIME

LEARNING OUTCOMES

After reading this chapter, you should be able to answer the following questions:

- What is the history of white-collar crime in this country?
- What is white-collar crime? What are the various kinds of white-collar crimes?
- How can white-collar and corporate crime be controlled?
- What is the history of organized crime in this country?
- How can organized crime be controlled?

WEB EXTRA 11-1

Introduction

In 2010, the highly acclaimed USA Network TV series *White Collar* began its second season. The show, which won praise from the *New York Times*,[1] *The Hollywood Reporter*,[2] and other media sources, follows the adventures of a convicted white-collar criminal who works for the FBI in order to stay out of prison. The series, known as "*Collar*" to its many fans, follows the adventures of Neal Caffrey, a convicted bond forger, who helps fictional FBI Agent Peter Burke capture other white-collar criminals using his expertise as an art and securities thief, counterfeiter, and racketeer; it has been described by critics as "a winsome, quick-paced caper that is part *Catch Me If You Can*, part *Shampoo*."[3] Reviewers said that *White Collar* "is packed with smart people who make things happen" and that the show is always "one step ahead of viewers' expectations."[4] Perhaps that explains fans' fascination with the show, which at its debut had 5.4 million reported viewers—a strong number for any television series.[5]

Part of *White Collar*'s success may be due to the American public's curiosity about white-collar crime and white-collar criminals, and notorious instances of white-collar offending have also fueled interest in the subject. Perhaps the best known white-collar criminal of the last few years is 70-year-old investment adviser Bernie Madoff, the architect of a huge Ponzi scheme (the fraudulent tactic of paying off early investors with later investors' money to encourage more and bigger investor risk) that cost investors at least $18 billion when the securities frauds that he perpetrated came to light in late 2008. Madoff, who is profiled in a box in this chapter, pleaded guilty in 2009 to 11 federal offenses including securities fraud, mail fraud, money laundering, and perjury and received a sentence of 150 years in federal prison.

As this book goes to press, ongoing prosecutions involving alleged white-collar offenses include the case of New York stock trader Zvi Goffer, charged with insider trading; 52-year-old Raj Rajaratnam, a Manhattan hedge fund executive originally from India reputed to be one of the world's richest men and also charged with insider trading; and 59-year-old Texas financier Robert Allen Stanford, charged with financial fraud and obstruction of justice. Keep up with these and other ongoing white-collar crime prosecutions via Ellen S. Podgor's *White Collar Crime Professor's Blog* at **Web Extra 11–1**.

A Brief History of White-Collar Crime

White-collar crime is not unique to the twenty-first century. Financial scandals have a long and ubiquitous history in the United States, sometimes involving even government regulators. In 1929, the Teapot Dome scandal, which embroiled the administration of President Warren Harding, began in 1921 when Secretary of the Interior Albert B. Fall secretly leased naval oil reserves at Teapot Dome, Wyoming, and Elk Hills, California, to developers without asking for competitive bids. A Senate investigation later revealed that large sums of federal money had been loaned to developers without interest. Fall was eventually fined and sent to prison, and a 1927 U.S. Supreme Court decision ordered the fields restored to the U.S. government.

The insider-trading scam of stock market tycoon Ivan Boesky and the securities fraud conviction of junk-bond king Michael Milken in the 1980s demonstrated again how fortunes could be amassed through white-collar law violations. Boesky was estimated to have netted a profit of $250 million for himself and a few close friends; Milken paid a $600 million fine—far less than the amount he is estimated to have reaped from illegal bond trading.

The nationwide savings and loan (S&L) disaster of the 1980s, which some have called the "biggest white-collar crime in history," serves as another example of white-collar crime. The S&L fiasco was the result of years of intentional mismanagement and personal appropriation of depositors' funds by institutional executives. Although the actual amount of money lost or stolen during the scandal may never be known, it has been estimated to run into the hundreds of billions of dollars. The collapse of just one such institution, Charles Keating's California-based Lincoln Savings and Loan Association, cost taxpayers—who were left to redeem the insolvent institution—approximately $2.5 billion, and the collapse of Neil Bush's Silverado Banking Savings and Loan in Denver cost nearly $1 billion.

> More money has been stolen at the point of a pen than at the point of a gun.
>
> —Woody Guthrie

Another type of white-collar crime sprang from the low interest rates characteristic of the early and mid-1990s. Sham banking operations flourished by offering high interest rates and

securities fraud

The theft of money resulting from intentional manipulation of the value of equities, including stocks and bonds. Securities fraud also includes theft from securities accounts and wire fraud.

WEB EXTRA 11-2

double-digit rates of return on investments, but such "phantom banks" evaporated as quickly as they were formed, leaving investors stunned and sometimes penniless.

The past decade has seen a number of infamous white-collar crime prosecutions, including those involving executives at the former energy trading giant Enron Corporation who had used complex off-balance-sheet partnerships to hide losses and inflate revenues. The company's collapse in 2001 set the stage both for massive reforms in the business and financial world and for federal and state investigations into the accounting practices and business dealings of all publicly traded companies in the United States. Share prices for Enron's stock grew quickly during 2000 as the company positioned itself as a major player in what appeared to be a lucrative energy-trading business. The business, which did not require that Enron own or produce any of the energy it traded, began to unravel in early 2001 when bankrupt California utility Pacific Gas and Electric Co. was unable to pay $570 million for energy that it had purchased, and Enron was subsequently unsuccessful in bids to extend its credit lines. In November 2001, Enron executives surprised stockholders when they revised the company's financial statements for the prior five years in order to account for hundreds of millions of dollars in losses that they had previously hidden, and a month later, Enron filed for Chapter 11 bankruptcy protection and laid off more than 4,000 workers. The bankruptcy wiped out at least

$24 billion in retirement plans, stock accounts, and mutual funds as the company's stock plummeted.

Enron's bankruptcy was followed by congressional hearings into the collapse of the company as well as by a U.S. Department of Justice investigation that wanted to know how five of the company's former officers had made over $300 million in profits from sales of company stock prior to bankruptcy while ordinary investors had lost everything. The company's former chairman, Kenneth Lay, was convicted in 2006 on numerous counts of securities and wire fraud along with other charges. Lay died of a heart attack before sentencing, and his convictions were later abated (a form of legal nullification) following federal precedent.

On July 21, 2002—less than a year after the collapse of Enron—WorldCom, Inc., a huge telecommunications company, filed for what was then the largest-ever U.S. bankruptcy. At least $11 billion of the company's money had been lost in an accounting fraud intended to save the failing company.[6] One month later, a federal grand jury indicted former WorldCom top executives Buford Yates and Scott Sullivan on charges of conspiracy, **securities fraud**, and false filings with the Securities and Exchange Commission (SEC).[7] Yates pleaded guilty and helped federal prosecutors build cases against others at the company; he was sentenced in 2005 to a year and a day in prison. Sullivan became the government's star witness at the criminal trial of former WorldCom chief executive officer Bernard Ebbers. Sullivan received a five-year sentence, but Ebbers was found guilty of nine counts of conspiracy, securities fraud, and false regulatory filings and was sent to prison for 25 years. For a list of *Time* magazine's "Top 10 Crooked CEOs" of recent years, visit **Web Extra 11–2**.

Allegations of criminal wrongdoing spread to other companies. In 2002, officials at cable television provider Adelphia Communications were charged with failing to adequately disclose loans and loan guarantees of $3.1 billion to the company's founder, John J. Rigas, and members of his family. About the same time, executives at a number of corporations—CMS Energy; Computer Associates International; Dynegy; Global Crossing; Halliburton; Kmart; Lucent Technologies; Network Associates; Qwest Communications International, Inc.; Reliant Resources; Trump Hotels and Casinos; Waste Management; and Xerox—were accused by the SEC, stockholders, and independent prosecutors of intentionally misstating revenues or hiding losses.

Matt Bomer, star of the USA Network's show *White Collar*. What is white-collar crime?

Source: David Giesbrecht/NBCU Photo Bank/AP Photo

■ **insider trading**
A type of equity trading based on confidential information about important events that may affect the price of the issue being traded.

■ **bank fraud**
Any fraud or embezzlement that occurs within or against financial institutions that are insured or regulated by the U.S. government. Fraud of financial institutions includes commercial-loan fraud, check fraud, counterfeit negotiable instruments, mortgage fraud, and false credit applications.

CRIME | in the NEWS

Obama Task Force Will Crack Down on Financial Crime

WASHINGTON—President Barack Obama is creating a multiagency task force to pursue criminals who bilked investors and consumers during the financial crisis.

The task force of top federal officials will work with state and local authorities to pursue financial fraud cases stemming from the crash of the housing market and the Wall Street meltdown. . . .

"Mortgages, securities, and corporate fraud schemes have eroded the public's confidence in the nation's financial markets and have led to a growing sentiment that Wall Street does not play by the same rules as Main Street," Attorney General Eric H. Holder, Jr., said.

The Financial Fraud Enforcement Task Force will attack what Holder called "unscrupulous executives, Ponzi scheme operators, and common criminals" in much the same way that a similar task force created in 2002 by former President George W. Bush went after corporate malfeasance following the accounting scandals at Enron Corp. and WorldCom Inc.

Obama's task force will take advantage of new antifraud powers and funding enacted by Congress last spring. The Fraud Enforcement and Recovery Act authorized $245 million annually in 2010 and 2011 to hire hundreds of prosecutors, agents, and other federal officials to pursue financial fraud. It also strengthened and expanded money-laundering laws and other statutes to apply to fraud committed by private mortgage lenders. . . .

Although the scope of the financial crisis was clear when Obama took office, Holder cautioned, "It would take time to coordinate an effort spread across numerous agencies and states. In the meantime, federal authorities have been vigorously pursuing financial fraud cases, which the task force would build on.

"We've all been doing things in the interim," Holder said, "but we thought that by putting our forces together, that we can be even more effective than we have been."

The new task force "brings a renewed focus and vigor" to financial fraud investigations, said David Zornow, a former federal prosecutor who heads the white-collar-crime group at Skadden, Arps, Slate, Meagher & Flom law firm.

The Justice Department will head the task force, with the Treasury Department, Housing and Urban Development, and the Securities and Exchange Commission serving on its steering committee.

"It is a way for us to mount an even better organized and more collaborative response to the pain and losses caused by the financial crisis,"

said Robert Khuzami, SEC's enforcement director. "The task force will improve our chances of identifying wrongdoers and thus restore confidence in our markets."

According to Khuzami, "The SEC, which has been severely criticized for missing warning signals about Bernard L. Madoff's multibillion-dollar Ponzi scheme, has reorganized and streamlined its enforcement efforts, and is launching special units to focus on types of financial fraud."

Discussion Questions

1. White-collar criminals were treated much more leniently during much of the twentieth century than they are today. Why?

2. What led to the recent change in public and official attitudes toward white-collar criminals?

President Barack Obama speaks to members of the press in the Rose Garden of the White House on April 27, 2010. How will the president's new task force fight white-collar crime?
Source: AFP Photo/Saul Loeb/NewsCom.com

Source: Jim Puzzanghera, "Obama Task Force Will Crack Down on Financial Crime," *Chicago Tribune*, November 17, 2009. © McClatchy-Tribune Information Services. All Rights Reserved. Reprinted with permission.

In 2002 insider trading threatened the home-decorating empire of Martha Stewart.

Also in 2002, ImClone founder Dr. Sam Waksal pleaded guilty to six federal charges of bank fraud and conspiracy involving **insider trading** (equity trading based on confidential information

that could affect stocks being traded) that threatened the home-decorating empire of Martha Stewart. Prosecutors alleged that Waksal had tipped off family members and friends, including Stewart and her stockbroker, that the Food and Drug Administration would not approve his company's experimental cancer drug, Erbitux.[8] Waksal, who admitted to **bank fraud** for forging the name of ImClone's chief attorney to a document

WEB EXTRA 11-3

■ **white-collar crime**
A violation of the criminal law committed by a person of respectability and high social status in the course of his or her occupation.

the **PROFESSOR** | **SPEAKS**

White-Collar Crime

MICHAEL M. WEHRMAN

Ohio University

Within Ponzi schemes, not all participants are victims. Early investors can earn the promised high returns, even if they're unaware that their money is not being properly invested. Some of Bernard Madoff's 'investors,' for example, came away with billions.

When I signed up to receive a free Xbox 360, I discovered how this was possible. An online company promised the game system if I did two things: (1) sign up for a business (e.g., video rental or music club), and (2) find eight more people to do the same thing. In total, the company earned revenue from nine people; but eight of them earned nothing. Only I earned something: an Xbox. If the other eight wanted to earn their own Xbox, they would each have had to find eight additional people to sign up (for a grand total of 72 persons involved, with only nine getting anything "free" out of it). In typical schemes, as they grow, more people become involved, with an increasingly smaller percentage getting anything meaningful out of it.

Bernard Madoff earned his early investors billions only because other, newer, people continued to join and invest in his firm. Later investors, however, lost virtually everything.

Source: Reprinted by permission of Michael M. Wehrman. Photo courtesy of Michael M. Wehrman. Logo courtesy of Ohio University.

securing a line of credit, was sentenced to seven years in prison, and Martha Stewart was ordered to spend five months behind bars.

Securities firms were pulled into the fray when Salomon Smith Barney (the investment arm of Citigroup, Inc.); Goldman Sachs Group, Inc.; Merrill Lynch & Co.; Deutsche Bank AG; and U.S. Bancorp's Piper Jaffray unit came under investigation by federal regulators on suspicion that they had created conflicts of interest in handing out shares in initial public offerings of companies that they supported financially to select stock-research analysts.[9] Regulators also charged the firms with providing biased research to mislead investors into buying stock in companies in which the firms had vested interests. Although some felt that criminal charges of securities fraud would be brought, an agreement between the SEC and the Wall Street firms in December 2002 ended the possibility of criminal prosecution and required the companies to pay $1.4 billion in fines.[10] Table 11–1 describes the terminology of white-collar crime. Learn more about white-collar crime and law enforcement's response from the National White Collar Crime Center via **Web Extra 11–3**. See the Crime in the News box for information on a presidential task force targeting financial crimes.

Understanding White-Collar Crime

Famed criminologist **Edwin H. Sutherland**, during his 1939 presidential address to the American Sociological Society, defined **white-collar crime** as any violation of the criminal law "committed by a person of respectability and high social status in the course of his occupation."[11] Many criminologists do not properly understand crime, Sutherland claimed, because they fail to recognize that the secretive violations of public and corporate trust by those in positions of authority are just as criminal as predatory acts committed by people of lower social standing.

Sutherland told those gathered for the address: "My thesis is that the traditional/conception(s) and explanations of crime [are] misleading and incorrect; that crime is in fact not closely correlated with poverty or with the psychopathic and sociopathic conditions associated with poverty, and that an adequate explanation of criminal behavior must proceed along quite different lines. The conventional explanations are invalid principally because they are derived from biased samples. The samples are biased in that they have not included vast areas of criminal behavior of persons not in the lower class."[12]

TABLE 11-1 | The Terminology of White-Collar Crime

Antitrust Violation

Any activity that illegally inhibits competition between companies and within an industry, such as price fixing and monopolies in restraint of trade. Antitrust violations are infractions of the Sherman Act (15 U.S.C. Sections 1–7) and the Clayton Act (15 U.S.C. Sections 12–27).

Bank Fraud (Financial Fraud or Financial Institution Fraud)

Any fraud or embezzlement that occurs within or against financial institutions that are insured or regulated by the U.S. government. Financial institution fraud includes commercial loan fraud, check fraud, counterfeit negotiable instruments, mortgage fraud, and false credit applications.

Bankruptcy Fraud

The misleading of creditors through the concealment and misstatement of assets. Bankruptcy fraud also involves illegal pressure on bankruptcy petitioners.

Economic Espionage/Trade-Secret Theft

The theft or misappropriation of proprietary economic information (trade secrets) from an individual, a business, or an industry.

Embezzlement

The unlawful misappropriation for personal use of money, property, or other thing of value entrusted to the offender's care, custody, or control.

Environmental Law Violation

Any business activity in violation of federal and state environmental laws, including the discharge of toxic substances into the air, water, or soil, especially when those substances pose a significant threat of harm to people, property, or the environment.

Government Fraud

Any fraud against the government, especially in connection with federal government contracting and federal and/or federally funded programs. Such programs include public housing, agricultural programs, defense procurement, and government-funded educational programs. Fraudulent activities involving government contracting include bribery in contracts or procurement, collusion among contractors, false or double billing, false certification of the quality of parts or of test results, and substitution of bogus or otherwise inferior parts.

Health-Care Fraud

Any fraudulent billing practice by health-care providers, including hospitals, home-health care, ambulance services, doctors, chiropractors, psychiatric hospitals, laboratories, pharmacies, and nursing homes, that affects health-care consumers, insurance providers, and government-funded payment providers such as Medicare and Medicaid. Fraudulent activities include receiving kickbacks, billing for services not rendered, billing for unnecessary equipment, and billing for services performed by a lesser qualified person.

Insider Trading

Any equity trading based on confidential information about important events that may affect the price of the issue being traded. Because confidential information confers advantages on those who possess it, federal law prohibits them from using that knowledge to reap profits or to avoid losses in the stock market.

Insurance Fraud

Any fraudulent activity by insurance applicants, policyholders, third-party claimants, or professionals who provide insurance services to claimants. Such fraudulent activities include inflating, or "padding," actual claims and fraudulent inducements to issue policies and/or establish a lower premium rate.

Kickback

The return of a certain amount of money from seller to buyer as a result of a collusive agreement.

Mail Fraud

The use of the U.S. mail in furtherance of criminal activity.

Money Laundering

The process of converting illegally earned assets, originating as cash, to one or more alternative forms to conceal such incriminating factors as illegal origin and true ownership.

Securities Fraud

The theft of money resulting from intentional manipulation of the value of equities, including stocks and bonds. Securities fraud also includes theft from securities accounts and wire fraud.

Tax Evasion

Any fraud committed by filing false tax returns or not filing tax returns at all.

Wire Fraud

The use of an electric or electronic communications facility to intentionally transmit a false and/or deceptive message in furtherance of a fraudulent activity.

References: Cynthia Barnett, *The Measurement of White-Collar Crime Using Uniform Crime Reporting Data*, FBI, Criminal Justice Information Services Division, http://www.fbi.gov/ucr/whitecollarforweb.pdf (accessed June 18, 2007); Clifford Karchmer and Douglas Ruch, "State and Local Money Laundering Control Strategies," *NIJ Research in Brief* (Washington, DC: National Institute of Justice, 1992); and Legal Information Institute, *White-Collar Crime: An Overview*, http://www.law.cornell.edu/topics/white_collar.html (accessed July 1, 2007).

LIBRARY EXTRA 11-1

According to Sutherland, "[The criminality of upper-class persons] has been demonstrated again and again in the investigations of land offices, railways, insurance, munitions, banking, public utilities, stock exchanges, the oil industry, real estate, reorganization committees, receiverships, bankruptcies and politics."[13] Sutherland also pointed to those he called "the robber barons" of the nineteenth century, citing Cornelius Vanderbilt's famous response to inquiries about his sometimes flagrantly illegal activities: "You don't suppose you can run a railroad in accordance with the statutes, do you?"[14]

In a later study still widely cited by criminologists, Sutherland reported on the frequency with which the nation's 70 largest corporations violated the law.[15] Each of the corporations he studied had been sanctioned by courts or by administrative commissions, and the typical corporation had an average of 14 decisions against it; 98% of corporations were recidivists (commit crime after crime), Sutherland said, and 90% could be called "habitual criminals" under the habitual-offender statutes that existed at the time of his study. "Sixty of the corporations [had] decisions against them for restraint of trade, fifty-four for infringements (generally, of patents), forty-four for unfair labor practices, twenty-seven for misrepresentation in advertising, twenty-six for [illegal] rebates, and forty-three for miscellaneous offenses."[16] He also found that of the 70 largest corporations studied, "thirty were either illegal in their origin or began illegal activities immediately after their origin."[17] Such businesses may have been built on price fixing or unregulated commodities offerings or via unlawful and clandestine negotiations with government regulators. The only real difference between modern-day white-collar criminals and those of the past, Sutherland claimed, is that today's criminals are more sophisticated. Although no hard-and-fast figures were available, Sutherland estimated that the "financial cost of white-collar crime is probably several times as great as the financial cost of all the crimes which are customarily regarded as the 'crime problem.'"[18]

> According to Sutherland, the criminality of upper-class persons has been demonstrated again and again.

Sutherland also noted that white-collar criminals are far less likely to be investigated, arrested, or prosecuted than other types of offenders and that when they are—on rare occasions—convicted, white-collar criminals are far less likely to receive prison terms than "common criminals." If they are sent to prison, the amount of time they are ordered to serve is far less than one would expect, given the amount of damage their crimes inflict on society. The deference shown to white-collar criminals, according to Sutherland, is due primarily to their social standing: They are well respected in their communities and take part in national affairs, and they are not seen as mean-spirited or even ill-intentioned. Private citizens who do not fully understand business affairs sometimes (wrongly) assume that those charged with white-collar crimes were unwittingly caught up in obscure government regulations or that government agencies chose to make examples of a few unfortunate businesspeople.

Criminologists have felt compelled for years to address the question "Is white-collar crime *crime*?" In 1987, writers asked, "Do persons of high standing commit crimes?"[19] Most criminologists today would answer the question with a resounding "Yes!" Members of the public were far slower to accept the notion that violations of the criminal law by businesspeople share conceptual similarities with street crime, but attitudes are changing as more headline-making charges are being filed against corporations and their representatives for illegal activities. Learn more about a specific case of white-collar crime at **Library Extra 11–1**.

Definitional Evolution of White-Collar Crime

One early writer on white-collar crime explained, "The chief criterion for a crime to be 'white-collar' is that it occurs as a part of, or a deviation from, the violator's occupational role."[20] This focus on the violator—rather than on the offense—in deciding whether to classify a crime as "white collar" was accepted by the 1967 President's Commission on Law Enforcement and Administration of Justice in its classic report, *The Challenge of Crime in a Free Society*: "The 'white-collar' criminal is the broker who distributes fraudulent securities, the builder who deliberately uses defective material, the corporation executive who conspires to fix prices, the legislator who peddles his influence and votes for private gain, or the banker who misappropriates funds in his keeping."[21] See the Criminal Profiles box about an executive involved in Ponzi schemes.

Over the past few decades, the concept of white-collar crime has undergone considerable refinement.[22] The reason, according to the U.S. Department of Justice, is that "the focus [in cases of white-collar crime] has shifted to the nature of the crime instead of the persons or occupations involved."[23] The methods used to commit white-collar crime, such as the use of computers and the special skills and knowledge necessary for attempted law violations, have resulted in a contemporary understanding of white-collar crime emphasizing the type of offense being committed rather than the social standing or occupational role of the person committing it. Some reasons for this shift are changes in the work environment and the business world; others are pragmatic: "The

CRIMINAL | PROFILES
Bernie Madoff

On July 24, 2009, convicted Ponzi schemer and formerly wealthy invest-ment counselor Bernard (Bernie) Madoff arrived by prison bus at the federal correctional institution in Butner, North Carolina, to begin serv-ing a 150-year sentence.[i] The 71-year-old Madoff had been convicted only days earlier of multiple fraud and securities violations stemming from a scheme in which he exploited thousands of clients who had en-trusted him with their money for over 20 years. Among his victims were some very wealthy people from places as diverse as New York City and Palm Beach, Florida.[ii]

Some estimates put losses to investors as high as $65 billion dollars—money that seemed to evaporate into thin air, and which investigators struggled to recover. By the time Madoff went to prison, only about $1.2 billion had been found, and insurance payments of around $500,000 had been made to investors.[iii] Madoff's scheme has been called "the largest investor fraud ever committed by a single person."[iv]

In fact, Madoff may not have actually invested any of his client's money, instead paying off redemptions from his fund with money taken in from new clients. The false account statements that Madoff issued to "investors" showed their accounts rapidly growing in value—outpacing the invest-ment results of even the most savvy investment managers. The stock mar-ket downturn of 2008, however, led to a record number of redemption requests—and when Madoff was unable to meet them, the game was up.

Born Bernard Lawrence Madoff on April 29, 1938, in Queens, New York, Madoff began his adult life as a plumber and also worked as a lifeguard and landscaper. He soon went to college, graduating from New York's Hofstra University in 1960 with a degree in political science. A year later he dropped out of Brooklyn Law School to become a stock-broker, eventually rising through the financial ranks to serve as a chair-man of the NASDAQ stock exchange. In 1960, Madoff founded his own firm, Bernard L. Madoff Investment Securities, LLC. He served as chair-man of that company until his arrest on December 11, 2008.

Doubts about Madoff preceded his arrest by at least ten years, as his firm had faced a number of investigations by the SEC, some of which had apparently been dropped by the SEC for lack of money.

At the time of this writing, only one other person—Madoff's longtime accountant, David Friehling—has been charged in connection with the fraud, although authorities suspect that others must have been involved.

Disgraced financier Bernard Madoff leaving the federal court in Manhattan after appearing at a bail hearing Monday, January 5, 2009, in New York City. Madoff was convicted of operating a Ponzi scheme that bilked investors out of $50 billion. He is currently serving a 150-year sentence at the medium-security Federal Correctional Institution in Butner, North Carolina. Was his sentence too harsh? Too lenient?
Source: Jason Decrow/Rapport/NewsCom.com

Madoff refused to cooperate in the investigation, claiming that he was the only person with knowledge of the scam. Federal prosecutors reached a settlement with Madoff's wife under which she abandoned claims to $85 million in assets that the couple had owned, leaving her with $2.5 mil-lion in cash. The couple's sons, Mark and Andrew, both of whom had worked with their father, continue to deny claims of any wrongdoing.

During the sentencing stage of the proceedings against him, Madoff apologized to his victims, saying, "I have left a legacy of shame . . . to my family and my grandchildren. This is something I will live in for the rest of my life. I'm sorry."[v]

Notes
  i. Zachery Kouwe, "Madoff Arrives at Federal Prison in North Carolina," *New York Times*, July 14, 2009, http://www.nytimes.com/2009/07/15/business/15madoff.html (accessed July 21, 2009).
 ii. Michael Moore, "Bernie Madoff," The 2009 Time 100, http://www.time.com/time/specials/packages/article/0,28804,1894410_1893837_1894189,00.html (accessed July 20, 2009).
iii. The Ticker, *Washington Post*, July 14, 2009; and Elizabeth Dwoskin, "Bernie Madoff's Accountant Charged, Pleads Not Guilty," *Village Voice*, July 17, 2009, http://blogs.villagevoice.com/runninscared/archives/2009/07/bernie_madoffs.php (accessed July 21, 2009).
 iv. "Topic: Bernard Madoff," *New York Post* (various dates), http://www.nypost.com/topics/topic.php?t=Bernard_Madoff (accessed August 12, 2009).
  v. "Transcript of Madoff's Sentencing Statement," *New York Post*, June 29, 2009, http://www.nypost.com/seven/06292009/news/regionalnews/partial_transcript_of_madoffs_sentencing_176718.htm (accessed August 12, 2009).

categorization of 'white-collar crime' as crime having a particu-lar modus operandi [committed in a manner that utilizes decep-tion and special knowledge of business practices and committed in a particular kind of economic environment] is of use in coor-dinating the resources of the appropriate agencies for purposes of investigation and prosecution."[24]

Between the early and later definitions of *white-collar crime*, many investigators refined its conceptual boundaries. **Herbert Edelhertz** defined *white-collar crime* as any "illegal act or series of illegal acts committed by nonphysical means and by concealment or guile, to obtain money or property, to avoid the payment or loss of money or property, or to obtain business or personal advantages."[25] **Gilbert Geis** grappled with the notion of "upper-world crime," which he called "a label designed to call attention to the violation of a variety of criminal statutes by persons who at the moment are generally not considered, in connection with

■ occupational crime
An act punishable by law that is committed through opportunity created in the course of a legal occupation.

WEB EXTRA 11–4
WEB EXTRA 11–5
LIBRARY EXTRA 11–2

THEORY | versus REALITY
White-Collar Crime: The Initial Statement

At least one eminent criminologist has called the concept of white-collar crime "the most significant development in criminology, especially since World War II."[i] The roots of the concept go back to 1939, when Edwin Sutherland first coined the term *white-collar crime* in his presidential address to the American Sociological Society. Details of that address are discussed elsewhere in this chapter. His speech concluded with the following five points:

1. White-collar criminality is real criminality, being in all cases in violation of the criminal law.

2. White-collar criminality differs from lower-class criminality principally in implementation of the criminal law, which segregates white-collar criminals administratively from other criminals.

3. The theories of the criminologists that crime is due to poverty or to psychopathic and sociopathic conditions statistically associated with poverty are invalid because, first, they are derived from samples which are grossly biased with respect to socioeconomic status; second, they do not apply to the white-collar criminals; and third, they do not even explain the criminality of the lower class, since the factors are not related to a general process characteristic of all criminality.

4. A theory of criminal behavior which will explain both white-collar criminality and lower-class criminality is needed.

5. A hypothesis of this nature is suggested in terms of differential association and social disorganization.

Discussion Questions

1. Why is white-collar crime possibly the most significant development in criminology since World War II?

2. Why did Sutherland have to remind people that "white-collar criminality is real criminality"? Why might some have thought otherwise?

Note
i. Donald J. Newman, "White-Collar Crime: An Overview and Analysis," *Law and Contemporary Problems*, Vol. 23, No. 4 (autumn 1958).
Source: Edwin Sutherland, "White-Collar Criminality," *American Sociological Review*, Vol. 5 (February 1940), pp. 1–12.

---

such violations, to be the 'usual' kind of underworld and/or psychologically aberrant offenders."[26] Many writers were quick to realize that "upperworld," or white-collar, crime might have its counterpart in certain forms of blue-collar crime committed by members of less prestigious occupational groups, so the term *blue-collar crime* emerged as a way of classifying the law-violating behavior of people involved in appliance and automobile repair, yard maintenance, house cleaning, and general installation services. See the Theory versus Reality box for more on definitions of white-collar crime.

In an effort to bring closure to the concept of work-related crime, the term **occupational crime**—"any act punishable by law that is committed through opportunity created in the course of an occupation which is legal"[27]—emerged as a kind of catchall category that included the job-related law violations of both white- and blue-collar workers. An excellent four-part typology of occupational crime is offered by **Gary S. Green** in his book *Occupational Crime*:[28]

1. **Organizational occupational crime**. An organizational occupational crime is committed for the benefit of an employer or organization, but only the employer or organization—not individual employees—benefits.

2. **State authority occupational crime**. A state authority occupational crime is committed by people exercising their state-based authority, is occupation specific, and can be committed only by officials in public office or those working for them.

3. **Professional occupational crime**. A professional occupational crime is committed by professionals while in their occupational capacity (such as physicians, attorneys, and psychologists).

4. **Individual occupational crime**. An individual occupational crime, committed by an individual acting alone, is a kind of catchall category that includes personal income-tax evasion, theft of goods and services by employees, and filing of false expense reports.

For an interesting presentation of white-collar and occupational crime typologies, visit the National Check Fraud Center and Cornell Law School's white-collar crime page via **Web Extras 11–4** and **11–5**. Learn more about white-collar crime and its measurement from **Library Extra 11–2**.

> The idea of occupational crime became a kind of catchall category.

Corporate Crime

Corporate malfeasance, another form of white-collar crime, has been called **corporate crime** and is defined as "a violation of a criminal statute either by a corporate entity or by its executives, employees, or agents acting on behalf of and for the benefit of the corporation, partnership, or other form of business entity."[29] Corporate crimes come in many forms, ranging from knowledge about automobile defects to price fixing and insider securities trading. Culpability, often resulting in civil suits against the corporation along with possible criminal prosecutions, is greatest when company officials can be shown to have

> Corporate crime is a violation of a criminal statute by a corporate entity or by its executives, acting on behalf of the corporation.

had advance knowledge about a defective product, dangerous conditions, or illegal employee behavior.

In 2002, the accounting firm of Arthur Andersen was convicted of obstruction of justice after its employees destroyed documents related to Enron Corporation audits; it was forced to relinquish its U.S. licenses and closed its American offices. Arthur Andersen had also provided accounting services for WorldCom, Inc., prior to the arrest of that company's chief financial officer and other executives;[30] in 2005, however, the firm was at least partially vindicated when its conviction was overturned by the U.S. Supreme Court, which found that the instructions given to the jury in the 2002 trial had been flawed.[31]

Power Fasterners, Inc., of Brewster, New York, was indicted in 2007 on charges of manslaughter by Massachusetts prosecutors after the epoxy products it manufactured failed in Boston's "Big Dig" tunnel in 2006, allowing 20 tons of concrete ceiling panels to collapse onto a car below, killing the driver.[32] In 2008, the company agreed to pay $16 million to settle a civil lawsuit brought against it in exchange for a promise by prosecutors to drop manslaughter charges.[33]

Kansas City pharmacist Robert R. Courtney, age 48, who pleaded guilty in 2002 to 20 felony counts charging him with the fraudulent distribution of diluted intravenous chemotherapy drugs to at least 34 patients. Other charges included tampering with consumer products, adulteration of drugs, and misbranding of drugs. Courtney, who is estimated to have made hundreds of thousands of dollars in the scheme, was caught when a drug salesman noticed that he was billing doctors for more medication than he was buying. His ten-year prison sentence was upheld in 2004 by the U.S. Court of Appeals for the Eighth Circuit. How does Sutherland's definition of *white-collar crime* apply in a case like this?
Source: AP Wide World Photos

Financial Crime

Most white-collar crimes are financial crimes, meaning illegal activities generally committed for monetary profit by businesses and those who run them. The FBI classified the following types of activities as financial crimes: corporate fraud, securities and commodities fraud, health-care fraud, mortgage fraud, insurance fraud, mass-marketing fraud, and money laundering.[34] We will discuss each in the pages that follow.

Corporate Fraud

The term **corporate fraud** refers to accounting schemes, self-dealing by corporate executives, and obstruction of justice as well as insider trading, kickbacks, and misuse of corporate property for personal gain. The majority of these cases pursued at the federal level are built on accounting schemes intended to deceive investors, auditors, and analysts about the financial health of a corporation. In addition to significant financial losses to investors, corporate fraud has the potential to cause damage to both investor confidence and the U.S. economy.

Corporate fraud sometimes involves the backdating of executive stock options under which the date of options is set to a time in the past when the price of the stock was lower than on the date the options were actually issued. Backdating stock options inflates the value of the options to the holder at the expense of regular shareholders.

■ **securities and commodities fraud**
A crime involving investments, such as stock-market manipulation, high-yield investment fraud (Ponzi schemes, pyramid schemes, and prime bank schemes), advance-fee fraud, hedge-fund fraud, commodities fraud, foreign-exchange fraud, and broker embezzlement.

■ **Ponzi scheme**
A form of high-yield investment fraud that uses money collected from new investors, rather than profits from the purported underlying business venture, to pay high rates of return promised to earlier investors.

Obstruction of justice occurs when activities are undertaken that are designed to conceal any of the types of criminal conduct noted here, particularly when the obstruction impedes the inquiries of the SEC, other regulatory agencies, and/or law enforcement agencies.

Securities and Commodities Fraud

Securities and commodities fraud includes crimes such as stock market manipulation, high-yield investment fraud (Ponzi schemes, pyramid schemes, and prime bank schemes), advance-fee fraud, hedge-fund fraud, commodities fraud, foreign-exchange fraud, and broker embezzlement.

Stock market manipulation schemes (commonly referred to as "pump and dumps") create artificial buying pressure for a targeted security, generally a low-volume stock in the over-the-counter securities market, that is largely controlled by the fraud perpetrators. This artificially increased trading volume unfairly increases the price of the targeted security (the "pump"), which is rapidly sold off into the inflated market created for the security by the fraud perpetrators (the "dump"), resulting in illicit gains for the perpetrators and losses for innocent third-party investors.

High-yield investment fraud takes various forms, all of which are characterized by offers of low- or no-risk investments that guarantee unusually high rates of return. **Ponzi schemes** use money collected from new investors, rather than business profits, to pay high rates of return promised to earlier investors, giving them the impression that this is a legitimate moneymaking enterprise when, in reality, investor monies are the only source of funding. The term *pyramid scheme* refers to money collected from newer victims of the fraud to pay earlier victims in order to provide a veneer of legitimacy; the victims themselves are induced to recruit more victims through the payment of recruitment commissions. *Prime bank schemes* (another form of high-yield investment fraud) induce victims to invest in financial instruments, allegedly issued by well-known institutions, offering risk-free opportunities for high rates of return. The benefits are supposedly the result of access to a secret worldwide exchange ordinarily open only to the world's largest financial institutions, but either such networks don't exist or the perpetrators don't have access to them, and the perpetrators keep the money with which they've been entrusted.

Advance-fee fraud encompasses a broad variety of schemes designed to induce victims into remitting up-front payments in exchange for the promise of goods, services, and/or prizes; victims are informed that in order to participate in this promising investment opportunity, they must first pay various taxes and/or fees—which go directly to the perpetrators. *Hedge-fund fraud* uses private investment partnerships that have generally experienced a relative lack of regulatory scrutiny, and the fraud perpetrated by fund managers can involve the overstatement or misappropriation of fund assets, overcharges for fund management fees, insider trading, market timing, and late trading.

Commodities fraud typically involves the deceptive or fraudulent sale of commodities investments (gold, silver, oil, copper, natural gas, and the like); false or deceptive sales practices are used to solicit victim funds for commodities transactions that either never occur or are inconsistent with the original sales promises. Commodities-market participants may also attempt to illegally manipulate the market for a commodity by fraudulently reporting price information or cornering the market to artificially increase the price of the targeted commodity.

Foreign-exchange fraud uses false or deceptive sales practices alleging high rates of return for minimal risk to induce victims to invest in the foreign-currency exchange market. The transactions never occur or are executed for the sole purpose of generating excessive trading commission—in breach of the trader's responsibilities to the client. Alternatively, individual currency traders employed by large financial institutions may illegally attempt to manipulate foreign-currency exchange prices to generate illicit trading profits for their own enrichment.

Schemes using *broker embezzlement* involve illicit, unauthorized actions by brokers to steal directly from their clients. These may be facilitated by the forging of client documents, the doctoring of account statements, or the unauthorized trading and fund transfers in violation of the broker's legal obligations to the client.

According to the FBI, the losses associated with these types of fraud range from the macroeconomic (erosion of investor confidence in capital markets) to the corporate (reduction in the economic health of corporations/industries due to decreased market capitalization) to the intensely personal (devastation of retirement and investment portfolios).[35] Victims of these kinds of fraud include government entities, corporations, financial institutions, pension funds, and individual investors.

Health-Care Fraud

All health-care programs are subject to fraud, with Medicare and Medicaid being most victimized. Estimates of fraudulent billings to health-care programs (public and private) are said to be between 3% and 10% of all health-care expenditures. According to the FBI, health-care fraud is not limited to any particular geographic area, targets large health-care programs (public and private) as well as beneficiaries, has become more sophisticated and complex over time, and is even being perpetrated by a number of organized-crime groups.

Estimates of fraudulent billings to health-care programs (public and private) are said to be between 3% and 10% of all health-care expenditures.

The FBI stated that "one of the most significant trends in recent health care fraud cases includes the willingness of medical professionals to risk patient harm in their schemes."[36] These cases involve health-care providers who conduct unnecessary surgeries, prescribe dangerous drugs without medical necessity, and engage in abusive or substandard care practices. Other schemes involve fraudulent billing for services not rendered and upcoding of charges for services provided.[37]

Mortgage Fraud

The federal government has reported a spike in the number of corporate-fraud cases involving subprime mortgage–lending companies[38] (businesses that lend to borrowers who do not qualify for loans from mainstream loan companies). The subprime market grew from 2% of all home mortgages in 1998 to 20% of mortgages in 2006, but as the housing market declined, subprime lenders were forced to buy back a number of non-performing loans. Many of these subprime lenders had relied on a continuous increase in real estate values to allow borrowers to refinance or sell their properties before going into default, but due to the slowdown in the housing market, loan defaults increased.

As subprime lenders suffered financial difficulties due to rising defaults, analyses of company financials by regulators identified instances of false accounting entries and fraudulently inflated assets and revenues. Federal investigations then determined that many now-bankrupt subprime lenders manipulated their reported loan-portfolio risks and used various accounting schemes to inflate and falsify their financial reports. In addition, before the value of these subprime lenders' stocks rapidly declined in value, some executives with insider information sold their equity positions and made illegal profits.

Mortgage fraud, which is not confined to the subprime market, involves material misstatements, misrepresentations, and/or omissions relating to the property or potential mortgage relied on by an underwriter or lender to fund, purchase, or insure a loan. As initial mortgage products are repackaged and sold on secondary markets, the process can conceal or distort the original fraud so that it is not reported, leading the FBI to explain that "the true level of mortgage fraud is largely unknown."[39]

Current mortgage fraud, according to the FBI, includes equity skimming, property flipping, and mortgage-debt elimination. *Equity skimming* uses corporate shell companies, corporate identity theft, and bankruptcy/foreclosure (or the threat of it) to dupe homeowners and investors. *Property flipping* involves purchasing properties and artificially inflating their value through false appraisals; the overvalued properties are then repurchased several times for a higher price by associates of the "flipper." After three or four sham sales, the properties are foreclosed on by victim lenders. Often flipped properties are ultimately repurchased for 50% to 100% of their original value. *Mortgage-debt elimination* uses e-mails or Web-based ads to promote the elimination of mortgage loans, credit-card debt, and other debt for an up-front fee to prepare documents to satisfy the debt, but these documents (typically referred to Declaration of Voidance, Bond for Discharge of Debt, Bill of Exchange, Due Bill, or Redemption Certificate) do not achieve debt-elimination goals; they only gain profit for the scammers.

Insurance Fraud

The U.S. insurance industry consists of thousands of companies and collects nearly $1 trillion in premiums each year, so its size makes it a prime target for criminal activity.[40] The Coalition against Insurance Fraud (CAIF) estimated that the cost of fraud in the industry is as high as $80 billion each year, a cost passed on to consumers in the form of higher premiums. The National Insurance Crime Bureau (NICB) calculated that insurance fraud raises the yearly cost of premiums by $300 for the average household.

Insurance fraud involving arson is also related to the mortgage crisis. Some distressed homeowners, property flippers, and other real estate investors have resorted to committing arson to avoid real estate foreclosure. The insurance policyholders for these properties receive otherwise-unobtainable proceeds/profits through the filing of false insurance claims.

With the downturn in the American and worldwide economies that started in the first decade of this century, workers' compensation fraud has soared. Workers' compensation insurance accounts for as much as 46% of small-business owners' operating expenses, so small-business owners have an incentive to shop for workers' compensation insurance on a regular basis. This has created an illicit opportunity for entities purporting to provide workers' compensation insurance to enter the marketplace, offer reduced premiums, and misappropriate funds without providing insurance, leaving injured and deceased victims without workers' compensation coverage to pay medical bills.

■ **money laundering**
The process of converting illegally earned assets from cash to one or more alternative forms to conceal factors such as illegal origin and true ownership.

■ **environmental crime**
A violation of the criminal law committed by businesses, business officials, organizational entities, and/or individuals that damages some protected or otherwise significant aspect of the natural environment.

Mass-Marketing Fraud

Mass-marketing fraud is a general term for any fraud connected with communications media such as telemarketing, mass mailings, and the Internet. Mass-marketing fraud takes a wide variety of forms that share a common theme: use of false and/or deceptive representations to induce potential victims to make advance fee-type payments to fraud perpetrators. Although there are no comprehensive statistics on the subject, it is estimated that mass-marketing frauds victimize millions of Americans each year and generate losses in the hundreds of millions of dollars. Following is a brief description of three key concepts and schemes associated with mass-marketing fraud:

1. **Nigerian letter fraud.** Victims of Nigerian letter fraud are contacted regarding substantial sums of money held in foreign accounts they are told is owed to them, and they are requested to pay various fees to secure the transfer of these monies to the United States; these fees are kept by the perpetrators. Victims also may be asked to act as U.S. agents in securing the release of such funds and are provided with counterfeit instruments to be cashed in order to pay any required fees, only to discover they must reimburse their financial institutions for cashing counterfeit instruments.

2. **Foreign lottery/sweepstakes fraud.** Victims are informed that they have won a substantial prize in a foreign lottery or sweepstakes but must remit payment for various taxes/fees to receive their winnings, and the taxes/fees are paid to the perpetrators. Victims may be given financial documents, supposedly representing a portion of the winnings, to be cashed in order to pay the required fees, only to discover they must reimburse their financial institutions for cashing counterfeit instruments.

3. **Overpayment fraud.** Victims who have advertised some item for sale are contacted by buyers who remit counterfeit instruments in excess of the purchase price for payment; the victims are told to cash the instruments, deduct any expenses, and return or forward the excess funds to an individual identified by the buyer, only to discover they must reimburse their financial institution for cashing counterfeit instruments.

Money Laundering

Money laundering is the process by which illegal gains are disguised as legal income. A more formal definition is offered by the National Institute of Justice for *money laundering*: "the process of converting illegally earned assets, originating as cash, to one or more alternative forms to conceal such incriminating factors as

illegal origin and true ownership."[41] In 2010 Wachovia Corporation (now part of Wells-Fargo & Co.) agreed to pay $160 million to settle federal charges that it failed to establish an adequate program to prevent money laundering through its facilities.[42] The plea resulted from transactions involving Wachovia and Mexican money exchanges between 2004 and 2007 that facilitated money transfers between the United States and Mexico; a federal investigation found that drug dealers routinely used them to move funds between the two countries.

Title 18, Section 1956, of the U.S. Criminal Code specifically prohibited what it called the "laundering of monetary instruments" and defined *money laundering* as "[efforts] to conceal or disguise the nature, the location, the source, the ownership, or the control of the proceeds of specified unlawful activity."[43] To assist in the identification of money launderers, a provision of the 1986 federal Money Laundering Control Act required that banks report to the government all currency transactions in excess of $10,000. The Bank Secrecy Act (BSA), formally known as the Currency and Foreign Transactions Reporting Act, required financial institutions to assist government agencies in detecting and preventing activities related to money laundering, to report cash transactions exceeding an aggregate amount of $10,000 daily per account, and to report suspicious financial activity. However, high-end money launderers know these requirements and routinely evade them by dealing in commodities like gold, by using foreign banks, or by making a series of smaller deposits and transfers, often involving numerous financial institutions. Reliable official estimates of the amount of money laundered in the United States are hard to establish. However, the Drug Enforcement Administration reported that estimates provided by the International Monetary Fund pegged worldwide money-laundering activities at between 2% and 5% of the world's gross domestic product, or about $600 billion annually.[44]

The problem of money laundering may be getting worse: A 2010 report by the Senate Permanent Subcommittee on Investigations found that billions of dollars are leaving the U.S. every year to be put into the flow of commerce and returned to this country as laundered capital.[45] The report also identified a number of individuals and organizations suspected of bringing millions of dollars from illegal activities into the country by funneling it through offshore accounts.

Environmental Crimes

A newer area of corporate and white-collar criminality defined in terms of violation of the criminal law is crimes against the environment.[46] **Environmental crimes** are violations of the

WEB EXTRA 11-6
WEB EXTRA 11-7
LIBRARY EXTRA 11-3

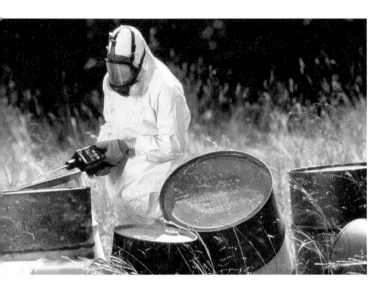

Cleanup workers monitoring toxic waste at an illegal dump site. Environmental crimes have recently become an area of special concern to criminologists. Why have such offenses only recently been recognized as crimes?

Source: Gabe Palmer/CORBIS-NY

criminal law, committed by businesses, business officials, organizational entities, and individuals, that damage some protected or otherwise significant aspect of the natural environment.

Whaling in violation of international conventions, for example, constitutes a form of environmental crime, as does intentional pollution. Sometimes negligence contributes to environmental criminality, as in the case of the 1,000-foot *Valdez* supertanker owned by Exxon Corporation which ran aground off the coast of Alaska in 1989, spilling 11 million gallons of crude oil over 1,700 miles of pristine coastline. In September 1994, an Alaskan civil jury ordered Exxon to pay $5 billion in punitive damages to 14,000 people affected by the spill and another $287 million in actual damages to commercial fishermen in the region; Exxon also agreed to pay $100 million in criminal fines.

British Petroleum Products North America, Inc. (BPPNA), pleaded guilty in 2007 to one felony count of violating the federal Clean Air Act; it was ordered to pay $50 million in fines and placed on three years of federal probation. The conviction stemmed from an explosion at the BPPNA Texas City refinery on March 23, 2005, that caused the deaths of 15 employees. The company admitted that several procedures required under the Clean Air Act for ensuring the integrity of safety equipment either had not been established or were being ignored.

The British Petroleum subsidiary BP Exploration Alaska (BPXA) pleaded guilty to one count of violating the federal

Clean Water Act as a result of a 2006 oil spill of 267,000 gallons at its facility on Alaska's North Slope.[47] Authorities charged that the spill occurred because company officials had conspired to save money by acting to conceal corrosion in a pipeline used to transfer oil and falsifying financial reports detailing money spent to fix the corrosion. The company agreed to pay a $20 million fine and was placed on three years' probation.[48]

The devastating fires set in oil fields throughout Kuwait by retreating Iraqi army troops during the Gulf War in 1991 provide an example of arson that resulted in global pollution while negatively affecting fossil-fuel reserves throughout much of the Middle East. These intentional fires, while properly classified as environmental criminality, also serve as an example of ecological terrorism because they were set for the purpose of political intimidation.

> **Environmental crimes damage some protected or significant aspect of the natural environment.**

Learn more about environmental crimes from the Duke Environmental Law and Policy Forum and the FBI at **Web Extras 11–6** and **11–7**; read about the conviction and sentencing of some defendants in environmental-crime prosecutions at **Library Extra 11–3**.

Terrorism and White-Collar Crime

Terrorist activity frequently involves some form of white-collar crime because terrorists need money for daily living expenses and for weapons, travel, and communications. Terrorist groups also frequently send a portion of the money acquired from illegal activities back to their home country or pass it along to those higher up the chain of command. Involvement in white-collar crime allows terrorist groups to maintain a significantly lower profile than if they raised funds through other crimes, such as bank robberies and illegal drug sales.

John Kane and April Wall, in a report prepared for the White Collar Crime Center, pointed out that "curtailing terrorist activity may be achieved through the combined efforts of nations, through legislation that criminalizes the financing of terrorism, modifications to regulations that govern non-profit or charity-based corporations, international cooperation, and a willingness of the international banking community to adhere to reporting rules designed to detect money laundering and suspicious activity" and that shell companies have been used by terrorist groups to receive and distribute money.[49] The term *shell companies* refers to entities engaged in legitimate activities to establish a good reputation in the business community and provide a veneer of legitimacy. They can launder funds by creating invoices for nonexistent products or services that then appear to be paid by another company in order to provide a channel for profits from illegal activities (such as insurance fraud or identity theft) to enter the legitimate flow of cash disguised as revenue from legitimate

activities. In 2001, for example, an American telecommunications company was indicted on charges of aiding members of al-Qaeda in preparation for the 9/11 terrorist attacks by handling more than $500,000 in monthly money transfers. Table 11–2 provides examples of the kinds of white-collar crimes associated with terrorism in recent years, along with information on federal criminal statutes that these kinds of activities violate.

TABLE 11–2 | White-Collar Crimes Associated with Terrorism Cases

TYPE OF OFFENSE	DESCRIPTION OF OFFENSE	STATUTE
Identification Document Fraud	Fraud in connection with identification documents	18 USC 1028
	Forgery or false use of passports	18 USC 1543
	Misuse of passports	18 USC 1544
	Fraud and misuse of visas, permits, and other documents	18 USC 1546
	Social Security fraud	42 USC 408
Financial Fraud	Bribery of public officials and witnesses	18 USC 201
	Counterfeited or forged securities of states and private entities	18 USC 513
	False statements on credit application	18 USC 1014
	Bank fraud	18 USC 1344
	Money laundering	18 USC 1956
	Unlicensed money-transmitting business	18 USC 1960
	Racketeering	18 USC 1962
	Transactions structured to evade reporting requirements	31 USC 5324
Mail and Wire Fraud	Mail fraud	18 USC 1341
	Fraud by wire, radio, or television	18 USC 1343
Credit-Card Fraud	Fraud in connection with access devices	18 USC 1029
Tax Fraud	Materially false income tax returns	26 USC 7206
	Corrupt endeavors to impede IRS laws	26 USC 7212
Immigration Fraud	Deportable alien	8 USC 1227
	Alien failing to report address change	8 USC 1305
	Alien smuggling	8 USC 1324
	Evasion of immigration laws	8 USC 1325
	False representations as U.S. citizen	18 USC 911
	Illegal alien	18 USC 922
	False statements regarding naturalization, citizenship, or alien registry	18 USC 1015
	Unlawful procurement of citizenship or naturalization	18 USC 1425
Other Related Charges	Aiding and abetting	18 USC 2
	Conspiracy to commit offenses against or defraud the U.S.	18 USC 371
	Materially false statements	18 USC 1001
	Perjury	18 USC 1621
	Provision of material support to terrorists	18 USC 2339
	Conspiracy to give or receive funds, goods, or services for designated terrorist	50 USC 595

Note: Subchapters are not listed.
Source: John Kane and April Wall, "Identifying the Links between White-Collar Crime and Terrorism," (Glen Allen, VA: National White Collar Crime Center, September 2004), p. 13.

Causes of White-Collar Crime

When Edwin H. Sutherland first coined the term *white-collar crime*, he wrote, "A hypothesis is needed that will explain both white-collar criminality and lower-class criminality";[50] his own answer was that "white-collar criminality, just as other systematic criminality, is learned."[51] He went on to apply elements of his famous theory of differential association (discussed in Chapter 6) to white-collar crime, saying that "it is learned in direct or indirect association with those who already practice the behavior."[52]

Other authors have since offered similar integrative perspectives. **Travis Hirschi** and **Michael Gottfredson** (whose work was discussed in Chapters 4 and 7), in an issue of the journal *Criminology* published half a century after Sutherland's initial work, wrote, "In this paper we outline a general theory of crime capable of organizing the facts about white-collar crime at the same time it is capable of organizing the facts about all forms of crime."[53] Their analysis of white-collar crime focused squarely on the development of the concept itself, suggesting that if we were not aware that the concept of white-collar crime arose "as a reaction to the idea that crime is concentrated in the lower class, there would be nothing to distinguish it from other [forms of crime]."[54] They continued, "It may be, then, that the discovery of white-collar criminals is important only in a context in which their existence is denied by theory or policy."[55] In other words, nothing is unusual about the idea of white-collar crime, but many people are simply loath to admit that high-status individuals also commit crimes.

Hirschi and Gottfredson went on to say that white-collar criminals are motivated by the same forces that drive other criminals: self-interest, pursuit of pleasure, and avoidance of pain. White-collar crimes do have special characteristics—they are less dangerous, they provide relatively large rewards, their rewards may follow quickly from their commission, any sanctions associated with them may be vague or only rarely imposed, and they may require only minimal effort from those with requisite skills.

Hirschi and Gottfredson concluded that criminologists err in assuming that white-collar criminality is common (or as common as the forms of criminality found among the lower classes). High educational levels, commitment to the status quo, personal motivation to succeed, deference to others, attention to conventional appearance, and other aspects of social conformity—all of which characterize those who operate at the white-collar level—are not the kinds of personal characteristics associated with crime commission. "In other words," stated Hirschi and Gottfredson,

"selection processes inherent to the high end of the occupational structure tend to recruit people with relatively low propensity to crime."

Another reason most criminologists are mistaken about the assumed high rate of white-collar criminality, Hirschi and Gottfredson told us, is because "white-collar researchers often take organizations as the unit of analysis" and confuse the crimes committed by organizational entities with those of individuals within those organizations.[56] Rates of white-collar offending tend to lump together the crimes of corporations with crimes committed by individual representatives of those organizations when making comparisons with the rate of criminal activity among blue-collar and other groups.

A complementary perspective by Australian criminologist **John Braithwaite** posited that white-collar criminals are frequently motivated by a disparity between corporate goals and the limited opportunities available to businesspeople through conventional business practices.[57] When pressured to achieve goals unattainable within the existing framework of laws and regulations surrounding their area of endeavor, innovative corporate officers may turn to crime to meet organizational demands.[58]

Braithwaite believed that a general theory covering both white-collar and other forms of crime can be developed by focusing on inequality as the central explanatory variable in all criminal activity.[59] Inequality, says Braithwaite, worsens both crimes of poverty motivated by the need to survive and crimes of wealth motivated by greed.

Braithwaite also suggested that corporate culture socializes budding executives into clandestine and frequently illegal behavioral modalities, making it easier for them to violate the law when pressures to perform mount, and the hostile relationship frequently existing between businesses and regulatory government agencies may further spur corporate officers to evade the law. Braithwaite emphasized his belief that the potential for shame associated with discovery—whether by enforcement agencies, the public, or internal corporate regulators—can have a powerful deterrent effect on most corporate executives because they are fundamentally conservative individuals who normally seek success through legitimate means.[60] Braithwaite recommended implementation of an "accountability model," which would hold all those responsible for corporate crimes accountable.[61] Rather than merely punishing corporations through fines, personal punishment meted out to corporate lawbreakers should have the potential to substantially reduce white-collar offending.[62]

In sum, Braithwaite contended that an integrated theory of organizational crime would include insights garnered from (1) strain theories, applied to the distribution of legitimate and

Personal punishment meted out to corporate lawbreakers should have the potential to substantially reduce white-collar offending.

illegitimate opportunities; (2) subcultural theory, applied to business subcultures; (3) labeling theory, applied to ways that stigmatization can foster the formation of a criminal subculture; and (4) control theory, applied to ways that potential white-collar offenders can be made accountable.[63] Learn more about white-collar crime at **Library Extra 11–4**.

Policy Issues to Curtail White-Collar and Corporate Crime

It is far easier to convict street criminals than white-collar criminals—it may even be difficult for prosecutors to show that a crime has occurred. "When someone breaks into a house and takes the TV and VCR," said Harvard University criminal law professor William Stuntz, "it's a matter of proving who did it. With white-collar crime, it's usually not even clear what happened."[64] Stuntz used Enron Corporation as an example, stating that "we know the broad outlines of what might have happened but not exactly what can be charged."[65]

White-collar crimes are difficult to investigate and prosecute for a number of other reasons. First, white-collar criminals are better educated than most other offenders and are better able to conceal their activities.[66] Second, cases against white-collar offenders for a continuing series of offenses (not a single crime) are often built on evidence only understandable to financial or legal experts, so it can be difficult to explain the evidence to jurors. Finally, because business executives often have salaries and bonuses in the millions of dollars as well as financial resources of an entire corporation at their disposal, they are able to hire excellent defense attorneys and can tie up the courts with motions and appeals not readily available to defendants with lesser resources.

In 2001, the atmosphere of distrust created by corporate criminals had become so severe that (then) President George W. Bush felt it necessary to make significant efforts to help restore investor confidence and bring order to American financial markets, so he created a federal Corporate Fraud Task Force within the U.S. Department of Justice. On July 30, 2002, he also signed the Sarbanes-Oxley Act (officially known as the Public Company Accounting Reform and Investor Protection Act), which set stiff penalties for corporate wrongdoers.

In 2007 the U.S. Department of Justice announced that activities of the task force had resulted in 1,236 fraud convictions, including those of 214 chief executive officers and 53 chief financial officers since 2002.[67] In announcing the convictions, (then) Attorney General Alberto Gonzales noted that "perhaps the most important accomplishment is the criminal conduct that never occurred because of the widespread deterrent effect" of the task force.[68]

The Sarbanes-Oxley Act, called the most far-reaching reform of American business practices since the time of Franklin Delano Roosevelt, authorized new funding for investigators and for development of new technologies to uncover corporate wrongdoing. Under the act, the SEC has the authority to bar dishonest corporate directors and officers from ever again serving in positions of corporate responsibility, penalties for obstructing justice and for shredding documents were greatly increased, corporate officers who profited illegally can be forced to return their gains to investors, and the maximum federal prison term for common types of corporate fraud was increased from five to 20 years.

The Sarbanes-Oxley Act also required chief executive officers and chief financial officers to personally vouch for the truth and fairness of their companies' financial disclosures and established an independent oversight board to regulate the accounting profession, to set clear standards to uphold the integrity of public audits, to investigate abuses, and to discipline offenders. The act prohibited auditing firms from providing consulting services that create conflicts of interest. Officials in public corporations are also barred from buying or selling stock during periods when employees are prevented from making stock transactions in their retirement or 401(k) accounts.

The Sarbanes-Oxley Act is comprised of 11 sections, including Title VIII (the Corporate and Criminal Fraud Accountability Act of 2002), Title IX (the White Collar Crime Penalty Enhancement Act of 2002), and Title XI (the Corporate Fraud Accountability Act of 2002). View the Sarbanes-Oxley Act in its entirety at **Web Extra 11–8**.

The Sarbanes-Oxley Act is the latest in a long line of federal legislation relating to the conduct of American business that extends back more than 100 years. Some early legislation included the 1890 Sherman Act, which eliminated restraints on trade and competition and prevented the development of trusts and monopolies in restraint of trade.[69] The 1914 Clayton Act prohibited mergers and acquisitions whose effect "may be substantially to lessen competition, or to tend to create a monopoly."[70]

WEB EXTRA 11–9
WEB EXTRA 11–10
WEB EXTRA 11–11
WEB EXTRA 11–12
WEB EXTRA 11–13
LIBRARY EXTRA 11–5

■ **organized crime**
The unlawful activity of members of a highly organized association engaged in supplying illegal goods and services, including gambling, prostitution, loan-sharking, narcotics, and racketeering.
■ **Mafia**
A criminal organization of Sicilian origin; also called *La Cosa Nostra*.
■ **La Cosa Nostra**
A criminal organization of Sicilian origin; also call *the Mafia*. The term literally means "our thing."

Two acts were enacted by federal legislators reeling from the effects of the Great Depression, which began with the stock market crash of 1929. The Securities Act of 1933, often referred to as the "truth in securities" law, had two basic objectives: (1) to require that investors receive financial and other significant information concerning securities being offered for public sale and (2) to prohibit deceit, misrepresentations, and other fraud in the sale of securities.[71] The Securities Exchange Act of 1934 resulted in the creation of the SEC and gave it broad authority over all aspects of the securities industry, including the power to register, regulate, and oversee brokerage firms, transfer agents, and clearing agencies as well as the nation's stock exchanges.[72] The act also identified and prohibited certain types of conduct in the markets, provided the SEC with disciplinary powers over regulated entities and persons associated with them, and empowered the SEC to require periodic reporting of information by companies with publicly traded securities.

Individual occupational crimes can be reduced by concerted enforcement and protective efforts, including enhanced IRS auditing programs, theft-deterrent systems, and good internal financial procedures. Consumer information services can help eliminate fraudulent business practices, and increases in both victim awareness and reporting can help target both individuals and businesses responsible for various forms of white-collar crime. However, Donald J. Newman observed that "if white-collar crime is intrinsic to and normative within the value structure of our society, then no punishment or treatment program will effectively eradicate it."[73] Gary S. Green pointed out that "professional occupational criminals will probably continue to enjoy immunity from prosecution. Hence, they are unlikely to be deterred by sanction or threat and are unlikely to be formally disqualified by their professional organizations. They will therefore feel free and be free to continue or begin their criminal activities."[74]

In the book *The Criminal Elite: The Sociology of White-Collar Crime*, **James William Coleman** suggested four areas of reform through which white-collar crime might be effectively addressed:[75] (1) ethical reform (including working to establish stronger, more persuasive codes of business ethics); (2) enforcement reform (including better funding for enforcement agencies); (3) structural reform (including changes in corporate structure to make white-collar crime more difficult to commit); and (4) political reform (centered on eliminating campaign contributions from corporations and businesses).

A number of corporate leaders are also calling for companies and business executives to develop an enhanced set of ethical standards for corporate responsibility that could be applied to the business world as a means of self-control. The Center for Innovation in Corporate Responsibility (CICR) suggested that companies replace the goal of improving their bottom line (profits) with the concept of the *triple bottom line*: "an innovative business approach which integrates financial, environmental, and social considerations into performance measurement and assessment."[76] A company's success should be judged in terms of what it contributes to society and how it protects the environment as well as by how much money it makes.

Learn more about corporate responsibility and ethical business practices from the Interfaith Center on Corporate Responsibility and the Center for Business Ethics and Social Responsibility at **Web Extras 11–9** and **11–10**; similar resources, including many government links, the American Institute of Certified Public Accountants's Antifraud and Corporate Responsibility Center, and the Carnegie Mellon Center for International Corporate Responsibility, can be found at **Web Extras 11–11** and **11–12**. Links to various corporate codes of ethics can be found online at **Web Extra 11–13**. A discussion about deterring white-collar crime can be found at **Library Extra 11–5**.

> A company's success should be judged in terms of what it contributes to society and how it protects the environment as well as by how much money it makes.

Organized Crime

When Americans think of **organized crime** (unlawful activities of a highly organized group engaged in supplying illegal goods and services), the **Mafia** and **La Cosa Nostra**, two terms referring to organized-crime groups of Sicilian origin, probably come to mind. For hundreds of years, secret societies—the products of extreme poverty, feudalism, a traditional disregard for the law, and national temperament—flourished in Italy.[77] Italian criminal organizations that came to the United States with the wave of

> ▓ **ethnic succession**
> The continuing process whereby one immigrant or ethnic group succeeds another by assuming its position in society.

European immigrants during the late nineteenth and early twentieth centuries included the Black Hand and the Mafia. The Black Hand (*La Mano Negro*) "specialized in the intimidation of Italian immigrants," typically extorting protection money and valuables, and became especially powerful in Detroit, St. Louis, Kansas City, and New Orleans.[78]

The Mafia worked to become a quasi-police organization in the Italian ghetto areas of the burgeoning American cities of the industrial era—often enforcing its own set of laws or codes when official intervention was lacking. Secret societies in Italy were all but expunged during the 1930s and early 1940s under Fascist dictator Benito Mussolini. Many *mafioso* (members of the Mafia) fled to the United States and set up criminal organizations here. They were vehemently anti-Fascist, sentiments that endeared them to American and Allied intelligence services during World War II, and following the war, *mafioso* leaders resumed their traditional positions of power in Italian society, and links grew between American criminal organizations and those in Italy.

In his comprehensive book *Organized Crime*, Howard Abadinsky, a professor of criminal justice at St. John's University, reported that the first mention of the Mafia in New York can be found in a *New York Times* article dated October 22, 1888.[79] The article quoted New York City police inspector Thomas Byrnes as saying that a murder victim named Antonio Flaccomio was "an Italian fruit dealer and a member of a secret society" who was executed by Carlo Quarteraro.[80] The society was called the Mafia; its members were fugitives from Sicily, an island in the south of Italy. "If one of the society commits a crime," Byrnes told reporters, "all the other members of the society are bound to shield and keep the crime secret under pain of death."[81]

A Rose by Any Other Name: La Cosa Nostra

Ethnic succession, the continuing process whereby one immigrant or ethnic group succeeds another through assumption of a particular position in society, has been a reality in organized crime as well as other aspects of American life. Organized criminal groups, including Jewish and Irish gangs, flourished in New York City prior to the arrival of large numbers of Italian immigrants in the late 1800s. Throughout the late nineteenth and early twentieth centuries, Jewish gangsters like Meyer Lansky, Benjamin "Bugsy" Siegel, "Dutch" Schultz, and Lepke Buchalter ran many of the rackets in New York City, only to have their places taken by Italian immigrants who arrived a few years later. Almost forgotten today is Arnold Rothstein, a famous Jewish gangster who was able to translate many ill-gotten gains into real estate holdings and other legitimate commercial ventures, who was called the "most important organizer and innovator" among Jewish criminal operatives in early-twentieth-century New York and the "Godfather" of organized crime in the city.[82] Italian American organized criminals were not immune to ethnic succession, and gangs of African Americans, Hispanics, and Asian Americans now run significant aspects of the drug trade and control other illicit activities in many parts of the country.

Attorney General Robert Kennedy describing a link between the Teamsters and organized crime. How influential is organized crime in American society today?

Source: UPI/CORBIS-NY

Organized criminal activity in the United States throughout much of the twentieth century was largely the domain of Italian American immigrants and their descendants, especially those of Sicilian descent. "To beat rival organizations, criminals of Sicilian descent reproduced the kind of illegal groups they had belonged to in the old country and employed the same rules to make them invincible."[83] It was not long before American Mafia leaders had taken over from their criminal predecessors, many of whom were either killed or forced to turn to more legitimate forms of enterprise.

It is both realistic and useful to discuss American organized crime primarily in terms of Sicilian American involvement, but two caveats must be stated. First, although many Sicilians who immigrated to this country had either ties to or experience with Mafia organizations in Italy, most did not and actually immigrated to America to escape Mafia despotism, becoming productive members of their adopted society. Those who involved themselves in organized crime created an organization known variously as the Mafia, the Outfit, the Mob, La Cosa Nostra ("our thing"), the syndicate, the organization, the crime cartel, and the confederation. Second, organized criminal enterprise in the United States today has moved in new directions, and criminal gangs come in many different "flavors."

Joseph Valachi, a member of the Genovese crime family, is generally credited with popularizing the term *Cosa Nostra* in 1963, when he used the term while testifying before the McClellan Committee, which was holding hearings on organized crime. Following the hearings, the name Cosa Nostra became increasingly popular with both the American press and the public and has at least partially replaced the term *Mafia* for Italian American criminal organizations.

The term *Mafia*, however, is still in widespread use, in the paragraphs that follow, Sicilian American organized criminal groups are referred to as both the Mafia and La Cosa Nostra—terms that have been used interchangeably by police investigators, the press, the public, and government commissions over the years.

> Organized criminal activity in the U.S. during much of the twentieth century was the domain of Italian American immigrants and their descendants.

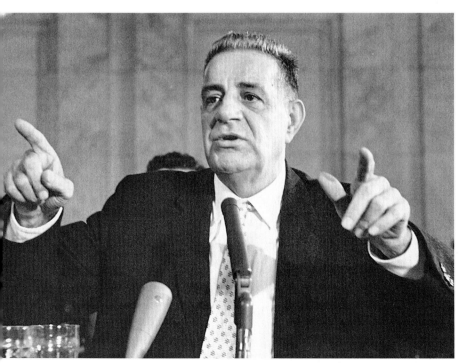

Mob informant Joseph Valachi testifying before Senate investigators in 1963.
How has organized crime changed since Valachi's time?
Source: Locs Mags (UPI)/CORBIS-NY

Prohibition and Official Corruption

By the 1920s, the influence of the Sicilian Mafia extended to most American cities, but it was the advent of Prohibition that gave the Mafia its vital financial foothold. In 1919, the U.S. Congress passed the Eighteenth Amendment to the U.S. Constitution that ushered in Prohibition and made the manufacture, transportation, and sale of alcoholic beverages illegal.

In many ways, the advent of Prohibition was a godsend for Mafia leaders. Prior to Prohibition, Mafia operations in American cities were small, concerned mostly with gambling, protection rackets, and loan-sharking. Many mafioso belonged to a brotherhood called Unione Siciliana, whose members were well versed in the manufacture of low-cost, high-proof, untaxed alcohol.[84] In addition, the existing infrastructure of organized crime permitted easy, efficient entry into the running and sale of contraband liquor.

▓ **Wickersham Commission**
A commission created by President Herbert Hoover in 1931
to improve justice system practices and to reinstate law's role in
civilized governance (officially known as the Commission on
Law Observance and Enforcement).

▓ **Kefauver Committee**
The popular name for the federal Special Committee to Investigate
Organized Crime in Interstate Commerce, formed in 1951.

Prohibition gave existing Mafia families the opportunity to accumulate unheralded wealth. As Abadinsky put it, "Prohibition enabled men who had been street thugs to become crime overlords."[85] Others described it this way: "Prohibition proved to be the catalyst that established the wealth and power of modern organized crime syndicates."[86] The huge profits from bootlegging led to the wholesale bribery of government officials and to the quick corruption of many law enforcement officers throughout the country. Nowhere was corruption more complete than in Chicago, where runners working for organized crime distributed illegal alcohol under police protection and corrupt city government officials received regular payoffs from criminal cartels.[87]

In 1929, (then) President Herbert Hoover appointed the National Commission on Law Observance and Enforcement, better known as the **Wickersham Commission** after its chairman, George Wickersham, which produced a series of 14 reports. Three of them—*Observance and Enforcement of Prohibition, Lawlessness in Law Enforcement*, and *The Police*—either mentioned or decried the corrupting influence Prohibition was having on professional law enforcement in America. The Eighteenth Amendment was repealed 14 years after it had been passed, and Prohibition ended.

Unfortunately, the heritage of Prohibition-associated corruption is still with us, frequently translating into officials "looking the other way" when drug operations and other forms of criminal enterprise take place in their locales. Official corruption has become an institutionalized part of American life in some parts of the country.[88]

In 1976, the Task Force on Organized Crime concluded that "all available data indicate that organized crime flourishes only where it has corrupted local officials."[89] Sometimes the roots of corruption reach far deeper: "The line between organized crime and corrupt officials is often unclear, at times nonexistent. In both Chicago and New York those who ran organized criminal activities, gambling and prostitution, were political figures and often elected officials."[90]

The Centralization of Organized Crime

The Prohibition era was a tumultuous time for American organized crime. Its leaders simultaneously grappled for the huge profits from the sale of illegal alcohol and worked to consolidate their power, so gang warfare was the order of the day. One of the most infamous gangland wars of all time erupted in Chicago in the mid-1920s, when Alphonse "Al" Capone, an up-and-coming thug, decided to make a citywide grab for power. Following a number of spectacular killings, Capone was successful in forging a crime syndicate and declared himself the leader of all Chicago's organized-crime families. His claim was mainly disputed by George "Bugs" Moran, who had inherited the leadership of a local gang, so Capone lured Moran's men to a garage on Chicago's East Side on the ruse that a truckload of bootleg liquor was soon to arrive, where they were surprised by five of Capone's executioners. Three uniformed men (dressed as police officers) ordered the Moran gang against the garage wall, and two plainclothes killers machine-gunned them to death. The killings, which became known as the Saint Valentine's Day massacre, established Capone as undisputed ruler of organized crime in Chicago.

Similar efforts at consolidation were made nationwide, and by the close of 1931, when the smoke had settled and the killings had stopped, the Mafia had become an integrated, coordinated criminal organization able to settle most disputes internally and capable of shielding its activities from the prying eyes of investigators. "In 1931 organized crime units across the United States formed into monopolistic corporations, and those corporations, in turn, linked themselves together in a monopolistic cartel."[91]

After 1931, Mafia activity went underground, and the Mafia's success at hiding its operations was so great that one expert wrote, "There is a considerable body of police opinion in the United States which holds that the Mafia in America died in September 1931, on 'Purge Day.'"[92] The 1967 President's Commission on Law Enforcement and Administration of Justice observed that Mafia activity remained nearly invisible and investigations of Mafia operations lay dormant until the 1950s: "After World War II there was little national interest in the problem [of organized crime] until 1950, when the U.S. Attorney General convened a national conference on organized crime."[93]

Organized crime reemerged into the national spotlight in 1951 when the federal Special Committee to Investigate Organized Crime in Interstate Commerce (better known as the **Kefauver Committee** after its chairman, Estes Kefauver) was formed.[94] It reported that "a nationwide crime syndicate known as the Mafia operate[s] in many large [American] cities, and the leaders of the Mafia usually control the most lucrative rackets in their cities."[95] Although the Kefauver Committee, which interviewed hundreds of witnesses, noted that it had "found it difficult to obtain reliable data concerning the extent of Mafia operation, the nature of Mafia organization, and the way it presently operates," it was able to reach the following conclusions:[96]

- A nationwide crime syndicate, known as the Mafia, exists, and its tentacles are found in many large cities.

- The American Mafia has international linkages that appear most clearly in connection with narcotics traffic.

- Mafia leaders are usually found in control of the most lucrative rackets in their cities.
- Indications suggest centralized direction and control in these rackets, but leadership appears to be based in a group rather than in a single individual.

Public interest in organized crime was again roused when authorities learned of a national meeting of at least 75 leaders of criminal cartels scheduled for November 1957. The meeting resulted in raids and the arrest of many well-known organized crime figures. In 1959, Joseph Bonanno and 26 others were convicted of obstruction of justice for their refusal to reveal the meeting's purpose, but their convictions were overturned in 1960 by the U.S. Second Circuit Court of Appeals, which reasoned in *United States* v. *Bufalino* that the suspects had been arrested without probable cause.[97]

A picture of Italian American organized criminal groups eventually emerged from years of federal investigations: "Today the core of organized crime in the United States consists of 24 groups operating as criminal cartels in large cities across the nation. Their membership is exclusively Italian, they are in frequent communication with each other, and their smooth functioning is insured by a national body of overseers. The wealthiest and most influential core groups operate in States including New York, New Jersey, Illinois, Florida, Louisiana, Nevada, Michigan, and Rhode Island." The report placed membership in organized crime at 5,000 nationwide and said that "each of the 24 groups is known as a 'family' with membership varying from as many as 700 men to as few as 20."[98]

Family organization was said to consist of (1) a boss, whose primary functions were described as "maintaining order and maximizing profits"; (2) an underboss, who was said to collect information for the boss and to relay messages to and from him; (3) the counselor, or consigliere, who served as an adviser; (4) numerous lieutenants, or *caporegime*, some of whom "serve as chiefs of operating units"; and (5) soldiers, or *soldati*, representing the lowest level of family membership who "operate a particular illicit enterprise," such as a loan-sharking operation, a lottery, or a smuggling operation. "Beneath the soldiers are large numbers of employees and agents who are not members of the family and not necessarily of Italian descent. These are people who do most of the actual work in the various enterprises." Unlike the family members who give them orders, "they have no buffers or other insulation from law enforcement." The structure of a typical Sicilian American organized-crime family is shown in Figure 11–1.

The President's Commission also found that organized-crime members swear allegiance to a code of conduct, which "stipulates that underlings should not interfere with the leaders' interests and should not seek protection from the police. They should be 'standup guys' who go to prison in order that the bosses may amass fortunes. The code gives leaders exploitative authoritarian power over everyone in the organization."

La Cosa Nostra Today

Some writers have maintained that at least 24 organized-crime families of Sicilian American heritage continue to operate throughout the United States today, with five operating out of New York: the Luciano/Genovese family (300–400 members), the Mineo/Gambino family (400–500 members), the Reina/Lucchese family (125 members), the Profaci/Colombo family (100 members), and the Bonanno family (75 members).[99]

Chicago is home to other influential Cosa Nostra families, including the Carlisi family (sometimes called the "Outfit"). The Scarfo organization (run by Nicodemo "Little Nicky" Scarfo)

> Organized-crime members swear allegiance to a code of conduct.

and the Stanfa organization operate in Philadelphia, and New Orleans serves as headquarters for the Marcello gang (headed by Carlos Marcello). Organized crime in New England is controlled by Ray Patriarca, Jr., and his henchmen; the Civella mob runs racketeering activities in Kansas City, Missouri. Learn more about Cosa Nostra families now operating in the United States at **Web Extra 11–14**.

Activities of Organized Crime

The 1976 federal Task Force on Organized Crime identified five types of activity that may qualify as organized crime—racketeering, vice operations, theft/fence rings, gangs, and terrorism—but whatever its source, money is the primary motivation for almost all organized criminal activity. Throughout the past half century, Sicilian American criminal cartels have continued to be involved in (1) establishment and control of both legalized and illicit forms of gambling, including lotteries, bookmaking, horse-race wagering, and bets on athletic contests; (2) loan-sharking, which involves the lending of money at rates far higher than legally prescribed limits; (3) large-scale drug trafficking; (4) fencing of stolen goods, including securities; (5) infiltration of legitimate businesses, including labor unions and corporations that can be used as quasi-legitimate fronts for money laundering and other activities; and (6) labor union racketeering via which legitimate businesses are intimidated through threats of strikes, walkouts, and sabotage.

■ **omertà**
The informal unwritten code of organized crime, which demands silence and loyalty of family members.

FIGURE 11-1 | A Typical Organized-Crime Family

Source: Adapted from the President's Commission on Law Enforcement and Administration of Justice, *The Challenge of Crime in a Free Society* (Washington, DC: U.S. Government Printing Office, 1967), p. 47.

In areas where lotteries began to be run by state government, organized crime's take from illegal gambling was reduced, so Sicilian American operatives moved into legitimate gambling, reportedly buying stakes in casinos in Nevada, New Jersey, and elsewhere. Although New Jersey has made Herculean efforts to keep organized crime from influencing casino operations in Atlantic City, some writers have claimed that "Local 54 of the Hotel Employees and Restaurant Employees Union, which represents 22,000 casino hotel employees, has long been dominated by the Bruno family of Philadelphia."[100]

Organized crime is involved in many other rackets besides gambling. For example, organized crime has become increasingly active in the illegal copying and distribution of copyrighted software, music, and other forms of recorded media, including videotapes, compact discs, DVDs, and cassette tapes. Elaborately staged and digitally recorded pornographic productions, including "snuff movies" (in which a sex "star" is actually killed on screen), and elements of child pornography can also be traced to organized criminal activity.

Code of Conduct

A strict unwritten code of conduct governing behavior among members of organized Sicilian American criminal groups, called **omertà** (meaning "manliness"), functions to concentrate power in

WEB EXTRA 11–15
LIBRARY EXTRA 11–6

■ **criminal enterprise**
A group of individuals with an identified hierarchy who are engaged in significant criminal activities.

Actor James Gandolfini, who played Tony Soprano in the HBO hit series *The Sopranos*. The popularity of shows like *The Sopranos* demonstrates America's fascination with organized crime and the lives of organized-crime figures. How does American culture view the "gangster"? How do classic gangster images support idealized notions of the "thug life" among some young people today?
Source: HBO/Picture Desk, Inc./Kobal Collection

the hands of crime bosses while ensuring their protection. Members are formally introduced to the code through an initiation ritual, which has changed little since it was brought to American shores by Sicilian immigrants well over a hundred years ago. Officials with one federal task force stated, "Those aspects of the code which prohibit appealing to outside authorities for justice while at the same time advocating great loyalty, respect and honor are probably most essential to the concentration of power in the hands of a few, and hence to exploitation of lower-status men by their leaders."[101]

Federal investigators and others studying organized crime have identified seven general features characteristic of the code that Mafia family members everywhere swear to:[102]

1. Do not be an informer. Do not "rat" on others, and do not sell out.

2. Be a member of the team. Be loyal to members of the organization.

3. Do not interfere with the interests of others. Do not rock the boat.

4. Be rational. Do not engage in battle if you cannot win.

5. Be a man of honor. Have class. Be independent.

6. Respect women and your elders.

7. Be a "stand-up" guy (stand-up guys take the "rap," shielding others). Keep your eyes and ears open and your mouth shut.

Like any informal unwritten code, omertà has many other implicit rules and is fraught with nuances fully understood only by those raised within its traditions. The code also imposes two clear and indisputable requirements on all family members: (1) obey your superiors and (2) keep silent. Failure to adhere closely to either rule means death. The 1967 President's Commission report stated it this way: "The basic principle of justice in the Sicilian Mafia, as in American organized crime, is deterrence from deviation by means of the threat of certain, swift, uniform and severe punishment."[103]

Omertà contains values similar to those found among career criminals everywhere. As one federal report explained, "There is a striking similarity between both the code of conduct and the enforcement machinery used in the confederation of organized criminals and the code of conduct and enforcement machinery which governs the behavior of prisoners."[104] Learn more about La Cosa Nostra at **Web Extra 11–15**. It's history is described in detail at **Library Extra 11–6**.

Organized Criminal Enterprises

The FBI defined a **criminal enterprise** as a group of individuals with an identified hierarchy, and extensive supporting networks, engaged in significant criminal activity. According to Howard Abadinsky, a hallmark of true criminal organizations is that they function independently of any of their members, including their leaders, and have continuity over time as personnel within them change.[105] Abadinsky mentioned the James Gang, which dissolved with the death of its leader, Jesse James, and then said that "when Al Capone was imprisoned fifty years later, the 'Capone Organization' continued, and in its more modern form (the 'Outfit') it continues to operate in Chicago."[106]

The terms *organized crime* and *criminal enterprise* are closely related and are often used interchangeably, but various federal criminal statutes have specifically defined the elements of a criminal enterprise that need to be proven in order to convict individuals or groups of individuals under those statutes. The federal

Continuing Criminal Enterprise statute defines a *criminal enterprise* as any group of six or more people—with one of the six occupying an organizing, supervisory, or management position—that generates substantial income or resources and is engaged in a continuing series of violations of Subchapters I and II of Chapter 13 of Title 21 of the U.S. Code (Chapter 13 is that portion of federal law concerned with drug-abuse prevention and control).[107]

> The terms *organized crime* and *criminal enterprise* are often used interchangeably.

State laws defining criminal enterprise are generally much more inclusive than federal statutes. The laws of New York, for example, stated that "the concept of criminal enterprise should not be limited to traditional criminal syndicates or crime families, and may include persons who join together in a criminal enterprise . . . for the purpose of corrupting . . . legitimate enterprises or infiltrating and illicitly influencing industries."[108] New York criminal statutes have defined *criminal enterprise* as "a group of persons sharing a common purpose of engaging in criminal conduct, associated in an ascertainable structure distinct from a pattern of criminal activity, and with a continuity of existence, structure and criminal purpose beyond the scope of individual criminal incidents."[109]

When people think of criminal enterprises, they often picture the Italian and Sicilian mafioso of television and popular movies, but the face of organized crime in the United States has changed, and its threat is broader and more complex than ever, with crimi-

A member of the Los Angeles 18th Street Gang posing near a street mural. What kinds of criminal activities attract the interest of street gangs?
Source: A. Ramey/PhotoEdit Inc.

nal enterprises of different origins (see **Web Extra 11–16**). Some especially noteworthy groups include:

- Russian mobsters who fled to the United States in the wake of the Soviet Union's collapse
- Groups from African countries like Nigeria that engage in drug trafficking and financial scams
- Chinese tongs, Japanese *Boryokudan*, and other Asian crime rings
- Enterprises based in Eastern European nations like Hungary and Romania

Many organized-crime groups of different nationalities—including Eurasian, Balkan, Asian, African, and Middle Eastern—currently operate in the United States or are targeting U.S. citizens from afar using the Internet and other technologies; we will describe each of these.

Eurasian Criminal Enterprises

The term *Eurasian organized crime* refers to organized-crime groups comprising criminals born in or with family ties to the former Soviet Union or Central or Eastern Europe.[110] Eurasian organized crime in the United States is rooted in the *Vory V Zakone* (meaning "thieves in law"), career criminals who banded together for support and profit in the Soviet prison system; their leaders operated outside the official Soviet system and were illegally paid to acquire scarce consumer goods and to divert raw materials and finished goods from production lines for the benefit of *Nomenklatura* (the educated elite) and criminals.

With the collapse of the Soviet Union in 1991, members of the *Vory V Zakone* joined with corrupt public officials to acquire control of industries and resources that were being privatized, which gave the criminal syndicate a one-time infusion of wealth and supplied the infrastructure with continuing cash flows and opportunities to launder criminal proceeds. In February 1993, Boris Yeltsin, the first elected president of the Federation of Russian States, said, "Organized crime has become the No. 1 threat to Russia's strategic interests and to national security. . . . Corrupted structures on the highest level have no interest in reform."

Organized-crime members first emerged in the West in the 1970s when so-called Soviet *Refuseniks* were allowed to immigrate to Europe, Israel, and the United States. Secreted among the *Refuseniks* were criminals who sought to exploit their newfound freedoms and helped major criminal groups expand to the West. When the Soviet Union collapsed, the people of the region were able to move about freely, many coming to join their criminal colleagues already in the United States and Western Europe.

Many organized-crime groups of different nationalities currently operate in the United States.

In the United States, Eurasian criminal organizations are heavily involved in health-care fraud, auto-insurance fraud, securities and investment fraud, money laundering, drug trafficking, extortion, auto theft, interstate transportation of stolen property as well as human smuggling and prostitution.

Balkan Criminal Enterprises

The term *Balkan organized crime* applies to criminal enterprises originating from or operating in Albania, Bosnia-Herzegovina, Bulgaria, Croatia, Greece, Kosovo, the former Yugoslav Republic of Macedonia, Romania, and Serbia and Montenegro and is an emerging threat in the United States today. The FBI noted that while several of these groups are active in various cities across the country, "they do not yet exhibit the established criminal sophistication of traditional Eurasian or La Cosa Nostra (LCN) organizations."

Organized crime in the rural areas of the Balkans sprang from traditional clan structures, which had large familial ties for protection and mutual assistance. Starting in the fifteenth century, clan relationships operated under the *kanun* (code), which values loyalty and *besa*, or secrecy. Each clan established itself in specific territories and controlled the criminal activities and illicit interests there, and the protection of these interests often led to violence between clans.

Years of communist rule led to black-market activities in the Balkans, but the impact of these activities was mostly limited to the region, but when Soviet-style communism collapsed in the late 1980s and early 1990s, Balkan organized-crime activities expanded. Within the Balkans, organized-crime groups infiltrated newly established democratic institutions, further expanding opportunities for criminal profits. Criminal markets once closed to Balkan groups suddenly opened, which led to the creation of an international criminal network.

Balkan criminal organizations have been active in the United States since the mid-1980s.[111] Initially, they were involved in low-level crimes, such as bank robberies, ATM burglaries, and home invasions. Later, ethnic Albanians affiliated themselves with established Mafia families in New York and acted as low-level participants; as their communities and presence became more established, they expanded their own organizations.

Balkan organized crime is not structured like the traditional Sicilian Mafia. The members brought their clan-like structure to the United States, meaning they are not clearly defined or organized but instead are grouped around central leaders, who maintain ties with the Balkan region while establishing close-knit communities in many cities across the nation. According to the FBI, "Albanian organized crime activities in the United States include gambling, money laundering, drug trafficking, human smuggling, extortion, violent witness intimidation, robbery, attempted murder, and murder" and are said to "have recently expanded into more sophisticated crimes including real estate fraud."[112]

Asian Criminal Enterprises

Asian criminal enterprises have been active in the United States since the early 1900s.[113] The first of these groups evolved from Chinese tongs—social organizations formed by early Chinese American immigrants. A century later, the criminalized tongs continue to thrive and have been joined by similar organizations with ties to East and Southeast Asia. The FBI has stated that "members of the most dominant Asian criminal enterprises affecting the United States have ties—either directly or culturally—to China, Korea, Japan, Thailand, the Philippines, Cambodia, Laos, and Vietnam."[114] Groups from the South Pacific island nations are also emerging as a threat.

Asian organized criminal groups rely on extensive networks of national and international criminal associates that are fluid and mobile, easily adapt to changes, have multilingual abilities, are sophisticated in their criminal operations, and have extensive financial capabilities. Some enterprises have commercialized their criminal activities and can be considered business firms, ranging from small family-run operations to large corporations.

Asian criminal enterprises have prospered due to communications technology, international travel, and the globalization of world economies. The FBI explained that "generous immigration policies have provided many members of Asian criminal enterprises the ability to enter and live on every populated continent in the world today undetected."[115]

Two categories of Asian criminal enterprises have been identified. Traditional criminal enterprises include the Chinese triads (or underground societies) based in Hong Kong, Taiwan, and Macau as well as the Japanese Yakuza or Boryokudan. Nontraditional criminal enterprises comprise criminally influenced Chinese tongs, triad affiliates, and other ethnic Asian street gangs found in several countries with sizable Asian communities.

Today's Asian criminal enterprises conduct traditional racketeering activities: extortion, murder, kidnapping, illegal gambling, prostitution, and loan-sharking. They also smuggle aliens, traffic in heroin and methamphetamine, commit financial fraud, steal autos and computer chips, produce counterfeit computer and clothing products, and launder money.

In this country, Asian criminal enterprises have been identified in more than 50 metropolitan areas but are more prevalent in

■ **transnational organized crime**
An unlawful activity undertaken and supported by organized
criminal groups operating across national boundaries.

WEB EXTRA 11–17
LIBRARY EXTRA 11–7

Boston, Chicago, Honolulu, Las Vegas, Los Angeles, Newark, New
Orleans, New York, Philadelphia, Portland, San Francisco, Seattle,
and Washington, D.C.

African Criminal Enterprises

African criminal enterprises have developed quickly since the
1980s due to advances in communications technology and the
globalization of the world's economies.[116] Easier international
travel, expanded world trade, and transnational financial transactions have enabled these groups to target international victims
and to develop criminal networks within prosperous countries
and regions. The political, social, and economic conditions in
African countries like Ghana, Liberia, and Nigeria also have
helped some enterprises expand globally.

African criminal enterprises actively operate in several major
metropolitan areas in the United States but are most prevalent in
Atlanta, Baltimore, Chicago, Dallas, Houston, Milwaukee, Newark,
New York, and Washington, D.C. Nigerian criminal enterprises are
the most significant group and operate in more than 80 countries
around the world. The FBI stated that "they are among the most
aggressive and expansionist international criminal groups and are
primarily engaged in drug trafficking and financial frauds."[117]

The most profitable activity for Nigerian groups is drug trafficking, primarily the delivery of cocaine from South America into Europe and South Africa and heroin from Southeast and Southwest
Asian into Europe and the United States (large populations of ethnic
Nigerians in India, Pakistan, and Thailand have given them direct access to 90% of the world's heroin production). Money laundering has
also helped establish Nigerian criminal enterprises around the world.

Nigerian groups are famous for their financial frauds, which
cost U.S. citizens, businesses, and government offices an estimated
$1 billion to $2 billion each year. Their schemes are diverse:
"insurance fraud involving auto accidents; healthcare billing
scams; life insurance schemes; bank, check, and credit card fraud;
advance-fee schemes known as 4-1-9 letters; and document fraud
to develop false identities." The Internet and e-mail have made
such crimes even more profitable and prevalent.

Middle Eastern Criminal Enterprises

The FBI has pointed out that "that some Middle Eastern criminal groups have no nexus to terror. Instead, these groups have the
same goals as any traditional organized crime ring—to make
money through illegal activities."[118] Middle Eastern criminal
enterprises originate from Afghanistan, Algeria, Bahrain, Egypt,
India, Iran, Iraq, Israel, Jordan, Kuwait, Lebanon, Libya, Morocco,
Oman, Pakistan, Qatar, Saudi Arabia, Syria, Tunisia, Turkey,
United Arab Emirates, and Yemen.

Middle Eastern criminal groups have been active in the
United States since the 1970s, tending to operate in areas with
significant Middle Eastern or Southwest Asian populations;
according to the FBI, they are most active in Illinois, Ohio, New
Jersey, and New York.

The FBI explained that these enterprises engage in "automobile theft, financial fraud, money laundering, interstate transportation of stolen property, smuggling, drug trafficking,
document fraud, health care fraud, identity fraud, cigarette smuggling, and the theft and redistribution of infant formula."[119] They
rely on extensive networks of international criminal associates
and can be highly sophisticated in their criminal operations; internationally, they thrive in Afghanistan, Canada, Iran, Pakistan,
Turkey, and the United Arab Emirates.

See **Web Extra 11–17** for a discussion of major organized
crime cases in the United States since the 1930s.

Transnational
Organized Crime

Transnational organized crime, referring to unlawful activity
undertaken and supported by organized criminal groups operating
across national boundaries and involving international criminal
enterprises, is emerging as one of the most pressing challenges of
the twenty-first century. (This topic is also discussed in Chapter 13,
and additional details can be found in **Library Extra 11–7**.)

In a conference in Seoul, Korea, former Assistant U.S. Attorney
General Laurie Robinson discussed transnational organized crime:
"The United States recognizes that we cannot confront crime in
isolation. With criminals' ability to cross international borders in a
few hours, and the advances of our modern age, such as the Internet and telecommunications, crime can no longer be viewed as just
a national issue. It is clear crime does not respect international
boundaries. It is clear crime is global. As recent economic trends
demonstrate, what happens in one part of the world impacts all the
rest. And crime problems and trends are no different."[120]

As early as 1995, delegates to the Ninth United Nations
Congress on the Prevention of Crime and the Treatment of
Offenders in Cairo, Egypt, agreed that transnational organized
crime is now a "major force in world finance, able to alter the
destinies of countries at critical stages of their economic development."[121] Participants in the conference identified the world's
major crime clans as the (1) Hong Kong–based Triads, (2) South
American cocaine cartels, (3) Italian Mafia, (4) Japanese Yakuza,
(5) Russian *Mafiya*, and (6) West African crime groups—each
of which extends its reach well beyond its home country. In

WEB EXTRA 11–18
WEB EXTRA 11–19
LIBRARY EXTRA 11–8
LIBRARY EXTRA 11–9

2010, the Tenth U.N. Congress adopted a Vienna Declaration committing member states to strengthening international cooperation in the fight against transnational crime.[122]

Russian organized crime is of special interest, both because it has grown quickly following the collapse of the Soviet Union and because it has taken root in the United States and in other countries outside the former Soviet sphere of influence. Within Russia, "rampant, unchecked organized crime has laid waste to noteworthy democratic reforms and contributed to an economic and moral meltdown within the 15 newly independent republics. Intelligence reports emanating out of Russia peg the numerical size of the Russian Mafia (*Mafiya*) at 100,000 members owing allegiance to 8,000 stratified crime groups who control 70–80% of all private business and 40% of the nation's wealth."[123] The 5,000-member drug-running organization *Solntsevskaya*, based in the Moscow suburb of Solntsevo, may be the largest organized-crime faction currently operating in Russia. Mafia leaders, or "made guys," are referred to as *vory v zakone*, which can be translated as "thieves in law"; the Russian word for godfather is *krestnii otets*, and soldiers are known as *boyevik*.

With the dissolution of Soviet-style controls between 1992 and 1994, the Russian mafia quickly seized control of the country's banking system through the investment of ill-gotten gains, money laundering, intimidation, fraud, murder, and the outright purchase of financial institutions. Between 1995 and 2000, 95 Russian bankers were murdered by *Mafiya* operatives and hundreds of reform-minded business leaders and investigative journalists were assassinated or kidnapped.[124] In September 2006, Russian Central Bank Deputy Chairman Andrei Kozlov was fatally shot as he left a soccer stadium in Moscow. He had been a crusader against money laundering and had suspended or withdrawn the licenses of dozens of banks. After Kozlov's death, President Vladimir Putin created a task force to combat financial crime.

The Analytical Center for Social and Economic Policies, a Russian think tank, estimated that four out of every five Russian businesses pay protection money to the mob.[125] In response to the wave of organized crime that Russia is currently experiencing, more than 25,000 private security firms have sprung up, but analysts have stated that few of these firms are legitimate and that many are fronts for Russian gangsters.[126]

Russian organized criminals differ from their counterparts in the United States because their ranks consist largely of ex-KGB officers, veterans of the 1979–1989 war in Afghanistan, underpaid military officers, and former Communist Party operatives who formed powerful economic alliances with traditional gangsters and black marketeers years ago. Some observers have noted that Russian organized crime seems to be a natural outgrowth of the corrupt practices of officials who operated in the days of strict Soviet control, combined with a huge underground criminal black market that had already developed a complex organizational structure long before the Soviet Union fell apart.[127]

While Russian organized crime profits from American-style activities like narcotics, prostitution, racketeering, and illicit gambling, it is also heavily involved in human trafficking, diversion and counterfeiting of popular Western goods (including software, video, and music duplication), and illicit arms sales and smuggling on a massive scale.

Over the past decade or two, hundreds of thousands of Russian citizens have immigrated to the United States. As U.S. officials have now discovered, many of these people were former black-market profiteers and hard-core offenders who had been released by the KGB from the Soviet gulag.[128]

Russian organized criminal groups operate out of 17 American cities in 14 states. "The FBI believes there are 15 separate organized crime groups and 4,000 hard-core Mafia criminals from the former Soviet Union at work in the U.S. They are engaged in money laundering, automobile theft, smuggling, contract murder, loan-sharking, medical insurance fraud, narcotics, and credit card and telecommunications fraud. The theft of electronic serial numbers from cellular phones and the duplication (cloning) of these PIN numbers have grown into a multimillion-dollar industry."[129]

The globalization of crime has necessitated the enhanced coordination of law enforcement efforts in different parts of the world and the expansion of American law enforcement activities beyond national borders. U.S. police agencies routinely send agents to assist law enforcement officers in other countries who are involved in transnational investigations. For additional information on transnational organized crime, see **Web Extra 11–18**. You can read more about transnational criminal organizations at **Library Extra 11–8** and learn more about organized crime in Russia via **Library Extra 11–9**. **Web Extra 11–19**

> The globalization of crime has necessitated the enhanced coordination of law enforcement efforts in different parts of the world.

LIBRARY EXTRA 11–10

■ **Racketeer Influenced and Corrupt Organizations (RICO)**
A statute that is part of the federal Organized Crime Control Act of 1970 whose goal is to combat criminal conspiracies.

■ **asset forfeiture**
The authorized seizure of money, negotiable instruments, securities, or other things of value. In federal antidrug laws, it is the authorization of judicial representatives to seize all monies, negotiable instruments, securities, and other things of value furnished or intended to be furnished by any person in exchange for a controlled substance, as well as all proceeds traceable to such an exchange.

provides a link to Radio Free Europe's Web site on high-profile killings in the post-Soviet period in Russia.

Organized Crime and the Law

For many years, American law enforcement agencies had few specialized weapons in the fight against organized crime, so they prosecuted organized criminal operatives under statutes directed at solitary offenders using laws against theft, robbery, assault, gambling, prostitution, drug abuse, and murder. Innovative prosecutors sometimes used other statutory resources in the drive to indict leaders of organized crime. For example, on October 17, 1931, Al Capone was convicted on various charges of income-tax evasion after federal investigators were able to show that he had paid no taxes on an income in excess of $1 million. Laws regulating the sale of alcohol and drugs and statutes circumscribing acts of prostitution have also been used against organized criminals, with varying degrees of success.

The first federal legislation aimed specifically at curtailing the activities of organized crime was known as the Hobbs Act, which encompassed a series of statutes passed beginning in 1946. The act made it a violation of federal law to engage in any form of criminal behavior that interfered with interstate commerce, criminalized interstate or foreign travel in furtherance of criminal activity, and made it a crime to use highways, telephones, or the mail in support of activities like gambling, drug trafficking, loan-sharking, and other forms of racketeering.

The single most important piece of federal legislation ever passed that specifically targeted activities of organized crime was the **Racketeer Influenced and Corrupt Organizations (RICO)** statute, part of the federal Organized Crime Control Act of 1970. The Organized Crime Control Act defined *organized crime* as "the unlawful activities of the members of a highly organized, disciplined association engaged in supplying illegal goods and services, including but not limited to gambling, prostitution, loansharking, narcotics, labor racketeering, and other unlawful activities of members of such organizations."[130] The RICO portion of the act brought together in one piece of legislation the diverse activities of American organized crime and made each punishable in a variety of new ways. RICO did not make racketeering itself illegal but focused on ill-gotten gains derived from such activities, specifying that it would be

Georgiy Gleyzer being escorted from the federal building in New York City. Gleyzer was arrested in connection with Russian mob activities and charged with terrorizing citizens of Russian communities in New York. What is the future of Russian organized crime in the United States?
Source: Suzanne Plunkett/AP Wide World Photos

unlawful for anyone involved in a pattern of racketeering to derive any income or proceeds from that activity.[131]

Punishments under RICO include **asset forfeiture**, which makes it possible for federal officials to seize the proceeds of those involved in racketeering. "Whoever violates any provision of this chapter shall be fined or imprisoned not more than 20 years (or for life if the violation is based on a racketeering activity for which the maximum penalty includes life imprisonment), or both, and shall forfeit to the United States, irrespective of any provision of State law any property derived from any proceeds that the person obtained, directly or indirectly, from racketeering activity or unlawful debt collection."[132] As a result, federal agents are empowered to seize the financial and other tangible fruits of organized criminal activity, including businesses; real estate; money; equities; gold and other commodities; vehicles, including airplanes and boats; and anything else that can be shown to have been acquired through a pattern of racketeering activity. Learn more at **Library Extra 11–10**.

Follow the author's tweets about the latest crime and justice news at **http://twitter.com/schmalleger.**

Policy Issues: The Control of Organized Crime

In a cogent analysis of organized crime, Gary W. Potter pointed out that "the question of what we [should] do about organized crime is largely predicated on how we conceptualize organized crime."[133] Potter criticized current policies for focusing "almost exclusively on *criminal* aspects of organized crime [because it is] the *organized* aspects of organized crime which offer the most useful data for formulating future policy."[134]

To understand organized crime and to deal effectively with it, according to Potter, we must study the social context in which it occurs—"organized crime is simply an integral part of the social, political, and economic system," according to Potter.[135] Any effective attack on organized crime should involve meeting the demands of the consumers of organized crime's products and services, which can be accomplished either by effectively punishing the consumers or by educating them about the perils of their own behavior.

Fighting corruption in politics and among law enforcement personnel and administrators is another track Potter suggested in the battle against organized crime. If organized crime has been successful at least partially because it has been able to corrupt local politicians and enforcement agents, then why not work to reduce corruption at the local level?

Howard Abadinsky recommended four approaches to the control of organized crime, each involving changes at the policy-making level:[136]

1. Increase the risk of involvement in organized crime by increasing the resources available to law enforcement agencies that fight organized crime.

2. Create more stringent laws to fight organized crime.

3. Reduce the economic lure of involvement in organized crime by making legitimate opportunities more readily available.

4. Decrease organized criminal opportunity through decriminalization or legalization.

Strict enforcement of existing laws is another strategy that has been used with considerable success by a number of federal and state law enforcement operations that have targeted organized crime.

One of the most spectacular mob trials was that of John "Dapper Don" Gotti, who took over control of New York's

Gambino crime family after orchestrating the murder of "Big Paul" Castellano in 1985. Over the years, Gotti had been arrested on many occasions and had been prosecuted at least five times for various offenses. His ability to escape conviction earned him the title "Teflon Don." That changed on April 2, 1992, when Gotti was convicted on 13 federal charges, including murder and racketeering, and sentenced to life in prison without possibility of parole. Gotti's major mistake was personally participating in several executions, including that of Castellano. After Gotti went to prison, his son, John, Jr., took over control of the family, but in 1999, he pleaded guilty to charges of bribery, extortion, gambling, fraud, tax evasion, and loan-sharking and was sentenced to six and a half years in prison.[137] After being released from prison, John, Jr. was tried on a number of racketeering charges, resulting in three hung juries, and following his last trial, he vowed to leave New York, saying he might move his family to the Midwest or to Florida; his father died of cancer at a federal prison hospital in 2002 at the age of 61.

The senior Gotti's downfall came at the hands of Salvatore "Sammy the Bull" Gravano, a former underboss in the Gambino crime family. Gravano, who admitted to 19 murders, shared family secrets with federal investigators in return for leniency and succor through the federal witness-protection program. Gravano

Salvatore "Sammy the Bull" Gravano. He admitted to 19 murders and has been called the "most significant witness in the history of organized crime." How has La Cosa Nostra been impacted by witnesses like Gravano?
Source: J. Markowitz/CORBIS-NY

spent days on the witness stand testifying against his former boss, and federal prosecutor Zachary Carter later called Gravano "the most significant witness in the history of organized crime."[138] In 1997, Gravano again assumed center stage when he testified in federal district court in Brooklyn as the star prosecution witness in the murder and racketeering trial of Vincent Gigante, reputed head of the powerful Genovese crime family. Gravano was assailed by defense lawyers for being a notorious liar and for leading "a life of lies," facts he largely admitted in his best-selling book, *Underboss*.[139] Although Gravano was sent to Phoenix, Arizona, under the witness-protection program, he found it hard to lead a straight life. In 2000, he was arrested on three separate occasions on drug-running and money-laundering charges and was also indicted by a New York federal grand jury and charged with financing and running a major Ecstasy drug ring in conjunction with an Israeli organized-crime syndicate.[140]

SUMMARY

- This chapter discusses white-collar and organized crime. The history of such crimes is replete with scandals, from the 1929 Teapot Dome scandal to the nationwide S&L fiasco of the 1980s, insider trading scams, illegalities of corporate executives, and corporate bankruptcies.

- Efforts to control white-collar and corporate crime have taken the form of federal legislation intended to lend greater transparency to financial business transactions. The Sarbanes-Oxley corporate reform bill set stiff penalties for corporate wrongdoers. Four additional areas of reform are discussed: ethical reform, enforcement reform, structural reform, and political reform.

- The terms *organized crime* and *criminal enterprise* are often used interchangeably. Various federal criminal statutes specifically define the elements of a criminal enterprise that need to be proven in order to convict individuals or groups under those statutes. Organized-crime groups of various nationalities—including Sicilian, Eurasian, Balkan, Asian, African, and Middle Eastern—are covered.

- Many organized criminals have a long tradition of criminal involvement, often including racketeering. Organized crime is a deviant subculture with a detailed and strict code of conduct, so organized criminal groups are committed to criminal activities and are unlikely to be easily affected by changes in the law.

KEY TERMS

asset forfeiture, 329

bank fraud, 304

corporate crime, 310

corporate fraud, 310

criminal enterprise, 324

environmental crimes, 313

ethnic succession, 319

insider trading, 304

Kefauver Committee, 321

La Cosa Nostra, 318

Mafia, 318

money laundering, 313

occupational crime, 309

omertà, 323

organized crime, 318

Ponzi scheme, 311

Racketeer Influenced and Corrupt Organizations (RICO), 329

securities and commodities fraud, 311

securities fraud, 303

transnational organized crime, 327

white-collar crime, 305

Wickersham Commission, 321

KEY NAMES

John Braithwaite, 316

James William Coleman, 318

Herbert Edelhertz, 308

Gilbert Geis, 308

Michael Gottfredson, 316

Gary S. Green, 309

Travis Hirschi, 316

Edwin H. Sutherland, 305

QUESTIONS FOR REVIEW

1. What are some examples of white-collar crime in American history?

2. What is white-collar crime? How did the idea of white-collar crime develop in the criminological literature?

3. How can white-collar and corporate crime be controlled? What are four areas of reform through which white-collar crime might be effectively addressed?

4. What is organized crime? How does it differ from white-collar crime?

5. What strategies does this chapter discuss for combating the activities of organized crime?

QUESTIONS FOR REFLECTION

1. What linkages, if any, might exist between white-collar and organized crime?

2. What types of white-collar crime has this chapter identified? Is corporate crime a form of white-collar crime? Is occupational crime a form of white-collar crime?

3. How would you describe a typical "traditional" organized crime family, as outlined in this chapter? Why does a crime family contain so many different "levels"?

4. What is money laundering? How might money laundering be reduced or prevented? Can you think of any strategies this chapter does not discuss for the reduction of money-laundering activities in the United States? If so, what are they?

PUBLIC ORDER AND DRUG CRIMES

LEARNING OUTCOMES

After reading this chapter, you should be able to answer the following questions:

- What can be said about the history of drugs, drug abuse, and drug-control legislation in the United States?

- What are the various categories of controlled substances described by federal law, and what is a dangerous drug?

- What is drug trafficking, and what efforts are being made to curtail it?

- What is the relationship among drug trafficking, drug abuse, and other forms of crime?

- What government strategies have been used to reduce the incidence of drug use in the United States?

- What is prostitution, and what are the various types of prostitutes identified in this chapter?

■ **psychoactive substance**
A substance that affects the mind, mental processes, or emotions.

Introduction

In 2009, *Forbes* magazine editors sparked anger among members of the Mexican government when they named Mexico's most wanted man, Joaquin "El Chapo" Guzman, to the magazine's list of the world's most powerful people.[1] Guzman, said to be in charge of one of the largest drug cartels in the world, is blamed for thousands of killings across Mexico. His place on the *Forbes* list put him ahead of Hugo Chavez, the president of Venezuela, and France's President Nicolas Sarkozy.[2] At only five feet tall, "Shorty" Guzman, age 51, has repeatedly embarrassed the Mexican government with his ability to escape from custody and to avoid capture, and his earnings from the drug trade are thought to number in the billions of dollars. The naming of Guzman to the *Forbes* list "not only goes against the efforts of the Mexican government, but the international fight to eliminate mafias and organized crime," said Luis Estrada, a spokesman for the Mexican Department of the Interior. "It's a justification for crime."

exception existed in the form of opium dens, which flourished in West Coast cities and eventually made their way across the country as a result of increased Asian immigration; some Chinese immigrants had brought opium products with them and introduced other segments of the American population to opium smoking.

Psychoactive substances (substances affecting mental processes and emotions) gained widespread acceptance during the hippie movement during the late 1960s and early 1970s, which was characterized by slogans like "If it feels good, do it" and "Tune in, turn on, drop out," promoting free love, personal freedom, experimentation with subjective states of consciousness, and "mind expansion."

One influential figure in the drug-inspired movement of the times was Harvard professor Timothy Leary, who formed the League of Spiritual Discovery in the mid-1960s, "an orthodox, psychedelic religion that permits the use of LSD and marijuana as sacraments by League members."[3] With the advent of the hippie era, marijuana, lysergic acid diethylamide (LSD), hashish,

History of Drug Abuse in the United States

Guzman's story illustrates the glamour sometimes associated with drug sales and drug trafficking, and his legend is told in popular Mexican *narcocorrido* songs that glorify drug dealers and the drug trade. Mexican drug traffickers and illicit drug use in the United States are closely linked and affect all segments of both Mexican and American society. Even more problematic is the fact that almost all forms of illicit drug use in America are associated with other forms of criminality. Drugs and their relationship to crime provide one of the most significant policy issues of our time.

The rampant, widespread use and abuse of mind- and mood-altering drugs, so commonplace in the United States today, is of relatively recent origin. Throughout the 1800s and early 1900s, the use of illegal drugs in America was mostly associated with artistic individuals and fringe groups and was almost exclusively confined to small groups of musicians, painters, poets, and other highly imaginative individuals seeking to enhance their creativity. One significant

A smoker in an opium den in Chinatown, San Francisco, circa 1925. How have American attitudes toward drugs changed over time?
Source: UPI/CORBIS-NY

■ **National Survey on Drug Use and Health (NSDUH)**
A national survey of illicit drug use among people 12 years of age and older that is conducted annually by the Substance Abuse and Mental Health Services Administration.

■ **Office of National Drug Control Policy (ONDCP)**
A national office charged by Congress with establishing policies, priorities, and objectives for the nation's drug-control program. ONDCP is responsible for annually developing and disseminating the *National Drug-Control Strategy*.

psilocybin, and peyote burst on the national scene as an ever-growing number of individuals began to view drugs as recreational substances and as more and more young people identified with the tenor of the period.

Extent of Drug Abuse

Data on drug abuse in the United States are available through a variety of sources, such as the *Monitoring the Future* (MTF) study, conducted by the University of Michigan's Institute for Social Research with funding from the National Institute on Drug Abuse at the National Institutes of Health; the **National Survey on Drug Use and Health (NSDUH)**, conducted annually by the Substance Abuse and Mental Health Services Administration (SAMHSA); the National Narcotics Intelligence Consumers Committee's *NNICC Report*, published in conjunction with the Drug Enforcement Administration (DEA); the National Institute of Justice (NIJ) quarterly Arrestee Drug Abuse Monitoring Program

The annual National Survey on Drug Use and Health is conducted by the Substance Abuse and Mental Health Services Administration.

report; the **Office of National Drug Control Policy (ONDCP)** *Pulse Check: National Trends in Drug Abuse*, which reports at least once a year on drug-use trends; and annual reports published by SAMHSA's Drug Abuse Warning Network.

According to NSDUH data released in 2010, an estimated 21.8 million Americans ages 12 and older were current users of illicit drugs in 2009, meaning they used an illicit drug at least once during the 30 days prior to being interviewed.[4] In 2009, as in prior years, men had higher rates of current illicit drug use than women (10.8% versus 6.6%), but, rates of nonmedical psychotherapeutic drug use were similar for males (3.1%) and females (2.4%).

Marijuana, the most commonly used illicit drug in 2009, was used by 77% of those reporting drug use. Approximately 58% of illicit drug users consumed only marijuana, 19% used marijuana and another illicit drug, and the remaining 23% used an illicit drug but not marijuana in the past month, so about 47% of current illicit drug users in 2009 (an estimated 9.2 million Americans) were users of illicit drugs other than marijuana and hashish, with or without the use of marijuana (see Figure 12–1).[5]

Of the 9.2 million users of illicit drugs other than marijuana, 7 million (representing 2.8% of the population ages 12 and older) were using psychotherapeutics nonmedically. Psychotherapeutics include pain relievers (5.2 million users), tranquilizers (1.3 million users), stimulants (1.2 million users), and sedatives (0.4 million users).

In 2009, an estimated 1.6 million Americans (0.8% of the population ages 12 and older) were current cocaine users, 702,000 were crack users, and 1.3 million Americans (or 0.4% of the population) were current hallucinogen users, including 555,000 Ecstasy users (0.2% of the population). Survey results also showed that an estimated 200,000 Americans (or 0.1% of the population) were current heroin users.

FIGURE 12-1 | The Past-Month Use of Selected Illicit Drugs among Persons Ages 12 and Older by Type of Drug, 2009
Source: Substance Abuse and Mental Health Services Administration, *National Survey on Drug Use and Health, 2009* (Washington, DC: U.S. Government Printing Office, 2010).

Of the 10% of youths (ages 12 to 17) who reported current use of illicit drugs in 2009, marijuana was the most common—7.3% of youths were current users of marijuana. The percentage using illicit drugs in the 30 days prior to being interviewed was slightly higher for boys (10.6%) than for girls (9.4%). In this age group, boys had a slightly higher rate of marijuana use than girls (8.3% versus 6.3%), but girls were somewhat more likely to use psychotherapeutics nonmedically than boys (3.5% versus 2.8%).

The highest rate of illicit drug use was found among people ages 18 to 25, with rates of current use around 20%. For this group, drug use was dominated by marijuana, with 16.3% reporting current marijuana use in 2009. As Figure 12–2 shows, rates of use generally declined in each successively older age group, with only 2.4% of people ages 55 to 59 and 0.7% of those ages 65 and older reporting current illicit use.

The NSDUH reported that rates of illicit drug use for major racial and ethnic groups in 2009 were 8.8% for whites, 7.9% for Hispanics, and 9.6% for blacks. The rates were highest among the American Indian/Alaska Native population (18.3%) and among people reporting multiple races (14.3%), and Asians had the lowest rate (3.7%).

The rate of illicit drug use in metropolitan areas was higher than in nonmetropolitan areas: 9.0% in large metropolitan areas, 8.8% in small metropolitan areas, and 7.3% in nonmetropolitan areas. Rural counties had a 4.6% rate of illicit drug use. The NSDUH and the MTF study showed a leveling or declining national trend in illicit drug use, marijuana use, and cigarette use among adolescents since 1997, following a period of significant increases in the early 1990s.

As in previous NSDUH data, the 2009 survey found that substance-abuse rates remained highly correlated with educational status: Among young adults 18 years and older, those who had not completed high school had the highest rate of abuse (10.2%), whereas college graduates had the lowest rate of abuse (6.1%), despite the fact that adults who had completed four years of college were more likely to have tried illicit drugs in their lifetime than adults who had not completed high school

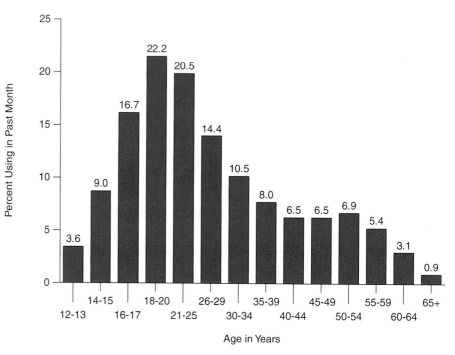

FIGURE 12-2 | Past-Month Illicit Drug Use among Persons Ages 12 and Older by Age, 2009

Source: Substance Abuse and Mental Health Services Administration, *National Survey on Drug Use and Health, 2009* (Washington, DC: U.S. Government Printing Office, 2010).

(51.8% versus 39.7%). Hence, it appears that the more education a person receives, the more likely he or she is to discontinue using drugs with age.

Current employment status was also found to be highly correlated with rates of illicit drug use. The NSDUH found that 17% of unemployed adults (ages 18 and older) were illicit drug users, compared with 8.0% of adults employed full time. Of all current illicit drug users ages 18 and older (19.3 million adults), 66.6% were employed either full time or part time.

If NSDUH results are accurate, they would seem to indicate that drug abuse is now substantially less of a problem than it was two decades ago. In 1979, the number of current illicit drug users was at its highest level, when estimates of current users reached 25 million; the largest ever annual estimate of marijuana use put routine users at 22.5 million in 1979, and the greatest cocaine use was estimated at 5.3 million in 1985—figures far greater than those of today. Growth of the American population over time gives the estimated decline even greater weight.

There are some methodological problems associated with any nationwide survey, and in recognition of these problems, NSDUH authors wrote, "Sample size, coverage, and validity

LIBRARY EXTRA 12–1
LIBRARY EXTRA 12–2
LIBRARY EXTRA 12–3

Dr. Timothy Leary, guru of the 1960s psychedelic movement.
Leary died in 1996, and his ashes were shot into space a year later. What was Leary's message?

Source: AP Photo/Walt Weis

problems are likely to be more pronounced for NSDUH estimates of heavy users than for other measures generated by the survey. Therefore, estimates of heavy use are considered conservative, and changes over time are generally not statistically significant. . . . Clearly there is considerable uncertainty about the size of the heavy drug-using population."[6] Read the latest NSDUH report at **Library Extra 12–1**.

Whereas the use of illicit drugs provides one measure of the drug problem facing our country, the ready availability of such drugs provides another. Data from the National Crime Victimization Survey (NCVS) showed that two of three students ages 12 to 19 reported ready availability of illegal drugs at their school.[7] Students in public schools reported a wider availability of drugs than those in private schools, and students in higher grades (9 through 12) reported more drugs available to them than those in the lower grades. Similar rates of availability were reported by white students (69% of whom said drugs were available to them at school), black students (67%), and students living in cities (66%), suburban areas (67%), and rural areas (71%).

Young People and Drugs

While NSDUH data provided a picture of drug abuse among all those 12 years of age and older, the National Institute on Drug Abuse's MTF study supplied data on drug abuse among junior high school and high school students, tracking twelfth-graders' illicit drug use, their perceived availability of drugs, and their attitudes toward drugs since 1975; in 1991, eighth- and tenth-graders were added to the survey. The 2009 survey gathered responses from over 50,000 students in more than 400 schools across the nation about lifetime use, past-year use, past-month use, and daily use of drugs, alcohol, cigarettes, and smokeless tobacco. For access to the full 2009 MTF data describing the use of many other drugs, including inhalants, view **Library Extra 12–2**. See the Theory versus Reality box for information on some college students' drinking patterns. **Library Extra 12–3** provides still more information.

MTF researchers noted that in the late twentieth century, illicit drug use among young Americans had reached very high levels. In 1975, when the MTF survey began, the majority of young people (55%) reported having used an illicit drug by the time they left high school, and this figure rose to two-thirds (66%) by 1981 before a long and gradual decline to 41% by 1992, the low point. After 1992, the proportion rose again, reaching a high of 55% in 1999, and stood at 47% in 2009.[8]

Because marijuana use is much more common than that of any other illicit drug, trends in marijuana use significantly influence the index of "any illicit drug use" reported by the survey. In 1975, over one-third (36%) of twelfth-graders had tried some illicit drug other than marijuana, a figure that rose to 43% by 1981 and then declined for a long period to a low of 25% in 1992. Some increases followed in the 1990s as the use of a number of drugs rose steadily, reaching 30% by 1997; then the rate fell to 24% in 2009.

> In the late twentieth century drug use among young Americans reached very high levels.

Marijuana has been the most widely used illicit drug throughout all the years of this study. Annual marijuana use peaked at 51% among twelfth-graders in 1979, following a rise that began during the 1960s, and then steadily declined for the next 13 years, bottoming out at 22% in 1992—a decline of more than half. The 1990s saw a resurgence in marijuana use. After a considerable increase, annual prevalence rates peaked in 1996 at the eighth-grade level and in 1997 at tenth- and twelfth-grade

Follow the author's tweets about the latest crime and justice news at **http://twitter.com/schmalleger**.

levels. Following the peak, there was a gradual decline among eighth-graders, but the decline appeared to halt in 2005, with an annual prevalence rate in 2009 about equal to that of 2004; in the upper grades, only a very modest decline occurred between 1997 and 2002, followed by a continuing gradual decline since.

Since the MTF survey began in 1975, between 83% and 90% of the members of every senior class have said they could get marijuana "fairly easily" or "very easily" if they wanted some, so marijuana has remained a highly accessible drug. Since 1991, when data became available for eighth- and tenth-graders, marijuana has become considerably less accessible to younger adolescents; however, in 2009 two-fifths of eighth-graders (40%) and almost three-quarters of all tenth-graders (69%) reported it as being accessible, compared to 81% of seniors.

Costs of Drug Abuse

The ONDCP estimated that Americans spent $64.8 billion to purchase illegal drugs in 2000 (see Figure 12–3).[9] The true costs of drug abuse are difficult to measure but would include expenditures for law enforcement activities intended to prevent drug growing, importation, and use; criminal justice case processing; drug-treatment programs; steps to prevent money laundering; and time lost from work as a result of drug involvement. More difficult to quantify, but

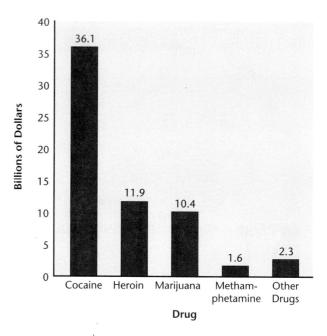

FIGURE 12-3 | The Annual Amount Spent on Illegal Drugs in the United States

Source: Office of National Drug Control Policy, *Drug Data Summary* (Washington, DC: ONDCP, 2003).

equally real, are other costs such as death and sickness resulting from exposure to controlled substances, drug-related crime, fragmentation of families and other relationships, changes in attitudes and worldview among the American population due to drug-crime fear, lost human potential, and the image of the United States on the world stage. In 2000, the last year for which Centers for Disease Control and Prevention (CDC) analyses of death-certificate data were available, there were 19,698 drug-induced deaths (deaths resulting from drug consumption, primarily overdose) in America.[10]

Americans spend about $65 billion on illegal drugs annually.

Acquired immunodeficiency syndrome (AIDS), many cases of which can be traced to intravenous drug use, has proved to be a costly disease in social terms. Researchers at the CDC have said that AIDS is already the leading cause of death of black and Hispanic men ages 25 to 44 (homicide is the second leading cause) and that AIDS "has become the second leading cause of death among black women aged 25 to 44."[11] The CDC listed 73 AIDS cases for every 100,000 black women but only five per 100,000 white women; of AIDS cases among minority women, 47% were traceable to intravenous drug use, while 37% appeared due to heterosexual intercourse.

A handout photo provided by a concert promoter of pop star Michael Jackson rehearsing for planned shows in London at the Staples Center on June 23, 2009, in Los Angeles, California. Jackson died two days later at the age of 50 in a hospital after going into cardiac arrest following the intravenous administration of a dangerous drug in his Los Angeles home. How can drugs be so attractive?

Source: Getty Images, Inc./Kevin Mazur/AEG

THEORY | versus REALITY

The Harvard Alcohol Study

In 1993, the Harvard School of Public Health conducted its first College Alcohol Study (CAS). The study surveyed a random sample of students at 140 colleges in 39 states and the District of Columbia. The study was the first national examination of the drinking patterns of college students.

The original CAS identified a style of drinking that study authors called "binge drinking." *Binge drinking* was defined as the consumption of five or more drinks in a row for men and four or more for women at least once in the two weeks preceding the survey. The CAS, with its emphasis on binge drinking, focused media attention on alcohol-related college deaths, including deaths from acute alcohol poisoning, falls, drownings, automobile accidents, fires, and hypothermia resulting from exposure to the elements. The study also led to passage of a congressional resolution to address binge drinking as a national problem and to the appointment of a National Institute on Alcoholism and Alcohol Abuse special task force on college drinking.

The CAS was repeated in 1997, 1999, and 2001. The study reported on the drinking behavior of four categories of students: (1) frequent binge drinkers—defined as those students who had binged three or more times in the past two weeks; (2) occasional binge drinkers—those students who had binged one or two times in the same period; (3) nonbinge drinkers—those students who had consumed alcohol in the past year but who had not binged in the previous two weeks; and (4) abstainers—those students who had not consumed alcohol in the past year.

The 2001 CAS surveyed students at 119 four-year colleges that also participated in the 1993, 1997, and 1999 studies. Responses in the four survey years were compared to determine trends in heavy alcohol use, alcohol-related problems, and encounters with college and community prevention efforts. In 2001, approximately two in five college students reported binge drinking, a rate almost identical to rates in the previous three surveys. Very little change in overall college binge drinking was observed in the surveys over

time, although a sharp rise in frequent binge drinking was noted among students attending all-women's colleges. The most significant finding, however, was an observed 18% increase in the college student population that reported driving under the influence of alcohol in the previous year (Figure 12–4).

The study also found that about 19% of surveyed students were abstainers and 23% were frequent binge drinkers. As in earlier studies, binge drinkers, and particularly frequent binge drinkers, were more likely than other students to experience alcohol-related problems. At colleges with high binge-drinking rates, students who did not binge drink were at high risk of experiencing the secondhand effects of others' heavy drinking. These secondhand effects included having study patterns interrupted, being kept awake at night, being insulted or humiliated, being subjected to unwanted sexual advances, and having to take care of drunken fellow students.

For the latest research reports based on CAS data, visit the Harvard School of Public Health's College Alcohol Study information page at www.hsph.harvard.edu/cas/AlcoholIndex.html. Additional information on binge drinking is available from the National Survey of Drug Use and Health (Figure 12–5).

Discussion Questions

1. Do you know students who consume alcohol on or off campus? If so, do you think that the College Alcohol Study categories provide a useful way of classifying the different kinds of drinking patterns among members of the student body?

2. What percentage of the student body at your school would you assign to each of the CAS categories?

3. Why might such categories be useful to policymakers?

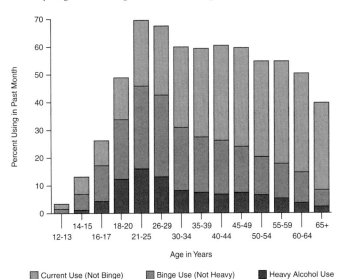

FIGURE 12-4 | Driving under the Influence of Alcohol in the Past Year among Persons Ages 16 and Older, by Age, 2008

Source: Office of Applied Studies, Substance Abuse and Mental Health Services Administration, *National Survey on Drug Use and Health, 2008*, http://oas .samhsa.gov/nsduh/2k8nsduh/gifs/Fig3-5.gif.

FIGURE 12-5 | Current, Binge, and Heavy Alcohol Use among Persons Ages 12 and Older, by Age, 2008

Source: Office of Applied Studies, Substance Abuse and Mental Health Services Administration, *National Survey on Drug Use and Health, 2008*, http://oas .samhsa.gov/nsduh/2k8nsduh/gifs/Fig3-1.gif.

References: Henry Weschler et.al., "Trends in College Binge Drinking during a Period of Increased Prevention Efforts: Findings from 4 Harvard School of Public Health College Alcohol Study Surveys: 1993–2001," http://www.hsph.harvard.edu/cas/Documents/trends/Trends.pdf (accessed July 10, 2007); Ralph Hingson et al., "Magnitude of Alcohol-Related Mortality and Morbidity among U.S. College Students Ages 18–24: Changes from 1998 to 2001," *Annual Review of Public Health*, Vol. 26 (2005), pp. 259–279; and Henry Weschler et al., "College Binge Drinking in the 1990s: A Continuing Problem: Results of the Harvard School of Public Health 1999 College Alcohol Study," http://www.hsph.harvard.edu/cas/rpt2000/CAS2000rpt.shtml (accessed January 15, 2009).

Follow the author's tweets about the latest crime and justice news at **http://twitter.com/schmalleger.**

Other costs, such as lost productivity due to drug abuse, were estimated to total $77.6 billion annually.[12] More than half the total ($43.8 billion) was estimated lost earnings due to drug-related crime victimization, and the remainder was estimated to be losses suffered by drug abusers themselves. Tables 12–1 and 12–2 show the estimated financial and social costs of illegal drug use in the United States per year. Table 12–1 includes dollar amounts spent on systemwide efforts at drug control, and Table 12–2 lists types of costs that are much more difficult to quantify.

TABLE 12-1 | Direct Costs of Illegal Drug Use

TYPE OF COST	MILLIONS
Federal drug expenditures	$12,630
Law enforcement[a]	3,200
Interdiction	2,600
International programs	1,150
Drug prevention	1,960
Drug treatment	3,720
State and local drug-crime expenditures	5,239
Enforcement of drug laws	2,007
Adjudication of drug-law violators	123
Correction of drug-law violators	3,071
State prisons	1,158
Local jails	890
Juvenile detention	224
Probation, pardon, and parole	677
Other corrections	122
Other criminal justice–related expenditures	38
Health-care costs for illegal drug users	2,272
Short-stay hospitals	1,242
Specialty institutions	570
Office-based physicians	52
Support services	201
Other professional services	17
Medical care for drug-related AIDS cases	126
Support services for drug-related AIDS cases	64
Total	$20,141

[a]Not all law enforcement categories are shown.
Source: Figures are the author's estimates from a variety of sources, including Office of National Drug Control Policy, *The National Drug Control Strategy, 2007* (Washington, DC: ONDCP, 2007); and Office of National Drug Control Policy, *National Drug Control Strategy: FY 2008 Budget Summary* (Washington, DC: ONDCP, 2007).

TABLE 12-2 | Indirect Costs of Illegal Drug Use

Criminal Justice Expenditures on Drug-Related Crime
* Costs to prosecute drug offenders
* Investigations of robberies, burglaries, and thefts for drug money, and adjudication and punishment of the offenders
* Investigations of assaults and homicides in the drug business (or by drug users who lost control), and adjudication and punishment of the offenders

Health-Care Costs
* Injuries resulting from drug-related child abuse or neglect
* Injuries from drug-related accidents
* Injuries from drug-related crime
* Premature death due to drug use
* Other medical care (including volunteer services and outpatient services, such as emergency room visits) for illegal drug users
* Antidrug resources used in nonhospital settings

Lost Productivity Costs
* Time away from work for drug-related accident victims
* Time away from work for drug-related crime victims
* Time away from work and homemaking to care for drug users and their dependents
* Drug-related educational problems and school dropouts
* Offenders incarcerated for drug-related or drug-defined crimes

Other Costs to Society
* Loss of property values due to drug-related neighborhood crime
* Property damaged or destroyed in fires and in workplace and vehicular accidents due to drug use
* Agricultural resources devoted to illegal drug cultivation or production
* Toxins introduced into air and water supplies by drug production
* Workplace drug-prevention programs, such as drug-testing and employee-assistance programs
* Training to avoid drug-related crime for potential victims
* Costs of pain and suffering for illegal drug users and their families and friends
* Private legal costs for drug-related issues

Source: National Institute on Drug Abuse and National Institute on Alcohol Abuse and Alcoholism, *The Economic Costs of Alcohol and Drug Abuse in the United States, 1992* (Washington, DC: U.S. Government Printing Office, 1998); Bureau of Justice Statistics, *Drugs, Crime and the Justice System: A National Report from the Bureau of Justice Statistics* (Washington, DC: U.S. Government Printing Office, December 1992); and *The Real Cost of the Drug War,* http://briancbennet.com (accessed October 1, 2004).

■ **addiction**
A chronic brain disease characterized by compulsive drug seeking and use despite harmful consequences.

■ **dangerous drug**
A controlled substance other than cocaine, opiates, and cannabis products. Amphetamines, LSD, methamphetamines, methcathinone, and phencyclidine (PCP), as well as designer drugs, are all considered dangerous drugs.

WEB EXTRA 12–1
LIBRARY EXTRA 12–4

Illegal Drugs and Drug Addiction

The term *drug addiction* is widely used but often not well understood. The National Institute on Drug Abuse (NIDA), a part of the National Institutes of Health, defined **addiction** as "a chronic, relapsing brain disease that is characterized by compulsive drug seeking and use, despite harmful consequences."[13] NIDA noted that people often underestimate the complexity of drug addiction, which leads to physical changes in the brain, resulting in modified structure and functioning of this crucial organ. NIDA researchers explained that brain imaging studies of drug-addicted individuals showed changes in areas of the brain that are critical to judgment, decision making, learning and memory, and behavior control.[14] Because it is a disease that impacts the brain, said NIDA, "stopping drug abuse is not simply a matter of willpower." Whether a person becomes addicted to drugs depends on a number of factors: the age at first use; the frequency of initial use, with genetic and environmental factors interacting with critical developmental stages; gender, ethnicity, and preexisting mental disorders; and social influences in the environment, such as peer pressure, physical and sexual abuse, stress, and parental involvement.[15] See the first Who's to Blame box in this chapter for a creative example of how drugs can affect two brothers differently.

Controlled substances are generally grouped according to both pharmacological and legal criteria into the following seven categories: stimulants, depressants, cannabis, narcotics, hallucinogens, anabolic steroids, and inhalants. A separate eighth category, dangerous drugs, provides a kind of legal and definitional catchall. The DEA used the term **dangerous drugs** to refer to "broad categories or classes of controlled substances other than cocaine, opiates, and cannabis products."[16] The seven major categories, as well as some of the drugs each contains, are described in the following paragraphs.[17] Table 12–3, from NIDA, summarizes the differences among the drug categories and shows the uses and effects of various types of controlled substances. Learn more about each type of drug at

> Controlled substances are generally grouped into seven categories: stimulants, depressants, cannabis, narcotics, hallucinogens, anabolic steroids, and inhalants.

Web Extra 12–1; read the federal statute describing the various categories of controlled substances at **Library Extra 12–4**.

Stimulants

Stimulants, including cocaine and crack cocaine, amphetamines like Dexedrine and Benzedrine, and methamphetamine, increase central nervous system activity, resulting in higher heart rate, elevated blood pressure, and increased mental activity. Legitimate uses of stimulants include increased alertness, reduced fatigue, weight control, and topical analgesic (pain-killing) action, but they are used illegally by people seeking to produce states of excitability and feelings of competence and power.

Cocaine is available in powdered form or as small "rocks" of crack. Crack cocaine, which is much less expensive than powdered cocaine, is made by mixing cocaine powder with water and baking soda or ammonia and is usually smoked in a crack pipe. Powdered cocaine is inhaled or snorted, but it may also be mixed with volatile chemicals and "freebased" or smoked or injected. Cocaine produces effects similar to other stimulants: euphoria, intense stimulation, psychic and physical well-being, and seemingly boundless energy. Cocaine highs are generally both more intense and more immediate than those produced by other drugs, but prolonged cocaine use can cause delusions, hallucinations, weight loss, and overall physical deterioration.

The American retail price of powdered cocaine is between $36,300 and $136,000 per pound. Crack cocaine sells for $3 to $40 per vial, each of which contains several small "rocks." The ONDCP estimated that the total annual amount spent on illegal cocaine in the United States is $36.1 billion.

Other stimulants include amphetamines, with street names like "bennies," "speed," and "uppers." Amphetamines produce mental alertness and increase the ability to concentrate and can also cause talkativeness, reduce fatigue, and result in wakefulness; they are used medically to treat narcolepsy, obesity, and some forms of brain dysfunction. Abuse produces irritability, overexhaustion, and—in cases of prolonged abuse—psychosis and death from cardiac arrest.

One drug that has caught the attention of many is methamphetamine ("speed," "meth," "crank"), a stimulant chemically related to other amphetamines but with stronger effects on the central nervous system. MDMA is used in pill form or in powdered form for snorting or injecting;[18] crystallized methamphetamine, known as "ice," "crystal," or "glass," is a more powerful form that is smokable. The effects of MDMA use include increased heart rate

TABLE 12-3 | Commonly Abused Drugs: Uses and Effects

SUBSTANCES: CATEGORY AND NAME	EXAMPLES OF COMMERCIAL AND STREET NAMES	DEA SCHEDULE[a]/WAYS ADMINISTERED[b]	INTOXICATION EFFECTS/POTENTIAL HEALTH CONSEQUENCES
Cannabinoids			
hashish	boom, chronic, gangster, hash, hash oil, hemp	I/swallowed, smoked	euphoria, slowed thinking and reaction time, confusion, impaired balance and coordination/cough, frequent respiratory infections; impaired memory and learning; increased heart rate, anxiety panic attacks; tolerance, addiction
marijuana	blunt, dope, ganja, grass, herb, joints, Mary Jane, pot, reefer, sinsemilla, skunk, weed	I/swallowed, smoked	
Depressants			
barbiturates	Amytal, Nembutal, Phenobarbital, Seconal: barbs, reds, red birds, phennies, tooies, yellows, yellow jackets	II, III, V/injected, swallowed	reduced anxiety; feeling of well-being; lowered inhibitions; slowed pulse and breathing; lowered blood pressure; poor concentration/fatigue; confusion; impaired coordination, memory, and judgment; addiction; respiratory depression and arrest; death for barbiturates—sedation, drowsiness/depression, unusual excitement, fever, irritability, poor judgment, slurred speech, dizziness, life-threatening withdrawal for benzodiazepines—sedation, drowsiness/dizziness for flunitrazepam—visual and gastrointestinal disturbances, urinary retention, memory loss for the time under the drug's effects for GHB—drowsiness, nausea/vomiting, headache, loss of consciousness, loss of reflexes, seizures, coma, death for methaqualone—euphoria/depression, poor reflexes, slurred speech, coma
benzodiazepines (other than flunitrazepam)	Ativan, Halcion, Librium, Valium, Xanax: candy, downers, sleeping pills, tranks	IV/injected, swallowed	
flunitrazepam[c]	Rohypnol: forget-me pill, Mexican Valium, R2, Roche, roofies, roofinol, rope, rophies	IV/swallowed, snorted	
GHB[c]	gamma-hydroxybutyrate: G, Georgia home boy, grievous bodily harm, liquid ecstasy	I/swallowed	
methaqualone	Parest, Quaalude, Sopor: ludes, mandrex, quad, quay	I/injected, swallowed	

Dissociative Anesthetics

Drug	Examples of Commercial and Street Names	DEA Schedule/How Administered	Intoxication Effects/Potential Health Consequences
ketamine	Ketalar SV: cat Valiums, K, Special K, vitamin K	III/injected, snorted, smoked	increased heart rate and blood pressure, impaired motor function/memory loss; numbness; nausea and vomiting — for ketamine—at high doses, delirium, depression, respiratory depression and arrest — for PCP and analogs—possible decrease in blood pressure and heart rate, panic, aggression, violence/loss of appetite, depression
PCP and analogs	phencyclidine: angel dust, boat, hog, love boat, peace pill	I, II/injected, swallowed, smoked	
Hallucinogens			
LSD	lysergic acid diethylamide: acid, blotter, boomers, cubes, microdot, yellow sunshines	I/swallowed, absorbed through mouth tissues	altered states of perception and feeling; nausea; persisting perception disorder (flashbacks) — for LSD and mescaline—increased body temperature, heart rate, blood pressure/loss of appetite, sleeplessness, numbness, weakness, tremors — for LSD—persistent mental disorders — for psilocybin—nervousness, paranoia
mescaline	buttons, cactus, mesc, peyote	I/swallowed, smoked	
psilocybin	magic mushroom, purple passion, shrooms	I/swallowed	
Opioids and Morphine Derivatives			
codeine	Empirin with Codeine, Fiorinal with Codeine, Robitussin A-C, Tylenol with Codeine: Captain Cody, Cody, schoolboy; (with glutethimide) doors & fours, loads, pancakes and syrup	II, III, IV, V/injected, swallowed	pain relief, euphoria, drowsiness/nausea, constipation, confusion, sedation, respiratory depression and arrest, tolerance, addiction, unconsciousness, coma, death — for codeine—less analgesia, sedation, and respiratory depression than morphine — for heroin—staggering gait
fentanyl and fentanyl analogs	Actiq, Duragesic, Sublimaze: Apache, China girl, China white, dance fever, friend, goodfella, jackpot, murder 8, Tango and Cash, TNT	I, II/injected, smoked, snorted	
heroin	diacetylmorphine: brown sugar, dope, H, horse, junk, skag, skunk, smack, white horse	I/injected, smoked, snorted	
morphine	Roxanol, Duramorph: M, Miss Emma, monkey, white stuff	II, III/injected, swallowed, smoked	
opium	laudanum, paregoric: big O, black stuff, block, gum, hop	II, III, V/swallowed, smoked	
oxycodone HCL	OxyContin: killer, O.C., Oxy	II/injected, swallowed, snorted	

(continued)

TABLE 12-3 | Commonly Abused Drugs: Uses and Effects   (*continued*)

SUBSTANCES: CATEGORY AND NAME	EXAMPLES OF COMMERCIAL AND STREET NAMES	DEA SCHEDULE^a/WAYS ADMINISTERED^b	INTOXICATION EFFECTS/POTENTIAL HEALTH CONSEQUENCES
hydrocodone bitartrate, acetaminophen	*Vicodin:* vike, Watson-387	II/swallowed	
Stimulants			
amphetamine	*Biphetamine, Dexedrine:* bennies, black beauties, crosses, hearts, LA turnaround, speed, truck drivers, uppers	II/injected, swallowed, smoked, snorted	*increased heart rate, blood pressure, and metabolism; feelings of exhilaration, energy; increased mental alertness/rapid or irregular heart beat; reduced appetite, weight loss, heart failure, nervousness, insomnia* *for amphetamine—rapid breathing/ tremor, loss of coordination; irritability, anxiousness, restlessness, delirium, panic, paranoia, impulsive behavior, aggressiveness, tolerance, addiction, psychosis* *for cocaine—increased temperature/chest pain, respiratory failure, nausea, abdominal pain, strokes, seizures, headaches, malnutrition, panic attacks*
cocaine	*Cocaine hydrochloride:* blow, bump, C, candy, Charlie, coke, crack, flake, rock, snow, toot	II/injected, smoked, snorted	
MDMA (methyl- enedioxymeth- amphetamine)	Adam, clarity, ecstasy, Eve, lover's speed, peace, STP, X, XTC	I/swallowed	*for MDMA—mild hallucinogenic effects, increased tactile sensitivity, empathic feelings/impaired memory and learning, hyperthermia, cardiac toxicity, renal failure, liver toxicity* *for methamphetamine—aggression, violence, psychotic behavior/ memory loss, cardiac and neurological damage; impaired memory and learning, tolerance, addiction* *for nicotine—additional effects attributable to tobacco exposure: adverse pregnancy outcomes; chronic lung disease, cardiovascular disease, stroke, cancer; tolerance, addiction*

Substance	DEA Schedule / How Administered	Examples of Commercial and Street Names	Intoxication Effects / Health Risks
methamphetamine	II/Injected, swallowed, smoked, snorted	Desoxyn: chalk, crank, crystal, fire, glass, go fast, ice, meth, speed	
methylphenidate	II/Injected, swallowed, snorted	Ritalin: JIF, MPH, R-ball, Skippy, the smart drug, vitamin R	
nicotine	not scheduled/smoked, snorted, taken in snuff and spit tobacco	cigarettes, cigars, smokeless tobacco, snuff, spit tobacco, bidis, chew	
Other Compounds			
anabolic steroids	III/injected, swallowed, applied to skin	Anadrol, Oxandrin, Durabolin, Depo-Testosterone, Equipoise: roids, juice	no intoxication effects/hypertension, blood clotting and cholesterol changes, liver cysts and cancer, kidney cancer, hostility and aggression, acne; in adolescents, premature stoppage of growth; in males, prostate cancer, reduced sperm production, shrunken testicles, and breast enlargement; in females, menstrual irregularities, development of beard, and other masculine characteristics
Dextromethorphan (DXM)	not scheduled/swallowed	Found in some cough and cold medications; Robotripping, Robo, Triple C	dissociative effects, distorted visual perceptions to complete dissociative effects/for effects at higher doses, see "dissociative anesthetics"
inhalants	not scheduled/inhaled through nose or mouth	Solvents (paint thinners, gasoline, glues), gases (butane, propane, aerosol propellants, nitrous oxide), nitrites (isoamyl, isobutyl, cyclohexyl): laughing gas, poppers, snappers, whippets	stimulation, loss of inhibition: headache: nausea or vomiting: slurred speech, loss of motor coordination: wheezing/unconsciousness, cramps, weight loss, muscle weakness, depression, memory impairment, damage to cardiovascular and nervous systems, sudden death

[a]Schedule I and II drugs have a high potential for abuse. They require greater storage security and have a quota on manufacturing, among other restrictions. Schedule I drugs are available for research only and have no approved medical use; Schedule II drugs are available only by prescription (unrefillable) and require a form for ordering. Schedule III and IV drugs are available by prescription, may have five refills in 6 months, and may be ordered orally. Some Schedule V drugs are available over the counter.

[b]Taking drugs by injection can increase the risk of infection through needle contamination with staphylococci, HIV, hepatitis, and other organisms.

[c]Associated with sexual assaults.

Source: National Institute on Drug Abuse.

LIBRARY EXTRA 12-5

WHO'S TO BLAME—The Individual or Society?

His Brother's Keeper

In March 2008, Nicole Smithfield received a letter from her former boyfriend, Derek Little. The letter came from the state's maximum-security prison where Derek was serving life without possibility of parole for the murder of his older brother, Hamilton. The brothers had grown up together and attended school in the same small town where Nicole lived. Derek began dealing drugs at age 13, bringing in a few dollars selling marijuana to some friends at school. By the time he was 24, Derek was operating one of the largest drug distribution networks in the county and bringing in thousands of dollars a week. He drove an expensive car, had the best clothes and high-tech gadgets, and carried a lot of cash with him wherever he went. People who knew him said that he also carried a 9-shot semiautomatic pistol strapped to his waist.

Hamilton took a different path and joined the army. He went to Afghanistan and then to Iraq for two tours of duty. One night, when he was home on leave, Hamilton stopped by his brother's house and an argument ensued. Hamilton wanted Derek to get out of the drug business and to turn his life around. "It's only a matter of time before you get arrested," Hamilton told his brother. "Do you want to spend the rest of your life in prison?"

"I'm too smart for that," Derek responded. "I've got too many layers (of dealers) protecting me. They'll never get anything on me."

"Yeah—but what about all the lives you're affecting? What about all the kids from our neighborhood who are getting strung out on drugs because of you? You're preying on society," Hamilton said, angry now. "And if you don't quit, I'll make you."

"What do you mean by that?" Derek asked, jumping out of his chair.

"I just think you need to stop, and if I have to, then I'll find a way to make you," Hamilton said, and left, beginning the walk home to his mother's mobile home less than a mile away.

According to evidence presented at his trial, that's when Derek got into his pickup truck and started down the road, accelerating to 80 mph before swerving onto the shoulder and hitting his brother. Hamilton's body flew 40 feet through the air before hitting the ground and then tumbled another 30 feet through the brush.

Prosecutors tried to present additional evidence showing that Derek was likely responsible for the deaths of three other people who had threatened him during the past two years, or who had said that they would turn him in to authorities—but the judge would not allow the jury to hear those claims. When the trial concluded, Derek was found guilty of killing his brother and sentenced to life in prison without the possibility of parole.

Think about it:

1. How is it that two brothers raised in the same environment might choose such different paths? What might explain their choices?

2. How would you explain the attraction that the drug trade seems to have for so many people in this country?

3. If you were able to set crime-control policies for the nation, how would you address the drug problem? Would you consider the decriminalization of any substances? If so, which ones and why? (See **Library Extra 12–5**.)

Note: Who's to Blame boxes provide fictionalized critical thinking opportunities, and are not actual cases.

and blood pressure, increased wakefulness, insomnia, increased physical activity, decreased appetite, and anxiety, paranoia, or violent behavior. The drug is easily made in simple home "laboratories" from readily available chemicals, and recipes describing how to produce the substance circulate on the Internet. Methamphetamine appeals to the abuser because it increases the body's metabolism, produces euphoria and alertness, and gives the user a sense of increased energy. Methamphetamine, an increasingly popular drug at raves (all-night dancing parties), is not physically addictive but can be psychologically addictive, with high doses or chronic use increasing users' nervousness, irritability, and paranoia. In 1996, the growing popularity of methamphetamine led to passage of the federal Comprehensive Methamphetamine Control Act (discussed in more detail later).

Depressants

The depressant family includes barbiturates, sedatives, and tranquilizers like Equanil, Librium, Nembutal, Phenobarbital, Quaalude, Seconal, Sopor, Thorazine, and Valium. Depressants are used legitimately for reduction of anxiety, for the treatment of psychological problems, and as mood elevators. Illegitimate users employ these substances to produce intoxication, to counter the effects of other drugs, or to treat themselves for drug withdrawal.

> The depressant family includes barbiturates, sedatives, and tranquilizers.

Depressants are often prescribed by physicians seeking to control patients' stress-related symptoms and to induce relaxed states and even sleep, and individuals who have experienced recent traumatic events may find that the temporary use of prescribed depressants helps to alleviate their psychic distress. If abused, however, depressants may lead to psychological dependence and addiction.

Cannabis

The cannabis category includes cannabis plants, hashish, hashish oil, marijuana, and sinsemilla—all of which are collectively termed *marijuana*. It (street names include "pot," "grass," and "weed") is a relatively mild nonaddictive drug with limited hallucinogenic properties whose primary active chemical is tetrahydrocannabinol. Although legitimate uses for cannabis have not been fully recognized, some research has suggested that the substance can be used in the treatment of pain and glaucoma and as a supplement to cancer treatments (cannabis appears to control the nausea associated with chemotherapy). Marijuana is used illegitimately to induce states of euphoria, gaiety, detachment, relaxation, intoxication, and focused awareness; time distortion,

Mexican drug lord Joaquin "Shorty" Guzman. Guzman was listed among the most powerful people in the world by *Forbes* in 2009. The vast amounts of money associated with the illegal drug trade have the potential to corrupt public officials and agents of drug control. How can that potential be reduced?
Source: AP Photo/Damian Dovarganes

increased sex drive, enhanced appetite, uncontrollable giddiness, and short-term memory loss tend to accompany its use.

Most of the marijuana consumed in the United States either is grown within the country or comes from Mexico. Although one marijuana plant produces between one and two pounds of dried leaves and stems, marijuana is generally sold to consumers in one-ounce bags; one pound of dried marijuana costs dealers $450 to $2,700, but users pay $25 to $1,000 per one-ounce bag, depending on the reputed potency of the particular variety they are purchasing. Single marijuana cigarettes (called "joints" and "reefers") sell for $1 to $5. The ONDCP estimated that the total amount spent on illegal marijuana in the United States is $10.4 billion annually.

Narcotics

Narcotics, including codeine, Dilaudid, heroin, methadone, morphine, and opium, have a number of legitimate uses, including pain relief, antidiarrheal action, and cough suppression. Street use of these drugs is intended to induce pleasure, euphoria, a lack of concern, and general feelings of well-being. Narcotics produce drowsiness and relaxation, accompanied by a dreamlike state of reverie, and are thought to mimic or enhance the activity of endorphins, proteins produced by the brain that control pain and influence other subjective experiences.

Heroin and morphine, generally sold as a white powder, are derived from opium and are usually injected into the body, although they may be smoked or eaten. Sometimes users inject these drugs under the skin, a practice called "skin-popping," but most addicts prefer direct intravenous injection for the immediate strong effects it produces.

One pound of 70% to 90% pure heroin sells in Southeast Asia for $2,700 to $5,000; at the wholesale level in the United States, the same substance brings $40,000 to $110,000 per pound, and mid-level dealers pay up to $270,000 for that amount. Dealers "cut" the drug, diluting it with a variety of other substances. "Once in the United States, heroin may be stepped on (diluted) as many as seven to ten times. What started out in some remote Asian laboratory as 99 percent pure heroin is cut with lactose (milk sugar, a by-product of milk processing), quinine, cornstarch, or almost any other powdery substance that will dissolve when heated. Ultimately, the heroin sold on the street is less than 10 percent pure and sometimes as little as 1 percent to 4 percent pure."[19] Street-level dealers sell diluted heroin in 0.1-gram single-dose bags for as much as $46 each, which translates into an effective retail price of more than $2 million per pound for imported heroin. ONDCP estimated that the total amount spent on heroin in the United States is $11.9 billion annually.

Although narcotics (including heroin) tend to be highly toxic when taken in large doses, frequent users build up tolerance and require ever larger doses for the desired effects. Physical addiction may result in drug dependence, and symptoms of withdrawal may appear if the drug is not available. Withdrawal symptoms include nervousness, restlessness, severe abdominal cramps, watery eyes, and nasal discharge; in later stages, there may be vomiting, diarrhea, weight loss, and pain in the large muscles of the body, especially the back and legs.

Hallucinogens

Hallucinogens, including drugs like belladonna, LSD, mandrake, Ectstasy (MDMA), mescaline, methylenedioxyamphetamine (MDA), peyote, phencyclidine (PCP), and psilocybin, have no official legitimate use. Street use of these drugs is intended to produce "mind expansion," hallucinations, creative mental states, and perceptual distortions—all of which have been popularly called "psychedelic experiences" or "trips."

The exact process by which hallucinogens act on the mind is not known, and the effects of these drugs are unpredictable. LSD "trips" may produce pleasurable hallucinations and sensations in users or may result in frightening experiences, during which uncontrollable nightmarish phantasms may appear to users who are no longer able to distinguish external reality from their own subjective states.

Anabolic Steroids

Anabolic steroids (the substances nandrolene, oxandrolene, oxymetholone, and stanozolol) are used legitimately for weight gain; for the treatment of arthritis, anemia, and connective-tissue disorder; and in the battle against certain forms of cancer. Some bodybuilders, professional athletes, and others seeking to build body bulk and increase strength have created a secondary market in steroids that has resulted in their ready availability through illegal channels of distribution.

Inhalants

Inhalants include a wide variety of psychotropic substances like acetate, amyl nitrite, butyl nitrite, carbon tetrachloride, chloroform, Freon, nitrous oxide, and toluene. They are highly volatile substances that generally act as central nervous system depressants and are found in fast-drying glues, nail-polish remover, room and car deodorizers, lighter fluid, paint thinner, kerosene, cleaning fluids, household sealants, and gasoline. Although some of these substances, such as amyl nitrate, chloroform, ether, and nitrous oxide, have legitimate medical uses, others are employed to produce a sense of light-headedness often described in colloquial terms as a "rush." The use of inhalants "can disturb vision, impair judgment, and reduce muscle and reflex control."[20]

Inhalants have been called "gateway drugs," meaning substances that can initiate young people into illicit drug use (Figure 12–6). Easy access to these chemicals is ensured by the fact that few inhalants are subject to legislative control beyond simple administrative regulations and are easily available on household shelves, in hardware stores, and on the shelves of general merchandisers.

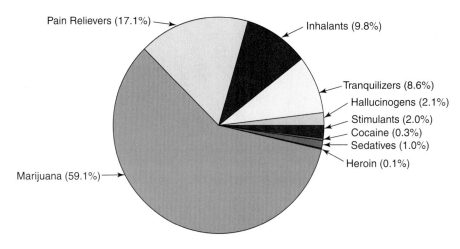

Pain Relievers (17.1%)
Inhalants (9.8%)
Tranquilizers (8.6%)
Hallucinogens (2.1%)
Stimulants (2.0%)
Cocaine (0.3%)
Sedatives (1.0%)
Heroin (0.1%)
Marijuana (59.1%)

3.1 Million Initiates of Illicit Drugs

FIGURE 12-6 | Drugs Used When Initiating Illicit Drug Use among Past-Year Initiates of Illicit Drugs Ages 12 or Older, 2009

Source: Substance Abuse and Mental Health Services Administration, *National Survey on Drug Use and Health, 2009* (Washington, DC: U.S. Government Printing Office, 2010).

■ **pharmaceutical diversion**
The process by which legitimately manufactured controlled substances are diverted for illicit use by illegal prescribing (physicians) and/or illegal dispensing (pharmacists).

■ **designer drug**
A new substance designed by slightly altering the chemical makeup of other illegal or tightly controlled drugs.

WEB EXTRA 12–2
LIBRARY EXTRA 12–6

■ **drug trafficking**
The manufacturing, distributing, dispensing, importing, and/or exporting of a controlled substance or a counterfeit substance.

Based on self-reports from members of surveyed households who were 12 years of age or older, an estimated 22.9 million Americans have used inhalants at some point in their lives, and more than 2.0 million have used these drugs within the past year.[21] In 2001, first-time inhalant users had a mean age of just 15.7 years—the youngest mean inhalant initiation age since 1963 and the youngest mean initiation age of any substance in the MTF survey.[22] Almost 12% of high school seniors have reported experimenting with some form of inhalant. Learn more about inhalants at the National Inhalant Prevention Coalition's Web site via **Web Extra 12–2**.

Pharmaceutical Diversion and Designer Drugs

The abuse of legitimately manufactured controlled substances is a major source of drug-related addiction and dependence, medical emergencies, and death. **Pharmaceutical diversion** occurs through illegal prescribing by physicians and illegal dispensing by pharmacists and their assistants. So-called doctor shopping (the process of finding a physician who is overly liberal in the type and amount of drug prescribed) and visits to numerous physicians for the purpose of collecting large quantities of prescribed medicines are practices that exacerbate the problem. Depressants (including antianxiety drugs such as Valium and Xanax, sedatives, and tranquilizers), stimulants, and anabolic steroids constitute the types of drugs most often diverted.

A number of drugs are manufactured in clandestine drug facilities, sometimes called "basement laboratories" because they are operated by individuals out of their homes. According to the NIJ, "Clandestine laboratories range from small crude operations in sheds, bathtubs, mobile homes, boats, and motel rooms to highly sophisticated operations with professional quality laboratory glassware and equipment."[23] **Designer drugs**, often made in basement labs, are so named

> Designer drugs are new substances designed by slightly altering the chemical makeup of controlled drugs.

because "they are new substances designed by slightly altering the chemical makeup of other illegal or tightly controlled drugs."[24] Designer drugs like Nexus, a new reputed aphrodisiac, usually fall under the rubric "synthetic narcotic" or "synthetic hallucinogen."

Opium, cocaine, and other naturally occurring psychoactive substances require the use of chemicals in step-by-step processes to make them ready for street-level distribution and consumption, and designer drugs also require a number of specifically identifiable chemicals in their production. The Chemical Diversion and Trafficking Act (CDTA) of 1988 placed the distribution of eight essential chemicals used in the production of illicit drugs, as well as 12 "precursor chemicals" (from which drugs could be made), under federal control; it also regulates the distribution of machines that can produce pharmaceutical capsules and tablets. In 1994, the Domestic Chemical Diversion Control Act added 32 other chemicals to the list, bringing the total number to 52 drug-related chemical substances under federal control.[25]

Drug Trafficking

In everyday usage, the phrase *drug trafficking* can have a variety of meanings, ranging from smuggling (the illegal shipment of controlled substances across state and national boundaries) to the legal sale of controlled substances. Technically speaking, **drug trafficking** includes manufacturing, distributing, dispensing, importing, and exporting (or possessing with intent to do the same) a controlled substance or a counterfeit substance.[26] Federal law enforcement agencies, in their effort to reduce trafficking, focus largely on the prevention of smuggling and the apprehension of smugglers. (See **Library Extra 12–6**.)

Drugs like cocaine, heroin, and LSD are especially easy to smuggle because relatively small quantities of these drugs can be adulterated with other substances to provide large amounts of illicit commodities for sale on the street. Figures 12–7 and 12–8 provide maps of major cocaine- and heroin-trafficking routes (sometimes called "pipelines") worldwide. Most cocaine that enters the United States originates in the Western Hemisphere, especially in the South American nations of Bolivia, Colombia, and Peru, and transportation routes into the United States include (1) shipment overland from South America through

Follow the author's tweets about the latest crime and justice news at **http://twitter.com/schmalleger**.

FIGURE 12-7 | Global Cocaine Trafficking: Major Countries of Origin and Routes of Transportation

Source: Adapted from the Office of National Drug Control Policy, *The National Drug Control Strategy: 2000 Annual Report* (Washington, DC: U.S. Government Printing Office, 2000), p. 78.

FIGURE 12-8 | Global Heroin Trafficking: Major Countries of Origin and Routes of Transportation

Source: Adapted from the Office of National Drug Control Policy, *The National Drug Control Strategy: 2000 Annual Report* (Washington, DC: U.S. Government Printing Office, 2000), p. 81.

WEB EXTRA 12–3
LIBRARY EXTRA 12–7

■ **Heroin Signature Program (HSP)**
A Drug Enforcement Administration program that identifies the geographic source of a heroin sample through the detection of specific chemical characteristics in the sample peculiar to the source area.

■ **drug-defined crime**
A violation of the laws prohibiting or regulating the possession, use, or distribution of illegal drugs.

■ **drug-related crime**
A crime in which drugs contribute to the offense (excluding violations of drug laws).

Central America, (2) direct shipments to U.S. ports concealed in containers or packed with legitimate products, (3) flights into the United States via commercial airplanes or in private aircraft, and (4) airdrops to vessels waiting offshore for smuggling into the United States.

Most cocaine entering the United States is smuggled aboard maritime vessels: fishing vessels with hidden compartments, cargo ships plying international waters, and even private submersibles. Annual seizures of cocaine in the United States total about 140 tons. In 2007, however, officials were surprised at the amount of cocaine seized when the U.S. Coast Guard cutter *Sherman* stopped the Panamanian cargo ship *Gatun* about 20 miles off of the California coast: 20 tons of cocaine, with an estimated street value of $600 million, was discovered and transported to the Coast Guard facility in Alameda to be destroyed.[27] The 14 crew members aboard the *Gatun* were Panamanians and Mexicans who were not armed and offered no resistance when stopped, and it was not immediately clear if any of them knew what cargo they were carrying.

Some trafficking methods are highly creative. "Unusual methods of concealment [include] cocaine concealed in a shipment of beach towels, inside spools of industrial thread, inside cans of lard, sealed within quartz crystals, in drums of fruit pulp, in fish meal, and in avocado paste. In addition, U.S. Customs Service and U.S. Fish and Wildlife officers seized several kilograms of cocaine from within a shipment of boa constrictors. The cocaine, wrapped in condoms, had been inserted into the snakes' intestines."[28]

The DEA follows heroin trafficking through its **Heroin Signature Program (HSP)**, which identifies the geographic source of a heroin sample through the laboratory detection of specific chemical characteristics in the sample peculiar to that area; the HSP employs special chemical analyses to identify and measure chemical constituents of a sample of seized heroin.

> The DEA's Heroin Signature Program identifies the geographic source of a heroin sample.

Results of the HSP have shown that 62% of heroin in the United States originates in South America, 17% in Southeast Asia, 16% in Southwest Asia, and 5% in Mexico. According to the DEA, most heroin originating in Southeast Asia is produced in the Golden Triangle area, which encompasses Burma, Laos, and Thailand. "[Shipments are] controlled by ethnic Chinese criminal groups while U.S.-based ethnic Chinese traffickers with links to these international criminal groups [are] the most prolific importers and distributors of Southeast Asian heroin [within the United States]."[29] HSP data were based on examination of over 800 random samples obtained through undercover purchases, domestic seizures, and seizures at U.S. ports of entry. Learn more about the DEA and the HSP at **Web Extra 12–3**; read about the different kinds of controlled substances at **Library Extra 12–7**.

Drugs and Crime

While the manufacture, sale, transportation, and use of controlled substances are themselves criminal, drugs and crime are also linked in other ways. The addict who is so habituated to the use of illegal drugs that he or she steals to support a habit, the drug importer who kills a rival dealer, and the offender who commits a criminal act due to the stimulation provided by drugs all provide examples of how drug abuse may be linked to other forms of criminal activity.

Recognizing these differences, the Bureau of Justice Statistics (BJS) distinguished between crimes that are drug defined and drug related. **Drug-defined crimes** are "violations of laws prohibiting or regulating the possession, use, or distribution of illegal drugs";[30] the costs of all drug-defined crimes are directly attributable to illegal drug use. **Drug-related crimes**, on the other hand, "are not violations of drug laws but are crimes in which drugs contribute to the offense."[31]

The U.S. Department of Justice has stated, "There is extensive evidence of the strong relationship between drug use and crime" supported by "a review of the evidence" that can be summarized in the following three points:[32]

1. Drug users report greater involvement in crime and are more likely than nonusers to have criminal records.

2. People with criminal records are much more likely than others to report being drug users.

3. Crimes rise in number as drug use increases.

One national initiative attempting to measure the degree to which criminal offenders use controlled substances is the

> ■ **Arrestee Drug Abuse Monitoring (ADAM) Program**
> A National Institute of Justice program that tracks trends in the prevalence and types of drug use among booked arrestees in urban areas.

WEB EXTRA 12-4
LIBRARY EXTRA 12-8

Arrestee Drug Abuse Monitoring (ADAM) Program, begun by the NIJ in 2000, which gathers data on drug use, drug and alcohol dependency and treatment, and drug-market participation among booked male arrestees (determined within 48 hours of arrest). ADAM data consist of information reported to interviewers by arrestees regarding their drug use as well as arrestees' urinalysis results, based on urine specimens collected from arrestees, sent to a central laboratory, and analyzed for the presence of ten drugs.

ADAM data are useful because they identify levels of drug use among arrestees, track changes in patterns of drug use, identify specific drugs of abuse in each jurisdiction, alert officials to trends in drug use and availability of new drugs, provide data to help understand the drug–crime connection, and evaluate law enforcement and jail-based programs and their effects.

ADAM's 2000 annual report (the last complete official document produced before program funding was suspended) showed that 64% of the adult male arrestees in 35 reporting American cities tested positive for drug use.[33] The range among female arrestees was even more pronounced, from a low of 22% in Laredo to 81% in New York City.[34]

Marijuana was the drug most commonly used by arrestees, followed by cocaine. The proportion of adult male arrestees testing positive for marijuana was greater than the rate for female adult arrestees in all sites. Adult male marijuana-positive rates ranged from 28.5% in Des Moines to 57% in Oklahoma City, and adult female marijuana-positive rates ranged from 17.2% in Laredo to 44.7% in Oklahoma City. At least 31% of adult male arrestees in a majority of sites tested positive for cocaine. Cocaine-positive rates for men ranged from 11% in Laredo to 49% in Atlanta, and cocaine-positive rates for women ranged from 7.8% in San Jose to 59.2% in Chicago.

Among juvenile detainees, marijuana was the most commonly used drug—more than six times higher than cocaine use for juvenile males and females alike. Among the sites that collect juvenile data, male detainees were more likely to test positive for the use of any drug than were female detainees; at every site, more than 40% of juvenile males and 20% of juvenile females tested positive for marijuana.

The use of opiates, such as heroin and opium, remained relatively low compared with the prevalence of marijuana and cocaine among adult arrestees.

Consistently high percentages of overall use among arrestees may mask differences in trends for specific drugs and in specific segments of the arrestee population. MDMA use among ADAM arrestees appeared to be concentrated mainly in the western part of the United States, particularly in Portland, Sacramento, Salt Lake City, San Diego, San Jose, and Spokane, where more than 20% of both the men and the women tested positive for the drug. The survey found that methamphetamine use among juvenile arrestees followed a pattern similar to that of adult arrestees in that it was more commonly used by females and was most often detected at sites in the West and Southwest. Learn more about ADAM at **Web Extra 12–4**, and read an ADAM publication online at **Library Extra 12–8**.

Other information on drug use by offenders at the time of the offense has come from the NCVS, which gathers data from victims of violent crime who are asked to report their impressions about offenders; for example, 33% of all victims of violent crime included in the survey reported that they believed their assailants were under the influence of drugs or alcohol at the time the crime occurred, and another 46% of victims stated that they did not know whether the offender was under the influence of drugs.

> Marijuana was the drug most commonly used by arrestees, followed by cocaine.

Offender self-reports of jail inmates collected by BJS researchers showed the following:[35]

- About 44% used illegal drugs in the month before the offense for which they were arrested.
- Roughly 30% used illegal drugs daily in the month before the offense.
- Around 27% used illegal drugs at the time of the offense.
- Cocaine and crack cocaine were the drugs most commonly abused by jail inmates.

Surveys of state prison inmates revealed much the same pattern: 61% said that they or their victims were under the influence of drugs or alcohol at the time of the offense, 50% reported that they were under the influence of alcohol or drugs, and 30% stated that their victims were under the influence of alcohol or drugs.[36] Nearly 40% of youths incarcerated in long-term state-operated facilities reported having been under the influence of illegal drugs at the time of their offense.[37] When self-reports of jail and state prison inmates were evaluated to determine the proportion reporting having ever used drugs, nearly 80% of adult inmates reported drug use, and 83% of incarcerated juveniles said they have used drugs at some point in their lives.[38]

Surveys of drug-related crime have also been conducted. Interviews with adult prison inmates revealed that 24% of female inmates and 16% of male inmates committed their offenses to get money to buy drugs and that approximately 30% of all robberies, burglaries, and thefts were committed to obtain drug money; 5% of murders resulted from such criminal activities.[39]

Illegal Drugs and Official Corruption

Sometimes the corrupting influence of lucrative drugs and drug money extends beyond street crime and street criminals, corrupting official agents of control, as the 1994 Mollen Commission study of police corruption in New York City discovered. It found that the severity of police corruption in New York City had worsened drastically since previous investigations into the subject. "Police have crossed the line into actively engaging in criminal activity including robbery, drug dealing and even a killing."[40] It called today's corrupt police "criminals in blue uniforms," contrasting the severity of their illegal activity with prior forms of corruption that simply involved turning a "blind eye" to crime.

Much illegal police activity was found to be drug related, with drug monies providing powerful incentives for corruption. Police officers in certain precincts banded together and regularly robbed drug dealers, sold drugs, and conducted illegal raids to confiscate additional drugs for personal gain.

It is not only police officers who face the threat of corruption from the lucrative rewards reaped from dealing drugs; in the mid-1990s, for example, 20 District of Columbia corrections officers and employees were given stiff prison sentences after being convicted of drug-smuggling activities. Even with those convictions, few believed that corruption in the city's prisons had been ended. U.S. District Judge Royce Lamberth, who sentenced the former officers, observed that "even as the latest prison guard drug ring was being shut down, corruption continues today as I sit in this courtroom."[41]

Social Policy and Drug Abuse

The history of drug-control policy in the United States is as interesting as it is diverse. Prior to 1907, any and all drugs could be bought and sold in the United States without restriction; manufacturers and distributors were not regulated or even required to disclose the contents of their products. Patent medicines of the time were trade secrets whose names were patented, although their ingredients were known to the manufacturers. The era of patent medicines began to end with enactment of the federal Pure Food and Drug Act of 1906, which required manufacturers to list their ingredients and specifically targeted mood-changing chemicals. Although the law required disclosure of the chemical composition of marketed substances, it did not outlaw them.

The Harrison Act, passed by Congress in 1914 as the first major piece of federal antidrug legislation, required anyone dealing in cocaine, heroin, morphine, opium, or their derivatives to register with the federal government and pay a tax of $1 per year, and it authorized the registration of only physicians, pharmacists, and other medical professionals, effectively outlawing street use of these drugs. By 1920, court rulings had severely curtailed the use of heroin for medical purposes, saying its prescribed use only prolonged addiction, marking the beginning of complete federal prohibition of a major drug.

In 1919, the Eighteenth Amendment to the U.S. Constitution, prohibiting the manufacture, sale, and transportation of alcoholic beverages, was ratified. Support for Prohibition began to wane not long after the amendment was enacted; objections stated that it gave the government too much power over people's personal lives, it was impossible to enforce, it corrupted agents of enforcement, and it made many bootleggers wealthy. The 1929 Great Depression magnified the effect of lost tax revenues from alcohol, so in 1933, Congress proposed and the states ratified the Twenty-First Amendment, which repealed Prohibition.

In 1937, passage of the Marijuana Tax Act effectively outlawed marijuana, a federal stance reinforced by the Boggs Act of 1951, which also mandated deletion of heroin from the list of medically useful substances and required its complete removal from all medicines. The 1956 Narcotic Control Act increased penalties for drug traffickers and made the sale of heroin to anyone under age 18 a capital offense.

The most comprehensive federal legislation to address controlled substances was the 1970 Comprehensive Drug Abuse Prevention and Control Act; Title 2 of that act is referred to as the Controlled Substances Act (CSA), which established five schedules that classified psychoactive drugs according to their medical use, degree of psychoactivity, and adjudged potential for abuse (Table 12–3 earlier in this chapter outlined the various drug schedules under federal law). Penalties under federal law are generally more severe for possession of higher-category substances (Schedule I being the highest) but vary by the amount possessed, the purpose of possession (sale or personal use), and the offender's criminal history.

Another federal initiative, the 1988 Anti-Drug Abuse Act, proclaimed the goal of a "drug-free America by 1995." Although many of the act's provisions were more rhetoric than substance, the act substantially increased penalties for recreational drug users and made weapons purchases by suspected drug dealers more difficult. The law also denied federal benefits—ranging from loans (such as federal student loans) to contracts and licenses—to federal drug convicts.

In 1991, steroids were added to the list of Schedule III controlled substances by congressional action. In 1996, the Drug-Induced Rape Prevention Act increased penalties for trafficking in the drug Rohypnol, which is known as the "date rape drug" because of its growing use:[42] "[Y]oung men put doses of the drug in women's drinks without their consent in order to lower their inhibitions."[43] It dissolves easily in drinks and can leave anyone who unknowingly consumes it unconscious for hours, making the person vulnerable to sexual assault. The drug is variously known as "roples," "roche," "ruffles," "roofies," and "rophies" on the street. Rohypnol (whose generic name is flunitrazepam) is a powerful sedative (seven to ten times more powerful than Valium) manufactured by Hoffmann-LaRoche Pharmaceuticals. A member of the benzodiazepine family of depressants, it is legally prescribed in 64 countries for insomnia and as a preoperative anesthetic; it is also readily available on the black market.

A tanning-bed repair shop where Modesto (California) Police and the Stanislaus Drug Enforcement Agency seized $1.5 million worth of marijuana plants from its back room in 2009. Why is California considering legalizing marijuana?
Source: ZUMA Press/NewsCom.com

Another date rape drug, gammahydroxybutyrate (GHB), has effects similar to those of Rohypnol. GHB, a central nervous system depressant, was once sold in health food stores as a performance enhancer for use by bodybuilders, but rumors that GHB stimulates muscle growth were never proved. The intoxicating effects of GHB soon became obvious, so in 1990, the Federal Drug Administration (FDA) banned the use of GHB except under the supervision of a physician. Learn more about abused drugs from the DEA via **Library Extra 12–9**.

Drug-Control Legislation

Drug-control legislation of note includes the Comprehensive Methamphetamine Control Act (CMCA) of 1996, relevant portions of the Violent Crime Control and Law Enforcement Act of 1994, and the 2006 Combat Methamphetamine Epidemic Act (CMEA).[44] The CMCA (1) contained provisions for the forfeiture and seizure of chemicals used in the manufacture of methamphetamine, (2) added iodine to the list of chemicals controlled under the Chemical Diversion and Trafficking Act of 1988 and the Domestic Chemical Diversion Control Act of 1993, (3) created new reporting requirements for distributors of combination products containing ephedrine, pseudoephedrine, and phenylpropanolamine, and (4) increased penalties for the manufacture and possession of equipment used to make controlled substances.

The far-reaching Violent Crime Control and Law Enforcement Act of 1994 included a number of drug-related provisions, including authorization of $1 billion in Edward Byrne Memorial Formula Grant Program monies to reduce or prevent juvenile drug- and gang-related activity in federally assisted low-income housing areas. It also provided $1.6 billion for direct funding to localities around the country for anticrime efforts, such as drug treatment, education, and jobs. Additionally, it provided $1 billion for drug-court programs, and established "drug-free zones" by increasing penalties for drug dealing in areas near playgrounds, school yards, video arcades, and youth centers.

The 2006 CMEA (passed as part of the USA PATRIOT Act Reauthorization of that same year[45]) placed significant restrictions on retail sales of over-the-counter products containing

> Recent drug-control legislation includes the 2006 Combat Methamphetamine Epidemic Act.

pseudoephedrine, used in the manufacture of methamphetamines. The CMEA allowed retailers without pharmacies to continue selling products containing pseudoephedrine only if they are sold from behind a service counter or locked

> ■ **interdiction**
> An international drug-control policy whose goal is to stop drugs from entering the country illegally.

THEORY | versus REALITY
Drug Courts and Public Policy

Since the 1980s, the drug epidemic in the United States and the adoption of tougher drug policies by lawmakers and officials have contributed to an abundance of drug cases on judicial dockets in many U.S. jurisdictions. About 20 years ago, in response to the ever-growing number of drug cases and the cycle of recidivism common among drug offenders, some state and local jurisdictions began experimenting with a new type of judicial proceeding known as "drug courts." Drug courts, which are generally used for nonviolent drug offenders, seek to identify eligible participants early in case processing. They offer an alternative to incarceration, which has not been effective in breaking the cycle of drugs and crime.

Drug-court programs, which may divert offenders from further handling by other official agencies, feature supervised treatment and periodic drug testing. Their purpose is to use the authority of the court to reduce crime by changing defendants' drug-using behavior. Defendants are typically diverted to drug-court programs in exchange for the possibility of dismissed charges or reduced sentences.

Judges who preside over drug-court proceedings monitor the progress of defendants through treatment programs via frequent status hearings—and they prescribe sanctions and rewards in collaboration with prosecutors, defense attorneys, treatment providers, and others. Treatment options are determined by the judge, who holds the offender personally and publicly accountable for treatment progress.

In exchange for the defendant's successfully completing treatment, the court may dismiss the original charge, reduce or set aside a previously imposed sentence, impose a lesser penalty, or dispense any combination of these options. Although some basic elements are common to many drug-court programs, the programs vary in terms of their approaches, participant eligibility, program requirements, type of treatment provided, sanctions and rewards, and other practices.

Treatment has been shown to work—if substance abusers stay involved. However, between 80% and 90% of conventional drug-treatment clients drop out before 12 months. By providing a structure that links supervision and treatment, drug courts work to exert legal pressure on defendants to enter and remain in treatment long enough to realize benefits. According to the NIJ, more than two-thirds of participants who begin treatment through a drug court complete it in a year or more—a six-fold increase in retention compared with programs outside the justice system.

Title V of the Violent Crime Control and Law Enforcement Act of 1994 (Public Law 103–322) specifically authorizes the awarding of federal grants for drug-court programs that include court-supervised drug treatment. In 1995, the federal Drug Courts Program Office was established to implement and support provisions of the act and has since funded the development and establishment of drug courts across the country.

A 2006 NIJ review of drug courts, which synthesized findings from five NIJ-funded studies, found that drug courts can substantially reduce recidivism and promote other positive outcomes. The review determined that the average investment per drug-court program participant was $5,928, while cost savings included $2,329 in avoided criminal justice system costs and $1,301 in reduced victimization costs over a 30-month period. The same review showed that overall, drug-court participants were rearrested (for any charge) less often than their counterparts in the comparison group (randomly selected from all felony drug cases that did not enter drug court): 53% versus 65%, respectively.

Discussion Questions

1. What is the purpose of drug courts? What do you think will be their future?

2. Do you think drug courts are a good idea? Why or why not?

Source: National Institute of Justice, *Drug Courts: The Second Decade* (Washington, DC: NIJ, 2006); Richard S. Gebelein, *Rebirth of Rehabilitation: Promise and Perils of Drug Courts* (Washington, DC: Department of Justice, 2000); Ken Wallentine, "Drug Courts: A Change in Tactics," *Police*, Vol. 24, No. 4 (April 2000), pp. 54–56; and U.S. General Accounting Office, *Drug Courts: Overview of Growth, Characteristics, and Results* (Washington, DC: GAO, 1997).

---

display case; consumers are prohibited from purchasing more than 9 grams of pseudoephedrine in any 30-day period. See the Theory versus Reality box for more information on drug courts.

Drug-Control Strategies

Major policy initiatives in the battle against illicit drugs have included (1) antidrug legislation and strict enforcement, (2) interdiction, (3) crop control, (4) asset forfeiture, and (5) antidrug education and drug treatment.[46] Current policy calls for strict enforcement of drug-control laws, although the emphasis has shifted from targeting users to arresting, prosecuting, and incarcerating distributors of controlled substances. Many employers no longer wait for drug-influenced problems to arise but instead require routine drug testing as a condition of employment and retention.

In 2006, nearly 1.9 million people were arrested for drug-law violations throughout the United States;[47] that arrest total was 1% lower than in 1998, 11% higher than the 1995 level, and 40% higher than in 1992.[48] Enforcement activities also included the seizure and destruction of illegal drugs and clandestine drug laboratories—in 2006, DEA agents destroyed 6,435 methamphetamine laboratories across the nation.[49]

Interdiction is an international drug-control policy aimed at stopping drugs from entering the country illegally. The

WEB EXTRA 12–5

WHO'S TO BLAME—The Individual or Society?

Gangs, Teenagers, and Peer Pressure

Fourteen-year-old Lakisha Jackson found herself in trouble with the law at her junior high school prom when her 18-year-old boyfriend, Jamal Carter, was caught smoking pot behind the curtain covering the school's stage. Jamal told off-duty police officers working the dance that the marijuana wasn't his, but that Lakisha had given it to him.

Jamal was known to the officers as a member of the Top 6 gang and bore a number of tattoos indicating his gang affiliation. Officers from the police department's juvenile division were called to the school, and both Lakisha and Jamal were taken to the police station for questioning. No additional drugs were found on either youth.

What bothered officers, however, was Lakisha's hostile attitude. While they expected that Jamal would refuse to say more than he already had about the source of the marijuana, they had hoped that Lakisha would either refute Jamal's story or tell them where she had gotten the substance. Lakisha, however, refused to say anything about the incident, calling the officers "pigs" and telling them to mind their own business. "I don't rat on nobody," was all she would volunteer.

A police psychologist who was present during the interviews later explained the youth's behavior in terms of gang and subcultural loyalties. "Even if this case involved a serious crime like a murder—maybe even especially then—you wouldn't get any cooperation from these kids," he said. "You can be sure that if they knew who committed a crime they wouldn't talk. It's not only part and parcel of their gang loyalties, but pretty much a value inherent in the subculture in which they've been raised. Maybe in another neighborhood things would be different—but not here."

Think about it:

1. Do you agree with the police psychologist? Is his explanation for why these youngsters won't talk to the police a plausible one, or is there likely to be some other explanation?

2. If the psychologist is correct in his assessment of the situation, then do you think that Lakisha and Jamal should "know better" than to let subcultural values influence them? Why or why not?

3. Are the police likely to get any more information from Lakisha or her boyfriend? Why or why not?

Note: Who's to Blame boxes provide fictionalized critical thinking opportunities, and are not actual cases.

Federal-Wide Drug Seizure System (FDSS) consolidates seizure reports from the FBI, DEA, U.S. Customs Service, U.S. Border Patrol, and U.S. Coast Guard. In 2006, federal agents seized 322,438 kilograms of marijuana, 69,826 kilograms of cocaine, and 805 kilograms of heroin.[50] More than half of all cocaine and much of the heroin, marijuana, and methamphetamine in the United States are thought to enter from Mexico. Southwestern borders of the United States are especially hard to police. Drugs cross the desert in armed pack trains as well as on the backs of human "mules"; they are also tossed over border fences and whisked away on foot or by vehicle.[51] Operators of ships find gaps in U.S.-Mexican interdiction coverage and position drugs close to the border for eventual transfer into the United States, and small boats in the Gulf of Mexico and the eastern Pacific deliver drugs directly into the United States. Instances of corruption in U.S. border agencies contribute to the difficulty in interdiction enforcement.

A third strategy, crop control, has both international and domestic aspects. During 2005, the DEA's Domestic Cannabis Eradication and Suppression Program was responsible for the elimination of 3,938,151 cultivated outdoor marijuana plants and 270,935 indoor marijuana plants as well as 11,922 arrests, 3,707 seized weapons, and $26,911,262 in seized assets.[52] Learn more about specific DEA domestic and overseas operations and task forces at **Web Extra 12–5**.

Asset forfeiture, another strategy in the battle against illegal drugs, is a legal procedure that authorizes judicial representatives to seize "all moneys, negotiable instruments, securities, or other things of value furnished or intended to be furnished by any person in exchange for a controlled substance [and] all proceeds traceable to such an exchange."[53] Unfortunately, asset forfeiture has at times been abused by enforcement agencies. U.S. Supreme Court decisions, however, now require that property owners be given notice of any pending seizures and be allowed the opportunity to respond to government charges.[54] The Court has also acted to restrain seizures of property far more valuable than the proceeds of the underlying crime with which the property owner has been charged.[55]

WEB EXTRA 12–6
LIBRARY EXTRA 12–10

Antidrug education and drug treatment have gained significant popularity. Those favoring education to attack the problem of drug abuse are quick to claim that other measures have not been effective in reducing the incidence of abuse. Many school-based programs have been built on the principles developed by the Drug Abuse Resistance Education (D.A.R.E.) model, which began as a joint effort of the Los Angeles Police Department and the Los Angeles Unified School District in 1983. D.A.R.E. uses uniformed police officers and other "experts" to explain issues of drug abuse to school-age children and attempts to build resistance to what might otherwise be perceived by youths as attractive drug-related activities; it focuses on developing competent decision-making skills, combating negative forms of peer pressure, and providing meaningful alternatives to drug use. Unfortunately, a number of studies have questioned the effectiveness of D.A.R.E.-type interventions, finding that their "effects on drug use, except for tobacco use, are nonsignificant."[56]

> A number of studies have questioned the effectiveness of D.A.R.E.-type programs.

The Office of National Drug Control Policy (ONDCP)

In 1988, with passage of the Anti-Drug Abuse Act, Congress established the ONDCP and endorsed as a national policy goal the creation of a drug-free America. The ONDCP mission is to establish policies, priorities, and objectives for the nation's drug-control program: to reduce illicit drug use, manufacturing, and trafficking; to reduce drug-related crime and violence; and to ameliorate drug-related health consequences. The director of ONDCP is charged with producing and publishing a *National Drug-Control Strategy* annual report that directs the nation's antidrug efforts and establishes a program, a budget, and guidelines for cooperation among federal, state, and local entities.

The *National Drug-Control Strategy* takes a long-term view of the nation's drug problem, focusing on prevention, treatment, research, law enforcement, protection of U.S. borders, drug-supply reduction, and international cooperation. Its goals are to educate young people about the dangers of illegal drugs, alcohol, and tobacco and to protect U.S. borders from drug incursion by sharing intelligence and using the latest technology. The Southwest border, a major gateway for illegal drugs, receives considerable attention,

but resources have also been allocated to close other avenues of drug entry, including the Virgin Islands, Puerto Rico, and the Canadian border as well as all airports and seaports; it also seeks to curtail illegal drug trafficking in the transit zone between source countries, and U.S.-led multinational efforts in the Caribbean, Central America, Europe, and the Far East are coordinated in an effort to exert maximum pressure on drug traffickers.

The United States continues to focus international drug-control efforts on source countries. International drug-trafficking organizations and their production and trafficking infrastructures are most concentrated, detectable, and vulnerable to effective law enforcement action in source countries. Also, the cultivation of coca and opium poppies and the production of cocaine and heroin are labor intensive, so cultivation and processing are relatively easier to disrupt than other aspects of the trade. International drug-control strategies seek to bolster source countries' resources, capabilities, and political will to reduce cultivation, attack production, interdict drug shipments, and disrupt and dismantle trafficking organizations, including their command and control structure and financial underpinnings.

Visit the ONDCP via **Web Extra 12–6**, and read the most recent *National Drug Control Strategy* in its entirety at **Library Extra 12–10**.

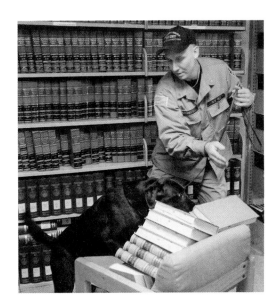

Sergeant Jeff Yurkiewicz of the Pennsylvania State Police K-9 unit leading his dog, Jake, through a search for drugs and contraband at the Allegheny County Jail in Pittsburgh. More than 20 dogs were brought in to sweep through the entire jail for drugs. How do controlled substances enter correctional facilities?
Source: AP Wide World Photos

CRIME | in the NEWS

Afghan Opium the Most Lethal Drug Worldwide, U.N. Says

MOSCOW—Afghan opium kills more people every year than any other drug on the planet, claiming up to 100,000 lives annually, according to a United Nations report released Wednesday.

Although U.S. officials have pointed to the last two years of lower production in Afghanistan, the country still produces 90 percent of the world's opium, which the report says now threatens to sow havoc in much of Central Asia.

"The catalog of casualties caused by Afghan narcotics is gruesome," Antonio Maria Costa, the executive director of the U.N. office on drugs and crime, says in a note in the report's summary. "We need to go back to the dramatic opium addiction in China a century ago to find comparable statistics." In addition to drug-related deaths, Afghan opium and heroin pay for weapons that anti-U.S. insurgents use to kill American troops.

From 2005 to 2008, Taliban insurgents in Afghanistan earned an average annual income of some $125 million from the opium trade, not including money gained from drug-processing facilities or other related business in neighboring Pakistan, according to the report.

The Afghan opium crop, used to produce heroin, dropped from 7,700 metric tons in 2008 to 6,900 this year, but because of massive overproduction, there are now more than 12,000 metric tons of opium in stockpiles, enough to meet world demand for more than two years. Criminal and insurgent groups probably are holding most of those reserves, the U.N. said.

The U.N.'s findings sounded a strong warning about the Central Asian opium-trafficking route, which has become a virtual conveyor belt for heroin between Afghanistan and Russia, referring to it as the "most sinister development yet."

"The perfect storm of drugs, crime and insurgency that has swirled around the Afghanistan-Pakistan border for years is heading for Central Asia," Costa said. "If quick preventive measures are not put into place, a big chunk of Eurasia could be lost."

Western inaction during the years after the 2001 U.S.-led invasion of Afghanistan opened the way for Afghan opium to fuel corruption throughout Afghanistan, turn Tajikistan into a borderline narco-state and create thousands of new addicts in Russia.

Russia is now the world's largest consumer of heroin, according to the U.N. report. At least 70 tons of Afghan heroin were consumed in Russia last year, the report says, more than three times the amount in the United States and Canada combined and higher than previous estimates.

The number of addicts in Russia has multiplied tenfold during the past decade, and there are now 30,000 to 40,000 Russian drug-related deaths each year, according to Russian government figures cited by the

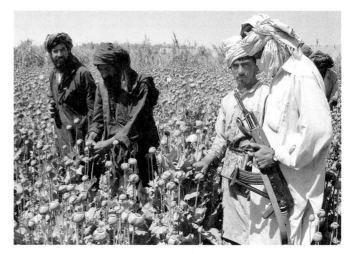

A Taliban militant holding an AK-47 automatic weapon (right) as farmers collect resin from poppies in an opium poppy field in Helmand province, southwest Afghanistan. Helmand province is one of the world's top opium-producing regions. How does this photo illustrate the link between illegal drugs and terrorism?
Source: AP Photo

report. Official Russian news services have said that up to 30,000 of those deaths are due to Afghan heroin.

Russian leaders repeatedly have voiced their anger about the lack of a Western crackdown on Afghan opium, and the issue was brought up during President Barack Obama's and Secretary of State Hillary Clinton's visits to Moscow this year.

In May, the head of Russia's federal drug-control service, Viktor Ivanov, said that about 180 Afghan drug cartels were trafficking heroin to Russia.

"The majority of these 180 drug cartels are based in the U.S. and NATO areas of responsibility," Ivanov said.

Discussion Questions

1. How does the production of opium and heroin "pay for weapons" used by Afghan anti-U.S. insurgents?

2. This article says that Afghan opium has turned "Tajikistan into a borderline narco-state." What is a narco-state?

Source: Tom Lasseter, "Afghan Opium the Most Lethal Drug Worldwide, U.N. Says," McClatchy Newspapers, October 21, 2009. © McClatchy-Tribune Information Services. All Rights Reserved. Reprinted with permission.

The Consequences of Drug Policy

There can be little doubt that the "war on drugs" has been a costly one. The federal government's 2008 drug-control budget was $12.961 billion, which represents an increase of $167 million (or 1.3%) over the fiscal year 2007 budget.[57] Broken down by priorities of ONDCP's national drug-control strategy, Priority 1 funding (stopping use before it starts with education and community action) totaled $1.6 billion, Priority 2 funding (healing America's drug users and getting treatment resources where they are needed) totaled $3 billion, and Priority 3 funding (disrupting the markets and attacking the economic basis of the drug trade) totaled $8.3 billion. Budget allocations for specific functions included $1.863 billion for prevention, $2.941 billion for treatment, $1.435 billion for international crop-control programs, $3.286 billion for interdiction, and $3.475 billion for law enforcement.

■ **decriminalization**
The redefinition of certain previously criminal behaviors as regulated activities that become "ticketable" instead of "arrestable."

■ **legalization**
The elimination of laws and criminal penalties associated with certain behaviors—usually the production, sale, distribution, and possession of a controlled substance.

LIBRARY EXTRA 12–11

U.S. law enforcement activities accounted for the lion's share of federal antidrug expenditures while demand-reduction programs absorbed the smallest part of the antidrug budget. Figure 12–9 depicts actual and projected federal drug-control spending by functional area for fiscal year 2008. When state monies spent on the control of illegal drugs and the enforcement of drug laws are added to funds spent on antidrug education, and personal and social costs of drug abuse are also included, the total cost of the "war on drugs" has been enormous.

The drug war has been costly in other ways as well. University of Delaware Professor James A. Inciardi described the situation, "As an outgrowth of the U.S. 'war on drugs' during the 1980s and early 1990s, all phases of the criminal justice process have become 'drug driven.'"[58] The same could be said of the nation's system of civil justice: "Although at first blush it may seem unrelated, the 'war on drugs' has had a major impact on the civil justice system at both the state and federal levels. Our courts, like all of government and commerce, are institutions of limited resources. To the extent that court resources must be diverted to deal with the enormous influx of drug prosecutions, these resources are not available to resolve civil matters. In some jurisdictions, drug cases account for as much as two-thirds of the criminal case filings. America's major cities have been especially affected."[59] In Los Angeles, for example, three-quarters of all criminal prosecutions are for drug charges or drug-related crimes.[60]

Strict enforcement combined with a "lock 'em up" philosophy has produced astonishingly high rates of imprisonment for drug

offenders. The proportion of federal prisoners who are sentenced drug offenders rose from 38% in 1986 to 53% in 1990 to 55% in 2005.[61] Part of the increase is due to congressional action that, beginning in 1986, required high mandatory minimum sentences in drug cases, so even first-time offenders were sentenced to long prison terms instead of probation. Approximately 70% of all first-time offenders, 85% of illegal immigrants, and 66% of female federal prisoners in federal prisons are serving drug sentences.[62]

> In some jurisdictions, drug cases account for as much as two-thirds of all criminal case filings.

Alternative Drug Policies

A number of alternative drug-control policies have been tried at both state and local levels (see **Library Extra 12–11**). Primary among them are **decriminalization** (redefinition of certain drug-related criminal activities as "ticketable") and **legalization** (elimination of criminal penalties for certain drug-related activities), both of which are "based on the assumption that drug abuse will never be eliminated."[63] Decriminalization typically reduces criminal penalties associated with the personal possession of a controlled substance; legalization eliminates "the laws and associated criminal penalties that prohibit its production, sale, distribution, and possession."[64] Put another way, decriminalization enhances personal freedoms, whereas legalization "is aimed at reducing the control that criminals have over the drug trade."[65]

Arguments in favor of drug legalization include the following:

- People should be permitted to do what they want as long as they don't harm others.
- Drug use is considered by many to be a "victimless crime," and existing drug laws make criminals out of otherwise law-abiding individuals.
- Keeping drugs illegal means they continue to be high-priced, so legalizing them could greatly lower the price.
- The expense of illicit drugs leads to the commission of many drug-related crimes, such as robbery and burglary, by users seeking to feed their habits. Legalize drugs, and many forms of crime will decline.

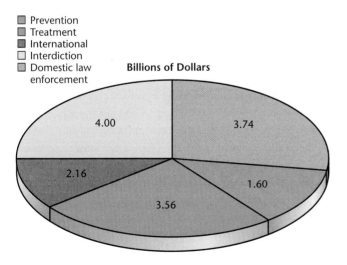

Prevention
Treatment
International
Interdiction
Domestic law enforcement

Billions of Dollars

4.00

3.74

2.16

1.60

3.56

FIGURE 12-9 | Federal Drug-Control Spending, 2010

Source: Office of the National Drug Control Policy, *National Drug Control Strategy: FY 2010 Budget Summary* (Washington, DC: ONDCP, March 2010), p. 1.

Follow the author's tweets about the latest crime and justice news at **http://twitter.com/schmalleger**.

- Legalizing drugs would reduce other forms of vice, such as prostitution, pornography, and gambling, because they are often engaged in to obtain money to purchase illegal drugs.

- Legalizing drugs would reduce the influence of criminal cartels involved in the production, transportation, and sale of controlled substances.

- Legalization would end the illegal status and associated high cost of drugs that indirectly victimize others, such as family members of drug abusers, property owners in drug-infested areas, and taxpayers footing the enforcement bill.

- Drug legalization would dramatically reduce the opportunity for official corruption frequently associated with the illicit drug trade.

- The legalization of drugs would result in increased tax revenues because drugs could be taxed just as alcohol and cigarettes are.

- The legalization of drugs would allow for better control of public health issues related to drug use.

If controlled substances were legalized, they could still be dispensed under controlled conditions (as in liquor stores), and those who use them injudiciously (as while driving a car) could still be penalized.

In 1996, California and Arizona voters passed resolutions legalizing the medical use of marijuana under certain circumstances. The thrust of California's Proposition 215 is contained in this

Drug use is considered by many to be a "victimless crime."

proposition: "(A) To ensure that seriously ill Californians have the right to obtain and use marijuana for medical purposes where medical use is deemed appropriate and has been recommended by a physician who has determined that the person's health would benefit from the use of marijuana in the treatment of cancer, anorexia, AIDS, chronic pain, spasticity, glaucoma, arthritis, migraine, or any other illness for which marijuana provides relief. (B) To ensure that patients and their primary caregivers who obtain and use marijuana for medical purposes upon the recommendation of a physician are not subject to criminal prosecution or sanction." Although the California law permits possession of marijuana for valid medicinal purposes, buying and selling the drug remain illegal, so legitimate users may have to grow their own supply or buy it on the black market.

Arizona law requires prescribing physicians to write a scientific opinion explaining why the drug is appropriate for a specific

Visitors to a cannabis festival in Amsterdam sampling marijuana from a bong. What are the advantages and disadvantages of drug legalization in the United States?
Source: Sjoerd Van Delden/AP Wide World Photos

patient, and a supportive second opinion is required before the drug can be legally used.

In 1999, Maine voters passed a limited referendum permitting some sick people to use small amounts of marijuana, and 26 other states and the District of Columbia have passed various laws and resolutions allowing therapeutic research programs involving the use of marijuana or asking the federal government to lift its ban on medical use of the drug.[66] In 2008, Michigan became the thirteenth state to legalize medical marijuana;[67] and Maine joined the ranks by enacting the Maine Medical Marijuana Act on November 3, 2009.[68] Consequently, 14 states now have laws allowing the use of marijuana for medical purposes.[69]

In May 2001, the U.S. Supreme Court prohibited California marijuana-growing clubs from distributing the drug to those who are ill or in pain, a ruling which effectivelyprohibited the use of medical marijuana in virtually all situations.[70] Federal agencies also announced that they would continue to enforce federal laws banning drug possession and use, even in states that provided for their medical use, but in 2009, the Obama administration initiated a policy of noninterference, saying that federal agencies would not arrest or prosecute medical marijuana suppliers and users who conform to state laws, a policy "designed to give a sense of prosecutorial priorities to U.S. Attorneys in the states that allow medical marijuana."[71]

As this book goes to press, voters in California are being given the opportunity to legalize the use and sale of marijuana.[72] The November 2, 2010, ballot initiative has the potential to fully legalize the recreational use of marijuana for

WEB EXTRA 12–7
LIBRARY EXTRA 12–12

prostitution
The act of engaging in sexual activity for money or its equivalent.

adults in California, although driving under the influence, public use of the drug, and appearing in public under the drug's influence would all still carry punitive consequences; it would also make it legal to grow small amounts of marijuana for personal use, and retailers would be able to sell up to one ounce of marijuana to individuals, subject to taxes and local regulations. The possibility of substantial tax revenues has generated much of the interest in marijuana legalization in California and elsewhere. *Time* magazine estimated that marijuana is currently California's largest cash crop, generating $14 billion a year in illegal sales, more than twice the revenue stream of the state's second largest agricultural commodities (milk and cream).[73] Over $1.3 billion in sales tax revenues could be brought into the cash-strapped state's coffers annually if marijuana sales were taxes;[74] additional savings of more than $1 billion would accrue to that state from not having to arrest, process, and house minor marijuana offenders. "We couldn't make this thing more available if we tried."[75]

Arguments against drug legalization include the following:

- Reducing official control over psychoactive substances is immoral and socially irresponsible and would result in heightened costs to society from drug abuse.

- Drug legalization would simply increase the types of problems now associated with alcohol abuse: lost time from work, drug-induced criminality (especially violence), loss of personal self-control, and severing of important social relationships.

- Drug laws are enforceable, and we are winning the "war on drugs"; the fact that laws are not *easily* enforceable is no reason to eliminate them.

Learn more about drug abuse and social policy at **Web Extra 12–7**.

Prostitution

Prostitution can be defined as the act of engaging in sexual activity for money. In heterosexual prostitution involving men as clients (or "johns") and women as sexual "service providers," the men can also be charged with and found guilty of the offense of prostitution. Except for parts of Nevada, prostitution is a criminal act in the United States and is generally classified as a misdemeanor.

In the United States, over 92,000 men, women, and juveniles are arrested yearly for the crime of prostitution.[76] The number of juveniles engaging in prostitution is estimated to be between 100,000 and 300,000 annually.

Morals Legislation

Laws against prostitution have a long and varied history in the United States. Underlying the statutes are fundamental questions about legislating morality. Whether and to what extent the criminal law should reflect and enforce the morality of the society it represents is one of the classic debates in criminal law literature. Most people agree that actions that harm others, as in the case of child prostitution, should be controlled, but not everyone sees prostitution, especially when willingly undertaken, as harmful (see **Library Extra 12–12**). See the Crime in the News box in this chapter for more information on child prostitution.

Some people argue that every organized society is permitted—even obligated—to enforce morality by means of criminal and other legal sanctions. Arguments in favor of criminalizing street prostitution can be seen in Table 12–4.

The classic statement that the law should not unnecessarily criminalize what are personal moral decisions that harm no one (other than possibly the person making them) was offered by the nineteenth-century English philosopher John Stuart Mill, who argued that society should interfere with an individual's freedom of action only "to prevent harm to others. His own good, either physical or moral, is not a sufficient warrant" for interference.[77]

A Typology of Prostitutes

There are many different venues where sexual services are sold: so-called red-light districts, commercial houses of prostitution, massage parlors, studios for nude photography, strip clubs, stag parties, and theaters for erotic dance.[78] Using location as the basis for a typology of prostitutes produces the categories of streetwalkers, bar/hotel prostitutes, call girls, and hotel/brothel prostitutes; others don't clearly fit any of these categories.

Streetwalkers are generally seen as the lowest class of prostitute because they solicit customers in public—often on foot and from curbside. They tend to be highly visible, and their dress is revealing, both of which advertise their services and entice customers. Streetwalkers, who perform their services in customers' cars, alleyways, nearby hotels, and darkened doorways, command the lowest prices and have little bargaining power over things like condom use and choice of sexual practices; they face the highest risk of harm from customers or others and run the highest risk of arrest.

Bar/hotel prostitutes work in bars, clubs, and hotels and may have a standing relationship with managers, bartenders, and security personnel, with whom they share their profits or for whom they provide "free" services. They tend to "work" conventions, sporting events, and business meetings. Desk clerks,

CRIME | in the NEWS

Child Prostitutes Not Receiving Needed Help

WASHINGTON—When the FBI announced a nationwide crackdown on child prostitution last month as part of a long-term initiative to combat domestic sex trafficking, it noted that 52 children had been rescued from "sexual slavery."

"It is repugnant that children in these times could be subjected to the great pain, suffering, and indignity of being forced into sexual slavery for someone else's profit," said Assistant Attorney General Lanny Breuer at the time.

But a month later none of those children is receiving the kind of help that experts say they require to overcome the trauma of their experiences, and some are still languishing in local juvenile detention centers.

Experts say the only way to ensure a good chance of recovery for these children is placement in a residential treatment program for such victims, of which there are only three in the United States: in New York, California and Georgia.

"When America's child prostitutes are identified by the FBI or police, they are incarcerated for whatever reason possible, whether it be an unrelated crime or 'material witness hold,'" said Lois Lee, founder of one of the three centers, Children of the Night in Los Angeles.

"Then they are dumped back in the dysfunctional home, ill equipped group home, or foster care, and (often) disappear back into the underground of prostitution with no voice."

Child-sex trafficking experts say that victims struggle to find the care they need once they escape an illicit industry that some estimate could involve as many as 300,000 U.S. children.

Asked about Lee's comments, Ian McCaleb, a spokesman for the Justice Department, said the department "uses a victim-centered approach that provides victims with the services they need in order to recover and to fully participate in the criminal justice process."

A report prepared for Health and Human Services in 2007 then found four residential treatment centers with a total of 45 beds for child prostitutes in the United States.

Interviews with the centers show that bed numbers remain low two years later.

New York–based Girls Educational and Mentoring Services has 12 beds. One of the four mentioned in the 2007 report, the Standing Against Global Exploitation Safe House in San Francisco, no longer has

Women sharing stories during a group session for former prostitutes at Veronica's Voice in Kansas City (Missouri). The organization helps victims of commercial sexual exploitation turn their lives around. What special issues face children who have been rescued from prostitution?
Source: AP Photo/Charlie Riedel

beds for trafficking victims, though it offers nonresidential care for victims and helps place them with foster families.

Melba Robinson, a program manager at Georgia's Center to End Adolescent Sexual Exploitation, said the center's Angela's House, which usually takes in girls on probation, is expanding from six beds to eight.

Still, with victims numbering in the thousands, advocates say there just aren't enough treatment options to go around.

Discussion Questions

1. Prostitution is sometimes called a "victimless" crime. What does that mean?

2. Why is childhood prostitution not "victimless"?

valets, and even discreet concierges sometimes refer clients to prostitutes, whose services are typically provided in the establishment, perhaps in a dark corner, a back room, or a hotel room rented by the customer or prostitute; the prices charged by bar/hotel prostitutes vary considerably according to the prestige of the establishment with which they are associated. A prostitute's risk of harm and arrest is low to moderate as long as the collaborative relationship with the establishment is maintained.

Call girls work for escort services—which advertise in flyers, in newspapers, in the yellow pages, on TV, and via the Internet (sometimes referred to as "cyberprostitution")—on an "outcall" basis and are not restricted to specific locales. Most call girls see

relatively well-to-do clients who prefer the anonymity of a referral service, and many customers are regulars who maintain a standing relationship with the service. Prostitutes are typically assigned by the agency to customers who may select them from pictures printed in brochures or posted on the Internet. Fees are often charged to credit cards by the customer before the girl is dispatched; on site, prostitutes may negotiate with the customer for specific services. Through this arrangement, the escort

> Most call girls see well-to-do clients who prefer the anonymity of a referral service.

TABLE 12-4 | Harms Caused by Street Prostitution

Moral and Nuisance Concerns
- Prostitution offends some citizens' moral standards.
- Prostitution is a nuisance to passersby and nearby residents and businesses.
- Prostitutes and clients offend uninvolved people when they solicit them.
- Juveniles who are less capable of making informed choices may become prostitutes.

Public Health Concerns
- Prostitutes and clients may spread sexually transmitted diseases such as syphilis, herpes, and AIDS.
- Used condoms, syringes, and other paraphernalia left on the ground are unsightly and potentially hazardous.
- Prostitutes without access to proper facilities may relieve themselves or bathe in public.

Personal Safety Concerns
- Clients may harm prostitutes.
- Clients or prostitutes may be defrauded, robbed, or assaulted.
- Pimps may financially and physically exploit prostitutes and clients.

Spillover-Effect Concerns
- Street prostitution and drug markets are often linked.
- Prostitution may provide a seedbed for organized crime.
- Prostitutes create parking and traffic problems where they congregate.
- Prostitution attracts strangers and criminals to a neighborhood.

Economic Concerns
- Legitimate businesses may lose customers who avoid the area because of prostitution.
- Prostitutes' presence may negatively affect the area's economy, reducing property values and limiting property use.

Civil Rights Concerns
- Prostitutes have rights that need to be protected.

Police-Integrity Concerns
- Policing prostitution creates special opportunities for police officers to engage in unethical conduct, such as taking payments in exchange for nonenforcement, because prostitutes, pimps, and clients are in weak positions to complain about police misconduct.

Source: Adapted from Michael S. Scott and Kelly Dedel, *Street Prostitution*, 2nd ed. (Washington, DC: Office of Community Oriented Policing Services, U.S. Department of Justice, 2006).

service tends to insulate itself from legal action, claiming that it simply arranged for companionship. Call girls depend on the agency to screen customers, which can be done by referrals from other agencies or by established clients with connections to the agency. Prices in this market segment reach the highest levels, and escorts have considerable bargaining power over such things as use of condoms and kinds of sexual services provided; call girls face the lowest risk of harm or arrest.

House or brothel prostitutes ply their trade in legal environments, which are limited to a few venues in the United States. Legalized prostitution, however, is common in a number of other countries, including Australia (where laws vary by state), New Zealand, the Netherlands (which outlaws pimping and trafficking of human beings), and Germany (where

advertising sex services remains illegal). In countries where prostitution is legal, it is still subject to health and locality controls as well as age and other restrictions. In such locales, prostitutes are generally licensed sex workers who pay taxes, belong to unions, and are eligible for government benefits such as unemployment wages and medical services. Some countries tolerate prostitution but restrict activities associated with it, such as pimping, operating brothels, and advertising services; others technically permit prostitution but have other kinds of restrictions making its practice difficult. In this latter category are countries like Brazil, Canada, Costa Rica, and Scotland. In Denmark, prostitution is legal, but profiting from it is not, and Sweden allows the selling of sexual services but criminalizes pimping and the purchasing of sex services (on the theory that such activity demeans women). In Japan, vaginal prostitution is illegal, but fellatio for money is not considered prostitution.

In the United States, brothel prostitution is an option in some rural counties in Nevada. Nevada's house prostitutes operate with posted fees and generally earn 40% to 60% of the revenue they generate. State law requires that they be fingerprinted, undergo regular health examinations, and keep financial records for tax purposes. All forms of prostitution are illegal in Nevada's Clark County (which contains Las Vegas). See the Criminal Profiles box on Heidi Fleiss, who ran a prostitution business in Hollywood and Los Angeles.

Clients of Prostitutes

About ten years ago, the NIJ undertook sponsorship of an extensive study conducted by Martin A. Monto of prostitutes' clients—commonly known as "johns"—that explored the sex-related behavior characteristic of men who solicited prostitutes.[79] The study, whose results were published in 2000, examined the effects of the First Offender Prostitution Program (FOPP) in San Francisco and similar programs in other cities.[80] These programs offered johns an opportunity to pay a fine and attend a daylong seminar rather than go to jail, and participants were advised that no further legal action would be taken against them if they successfully avoided rearrest for a year, but if there was a subsequent offense, they would be prosecuted for the new offense and the original charge would be reinstated.

Monto surveyed 1,291 men arrested for soliciting street prostitutes before they participated in FOPP or similar programs in Las Vegas, Nevada; Portland, Oregon; and Santa Clara, California. He collected data on their reasons for use of prostitutes, their attitudes regarding violence against women, and the consequences of their views of sex as a commodity. Monto found that 72% of the men, who ranged in age from 18 to 84 years (median age of 37), had attended some college and were less likely to be married than other men. Although their motives for seeking sex with a prostitute differed, there were similarities among certain groups: Married clients and college graduates more often wanted a different kind of sex than they had with their regular partners; unmarried clients and those without college degrees felt shy and awkward when trying to meet women but did not feel intimidated by prostitutes.

Researcher Monto also explored men's attitudes toward rape myths (discussed in Chapter 9). Less than 0.5% of the men surveyed indicated acceptance of the majority of rape myths, but 20% demonstrated acceptance of four or more of them. Although the evidence wasn't clear, researchers believed that it was this latter group that may be responsible for perpetrating violent acts against women for hire.

Concerning the degree to which clients regarded sexuality as a commercial commodity, Monto found that the greater a client's belief that women and sex were commercial products, the more frequently he would visit prostitutes. This mind-set was also a strong predictor of the acceptance of rape myths, less frequent condom use with prostitutes, and a disinclination to view prostitution as a demeaning profession for women.

Monto and his colleagues also studied the recidivism of those clients who participated in the San Francisco and Portland FOPPs. Although both programs had a recidivism rate of about 2%, researchers acknowledged that conclusions about the programs' efficacy in reducing recidivism were hampered by a lack of available baseline data for comparative purposes. Read Monto's entire 80-page report on street prostitution at **Library Extra 12–13**.

> The greater a man's belief that women and sex were commercial products, the more frequently he would visit prostitutes.

Feminist Perspectives on Prostitution

Prostitution represents a significant issue in today's feminist thought. Some feminist thinkers argue that prostitution exploits and demeans women and subjects them to the dangers of violence and disease. Andrea Dworkin, an ex-prostitute and antipornography crusader, wrote that commercial sex is a form of rape perpetrated by poverty and frequent overt violence (often by pimps).[81]

Others take a different approach, saying that selling sex need not be inherently exploitative and might actually be liberating because it fulfills a woman's rights to control her body and her sexuality; they see prostitution as legitimate sex work and argue for the legalization of prostitution (with added protections for those who choose sex work as a trade). The redefinition of prostitution as sex work has been accompanied by the development of an activist movement comprising organizations such Call Off Your Old Tired Ethics (COYOTE). COYOTE, founded in 1973, advocates for the repeal of prostitution laws and an end to the stigma associated with sex work.

CRIMINAL | PROFILES

Heidi Lynne Fleiss

Heidi Fleiss's notorious high-priced prostitution ring was the stuff of Hollywood lore, but no more so than her arrest, trial, incarceration, and post-release emergence as an unrepentant sex entrepreneur.[i] Fleiss was initially arrested in June 1993 on state charges that included five counts of pandering and one count of narcotics possession. On July 28, 1994, during her California trial, she was indicted by a federal grand jury on charges of income tax evasion, money laundering, and conspiracy.

Fleiss was convicted in federal court of income tax evasion, money laundering, and eight counts of conspiracy in August 1995. She also pled guilty in state court to the pandering charges. The combined sentences resulted in her serving three years in prison.

Born in Los Angeles on December 30, 1965, Heidi Fleiss showed a precocious flair for business as early as age 12. A popular and responsible babysitter, she soon found herself with more job offers than she could handle herself, so she established a babysitting service by hiring her friends from school to handle some of the jobs. She, of course, got a cut of all the fees.[ii]

Her school performance, however, did not keep pace with her business enterprise. Low grades in junior high and high school ultimately led to her dropping out in the tenth grade. For the next few years, she held a variety of low-wage jobs. Fleiss's aspirations never wavered, however, and she was constantly on the lookout for the right opportunity.

That opportunity came when she and a friend attended a party at 61-year-old millionaire financier Bernie Cornfeld's estate. Impressed with Fleiss, Cornfeld hired her as his personal secretary, an arrangement that, in short order, evolved into a personal relationship. Fleiss sought to deepen the relationship to a live-in level, which she hoped would result in her enjoying a financially secure life of privilege and hedonistic pursuits. Cornfeld, however, had a well-known appetite for classical beauties, which he enthusiastically indulged. His continued dalliances signaled an unwillingness to remain in a monogamous relationship, and the couple eventually broke up.

Still, Fleiss walked away with newly acquired business skills learned from associating with Cornfeld and his friends. A chance meeting with the reigning queen madam of the Los Angeles area, Madam Alex, gave Fleiss entrée to the sex industry.

Madam Alex was, at that time, looking for a replacement to take over her business operations so that she could live a privileged retirement. Fleiss's business acumen fit the bill so well that she increased Madam Alex's profits by more than 400%. But when Madam Alex proved to be less than generous in sharing her largess, Fleiss went off on her own.

Renowned Hollywood Madame Heidi Fleiss at the Melbourne, Australia, Stock Exchange for the start of trading of "The Daily Planet" bordello—the first brothel in the world to be listed on a national stock exchange. For years, Fleiss's prostitution business had catered to the rich and famous in Hollywood and Los Angeles, but she spent 20 months in prison after being convicted in 1995 on federal charges of conspiracy, tax evasion, and money laundering. Should Fleiss have received a longer sentence?

Source: Regis Martin/Getty Images

And the rest is sex industry history. Ultimately, Fleiss's client base included top producers, directors, and movie stars from the Hollywood scene, as well as some of the world's most famous (and wealthiest) men. Business tycoons, Middle Eastern sheiks, members of royalty, and various heads of state are counted among those to whom she provided women for sexual services.[iii]

Since her release from prison, Fleiss has parlayed her notoriety into a series of successful business ventures, including a men's apparel store in Los Angeles called "Heidi's Wear." A book (*Pandering*), a DVD (*Sex Tips*), a Web site, and repeated appearances on late-night talk shows have kept her in the public eye. Ever the sensationalist, Fleiss's current project, which she describes as a "stud farm,"[iv] involves converting a brothel in southern Nevada into a resort staffed by male prostitutes to service Fleiss's hoped-for female customers.[v]

Notes

i. "Then & Now: Heidi Fleiss," CNN, June 19, 2005, http://www.cnn.com/2005/US/02/28/cnn25.tan.fleiss (accessed June 1, 2010).

ii. Rachael Bell, "Heidi Fleiss: The Million Dollar Madam," CourtTV Crime Library, http://www.crimelibrary.com/notorious_murders/celebrity/heidi_fleiss/index.html (accessed June 1, 2010).

iii. Ibid.

iv. "Fleiss Plans Makeover for Nevada Brothel," *USA Today*, November 16, 2005, http://www.usatoday.com/life/people/2005-11-16-fleiss_x.htm (accessed June 1, 2007).

v. Steve Friess, "Betting on the Studs," *Newsweek*, December 12, 2005, http://www.msnbc.msn.com/id/10313009/site/newsweek (accessed June 1, 2007).

Feminists who believe that prostitution is inherently exploitative reject the idea that prostitution can be reformed. The assumptions that women exist for men's sexual enjoyment, that all men need sex, and that women's bodily integrity and sexual pleasure are irrelevant underlie the whole idea of prostitution, making it an inherently exploitative sexist practice. One feminist argument against Dworkin's position is that prostitution is exploiting men more than it exploits women.

In an interesting critique of what he calls "extreme radical feminist theory," as represented by the writings of Dworkin and others, sociologist Ronald Weitzer of George Washington University listed four core claims characterizing this body of literature:[82]

1. Prostitution involves male domination and exploitation of women regardless of historical time period, societal context, or legal status.

2. Violence is omnipresent in prostitution.

3. Female prostitutes lack agency (they cannot actively make choices about whether or not to stay in prostitution).

4. Legalization or decriminalization would only make the situation worse.

Weitzer saw these claims as counterproductive because they tend to stifle debate over prostitution and effectively divert research programs through what he calls "considerable ideological contamination of our understanding of prostitution."[83] Extreme feminists have contributed to a growing moral panic over prostitution by tying it to sex trafficking and the trafficking of children for sex. Many of the radicals' claims, explained Weitzer, are simply false; violence is not inevitably associated with prostitution, some prostitutes (especially those engaged in legal prostitution) see themselves positively, and prostitution can be lawfully organized in ways that protect the prostitutes' health, rights, and freedoms.

Legalization and Decriminalization of Prostitution

A number of arguments have been made in favor of legalizing or decriminalizing prostitution. Under legalization, women beyond a specified age would be able to offer paid sexual services with few restrictions (as in parts of Nevada). Decriminalization would significantly reduce the criminal penalties associated with prostitution but would still regulate the practice and might require counseling and alternative employment programs for women in that line of work in an effort to curtail the practice (**Library Extra 12–14**).

Those who argue in favor of legalization say that keeping prostitution illegal tends to force prostitution out of areas where it might naturally be found (certain hotels, massage parlors) and onto the streets and into other parts of the community and that prostitutes will continue to be viewed as easy targets for pimps, sex offenders, and violent predators. Legalization of prostitution would free up law enforcement resources to be used in the prevention and investigation of more serious types of crime. Those who argue against legalization say that legalization promotes other crimes like sex trafficking and that it will expand the sex industry rather than eliminate it.[84]

> Legalization of prostitution would free up law enforcement resources to be used in the investigation of more serious types of crime.

SUMMARY

- Drug abuse has a long and varied history in American society, from the use of illegal drugs by artistic individuals seeking to enhance their creativity to citizens using medicinal elixirs containing cocaine, alcohol, and opium. Policy responses to drug abuse have been equally diverse.

- Controlled substances are grouped into seven categories: stimulants, depressants, cannabis, narcotics, hallucinogens, anabolic steroids, and inhalants. A separate eighth category, dangerous drugs, provides a kind of legal and definitional catchall. The Controlled Substances Act established five schedules of federally controlled substances based on the effects of a drug and its potential for abuse.

- Drug trafficking includes manufacturing, distributing, dispensing, importing, and exporting (or possessing with intent to do the same) a controlled substance or a counterfeit substance. Federal law enforcement agencies focus on the prevention of smuggling and the apprehension of smugglers.

- Drug users commit both property and personal crimes to acquire the money necessary to continue drug use, and drug traffickers use violence and intimidation to gain access to profitable drug markets.

- Strategies to reduce the flow of illegal drugs into this country are supplemented with programs of education and treatment to reduce the demand for controlled substances. Major policy initiatives have included (1) antidrug legislation and strict enforcement, (2) interdiction, (3) crop control, (4) forfeiture, and (5) antidrug education and drug treatment.

- Prostitution is a morals offense. Using location as the basis for a typology of prostitutes results in the categories of streetwalkers, bar/hotel prostitutes, call girls, and hotel/brothel prostitutes, as well as others who don't fit any of these categories.

KEY TERMS

addiction, 341

Arrestee Drug Abuse Monitoring (ADAM) Program, 352

dangerous drug, 341

decriminalization, 359

designer drug, 349

drug-defined crime, 351

drug-related crime, 351

drug trafficking, 349

Heroin Signature Program (HSP), 351

interdiction, 355

legalization, 359

National Survey on Drug Use and Health (NSDUH), 335

Office of National Drug Control Policy (ONDCP), 335

pharmaceutical diversion, 349

prostitution, 361

psychoactive substance, 334

QUESTIONS FOR REVIEW

1. What can be said about the history of drugs, drug abuse, and drug-control legislation in the United States?

2. What are the various categories of controlled substances described by federal law? What is a dangerous drug?

3. What is drug trafficking, and what efforts are being made to curtail it?

4. What is the relationship among drug trafficking, drug abuse, and other forms of crime?

5. What government strategies have been used to reduce the incidence of drug use in the United States?

6. What is prostitution? What are the various types of prostitutes identified in this chapter?

QUESTIONS FOR REFLECTION

1. This book emphasizes the theme of social problems versus social responsibility. Which of the social policy approaches to controlling drug abuse discussed in this chapter (if any) appear to be predicated on a social problems approach? Which (if any) are predicated on a social responsibility approach? Explain the nature of the relationship.

2. What are some of the costs of illicit drug use in the United States today? Which costs can be more easily reduced than others? How would you reduce the costs of illegal drug use?

3. What is the difference between decriminalization and legalization? Should drug use remain illegal? What do you think of the arguments in favor of legalization? Those against?

4. What is asset forfeiture? How has asset forfeiture been used in the fight against illegal drugs? How have U.S. Supreme Court decisions limited federal asset seizures? Do you agree that such limitations were necessary? Why?

5. How is prostitution like other crimes? How does it differ?

6. Do you think that prostitution should be legalized? Why or why not?

CHAPTER 13

TECHNOLOGY AND CRIME

LEARNING OUTCOMES

After reading this chapter, you should be able to answer the following questions:

- How does advancing technology produce new forms of crime?

- How does high technology provide new criminal opportunities?

- What different types of cybercriminals does this chapter describe?

- What is identity theft, and how can identities be stolen?

- What new technologies are being used in today's fight against crime?

- What is being done to combat cybercrime and to secure the Internet today?

- What are some of the personal freedoms that are threatened by today's need for advanced security?

Follow the author's tweets about the latest crime and justice news at http://twitter.com/schmalleger.

Introduction

In 2010 a new term, *cyberbanging*—referring to the use of the Internet and social networking Web sites by street gangs to tout their exploits, recruit new members, post threats, and socialize—entered the law enforcement lexicon. Videos and lyrics glorifying gang activities can be found on Facebook, MySpace, and Twitter, and some gangs have their own home pages and even run their own servers.[1] "Gangs are going to use any form of communication they can," stated George W. Knox, director of the National Gang Crime Research Center, "including Twitter, including Facebook."[2] Law enforcement experts have said that gangs sometimes use social networking sites to circumvent court injunctions forbidding members from meeting face-to-face. Not to be outdone, police agencies and criminal prosecutors have begun scouring social networking sites looking for evidence they can use to disrupt gang activities or to prosecute gang members for crimes they've committed. "Five years ago we would find evidence in a gang case on the Internet and say, 'Wow!'" Bruce Riordan, director of antigang operations for the Los Angeles City Attorney's office commented. "Well, there's no more 'Wow' anymore. It's much more routine."[3]

The Advance of Technology

Technology and crime have always been closely linked. The con artist who uses a telephone in a financial scam, the robber who uses a firearm and drives a getaway car, even the murderer who wields a knife—all employ at least rudimentary forms of technology in the crimes they commit. Technology can be employed by both crime fighters and lawbreakers. Early forms of technology, including the telegraph, telephone, and automobile, were embraced by agents of law enforcement as soon as they became available. Evidence derived from fingerprint and ballistics analysis is routinely employed by prosecutors; and emerging technologies promise to keep criminologists and law enforcement agents in step with high-tech offenders.

As technology advances, it facilitates new forms of behavior, so we can be certain that tomorrow's crimes will differ from those of today. Personal crimes of violence and traditional property crimes will continue to occur, but advancing technology will create new and as-yet unimaginable opportunities for criminals positioned to take advantage of it and of the power it will afford.

Bret and Sammy of the Sammy4U show adult Web site, which broadcasts the daily activities of nudists on the Internet. Bret and Sammy (a former stripper) work out of their home in Florida using video-streaming technology. Should the federal government regulate such productions?
Source: Preston C. Mack

A frightening preview of such possibilities was seen during the collapse of the Soviet Union when the resulting social disorganization made the acquisition of fissionable materials, stolen from Soviet stockpiles, simple for even relatively small outlaw organizations. In what is a nightmare for authorities throughout the world, Middle Eastern terrorist groups are making forceful efforts to acquire former Soviet nuclear weapons and the raw materials necessary to manufacture their own bombs, and some evidence suggests that nuclear weapons parts may have already been sold to wealthy international drug cartels and organized criminal groups, who could hoard them to use as bargaining chips against possible government prosecution.

High Technology and Criminal Opportunity

The twenty-first century has been described by some as the epitome of the postindustrial information age. Information is vital to the success of any endeavor, and certain forms of information hold nearly incalculable value. Patents on new products, chemical compositions of innovative and effective drugs, corporate marketing strategies, and financial resources of competing corporations are all forms of information whose illegitimate access might

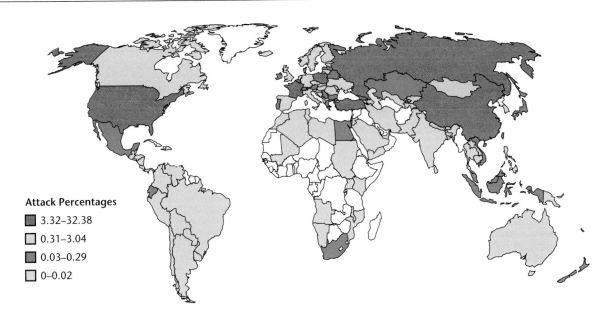

Attack Percentages
- ■ 3.32–32.38
- □ 0.31–3.04
- ■ 0.03–0.29
- □ 0–0.02

FIGURE 13-1 | Global Cyberthreat Map

Source: Courtesy Websense, Inc., *Global Threat Map 2010*.

bestow unfair advantages on unscrupulous competitors. Imagine the financial wealth and market share that would accrue to the first pharmaceutical company to patent a true AIDS cure or an effective treatment for bird flu and the potential profitability inherent in the information describing the chemical composition of that drug (especially to a competitor, who might be able to beat the legitimate originator of the substance to the patent desk or who might use stolen information in a later bid to challenge patents already issued).

High-tech criminals seeking illegitimate access to computerized information and to the databases that contain it have taken a number of routes (Figure 13–1). One is the path of direct access, by which office workers or corporate spies, planted as seemingly innocuous employees, violate positions of trust and use otherwise legitimate work-related entry to a company's computer resources to acquire wanted information, stealing data during business hours under the guise of normal work routines.

Another path of illegal access, called "computer trespass," involves remote access to targeted machines. Anyone equipped with a home computer and some knowledge about computer modems, telecommunications, and log-on procedures has easy access to numerous computer systems across the country because many of these systems have few (if any) security procedures in place. In one case, a Silicon Valley software company learned that a fired software developer had been using a telephone connection to enter the company's computers. By the time she was caught, she had copied several million dollars' worth of the company's programs.[5] It was later learned that the stolen software had been slated for illicit transmission to collaborators in Taiwan, and if the scheme had succeeded, thousands of pirated copies of the software would have been distributed at great financial loss to the legitimate copyright owners.

More exotic techniques used to steal data stored in computers extend to reading the electromagnetic radiation produced by electromagnetic field (EMF) decoders, which were originally developed for military purposes and can scan radio-frequency emanations generated by all types of computers; keystroke activity, internal chip-processed computations, disk reads, and the like can all be detected and interpreted at a distance under favorable conditions. Computers secured against such passively invasive practices are rarely found in the commercial marketplace because those available to commercial organizations generally conform to a security standard developed by the U.S. military called **TEMPEST**, created

> The cyberthreat is one of the most serious economic and national security challenges we face as a nation. . . .
>
> —President Barack Obama[4]

■ **hacker**
A person who uses computers for exploration and exploitation.
■ **computer virus**
A computer program designed to invade computer systems and either modify the way they operate or alter the information they store.

LIBRARY EXTRA 13–1

■ **cybercrime**
Any crime that involves the use of computers or the manipulation of digital data as well as any violation of a federal or state cybercrime statute.

under a U.S. Department of Defense program seeking to develop methods of reducing or eliminating unintended electronic emissions from computers and other electromagnetic devices. The newer wireless networking has rekindled fears of data theft.

Some cybercriminals intend simply to destroy or alter data without otherwise accessing or copying the information. Disgruntled employees, mischievous computer **hackers** (people who use a computer for exploration or exploitation), business competitors, and others have varied degrees of interest in destroying a company's records or computer capabilities.

In 1988, in the first criminal prosecution of a person accused of creating a **computer virus** (a computer program designed to secretly invade computer systems and modify the way they operate or alter the information they store), Texas programmer Donald Gene Burleson was arrested for allegedly infecting a former employer's computer with a program designed to destroy the information it contained.

> ## The person most likely to invade your computer is currently on your payroll.

Since Burleson's arrest, many imitators have taken similar paths of revenge. According to Richard Baker, author of the respected *Computer Security Handbook,* "The greatest threat to your computers and data comes from inside your company, not outside. The person most likely to invade your computer is not a gawky youngster in some other part of the country but an employee who is currently on your payroll."[6]

Cybercrime refers to any crime that involves the use of computers or the manipulation of digital data as well as any violation of a federal or state cybercrime statute. Many argue that only those crimes that employ computer technology as central to their commission and that could not be committed without it may properly be called "cybercrimes."

A Federal Bureau of Investigation typology distinguishes among five types of computer crimes: (1) internal computer crimes, such as viruses; (2) Internet and telecommunications crimes, including illegal hacking; (3) support of criminal enterprises, such as databases supporting drug distribution; (4) computer-manipulation crimes, such as embezzlement; and (5) hardware, software, and information theft.[7] Table 13–1 lists these five categories, with additional examples of each. Learn more about cybercrime typologies by reading **Library Extra 13–1**.

An estimate by the U.S. Secret Service in conjunction with the Cybersecurity Center (CERT) at Carnegie Mellon University

TABLE 13-1	Categories of CyberCrime
Internal Cybercrimes (Malware)
Trojan horses
Logic bombs
Trapdoors
Viruses
Internet and Telecommunications Crimes
Phone phreaking
Hacking
Denial of service attacks
Illegal Web sites
Dissemination of illegal material (such as child pornography)
Misuse of telephone systems
Theft of telecommunications services
Illegal eavesdropping
Illegal Internet-based gambling
Support of Criminal Enterprises
Databases to support drug distribution
Databases to support loan-sharking
Databases to support illegal gambling
Databases to keep records of illegal client transactions
Electronic money laundering
Communications in furtherance of criminal conspiracies
Computer-Manipulation Crimes
Embezzlement
Electronic fund-transfer fraud
Other fraud/phishing
Extortion threats/electronic terrorism
Hardware, Software, and Information Theft
Software piracy (Warez)
Theft of computers
Theft of microprocessor chips
Theft of trade secrets and proprietary information
Identity theft

put the annual cost of cybercrime at around $666 million.[8] Another industry group, the Computer Security Institute (CSI), surveyed 313 business organizations and found that cybercrimes

■ **software piracy**
The unauthorized and illegal copying of software programs.

■ **phone phreak**
A person who uses switched, dialed-access telephone services for exploration and exploitation.

WEB EXTRA 13–1

Coincidence or espionage? Before the dissolution of the Soviet Union, Eastern bloc scientists succeeded in building a copy of the American space shuttle (pictured here). Experts suspected that the Soviet model would not have been possible without information stolen from U.S. research archives. Why is technology difficult to protect?

Source: Phil Sandlin-Canapress Photo Service/AP Wide World Photos (left); Terry Renna-Canapress Photo Service/AP Wide World Photos (right)

example, it is estimated that 82% has been illegally copied. Learn more about software piracy from the Business Software Alliance via **Web Extra 13–1**.

According to some experts, losses like these may be just the beginning. One technological visionary observed, "Our society is about to feel the impact of the first generation of children who have grown up using computers. The increasing sophistication of hackers suggests that computer crime will soon soar, as members of this new generation are tempted to commit more serious offenses."[13]

While the theft or damage of information represents one area of criminal activity, using different technologies in direct furtherance of criminal enterprises constitutes another and is as varied as the technologies themselves. Nuclear blackmail may represent the extreme technologically based criminal threat, whereas telephone fraud and phone phreaking are examples of low-end crimes that depend on modern technology for their commission.

cost companies an average of $168,000 each in 2006.[9] A 2009 survey by the Ponemon Institute, however, found per-company losses as high as $6.7 million from data breaches at 43 large organizations in 2008.[10]

Software piracy, the unauthorized and illegal copying of software programs, is rampant, and global estimates of lost revenues due to pirated software (known as "Warez" in the computer underground) dwarfed those cybercrime amounts. The Software and Information Industry Association (SIIA) distinguishes among various forms of software piracy, including Internet piracy and software counterfeiting.[11]

According to the Business Software Alliance, global losses from software piracy totaled nearly $51.4 billion in 2009.[12] The Alliance notes that 43% of software in use worldwide is illegally copied. Some countries have especially high rates of illegal use. Of all the computer software in use in China, for

One of the earliest forms of cybercrime was committed by **phone phreaks**, who use special dial-up access codes and other restricted technical information to avoid long-distance charges; some are able to place calls from pay phones, whereas others fool telephone equipment into billing other callers. "Many organizations discover they have been victims of telephone fraud only after their telephone bill arrives in a carton instead of an envelope."[14]

Another form of phone phreaking emerged that involved the electronic theft of cellular telephone numbers and access codes. Thieves armed with simple mail-order scanners and low-end computers can "literally grab a caller's phone number and identification number out of the air."[15] According to some experts, "Those numbers are [then] used to program computer

■ **phishing**

An Internet-based scam to steal valuable information such as credit-card numbers, Social Security numbers, user IDs, and passwords.

WEB EXTRA 13–2
LIBRARY EXTRA 13–2

chips, which are placed inside other cellular phones—or 'clones'—so the long-distance calls appear on the victim's bill."[16]

Developments in voice-over Internet protocol (VoIP) technology have made the theft of telecommunications services less lucrative but have also opened the door to new kinds of crimes. The U.S. Department of Justice (DOJ) has gone on record as being concerned about the fast growth of VoIP communications services because they make surveillance and wiretapping difficult and can facilitate "drug trafficking, organized crime and terrorism."[17] Laura Parsky, a deputy assistant attorney general in the DOJ, told investigators at a recent Senate hearing, "If legal loopholes allow criminals to use new technologies to avoid law enforcement detection, they would use these technologies to coordinate terrorist attacks, to sell drugs throughout the United States and to pass along national security secrets to our enemies." The hearing was held to consider changes to the proposed VoIP Regulatory Freedom Act, which might require telecommunications providers to build "back doors" into VoIP networks that would allow for court-ordered wiretaps to be successfully enforced.

Another form of high-technology fraud is termed **phishing** (pronounced "fishing"), a scam that uses official-looking e-mail messages to steal valuable information such as credit-card numbers, Social Security numbers, user IDs, and passwords from victims. The e-mail messages appear to come from a user's bank, credit-card company, retail store, or Internet service provider (ISP) and generally inform the recipient that some vital information in his or her account urgently needs to be updated. Those who respond are provided with an official-looking Web form on which they can enter their private financial information; once the information is submitted, it enters the phisher's database.

The Anti-Phishing Working Group—a coalition of banks and ISPs—estimated that a typical phishing scheme reaches up to 1 million e-mail inboxes and had identified more than 55,600 different phishing Web sites as of June 2007.[18] Some observers have noted that in addition to losses suffered by individuals and institutions, phishing has the potential to threaten the viability of e-commerce and to call into question the safety of all Web-based financial transactions.[19]

The federal Violent Crime Control and Law Enforcement Act of 1994 made it illegal to use interstate telephone lines in furtherance of telemarketing fraud and expanded federal jurisdiction to cover cases of insurance fraud and fraud committed against the elderly, even when such crimes do not

> The world isn't run by weapons anymore, or energy, or money. It's run by ones and zeros—little bits of data—it's all electrons. . . .
> —*Sneakers*

involve use of the mail or telephone. Learn more about telemarketing fraud and Internet-based fraud at the National Fraud Information Center via **Web Extra 13–2**; read an important criminological discourse on cybercrime via **Library Extra 13–2**.

Technology and Criminal Mischief

Not all cybercrime is committed for financial gain. Some types of cybercrime—the creation and transmission of destructive computer viruses, "worms," spyware, and other malicious forms of programming code (often called *malware*)—might better be classified as "criminal mischief." These types of activities are typically associated with young, technologically sophisticated males

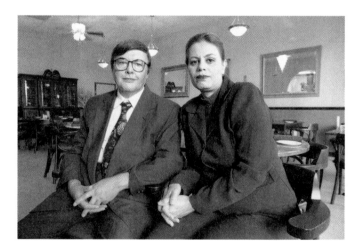

Dr. Ali-Reza Ghasemi and his wife, Shahla Ghasemi, of Tampa (Florida). They lost $400,000 to an advance-fee scheme on the Internet. Advance-fee schemes (often called Nigerian e-mail fraud because many of the messages appear to come from Nigeria) promise victims a lot of money in return for advancing fees to cover legal services and transfer of funds. How can you tell when an e-mail message is likely to be a fraud?
Source: William S. Speer/Bloomberg News

1	**Mydoom (2004)** *Estimated damage: $38.5 billion*
2	**Sobig.F (2003)** *Estimated damage: $30 billion*
3	**Klez (2001)** *Estimated damage: $18.9 billion*
4	**Sasser (2004)** *Estimated damage: $14.8 billion*
5	**ILOVEYOU, AKA Loveletter and The Love Bug (2000)** *Estimated damage: $8.75–$15 billion*
6	**Backdoor.Zagaban (2005)** *Estimated damage: unknown, but thought to be in the billions of dollars*
7	**Blaster (2003)** *Estimated damage: $5 to $10 billion*
8	**Code Red (2001)** *Estimated damage: $2.6 billion*
9	**Slammer (2003)** *Estimated damage: unknown, but thought to total in the billions of dollars*
10	**Storm (2007)** *Estimated damage: $1 billion in lost productivity*

FIGURE 13-2 | The Ten Most Damaging Computer Viruses and Worms

References: Buzzle.com, "The Most Damage Causing Computer Viruses Revealed," http://www.buzzle.com/articles/the-most-damage-causing-computer-virusesrevealed.html (accessed October 22, 2010); Christopher Null, "The Worst Computer Viruses of All Time," Yahoo! Tech, http://tech.yahoo.com/blogs/null (accessed October 22, 2010); and George Jones, "The 10 Most Destructive PC Viruses of All Time," Tech Web, July 5, 2006, http://www.techweb.com/tech/160200005 (accessed June 26, 2010).

seeking a kind of clandestine recognition from their computer-savvy peers. Cybercrimes committed by youthful idealistic offenders may represent a new form of juvenile delinquency—one aimed at expressing dissatisfaction with the status quo (see **Library Extra 13–3**).

Computer viruses have shown signs of becoming effective terrorist-like tools in the hands of young, disaffected "technonerds" intent on attacking or destroying existing social institutions. A computer virus is simply a computer program that is designed to secretly invade computer systems, changing the way in which they run or the content they store.[20] Other types of destructive programs are called logic bombs, worms, and Trojan horse routines. Distinctions among these programs are based on either the way they infect targeted machines or the way they behave once they have managed to find their way into a computer. Figure 13–2 provides an overview of some of the most damaging computer viruses and worms.

Viruses may spread from one machine to another via modem or high-speed cable and digital subscriber line (DSL) connections (when files are downloaded) and through networks or direct links, DVDs, flash drives, CD-ROMs, or magnetic or optical backup media. Most viruses hide inside executable computer software, in the so-called boot sectors of storage media. Rogue codes known as "macro viruses" have also been secreted in text documents; the most famous of these, the Concept virus, affects users of Microsoft's Word software. Hypertext markup language (HTML) files, which form the backbone of the World Wide Web, may be infected with viruses lurking inside Java script or Macromedia Shockwave–generated code, and some users worry that "cookies" (small programs sent to users' machines by servers on the Web) may spread viruses.

Viruses infect not only desktop and laptop machines but also popular handheld devices, including personal digital assistants (PDAs) and mobile phones. In 2000, a Swedish software developer accidentally released Liberty Crack, a disabling software code that enters handheld devices like the Palm and Handspring products.[21]

Perhaps the most insidious forms of destructive programming making the rounds of the computer world are polymorphic viruses, which use advanced encryption techniques to assemble varied (yet entirely operational) clones of themselves and have the ability to alter themselves once they have infected a computer. This strategy is effective in circumventing most security devices that depend on scanning techniques to recognize viral signatures—when viruses change, they can no longer be recognized. In typical leapfrog fashion, as when crime-fighting techniques are overtaken and surpassed by new technologies favoring lawbreakers and then later regain ascendancy, polymorphic viruses have largely rendered signature-based antivirus-scanning technologies obsolete.

Although many hardware devices and software products now on the market offer some degree of virus protection to individual and commercial users, new viruses are constantly being created that may soon have the ability to circumvent all security procedures now in place. The only fully effective technique for

CRIME | in the NEWS

Gangs Turn to Social Media

Gang members in Oklahoma have begun using cell phones and text messaging to conduct criminal activities, and Internet social media such as Facebook and YouTube to recruit members as young as second-graders, according to a survey of gang activity in the state. The survey, a follow-up to a study in 2006, shows Oklahoma's increase in gang members the past three years is relatively small compared with the rest of the country. But youth in the state are joining gangs at an earlier age, and gang members are becoming more prone to violent actions.

As a result, the entire community, not just law enforcement, must address the gang issues facing Oklahoma, said Michael Wilds, an associate professor of criminal justice and legal studies at Northeastern State University, the author of the report. "You're seeing more recruiting done to the younger population," said Wilds.

Oklahoma City and Tulsa officers reported gang members as young as ten years old, compared with the youngest being identified as 12 years old three years ago. Oklahoma City officers reported that some youngsters are recruited as young as 8 years old, the survey states.

Officers reported Oklahoma gangs are becoming more sophisticated in conducting criminal operations by using Internet social networking sites to recruit new members. They are also using cell phones and text messaging for communications related to criminal activities such as drug manufacturing and distribution routes, the survey found.

Gang members are also using cell phones and international dialing to maintain contact with incarcerated gang members or gang members who have been deported to Mexico, Columbia, El Salvador, and other Central American countries.

State law enforcement agencies and district attorneys reported 1,026 gangs in 2009, a 2% increase compared with the 1,006 gangs reported in 2006, the report shows. Wilds also did the 2006 report.

Law officers reported 13,512 gang members in the state, an increase of 0.26% compared with the 13,477 gang members reported in 2006. Nationally, gang members increased 25%, according to the National Gang Threat Assessment.

Wilds said the 2009 numbers are more accurate because law enforcement officers have had increased training and are more accurate in identifying gang members.

"The officers that first thought four people walking around with a baseball bat were gang members—no, they were baseball players," he said.

About 60% of the police chiefs, sheriffs, and district attorneys who were mailed surveys responded, or 378 of 635, Wilds said. The survey was paid for by the state District Attorneys Council.

Similar to the 2006 survey, the newest survey shows the major criminal gangs operating in Oklahoma are the Crips, Bloods, Hoover Crips, white supremacist groups, and various Hispanic gangs.

A prisoner charged with murdering a corrections officer who took him to a hospital appointment in Utah. Curtis Allgier, a neo-Nazi affiliated with the Aryan Brotherhood, is alleged to have wrestled the guard's gun from him and shot him; he then carjacked a vehicle and led police on a chase before being apprehended. Why are street gangs turning to the Internet?

Source: Splash News & Pictures/NewsCom.com

Oklahoma City and Tulsa officers reported "third-generation" gang members, where son, dad, and grandfather all belong to the same criminal gang.

Only 15 of the state's 77 counties reported no gangs in 2009 compared with 19 counties three years ago.

"They're not afraid of hurting people," Wilds said. "Now we're more aware that many of the drive-by shootings are in fact related to gang activity as well as meth activity–type drugs. Gangs are getting a little bit more lethal . . . more bold in their criminal activities."

Discussion Questions

1. How might criminal gangs make use of social media such as Facebook?

2. How might the use of social media by criminal street gangs potentially impact other users of social media?

avoiding viral contamination is the complete and total isolation of computer equipment—a strategy as unlikely to be maintained as it is to be implemented. Once certain forms of malicious software code have successfully invaded a computer, they can take over the machine and use it to either send additional copies of themselves or send spam and other information (including the

legitimate user's personal information) to various places on the Internet.

In 2010, international law enforcement and security officials shut down the Mariposa botnet, one of the largest networks of co-opted computers ever discovered.[22] At its peak, the Mariposa botnet, which used compromised computers to

■ **Cyber Security Enhancement Act (CSEA)**
A federal law found in the Homeland Security Act of 2002 that directs the U.S. Sentencing Commission to take specific factors into account in creating new sentencing guidelines for cybercriminals.

■ **Digital Theft Deterrence and Copyright Damages Improvement Act**
A 1999 federal law (Public Law 106–160) that amends Section 504(c) of the Copyright Act by increasing the amount of damages that could be awarded in cases of copyright infringement.

WEB EXTRA 13-3

■ **No Electronic Theft Act (NETA)**
A 1997 federal law (Public Law 105–147) that criminalizes the willful infringement of copyrighted works, including by electronic means, even when the infringing party derives no direct financial benefit from the infringement (such as when pirated software is freely distributed online).

identify and capture sensitive personal and financial information for malware creators, was able to install itself on 12.7 million computers worldwide. Learn more about botnets, computer viruses, and malware at **Web Extra 13–3**.

Cybercrime and the Law

In the early years of computer-based information systems, most U.S. jurisdictions often tried to prosecute unauthorized computer access under preexisting property-crime statutes, such as burglary and larceny laws. Because stealing a computer is quite different from simply copying or altering some of its information, juries frequently could not understand the applicability of such laws to high-tech crimes and computer criminals were exonerated. As a result, all states and the federal government developed cybercrime statutes specifically applicable to invasive activities aimed at illegally accessing stored information. Federal statutes included (1) the Cyber Security Enhancement Act of 2002;[23] (2) the Digital Theft Deterrence and Copyright Damages Improvemsent Act of 1999;[24] (3) the No Electronic Theft Act of 1997;[25] (4) the Communications Decency Act as amended; (5) the Computer Fraud and Abuse Act of 1984[26] and its amendments, especially Section 290001 of Title 29 of the Violent Crime Control and Law Enforcement Act of 1994, known as the Computer Abuse Amendments Act of 1994; (6) the Electronic Communications Privacy Act of 1986; (7) the National Stolen Property Act;[27] and (8) the Federal Wiretap Act of 1968.

Federal laws protect both equipment owned by the federal government or financial institutions and computers accessed across state lines without prior authorization.[28] The U.S. Criminal Code, Title 18, Section 1030(a), defined as criminal the intentional unauthorized access to a computer used exclusively by the federal government or any other computer used by the government when such conduct affects the government's use. It also made criminal the intentional and unauthorized access to two or more computers in different states and conduct that alters or destroys information and causes loss to one or more parties in excess of $1,000.[29] Punishment specified under federal law is a maximum sentence of five years and a fine of up to $250,000 upon conviction. The Computer Abuse Amendments Act of 1994 added the provision that "any person who suffers damage

or loss by reason of a violation of [this] section may maintain a civil action against the violator to obtain compensatory damages and injunctive relief or other equitable relief,"[30] which is intended to support civil actions in federal court against cybercriminals by those suffering monetary losses as a result of cybercrimes.

The 2002 **Cyber Security Enhancement Act (CSEA)**, part of the Homeland Security Act of 2002, directed the U.S. Sentencing Commission to take several factors into account in creating new sentencing guidelines for cybercriminals.[31] The commission should consider not only how large the financial losses caused by cybercrime were but also what the level of planning involved in the offense was,

> The 2002 Cyber Security Enhancement Act (CSEA), provides substantial new penalties for cybercriminals.

whether the crime was committed for commercial or private advantage, and whether malicious intent existed on the part of the perpetrator; cybercriminals can face life in prison if they put human lives in jeopardy. The law intends to help deter cybercrime by subjecting cybercriminals to substantial criminal penalties, makes it easier for law enforcement agencies to obtain investigative information from ISPs, and shields from lawsuits ISPs that hand over user information to law enforcement officers without a warrant—but that information should pose an immediate risk of injury or death.

The 1999 **Digital Theft Deterrence and Copyright Damages Improvement Act** amended Section 504(c) of the Copyright Act and increased the amount of damages that could be awarded in cases of copyright infringement, a crime intimately associated with software piracy. Enacted in 1997, the **No Electronic Theft Act (NETA)** criminalized the willful infringement of copyrighted works, including by electronic means, even when the infringing party derives no direct financial benefit from the infringement (such as when pirated software is freely distributed online). In keeping with requirements of NETA, the U.S. Sentencing Commission enacted amendments to its guidelines on April 6, 2000, to increase penalties associated with electronic theft.

■ **Communications Decency Act (CDA)**
A 1996 federal statute labeled Title 5 of the federal Telecommunications Act of 1996 (Public Law 104–104, 110 Stat. 56) that seeks to protect minors from harmful material on the Internet and that criminalizes the knowing transmission of obscene or indecent messages to any recipient under 18 years of age. In 1997, in *Reno* v. *ACLU* (521 U.S. 844), the U.S. Supreme Court found the bulk of the CDA to be unconstitutional, ruling that it contravenes First Amendment free speech guarantees.

In 1996, President Bill Clinton signed into law the **Communications Decency Act (CDA)**, Title 5 of the Telecommunications Act of 1996, to protect minors from harmful material on the Internet.[32] A portion of the CDA criminalized the knowing transmission of obscene or indecent messages to any recipient under 18 years of age. Another section prohibited the sending or displaying to a person under age 18 any message "that, in context, depicts or describes, in terms patently offensive as measured by contemporary community standards, sexual or excretory activities or organs." The law provided acceptable defenses for those who took "good faith effective actions" to restrict access by minors to prohibited communications and for those who restricted such access by requiring certain designated forms of age proof, such as a verified credit card or an adult identification number.

Shortly after the law was passed, the American Civil Liberties Union (ACLU) and a number of other plaintiffs filed suit against the federal government, challenging the constitutionality of the law's two provisions relating to the transmission of obscene materials to minors. In 1996, a three-judge federal district court entered a preliminary injunction against enforcement of both challenged provisions, ruling that they contravened First Amendment guarantees of free speech. The government then appealed to the U.S. Supreme Court. The Court's 1997 decision in **Reno v. ACLU** upheld the lower court's ruling and found that the CDA's "indecent transmission" and "patently offensive display" provisions abridged "the freedom of speech" protected by the First Amendment.[33] Justice John Paul Stevens wrote for the majority: "It is true that we have repeatedly recognized the governmental interest in protecting children from harmful materials. But that interest does not justify an unnecessarily broad suppression of speech addressed to adults."

Most other federal legislation aimed at keeping online pornography away from children has not fared any better when reviewed by the Court, so it remains to be seen whether the 1998 Child Online Protection Act (COPA) can be modified to meet Court muster. Although the Children's Internet Protection Act (CIPA), which requires public and school libraries receiving certain kinds of federal funding to install pornography filters on their Internet-linked computers, was approved, most observers acknowledge that the Court has placed the Internet in the same category as newspapers and other print media, where almost no regulation is permitted.

The cybercrime laws of individual states are rarely modeled after federal legislation, so they contain great variation. Texas law criminalized "breach of computer security," which occurs when an individual "knowingly accesses a computer, computer network, or computer system without the effective consent of the owner [or when someone] intentionally or knowingly gives a password, identifying code, personal identification number, debit card number, bank account number, or other confidential information about a computer security system to another person without the effective consent of the person employing the computer security system to restrict access to a computer, computer network, computer system, or data."[34]

Virginia specifically defined *cybercrime* according to the following categories: "theft of computer services, computer invasion of privacy, computer trespass, computer fraud, [and] personal trespass by computer" (via which physical injury accrues to someone by virtue of unauthorized access to a computer, as may happen in the case of disruption of utility services).[35]

Ambiguities in existing cybercrime laws, complicated by rapid changes in technology, can make it difficult even to tell when a crime has occurred. In 1995, 20-year-old University of Michigan student Jacob Alkhabaz (aka Jake A. Baker) became the first person ever indicted for writing something on the Internet when he was arrested by the FBI and charged with five counts of interstate transmission of threats;[36] he had posted a series of stories on the Internet about his fantasy of torturing, raping, and murdering a female classmate. His messages contained the following: "Just thinking about it anymore doesn't do the trick. I need to do it." "Torture is foreplay, rape is romance, snuff (killing) is climax."[37]

Although Alkhabaz might have been punished by a sentence of up to five years in prison, Detroit U.S. District Judge Avern Cohn threw out the charges after Alkhabaz had spent 29 days in jail, ruling that Alkhabaz's violent-sounding Internet writings were protected under the free speech clause of the U.S. Constitution.[38] Alkhabaz had been charged with communicating threats rather than cybercrime because his activities were not specifically covered under federal cybercrime laws. If they had been, a different verdict might have resulted.

Future illegitimate activities employing computer equipment may not always be adequately covered by existing laws, but

> The cybercrime laws of individual states contain great variation.

WEB EXTRA 13-4
LIBRARY EXTRA 13-4

■ **computer-related crime**
An illegal act using computer technology in its perpetration, investigation, or prosecution.
■ **computer abuse**
An unlawful incident associated with computer technology in which a victim suffers loss or a perpetrator reaps benefit.

■ **cyberspace**
The computer-created matrix of virtual possibilities, including online services, in which human beings interact with one another and with the technology itself.

some crimes committed with the use of a computer may be more appropriately prosecuted under traditional laws. For that reason, some experts distinguish among cybercrime (defined earlier) and two other types. **Computer-related crime** is "any illegal act for which knowledge of computer technology is involved for its investigation, perpetration, or prosecution," whereas **computer abuse** is said to be "any incident without color of right associated with computer technology in which a victim suffered or could have suffered loss and/or a perpetrator by intention made or could have made gain."[39] Learn more about digital crime of all kinds from the Computer Crime and Intellectual Property Section (CCIPS) of the Criminal Division of the DOJ via **Web Extra 13–4**.

A Profile of Cybercriminals

In 1997, FBI agents arrested Adam Quinn Pletcher, age 21, and charged him with trying to extort $5.25 million from Microsoft founder and chairman, Bill Gates.[40] Pletcher, a loner from Illinois who spent hour after hour in front of his computer, allegedly sent several letters to Gates demanding money and threatening to kill him or his wife, Melinda, if Gates did not respond to an America Online service known as "NetGirl." The service, an online dating forum, was to serve as a secure medium for the exchange of messages between Gates and the extortionist. FBI agents nabbed Pletcher after he sent a disk to Gates that held erased files containing the names of Pletcher's parents. By all accounts, Pletcher was a hacker—a technologically sophisticated loner.

It is from hacker subculture that cybercriminals tend to come because hackers and hacker identities are the products of **cyberspace**, a realm that exists only within electronic networks where computer technology and human psychology meet. For many hackers, cyberspace provides the opportunity for impersonal interpersonal contact, technological challenges, and game playing. Fantasy role-playing games are popular among hackers and may engross many "wave riders," who appear to prefer what is called "virtual reality" to the external physical and social worlds around them: "Cyberspace is hacker heaven."[41]

No one knows the actual identity of many of these people, but computer-security experts have come up with a rough profile of the average hacker.[42] He is a male between the ages

Simon Vallor, the 22-year-old Welsh Web site designer who was sentenced to two years in prison in 2002 for creating mass-mailer computer viruses. His viruses, named Gokar, Redesi, and Admirer, infected more than 27,000 computers and spread to 42 different countries. Should those who write malicious computer code be sent to prison?
Source: Stefan Rousseau/PA Photos

of 16 and 25 who lives in the United States, is a computer user but not a programmer, and hacks with software written by others; his primary motivation is to gain access to Web sites and computer networks, not to profit financially (see the Who's to Blame box).

The History and Nature of Hacking

Some authors have suggested that computer hacking began with the creation of the interstate phone system and direct dialing, implemented by AT&T in the late 1950s.[43] Early switching devices used audible tones that were easily duplicated by electronics hobbyists, and "blue boxes" capable of emulating such tones quickly entered the illicit marketplace. A form of illegal telephone access that has come to the fore is voice-mail hacking. Private voice-mail boxes used for storing verbal messages have become the targets of corporate raiders and young vandals alike. See **Library Extra 13–4** for a discussion of self-defense in cyberspace.

WHO'S TO BLAME—The Individual or Society?

Criminal Activity or Mischievous Gaming?

Late last year, Kelvin Mutchnak was arrested and charged under federal law with interfering with the operation of computers owned by the federal government. The computers, mostly Apple Mac Pros, ran Apple's latest operating system, popularly referred to as Mac OS X Snow Leopard, and were located in Veterans Administration (VA) hospitals across the country.

Mutchnak was especially taken with the long-standing popular impression that Apple's operating system was secure and impenetrable—a myth that computer hackers had long known was untrue, but which Apple corporate officials had done little to dispel. The feeling of those who worked for Apple, Mutchnak concluded, was that the popular myth could help sell computers. Nonetheless, most hackers continued to focus their efforts on Microsoft's Windows operating system because of its greater popularity, and because it was easier to hack. Since the advent of Windows Vista in 2006, however, and with the introduction of Macintosh computers able to dual-boot both Vista and Leopard, and able to run both simultaneously, attention in the hacker community had increasingly turned to identifying backdoors into the Macintosh operating system.

Soon Mutchnak was devoting all of his spare time to dispelling Apple's myth of invincibility, and to writing malware—malicious software code—that could successfully invade almost any of Apple's higher-end computers that were connected to the Internet.

After writing a malicious script that he could insert into a tiny QuickTime video, Mutchnak sent the video as an e-mail attachment to VA hospital computers, making the e-mail look as though it contained administrative data that would be of significance to people in charge of the facilities. Although the e-mail had to be opened and the video file clicked on, and although the person reading the e-mail had to be logged in under an administrative account (most, he found, were), Mutchnak's plan was very successful, and soon most Macintosh computers in federally run hospitals across the country were infected. Unfortunately for Mutchnak, however, federal anticyberterrorism officials had been running a drill responding to a mock cyberterrorism attack when his e-mail made its way onto the Net. Within minutes of its release, Mutchnak's malicious e-mail had been traced to the IP address assigned to his home by his ISP.

A warrant for his arrest was drawn up, and Mutchnak was arrested by federal agents who charged him with violating various federal computer crime laws, including one meant to deter terrorists.

Think about it:

1. Do you believe that Mutchnak saw his activity as criminal? As terrorist activity? If not, how did he perceive it?

2. Was Mutchnak, as he claimed, doing a service by showing weaknesses in parts of the nation's computer infrastructure?

3. Might there have been other ways for Mutchnak to make his point? Would those ways have been as effective as the computer mischief in which he engaged? Why or why not?

Note: Who's to Blame boxes provide fictionalized critical thinking opportunities, and are not actual cases.

Voice-mail fraud, another form of telephone crime, involves schemes in which mailbox access codes are shared in such a way that callers to toll-free numbers can leave messages for one another in voice-mail boxes, thereby avoiding personal long-distance charges.[44] Companies that provide access to voice-mail systems through toll-free numbers often learn of the need for access-code security only after they have been victimized by such schemes.

Hackers can be distinguished both by their purpose and by their method of operation, but such categorization is descriptive; distinctions can also be made on the basis of personality and lifestyle. Some experts have suggested that hackers can be grouped according to psychological characteristics:[45]

- **Pioneers**. Individuals who are fascinated by the evolving technology of telecommunications and explore it without knowing exactly what they are going to find are called pioneers; few hard-core criminals are found among this group.

- **Scamps**. Hackers with a sense of fun, with no intention to harm, are referred to as scamps.

- **Explorers**. Explorers are hackers motivated by their delight in discoveries associated with breaking into new computer systems—the farther away geographically such systems are from the hackers' physical locations or the more secure such systems are, the greater the excitement associated with breaking into them.

- **Game players**. Game players enjoy defeating software or system copy protection and may seek to illegally access computer systems with games to play. Hacking itself becomes a game for this sort of hacker.

- **Vandals**. Malicious hackers who deliberately cause damage with no apparent gain for themselves are called vandals. The original 414 Gang in Milwaukee, which broke into the Sloan-Kettering Cancer Institute's computers and wiped out patient records, is an example of this type of hacker.

WEB EXTRA 13–5

- **Addicts**. Classic computer nerds who are addicted to hacking and to computer technology are addicts. They may also be addicted to illicit drugs (some hacker bulletin board systems post information on drugs as well as on modems, passwords, and vulnerable systems).

Psychologist Percy Black argued for the existence of an underlying theme in all cases of hacking, calling it "the search for a feeling of power, possibly stemming from a deep-seated sense of powerlessness."[46] Hacking may serve as compensation for feelings of personal inferiority; by challenging the machine and by winning against machine culture, hackers go through a kind of rite of passage into adulthood, whereby they prove themselves capable of success.

Because most hackers are young adolescent males, it is important to realize that "their other favorite risky business is the time-honored adolescent sport of trespassing. They insist on going where they don't belong. But then teen-age boys have been proceeding uninvited since the dawn of human puberty. It seems hard-wired. The only innovation is in the new form of the forbidden zone and the means of getting in it."[47]

Unfortunately, not all computer hackers are simply kids trying their hand at beating technological challenges. Many are "high-tech computer operators using computers to engage in unlawful conduct."[48] Learn more about hackers and information security at the CERT Coordination Center, which can be reached via **Web Extra 13–5**.

Many technologically sophisticated professional criminals are also operating today by using diverse types of high technology for serious criminal activity, the theft of money being one major goal. Some years ago, technologically sophisticated thieves in New York City rolled a fake automated teller machine (ATM) into the local Buckland Hills shopping mall. Although the machine did not dispense money, it did record the information contained on the magnetic strips of legitimate banking cards as well as the personal information numbers (PINs) inserted by would-be customers. Armed with the necessary codes for legitimate accounts, the thieves then fabricated their own cards and used them to withdraw thousands of dollars from real ATM machines across the city.

Most people probably think of money as dollar bills, but money today is really only information—information stored in a computer network, located within the physical confines of a bank but also as bits and bytes of data on ISP machines. Typical financial customers give little thought to the fact that very little "real" money is held by their bank, brokerage house, mutual fund, or commodities dealer, nor do they consider the threats to their financial well-being by activities like electronic theft or the sabotage of existing accounts. Unfortunately, that threat is very real. Cybercriminals who are equipped with enough information or are able to ferret out the data they need can quickly and easily send vast amounts of money anywhere in the world. Although billions of dollars' worth of electronic transactions occur every day, no reliable estimates exist on the losses suffered in such transactions due to the activities of technologically adept criminal perpetrators because sophisticated high-tech thieves are so effective at eluding apprehension and even detection that reliable loss figures are impossible to ascertain.

Web sites can also facilitate criminal activity. U.S. Customs Service agents involved in Operation Longarm carried out raids on child pornographers and suspected pedophiles in 18 states using names taken from a pedophile site. According to the Customs Service, the computerized transmission of illegal pornography among pedophiles is rapidly becoming more popular than smutty magazines.[49] On June 18, 2007, British police, aided by U.S. investigators, arrested 200 suspects in an Internet pornography ring that streamed live video of children being sexually abused. The ring involved more than 700 suspects worldwide, and authorities in 35 countries participated in the investigation; 31 children were rescued as a result of the operation, some of them only a few months old.[50]

> Money today is really only information stored in a computer network as bits and bytes of data.

Cybercrime as a Form of White-Collar Crime

A number of analysts have suggested that cybercrime is merely a new form of white-collar crime or maybe its ultimate expression (white-collar crime is discussed in detail in Chapter 11). Donn B. Parker, author of the National Institute of Justice (NIJ) *Computer Crime: Criminal Justice Research Manual*, compared white-collar criminals with computer criminals, stating that both share certain "common criminal behavior-related issues":[51]

- Both types of acts are often committed through nonviolent means, although certain industrial-, consumer-, and environment-related crimes have life-threatening consequences.

- Access to computers or computer storage media, through employment-related knowledge or technical skills, is often needed.

- These acts generally involve information manipulations that either directly or indirectly create profits or losses.

■ **identity theft**
The unauthorized use of another individual's personal information to commit fraud.

- These crimes can be committed by an individual, by several individuals working in collusion, or by organizations, with the victims in the last case ranging from individual clients to customers to employees in other organizations.

See the Criminal Profiles box for the story of a convicted hacker who became an author.

According to Parker, cybercrime and white-collar crime also share the following similarities:

- These crimes are difficult to detect, with discovery often started by accident or by customer complaint rather than as the result of direct investigation.

- The general public views many of these acts as less serious than crimes involving physical violence.

- These crimes cost individuals, organizations, and society large amounts of money and other resources.

- Prevention of these crimes requires a combination of legal, technical, managerial, security, and audit-monitoring controls.

Identity Theft

Identity theft—the misuse of another individual's personal information to commit fraud—is a special kind of larceny that often makes headlines and that appears to be rapidly growing in both scope and frequency.[52] It involves obtaining credit, merchandise, or services by fraudulent personal representation.

The DOJ notes that "the advent of information technology and computer literacy has joined with the accessibility of personal information to produce a rapid increase in identity theft as the method of choice for criminals."[53] The DOJ also says that the lack of severe consequences and the inconsistencies in investigation and in prosecution have all added to the value of identity theft for offenders. Individuals often learn that they are victims of identity theft only after they are denied credit or employment or when a debt collector seeking payment for a debt they did not incur contacts them. One of the most threatening aspects of identity theft is its potential relationship to international terrorism, and even where terrorism is not involved, identity theft could be used by transnational crime rings.

The misuse of stolen personal information can be classified into two broad categories: existing account fraud and new account fraud. *Existing account fraud* occurs when thieves obtain account information involving credit, brokerage, banking, or utility accounts that are already open; it is typically less costly but more prevalent. A stolen credit card may lead to thousands of dollars in fraudulent charges, but the card generally will not provide a thief with enough information to establish a false identity. Moreover, most credit-card companies do not hold consumers liable for fraudulent charges, and federal law caps liability of victims of credit-card theft at $50.

In *new account fraud*, identity thieves use personal information, such as a Social Security number, birth date, and home address, to open new accounts in the victim's name, make charges indiscriminately, and then disappear. While this type of identity theft is less likely to occur, it imposes much greater costs and hardships on the victim. In addition, identity thieves sometimes use stolen personal information to obtain government, medical, or other benefits to which the criminal is not legally entitled.

In addition to the losses that result when identity thieves misuse existing accounts or fraudulently open new accounts, monetary costs of identity theft include indirect costs to businesses for fraud prevention and for mitigation of any harm (for example, mailing notices to consumers and upgrading systems). Individual victims often suffer indirect financial costs, such as paying the costs incurred in civil litigation initiated by creditors and overcoming the many obstacles they face in obtaining or retaining credit. Victims of nonfinancial identity theft such as health-care-related or criminal-record fraud, face other types of harm and frustration.

Consumers' fears of becoming victims of identity theft can also harm the digital economy. In a 2006 online survey conducted by the Business Software Alliance and Harris Interactive, nearly 30% of adults interviewed said that security fears caused them to shop online less or not at all during the 2005–2006 holiday season.[54] A Cyber Security Industry Alliance survey found that 48% of consumers avoided making purchases on the Internet because they feared that their financial information might be stolen.[55]

> Consumers' fears of becoming victims of identity theft can harm the digital economy.

Identity theft became a federal crime in 1998 with the passage of the Identity Theft and Assumption Deterrence Act, which made it a crime whenever anyone "knowingly transfers or uses, without lawful authority, a means of identification of another person with the intent to commit, or to aid or abet, any unlawful activity that constitutes a violation of federal law, or that constitutes a felony under any applicable state or local law."[56]

The 2004 Identity Theft Penalty Enhancement Act added two years to federal prison sentences for criminals convicted of using stolen credit-card numbers and other personal data to commit crimes.[57] It also prescribed prison sentences for those who use identity theft to commit other crimes, including terrorism, and increased penalties for defendants who exceed or abuse the authority of their position to unlawfully obtain or misuse means of personal identification.

CRIMINAL | PROFILES

Kevin Mitnick

At the time of his arrest in February 1995, Kevin Mitnick was the most wanted computer criminal in U.S. history. His crimes included wire fraud, computer fraud, and wire communication interception, and the cost to his victims included millions of dollars in lost licensing fees, marketing delays, lost research and development, and the costs of repairing compromised computer systems.[i]

Cloned cellular telephones, hacker software programs, "sniffer" devices, and so-called social engineering were the tools Mitnick used to conduct the computer crime spree that launched a lengthy investigation beginning in 1992. The evidence amassed by the FBI during its three-year probe was sufficient to force Mitnick to accept a plea bargain rather than risk more severe penalties by going to trial.[ii] His corporate victims included a number of Fortune 500 companies, and he used University of Southern California computer systems to hide software code and obscure his identity.

Born August 6, 1963, and a product of a blue-collar upbringing in California's San Fernando Valley, Mitnick's 1981 juvenile arrest for stealing computer manuals led to his being placed on probation. The experience had little deterrent effect, however, as evidenced by his subsequent arrests in 1989 (for possession of unauthorized access devices) and in 1992 (for allegedly hacking into California Department of Motor Vehicles computers).[iii]

It is said that Mitnick served as the inspiration for the 1983 film *War Games* by breaking into the U.S. Department of Defense's North American Defense Command (NORAD) computers in 1982.[iv]

An intriguing element of Mitnick's case was the manner in which he was finally caught. Computer expert Tsutomu Shimomura, infuriated after Mitnick hacked into and stole information from his home computer, employed a dramatic cybersleuthing effort to track Mitnick down, resulting in Mitnick's arrest by the FBI in a Raleigh, North Carolina, apartment complex.

As a result of his 1995 arrest, Mitnick spent more than five years in prison, with more than eight months of it in solitary confinement. Now in his early forties, a significantly matured Mitnick has done a 180-degree turnaround in his approach to computer security. On March 1, 2000, he testified before the U.S. Senate's Governmental Affairs Committee, during which he suggested that the millions of dollars corporations spend on firewalls and secure access devices are negated by the "the weakest link in the security chain: the people who

Hacker-turned-author Kevin Mitnick posing for a portrait in 2002 in Las Vegas. Barred by the terms of his probation from using computers, ex-convict Mitnick turned to writing about them, baring the tricks of his former trade of hacking in a book titled *The Art of Deception.* Mitnick was granted an exemption to use a computer to write his book. What is he doing today?
Source: Joe Cavaretta/AP Wide World Photos

use, administer and operate computer systems."[v] Mitnick regaled the committee with tales of his use of "social engineering" (what he defines as "using manipulation, influence, and deception to get a trusted insider to release information and to perform some sort of action item") that enables a hacker to successfully attack the insider's own computer system.

Mitnick now heads up a highly successful computer consulting firm which specializes in advising on computer security issues. He suggests that it is easier to hack today than it was years ago, citing social engineering as still an extraordinarily effective technique for computer exploit. Mitnick's message is clear: Notwithstanding tremendous advances in both hardware and software security measures, the weak link is still the human element.[vi]

Notes

i. "Kevin Mitnick Sentenced to Nearly Four Years in Prison," U.S. Department of Justice Press Release, August 9, 1999; and "Computer Hacker Ordered to Pay Restitution to Victim Companies Whose Systems Were Compromised," U.S. Attorney's Office, Central District of California, August 9, 1999, http://www.cybercrime.gov/mitnick.htm (accessed June 2, 2010).

ii. Ibid.

iii. John Christensen, "The Trials of Kevin Mitnick," CNN, March 18, 1999, http://www.cnn.com/SPECIALS/1999/mitnick.background (accessed June 2, 2010).

iv. Ibid.

v. Elizabeth Wasserman, "Mitnick Schools Feds on Hacking 101," CNN, March 3, 2000, http://archives.cnn.com/2000/TECH/computing/03/03/mitnick.the.prof/mitnick.the.prof.html (accessed June 2, 2007).

vi. "A Convicted Hacker Debunks Some Myths," CNN, October 13, 2005, http://www.cnn.com/2005/TECH/internet/10/07/kevin.mitnick.cnna (accessed June 2, 2010).

LIBRARY EXTRA 13–5
LIBRARY EXTRA 13–6

The Incidence of Identity Theft

In 2007, the Bureau of Justice Statistics (BJS) reported its second statistical overview of identity theft in information derived from the National Crime Victimization Survey (NCVS).[58] For statistical-reporting purposes, BJS defined *identity theft* to include the following three behaviors: (1) the unauthorized use or attempted use of existing credit cards; (2) the unauthorized use or attempted use of other existing accounts such as checking accounts; and (3) the misuse of personal information to obtain new accounts or loans or to commit other crimes.

BJS surveyors found that at least one member of 5.5% of all households had been the victim of identity theft during the previous year, and the most common type of identity theft uncovered was the unauthorized use of credit cards, experienced by 2.96 million households in the 12-month period covered by the survey. About 1.6 million households reported being victimized by the theft of an existing account other than a credit-card account, such as the use or attempted use of a cell phone account, bank account, or debit/check card account without permission. Approximately 1 million households were victimized by the use of personal information to obtain new credit cards or loans, run up debts, open other accounts, or otherwise commit theft, fraud, or some other crime; the identity theft experienced by more than 790,000 households encompassed two or more types of thefts.

The BJS survey also revealed that about one in six victimized households had to pay higher interest rates as the result of identity theft, and one in nine households was denied phone or utility service as a consequence of being victimized. About 7% of victimized households were turned down for insurance or had to pay higher rates, 5% became the subject of a civil suit or judgment, 4% became the subject of a criminal investigation, and about 20% reported other kinds of problems.

> At least one member of 5.5% of all households has been the victim of identity theft during the previous year.

Among households sustaining a loss whose amount was known, about 5% reported losing more than $5,000, but 66% reported losing less than $500; the average amount of money involved in any type of identity theft in which there was a loss was put at $1,620. For households experiencing misuse of personal information, the average loss was $4,850, and it was $2,460 for households experiencing multiple types of theft at the same time. Learn more about identity theft from the Bureau of Justice Assistance at **Library Extra 13–5**.

Who Are Identity Thieves?

Unlike some groups of criminals, identity thieves cannot be readily classified because victims are not usually in a position to know who stole or misused their information.[59] Based on the Federal Trade Commission (FTC) survey of identity theft, only 14% of victims claim to know the perpetrator, who may be a family member, friend, or in-home employee. Identity thieves can act alone or as part of a criminal enterprise, and each poses unique threats to the public.

According to law enforcement agencies, identity thieves often have no prior criminal background and sometimes have preexisting relationships with the victims. Identity thieves have been known to prey on people they know, including coworkers, senior citizens for whom they are serving as caretakers, and even family members. Some identity thieves rely on unsophisticated techniques, such as stealing mail from homeowners' mailboxes or taking trash containing financial documents, and in some jurisdictions, identity theft by illegal immigrants has resulted in passport, employment, and Social Security fraud. Occasionally, small clusters of individuals with no significant criminal records work together in a loosely knit fashion to obtain personal information and even to create false or fraudulent documents.[60]

Law enforcement agencies around the country have observed a steady increase in the involvement of groups and organizations of repeat offenders or career criminals in identity theft. Some of these groups—including national gangs such as the Hell's Angels and MS-13—are formally organized, have a hierarchical structure, and are well known to law enforcement because of their long-standing involvement in other major crimes such as drug trafficking. Other groups are more loosely organized but have taken advantage of the Internet to contact each other and then organize and coordinate their identity thefts more efficiently; members of these groups often are located in different countries and communicate primarily via the Internet. Some groups have a real-world connection with one another and share a nationality or ethnic group.

What Can Be Done about Identity Theft?

In 2006, the federal Office of Community Oriented Policing Services (the COPS Office), in conjunction with the Major Cities Chiefs Association (MCCA), released a report titled *A National Strategy to Combat Identity Theft*, which is available as **Library Extra 13–6**. It recognized identity theft as a pervasive crime that requires cooperation among law enforcement agencies, the federal and state governments, and citizens in order to

WEB EXTRA 13-6
LIBRARY EXTRA 13-7
LIBRARY EXTRA 13-8
LIBRARY EXTRA 13-9

develop a comprehensive and effective response and suggested six components of an effective national strategy for preventing and responding to the crime of identity theft:

1. **Public-awareness campaigns**. Public education has proven highly successful in the past to curtail national levels of alcohol and cigarette use.

2. **Victim assistance**. Frequently, victimization focuses on dollar loss and dismisses the emotional trauma or time needed to restore records and identity.

3. **Partnership and collaboration**. A staple for police departments, private industry, and others following the September 11 terrorist attacks, collaboration is also vital to the issue of identity theft. Many permutations and combinations are available when one considers the different functions within a jurisdiction—a single function across jurisdictions, such as a statewide or regional collaboration, or multiple functions across several jurisdictions.

4. **Legislation**. Legislative action is needed for several reasons: Private industry may not be willing to enact certain protections without a federal government mandate, or local police agencies may overlook the significance of taking identity theft reports, no matter how minor, to feed into a larger data bank for analysis.

5. **Information protection**. Protecting information is critical, and those combating identity theft should be as imaginative as needed.

6. **Training**. There was no doubt throughout the project that training is paramount, especially for police officers, investigators, and prosecutors.

On May 10, 2006, President George W. Bush established the President's Task Force on Identity Theft via Executive Order 13402. In forming the task force, the president called for a coordinated approach among government agencies to combat identity theft and to craft a strategic plan to make the federal government's efforts regarding identity theft more effective and efficient in the areas of awareness, prevention, detection, and prosecution. The task force, chaired by (then) Attorney General Alberto R. Gonzales and cochaired by FTC Chairman Deborah Platt Majoras, released its report in mid-2007 that said, "Identity theft depends on access to consumer data. Reducing the opportunities for thieves to get the data is critical to fighting the crime. Government, the business community, and consumers have roles to play in protecting data."[61] The task force made a number of recommendations to combat identity theft:

- Decrease the unnecessary use of Social Security numbers in the public sector by developing alternative strategies for identity management.

- Establish national standards to require private-sector entities to safeguard the personal data they compile and maintain and to provide notice to consumers when a breach occurs that poses a significant risk of identity theft.

- Have federal agencies implement a broad, sustained awareness campaign to educate consumers, the private sector, and the public sector on deterring, detecting, and defending against identity theft.

- Create a National Identity Theft Law Enforcement Center to allow law enforcement agencies to coordinate their efforts and information more efficiently and to investigate and prosecute identity thieves more effectively.

- Ensure that government agencies work together to provide victims with the knowledge, tools, and assistance needed to minimize the damage and begin the recovery process.

- Provide specialized training about victim recovery to first responders and others offering direct assistance to victims of identity theft.

- Create and distribute an ID Theft Victim Statement of Rights.

- Amend criminal restitution statutes to ensure that victims recover the value of time spent in trying to remediate the harms suffered.

- Assess whether to implement a national system that allows victims to obtain an identification document for authentication purposes.

Learn more about identity thieves and how they operate via the Identity Theft Resource Center at **Web Extra 13–6**, and read about how to prevent your own victimization and what to do if your identity is stolen via **Library Extras 13–7, 13–8**, and **13–9**.

Technology in the Fight against Crime

Technology is a double-edged sword: It arms evildoers with potent new weapons of crime commission, yet it provides police agencies and criminal justice personnel with powerful tools useful in the battle against crime. Criminally useful or evasive technologies and law enforcement capabilities commonly leapfrog one another. Consider traffic radar, which has gone from early always-on units through trigger-operated radar devices to today's sophisticated laser-based speed-measuring apparatus—each change being an attempt by enforcement agencies to keep a step ahead of increasingly sophisticated radar-detection devices marketed to drivers.

■ **DNA profiling**
The use of biological residue found at a crime scene for genetic comparisons in aiding the identification of criminal suspects.

Although cutting-edge laser units are invisible to most radar detectors, laser radar detectors *do* exist; their usefulness is open to debate because they generally alert the speeding driver too late. Radar-jamming devices and laser jammers are also now used by people apparently intent on breaking speed-limit laws. Not to be outdone, suppliers to law enforcement agencies have created radar-detector detectors, which are used by authorities in states where radar detectors have been outlawed.[62]

Other potent technologies in law enforcement today are computer databases of known offenders (including public access to sex-offender databases), machine-based expert systems, cellular communications, video surveillance (often combined with face-recognition technology), electronic eavesdropping, deoxyribonucleic acid (DNA) analysis, and less-lethal weapons.

Criminal technologies and law enforcement capabilities leapfrog one another.

Transponder-based automated vehicle location (AVL) systems now use patrol car–based transmitters in tandem with orbiting global positioning satellites (GPS) to pinpoint locations of police vehicles to within 50 feet so that dispatchers can better allocate available resources on a given shift and be able to substantially reduce police response times in crisis situations. (Chip-based transponders are also installed in private vehicles to deter thieves and to help trace stolen automobiles.)

In jurisdictions with computer-aided dispatch (CAD) systems, police dispatchers are prompted by computers for important information that allows them to distinguish a location (such as a particular McDonald's). CAD systems also quickly provide information about how often officers have been called to a given site and can tell responding officers what they might expect to find based on past calls from that location.

More innovative crime-fighting technologies are becoming available. The "Spiderman snare," being tested for its usefulness in incapacitating fleeing suspects, is a 16-foot-wide net that is compressed into a small shotgun-like shell. The net has small weights at its circumference and wraps itself around its target after being fired. The snare's impact is harmless, and test subjects report being able to watch with open eyes as the net wraps around them. A special-frequency disco-like strobe light quickly disorients human targets by causing intense dizziness, leaving subjects unable to resist cuffing and arrest (operators wear special glasses designed to counter the influence of the light). Because high-speed chases pose a substantial danger to the public, scientists have developed an electromagnetic pulsing device that can be used to temporarily disable a vehicle's electrical system, causing the engine to stall.

The prototype is said to be safe enough to use on vehicles driven by those wearing pacemakers.

As new technologies are developed, their potential usefulness in law enforcement activities is evaluated by the FBI, the NIJ, and other agencies. NIJ's Technology Assessment Program (TAP) focuses on four areas of advancing technology: protective equipment, such as bullet-proof vests and other body armor; forensic sciences, including advances in DNA technology; transportation and weapons, such as electronic stun guns and other less-lethal weapons; and communications and electronics, including computer security and electronic eavesdropping. Other groups, such as the National Computer Security Association, the American Cryptography Association, and the American Society for Industrial Security, bring more specialized high-tech expertise to the private-security and public law enforcement professions.

DNA Technology

On January 16, 2001, Christopher Ochoa, age 34, was released from a Texas prison after serving 13 years for a murder he did not commit.[63] Ochoa had confessed to the rape and murder of 20-year-old Nancy DePriest at a Pizza Hut in Austin in 1988; although Ochoa later said he had been coerced by homicide detectives into confessing, no one believed him. A decade after he began serving a life sentence, law students at the Wisconsin Innocence Project at the University of Wisconsin–Madison took an interest in his case, studied surviving information, and concluded that DNA evidence conclusively proved that someone else had killed DePriest. The students and their law professor took the evidence to District Judge Bob Perkins, who called the case "a fundamental miscarriage of justice" and ordered Ochoa set free. According to authorities, evidence of DePriest's murder now points to Texas inmate Achim Joseph Marino, who confessed to her murder in 1996 following a religious conversion. Marino, currently serving three life sentences for other crimes, has provided investigators with the gun and handcuffs used to commit the crime. The law students involved in the case used **DNA profiling**, matching DNA samples taken from mouth swabs of Marino with the DNA found in semen taken from the victim's body. Without DNA profiling, Ochoa would still be in prison, and DePriest's real killer would be unknown.

A person's genetic code is contained in his or her DNA, whose composition is unique to each individual (except in the case of identical twins). DNA samples can be taken from blood, hair, semen, saliva, or even small flakes of skin left at the scene of a crime. After processing, DNA profiles appear like bar codes on film negatives, codes that can exonerate a suspect or provide nearly irrefutable evidence of guilt.

■ **_Daubert_ standard**
A test of scientific acceptability applicable to the gathering of evidence in criminal cases.

DNA evidence is long lasting—fossilized DNA is now being used to reconstruct genetic maps of long-extinct plant and animal species. Although DNA analysis is theoretically possible using only a single cell, most reputable DNA laboratories require a considerably greater quantity of material to conduct an effective analysis, but that could change. Using a Nobel Prize–winning technique called "polymerase chain-reaction technology," minute strands of DNA can be effectively amplified so that even the identity of a person taking a single puff from a cigarette can be accurately established. Although the cost and complexity are prohibitive, these technological advances are expected to be available to a range of forensic analysts.

The National Research Council called DNA profiling "a highly reliable forensic tool" but admits that it is not infallible.[64] Obvious differences in scrutinized DNA samples can easily eliminate a suspect, but testing provides less certainty with positive identification, with human error in conducting the tests being perhaps the greatest threat to reliable results. At least 20 states and the federal government generally accept DNA evidence in criminal trials. Other jurisdictions, including California, are less clear in their recognition of DNA testing, and trial judges in those states may offhandedly exclude the use of such evidence when experts disagree as to its validity.

In 1993, the U.S. Supreme Court, in the civil case of **_Daubert_ v. _Merrell Dow Pharmaceuticals, Inc._**, revised the criteria for the admissibility of scientific evidence;[65] the ruling rejected the previous admissibility standard established in the 1923 case of **_Frye_ v. _United States_**.[66] The _Daubert_ Court ruled that the older _Frye_ standard, requiring "general acceptance" of a test or procedure by the relevant scientific community, "is not a necessary precondition to the admissibility of scientific evidence," which is established by Rule 402 of the _Federal Rules of Evidence_, published after _Frye_ and superseding it. Rule 402 says that "all relevant evidence is admissible [in a trial], except as otherwise provided by the Constitution of the United States, by Act of Congress, by these Rules, or by other rules prescribed by the Supreme Court pursuant to statutory authority."[67] The Court said that although "the _Frye_ test was displaced by the Rules of Evidence, [it] does not mean that the Rules themselves place no limits on the admissibility of purportedly scientific evidence. Nor is the trial judge disabled from screening such evidence. To the contrary, under the Rules the trial judge must ensure that any and all scientific testimony or evidence admitted is not only relevant, but reliable." The real test for the admissibility of scientific expert testimony is for the trial judge to decide "at the outset whether the expert is proposing to testify to (1) scientific knowledge that (2) will assist the trier of fact to understand or determine a fact in issue." The Court

concluded that the trial judge's task is one of "ensuring that an expert's testimony both rests on a reliable foundation and is relevant to the task at hand. Pertinent evidence based on scientifically valid principles will satisfy those demands."

The plaintiffs in _Daubert_ were not arguing the merits of DNA testing but were claiming that the drug Bendectin caused birth defects, but the **_Daubert_ standard** eased the criteria for the introduction of scientific evidence at both civil and criminal trials—and effectively cleared the way for the use of DNA evidence in the courtroom.[68] The _Daubert_ Court found that the following factors may be used to determine whether a form of scientific evidence is reliable:

- It has been subjected to testing.
- It has been subjected to peer review.
- It has known or potential rates of error.
- It has standards controlling application of the techniques involved.

One observer, discussing the quality of DNA identification methods, noted, "The challenges today are no longer technical; instead they lie in taking the technology and building a meaningful legal infrastructure around it."[69] As DNA evidence is accepted throughout jurisdictions nationwide and worldwide, digitized forensic DNA databases (similar to widely used fingerprint archives) are useful at the state and national levels, and a number of states and the federal government (through the FBI laboratory) already have them. In 1998 the FBI announced that its National DNA Index System (NDIS)—which enables U.S. forensic laboratories to exchange and compare DNA profiles electronically, thereby linking unsolved serial violent crimes to each other and to known offenders—had begun operation.[70] By June 1998, all 50 states had passed legislation requiring convicted offenders to provide samples for DNA databases, and all states have been invited to participate in NDIS. The federal DNA Identification Act of 1994 authorized the FBI to establish DNA indexes for (1) offenders convicted of crimes, (2) samples recovered from crime scenes, and (3) samples recovered from unidentified human remains.[71] There is the potential for coordination between the federally funded multibillion-dollar Human Genome Project and forensic DNA programs, which could lead to explosive growth in the use of DNA in criminal case processing.

In 1995 the British police, operating under a new nationwide crime bill, became the first national police force in the world to begin routine collection of DNA samples from anyone involved in a "recordable" offense (a serious crime).[72] It appears that genetic profiling will become one of the most significant crime-fighting

LIBRARY EXTRA 13–10
LIBRARY EXTRA 13–11

technologies of the twenty-first century. "Genetic profiling—the use of biotechnology to identify the unique characteristics of an individual's DNA—is about to become as prevalent as the Breathalyzer and more important than the fingerprint."[73]

In 1996, the NIJ released a comprehensive report, titled *Convicted by Juries, Exonerated by Science*, on the applicability of DNA testing to criminal case processing, calling DNA testing "the most important technological breakthrough of twentieth-century forensic science" and providing a detailed review of 28 cases in which postconviction DNA evidence exonerated defendants who had been sentenced to lengthy prison terms.[74] The 28 cases were selected on the basis of a detailed examination of records that indicated the convicted defendants might have actually been innocent. The men in the study had served, on average, seven years in prison, and most had been tried and sentenced prior to the widespread availability of reliable DNA testing. "Momentum is growing, spurred in part by the public's education from the Simpson trial, for DNA testing in criminal cases. Juries may begin to question cases where the prosecutor does not offer 'conclusive' DNA test results if the evidence is available for testing. More defense attorneys in court-appointed cases may file motions for DNA testing and request the State to pay for the tests."[75] Learn more about the science behind forensic DNA testing and how it has been used to convict as well as exonerate criminal defendants at **Library Extra 13–10**. An assessment of its likely future is available as **Library Extra 13–11**.

> Genetic profiling will become one of the most significant crime-fighting technologies of the twenty-first century.

Computers as Crime-Fighting Tools

The widespread use of computers and computer applications in a diversity of professions has been one of the most far-reaching social phenomena of recent years. Computers assist in the design of new technologies and aid in the assignment of resources to problem areas: Police departments, prisons, and courts now employ computer software to schedule facilities and personnel; to keep track of defendants, witnesses, and cases; and to keep account of budgetary matters.

Computers also connect people. The Internet contains a large number of law enforcement–oriented blogs and discussion groups and provides access to United Nations and worldwide crime data through its link to the United Nations Criminal Justice Information Network (uncjin.org). Other computer services offer access to security information and to software useful in law enforcement administration. Specialized Web sites, such as the Society of Police Futurists International's home page (policefuturists.org), the International Association of Chiefs of Police site (theiacp.org), and the SEARCH Group (search.org), link law enforcement professionals and criminologists throughout the country.

Other innovative computer technologies—the automated fingerprint identification system (AFIS) with interstate and international links, a computerized crime-scene simulation and reenactment, expert systems, and online clearinghouses with data on criminal activity and offenders—facilitate the work of law enforcement agents. AFIS allows investigators to match a suspect's fingerprints against stored records in a matter of minutes (instead of weeks or months) because its computers are able to compare and eliminate many thousands of fingerprints per second, sometimes leading to the identification of a suspect in a short time. "Live-scan" technology permits easy inkless digitizing of fingerprints from suspects, and the Bureau of Alcohol, Tobacco, and Firearms has new software that takes a 360-degree picture of a bullet's ballistic characteristics and then compares them with others stored in a database to isolate a small universe of potential matches.

Once crime-related information or profiles of criminal offenders have been generated, they are typically stored in a database and made accessible to law enforcement agencies at other sites. Some widely used online criminal information services include the FBI's National Crime Information Center, the Violent Criminal Apprehension Program, and the Police Executive Research Forum's information-sharing network called METAPOL. Other specialized database programs now track inner-city gang activity and gang membership, contain information on known sexual predators, and describe missing children.

PC radios, combinations of laptop computers and police radios, provide another high-tech weapon in the "war on crime." These devices were initially tested by the Baltimore (Maryland) Police Department, and mobile data terminals placed in police cars are proving useful in the apprehension of both traffic violators and more serious offenders. Officers use PC radios to (1) obtain motor vehicle information, (2) get detailed information when answering a call, and (3) report incidents either by saving

■ **expert system**
A system of computer hardware and software that attempts to duplicate the decision-making processes used by skilled investigators in the analysis of evidence and in the recognition of patterns that such evidence might represent.

■ **data encryption**
The process by which information is encoded, making it unreadable to all but its intended recipients.

■ **threat analysis**
A thorough assessment of the perils facing an organization.

■ **audit trail**
A record of computer activities that enables auditors to reconstruct and review the sequence of activities surrounding each event in one or more related transactions from inception to output of final results back to inception.

data on disk or by transmitting them to other locations such as police headquarters. PC radios have also helped mislead drug dealers, who routinely use police scanners to keep abreast of enforcement activities, because the digitized transmissions consist of machine code that cannot be easily read by drug dealers or other criminals trying to outguess the police.

Expert systems deploy machine-based artificial intelligence to duplicate decision-making processes used by skilled investigators in the analysis of evidence and in the recognition of patterns that such evidence might represent to draw conclusions and make recommendations to police investigators and others interested in solving problems related to crime and its commission. One system being used by the FBI's National Center for the Analysis of Violent Crime (NCAVC) attempts to profile serial killers by matching clues left at a crime scene with individual personality characteristics. While the NCAVC system is becoming increasingly sophisticated, it has not yet replaced human investigators. "There is certainly no possibility that the system we are devising will ever replace skilled human profilers. Rather, the system will function as a profiler's assistant or consultant."[76] A number of other specialized computer programs, such as ImAger (by Face Software, Inc.) and Compusketch (by Visatex Corporation), assist police artists in rendering composite images of suspects and missing victims.

Combating Cybercrime

In 1982, sales of information security software products to private companies and government agencies totaled only $51 million; by 1997, expenditures exceeded $425 million; and by 2003, they had grown to $1.17 billion.[77] Research conducted by Infonetics Research indicated that worldwide network-security appliance and software sales reached more than $4.5 billion in 2006 and surpassed $5.6 billion in 2009.[78] Among the products are **data encryption** (the process of encoding information so that it is unreadable to all but its intended recipients), keylog detectors, and Web servers supporting major security protocols.

Software alone is not enough—any effective program intended to secure an organization's operation against the threat of high-tech crime must be built on a realistic **threat analysis** (also called *risk analysis*) involving a thorough assessment of the perils facing the organization. Some risks, such as floods, tornadoes, hurricanes, and earthquakes, arise from natural events and

are often unpredictable. Others, including fires, electrical outages, and disruptions in public services, may be of human origin but are equally difficult to presage. Theft, employee sabotage, and terrorist attacks constitute yet another category of risk—those brought about by intentional human intervention. Responses to unpredictable threats can nonetheless be planned, and strategies for dealing with almost any kind of risk can be implemented. Unless an organization adequately assesses the threats to its continuing operation, it will be unable to formulate a plan to deal effectively with such risks, so threat analysis is a must for organizations preparing to meet the many diverse challenges of today's world.

Once specific threats are identified, strategies tailored to dealing with them can be introduced. One powerful tool useful in identifying instances of computer crime is the **audit trail**, "a sequential record of system activities that enables auditors to reconstruct, review, and examine the sequence of states and activities surrounding each event in one or more related transactions from inception to output of final results back to inception."[79] Audit trails, which are recorded in computer memory, trace and record the activities of computer operators and facilitate the apprehension of cybercriminals.

Although most large companies and financial institutions have fairly extensive computer-security programs, few small businesses, schools, hospitals, and individuals have any real understanding of their need for computer security. "What is surprising about computer crime," explained computer-security expert Kenneth Rosenblatt, "is how little is being done to deter it: Industry will not beef up security, the police are not equipped to catch electronic thieves, and judges do not hand down the kind of sentences that will impress would-be computer criminals. New strategies are urgently needed."[80]

Police Investigations of Cybercrime and Cybercriminals

In the past, few police departments had either the time or the qualified personnel to effectively investigate crimes committed by cybercriminals, even with new laws for backup. When it comes to cybercrime investigations, one technology expert concluded, "Police departments are simply unsuited to the task."[81] Although specialized cybercrime units have been created in some jurisdictions, they are often poorly funded and seriously understaffed.

WEB EXTRA 13-7
LIBRARY EXTRA 13-12

■ **DCS–3000**
An FBI-developed network diagnostic tool that is capable of assisting in criminal investigations by monitoring and capturing large amounts of Internet traffic. It was originally called *Carnivore.*

Most state and local police departments do not have personnel skilled in the investigation of cybercrimes, most officers know little about tracing the activities of cybercriminals, and some police investigators find it difficult to understand how a crime can actually have occurred when nothing at the scene appears to be missing or damaged. Police departments also sometimes intentionally avoid cybercrime investigations because they can be complex and demanding, thinking that the amount of time and money spent on cybercrime investigations could better be spent elsewhere. Cybercrime investigations can also cross state lines, involving a number of telecommunications companies and other services. Additionally, investigators who spend a lot of time on cybercrimes tend to not be promoted as readily as those in homicide and property-crime divisions, and personnel who are truly skilled in computer applications are apt to take jobs with private industries where pay scales are far higher than in police work. As a consequence, many police departments and their investigators frequently accord cybercrime a low priority, focusing instead on highly visible offenses, such as murder and rape, and seeing cybercrime victims as too wealthy to be seriously affected by the crimes they experience.

But the situation has been changing, thanks to federal intervention. In 1992, the FBI formed a National Computer Crime Squad (NCCS);[82] its job was to investigate violations of the federal Computer Fraud and Abuse Act of 1984 and other federal cybercrime laws.[83] Most of the FBI's larger offices established their own cybercrime squads to conduct high-tech investigations in the areas they served. Prior to the creation of the Department of Homeland Security (DHS), the FBI's Washington Field Office housed the agency's Infrastructure Protection and Computer Intrusion Squad (IPCIS), which was responsible for investigating unauthorized intrusions into major computer networks belonging to telecommunications providers, private corporations, U.S. government agencies, and public and private educational facilities;[84] the squad, whose duties have now been transferred to DHS, also investigated the illegal interception of signals (especially cable and satellite signal theft) and the infringement of copyright laws related to software.

The Computer Crime and Intellectual Property Section (CCIPS) began in 1991 as the DOJ's Computer Crime Unit. The CCIPS staff consisted of about two dozen lawyers focusing exclusively on the issues raised by cybercrime and intellectual-property crime. They worked closely on cybercrime cases with assistant U.S. attorneys known as "computer and telecommunications coordinators" in U.S. attorney's offices around the country.[85] CCIPS attorneys have taken a leading role in litigating some cybercrime and intellectual-property investigations and

> **Police departments sometimes intentionally avoid cybercrime investigations because they can be complex and demanding.**

a coordinating role in some national investigations, and U.S. assistant attorneys have advised federal prosecutors and law enforcement agents, commented on and proposed legislation, coordinated international efforts to combat cybercrime, litigated cases, and trained federal law enforcement groups. One of the first large-scale federal cybercrime operations took place in 1997 when FBI agents raided the homes and offices of about a dozen Web masters suspected of pirating software in eight cities across the country. The operation, code-named Cyber Strike, resulted from NCCS monitoring of Internet chat channels and file transfers over the Internet.[86] Visit CCIPS via **Web Extra 13–7.**

Automated monitoring of network traffic is an area of considerable interest to law enforcement officials. One network "sniffer" created by the FBI called DCS–1000 (previously known as "Carnivore") was a diagnostic tool intended to assist in criminal investigations by monitoring and capturing large amounts of Internet traffic. DCS–1000 was installed by FBI agents in ISP data centers as the need arose to monitor the electronic communications of individuals suspected of federal crimes like terrorism. The Carnivore/DCS–1000 initiative was later renamed **DCS–3000** and changed its focus to intercepting suspect personal communications services delivered via wireless services. Learn more about the challenges facing American law enforcement agencies when it comes to cybercrime and Internet-related crime by reading **Library Extra 13–12.**

While any effective policy for dealing with cybercrime and high-tech crime must recognize the issues associated with personal freedoms and individual rights in the information age, a second aspect of effective policy necessarily relates to crime control: How can high-tech criminals be deterred? If they succeed in committing criminal acts, how can they be reformed? Kenneth Rosenblatt, who focused on cybercrimes during his work as a California district attorney, suggested three effective sanctions to deter high-tech offenders:[87] confiscating equipment used to commit cybercrimes, limiting the offender's use of computers, and restricting the offender's freedom to accept jobs involving computers. Such penalties could be supplemented by a few days or weeks in a county jail, with longer periods of incarceration applicable in serious cases. "In my experience, one of the best ways to hurt computer offenders, especially young hackers, is to take away their toys."[88]

■ Internet
The world's largest computer network for moving data and making information accessible.

WEB EXTRA 13–8

Cybercrime and Internet Security

America is a service-oriented, information-rich society. John Naisbitt, author of *Megatrends*, explained it this way: "The transition from an industrial to an information society does not mean manufacturing will cease to exist or become unimportant. Did farming end with the industrial era? Ninety percent of us produced 100 percent of the food in the agricultural era; now 3 percent of us produce 100 percent. In the information age, the focus of manufacturing will shift from the physical to more intellectual functions on which the physical depends."[89]

Although goods and materials will always need to be created, transported, and distributed, it is information that forms the lifeblood of the new world order and is a very valuable resource, comparable to (or exceeding) natural resources like oil, gas, coal, and gold. According to Naisbitt, "Information is an economic entity because it costs something to produce and because people are willing to pay for it."[90] Nations that are able to effectively manage valuable information and make it accessible to their citizens experience enhanced productivity and greater wealth. Moving information safely and securely is important, and today a large part of that is done on the **Internet**, the world's largest computer network. It began with the linkage of military and scientific computer facilities already existing on the Arpnet and Milnet and today consists of a vast resource of tens of thousands of computers around the world all linked together as a way of moving data quickly and making information accessible to masses of citizens.

The Internet provides some amazing and constantly growing capabilities: Web sites, e-mail, mailing lists, newsgroups, and file-transfer capability. Internet access was originally restricted to commercial users, researchers, and university personnel, but access to the Internet is now routinely available through ISPs that furnish Internet access to anyone able to pay the monthly fee. Web browsers combine with search engines like Google to make it easy to search the tremendous amount of information on the Web and to interact with other Internet users.

As the Internet has grown, it has been targeted by hackers and cybercriminals, some of whom have introduced rogue computer programs into the network's machines. In 1988, the infamous Internet "worm" written by Cornell University graduate student Robert T. Morris, Jr., circulated through computers connected to the Internet, effectively disabling many of them. Morris was later arrested, sentenced to 400 hours of community service and three years of probation, and was fined $10,000. Since then, many other hackers have exploited loopholes in the software and hardware supporting the Internet.

In response to the growing threat to the nation's information systems, President Clinton created the Commission on Critical Infrastructure Protection, which was charged with assessing threats to the nation's computer networks and recommending policies to protect them.[91] Security issues related to information systems that control the nation's telecommunications, electric power, oil and gas, banking and finance, transportation, water supply, emergency services, and government operations were studied by the commission. Its October 1997 report proposed (1) establishing an Information Analysis and Warning Center to collect information on computer-security breaches in industry and government; (2) creating legislation to permit private companies to conduct special background checks when hiring computer experts for sensitive positions; (3) creating a White House office to coordinate the information security roles of government, including the departments of Commerce, Defense, Energy, Justice, Treasury, and Transportation; and (4) quadrupling research on cyberspace security to $1 billion by the year 2004.[92]

The National Infrastructure Protection Center (NIPC), created in 1998 and located at the FBI's headquarters in Washington, D.C., served as the federal government's center for threat assessment, warnings, investigation, and response for threats or attacks against the nation's critical infrastructures. Its successor, the Office of Infrastructure Protection (IP), operates today within the DHS. Visit the IP Office via **Web Extra 13–8**.

In February 2000, the President's Working Group on Unlawful Conduct on the Internet released a report titled *The Electronic Frontier: The Challenge of Unlawful Conduct Involving the Use of the Internet*.[93] The group reported that "similar to the technologies that have preceded it, the Internet provides a new tool for wrongdoers to commit crimes, such as fraud, the sale or distribution of child pornography, the sale of guns or drugs or other regulated substances without regulatory protections, or the unlawful distribution of computer software or other creative material protected by intellectual property rights."

The group said that "although the precise extent of unlawful conduct involving the use of computers is unclear, the rapid growth of the Internet and e-commerce has made such unlawful conduct a critical priority for legislators, policymakers, industry, and law enforcement agencies." Because of the Internet's potential to reach vast audiences easily, the potential scale of unlawful conduct is equally wide.

Cybercriminals are no longer hampered by the existence of national or international boundaries because information and property can be easily transmitted through communications and data networks. A computer server running a Web page designed to defraud senior citizens might be located in Thailand, but

WEB EXTRA 13-9
WEB EXTRA 13-10
LIBRARY EXTRA 13-13
LIBRARY EXTRA 13-14

victims of the scam could be scattered throughout the world. Evidence of a crime can be stored at a remote location, either for concealment of the crime from law enforcement or due to the design of the network. "A cyberstalker in Brooklyn, New York, may send a threatening e-mail to a person in Manhattan. If the stalker routes his communication through Argentina, France, and Norway before reaching his victim, the New York Police Department may have to get assistance from the Office of International Affairs at the Department of Justice in Washington, D.C., which, in turn, may have to get assistance from law enforcement in (say) Buenos Aires, Paris, and Oslo just to learn that the suspect is in New York." In this example, the working group points out, the perpetrator needs no passport and passes through no checkpoints as he commits his crime, while law enforcement agencies are burdened with cumbersome mechanisms for international cooperation—mechanisms that often derail or slow investigations. Because the gathering of information in other jurisdictions and internationally is crucial to investigating and prosecuting cybercrimes, the President's Working Group concluded that "all levels of government will need to develop concrete and reliable mechanisms for cooperating with each other." Read the entire text of *The Electronic Frontier* via **Web Extra 13-9**.

In September 2003, the U.S. government established the United States Computer Emergency Readiness Team (US–CERT), a partnership between DHS and public and private sectors to protect the nation's Internet infrastructure and to coordinate defenses against cyberattacks across the nation. US–CERT is in charge of the National Cyber Alert System: "America's first cohesive national cyber security system for identifying, analyzing, and prioritizing emerging vulnerabilities and threats."[94] The Cyber Alert System relays computer-security updates and warning information to anyone who subscribes to its bulletins and provides all citizens—from computer-security professionals to home-computer users with basic skills—with free, timely, actionable information to better secure their computer systems. Visit US–CERT at **Web Extra 13–10**.

After taking office, President Barack Obama identified cybersecurity as one of the most serious economic and national-security challenges facing the United States and noted that the country was not adequately prepared to counter cybersecurity threats. In May 2009, the president decided to implement recommendations from the Comprehensive National Cybersecurity Initiative (CNCI), which had been launched by President George W. Bush in January 2008.[95] In December 2009, President Obama announced the appointment of Howard A. Schmidt as White House Cybersecurity Coordinator.[96] Schmidt, who served as chief security officer for Microsoft and eBay, was charged with coordinating cybersecurity activities across the federal government. Learn more about the CNCI at **Library Extra 13-13**, and read about new legislation to address the problem of cybercrime at **Library Extra 13–14**.

Policy Issues: Personal Freedoms in the Information Age

The continued development of telecommunications resources has led not only to concerns about security and data integrity but also to expanding interest in privacy, free speech, and personal freedoms. While the First and Fourth Amendments of the Constitution guarantee each of us freedom of speech and security in our "persons, houses, papers, and effects, against unreasonable searches and seizures," it is understandably silent on the subject of electronic documents and advanced forms of communication facilitated by technologies that did not exist at the time of the Constitutional Convention.

Within the context of contemporary society, we are left to ask, "What is speech? What are papers? Do electronic communications qualify for protection under the First Amendment?" In an era when most houses are wired for telephones and many support data links that extend well beyond voice capabilities, it becomes necessary to ask what constitutes someone's "speech" or "home." Questions abound: Does e-mail qualify as speech? Where does the concept of a home begin and end for purposes of constitutional guarantees? Do activities within the home that can be accessed from outside it (as when a Web site is run out of a home) fall under the same constitutional guarantees as a private conversation held in the physical confines of a house?

These and questions like them will be debated for years to come. In 1990, concerned individuals banded together to form the Electronic Frontier Foundation (EFF), a citizens' group funded by private contributions with the task of actively assisting in refining notions of privacy and legality as they relate to telecommunications and other computer-based media. Mitch Kapor, EFF cofounder and former president of Lotus Development Corporation, explained, "It is becoming increasingly obvious that the rate of technology

> Do electronic communications qualify for protection under the First Amendment?

WEB EXTRA 13-11

advancement in communications is far outpacing the establishment of appropriate cultural, legal and political frameworks to handle the issues that are arising."[97]

The EFF, which also supports litigation in the public interest, has been an active supporter of the advocacy group Computer Professionals for Social Responsibility (CPSR), which maintains a Computing and Civil Liberties Project much in keeping with EFF's purpose. Visit the EFF on the Web via **Web Extra 13-11**.

SUMMARY

Technology and criminology have always been closely linked—as technology advances, it facilitates new forms of criminal behavior.

- High-technology offenses can dramatically change our understanding of crime. Some forms of high-tech crime, committed without regard for national borders or even the need for physical travel, hold dangers never before imagined.

- High technology provides new criminal opportunities by making available to perpetrators new tools and advanced techniques useful in the commission of crime, and by contributing to the development of items of value, like computer codes, that did not previously exist.

- Hackers can be pioneers (those fascinated by the evolving technology of telecommunications and its exploration), scamps (those with a sense of fun and no intent to harm), explorers (those motivated by personal delight in discoveries associated with breaking into new systems), game players (those whose joy is in defeating software or copyright protection), vandals (those with the goal of intentional damage without personal apparent gain), and/or addicts (those computer nerds addicted to hacking and computer technology).

- The combination of information technology and easy accessibility of personal information has produced a rapid increase in identity theft (misuse of another individual's personal information to commit fraud).

- Technology in law enforcement today involves computer databases of known offenders, expert systems, cellular communications, video surveillance and face-recognition technology, electronic eavesdropping, DNA analysis, and less-lethal weapons.

- Any effective program to combat cybercrime and secure an organization against the threat of high-tech crime must use threat analysis. Once specific threats are identified, strategies tailored to dealing with them can be implemented.

- Efforts to control high-tech crime through criminal investigation and prosecution impact issues of individual rights, from free speech to technological privacy in the context of digital interconnectedness. There will need to be an acceptable balance between constitutional guarantees of continued freedom of access to legitimate high-tech activities and effective enforcement initiatives for the massive threat high-tech crimes represent.

KEY TERMS

audit trail, 389

Communications
   Decency Act (CDA), 378

computer abuse, 379

computer-related
   crime, 379

computer virus, 372

cybercrime, 372

Cyber Security
   Enhancement Act
   (CSEA), 377

cyberspace, 379

data encryption, 389

Daubert standard, 387

DCS–3000, 390

Digital Theft Deterrence
   and Copyright Damages
   Improvement Act, 377

DNA profiling, 386

expert system, 389

hacker, 372

identity theft, 382

Internet, 391

No Electronic Theft Act
   (NETA), 377

phishing, 374

phone phreak, 373

software piracy, 373

TEMPEST, 371

threat analysis, 389

QUESTIONS FOR REVIEW

1. How does advancing technology produce new forms of crime?

2. How does high technology provide new criminal opportunities?

3. What different types of cybercriminals does this chapter describe?

4. What is identity theft, and how can identities be stolen?

5. What new technologies are being used in today's fight against crime?

6. What is being done to combat cybercrime and to secure the Internet today?

7. What are some personal freedoms that are threatened by today's need for advanced security?

QUESTIONS FOR REFLECTION

1. This book emphasizes the theme of social problems versus social responsibility. Which perspective better explains the involvement of capable individuals in criminal activity necessitating high-tech skills? What is the best way to deal with such criminals?

2. What is the difference between high-tech crime and traditional forms of criminal activity? Will the high-tech crimes of today continue to be the high-tech crimes of tomorrow? Why?

3. What forms of high-tech crime can you imagine that this chapter has not discussed? Describe each briefly.

4. Do you believe that high-tech crimes will eventually surpass the abilities of enforcement agents to prevent or solve them? Why?

5. What different kinds of high-tech offenders can you imagine? What is the best way to deal with each type of offender? Give reasons for your answers.

CHAPTER 14

GLOBALIZATION AND TERRORISM

LEARNING OUTCOMES

After reading this chapter, you should be able to answer the following questions:

- What is globalization, and how does it impact contemporary transnational criminal activity?

- What is comparative criminology, and what are the advantages of a comparative approach to the study of crime and criminals?

- What is terrorism, and what are the various types of terrorism that this chapter discusses?

■ **globalization**
A process of social homogenization by which the experiences of everyday life, marked by the diffusion of commodities and ideas, can foster a standardization of cultural expressions around the world.

■ **transnational organized crime**
Any unlawful activity undertaken and supported by organized criminal groups operating across national boundaries; also called *transnational crime.*

Introduction

In 2007, officials of Cincinnati-based Chiquita Brands International admitted in federal court that executives with the company had paid protection money to Colombian terrorists to help secure their most profitable banana-growing operations.[1] Under a plea arraignment, the company pleaded guilty to one count of doing business with a terrorist organization—a crime under federal law—and paid a $25 million fine, but the deal allowed the identities of several senior executives involved in the illegal protection payments to remain anonymous. Attorneys for Chiquita said that the company was forced to make the payments and was acting only to ensure the safety of its workers.

Globalization

The payment of protection monies to a South American terrorist organization by an Ohio-based banana importer illustrates the complexity of contemporary international business operations, which often occur amid intricate political situations and which can be impacted by the interests of a wide variety of groups. On a global scale, society is experiencing a period of unprecedented change in both substance and pace. Sequences of events are no longer occurring in relative isolation and are happening ever more quickly; there is greater simultaneity of occurrences, swifter interpenetration of various groups, and increased feedback of one set of changes on another.[2]

The increasing integration of previously isolated events in all spheres of endeavors impacts people far and wide. The economist Thomas L. Friedman said that globalization will likely be the most pervasive influence affecting the entire world in the first part of the twenty-first century;[3] **globalization** can be defined as a process of social homogenization by which the experiences of everyday life, marked by the diffusion of commodities and ideas, can foster a standardization of cultural expressions around the world.[4] Globalization, occurring in communications, economics, science, education, and business, involves the progressive erosion of the influence of nation-states and the rise in influence of global decision makers at both public and private levels.

Globalization makes it impossible for policymakers to ignore criminal activities in other parts of the world, especially crimes perpetrated by transnational criminal and terrorist organizations. **Transnational organized crime** (also called *transnational crime*) refers to unlawful activity undertaken and supported by organized

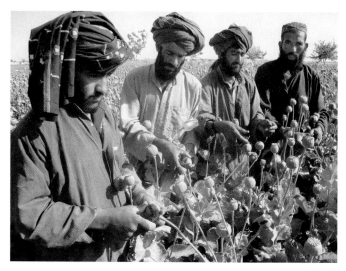

Afghans collecting resin from a poppy field in Lashkar Gah, south of Kabul, Afghanistan, in 2007. Afghanistan is one of the top producers of opium in the world, where its growth is largely controlled by Taliban militia who either befriend or intimidate local poppy growers. Much of the heroin manufactured from opium produced in Afghanistan is sold in the United States, completing an international cycle that forms one aspect of globalization and serves as a source of funds for the ongoing Taliban resistance in Afghanistan. How can the cycle be broken?
Source: Abdul Khaliq/AP Wide World Photos

criminal groups operating across national boundaries. The growing globalization of crime has necessitated the enhanced coordination of law enforcement efforts in different parts of the world and the expansion of American law enforcement activities beyond national borders.

Transnational Crimes

According to the National Institute of Justice (NIJ), transnational crime groups have profited more from globalization than legitimate businesses, which are subject to domestic and host country laws and regulations, pointing out that transnational criminal syndicates and networks, abetted by official corruption, blackmail, and intimidation, can use open markets and open societies to their full advantage.[5] The list of transnational crimes is long and ranges from relatively simple fraudulent e-mail and phishing schemes that are globally perpetrated to the much more dangerous and threatening illegal trafficking in human beings, human organs, and illicit drugs. Included are the activities of multinational drug cartels, the support

■ **human smuggling**
A type of illegal immigration in which an agent is paid to help a person cross a border clandestinely.

of terrorist groups by criminal organizations seeking armed protection, and well-funded and politically sophisticated efforts by organized criminal groups seeking to supplant the ruling regime in countries or regions with others sympathetic to their operations.

No one is immune from the economic effects of transnational crime, and some of the threats hit close to U.S. borders. The entire 32-member police force of Villa Madero, in Mexico's Michoacán state, resigned or failed to show up for work after being threatened by drug traffickers;[6] members of the town's police force complained about a lack of weapons and communications equipment needed to protect themselves and the town's citizens. In some parts of Mexico, the local police have had to be disarmed because of fears that they are taking bribes and working with drug traffickers. Larry Birns, director of the Council on Hemispheric Affairs and an expert on Mexican affairs, stated that Mexican drug cartels have wrested control of what the United Nations (UN) has estimated is an annual $142 billion Central American drug-trafficking operation from Colombians.[7] "President Felipe Calderon may be the consti-

> **No one is immune to the economic effects of transnational crime.**

tutionally elected leader of the nation, but in reality, drug cartels and warlords exercise *de facto* authority over much of the [country]."[8]

Mexican drug traffickers, wearing what appear to be Mexican military uniforms, have made armed incursions into the United States.[9] The not-infrequent beheadings of reporters and others who speak out against drug-related corruption, as well as assassinations or attempted assassinations of Mexican political leaders opposed to the drug trade, have raised alarms about the future of the Mexican political system.[10] In a World Press analysis of the current situation titled "The Government and the Drug Lords: Who Rules Mexico?"[11] Birns pointed out that "there have been a growing number of assassinations, which most likely can be attributed to the drug cartels 'punishing' the government." Even Mexican President Calderon has admitted that he and his family have received death threats due to his highly publicized stand against drug-trafficking.

Human Smuggling and Trafficking

According to the UN, smuggling of persons and human trafficking, two distinct crimes, are two of the fastest-growing areas of international criminal activity today[12] (Figures 14–1 and 14–2). The U.S. State Department defined **human smuggling** as "the facilitation, transportation, attempted transportation or illegal

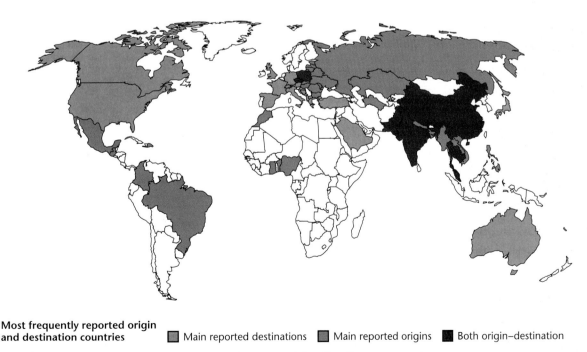

Most frequently reported origin and destination countries ■ Main reported destinations ■ Main reported origins ■ Both origin–destination

FIGURE 14-1 | Human Trafficking—Countries of Origin and Destination

Source: United Nations Office on Drugs and Crime (UNODC), *Trafficking in Persons: Global Patterns* (April 2006), p. 17, http://www.unodc.org. Reprinted by permission.

▨ **trafficking in persons (TIP)**
The exploitation of unwilling or unwitting people through force, coercion, threat, or deception.

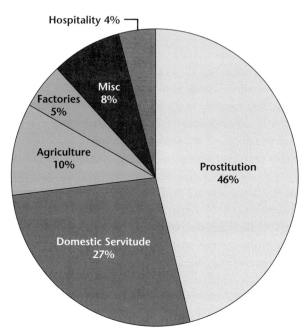

FIGURE 14-2 | Human Trafficking into the United States—Endpoint Sectors

Source: Adapted from Free the Slaves and the Human Rights Center, University of California, Berkeley, *Hidden Slaves, Forced Labor in the United States* (September, 2004), http://web.archive.org/web/20070830033751/ http://freetheslaves.net/files/Hidden_Slaves.pdf (accessed August 1, 2009), p. 14.

but abandoned the truck about 100 miles from its destination; the victims died of dehydration, overheating, and suffocation in the Texas heat before the truck was discovered and its doors opened.

Trafficking in persons (TIP)—the exploitation of unwilling or unwitting people through force, coercion, threat, or deception—can be compared to modern-day slavery, prompting Secretary of State Condoleezza Rice to say that "defeating human trafficking is a great moral calling of our day."[15] Trafficking can involve human rights abuses such as debt bondage, deprivation of liberty, or lack of control over freedom and labor and is often undertaken for sexual or labor exploitation.

> Officials estimate that 800,000 to 900,000 victims are trafficked globally each year.

U.S. government officials have estimated that 800,000 to 900,000 victims are trafficked globally each year, with 7,500 to 18,500 being trafficked into the United States.[16] Women and children, the largest group of victims, are often physically and emotionally abused. Although TIP is often an international crime involving the crossing of borders, it is important to note that TIP

entry of a person(s) across an international border, in violation of one or more country's laws, either clandestinely or through deception, such as the use of fraudulent documents"; in other words, it refers to illegal immigration in which an agent is involved for payment to help a person cross a border clandestinely.[13] Human smuggling may be conducted to obtain financial or other benefits for the smuggler, although sometimes people engage in smuggling for other motives, such as to reunite their families. It generally occurs with the consent of the persons being smuggled, who often pay a smuggler for his or her services, and once in the country they've paid to enter, they usually no longer are in contact with the smuggler. The U.S. State Department noted that the vast majority of people who are assisted in illegally entering the United States annually are smuggled rather than trafficked.

Although smuggling might not involve active coercion, it can be deadly. In January 2007, truck driver Tyrone Williams, a 36-year-old Jamaican citizen living in Schenectady, New York, was sentenced to life in prison for causing the deaths of 19 illegal immigrants in the nation's deadliest known incident of human smuggling.[14] Williams locked more than 70 immigrants in a container truck during a trip from South Texas to Houston

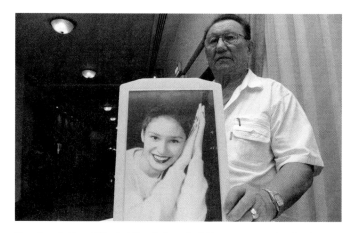

Russian father Nikolai Rantchev holding up a portrait of his dead daughter, Oxana, at a hotel in Nicosia on November 20, 2008, during a conference on human trafficking. Only days after Oxana left Russia for the Mediterranean island of Cyprus, duped into thinking she would work as a translator, her body was found slumped at the foot of a building. Her father, a former Soviet army officer, believes she was killed by human traffickers who wanted to turn her into a sex slave. What different forms does human trafficking take?

Source: AFP Photo/Stefanos Kouratzis/NewsCom.com

victims can also be trafficked within their own countries and communities, as when traffickers move victims between locations within the same country and/or sell them to other trafficking organizations.

The International Labor Organization (ILO), the UN agency charged with addressing labor standards, employment, and social protection issues, estimated that there are 12.3 million people in forced labor, bonded labor, forced child labor, and sexual servitude throughout the world;[17] other estimates have ranged as high as 27 million.[18]

It is sometimes difficult to distinguish between smuggling and trafficking because trafficking may include an element of smuggling (that is, the illegal crossing of a national border), and some trafficking victims may believe they are being smuggled when they are really being trafficked but are unaware of their eventual fate. For example, women trafficked for sexual exploitation thought they were agreeing to work in legitimate industries for decent wages, part of which they would pay to the trafficker who smuggled them, not knowing the trafficker would keep them in bondage, subject them to physical force or sexual violence, force them to work in the sex trade, and take most or all of their income.

The U.S. Department of State's 2007 *Trafficking in Persons* report explained that "human trafficking is a multi-dimensional threat. It deprives people of their human rights and freedoms, it increases global health risks, and it fuels the growth of organized crime. [At the individual level,] human trafficking has a devastating impact on individual victims, who often suffer physical and emotional abuse, rape, threats against self and family, document theft, and even death."[19]

The distinctions between smuggling and trafficking are sometimes subtle, but the key components generally distinguishing the two are the fraud, force, and/or coercion necessary for trafficking but not used in smuggling. But under U.S. law, if the person is under age 18 and is induced to perform a commercial sex act, then it is considered trafficking, regardless of whether fraud, force, or coercion is involved. Table 14–1 provides a guide to distinguishing criminal trafficking from smuggling.

According to the UN, human smuggling and trafficking have become a worldwide industry affecting millions of people and involving billions of dollars.[20] Many of the routes used by smugglers—from Mexico and Central America to the United States, from West Asia through Greece and Turkey to Western Europe, and within East and Southeast Asia—have become well established and are widely known. The UN has attributed the flourishing smuggling routes to weak legislation, lax border controls, corrupt officials, and organized crime's power and influence. While there are significant differences between human smuggling and TIP, the underlying conditions that give rise to both are similar: extreme poverty, lack of economic opportunity, civil unrest, and political uncertainty.

TABLE 14-1 | Differences between Human Trafficking and Smuggling

TRAFFICKING	SMUGGLING
Trafficking contains an element of force, fraud, or coercion (actual, perceived, or implied). (Force, fraud, or coercion is not required if the person is under age 18 and is involved in commercial sex acts.)	The person being smuggled is generally cooperating.
Trafficking involves forced labor and/or exploitation.	Smuggling involves no forced labor or other exploitation.
Persons trafficked are victims.	Persons smuggled are not victims; they are violating the law.
Trafficked persons are enslaved, are subjected to limited movement or isolation, and have their documents confiscated.	Smuggled persons are free to leave, change jobs, etc.
Trafficking need not involve the actual movement of the victim.	Smuggling facilitates the illegal transportation of the person from one country into another.
Trafficking does not need to cross an international border.	Smuggling always crosses an international border.
Trafficked persons must be involved in labor/services or commercial sex acts (that is, must be "working").	Smuggled persons must be attempting entry or already be in a country illegally.

Note: This table is meant to be conceptual and is not intended to provide precise legal distinctions between trafficking and smuggling.
Source: Adapted from U.S. Department of State, Bureau for International Narcotics and Law Enforcement Affairs, Human Smuggling and Trafficking Center, *Distinctions between Human Smuggling and Human Trafficking* (Washington, DC: January 1, 2005).

■ **sex trafficking**
The recruitment, harboring, transportation, provision, or obtaining of a person for the purpose of a commercial sex act.

WEB EXTRA 14-1
LIBRARY EXTRA 14-1

Federal Immigration and Trafficking Legislation

The United States had open national borders until the 1880s, when limited federal controls on immigration began. One of the nation's first immigration laws was the Chinese Exclusion Act, which became law in 1882 and was enforced for ten years; it was enacted in response to large numbers of Chinese male laborers who had immigrated to the western United States in the mid-1800s looking for work and often took jobs on railroads and in the mining industry.

A more comprehensive piece of federal immigration legislation was the 1924 Immigration Act limiting the number of immigrants who could be admitted from any one country to 2% of the number of people from that country who were already living here (calculated using the Census of 1890). The law also barred immigration from specific parts of the Asia-Pacific Triangle, including Cambodia, China, Japan, Korea, Laos, the Philippines, and Thailand. The Immigration and Nationality Act (INA) of 1952, establishing the Immigration and Naturalization Service (INS) while continuing numerical ethnic quotas, provided criminal penalties for anyone bringing or attempting to bring unauthorized aliens into the United States;[21] 13 years later, the Immigration and Nationality Act amendments of 1965 abolished quotas based on ethnicity.[22] The Homeland Security Act of 2002 (HSA) dissolved the INS and transferred most of its functions to three branches of the Department of Homeland Security (DHS): Citizenship and Immigration Services (CIS), Customs and Border Protection (CBP), and Immigration and Customs Enforcement (ICE).

Recognizing that human smuggling and TIP were serious social issues, Congress passed the Trafficking Victims Protection Act of 2000 (TVPA), which addressed the significant problem of TIP for the purposes of having people commit commercial sex acts (termed **sex trafficking**) and of subjecting them to involuntary servitude, peonage, or debt bondage and increased the protections afforded victims of trafficking.[23] The TVPA specified severe forms of trafficking: "(a) sex trafficking in which a commercial sex act is induced by force, fraud, or coercion, or in which the person induced to perform such an act has not attained 18 years of age; or (b) the recruitment, harboring, transportation, provision, or obtaining of a person for labor or services, through the use of force, fraud, or coercion for the purpose of subjection to involuntary servitude, peonage, debt bondage, or slavery."[24]

Under the TVPA, human trafficking does not require the crossing of an international border or even the transportation of victims from one locale to another because victims of certain forms of trafficking are not just illegal aliens but also U.S. citizens, legal residents, or visitors. Victims do not have to be women or children; they may also be adult males.

The Trafficking Victims Protection Reauthorization Act (TVPRA) of 2003 added a new initiative to the original law to collect foreign data on trafficking investigations, prosecutions, convictions, and sentences. Its 2006 data showed that reporting jurisdictions prosecuted 5,808 persons for trafficking-related offenses and secured 3,160 convictions, the lowest number of reported foreign prosecutions since reporting began in 2003.[25] The number of alleged human-trafficking incidents in the United States in 2007–2008 is shown in Table 14–2.

Section 7202 of the Intelligence Reform and Terrorism Prevention Act of 2004 established the Human Smuggling and Trafficking Center within the U.S. State Department, and the secretary of state, the secretary of DHS, the attorney general, and members of the national Intelligence Community oversee it. The center was created to achieve greater integration and overall effectiveness in the U.S. government's enforcement of issues related to human smuggling, TIP, and criminal support of clandestine terrorist travel. Visit the Human Smuggling and Trafficking Center at **Web Extra 14–1**, and read the U.S. Department of State's 319-page 2009 *Trafficking in Persons Report* at **Library Extra 14–1**.

TABLE 14-2 | Number of Alleged Human-Trafficking Incidents in the U.S., 2007-2008

TYPE OF HUMAN-TRAFFICKING INCIDENT	NUMBER	TOTAL INCIDENTS (PERCENT)
All incidents[a]	1,229	100.0
Sex trafficking	**1,018**	**82.8**
Forced prostitution	596	48.5
Child sex trafficking	391	31.8
Other sex trafficking	31	2.5
Labor trafficking	**146**	**11.9**
Other	65	5.3

[a]One trafficking incident may involve many victims.
Source: Tracey Kyckelhahn, Allen J. Beck, and Thomas H. Cohen, *Characteristics of Suspected Human Trafficking Incidents, 2007-2008* (Washington, DC: Bureau of Justice Statistics, 2009), p. 1.

■ **comparative criminology**
The cross-national study of crime.

■ **comparative criminologist**
A criminologist involved in the cross-national study of crime.

LIBRARY EXTRA 14–2

■ **ethnocentrism**
The phenomenon of "culture-centeredness" by which one uses one's own culture as a benchmark against which to judge all other patterns of behavior.

Globalization and Comparative Criminology

The globalization of crime has led to a resurgence of interest in **comparative criminology**, the study of crime on a cross-national level. When **comparative criminologists** compare crime patterns in one country with those in another, theories and policies that have been taken for granted can be reevaluated in the light of world experience. "The challenge for comparative criminologists is to develop theories with increased specificity while managing to construct them in such a way that they can be applied across more than one culture or nation-state. This eventually must demand that theories be developed to conceptualize societies as totalities and that theories that manage to provide a world context in which total societies behave be further constructed."[26]

> Comparative criminologists compare crime patterns in one country with those in another.

Some have used the term *globalization of knowledge* to describe the increase in understanding that results from the sharing of information between cultures, a factor beginning to play a significant role in both the process of theory formation within criminology and the development of American crime-control policies. "Globalization will make it increasingly difficult for nation-states to ignore the criminal justice information of other countries. Politicians and influential bureaucrats increasingly will be forced to answer as to why their country displays crime rates, prosecution rates, incarceration rates, or rates of violence or gun ownership that are strikingly different from similar countries."[27]

Recipient of the prestigious Vollmer Award in Criminology Franklin E. Zimring, of the University of California–Berkeley, addressed the American Society of Criminology, telling the assembly that "over the past decade I have become convinced that transnational comparisons are a necessary part of virtually all serious work in criminal justice and the study of criminal behavior."[28] Zimring went on to bemoan the fact that American criminology had been self-obsessed and "particularly inattentive to the value and necessity to transnational comparisons;" he saw comparative efforts as providing a context for evaluating knowledge and reviewing observations, and he demonstrated that the U.S. crime decline during the 1990s was not unique to America but had also occurred in Canada at exactly the same time. "Whatever was driving the decline in the United States was also operating in Canada."[29] Read more about global crime at **Library Extra 14–2**.

Comparative Criminology and Ethnocentrism

One important issue facing comparative criminologists is **ethnocentrism** (culture-centeredness, or the use of a person's own culture as a benchmark for other cultures' behaviors), which can interfere with their work in a number of ways, including how crime statistics are gathered, analyzed, and presented. Researchers can avoid being ethnocentric by realizing that it is quite common for people to regard processes and methods they are familiar with as somehow superior or more desirable than others they are less familiar with.

Because people are socialized from birth into a particular culture, they tend to prefer their own culture's way of doing things—native behavioral patterns, values, beliefs, and customs are seen as natural and better than foreign ones. People tend to think that their religion holds a spiritual edge over other religions, that their values and ethical sense are superior to those of others, and that the fashions they wear, the language they speak, and the rituals of daily life in which they participate are somehow better than comparable practices elsewhere. Ethnocentric individuals rarely stop to think that people in other parts of the world frequently cling to their own values, beliefs, and standards of behavior with just as much fervor; in other words, ethnocentrism is not a uniquely American phenomenon.

American students of criminology have begun to closely examine crime in other cultures, although not all societies are equally open and it is not always easy to explore them. In some societies, even the *study* of crime is taboo, so data-gathering strategies taken for granted in Western culture may not be well received elsewhere. Difficulties also arise in the comparison of crime rates from one country to another because of (1) differences in the given definitions of a crime, (2) diverse crime-reporting practices, and (3) political, social, economic, and other influences on the reporting of statistics to international agencies.[30]

Definitional Issues in Reporting Crime

Definitional differences create what may be the biggest problem in reporting crime (see the Theory versus Reality box). For cross-national comparisons of crime data to be meaningful, it is

CRIME | in the NEWS

Terrorism Recruiting on U.S. Soil

WASHINGTON—Federal authorities [recently] unsealed criminal charges against eight suspects in an expanding investigation into an alleged U.S.-based recruitment network sending young men to fight in Somalia, making it one of the largest militant operations uncovered on U.S. soil since the Sept. 11, 2001, attacks.

The charges, filed in federal court in Minneapolis, disclosed how some older and well-respected members of the Somali-American community were luring younger men to fight with a Somali group affiliated with al-Qaeda known as al-Shabaab, or "The Youth."

The alleged offenses include providing financial support to those who traveled to Somalia to fight; attended terrorist training camps operated by al-Shabaab; and fought with al-Shabaab against the U.S.-backed transitional government there, as well as Ethiopian government forces and African Union troops.

The recruitment of young people from Minneapolis and other U.S. communities to fight for militant extremists in Somalia "has been the focus of intense investigation for many months," said Assistant Attorney General for National Security David Kris.

The new charges bring the total of men charged in connection with the case in Minnesota to 14. Several of the newly disclosed defendants are believed outside the United States.

At least 20 young men, all but one of Somali descent, are believed to have left the Minneapolis area and traveled to Somalia between September 2007 and October 2009, according to court documents and interviews.

They were trained by Somali, Arab, and Western instructors in the use of small arms, machine guns, rocket-propelled grenades, and military-style tactics, authorities said. They said the recruits were also indoctrinated with "anti-Ethiopian, anti-American, anti-Israeli, and anti-Western beliefs."

One of them, Shirwa Ahmed, left in 2007, attended al-Shabaab training camps and then took part in one of five simultaneous suicide attacks on targets in northern Somalia in October 2008.

Until Monday, the public aspects of the investigation focused on the young Somalis who had gone overseas to fight. But the newly unsealed court documents provide a wealth of detail about how some of their peers and elders allegedly recruited the young men, in some cases by exhorting them to fight for their homeland, and in other cases to fight for jihad, or holy war against the West and what they describe as its puppet government in Mogadishu.

"Instead of the kids going over there as cannon fodder, this identifies some of the recruiters behind them," one federal law enforcement official said of the new charges. He spoke on the condition of anonymity because he was not authorized to discuss the ongoing investigation.

Federal authorities say they are particularly concerned that some of the men who receive training in guerilla warfare and terrorism tactics in Somalia might return home to the United States and launch an

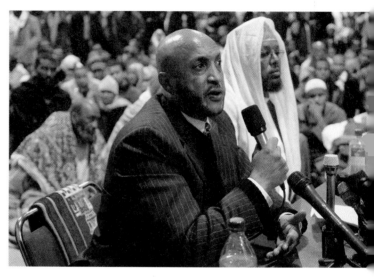

Attorney Mahir Sherif and Abdirahman Ahmed, leader of the Abubakar As-Saddique Islamic Center in Minneapolis, speaking at a 2008 press conference held at the Minneapolis Convention Center. They were addressing charges that several young Muslim Somali men from their area have been recruited by terror groups in Somalia to fight in that country's civil war. What tools do terrorist organizations use to recruit in the United States?
Source: AP Photo/Dawn Villella

attack, citing at least one recent case in Australia. And they say they have found evidence of support and finance cells for the network in several U.S. cities.

"It's always troubling when you find indications of a terrorist recruitment and training operation with structure, organization, and continuity, because those are the makings of an effective terrorist cell," said Kenneth Wainstein, who tracked the threat of Somali Americans fighting overseas as head of counterterrorism and homeland security in the Bush administration White House until earlier this year.

"And while that terrorism may be focused today in the Horn of Africa, which is troubling enough, that same operation could conceivably be directed at us or our allies in the future," said Wainstein....

Discussion Questions

1. Why are U.S. authorities concerned about young men leaving this country to fight in Somalia?

2. How can the types of activities described here best be prevented?

WEB EXTRA 14–2
WEB EXTRA 14–3
WEB EXTRA 14–4
LIBRARY EXTRA 14–3
LIBRARY EXTRA 14–4
LIBRARY EXTRA 14–5

essential that the reported data share conceptual similarities, but that is often not the case because nations report offenses according to the legal criteria by which their arrests are made and under which their prosecution can occur. Switzerland includes bicycle thefts in its reported data on what we call "auto theft" because Swiss data gathering focuses more on the concept of personal transportation than on the type of stolen vehicle; the Netherlands has no crime category for robberies, counting them as thefts; Japan classifies an assault resulting in death as an assault or an aggravated assault, not as a homicide; Greek rape statistics include crimes of sodomy, lewdness, seduction of a child, incest, and prostitution, and China reports only robberies and thefts that involve citizens' property, using crimes against state-owned property as a separate category.

Reporting practices vary substantially among nations. The International Criminal Police Organization (INTERPOL) and the UN are the only international organizations that regularly collect crime statistics from a large number of countries, and both can only request data and have no way of checking on the accuracy of those data. Many countries do not disclose the requested information, and those that do sometimes make only partial reports; in general, small countries are more likely to report than large ones, and nonsocialist countries are more likely to report than are socialist nations.

International comparisons are also difficult because complete up-to-date data are not easy to acquire, since the information made available to agencies like INTERPOL and the UN is reported at different times and according to schedules varying from nation to nation. In addition, official UN crime surveys are conducted infrequently at the international level (as of 2006, only nine surveys have been undertaken).[31]

Economic differences among countries compound these difficulties. Auto-theft statistics between countries like the United States and China need to be placed in an economic as well as a demographic context. The United States has two automobiles for every three people, but China has only one car for every 100 of its citizens, so for the Chinese auto-theft rate to equal that of the United States, every automobile in the country would have to be stolen nearly twice each year!

Crime statistics also reflect social and political contexts, with some nations not accurately reporting the frequency of certain kinds of culturally reprehensible crimes. Communist countries appear loathe to report crimes like theft, burglary, and robbery because the very existence of such offenses might appear to demonstrate felt inequities within the communist system, and the social norms in some societies may make it almost impossible for women to report cases of rape or sexual abuse, whereas in others, women are encouraged to come forward.

With all these caveats in mind, it can still be instructive to look at crime rates in other countries and attempt comparisons with U.S. crime rates. As mentioned earlier, a useful tool for international crime rate comparisons is *The Ninth United Nations Survey on Crime Trends and the Operations of Criminal Justice System,* which covers the years 2003–2004. To some, U.S. violent crime rates seem high compared with violent crime rates of other developed countries, but American crime rates are far from the highest in the world, and UN surveys typically place U.S. crime rates well below world highs.

> **Definitional differences create the biggest problem in reporting crime.**

While lawless areas without strong central governments and countries experiencing strong social upheaval might be expected to have high violent crime rates, some other parts of the world do, too. Murder rates in Colombia and South Africa are more than twelve times that of the United States, Russia has a murder rate that is almost four times the U.S. rate, and homicide rates in Mexico are more than three times as great as those in the United States. The rate of reported rape in South Africa is four times that of the United States, whereas Canada and Australia have rape rates more than double the U.S. figure. Spain has a robbery rate many times higher than that of the United States, and at least a few countries have rates of assault that are greater than that reported in the United States.

See more international crime statistics at **Web Extra 14–2**, and visit the NIJ International Center at **Web Extra 14–3**. The comprehensive Global Criminology Web site run by Professor Robert W. Winslow at San Diego State University can be found at **Web Extra 14–4**. Read an intriguing paper on comparative criminology at **Library Extra 14–3**; the *Ninth United Nations Survey on Crime Trends*, covering 64 countries, is available at **Library Extra 14–4**; and the *European Sourcebook of Crime and Criminal Justice Statistics* can be accessed via **Library Extra 14–5**.

Terrorism

The most infamous attack of international terrorism to date took place on September 11, 2001, when members of Osama Bin Laden's al-Qaeda Islamic terrorist organization attacked New York City's World Trade Center and the Pentagon using commandeered jetliners. Following the attacks, which left more than 3,000 people dead and resulted in billions of dollars' worth of property damage, the United States declared a worldwide war on international terrorism.[32] See the Criminal Profiles box for more information on one of the 9/11 attackers.

■ **terrorism**
An act of premeditated, politically motivated violence perpetrated against a noncombatant target by a subnational group or clandestine agent.

THEORY | versus REALITY
UN Offense Definitions

The UN Office on Drugs and Crime regularly conducts a survey of international crime trends. The latest such survey, the ninth, covers the years 2003–2004. In an effort to standardize reporting practices, the UN provides the following crime definitions to guide survey participants:

Intentional homicide may be understood to mean death deliberately inflicted on a person by another person, including infanticide.

Non-intentional homicide may be understood to mean death not deliberately inflicted on a person by another person. That includes the crime of manslaughter but excludes traffic accidents that result in the death of persons.

Assault may be understood to mean physical attack against the body of another person, including battery but excluding indecent assault. Some criminal or penal codes distinguish between aggravated assault and simple assault, depending on the degree of resulting injury. If such a distinction is made in your country, please provide the relevant data for aggravated assault under the category "Major assault." Under the category "Total assault" should be included data on both aggravated assault (i.e., major assault) and simple assault. Please provide the main criterion for distinguishing between aggravated assault and simple assault if such a distinction is made in your country.

Rape may be understood to mean sexual intercourse without valid consent. Please indicate whether statutory rape is included in the data provided. If, in your country, a distinction is made between sexual assault and actual penetration, please provide relevant information.

Robbery may be understood to mean the theft of property from a person, overcoming resistance by force or threat of force.

Theft may be understood to mean the removal of property without the property owner's consent. "Theft" excludes burglary and house-breaking as well as theft of a motor vehicle. Some criminal and penal codes distinguish between grand and petty theft, depending on the value of the goods and property taken from their rightful owner. If such a distinction is made in your country, please provide the relevant

data for grand theft under the category "Major theft." The category "Total theft" should include data on both grand theft (i.e., major theft) and petty theft. Please provide the main criterion for distinguishing between grand theft and petty theft if such a distinction is made in your country.

Automobile theft may be understood to mean the removal of a motor vehicle without the consent of the owner of the vehicle.

Burglary may be understood to mean unlawful entry into someone else's premises with the intention to commit a crime. . . .

Embezzlement may be understood to mean the wrongful appropriation of another person's property that is already in the possession of the person doing the appropriating.

Drug-related crimes may be understood to mean intentional acts that involve the cultivation, production, manufacture, extraction, preparation, offering for sale, distribution, purchase, sale, delivery on any terms whatsoever, brokerage, dispatch, dispatch in transit, transport, importation, exportation and possession of internationally controlled drugs.

Recorded crimes may be understood to mean the number of penal code offences or their equivalent (i.e., various special law offences), but excluding minor road traffic offences and other petty offences, brought to the attention of the police or other law enforcement agencies and recorded by one of those agencies.

If the categories above are not fully compatible with the legal code in your country, please try to adjust the data as far as possible. Alternatively, you may indicate what kinds of crime are included in your statistics that might be comparable to the categories suggested or how the comparable types of crime are defined in your country.

View the entire *United Nations Survey on Crime Trends* questionnaire online at www.justicestudies.com/pubs/unsurvey.pdf. The UN *Criminal Justice Assessment Toolkit* is available at http://justicestudies.com/pubs/untoolkit.pdf.

Source: United Nations Office on Drugs and Crime, *Questionnaire for the Ninth United Nations Survey on Crime Trends and the Operations of Criminal Justice Systems* (New York: UN, 2005). Reprinted by permission.

The U.S. Department of State defined **terrorism** as "premeditated, politically motivated violence perpetrated against noncombatant targets by subnational groups or clandestine agents, usually intended to influence an audience."[33] Paul Pillar, former deputy chief of the Central Intelligence Agency (CIA) Counterterrorist Center, identified four key features of terrorism that distinguish it from other forms of violence[34] (see Table 14–3).

Terrorist acts are inherently criminal because they violate the law (local, state, and federal laws against terrorism), involve criminal activity (hijacking, kidnapping, arson), and produce

> Terrorist acts are inherently criminal because they violate the law, involve criminal activity, and produce criminal results.

criminal results (homicide, property destruction). The primary distinction between violent criminal acts and acts of terrorism has to do with the political motivation or social ideology of the offender;[35] bombings, hostage taking, and other similar terrorist-like acts

CRIMINAL | PROFILES
Mohammed Atta

This profile box is somewhat different from those in previous chapters. Background information regarding Mohammed Atta, the subject of this box, is sparse, unreliable, and rife with conflicting claims. Given that Atta trained as a terrorist, came from the Middle East, and likely made efforts to live a life "under the radar," it is unsurprising that extensive research into Atta's pre-9/11 life yields little information about which one can feel confident. Although some facts about Atta's life are verifiable, many of the available sources appear to be speculative or outright rumor.

We know, for example, that Atta was born in Kafr El Sheikh in Egypt's Nile Delta, grew up in Cairo, and received an undergraduate degree in architecture from Cairo University. He is known to have resided in Germany from 1993 to 1999, where he pursued an urban planning degree at the University of Harburg-Hamburg. Reliable records also show that he was a licensed pilot who moved to Venice, Florida, in 2000 to pursue additional flight training at Huffman Aviation International. Records and witness information tell us that he was a committed fundamentalist Muslim.[i] We can conclude that he was intensely motivated by personal ideals, zealous and spiritual beliefs, most of which were acquired through his life experiences.

Other claims, however, cannot be as readily confirmed. For example, England's *Telegraph* online daily newspaper reported on December 13, 2003, that documents it had obtained showed that during the summer of 2001 Atta underwent an intensive three-day "work programme" in Baghdad under the tutelage of notorious Palestinian terrorist Abu Nidal. The handwritten, top secret memo the *Telegraph* had acquired was, ostensibly, prepared by the former head of Iraq's Intelligence Service and submitted to then–President Saddam Hussein. The memo purportedly lauds Atta's "extraordinary effort" in preparing to lead the team that would be "responsible for attacking the targets that we have agreed to destroy."[ii] Numerous subsequent investigations, however—including the U.S. government's own 9/11 Commission—have failed to confirm a direct link between Hussein's Iraqi government and the al Qaeda terrorist group of which Atta was a member and which later claimed responsibility for the World Trade Center attacks.[iii]

In Atta's case, extensive scrutiny of existing information sources reveals a confusing and often conflicting profile of a man whose movements and

September 11 hijacker Mohammed Atta. Why do we know so little about him?
Source: Portland (Maine) Police Department/AP Wide World Photos

activities during the period immediately preceding the World Trade Center attacks cannot be reliably confirmed. Available news reports starkly conflict with official documents. Some government agency documents conflict with the documentary evidence provided by other government agencies. "Highly reliable" information reported by reputable news sources in the period immediately following the attacks has subsequently proven to be almost completely inaccurate. It is the nature of the terrorists' nether world. Secrecy, disinformation, obfuscation, and orchestrated confusion are tools of the trade in such an environment.

The life experiences and complex motivations of terrorists do not fit the motivational patterns of the (for lack of a better word) *ordinary* criminals described in previous chapters. Those seeking to understand terrorist behavior would probably be best served by examining the cultural, educational, ideological, and religious influences that shape the terrorists' world views, as those same views also serve to justify in the terrorist's mind even the most horrendous behavior in their pursuit of "correcting" perceived wrongs.

Notes

i. John Hooper, "The Shy, Caring, Deadly Fanatic," *The Observer* (Hamburg), September 23, 2001, http://observer.guardian.co.uk/waronterrorism/story/0,,556630,00.html (accessed June 3, 2007).

ii. Con Coughlin, "Terrorist behind September 11 Strike Was Trained by Saddam," *Telegraph* (United Kingdom), December 13, 2003, http://www.telegraph.co.uk/news/main.jhtml?xml=/news/2003/12/14/wterr14.xml&sSheet=/portal/2003/12/14/ixportaltop.html (accessed June 3, 2007).

iii. Walter Pincus and Dana Milbank, "Al-Qaeda-Hussein Link Is Dismissed," *Washington Post*, June 17, 2004, http://www.washingtonpost.com/wp-dyn/articles/A47812-2004Jun16.html (accessed June 3, 2007).

■ **domestic terrorism**
The unlawful use of force or violence by an individual or group based and operating entirely within the United States and its territories, without foreign influence, directed at the U.S. government, the civilian population, or any segment thereof for political or social objectives.

■ **international terrorism**
The unlawful use of force or violence by an individual or group with a connection to a foreign power or whose activities transcend national boundaries against people or property to intimidate or coerce a government, the civilian population, or any segment thereof for political or social objectives.

TABLE 14-3 | Characteristics of Terrorism

TERRORISM	OTHER FORMS OF VIOLENCE
Premeditated or planned	Impulsive or initiated by rage
Motivated by politics (intended to change the existing political order)	Perpetrated for criminal gain (illicit personal or financial benefit)
Aimed at civilians	Aimed at military targets or combat-ready troops
Carried out by subnational groups	Perpetrated by private individuals or the army of a country

undertaken for mere individual or pecuniary gain, without political or social objectives, do not qualify as "terrorism."

Not all terrorists share the same motivation. The Washington, D.C.–based Council on Foreign Relations offered a typology of terrorism consisting of six types of terrorists: (1) nationalist terrorists, (2) religious terrorists, (3) state-sponsored terrorists, (4) left-wing terrorists, (5) right-wing terrorists, and (6) anarchist terrorists.[36] According to the council, *nationalist terrorists* seek to form a separate state of their own and frequently depict their activities as a fight for liberation, usually from a political entity portrayed as unfair and repressive. According to the council, such groups are "among the most successful at winning international sympathy and concessions."

Religious terrorists pursue their own vision of the divine will and use violence intended to bring about social and cultural changes in keeping with that vision. The claims of religious terrorists are hard to counter in the minds of their followers, and such groups are rarely open to accommodation or compromise. Bruce Hoffman, director of the Washington office of RAND (formerly the RAND Corporation) noted that the most extreme religious terrorists can sanction "almost limitless violence against a virtually open-ended category of targets: that is, anyone who is not a member of the terrorists' religion or religious sect."[37] *State-sponsored terrorists* are deliberately used by radical states as foreign policy tools or (as Hoffman put it) as "a cost-effective way of waging war covertly, through the use of surrogate warriors or 'guns for hire.'" State-sponsored terrorist

organizations are discussed in greater detail later in this chapter.

Left-wing terrorists seek to destroy economies based on free enterprise and to replace them with socialist or communist economic systems; *right-wing terrorists* are motivated by fascist ideals and work toward the dissolution of democratic governments, and their leaders seek personal political power and often envision themselves as likely candidates for the role of beneficent dictator. *Anarchist terrorists* are revolutionaries who seek to overthrow all established forms of government. Table 14–4 shows groups that are representative of each kind of terrorism, and a glance at the table shows that some groups, such as Hezbollah (a religiously motivated terrorist organization that has received financial support from Iran), may fit into more than one category.

Other kinds of terrorist typologies can also be described. The United States has to deal with two types of terrorism: domestic and international. **Domestic terrorism** refers to the unlawful use of force or violence by an individual or a group based and operating entirely within the United States and its territories, without foreign direction; its acts are directed at elements of the U.S. government or population.[38] **International terrorism**, in contrast, is the unlawful use of force or violence by an individual or a group that has a connection to a foreign power or whose activities transcend national boundaries against persons or property to intimidate or coerce a government, the civilian population, or any segment of it to further political or social objectives.[39]

> The United States has to deal with two types of terrorism: domestic and international.

TABLE 14-4 | Types of Terrorist Groups

NATIONALIST	RELIGIOUS	STATE-SPONSORED	LEFT-WING	RIGHT-WING	ANARCHIST
Basque Fatherland and Liberty, Irish Republican Army, Kurdistan Workers' Party	Al-Qaeda, Aum Shinrikyo (Japan), HAMAS, Hezbollah	Abu Nidal Organization (Syria, Libya), Hezbollah (backed by Iran), Japanese Red Army (Libya)	Baader-Meinhof Gang (Germany), Japanese Red Army, Red Brigades (Italy)	Neo-Nazis, skinheads, white supremacists	Some contemporary antiglobalization groups

Source: Derived from information provided by the Council on Foreign Relations and the Markle Foundation, *Types of Terrorism*, http://www.terrorismanswers.com/terrorism/types.html, *and* http://www.cfr.org/issue/135/terrorism.html (accessed January 10, 2006, and July 10, 2010).

International terrorism is sometimes incorrectly called *foreign terrorism*, a term that refers only to acts of terrorism occurring outside the United States.

International Terrorism

According to the National Counterterrorism Center (NCTC), approximately 11,000 terrorist attacks occurred around the world against noncombatants during 2009, resulting in almost 15,000 deaths (Figures 14–3 and 14–4).[40] The largest number of terrorist incidents and deaths reported in 2009 occurred in the Middle East and South Asia, which accounted for 90% of the high-casualty attacks that killed ten or more people. Of the 11,000 reported attacks, about 2,500 of them occurred in Iraq, where approximately 3,650 fatalities were reported.

Sunni extremists were identified with about one-half of all attacks worldwide in 2009. The Taliban claimed credit for the largest number of attacks causing the highest number of fatalities. Al-Shabaab was the second deadliest group, followed by al-Qa'ida in Iraq as the third deadliest group.

A significant number of victims of terrorist attacks in 2009 were Muslim. Almost 58,000 individuals worldwide were either killed or injured by terrorist attacks in 2009, and well over 50% were Muslims. Most were victims of Sunni extremist attacks in Iraq, Pakistan, and Afghanistan. View the latest edition of the National Counterterrorism Center's *Report on Terrorism* via **Library Extra 14–6**.

Experts warn that the United States may soon suffer from more incidents of international terrorism. As one terrorism expert explained, "As long as the United States remains actively engaged in the world, as it clearly must, there will be governments and groups committed to the use of violence to attack U.S. interests and further their own political goals."[41]

Domestic Terrorism

The 1995 terrorist bombing of the Alfred P. Murrah federal building in downtown Oklahoma City, in which 168 people died and hundreds more were wounded, demonstrated just how vulnerable the United States was to terrorist attacks from

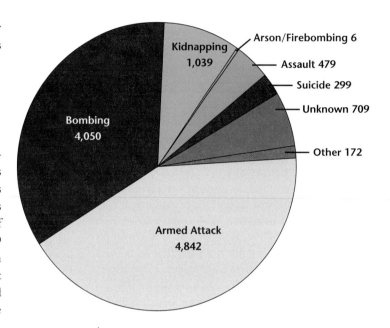

FIGURE 14-3 | Worldwide Terrorism Attacks by Method, 2009

Source: National Counterterrorism Center, *2009 Report on Terrorism* (Washington, DC: NCTC, 2010), http://www.nctc.gov/witsbanner/docs/2009_report_on_terrorism.pdf (accessed August 28, 2010), p. 22.

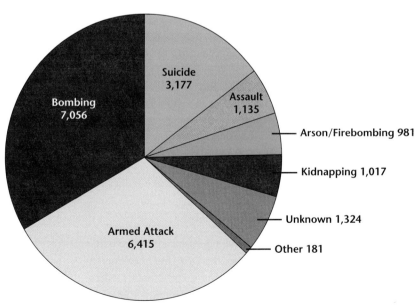

Note: 14,971 Total Deaths. Some double counting may occur when multiple methods are used.

FIGURE 14-4 | Worldwide Deaths from Terrorist Attacks by Method of Attack, 2009

Source: National Counterterrorism Center, *2009 Report on Terrorism* (Washington, DC: NCTC, 2010), http://www.nctc.gov/witsbanner/docs/2009_report_on_terrorism.pdf (accessed August 28, 2010), p. 15.

Follow the author's tweets about the latest crime and justice news at http://twitter.com/schmalleger.

WHO'S TO BLAME—The Individual or Society?

The Making of a Suicide Bomber

Khaled Al-Rasheed was born in New York City to Egyptian parents and repeatedly visited the Middle East with his father. His last trip was in 2008 when Khaled spent part of the summer with his grandparents near the world-famous Aswan dam. Although his American passport didn't show it, Khaled, a Muslim, had traveled extensively throughout the Arab world while he was growing up, sometimes in the company of his father, and sometimes with his grandfather.

He had seen firsthand the damage done by the first Gulf War in 1991, much of which hadn't been repaired by the time he first visited the region. He had also experienced the resentment festering among the huge non-Arab populations in Saudi Arabia and Kuwait, where oil money paid for the extravagant lifestyles of the royal families but didn't find its way into the hands of the working class.

By the time he was 15, he had befriended a group of radical young Islamists living in Jordan, who blamed the problems in the Middle East on the Great Satan—their name for America. "Americans are stealing our region's wealth," he was told, "and polluting the holy land with their vice and nonbelief."

Returning to the United States in the fall of 2008, Khaled had become radicalized and was ready to strike a blow in what he saw as a worldwide holy war against nonbelievers. As a U.S. citizen, he could travel easily in and out of the country, and on one of his trips he was able to smuggle in the equipment necessary to manufacture a new kind of explosive—one that could be packed into condoms and swallowed like the heroin and cocaine that often crossed the country's southern borders. Equipped with a small blasting-cap whose thin wire ran up the esophagus and into his mouth, the last charge to be swallowed could be set off by simply biting down on a tiny switch clenched between Khaled's molars. The device, which used very little metal, was virtually undetectable.

One day, Khaled swallowed six explosive-filled condoms, passed through security, and boarded a plane at New York's John F. Kennedy airport. Once the plane, bound for Los Angeles, was airborne, Khaled bit down on the detonator. To his surprise, nothing happened. An hour into the flight, however, one of the swallowed condoms ruptured, and Khaled became violently ill as its contents entered his digestive system. Taken off the plane when it landed in Los Angeles, he was taken to a hospital where the explosives were discovered. An operation saved his life, and he recovered in the medical wing of the Los Angeles County Men's Central Jail.

Think about it:

1. What does it mean to say, as this scenario does, that "Khaled had become radicalized"? Might the term be applied to other kinds of offenders? If so, which ones?

2. How could someone like Khaled, born in America, be so taken with a foreign ideology?

3. If you were in charge of policy making for America's "war on terror," what would you want to see happen to Khaled?

4. If you were a judge in charge of sentencing Khaled for his attempted terrorist attack, what kind of sentence would you give him? Is there any chance that he might be rehabilitated? What does "rehabilitation" mean in this context?

Note: Who's to Blame boxes provide fictionalized critical thinking opportunities, and are not actual cases.

domestic sources. The nine-story building—which included offices of the Social Security Administration, the Drug Enforcement Administration, the Secret Service, and the Bureau of Alcohol, Tobacco, and Firearms as well as a day-care center called America's Kids—was devastated by the homemade bomb. The device (made of fertilizer and diesel fuel) used in the attack, estimated to have weighed approximately 1,200 pounds, was left in a parked rental truck on the 5th Street side of the building, and the blast left a crater 30 feet wide and 8 feet deep and spread debris over a ten-block area.

In June 1997, a federal jury found 29-year-old Timothy McVeigh guilty of 11 counts ranging from conspiracy to first-degree murder in the bombing. Jurors concluded that McVeigh had conspired with Terry Nichols, a friend he had met while both were in the army, and with unknown others to use a truck bomb to destroy the Murrah building. Prosecutors argued that the attack was intended to avenge the 1993 assault on David Koresh's Branch Davidian complex in Waco (Texas) that left 78 cult members dead and happened two years to the day before the Oklahoma City attack. Following the

LIBRARY EXTRA 14–7

▣ **cyberterrorism**
A form of terrorism that makes use of high technology, especially computer technology and the Internet, in planning and carrying out terrorist attacks.

▣ **infrastructure**
The basic facilities, services, and installations needed for the functioning of a community or society, such as its transportation and communications systems, water and power lines, and public institutions.

guilty verdicts, McVeigh was sentenced to die.[42] His coconspirator, Terry Nichols, was convicted of eight counts of involuntary manslaughter but escaped the death penalty. In late 1999, McVeigh requested that all appeals on his behalf be dropped and that an execution date be set, and he was executed at the Terre Haute (Indiana) federal correctional facility on June 11, 2001.

A less-lethal but still frightening series of terrorist incidents in late 2001 and early 2002 involved the mailing of letters laced with weapons-grade (highly dispersible) anthrax that were sent to members of Congress and to the news media, causing the deaths of five people and sickening at least 17 others, and that resulted in the shutdown of contaminated mail facilities and government buildings.[43] From the initial reports in New York and Florida in early September and October 2001 to the discovery of anthrax spores in a letter mailed to the U.S. Senate on October 15, a series of escalating safety concerns about opening, handling, and even being in the proximity of mail—especially in government offices in Washington, D.C.—led to disruptions in and even total curtailments of mail delivery service at many federal agencies. No agency was hit harder than the Department of Justice, where anthrax was found in a central mail facility.[44] The attacks turned mail delivery into a potentially lethal experience. Widespread testing of exposed locations and the irradiation treatment of all undelivered mail followed, and it was months before full mail service was restored to all government offices. See **Library Extra 14–7** for a discussion of measures meant to curtail domestic terrorism.

Cyberterrorism

There is a new kind of threat called **cyberterrorism**, a form of terrorism that makes use of high technology, especially computers, the Internet, and the World Wide Web, for planning and carrying out terrorist attacks. Most common forms of terrorism target people and things—the physical world; cyberterrorism targets software, information, and communications—the virtual world. The term *cyberterrorism* was coined in the 1980s by Barry Collin, a senior research fellow at the Institute for Security and Intelligence in California who used it to refer to the convergence of cyberspace and terrorism.[45] It was later popularized by a 1996

> **Cyberterrorism makes use of high technology in planning and carrying out terrorist attacks.**

A surveillance photo released by the Brooklyn U.S. Attorney's Office showing an unidentified police informant (right) with alleged bomb plotter Shahawar Matin Siraj (center) and his alleged coconspirator, James Elshafay, in New York City on August 21, 2004. Siraj, age 23, was arrested on the eve of the 2004 Republican National Convention on charges that he wanted to attack a subway station in Herald Square, a dense shopping district in the city that includes Macy's department store. What is the nature of the threat represented by "homegrown" terrorists like Siraj, and how does it differ from that represented by international terrorist organizations like Al-Qaeda?
Source: Brooklyn U.S. Attorney's Office/HO/AP Wide World Photos

RAND report that warned of an emerging "new terrorism" being implemented by terrorist groups organizing and using technology; it warned of a coming "netwar," or "infowar," consisting of coordinated cyberattacks on our nation's economic, business, and military infrastructures.[46] A country's **infrastructure** consists of the basic facilities, services, and installations needed for its functioning, such as transportation and communications systems, water and power lines, and institutions serving the public (banks, schools, post offices, prisons).[47]

Following the RAND report, (then) President Bill Clinton announced the formation of the President's Commission on Critical Infrastructure Protection (PCCIP) to study the critical components of the support systems of the nation, determine their vulnerabilities to a wide range of threats, and propose a strategy for protecting them in the future.[48] Eight critical infrastructure components were identified: telecommunications, banking and finance, electrical power, oil and gas distribution and storage, water supply, transportation, emergency services, and government services.[49] PCCIP was the first national effort to address the vulnerabilities created by the information age.[50]

Earlier in 1998, the federal National Infrastructure Protection Center (NIPC) was created to serve as a focal point within the U.S. government for threat assessment, warning, investigation, and response to threats or attacks against the nation's critical infrastructure. NIPC functions have since been assumed by various groups within the DHS Information Analysis and Infrastructure Protection (IAIP) Directorate.

The Critical Infrastructure Assurance Office (CIAO) was created by a Presidential Decision Directive in May 1998 to coordinate the federal government's initiatives on critical infrastructure protection, and its responsibilities expanded in 2001 when (then) President George W. Bush signed an executive order establishing the President's Critical Infrastructure Protection Board (PCIPB).[51] In September 2002, the board released a study called *The National Strategy to Secure Cyberspace*, which stated that "for the United States, the Information Technology Revolution quietly changed the way business and government operate. Without a great deal of thought about security, the nation shifted the control of essential processes in manufacturing, utilities, banking, and communications to networked computers. As a result, the cost of doing business dropped and productivity skyrocketed."[52] The board found that "our economy and national security are fully dependent upon information technology and the information infrastructure. A network of networks directly supports the operation of all sectors of our economy—energy (electric power, oil and gas), transportation (rail, air, merchant marine), finance and banking, information and telecommunications, public health, emergency services, water, chemical, defense industrial base, food, agriculture, and postal and shipping. The reach of these computer networks exceeds the bounds of cyberspace. They also control physical objects such as electrical transformers, trains, pipeline pumps, chemical vats, radars, and stock markets."[53] In 2003, the functions of the CIAO were transferred to the National Cyber Security Division (NCSD) of the newly created DHS; the creation of NCSD improved protection of critical cyberassets by "maximizing and leveraging the resources" of previously separate offices.[54]

Scenarios describing cyberterrorism possibilities are imaginative and diverse, ranging from a successful cyberterrorist attack on the nation's air traffic control system, causing multiple airplanes to collide in midair, to an attack on food and cereal processing plants, drastically altering the levels of certain nutritional supplements to sicken or kill a large proportion of our nation's young children. Other terrorist attacks could cause the country's power grid to collapse or could muddle the records and transactions of banks and stock exchanges. The possibilities are almost endless.

In an effort to protect its vital interests from future acts of terrorism, the U.S. government has built a whole new Internet of its own. Dubbed "GovNet," the service is a private voice and data network based on the Internet Protocol (IP) that has no connectivity with commercial or public networks and is physically and electronically separate from existing Internet routers and gateways; a key feature of this network is that it must be able to perform its functions with no risk of penetration or disruption from users on other networks.[55] The idea for GovNet was first offered by Richard Clarke, President Bush's cybersecurity adviser, in late 2001: "We'll be working to secure our cyberspace from a range of possible threats, from hackers to criminals to terrorist groups, to foreign nations, which might use cyber war against us."[56] **Library Extra 14–8** provides additional insight into the issue of cyberterrorism.

Terrorism and Technology

The technological sophistication of state-sponsored terrorist organizations is rapidly increasing. Handguns and even larger weapons are now being manufactured out of plastic polymers and ceramics; they are capable of firing Teflon-coated, armor-piercing hardened ceramic bullets and are extremely powerful as well as impossible to discern with metal detectors. The black market makes available other sinister items, including liquid metal embrittlement (LME), a chemical that slowly weakens any metal it contacts, which some experts say could be applied with a felt-tipped marker to fuselage components in domestic aircraft, causing delayed structural failure.[57] Backpack-type electromagnetic pulse generators may be used by terrorists who would carry them into major cities, set them up next to important computer installations, and activate them to wipe out billions of items of financial, military, or other information now stored on magnetic media. International terrorists, along with the general public, have easy access to maps and other information that could be used to cripple the nation. The approximately 500 extremely high-voltage (EHV) transformers on which the nation's electric grid depends, for example, are largely undefended but have been specified with extreme geographic accuracy on easily available Web-based power-network maps.

It is clear that at least some terrorist organizations are seeking to obtain weapons of mass destruction (WMDs) for possible chemical, biological, radiological, and nuclear threats. A CIA report made public in 2003 warned that al-Qaeda's end goal is to use WMDs and noted that the group had "openly expressed its desire to produce nuclear weapons" and that sketches and documents recovered from an al-Qaeda facility in Afghanistan contained plans for a crude nuclear device.[58] A 2008 report by the federal Commission on the Prevention of Weapons of Mass

WEB EXTRA 14–5
WEB EXTRA 14–6
LIBRARY EXTRA 14–9

Destruction Proliferation and Terrorism contained the frightening conclusion that "unless the world community acts decisively and with great urgency, it is more likely than not that a weapon of mass destruction will be used in a terrorist attack somewhere in the world by the end of 2013."[59] Earlier in 2003, a study by Harvard University researchers found that the United States and other countries were moving too slowly in efforts to help Russia and other former Soviet-bloc nations destroy poorly protected nuclear material and warheads left over from the cold war; the study also warned that most civilian nuclear reactors in Eastern Europe are "dangerously insecure."[60] Experts said the amount of plutonium needed to make one bomb can be smuggled out of a supposedly secure area in a briefcase or even in the pocket of an overcoat.

Biological weapons were banned by the 1975 international Biological Weapons Convention (BWC),[61] but a biocrime called *bioterrorism*—defined by the Centers for Disease Control and Prevention (CDC) as the "intentional or threatened use of viruses, bacteria, fungi, or toxins from living organisms to produce death or disease in humans, animals, or plants"[62]—is of considerable concern today. The infamous anthrax letters mailed to at least four people in the United States in 2001 (discussed earlier) provide an example of a bioterrorism incident intended to create widespread fear among Americans; five people (including mail handlers) died, and 23 others were infected.[63] Other possible bioterrorism agents include botulism toxin, brucellosis, cholera, glanders, plague, ricin, smallpox, and tularemia Q fever as well as a number of viral agents like viral hemorrhagic fevers and severe acute respiratory syndrome (SARS). Experts fear that technologically savvy terrorists could create their own novel bioweapons through bioengineering, a process that uses snippets of made-to-order DNA, the molecular code on which life is based.[64] Learn more about biological agents via the CDC Web site at **Web Extra 14–5**, and visit the Center for the Study of Bioterrorism via **Web Extra 14–6**. An intriguing paper on the topic of bioterrorism from the CDC is available as **Library Extra 14–9**.

> The technological sophistication of state-sponsored terrorist organizations is rapidly increasing.

The War on Terrorism

During the first years of the Bush presidency, terrorist attacks and corporate scandals demanded the attention of federal legislators and the Oval Office, and three important legislative initiatives resulted. The USA PATRIOT Act was rushed through Congress in response to the September 11, 2001, attacks on the World Trade Center and the Pentagon ("USA PATRIOT" stands for "Uniting and Strengthening America by Providing Appropriate Tools Required to Intercept and Obstruct Terrorism") and became law on October 26, 2001.[65] The Sarbanes-Oxley Act was signed into law on July 30, 2002, as a response to a series of corporate bankruptcies and a declining stock market brought on by the misdeeds of executives at a number of the nation's large corporations; it established new requirements for corporate governance and set stiff criminal punishments for violators (the act is discussed more fully in Chapter 14). The Homeland Security Act of 2002 became law on November 25, 2002, and created a new cabinet-level department charged with helping to prevent, protect against, and respond to acts of terrorism on American soil (the DHS), and it restructured the executive branch of the federal government.

USA PATRIOT Act

Like the Homeland Security Act, the USA PATRIOT Act was designed to fight terrorism, but it contained provisions that applied to other forms of criminal activity as well. The act permitted longer jail terms for certain suspects arrested without a warrant, broadened "sneak and peak" search authority (searches conducted without notice), enhanced the power of prosecutors, and increased the ability of federal authorities to tap phones (including wireless devices), share intelligence information, track Internet usage, crack down on money laundering, and protect the country's borders.

The USA PATRIOT Act is not a stand-alone law—it amends various federal statutes and rules: federal Wiretap Statute,[66] the Bank Secrecy Act of 1970,[67] the federal Pen Register and Trap and Trace Statute,[68] the Electronic Communications Privacy Act (ECPA),[69] the Foreign Intelligence Surveillance Act of 1978 (FISA),[70] the Federal Rules of Criminal Procedure,[71] immigration laws, and the Family Education Rights and Privacy Act (FERPA).[72] The act led some to question whether the government unfairly expanded police powers at the expense of individual rights and civil liberties. Prior to passage, the legislation had been questioned by the American Civil Liberties Union (ACLU), which feared it would substantially reduce the constitutional rights of individuals facing justice system processing. After the bill became law, the ACLU pledged to work with the president and law enforcement agencies across the country "to ensure that civil liberties in America are not eroded."[73] Some of the law's strictest provisions were slated to "sunset" at the end of 2005, but most were renewed by congressional action before they could expire.

Department of Homeland Security

The Homeland Security Act of 2002, enacted to protect America against terrorism, established the federal DHS, which is also charged with protecting the nation's critical infrastructure against a terrorist attack.[74] The director is a member of the president's Cabinet.

Experts have said that the creation of DHS is the most significant transformation of the U.S. government since 1947, when President Harry S. Truman merged the various branches of the armed forces into the Department of Defense in an effort to better coordinate the nation's defense against military threats.[75] DHS coordinates the activities of 22 disparate domestic agencies by placing administration of those agencies under five directorates or departmental divisions:

1. **Border and Transportation Security (BTS)**. The BTS is responsible for maintaining security of the nation's borders and transportation systems. It assumed the border-security functions of the former Immigration and Naturalization Service.[76]

2. **Emergency Preparedness and Response (EPR)**. The EPR works to ensure that the nation is prepared for, and able to recover from, terrorist attacks and natural disasters.

3. **Science and Technology (S&T)**. The S&T directorate coordinates the department's efforts in research and development, including preparing for and responding to the full range of terrorist threats involving weapons of mass destruction.

4. **Information Analysis and Infrastructure Protection (IAIP)**. The IAIP merges under one roof the functions of identifying and assessing a broad range of intelligence information concerning threats to the homeland, issuing timely warnings, and taking appropriate preventive and protective action.

5. **Management**. The Management Directorate is responsible for budgetary, managerial, and personnel issues within DHS.

Besides the five directorates, several other critical agencies have been folded into the new department or were created:[77]

- **U.S. Coast Guard (USCG)**. The commandant of the USCG reports directly to the secretary of DHS, but the USCG also works closely with the undersecretary of BTS and maintains its existing identity as an independent military service. Upon declaration of war or when the president so directs, the USCG would operate as an element of the Department of Defense, consistent with existing law.

- **U.S. Secret Service**. The primary mission of the Secret Service is the protection of the president and other government leaders and the security for designated national events. The Secret Service is also the primary agency responsible for protecting U.S. currency from counterfeiters and safeguarding Americans from credit-card fraud.

- **Bureau of Citizenship and Immigration Services**. While the BTS is responsible for enforcing our nation's immigration laws, the newly created Bureau of Citizenship and Immigration Services dedicates its energies to providing efficient immigration services and easing the transition to American citizenship.

- **Office of State and Local Government Coordination**. The Office of State and Local Government Coordination ensures close coordination among local, state, and federal governments to ensure an effective terrorism-prevention effort and to provide quick responses to terrorist incidents.

- **Office of Private Sector Liaison**. The Office of Private Sector Liaison provides the business community with a direct line of communication to DHS by working directly with individual businesses and through trade associations and other nongovernmental organizations to foster dialogue between the private sector and DHS on the full range of issues and challenges that America's businesses face today.

- **Office of Inspector General**. The Office of Inspector General serves as an independent and objective inspection, audit, and investigative body to promote effectiveness, efficiency, and economy in DHS programs and operations and to prevent and detect fraud, abuse, mismanagement, and waste.

Figure 14–5 shows the organizational chart for the DHS. You can reach DHS on the Web via **Web Extra 14–7**.

Terrorism Commissions and Reports

A number of government and private groups have issued reports on terrorism and America's preparedness to deal with threats of terrorism, one of the most important being the Gilmore Commission (officially known as the Advisory Panel to Assess Domestic Response Capabilities for Terrorism Involving Weapons of Mass Destruction), established by Section 1405 of the National Defense Authorization Act for Fiscal Year 1999.[78] That act directed

LIBRARY EXTRA 14-10
LIBRARY EXTRA 14-11
LIBRARY EXTRA 14-12

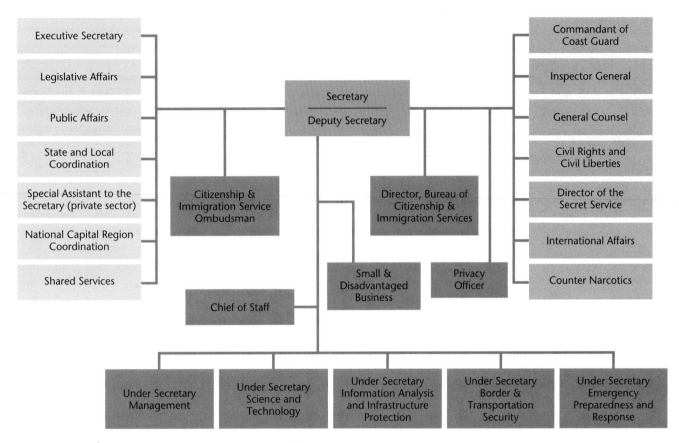

FIGURE 14-5 | Department of Homeland Security

Source: Department of Homeland Security.

that a federally funded research and development center provide research, analytical, and other support to the advisory panel during the course of its activities and deliberations.

Under contract with the Department of Defense, RAND provided that support and was the corporate author of three annual Gilmore Commission reports to the president and Congress that have been issued. The first, published on December 15, 1999, provided an in-depth overview of terrorist threats facing the United States. The second report, on December 14, 2000, focused on the need for a national antiterrorism strategy encompassing the full spectrum of deterrence, prevention, preparedness, and response and called for coordination among state and local officials to address intelligence, law enforcement, fire services, public health, and emergency medical and emergency management issues involved in the fight against terrorism. The third Gilmore Commission report, published

> A number of government and private groups have issued reports on terrorism.

on December 15, 2001 (the first to be released after the events of September 11, 2001), emphasized the need for improvements in state and local response capabilities, enhanced immigration standards and better border control, improved security against cyberattacks, and an expanded role for the military in fighting terrorism. The three Gilmore Commission reports are available in their entirety as **Library Extras 14–10, 14–11,** and **14–12.**

Another important group, the U.S. Commission on National Security in the 21st Century (also known as the Hart-Rudman Commission) has reported in three phases:

- **Phase I report—New World Coming: American Security in the 21st Century (September 15, 1999).** The Phase I report discussed relevant economic, technological, and intellectual influences throughout the global community and underscored the powerful forces of social and political fragmentation occurring in many places in the world. This new world order requires a new and comprehensive U.S. international strategy.

LIBRARY EXTRA 14–13
LIBRARY EXTRA 14–14
LIBRARY EXTRA 14–15
LIBRARY EXTRA 14–16
LIBRARY EXTRA 14–17

Members of the National Commission on Terrorist Attacks upon the United States (aka the 9/11 Commission) (from left): Thomas H. Kean, Lee H. Hamilton, Fred F. Fielding, Bob Kerrey, John F. Lehman, and Richard Ben-Veniste. The commission's report, released on July 22, 2004, called for a major overhaul of U.S. intelligence agencies and a realignment of federal expenditures on homeland security. Acts of terrorism generally involve a multitude of criminal law violations. What crimes were committed by the terrorists who attacked the World Trade Center and the Pentagon?
Source: Doug Mills/*New York Times*

- **Phase II report—Seeking a National Strategy: A Concert for Preserving Security and Promoting Freedom (April 15, 2000)**. The Phase II report suggested U.S. antiterrorism priorities for the future: defending the homeland; maintaining America's internal social cohesion, economic competitiveness, technological ingenuity, and military strength; assisting with the macroeconomic and political integration of key major powers, such as China, Russia, and India; promoting growth of the global economy; establishing needed international laws and agreements; adapting existing alliances to meet new challenges; and helping sustain international stability.

- **Phase III report—Roadmap for National Security (January 31, 2001)**. The Phase III report examined multiple potential threats to homeland security, emphasized the need to capitalize on America's strengths in the sciences and education, and suggested that the human requirements needed for adequate national security are not being met.

All three reports are available in their entirety as **Library Extras 14–13**, **14–14**, and **14–15**.

After leaving Congress, former Senators Gary Hart and Warren Rudman collaborated on a follow-up antiterrorism report sponsored by the Washington, D.C.–based Council on Foreign Relations titled *America Still Unprepared—America Still in Danger.*[79] It concluded that the United States remained "dangerously unprepared" to prevent or respond to attacks by well-organized terrorist groups. "America's own ill-prepared response could hurt its people to a much greater extent than any single attack by a terrorist."

The National Commission on Terrorism (known as the Bremmer Commission) was established under the federal Omnibus Consolidated and Emergency Supplemental Appropriations Act of 1999 to review and assess the laws, regulations, policies, directives, and practices relating to combating international terrorism directed against the United States as well as to recommend changes needed to improve U.S. counterterrorism performance.[80] The commission's June 7, 2000, report, titled *Countering the Changing Threat of International Terrorism*, outlined the changing face of international terrorism and offered diplomatic, intelligence, and law enforcement options for addressing that threat; it is available in its entirety as **Library Extra 14–16**.

On July 22, 2004, the National Commission on Terrorist Attacks upon the United States (the 9/11 Commission) released its highly anticipated 567-page report, which said that the September 11 attacks should have come as no surprise because the U.S. government had received clear warnings that Islamic terrorists were planning to strike at targets in the United States. The report stated that the United States was still not properly prepared to adequately deal with

> The 9/11 Commission said that the September 11 attacks should have come as no surprise.

terrorist threats and called for the creation of a new federal intelligence-gathering center to unify more than a dozen federal agencies gathering terrorism-related intelligence at home and abroad. The report also commented that the United States and other economically advanced nations should create a global strategy of diplomacy and public relations to counter Islamic terror networks and to defeat their ideology. "To Muslim parents, terrorists like bin Laden have nothing to offer their children but visions of violence and death. America and its friends have the advantage—our vision can offer a better future." The entire 567-page report is available as **Library Extra 14–17**.

In December 2008, the Commission on the Prevention of Weapons of Mass Destruction Proliferation and Terrorism

LIBRARY EXTRA 14–18
LIBRARY EXTRA 14–19
LIBRARY EXTRA 14–20
WEB EXTRA 14–8

■ **foreign terrorist organization (FTO)**
A foreign organization that engages in terrorist activity threatening the security of U.S. nationals or the national security of the United States and that is so designated by the U.S. secretary of state.

(mentioned earlier) reported to Congress on the threat from terrorists seeking to obtain and deploy biological and nuclear weapons; its report focused on weapons with the "greatest potential to kill in the most massive numbers."[81] It contained more than a dozen recommendations, including the following: "[The United States must] accelerate integration of effort among the counterproliferation, counterterrorism, and law enforcement communities to address WMD proliferation and terrorism issues; strengthen expertise in the nuclear and biological fields; prioritize pre-service and in-service training and retention of people with critical scientific, language, and foreign area skills; and ensure that the threat posed by biological weapons remains among the highest national intelligence priorities for collection and analysis." The commission went on to say, "The United States must build a national security workforce for the 21st century."[82] Read the commission's full 160-page report at **Library Extra 14–18**.

Countering of the Terrorist Threat

The U.S. Department of State, in its publication *Patterns of Global Terrorism*, made a number of policy recommendations for use in the fight against international terrorism. One of the most significant was that "Money is like oxygen to terrorists, and it must be choked-off."[83] In September 2001, President George W. Bush issued an executive order imposing stiff penalties on anyone providing financial support to terrorists or their organizations.[84] The order also blocked the assets of designated individuals and organizations linked to global terrorism; prohibited financial transactions with the terrorist groups, leaders, and corporate and charitable fronts listed in the order; and established America's ability to block the U.S. assets of (and deny access to U.S. markets to) any foreign banks refusing to freeze terrorists' assets.

In 2003, the White House released its official *National Strategy for Combating Terrorism*, which included a multipronged initiative aimed at reducing both the threat severity and international reach of international terrorist organizations.[85] Following are its goals:

- Defeat terrorists and their organizations by identifying, locating, and destroying them.

- Deny sponsorship, support, and sanctuary to terrorists by helping other nations fulfill their responsibilities and obligations to combat terrorism.

- Diminish the underlying conditions that terrorists seek to exploit by resolving regional disputes; by fostering economic, social, and political development; by encouraging market-based economies; by supporting good governance and the rule of law; and by "winning the war of ideas" to ensure that ideologies that promote terrorism do not find fertile ground in any nation.

- Defend U.S. citizens and interests at home and abroad by implementing strong and effective security measures and by enhancing measures intended to ensure the integrity, reliability, and availability of critical physical and information-based infrastructures (including transportation and information systems).

The July 2004 report of the 9/11 Commission proposed sweeping changes within the U.S. intelligence community, including the creation of the position of a national intelligence director (NID), and then the Intelligence Reform and Terrorism Prevention Act of 2004 (IRTPA) facilitated the creation of the NCTC under the newly created position of NID.[86] The NID would act as the principal adviser to the president, the National Security Council, and the Homeland Security Council for intelligence matters related to national security, and the NCTC would serve as the primary organization for integrating and analyzing all intelligence pertaining to terrorism and counterterrorism and for conducting strategic counterterrorism operational planning.[87] Learn more about countering terrorist threats at **Library Extra 14–19**, and the *National Strategy* is available in its entirety at **Library Extra 14–20**. Visit the NCTC at **Web Extra 14–8**.

Foreign Terrorist Organizations

From the late 1970s to the mid-1990s, U.S. antiterrorism policy focused largely on deterring and punishing state sponsors of terrorism as opposed to terrorist groups themselves.[88] In 1996, passage of the federal Anti-Terrorism and Effective Death Penalty Act signaled an important shift in policy:[89] It recognized the transnationalism of many terrorist organizations, created a legal category of **foreign terrorist organizations (FTOs)**, and banned funding, granting of visas, and other material support to such organizations and their members. The USA PATRIOT Act extended and strengthened the provisions of that legislation.[90]

Federal law has required that any organization considered for FTO designation must (1) be *foreign* and engage in terrorist activity as defined in Section 212(a)(3)(B) of the Immigration

LIBRARY EXTRA 14–21

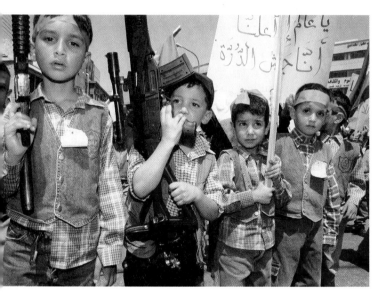

Palestinian boys wearing green ribbons on their heads in support of HAMAS and brandishing plastic rifles as they march through the streets of the West Bank town of Nablus in a protest rally against Israeli aggression. Some argue that terrorists already control the hearts and minds of young people in many parts of the world. What can be done to change that?
Source: Nasser Ishtayeh/AP Wide World Photos

and Nationality Act;[91] it must also threaten the security of U.S. nationals *or* the national security (national defense, foreign relations, *or* economic interests) of the United States. The U.S. Department of State has the authority to designate any group external to the United States as an FTO based on an exhaustive interagency review in which all evidence of a group's activity, from both classified and open sources, is scrutinized; the State Department, working closely with the Justice and Treasury Departments and the intelligence community, would prepare a detailed "administrative record" documenting the terrorist activity of the designated FTO. Under federal law, FTO designations are subject to judicial review, and in the event of a challenge to a group's FTO designation in federal court, the U.S. government would rely on the administrative records containing classified intelligence information to defend the designation decision. FTO designations expire in two years unless renewed.

Once an organization has been designated an FTO, a number of legal consequences ensue. It becomes unlawful for a person in the United States or subject to the jurisdiction of the United States to provide funds or other material support to a designated FTO, and representatives and certain members of a designated FTO can be denied visas or kept from entering the United States if they are aliens. Also U.S. financial institutions must block funds of designated FTOs and their agents and report the blockage to the Office of Foreign Assets Control in the U.S. Department of the Treasury. Designated FTOs can be found in Table 14–5.

The State Department also has the authority to designate selected foreign governments as *state sponsors of international terrorism*, and four countries currently are so designated: Cuba, Iran, Sudan, and Syria. Cuba continues to be a safe haven for several terrorists and U.S. fugitives and maintains ties to state sponsors of terrorism and Latin American insurgents. Iran remains the most active state sponsor of terrorism in the world: Iran's Islamic Revolutionary Guard Corps (IRGC) and the Ministry of Intelligence and Security (MOIS) continue to be involved in the planning and support of terrorist acts and aid a variety of groups that use terrorism to pursue their goals, and the Iranian government continues to provide support to numerous terrorist groups, including the Lebanese Hezbollah, HAMAS, and the Palestine Islamic Jihad (PIJ), all of which seek to undermine Middle East peace negotiations through the use of terrorism. Since 2007, Sudan has provided shelter for members of al-Qaeda, the Lebanese Hezbollah, al-Gama'a al-Islamiyya, Egyptian Islamic Jihad, the PIJ, and HAMAS in spite of being engaged in a counterterrorism dialogue with the United States since mid-2000. Syria offers safe haven and support to several terrorist groups, some of which oppose the Middle East peace negotiations. Learn more about terrorist activities in individual countries from the Department of State's Country Reports on Terrorism via **Library Extra 14–21**.

> The State Department has the authority to designate foreign governments as state sponsors of international terrorism.

The 2001 USA PATRIOT Act created a Terrorist Exclusion List (TEL) with immigration consequences for groups on the list.[92] The federal government may deport aliens living in the United States who provide material assistance to organizations listed on the TEL and may refuse entry to the country to anyone who assists or solicits assistance for those organizations.

At the individual level, the U.S. government's Terrorist Identities Datamart Environment (TIDE) serves as a central repository of information on international terrorist identities.[93] TIDE supports the federal government's various terrorist screening systems or "watchlists" and the U.S. Intelligence Community's overall counterterrorism efforts. The Terrorist Identities Group (TIG), located in NCTC's Information Sharing and Knowledge

WEB EXTRA 14-9
WEB EXTRA 14-10
WEB EXTRA 14-11

TABLE 14-5 | Designated Foreign Terrorist Organizations

Abu Nidal Organization (ANO)
Abu Sayyaf Group (ASG)
Al-Aqsa Martyrs Brigade
Al-Qaeda
Ansar al-Islam (AI)
Armed Islamic Group (GIA)
Asbat al-Ansar
Aum Shinrikyo
Basque Fatherland and Liberty (ETA)
Communist Party of Philippines/New People's Army (CPP/NPA)
Al-Gama's al-Islamiyya (also called Islamic Group (IG))
HAMAS (Islamic Resistance Movement)
Harakat ul Mujahidin (HUM)
Hezbollah (also called Party of God)
Islamic Movement of Uzbekistan (IMU)
Jaish-e-Mohammed (JEM)
Jemaah Islamiya (JI)
Al-Jihad (also called Egyptian Islamic Jihad (EIJ))
Kahane Chai (Kach)
Kongra-Gel (KGK; formerly Kurdistan Workers' Party (PKK, KADEK))
Lashkar-e-Tayyiba (LT)
Lashkar I Jhangvi (LJ)
Liberation Tigers of Tamil Eelam (LTTE)
Mujahedin-e Khalq Organization (MEK or MKO)
National Liberation Army (ELN) of Colombia
Palestine Islamic Jihad (PIJ)
Palestine Liberation Front (PLF)
Popular Front for the Liberation of Palestine (PFLP)
Popular Front for the Liberation of Palestine—General Command (PFLP-GC)
Real IRA (RIRA)
Revolutionary Armed Forces of Colombia (FARC)
Revolutionary Nuclei (RN)
Revolutionary Organization 17 November (17 November)
Revolutionary People's Liberation Party/Front (DHKP/C)
Salafist Group for Call and Combat (GSPC)
Sendero Luminoso (SL; also called Shining Path)
United Self-Defense Forces/Group of Colombia (AUC)

Note: For more detailed descriptions of these organizations, see the National Counterterrorism Center, *2007 Report on Terrorism*, http://www.terrorisminfo.mipt.org/GetDoc.asp?id=6051&type=d; and the U.S. Department of State's *Country Reports on Terrorism*, http://www.terrorisminfo.mipt.org/GetDoc.asp?id=6047&type=d.

Development Directorate (ISKD), is responsible for building and maintaining TIDE, whose database includes all information the U.S. government has on the identities of individuals who are known or lawfully suspected to be or who have been involved in terrorism-related activities. Federal agencies nominate individuals based on evaluations of available intelligence and law enforcement antiterrorism information; then federal data analysts create and enhance TIDE records based on their review of those nominations and daily transmit those data to the Terrorist Screening Center (TSC) for use in the government's consolidated watchlist. The watchlist supports screening processes to detect and interdict known and suspected terrorists at home and abroad and is used to create and maintain the Transportation Security Administration's "no-fly list," the Department of State's visa database, and other similar databases.

Present U.S. policy focuses largely on terrorist organizations like al-Qaeda and their affiliated networks and state supporters.[94] New brands of terrorists—individuals who not affiliated with any established terrorist organization who are apparently not agents of any state sponsor—are also emerging; for example, the terrorist Ramzi Ahmed Yousef, believed to have masterminded the 1993 World Trade Center bombing, apparently did not belong to any larger established terrorist group, although he may have had some ties to al-Qaeda operatives. The worldwide threat of individual or "boutique" terrorism and "spontaneous" terrorist activity, such as the bombing of bookstores in the United States after Ayatollah Khomeini's death edict against British author Salman Rushdie, appears to be on the increase. Because the U.S. international counterterrorism policy framework has been sanctions oriented and has traditionally sought to pin responsibility on state sponsors, changes in policy are being considered and implemented.

Another problem surfacing in the wake of incidents associated with Islamic fundamentalist groups is how to condemn and combat such terrorist activity—and the extreme and violent ideology of specific radical groups—without appearing to be anti-Islamic in general. A desire to punish a state for supporting international terrorism may also conflict with other foreign policy objectives involving that nation. Learn more about terrorism from the Terrorism Research Center via **Web Extra 14–9** and the Lawson Terrorism Information Center at **Web Extra 14–10**, or visit the NCTC via **Web Extra 14–11**.

The Future of Terrorism

The Congressional Research Service identified three trends in modern terrorism.[95] The first trend—one that makes terrorism especially difficult to combat—is toward loosely organized, self-financed international terrorist networks. The second is toward terrorism that is religiously or ideologically motivated, and groups using religion as a pretext (such as radical Islamic fundamentalist groups) pose serious terrorist threats of varying kinds to U.S. interests and call upon other like-minded people throughout the world to join their causes. The third trend is the recent growth of cross-national links among different terrorist organizations, which may involve combinations of military training, funding, technology transfer, and political advice. The Congressional Research cited intelligence reports showing, for example, that Chechen rebels have been trained in al-Qaeda terrorist camps in Afghanistan and even in Chechnya itself; al-Qaeda funding reputedly helped establish the Islamic separatist group Abu Sayyaf in the Philippines; and some intelligence reports have suggested the possibility of mid- and low-level cooperation between al-Qaeda and the Lebanese Hezbollah in weapons smuggling, money laundering, and training for terrorist operations.

Looming over the entire issue of international terrorism is a trend toward proliferation of WMDs. Iran has been aggressively seeking nuclear arms capability; Iraq is thought to be stockpiling chemical and biological agents and rebuilding its nuclear weapons program. North Korea has admitted to having a clandestine program for uranium enrichment, and indications have also surfaced that al-Qaeda has attempted to acquire chemical, biological, radiological, and nuclear weapons. Stakes in the war against international terrorism are increasing, and margins for error in selecting appropriate policy instruments or combinations of them to prevent terrorist attacks are diminishing.

> Looming over the issue of international terrorism is the proliferation of WMDs.

SUMMARY

- Globalization refers to the increasing integration of previously isolated events in all areas of life and to its effects on people throughout the world. Globalization makes it impossible for U.S. policymakers to ignore criminal activity in other parts of the world. Transnational crime refers to unlawful activity undertaken and supported by organized criminal groups operating across national boundaries whose activities include fraudulent e-mail and phishing schemes, drug running, sex tourism, illegal trafficking in human beings and human organs, and international trade in weapons of mass destruction.

- Comparative criminology is the study of crime on a cross-national level. By comparing crime patterns in one country with those in another, accepted local theories can be reevaluated in light of world experiences. *Globalization of knowledge*, a term describing the increased understanding due to sharing of information among cultures, plays a significant role in both criminological theory formation and American crime-control policies. Ethnocentrism, or culture-centeredness, can interfere with the work of comparative criminologists in gathering, analyzing, and presenting crime statistics by causing those statistics to only reflect the social and political arenas in which they were generated.

- Terrorism is politically motivated violence planned and perpetrated against noncombatant targets by subnational groups or clandestine agents to bring about change in an existing social order, often with the threat of massive destruction and large numbers of casualties. Domestic and international terrorism are two main forms of terrorism; specific terrorist activities include cyberterrorism and attacks on information-management segments of our nation's critical infrastructure. The vigilance required to prevent both domestic and international terrorism has resulted in new laws restricting some freedoms that many Americans had previously taken for granted.

KEY TERMS

comparative criminologist, 401

comparative criminology, 401

cyberterrorism, 409

domestic terrorism, 406

ethnocentrism, 401

foreign terrorist organization (FTO), 415

globalization, 396

human smuggling, 397

infrastructure, 409

international terrorism, 406

sex trafficking, 400

terrorism, 404

trafficking in persons (TIP), 398

transnational organized crime, 396

QUESTIONS FOR REVIEW

1. What is globalization? How does it impact transnational criminal activity in the world today?

2. What is comparative criminology? What are the advantages of a comparative approach in the study of criminology?

3. What is terrorism? What types of terrorism does this chapter discuss?

QUESTIONS FOR REFLECTION

1. What are the advantages of a comparative perspective in criminology? Are there any disadvantages? If so, what are they?

2. What types of terrorism has this chapter identified? Are there any that it might have missed? If so, what are they?

3. Has the "war against terror" affected you personally? If so, how?

4. Has the average American had to sacrifice any rights or freedoms in the fight against terrorism? If so, what rights or freedoms have been sacrificed?

5. Is it true that the only way to secure freedom is to curtail it during times of national crisis? Why or why not?

EPILOGUE

FUTURE DIRECTIONS

LEARNING OUTCOMES

After reading this epilogue, you should be able to answer the following questions:

- What techniques are used in the field of futures research for assessing the future?

- What are some likely future crimes, and how will future criminal activity differ from criminal activity today?

- What can be predicted about the future of criminological theorizing?

■ **future criminology**
The study of likely futures as they impinge on crime and its control.
■ **futurist**
One who studies the future.

WEB EXTRA EP–1
LIBRARY EXTRA EP–1
LIBRARY EXTRA EP–2

Introduction

Canadian criminologist Gwynn Nettler once told a story of two people passing on a street in New York City.[1] One carried a pint of whiskey; the other had $100 in gold coins. In March 1933, near the end of the Prohibition era, the person with the alcohol would have been committing a crime, but the person carrying the gold would have been regarded as law-abiding. A year later, however, the same two people passing on the street would have occupied exactly the opposite legal positions: The repeal of Prohibition legalized carrying whiskey in most places, but gold hoarding became a federal crime in 1934 and remained so until 1974.

It is easy to look back in time and assess the legal standing of people like those in Nettler's story, but predicting what crimes the future will bring is far more difficult. The future is an abstract concept through which human beings bring symbolic order to the present and meaning to past endeavors.[2] From our present point of view, multiple futures exist, each of which is more or less probable and may or may not come to pass. In other words, the future contains an almost limitless number of possibilities, any of which might unfold but only a few of which actually will. Those who study the future are called **futurists**, and their task is to effectively distinguish among these impending possibilities, assessing the likelihood of each and making more or less realistic forecasts based on such assessments. **Future criminology** is the study of likely futures as they relate to crime and its control, and futurists working in the area of criminology try to imagine how crime will appear in both the near and the distant future.

Some assumptions about the future, such as estimates of future world populations, can be based on existing and highly credible public or private statistics and mathematical analyses of trends, but others are more intuitive and result from the integration of a wide range of diverse materials derived from many different sources. As one futurist explained, "Before we can plan the future, we must make some assumptions about what that future will be like. Assumptions about the future are not like assumptions in a geometry exercise. They are not abstract statements from which consequences can be derived with mathematical precision. But we need to make some assumptions about the future in order to plan it, prepare for it, and prevent undesired events from happening."[3]

Best known among groups that study the future is the World Future Society, which publishes *The Futurist*, a journal of well-considered essays about probable futures. Individual futurists who have become well known to the general public include Alvin Toffler, author of the trilogy of futurist titles *Future Shock*,[4] *Powershift*,[5] and *The Third Wave*;[6] John Naisbitt, author of *Megatrends: Ten New Directions Transforming Our Lives*;[7] Peter F. Drucker, author of *Management Challenges for the 21st Century*[8] and *Post-Capitalist Society*;[9] and Francis Fukuyama, author of *Our Posthuman Future*[10] and *The End of History and the Last Man*.[11]

Within criminology, the Society of Police Futurists International (PFI), representing the cutting edge of research into future crime-control policy, evolved from a conference of approximately 250 educators and practitioners representing most states and 20 different nations that was held at the FBI National Academy in Quantico, Virginia, in 1991; the society's Millennium Conference was held at the National Academy in July 2000. PFI members apply the principles of futures research to gain an understanding of the world as it is likely to be in the future.[12]

In 2002, PFI joined with the FBI to create the Futures Working Group (FWG), whose aim is to "develop and encourage others to develop forecasts and strategies to ethically maximize the effectiveness of local, state, federal, and international law enforcement bodies as they strive to maintain peace and security in the 21st century."[13] A report by the FWG foresaw a future in which the increasing effects of globalization would lead to a world of new crimes, like energy smuggling, and produce conditions whereby what is good economically for oneself or one's company may not be good for one's country.[14] The FWG has regarded the Internet as highly influential in shaping the future of the social world: "The biggest change that the Information Age may bring about is the redefinition of boundaries. The boundaries between criminal syndicates, terrorist groups, and gangs will continue to disappear. Physical boundaries will be replaced by electronic and philosophical ones as individuals discover new virtual communities."[15] Learn more about the PFI at its Web site via **Web Extra EP–1**, and read the FWG's publication *Policing 2020: Exploring the Future of Crime, Communities, and Policing* at **Library Extra EP–1**. Also available on the PFI Web site is *The Joint Operational Environment: The World Through 2030 and Beyond*, a publication of the U.S. Joint Forces Command, which can be viewed at **Library Extra EP–2**.

Another group actively attempting to discern the future is the United Kingdom's government-led Foresight program, which "brings people, knowledge and ideas together to look ahead and prepare for the future."[16] Foresight's Crime Prevention

> The Society of Police Futurists International represents the cutting edge of research into future crime-control policy.

WEB EXTRA EP-2

Panel released a report in 2001 titled *Just around the Corner* that focused on the year 2020 and provided a summation of the views of 60 experts given three tasks: to describe crimes of the near future, to identify methods to reduce and detect those crimes, and to decide what role science and technology will play in future criminality and crime prevention.[17] According to Foresight's Crime Prevention Panel, a number of social characteristics will affect future crimes in Great Britain and throughout the world, including what the panel called "individuality and independence." The panel believed that greater individuality and personal independence will arise as traditional family forms decline over the next decade or two. Once traditional families no longer provide the "foundation" of society and more people find themselves living in single-person households, "there will be more self-centered, self-indulgent and hedonistic psychologies." Traditional limits on antisocial behavior will erode, the panel predicted, as individuals gravitate toward membership in likeminded groups, many of which "may reinforce rather than challenge anti-social views."

A second social characteristic that will affect crime in the future, according to the panel, is what it termed "Information Communication Technology (ICT) usage." The panel predicted that crimes like electronic theft and fraud will occur with increasing rapidity, reducing the likelihood that offenders will be caught, and Web sites will become highly targeted properties, with sites in English being the hardest hit. Such attacks will require that digital evidence in courts be increasingly accepted and that jurors, judges, and attorneys be educated in relevant technologies.

Technology is also leading to the growth of an impersonal society in which people meet and interact in virtual space rather than in physical society. As a consequence, physical space may become an increasingly hostile and dangerous place, what the panel termed "a dehumanized environment" in which "people may become less 'real' to one another leading to more extreme reactions, interactions and the reluctance to intervene in conflicts."

A third social characteristic, according to the panel, that is relevant to understanding and predicting future forms of criminality and that is having an impact on much of society—including technology, commerce, communication, and crime—is globalization, the increasingly international character of social life. "Already, crimes on the Internet, drug dealing, and smuggling show the power of global crime and the difficulties it poses for local level law enforcement." Local crimes and small-time perpetrators will be replaced or supplemented by crimes and criminal groups with global scope.

William L. Tafoya, founder of the Society of Police Futurists International (PFI). Regarded by many in the field as a visionary, Dr. Tafoya is a retired FBI special agent, teaching at the University of New Haven. What are the goals of PFI?
Source: Dr. William Tafoya. Reprinted with permission

The panel noted that criminal organizations, like organizations everywhere, "are adapting to the opportunities offered by the flexibility of the Internet." Modern technology offers individuals new opportunities to commit crimes that may be virtually unsolvable: "The clear danger is being at the mercy of a small technologically knowledgeable elite." At the same time, the panel warned, large numbers of people either won't have the opportunity to acquire advanced technological skills or won't be able to learn them; the consequence will be a technologically disenfranchised underclass whose existence will "further fuel crime and reduce the opportunities for access to mainstream society."

For more details about Foresight and for access to the complete report of Foresight's Crime Prevention Panel, visit **Web Extra EP-2**.

■ **futures research**
A type of multidisciplinary operations research that facilitates long-range planning based on (1) forecasting supported by mathematical models, (2) cross-disciplinary treatment of subject matter, (3) expert judgments, and (4) systems-analytical approach to problems.

■ **trend extrapolation**
A technique of futures research that makes future predictions based on the projection of existing trends.

■ **cross-impact analysis**
A technique of futures research that attempts to analyze one trend or event in light of the occurrence or nonoccurrence of a series of related events.

■ **Delphi Method**
A technique of futures research that uses repetitive questioning of experts to refine predictions.

■ **environmental scanning**
A technique of futures research that tries to identify future developments (trends or events) that could plausibly occur over a given period of time and that might affect one's area of concern.

■ **scenario writing**
A technique of futures research intended to predict future outcomes that builds on environmental scanning by attempting to assess the likelihood of possible outcomes once important trends have been identified.

Techniques of Futures Research

Futures research has been described as "a multidisciplinary branch of operations research [whose principal aim] is to facilitate long-range planning based on (1) forecasting from the past supported by mathematical models, (2) cross-disciplinary treatment of its subject matter, (3) systematic use of expert judgment, and (4) a systems-analytical approach to its problems."[18] In the words of PFI founder **William L. Tafoya**, "Futures research offers both the philosophy and the methodological tools to analyze, forecast, and plan in ways rarely seen [in crime-control planning]. Guided by insight, imagination, and innovation, a new perspective awaits criminal justice professionals willing to attempt creative new approaches to dealing with crime and criminals."[19]

Central to futures research is a futurist perspective built around five principles:[20]

1. The future is determined by a combination of factors, not the least of which is human choice; what we decide today will have a significant effect tomorrow.

2. There are alternative futures, so a range of decisions and planning choices is always available in the present.

3. We operate in an interdependent, interrelated system, with any major decision, development, or force affecting one part of the system having the possibility of affecting the entire system.

4. Tomorrow's problems are developing today. Minor problems ignored today may have catastrophic consequences even a few years from now, so distinct trends and developments and even gradual changes cannot be ignored.

5. We should regularly develop possible responses to potential changes and monitor trends and developments, and we should not hesitate to use our collective creativity and judgment to develop forecasts, projections, and predictions—or to take action.

The techniques of futures research are many and varied. Perhaps the simplest is **trend extrapolation**, making future predictions based on the projection of existing trends. The technique of **cross-impact analysis** attempts to analyze one trend or event in light of the occurrence or nonoccurrence of a series of related events.[21] The social consequences of the aging baby-boomer population, for example, will be intimately affected by the future economic health of the U.S. economy, along with the availability of medical and social programs to care for geriatric segments of the population.

The **Delphi Method**, developed at RAND by Olaf Helmer and Norman Dalkey, involves four steps designed to elicit expert opinions until a general consensus is reached: (1) problem identification, (2) development of an expert panel, (3) questions directed at the panel, and (4) collection and synthesis of responses. The Delphi Method does not stop with one iteration of this sequence but provides feedback to the experts and allows them to refine their responses.

Simulations and models attempt to replicate the system under study by reproducing its conditions in a form that can be readily manipulated to assess possible outcomes. A wind tunnel, for example, provides an environment in which models of airplanes can be tested. Many of today's simulations are based on mathematical models and make use of computer technology in an effort to create simulated environments, and this is also true of demographic and economic models, which are sometimes used to predict future criminality.

Environmental scanning is a targeted effort to collect as much information as possible in "a systematic effort to identify in an elemental way future developments (trends or events) that could plausibly occur over the time horizon of interest" and that might affect one's area of concern because it is impossible to predict the future without having an informed sense of what is happening now, especially where important trends are concerned.[22] The technique of **scenario writing** builds on environmental scanning by attempting to assess the likelihood of a variety of possible outcomes once important trends have been identified, develops a list of possible futures, and assigns each a degree of probability or likelihood; while not necessarily predicting

> The Delphi Method elicits expert opinions until a general consensus is reached.

WEB EXTRA EP-3

▓ **strategic assessment**
A technique of futures research that assesses the risks and
opportunities facing those who plan for the future.

a specific future, scenario writers tend to highlight a range of possible outcomes. **Strategic assessment** provides an appreciation
of the risks and opportunities facing those who plan for the
future. Whatever techniques a futurist employs, it is important to
remember that techniques are no better than the data they use.

A comprehensive futures research approach might identify an
important trend showing affluent middle- and upper-class citizens
fleeing cities and suburbs for the safety of enclosed residential
enclaves surrounded by secure perimeters and patrolled by paid
private-security personnel. Many likely scenarios could then be
envisioned: a further decline in America's cities as the moneyed
classes abandon them, continued growth of street and property
crimes in metropolitan areas, and rampant victimization of the
urban working poor. Although crime-control strategies might be
developed to counter the imagined threat to cities, many risks
must be considered in any planning. A serious decline in the value
of the dollar could cause gated communities to unravel and could
create a shortfall of tax dollars needed to pay for enhanced policing in cities, or a new influx of large immigrant populations would
likely add to the burgeoning number of inner-city dwellers,
which would be another new dimension to overall crime-control
planning. Futurists who have made their mark on criminology include Georgette Bennett; Bernard Levin; Richter H. Moore, Jr.;
Allen Sapp; Gene Stephens; and William Tafoya. Their work, other
emerging theoretical explanations for crime, and new suggestions
for crime-control policy are discussed in this chapter. Learn more
via **Web Extra EP–3**.

Future Crimes

Murder, rape, robbery, and the other types of "everyday" crime
that have become mainstays of contemporary criminological
analysis will continue to occur in the future, but other emergent
forms of criminality will grow in frequency and number. Joseph
F. Coates, president of the future-oriented think tank of Coates
& Jarratt, predicted that by the year 2025, "socially significant
crime—that is, the crimes that have the widest negative effects—
in the advanced nations will be increasingly economic and computer based. Examples include disruption of business, theft,
introduction of maliciously false information, and tampering

with medical records, air traffic control, or national-security
systems."[23] Another futurist predicted that "the top guns of
twenty-first-century criminal organizations will be educated,
highly sophisticated, computer-literate individuals who can
wield state-of-the-art information technology to the best advantage—for themselves and for their organizations."[24]

In a wide-ranging overview of future crimes, **Richter H.
Moore, Jr.**, painted a picture of future criminality that included
many dimensions: "Computer hackers are changing bank
records, credit accounts and reports, criminal-history files, and
educational, medical, and even military records."[25] Identity
manipulation will be a nexus of future criminality. "By the
twenty-first century," Moore wrote, "genetic-based records will
include a birth-to-death dossier of a person and will be the
method of criminal identification." The U.S. military is presently
using genetic testing to assign unique identification codes to each
of its soldiers; in the event of war, such codes enable the identification of human remains from as little as a single cell. DNA
coding may form the basis for nearly foolproof identification
technologies, taking the science of personal identification beyond fingerprinting, blood-type matching, or photography. The
science of bioengineering, now undergoing clinical trials in the
treatment of various diseases, could also be clandestinely employed for illegal modifications of human DNA, with the goal of
effectively altering a person's identity, and the theft of computer-
based genetic identification records could make it possible for
one person to effectively imitate another in our future society.

Moore described many other crimes of the future. Within a
few decades, "criminal organizations will be able to afford their
own satellites." Drug trafficking and money laundering could be
coordinated via satellite communications, couriers and shipments
could be tracked, and satellite surveillance could provide alerts of
enforcement activity. Moore went on to say that "prostitution
rings will use modern technology to coordinate global activities"
and that children and fetuses may "become subject to unlawful
trafficking." The illegal disposal of toxic materials, an activity already perpetrated by organized crime, may become even more
profitable for criminal entrepreneurs as many more hazardous
substances are produced in the face of ever-tighter controls.
The supply of nuclear materials and military-quality armaments
to "private armies, terrorists, hate groups, questionable regimes,

LIBRARY EXTRA EP–3
WEB EXTRA EP–4

independent crime groups, and individual criminals" will be a fact of life in the twenty-first century, as will the infiltration of governments and financial institutions by sophisticated criminals whose activities are supported by large illegally acquired fortunes.

Georgette Bennett, whose seminal book *Crimewarps* was published in 1987 and helped establish the study of criminal futures, predicted that American society will experience major changes (many of which have since happened) in both what society considers criminal and who future offenders will be:[26]

- Declines in street crimes, such as robbery and assault

- Increases in white-collar crimes, especially high-technology crimes

- Increased involvement of women in crime

- Increased crime commission among the elderly

- Shifts in high crime rates from the Frost Belt to the Sun Belt

- Safer cities but increased criminal activity in small towns and rural areas

The U.S. Joint Forces Command had this to say about future crimes in its publication *The Joint Operational Environment: The World through 2030 and Beyond*:

> Criminal organizations and elements will take advantage of information and communication technologies and the proliferation of weapons to develop very sophisticated capabilities. The destructive social, economic, and political impact of crime will increase in both its severity and sophistication. Transnational criminal activity, fueled by global connections to money and arms, will blur the lines between traditional military action and criminal activities. Criminal organizations will continue to form strategic alliances with states and nonstate actors, including terrorists. Terrorists and criminals will also be active in such an environment, ready to exploit the situation for their respective gains. United States joint forces, combined with law enforcement and intelligence activities in a collaborative information environment, will have to deal both with enemy military forces and [with] other nontraditional forces, such as criminal organizations, terrorists, or religious fanatics, who will seek to profit from instability.[27]

Learn more about the changing nature of crime in America via **Library Extra EP–3** and **Web Extra EP–4**.

New Criminologies

Along with futures research, emerging criminological theories provide a picture of what criminology will be like in the years and decades to come. In an intriguing article, Illinois State University criminal justice professor L. Edward Wells suggested that "when it comes to explaining crime, we seem to have an embarrassment of riches but a poverty of results."[28] In other words, although many explanations for criminal behavior have come and gone, "none has proven noticeably more effective in explaining, predicting, or controlling crime."[29] But that may be about to change, according to Wells. Contemporary criminological theorizing is interdisciplinary and conservative in its approach to crime causation, and major changes in the premises on which criminological theories are built are unlikely without significant ideological shifts or changes in basic components of the social structure, such as the economy, the political system, or the family, but significant social change creates the need for new theoretical formulations. "Legal events in the 1960s and 1970s changed abortion from a criminal act to a routine medical procedure."[30] An aversion to even minor physical force may require a redefinition of crimes like child abuse, spousal abuse, elder abuse, and sexual aggression. Both of these examples point to our basic understanding of criminal violence undergoing fundamental modifications that will result in a concomitant change in our attempts to theorize about its causes.

Wells saw similar possibilities for theoretical change due to advances in scientific knowledge. For example, if research on the human genome yields definitive evidence that some forms of aggression and violence are biologically grounded, that would provide the basis for an entirely new group of biological explanations for at least certain forms of criminal activity.

> Significant social change creates the need for new theoretical formulations.

Based on emerging explanations of crime, Wells made a number of specific predictions about new criminological theories:[31]

- They will be more eclectic and less tied to a single theoretical tradition or discipline.

- They will be more comparative and less confined to a single society or single dominant group within society.

- They will be predominantly individualistic, rather than collective, and voluntaristic, rather than deterministic.

- They will be more applied and more pragmatic in orientation.

- They will be more focused on explaining white-collar crime.

- They will reflect a renewed appreciation for the biological foundations of human behavior, assigning more theoretical substance to biological and medical factors.

From about 1960 to 1985, criminological theory building fell by the wayside as a generation of criminologists trained in quantitative analysis repeatedly tested existing ideas at the expense of developing new ones, but in the mid-1980s, a dynamic new era of theory building was unleashed. Frank P. Williams III and Marilyn D. McShane explained, "As if the restraints on theory building had created a pent-up demand, criminologists began exploring new theoretical constructs during the 1980s. Slowly at first, and then with great rapidity, theoretical efforts began to emerge."[32]

A number of these new approaches, including postmodernism, feminist criminology, and peacemaking criminology, were discussed in previous chapters. One more perspective that deserves special attention is what David P. Farrington termed the "risk factor prevention paradigm."[33] Farrington explained, "The basic idea of the paradigm is very simple: Identify the key risk factors for offending and implement prevention methods designed to counteract them." Farrington said that the risk factor prevention paradigm, which experienced "an enormous increase in influence in criminology" during the 1990s, is especially important because it holds the potential for guiding criminological research, crime-control policy, and theoretical development well into the twenty-first century. The main challenges for the paradigm "are to determine which risk factors are causes, to establish what are protective factors, to identify the active ingredients of multiple component interventions, to evaluate the effectiveness of area-based intervention programs, and to assess the monetary costs and benefits of interventions."

Crime-Control Policies of the Future

The well-known futurist **Gene Stephens** observed that "crime is increasing worldwide, and there is every reason to believe the trend will continue."[34] Street crimes are greatly escalating in formerly communist countries throughout Eastern Europe and in other European nations, such the United Kingdom and those in Scandinavia. Stephens explained that even though some official measures show crime is currently on the decline in the United States, America was one of the first nations to experience a rapid

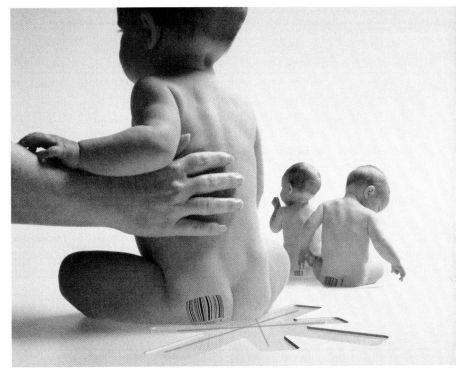

A surrealistic image of bar-coded babies, reflecting the highly controversial subject of human cloning. Should human cloning be legal?
Source: Ron Lowery/Windsock Media

rise in criminality because it was the most advanced nation on the globe. It was a highly diverse, multicultural, industrialized, and democratic society; it strongly supported individual freedoms; and it fostered a strong sense of personal independence among its citizens.

Multiculturalism and heterogeneity, according to Stephens, increase anomie, so previously isolated homogeneous societies like those of Japan, Denmark, China, and Greece face a growing cultural diversity due to international migration, expansion of new social ideals, and increases in foreign commerce. "Heterogeneity in societies will be the rule in the twenty-first century, and failure to recognize and plan for such diversity can lead to serious crime problems, especially in emerging multicultural societies." Stephens's thesis is best summarized in this passage from his work—"The connection between crime and culture cannot be overemphasized: There are high-crime and low-crime cultures around the world. In the years ahead, many low-crime cultures may become high-crime cultures because of changing world demographics and politicoeconomic systems. In general, heterogeneous populations in which people have lots of political freedom (democracy) and lots of economic choice (capitalism) are prime candidates for crime unless a good socialization system is created and maintained."

Homogeneous nations—in which citizens share backgrounds, life experiences, and values—produce citizens who are generally capable of complying with the wishes of the majority and who can legislate controls over behavior that are not difficult for most citizens to respect. In such societies, a tradition of discipline, a belief in the laws, and an acceptance of personal responsibility are typically the norm.

Diverse societies suffer from constant internal conflict, much of it focusing on acceptable ways of living and working. Heterogeneous societies tend to place a strong emphasis on individualism, and disagreement about the law and social norms is rife. Characteristic of such cultures is the fact that lawbreakers tend to deny responsibility and go to great lengths to avoid capture and conviction. Stephens pointed out that in some highly homogeneous cultures, such as Japan, those who break norms will often punish themselves, even if their transgressions are not publicly discovered but that such self-punishing behavior would be almost unthinkable in an advanced heterogeneous society like that of the United States. "Some nations, such as the United States, face pervasive *anomie* due to their lack of restraints on human desires."

Heterogeneity can arise in numerous ways, in both heterogeneous and homogeneous societies. One source of increasingly important differences in American society is the growth of a technological culture with two distinct groups: those who are technologically capable and those who are incapable of utilizing modern technology. To these two groups, we could add a third: the technologically aware, those who realize the importance of technology but who—because of age, lack of education, poverty, or other life circumstances—have not yet acquired the skills necessary to participate fully in what our highly technological society has to offer. According to Stephens: "More people are turning to street crime and violence because they find themselves unprepared, educationally or emotionally, to cope with the requirements for success in the new era."

Another reason that crime rates are high in increasingly heterogeneous societies is that such societies often display a lack of consistent child-care philosophies and child-rearing methods. "In some societies," stated Stephens, "parents are seen as primarily responsible for their children, but all citizens share in that responsibility, since everyone's welfare is affected by the proper socialization of each child."

> ## Diverse societies suffer from constant internal conflict.

In others, children are viewed as the parents' property, and little is expected of parents other than that they be biologically capable of reproducing; no requirements are set for parental knowledge, skills, income, education, and so on. Stephens described child-rearing practices in those societies as "helter-skelter, catch-as-catch-can child care." Lacking child-rearing standards in which the majority of members of society can meaningfully participate, heterogeneous societies tend to produce adults who are irresponsible and who do not adhere to legal or other standards of behavior.

Future crimes will be plentiful, with countries around the world experiencing explosive growth in their crime rates. Stephens commented, "The United States was the first industrialized, democratic, heterogeneous nation and thus the first to face the crime problems associated with *anomie*." Now other nations are undergoing increased modernization, with many entering the postmodern era previously occupied solely by the United States. "We can theorize that crime will be a growth industry in many countries as they find themselves gripped by the same social forces that have long affected the United States."

Other authors have also attempted to describe crime-control issues that may face future policymakers.[35] Moore identified the following seven issues that are likely to concern crime-control planners in the near future:[36]

1. **New criminal groups**. "Groups such as Colombian drug cartels, Jamaican posses, Vietnamese gangs, various Chinese groups, and Los Angeles black street gangs are now a much bigger concern than the Mafia," and the criminal activity and influence of these new groups are growing rapidly. Traditional law enforcement responses, such as those developed to deal with Italian American Mafia organizations, may be inappropriate in the face of the new challenges these groups represent.

2. **Language barriers**. "U.S. law-enforcement officials now find themselves hampered by a lack of understanding about the language and culture of some of the new criminal groups [operating in America.]" Cuban, Mexican, Colombian, Japanese, and Chinese criminals and criminal organizations are becoming commonplace, and such groups are increasingly involved in international communications and travel.

3. **Distrust by ethnic communities**. More recent immigrant groups have been slow to assimilate into American culture and society, strongly holding on to native identities and distancing themselves from formal agencies of social

■ *Kriminalpolitik*
The political handling of crime; also a criminology-based social policy.

control, such as the police. "In many of their countries of origin, new immigrants see police as corrupt, self-serving individuals, a viewpoint often not without foundation." A distrust of police and government representatives is nearly instinctual for members of such groups, making the work of law enforcement within the context of immigrant communities challenging and often difficult.

4. **Greater reliance on community involvement**. "[D]ue to the increasing costs of electronic surveillance, informant programs, undercover operations, and witness-protection programs, police are now encouraging community members to become more involved in their own security." The involvement of private citizens in the battle against crime may be the only realistic solution to the problem; neighborhood watch programs, community volunteers in criminal justice organizations, and other neighborhood self-help programs such as school- and church-based education all may have a part in the future of neighborhood-based crime-control policy.

5. **More marketplace regulation**. Decriminalization and legalization will be of increasingly greater concern to future legislators, who will focus on regulating the marketplace for criminal activities like gambling, drug trafficking, and prostitution.

6. **Reduced public demand**. Future crime-control policies will aim to reduce involvement in criminal activity by providing better education and mandating other policies that will lower the demand for drugs and other illegal services.

7. **Increased treatment**. In the future, a greater emphasis will be placed on the treatment of all forms of criminality, including drug abuse, gambling, and rape. This approach contrasts with today's "get tough" policies.

Learn more about possible crime-control policies of the future from **Library Extra EP-4**.

Can We Solve the Problem of Crime?

In 1956, European writer Hermanus Bianchi emphasized what he saw as the difference between criminology and what he termed *Kriminalpolitik*, meaning the political handling of crime or a criminology-based social policy.[37] Criminology should be considered a "metascience" or "a science of wider scope [than that of criminal law, jurisprudence, criminal justice, or correc-

tions] whose terminology can be used to clarify the conceptions of its subdisciplines. Far from being a mere auxiliary to the criminal law, it is therefore superior to it."[38] Bianchi believed that if criminology were to remain pure, it could not afford to "sully its hands" with political concerns.

Today, the image esteemed by criminologists and the expectations they hold for their discipline are quite different than in Bianchi's time. Many criminologists expect to work hand in hand with politicians and policymakers forging crime-control agendas based on scientific knowledge and criminological theorizing and would say that this change in attitude represents a maturation of the discipline of criminology.

Whether effective crime-control policies can ever be implemented is a different matter. A number of critics have argued that only drastic policy-level changes can address the real issues underlying high rates of crime and criminal activity; drug legalization, elimination of guns throughout America, nightly curfews, and closer control of media violence may be necessary before crime can be curbed. "Reforms that substantially will lower the crime rate are unlikely because of cultural taboos," commented Lawrence Friedman, a Stanford University law professor and author of the book *Crime and Punishment in American History*.[39] "If you add up all the taboos we have—against legalization of drugs, real gun control, paying taxes for social programs we might at least try—it's hard not to come to the conclusion that there isn't much we can do about crime." Many existing taboos are rooted in citizens' demands for individual freedoms. "At one time in South Korea," explained Friedman, "they had an absolute curfew between midnight and 5 A.M. The police kept everyone off the streets. It was as hard on burglars as other citizens and very effective at squelching crime. But most Americans would consider that an unacceptable inroad on their personal lives."[40]

Complicating the picture further are the numerous interest groups, each with its own agenda, that are clamoring to be heard by policymakers. Robert D. Pursley, professor of criminal justice at Buffalo State College, stated, "Our nation's efforts to deal with crime remind us that crime, among other things, is a highly political issue that has been transformed into a racially volatile subject. This issue provides an excellent window into political policymaking. Opposing ideological lines have divided our efforts to develop comprehensive anticrime programs. Deep fissures in our social fabric have contributed to conflicting attitudes about crime and its control."[41]

Racial divisiveness has created one of those fissures. According to Pursley, "Our anticrime programs and studies of traditional street crimes, especially those involving violence, show that such crimes are disproportionately the acts of young

Follow the author's tweets about the latest crime and justice news at http://twitter.com/schmalleger.

African-American males. So long as black men commit violent crimes at a rate that is six to eight times higher than that found among whites and three to four times higher than that among Latino males, race and crime will be threads of the same cloth. These facts have become unpopular and certainly not politically correct to discuss in certain circles, but they remain facts. No attempt to silence those who raise such issues by denouncing them as 'racists' can conceal these statistics."[42]

For some groups in some locales, violations of the criminal law are simply part of the landscape. Among certain segments of the American population, crime may be an accepted way of doing business, and criminal activity, even when discovered, might not necessarily be stigmatizing. Those who commit crimes could continue to hold positions of prestige or highly visible public offices if their constituencies fail to condemn their illicit behavior and may even serve as role models—albeit dubious role models—to youngsters. Although such a perspective is undoubtedly a minority point of view, it seriously impacts the ability of policymakers to establish consistent policies in the battle against crime.

Symbolism and Crime-Control Policy

When all the political crime-fighting rhetoric has ended and all the dollars have been spent, most expect that crime will still be with us. Many analysts of the contemporary scene see all crime-control policies, especially at the federal level, as largely symbolic. Nancy E. Marion, professor of political science at the University of Akron, stated that "many of the policies supported by the federal government may in actuality be symbolic gestures to appease the public rather than attempts to reduce crime. One reason for the presence of symbolic policies is simply that the federal government cannot reduce crime— it is not within the government's capacity to do so."[43] Marion went on to say that congressional power is fragmented through the influence of special interest groups, so the potential of crime-control initiatives is effectively dispersed by the time any legislation is enacted. In addition, the American political system is decidedly shortsighted, focusing only on issues that are likely to win elections. Changes in incumbents (often every two to four years), as well as continual modifications of laws, enforcement practices, and criminal sanctions, make it impossible to establish consistent crime-control policies.

A Democratic president may hold office for four years but be followed by a Republican president, and there is a nearly continuous shuffling of cabinet members, senators, representatives, U.S. Supreme Court justices, agency heads, and federal judges; similar changes occur at the state level. Without a consistent long-term national and/or interstate approach to crime fighting, crime rates can never be substantially impacted by federal and/or state policies.

Even some consistent crime-control policies that do exist may be inaccurate. According to Marion, "One reason we cannot stop crime in the United States is because many elements of the crime problem we believe to be true simply are not. Because of the way crime is presented in the media, crime events 'become distorted and are given unprecedented social consideration.' These myths help to sustain our views of crime, criminals, and the system as a whole."[44] Part of the mythology of crime is the belief in criminological theories that have limited usefulness, but another problem flows from our inability to effectively conceptualize crime itself. Laws may merely reflect moral conceptions of the political majority, so both morality and law are subject to change, making it difficult to accurately define *crime*. Hence, as critics of contemporary crime-fighting policies have indicated, if we do not fully understand what crime is or what causes it, how can we create an effective policy for controlling it?

> The American political system is decidedly shortsighted.

Some people have said that the answer may be found in increased expenditures on criminological research. According to Alfred Blumstein, "That we are in this confused state is not surprising when we recognize that the nation spends less than $25 million per year for research at the National Institute of Justice on the problem that seems to be the nation's greatest concern. Contrast this with $11 billion for health research at the National Institutes of Health, $600 million on mental health, and $165 million for dental research. With so small a research effort, it is not surprising that we reach out for programs with little ability to assess the impact that they might have on the intended objective, and that we operate in a pre-Galilean mode when we debate crime policy."[45] In the FWG's report *Policing 2020*, Carl J. Jensen and **Bernard H. Levin** summarized it this way: "In a rapidly changing world, those who play catch-up will never catch up."[46]

KEY TERMS

cross-impact analysis, 424

Delphi Method, 424

environmental scanning, 424

future criminology, 422

futurist, 422

futures research, 424

Kriminalpolitik, 429

scenario writing, 424

strategic assessment, 425

trend extrapolation, 424

KEY NAMES

Georgette Bennett, 426

Bernard H. Levin, 430

Richter H. Moore, Jr., 425

Gene Stephens, 427

William L. Tafoya, 424

QUESTIONS FOR REVIEW

1. What techniques are used in the field of futures research for assessing the future?

2. What are some likely future crimes, and how will future criminal activity differ from criminal activity today?

3. What can be predicted about the future of criminological theorizing?

QUESTIONS FOR REFLECTION

1. This book emphasizes the theme of social problems versus social responsibility. Which perspective do you think will be more dominant in twenty-first-century crime-control planning? Why?

2. Do you believe it is possible to know the future? What techniques are identified in this chapter for assessing possible futures? Which one of these do you think holds the most promise? Why?

3. What kinds of crime-control policies do you think the future will bring? Will they be consistent with present understandings of civil liberties? Why or why not?

Glossary

acquaintance rape A rape characterized by a prior social, though not necessarily intimate or familial, relationship between the victim and the perpetrator.

addiction A chronic brain disease characterized by compulsive drug seeking and use despite harmful consequences.[1]

administrative law Law that regulates many daily business activities. Violations of these regulations generally result in warnings or fines, depending on their adjudged severity.

adolescence-limited offender A juvenile offender who abandons delinquency upon maturity.

Age of Reason See **Enlightenment**.

aggravated assault (UCR) An unlawful attack by one person upon another for the purpose of inflicting severe or aggravated bodily injury. See also **simple assault**.

alloplastic adaptation A form of adjustment that results from changes in the environment surrounding an individual.

androcentricity A male-dominated perspective, as in the case of criminologists who study only the criminality of males.

anomie A social condition in which norms are uncertain or lacking.

anomie theory See **strain theory**.

Anti-Drug Abuse Act A federal law (Public Law 99–570) enacted in 1986 that established new federal mandatory minimum sentences for drug offenses.

antisocial (asocial) personality An individual who is unsocialized and whose behavior pattern brings him or her into repeated conflict with society.

antisocial personality disorder (ASPD) A psychological condition exhibited by an individual who is unsocialized and whose behavior pattern brings him or her into conflict with society.[2]

applied research Any research based on scientific inquiry that is designed and carried out with practical applications in mind.

Arrestee Drug Abuse Monitoring (ADAM) Program A National Institute of Justice program that tracks trends in the prevalence and types of drug use among booked arrestees in urban areas.

arson The willful or malicious burning (or attempt to burn), with or without intent to defraud, of a house, public building, motor vehicle or aircraft, or personal property of another.

asocial personality See **antisocial personality**.

assault See **aggravated assault; simple assault**.

asset forfeiture The authorized seizure of money, negotiable instruments, securities, or other things of value. In federal antidrug laws, it is the authorization of judicial representatives to seize all monies, negotiable instruments, securities, or other things of value furnished or intended to be furnished by any person in exchange for a controlled substance, as well as all proceeds traceable to such an exchange.

atavism A term used by Cesare Lombroso to suggest that criminals are physiological throwbacks to earlier stages of human evolution. The term is derived from the Latin term *atavus*, which means "ancestor."

attachment theory A social-psychological perspective on delinquent and criminal behavior that holds that the successful development of secure attachment between a child and his or her primary caregiver provides the basic foundation for all future psychological development.

audit trail A record of computer activities that enables auditors to reconstruct and review the sequence of activities surrounding each event in one or more related transactions from inception to output of final results back to inception.

autoplastic adaptation A form of adjustment that results from changes within an individual.

bank fraud Any fraud or embezzlement that occurs within or against financial institutions that are insured or regulated by the U.S. government. Fraud of financial institutions includes commercial-loan fraud, check fraud, counterfeit negotiable instruments, mortgage fraud, and false credit applications.

behavioral genetics The study of genetic and environmental contributions to individual variations in human behavior.

behavior theory A psychological perspective that posits that behavior that is rewarded will increase in frequency and behavior that is punished will decrease.

bias crime See **hate crime**.

biological theory A theory that maintains that the basic determinants of human behavior, including criminality, are constitutionally or physiologically based and often inherited.

biopsychology A field of study that combines the principles of psychology with those of neuroscience and biology. It examines how thoughts and behavior are mediated by interaction between the brain (especially neurotransmitters) and the environment. It is also called *behavioral psychology* and *behavioral neuroscience*.

biosocial criminology A theoretical perspective that sees the interaction between biology and the environment as key to understanding human behavior, including criminality.

booster A frequent shoplifter.

born criminal An individual who is born with a genetic predilection toward criminality.

bourgeoisie The "haves," or the class of people who own the means of production in the Marxist theory.

Brady Handgun Violence Prevention Act A federal law (Public Law 103–159) enacted in 1993 that initiated a national background checking system for all potential gun purchasers.

Brawner rule A somewhat vague rule for determining insanity created in the 1972 federal court case of *United States* v. *Brawner* (471 F.2d 969), since superseded by statute, that asks the jury to decide whether the defendant could be justly held responsible for the criminal act with which he or she stands charged in the face of any claims of insanity or mental incapacity.

broken windows thesis A perspective on crime causation that holds that physical deterioration in an area leads to increased concerns for personal safety among area residents and to higher crime rates in that area.

burglary The trespassory breaking and entering of the dwelling house of another in the nighttime with the intent to commit a felony; also the unlawful entry of a structure to commit a felony or a theft.

burglary (UCR) The unlawful entry of a structure to commit a felony or a theft.

Cambridge Study in Delinquent Development A longitudinal (life course) study of crime and delinquency tracking a cohort of 411 boys born in London in 1953.

capable guardian One who effectively discourages crime.

capital punishment The legal imposition of a sentence of death upon a convicted offender; also called *death penalty.*

carjacking The stealing of a car while it is occupied.

Chicago Area Project A program originating at the University of Chicago during the 1930s that focused on urban ecology and that attempted to reduce delinquency, crime, and social disorganization in transitional neighborhoods.

Chicago School of criminology An ecological approach to explaining crime that examines how social disorganization contributes to social pathology.

child sexual abuse (CSA) A term encompassing a variety of criminal and civil offenses in which an adult engages in sexual activity with a minor, exploits a minor for purposes of sexual gratification, or exploits a minor sexually for purposes of profit.

civil law The body of law that regulates arrangements between individuals, such as contracts and claims to property.

Classical School A criminological perspective of the late 1700s and early 1800s that had its roots in the Enlightenment and that held that humans are rational beings, that crime is the result of the exercise of free will, and that punishment can be effective in reducing the incidence of crime to the degree it negates the pleasure to be derived from crime commission.

clearance rate The proportion of reported or discovered crimes within a given offense category that are solved.

Code of Hammurabi An early set of laws established by the Babylonian king Hammurabi, who ruled the ancient city from 1792 to 1750 B.C.

cohort A group of individuals having certain significant social characteristics in common, such as gender and date and place of birth.

cohort analysis A social scientific technique that studies a population with common characteristics over time. Cohort analysis usually begins at birth and traces the development of cohort members until they reach a certain age.

Commission on Law Observance and Enforcement See **Wickersham Commission**.

common law Law originating from usage and custom rather than from written statutes. The term refers to nonstatutory customs, traditions, and precedents that help guide judicial decision making.

Communications Decency Act (CDA) A 1996 federal statute labeled Title 5 of the federal Telecommunications Act of 1996 (Public Law 104–104, 110 Stat. 56) that seeks to protect minors from harmful material on the Internet and that criminalizes the knowing transmission of obscene or indecent messages to any recipient under 18 years of age. In 1997, in *Reno* v. *ACLU* (521 U.S. 844), the U.S. Supreme Court found the bulk of the CDA to be unconstitutional, ruling that it contravenes First Amendment free speech guarantees.

comparative criminologist A criminologist involved in the cross-national study of crime.

comparative criminology The cross-national study of crime.

Comprehensive Crime Control Act A far-reaching federal law (Public Law 98–473) enacted in 1984 that mandated new federal sentencing guidelines, eliminated parole at the federal level, limited the use of the insanity defense in federal criminal courts, and increased federal penalties associated with drug dealing.

computer abuse An unlawful incident associated with computer technology in which a victim suffers loss or a perpetrator reaps benefit.[3]

computer crime Any violation of a federal or state computer crime statute. The term is now being replaced with *cybercrime.*

computer-related crime An illegal act using computer technology in its perpetration, investigation, or prosecution.

computer virus A program designed to invade computer systems and either modify the way they operate or alter the information they store.

conditioning A psychological principle that holds that the frequency of any behavior can be increased or decreased through reward, punishment, or association with other stimuli.

conduct norm A shared expectation of a social group relative to personal conduct.

confidentiality See **data confidentiality**.

conflict perspective An analytical perspective on social organization that holds that conflict is a fundamental aspect of social life and can never be fully resolved.

confounding effect A rival explanation or competing hypothesis that is a threat to the internal or external validity of a research design.

consensus perspective An analytical perspective on social organization that holds that most members of society agree about what is right and wrong and that the various elements of society work together toward a common vision of the greater good.

constitutional theory A theory that explains criminality by reference to offenders' body types, inheritance, genetics, or external observable physical characteristics.

constitutive criminology The study of the process by which human beings create an ideology of crime that sustains the notion of crime as a concrete reality.

containment An aspect of the social bond that acts as a stabilizing force to prevent individuals from committing crimes and that keeps them from engaging in deviance.

containment theory A form of control theory that suggests that a series of both internal and external factors contributes to law-abiding behavior.

control group A group of experimental subjects that, although the subject of measurement and observation, is not exposed to the experimental intervention.

controlled experiment An experiment that attempts to hold conditions (other than the intentionally introduced experimental intervention) constant.

control ratio The amount of control to which a person is subject versus the amount of control that person exerts over others.

control theory See **social control theory**.

convict criminology A radical paradigm consisting of writings on criminology by convicted felons and ex-inmates who have acquired academic credentials or who are associated with credentialed others; also called *alternative criminology*.

corporate crime A violation of a criminal statute by an organization or its executives, employees, or agents acting on its behalf and for its benefit.[4]

corporate fraud A type of organizational fraud, such as accounting schemes, self-dealing by corporate executives, obstruction of justice, insider trading, kickbacks, and misuse of corporate property for personal use.

correctional psychology The branch of forensic psychology concerned with the diagnosis and classification of offenders, the treatment of correctional populations, and the rehabilitation of inmates and other law violators.

correlation A causal, complementary, or reciprocal relationship between two measurable variables. See also **statistical correlation**.

Cosa Nostra A criminal organization of Sicilian origin (literally means "our thing"); also called *the Mafia, the Outfit, the Mob, the syndicate*, or simply *the organization*.

crime Any human conduct in violation of the criminal laws of the federal government or a local jurisdiction with the power to make such laws.

crime typology A classification of crimes along a particular dimension, such as legal categories, offender motivation, victim behavior, or characteristics of individual offenders.

Crime Victims' Rights Act A 2004 federal law that establishes statutory rights for victims of federal crimes and gives victims the necessary legal authority to assert those rights in federal courts.

criminal anthropology The scientific study of the relationship between human physical characteristics and criminality.

criminal behavior A method used to gain valued resources from others by exploiting or deceiving them.[5]

criminal career The longitudinal sequence of crimes committed by an individual offender.

criminal enterprise A group of individuals with an identified hierarchy engaged in significant criminal activities.

criminal homicide The illegal killing of one human being by another.

criminal homicide (UCR) The UCR category that includes and is limited to all offenses of causing the death of another person without justification or excuse.

criminalist A specialist in the collection and examination of the physical evidence of crime.

criminality A behavioral predisposition that disproportionately favors criminal activity.

criminality index The actual extent of the crime problem in a society. The criminality index is computed by adding the actual crime rate and the latent crime rate.

criminalize To make illegal.

criminal justice The scientific study of crime, the criminal law, and components of the criminal justice system, including the police, courts, and corrections.

criminal justice system The various agencies of justice, especially the police, courts, and corrections, whose goal it is to apprehend, convict, punish, and rehabilitate law violators.

criminal law The body of law that regulates actions that have the potential to harm the interests of the state or the federal government.

criminaloid A term used by Cesare Lombroso to describe the occasional criminal who is enticed into criminality primarily by environmental influences.

criminal psychology The application of the science and profession of psychology to questions and issues relating to law and the legal system; also called *forensic psychology*.

criminal receiver See **fence**.

criminologist One who is trained in the field of criminology; also one who studies crime, criminals, and criminal behavior.

criminology An interdisciplinary profession built around the scientific study of crime and criminal behavior, including their forms, causes, legal aspects, and control.

criminology of place A perspective that emphasizes the importance of geographic location and architectural features as they are associated with the prevalence of criminal victimization; also called *environmental criminology*.

critical criminology A perspective that holds that crime is the natural product of a capitalist system.

cross-impact analysis A technique of futures research that attempts to analyze one trend or event in light of the occurrence or nonoccurrence of a series of related events.

cultural transmission The idea that delinquency is transmitted through successive generations of people living in an area through the same process of social communication as languages, roles, and attitudes are transmitted.

culture conflict theory A sociological perspective on crime that suggests that the root cause of criminality can be found in a clash of values between variously socialized groups over what is acceptable or proper behavior; also called *cultural deviance theory*.

cybercrime Any crime that involves the use of computers or the manipulation of digital data as well as any violation of a federal or state cybercrime statute.

Cyber Security Enhancement Act (CSEA) A federal law found in the Homeland Security Act of 2002 that directs the U.S. Sentencing Commission to take specific factors into account in creating new sentencing guidelines for cybercriminals.

cyberspace The computer-created matrix of virtual possibilities, including online services, in which human beings interact with one another and with the technology itself.

cyberstalking An array of high-technology options, including e-mail and the Internet, that an offender uses to harass or "follow" another individual.

cyberterrorism A form of terrorism that makes use of high technology, especially computer technology and the Internet, in planning and carrying out terrorist attacks.

cycloid A term developed by Ernst Kretschmer to describe a particular relationship between body build and personality type. The cycloid personality, which was associated with a heavyset, soft type of body, was said to vacillate between normality and abnormality.

dangerous drug A controlled substance other than cocaine, opiates, and cannabis products. Amphetamines, LSD, methamphetamines, methcathinone, and phencyclidine (PCP), as well as designer drugs, are all considered dangerous drugs.

dangerousness The likelihood that a given individual will later harm society or others. Dangerousness is often measured in terms of recidivism, or the likelihood of new crime commission or rearrest for a new crime within a five-year period following arrest or release from confinement.

dark figure of crime The numerical total of unreported crimes not reflected in official crime statistics.

data confidentiality The ethical requirement of social scientific research to protect the confidentiality of individual research participants while preserving justified research access to the information participants provide.

data encryption The process by which information is encoded, making it unreadable to all but its intended recipients.

date rape The unlawful forced sexual intercourse with a woman against her will that occurs within the context of a dating relationship.

Daubert **standard** A test of scientific acceptability applicable to the gathering of evidence in criminal cases.

DCS–3000 An FBI-developed network diagnostic tool that is capable of assisting in criminal investigations by monitoring and capturing large amounts of Internet traffic.

death penalty See **capital punishment**.

deconstructionist theory A postmodern perspective that challenges existing criminological theories in order to debunk them and that works toward replacing traditional ideas with concepts seen as more appropriate to the postmodern era.

decriminalization The redefinition of certain previously criminal behaviors as regulated activities that become "ticketable" instead of "arrestable."

defensible space The range of mechanisms that combine to bring an environment under the control of its residents.

Delphi Method A technique of futures research that uses repetitive questioning of experts to refine predictions.

demographics The characteristics of population groups, usually expressed in statistical fashion.

demography The study of the characteristics of population groups.

descriptive statistics The statistics that describe, summarize, or highlight the relationships within data that have been gathered.

designer drug A new substance designed by slightly altering the chemical makeup of other illegal or tightly controlled drugs.[6]

desistance A person's cessation of criminal activity or termination of a period of involvement in offending behavior.

desistance phenomenon The observable decrease in crime rates that is invariably associated with age.

determinate sentencing A criminal punishment strategy that mandates a specified and fixed amount of time to be served for every offense category. Under the strategy, for example, all offenders convicted of the same degree of burglary would be sentenced to the same length of time behind bars. It is also called *fixed sentencing*.

deterrence The prevention of crime. See also **general deterrence; specific deterrence**.

deterrence strategy A crime-control strategy whose goal is to lessen motivation for a crime by increasing the perceived sureness or severity of its penalty.[7]

deviant behavior Any human activity that violates social norms.

differential association The sociological thesis that criminality, like any other form of behavior, is learned through a process of association with others who communicate criminal values.

differential identification theory An explanation for crime and deviance that holds that people pursue criminal or deviant behavior to the extent that they identify themselves with real or imaginary people from whose perspective their criminal or deviant behavior seems acceptable.

Digital Theft Deterrence and Copyright Damages Improvement Act A 1999 federal law (Public Law 106–160) that amends Section 504(c) of the Copyright Act increasing the amount of damages that could be awarded in cases of copyright infringement.

disclosure (of research methods) The provision of information to potential subjects informing them of the nature of the research methods to be used by the social scientific study in which their involvement is planned.

discrediting information Any information that is inconsistent with the managed impressions being communicated in a given situation.

displacement A shift of criminal activity from one location to another.

displastic A mixed group of offenders described by constitutional theorist Ernst Kretschmer as highly emotional and often unable to control themselves. They were thought to commit mostly sexual offenses and other crimes of passion.

distributive justice The rightful, equitable, and just distribution of rewards within a society.

dizygotic (DZ) twin A twin who develops from a separate ovum and who carries the genetic material shared by siblings.

DNA fingerprinting See **DNA profiling**.

DNA profiling The use of biological residue found at a crime scene for genetic comparisons in aiding the identification of criminal suspects.

domestic terrorism The unlawful use of force or violence by an individual or group based and operating entirely within the United States and its territories, without foreign influence, directed at the U.S. government, the civilian population, or any segment thereof for political or social objectives.[8]

dramaturgical perspective A theoretical point of view that depicts human behavior as centered around the purposeful management of interpersonal impressions; also called *dramaturgy*.

dramaturgy See **dramaturgical perspective**.

drug-defined crime A violation of the laws prohibiting or regulating the possession, use, or distribution of illegal drugs.

drug-related crime A crime in which drugs contribute to the offense (excluding violations of drug laws).

drug trafficking The manufacturing, distributing, dispensing, importing, and/or exporting of a controlled substance or a counterfeit substance.[9]

Durham rule A standard for judging legal insanity that holds that an accused is not criminally responsible if his or her unlawful act was the product of mental disease or mental defect.

ecological theory A type of sociological approach that emphasizes demographics (the characteristics of population groups) and geographics (the mapped location of such groups relative to one another) and that sees the social disorganization that characterizes delinquency areas as a major cause of criminality and victimization.

ectomorph A body type originally described as thin and fragile, with long, slender, poorly muscled extremities and delicate bones.

ego The reality-testing part of the personality; also called the *reality principle*. More formally, it is the personality component that is conscious, most immediately controls behavior, and is most in touch with external reality.[10]

electroencephalogram (EEG) The electrical measurement of brain wave activity.

encryption See **data encryption**.

endomorph A body type originally described as soft and round or overweight.

Enlightenment A social movement that arose during the eighteenth century and that built upon ideas like empiricism, rationality, free will, humanism, and natural law; also called *Age of Reason.*

environmental crime A violation of the criminal law committed by businesses, business officials, organizational entities, and/or individuals that damages some protected or otherwise significant aspect of the natural environment.

environmental criminology A perspective that emphasizes the importance of geographic location and architectural features as they are associated with the prevalence of criminal victimization; also called *criminology of place.*

environmental scanning A technique of futures research. It is a "systematic effort to identify in an elemental way future developments (trends or events) that could plausibly occur over the time horizon of interest."[11]

ethnic succession The continuing process whereby one immigrant or ethnic group succeeds another by assuming its position in society.

ethnocentrism The phenomenon of "culture-centeredness" by which one uses one's own culture as a benchmark against which to judge all other patterns of behavior.

eugenic criminology A perspective that holds that the root causes of criminality are passed from generation to generation in the form of "bad genes."

eugenics The study of hereditary improvement by genetic control.

evidence based Any evidence built on scientific findings, especially practices and policies founded on the results of randomized, controlled experiments.

evidence-based criminology A form of contemporary criminology that makes use of rigorous social scientific techniques, especially randomized, controlled experiments and the systematic review of research results; also called *knowledge-based criminology.*

evolutionary ecology An approach to understanding crime that draws attention to the ways people develop over the course of their lives.

experiment See **controlled experiment; quasi-experimental design**.

experimental criminology See **evidence-based criminology**.

expert system A system of computer hardware and software that attempts to duplicate the decision-making processes used by skilled investigators in the analysis of evidence and in the recognition of patterns that such evidence might represent.

exposure-reduction theory A theory of intimate homicide that claims that a decline in domesticity, accompanied by an improvement in the economic status of women and a growth in domestic violence resources, explains observed decreases in intimate-partner homicide.

expressive crime A criminal offense that results from acts of interpersonal hostility, such as jealousy, revenge, romantic triangles, and quarrels.

external validity The ability to generalize research findings to other settings.

felony A serious criminal offense, specifically one punishable by death or by incarceration in a prison facility for a year or more.

felony murder An unlawful homicide that occurs during the commission or attempted commission of a felony or certain felonies specified by law.

feminist criminology A corrective model intended to redirect the thinking of mainstream criminologists to include gender awareness.

fence An individual or a group involved in the buying, selling, and distribution of stolen goods.

first-degree murder A criminal homicide that is planned or involves premeditation.

focal concern A key value of any culture, especially a delinquent subculture.

folkways A time-honored custom. Although folkways carry the force of tradition, their violation is unlikely to threaten the survival of the group. See also **mores**.

forcible rape (UCR) The carnal knowledge of a female forcibly and against her will. Assaults or attempts to commit rape by force or threat of force are also included in the UCR definition; however, statutory rape (without force) and other sex offenses are excluded.

foreign terrorist organization (FTO) A foreign organization that engages in terrorist activity threatening the security of U.S. nationals or the national security of the United States and that is so designated by the U.S. secretary of state.

forensic psychiatry A branch of psychiatry having to do with the study of crime and criminality.

forensic psychology The application of the science and profession of psychology to questions and issues relating to law and the legal system; also called *criminal psychology.*

forfeiture See **asset forfeiture**.

frustration-aggression theory A theory that holds that frustration, which is a natural consequence of living, is a root cause of crime. Criminal behavior can be a form of adaptation when it results in stress reduction.

future criminology The study of likely futures as they impinge on crime and its control.

futures research "A multidisciplinary branch of operations research [whose principal aim] is to facilitate long-range planning based on (1) forecasting from the past supported by mathematical models, (2) cross-disciplinary treatment of its subject matter, (3) systematic use of expert judgments, and (4) a systems-analytical approach to its problems."[12]

futurist One who studies the future.

gateway offense An offense, usually fairly minor in nature, that leads to more serious offenses.

gender gap The observed differences between male and female rates of criminal offending in a given society.

general deterrence A goal of criminal sentencing that seeks to prevent others from committing crimes similar to the one for which a particular offender is being sentenced.

general strain theory (GST) A perspective that suggests that law-breaking behavior is a coping mechanism enabling those who engage in it to deal with the socioemotional problems generated by negative social relations.

general theory A theory that attempts to explain all (or at least most) forms of criminal conduct through a single overarching approach.

general theory of crime A perspective on crime, developed by Travis Hirschi and Michael Gottfredson, that asserts "that the operation of a single mechanism, low self-control, accounts for 'all crime, at all times,' [including] acts ranging from vandalism to homicide, from rape to white-collar crime."[13]

genetic determinism The belief that genes are the major determining factor in human behavior.

globalization A process of social homogenization that everyday experiences can foster by standardized cultural expressions through the diffusion of goods and ideas around the world.[14]

guilty but mentally ill (GBMI) A finding that offenders are guilty of the criminal offense with which they are charged, but because of their prevailing mental condition, they are generally sent to psychiatric hospitals for treatment rather than to prison. Once they have been declared cured, such offenders can be transferred to correctional facilities to serve out their sentences.

habitual offender statute A law intended to keep repeat criminal offenders behind bars. These laws sometimes come under the "three strikes and you're out" rubric.

hacker A person who uses computers for exploration and exploitation.

hard determinism The belief that crime results from forces beyond the control of the individual.

hate crime A criminal offense in which the motive is hatred, bias, or prejudice based on the actual or perceived race, color, religion, national origin, ethnicity, gender, or sexual orientation of another individual or group of individuals.

Hate Crimes Sentencing Enhancement Act A federal law (28 U.S. Code, Section 994) enacted in 1994 as part of the Violent Crime Control and Law Enforcement Act that required the U.S. Sentencing Commission to increase penalties for crimes in which the victim was chosen due to actual or perceived color, ethnicity, religion, gender, disability, or sexual orientation.

hedonistic calculus The belief, first proposed by Jeremy Bentham, that behavior holds value to any individual undertaking it according to the amount of pleasure or pain it can be expected to produce for that person. See also **utilitarianism**.

heritability A statistical construct that estimates the amount of variation in the traits of a population that is attributable to genetic factors.

Heroin Signature Program (HSP) A Drug Enforcement Administration program that identifies the geographic source of a heroin sample through the detection of specific chemical characteristics in the sample peculiar to the source area.

homicide The killing of one human being by another.

household crime (NCVS) An attempted or completed crime that does not involve confrontation, such as burglary, motor vehicle theft, and household larceny.

human agency The active role that people take in their lives; the fact that people are not merely subject to social and structural constraints but actively make choices and decisions based on the alternatives they see before them.

human development The relationship between the maturing individual and his or her changing environment, as well as the social processes that the relationship entails.

human ecology The interrelationship between human beings and the physical and cultural environments in which they live.

human smuggling A type of illegal immigration in which an agent is paid to help a person cross a border clandestinely.[15]

human trafficking See **trafficking in persons**.

hypoglycemia A medical condition characterized by low blood sugar.

hypothesis An explanation accounting for a set of facts that can be tested by further investigation.[16]

id The aspect of the personality from which drives, wishes, urges, and desires emanate. More formally, this division of the psyche is associated with instinctual impulses and demands for immediate satisfaction of primitive needs.[17]

identity theft The unauthorized use of another individual's personal information to commit fraud.

illegitimate opportunity structure A subcultural pathway to success that the wider society disapproves of.

impression management The intentional enactment of practiced behavior that is intended to convey to others one's desirable personal characteristics and social qualities.

incapacitation The use of imprisonment or other means to reduce the likelihood that an offender will be capable of committing future offenses.

individual-rights advocate One who seeks to protect personal freedoms in the face of criminal prosecution.

inferential statistics Any statistics that specify how likely findings are to be true for other populations or in other locales.

informed consent The ethical requirement of social scientific research that research subjects be informed as to the nature of the research about to be conducted, their anticipated role in it, and the uses to which the data they provide will be put.

infrastructure The basic facilities, services, and installations needed for the functioning of a community or society, such as its transportation and communications systems, water and power lines, and public institutions.[18]

insanity (legal) A legally established inability to understand right from wrong or to conform one's behavior to the requirements of the law.

insanity (psychological) A persistent mental disorder.[19]

insider trading A type of equity trading based on confidential information about important events that may affect the price of the issue being traded.

institutional robbery A robbery that occurs in a commercial setting, such as a convenience store, gas station, and bank.

instrumental crime A goal-directed offense that involves some degree of planning by the offender and little or no precipitation by the victim.

instrumental Marxism A perspective that holds that those in power intentionally create laws and social institutions that serve their own interests and keep others from becoming powerful.

integrated theory An explanatory perspective that merges (or attempts to merge) concepts drawn from different sources.

interactional theory A theoretical approach to exploring crime and delinquency that blends social control and social learning perspectives.

interactionist perspective See **social process theory**.

interdiction An international drug-control policy whose goal is to stop drugs from entering the country illegally.

internal validity The certainty that experimental interventions did indeed cause the changes observed in the study group; also the control over confounding factors that tend to invalidate the results of an experiment.

international terrorism The unlawful use of force or violence by an individual or group with a connection to a foreign power or whose activities transcend national boundaries against people or property to intimidate or coerce a government, the civilian population, or any segment thereof for political or social objectives.[20]

Internet The world's largest computer network for moving data and making information accessible.

intersubjectivity A scientific principle that requires that independent observers see the same thing under the same circumstances for observations to be regarded as valid.

intimate-partner assault A gender-neutral term used to characterize assaultive behavior that takes place between individuals involved in an intimate relationship.

irresistible-impulse test A standard for judging legal insanity that holds that a defendant is not guilty of a criminal offense if the person, by virtue of his or her mental state or psychological condition, was not able to resist committing the crime.

jockey A professional car thief involved in calculated steal-to-order car thefts.

joyriding An opportunistic car theft, often committed by a teenager, for fun or thrills.

Juke family A well-known "criminal family" studied by Richard L. Dugdale.

just deserts model The notion that criminal offenders deserve the punishment they receive at the hands of the law and that punishments should be appropriate to the type and severity of crime committed.

justice model A contemporary model of imprisonment in which the principle of just deserts forms the underlying social philosophy.

Kallikak family A well-known "criminal family" studied by Henry H. Goddard.

Kefauver Committee The popular name for the federal Special Committee to Investigate Organized Crime in Interstate Commerce, formed in 1951.

Kriminalpolitik The political handling of crime; also a criminology-based social policy.

labeling theory An interactionist perspective that sees continued crime as a consequence of limited opportunities for acceptable behavior that follow from the negative responses of society to those defined as offenders; also called *social reaction theory*.

La Cosa Nostra A criminal organization of Sicilian origin; also called *Mafia*. The term literally means "our thing."

larceny The unlawful taking or attempted taking of property (other than a motor vehicle) from the possession of another, by stealth, without force or deceit, with intent to permanently deprive the owner of the property.

larceny-theft (UCR) The unlawful taking, carrying, leading, or riding away of property (other than a motor vehicle) from the possession or constructive possession of another (attempts are included).

latent crime rate A rate of crime calculated on the basis of crimes that would likely be committed by those who are in prison or jail or who are otherwise incapacitated by the justice system.

law-and-order advocate One who suggests that under certain circumstances involving criminal threats to public safety, the interests of society should take precedence over individual rights.

Law Enforcement Assistance Administration (LEAA) A federal program, established under Title 1 of the Omnibus Crime Control and Safe Streets Act of 1967, designed to provide assistance to police agencies.

learning theory See **social learning theory**.

left realism A conflict perspective that insists on a pragmatic assessment of crime and its associated problems; also called *radical realism* or *critical realism*.

left-realist criminology An approach to criminology based on ideas inherent in the perspective of left realism.

legalization The elimination of laws and criminal penalties associated with certain behaviors—usually the production, sale, distribution, and possession of a controlled substance.

liberal feminism A feminist perspective in criminology that sees gender-role socialization as the primary source of women's oppression.

life course The different pathways through the age-differentiated life span; also the course of a person's life over time.

life course persister An offender who, as a result of neuropsychological deficits combined with poverty and family dysfunction, displays patterns of misbehavior throughout life.

life course perspective A perspective that draws attention to the fact that criminal behavior tends to follow a distinct pattern across the life cycle; also called *life course criminology*.

lifestyle theory Another term for the routine activities approach of Lawrence Cohen and Marcus Felson. See also **routine activities theory**.

Mafia A criminal organization of Sicilian origin; also called *La Cosa Nostra*.

mala in se An act that is thought to be wrong in and of itself.

mala prohibita An act that is wrong only because it is prohibited.

Marxist criminology A perspective on crime and crime causation based on the writings of Karl Marx.

Marxist feminism A perspective in feminist criminology that sees the oppression of women as caused by their subordinate class status within capitalist societies.

masculinity hypothesis The belief that, over time, men and women will commit crimes that are increasingly similar in nature, seriousness, and frequency. Increasing similarity in crime commission was predicted to result from changes in the social status of women.

mass murder The illegal killing of four or more victims at one location within one event.

mesomorph A body type described as athletic and muscular.

meta-analysis A study that combines the results of other studies about a particular topic of interest; a comprehensive and systematic review of other studies.

metatheory A theory about theories and the theorizing process.

misdemeanor A criminal offense that is less serious than a felony and is punishable by incarceration, usually in a local confinement facility, typically for a year or less.

M'Naughten rule A standard for judging legal insanity that requires that offenders not know what they were doing, or if they did, that they not know it was wrong.

modeling theory A form of social learning theory that asserts that people learn how to act by observing others.

money laundering The process of converting illegally earned assets from cash to one or more alternative forms to conceal factors such as illegal origin and true ownership.[21]

Monitoring the Future A national self-report survey on drug use that has been conducted since 1975.

monozygotic (MZ) twin One of two twins who develop from the same egg and who carry virtually the same genetic material.

moral enterprise The efforts made by an interest group to have its sense of moral or ethical propriety enacted into law.

mores The behavioral proscriptions covering potentially serious violations of a group's values. Examples include strictures against murder, rape, and robbery. See also **folkways**.

motor vehicle theft (UCR) The theft or attempted theft of a motor vehicle. In the FBI's definition, this offense category includes the stealing of automobiles, trucks, buses, motorcycles, motor scooters, and snowmobiles.

murder An unlawful homicide.

National Advisory Commission on Criminal Justice Standards and Goals A federal body commissioned in 1971 by President Richard Nixon to examine the nation's criminal justice system and to set standards and goals to direct the development of the nation's criminal justice agencies.

National Crime Victimization Survey (NCVS) A survey conducted annually by the Bureau of Justice Statistics that provides data on surveyed households that report they were affected by crime.

National Incident-Based Reporting System (NIBRS) An enhanced statistical-reporting system to collect data on each incident and arrest within 22 crime categories.

National Survey on Drug Use and Health (NSDUH) A national survey of illicit drug use among people 12 years of age and older that is conducted annually by the Substance Abuse and Mental Health Services Administration.

National Violence against Women (NVAW) Survey A national survey of the extent and nature of violence against women conducted between November 1995 and May 1996 funded through grants from the National Institute of Justice and the U.S. Department of Health and Human Services National Center for Injury Prevention and Control.

National Youth Survey (NYS) A longitudinal panel study of a national sample of 1,725 individuals that measured self-reports of delinquency and other types of behavior.

natural law The philosophical perspective that certain immutable laws are fundamental to human nature and can be readily ascertained through reason. Human-made laws, in contrast, are said to derive from human experience and history—both of which are subject to continual change.

natural rights The rights that, according to natural law theorists, individuals retain in the face of government action and interests.

negative affective state An adverse emotion such as anger, fear, depression, and disappointment that derives from the experience of strain.

negligent homicide The act of causing the death of another person by recklessness or gross negligence.

neoclassical criminology A contemporary version of classical criminology that emphasizes deterrence and retribution, with reduced emphasis on rehabilitation.

neurosis A functional disorder of the mind or of the emotions involving anxiety, phobia, or other abnormal behavior.

No Electronic Theft Act A 1997 federal law (Public Law 105–147) that criminalizes the willful infringement of copyrighted works, including by electronic means, even when the infringing party derives no direct financial benefit from the infringement (such as when pirated software is freely distributed online). In keeping with requirements of the NETA, the U.S. Sentencing Commission enacted amendments to its guidelines on April 6, 2000, to increase penalties associated with electronic theft.

nonprimary homicide A murder that involves victims and offenders who have no prior relationship and that usually occurs during the course of another crime such as robbery.

nothing-works doctrine The belief popularized by Robert Martinson in the 1970s that correctional treatment programs have little success in rehabilitating offenders.

nurturant strategy A crime-control strategy that attempts "to forestall development of criminality by improving early life experiences and channeling child and adolescent development" in desirable directions.[22]

occasional offender A criminal offender whose offending patterns are guided primarily by opportunity.

occupational crime Any act punishable by law that is committed in the course of an individual's legal occupation.[23]

offense A violation of the criminal law or, in some jurisdictions, a minor crime, such as jaywalking, sometimes described as "ticketable."

offense specialization A preference for engaging in a certain type of offense to the exclusion of others.

Office of Juvenile Justice and Delinquency Prevention (OJJDP) A national office that provides monetary assistance and direct victim-service programs for juvenile courts.

Office of National Drug Control Policy (ONDCP) A national office charged by Congress with establishing policies, priorities, and objectives for the nation's drug-control program. ONDCP is responsible for developing and disseminating the *National Drug-Control Strategy*.

omertà The informal unwritten code of organized crime, which demands silence and loyalty, among other things, of family members.

Omnibus Anti-Drug Abuse Act A federal law (Public Law 100–690) enacted in 1988 that substantially increased federal penalties for recreational drug users and created a new cabinet-level position (known unofficially as the drug czar) to coordinate the drug-fighting efforts of the federal government.

Omnibus Crime Control and Safe Streets Act A federal law enacted in 1967 to eliminate the social conditions that create crime and to fund many anticrime initiatives nationwide.

operant behavior Any behavior that affects the environment in such a way as to produce responses or further behavioral cues.

operationalization The process by which concepts are made measurable.

opportunity structure A path to success. Opportunity structures may be of two types: legitimate and illegitimate.

organized crime The unlawful activities of the members of a highly organized, disciplined association engaged in supplying illegal goods and services, including gambling, prostitution, loan-sharking, narcotics, and labor racketeering.[24]

Panopticon A prison designed by Jeremy Bentham that was to be a circular building with cells along the circumference, each clearly visible from a central location staffed by guards.

paradigm An example, a model, or a theory.

paranoid schizophrenic A schizophrenic individual who suffers from delusions and hallucinations.

Part I offenses The crimes of murder, rape, robbery, aggravated assault, burglary, larceny, and motor vehicle theft, as defined under the FBI's Uniform Crime Reporting Program; also called *major crimes*.

Part II offenses The less serious offenses as identified by the FBI for the purpose of reporting arrest data.

participant observation A strategy in data gathering in which the researcher observes a group by participating, to varying degrees, in the activities of the group.[25]

participatory justice A relatively informal type of criminal justice case processing that makes use of local community resources rather than requiring traditional forms of official intervention.

patriarchy The tradition of male dominance.

peacemaking criminology A perspective that holds that crime-control agencies and the citizens they serve should work together to alleviate social problems and human suffering and thus reduce crime.

peace model An approach to crime control that focuses on effective ways for developing a shared consensus on critical issues that could seriously affect the quality of life.

penal couple A term that describes the relationship between offender and victim; also the two individuals most involved in the criminal act: the offender and the victim.

persistence The act of continuing in crime; also continual involvement in offending.

persistent thief One who continues in common law types of property crimes despite no better than an ordinary level of success.

personal robbery A robbery that occurs on the highway or street or in a public place (also called *mugging*) or that occurs in a residence.

pharmaceutical diversion The process by which legitimately manufactured controlled substances are diverted for illicit use.

phenomenological criminology The study of crime as a social phenomenon that is created through a process of social interaction.

phenomenology The study of the contents of human consciousness without regard to external conventions or prior assumptions.

phishing An Internet-based scam whose goal is to steal valuable personal information such as credit-card or Social Security numbers, user IDs, and passwords.[26]

phone phreak A person who uses switched, dialed-access telephone services for exploration and exploitation.

phrenology The study of the shape of the head to determine anatomical correlates of human behavior.

piracy See **software piracy**.

pluralist perspective An analytical approach to social organization that holds that a multiplicity of values and beliefs exists in any complex society but that most social actors agree on the usefulness of law as a formal means of dispute resolution.

positivism The application of scientific techniques to the study of crime and criminals.

postcrime victimization Any problem that tends to follow from initial victimization; also called *secondary victimization*.

postmodern criminology A brand of criminology that developed following World War II and that builds on the tenets inherent in postmodern social thought.

postmodern feminism A perspective within modern criminology that questions the social construction of concepts that are typically used in any discussion of crime and justice.

power-control theory A perspective that holds that the distribution of crime and delinquency within society is to some degree founded upon the consequences that power relationships within the wider society hold for domestic settings and for the everyday relationships among men, women, and children within the context of family life.

primary deviance The initial deviance often undertaken to deal with transient problems in living.

primary homicide A murder involving a family member, friend, or acquaintance.

primary research Any research characterized by original and direct investigation.

professional criminal A criminal offender who makes a living from criminal pursuits, is recognized by other offenders as professional, and engages in offending that is planned and calculated.

Project on Human Development in Chicago Neighborhoods (PHDCN) An intensive study of Chicago neighborhoods employing longitudinal evaluations to examine the changing circumstances of people's lives in an effort to identify personal characteristics that may lead toward or away from antisocial behavior.

proletariat The "have-nots," or the working class in Marxist theory.

prosocial bond A bond between the individual and the social group that strengthens the likelihood of conformity. Prosocial bonds are characterized by attachment to conventional social institutions, values, and beliefs.

prostitution The offering of one's self for hire for the purpose of engaging in sexual relations, or the act or practice of engaging in sexual activity for money or its equivalent.

protection/avoidance strategy A crime-control strategy whose goal is to reduce criminal opportunities by changing people's routine activities, increasing guardianship, or incapacitating convicted offenders.[27]

psychiatric criminology Any theory that is derived from the medical sciences, including neurology, and that, like other psychological theories, focuses on the individual as the unit of analysis. Psychiatric theories form the basis of psychiatric criminology. See also **forensic psychiatry**.

psychiatric theory A theory derived from the medical sciences, including neurology, and that, like other psychological theories, focuses on the individual as the unit of analysis.

psychoactive substance A substance that affects the mind, mental processes, or emotions.

psychoanalysis The theory of human psychology founded by Sigmund Freud on the concepts of the unconscious, resistance, repression, sexuality, and the Oedipus complex.[28]

psychoanalytic criminology A psychiatric approach developed by Sigmund Freud that emphasizes the role of personality in human behavior and which sees deviant behavior as the result of dysfunctional personalities.

psychological profiling The attempt to categorize, understand, and predict the behavior of certain types of offenders based on behavioral clues they provide.

psychological theory A theory derived from the behavioral sciences that focuses on the individual as the unit of analysis. Psychological theories place the locus of crime causation within the personality of the individual offender.

psychopath An individual who has a personality disorder, especially one manifested in aggressively antisocial behavior, and who is lacking in empathy; also called *sociopath*.

psychopathology A psychological disorder that causes distress for either the individual or someone in the individual's life.[29] It is also the study of pathological mental conditions (mental illness).

psychopathy A personality disorder characterized by antisocial behavior and lack of affect.

psychosis A form of mental illness in which sufferers are said to be out of touch with reality.

psychotherapy A form of psychiatric treatment based on psychoanalytical principles and techniques.

public policy A course of action that government takes in an effort to solve a problem or to achieve an end.

punishment An undesirable behavioral consequence likely to decrease the frequency of occurrence of that behavior.

pure research Any research undertaken simply for the sake of advancing scientific knowledge.

qualitative method A research technique that produces subjective results or results that are difficult to quantify.

quantitative method A research technique that produces measurable results.

quasi-experimental design An approach to research that, although less powerful than experimental designs, is deemed worthy of use when better designs are not feasible.

Racketeer Influenced and Corrupt Organizations (RICO) A statute that was part of the federal Organized Crime Control Act of 1970 and that is intended to combat criminal conspiracies.

radical criminology A perspective that holds that the causes of crime are rooted in social conditions that empower the wealthy and the politically well organized but disenfranchise the less fortunate; also called *critical criminology* and *Marxist criminology*.

radical feminism A perspective that holds that any significant change in the social status of women can be accomplished only through substantial changes in social institutions such as the family, law, and medicine. Radical feminism argues, for example, that the structure of current legal thinking involves what is fundamentally a male perspective, which should be changed to incorporate women's social experiences and points of view.

randomization The process whereby individuals are assigned to study groups without biases or differences resulting from selection.

rape (NCVS) The carnal knowledge through the use of force or the threat of force, including attempts. Statutory rape (without force) is excluded. Both heterosexual and homosexual rape are included.

rape (UCR) See **forcible rape**.

rape myth A false assumption about rape such as "When a woman says no, she really means yes." Rape myths characterize much of the discourse surrounding sexual violence.

rape-shield law A statute providing for the protection of rape victims by ensuring that defendants do not introduce irrelevant facts about the victim's sexual history into evidence.

rational choice theory A perspective that holds that criminality is the result of conscious choice and that predicts that individuals choose to commit crime when the benefits outweigh the costs of disobeying the law.

reaction formation The process by which a person openly rejects that which he or she wants or aspires to but cannot obtain or achieve.

realist criminology See **left realism**.

recidivism The repetition of criminal behavior.

recidivism rate The percentage of convicted offenders who have been released from prison and who are later rearrested for a new crime, generally within five years following release. See also **dangerousness**.

reintegrative shaming A form of shaming, imposed as a sanction by the criminal justice system, that is thought to strengthen the moral bond between the offender and the community.

relative deprivation A sense of social or economic inequality experienced by those who are unable, for whatever reason, to achieve legitimate success within the surrounding society.

replicability A scientific principle that holds that valid observations made at one time can be made again later if all other conditions are the same.

research The use of standardized, systematic procedures in the search for knowledge.[30]

research design The logic and structure inherent in an approach to data gathering.

resilience The psychological ability to successfully cope with severe stress and negative events.

restitution A criminal sanction, especially the payment of compensation by the offender to the victim.

restorative justice A postmodern perspective that stresses "remedies and restoration rather than prison, punishment and victim neglect."[31]

retribution The act of taking revenge on a criminal perpetrator.

reward A desirable behavioral consequence likely to increase the frequency of occurrence of that behavior.

risk analysis See **threat analysis**.

robbery (UCR) The taking of or attempting to take anything of value from the care, custody, or control of a person or persons by force or threat of force or violence or by putting the victim in fear.

routine activities theory A brand of rational choice theory that suggests that lifestyles contribute significantly to both the volume and the type of crime found in any society; also called *lifestyle theory*.

scenario writing A technique intended to predict future outcomes that builds on environmental scanning by attempting to assess the likelihood of a variety of possible outcomes once important trends have been identified.

schizoid A person characterized by schizoid personality disorder. Such disordered personalities appear to be aloof, withdrawn, unresponsive, humorless, dull, and solitary to an abnormal degree.

schizophrenic A mentally ill individual who is out of touch with reality and who suffers from disjointed thinking.

secondary deviance Any deviant behavior that results from official labeling and from association with others who have been so labeled.

secondary research A new evaluation of existing information that had been collected by other researchers.

secondary victimization See **postcrime victimization**.

second-degree murder A criminal homicide that is unplanned and that is often described as a "crime of passion."

securities fraud The theft of money resulting from intentional manipulation of the value of equities, including stocks and bonds. Securities fraud also includes theft from securities accounts and wire fraud.

selective disinhibition A loss of self-control due to the characteristics of the social setting, drugs or alcohol, or a combination of both.

selective incapacitation A social policy that seeks to protect society by incarcerating the individuals deemed to be the most dangerous.

self-control A person's ability to alter his or her own mental and emotional states and behavioral responses.

self-report survey A survey in which anonymous respondents, without fear of disclosure or arrest, are asked to confidentially report any violations of the criminal law that they have committed.

separation assault Any violence inflicted by partners on significant others who attempt to leave an intimate relationship.

serial murder A criminal homicide that involves the killing of several victims in three or more separate events.

sex trafficking The recruitment, harboring, transportation, provision, or obtaining of a person for the purpose of a commercial sex act.

sibling offense An offense or incident that culminates in homicide. The offense or incident may be a crime, such as robbery, or an incident that meets a less stringent criminal definition, such as a lover's quarrel involving assault or battery.

simple assault (NCVS) An attack without a weapon, resulting either in minor injury or in undetermined injury requiring less than two days of hospitalization. See also **aggravated assault**.

situational choice theory A brand of rational choice theory that views criminal behavior "as a function of choices and decisions made within a context of situational constraints and opportunities."[32]

situational crime prevention A social policy approach whose goal is to develop greater understanding of crime as well as more effective crime-prevention strategies by focusing on physical, organizational, and social environments that make crime possible.[33]

snitch An amateur shoplifter.

social bond The link, created through socialization, between individuals and the society of which they are a part.

social capital The degree of positive relationships with others and with social institutions that individuals build up over the course of their lives.

social class A distinction made between individuals on the basis of important defining social characteristics.

social contract The Enlightenment-era concept that human beings abandon their natural state of individual freedom to join together and form society. In the process of forming a social contract, individuals surrender some freedoms to society as a whole, and government, once formed, is obligated to assume responsibilities toward its citizens and to provide for their protection and welfare.

social control theory A perspective that predicts that when social constraints on antisocial behavior are weakened or absent, delinquent behavior emerges. Rather than stressing causative factors in criminal behavior, social control theory asks why people actually obey rules instead of breaking them.

social development perspective An integrated view of human development that examines multiple levels of maturation simultaneously, including the psychological, biological, familial, interpersonal, cultural, societal, and ecological levels.

social disorganization A condition said to exist when a group is faced with social change, uneven development of culture, maladaptiveness, disharmony, conflict, and lack of consensus.

social disorganization theory A perspective on crime and deviance that sees society as a kind of organism and crime and deviance as a kind of disease or social pathology. Theories of social disorganization are often associated with the perspective of social ecology and with the Chicago School of criminology, which developed during the 1920s and 1930s.

social ecology An approach to criminological theorizing that attempts to link the structure and organization of a human community to interactions with its localized environment.

social epidemiology The study of social epidemics and diseases of the social order.

Socialist feminism A perspective within modern criminology that sees gender oppression as a consequence of the interaction between the economic structure of society and gender-based roles.

socialization The lifelong process of social experience whereby individuals acquire the cultural patterns of their society.

social learning theory A perspective that places primary emphasis on the role of communication and socialization in the acquisition of learned patterns of criminal behavior and the values that support that behavior; also called *learning theory*.

social life The ongoing and (typically) structured interaction that occurs between persons in a society, including socialization and social behavior in general.

social pathology A concept that compares society to a physical organism and that sees criminality as an illness.

social policy A government initiative, program, or plan intended to address problems in society. The "war on crime," for example, is a kind of generic (large-scale) social policy—one consisting of many smaller programs.

social problems perspective The belief that crime is a manifestation of underlying social problems, such as poverty, discrimination, pervasive family violence, inadequate socialization practices, and the breakdown of traditional social institutions.

social process The interaction between and among social institutions, individuals, and groups.

social process theory A theory that asserts that criminal behavior is learned in interaction with others and that socialization processes that occur as the result of group membership are the primary route through which learning occurs; also called *interactionist perspective*.

social relativity The notion that social events are differently interpreted according to the cultural experiences and personal interests of the initiator, the observer, or the recipient of that behavior.

social responsibility perspective The belief that individuals are fundamentally responsible for their own behavior and that they choose crime over other, more law-abiding courses of action.

social structure The pattern of social organization and the interrelationships among institutions characteristic of a society.

social structure theory A theory that explains crime by reference to some aspect of the social fabric. These theories emphasize relationships among social institutions and describe the types of behavior that tend to characterize groups of people rather than individuals.

sociobiology "The systematic study of the biological basis of all social behavior."[34]

sociological theory A perspective that focuses on the nature of the power relationships that exist between social groups and on the influences that various social phenomena bring to bear on the types of behaviors that tend to characterize groups of people.

sociopath See **psychopath**.

soft determinism The belief that human behavior is the result of choices and decisions made within a context of situational constraints and opportunities.

software piracy The unauthorized and illegal copying of software programs.

somatotyping The classification of human beings into types according to body build and other physical characteristics.

specific deterrence A goal of criminal sentencing that seeks to prevent a particular offender from engaging in repeat criminality.

spousal rape The rape of one spouse by the other. The term usually refers to the rape of a woman by her husband.

stalking A course of conduct directed at a specific person that involves repeated visual or physical proximity; nonconsensual communication; verbal, written, or implied threats; or a combination thereof that would cause a reasonable person fear as well as a constellation of behaviors involving repeated and persistent attempts to impose on another person unwanted communication and/or contact.

state-organized crime Any act defined by law as criminal that is committed by a state official during his or her work as a representative of the state.[35]

statistical correlation The simultaneous increase or decrease in value of two numerically valued random variables.[36]

statistical school A criminological perspective with roots in the early 1800s that seeks to uncover correlations between crime rates and other types of demographic data.

statute A formal written enactment by a legislative body.[37]

statutory law Law in the form of statutes or formal written strictures made by a legislature or governing body with the power to make law.

stigmatic shaming A form of shaming, imposed as a sanction by the criminal justice system, that is thought to destroy the moral bond between the offender and the community.

strain theory A sociological approach that posits a disjuncture between socially and subculturally sanctioned means and goals as the cause of criminal behavior; also called *anomie theory*.

strategic assessment A technique that assesses the risks and opportunities facing those who plan for the future.

structural Marxism A perspective that holds that the structural institutions of society influence the behavior of individuals and groups by virtue of the type of relationships created. The criminal law, for example, reflects class relationships and serves to reinforce those relationships.

subcultural theory A sociological perspective that emphasizes the contribution made by variously socialized cultural groups to the phenomenon of crime.

subculture A collection of values and preferences that is communicated to subcultural participants through a process of socialization.

sublimation The psychological process whereby one aspect of consciousness comes to be symbolically substituted for another.

substantial-capacity test A standard for judging legal insanity that requires that a person lack the mental capacity needed to understand the wrongfulness of his or her act or to conform his or her behavior to the requirements of the law.

superego The moral aspect of the personality; much like the conscience. According to Freud, this part of the psyche develops by incorporating the community's (perceived) moral standards, is mainly unconscious, and includes the conscience.[38]

supermale A male individual displaying the XYY chromosome structure.

superpredator A member of a new generation of juveniles "who [is] coming of age in actual and 'moral poverty' without the benefits of parents, teachers, coaches and clergy to teach [him or her] right from wrong and show [him or her] 'unconditional love.' "[39] The term is often applied to inner-city youths.

survey research A social science data-gathering technique that involves the use of questionnaires.

tagging The process whereby an individual is negatively defined by agencies of justice; also called *labeling*.

target hardening The reduction in criminal opportunity for a particular location, generally through the use of physical barriers, architectural design, and enhanced security measures.

technique of neutralization A culturally available justification that can provide criminal offenders with the means to disavow responsibility for their behavior.

TEMPEST A standard developed by the U.S. government that requires that electromagnetic emanations from computers designated as "secure" be below levels that would allow radio receiving equipment to read the data being computed.

terrorism Any premeditated, politically motivated violence perpetrated against noncombatant targets by subnational groups or clandestine agents, usually intended to influence an audience.[40]

test of significance A statistical technique intended to provide researchers with confidence that their results are, in fact, true and not the result of sampling error.

testosterone The primary male sex hormone produced in the testes. Its function is to control secondary sex characteristics and sexual drive.

Thanatos A death wish.

theory A series of interrelated propositions that attempt to describe, explain, predict, and ultimately control some class of events. A theory gains explanatory power from inherent logical consistency and is "tested" by how well it describes and predicts reality.

threat analysis A complete and thorough assessment of the kinds of perils facing an organization; also called *risk analysis*.

three-strikes legislation A criminal statute that mandates life imprisonment for criminals convicted of three violent felonies or serious drug offenses.

total institution A facility from which individuals can rarely come and go and in which communal life is intense and circumscribed. Individuals in total institutions tend to eat, sleep, play, learn, and worship together.

trafficking in persons (TIP) The exploitation of unwilling or unwitting people through force, coercion, threat, or deception.

transnational organized crime Any unlawful activity undertaken and supported by organized criminal groups operating across national boundaries.

trend extrapolation A technique of futures research that makes future predictions based on the projection of existing trends.

truth in sentencing A close correspondence between the incarceration sentence given the offender and the time actually served prior to prison release.[41]

Twelve Tables Early Roman laws written circa 450 B.C. that regulated family, religious, and economic life.

unicausal The characteristic of having one cause. Unicausal theories posit only one source for all that they attempt to explain.

Uniform Crime Reporting Program (UCR) A Federal Bureau of Investigation data-gathering initiative that provides an annual tally of statistics consisting primarily of information on crimes reported to the police and on arrests.

utilitarianism See **hedonistic calculus**.

variable A concept that can undergo measurable changes.

verstehen The kind of subjective understanding that can be achieved by criminologists who immerse themselves in the everyday world of the criminals they study.

victim-impact statement A written document that describes the losses, suffering, and trauma experienced by the crime victim or by the victim's survivors. In jurisdictions where victim-impact statements are used, judges are expected to consider them in arriving at an appropriate sentence for the offender.

victimization rate (NCVS) A measure of the occurrence of victimizations among a specified population group. For personal crimes, the rate is based on the number of victimizations per 1,000 residents age 12 or older. For household crimes, the victimization rates are calculated using the number of incidents per 1,000 households.

victimogenesis The contributory background of a victim as a result of which he or she becomes prone to victimization.

victimology The study of victims and their contributory role, if any, in crime causation.

victim-precipitated homicide A killing in which the victim was the first to commence the interaction or was the first to resort to physical violence.

victim precipitation Any contribution made by the victim to the criminal event, especially something that led to its initiation.

victim proneness An individual's likelihood of victimization.

Victims of Crime Act (VOCA) A federal law enacted in 1984 that established the federal

Crime Victims Fund. The fund uses monies from fines and forfeitures collected from federal offenders to supplement state support of local victims' assistance programs and state victims' compensation programs.

victim-witness assistance program A program that counsels victims, orients them to the justice process, and provides a variety of other services, such as transportation to court, child care during court appearances, and referrals to social services agencies.

Violence against Women Act (VAWA) A federal law enacted as a component of the 1994 Violent Crime Control and Law Enforcement Act and intended to address concerns about violence against women. The law focused on improving the interstate enforcement of protection orders, providing effective training for court personnel involved with women's issues, improving the training and collaboration of police and prosecutors with victim service providers, strengthening law enforcement efforts to reduce violence against women, and increasing services to victims of violence. President Clinton signed the reauthorization of this legislation, known as the Violence against Women Act 2000, into law on October 28, 2000.

Violent Crime Control and Law Enforcement Act A federal law (Public Law 103–322) enacted in 1994 that authorized spending billions of dollars on crime prevention, law enforcement, and prison construction. It also outlawed the sale of certain types of assault weapons and enhanced federal death-penalty provisions.

Violent Criminal Apprehension Program (VICAP) The program of the Federal Bureau of Investigation focusing on serial murder investigations and the apprehension of serial killers.

virus See **computer virus**.

white-collar crime Any violation of the criminal law committed by a person of respectability and high social status in the course of his or her occupation.

Wickersham Commission A commission (officially known as the Commission on Law Observance and Enforcement) created by President Herbert Hoover in 1931 whose mandate was to improve justice system practices and to reinstate law's role in civilized governance. The commission made recommendations concerning the nation's police forces and described how to improve policing throughout America.

workplace violence The crimes of murder, rape, robbery, and assault committed against persons who are at work or on duty.

Notes

CHAPTER 1: WHAT IS CRIMINOLOGY?

1. Chris Balish, "NCIS Honored as Top Scripted TV Series," March 23, 2010, http://ontheredcarpet.typepad.com/ontheredcarpet/2010/03/crime-drama-ncis-honored-as-top-scripted-tv-series.html (accessed August 2, 2010).

2. CTV Global Media, "CSI: Miami," http://www.ctv.ca/servlet/ArticleNews/show/CTVShows/1064338847511_59746366 (accessed March 10, 2007).

3. Gerard Gilbert, "CSI: The Cop Show That Conquered the World," The (London) Independent, December 19, 2006, http://www.findarticles.com/p/articles/mi_qn4158/is_20061219/ai_n17081057 (accessed March 10, 2007).

4. From the standpoint of the law, the proper word is conduct rather than behavior because the term conduct implies intentional and willful activity, whereas behavior refers to any human activity—even that which occurs while a person is unconscious, as well as that which is unintended.

5. Paul W. Tappan, "Who Is the Criminal?" American Sociological Review, Vol. 12 (1947), pp. 96–102.

6. Edwin Sutherland, Principles of Criminology, 4th ed. (New York: Lippincott, 1947).

7. In 1996, for example, euthanasia advocate Dr. Jack Kevorkian was arrested and unsuccessfully prosecuted in Michigan on charges of violating the state's common law against suicide.

8. John F. Galliher, Criminology: Human Rights, Criminal Law, and Crime (Upper Saddle River, NJ: Prentice Hall, 1989), p. 2.

9. C. D. Shearing, "Criminologists Must Broaden Their Field of Study beyond Crime and Criminals," in R. Boostrom, ed., Enduring Issues in Criminology (San Diego, CA: Greenhaven, 1995).

10. Ezzat Fattah, Introduction to Criminology (Burnaby, British Columbia: School of Criminology, Simon Fraser University, 1989).

11. Hermann Mannheim, Comparative Criminology (Boston: Houghton Mifflin, 1965).

12. Ron Claassen, "Restorative Justice: Fundamental Principles," http://www.fresno.edu/pacs/rjprinc.htm (accessed May 5, 2007).

13. H. Schwendinger and J. Schwendinger, "Defenders of Order or Guardians of Human Rights?" in I. Taylor, P. Walton, and J. Young, eds., Critical Criminology (London: Routledge and Kegan Paul, 1975).

14. Ibid.

15. Jeffrey H. Reiman, The Rich Get Richer and the Poor Get Prison, 4th ed. (Boston: Allyn & Bacon, 1997).

16. Fattah, Introduction to Criminology.

17. Matthew Robinson, "Defining 'Crime,'" http://www.appstate.edu/~robinsnmb/smokeharms.htm (accessed November 4, 2006).

18. Piers Beirne and James W. Messerschmidt, Criminology (San Diego, CA: Harcourt Brace Jovanovich, 1991), p. 20.

19. Susan Spencer-Wendel, "Let 'Em Sag, Judge Rules on Riviera Beach's No-Baggy-Pants Law," The Palm Beach Post, April 22, 2009, http://www.palmbeachpost.com/localnews/content/local_news/epaper/2009/04/22/0422saggy.html (accessed March 24, 2010).

20. "State Assemblyman Felix Ortiz Takes on Salt," 1010 Wins, March 11, 2010, http://www.1010wins.com/B-klyn-Dem-Wants-Salt-Banned-from-Restaurant-Food/6551054 (accessed April 2, 2010).

21. "Girl, 12, Arrested in New York for Doodling on School Desk," USA Today, February 5, 2010, http://www.usatoday.com/news/nation/2010-02-05-girl-arrested-doodling_N.htm (accessed March 30, 2010).

22. The American Heritage Dictionary on CD-ROM (Boston: Houghton Mifflin, 1992).

23. The American Heritage Dictionary of the English Language, 3rd ed. (Boston: Houghton Mifflin, 1996).

24. This list is not meant to be exclusive. There are many other journals in the field, too many to list here.

25. Piers Beirne, Inventing Criminology (Albany: State University of New York Press, 1993).

26. See also Paul Topinard, Anthropology (London: Chapman and Hall, 1894).

27. Joseph F. Sheley, Criminology: A Contemporary Handbook (Belmont, CA: Wadsworth, 1991), p. xxiii.

28. Edwin H. Sutherland, Criminology (Philadelphia: Lippincott, 1924), p. 11.

29. Edwin H. Sutherland, Principles of Criminology (Chicago: University of Chicago Press, 1934).

30. "Sutherland, Edwin H.," Encyclopedia of Criminology, http://www.fitzroydearborn.com/chicago/criminology/sample-sutherlandedwin.asp (accessed November 15, 2007).

31. Edwin H. Sutherland and Donald R. Cressey, Criminology, 9th ed. (Philadelphia: Lippincott, 1974), p. 3.

32. Gennaro F. Vito and Ronald M. Holmes, Criminology: Theory, Research, and Policy (Belmont, CA: Wadsworth, 1994), p. 3.

33. Clemens Bartollas and Simon Dinitz, Introduction to Criminology: Order and Disorder (New York: Harper & Row, 1989), p. 548.

34. Marvin E. Wolfgang and Franco Ferracuti, The Subculture of Violence: Towards an Integrated Theory in Criminology (London: Tavistock, 1967).

35. European Society of Criminology, Constitution, Section 1 (d), http://www.esc-eurocrim.org/constitution.shtml (accessed July 10, 2007).

36. Jack P. Gibbs, "The State of Criminological Theory," Criminology, Vol. 25, No. 4 (November 1987), pp. 822–823.

37. Jim Short, "President's Message: On Communicating, Crossing Boundaries and Building Bridges," The Criminologist, Vol. 22, No. 5 (September/October 1997), p. 1.

38. Available through Sage Publications, Thousand Oaks, CA.

39. Piers Beirne and Colin Sumner, "Editorial Statement," Theoretical Criminology, Vol. 1, No. 1 (February 1997), pp. 5–11.

40. There are, however, those who deny that criminology deserves the name discipline. See, for example, Don C. Gibbons, Talking about Crime and Criminals: Problems and Issues in Theory Development in Criminology (Upper Saddle River, NJ: Prentice Hall, 1994), p. 3.

41. Charles F. Wellford, "Controlling Crime and Achieving Justice: The American Society of Criminology 1996 Presidential Address," *Criminology*, Vol. 35, No. 1 (1997), p. 1.

42. Gibbons, *Talking about Crime and Criminals*, p. 4.

43. Sutherland, *Principles of Criminology*.

44. Don M. Gottfredson, "Criminological Theories: The Truth as Told by Mark Twain," in William S. Laufer and Freda Adler, eds., *Advances in Criminological Theory*, Vol. 1 (New Brunswick, NJ: Transaction, 1989), p. 1.

45. Gregg Barak, *Integrating Criminologies* (Boston: Allyn & Bacon, 1998), p. 5.

46. Don C. Gibbons, "Talking about Crime: Observations on the Prospects for Causal Theory in Criminology," *Criminal Justice Research Bulletin* (Sam Houston State University), Vol. 7, No. 6 (1992).

47. Ibid.

48. Not all studies support such a policy, however. See, for example, P. R. Marchant, "A Demonstration That the Claim That Brighter Lighting Reduces Crime Is Unfounded," *British Journal of Criminology*, Vol. 44, No. 3 (2004), p. 441.

49. "Editorial: In Denial about On-screen Violence," *New Scientist*, April 21, 2007, p. 5.

50. Congressional Public Health Summit, *Joint Statement on the Impact of Entertainment Violence on Children*, July 26, 2000.

51. Federal Trade Commission, *Marketing Violent Entertainment to Children* (Washington, DC: U.S. Government Printing Office, 2000).

52. Sue Pleming, "U.S. Report Says Hollywood Aims Violence at Kids," Reuters, September 11, 2000.

53. "Editorial: In Denial about On-Screen Violence," *New Scientist*, April 21, 2007, http://www.newscientist.com/channel/opinion/mg19426003.600-editorial-in-denial-about-onscreen-violence.html (accessed August 1, 2007).

54. Alfred Blumstein, "Making Rationality Relevant: The American Society of Criminology 1992 Presidential Address," *Criminology*, Vol. 31, No. 1 (February 1993), p. 1.

55. Ibid.

56. Lydia Saad, "Crime Tops List of Americans' Local Concerns," Gallup Organization, June 21, 2000, http://www.gallup.com/poll/releases/pr000621.asp (accessed February 20, 2004).

57. For an especially good discussion of this issue, see Theodore Sasson, *Crime Talk: How Citizens Construct a Social Problem* (Hawthorne, NY: Aldine de Gruyter, 1995).

58. John P. Crank, *Understanding Police Culture* (Cincinnati, OH: Anderson, 1998), p. 15.

59. Public Law 103–322.

60. For a good overview of this issue, see Wesley G. Skogan, ed., *Reactions to Crime and Violence: The Annals of the American Academy of Political and Social Science* (Thousand Oaks, CA: Sage, 1995).

61. For an excellent discussion of crime as a social event, see Leslie W. Kennedy and Vincent F. Sacco, *Crime Counts: A Criminal Event Analysis* (Toronto: Nelson Canada, 1996).

62. For a good discussion of the social construction of crime, see Leslie T. Wilkins, "On Crime and Its Social Construction: Observations on the Social Construction of Crime," *Social Pathology*, Vol. 1, No. 1 (January 1995), pp. 1–11.

63. For a parallel approach, see Terance D. Miethe and Robert F. Meier, *Crime and Its Social Context: Toward an Integrated Theory of Offenders, Victims, and Situations* (Albany: State University of New York Press, 1995).

64. Joan McCord, "Family Relationships, Juvenile Delinquency, and Adult Criminality," *Criminology*, Vol. 29, No. 3 (August 1991), pp. 397–417.

65. Elizabeth Candle and Sarnoff A. Mednick, "Perinatal Complications Predict Violent Offending," *Criminology*, Vol. 29, No. 3 (August 1991), pp. 519–529.

66. Carol W. Kohfeld and John Sprague, "Demography, Police Behavior, and Deterrence," *Criminology*, Vol. 28, No. 1 (February 1990), pp. 111–136.

67. Leslie W. Kennedy and David R. Forde, "Routine Activities and Crime: An Analysis of Victimization in Canada," *Criminology*, Vol. 28, No. 1 (February 1990), p. 137.

68. William G. Doerner, "The Impact of Medical Resources on Criminally Induced Lethality: A Further Examination," *Criminology*, Vol. 26, No. 1 (February 1988), pp. 171–177.

69. Ibid., p. 177.

70. Jeff Ferrell, "Criminological *Verstehen*: Inside the Immediacy of Crime," *Justice Quarterly*, Vol. 14, No. 1 (1997), p. 11.

71. James F. Gilsinan, "They Is Clowning Tough: 911 and the Social Construction of Reality," *Criminology*, Vol. 27, No. 2 (May 1989), pp. 329–344.

72. See, for example, Miethe and Meier, *Crime and Its Social Context*.

73. For a good discussion of the historical development of criminology, see Leon Radzinowicz, *In Search of Criminology* (Cambridge: Harvard University Press, 1962).

74. As quoted in W. Wayt Gibbs, "Trends in Behavioral Science: Seeking the Criminal Element," *Scientific American*, Vol. 272, No. 3 (March 1995), pp. 100–107.

75. Wellford, "Controlling Crime and Achieving Justice," p. 4.

CHAPTER 2: WHERE DO THEORIES COME FROM?

1. "Florida Town Casts Out Satan," CNN, January 29, 2002, http://cnn.com/2002/US/01/29/town.satan (accessed June 3, 2007).

2. Mike Schneider, "Mayor Bans Satan from Florida Town," Associated Press, April 15, 2002.

3. Alex Leary, "ACLU Action Lands Satan on Inglis Meeting Agenda," *St. Petersburg Times* online, January 25, 2002, http://www.sptimes.com/2002/01/25/TampaBay/ACLU_action_lands_Sat.shtml (accessed May 7, 2007).

4. "Inglis, Florida," *Wikipedia*, http://en.wikipedia.org/wiki/Inglis,_Florida (accessed May 7, 2007).

5. The Carpetbagger Report, "An Interesting Update on Inglis, Fla., and Its Campaign against Satan," March 15, 2004, http://www.thecarpetbaggerreport.com/archives/1403.html (accessed May 7, 2007).

6. Lawrence W. Sherman, *Evidence-Based Policing* (Washington, DC: Police Foundation, 1998), p. 4.

7. David Weisburd, Lorraine Mazerolle, and Anthony Petrosino, "The Academy of Experimental Criminology: Advancing Randomized Trials in Crime and Justice," http://www.crim.upenn.edu/aec/AECCriminologist417.doc (accessed May 20, 2010).

8. David P. Farrington, Lloyd Ohlin, and James Q. Wilson, *Understanding and Controlling Crime* (New York: Springer-Verlag, 1986).

9. Lawrence W Sherman, *Policing Domestic Violence* (New York: Free Press, 1992).

10. Anthony Petrosino et al., "Toward Evidence-Based Criminology and Criminal Justice," *International Journal of Comparative Criminology*, Vol. 3 (2003).

11. American Society of Criminology, "The ASC Announces a New Division: The Division of Experimental Criminology," https://www.asc41.com/DECannouncement.html (accessed April 7, 2010).

12. David Weisburd, "Editor's Introduction," *Journal of Experimental Criminology*, Vol. 1 (2005), p. 3.

13. John H. Laub, "The Life Course of Criminology in the United States: The American Society of Criminology 2003 Presidential Address," *Criminology*, Vol. 42, No. 1 (February 2004), pp. 1-26.

14. Ibid., p. 7.

15. Ibid.

16. As discussed by Piers Beirne and Colin Summer, "Editorial Statement," *Theoretical Criminology: An International Journal*, Vol. 1, No. 1 (February 1997), pp. 5–11.

17. Hermann Mannheim, *Comparative Criminology* (Boston, MA: Houghton Mifflin, 1967), p. 20.

18. Details for this story come from Paul Stokes, "Extra Police Put on the Beat for Full Moon," *The Telegraph*, June 7, 2006, http://www.telegraph.co.uk/news/main.jhtml?xml=/news/2007/06/06/nmoon106.xml (accessed July 12, 2007).

19. Don M. Gottfredson, "Criminology Theories: The Truth as Told by Mark Twain," in William S. Laufer and Freda Adler, eds., *Advances in Criminological Theory*, Vol. 1 (New Brunswick, NJ: Transaction, 1989), p. 3.

20. Kenneth R. Hoover, *The Elements of Social Scientific Thinking*, 5th ed. (New York: St. Martin's, 1992), p. 34.

21. Ibid., p. 35.

22. Todd Clear, "Policy and Evidence: The Challenge to the American Society of Criminology—2009 Presidential Address to the American Society of Criminology," *Criminology*, Vol. 48, No. 1 (2010), p. 6.

23. Ibid.

24. Susette M. Talarico, *Criminal Justice Research: Approaches, Problems and Policy* (Cincinnati: Anderson, 1980), p. 3.

25. Ibid.

26. For a good review of secondary research, see J. H. Laub, R. J. Sampson, and K. Kiger, "Assessing the Potential of Secondary Data Analysis: A New Look at the Gluecks' Unraveling Juvenile Delinquency Data," in Kimberly L. Kempf, ed., *Measurement Issues in Criminology* (New York: Springer-Verlag, 1990), pp. 241–257; and Robert J. Sampson and John H. Laub, *Crime in the Making* (Cambridge: Harvard University Press, 1993).

27. Sampson and Laub, *Crime in the Making*, p. 3.

28. Larry S. Miller and John T. Whitehead, *Introduction to Criminal Justice Research and Methods* (Cincinnati: Anderson, 1996).

29. *The American Heritage Dictionary of the English Language*, 4th ed., (Chicago: Houghton Mifflin Harcourt Publishing Company, 2010), http://www.yourdictionary.com/hypothesis.

30. Donald T. Campbell and Julian C. Stanley, *Experimental and Quasi-Experimental Designs for Research* (Chicago: Rand-McNally, 1966), p. 35.

31. Ibid., p. 5, from which many of the descriptions that follow are adapted.

32. Ibid., p. 34.

33. According to Denise C. Gottfredson, "[M]idnight basketball programs are not likely to reduce crime." Gottfredson cites research (J. G. Ross et al., "The Effectiveness of an After-School Program for Primary Grade Latchkey Students on Precursors of Substance Abuse," *Journal of Community Psychology*, OSAP Special Issue [1992], pp. 22–38) showing that such programs may actually increase the risk for delinquency by increasing risk taking and impulsiveness. See Denise C. Gottfredson, "School-Based Crime Prevention," in Lawrence W. Sherman et al., *Preventing Crime: What Works, What Doesn't, What's Promising* (Washington, DC: National Institute of Justice, 1998), http://www.ncjrs.org/works/chapter5.htm (accessed June 15, 2004).

34. Shawn Bushway and David Weisburd, "Acknowledging the Centrality of Quantitative Criminology in Criminology and Criminal Justice," *The Criminologist*, Vol. 31, No. 4 (2006), p. 1.

35. Lawrence W. Sherman et al., *Evidence-Based Crime Prevention* (New York: Routledge, 2002).

36. Frank E. Hagan, *Research Methods in Criminal Justice and Criminology*, 6th ed. (New York: Allyn & Bacon, 2003).

37. Jeff Ferrell, "Criminological *Verstehen*: Inside the Immediacy of Crime," *Justice Quarterly*, Vol. 14, No. 1 (1997), p. 11.

38. William Foote Whyte, *Street Corner Society: The Social Structure of an Italian Slum* (Chicago: University of Chicago Press, 1943), pp. v–vii.

39. Ibid., p. vii.

40. Hagan, *Research Methods in Criminal Justice and Criminology*.

41. Nicole Vanden Heuvel, *Directory of Criminal Justice Information Sources*, 8th ed. (Washington, DC: National Institute of Justice, 1992), p. 145.

42. Hagan, *Research Methods in Criminal Justice and Criminology*.

43. Hoover, *The Elements of Social Scientific Thinking*, p. 34.

44. Abraham Kaplan, *The Conduct of Inquiry: Methodology for Behavioral Science* (San Francisco: Chandler, 1964), p. 134.

45. Ibid.

46. See American Society of Criminology, "Critical Criminal Justice Issues," 1994; available from the National Institute of Justice via http://www.ncjrs.gov/App/AbstractDB/AbstractDBDetails.aspx?id=158837.

47. Avshalom Caspim et al., "Are Some People Crime-Prone? Replications of the Personality-Crime Relationship across Countries, Genders, Races, and Methods," *Criminology*, Vol. 32, No. 2 (May 1994), pp. 162–195.

48. Kaplan, *The Conduct of Inquiry*, p. 172.

49. As with almost anything else, qualitative data can be assigned to categories, and the categories can be numbered. Hence, qualitative data can be quantified, although the worth of such effort is subject to debate.

50. Sanyika Shakur, *Monster: The Autobiography of an L.A. Gang Member* (New York: Penguin, 1993), pp. 45–46.

51. Ibid, p. xiv.

52. Ferrell, "Criminological *Verstehen*," p. 10.

53. Academy of Criminal Justice Sciences, *Code of Ethics*, Section 18.

54. Ibid., Section 19.

55. National Institute of Justice, *Protecting Human Subjects*, http://www.ojp.usdoj.gov/nij/humansubjects (accessed June 16, 2007).

56. Ferrell, "Criminological *Verstehen*," p. 8.

57. Hagan, *Research Methods in Criminal Justice and Criminology*.

58. Ibid.

59. See Dennis Cauchon, "Study Critical of D.A.R.E. Rejected," *USA Today*, October 4, 1994, p. 2A.

60. See Susan T. Ennett et al., "How Effective Is Drug Abuse Resistance Education? A Meta-Analysis of Project DARE Outcome Evaluations," *American Journal of Public Health*, Vol. 84, No. 9 (September 1994), pp. 1394–1401.

61. Susan T. Ennett et al., "Long-Term Evaluation of Drug Abuse Resistance Education," *Addictive Behaviors*, Vol. 19, No. 2 (1994), pp. 112–125.

62. Donald R. Lynam and Richard Milich, "Project DARE: No Effects at 10-Year Follow-Up," *Journal of Consulting and Clinical Psychology*, Vol. 67, No. 4 (August 1999), pp. 590–593.

63. Kevin Helliker, "The Case for Alcoholics Anonymous: It Works Even If the Science Is Lacking," *Wall Street Journal*, October 17, 2006, p. D1.

64. American Society of Criminology, *Draft Code of Ethics*, Section II, paragraph 7 (unpublished manuscript).

65. Faye S. Taxman, "Research and Relevance: Lessons from the Past, Thoughts for the Future," *Criminology and Public Policy*, Vol. 3, No. 2 (March 2004), p. 170.

66. Julian Leigh, "Mandatory Arrest Laws Can Reduce Domestic Violence," in Tamara L. Roleff, ed., *Domestic Violence: Opposing Viewpoints* (San Diego, CA: Greenhaven Press, 2000).

67. James Austin, "Why Criminology Is Irrelevant," *Criminology and Public Policy*, Vol. 2, No. 3 (July 2003), pp. 557–564.

68. Robert M. Bohm, "On the State of Criminal Justice: 1993 Presidential Address to the Academy of Criminal Justice Sciences," *Justice Quarterly*, Vol. 10, No. 4 (December 1993), p. 537.

69. National Institute of Justice, "Critical Criminal Justice Issues: Task Force Reports From the American Society of Criminology," an NIJ Report (May 1997).

70. The Campaign for an Effective Crime Policy, *The Impact of Three Strikes and You're Out Laws: What Have We Learned?* (Washington, DC: CECP, 1997).

71. Fox Butterfield, no headline, *New York Times News Service* Online, April 16, 1997.

72. Sherman et al., *Preventing Crime*.

73. Lawrence W. Sherman, "Evidence and Liberty: The Promise of Experimental Criminology," *Criminology & Criminal Justice*, Vol. 9, No. 1 (2009), pp. 5–28. Copyright © 2009, SAGE Publications. Reprinted by Permission of SAGE and the author.

74. Patricia Van Voorhis et al., "The Impact of Family Structure and Quality on Delinquency: A Comparative Assessment of Structural and Functional Factors," *Criminology*, Vol. 26, No. 2 (May 1988), pp. 235–261.

75. David F. Greenberg, "Comparing Criminal Career Models," *Criminology*, Vol. 30, No. 1 (February 1992), pp. 132–140.

76. This list of journals is representative at best. For a much more complete list, see Michael S. Vaughn et al., "Journals in Criminal Justice and Criminology: An Updated and Expanded Guide for Authors," *Journal of Criminal Justice Education*, Vol. 15, No. 1 (spring 2004), pp. 61–192.

77. American Psychological Association, *Publication Manual of the American Psychological Association*, 5th ed. (Washington, DC: APA, 2001).

78. William Strunk, Jr., and E. B. White, *The Elements of Style*, 4th ed. (New York: Longman, 2000).

79. Mary-Claire van Leunen, *A Handbook for Scholars*, rev. ed. (Oxford: Oxford University Press, 1992).

CHAPTER 3: CLASSICAL AND NEOCLASSICAL THOUGHT

1. Eliot Kleinberg, "Mentally Ill Man Taken Back to Jail after 50th Arrest," *The Palm Beach Post*, February 6, 2010, p. 1B.

2. William Graham Sumner, *Folkways* (New York: Dover, 1906).

3. Marvin Wolfgang, "The Key Reporter," *Phi Beta Kappa*, Vol. 52, No. 1.

4. Roman influence in England had ended by A.D. 442, according to Crane Brinton, John B. Christopher, and Robert L. Wolff, *A History of Civilization*, 3rd ed., Vol. 1 (Upper Saddle River, NJ: Prentice Hall, 1967), p. 180.

5. Howard Abadinsky, *Law and Justice* (Chicago: Nelson-Hall, 1988), p. 6.

6. Edward McNall Burns, *Western Civilization*, 7th ed. (New York: W. W. Norton, 1969).

7. Ibid.

8. Brinton, Christopher, and Wolff, *A History of Civilization*, p. 274.

9. Harry V. Jaffa and Ernest van den Haag, "Of Men, Hogs, and Law: If Natural Law Does Not Permit Us to Distinguish between Men and Hogs, What Does?" *National Review*, February 3, 1992, p. 40.

10. Abraham Lincoln, Speech on the Kansas-Nebraska Act, October 16, 1854.

11. Referred to in official transcripts as Rudolf Franz Ferdinand Hoess.

12. International Military Tribunal, "One Hundred and Eighth Day, Monday, 4/15/1946, Part 03," in *Trial of the Major War Criminals before the International Military Tribunal*, Vol. XI. Proceedings: 4/8/1946–4/17/1946 (Nuremberg: International Military Tribunal, 1943), pp. 398–400.

13. The quotations attributed to Beccaria in this section are from Cesare Beccaria, *Essay on Crimes and Punishments* (Livorno, Italy; Tipografia Coltellini, 1764).

14. The quotations attributed to Bentham in this section are from Bentham, *An Introduction to the Principles of Morals and Legislation* (Oxford: Clarendon Press, 1907); reprint of the 1823 edition, first printed 1780.

15. R. Martinson, "What Works: Questions and Answers about Prison Reform," *Public Interest*, No. 35 (1974), pp. 22–54.

16. James Q. Wilson, *Thinking about Crime* (New York: Vintage, 1975).

17. David Fogel, *We Are the Living Proof: The Justice Model of Corrections* (Cincinnati: Anderson, 1975).

18. Conrad P. Rutkowski, "Fogel's 'Justice Model': Stop Trying to Reform. Punish, but Treat All Alike," *Illinois Issues*, February 1976.

19. Felton M. Earls and Albert J. Reiss, *Breaking the Cycle: Predicting and Preventing Crime* (Washington, DC: National Institute of Justice, 1994), p. 49.

20. L. E. Cohen and Marcus Felson, "Social Change and Crime Rate Trends: A Routine Activity Approach," *American Sociological Review*, Vol. 44, No. 4 (August 1979), pp. 588–608. Also see Marcus Felson and L. E. Cohen, "Human Ecology and Crime: A Routine Activity Approach," *Human Ecology*, Vol. 8, No. 4 (1980), pp. 389–406; Marcus Felson, "Linking Criminal Choices, Routine Activities, Informal Control, and Criminal Outcomes," in Derek B. Cornish and Ronald V. Clarke, eds., *The Reasoning Criminal: Rational Choice Perspectives on Offending* (New York: Springer-Verlag, 1986), pp. 119–128; and Ronald V. Clarke and Marcus Felson, eds., *Advances in Criminological Theory: Routine Activity and Rational Choice* (New Brunswick, NJ: Transaction, 1993).

21. Cohen and Felson, "Social Change and Crime Rate Trends," p. 595.

22. For a test of routine activities theory as an explanation for victimization in the workplace, see John D. Wooldredge, Francis T. Cullen, and Edward J. Latessa, "Victimization in the Workplace: A Test of Routine Activities Theory," *Justice Quarterly*, Vol. 9, No. 2 (June 1992), pp. 325–335.

23. Marcus Felson, *Crime and Everyday Life: Insight and Implications for Society* (Thousand Oaks, CA: Pine Forge Press, 1994).

24. Gary LaFree and Christopher Birkbeck, "The Neglected Situation: A Cross-National Study of the Situational Characteristics of Crime," *Criminology*, Vol. 29, No. 1 (February 1991), p. 75.

25. Ronald V. Clarke and Derek B. Cornish, eds., *Crime Control in Britain: A Review of Police and Research* (Albany: State University of New York Press, 1985), p. 8.

26. Ronald V. Clarke, "Situational Crime Prevention—Everybody's Business," paper presented at the 1995 Australian Crime Prevention Council conference, http://barney.webace.com.au/~austcpc/conf95/clarke.htm (accessed December 2, 2000).

27. See Derek B. Cornish and Ronald V. Clarke, "Understanding Crime Displacement: An Application of Rational Choice Theory," *Criminology*, Vol. 25, No. 4 (November 1987), p. 933.

28. See Tomislav V. Kovandzic, Lynne M. Vieraitis, and Denise Paquette Boots, "Does the Death Penalty Save Lives? New Evidence from State Panel Data, 1977 to 2006," *Criminology and Public Policy*, Vol. 8, No. 4 (2009), pp. 803–843.

29. Werner Einstadter and Stuart Henry, *Criminological Theory: An Analysis of Its Underlying Assumptions* (Fort Worth, TX: Harcourt Brace, 1995), p. 70.

30. For a history of the development of the concept of situational crime prevention, see R. V. Clarke, ed., *Situational Crime Prevention: Successful Case Studies*, 2nd ed. (New York: Harrow and Heston, 1997); R. V. Clarke and J. Eck, *Become a Problem-Solving Crime Analyst* (London: Jill Dando Institute of Crime Science, University College London, 2003); and R. Wortley, "A Classification of Techniques for Controlling Situational Precipitators of Crime," *Security Journal*, Vol. 14 (2001), pp. 63–82.

31. Daniel J. Curran and Claire M. Renzetti, *Theories of Crime* (Boston: Allyn & Bacon, 1994), p. 18.

32. Jack Katz, *Seductions of Crime: Moral and Sensual Attractions in Doing Evil* (New York: Basic Books, 1988), p. 8.

33. Ibid., p. 3.

34. Ibid., p. 76.

35. Ibid., p. 71.

36. Bill McCarthy, "Not Just 'for the Thrill of It': An Instrumentalist Elaboration of Katz's Explanation of Sneaky Thrill Property Crimes," *Criminology*, Vol. 33, No. 4 (1995), pp. 519–538.

37. The quotations attributed to Weisburd in this section are from David Weisburd, "Reorienting Crime Prevention Research and Policy: From the Causes of Criminality to the Context of Crime," NIJ Research Report (Washington, DC: National Institute of Justice, June 1997).

38. See P. Brantingham and P. Brantingham, "Situational Crime Prevention in Practice," *Canadian Journal of Criminology* (January 1990), pp. 17–40; and R. V. Clarke, "Situational Crime Prevention: Achievements and Challenges," in M. Tonry and D. Farrington, eds., *Building a Safer Society: Strategic Approaches to Crime Prevention, Crime and Justice: A Review of Research*, Vol. 19 (Chicago: University of Chicago Press, 1995).

39. Quotes in this paragraph and the next are taken from Weisburd, "Reorienting Crime Prevention Research and Policy."

40. See, for example, J. E. Eck and D. Weisburd, eds., *Crime and Place: Crime Prevention Studies*, Vol. 4 (Monsey, NY: Willow Tree Press, 1995).

41. Marcus Felson and Ronald V. Clarke, *Opportunity Makes the Thief: Practical Theory for Crime Prevention* (London: British Home Office, 1998), p. 33.

42. Ibid.

43. Laura J. Moriarty and James E. Williams, "Examining the Relationship between Routine Activities Theory and Social Disorganization: An Analysis of Property Crime Victimization," *American Journal of Criminal Justice*, Vol. 21, No. 1 (1996), pp. 43–59.

44. Ibid., p. 43.

45. Ibid., p. 46.

46. M. Lyn Exum, "The Application and Robustness of the Rational Choice Perspective in the Study of Angry Intentions to Aggress," *Criminology*, Vol. 40, No. 4 (2002), p. 933, citing Allen E. Liska and Stephen F. Messner, *Perspectives on Crime and Deviance*, 3rd ed. (Upper Saddle River, NJ: Prentice Hall, 1999).

47. Dolf Zillman, *Hostility and Aggression* (Hillsdale, NJ: Lawrence Erlbaum Associates, 1979), p. 279.

48. David Lee and Justin McCrary, "Crime, Punishment, and Myopia," NBER Working Paper No. W11491 (Cambridge, MA: National Bureau of Economic Research, 2005). Available at SSRN: http://ssrn.com/abstract=762770.

49. Ibid.

50. Francesco Drago, Roberto Galbiati, and Pietro Vertova, "The Deterrent Effects of Prison: Evidence from a Natural Experiment," *Journal of Political Economy*, Vol. 117 (2009), pp. 257–280.

51. Kenneth D. Tunnell, "Choosing Crime: Close Your Eyes and Take Your Chances," *Justice Quarterly*, Vol. 7 (1990), pp. 673–690.

52. See R. Barr and K. Pease, "Crime Placement, Displacement and Deflection," in M. Tonry and N. Morris, eds., *Crime and Justice: A Review of Research*, Vol. 12 (Chicago: University of Chicago Press, 1990).

53. For a good summation of target hardening, see Ronald V. Clarke, *Situational Crime Prevention* (New York: Harrow and Heston, 1992).

54. For a good summation of studies on displacement, see R. Hesseling, "Displacement: A Review of the Empirical Literature," in R. V. Clarke, ed., *Crime Prevention Studies*, Vol. 3 (Monsey, NY: Willow Tree Press, 1994).

55. C. S. Lewis, "The Humanitarian Theory of Punishment," *Res Judicatae*, Vol. 6 (1953), pp. 224–225.

56. Tracey L. Snell, *Capital Punishment, 1999* (Washington, DC: Bureau of Justice Statistics, 2000).

57. See, for example, W. C. Bailey, "Deterrence and the Death Penalty for Murders in Utah: A Time Series Analysis," *Journal of Contemporary Law*, Vol. 5, No. 1 (1978), pp. 1–20; and William Bailey, "An Analysis of the Deterrent Effects of the Death Penalty for Murder in California," *Southern California Law Review*, Vol. 52, No. 3 (1979), pp. 743–764.

58. See, for example, B. E. Forst, "The Deterrent Effect of Capital Punishment: A Cross-State Analysis of the 1960s," *Minnesota Law Review*, Vol. 61 (1977), pp. 743–764.

59. Scott H. Decker and Carol W. Kohfeld, "Capital Punishment and Executions in the Lone Star State: A Deterrence Study," *Criminal Justice Research Bulletin* (Criminal Justice Center, Sam Houston State University), Vol. 3, No. 12 (1988).

60. Tomislav V. Kovandzic, Lynne M. Vieraitis, and Denise Paquette Boots, "Does the Death Penalty Save Lives? New Evidence from State Panel Data, 1977 to 2006," *Crime and Public Policy*, Vol. 8, No. 4 (2009), p. 803.

61. See Gordon Tullock, *The Logic of the Law* (New York: Basic Books, 1971).

62. Information and quotes in this paragraph are from the Death Penalty Information Center's Web site, http://www.deathpenaltyinfo.org (accessed December 15, 2007).

63. *Racial Disparities in Federal Death Penalty Prosecutions 1988–1994*, Staff Report by the Subcommittee on Civil and Constitutional Rights, Committee on the Judiciary, 103rd Congress, Second Session, prepared with the assistance of the Death Penalty Information Center, March 1994.

64. As some of the evidence presented before the Supreme Court in *Furman* v. *Georgia*, 408 U.S. 238 (1972), suggested.

65. *McCleskey* v. *Kemp*, 481 U.S. 279 (1987).

66. Formerly known as the National Committee to Prevent Wrongful Executions.

67. The Constitution Project, *Mandatory Justice: Eighteen Reforms to the Death Penalty* (Washington, DC: The Constitution Project, 2001).

68. Edward Connors et al., *Convicted by Juries, Exonerated by Science: Case Studies in the Use of DNA Evidence to Establish Innocence after Trial* (Washington, DC: National Institute of Justice, 1996).

69. Texas Defender Service, *A State of Denial: Texas Justice and the Death Penalty* (Houston, TX: TDS, 2000), www.texasdefender.org/study (accessed January 5, 2005).

70. U.S. Department of Justice, *The Federal Death Penalty System: A Statistical Survey—1988–2000* (Washington, DC: U.S. Department of Justice, 2000).

71. James S. Liebman, Jeffrey Fagan, and Valerie West, "A Broken System: Error Rates in Capital Cases, 1973–1995," Columbia Law School, Public Law Research Paper No. 15 (June 2000); http://www.law.columbia.edu/instructionalservices/liebman (accessed September 10, 2010).

72. "Released" in this context means exonerated or determined to be innocent. The definition of *innocence* used by the Death Penalty Information Center in placing defendants on the list is that they had been convicted and sentenced to death and that subsequently either (1) their conviction was overturned and they were acquitted at a retrial or all charges were dropped or (2) they were given an absolute pardon by the governor of the relevant state based on new evidence of innocence.

73. Jeffrey L. Kirchmeier, "Another Place beyond Here: The Death Penalty Moratorium Movement in the United States," *University of Colorado Law Review*, Vol. 70, No. 1 (2002), pp. 1–116.

74. Governor's Commission on Capital Punishment, *Report of the Governor's Commission on Capital Punishment* (April 2002), from which material in this paragraph is taken, http://www.idoc.state.il/us.ccp.ccp/reports/commission_report (accessed January 21, 2007).

75. Governor's Press Office, State of Maryland, "Governor Glendening Issues a Stay of Execution in the Case of Wesley Eugene Baker," May 9, 2002, http://www.gov.state.md.us/gov/press/2002/may/html/baker.html (accessed January 30, 2005).

76. *Gregg* v. *Georgia*, 428 U.S. 153 (1976).

77. "Massachusetts Panel Offers Limited Death Penalty Plan," *Criminal Justice Newsletter*, May 17, 2004, p. 1.

78. "New Jersey Suspends Death Penalty Pending a Task Force Review," *Criminal Justice Newsletter*, January 17, 2006, p. 8.

79. Title IV of the Justice for All Act of 2004.

80. At the time the legislation was enacted, Congress estimated that 300,000 rape kits remained unanalyzed in police department evidence lockers across the country.

81. The act also provides funding for the DNA Sexual Assault Justice Act (Title III of the Justice for All Act of 2004) and the Rape Kits and DNA Evidence Backlog Elimination Act of 2000 (42 U.S.C. 14135), authorizing more than $500 million for programs to improve the capacity of crime labs to conduct DNA analysis, reduce non-DNA backlogs, train evidence examiners, support sexual assault forensic examiner programs, and promote the use of DNA to identify missing persons.

82. In those states that accept federal monies under the legislation.

83. The Clark County (Indiana) Prosecutor's Office, "Roger Keith Coleman," http://www.clarkprosecutor.org/html/death/US/coleman175.htm (accessed May 20, 2007).

84. Lawrence W. Sherman, "Reason for Emotion: Reinventing Justice with Theories, Innovations and Research: 2002 ASC Presidential Address," *Criminology*, Vol. 41, No. 1 (2003), pp. 1–38.

85. Ibid., p. 8.

86. Heather C. West, *Prisoners at Yearend 2009-Advance Counts* (Washington, DC: Bureau of Justice Statistics, 2010).

87. Marvin Wolfgang, Thorsten Sellin, and Robert Figlio, *Delinquency in a Birth Cohort* (Chicago: University of Chicago Press, 1972).

88. Sherman, "Reason for Emotion," p. 7.

89. Randy Martin, Robert J. Mutchnick, and W. Timothy Austin, *Criminological Thought: Pioneers Past and Present* (New York: Macmillan, 1990), p. 17.

90. Ibid., p. 18.

CHAPTER 4: BIOLOGICAL ROOTS OF CRIMINAL BEHAVIOR

1. "Brain Tumour Causes Uncontrollable Paedophilia," *New Scientist*, October 21, 2002, http://www.newscientist.com/news/news.jsp?iD=NS99992943 (accessed September 12, 2010).

2. Alwyn Barr, "Charles Joseph Whitman," *The Handbook of Texas Online* (University of Texas at Austin), http://www.tsha.utexas.edu/handbook/online/articles/view/WW/fwh42.html (accessed February 2, 2007).

3. A. Raine et al., "Corpus Callosum Abnormalities in Psychopathic Antisocial Individuals," *Archives of General Psychiatry*, Vol. 60, No. 11 (November 2003), pp. 1134–1142.

4. See, for example, Henrik Soderstrom et al., "Reduced Regional Cerebral Blood Flow in Non-psychotic Violent Offenders," *Psychiatry Research*, Vol. 98 (2000), pp. 29–41; and Antoine Bechara et al., "Insensitivity to Future Consequences Following Damage to Human Prefrontal Cortex," *Cognition*, Vol. 50, No. 7 (1994), pp. 7–15.

5. Jose Leon-Carrion and Francisco Javier Chacartegui Ramos, "Blows to the Head during Development Can Predispose to Violent Criminal Behaviour: Rehabilitation of Consequences of Head Injury Is a Measure for Crime Prevention," *Brain Injury*, Vol. 17, No. 3 (March 2003), pp. 207–216.

6. See, for example, Ann Pytkowicz Streissguth et al., "Fetal Alcohol Syndrome in Adolescents and Adults," *Journal of the American Medical Association*, Vol. 265, No. 15 (April 17, 1991).

7. C. Ray Jeffery, "Biological Perspectives," *Journal of Criminal Justice Education*, Vol. 4, No. 2 (fall 1993), pp. 292–293.

8. Anthony Walsh, "Biological Theories of Criminal Behavior," in Richard A. Wright and J. Mitchell Miller, eds., *Encyclopedia of Criminology*, Vol. 1 (New York: Routledge, 2005), p. 106.

9. Ibid.

10. Ibid.

11. C. Ray Jeffery, "Genetics, Crime and the Canceled Conference," *Criminologist*, Vol. 18, No. 1 (January/February 1993), pp. 1–8.

12. Anastasia Toufexis, Hannah Bloch, and Dick Thompson, "Seeking the Roots of Violence," *Time*, April 19, 1993, p. 53, http://www.time.com/time/magazine/article/0,9171,978275,00.html (accessed August 5, 2010).

13. C. Ray Jeffery, "The Genetics and Crime Conference Revisited," *Criminologist*, Vol. 21, No. 2 (March/April 1996), p. 3.

14. Taken from "Hope for the 'Hopeless,'" *Crime Times*, Vol. 10, No. 2 (2004), p. 2.

15. Jeffery, "Biological Perspectives," p. 298.

16. Konrad Lorenz, *On Aggression* (New York: Harcourt, Brace and World, 1966).

17. Ibid., p. 23.

18. Ibid., p. 38.

19. Ibid., p. 249.

20. Ibid.

21. Cesare Lombroso, "Introduction," in Gina Lombroso-Ferrero, *Criminal Man According to the Classification of Cesare Lombroso* (1911; reprint, Montclair, NJ: Patterson Smith, 1972), p. xiv.

22. Charles Darwin, *Descent of Man: And Selection in Relation to Sex*, rev. ed. (London: John Murray, 1874), p. 137.

23. Auguste Comte, *A System of Positive Polity*, trans. John Henry Bridges (New York: Franklin, 1875; originally published in four volumes, 1851–1854).

24. See K. L. Henwood and N. F. Pidgeon, "Qualitative Research and Psychological Theorising," *British Journal of Psychology*, Vol. 83 (1992), pp. 97–111.

25. Lombroso, "Introduction," in Lombroso-Ferrero, *Criminal Man According to the Classification of Cesare Lombroso*, p. xv.

26. The English-language version appeared in 1895 as Cesare Lombroso, *The Female Offender* (New York: D. Appleton, 1895).

27. Marvin Wolfgang, "Cesare Lombroso," in Hermann Mannheim, *Pioneers in Criminology*, 2nd ed. (Montclair, NJ: Patterson Smith, 1972), p. 254.

28. Charles Goring, *The English Convict: A Statistical Study* (London: His Majesty's Stationery Office, 1913; reprint, Montclair, NJ: Patterson Smith, 1972), p. 15.

29. Ibid.

30. Earnest A. Hooton, *Crime and the Man* (Cambridge: Harvard University Press, 1939; reprint, Westport, CT: Greenwood Press, 1972).

31. Ibid., p. 75.

32. Ibid., p. 388.

33. Earnest A. Hooton, *The American Criminal: An Anthropological Study* (Cambridge: Harvard University Press, 1939).

34. Stephen Schafer, *Theories in Criminology: Past and Present Philosophies of the Crime Problem* (New York: Random House, 1969), p. 187.

35. L. Arseneault et al., "Minor Physical Anomalies and Family Adversity as Risk Factors for Violent Delinquency in Adolescence," *American Journal of Psychiatry*, Vol. 157, No. 6 (June 2000), pp. 917–923.

36. William H. Sheldon, *Varieties of Delinquent Youth* (New York: Harper & Brothers, 1949).

37. Ibid.

38. Sheldon Glueck and Eleanor Glueck, *Unraveling Juvenile Delinquency* (Cambridge: Harvard University Press, 1950).

39. D. Hill and W. Sargent, "A Case of Matricide," *Lancet*, Vol. 244 (1943), pp. 526–527.

40. William Dufty, *Sugar Blues* (Pandor, PA: Chilton, 1975).

41. See Court TV's Crime Library, "Twinkies as a Defense," http://www.crimelibrary.com/criminal_mind/psychology/insanity/7.html (accessed August 8, 2007).

42. Nanci Hellmich, "Sweets May Not Be Culprit in Hyper Kids," *USA Today*, February 3, 1994, p. 1A (reporting on a study published in the *New England Journal of Medicine*).

43. Ibid., p. 1A.

44. See Adrian Raine et al., "Prefrontal Glucose Deficits in Murderers Lacking Psychosocial Deprivation," *Neuropsychiatry, Neuropsychology, and Behavioral Neurology*, Vol. 11, No. 1 (1998), pp. 1–7; and Adrian Raine et al., "Selective Reductions in Prefrontal Glucose Metabolism in Murderers," *Biological Psychiatry*, Vol. 36 (September 1, 1994), pp. 319–332.

45. "PET Study: Looking inside the Minds of Murderers," *Crime Times*, Vol. 1, No. 1–2 (1995), http://www.crime-times.org/95a/w95ap1.htm (accessed November 15, 2006).

46. Ibid.

47. Raine et al., "Selective Reductions in Prefrontal Glucose Metabolism in Murderers."

48. See, for example, A. R. Mawson and K. J. Jacobs, "Corn Consumption, Tryptophan, and Cross National Homicide Rates," *Journal of Orthomolecular Psychiatry*, Vol. 7 (1978), pp. 227–230; and A. Hoffer, "The Relation of Crime to Nutrition," *Humanist in Canada*, Vol. 8 (1975), p. 8.

49. See, for example, C. Hawley and R. E. Buckley, "Food Dyes and Hyperkinetic Children," *Academy Therapy*, Vol. 10 (1974), pp. 27–32; and Alexander Schauss, *Diet, Crime and Delinquency* (Berkeley, CA: Parker House, 1980).

50. "Special Report: Measuring Your Life with Coffee Spoons," *Tufts University Diet and Nutrition Letter*, Vol. 2, No. 2 (April 1984), pp. 3–6.

51. See, for example, "Special Report: Does What You Eat Affect Your Mood and Actions?" *Tufts University Diet and Nutrition Letter*, Vol. 2, No. 12 (February 1985), pp. 4–6.

52. See *Tufts University Diet and Nutrition Newsletter*, Vol. 2, No. 11 (January 1985), p. 2; and "Special Report: Why Sugar Continues to Concern Nutritionists," *Tufts University Diet and Nutrition Letter*, Vol. 3, No. 3 (May 1985), pp. 3–6.

53. A. Hoffer, "Children with Learning and Behavioral Disorders," *Journal of Orthomolecular Psychiatry*, Vol. 5 (1976), p. 229.

54. I. B. Helland et al., "Maternal Supplements with Very-Long-Chain Omega-3 Fatty Acids during Pregnancy and Lactation Augment Children's IQ at 4 Years of Age," *Pediatrics*, Vol. 111, No. 1 (January 2003), pp. 39–44.

55. C. Iribarren et al., "Dietary Intake of Omega-3, Omega-6 Fatty Acids and Fish: Relationship with Hostility in Young Adults—The CARDIA Study," *European Journal of Clinical Nutrition*, Vol. 50, No. 1 (January 2004), pp. 24–31.

56. David Benton, "The Impact of Diet on Anti-Social, Violent and Criminal Behaviour," *Neuroscience and Biobehavioral Reviews*, Vol. 31 (2007), pp. 752–774.

57. C. Bernard Gesch et al., "Influence of Supplementary Vitamins, Minerals and Essential Fatty Acids on the Antisocial Behaviour of Young Adult Prisoners: Randomized, Placebo-Controlled Trial," *British Journal of Psychiatry*, Vol. 181 (July 2002), pp. 22–28.

58. S. Schoenthaler and I. D. Bier, "Addiction and Criminal Behaviour," in J. Brostoff and S. Challacombe, eds., *Food Allergy and Intolerance*, 2nd ed. (London: W. B. Saunders, 2002), pp. 985–1000.

59. Roger D. Masters, Brian Hone, and Anil Doshi, "Environmental Pollution, Neurotoxicity, and Criminal Violence," in J. Rose, ed., *Environmental Toxicology* (London and New York: Gordon and Breach, 1997).

60. Peter Montague, "Toxics and Violent Crime," *Rachel's Environment and Health Weekly*, No. 551 (June 19, 1997).

61. See, for example, Jeffrey Halperin et al., "Serotonergic Function in Aggressive and Nonaggressive Boys with ADHD," *American Journal of Psychiatry*, Vol. 151, No. 2 (February 1994), pp. 243–248.

62. Masters, Hone, and Doshi, "Environmental Pollution, Neurotoxicity, and Criminal Violence."

63. See, for example, Rick Nevin, "How Lead Exposure Relates to Temporal Changes in IQ, Violent Crime, and Unwed Pregnancy," *Environmental Research*, Vol. 83, No. 1 (May 2000), pp. 1–22.

64. Quoted in Alison Motluck, "Pollution May Lead to a Life of Crime," *New Scientist*, Vol. 154, No. 2084 (May 31, 1997), p. 4.

65. Don Cherek and Scott Lane, "Effects of d,1-Fenfluramine on Aggressive and Impulsive Responding in Adult Males with a History of Conduct Disorder," *Psychopharmacology*, Vol. 146 (1999), pp. 473–481.

66. Ibid.

67. See Alexander G. Schauss, "Tranquilizing Effect of Color Reduces Aggressive Behavior and Potential Violence," *Journal of Orthomolecular*

Psychiatry, Vol. 8, No. 4 (1979), pp. 218–221; and David Johnston, "Is It Merely a Fad, or Do Pastel Walls Stop Jail House Brawls?" *Corrections Magazine*, Vol. 7, No. 3 (1981), pp. 28–32.

68. Questions were raised, however, about the long-term effects of confinement in pink cells, and some researchers suggested that extended exposure to the color pink could generate suicidal impulses.

69. L. Goldschmidt, N. L. Day, and G. A. Richardson, "Effects of Prenatal Marijuana Exposure on Child Behavior Problems at Age 10," *Neurotoxicology and Teratology*, Vol. 22, No. 3 (May/June 2000), pp. 325–336.

70. David Fergusson, Lianne Woodward, and L. John Horwood, "Maternal Smoking during Pregnancy and Psychiatric Adjustment in Late Adolescence," *Archives of General Psychiatry*, Vol. 55 (August 1998), pp. 721–727.

71. Jacob F. Orlebeke, Dirk L. Knol, and Frank C. Verhulst, "Increase in Child Behavior Problems Resulting from Maternal Smoking during Pregnancy," *Archives of Environmental Health*, Vol. 52, No. 4 (July/August 1997), pp. 317–321.

72. Travis C. Pratt, Jean Marie McGloin, and Noelle E. Fearn, "Maternal Cigarette Smoking during Pregnancy and Criminal/Deviant Behavior: A Meta-Analysis," *International Journal of Offender Therapy and Comparative Criminology*, Vol. 50, No. 6 (2006), pp. 672–690.

73. See, for example, Ann Pytkowicz Streissguth et al., "Fetal Alcohol Syndrome in Adolescents and Adults," *Journal of the American Medical Association*, Vol. 265, No. 15 (April 17, 1991).

74. Tresa M. Roebuck, Sarah N. Mattson, and Edward P. Riley, "Behavioral and Psychosocial Profiles of Alcohol-Exposed Children," *Alcoholism: Clinical and Experimental Research*, Vol. 23, No. 6 (June 1999), pp. 1070–1076.

75. "Flu in Pregnancy Changes Fetal Brain," *New Scientist*, January 30, 2010, p. 15.

76. See, for example, R. T. Rada, D. R. Laws, and R. Kellner, "Plasma Testosterone Levels in the Rapist," *Psychosomatic Medicine*, Vol. 38 (1976), pp. 257–268.

77. "The Insanity of Steroid Abuse," *Newsweek*, May 23, 1988, p. 75.

78. Dan Olweus et al., "Testosterone, Aggression, Physical and Personality Dimensions in Normal Adolescent Males," *Psychosomatic Medicine*, Vol. 42 (1980), pp. 253–269.

79. Richard Udry, "Biosocial Models of Adolescent Problem Behaviors," *Social Biology*, Vol. 37 (1990), pp. 1–10.

80. Dan Olweus, "Testosterone and Adrenaline: Aggressive Antisocial Behavior in Normal Adolescent Males," in Sarnoff A. Mednick, Terrie E. Moffitt, and Susan A. Stack, eds., *The Causes of Crime: New Biological Approaches* (Cambridge: Cambridge University Press, 1987), pp. 263–282.

81. Alan Booth and D. Wayne Osgood, "The Influence of Testosterone on Deviance in Adulthood: Assessing and Explaining the Relationship," *Criminology*, Vol. 31, No. 1 (1993), p. 93.

82. E. G. Stalenheim et al., "Testosterone as a Biological Marker in Psychopathy and Alcoholism," *Psychiatry Research*, Vol. 77, No. 2 (February 1998), pp. 79–88.

83. Paul C. Bernhardt, "Influences of Serotonin and Testosterone in Aggression and Dominance: Convergence with Social Psychology," *Current Directions in Psychological Science*, Vol. 6, No. 2 (April 1997), pp. 44–48.

84. Michelle M. Wirth and Oliver C. Schultheiss, "Basal Testosterone Moderates Responses to Anger Faces in Humans," *Physiology and Behavior*, Vol. 90 (2007), pp. 496–505.

85. Ibid., p. 502.

86. Richard Udry, Luther Talbert, and Naomi Morris, "Biosocial Foundations for Adolescent Female Sexuality," *Demography*, Vol. 23 (1986), pp. 217–227.

87. James M. Dabbs, Jr., and Marian F. Hargrove, "Age, Testosterone, and Behavior among Female Prison Inmates," *Psychosomatic Medicine*, Vol. 59 (1997), pp. 447–480.

88. A. Maras et al., "Association of Testosterone and Dihydrotestosterone with Externalizing Behavior in Adolescent Boys and Girls, *Psychoneuroendocrinology*, Vol. 28, No. 7 (October 2003), pp. 932–940.

89. *Regina v. English*, unreported, Norwich Crown Court, November 10, 1981.

90. "Drunk Driving Charge Dismissed: PMS Cited," *Fayetteville* (NC) *Observer-Times*, June 7, 1991, p. 3A.

91. Toufexis, Bloch, and Thompson, "Seeking the Roots of Violence."

92. Terrie E. Moffitt et al., "Whole Blood Serotonin Relates to Violence in an Epidemiological Study," *Biological Psychiatry*, Vol. 43, No. 6 (March 15, 1998), pp. 446–457.

93. Ibid.

94. H. Soderstrom et al., "New Evidence for an Association between the CSF HVA:5–HIAA Ratio and Psychopathic Traits," *Journal of Neurology, Neurosurgery and Psychiatry*, Vol. 74 (2003), pp. 918–921.

95. Keith McBurnett et al., "Low Salivary Cortisol and Persistent Aggression in Boys Referred for Disruptive Behavior," *Archives of General Psychiatry*, Vol. 57, No. 1 (January 2000), pp. 38–43.

96. Ibid.

97. See E. G. Stalenheim, L. von Knorring, and L. Wide, "Serum Levels of Thyroid Hormones as Biological Markers in a Swedish Forensic Psychiatric Population," *Biological Psychiatry*, Vol. 43, No. 10 (May 15, 1998), pp. 755–761; and P. O. Alm et al., "Criminality and Psychopathy as Related to Thyroid Activity in Former Juvenile Delinquents," *Acta Psychiatrica Scandinavica*, Vol. 94, No. 2 (August 1996), pp. 112–117.

98. Michael Kosfeld et al., "Oxytocin Increases Trust in Humans," *Nature*, Vol. 435 (June 2005), pp. 673–676.

99. "'Trust' Hormone Identified," *Red Herring*, June 2, 2005.

100. J. Rotton and E. G. Cohn, "Weather, Climate, and Crime," in R. Bechtel and E. Churchman, eds., *The 2002 Handbook of Environmental Psychology* (New York: Wiley, 2002), pp. 461–498.

101. E. G. Cohn and J. Rotton, "Assault as a Function of Time and Temperature: A Moderator-Variable Time-Series Analysis," *Journal of Personality and Social Psychology*, Vol. 72 (1997), pp. 1322–1334.

102. J. Rotton and E. G. Cohn, "Violence as a Curvilinear Function of Temperature in Dallas: A Replication," *Journal of Personality and Social Psychology*, Vol. 78 (2000), pp. 1074–1081.

103. E. G. Cohn and J. Rotton, "Weather, Seasonal Trends, and Property Crimes in Minneapolis, 1987–1988: A Moderator-Variable Time-Series Analysis of Routine Activities," *Journal of Environmental Psychology*, Vol. 20 (2000), pp. 257–272.

104. J. Rotton and E. G. Cohn, "Temperature, Routine Activities, and Domestic Violence: A Reanalysis," *Victims and Violence*, Vol. 16 (2001), pp. 203–215.

105. J. Rotton and E. G. Cohn, "Weather, Disorderly Conduct, and Assaults: From Social Contact to Social Avoidance," *Environment and Behavior*, Vol. 32 (2000), pp. 649–671.

106. Thomas J. Schory et al., "Barometric Pressure, Emergency Psychiatric Visits, and Violent Acts," *Canadian Journal of Psychiatry*, Vol. 48 (October 2003), pp. 624–627.

107. Richard Louis Dugdale, *The Jukes: A Study in Crime, Pauperism, Disease, and Heredity*, 3rd ed. (New York: G. P. Putnam's Sons, 1895).

108. Arthur H. Estabrook, *The Jukes in 1915* (Washington, DC: Carnegie Institute of Washington, 1916).

109. Henry Herbert Goddard, *The Kallikak Family: A Study in the Heredity of Feeblemindedness* (New York: Macmillan, 1912).

110. See Nicole Hahn Rafter, *Creating Born Criminals* (Urbana: University of Illinois Press, 1997).

111. See Nicole Hahn Rafter, ed., *White Trash: The Eugenics Family Studies, 1877–1919* (Boston: Northeastern University Press, 1988).

112. *Buck v. Bell*, 274 U.S. 200, 207 (1927).

113. Sir Julian Huxley, "How Can Man Improve Man?" *New Scientist*, June 15, 1962.

114. P. A. Jacobs, M. Brunton, and M. Melville, "Aggressive Behavior, Mental Subnormality, and the XYY Male," *Nature*, Vol. 208 (1965), p. 1351.

115. *Webster's* defines *karyotype* as "a photomicrograph of metaphase chromosomes in a standard array" (*Webster's II New College Dictionary* [Chicago, IL: Houghton Mifflin Harcourt, 2005], p. 618).

116. See David A. Jones, *History of Criminology: A Philosophical Perspective* (Westport, CT: Greenwood Press, 1986), p. 124.

117. Many of these characteristics have been summarized in J. Katz and W. Chambliss, "Biology and Crime," in J. F. Sheley, ed., *Criminology* (Belmont, CA: Wadsworth, 1991), pp. 245–272.

118. As reported by S. A. Mednick and J. Volavka, "Biology and Crime," in N. Morris and M. Tonry, *Crime and Justice: An Annual Review of Research*, Vol. 2 (Chicago: University of Chicago Press, 1980), pp. 85–158; and D. A. Andrews and James Bonta, *The Psychology of Criminal Conduct* (Cincinnati: Anderson, 1994), pp. 126–127.

119. T. Sarbin and J. Miller, "Demonism Revisited: The XYY Chromosomal Anomaly," *Issues in Criminology*, Vol. 5 (1970), p. 199.

120. Geoffrey Cowley and Carol Hallin, "The Genetics of Bad Behavior: A Study Links Violence to Heredity," *Newsweek*, November 1, 1993, p. 57.

121. See Joseph D. McInerney, "Genes and Behavior: A Complex Relationship," *Judicature*, Vol. 83, No. 3 (November–December 1999).

122. Sir Francis Galton, *Inquiry into Human Faculty and Its Development*, 2nd ed. (London: J. M. Dent and Sons, 1907).

123. Johannes Lange, *Verbrechen als Schicksal* (Leipzig: Georg Thieme, 1929).

124. Karl O. Christiansen, "A Preliminary Study of Criminality among Twins," in Sarnoff Mednick and Karl Christiansen, eds., *Biosocial Bases of Criminal Behavior* (New York: Gardner Press, 1977).

125. The Minnesota Twin Family Study, http://www.psych.umn.edu/psylabs/mtfs (accessed August 10, 2007).

126. T. J. Bouchard et al., "Sources of Human Psychological Differences: The Minnesota Study of Twins Reared Apart," *Science*, Vol. 250, No. 4978 (1990), pp. 223–228.

127. Edwin J. C. G. van den Oord, Dorret I. Boomsma, and Frank C. Verhulst, "A Study of Problem Behaviors in 10- to 15-Year-Old Biologically Related and Unrelated International Adoptees," *Behavior Genetics*, Vol. 24, No. 3 (1994), pp. 193–205.

128. Peter McGuffin and Anita Thapar, "Genetic Basis of Bad Behaviour in Adolescents," *Lancet*, Vol. 350 (August 9, 1997), pp. 411–412.

129. Wendy Slutske et al., "Modeling Genetic and Environmental Influences in the Etiology of Conduct Disorder: A Study of 2,682 Adult Twin Pairs," *Journal of Abnormal Psychology*, Vol. 106, No. 2 (1997), pp. 266–279.

130. Louise Arseneault et al., "Strong Genetic Effects on Cross-Situational Antisocial Behaviour among 5-Year-Old Children According to Mothers, Teachers, Examiner-Observers, and Twins' Self-Reports," *Journal of Child Psychology and Psychiatry*, Vol. 44, No. 6 (September 2003), pp. 832–848.

131. Ibid.

132. Jeanette Taylor et al., "Genetic and Environmental Influences on Psychopathy Trait Dimensions in a Community Sample of Male Twins," *Journal of Abnormal Child Psychology*, Vol. 31, No. 6 (December 2003), pp. 633–645.

133. Much of the information and some of the wording in this section come from the National Human Genome Research Institute's Web page, http://www.nhgri.nih.gov/HGP (accessed November 16, 2007).

134. Rick Weiss, "Genome Project Completed," *Washington Post*, April 15, 2003, p. A6.

135. James Watson and Francis Crick, "Molecular Structure of Nucleic Acids: A Structure for Deoxyribose Nucleic Acid," *Nature*, Vol. 171 (April 1953), p. 737.

136. Quoted in Tim Friend, "Violence Linked to Gene Defect: Pleasure Deficit May Be the Spark," *USA Today*, May 9, 1996. See the original research at Kenneth Blum et al., "Reward Deficiency Syndrome," *American Scientist*, Vol. 84 (March/April 1996), pp. 132–145, http://www.sigmaxi.org/amsci/Articles/96Articles/Blum-full.html (accessed January 5, 2005).

137. A. E. Baum et al., "A Genome-Wide Association Study Implicates Diacylglycerol Kinase Eta (DGKH) and Several Other Genes in the Etiology of Bipolar Disorder," *Molecular Psychiatry*, advance online publication, http://doi:10.1038/sj.mp.4002012 (accessed May 8, 2007).

138. Katie Moisse, "Communication Breakdown in Brain Caused by a Gene Defect May Contribute to Schizophrenia," *Scientific American*, April 1, 2010, http://www.scientificamerican.com/article.cfm?id=schizophrenia-gene-mechanism (accessed May 20, 2010). See also

Torfi Sigurdsson et al., "Impaired Hippocampal-Prefrontal Synchrony in a Genetic Mouse Model of Schizophrenia," *Nature*, Vol. 464, No. 7289 (2010), pp. 763–667.

139. National Institute on Drug Abuse, "Genetics of Addiction: A Research Update from the National Institute on Drug Abuse," http://www.drugabuse.gov/tib/genetics.html (accessed May 1, 2010).

140. McInerney, "Genes and Behavior."

141. See "The Genome Changes Everything: A Talk with Matt Ridley," http://www.edge.org/3rd_culture/ridley03/ridley_print.html (accessed February 10, 2007).

142. Matt Ridley, "What Makes You Who You Are?" *Time*, June 2, 2003, pp. 55–63.

143. "Genes Are So Liberating," *New Scientist*, May 17, 2003, http://www.newscientist.com/hottopics/humannature/article.jsp?id=2395520=The%20brain (accessed January 9, 2007).

144. Jeffery, "Biological Perspectives," p. 300.

145. Leanne Fiftal Alarid et al., "Women's Roles in Serious Offenses: A Study of Adult Felons," *Justice Quarterly*, Vol. 13, No. 3 (September 1996), pp. 432–454.

146. Federal Bureau of Investigation, *Crime in the United States, 2006* (Washington, DC: U.S. Department of Justice, 2007).

147. Freda Adler, *Sisters in Crime: The Rise of the New Female Criminal* (New York: McGraw-Hill, 1975).

148. Darrell J. Steffensmeier, "Sex Differences in Patterns of Adult Crime, 1965–1977: A Review and Assessment," *Social Forces*, Vol. 58 (1980), pp. 1098–1099.

149. FBI, *Crime in the United States, 2000*, as computed by the author.

150. See, for example, D. H. Fishbein, "The Psychobiology of Female Aggression," *Criminal Justice and Behavior*, Vol. 19 (1992), pp. 99–126.

151. Robbin S. Ogle, Daniel Maier-Katin, and Thomas J. Bernard, "A Theory of Homicidal Behavior among Women," *Criminology*, Vol. 33, No. 2 (1995), pp. 173–193.

152. Ibid., p. 177.

153. Ibid., p. 179.

154. Arthur Fisher, "A New Synthesis Comes of Age," *Mosaic*, Vol. 22, No. 1 (spring 1991), pp. 2–9.

155. The quotations attributed to Wilson in this section are from Edward O. Wilson, *Sociobiology: The New Synthesis* (Cambridge: Belknap Press of Harvard University Press, 1975).

156. Wilson, *Sociobiology*, p. 327.

157. Research by Martin Daly and Margo Wilson of McMaster University in Hamilton, Canada, as reported in Arthur Fisher, "A New Synthesis II: How Different Are Humans?" *Mosaic*, Vol. 22, No. 1 (spring 1991), p. 14.

158. Fisher, "A New Synthesis II," p. 11.

159. John H. Beckstrom, *Evolutionary Jurisprudence: Prospects and Limitations on the Youth of Modern Darwinism throughout the Legal Process* (Urbana: University of Illinois Press, 1989).

160. John Madison Memory, "Sociobiology and the Metamorphoses of Criminology: 1978–2000," unpublished manuscript.

161. Ibid., p. 11.

162. Ibid., p. 33.

163. See also Arnold L. Lieber, *The Lunar Effect: Biological Tides and Human Emotions* (Garden City, NY: Anchor, 1978).

164. James Q. Wilson and Richard J. Herrnstein, *Crime and Human Nature* (New York: Simon & Schuster, 1985).

165. Quoted in Karen J. Winkler, "Criminals Are Born as Well as Made, Authors of Controversial Book Assert," *Chronicle of Higher Education*, January 16, 1986, p. 5.

166. Wilson and Herrnstein, *Crime and Human Nature*.

167. Winkler, "Criminals Are Born as Well as Made," p. 8.

168. Anthony Walsh, *Biosocial Criminology: Introduction and Integration* (Cincinnati: Anderson, 2002), p. vii.

169. "Childhood Abuse Hurts the Brain," *Harvard University Gazette*, May 22, 2003, http://www.news.harvard.edu/gazette/2003/05.22/01-brain.html (accessed June 4, 2010).

170. Ibid.

171. Antoine Lutz et al., "Long-Term Meditators Self-Induce High-Amplitude Gamma Synchrony during Mental Practice," *Proceedings of the National Academy of Sciences*, Vol. 101, No. 46 (November 16, 2004), pp. 16369–16373.

172. Jeffrey M. Schwartz and Sharon Begley, *The Mind and the Brain: Neuroplasticity and the Power of Mental Force* (New York: Regan Books, 2002).

173. Walsh, *Biosocial Criminology*, p. ix.

174. Ibid.

175. Gennaro F. Vito, Jeffrey R. Maahs, and Ronald M. Holmes, *Criminology: Theory, Research, and Policy* (Boston: Jones and Bartlett, 2007), p. 100.

176. Terrie E. Moffitt, "Adolescence-Limited and Life-Course-Persistent Antisocial Behavior: A Developmental Taxonomy," *Psychological Review*, Vol. 100, No. 4 (1993), pp. 674–701.

177. Adapted from C. Tittle, "Theoretical Developments in Criminology," *The Nature of Crime: Continuity and Change*, Vol. 1 (Washington, DC: National Institute of Justice, 2000), pp. 51–101.

178. Moffitt, "Adolescence-Limited and Life-Course-Persistent Antisocial Behavior," pp. 674–701.

179. Avshalom Caspi et al., "Role of Genotype in the Cycle of Violence in Maltreated Children," *Science*, Vol. 298, No. 2 (August 2002), p. 851.

180. Ibid.

181. Nilsson Oreland et al., "Monoamine Oxidases: Activities, Genotypes and the Shaping of Behaviour," *Journal of Neural Transmission*, April 12, 2007; and Rickard L. Sjöberg, et al., "Adolescent Girls and Criminal Activity: Role of MAOA-LPR Genotype and Psychosocial Factor," *American Journal of Medical Genetics Part B: Neuropsychiatric Genetics*, Vol. 144B, No. 2 (October 2006), pp. 159–164.

182. For more information on the Dunedin Multidisciplinary Health and Development Study, see T. E. Moffitt et al., *Sex Differences in Antisocial Behavior: Conduct Disorder, Delinquency and Violence in the*

Dunedin Longitudinal Study (Cambridge: Cambridge University Press, 2001). Visit the Dunedin Multidisciplinary Health and Development Research Unit on the Web at http://healthsci.otago .ac.nz/dsm/dmhdru.

183. See, for example, M. Rutter, H. Giller, and A. Hagell, *Antisocial Behavior by Young People* (Cambridge: Cambridge University Press, 1998).

184. Kevin M. Beaver, Matt DeLisi, Michael G. Vaughn, and John Paul Wright, "The Intersection of Genes and Neuropsychological Deficits in the Prediction of Adolescent Delinquency and Low Self-Control," *International Journal of Offender Therapy and Comparative Criminology*, Vol. 20, No. 10, (2008), p. 17.

185. Hans J. Eysenck, *Crime and Personality* (Boston: Houghton Mifflin, 1964).

186. Hans J. Eysenck, "Personality and Criminality: A Dispositional Analysis," in William S. Laufer and Freda Adler, eds., *Advances in Criminology Theory*, Vol. 1 (New Brunswick, NJ: Transaction, 1989), p. 90.

187. Eysenck, *Crime and Personality*, pp. 35–36.

188. Ibid., p. 92.

189. Jerome H. Barkow, Leda Cosmides, and John Tooby, eds., *The Adapted Mind: Evolutionary Psychology and the Generation of Culture* (New York: Oxford University Press, 1992).

190. Steven Pinker, *The Blank Slate: The Modern Denial of Human Nature* (New York: Viking, 2002).

191. Quotes in the following list are taken from Jeffery, "Biological Perspectives," p. 303.

192. Ibid.

193. *Buck v. Bell*, 274 U.S. 200, 207 (1927).

194. Toufexis, Bloch, and Thompson, "Seeking the Roots of Violence," p. 53.

195. Gary LaFree and Katheryn K. Russell, "The Argument for Studying Race and Crime," *Journal of Criminal Justice Education*, Vol. 4, No. 2 (fall 1993), p. 279.

196. Lee Ellis and Anthony Walsh, "Gene-Based Evolutionary Theories in Criminology," *Criminology*, Vol. 35, No. 2 (1997), pp. 229–230.

197. Rafter, *Creating Born Criminals*.

198. Glenn D. Walters and Thomas W. White, "Heredity and Crime: Bad Genes or Bad Research?" *Criminology*, Vol. 27, No. 3 (1989), pp. 455–485. See also P. A. Brennan and S. A. Mednick, "Reply to Walters and White: Heredity and Crime," *Criminology*, Vol. 28, No. 4 (November 1990), pp. 657–661.

199. Ibid., p. 476.

200. Ibid., p. 478.

CHAPTER 5: PSYCHOLOGICAL AND PSYCHIATRIC FOUNDATIONS OF CRIMINAL BEHAVIOR

1. "Police Fear Killings Span 10 Years," *USA Today*, July 26, 1991, p. 3A.

2. "Mutilator 'Seemed So Natural,'" *Fayetteville (NC) Observer-Times*, July 28, 1991, p. 7A.

3. "Doctor: Dahmer Wanted to Freeze-Dry a Victim," *Fayetteville (NC) Observer-Times*, February 13, 1992, p. 7A.

4. "Psychiatrist: Dahmer Lacked Will to Stop," *Fayetteville (NC) Observer-Times*, February 4, 1992, p. 5A.

5. "Dahmer: 936 Years for 'Holocaust,'" *USA Today*, February 18, 1992, p. 1A.

6. D. A. Andrews and James Bonta, *The Psychology of Criminal Conduct* (Cincinnati: Anderson, 1994), p. 69.

7. See Adrian Raine, *The Psychopathology of Crime: Criminal Behavior as a Clinical Disorder* (Orlando, FL: Academic Press, 1993).

8. American Board of Forensic Psychology, http://www.abfp.com/brochure.html (accessed November 22, 2007).

9. See the American Academy of Psychiatry and the Law, http://www.cc.emory.edu/AAPL (accessed December 20, 2007).

10. Cathy Spatz Widom and Hans Toch, "The Contribution of Psychology to Criminal Justice Education," *Journal of Criminal Justice Education*, Vol. 4, No. 2 (fall 1993), p. 253.

11. Curt R. Bartol, *Criminal Behavior: A Psychosocial Approach*, 3rd ed. (Upper Saddle River, NJ: Prentice Hall, 1991), p. 16.

12. For additional information, see S. Giora Shoham and Mark C. Seis, *A Primer in the Psychology of Crime* (New York: Harrow and Heston, 1993); and Frederic L. Faust, "A Review of *A Primer in the Psychology of Crime*," *Social Pathology*, Vol. 1, No. 1 (January 1995), pp. 48–61.

13. Laurence Steinberg, "The Juvenile Psychopath: Fads, Fictions, and Facts," *National Institute of Justice Perspectives on Crime and Justice: 2001 Lecture Series*, Vol. 5 (Washington, DC: NIJ, 2002), pp. 35–64.

14. Ibid.

15. Nicole Hahn Rafter, "Psychopathy and the Evolution of Criminological Knowledge," *Theoretical Criminology*, Vol. 1, No. 2 (May 1997), p. 236.

16. Nolan D. C. Lewis, "Foreword," in David Abrahamsen, *Crime and the Human Mind* (New York: Columbia University Press, 1944; reprint, Montclair, NJ: Patterson Smith, 1969), p. vii.

17. As noted by Rafter, "Psychopathy and the Evolution of Criminological Knowledge." See Richard von Krafft-Ebing, *Psychopathia Sexualis* (1886; reprint, New York: Stein and Day, 1965); and Richard von Krafft-Ebing, *Textbook of Insanity* (Germany, 1879; reprint, Philadelphia: F. A. Davis, 1904).

18. Bernard H. Glueck, *Studies in Forensic Psychiatry* (Boston: Little, Brown, 1916).

19. William Healy, *The Individual Delinquent* (Boston: Little, Brown, 1915).

20. Early writings about the psychopathic personality focused almost exclusively on men, and most psychiatrists appeared to believe that very few women (if any) possessed such traits.

21. Hervey M. Cleckley, *The Mask of Sanity*, 4th ed. (St. Louis, MO: C. V. Mosby, 1964).

22. Quoted in Joseph P. Newman and Chad A. Brinkley, "Psychopathy: Rediscovering Cleckley's Construct," *Psychopathology Research*, Vol. 9, No. 1 (March 1998).

23. Gwynn Nettler, *Killing One Another* (Cincinnati: Anderson, 1982).

24. Robert D. Hare, "Checklist for the Assessment of Psychopathy in Criminal Populations," in M. H. Ben-Aron, S. J. Hucker, and C. D. Webster, eds., *Clinical Criminology* (Toronto: University of Toronto, Clarke Institute of Psychiatry, 1985), pp. 157–167.

25. See Steinberg, "The Juvenile Psychopath," from which some of the wording in this paragraph is adapted.

26. Kent A. Kiehl et al., "Temporal Lobe Abnormalities in Semantic Processing by Criminal Psychopaths as Revealed by Functional Magnetic Resonance Imaging," *Psychiatry Research: Neuroimaging*, Vol. 130 (2004), pp. 27–42.

27. Ibid.

28. Julia C. Keller, "Aha! Study Finds Eureka Moments Light Up Brain," *Science and Theology News*, June 2004, http://www.stnews.org/feat_aha_0604.html (accessed December 12, 2006).

29. Bertine Lahuis, Chantal Kemmer, and Herman Van Engeland, "Magnetic Resonance Imaging Studies on Autism and Childhood-Onset Schizophrenia in Children and Adolescents," *Acta Neuropsychiatrica*, Vol. 15, No. 3 (June 2003), p. 140.

30. Ivan Semeniuk, "How We Tell Right from Wrong: An Interview with Marc Hauser," *New Scientist*, March 3, 2007, p. 44.

31. Michael Caldwell et al., "Treatment Response of Adolescent Offenders with Psychopathy Features: A 2-Year Follow-Up," *Criminal Justice and Behavior*, Vol. 33, No. 5 (2006), pp. 571–576.

32. Peter Aldhous, "Violent, Antisocial, Past Redemption?" *New Scientist*, April 14, 2007, pp. 8–9.

33. American Psychiatric Association, *Diagnostic and Statistical Manual of Mental Disorders,* 2nd ed. (Washington, DC: American Psychiatric Association, 1968).

34. Ibid., p. 43.

35. See Internet Mental Health, "Disorders: European Description," http://www.mentalhealth.com/icd (accessed January 5, 2007).

36. Robert D. Hare, "Psychopathy and Antisocial Personality Disorder: A Case of Diagnostic Confusion," *Psychiatric Times*, Vol. 13, No. 2 (February 1996).

37. Albert I. Rabin, "The Antisocial Personality—Psychopathy and Sociopathy," in Hans Toch, ed., *Psychology of Crime and Criminal Justice* (Prospect Heights, IL: Waveland, 1979), p. 330.

38. Especially applicable is Hare's Revised Psychopathy Checklist, also called the Psychopathy Checklist–Revised (PCL–R). The PCL–R provides a numerical score reflecting the degree to which a person's symptoms match the traditional clinical conception of psychopathy. This score can be statistically analyzed into two factors: one covering attitudes and feelings and the other covering socially deviant behavior.

39. For research in this area, see A. Tengstrom et al., "Psychopathy (PCL–R) as a Predictor of Violent Recidivism among Criminal Offenders with Schizophrenia in Sweden," *Law and Behavior*, Vol. 24, No. 1 (2000), pp. 45–58. For additional information, see V. L. Quinsey et al., *Violent Offenders: Appraising and Managing Risk* (Washington, DC: American Psychological Association, 1998); and V. L. Quinsey, M. E. Rice, and G. T. Harris, "Actuarial Prediction of Sexual Recidivism," *Journal of Interpersonal Violence*, Vol. 10, No. 1 (1995), pp. 85–105.

40. R. D. Hare, *Psychopathy: Theory and Research* (New York: John Wiley and Sons, 1970).

41. L. N. Robins, *Deviant Children Grow Up* (Baltimore: Williams and Wilkins, 1966).

42. S. B. Guze, *Criminality and Psychiatric Disorders* (New York: Oxford University Press, 1976).

43. S. Hodgins and G. Cote, "The Prevalence of Mental Disorders among Penitentiary Inmates in Quebec," *Canada's Mental Health*, Vol. 38 (1990), pp. 1–4. Note: Categories are not mutually exclusive.

44. H. Prins, *Offenders, Deviants or Patients? An Introduction to the Study of Socio-Forensic Problems* (London: Tavistock, 1980).

45. Abrahamsen, *Crime and the Human Mind*, p. vii.

46. P. Q. Roche, *The Criminal Mind: A Study of Communications between Criminal Law and Psychiatry* (New York: Grove Press, 1958), p. 52.

47. "Nationline: Book Thief," *USA Today*, August 1, 1991, p. 3A.

48. Marti Olsen Laney, *The Hidden Gifts of the Introverted Child* (New York: Workman Publishing, 2006).

49. Mark Solms, "Freud Returns," *Scientific American*, Vol. 290, No. 5 (May 2004), pp. 82–90.

50. Eric R. Kandel, "Biology and the Future of Psychoanalysis: A New Intellectual Framework for Psychiatry Revisited," *American Journal of Psychiatry*, Vol. 156 (April 1999), pp. 505–524.

51. Anne Sciater, "Torturer-Killer Wants to Die Today, as Scheduled," *USA Today*, April 15, 1997, p. 2A.

52. Nettler, *Killing One Another*, p. 159.

53. Ibid., p. 155.

54. Abrahamsen, *Crime and the Human Mind*, p. 99.

55. Ibid., p. 100.

56. J. Dollard et al., *Frustration and Aggression* (New Haven, CT: Yale University Press, 1939).

57. Carl Weiser, "This Is What You Get for Firing Me!" *USA Today*, January 28, 1993, p. 3A.

58. Andrew F. Henry and James F. Short, Jr., *Suicide and Homicide: Economic, Sociological, and Psychological Aspects of Aggression* (Glencoe, IL: Free Press, 1954).

59. Stewart Palmer, *A Study of Murder* (New York: Crowell, 1960).

60. Abrahamsen, *Crime and the Human Mind*, p. 26.

61. Nancy Gibbs, "The Devil's Disciple," *Time*, January 11, 1993, p. 40.

62. Seymour L. Halleck, *Psychiatry and the Dilemmas of Crime: A Study of Causes, Punishment and Treatment* (Berkeley: University of California Press, 1971).

63. Ibid., p. 77.

64. Ibid., p. 80.

65. Ibid.

66. Ibid.

67. Arnold S. Linsky, Ronet Bachman, and Murray A. Straus, *Stress, Culture, and Aggression* (New Haven, CT: Yale University Press, 1995).

68. Ibid., p. 7.

69. Adapted from Richard Danielson, "Programmed to Kill," *St. Petersburg Times*, March 22, 2000, http://www.sptimes.com/News/032200/Floridian/Programmed_to_kill.shtml (accessed December 5, 2005).

70. Ibid.

71. *Video Software Dealers Assoc.* v. *Schwarzenegger*, Ninth Circuit, Case No. 07-16620 (2009).

72. Gabriel Tarde, *The Laws of Imitation*, trans. E. C. Parsons (1890; reprint, Gloucester, MA: Peter Smith, 1962).

73. Albert Bandura, "The Social Learning Perspective: Mechanisms of Aggression," in Hans Toch, ed., *Psychology of Crime and Criminal Justice* (Prospect Heights, IL: Waveland, 1979), p. 198.

74. Ibid.

75. Ibid., p. 199.

76. M. M. Lefkowitz et al., "Television Violence and Child Aggression: A Follow-Up Study," in G. A. Comstock and E. A. Rubinstein, eds., *Television and Social Behavior*, Vol. 3 (Washington, DC: U.S. Government Printing Office, 1972), pp. 35–135.

77. C. A. Anderson et al., "Violent Video Game Effects on Aggression, Empathy, and Prosocial Behavior in Eastern and Western Countries," *Psychological Bulletin*, Vol. 136 (2010), pp. 151–173.

78. Widom and Toch, "The Contribution of Psychology to Criminal Justice Education."

79. Ibid., p. 253.

80. C. R. Hollin, *Psychology and Crime: An Introduction to Criminological Psychology* (London: Routledge, 1989), p. 42.

81. Widom and Toch, "The Contribution of Psychology to Criminal Justice Education," p. 254.

82. See Mary D. Salter Ainsworth, "John Bowlby, 1907–1990," *American Psychologist*, Vol. 47 (1992), p. 668.

83. John Bowlby, "The Nature of the Child's Tie to Its Mother," *International Journal of Psycho-Analysis*, Vol. 39 (1958), pp. 350–373.

84. See John Bowlby, *Maternal Care and Mental Health*, World Health Organization Monograph (1951); and John Bowlby, *A Secure Base* (New York: Basic Books, 1988).

85. Bowlby, *A Secure Base*, p. 11.

86. David P. Farrington and Donald J. West, "Effects of Marriage, Separation, and Children on Offending by Adult Males," *Current Perspectives on Aging and the Life Cycle*, Vol. 4 (1995), pp. 249–281.

87. Stephen A. Cernkovich and Peggy C. Giordano, "Family Relationships and Delinquency," *Criminology*, Vol. 25 (1987), pp. 295–313.

88. Roy F. Baumeister and Julie Juola Exline, "Self-Control, Morality, and Human Strength," *Journal of Social and Clinical Psychology*, Vol. 19, No. 1 (April 2000), pp. 29–42.

89. Ibid.

90. See R. F. Baumeister, T. F. Heatherton, and D. Tice, *Losing Control: How and Why People Fail at Self-Regulation* (San Diego, CA: Academic Press, 1994).

91. Teresa C. LaGrange and Robert A. Silverman, "Low Self-Control and Opportunity: Testing the General Theory of Crime as an Explanation for Gender Differences in Delinquency," *Criminology*, Vol. 37, No. 1 (1999), p. 41.

92. M. R. Gottfredson and Travis Hirschi, *A General Theory of Crime* (Stanford, CA: Stanford University Press, 1990).

93. Carter Hay and Walter Forrest, "The Development of Self-Control: Examining Self-Control Theory's Stability Thesis," *Criminology*, Vol. 44, No. 4 (November 2006), pp. 739–772.

94. Ibid.

95. Constance L. Chapple, "Self-Control, Peer Relations, and Delinquency," *Justice Quarterly*, Vol. 22, No. 1 (March 2005), pp. 89–106.

96. Ibid., p. 101.

97. Douglas Longshore, "Self-Control and Criminal Opportunity: A Prospective Test of the General Theory of Crime," *Social Problems*, Vol. 45, No. 1 (February 1998), pp. 102–114.

98. Gottfredson and Hirschi, *A General Theory of Crime*, p. 88.

99. Longshore, "Self-Control and Criminal Opportunity."

100. Harold G. Grasmick et al., "Testing the Core Empirical Implications of Gottfredson and Hirschi's General Theory of Crime," *Journal of Research in Crime and Delinquency*, Vol. 30 (1993), pp. 5–29.

101. Citing Gottfredson and Hirschi, *A General Theory of Crime*, p. 89.

102. Travis C. Pratt and Francis T. Cullen, "The Empirical Status of Gottfredson and Hirschi's General Theory of Crime: A Meta-Analysis," *Criminology*, Vol. 38, No. 3 (2000), pp. 931–964.

103. Carter Hay, "Parenting, Self-Control, and Delinquency: A Test of Self-Control Theory," *Criminology*, Vol. 39, No. 3 (2001), pp. 707–736.

104. Ibid., p. 725.

105. Karen L. Hayslett-McCall and Thomas J. Bernard, "Attachment, Masculinity, and Self-Control: A Theory of Male Crime Rates," *Theoretical Criminology*, Vol. 6, No. 1 (February 2002), pp. 5–33.

106. In civil proceedings, however, the state may confine a mentally ill person if it shows "by clear and convincing evidence that the individual is mentally ill and dangerous." *Jones* v. *United States*, 463 U.S. 354 (1983).

107. *Foucha* v. *Louisiana*, 504 U.S. 71 (1992), Justices Kennedy and Rehnquist's dissenting opinion.

108. *Leland* v. *Oregon*, 343 U.S. 790 (1952).

109. *Riggins* v. *Nevada*, 504 U.S. 127 (1992).

110. *Sell* v. *United States*, 123 S.Ct. 2174 (2003).

111. U.S. Code, Title 18, Section 17.

112. See, for example, *United States* v. *Pohlot*, 827 F.2d 889, 897 (3d Cir. 1987), *cert. denied*, 484 U.S. 1011 (1988).

113. U.S. Code, Title 18, Section 401.

114. U.S. Code, Title 18, Sections 17 and 4242(b).

115. *Terrance Frank* v. *United States*, 113 S.Ct. 363 (1992).

116. P.L. 98–473, Title II, Section 403(a), 98 Stat. 2057.

117. Halleck, *Psychiatry and the Dilemmas of Crime*, p. 213.

118. *Durham* v. *United States*, 214 F.2d 862 (D.C. Cir. 1954).

119. American Law Institute, *Model Penal Code: Official Draft and Explanatory Notes* (Philadelphia: American Law Institute, 1985).

120. *United States* v. *Brawner*, 471 F.2d 969 (D.C. Cir. 1972).

121. Quotes in this paragraph are based on the following: June 25, 1948, Ch. 645, 62 Stat. 855; October 12, 1984, P.L. 98–473, Title II, Section 403(a), 98 Stat. 2059; November 18, 1988, P.L. 100–690, Title VII, Section 7043, 102 Stat. 4400.

122. See, for example, D. P. Farrington, "Childhood Aggression and Adult Violence: Early Precursors and Later Life Outcomes," in D. J. Pepler and K. H. Rubin, eds., *The Development and Treatment of Childhood Aggression* (Hillsdale, NJ: Erlbaum, 1990), pp. 2–29; and R. E. Tremblay et al., "Early Disruptive Behavior: Poor School Achievement, Delinquent Behavior and Delinquent Personality: Longitudinal Analyses," *Journal of Consulting and Clinical Psychology*, Vol. 60, No. 1 (1992), pp. 64–72.

123. R. Loeber, "Questions and Advances in the Study of Developmental Pathways," in D. Cicchetti and S. Toth, eds., *Models and Integration: Rochester Symposium on Developmental Psychopathology* (Rochester, NY: University of Rochester Press, 1991), pp. 97–115.

124. "State Probing Release of Molester Now Charged with Murder," United Press International wire service, Southwestern edition, September 24, 1993.

125. "Texas Executes Convicted Killer Who Waived Appeals," Reuters, Western edition, November 10, 1993.

126. Christine Spolar, "California Town Cries as Polly Klaas Is Found; Twice-Convicted Suspect Faces Murder, Kidnapping Charges in Abduction of 12-Year-Old," *Washington Post* wire service, December 6, 1993.

127. Jennifer L. White et al., "How Early Can We Tell? Predictors of Childhood Conduct Disorder and Adolescent Delinquency," *Criminology*, Vol. 28, No. 4 (1990), pp. 507–528.

128. Daniel S. Nagin and David P. Farrington, "The Stability of Criminal Potential from Childhood to Adulthood," *Criminology*, Vol. 30, No. 2 (1992), pp. 235–260.

129. Paul Gendreau, Tracy Little, and Claire Goggin, "A Meta-Analysis of the Predictors of Adult Offender Recidivism: What Works!" *Criminology*, Vol. 34, No. 4 (November 1996), pp. 575–607.

130. For one of the first and still definitive works in the area of selective incapacitation, see Peter Greenwood and Allan Abrahamsen, *Selective Incapacitation* (Santa Monica, CA: RAND, 1982).

131. M. A. Peterson, H. B. Braiker, and S. M. Polich, *Who Commits Crimes?* (Cambridge, MA: Oelgeschlager, Gunn and Hain, 1981).

132. Jeremy Travis, "But They All Come Back," papers from the Executive Session on Sentencing and Corrections, No. 7 (Washington, DC: National Institute of Justice, 2000).

133. J. Monahan, *Predicting Violent Behavior: An Assessment of Clinical Techniques* (Beverly Hills, CA: Sage, 1981).

134. The 1984 Amendment to Section 200 of Title II (Sections 200–2304) of P.L. 98–473 is popularly referred to as the "1984 Comprehensive Crime Control Act."

135. U.S. Sentencing Commission, *Federal Sentencing Guidelines Manual* (Washington, DC: U.S. Government Printing Office, 1987), p. 10.

136. Jill Peay, "Dangerousness—Ascription or Description," in M. P. Feldman, ed., *Violence*, Vol. 2 of *Developments in the Study of Criminal Behavior* (New York: John Wiley and Sons, 1982), p. 211, citing N. Walker, "Dangerous People," *International Journal of Law and Psychiatry*, Vol. 1 (1978), pp. 37–50.

137. See, for example, Gottfredson and Hirschi, *A General Theory of Crime*; and Travis Hirschi and Michael Gottfredson, "Age and the Explanation of Crime," *American Journal of Sociology*, Vol. 89 (1983), pp. 552–584.

138. David F. Greenberg, "Modeling Criminal Careers," *Criminology*, Vol. 29, No. 1 (1991), p. 39.

139. Andrews and Bonta, *The Psychology of Criminal Conduct*.

140. Ibid., p. 1.

141. Ibid.

142. Ibid., pp. 20–21.

143. Ibid., p. 227.

144. Ibid.

145. Ibid., p. 236.

146. Interview by Amy Goldman, February 27, 1998, http://www.serialkillers.net/interviews/jdouglas2bak.html (accessed December 20, 2000).

147. Robert R. Hazelwood and John E. Douglas, "The Lust Murderer," *FBI Law Enforcement Bulletin*, April 1980.

148. Ibid.

149. Ibid.

CHAPTER 6: SOCIAL STRUCTURE THEORIES

1. C. Belfield and H. Levin, *High School Dropouts and the Economic Losses from Juvenile Crime in California* (Santa Barbara: California Dropout Research Project, 2009), http://cdrp.ucsb.edu/dropouts/download.php?file=researchreport16.pdf (accessed April 25, 2010).

2. Ibid., p. 2.

3. Ibid.

4. Annie E. Casey Foundation, "High School Dropouts Cost California More Than $1 Billion," *Juvenile Justice News*, December, 2009, http://www.aecf.org/MajorInitiatives/JuvenileDetentionAlternativesInitiative/Resources/Dec09newsletter/JJNews3.aspx (accessed August 12, 2010).

5. Charles R. Tittle, "Theoretical Developments in Criminology," *Criminal Justice 2000* (Washington, DC: National Institute of Justice, 2000), p. 70.

6. See Anthony Walsh, *Biosocial Criminology: Introduction and Integration* (Cincinnati: Anderson, 2002).

7. Emile Durkheim, *The Division of Labor in Society*, trans. George Simpson (1893; reprint, New York: Free Press, 1947).

8. Ferdinand Toennies, *Community and Society*, trans. Charles P. Loomis (1887; reprint, East Lansing: Michigan State University Press, 1957).

9. Georg Simmel, "The Metropolis and Mental Life," in Donald N. Levine, ed., *On Individuality and Social Forms* (Chicago: University of Chicago Press, 1903).

10. Durkheim, *The Division of Labor in Society*, p. 80.

11. W. I. Thomas and Florian Znaniecki, *The Polish Peasant in Europe and America* (Boston: Gorham, 1920).

12. Robert Park and Ernest Burgess, *The City* (Chicago: University of Chicago Press, 1925).

13. "Human Ecology," *Encyclopaedia Britannica* online, http://britannica.com (accessed March 7, 2007).

14. Peter Haggett, "Human Ecology," in Alan Bullock and Oliver Stallybrass, eds., *The Fontana Dictionary of Modern Social Thought* (London: Fontana, 1977), p. 187.

15. For an excellent contemporary review of measuring the extent of social disorganization, see Barbara D. Warner and Glenn L. Pierce, "Reexamining Social Disorganization Theory Using Calls to the Police as a Measure of Crime," *Criminology*, Vol. 31, No. 4 (November 1993), pp. 493–513.

16. Edwin M. Lemert, *Social Pathology* (New York: McGraw-Hill, 1951), p. 3.

17. Ibid., p. 7.

18. Clifford R. Shaw et al., *Delinquency Areas* (Chicago: University of Chicago Press, 1929).

19. David Matza, *Becoming Deviant* (Upper Saddle River, NJ: Prentice Hall, 1969).

20. Lawrence W. Sherman, Patrick R. Gartin, and Michael E. Buerger, "Hot Spots of Predatory Crime: Routine Activities and the Criminology of Place," *Criminology*, Vol. 27, No. 1 (1989), pp. 27–55.

21. Rodney Stark, "Deviant Places: A Theory of the Ecology of Crime," *Criminology*, Vol. 25, No. 4 (1987), p. 893.

22. Ibid.

23. James Q. Wilson and George Kelling, "Broken Windows," *Atlantic Monthly*, March 1982, pp. 1–11.

24. David Thacher, "Order Maintenance Reconsidered: Moving beyond Strong Causal Reasoning," *Journal of Criminal Law and Criminology*, Vol. 94, No. 2 (2004), pp. 381–414.

25. James Q. Wilson and George L. Kelling, "Broken Windows: The Police and Neighborhood Safety," *Atlantic Monthly*, March 1982, http://www.theatlantic.com/politics/crime/windows.htm (accessed January 10, 2005).

26. Oscar Newman, *Architectural Design for Crime Prevention* (Washington, DC: U.S. Department of Justice, 1973). See also Oscar Newman, *Creating Defensible Space* (Washington, DC: Office of Housing and Urban Development, 1996).

27. Oscar Newman, *Defensible Space: Crime Prevention through Urban Design* (New York: Macmillan, 1972), p. 3. See also Ralph B. Taylor and Adele V. Harrell, *Physical Environment and Crime* (Washington, DC: National Institute of Justice, May 1996).

28. Sherman, Gartin, and Buerger, "Hot Spots of Predatory Crime," p. 31.

29. Ibid., p. 49.

30. Bernard E. Harcourt, *Illusion of Order: The False Promise of Broken Windows Policing* (Cambridge: Harvard University Press, 2001).

31. Robert J. Sampson and Stephen W. Radenbush, "Systematic Social Observation of Public Spaces: A New Look at Disorder in Urban Neighborhoods," *American Journal of Sociology*, Vol. 105 (1999), p. 603.

32. Thacher, "Order Maintenance Reconsidered," p. 386.

33. Thomas M. Arvanites and Robert H. Defina, "Business Cycles and Street Crime," *Criminology*, Vol. 44, No. 1 (2006), pp. 141.

34. Emile Durkheim, *Suicide: A Study in Sociology* (New York: Free Press, 1897).

35. Robert K. Merton, "Social Structure and Anomie," *American Sociological Review*, Vol. 3, No. 5 (October 1938), pp. 672–682; and Robert K. Merton, *Social Theory and Social Structure*, rev. ed. (New York: Free Press, 1957).

36. Merton, "Social Structure and Anomie," p. 681.

37. Thomas M. Arvanites and Robert H. Defina, "Business Cycles and Street Crime," *Criminology*, Vol. 44, No. 1 (2006), pp. 139–164.

38. Steven F. Messner and Richard Rosenfeld, *Crime and the American Dream* (Belmont, CA: Wadsworth, 1994), p. 68.

39. J. Blau and P. Blau, "The Cost of Inequality: Metropolitan Structure and Violent Crime," *American Sociological Review*, Vol. 147 (1982), pp. 114–129.

40. Masahiro Tsushima, "Economic Structure and Crime: The Case of Japan," *Journal of Socio-Economics*, Vol. 25, No. 4 (winter 1996), p. 497.

41. Thomas F. Pettigrew, "Applying Social Psychology to International Social Issues," *Journal of Social Issues* (winter 1998), pp. 663–676.

42. Robert Agnew, "Foundation for a General Strain Theory of Crime and Delinquency," *Criminology*, Vol. 30, No. 1 (February 1992), pp. 47–87.

43. Adapted from Robert Agnew, *Pressured into Crime: An Overview of General Strain Theory* (Los Angeles: Roxbury, 2006), pp. 193–196.

44. Ibid., p. 60.

45. Agnew, "Foundation for a General Strain Theory of Crime and Delinquency."

46. Ibid., p. 48.

47. Raymond Paternoster and Paul Mazerolle, "General Strain Theory and Delinquency: A Replication and Extension," *Journal of Research in Crime and Delinquency*, Vol. 31, No. 3 (1994), pp. 235–263.

48. Robert Agnew and Helene Raskin White, "An Empirical Test of General Strain Theory," *Criminology*, Vol. 30, No. 4 (1992), pp. 475–499.

49. Lisa M. Broidy, "A Test of General Strain Theory," *Criminology*, Vol. 39, No. 1 (2002), pp. 9–35.

50. Ibid., p. 29.

51. Ibid.

52. Robert Agnew et al., "Strain, Personality Traits, and Delinquency: Extending General Strain Theory," *Criminology*, Vol. 40, No. 1 (2002), pp. 43–71.

53. Ibid., p. 47.

54. Thorsten Sellin, *Culture Conflict and Crime* (New York: Social Science Research Council, 1938).

55. Sellin, *Culture Conflict and Crime*, p. 68.

56. Frederic M. Thrasher, *The Gang* (Chicago: University of Chicago Press, 1927).

57. William F. Whyte, *Street Corner Society: The Social Structure of an Italian Slum* (Chicago: University of Chicago Press, 1943).

58. The quotations attributed to Miller in these paragraphs are from Walter Miller, "Lower Class Culture as a Generating Milieu of Gang Delinquency," *Journal of Social Issues*, Vol. 14, No. 3 (1958), pp. 5–19.

59. Gresham Sykes and David Matza, "Techniques of Neutralization: A Theory of Delinquency," *American Sociological Review*, Vol. 22 (December 1957), pp. 664–670.

60. See Volkan Topalli, "When Being Good Is Bad: An Expansion of Neutralization Theory," *Criminology*, Vol. 43 (2005), p. 797.

61. As cited in Volkan Topalli, "When Being Good Is Bad," p. 797.

62. David Matza, *Delinquency and Drift* (Piscataway, New Jersey: Transaction, 1990), p. 28.

63. Robert Agnew, "The Techniques of Neutralization and Violence," *Criminology*, Vol. 32, No. 4 (1994), p. 555.

64. Ibid.

65. Topalli, "When Being Good Is Bad."

66. Ken Levi, "Becoming a Hit Man: Neutralization in a Very Deviant Career," *Urban Life*, Vol. 10 (1981), pp. 47–63.

67. Lois Presser, "Remorse and Neutralization among Violent Male Offenders," *Justice Quarterly*, Vol. 20, No. 4 (2003), pp. 801–825.

68. Orly Turgeman-Goldschmidt, "The Rhetoric of Hackers' Neutralizations," in Frank Schmalleger and Michale Pittaro, eds., *Crimes of the Internet* (Upper Saddle River, NJ: Prentice Hall, 2008).

69. See, for example, Dorothy E. Denning, "Activism, Hacktivism, and Cyberterrorism: The Internet as a Tool for Influencing Foreign Policy," *Computer Security Journal*, Vol. 16 (2000), pp. 15–35; and Tim Jordan and Paul Taylor, *Hacktivism and Cyberwars: Rebels with a Cause?* (New York: Routledge, 2004).

70. Franco Ferracuti and Marvin Wolfgang, *The Subculture of Violence: Toward an Integrated Theory of Criminology* (London: Tavistock, 1967).

71. Ferracuti and Wolfgang, *The Subculture of Violence*.

72. Ibid., p. 151.

73. Ibid, pp. 159–160.

74. For an excellent review of the literature, see F. Frederick Hawley, "The Southern Violence Construct: A Skeleton in the Criminological Closet," paper presented at the annual meeting of the American Society of Criminology, 1988.

75. Bertram Wyatt-Brown, *Southern Honor: Ethics and Behavior in the Old South* (Oxford: Oxford University Press, 1983).

76. James W. Clarke, *The Lineaments of Wrath: Race, Violent Crime, and American Culture* (New Brunswick, NJ: Transaction, 1998), p. 4.

77. Ibid.

78. Franklin Zimring et al., "Punishing Homicide in Philadelphia: Perspectives on the Death Penalty," *University of Chicago Law Review*, Vol. 43 (1976), pp. 227–252.

79. Richard A. Cloward and Lloyd E. Ohlin, *Delinquency and Opportunity: A Theory of Delinquent Gangs* (Glencoe, IL: Free Press, 1960).

80. Ibid., p. 7.

81. Ibid., p. 13.

82. Ibid., p. 16.

83. Ibid., p. 19.

84. Ibid., p. 3.

85. Ibid., p. 37.

86. Ibid., pp. 12–13.

87. Albert Cohen, *Delinquent Boys: The Culture of the Gang* (New York: Free Press, 1955), p. 13.

88. Ibid.

89. Donald J. Shoemaker, *Theories of Delinquency: An Examination of Explanations of Delinquent Behavior* (New York: Oxford University Press, 1984), p. 102, citing Cohen.

90. Cohen, *Delinquent Boys*, p. 76.

91. Ibid., p. 121.

92. Shoemaker, *Theories of Delinquency*, p. 105.

93. Elijah Anderson, *The Code of the Street: Decency, Violence, and the Moral Life of the Inner City* (New York: W. W. Norton, 1990).

94. Arlen Egley, Jr., James C. Howell, and John P. Moore, *Highlights of the 2008 National Youth Gang Survey* (Washington, DC: OJJDP, March 2010), from which some of the wording in this section is adapted.

95. National Gang Crime Research Center, *Achieving Justice and Reversing the Problem of Gang Crime and Gang Violence in America Today: Preliminary Results of the Project Gangfact Study* (Chicago: National Gang Crime Research Center, 1996).

96. Carl Rogers, "Children in Gangs," in *Criminal Justice, 1993–94* (Guilford, CT: Dushkin, 1993), pp. 197–199.

97. "Youths Match Power, Fear, Guns," *Fayetteville (NC) Observer-Times*, September 6, 1993, p. 2A.

98. The quotations attributed to Curry and Spergel in this section are from G. David Curry and Irving A. Spergel, "Gang Homicide, Delinquency, and Community," *Criminology*, Vol. 26, No. 3 (1988), pp. 381–405.

99. Ibid., p. 401.

100. Finn-Aage Esbensen, "A National Gang Strategy," in J. Mitchell Miller and Jeffrey P. Rush, eds., *Gangs: A Criminal Justice Approach* (Cincinnati: Anderson, 1996).

101. Cited in Mary H. Glazier, review of J. Mitchell Miller and Jeffrey P. Rush, eds., *Gangs: A Criminal Justice Approach*, in *Criminologist* (July/August 1996), p. 29.

102. Joan McCord and Kevin P. Conway, *Co-Offending and Patterns of Juvenile Crime* (Washington, DC: National Institute of Justice), p.1.

103. Steven Schlossman et al., *Delinquency Prevention in South Chicago: A Fifty-Year Assessment of the Chicago Area Project* (Santa Monica, CA: RAND, 1984).

104. J. Robert Lilly, Francis T. Cullen, and Richard A. Ball, *Criminological Theory: Context and Consequences* (Newbury Park, CA: Sage, 1989), p. 80.

105. Lamar T. Empey, *American Delinquency: Its Meaning and Construction* (Homewood, IL: Dorsey, 1982), p. 243.

106. See James DeFronzo, "Welfare and Burglary," *Crime and Delinquency*, Vol. 42 (1996), pp. 223–230.

107. Since overall rates of crime rose throughout much of the 1970s and 1980s, the effectiveness of such programs remains very much in doubt.

108. Public Law 104–193 (August 22, 1996).

109. Section 103 of the Welfare Reform Act of 1996.

110. See, for example, George L. Kelling, "Crime Control, the Police, and Culture Wars: Broken Windows and Cultural Pluralism," in National Institute of Justice, *Perspectives on Crime and Justice: 1997–1998 Lecture Series* (Washington, DC: National Institute of Justice, 1998).

111. Robert J. Bursik, "Social Disorganization and Theories of Crime and Delinquency: Problems and Prospects," *Criminology*, Vol. 26, No. 4 (1988), p. 519.

112. Stephen J. Pfohl, *Images of Deviance and Social Control* (New York: McGraw-Hill, 1985), p. 167.

113. Travis Hirschi, in review of Delbert S. Elliott, David Huizinga, and Suzanne S. Ageton, *Explaining Delinquency and Drug Use*, in *Criminology*, Vol. 25, No. 1 (February 1987), p. 195.

114. John Hagan, "Defiance and Despair: Subcultural and Structural Linkages between Delinquency and Despair in Life Course," *Social Forces*, Vol. 76, No. 1 (September 1997), p. 119.

115. Ibid.

116. Gwynn Nettler, *Killing One Another* (Cincinnati: Anderson, 1982), p. 67.

117. Margaret Anderson, "Review Essay: Rape Theories, Myths, and Social Change," *Contemporary Crises*, Vol. 5 (1983), p. 237.

118. Bradley R. Entner Wright et al., "Reconsidering the Relationship between SES and Delinquency: Causation but Not Correlation," *Criminology*, Vol. 37, No. 1 (February 1999), pp. 175–194.

119. R. Larzelre and G. R. Patterson, "Parental Management: Mediator of the Effect of Socioeconomic Status on Early Delinquency," *Criminology*, Vol. 28 (1990), pp. 301–323.

120. Nettler, *Killing One Another*, p. 54.

121. James Q. Wilson, *The Moral Sense* (New York: Free Press, 1993).

CHAPTER 7: THEORIES OF SOCIAL PROCESS AND SOCIAL DEVELOPMENT

1. Details for this story come from Kirk Johnson, "Columbine Evidence Is Placed on Chilling Public Display," *New York Times*, February 27, 2004, http://www.carleton.ca/law/outlines/f03/3307bv-f03-ColumbineEvidence-mcnaught.html (accessed January 5, 2007); and Robert Weller, "Authorities Had Many Contacts with Killers before Columbine Massacre," *Denver Post*, February 27, 2004, http://www.denverpost.com/Stories/0,1413,36~53~1981294,00.html (accessed January 5, 2007).

2. "Columbine Evidence Shown," *Richmond Times-Dispatch*, February 27, 2004, http://www.timesdispatch.com/servlet/Satellite?pagename=RTD/MGArticle/RTD_BasicArticle&c=MGArticle&cid=1031773924178 (accessed January 5, 2007).

3. "Columbine Report Stirs Anger," CBS News, February 26, 2004, http://www.cbsnews.com/stories/2003/10/22/national/main579500.shtml (accessed January 5, 2007).

4. Fight Crime, Invest in Kids, *Bullying Prevention Is Crime Prevention* (Washington, DC: Fight Crime, 2003).

5. "Columbine: Were There Warnings?" CBS News, February 26, 2004, http://www.cbsnews.com/stories/2004/02/26/national/main602460.shtml (accessed January 5, 2007).

6. Edwin Sutherland, *Principles of Criminology*, 3rd ed. (New York: Lippincott, 1939).

7. Edwin Sutherland, *Principles of Criminology*, 4th ed. (New York: Lippincott, 1947), pp. 6–7.

8. Robert Burgess and Ronald L. Akers, "A Differential Association–Reinforcement Theory of Criminal Behavior," *Social Problems*, Vol. 14 (1966), pp. 363–383.

9. Ibid., p. 364.

10. Ronald L. Akers, *Deviant Behavior: A Social Learning Approach* (Belmont, CA: Wadsworth, 1973).

11. Ibid.

12. Ronald L. Akers, *Social Learning and Social Structure: A General Theory of Crime and Deviance* (Boston: Northeastern University Press, 1998).

13. Ronald L. Akers, *Deviant Behavior: A Social Learning Approach*, 3rd ed. (Belmont, CA: Wadsworth, 1985), pp. 40–41.

14. Gang Lee, Ronald L. Akers, and Marian J. Borg, "Social Learning and Structural Factors in Adolescent Substance Use," *Western Criminology Review*, Vol. 5, No. 1 (2004), p. 17.

15. Daniel Glaser, "Differential Association and Criminological Prediction," *Social Problems*, Vol. 8 (1960), pp. 6–14.

16. Daniel Glaser, "Differential Identification," in Henry N. Pontel, ed., *Social Deviance: Readings in Theory and Research*, 3rd ed. (Upper Saddle River, NJ: Prentice Hall 1999), p. 146.

17. Charles R. Tittle, "Theoretical Developments in Criminology," in National Institute of Justice, ed.," *The Nature of Crime: Continuity and Change*, Vol. 1 of *Criminal Justice 2000* (Washington, DC: National Institute of Justice, 2000), p. 65.

18. For a good overview of social control approaches, see George S. Bridges and Martha Myers, eds., *Inequality, Crime, and Social Control* (Boulder, CO: Westview Press, 1994).

19. Walter C. Reckless, *The Crime Problem*, 4th ed. (New York: Appleton-Century-Crofts, 1967).

20. Ibid., p. 470.

21. Ibid.

22. Ibid., p. 475.

23. Ibid.

24. Howard B. Kaplan, "Self-Derogation and Violence," paper presented at the first meeting of the International Society for Research on Aggression, Toronto, 1974. See also Howard B. Kaplan and A. D. Pokorny, "Self-Derogation as an Antecedent of Suicidal Responses," paper presented at the Eighth International Congress on Suicide Prevention and Crisis Intervention, Jerusalem, October 19–22, 1975.

25. Howard B. Kaplan, *Deviant Behavior in Defense of Self* (New York: Academic Press, 1980).

26. M. Rosenberg, C. Schooler, and C. Schoenbach, "Self-Esteem and Adolescent Problems: Modeling Reciprocal Effects," *American Sociological Review*, Vol. 54 (1989), pp. 1004–1018.

27. L. E. Wells, "Self-Enhancement through Delinquency: A Conditional Test of Self-Derogation Theory," *Journal of Research in Crime and Delinquency*, Vol. 26, No. 3 (1989), pp. 226–252.

28. K. Leung and F. Drasgow, "Relation between Self-Esteem and Delinquent Behavior in Three Ethnic Groups: An Application of Item Response Theory," *Journal of Cross-Cultural Psychology*, Vol. 17, No. 2 (1986), pp. 151–167.

29. G. Calhoun, Jr., S. Connley, and J. A. Bolton, "Comparison of Delinquents and Non-Delinquents in Ethnicity, Ordinal Position and Self-Perception," *Journal of Clinical Psychology*, Vol. 40, No. 1 (1984), pp. 323–328.

30. D. Oyserman and H. R. Markus, "Possible Selves in Balance: Implications for Delinquency," *Journal of Social Issues*, Vol. 46, No. 2 (1990), pp. 141–157.

31. Daphna Oyserman and Hazel Markus, "The Sociocultural Self," in J. Suls, ed., *Psychological Perspectives on the Self*, Vol. 4 (Hillsdale, NJ: Erlbaum, 1993), pp. 187–220.

32. Travis Hirschi, *Causes of Delinquency* (Berkeley: University of California Press, 1969).

33. Tittle, "Theoretical Developments in Criminology," p. 65.

34. Hirschi, *Causes of Delinquency*.

35. Ibid.

36. Ibid.

37. Ibid.

38. Ibid.

39. Ibid.

40. Ibid.

41. Michael Gottfredson and Travis Hirschi, *A General Theory of Crime* (Stanford, CA: Stanford University Press, 1990).

42. See also Michael R. Gottfredson and Travis Hirschi, "Criminality and Low Self-Control," in John E. Conklin, ed., *New Perspectives in Criminology* (Boston: Allyn & Bacon, 1996).

43. Werner Einstadter and Stuart Henry, *Criminological Theory: An Analysis of Its Underlying Assumptions* (Fort Worth, TX: Harcourt Brace, 1995), p. 189.

44. Charles R. Tittle, *Control Balance: Toward a General Theory of Deviance* (Boulder, CO: Westview Press, 1995).

45. For an excellent summation of control–balance theory, see Alex R. Piquero and Matthew Hickman, "An Empirical Test of Tittle's Control Balance Theory," *Criminology*, Vol. 37, No. 2 (1999), pp. 319–341.

46. Tittle, *Control Balance*, p. 181.

47. Piquero and Hickman, "An Empirical Test of Tittle's Control Balance Theory," p. 327.

48. Tittle, *Control Balance*, p. 95. For a good critique of control–balance theory, see Joachim J. Savelsberg, "Human Nature and Social Control in Complex Society: A Critique of Charles Tittle's Control Balance," *Theoretical Criminology*, Vol. 3, No. 3 (August 1999), pp. 331–338.

49. "Killer's Admission to Law School Criticized," *Fayetteville (NC) Observer-Times*, September 12, 1993, p. 14A.

50. See the biography of James Hamm at the Middle Ground Prison Reform, Inc., Web site, http://www.middlegroundprisonreform.org/hamm (accessed January 10, 2007).

51. Frank Tannenbaum, *Crime and the Community* (New York: Atheneum Press, 1938), pp. 17–18.

52. Ibid., p. 19.

53. Edwin M. Lemert, *Social Pathology: A Systematic Approach to the Theory of Sociopathic Behavior* (New York: McGraw-Hill, 1951), p. 76.

54. Ibid.

55. Howard Becker, *Outsiders: Studies in the Sociology of Deviance* (New York: Free Press, 1963).

56. Ibid., p. 1.

57. Ibid., p. 9.

58. Ibid., p. 147.

59. Ibid., pp. 37–38.

60. Jon Gunnar Bernburg and Marvin D. Krohn, "Labeling, Life Chances, and Adult Crime: The Direct and Indirect Effects of Official Intervention in Adolescence on Crime in Early Adulthood," *Criminology*, Vol. 41, No. 4 (2003), pp. 1287–1318.

61. Robert J. Sampson and John H. Laub, "A Life-Course Theory of Cumulative Disadvantage and the Stability of Delinquency," in Terence P. Thornberry, ed., *Developmental Theories of Crime and Delinquency* (New Brunswick, NJ: Transaction, 1997).

62. Jon Gunnar Bernburg and Marvin D. Krohn, "Labeling, Life Chances, and Adult Crime."

63. Legal Action Center, *After Prison: Roadblocks to Reentry* (2008), http://lac.org/roadblocks-to-reentry.

64. Mike S. Adams, "Labeling and Differential Association: Towards a General Social Learning Theory of Crime and Deviance," *American Journal of Criminal Justice*, Vol. 20, No. 2 (1996), pp. 147–164.

65. Ibid., p. 160.

66. John Braithwaite and Heather Strang, *The Right Kind of Shame for Crime Prevention*, RISE Working Papers, Number 1 (Australian National University, 1997), http://www.aic.gov.au/rjustice/rise/working/risepap1.html (accessed March 11, 2005).

67. A number of papers have been released in the Reintegrative Shaming Experiments (RISE) series. They include Braithwaite and Strang, *The Right Kind of Shame for Crime Prevention*; Heather Strang and Lawrence W. Sherman, *The Victim's Perspective* (Canberra: Australian National University, 1997); Lawrence W. Sherman and Geoffrey C. Barnes, *Restorative Justice and Offenders' Respect for the Law* (Canberra: Australian National University, 1997); and Lawrence W. Sherman and Heather Strang, *Restorative Justice and Deterring Crime* (Canberra: Australian National University, 1997).

68. John Braithwaite and Heather Strang, *Restorative Justice and Offenders' Respect for the Law*, RISE Working Papers, Number 3 (Australian National University, 1997), http://www.aic.gov.au/rjustice/rise/working/risepap3.html (accessed March 11, 2005).

69. Ibid.

70. Erving Goffman, *The Presentation of Self in Everyday Life* (Garden City, NY: Doubleday, 1959).

71. Goffman, *The Presentation of Self in Everyday Life*, pp. 9–10.

72. Erving Goffman, *Stigma: Notes on the Management of Spoiled Identity* (Upper Saddle River, NJ: Prentice Hall, 1963).

73. Ibid., p. 5.

74. Ibid., p. 138.

75. Erving Goffman, *Asylums: Essays on the Social Situation of Mental Patients and Other Inmates* (Garden City, NY: Anchor, 1961).

76. P.L. 93–415; 42 U.S. Code Section 5667e.

77. See, for example, Information Technology International's initial report data at http://www.itiincorporated.com/showpage.asp?sect=proj&pid=6 (accessed June 8, 2007).

78. See Kevin Haggerty et al., *Preparing for the Drug Free Years* (Washington, DC: Office of Juvenile Justice and Delinquency Prevention, 1999), http://www.ncjrs.org/html/jjbulletin/9907/theo.html (accessed March 11, 2005).

79. Haggerty et al., *Preparing for the Drug Free Years.*

80. Material in this paragraph is adapted from Finn-Aage Esbensen, "Preventing Adolescent Gang Involvement," *OJJDP Juvenile Justice Bulletin* (Washington, DC: Office of Juvenile Justice and Delinquency Prevention, September 2000).

81. See R. E. Tremblay et al., "From Childhood Physical Aggression to Adolescent Maladjustment: The Montreal Prevention Experiment," in R. D. Peters and R. J. McMahon, *Preventing Childhood Disorders, Substance Abuse, and Delinquency* (Thousand Oaks, CA: Sage, 1996), pp. 268–298.

82. Randy Martin, Robert J. Mutchnick, and W. Timothy Austin, *Criminological Thought: Pioneers Past and Present* (New York: Macmillan, 1990), p. 368.

83. Laurie Taylor, "Erving Goffman," *New Society,* (December 1968), p. 836.

84. George Psathas, "Ethnomethods and Phenomenology," in Donald McQuarie, ed., *Readings in Contemporary Sociological Theory: From Modernity to Post-Modernity* (Toronto: Prentice Hall Canada, 1999).

85. For some influential writings of the period, see K. F. Riegel, "Toward a Dialectical Theory of Development," *Human Development*, Vol. 18 (1975), pp. 50–64; and U. Bronfenbrenner, *The Ecology of Human Development* (Cambridge: Harvard University Press, 1979).

86. R. M. Lerner, "Early Adolescence: Towards an Agenda for the Integration of Research, Policy and Intervention," in R. M. Lerner, ed., *Early Adolescence: Perspectives on Research, Policy, and Intervention* (Hillsdale, NJ: Erlbaum, 1993), pp. 1–13.

87. See T. P. Thornberry, *Developmental Theories of Crime and Delinquency* (Piscataway, NJ: Transaction, 1997).

88. Elaine Eggleston Doherty, "Self-Control, Social Bonds, and Desistance," *Criminology*, Vol. 44, No. 4 (November 2006), pp. 807–808.

89. A. Blumstein et al., eds., *Criminal Careers and Career Criminals* (Washington, DC: National Academy Press, 1986).

90. See Alfred Blumstein et al., "Introduction: Studying Criminal Careers," in Blumstein et al., eds., *Criminal Careers and Career Criminals*, p. 12.

91. Blumstein et al., *Criminal Careers and Career Criminals.*

92. Robert J. Sampson and John H. Laub, *Crime in the Making: Pathways and Turning Points through the Life Course* (Cambridge: Harvard University Press, 1993).

93. G. H. Elder, Jr., "Perspectives on the Life-Course," in G. H. Elder, Jr., ed., *Life-Course Dynamics* (Ithaca, NY: Cornell University Press, 1985).

94. Philip W. Harris, Wayne N. Welsh, and Frank Butler, "A Century of Juvenile Justice," in *Criminal Justice 2000*, Vol. 1 (Washington, DC: National Institute of Justice, 2000).

95. Elder, *Life-Course Dynamics.*

96. Robert J. Sampson and John H. Laub, "Understanding Variability in Lives through Time: Contributions of Life-Course Criminology," in Alex Piquero and Paul Mazerolle, eds., *Life-Course Criminology: Contemporary and Classic Readings* (Belmont, CA: Wadsworth, 2001), p. 243.

97. Marc LeBlanc and Rolf Loeber, "Developmental Criminology Updated," in Michael Tonry, ed., *Crime and Justice: A Review of Research*, Vol. 23 (Chicago: University of Chicago Press, 1998).

98. Adapted from Harris, Welsh, and Butler, "A Century of Juvenile Justice," p. 379.

99. Glen H. Elder, Jr., "Time, Human Agency, and Social Change: Perspectives on the Life Course," *Social Psychology Quarterly*, Vol. 57, No. 1 (1994), pp. 4–15.

100. Glen H. Elder, Jr. and Monica Kirkpatrick Johnson, "The Life Course and Aging: Challenges, Lessons, and New Directions," in Richard A. Settersten, Jr., *Invitation to the Life Course: Toward New Understandings of Later Life* (Amityville, NY: Baywood Publishing, 2002), pp. 49–84.

101. See, for example, the collected papers of Sheldon Glueck, 1916–1972, which are part of the David L. Bazelon collection at Harvard University Law School (Cambridge, MA). Results of the Gluecks' work were reported in S. Glueck and E. Glueck, *Unraveling Juvenile Delinquency* (New York: The Commonwealth Fund, 1950).

102. Sheldon Glueck and Eleanor Glueck, *Delinquents and Nondelinquents in Perspective* (Cambridge: Harvard University Press, 1968).

103. John H. Laub and Robert J. Sampson, "Urban Poverty and the Family Context of Delinquency: A New Look at Structure and Process in a Classic Study," *Child Development*, Vol. 65 (1994), pp. 523–540. See also John H. Laub and Robert J. Sampson, "Turning Points in the Life Course: Why Change Matters to the Study of Crime," *Criminology*, Vol. 31, No. 3 (1993), pp. 301–325; and Robert J. Sampson and John H. Laub, "Crime and Deviance in the Life Course," *Annual Review of Sociology*, Vol. 18 (1992), pp. 63–84.

104. See John H. Laub and Leana C. Allen, "Life Course Criminology and Community Corrections," *Perspectives*, Vol. 24, No. 2 (spring 2000), pp. 20–29.

105. Sampson and Laub, "Crime and Deviance in the Life Course," pp. 63–84.

106. John H. Laub, "The Life Course of Criminology in the United States: The American Society of Criminology 2003 Presidential Address," *Criminology*, Vol. 42, No. 1 (2004), pp. 1–26.

107. G. B. Trasler, "Aspects of Causality, Culture, and Crime," paper presented at the Fourth International Seminar at the International Centre of Sociological, Penal and Penitentiary Research and Studies, Messina, Italy, 1980.

108. Laub and Sampson, "Turning Points in the Life Course."

109. Ibid.

110. Bradley R. Entner Wright et al., "The Effects of Social Ties on Crime Vary by Criminal Propensity: A Life-Course Model of Interdependence," *Criminology*, Vol. 39, No. 2 (2001), pp. 321–348.

111. See Laub and Allen, "Life Course Criminology and Community Corrections," pp. 20–29.

112. Sampson and Laub, *Crime in the Making*.

113. Matthew G. Yeager, "Life-Course Study of Released Prisoners Suggests Importance of Employment for Offender Reintegration and Community Safety," *Offender Programs Report*, Vol. 7, No. 2 (July–August 2003), pp. 1, 28–32.

114. Robert J. Sampson, John H. Laub, and Christopher Wimer, "Does Marriage Reduce Crime? A Counterfactual Approach to Within-Individual Causal Effects," *Criminology*, Vol. 44, No. 3 (2006), pp. 465–508.

115. Ronald L. Simons et al., "A Test of Life-Course Explanations for Stability and Change in Antisocial Behavior from Adolescence to Young Adulthood," *Criminology*, Vol. 40, No. 2 (2002), pp. 401–434.

116. Marvin E. Wolfgang, "Crime in a Birth Cohort," *Proceedings of the American Philosophical Society*, Vol. 117, No. 5 (Oct. 25, 1973), pp. 404–411.

117. A. Quetelet, *A Treatise on Man and the Development of His Facilities* (Gainesville, FL: Scholars Facsimiles and Reprints, 1969).

118. Sheldon Glueck and Eleanor Glueck, *Later Criminal Careers* (New York: The Commonwealth Fund, 1937), p. 105.

119. Walter R. Grove, "The Effect of Age and Gender on Deviant Behavior: A Biopsychosocial Perspective," in Alice S. Rossi, ed., *Gender and the Life Course* (New York: Aldine, 1985).

120. Ibid., p. 128.

121. See David P. Farrington, "The Twelfth Jack Tizard Memorial Lecture: The Development of Offending and Antisocial Behavior from Childhood—Key Findings from the Cambridge Study in Delinquent Development," *Journal of Child Psychology and Psychiatry*, Vol. 360 (1995), pp. 929–964; and Donald J. West and David P. Farrington, *The Delinquent Way of Life: Third Report of the Cambridge Study in Delinquent Development* (London: Heinemann, 1977).

122. David P. Farrington, "Explaining and Preventing Crime: The Globalization of Knowledge—The American Society of Criminology 1999 Presidential Address," *Criminology*, Vol. 38, No. 1 (February 2000), pp. 1–24.

123. Piquero and Mazerolle, *Life-Course Criminology*, p. xv.

124. Rolf Loeber and Marc LeBlanc, "Toward a Developmental Criminology," in M. Tonry and N. Morris, eds., *Crime and Justice: A Review of Research*, Vol. 12 (Chicago: University of Chicago Press, 1990).

125. Stephanie R. Hawkins et al., *Resilient Girls: Factors That Protect against Delinquency* (Washington, DC: Office of Justice Programs, 2009), p. 1.

126. Ibid., p. 9.

127. Marvin Wolfgang, Robert Figlio, and Thorsten Sellin, *Delinquency in a Birth Cohort* (Chicago: University of Chicago Press, 1972).

128. Marvin Wolfgang, Terence Thornberry, and Robert Figlio, *From Boy to Man, from Delinquency to Crime* (Chicago: University of Chicago Press, 1987).

129. Steven P. Lab, "Analyzing Change in Crime and Delinquency Rates: The Case for Cohort Analysis," *Criminal Justice Research Bulletin*, Vol. 3, No. 10 (Huntsville, TX: Sam Houston State University, 1988), p. 2.

130. Lawrence E. Cohen and Richard Machalek, "A General Theory of Expropriative Crime: An Evolutionary Ecological Approach," *American Journal of Sociology*, Vol. 94, No. 3 (1988), pp. 465–501; and Lawrence E. Cohen and Richard Machalek, "The Normalcy of Crime: From Durkheim to Evolutionary Ecology," *Rationality and Society*, Vol. 6 (1994), pp. 286–308.

131. Bryan Vila, "Human Nature and Crime Control: Improving the Feasibility of Nurturant Strategies," *Politics and the Life Sciences*, Vol. 16, No. 1 (March 1997), pp. 3–21.

132. Ibid.

133. Terence Thornberry, "Toward an Interactional Theory of Delinquency," *Criminology*, Vol. 25 (1987), pp. 863–891.

134. See Terence P. Thornberry et al., "Delinquent Peers, Beliefs, and Delinquent Behavior: A Longitudinal Test of Interactional Theory," *Criminology*, Vol. 32, No. 1 (1994), pp. 47–53.

135. Terence P. Thornberry et al., "Testing Interactional Theory: An Examination of Reciprocal Causal Relationships among Family, School and Delinquency," *Journal of Criminal Law and Criminology*, Vol. 82 (1991), pp. 3–35.

136. Carolyn Smith and Terence P. Thornberry, "The Relationship between Childhood Maltreatment and Adolescent Involvement in Delinquency," *Criminology*, Vol. 33, No. 4 (1995), pp. 451–477.

137. Suman Kakar, "Youth Gangs and Their Families: Effects of Gang Membership on Their Families' Subjective Well-Being," *Journal of Crime and Justice*, Vol. 21 (1998), pp. 157–171.

138. Barbara Tatem Kelley et al., *Developmental Pathways in Boys' Disruptive and Delinquent Behavior* (Washington, DC: Office of Juvenile Justice and Delinquency Prevention, December 1997).

139. R. Loeber and D. F. Hay, "Developmental Approaches to Aggression and Conduct Problems," in M. Rutter and D. F. Hay, eds., *Development through Life: A Handbook for Clinicians* (Oxford, England: Blackwell Scientific, 1994).

140. Ibid.

141. The Causes and Correlates of Delinquency study is being conducted by Terence P. Thornberry of the Rochester Youth Development Study at the State University of New York at Albany, New York; Rolf Loeber of the Pittsburgh Youth Study at the University of Pittsburgh; and David Huizinga of the Denver Youth Survey at the University of Colorado.

142. Adapted from Katharine Browning et al., "Causes and Correlates of Delinquency Program," *OJJDP Fact Sheet* (Washington, DC: U.S. Department of Justice, April 1999).

143. Compiled from Katharine Browning and Rolf Loeber, "Highlights of Findings from the Pittsburgh Youth Study," *OJJDP Fact Sheet* (Washington, DC: U.S. Department of Justice, February 1999); Katharine Browning, Terence P. Thornberry, and Pamela K. Porter,

"Highlights of Findings from the Rochester Youth Development Study," *OJJDP Fact Sheet* (Washington, DC: U.S. Department of Justice, April 1999); and Katharine Browning and David Huizinga, "Highlights of Findings from the Denver Youth Survey," *OJJDP Fact Sheet* (Washington, DC: U.S. Department of Justice, April 1999).

144. Browning and Huizinga, "Highlights of Findings from the Denver Youth Survey."

145. Family and Youth Services Bureau, *Understanding Youth Development: Promoting Positive Pathways of Growth* (Washington, DC: U.S. Department of Health and Human Services, 2000).

146. Quotations in the following list are taken from Kelley et al., *Developmental Pathways in Boys' Disruptive and Delinquent Behavior.*

147. Ibid., p. 14.

148. See Felton J. Earls and Albert J. Reiss, *Breaking the Cycle: Predicting and Preventing Crime* (Washington, DC: National Institute of Justice, 1994), http://www.ncjrs.org/txtfiles/break.txt (accessed March 12, 2006).

149. Ibid.

150. Ibid.

151. Adapted from the MacArthur Foundation, "The Project on Human Development in Chicago Neighborhoods," http://www.macfound.org/research/hcd/hcd_5.htm (accessed January 5, 2006).

152. "Study of Chicago Finds Neighborhood Efficacy Explains Reductions in Violence," Project on Human Development in Chicago Neighborhoods press release, http://phdcn.harvard.edu/press/index.htm (accessed January 5, 2006).

153. Vila, "Human Nature and Crime Control," p. 10.

154. Robert W. Sweet, Jr., "Preserving Families to Prevent Delinquency," *Office of Juvenile Justice and Delinquency Prevention Model Programs, 1990* (Washington, DC: U.S. Department of Justice, April 1992).

155. Ibid.

156. Farrington, "The Twelfth Jack Tizard Memorial Lecture," p. 929.

CHAPTER 8: SOCIAL CONFLICT THEORIES

1. Much of the information in this paragraph comes from "Troubling Portrait Emerges of Pilot Who Crashed into Texas Building," FOXNews.com, February 18, 2010, http://www.foxnews.com/us/2010/02/18/troubling-portrait-emerges-pilot-crashed-texas-building (accessed April 27, 2010).

2. "Communism," *Encyclopedia Britannica* online, http://britannica.com (accessed January 3, 2007).

3. Raymond J. Michalowski, "Perspectives and Paradigm: Structuring Criminological Thought," in Robert F. Meier, ed., *Theory in Criminology* (Beverly Hills, CA: Sage, 1977), pp. 17–39.

4. Roscoe Pound, *Social Control through the Law: The Powell Lectures* (Hamden, CT: Archon, 1968), pp. 113–114.

5. Although Pound's postulates originally referred only to men, we have here used the now-conventional phrase "men and women" throughout the postulates to indicate that Pound was speaking of everyone within the social group. No other changes to the original postulates have been made.

6. Adapted from Michalowski, "Perspectives and Paradigm."

7. William Bonger, *Criminality and Economic Conditions* (Bloomington: Indiana University Press, 1969). It was originally published in Amsterdam as *Criminalite et Conditions Economiques* (1905) and was translated into English in 1916.

8. Georg Simmel, *Conflict and the Web of Group Affiliations* (New York: Free Press, 1964). It was originally published in 1908.

9. Adapted from Michalowski, "Perspectives and Paradigm."

10. Richard Quinney, *Class, State, and Crime: On the Theory and Practice of Criminal Justice* (New York: David McKay, 1977).

11. Vance Packard, *The Status Seekers* (London: Harmondsworth, 1961).

12. George B. Vold, *Theoretical Criminology* (New York: Oxford University Press, 1958).

13. Ibid., p. 205.

14. Ibid., pp. 208–209.

15. Ralf Dahrendorf, *Class and Class Conflict in Industrial Society* (Stanford, CA: Stanford University Press, 1959).

16. Ralf Dahrendorf, "Out of Utopia: Toward a Reorientation of Sociological Analysis," *American Journal of Sociology,* Vol. 64 (1958), pp. 115–127.

17. Austin Turk, *Criminality and Legal Order* (Chicago: Rand McNally, 1969), p. vii.

18. Ibid.

19. William J. Chambliss, "Toward a Political Economy of Crime," in C. Reasons and R. Rich, eds., *The Sociology of Law* (Toronto: Butterworth, 1978), p. 193.

20. William Chambliss and Robert T. Seidman, *Law, Order, and Power* (Reading, MA: Addison-Wesley, 1971), p. 33.

21. Adapted from ibid., pp. 473–474.

22. William J. Chambliss, *Crime and the Legal Process* (New York: McGraw-Hill, 1969), p. 88.

23. Chambliss, "Toward a Political Economy of Crime."

24. Ibid.

25. Ibid.

26. Richard Quinney, *Critique of the Legal Order: Crime Control in Capitalist Society* (Boston: Little, Brown, 1974), p. 16.

27. Quinney, *Class, State, and Crime*, p. 58.

28. Ibid.

29. Ibid., p. 61.

30. Ibid., p. 65.

31. Jeffrey H. Reiman, *The Rich Get Richer and the Poor Get Prison: Ideology, Class and Criminal Justice*, 6th ed. (Boston: Allyn & Bacon, 2000).

32. Gresham M. Sykes, "Critical Criminology," *Journal of Criminal Law and Criminology,* Vol. 65 (1974), pp. 206–213.

33. David A. Jones, *History of Criminology: A Philosophical Perspective* (Westport, CT: Greenwood, 1986), p. 200.

34. The quotations attributed to Currie in this section are from Elliott Currie, "Market, Crime, and Community," *Theoretical Criminology*, Vol. 1, No. 2 (May 1997), pp. 147–172.

35. Michael J. Lynch and W. Byron Groves, *A Primer in Radical Criminology*, 2nd ed. (Albany, NY: Harrow & Heston, 1989), p. 126.

36. Ibid., p. 128.

37. Raymond J. Michalowski, *Order, Law, and Crime: An Introduction to Criminology* (New York: Random House, 1985), p. 410.

38. Lynch and Groves, *A Primer in Radical Criminology*, p. 130.

39. William V. Pelfrey, *The Evolution of Criminology* (Cincinnati: Anderson, 1980), p. 86.

40. For a good overview of critiques of radical criminology, see J. F. Galliher, "Life and Death of Liberal Criminology," *Contemporary Crisis*, Vol. 2, No. 3 (July 1978), pp. 245–263.

41. Jackson Toby, "The New Criminology Is the Old Sentimentality," *Criminology*, Vol. 16 (1979), pp. 516–526.

42. Ibid.

43. Hermann Mannheim, *Comparative Criminology* (Boston: Houghton Mifflin, 1965), p. 445.

44. Carl Klockars, "The Contemporary Crisis of Marxist Criminology," *Criminology*, Vol. 16 (1979), pp. 477–515.

45. Ibid.

46. Werner Einstadter and Stuart Henry, *Criminological Theory: An Analysis of Its Underlying Assumptions* (Toronto: Harcourt, 1995), p. 233.

47. For an excellent review of critical realism in a Canadian context, see John Lowman and Brian D. MacLean, eds., *Realist Criminology: Crime Control and Policing in the 1990s* (Toronto: University of Toronto Press, 1994).

48. Daniel J. Curran and Claire M. Renzetti, *Theories of Crime* (Boston: Allyn & Bacon, 1994), p. 283.

49. See M. D. Schwartz and W. S. DeKeseredy, "Left Realist Criminology: Strengths, Weaknesses, and the Feminist Critique," *Crime, Law, and Social Change*, Vol. 15, No. 1 (January 1991), pp. 51–72; W. S. DeKeseredy and B. D. MacLean, "Exploring the Gender, Race, and Class Dimensions of Victimization: A Left Realist Critique of the Canadian Urban Victimization Survey," *International Journal of Offender Therapy and Comparative Criminology*, Vol. 35, No. 2 (summer 1991), pp. 143–161; and W. S. DeKeseredy and M. D. Schwartz, "British and U.S. Left Realism: A Critical Comparison," *International Journal of Offender Therapy and Comparative Criminology*, Vol. 35, No. 3 (fall 1991), pp. 248–262.

50. See Jock Young, "The Failure of Criminology: The Need for a Radical Realism," in R. Matthews and J. Young, eds., *Confronting Crime* (Beverly Hills, CA: Sage, 1986), pp. 4–30; Jock Young, "The Tasks of a Realist Criminology," *Contemporary Crisis*, Vol. 11, No. 4 (1987), pp. 337–356; and Jock Young, "Radical Criminology in Britain: The Emergence of a Competing Paradigm," *British Journal of Criminology*, Vol. 28 (1988), pp. 159–183.

51. D. Brown and R. Hogg, "Essentialism, Racial Criminology, and Left Realism," *Australian and New Zealand Journal of Criminology*, Vol. 25 (1992), pp. 195–230.

52. Roger Matthews and Jock Young, "Reflections on Realism," in Jock Young and Roger Matthews, eds., *Rethinking Criminology: The Realist Debate* (Newbury Park, CA: Sage, 1992).

53. Don C. Gibbons, *Talking about Crime and Criminals: Problems and Issues in Theory Development in Criminology* (Upper Saddle River, NJ: Prentice Hall, 1994), p. 170.

54. Piers Beirne and James W. Messerschmidt, *Criminology* (New York: Harcourt Brace Jovanovich, 1991), p. 501.

55. Gibbons, *Talking about Crime and Criminals*, p. 165, citing Loraine Gelsthorpe and Alison Morris, "Feminism and Criminology in Britain," *British Journal of Criminology* (spring 1988), pp. 93–110.

56. Sally S. Simpson, "Feminist Theory, Crime and Justice," *Criminology*, Vol. 27, No. 4 (1989), p. 605.

57. Roslyn Muraskin and Ted Alleman, eds., *It's a Crime: Women and Justice* (Upper Saddle River, NJ: Prentice Hall, 1993), p. 1.

58. As stated in Amanda Burgess-Proctor, "Intersections of Race, Class, Gender, and Crime: Future Directions for Feminist Criminology," *Feminist Criminology*, Vol. 1, No. 27 (2006), p. 29.

59. Carol Pateman, "Feminist Critiques of the Public/Private Dichotomy," in Anne Phillips, ed., *Feminism and Equality* (Oxford, England: Blackwell, 1987).

60. F. P. Williams III and M. D. McShane, *Criminological Theory* (Upper Saddle River, NJ: Prentice Hall, 1994), p. 238.

61. Ibid.

62. Amanda Burgess-Proctor, "Intersections of Race, Class, Gender, and Crime," p. 29.

63. James W. Messerschmidt, *Capitalism, Patriarchy and Crime: Toward a Socialist Feminist Criminology* (Totowa, NJ: Rowman and Littlefield, 1986).

64. Freda Adler, *Sisters in Crime: The Rise of the New Female Criminal* (New York: McGraw-Hill, 1975).

65. Rita J. Simon, *Women and Crime* (Lexington, MA: Lexington Books, 1975).

66. Carol Smart, *Women, Crime and Criminology: A Feminist Critique* (London: Routledge, 1977).

67. Kathleen Daly and Meda Chesney-Lind, "Feminism and Criminology," *Justice Quarterly*, Vol. 5, No. 5 (December 1988), p. 527.

68. The following list is adapted from ibid., pp. 497–535.

69. Susan Caulfield and Nancy Wonders, "Gender and Justice: Feminist Contributions to Criminology," in Gregg Barak, ed., *Varieties of Criminology: Readings from a Dynamic Discipline* (Westport, CT: Praeger, 1994), pp. 213–229.

70. John Hagan, *Structural Criminology* (New Brunswick, NJ: Rutgers University Press, 1989), p. 130.

71. Ibid.

72. Daly and Chesney-Lind, "Feminism and Criminology," p. 506.

73. Ibid.

74. Ibid., p. 514.

75. For an intriguing analysis of how existing laws tend to criminalize women and their reproductive activities, see Susan O. Reed, "The Criminalization of Pregnancy: Drugs, Alcohol, and AIDS," in

Muraskin and Alleman, eds., *It's a Crime*, pp. 92–117; and Drew Humphries, "Mothers and Children, Drugs and Crack: Reactions to Maternal Drug Dependency," in Muraskin and Alleman, eds., *It's a Crime*, pp. 131–145.

76. Dawn H. Currie, "Feminist Encounters with Postmodernism: Exploring the Impasse of the Debates on Patriarchy and Law," *Canadian Journal of Women and Law*, Vol. 5, No. 1 (1992), p. 10.

77. For an excellent overview of feminist theory in criminology and for a comprehensive review of research regarding female offenders, see Joanne Belknap, *The Invisible Woman: Gender, Crime and Justice* (Belmont, CA: Wadsworth, 1996).

78. Such studies are still ongoing and continue to add to the descriptive literature of feminist criminology. See, for example, Deborah R. Baskin and Ira Sommers, "Female Initiation into Violent Street Crime," *Justice Quarterly*, Vol. 10, No. 4 (December 1993), pp. 559–583; Scott Decker et al., "A Woman's Place Is in the Home: Females and Residential Burglary," *Justice Quarterly*, Vol. 10, No. 1 (March 1993), pp. 143–162; and Jill L. Rosenbaum, "The Female Delinquent: Another Look at the Role of the Family," in Muraskin and Alleman, eds., *It's a Crime*, pp. 399–420.

79. Ronald L. Akers, *Criminological Theories: Introduction and Evaluation* (Los Angeles: Roxbury, 1994), p. 39.

80. Karen Heimer, "Changes in the Gender Gap in Crime and Women's Economic Marginalization," in *The Nature of Crime: Continuity and Change*, Vol. 1 of *Criminal Justice 2000* (Washington, DC: National Institute of Justice, 2000), p. 428.

81. Daly and Chesney-Lind, "Feminism and Criminology," p. 512.

82. Citing Allison Morris, *Women, Crime and Criminal Justice* (New York: Blackwell, 1987).

83. Gregg Barak, "Introduction: Criminological Theory in the 'Postmodernist' Era," in Gregg Barak, ed., *Varieties of Criminology*, pp. 1–11.

84. Joycelyn M. Pollock, *Criminal Women* (Cincinnati: Anderson, 1999), p. 146.

85. See, for example, Stuart Henry and Dragan Milovanovic, *Constitutive Criminology: Beyond Postmodernism* (London: Sage, 1995); and Milovanovic, *Postmodern Criminology* (New York: Routledge, 1997).

86. Milovanovic, *Postmodern Criminology*.

87. Henry and Milovanovic, *Constitutive Criminology*, p. 118.

88. Werner Einstadter and Stuart Henry, *Criminological Theory: An Analysis of Its Underlying Assumptions* (Fort Worth, TX: Harcourt Brace, 1995).

89. Ian Taylor, Paul Walton, and Jock Young, *The New Criminology: For a Social Theory of Deviance* (London: Routledge, 1973); and Ian Taylor, Paul Walton, and Jock Young, *Critical Criminology* (London: Routledge, 1975).

90. Ian Taylor, "Crime and Social Criticism," *Social Justice*, Vol. 26, No. 2 (1999), p. 150.

91. Ibid.

92. For examples of how this might be accomplished, see F. H. Knopp, "Community Solutions to Sexual Violence: Feminist/Abolitionist Perspectives," in Harold E. Pepinsky and Richard Quinney, eds.,

Criminology as Peacemaking (Bloomington: Indiana University Press, 1991), pp. 181–193; and S. Caringella-MacDonald and D. Humphries, "Sexual Assault, Women, and the Community: Organizing to Prevent Sexual Violence," in Pepinsky and Quinney, eds., *Criminology as Peacemaking*, pp. 98–113.

93. Richard Quinney, "Life of Crime: Criminology and Public Policy as Peacemaking," *Journal of Crime and Justice*, Vol. 16, No. 2 (1993), pp. 3–9.

94. See, for example, Harold E. Pepinsky, "This Can't Be Peace: A Pessimist Looks at Punishment," in W. B. Groves and G. Newman, eds., *Punishment and Privilege* (Albany, NY: Harrow and Heston, 1986); Harold E. Pepinsky, "Violence as Unresponsiveness: Toward a New Conception of Crime," *Justice Quarterly*, Vol. 5 (1988), pp. 539–563; and Pepinsky and Quinney, eds., *Criminology as Peacemaking*.

95. See, for example, Richard Quinney, "Crime, Suffering, Service: Toward a Criminology of Peacemaking," *Quest*, Vol. 1 (1988), pp. 66–75; Richard Quinney, "The Theory and Practice of Peacemaking in the Development of Radical Criminology," *Critical Criminologist*, Vol. 1, No. 5 (1989), p. 5; and Richard Quinney and John Wildeman, *The Problem of Crime: A Peace and Social Justice Perspective*, 3rd ed. (Mayfield, CA: Mountain View Press, 1991)—originally published as *The Problem of Crime: A Critical Introduction to Criminology* (New York: Bantam, 1977).

96. All of these themes are addressed, for example, in Pepinsky and Quinney, eds., *Criminology as Peacemaking*.

97. Quinney and Wildeman, *The Problem of Crime*, pp. vii–viii.

98. Bo Lozoff and Michael Braswell, *Inner Corrections: Finding Peace and Peace Making* (Cincinnati: Anderson, 1989).

99. Clemens Bartollas and Michael Braswell, "Correctional Treatment, Peacemaking, and the New Age Movement," *Journal of Crime and Justice*, Vol. 16, No. 2 (1993), pp. 43–58.

100. Ibid.

101. For a good overview of such programs, see Thomas E. Carbonneau, *Alternative Dispute Resolution: Melting the Lances and Dismounting the Steeds* (Chicago: University of Illinois Press, 1989).

102. Peter Finn and Andrea K. Newlyn, *Miami's "Drug Court": A Different Approach* (Washington, DC: National Institute of Justice, June 1993), p. 2.

103. Fay Honey Knopp, "Community Solutions to Sexual Violence: Feminist-Abolitionist Perspectives," in Pepinsky and Quinney, eds., *Criminology as Peacemaking*, p. 183.

104. Ibid.

105. Daniel Van Ness and Karen Heetderks Strong, *Restoring Justice* (Cincinnati: Anderson, 1997), p. 31.

106. Stephen C. Richards, "Introducing the New School of Convict Criminology," *Social Justice*, Vol. 28, No. 1 (2001), p. 177.

107. J. I. Ross and S. C. Richards, *Convict Criminology* (Belmont, California: Thomson Wadsworth, 2002).

108. Stephen C. Richards and Jeffrey Ian Ross, "Convict Criminology," in Richard A. Wright and J. Mitchell Miller, eds., *Encyclopedia of Criminology*, Vol. 1 (New York: Routledge, 2005), pp. 232–236.

109. Ibid.

110. John Irwin, *The Felon* (Upper Saddle River, NJ: Prentice Hall, 1970).

111. K. C. Carceral et al., *Behind a Convict's Eyes: Doing Time in a Modern Prison* (New York: Wadsworth, 2003).

112. K. C. Carceral and Thomas J. Bernard, *Prison, Inc.: A Convict Exposes Life inside a Private Prison* (New York: New York University Press, 2006).

113. The following list is adapted from Richards and Ross, "Convict Criminology"; and Matthew B. Robinson, *Justice Blind: Ideals and Realities of American Criminal Justice*, 2nd ed. (Upper Saddle River, NJ: Prentice Hall, 2005).

CHAPTER 9: CRIMES AGAINST PERSONS

1. Access NCJRS on the Web at http://www.ncjrs.gov.

2. Jennifer L. Truman and Michael R. Rand, *Criminal Victimization, 2009* (Washington, DC: Bureau of Justice Statistics, 2010).

3. Jennifer L. Truman and Michael R. Rand, *Criminal Victimization, 2009* (Washington, DC: Bureau of Justice Statistics, 2010); and Patsy A. Klaus, *Crime and the Nation's Households, 2003* (Washington, DC: Bureau of Justice Statistics, 2004).

4. See FBI, "About the UCR Program," http://www.fbi.gov/ucr/05cius/about/about_ucr.html (accessed July 10, 2010).

5. Federal Bureau of Investigation, *Crime in the United States, 2006* (Washington, DC: U.S. Department of Justice, 2007).

6. The President's Commission on Law Enforcement and Administration of Justice, *The Challenge of Crime in a Free Society* (Washington, DC: U.S. Government Printing Office, 1967). The President's Commission relied on UCR data, and the other crime statistics reported in this section come from UCRs for various years.

7. Frank E. Hagan, *Research Methods in Criminal Justice and Criminology*, 5th ed. (Boston: Allyn & Bacon, 2000).

8. The coining of the term *dark figure of crime* is sometimes attributed to Michael Gottfredson. See Michael Gottfredson, "Substantive Contributions of Victimization Surveys," in Michael Tonry and Norval Morris, eds., *Crime and Justice: An Annual Review of Research*, Vol. 7 (Chicago: University of Chicago Press, 1986).

9. Terence P. Thornberry and Marvin D. Krohn, "The Self-Report Method for Measuring Delinquency and Crime," *Criminal Justice 2000* (Washington, DC: National Institute of Justice, 2000), p. 34.

10. National Institute on Drug Abuse, *Monitoring the Future: National Results on Adolescent Drug Use—Overview of Key Findings, 2006* (Rockville, MD: U.S. Department of Health and Human Services, 2007).

11. Terance D. Miethe and Richard C. McCorkle, *Crime Profiles: The Anatomy of Dangerous Persons, Places, and Situations* (Los Angeles: Roxbury, 1998), p. 2.

12. This and other statistics in this section come from Federal Bureau of Investigation, *Crime in the United States, 2009* (Washington, DC: U.S. Department of Justice, 2010).

13. Marvin Wolfgang and Franco Ferracuti, *The Subculture of Violence: Towards an Integrated Theory in Criminology* (1967; reprint, Beverly Hills, CA: Sage, 1982).

14. Marc Reidel and Margaret A. Zahn, *The Nature and Patterns of American Homicide* (Washington, DC: U.S. Government Printing Office, 1985). See also Margaret A. Zahn and P. C. Sagi, "Stranger Homicide in Nine American Cities," *Journal of Criminal Law and Criminology*, Vol. 78, No. 2 (1987), pp. 377–397.

15. Kirk R. Williams and Robert L. Flewelling, "The Social Production of Criminal Homicide: A Comparative Study of Disaggregated Rates in American Cities," *American Sociological Review*, Vol. 53, No. 3 (1988), pp. 421–431.

16. Lynne A. Curtis, *American Violence and Public Policy* (New Haven, CT: Yale University Press, 1985); and Lynne A. Curtis, *Violence, Race and Culture* (Lexington, MA: Lexington Books, 1975).

17. Claude S. Fisher, "Toward a Subcultural Theory of Urbanism," *American Journal of Sociology*, Vol. 80 (1975), p. 1335.

18. Steven Messner, "Poverty, Inequality and Urban Homicide Rate," *Criminology*, Vol. 20 (1982), pp. 103–114; and Steven Messner, "Regional and Racial Effects on the Urban Homicide Rate," *American Journal of Sociology*, Vol. 88 (1983), pp. 997–1007.

19. Robert Sampson, "Neighborhood Family Structure and the Risk of Personal Victimization," in James Byrne and Robert J. Sampson, eds., *The Social Ecology of Crime* (New York: Springer-Verlag, 1985); and Robert J. Sampson, "Structural Sources of Variation in Race-Age Specific Rates of Offending across Major U.S. Cities," *Criminology*, Vol. 23, No. 4 (1985), pp. 647–673.

20. S. Hackney, "Southern Violence," in H. D. Graham and T. R. Gurr, eds., *History of Violence in America: Report of the Task Force on Historical and Comparative Perspectives to the National Commission on the Causes and Prevention of Violence* (New York: Bantam, 1960), pp. 505–528; and L. W. Shannon, "The Spatial Distribution of Criminal Offenses by States," *Journal of Criminal Law, Criminology, and Police Science*, Vol. 45 (1954), pp. 264–273.

21. Hackney, "Southern Violence"; and Wolfgang and Ferracuti, *The Subculture of Violence*.

22. R. D. Gastil, "Homicides and a Regional Culture of Violence," *American Sociological Review*, Vol. 36 (1971), pp. 412–427; and Hackney, "Southern Violence."

23. Colin Loftin and R. H. Hill, "Regional Subculture and Homicide: A Comparison of the Gastil-Hackney Thesis," *American Sociological Review*, Vol. 39 (1974), pp. 714–724.

24. Ibid.

25. Marvin E. Wolfgang, *Patterns in Criminal Homicide* (New York: Wiley, 1958).

26. Ibid.

27. Rosert Nash Parker and Dwayne M. Smith, "Deterrence, Poverty and Type of Homicide" *American Journal of Sociology*, Vol. 85 (1979), pp. 614–624; and M. Dwayne Smith and Robert Nash Parker, "Types of Homicide and Variation in Regional Rates," *Social Forces*, Vol. 59 (1980), pp. 136–147.

28. The distinction between expressive and instrumental crimes has been incorporated into much research on different crimes. This approach originated in the work of Richard Block and Franklin Zimring, "Homicide in Chicago, 1965–1970," *Journal of Research in Crime and Delinquency*, Vol. 10 (1973), pp. 1–12.

29. Williams and Flewelling, "The Social Production of Criminal Homicide."

30. Laura Dugan, Daniel S. Nagin, and Richard Rosenfeld, "Explaining the Decline in Intimate Partner Homicide," *Homicide Studies*, Vol. 3, No. 3 (1999), p. 189.

31. Ibid., p. 208.

32. Wolfgang, *Patterns in Criminal Homicide*.

33. Richard Rosenfeld, "Changing Relationships between Men and Women: A Note on the Decline in Intimate Partner Homicide," *Homicide Studies*, Vol. 1, No. 1 (1997), pp. 72–83.

34. Wolfgang, *Patterns in Criminal Homicide*, p. 2.

35. Ibid., p. 9.

36. Ibid.

37. Philip J. Cook and Mark H. Moore, "Guns, Gun Control, and Homicide," in M. Dwayne Smith and Margaret A. Zahn, eds., *Studying and Preventing Homicide: Issues and Challenges* (Thousand Oaks, CA: Sage, 1999), p. 252.

38. Ibid., p. 254.

39. Ibid., p. 266.

40. Reprinted as Paul J. Goldstein, "The Drugs/Violence Nexus: A Tripartite Conceptual Framework," in James A. Inciardi and Karen McElrath, eds., *The American Drug Scene* (Los Angeles: Roxbury, 1995).

41. Auerhahn and Parker, "Drugs, Alcohol, and Homicide."

42. Ibid.

43. Ibid., p. 108.

44. Ibid.

45. Robert Nash Parker, "Bringing 'Booze' Back In: The Relationship between Alcohol and Homicide," *Journal of Research in Crime and Delinquency*, Vol. 32, No. 1 (1995), pp. 3–38.

46. Ibid., p. 4.

47. Ibid., p. 25.

48. Cheryl L. Maxsong, M. A. Gordon, and Malcolm W. Klein, "Differences between Gang and Nongang Homicides," *Criminology*, Vol. 23, No. 2 (1985), pp. 209–222.

49. Richard Rosenfeld, Timothy M. Bray, and Arlen Egley, "Facilitating Violence: A Comparison of Gang-Motivated, Gang-Affiliated, and Nongang Youth Homicides," *Journal of Quantitative Criminology*, Vol. 15, No. 4 (1999), pp. 495–516.

50. Ibid., p. 513.

51. "Experts Say Method of Man Accused of Luring, Killing Women Rare," Associated Press, November 30, 2009.

52. Marisol Bello, "Families Wait for Victims' ID's," *USA Today*, November 6, 2009, p. 3A.

53. Bureau of Justice Statistics, *Report to the Nation on Crime and Justice*, 2nd ed. (Washington, DC: U.S. Government Printing Office, 1988), p. 4.

54. James Alan Fox and Jack Levin, "Multiple Homicide: Patterns of Serial and Mass Murder," in Michael Tonry, ed., *Crime and Justice: A Review of Research*, Vol. 23 (1998), p. 413.

55. Ibid.

56. James Alan Fox and Jack Levin, "Serial Murder: Myths and Realities," in Smith and Zahn, eds., *Studying and Preventing Homicide*, pp. 79–96.

57. Ibid.

58. Fox and Levin, "Multiple Homicide."

59. Ibid., p. 413.

60. Ibid., p. 415.

61. Ibid.

62. Ibid.

63. Ronald Holmes and J. DeBurger, "Profiles in Terror: The Serial Murderer," *Federal Probation*, Vol. 49, No. 3 (1985), pp. 29–34.

64. Fox and Levin, "Serial Murder."

65. James DeFronzo et al., "Male Serial Homicide: The Influence of Cultural and Structural Variables," *Homicide Studies*, Vol. 11, No. 3 (2007).

66. Stephen T. Holmes, Eric Hickey, and Ronald M. Holmes, "Female Serial Murderesses: Constructing Different Typologies," *Journal of Contemporary Criminal Justice*, Vol. 7, No. 4 (1991), pp. 245–256.

67. Ibid.

68. Ibid.

69. Michael D. Kelleher and C. L. Kelleher, *Murder Most Rare: The Female Serial Killer* (Westport, CT: Praeger, 1998).

70. Ibid., p. 11.

71. Ibid., p. 7.

72. Fox and Levin, "Multiple Homicide."

73. Ibid., p. 428.

74. Ibid.

75. Thomas O'Reilly-Fleming, "The Evolution of Multiple Murder in Historical Perspective," in Thomas O'Reilly-Fleming, ed., *Serial and Mass Murder: Theory, Research, and Policy* (Toronto: Canadian Scholars' Press, 1996).

76. Jack Levin and James Alan Fox, "A Psycho-Social Analysis of Mass Murder," in O'Reilly-Fleming, ed., *Serial and Mass Murder*, p. 65.

77. Ibid., p. 66.

78. Ibid.

79. Ibid., p. 69.

80. Ibid.

81. Ibid., p. 69.

82. James Alan Fox and Jack Levin, *Overkill: Mass Murder and Serial Killing Exposed* (New York: Plenum, 1994).

83. See James L. Knoll, "Mass Murderers and the Psychology of Revenge," *Criminal Justice Research Review*, March/April 2010, pp. 58–63. The term *pseudocommando* was apparently first used by P. Dietz in the publication, "Mass, Serial, and Sensational Homicides," *Bulletin of the New York Academy of Medicine*, Vol. 62, No. 5 (1986), pp. 477–491.

84. Paul E. Mullen, "Schizophrenia and Violence: From Correlations to Preventive Strategies," *Advances in Psychiatric Treatment*, Vol. 12 (2006), pp. 239–248.

85. For an overview of the measurement of rape in national surveys, see Debra S. Kelley, "The Measurement of Rape," in James F. Hodgson and Debra S. Kelley, eds., *Sexual Violence: Policies, Practices,*

and Challenges in the United States and Canada (New York: Praeger, 2001). For a more detailed exploration of this topic, see Bonnie S. Fisher and Francis T. Cullen, "Measuring the Sexual Victimization of Women: Evolution, Current Controversies, and Future Research," in Criminal Justice 2000: Measurement and Analysis of Crime and Justice (Washington, DC: U.S. Department of Justice, Office of Justice Programs, 2000).

86. FBI, Crime in the United States, 2009.

87. Jennifer L. Truman and Michael R. Rand, Criminal Victimization, 2009 (Washington, DC: Bureau of Justice Statistics, 2010).

88. Diana E. H. Russell and Rebecca M. Bolen, The Epidemic of Rape and Child Sexual Abuse in the United States (Thousand Oaks, CA: Sage, 2000). See also Mary P. Koss, "The Underdetection of Rape: Methodological Choices Influence Incidence Estimates," Journal of Social Issues, Vol. 48, No. 1 (1992), pp. 61–75; and Mary P. Koss, "The Measurement of Rape Victimization in Crime Surveys," Criminal Justice and Behavior, Vol. 23 (1996), pp. 55–69.

89. Patricia Tjaden and Nancy Thoennes, Prevalence, Incidence, and Consequences of Violence against Women: Findings from the National Violence against Women Survey (Washington, DC: National Institute of Justice and Centers for Disease Control and Prevention, 1991).

90. Martha R. Burt, "Cultural Myths and Supports for Rape," Journal of Personality and Social Psychology, Vol. 38 (1980), pp. 217–230.

91. For example, see Mary P. Koss et al., "Nonstranger Sexual Aggression: A Discriminant Analysis of the Psychological Characteristics of Undetected Offenders," Sex Roles, Vol. 12 (1985), pp. 981–992.

92. Martha R. Burt, "Rape Myths," in Andrea Parrot and Laurie Bechhofer, eds., Acquaintance Rape: The Hidden Crime (New York: John Wiley & Sons, 1991).

93. Gary LaFree, Rape and Criminal Justice: The Social Construction of Sexual Assault (Belmont, CA: Wadsworth, 1989). See also Jeanne C. Marsh, Alison Geist, and Nathan Caplan, Rape and the Limits of Law Reform (Boston: Auburn, 1982).

94. Harriet R. Galvin, "Shielding Rape Victims in the State and Federal Courts: A Proposal for the Second Decade," Minnesota Law Review, Vol. 70 (1986), pp. 763–916.

95. Cassia Spohn and Julie Horney, Rape Law Reform: A Grassroots Revolution and Its Impact (New York: Plenum, 1992).

96. Ibid., p. 21.

97. Ibid.

98. Ibid.

99. Ibid.

100. Ibid.

101. Julie Horney and Cassia Spohn, "Rape Law Reform and Instrumental Change in Six Urban Jurisdictions," Law and Society Review, Vol. 25, No. 1 (1991), pp. 117–153.

102. Spohn and Horney, Rape Law Reform.

103. Ibid., p. 162.

104. Ibid., p. 129.

105. E. J. Kanin, "Male Aggression in Dating-Courtship Relations," American Journal of Sociology, Vol. 63 (1957), cited in Martin D.

Schwartz and Molly S. Leggett, "Bad Dates or Emotional Trauma? The Aftermath of Campus Sexual Assault," Violence against Women, Vol. 5, No. 3 (1999), pp. 197–204.

106. See Frances P. Bernat, "Rape Law Reform," in James F. Hodgson and Debra S. Kelley, eds., Sexual Violence: Policies, Practices, and Challenges in the United States and Canada (New York: Praeger, 2001).

107. Public Law 102–325, Section 486(c).

108. Carol Bohmer and Andrea Parrot, Sexual Assault on Campus: The Problem and the Solution (New York: Lexington Books, 1993), pp. 15–16.

109. Mary P. Koss, C. J. Gidycz, and N. Wisniewski, "The Scope of Rape: Sexual Aggression and Victimization in a National Sample of Students in Higher Education," Journal of Consulting and Clinical Psychology, Vol. 55 (1987), pp. 162–170.

110. Mary P. Koss, "Hidden Rape: Sexual Aggression and Victimization in a National Sample of Students in Higher Education," in Patricia Searles and Ronald J. Berger, eds., Rape and Society: Readings on the Problem of Sexual Assault (Boulder, CO: Westview Press, 1995).

111. B. L. Yegidis, "Date Rape and Other Forced Sexual Encounters among College Students," Journal of Sex Education and Therapy, Vol. 12 (1986), pp. 51–54.

112. Patricia Yancey Martin and Robert A. Hummer, "Fraternities and Rape on Campus," Gender and Society, Vol. 3, No. 4 (1989), p. 462.

113. Ibid.

114. Diana E. H. Russell, Rape in Marriage (Bloomington: Indiana University Press, 1990).

115. Lisa M. Cuklanz, Rape on Trial: How the Mass Media Construct Legal Reform and Social Change (Philadelphia: University of Pennsylvania Press, 1996).

116. Ibid., p. 53.

117. Ibid., p. 62.

118. David Finkelhor and Kersti Yllo, "Forced Sex in Marriage," Crime and Delinquency, Vol. 28, No. 3 (1982), pp. 459–478.

119. Russell, Rape in Marriage.

120. Ibid., p. 133.

121. Charles Crawford, "Sexual Assault behind Bars: The Forgotten Victims," in Hodgson and Kelley, eds., Sexual Violence.

122. Cindy Struckman-Johnson et al., "Sexual Coercion Reported by Men and Women in Prison," Journal of Sex Research, Vol. 33, No. 1 (1996), pp. 67–76.

123. Susan Brownmiller, Against Our Will: Men, Women, and Rape (New York: Simon & Schuster, 1975).

124. Dianne Herman, "The Rape Culture," in Jo Freeman, ed., Women: A Feminist Perspective (Palo Alto, CA: Mayfield, 1984).

125. Catherine MacKinnon, Toward a Feminist Theory of the State (Cambridge: Harvard University Press, 1989); and Catherine MacKinnon, Only Words (Cambridge: Harvard University Press, 1993).

126. See Andrea Dworkin, Pornography: Men Possessing Women (New York: Plenum, 1981); Andrea Dworkin, "Questions and Answers," in Diana E. H. Russell, ed., Making Violence Sexy: Feminist Views on Pornography (New York: Teachers College Press, 1993); and Andrea

Dworkin, "Against the Male Flood: Censorship, Pornography, and Equality," in Patricia Smith, ed., *Feminist Jurisprudence* (New York: Oxford University Press, 1993).

127. Robin Morgan, *The Word of a Woman: Feminist Dispatches, 1968–1992* (New York: W. W. Norton, 1992), p. 88.

128. Brownmiller, *Against Our Will.*

129. James W. Messerschmidt, *Masculinities and Crime: Critique and Reconceptualization of Theory* (Lanham, MD: Rowman and Littlefield, 1993).

130. Ngaire Naffine, *Feminism and Criminology* (Philadelphia: Temple University Press, 1996), p. 101.

131. Diana Scully and Joseph Marolla, "Riding the Bull at Gilley's: Convicted Rapists Describe the Rewards of Rape," *Social Problems,* Vol. 32, No. 2 (1985), p. 252.

132. Nicholas Groth, *Men Who Rape: The Psychology of the Offender* (New York: Plenum, 1979).

133. Scully and Marolla, "Riding the Bull at Gilley's."

134. Scully and Marolla, "Riding the Bull at Gilley's."

135. Russell, *Rape in Marriage.*

136. Larry Baron and Murray A. Straus, *Four Theories of Rape in American Society: A State-Level Analysis* (New Haven, CT: Yale University Press, 1989).

137. For examples, see Peggy Reeves Sanday, "The Socio-Cultural Context of Rape: A Cross-Cultural Study," *Journal of Social Issues,* Vol. 37 (1981), pp. 5–27.

138. Baron and Straus, *Four Theories of Rape in American Society.*

139. Robert T. Sigler, Ida M. Johnson, and Etta F. Morgan, "Forced Sexual Intercourse: Contemporary Views," in Roslyn Muraskin, ed., *It's a Crime: Women and Justice* (Upper Saddle River, NJ: Prentice Hall, 2000), p. 352.

140. Randy Thornhill, "The Biology of Human Rape," *Jurimetrics,* Vol. 39, No. 2 (1999), p. 138.

141. Randy Thornhill and Craig T. Palmer, *A Natural History of Rape* (Cambridge: MIT Press, 2000), p. 53.

142. Martin Daly and Margo Wilson, *Homicide* (New York: Aldine De Gruyter, 1988), p. 140.

143. Thornhill and Palmer, *A Natural History of Rape,* p. 199. See also Katharine K. Baker, "What Rape Is and What It Ought Not to Be," *Jurimetrics,* Vol. 30, No. 3 (1999), p. 233.

144. R. R. Hazelwood and A. N. Burgess, eds., *Practical Aspects of Rape Investigation: A Multidisciplinary Approach* (New York: CRC Press, 1995).

145. Dennis J. Stevens, *Inside the Mind of a Serial Rapist* (San Francisco: Austin and Winfield, 1999), p. 39.

146. Diana Scully, *Understanding Sexual Violence: A Study of Convicted Rapists* (New York: Routledge, 1990).

147. Ibid., p. 59.

148. Ibid.

149. Ibid.

150. Kim Curtis, "Child Psychiatrist Accused of Molesting," *USA Today,* April 6, 2007.

151. Robert A. Prentky, Raymond A. Knight, and Austin F. S. Lee, *Child Sexual Molestation: Research Issues* (Washington, DC: National Institute of Justice, 1997), p. 1.

152. G. G. Abel et al., "Self-Reported Sex Crimes of Nonincarcerated Paraphiliacs," *Journal of Interpersonal Violence,* Vol. 2 (1987), pp. 3–25.

153. Child Molestation Research and Prevention Institute, "Some Facts," http://www.childmolestationprevention.org (accessed June 5, 2007).

154. Abel et al., "Self-Reported Sex Crimes of Nonincarcerated Paraphiliacs."

155. B. M. Maletzky, "Factors Associated with Success and Failure in the Behavioral and Cognitive Treatment of Sexual Offenders," *Annals of Sex Research,* Vol. 6 (1993), pp. 241–258.

156. Prentky, Knight, and Lee, *Child Sexual Molestation,* from which much of the information and some of the wording in this section are taken.

157. Ibid.

158. A. Nicholas Groth, W. F. Hobson, and T. S. Gary, "The Child Molester: Clinical Observations," *Journal of Social Work and Child Sexual Abuse,* Vol. 1, No. 2 (1982), pp. 129–144.

159. Prentky, Knight, and Lee, *Child Sexual Molestation.*

160. Ibid.

161. Ibid.

162. R. A. Prentky and R. A. Knight, "Age of Onset of Sexual Assault: Criminal and Life History Correlates," in G. C. N. Hall et al., eds., *Sexual Aggression: Issues in Etiology, Assessment, and Treatment* (Washington, DC: Taylor & Francis, 1993), pp. 43–62.

163. Prentky, Knight, and Lee, *Child Sexual Molestation.*

164. Details for this story come from "Robber Sentenced for Shooting Pregnant Teller," http://crime.about.com/b/2010/02/15/robber-sentenced-for-shooting-pregnant-teller.htm (accessed April 29, 2010).

165. Note that while purse snatching and pocket picking involve the express goal of taking someone's property, they are classified as property crimes because they do not involve the same type of direct contact with the victim as does robbery.

166. Terance D. Miethe and David McDowall, "Contextual Effects in Models of Criminal Victimization," *Social Forces,* Vol. 71, No. 3 (1993), pp. 741–760.

167. Miethe and McCorkle, *Crime Profiles.*

168. Scott A. Hendricks et al., "A Matched Case-Control Study of Convenience Store Robbery Risk Factors," *Journal of Occupational and Environmental Medicine,* Vol. 41, No. 11 (1999), p. 995.

169. Richard T. Wright and Scott H. Decker, *Armed Robbers in Action: Stickups and Street Culture* (Boston: Northeastern University Press, 1997), p. 88.

170. Floyd Feeney, "Robbers as Decision Makers," in Derek B. Cornish and Ronald V. Clarke, eds., *The Reasoning Criminal* (New York: Springer-Verlag, 2009).

171. Brian A. Reaves, *Using NIBRS Data to Analyze Violent Crime* (Washington, DC: U.S. Department of Justice, Office of Justice Programs, Bureau of Justice Statistics, 1993).

172. FBI, *Crime in the United States, 2009*.

173. Ibid.

174. Thomas Gabor et al., *Armed Robbery: Cops, Robbers, and Victims* (Springfield, IL: Charles C. Thomas, 1987).

175. Mark A. Peterson and Harriet B. Braiker, *Doing Crime: A Survey of California Prison Inmates* (Santa Monica, CA: RAND Corporation, 1980).

176. Mark A. Peterson and Harriet B. Braiker, *Who Commits Crimes: A Survey of Prison Inmates* (Boston: Oelgeschlager, Gunn, and Hain, 1981).

177. Martha J. Smith and Ronald V. Clarke, "Crime and Public Transport," in Michael Tonry, ed., *Crime and Justice: A Review of Research*, Vol. 27 (Chicago: University of Chicago Press, 2000), pp. 169–234.

178. Ibid.

179. Ibid.

180. Ibid., p. 181.

181. Ibid., p. 182.

182. Derek Cornish, "The Procedural Analysis of Offending and Its Relevance for Situational Prevention," in Ronald V. Clarke, ed., *Crime Prevention Studies*, Vol. 3 (Monsey, NY: Criminal Justice Press, 1994), cited in Smith and Clarke, "Crime and Public Transport," in Tonry, ed., *Crime and Justice*, p. 181.

183. Smith and Clarke, "Crime and Public Transport," p. 181.

184. "Supreme Court Lets Taxi-Stop Rulings Stand: NYC Searchers Too Intrusive, but Boston Sweeps Legal," APBnews.com, December 4, 2000, http://www.apbnews.com/newscenter/breakingnews/2000/12/04/taxi1204_01.html (accessed January 14, 2001).

185. Feeney, "Robbers as Decision Makers."

186. Ibid., p. 59.

187. Bruce A. Jacobs and Richard Wright, "Stick-Up, Street Culture, and Offender Motivation," *Criminology*, Vol. 37, No. 1 (1999), p. 150.

188. S. Morrison and I. O'Donnell, "An Analysis of the Decision Making Processes of Armed Robbers," in R. Homel, ed., *The Politics and Practice of Situational Crime Prevention*, Vol. 5 of *Crime Prevention Studies* (Monsey, NY: Criminal Justice Press, 1996). See also Gabor et al., *Armed Robbery*.

189. Jacobs and Wright, "Stick-Up, Street Culture, and Offender Motivation."

190. Ibid., pp. 167–168.

191. Trevor Bennett and Fiona Brookman, "A Qualitative Study of the Role of Violence in Street Crime," reported in Annika Howard, "Street Robbery Is Not Just about Money," *Medical News Today*, http://www.medicalnewstoday.com/printerfriendlynews.php?newsid=57730, December 1, 2006 (accessed August 24, 2007).

192. Richard T. Wright and Scott H. Decker, *Armed Robbers in Action: Stickups and Street Culture* (Boston: Northeastern University Press, 1997), p. 62.

193. Ibid., p. 63.

194. Ibid.

195. Ibid., p. 66.

196. Bruce A. Jacobs, Volkan Topalli, and Richard Wright, "Managing Retaliation: Drug Robbery and Informal Sanction Threats," *Criminology*, Vol. 38, No. 1 (2000), p. 173.

197. Ibid.

198. Ibid., p. 177.

199. Ibid.

200. Wright and Decker, *Armed Robbers in Action*, p. 67.

201. Jacobs, Topalli, and Wright, "Managing Retaliation," p. 180.

202. Ibid., p. 185.

203. Ibid.

204. Ibid., p. 172.

205. Ibid., p. 194.

206. Ibid.

207. Miller, "Up It Up," p. 37.

208. FBI, *Crime in the United States, 2009*, based on arrests.

209. Miller, "Up It Up," p. 47.

210. Ibid.

211. Reiss and Roth, eds., *Understanding and Preventing Violence*, p. 3.

212. James Garbarino, *Lost Boys: Why Our Sons Turn Violent and How We Can Save Them* (New York: Free Press, 1999), p. 25.

213. Miethe and McCorkle, *Crime Profiles*.

214. Ibid., p. 27.

215. Jennifer L. Truman and Michael R. Rand, *Criminal Victimization, 2009* (Washington, DC: Bureau of Justice Statistics, 2010).

216. Callie Marie Rennison, *Criminal Victimization, 1999: Changes 1998–1999 with Trends 1993–1999* (Washington, DC: U.S. Department of Justice, Office of Justice Programs, 2000).

217. Robert J. Sampson, "Personal Violence by Strangers: An Extension and Test of Predatory Victimization," *Journal of Criminal Law and Criminology*, Vol. 78, No. 2 (1987), p. 342.

218. Marc Riedel and Roger K. Przybylski, "Stranger Murders and Assault: A Study of a Neglected Form of Stranger Violence," in Anna Victoria Wilson, ed., *Homicide: The Victim/Offender Connection* (Cincinnati: Anderson, 1993).

219. Ibid., p. 376.

220. Ibid.

221. Ibid.

222. Richard J. Gelles, *The Violent Home: A Study of Physical Aggression between Husbands and Wives* (Beverly Hills, CA: Sage, 1974).

223. Michael Hindelang, *Criminal Victimization in Eight American Cities* (Cambridge, MA: Ballinger, 1976).

224. Evan Stark, A. Flitcraft, and W. Frazier, "Medicine and Patriarchal Violence: The Social Construction of a Private Event," *International Journal of Health Service*, Vol. 9, No. 3 (1979), pp. 461–493.

225. Murray A. Straus, "The National Family Violence Surveys," in Murray A. Straus and Richard J. Gelles, eds., *Physical Violence in American Families: Risk Factors and Adaptations to Violence in 8,145 Families* (New Brunswick, NJ: Transaction, 1990).

226. Murray A. Straus, "The Conflict Tactics Scales and Its Critics: An Evaluation and New Data on Validity and Reliability," in Straus and Gelles, eds., *Physical Violence in American Families*.

227. Murray A. Straus and Richard J. Gelles, "How Violent Are American Families? Estimates from the National Family Violence Research and Other Studies," in G. Hotaling, ed., *New Directions in Family Violence Research* (Newbury Park, CA: Sage, 1988).

228. Federal Bureau of Investigation, *Crime in the United States, 2006*.

229. Ibid.

230. Ibid.

231. Neil Websdale, *Rural Woman Battering and the Justice System* (Thousand Oaks, CA: Sage, 1997).

232. Martha R. Mahoney, "Legal Issues of Battered Women: Redefining the Issue of Separation," *Michigan Law Review*, Vol. 90, No. 1 (1991), p. 6.

233. Websdale, *Rural Woman Battering and the Justice System*.

234. James Ptacek, *Battered Women in the Courtroom* (Boston: Northeastern University Press, 1999).

235. Ibid., p. 29.

236. Ibid., p. 82.

237. Ibid.

238. Bob Drogin and Faye Fiore, "Retracing Steps of Suspected Fort Hood Shooter, Nidal Malik Hasan," *Los Angeles Times*, November 7, 2007 (accessed May 3, 2010).

239. Shaila Dewan, Stephanie Saul, and Katie Zezima, "For Professor, Fury Just Beneath the Surface," *New York Times*, February 21, 2010.

240. Federal Bureau of Investigation, *Workplace Violence: Issues in Response* (Quantico, VA: FBI, 2004), from which the quotes and information in this section are taken.

241. Some of the wording in this paragraph is adapted from ibid., p. 13.

242. Some of the wording in this paragraph is adapted from ibid., p. 14.

243. Detis T. Duhart, *Violence in the Workplace, 1993–99* (Washington, DC: Bureau of Justice Statistics, 2001).

244. National Institute for Occupational Safety and Health, *Violence in the Workplace: Risk Factors and Prevention Strategies*, July 1996, http://www.cdc.gov/niosh/violcont.html (accessed July 21, 2006).

245. Ibid.

246. Kevin Johnson and David Jackson, "Holocaust Museum Killing Stuns Nation," *USA Today*, June 11, 2009.

247. 28 U.S.C.A., Section 534.

248. Public Law 103–322.

249. Bureau of Justice Assistance, *Addressing Hate Crimes: Six Initiatives That Are Enhancing the Efforts of Criminal Justice Practitioners* (Washington, DC: U.S. Department of Justice, 2000).

250. Matthew Shepard and James Byrd, Jr., Hate Crimes Prevention Act, H.R. 2647.

251. FBI, *Crime in the United States, 2009* (Washington, DC: U.S. Government Printing Office, 2010).

252. James B. Jacobs and Kimberly A. Potter, "Hate Crimes: A Critical Perspective," in Michael Tonry, ed., *Crime and Justice: A Review of Research* (Chicago: University of Chicago Press, 1997), p. 19.

253. "FBI: Man Arrested in ESPN Reporter Nude Video Case Has Buffalo Connection," WKBW-TV News, http://www.msnbc.com/id/33152457 (accessed May 4, 2010).

254. "Sheriff: Accused Jewel Stalker Says God Led Him," Associated Press, September 22, 2009.

255. Violence against Women Grants Office, *Stalking and Domestic Violence: The Third Annual Report to Congress under the Violence against Women Act* (Washington, DC: Violence against Women Grants Office, 1998).

256. Ibid., p. 6.

257. Ibid.

258. Katrina Baum, Shannan Catalano, and Michael Rand, *Stalking Victimization in the United States* (Washington, DC: Bureau of Justice Statistics, 2009).

259. Ibid.

260. Patricia Tjaden and Nancy Thoennes, *Stalking in America: Findings from the National Violence against Women Survey* (Washington, DC: National Institute of Justice, 1998).

261. Paul E. Mullen et al., "Assessing and Managing the Risks in the Stalking Situation," *Journal of the American Academy of Psychiatry and Law*, Vol. 34 (2006), pp. 439–450; and Paul E. Mullen et al., "Study of Stalkers," *American Journal of Psychiatry*, Vol. 156 (August 1999), pp. 1244–1249.

262. Ibid.

263. Ibid., p. 8.

264. Ibid. See also P. Tjaden and N. Thoennes *Extent, Nature, and Consequences of Intimate Partner Violence: Findings from the National Violence Against Women Survey* (Washington, DC: U.S. Department of Justice, 2000).

265. Tjaden and Thoennes, *Stalking in America*.

266. Ibid., p. 8.

267. Ibid., p. 10.

268. Ibid.

269. Ibid.

270. T. Gregorie, *Cyberstalking: Dangers on the Information Highway* (Arlington, VA: National Center for Victims of Crime, 2000).

271. Janet Reno, *Cyberstalking: A New Challenge for Law Enforcement and Industry—A Report from the U.S. Attorney General to the Vice President* (Washington, DC: U.S. Department of Justice, 1999).

CHAPTER 10: CRIMES AGAINST PROPERTY

1. William Spain, "Art Crime of the Century Still Frustrates: Empty Frames Still Hang in Boston Museum," APB News, June 16, 2000, http://apbnews.com/newscenter/breakingnews/2000/06/16/artcrime_gardner0161_01.html (accessed December 1, 2000).

2. William Spain, "Inside the World of Art Theft: Trade Ranks Third after Drugs, Arms Sales," APB News, June 16, 2000, http://apbnews.com/newscenter/breakingnews/2000/06/16/artcrime0616_01.html (accessed September 3, 2004).

3. Ibid.

4. Ibid.

5. Ibid.

6. Cited in Thomas Gabor, *Everybody Does It! Crime by the Public* (Toronto: University of Toronto Press, 1994), p. 11.

7. Edwin Sutherland, *The Professional Thief* (Chicago, IL: University of Chicago Press, 1937), p. 172.

8. Neal Shover, *Great Pretenders: Pursuits and Careers of Persistent Thieves* (Boulder, CO: Westview, 1996). p. xiii.

9. Ibid., pp. xii–xiii.

10. Ibid., p. 63.

11. Mark S. Fleisher, *Beggars and Thieves: Lives of Urban Street Criminals* (Madison: University of Wisconsin Press, 1995).

12. Malcolm W. Klein, "Offense Specialization and Versatility among Juveniles," *British Journal of Criminology*, Vol. 24 (1984), pp. 185–194.

13. Ibid., p. 186.

14. Neil Shover, "Burglary," in Michael Tonry, ed., *Crime and Justice: A Review of Research* (Chicago: University of Chicago Press, 1991).

15. See Shover, *Great Pretenders*; and Shover, "Burglary."

16. John R. Hepburn, "Occasional Property Crime," in Robert F. Meier, ed., *Major Forms of Crime* (Beverly Hills, CA: Sage, 1984).

17. Ibid., p. 76.

18. Richard T. Wright and Scott H. Decker, *Burglars on the Job: Streetlife and Residential Break-Ins* (Boston: Northeastern University Press, 1994), p. 35.

19. See Center for Problem-Oriented Policing, "Crime Analysis for Problem Solvers in 60 Small Steps," from which the wording for this definition is taken, http://www.popcenter.org/learning/60steps/index.cfm?stepNum=10 (accessed May 31, 2007).

20. Neil Alan Weiner, "Violent Criminal Careers and 'Violent Career Criminals': An Overview of the Research Literature," in Neil Alan Weiner and Marvin E. Wolfgang, eds., *Violent Crime, Violent Criminals* (Newbury Park, CA: Sage, 1989), p. 39.

21. A. Blumstein et al., eds., *Criminal Careers and "Career Criminals,"* 2 vols. (Washington, DC: National Academy Press, 1986).

22. D. S. Elliott, "Serious Violent Offenders: Onset, Developmental Course, and Termination: 1993 Presidential Address," *Criminology*, Vol. 32, No. 1 (1994), pp. 1–22. See also D. S. Elliott, D. Huizinga, and B. Morse, "Self-Reported Violent Offending: A Descriptive Analysis of Juvenile Violent Offenders and Their Offending Careers," *Journal of Interpersonal Violence*, Vol. 1, No. 4 (1987), pp. 472–514.

23. Michael R. Gottfredson and Travis Hirschi, "Science, Public Policy, and the Career Paradigm," *Criminology*, Vol. 26 (1988), pp. 37–55.

24. Fleisher, *Beggars and Thieves*, p. 11.

25. Ibid., p. 10.

26. Ibid., p. 11.

27. Dermot Walsh, "Victim Selection Procedures among Economic Criminals: The Rational Choice Perspective," in Derek B. Cornish and Ronald V. Clarke, eds., *The Reasoning Criminal: Rational Choice Perspectives on Offending* (New York: Springer-Verlag, 1986), p. 40.

28. Ibid., p. 50.

29. Thomas Bennett and Richard Wright, *Burglars on Burglary* (Aldershot, Hants, England: Gower, 1984).

30. Walsh, "Victim Selection Procedures among Economic Criminals," p. 50.

31. Neil Shover and David Honaker, "The Socially Bounded Decision Making of Persistent Property Offenders," *Howard Journal*, Vol. 31, No. 4 (1992), p. 290.

32. Ramona R. Rantala and Thomas J. Edwards, *Effects of NIBRS on Crime Statistics* (Washington, DC: Office of Justice Programs, 2000), p. 12.

33. President's Commission on Law Enforcement and Administration of Justice, *The Challenge of Crime in a Free Society* (New York: Avon, 1968), p. 64.

34. David Barry, "Thieves Peel Off with 1,200 Orange Trees: Culprits Strike California Groves at Night," APB News, November 27, 2000, http://www.apbnews.com/newscenter/breakingnews/2000/11/27/trees1127_01.html (accessed December 1, 2000).

35. Federal Bureau of Investigation, *Crime in the United States, 2009* (Washington, DC: U.S. Department of Justice, 2010).

36. Bureau of Justice Statistics, *Criminal Victimization, 1999* (Washington, DC: BJS, 2000), Table 84.

37. Richard C. Hollinger and Lynn Langton, *2003 National Retail Security Survey: Final Report* (Tallahassee: University of Florida, 2004).

38. Gabor, *Everybody Does It!* p. 80.

39. "Worker Theft Robs Firms of Far More Than Shoplifters Do," *Kansas City Star*, February 27, 2010, http://www.kansascity.com/2010/02/27/1778475/thefts-by-employees-are-a-big.html (accessed May 3, 2010).

40. Lloyd W. Klemke, *The Sociology of Shoplifting: Boosters and Snitches Today* (Santa Barbara, CA: Greenwood, 1992), p. 16.

41. Silverman, "Crime and Punishment."

42. "Ryder Sentenced, No Prison Time," *USA Today*, December 9, 2002, http://www.usatoday.com/life/2002_12_06_winona_sentenced_x.htm (accessed January 5, 2006).

43. Klemke, *The Sociology of Shoplifting*.

44. Lloyd W. Klemke, "Exploring Juvenile Shoplifting," *Sociology and Social Research*, Vol. 67, No. 1 (1982), pp. 59–75.

45. Mary Owen Cameron, *The Booster and the Snitch: Department Store Shoplifting* (New York: Free Press of Glencoe, 1964).

46. Klemke, "Exploring Juvenile Shoplifting," p. 62.

47. JoAnn Ray, "Every Twelfth Shopper: Who Shoplifts and Why?" *Social Casework*, Vol. 68 (1987).

48. Klemke, "Exploring Juvenile Shoplifting," p. 71.

49. Ibid. For support for this point, see also Robert Sampson and John Laub, "Crime and Deviance over the Life Course: The Salience of Adult Social Bonds," *American Sociological Review*, Vol. 55, No. 5 (1990), pp. 609–627; and David Farrington, "Age and Crime," in Michael Tonry and Norval Morris, eds., *Crime and Justice: An Annual Review of Research*, Vol. 7 (Chicago: University of Chicago Press, 1986).

50. J. Kivivuori, "The Case of Temporally Intensified Shoplifting Behavior," *British Journal of Criminology*, Vol. 38, No. 4, p. 678.

51. Terrie Moffitt, "Adolescence-Limited and Life-Course Persistent Antisocial Behavior: A Developmental Taxonomy," *Psychological Review*, Vol. 100, No. 4 (1993), pp. 674–701.

52. Kivivuori, "The Case of Temporally Intensified Shoplifting."

53. Frederick M. Thrasher, *The Gang: A Study of 1,313 Gangs in Chicago* (Chicago: University of Chicago Press, 1927).

54. Kenneth D. Tunnell, *Choosing Crime: The Criminal Calculus of Property Offenders* (Chicago: Nelson-Hall, 1992), p. 122.

55. Cameron, *The Booster and the Snitch*.

56. Richard H. Moore, "Shoplifting in Middle America: Patterns and Motivational Correlates," *International Journal of Offender Therapy and Comparative Criminology*, Vol. 23, No. 1 (1984), pp. 55–64.

57. Frank J. McShane and Barrie A. Noonan, "Classification of Shoplifters by Cluster Analysis," *International Journal of Offender Therapy and Comparative Criminology*, Vol. 37, No. 1 (1993), pp. 29–40.

58. Ibid., p. 35.

59. Ibid., p. 36.

60. Ibid.

61. Jack Katz, *Seductions of Crime: Moral and Sensual Attractions in Doing Evil* (New York: Basic Books, 1988).

62. Ibid., p. 9.

63. Marcus Felson, *Crime and Everyday Life* (Thousand Oaks, CA: Pine Forge, 1998), p. 75.

64. Student Right to Know and Campus Security Act of 1990 (aka "The Clery Act"), Public Law 101–542.

65. Magnus Seng, "Theft on Campus: An Analysis of Larceny-Theft at an Urban University," *Journal of Crime and Justice*, Vol. 19, No. 1 (1996), p. 34.

66. Ibid., p. 36.

67. Ibid., 40.

68. Elizabeth Ehrhardt Mustaine and Richard Tewksbury, "Predicting Risks of Larceny Theft Victimization: A Routine Activity Analysis Using Refined Lifestyle Measures," *Criminology*, Vol. 36, No. 4 (1998), pp. 829–858.

69. Ibid., p. 852.

70. FBI, *Crime in the United States, 2009*.

71. BJS, *Criminal Victimization, 1999*, Tables 87 and 89.

72. Ibid.

73. Ibid.

74. Felson, *Crime and Everyday Life*, p. 32.

75. Jennifer L. Truman and Michael R. Rand, *Criminal Victimization, 2009* (Washington, DC: Bureau of Justice Statistics, 2010).

76. Ibid.

77. Caroline Wolf Harlow, *Motor Vehicle Theft* (Washington, DC: Bureau of Justice Statistics, 1988).

78. Kevin Blake, "What You Should Know about Car Theft," *Consumer's Research*, October 1995, cited in Terance D. Miethe and Richard McCorkle, *Crime Profiles: The Anatomy of Dangerous Persons, Places, and Situations* (Los Angeles: Roxbury, 1998), p. 156.

79. "Japanese Cars Top Thieves' Wish Lists," APB News, November 14, 2000, http://www.apbnews.com/newscenter/breakingnews/2000/11/14/cartheft/1114_01.htm (accessed December 1, 2000).

80. Ibid.

81. Miethe and McCorkle, *Crime Profiles*.

82. Public Law No. 98–547, 98 Stat. 2754 (1984).

83. Patricia M. Harris and Ronald V. Clarke, "Car Chopping, Parts Marking and the Motor Vehicle Theft Law Enforcement Act of 1984," *Sociology and Social Research*, Vol. 75 (1991).

84. Ibid., p. 228.

85. Joanna Sallybanks and Nerys Thomas, "Thefts of External Vehicle Parts: An Emerging Problem," *Crime Prevention and Community Safety: An International Journal*, Vol. 2 (2000), pp. 17–22.

86. Ibid., p. 18.

87. Miethe and McCorkle, *Crime Profiles*, p. 156.

88. Michael Gottfredson and Travis Hirschi, *A General Theory of Crime* (Stanford, CA: Stanford University Press, 1990), p. 35.

89. Ronald V. Clarke and Patricia M. Harris, "Auto Theft and Its Prevention," in Tonry, ed., *Crime and Justice*.

90. Miethe and McCorkle, *Crime Profiles*; and Clarke and Harris, "Auto Theft and Its Prevention."

91. William W. Wattenberg and James Balliestri, "Automobile Theft: A Favored Group Delinquency," *American Journal of Sociology*, Vol. 57 (1952).

92. Miethe and McCorkle, *Crime Profiles*.

93. For research reporting no effect of social class, see Charles H. McCaghy, Peggy C. Giordano, and Trudy Knicely Henson, "Auto Theft: Offender and Offense Characteristics," *Criminology*, Vol. 15 (1977), pp. 367–385.

94. Pierre Trembley, Yvan Clermont, and Maurice Cusson, "Jockeys and Joyriders: Changing Patterns in Car Theft Opportunity Structures," *British Journal of Criminology*, Vol. 34, No. 3 (1994), p. 314.

95. Ibid.

96. Clarke and Harris, "Auto Theft and Its Prevention," p. 23.

97. President's Commission, *The Challenge of Crime in a Free Society*, p. 64.

98. Herbert Koppel, *Lifetime Likelihood of Victimization* (Washington, DC: Bureau of Justice Statistics, 1987).

99. FBI, *Crime in the United States, 2009*.

100. Ibid.

101. Shover, *Great Pretenders*, p. 64.

102. Shover, "Burglary."

103. For representative examples of this perspective, see Michael J. Hindelang, *Criminal Victimization in Eight American Cities* (Cambridge, MA: Ballinger, 1978); and Michael J. Hindelang, Michael R. Gottfredson, and James Garolfalo, *Victims of Personal Crime: An Empirical Foundation for a Theory of Personal Victimization* (Cambridge, MA: Ballinger, 1978).

104. For representative discussions of this perspective, see Lawrence E. Cohen and Marcus Felson, "Social Change and Crime Rate Trends: A Routine Activity Approach," *American Sociological Review*, Vol. 44 (1979), pp. 588–607; and Marcus Felson and Lawrence E. Cohen, "Human Ecology and Crime: A Routine Activity Approach," *Human Ecology*, Vol. 8 (1980), pp. 398–405.

105. Marcus Felson, "Linking Criminal Choices, Routine Activities, Informal Control, and Criminal Outcomes," in Derek B. Cornish and Ronald V. Clarke, eds., *The Reasoning Criminal: Rational Choice Perspectives on Offending* (New York: Springer-Verlag, 1986), p. 127.

106. Lawrence E. Cohen and David Cantor, "Residential Burglary in the United States: Life-Style and Demographic Factors Associated with the Probability of Victimization," *Journal of Research in Crime and Delinquency*, Vol. 18, No. 1 (1981), pp. 113–127.

107. Robert J. Sampson and John D. Wooldredge, "Linking the Micro- and Macro-Level Dimensions of Lifestyle-Routine Activity and Opportunity Models of Predatory Victimization," *Journal of Quantitative Criminology*, Vol. 3 (1987), pp. 371–393.

108. Ibid.

109. Mike Maguire, *Burglary in a Dwelling* (London: Heinemann, 1982), cited in Shover, "Burglary," p. 89.

110. Shover, "Burglary," p. 90.

111. Ibid., p. 91.

112. Miethe and McCorkle, *Crime Profiles*.

113. Bureau of Justice Statistics, *Criminal Victimization, 1999*, Table 59.

114. Tunnell, *Choosing Crime*, p. 5.

115. See Paul F. Cromwell, James N. Olson, and D'Aunn Wester Avary, *Breaking and Entering: An Ethnographic Analysis of Burglary* (Newbury Park, CA: Sage, 1991); and Wright and Decker, *Burglars on the Job*.

116. Cromwell, Olson, and Avary, *Breaking and Entering*.

117. Wright and Decker, *Burglars on the Job*.

118. Ibid., p. 38.

119. Ibid., pp. 45–46.

120. Ibid., p. 47.

121. Wright and Decker, *Burglars on the Job*, p. 51.

122. Ibid.

123. Ibid., p. 56.

124. Ibid.

125. Katz, *Seductions of Crime*, p. 79.

126. Tunnell, *Choosing Crime*, p. 41.

127. Wright and Decker, *Burglars on the Job*, p. 63.

128. Ibid.

129. Wright and Decker, *Burglars on the Job*, p. 72.

130. Ibid., p. 73.

131. Shover, "Burglary," p. 83.

132. Ibid., p. 80.

133. Ibid., p. 110.

134. Ibid., p. 113.

135. Ibid., p. 86.

136. Bureau of Justice Statistics, *Criminal Victimization, 1999*, Tables 81 and 83.

137. Ibid., Tables 87 and 89.

138. Laura Dugan, "The Effect of Criminal Victimization on a Household's Moving Decision," *Criminology*, Vol. 37, No. 4 (1999), pp. 903–930.

139. Eric Baumer et al., "The Influence of Crack Cocaine on Robbery, Burglary, and Homicide Rates: A Cross-City, Longitudinal Analysis," *Journal of Research in Crime and Delinquency*, Vol. 35, No. 3 (1998), pp. 316–340.

140. Ibid., p. 317.

141. Ibid.

142. Ibid., p. 319.

143. Louis B. Schlesinger and Eugene Revitch, "Sexual Burglaries and Sexual Homicide: Clinical, Forensic, and Investigative Considerations," *Journal of the American Academy of Psychiatry and the Law*, Vol. 27, No. 2 (1999), p. 228.

144. Ibid., p. 232.

145. Mark Warr, "Rape, Burglary, and Opportunity," *Journal of Quantitative Criminology*, Vol. 4, No. 3 (1988), pp. 275–288.

146. Ibid., pp. 217–218.

147. Ibid., p. 287.

148. Ibid., p. 286.

149. Darrell J. Steffensmeier, *The Fence: In the Shadow of Two Worlds* (Savage, MD: Rowman and Littlefield, 1986), p. 10.

150. Ibid., p. 9.

151. Ibid. See also Wright and Decker, *Burglars on the Job*.

152. Steffensmeier, *The Fence*, p. 9.

153. Ibid.

154. Carl B. Klockars, *The Professional Fence* (New York: Free Press, 1974).

155. Steffensmeier, *The Fence*.

156. Ibid., p. 13.

157. Ibid.

158. Cromwell, Olson, and Avary, *Breaking and Entering*.

159. Wright and Decker, *Burglars on the Job*, p. 167.

160. Shover, "Burglary," p. 103.

161. Wright and Decker, *Burglars on the Job*, p. 169.

162. Steffensmeier, *The Fence*, p. 25.

163. Ibid., p. 23.

164. Ibid., p. 21.

165. Wright and Decker, *Burglars on the Job*, p. 179.

166. Ibid., pp. 175–176.

167. Cromwell, Olson, and Avary, *Breaking and Entering*, p. 74.

168. Ibid., p. 75.

169. Cromwell, Olson, and Avary, *Breaking and Entering*, p. 76.

170. Ibid., p. 77.

171. Ibid.

172. Stuart Henry, *The Hidden Economy: The Context and Control of Borderline Crime* (Oxford, England: Martin Robertson, 1978).

173. FBI, *Crime in the United States, 2009*.

174. Ibid.

175. Sarah A. Soule and Nella Van Dyke, "Black Church Arson in the United States, 1989–1996," *Ethnic and Racial Studies*, Vol. 22, No. 4 (1999), p. 725.

176. Public Law 104–155.

177. "Report Issued on Church Burnings," *Christian Century*, Vol. 114, No. 19 (June 18, 1997).

178. Ken Brownlee, "Ignoring Juvenile Arson Is Like Playing with Fire," *Claims*, Vol. 48, No. 3 (March 2000), p. 106.

179. Ibid.

180. FBI, *Crime in the United States, 2004* (Washington, DC: U.S. Department of Justice, 2005).

181. Eileen M. Garry, *Juvenile Firesetting and Arson*, Office of Juvenile Justice and Delinquency Prevention Fact Sheet 51 (Washington, DC: Office of Juvenile Justice and Delinquency Prevention, 1997).

182. Ibid., p. 1.

CHAPTER 11: WHITE-COLLAR AND ORGANIZED CRIME

1. Gina Bellafante, "Con Man and Cops, with I.Q. to Spare," *New York Times*, October 22, 2009, www.nytimes.com/2009/10/23/arts/television/23white.html (accessed May 18, 2010).

2. Randee Dawn, "White Collar TV Review," *Hollywood Reporter*, October 20, 2009, http://www.hollywoodreporter.com/hr/tv-reviews/white-collar-tv-review-1004026273.story (accessed May 18, 2010).

3. Bellafante, "Con Man and Cops."

4. Dawn, "White Collar TV Review."

5. "White Collar Premiere Averages 5.4 Million Viewers," By the Numbers, http://tvbythenumbers.com/2009/10/26/white-collar-premiere-averages-5-4-million-viewers/31572 (accessed May 18, 2010).

6. Barnaby J. Feder and Seth Schiesel, "WorldCom Finds $3.3 Billion More in Irregularities," *New York Times*, August 9, 2002, p. 1A.

7. Deborah Solomon, Jerry Markson, and Susan Pulliam, "WorldCom's Sullivan, Yates Are Indicted by Grand Jury," *Wall Street Journal*, August 28, 2002.

8. Devlin Barrett, "Waksal Pleads Guilty to Six Charges," Associated Press, October 15, 2002.

9. "Analyzing the Analysts: More Trouble for Street," *Wall Street Journal*, August 2, 2002, http://online.wsj.com/page/0,,2_0807,00.html (accessed January 23, 2006).

10. Thor Valdmanis, "Some Investors Balk at $1.4 Billion Wall Street Deal," *USA Today*, December 23, 2002, http://www.usatoday.com/money/companies/regulation/2002–12–23-settle_x.htm (accessed February 28, 2007).

11. Edwin H. Sutherland, "White-Collar Criminality," *American Sociological Review*, Vol. 5, No. 1 (February 1940), pp. 2–10.

12. Ibid.

13. Ibid.

14. Edwin H. Sutherland, "White-Collar Criminality," in Gilbert Geis, ed., *White Collar Criminal: The Offender in Business and the Professions* (Piscataway, NJ: Transaction Publishers, 2006) p. 41.

15. Edwin H. Sutherland, "Crime of Corporations," in Albert Cohen, Alfred Lindesmith, and Karl Schuessler, eds., *The Sutherland Papers* (Bloomington: Indiana University Press, 1956), pp. 78–96.

16. Ibid.

17. Ibid.

18. Sutherland, "White-Collar Criminality."

19. Travis Hirschi and Michael Gottfredson, "Causes of White-Collar Crime," *Criminology*, Vol. 25, No. 4 (1987), p. 952.

20. Donald J. Newman, "White-Collar Crime: An Overview and Analysis," *Law and Contemporary Problems*, Vol. 23, No. 4 (autumn 1958).

21. President's Commission on Law Enforcement and Administration of Justice, *The Challenge of Crime in a Free Society* (Washington, DC: U.S. Government Printing Office, 1967), p. 47.

22. For excellent reviews of the evolution of the concept of white-collar crime, see K. Schlegel and D. Weisburd, "White-Collar Crime: The Parallax View," in Kip Schlegel and David Weisburd, eds., *White-Collar Crime Reconsidered* (Boston: Northeastern University Press, 1992), pp. 3–27; and K. Schlegel and D. Weisburd, "Returning to the Mainstream: Reflections on Past and Future White-Collar Crime Study," in Schlegel and Weisburd, eds., *White-Collar Crime Reconsidered*, pp. 352–365.

23. Task Force on Organized Crime, *Organized Crime* (Washington, DC: U.S. Government Printing Office, 1976).

24. Ibid.

25. Herbert Edelhertz, *The Nature, Impact and Prosecution of White-Collar Crime* (Washington, DC: National Institute of Law Enforcement and Criminal Justice, 1970).

26. Gilbert Geis, "Upperworld Crime," in Abraham S. Blumberg, ed., *Current Perspectives on Criminal Behavior: Original Essays on Criminology* (New York: Alfred A. Knopf, 1974).

27. Gary S. Green, *Occupational Crime* (Chicago: Nelson-Hall, 1990).

28. Ibid.

29. Michael L. Benson, Francis T. Cullen, and William J. Maakestad, *Local Prosecutors and Corporate Crime* (Washington, DC: National Institute of Justice, 1993).

30. Jonathan D. Glater and Kurt Eichenwald, "Audit Lapse at WorldCom Puzzles Some," *New York Times*, June 28, 2002, p. 1C.

31. *Arthur Andersen LLP v. United States*, 544 U.S. 696 (2005).

32. "Epoxy Company Indicted for Manslaughter in Big Dig Death," *Tollroads News*, August 8, 2007, http://www.tollroadsnews.com/node/3063 (accessed April 10, 2010).

33. "Epoxy Company to Pay Millions in Big Dig Collapse," WBZ-TV, December 17, 2008, http://wbztv.com/bigdig/big.dig.agreement.2.889425.html (accessed April 9, 2010).

34. Federal Bureau of Investigation, *Financial Crimes Report to the Public, Fiscal Year 2007*, http://www.fbi.gov/publications/financial/fcs_report2007/financial_crime_2007.htm#financial (accessed May 10, 2010), from which much of the material in this section is derived.

35. Ibid.

36. Ibid.

37. Ibid.

38. Ibid.

39. Ibid.

40. Ibid.

41. Clifford Karchmer and Douglas Ruch, "State and Local Money Laundering Control Strategies," *NIJ Research in Brief* (Washington, DC: National Institute of Justice, 1992), p. 1.

42. "Wachovia to Pay $160M Settlement," *Business Journal*, March 18, 2010, http://www.bizjournals.com/triad/stories/2010/03/15/daily30.html (accessed May 2, 2010).

43. U.S. Code, Title 18, Section 1956.

44. U.S. Drug Enforcement Administration, "Money Laundering," http://www.usdoj.gov/dea/programs/money.htm (accessed June 18, 2007).

45. See Bernie Becker, "U.S. Report Details Money Laundering," *The New York Times*, February 4, 2010, http://dealbook.blogs.nytimes.com/2010/02/04/us-report-details-money-laundering (accessed August 24, 2010).

46. Of course, environmental damage inflicted by corporations may not only violate criminal statutes but also result in civil liability.

47. "Alaska Hit by 'Massive' Oil Spill," BBC News, March 11, 2006, http://news.bbc.co.uk/2/hi/americas/4795866.stm (accessed May 2, 2010).

48. "BP Fined $60 Million for Alaska Oil Spill, Texas Air Toxics," Environment News Service, November 1, 2007, http://www.ens-newswire.com/ens/nov2007/2007-11-01-095.asp (accessed May 2, 2010).

49. John Kane and April Wall, "Identifying the Links between White-Collar Crime and Terrorism," National White Collar Crime Center, September 2004.

50. Sutherland, "White-Collar Criminality."

51. Ibid.

52. Ibid.

53. Hirschi and Gottfredson, "Causes of White-Collar Crime," p. 949.

54. Ibid., p. 951.

55. Ibid., p. 956.

56. Ibid.

57. Braithwaite began many of his studies of white-collar crime with investigations into the criminal activities of pharmaceutical company executives. See, for example, John Braithwaite, *Corporate Crime in the Pharmaceutical Industry* (London: Routledge and Kegan Paul, 1984).

58. For a test of this thesis, see Anne Jenkins and John Braithwaite, "Profits, Pressure and Corporate Lawbreaking," *Crime, Law, and Social Change*, Vol. 20, No. 3 (1993), pp. 221–232.

59. John Braithwaite, "Poverty, Power, White-Collar Crime and the Paradoxes of Criminological Theory," *Australian and New Zealand Journal of Criminology*, Vol. 24, No. 1 (1991), pp. 40–48.

60. John Braithwaite and Gilbert Geis, "On Theory and Action for Corporate Crime Control," *Crime and Delinquency*, Vol. 28, No. 2 (1982), pp. 292–314. See also Brent Fisse and John Braithwaite, *The Impact of Publicity on Corporate Offenders* (Albany: State University of New York Press, 1983).

61. Brent Fisse and John Braithwaite, "Accountability and the Control of Corporate Crime: Making the Buck Stop," in Mark Findlay and Russell Hogg, eds., *Understanding Crime and Criminal Justice* (North Ryde, Australia: Law, 1988), pp. 93–127.

62. Brent Fisse and John Braithwaite, *Corporations, Crime and Accountability* (New York: Cambridge University Press, 1994).

63. John Braithwaite, "Criminological Theory and Organizational Crime," *Justice Quarterly*, Vol. 6, No. 3 (1989), pp. 333–358.

64. Joan Biskupic, "Why It's Tough to Indict CEOs," *USA Today*, July 24, 2002, p. 1A.

65. Ibid.

66. Ibid.

67. John R. Wilke, *Wall Street Journal* Online, July 17, 2007, http://online.wsj.com/article/SB118469845609569168.html (accessed September 1, 2007).

68. Ibid.

69. U.S. Code, Title 15, Section 1.

70. U.S. Code, Title 15, Sections 12–27.

71. U.S. Code, Title 15, Section 77.

72. U.S. Code, Title 15, Section 78.

73. Newman, "White-Collar Crime."

74. Green, *Occupational Crime*, p. 256.

75. James William Coleman, *The Criminal Elite: The Sociology of White-Collar Crime*, 3rd ed. (New York: St. Martin's Press, 1994).

76. This information is taken from the Center for Innovation in Corporate Responsibility's home page, http://www.cicr.net (accessed January 2, 2007).

77. Much of the information in this section comes from Julian Symons, *A Pictorial History of Crime* (New York: Bonanza, 1966).

78. Ibid.

79. Howard Abadinsky, *Organized Crime*, 9e (New York: Wadsworth, 2009).

80. The original article is available in the *New York Times* Online archive at http://query.nytimes.com/mem/archive-free/pdf?_r=1&res=9506EED61F38E033A25751C2A9669D94699FD7CF.

81. "By Order of the Mafia," *New York Times*, October 22, 1888, http://query.nytimes.com/mem/archive-free/pdf?_r=1&res=9506EED61F38E033A25751C2A9669D94699FD7CF (accessed April 10, 2010).

82. Ibid., p. 112.

83. Luigi Barzini, *The Italians* (New York: Atheneum, 1965).

84. Abadinsky, *Organized Crime*.

85. Abadinsky, *Organized Crime*, p. 173.

86. Ibid.

87. John Kilber, *Capone: The Life and World of Al Capone* (Greenwich, CT: Fawcett, 1971).

88. See Mark H. Haller, "Illegal Enterprise: A Theoretical and Historical Interpretation," *Criminology*, Vol. 28, No. 2 (May 1990), p. 209.

89. President's Commission on Law Enforcement and Administration of Justice, *Task Force Report: Organized Crime* (Washington, DC: U.S. Government Printing Office, 1967).

90. Anthony E. Simpson, *The Literature of Police Corruption* (New York: John Jay Press, 1977).

91. Robert W. Ferguson, *The Nature of Vice Control in the Administration of Justice* (St. Paul, MN: West, 1974), p. 379.

92. Symons, *A Pictorial History of Crime*, p. 226.

93. President's Commission, *The Challenge of Crime in a Free Society*, p. 196.

94. Special Committee to Investigate Organized Crime in Interstate Commerce, U.S. Senate, 82nd Congress, 1951.

95. President's Commission, *The Challenge of Crime in a Free Society*, p. 192, citing the Kefauver Committee report.

96. Ibid.

97. *United States* v. *Bufalino*, 285 F.2d. 408 (2nd. Cir. 1960).

98. The quotations attributed to the 1967 President's Commission report in this section are from President's Commission, *The Challenge of Crime in a Free Society*, p. 195.

99. This information is taken from Abadinsky, *Organized Crime*.

100. Ibid.

101. President's Commission on Law Enforcement and Administration of Justice, *Task Force Report: Organized Crime* (Washington, DC: U.S. Government Printing Office, 1967).

102. See, for example, "Corleone Family Rules," http://www.webmaze.com/memberpages/doncorleone/rules.html (accessed April 2, 2007). See also "Santino's Mafia Code," http://organizedcrime.about.com/newsissues/organizedcrime/blsantino_1.htm (accessed April 2, 2007).

103. President's Commission, *The Challenge of Crime in a Free Society*.

104. President's Commission, *Task Force Report: Organized Crime*, p. 41.

105. Abadinsky, *Organized Crime*.

106. Ibid., p. 5.

107. U.S. Code, Title 21, Section 848(c)(2).

108. New York Penal Law, Section 460.00.

109. New York Penal Law, Section 460.10(3).

110. Much of the information and the quotes in this section come from FBI, "Organized Crime: Eurasian Organized Crime," http://www.fbi.gov/hq/cid/orgcrime/eocindex.htm (accessed May 20, 2010).

111. Ibid.

112. Ibid.

113. Much of the information and the quotes in this section come from FBI, "Organized Crime: Asian Criminal Enterprises," http://www.fbi.gov/hq/cid/orgcrime/asiancrim.htm (accessed May 20, 2010).

114. Ibid.

115. Ibid.

116. Much of the information and the quotes in this section come from FBI, "Organized Crime: African Criminal Enterprise," http://www.fbi.gov/hq/cid/orgcrime/africancrim.htm (accessed May 20, 2010).

117. Ibid.

118. Much of the information and the quotes in this section come from FBI, "Organized Crime: Middle Eastern Criminal Enterprises," http://www.fbi.gov/hq/cid/orgcrime/middle_eastern.htm (accessed May 20, 2010).

119. Ibid.

120. Laurie Robinson, address given at the Twelfth International Congress on Criminology, Seoul, South Korea, August 28, 1998.

121. See United Nations Office on Drugs and Crime, *United Nations Congresses on Crime Prevention and Criminal Justice 1955-2010: 55 Years of Achievement* (New York: United Nations Information Service, 2011).

122. Ibid.

123. Richard Lindberg and Vesna Markovic, *Organized Crime Outlook in the New Russia: Russia Is Paying the Price of a Market Economy in Blood*, Search International, http://www.search-international.com/Articles/crime/russiacrime.htm (accessed January 4, 2007).

124. Ibid.

125. Gary T. Dempsey, "Is Russia Controlled by Organized Crime?" *USA Today*, May 1999.

126. Lindberg and Markovic, *Organized Crime Outlook in the New Russia*.

127. Dempsey, "Is Russia Controlled by Organized Crime?"

128. Lindberg and Markovic, *Organized Crime Outlook in the New Russia*.

129. Ibid.

130. P.L. 91-452, 84 Stat. 922.

131. For a cogent analysis of RICO, see Cliff Roberson, "RICO Is 40 Years Old," *Professional Issues in Criminal Justice*, Vol. 5, No. 1 (2010), http://kucampus.kaplan.edu/documentstore/Docs10/pdf/CJ/PICJ/PICJ_V5N1_Roberson_55_66.pdf (accessed May 2, 2010), pp. 55–66.

132. 18 U.S.C. Section 1961–1968.

133. Gary W. Potter, *Criminal Organizations: Vice, Racketeering, and Politics in an American City* (Prospect Heights, IL: Waveland, 1994), p. 183.

134. Ibid.

135. Ibid.

136. Abadinsky, *Organized Crime*.

137. "'Junior' Gotti Gets Nearly 6 1/2 Years," Associated Press, September 3, 1999.

138. "5-Year Prison Term for Mafia Turncoat," *USA Today*, September 27, 1994, p. 3A.

139. Peter Maas, *Underboss: Sammy the Bull Gravano's Story of Life in the Mafia* (New York: HarperCollins, 1997). According to Ronald Kuby, an attorney suing Gravano to reclaim book royalties under New York's "Son of Sam" law, a roundabout method had been used to pay Gravano in order to avoid the provisions of the law. Kuby claimed that documents would show that author Peter Maas, Gravano, HarperCollins, and International Creative Management (the agent for the book) had conspired to hide payments made to Gravano. To learn more about the case, visit http://www.crimelibrary.com/gangsters2/gravano/24.htm.

140. "'Sammy the Bull' Faces More Drug Charges," Associated Press, December 21, 2000.

CHAPTER 12: PUBLIC ORDER AND DRUG CRIMES

1. E. Eduardo Castillo, "Mexico Angered by Drug Lord's Spot on Forbes List," Associated Press, November 13, 2009.

2. "Mexico Drug Lord on Forbes Rich List with $1 Billion," Reuters, March 11, 2009.

3. This quote is taken from http://librearts.com/wsn8439.html (accessed September 21, 2007).

4. Data in this section are derived from Substance Abuse and Mental Health Services Administration, *2009 National Survey on Drug Use and Health* (Rockville, MD: SAMHSA, 2010).

5. Numbers total more than 100% because of rounding.

6. Drug Enforcement Administration, *Overview of Drug Use in the United States,* www.dea.gov/stats/overview.htm (accessed April 8, 2007).

7. Bureau of Justice Statistics, *Drug and Crime Facts, 1993* (Washington, DC: U.S. Department of Justice, August 1994).

8. Information in this section comes from National Institute on Drug Abuse, *Monitoring the Future: National Results on Adolescent Drug Use—Overview of Key Findings, 2009* (Bethesda, MD: National Institutes of Health, 2010).

9. Office of National Drug Control Policy, *Drug Data Summary Fact Sheet* (Washington, DC: ONDCP, March 2003), http://www .whitehousedrugpolicy.gov/pdf/drug_datasum.pdf (accessed May 18, 2007).

10. Ibid.

11. Mike Cooper, "CDC Charts Impact of AIDS among Blacks, Hispanics," Reuters, September 8, 1994.

12. National Institute on Drug Abuse and National Institute on Alcohol Abuse and Alcoholism, *The Economic Costs of Alcohol and Drug Abuse in the United States, 1992* (Washington, DC: U.S. Government Printing Office, 1998).

13. National Institute on Drug Abuse, *The Science of Addiction: Drugs, Brains, and Behavior* (Washington, DC: U.S. Department of Health and Human Services, 2007), p. 5.

14. National Institute on Drug Abuse, "NIDA InfoFacts: Understanding Drug Abuse and Addiction," http://www.drugabuse.gov/ infofacts/understand.html (accessed May 10, 2010).

15. Ibid.

16. National Narcotics Intelligence Consumers Committee, *The NNICC Report, 1996: The Supply of Illicit Drugs to the United States* (Arlington, VA: Drug Enforcement Administration, 1997), p. 69.

17. Most of the information in the paragraphs that follow is taken from ibid. and from the Office of National Drug Control Policy, *Pulse Check: Trends in Drug Abuse, January–June 1998* (Washington, DC: ONDCP, 1998).

18. Much of the information in this section comes from the National Institute on Drug Abuse's Web site, http://www.nida.nih.gov, (accessed January 6, 2007), and from the Office of National Drug Control Policy, *Pulse Check: Special Report; Methamphetamine Trends in Five Western States and Hawaii* (Washington, DC: ONDCP, 1997).

19. James A. Inciardi, *The War on Drugs II* (Mountain View, CA: Mayfield, 1992), p. 69.

20. Michael D. Lyman and Gary W. Potter, *Drugs in Society: Causes, Concepts and Control* (Cincinnati: Anderson, 1991), p. 45.

21. National Inhalant Prevention Coalition Web site, http://www .inhalants.org (accessed January 6, 2007).

22. Ibid.

23. Sherry Green, *Preventing Illegal Diversion of Chemicals: A Model Statute* (Washington, DC: National Institute of Justice, November 1993), p. 2.

24. Ibid., p. 79.

25. The provisions of the Domestic Chemical Diversion Control Act of 1993 became effective April 16, 1994.

26. Federal law and precedent have contributed to this definition.

27. National Briefing: "Largest Drug Seizure at Sea," *New York Times,* April 24, 2007, http://query.nytimes.com/gst/fullpage.html ?res=9801EEDD143EF937A15757C0A9619C8B63 (accessed May 10, 2007).

28. National Narcotics Intelligence Consumers Committee, *The NNICC Report, 1993* (Washington, DC: U.S. Government Printing Office, 1994).

29. Ibid., p. 35.

30. Bureau of Justice Statistics, *Drugs, Crime and the Justice System* (Washington, DC: U.S. Government Printing Office, 1992), p. 2.

31. Ibid.

32. Ibid., p. 2.

33. National Institute of Justice, *Arrestee Drug Abuse Monitoring (ADAM) Program: 2000 Annual Report* (Washington, DC: NIJ, 2003). One additional report was produced about the same time using somewhat later data: Zhiwei Zhang, *Drug and Alcohol Use and Related Matters Among Arrestees, 2003* (Washington, DC: NIJ, 2003).

34. Much of the material in this section is adapted from National Institute of Justice, Office of Justice Programs, "Study Shows Substantial Levels of Drug Use among Arrestees across the Nation," *OJP News,* July 20, 2000.

35. Bureau of Justice Statistics, *Drug and Crime Facts, 1993,* pp. 4–5.

36. Ibid.

37. Ibid.

38. Ibid.

39. Ibid.

40. "Study: Bad NYC Cops 'Criminals in Blue,'" United Press International wire service, Northeastern edition, July 7, 1994.

41. "Judgment on Corrections," *Washington Post* wire service, July 5, 1994.

42. Public Law 104–305.

43. "'Rophies' Reported Spreading Quickly throughout the South," *Drug Enforcement Report,* June 23, 1995, pp. 1–5.

44. Part of the USA PATRIOT Act Reauthorization Act (Public Law 109–177).

45. Public Law 109–177.

46. For an excellent overview of policy initiatives in the area of drug control, see Doris Layton MacKenzie and Craig D. Uchida, *Drugs and Crime: Evaluating Public Policy Initiatives* (Thousand Oaks, CA: Sage, 1994).

47. Federal Bureau of Investigation, *Crime in the United States, 2006* (Washington, DC: U.S. Department of Justice, 2007).

48. Ibid.

49. Drug Enforcement Administration, "Maps of Methamphetamine Lab Incidents," http://www.usdoj.gov/dea/concern/map_lab_seizures .html (accessed July 7, 2007).

50. Drug Enforcement Administration, "Stats & Facts," http://www.usdoj.gov/dea/statistics.html#seizures (accessed May 18, 2007).

51. Office of National Drug Control Policy, *National Drug Control Strategy: 2007 Annual Report* (Washington, DC: The White House, 2007), p. 89.

52. Drug Enforcement Administration, *National Drug Threat Assessment, 2007*, http://www.usdoj.gov/dea/concern/18862/marijuana.htm (accessed January 5, 2007).

53. 21 U.S. Code, Section 881(a)(6).

54. *United States v. James Daniel Good Real Property*, 510 U.S. 43, 81–82 (1993).

55. *Austin v. United States*, 113 S.Ct. 2801, 15 L.Ed.2d 448 (1993).

56. Fox Butterfield, *New York Times* news service, http://www.nytimes.com (accessed April 16, 1997), citing Office of Justice Programs, *Preventing Crime: What Works, What Doesn't, What's Promising* (Washington, DC: U.S. Department of Justice, 1997).

57. Much of the information in this section comes from Office of National Drug Control Policy, *National Drug Control Strategy: FY 2008 Budget Summary* (Washington, DC: ONDCP, 2007).

58. James A. Inciardi, *Criminal Justice* (Orlando, FL: Harcourt Brace Jovanovich, 1993), p. v.

59. J. Michael McWilliams, "Setting the Record Straight: Facts about Litigation Costs and Delay," *Business Economics*, Vol. 27, No. 4 (October 1992), p. 19.

60. Ibid.

61. Paige M. Marrison and Allen J. Beck, *Prisoners in 2005* (Washington, DC: U.S. Bureau of Justice Statistics, November 2006).

62. "Who Is in Federal Prison?" *Washington Post*, October 3, 1994.

63. Lyman and Potter, *Drugs in Society*, p. 316.

64. Inciardi, *The War on Drugs II*, p. 239.

65. Lyman and Potter, *Drugs in Society*, p. 316.

66. *Newsweek*, February 3, 1997, pp. 20–23.

67. Charlie Cain, "Stem Cell, Medical Marijuana Props Approved," *Detroit News*, November 5, 2008.

68. LD 975, Maine Medical Marijuana Act.

69. "New Medical Pot Policy Will Only Target State Lawbreakers," *USA Today*, October 19, 2009.

70. *United States v. Oakland Cannabis Buyers, Cooperative*, 532 U.S. 483 (2001).

71. "Medical Marijuana Arrest Guidelines Eased," CBS News, October 19, 2009, http://www.cbsnews.com/stories/2009/10/19/politics/main5395248.shtml (accessed May 20, 2010).

72. Dan Whitcomb, "Marijuana Legalization Will Be on California Ballot," Reuters, March 25, 2010.

73. Alison Stateman, "Can Marijuana Help Rescue California's Economy?" *Time*, March 13, 2009, http://www.time.com/time/nation/article/0,8599,1884956,00.html (accessed May 10, 2010).

74. Ibid.

75. Ibid.

76. Federal Bureau of Investigation, *Crime in the United States, 2006*.

77. John Stuart Mill, *On Liberty* (1859), chapter 1.

78. Much of the information in this section is derived from the Law Library: American Law and Legal Information, "Typology of Prostitution," *Crime and Justice*, Vol. 3, http://law.jrank.org/pages/1879/Prostitution-Typology-prostitution.html (accessed July 10, 2007).

79. Marilyn C. Moses, "Understanding and Applying Research on Prostitution," *NIJ Journal*, No. 255 (November 2006), http://www.ojp.usdoj.gov/nij/journals/255/prostitution_research.html (accessed July 25, 2007).

80. Martin A. Monto, *Focusing on the Clients of Street Prostitutes: A Creative Approach to Reducing Violence against Women*, final report submitted to the National Institute of Justice, Washington, DC: June 9, 2000, http://www.ncjrs.gov/pdffiles1/nij/grants/182860.pdf (accessed July 25, 2007).

81. Andrea Dworkin, *Intercourse* (New York: Free Press, 1987).

82. Ronald Weitzer, "The Growing Moral Panic over Prostitution and Sex Trafficking," *The Criminologist*, Vol. 30, No. 5 (September/October, 2005), pp. 1 and 3.

83. Ibid.

84. Janice G. Raymond, "10 Reasons for Not Legalizing Prostitution," Coalition against Trafficking in Women International, March 25, 2003, http://www.raperelishelter.bc.ca/issues/prostitution_legalizing.html (accessed July 25, 2007).

CHAPTER 13: TECHNOLOGY AND CRIME

1. Tony Castro, "Valley Gangs Leave Trail on Web," *Los Angeles Daily News*, December 5, 2009, www.dailynews.com/news/ci_13931149 (accessed May 12, 2010).

2. Ibid.

3. Ibid.

4. The White House, *The Comprehensive National Security Initiative*, http://www.whitehouse.gov/cybersecurity/comprehensive-national-cybersecurity-initiative.

5. Kenneth Rosenblatt, "Deterring Computer Crime," *Technology Review*, Vol. 93, No. 2 (February/March 1990), pp. 34–41.

6. Richard H. Baker, *The Computer Security Handbook* (Blue Ridge Summit, PA: TAB Books, 1985).

7. Catherine H. Conly and J. Thomas McEwen, "Computer Crime," *NIJ Reports*, January/February 1990.

8. David McGuire, "Study: Online Crime Costs Rising," *Washington Post*, May 24, 2004, http://www.washingtonpost.com/wp-dyn/articles/A53042-2004May24.html (accessed July 30, 2005).

9. Dan Briody, "Keep Out," *Inc.*, March 2007, http://www.inc.com/magazine/20070301/technology-security.html (accessed June 17, 2007).

10. Ponemon Institute, *Fourth Annual U.S. Cost of Data Breach Study: Benchmark Study of Companies* (Traverse City, MI: Ponemon Institute, January 2009), p. 4.

11. Software and Information Industry Association, *Report on Global Software Piracy 2000*, http://www.siia.net/piracy/pubs/piracy2000.pdf, p. 7.

12. Business Software Alliance, *Seventh Annual BSA/IDC Global Software Piracy Study* (BSA, May 2010), http://portal.bsa.org/globalpiracy2009/index.html (accessed August 28, 2010).

13. Gary H. Anthes, "Software Pirates' Booty Topped $13B, Study Finds," *Computerworld*, January 6, 1997, p. 24.

14. Stephen R. Purdy, "Protecting Your Telephone Systems against Dial-Tone Thieves," *Infosecurity News*, July/August 1993, p. 43.

15. Paul Keegan, "High Tech Pirates Collecting Phone Calls," *USA Today*, September 23, 1994, p. 4A.

16. Ibid.

17. Fraser Lovatt, "U.S. Department of Justice: VoIP Fosters Crime, Drugs and Terrorism," Digital-Lifestyles.info, June 18, 2004, http://digital-lifestyles.info/display_page.asp?section=business&id=1318 (accessed August 1, 2006).

18. The Anti-Phishing Working Group, "Phishing Activity Trends," http://www.antiphishing.org/reports/apwg_report_april_2007.pdf (accessed June 17, 2007).

19. Gregg Keizer, "Gartner: Phishing Attacks Threaten E-Commerce," Security Pipeline.com, www.securitypipeline.com/news/20000036 (accessed July 30, 2007).

20. This and most other definitions related to cybercrime in this chapter are taken from Donn B. Parker, *Computer Crime: Criminal Justice Resource Manual* (Washington, DC: National Institute of Justice, 1989).

21. "Palm, Other Handheld Devices to Face Virus Threats," Reuters, August 31, 2000, http://www.bostonherald.com/business/technology/palm08312000.htm (accessed January 11, 2006).

22. Joseph Menn, "Police Shut Down Hacker Ring," *Financial Times*, March 4, 2010.

23. Public Law 107–296 (Homeland Security Act), Section 225.

24. Public Law 106–160.

25. Public Law 105–147.

26. U.S. Code, Title 18, Section 1030.

27. Public Law 104–294 as amended by the National Information Infrastructure Protection Act of 1996.

28. U.S. Code, Title 18, Section 1029.

29. M. Gemiganni, "Viruses and Computer Law," *Communications of the ACM*, Vol. 32 (June 1989), p. 669.

30. Section 290001(a) of Pub. L. 103-322, as amended by Pub. L. 104-294, title VI, Sec. 604(b)(34).

31. Section 225 of the Homeland Security Act of 2002 (H.R. 5710).

32. The following quotes are taken from Public Law 104–104, 110 Stat. 56.

33. *Reno v. ACLU*, 521 U.S. 844 (1997).

34. Texas Penal Code, Section 33.01.

35. Virginia Criminal Code, Sections 18.2–152.2 through 18.2–152.7.

36. Brian S. Akre, "Internet-Torture," Associated Press, February 10, 1995.

37. Ibid.

38. Jim Schaefer and Maryanne George, "Internet User's Charges Dismissed—U.S. Criticized for Pursuing U-M Case," *Detroit Free Press*, June 22, 1995.

39. Parker, *Computer Crime*.

40. Steve Miletich, no title, *Seattle Post-Intelligencer*, via Simon & Schuster NewsLink Online, May 21, 1997.

41. Paul Saffo, "Desperately Seeking Cyberspace," *Personal Computing*, May 1989, p. 247.

42. John Markoff, "Cyberpunks," *New York Times Upfront*, Vol. 132, No. 15 (March 27, 2000), pp. 10–14.

43. J. Bloombecker, "A Security Manager's Guide to Hacking," *DATAPRO Reports on Information Security*, Report IS35–450–101, 1986.

44. For more information, see Ronald R. Thrasher, "Voice-Mail Fraud," *FBI Law Enforcement Bulletin*, July 1994, pp. 1–4.

45. J. Maxfield, "Computer Bulletin Boards and the Hacker Problem," *EDPACS: The Electric Data Processing Audit, Control and Security Newsletter* (Arlington, VA: Automation Training Center, October 1985).

46. Percy Black, personal communication, 1991, as cited in M. E. Kabay, "Computer Crime: Hackers" (undated electronic manuscript).

47. John Perry Barlow, "Crime and Puzzlement: In Advance of the Law on the Electronic Frontier," *Whole Earth Review* (fall 1990), p. 44.

48. Ibid.

49. "Computer Porn," *Time*, March 15, 1993, p. 22.

50. Details for this story come from "Britain, U.S. Break Up Online Pedophile Ring," http://www.msnbc.msn.com/id/19288057 (accessed June 18, 2007).

51. Parker, *Computer Crime*.

52. President's Identity Theft Task Force, *Combating Identity Theft: A Strategic Plan* (Washington, DC: U.S. Department of Justice, 2007), from which much of the information comes and some of the wording is taken or adapted.

53. Office of Community Oriented Policing Services, *A National Strategy to Combat Identity Theft* (Washington, DC: COPS Office, 2006), from which the quote and some of the material in this section are taken.

54. See Business Software Alliance, "Consumer Confidence in Online Shopping Buoyed by Security Software Protection, BSA Survey Suggests," January 12, 2006, http://www.bsacybersafety.com/news/2005-Online-Shopping-Confidence.cfm (accessed May 10, 2010).

55. See Cyber Security Industry Alliance, "Internet Security Voter Survey," June 2005, https://www.csialliance.org/publications/surveys_and_polls/CSIA_Internet_Security_Survey_June_2005.pdf (accessed May 10, 2010).

56. U.S. Code, Title 18, Section 1028.

57. H.R. 1731 (2004).

58. Katrina Baum, *Identity Theft, 2005* (Washington, DC: Bureau of Justice Statistics, 2007).

59. The information and some of the wording in this section are taken from *Combating Identity Theft: A Strategic Plan*.

60. U.S. Attorney's Office, Southern District of Florida, press release, July 19, 2006, http://www.usdoj.gov/usao/fls/PressReleases/060719-01.html (accessed May 9, 2009).

61. Ibid., pp. 22–51.

62. For insight into how security techniques often lag behind the abilities of criminal perpetrators in the high-technology arena, see James A. Fagin, "Computer Crime: A Technology Gap," *International Journal of Comparative and Applied Criminal Justice*, Vol. 15, Nos. 1 and 2 (spring/fall 1991), pp. 285–297.

63. "DNA Frees Man Sentenced to Life," Associated Press, January 16, 2001, www.msnbc.com/news/517172.asp (accessed January 17, 2005).

64. Michael Schrage, "Today, It Takes a Scientist to Catch a Thief," *Washington Post*, March 18, 1994.

65. *Daubert v. Merrell Dow Pharmaceuticals, Inc.*, 509 U.S. 579 (1993).

66. *Frye* v. *United States*, 54 App. D.C. 46, 47, 293 F. 1013, 1014 (1923).

67. Federal Rules of Evidence, Article IV, Rule 402.

68. For the application of *Daubert* to DNA technology, see Barry Sheck, "DNA and *Daubert*," *Cardozo Law Review*, Vol. 15 (1994), p. 1959.

69. Schrage, "Today, It Takes a Scientist to Catch a Thief."

70. FBI press release, October 13, 1998, http://www.fbi.gov/pressrm/pressrel/pressrel98/dna.htm (accessed January 22, 2003).

71. U.S. Code, Title 42, Section 14132.

72. "British Police to Use DNA to Catch Burglars," Reuters, June 16, 1994.

73. Schrage, "Today, It Takes a Scientist to Catch a Thief."

74. Edward Connors et al., *Convicted by Juries, Exonerated by Science: Case Studies in the Use of DNA Evidence to Establish Innocence after Trial* (Washington, DC: National Institute of Justice, 1996).

75. Ibid.

76. Roland Reboussin, "An Expert System Designed to Profile Murderers," in Frank Schmalleger, ed., *Computers in Criminal Justice: Issues and Applications* (Bristol, IN: Wyndham Hall Press, 1990), p. 239.

77. Japan Electronics Industry Association, *Industry Monitor: High-Tech Sector*, "Security Software Demand to Show Strong Growth—Week Ended June 27, 2004," http://www.irstreet.com/top/im/im20040627.pdf (accessed July 30, 2006).

78. Infonetics Research, "Strong Growth Expected for Security Appliance and Software Markets," March 9, 2009 http://www.infonetics.com/pr/2010/4Q09-Network-Security-Content-Security-Market-Highlights.asp (accessed October 2, 2010).

79. Parker, *Computer Crime*, p. xiii.

80. Kenneth Rosenblatt, "Deterring Computer Crime," *Technology Review*, Vol. 93, No. 2 (February/March 1990), pp. 34–41.

81. Ibid.

82. The NCCS can be found at http://www.fbi.gov/programs/nccs/comcrim.htm.

83. Ibid., as modified in 1986, 1988, and later years.

84. This is adapted from the FBI's Washington Field Office Infrastructure Protection and Computer Intrusion Squad home page at http://www.fbi.gov/programs/ipcis/ipcis.htm.

85. This is adapted from the Computer Crime and Intellectual Property Section of the Criminal Division of the U.S. Department of Justice's home page at http://www.cybercrime.gov.

86. Wylie Wong, "FBI Targets BBS Operators, Seizes Hardware in Software Piracy Sting," *Computerworld*, February 3, 1997, p. 24.

87. Rosenblatt, "Deterring Computer Crime."

88. Ibid.

89. John Naisbitt, *Megatrends: Ten New Directions Transforming Our Lives* (New York: Warner, 1982), p. 36.

90. Ibid.

91. Gary H. Anthes, "White House Launches Cybershield," *Computerworld*, July 22, 1996, p. 29.

92. M. J. Zuckerman, "Clinton to Get Cyberterror Plan," *USA Today*, October 9, 1997, p. 1A.

93. The quotations attributed to the President's Working Group in this section are from President's Working Group on Unlawful Conduct on the Internet, *The Electronic Frontier: The Challenge of Unlawful Conduct Involving the Use of the Internet* (Washington, DC: White House, 2000), http://www.usdoj.gov/criminal/cybercrime/unlawful.htm (accessed April 16, 2007).

94. United States Computer Emergency Readiness Team, "About Us," http://www.us-cert.gov/aboutus.html (accessed August 1, 2007).

95. National Security Presidential Directive 54; Homeland Security Presidential Directive 23 (NSPD-54/HSPD-23).

96. "Introducing the New Cybersecurity Coordinator," White House Blog, December 22, 2009, http://www.whitehouse.gov/blog/2009/12/22/introducing-new-cybersecurity-coordinator (accessed May 12, 2010).

97. S. Mace, "Kapor and Wozniak Establish Electronic Policy Foundation," *InfoWorld*, Vol. 12, No. 29 (July 16, 1990), p. 6.

CHAPTER 14: GLOBALIZATION AND TERRORISM

1. "Chiquita Pleads Guilty to Paying Terrorists to Protect Workers," Associated Press, March 19, 2007, http://www.usatoday.com/money/industries/food/2007-03-19-chiquita-terrorism_N.htm.

2. Adapted from John McHale, "Futures Critical: A Review," in *Human Futures: Needs, Societies, Technologies* (Guildford, Surrey, UK: IPC Business Press Limited, 1974), p. 13.

3. Thomas L. Friedman, *The Lexus and the Olive Tree* (New York: Anchor, 2000).

4. Adapted from "Globalization," *Encyclopedia Britannica, 2007*, Encyclopedia Britannica, http://www.britannica.com/eb/article?eu5369857 (accessed July 23, 2007).

5. National Institute of Justice, *Asian Transnational Organized Crime and Its Impact on the United States* (Washington, DC: NIJ, 2007).

6. "Mexico: Drug Cartels a Growing Threat," World Press, November 2, 2006, http://www.worldpress.org/Americas/2549.cfm (accessed July 9, 2007).

7. Ibid., citing United Nations sources.

8. Larry Birns and Alex Sánchez, "The Government and the Drug Lords: Who Rules Mexico?" World Press, April 23, 2007, http://www.worldpress.org/Americas/2763.cfm (accessed June 4, 2007).

9. Kevin Mooney, "Mexican Soldiers Freelancing for Drug Cartels on U.S. Soil," Cybercast news service, December 21, 2006,

http://www.cnsnews.com/ViewNation.asp?Page=/Nation/archive/200612/NAT20061221a.html (accessed July 7, 2007).

10. "Severed Head of Mexican Politician Dumped Outside Newspaper's Office," Associated Press, http://www.foxnews.com/story/0,2933,275713,00.html (accessed July 7, 2007).

11. Larry Birns and Alex Sánchez, "The Government and the Drug Lords."

12. Bureau for International Narcotics and Law Enforcement Affairs, Human Smuggling and Trafficking Center, *Distinctions between Human Smuggling and Human Trafficking* (Washington, DC: The Bureau, January 2005).

13. Raimo Väyrynen, "Illegal Immigration, Human Trafficking, and Organized Crime," United Nations University/World Institute for Development Economics Research, Discussion Paper No. 2003/72 (October 2003), p. 16.

14. Details for this story come from "Immigrant Smuggler Faulted in 19 Deaths Sentenced to Life in Prison," Associated Press, January 18, 2007, http://www.usatoday.com/news/nation/2007-01-18-smuggler_x.htm.

15. Office of the Under Secretary for Democracy and Global Affairs, *Trafficking in Persons Report* (Washington, DC: U.S. Department of State, June 2007).

16. Ibid.

17. Ibid.

18. Ibid.

19. *Trafficking in Persons Report*, p. 5.

20. Ibid.

21. U.S. Code, Title 8, Section 1324.

22. Public Law 89–236.

23. Trafficking Victims Protection Act of 2000, Division A of Public Law 106–386, Section 108, as amended.

24. *Trafficking in Persons Report*, p. 7.

25. Ibid.

26. Gregory J. Howard, Graeme Newman, and William Alex Pridemore, "Theory, Method, and Data in Comparative Criminology," in David Duffee, ed., *Measurement and Analysis of Criminal Justice*, Vol. 4 of *Criminal Justice 2000* (Washington, DC: National Institute of Justice, 2000), p. 189.

27. Ibid.

28. Franklin E. Zimring, "The Necessity and Value of Transnational Comparative Study: Some Preaching from a Recent Convert," *Criminology and Public Policy*, Vol. 5, No. 4 (2006), pp. 615–622.

29. Ibid.

30. See United Nations Office on Drugs and Crime, "Compiling and Comparing International Crime Statistics," http://www.unodc.org/en/crime_cicp_surveys_3.html (accessed June 5, 2007).

31. For information about the latest survey, see *The Ninth United Nations Survey on Crime Trends and the Operations of Criminal Justice Systems* (New York: United Nations, 2006), http://www.unodc.org/unodc/en/crime_clip_surveys.html (accessed July 10, 2006).

32. As of January 1, 2003, the New York City Office of Emergency Management said that 2,795 people died in the attacks on the World Trade Center; another 184 people died in the attack on the Pentagon (including those aboard the crashed airliner), and 44 people died aboard hijacked United Airlines Flight 93 that crashed in a Pennsylvania field.

33. U.S. Department of State, *Patterns of Global Terrorism, 2001* (Washington, DC: U.S. Government Printing Office, 2002), http://www.state.gov/s/ct/rls/pgtrpt/2001/ (accessed January 2, 2003). Until 2004, *Patterns of Global Terrorism* was made available to the public annually by the U.S. Department of State; as of 2004, however, the report became unavailable after its methodology was challenged by the Bush administration.

34. Paul R. Pillar, *Terrorism and U.S. Foreign Policy* (Washington, DC: Brookings Institution, 2001).

35. See Michael J. Lynch and W. Byron Groves, *A Primer in Radical Criminology* (Monsey, NY: Willow Tree Press, 1990); and Michael J. Lynch et al., *The New Primer in Radical Criminology: Critical Perspectives on Crime, Power and Identity* (Monsey, NY: Willow Tree Press, 2000).

36. Council on Foreign Relations and the Markle Foundation, *Types of Terrorism*, http://www.terrorismanswers.com/terrorism/types.html (accessed January 10, 2007).

37. Bruce Hoffman, *Inside Terrorism* (New York: Columbia University Press, 1998), p. 91.

38. Adapted from *FBI Policy and Guidelines: Counterterrorism*, http://www.fbi.gov/contact/fo/jackson/cntrterr.htm (accessed March 4, 2006).

39. Adapted from *FBI Policy and Guidelines: Counterterrorism*.

40. National Counterterrorism Center, *2009 Report on Terrorism* (Washington, DC: NCTC, 2010), from which much of the information in this section is taken.

41. Peter Flory, "Terrorism Must Continue to Be a Top Priority," *Insight on the News*, Vol. 10, No. 21 (May 23, 1994), pp. 37–38.

42. The death penalty was imposed for the first-degree murders of eight federal law enforcement agents who were at work in the Murrah Building at the time of the bombing. While the killings violated Oklahoma law, only the killings of the federal agents fell under federal law, which makes such murders capital offenses.

43. Scott Shane, "A Year Later, Clues on Anthrax Still Few," SunSpot.Net, October 9, 2002, http://www.sunspot.net/news/printedition/balte.anthrax09oct09001612,0,6275426.story?coll=bal%2Dpe%2Dasection (accessed January 21, 2003).

44. U.S. Department of Justice, Office of Information and Privacy, FOIA Post, "Anthrax Mail Emergency Delays FOIA Correspondence," http://www.usdoj.gov/oip/foiapost/2001foiapost21.htm (accessed January 31, 2003).

45. See Barry Collin, "The Future of Cyberterrorism," *Crime and Justice International* (March 1997), pp. 15–18.

46. John Arquilla and David Ronfeldt, *The Advent of Netwar* (Santa Monica, CA: RAND, 1996).

47. Adapted from Dictionary.com, http://dictionary.reference.com/search?q=infrastructure (accessed January 10, 2007).

48. The PCCIP was established by Executive Order 13010.

49. Dorothy E. Denning, "Activism, Hactivism, and Cyberterrorism: The Internet as a Tool for Influencing Foreign Policy," paper presented at the Internet and International Systems: Information Technology and American Foreign Policy Decisionmaking Workshop, San Francisco, CA, December 10, 2001.

50. Critical Infrastructure Assurance Office, "Resource Library," http://www.ciao.gov/resource/index.html (accessed January 10, 2002).

51. Executive Order 13231 (Critical Infrastructure Protection in the Information Age), October 16, 2001.

52. President's Critical Infrastructure Protection Board, *The National Strategy to Secure Cyberspace* (Washington, DC: U.S. Government Printing Office, September 18, 2002), p. 3.

53. Ibid.

54. "Ridge Creates New Division to Combat Cyber Threats," Department of Homeland Security press release, June 6, 2003, http://www.dhs.gov/dhspublic/display?content=916 (accessed September 20, 2006).

55. U.S. General Services Administration, "GovNet Planned to Protect Critical Government IT Functions from Cyber Attacks," GSA news release number 9890, October 10, 2001, http://w3.gsa.gov/web/x/publicaffairs.nsf/dea168abbe828fe9852565c600519794/1c10e9ac670553b885256ae100668beb?OpenDocument (accessed January 21, 2005).

56. "U.S. Plans New Secure Government Internet," Associated Press, October 11, 2001.

57. Technological devices described in this section are discussed in G. Gordon Liddy, "Rules of the Game," *Omni*, January 1989, pp. 43–47, 78–80.

58. CIA Directorate of Intelligence, *Terrorist CBRN: Materials and Effects* (Washington, DC: CIA, 2003).

59. Commission on the Prevention of Weapons of Mass Destruction Proliferation and Terrorism, *World at Risk: The Report of the Commission on the Prevention of WMD Proliferation and Terrorism* (Washington, DC: The Commission, 2008), p. xv.

60. Matthew Bunn, Anthony Wier, and John P. Holden, *Controlling Nuclear Warheads and Materials: A Report Card and Action Plan* (Cambridge: Nuclear Threat Initiative and Harvard University, 2003).

61. *Fact Sheet: The Biological Weapons Convention* (Washington, DC: Bureau of Arms Control, 2002), http://www.state.gov/t/ac/rls/fs/10401.htm (accessed August 8, 2006).

62. Ali S. Kahn et al., *Biological and Chemical Terrorism: Strategic Plan for Preparedness and Response* (Atlanta, GA: Centers for Disease Control, April 21, 2000), http://www.cdc.gov/mmwr/preview/mmwrhtml/rr4904a1.htm (accessed August 2, 2007).

63. Council on Foreign Relations, "Terrorism: Questions and Answers—The Anthrax Letters," http://www.terrorismanswers.com/weapons/anthraxletters.html (accessed August 3, 2006).

64. See Rick Weiss, "DNA by Mail: A Terror Risk," *Washington Post*, July 18, 2002.

65. Public Law 107–56.

66. U.S. Code, Title 18, Sections 2510–2522.

67. Public Law 91–508, Title I.

68. U.S. Code, Title 18, Sections 3121–3127.

69. U. S. Code, Title 18, Sections 2701–2712.

70. U. S. Code, Title 50, Sections 1801–1811.

71. See, especially, Rules 41 and 41a (Search Warrants).

72. U. S. Code, Title 20, Section 1232g; 34 C.F.R. Part 99.

73. Stefanie Olsen, "PATRIOT Act Draws Privacy Concerns," CNET News.com, October 26, 2001, http://news.cnet.com/news/0–1005–200–7671240.htm?tag=rltdnws (accessed November 3, 2002).

74. Public Law 107–296.

75. U.S. Department of Homeland Security, "DHS Organization: Building a Secure Homeland," http://www.dhs.gov/dhspublic/theme_home1.jsp (accessed August 2, 2004).

76. On March 1, 2003, the Immigration and Naturalization Service became part of the U.S. Department of Homeland Security, and its functions were divided into various bureaus within that department.

77. The information in this section comes from U.S. Department of Homeland Security, "DHS Organization: Department Components," http://www.dhs.gov/dhspublic/display?theme=9&content=858 (accessed August 2, 2006).

78. Public Law 105–261.

79. Gary Hart, Warren B. Rudman, and Stephen E. Flynn, *America Still Unprepared—America Still in Danger* (Washington, DC: Council on Foreign Relations, 2002).

80. Public Law 105–277.

81. Commission on the Prevention of Weapons of Mass Destruction Proliferation and Terrorism, *World at Risk*, pp. xv, xvi.

82. Ibid., p. xxvi.

83. U.S. Department of State, *Patterns of Global Terrorism 2001* (Washington, DC: U.S. Government Printing Office, 2002), http://www.state.gov/s/ct/rls/pgtrpt/2001 (accessed January 2, 2003). Previously available annually, *Patterns of Global Terrorism* has been superseded by the National Counterterrorism Center's yearly *Report on Terrorist Incidents*, http://www.terrorisminfo.mipt.org/pdf/Country-Reports-Terrorism-2006-NCTC-Annex.pdf.

84. Executive Order 13224.

85. National Security Council, *National Strategy for Combating Terrorism* (Washington, DC: The White House, 2006).

86. The NCTC was established by Executive Order in 2004, although Congress codified the NCTC in the Intelligence Reform and Terrorism Prevention Act of 2004 (IRTPA) and placed the NCTC within the Office of the Director of National Intelligence.

87. National Counterterrorism Center, *NCTC and Information Sharing* (Washington, DC: NCTC, 2006), p. I, from which some of the wording in this paragraph is taken.

88. Congressional Research Service, *Terrorism, the Future, and U.S. Foreign Policy* (Washington, DC: Library of Congress, April 11, 2003), from which the material in this section is derived.

89. Public Law 104–132.

90. Public Law 107–56.

91. U.S. Code, Title 8, Section 1-1599.

92. Public Law 107–56.

93. Information in this paragraph is taken from National Counterterrorism Center, "Terrorist Identities Datamart Environment (TIDE)," May 20, 2007, http://www.nctc.gov/docs/Tide_Fact_Sheet.pdf (accessed June 11, 2007).

94. Information in this paragraph comes from *Terrorism, the Future, and U.S. Foreign Policy*, p. 6.

95. Congressional Research Service, *Terrorism, the Future, and U.S. Foreign Policy*, p. 5.

EPILOGUE: FUTURE DIRECTIONS

1. This story is adapted from Gary LaFree et al., "The Changing Nature of Crime in America," in Gary LaFree, ed., *The Nature of Crime—Continuity and Change*, Vol. 3 of *Criminal Justice 2000* (Washington, DC: National Institute of Justice, 2000).

2. Darlene E. Weingand, "Futures Research Methodologies: Linking Today's Decisions with Tomorrow's Possibilities," paper presented at the Sixty-First International Federation of Library Associations and Institutions annual conference, August 20, 1995, http://www.ifla.org/IV/ifla61/61-weid.htm (accessed June 16, 1998, and July 10, 2007).

3. Joseph F. Coates, "The Highly Probable Future: 83 Assumptions about the Year 2025," *Futurist*, Vol. 28, No. 4 (July/August 1994), p. 51.

4. Alvin Toffler, *Future Shock* (New York: Random House, 1970).

5. Alvin Toffler, *Powershift: Knowledge, Wealth and Violence at the Edge of the 21st* Century (New York: Bantam Books, 1990).

6. Alvin Toffler, *The Third Wave* (New York: Bantam, 1981).

7. John Naisbitt, *Megatrends: Ten New Directions Transforming Our Lives* (New York: Warner, 1982).

8. Peter F. Drucker, *Management Challenges for the 21st Century* (New York: Harper, 1999).

9. Peter F. Drucker, *Post-Capitalist Society* (New York: Harper, 1994).

10. Francis Fukuyama, *Our Posthuman Future: Consequences of the Biotechnology Revolution* (New York: Farrar, Straus and Giroux, 2002).

11. Francis Fukuyama, *The End of History and the Last Man* (New York: Avon Books, 1992).

12. Although this chapter cannot cover all future aspects of the criminal justice system, readers are referred to C. J. Swank, "Police in the Twenty-First Century: Hypotheses for the Future," *International Journal of Comparative and Applied Criminal Justice*, Vol. 17, Nos. 1 and 2 (spring/fall 1993), pp. 107–120, for an excellent analysis of policing in the future.

13. Joseph A. Schafer, ed., *Policing 2020: Exploring the Future of Crime, Communities, and Policing* (Quantico, VA: Futures Working Group, 2007).

14. Ibid.

15. Ibid., p. 32.

16. Foresight, http://www.foresight.gov.uk (accessed March 22, 2007).

17. The quotations attributed to the panel in this section are from Foresight Crime Prevention Panel, *Just around the Corner: A Consultation Document*, http://www.foresight.gov.uk/servlet/DocViewer/docnoredirect=883 (accessed January 22, 2007).

18. Society of Police Futurists International, *PFI: The Future of Policing*, no date.

19. William L. Tafoya, "Futures Research: Implications for Criminal Investigations," in James N. Gilbert, ed., *Criminal Investigation: Essays and Cases* (Columbus, OH: Charles E. Merrill, 1990), p. 214.

20. Frederick R. Brodzinski, "The Futurist Perspective and the Managerial Process," *Utilizing Futures Research*, No. 6 (1979), pp. 8–19.

21. Weingand, "Futures Research Methodologies."

22. George F. Cole, "Criminal Justice in the Twenty-First Century: The Role of Futures Research," in John Klofas and Stan Stojkovic, eds., *Crime and Justice in the Year 2010* (Belmont, CA: Wadsworth, 1995).

23. Joseph F. Coates et al., *2025: Scenarios of U.S. and Global Society Reshaped by Science and Technology* (Winchester, VA: Oakhill Press, 1997).

24. Richter H. Moore, Jr., "Wiseguys: Smarter Criminals and Smarter Crime in the Twenty-First Century," *Futurist*, Vol. 28, No. 5 (September/October 1994), p. 33.

25. The quotations attributed to Moore in this section are from ibid., pp. 33–37.

26. Georgette Bennett, *Crimewarps: The Future of Crime in America* (Garden City, NY: Anchor/Doubleday, 1987).

27. U.S. Joint Forces Command, *The Joint Operational Environment: The World through 2030 and Beyond*, CreateSpace, 2007.

28. L. Edward Wells, "Explaining Crime in the Year 2010," in Klofas and Stojkovic, eds., *Crime and Justice in the Year 2010*, pp. 36–61.

29. Ibid.

30. Ibid., pp. 48–49.

31. Ibid.

32. Frank P. Williams III and Marilyn D. McShane, *Criminological Theory*, 2nd ed. (Upper Saddle River, NJ: Prentice Hall, 1994), p. 257.

33. The quotations attributed to Farrington in this section are from David P. Farrington, "Explaining and Preventing Crime: The Globalization of Knowledge," *Criminology*, Vol. 38, No. 1 (February 2000), pp. 1–24.

34. The quotations attributed to Stephens in this section are from Gene Stephens, "The Global Crime Wave," *Futurist*, Vol. 28, No. 4 (July/August 1994), pp. 22–29.

35. For an interesting and alternative view of the future—one that evaluates what might happen if the insight provided by feminist perspectives on crime were implemented—see M. Kay Harris, "Moving into the New Millennium: Toward a Feminist Vision of Justice," in Barry W. Hancock and Paul M. Sharp, eds., *Public Policy, Crime, and Criminal Justice*, 2nd ed. (Upper Saddle River, NJ: Prentice Hall, 2000), pp. 407–419.

36. The quotations in the numbered list are taken from Moore, "Wiseguys," p. 33.

37. Hermanus Bianchi, *Position and Subject-Matter of Criminology* (Amsterdam: North-Holland, 1956).

38. Hermann Mannheim, *Comparative Criminology* (New York: Houghton Mifflin, 1965), p. 18.

39. Lawrence Friedman, *Crime and Punishment in American History* (New York: Basic Books, 1993).

40. "Can Anything Really Be Done?" *USA Today* magazine, Vol. 122, No. 2587 (April 1994), p. 6.

41. Robert D. Pursley, *Introduction to Criminal Justice*, 6th ed. (New York: Macmillan, 1991), p. 677.

42. Ibid.

43. Nancy E. Marion, *A History of Federal Crime Control Initiatives, 1960–1993* (Santa Barbara, CA: Greenwood, 1994), p. 244.

44. Ibid., p. 249.

45. Alfred Blumstein, "Seeking the Connection Between Crime and Punishment," *Jobs and Capital*, Winter 1995, pp. 23–27.

46. Carl J. Jensen and Bernard H. Levin, "The World of 2020: Demographic Shifts, Cultural Change, and Social Challenge," in Schafer, *Policing 2020*, p. 33.

GLOSSARY

1. National Institute on Drug Abuse, *The Science of Addiction: Drugs, Brains, and Behavior* (Washington, DC: U.S. Department of Health and Human Services, 2007).

2. American Board of Forensic Psychology, http://www.abfp.com/brochure.html (accessed November 22, 2009).

3. This and other cybercrime-related terms are adapted from Donn B. Parker, *Computer Crime: Criminal Justice Resource Manual* (Washington, DC: National Institute of Justice, 1989).

4. Michael L. Benson, Francis T. Cullen, and William J. Maakestad, *Local Prosecutors and Corporate Crime* (Washington, DC: National Institute of Justice, 1993).

5. Adapted from Anthony Walsh, *Biosocial Criminology: Introduction and Integration* (Cincinnati: Anderson, 2002), p. 59.

6. James A. Inciardi, *The War on Drugs II* (Mountain View, CA: Mayfield, 1992).

7. Bryan Vila, "A General Paradigm for Understanding Criminal Behavior: Extending Evolutionary Ecological Theory," *Criminology*, Vol. 32, No. 3 (August 1994), pp. 311–359.

8. Adapted from Federal Bureau of Investigation, *FBI Policy and Guidelines: Counterterrorism*, http://www.fbi.gov/contact/fo/jackson/cntrterr.htm (accessed January 15, 2010).

9. Bureau of Justice Statistics, *Drugs, Crime and the Justice System* (Washington, DC: U.S. Department of Justice, December 1992).

10. *American Heritage Dictionary and Electronic Thesaurus* (Boston: Houghton Mifflin, 1987).

11. George F. Cole, "Criminal Justice in the Twenty-First Century: The Role of Futures Research," in John Klofas and Stan Stojkovic, eds., *Crime and Justice in the Year 2010* (Belmont, CA: Wadsworth, 1995).

12. Society of Police Futurists International, *PFI: The Future of Policing*, no date.

13. Teresa C. LaGrange and Robert A. Silverman, "Low Self-Control and Opportunity: Testing the General Theory of Crime as an Explanation for Gender Differences in Delinquency," *Criminology*, Vol. 37, No. 1 (1999), p. 41.

14. Adapted from "Globalization," *Encyclopedia Britannica, 2007*, Encyclopedia Britannica, http://www.britannica.com/eb/article?eu5369857 (accessed July, 23, 2007).

15. Raimo Väyrynen, "Illegal Immigration, Human Trafficking, and Organized Crime," United Nations University/World Institute for Development Economics Research, Discussion Paper No. 2003/72 (October 2003).

16. *American Heritage Dictionary and Electronic Thesaurus.*

17. Ibid.

18. Adapted from Dictionary.com, http://dictionary.reference.com/search?1q=infrastructure (accessed January 10, 2003).

19. *American Heritage Dictionary and Electronic Thesaurus.*

20. Adapted from Federal Bureau of Investigation, *FBI Policy and Guidelines.*

21. Clifford Karchmer and Douglas Ruch, "State and Local Money Laundering Control Strategies," *NIJ Research in Brief* (Washington, DC: National Institute of Justice, 1992).

22. Vila, "A General Paradigm for Understanding Criminal Behavior."

23. Gary S. Green, *Occupational Crime* (Chicago: Nelson-Hall, 1990).

24. The Omnibus Crime Control Act of 1970, Pub. L. 90–351, Title I, Section 101.

25. Frank E. Hagan, *Research Methods in Criminal Justice and Criminology* (New York: Macmillan, 1993).

26. "Phishing," TechWeb's *TechEncyclopedia*, http://www.techweb.com/encyclopedia/defineterm?term=phishing (accessed July 30, 2010).

27. Bryan Vila, "Human Nature and Crime Control: Improving the Feasibility of Nurturant Strategies," *Politics and the Life Sciences* (March 1997), pp. 3–21.

28. *American Heritage Dictionary and Electronic Thesaurus.*

29. Laurence Steinberg, "The Juvenile Psychopath: Fads, Fictions, and Facts," *National Institute of Justice Perspectives on Crime and Justice: 2001 Lecture Series*, Vol. 5 (Washington, DC: National Institute of Justice, 2002), pp. 35–64.

30. Abraham Kaplan, *The Conduct of Inquiry: Methodology for Behavioral Science* (San Francisco: Chandler, 1964).

31. Fay Honey Knopp, "Community Solutions to Sexual Violence: Feminist-Abolitionist Perspectives," in Harold Pepinsky and Richard Quinney, eds., *Criminology as Peacemaking* (Bloomington: Indiana University Press, 1991), p. 183.

32. Ronald V. Clarke and Derek B. Cornish, eds., *Crime Control in Britain: A Review of Police and Research* (Albany: State University of New York Press), p. 8.

33. David Weisburd, "Reorienting Crime Prevention Research and Policy: From the Causes of Criminality to the Context of Crime," *NIJ Research Report* (Washington, DC: National Institute of Justice, June 1997).

34. Edward O. Wilson, *Sociobiology: The New Synthesis* (Cambridge: Harvard University Press, Belknap Press, 1975).

35. William J. Chambliss, "State-Organized Crime—The American Society of Criminology, 1988 Presidential Address," *Criminology*, Vol. 27, No. 2 (1989), pp. 183–208.

36. *American Heritage Dictionary and Electronic Thesaurus.*

37. Henry Campbell Black, *Black's Law Dictionary*, 6th ed. (St. Paul, MN: West, 1990).

38. *American Heritage Dictionary and Electronic Thesaurus.*

39. See John J. DiIulio, Jr., "The Question of Black Crime," *Public Interest* (fall 1994), pp. 3–12. The term *superpredator* is generally attributed to DiIulio.

40. U.S. Department of State, *Patterns of Global Terrorism, 2001* (Washington, DC: U.S. Government Printing Office, 2002), http://www.state.gov/s/ct/rls/pgtrpt/2001 (accessed January 2, 2003).

41. Lawrence A. Greenfeld, "Prison Sentences and Time Served for Violence," *Bureau of Justice Statistics Selected Findings*, No. 4, April 1995.

Name Index

Subject Index

Criminology-Related Websites

Academy of Experimental Criminology (AEC)
http://www.crim.upenn.edu/aec/about.htm
The Academy of Experimental Criminology was founded in 1999 to recognize successful randomized, controlled field experiments in criminology. The academy publishes the *Journal of Experimental Criminology*.

American Society of Criminology (ASC)
http://www.asc41.com
The ASC is an international organization concerned with scholarly, scientific, and professional knowledge concerning the etiology, prevention, control, and treatment of crime and delinquency.

Australian Institute of Criminology (AIC)
http://www.aic.gov.au
The Australian Institute of Criminology serves as the national center for the study of crime and criminal justice in Australia and for the dissemination of information in the areas of criminology and criminal justice. AIC makes its Trends & Issues in Crime and Criminal Justice Series available through its website. The series provides studies and information for decision makers to assist in the promotion of justice and the prevention of crime.

Restoration Justice
http://www.barjproject.org
Restoration Justice is a national initiative of the Office of Juvenile Justice and Delinquency Prevention (OJJDP). It works with communities and criminal justice agencies to provide training, education, technical assistance, evaluation, and research on emerging law enforcement and restorative justice practices. Its website contains PDF versions of project newsletters, as well as a listing of project publications.

British Society of Criminology (BSC)
http://www.britsoccrim.org
The Society is Britain's major professional criminology organization, working to further the interests and knowledge of both academic and professional people engaged in any aspect of teaching, research, or public education about crime, criminal behavior, and the criminal justice system in the United Kingdom.

Campbell Collaboration's Crime and Justice Coordinating Group (CCJG)
http://www.campbellcollaboration.org/crime_and_justice/index.php
The Crime and Justice Coordinating Group is an international network of researchers that prepares, updates, and rapidly disseminates systematic reviews of high-quality research conducted worldwide on effective methods to reduce crime and delinquency and improve the quality of justice.

Center for Restorative Justice and Peacemaking
http://rjp.umn.edu
The Center is "committed to the development of community-based responses to crime and violence that strengthen social harmony and individual healing through dialogue, repair of harm, and peace-building by providing technical assistance, training, and research in support of restorative dialogue practices." Its website provides the full text of several of the Center's publications as well as an annotated bibliography of restorative justice materials.

Center for the Study and Prevention of Violence (CSPV)
http://www.colorado.edu/cspv
The CSPV, a research program of the Institute of Behavioral Science at the University of Colorado at Boulder, was founded to provide informed assistance to groups committed to understanding and preventing violence, particularly adolescent violence.

Computer Crime and Intellectual Property Section (U.S. Department of Justice)
http://www.cybercrime.gov
The Computer Crime and Intellectual Property Section (CCIPS) of the U.S. Department of Justice is responsible for implementing the Department's national strategies in combating computer and intellectual property crimes worldwide.

Crime Library, tru TV
http://www.crimelibrary.com
tru TV's Crime Library is a rapidly growing collection of more than 600 nonfiction feature stories on major crimes, criminals, trials, forensics, and criminal profiling by prominent writers. The stories focus mostly on recent crimes, but an expanding collection also delves into historically notorious characters, dating back to the 1400s and spanning the globe.

Crime Mapping Research Center
http://www.ojp.usdoj.gov/nij/maps
The Mapping and Analysis for Public Safety (MAPS) program at the National Institute of Justice supports research into spatial aspects of crime, spatial data analysis, mapping, and analysis for evaluating programs and policy, as well as development of mapping, data sharing, and spatial analysis tools.

Crime Times
http://www.crime-times.org
An electronic journal fostering the effort to learn about the brain dysfunction that underlies much delinquency and criminality. The site provides research reviews and information on biological causes of disordered, criminal, and psychopathic behavior.

Critical Criminology Division of the ASC
http://www.critcrim.org
The ASC Division on Critical Criminology fosters research and theory development in the field of critical criminology, which is widely recognized as one of the major paradigms in criminology. The division also provides access to the online edition of the journal *The Critical Criminologist*.

Domestic Violence and Sexual Assault Data Resource Center
http://www.jrsa.org/dvsa-drc
The Domestic Violence and Sexual Assault Data Resource Center provides information on state-collected data. Funded by the National Institute of Justice, the center's website includes national summaries, state-by-state information, lists of related reports, and a list of national and state contacts.

Drug and Alcohol Services Information System (DASIS)
http://oas.samhsa.gov/dasis.htm
DASIS is the primary source of national data on substance abuse treatment. It has three components available online: National Survey of Substance Abuse Treatment Services (N-SSATS), Treatment Episode Data Set (TEDS), and Inventory of Substance Abuse Treatment Services (I-SATS).

European Society of Criminology
http://www.esc-eurocrim.org
The European Society of Criminology, founded in 2000, works to bring together persons actively engaged in research, teaching, and/or practice in the field of criminology.

Financial Crimes Enforcement Network (FinCEN)
http://www.fincen.gov
The Financial Crimes Enforcement Network is designed to help in the fight against money laundering. The FinCEN works to maximize information sharing among law enforcement agencies and its other partners in the regulatory and financial communities.

Homicide Research Working Group (HRWG)
http://homicideworkinggroup.cos.ucf.edu/
The HRWG provides a clearinghouse for homicide research from many disciplines. It was created by homicide experts from criminology, public health, demography, geography, medicine, sociology, criminal justice, and a variety of other disciplines.

Identity Theft Resource Center (ITRC)
http://www.idtheftcenter.org
The ITRC is a nonprofit program dedicated exclusively to solving the problem of identity theft. Its website includes information on current laws that address the issue of identity theft, up-to-date studies, and links to relevant organizations.